D0679988

COMMERCIAL LAW

If you're serious about exam success, it's time to *Concentrate!*

Commercial Law Concentrate, Eric Baskind

This high quality revision and study guide, with clear, succinct coverage of all the key topics, will help you to quickly grasp the fundamental principles of commercial law and feel confident for the exam.

* Key cases and legal principles are clearly presented for easy reference

* Key Facts lists help you remember the essential points of a topic

* Sample questions with outline answers provide guidance on how to structure a good answer

* *Looking for extra marks?* gives you advice on how to impress examiners

* Practical examples relate contract law to real life

* A glossary of key terms provides useful definitions

@ Visit **www.oxfordtextbooks.co.uk/ orc/concentrate/**

Additional online resources accompany *Commercial Law Concentrate* so you can:

→ check your knowledge of key cases with the interactive flashcards;

→ test your understanding of terms and concepts with the interactive glossary; and

→ understand your marks with guidance on answering essay and problem questions.

concentrate!

Each guide in the series shows you what to expect in your exam, what examiners are looking for, and how to achieve extra marks.

→ Written by experts
→ Developed with students
→ Designed for success

Buy yours from your campus bookshop, online, or direct from OUP

www.oxfordtextbooks.co.uk/law/revision

COMMERCIAL LAW

Eric Baskind

Senior Lecturer in Law, Liverpool John Moores University

Greg Osborne

Senior Lecturer in Law, University of Portsmouth

Lee Roach

Senior Lecturer in Law, University of Portsmouth

OXFORD

UNIVERSITY PRESS

OXFORD
UNIVERSITY PRESS

Great Clarendon Street, Oxford, OX2 6DP,
United Kingdom

Oxford University Press is a department of the University of Oxford.
It furthers the University's objective of excellence in research, scholarship,
and education by publishing worldwide. Oxford is a registered trade mark of
Oxford University Press in the UK and in certain other countries

© Eric Baskind, Greg Osborne, Lee Roach 2013

The moral rights of the authors have been asserted

Impression: 1

All rights reserved. No part of this publication may be reproduced, stored in
a retrieval system, or transmitted, in any form or by any means, without the
prior permission in writing of Oxford University Press, or as expressly permitted
by law, by licence or under terms agreed with the appropriate reprographics
rights organization. Enquiries concerning reproduction outside the scope of the
above should be sent to the Rights Department, Oxford University Press, at the
address above

You must not circulate this work in any other form
and you must impose this same condition on any acquirer

Public sector information reproduced under Open Government Licence v1.0
(http://www.nationalarchives.gov.uk/doc/open-government-licence/open-government-licence.htm)

Crown Copyright material reproduced with the permission of the
Controller, HMSO (under the terms of the Click Use licence)

British Library Cataloguing in Publication Data

Data available

ISBN 978–0–19–966423–8

Printed in Great Britain by
Ashford Colour Press Ltd, Gosport, Hampshire

Links to third party websites are provided by Oxford in good faith and
for information only. Oxford disclaims any responsibility for the materials
contained in any third party website referenced in this work.

All persons referred to in the example boxes are fictitious and any resemblance to
real persons, existing or otherwise, is purely coincidental.

preface

Writing a brand new commercial law text can be a daunting task. Although the commercial law textbook market is not as saturated as that of other legal subjects, many of the texts that exist are renowned for their comprehensiveness and rigour, and for the eminence of their authors. This book aims to join their august company through providing a similar level of rigour and coverage, but also by providing a fresh and engaging discussion of the topic. To this end, the book provides a number of features that aim to help students better identify and discuss key cases and statutory provisions. Definition boxes and link boxes help students understand the terminology of the subject and the ways in which various commercial law topics interact with one another. Throughout the text, a fictional company (ComCorp Ltd) is used to provide examples of the problems that the law aims to regulate and how the law is applied in practice. Through these, and other features, it is hoped that students will better appreciate the intricacies of the topic and its application in the marketplace and on the high street. In addition, the accompanying Online Resource Centre will provide further resources and updates on the topics covered in the book, as well as providing bonus chapters on competition law, insurance law, and consumer credit.

Some points should be noted relating to the style of the text:

- Section 6 of the Interpretation Act 1978 provides that, in relation to statutory interpretation, unless otherwise stated, the masculine shall also indicate the feminine. This text follows the same rule and, accordingly, 'he', 'him', and 'his' shall, unless otherwise stated, also be taken to mean 'she', 'her', and 'hers', respectively.

- The term 'claimant' is used throughout, except where an original quote uses the term 'plaintiff', in which case, the original term remains.

- As many law schools now require their students to cite legal sources using OSCOLA, this text follows OSCOLA, as opposed to OUP's normal house style. A guide on how to use OSCOLA can also be found in the accompanying Online Resource Centre.

The authors offer their thanks to the publishing team at OUP, especially Tom Young, Emily Uecker, Hannah Marsden, and Jacqueline Senior. Additionally our thanks go to Kate Whetter and Deborah Hey. The authors would also like to thank the anonymous reviewers for their invaluable comments and feedback.

The division of labour for this edition has been as follows: Lee Roach held overall editorial responsibility and wrote Chapter 1 and Chapters 3 to 9; Greg Osborne wrote Chapter 2 and Chapters 18 to 26; Eric Baskind wrote Chapters 10 to 17.

The authors have stated the law, as it is understood by them, as of March 2013. With the kind indulgence of the publisher, minor amendments have been made at proof stage to accommodate subsequent changes in the law.

Eric Baskind
Greg Osborne
Lee Roach
March 2013

guide to the book

This guide outlines the key features of the book that have been devised to make the learning experience easier and more enjoyable for you. This brief overview explains the features and how to make the most of them for effective study of the law in a commercial environment.

Features to aid learning

INTRODUCTION

This chapter is the first of four dealing with the la
In addition, Chapter 25 is also relevant, since it de
mechanisms for payment in international sales contr
After identifying what amounts to an internationa
in which the nature of the law of international sale

Introductions at the start of each chapter outline the practical relevance of that particular area of law and how it will relate to you as a student of commercial law.

Eg ComCorp Ltd

ComCorp is looking to acquire several pieces of art to display in th
headquarters. Daniella, an art dealer, purchases a number of pai
She informs the gallery that she is purchasing the paintings on be
is not the case—she has not been appointed as ComCorp's ag
to act on ComCorp's behalf. Upon discovering this, the gallery
contracts of sale. ComCorp, however, upon discovering that D

Example boxes feature a fictional company (ComCorp Ltd) that is referred to throughout the book. As you work through the text, the activities that ComCorp engages in, and the problems that it faces, will demonstrate to you how the law operates in practice.

→ **FOB contract:**
A free on board
contract, under which
the buyer arranges
for the shipment
and insurance of the
goods. With such a
contract, as soon as
the goods are loaded
onto the vessel, the

especially in the case of a
the buyer by a route involv
to insure the goods, the seller must giv
to insure them during their sea transit.
risk during such sea transit, although t

Definition boxes highlight and explain all of the new terms that you will come across within the text.

isha Ltd (The Hong Kong Fir),[19] the
*v*ide a seaworthy ship was, in the
n, so that the legal effect of the
each of the duty which deprives
ie benefit of the contract will be

 Hong Kong Fir and the innominate term is discussed at p 223

Link boxes are cross-references to other areas of the textbook with page references to highlight fundamental connections across the chapters, thereby aiding your understanding of the overarching themes.

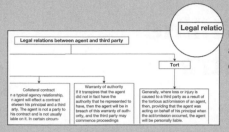

Diagrams summarize the more complex areas of the law to provide a clear and concise visual overview.

> *Overbrooke Estates Ltd v Glencombe Properti Ltd* [1974] 1 WLR 1335 (Ch)
>
> **FACTS:** Overbrooke Estates Ltd (the principal) put up a piece of property for by auction. Prior to the auction, Glencombe Properties Ltd was sent a copy of the auctioneer's general conditions of sale, which stated that '[t]he vendors do not make or give and neither the auctioneers nor any person in the employment of the auctioneers has any authority to make or give any representation or warranty in relation to these properties'. At the auction, the auctioneer (the agent) told Glencombe that neither the local authority nor Greater London Council had plans for the property and were not interested in compulsorily purchasing it. Glencombe bought the property, but subsequently discovered from the local authority that the property was within an area that would be subject to a slum clearance programme. Upon discovering this, Glencombe stopped the payment and refused to honour the contract. Overbrooke sought specific performance, and Glencombe

Case boxes provide clear and thorough explanations and, where appropriate, commentary of the key facts and judgments of notable cases, which will help to develop an effective understanding of the application, effectiveness, and relevance of the law.

Conclusion

This chapter has introduced an important concept documentary sale, under which the mechanics of the completion delivery of documents both by the seller, with documents relating buyer, with documents representing payment. Particular forms documentary approach to completion, so much so that with Cif is that the seller must tender a bill of lading and a policy of in

Conclusions at the end of each chapter highlight the essential areas of the law. These also help you to focus your study, not to mention making great revision aids!

Practice questions

1. Do you consider that the principles of *nemo dat* strike ept the original owner of the goods and the innocent purchaser?

2. ComCorp opens a new office and needs to purchase some co six computers from Chris, who advertises himself as a local c fact, Chris is a rogue and has stolen the computers from his Sales lc. Chris delivers and installs the com uters in Co

Practice questions are provided at the end of each chapter to help you to check your understanding of the chapter and assess your own progress.

Further reading

Patrick S Atiyah, '*Couturier v Hastie* and the Sale of Non-Ex
• Argues that section 6 of the SGA 1979 merely lays down a rule of co may be ousted by the contrary intention of the parties.

Celia Battersby, 'Frustration: A Limited Future' (1990) 134 SJ 354
• Discusses the strict limits of the application of the doctrine of frustrati

Ewan McKendrick, 'The Construction of Force Majeure Clauses and Self-

Further reading references conclude each chapter. Annotated, they point you in the direction of articles, textbooks, reports, and websites that develop the issues discussed in the chapter.

guide to the Online Resource Centre

This book is accompanied by a fully integrated Online Resource Centre that provides a whole host of additional resources to support you in your studies, and to advance your understanding of the topics.

www.oxfordtextbooks.co.uk/orc/baskind

Oxford University Press's Online Resource Centres are developed to provide lecturers and students with ready-to-use teaching and learning resources. They are free of charge, designed specifically to complement the textbook, and offer additional materials that are suited to electronic delivery.

If you would like advice or help at any point, do not hesitate to contact our ORC helpdesk at: **orc.help@oup.com**.

Updates

Ensure that you're kept up to date with the latest developments by checking this page for the latest updates from the author team.

Further reading lists

A selection of further reading, chosen by the authors and organized by chapter, allows you to research those topics that are of particular interest to you and find the most appropriate material to develop your knowledge of the law detailed in the chapter. Links are provided to all the websites referred to in the book to allow for easy access and reference.

Self-test questions

Test yourself with the self-test questions written for each chapter. Feedback for each question and page references to the textbook are provided to direct you back to the content.

Flashcard glossary

Flashcard glossaries offering manageable definitions of key terms and legislation are available for your ease of reference. Flashcards are available via your Internet browser or mobile device and can be easily downloaded for convenient use.

Problem and essay questions with answer guidance

Try the further problem and essay questions for each chapter to practice the technique of answering problem questions, then check the authors' answer guidance.

Bonus chapters

Three bonus chapters provide comprehensive coverage of some more specialist areas of commercial law. The topics covered are insurance law, consumer credit, and competition law.

These chapters are available free of charge to all readers of the book. To access them please follow the instructions below:

1. Go to: **www.oxfordtextbooks.co.uk/orc/baskind/**

2. Click on the 'bonus chapters' link.

3. Enter the login details opposite (case sensitive).

Username: Baskind1e
Password: CommercialLaw01

contents in brief

PART I: An introduction to commercial law

PART II: The law of agency

PART III: The law relating to the domestic sale of goods

PART IV: The law relating to the international sale of goods

PART V: Methods of payment, security, and finance

ONLINE CHAPTERS

Visit the **Online Resource Centre** that accompanies this book to access these chapters and other useful materials: www.oxfordtextbooks.co.uk/orc/baskind/

detailed contents

PART I: An introduction to commercial law

PART II: The law of agency

PART III: The law relating to the domestic sale of goods

**PART IV: The law relating to the international
sale of goods**

ONLINE CHAPTERS

(a) Aspects of consumer credit

(b) Principles of insurance law

(c) Aspects of competition law

Visit the **Online Resource Centre** that accompanies this book to access these chapters and other useful materials: www.oxfordtextbooks.co.uk/orc/baskind/

table of cases

table of legislation

*References in **bold** are fully discussed as 'Key provisions'.*

table of legislation from other jurisdictions

table of statutory instruments

table of European legislation

table of international treaties and conventions

abbreviations

The following is a list of abbreviations used in this text.

BACS	Bankers Automated Clearing Services
c&f	cost and insurance
CFR	cost and freight
CHAPS	Clearing House Automated Payment System
Cif	cost, insurance, freight
CIP	carriage and insurance paid to
CISG	United Nations Convention on Contracts for the International Sale of Goods (the Vienna Convention)
COGSA 1992	Carriage of Goods by Sea Act 1992
CPA 1987	Consumer Protection Act 1987
CPT	carriage paid to
DAF	delivered at frontier
DAP	delivered at place
DAT	delivered at terminal
DEQ	delivered ex-quay
DES	delivered ex-ship
DDP	delivered duty paid
DOU	delivered duty unpaid
DTI	Department of Trade and Industry
EC	European Community
ECJ	European Court of Justice
EEC	European Economic Community
EU	European Union
Exw	ex-works
FA 1889	Factors Act 1889
Fas	free alongside ship
FCA	free carrier
Fob	free on board
Fobs	free on board stowed
Fobst	free on board stowed and trimmed
Fobt	free on board trimmed
HPA 1964	Hire Purchase Act 1964
ICC	International Chamber of Commerce or (depending on context) Institute Cargo Clauses
LLP	limited liability partnership
SG	ships and goods
SGA 1893	Sale of Goods Act 1893
SGA 1979	Sale of Goods Act 1979
UCP	Uniform Customs and Practice
UCTA 1977	Unfair Contract Terms Act 1977
URC	Uniform Rules for Collections

PART I

An introduction to commercial law

An introduction to commercial law

- What is commercial law?
- History and development of commercial law

- Sources of commercial law

What is commercial law?

It is customary for a commercial law text to begin by posing the question 'What is commercial law?' However, perhaps a better opening question is to ask whether or not commercial law as a distinct legal topic actually exists. The following much-quoted passage from Professor Sir Roy Goode indicates that, depending on the scope of the question, the answer may in fact be no:

> Does commercial law exist? Are there unifying principles which bind the almost infinite variety of transactions in which businessmen engage, marking these off from other types of contract?...If by commercial law we mean a relatively self-contained, integrated body of principles and rules peculiar to commercial transactions, then we are constrained to say that this is not to be found in England.[1]

If no such unifying principles exist, then commercial law as a distinct topic cannot be said to exist, and it will merely amount to a 'label which is useful for gathering together diverse material with no obvious home of its own, so as to aid exposition on a lecture course or in a textbook, or for the better organisation of the business of the High Court of Justice...but no more'.[2]

The vast majority of commentators (including Goode), however, firmly believe that such unifying principles do exist (these are discussed later in this chapter) and that not only is commercial law a distinct topic, but that it is one that 'flourishes...adapting itself constantly to new business procedures, new instruments, new demands'.[3] Unfortunately, whilst there is little doubt that commercial law exists, it is much more difficult to define its parameters as, unlike other countries, the UK has not sought to establish a commercial law code. Instead our body of commercial law can be found in a collection of 'ill-assorted statutes bedded down on an amorphous mass of constantly shifting case law'.[4]

---

1. Roy Goode and Ewan McKendrick, *Goode on Commercial Law* (4th edn, Penguin 2010) 1347.
2. Len S Sealy and Richard JA Hooley, *Commercial Law: Text, Cases and Material* (4th edn, OUP 2009) 6.
3. Roy Goode and Ewan McKendrick, *Goode on Commercial Law* (4th edn, Penguin 2010) 1347.
4. ibid.

So, if commercial law does exist, then what is it? The scope of the subject has ensured that no universally accepted definition exists, but numerous definitions have been advanced, including the following:

- Goode has defined commercial law as 'that branch of law which is concerned with rights and duties arising from the supply of goods and services in the way of trade'[5] and as 'the totality of the law's response to the needs and practices of the mercantile community'.[6]

- Gutteridge states that commercial law encapsulates 'the special rules which apply to contracts for the sale of goods and to such contracts as are ancillary thereto, namely contracts for the carriage and insurance of goods and contracts the main purpose of which is to finance the carrying out of contracts of sale'.[7]

- Sealy and Hooley state that '[c]ommercial law is the law of commerce. It is concerned with commercial transactions, i.e. transactions in which both parties deal with each other in the course of business.'[8]

It is clear from these definitions that no author has sought to provide a precise and specific definition of what commercial law is, preferring instead to offer broad comments about the scope and purposes of the subject. This is both unsurprising and welcome. It is unsurprising as the sheer scope and breadth of commercial law ensures that it is not amenable to a succinct, yet exhaustive definition. It is welcome because the topic is one that must constantly evolve. As Sealy and Hooley state:

> Commercial law is a pragmatic and responsive subject which looks to facilitate the commercial practices of the business community. As those practices change and develop, often to accommodate new technology, the contents of commercial law may change and develop with them. A rigid definition of the scope of the subject would only inhibit this process.[9]

Accordingly, a precise and rigid definition of commercial law is of little aid. Perhaps what is more important is an understanding of the purposes of commercial law or, as Goode referred to them in the passage discussed previously, the 'unifying principles'.

Principles of commercial law

It has been stated that '[t]he primary function of commercial law...is to accommodate the legitimate practices and expectations of the business community in relation to their commercial dealings'.[10] This leads us to ask what the expectations of the business community are. Four principal expectations can be identified, namely (i) predictability; (ii) flexibility; (iii) party autonomy; and (iv) efficient dispute resolution.

---

5. ibid 8.   6. ibid 1347.

7. Harold C Gutteridge, 'Contract and Commercial Law' (1935) 51 LQR 91, 91.

8. Len S Sealy and Richard JA Hooley, *Commercial Law: Text, Cases and Material* (4th edn, OUP 2009) 4.

9. ibid.

10. Roy Goode, 'The Codification of Commercial Law' (1988) 14 Mon LR 135, 148.

Predictability[11]

As Lord Mansfield has stated '[i]n all mercantile transactions, the great objective should be certainty'.[12] Commercial transactions can require a significant amount of planning and it is important that business persons can engage in transactions without undue fear that those transactions will be set aside. In order for this to be the case, commercial law must exhibit several characteristics:

- The law must be clear. If a statute is drafted poorly or if the reasoning behind a legal judgment is vague, ambiguous, or misguided, then business persons will be unable to rely on it. This is even more important where a transaction is standard and is entered into many times, or where the subject matter of a transaction is of high value or unique.

- The law must be applied consistently and set aside sparingly. Whilst the law must be free to develop to deal with evolving situations, businesses must be free to transact on the basis that settled law will not be changed without due reason.

Litigation is expensive, and predictable law helps businesses organize their activities so as to avoid costly legal breaches. Should a dispute arise, predictable law helps the dispute to be resolved more speedily and cheaply. In some cases, however, applying the law in a predictable fashion may lead to an unfair result being imposed on one or more of the parties. In such a case, should fairness or predictability be the dominant consideration? Goode is firmly of the opinion that the latter consideration will usually triumph:

> in a contest between contract and equity in a commercial dispute, contract wins almost every time; and I suspect that one reason why foreigners so frequently select English law, rather than Continental law, to govern their contracts and English courts to adjudicate their disputes is that they know where they stand on the law and can rely on judges experienced in commercial transactions to give effect to their understanding.[13]

However, this does not mean that the law always favours predictability over fairness. For example, s 14(2) of the Sale of Goods Act 1979 implies a term into contracts of sale providing that goods will be of satisfactory quality. Clearly, the word 'satisfactory' is a very wide term and it may be difficult to predict whether or not a product that has some form of imperfection will be deemed unsatisfactory by the courts. However, this lack of predictability is an unfortunate, but necessary, consequence of the need for s 14(2) to be flexible and to provide a fair outcome for purchasers of goods.

Section 14(2) is discussed at p 362

Flexibility

Whilst the business community desires laws that are certain and predictable, it is also important that the law is flexible so that it can react to evolving and novel commercial practices. The problem that arises is that laws that are predictable are often

---

11. Many texts use the term 'certainty', but, as Goode correctly notes (see Roy Goode, 'The Codification of Commercial Law' (1988) 14 Mon LR 135, 150), litigation is rarely certain and so the term 'predictability' is preferable.

12. *Vallejo v Wheeler* (1774) 1 Cowp 143, 153.

13. Roy Goode, 'The Codification of Commercial Law' (1988) 14 Mon LR 135, 149.

inflexible, and laws that are flexible are often unpredictable, but the businessperson 'wishes to have his cake and eat it; to be given predictability on the one hand and flexibility to accommodate new practices and developments on the other'.[14] Striking a balance between predictability and flexibility is a difficult task and one that the courts are not always best placed to undertake.

Commercial law aims to provide flexibility in two ways. First, the law affords businesses considerable party autonomy (this is discussed in the next paragraph). Second, the courts can recognize and give effect to the customs, practices and trade usages of the business community. Custom and usage as a source of law is discussed later in this chapter.

Custom and usage as a source of commercial law is discussed at p 13

Party autonomy

Lord Devlin has stated that '[t]he function of the commercial law is to allow, so far as it can, commercial men to do business in the way they want to do it'.[15] This results in the courts giving significant weight to two legal concepts:

1. *Freedom of contract*: The parties are free to agree the terms of the contract that will govern their relationship or, to put it more simply, 'businessmen should be free to make their own law'.[16]

2. *Sanctity of contract*: As the parties are free to contract, it follows that the courts should give effect to the terms of the contract and should not be quick to invalidate contractual terms freely entered into. Accordingly, the courts will seek to uphold commercial contracts, unless the terms are overly restrictive or oppressive, in breach of statute, or if they offend principles of public policy.

By upholding the validity of contracts freely entered into by the parties, the law is made more certain, as the parties can expect their bargains to be upheld. This in turn 'facilitates the conduct of trade',[17] or as Lord Goff famously stated:

> Our only desire is to give sensible commercial effect to the transaction. We are there to help businessmen, not to hinder them: we are there to give effect to their transactions, not to frustrate them: we are there to oil the wheels of commerce, not to put a spanner in the works, or even grit in the oil.[18]

However, the law's respect for party autonomy is not absolute and, over the past forty years, Parliament has passed several notable pieces of legislation that strongly curtail freedom of contract in certain areas, with notable examples being the Consumer Credit Act 1974, the Unfair Contract Terms Act 1977, and the Unfair Terms in Consumer Contracts Regulations 1999.[19] In turn, these statutes have resulted in increased intervention from the courts in certain areas. However, as Bradgate correctly notes, these statutes tend to apply more to consumer cases and not to what he terms 'pure' commercial law cases.[20] For example, certain provisions of the Unfair Contract Terms Act 1977 do not apply to many forms of commercial contract, such

---

14. ibid 150.   15. *Kum v Wah Tat Bank Ltd* [1971] 1 Lloyd's Rep 439 (PC) 444.
16. Roy Goode, 'The Codification of Commercial Law' (1988) 14 Mon LR 135, 149.
17. *Schroeder Music Publishing Co Ltd v Macaulay* [1974] 1 WLR 1308 (HL) 1316 (Lord Diplock).
18. Lord Goff, 'Commercial Contracts and the Commercial Court' [1984] LMCLQ 382, 391.
19. SI 1999/2083.
20. Robert Bradgate, *Commercial Law* (3rd edn, OUP 2005) 6.

as (i) contracts of insurance; (ii) contracts involving the creation of patents, trade-marks, and copyrights; (iii) charterparties; and (iv) contracts involving the carriage of goods by ship or hovercraft.[21]

> **charterparty:** a written agreement whereby a person hires a ship, usually for the purpose of transporting goods

Efficient dispute resolution

A sound system of commercial law should aim to minimize the number of cases that need to go to court, and UK commercial law's availability of self-help remedies (such as the exercise of liens, or the ability to rescind contracts) can help achieve this. There will, however, always be instances when recourse to the courts is unavoidable and, in such cases, it is important that the parties have access to a system of dispute resolution that is quick and inexpensive. The law's answer is to provide a specialist court, namely the Commercial Court.

> **lien:** the right to hold the property of another until an obligation is satisfied

The Commercial Court was formally established in 1970[22] and is a separate court of the Queen's Bench Division of the High Court. It consists of around fifteen nomin-ated judges, all of whom are experts in commercial law matters and will hear cases relating to both national and international disputes. In line with the earlier discus-sion, the procedures of the Commercial Court[23] tend to be more flexible than those of the High Court generally (for example, many of the rules relating to case man-agement in the High Court do not apply to the Commercial Court). The work of the Commercial Court is often extremely complex, with around 80 per cent of its cases involving a party that derives from outside the Court's jurisdiction.[24] The reason for this is that many parties choose to resolve their disputes in the Commercial Court and, as such, it is inundated with work (which is another reason why it is granted its own flexible procedural rules).

History and development of commercial law

Origins

The origins of our system of commercial law can be found in a medieval body of laws known as the *lex mercatoria*. Throughout the Middle Ages, merchants would travel throughout Europe engaging in trade at fairs and markets. If a dispute arose, it was important that it could be resolved quickly, and in accordance with the cus-toms of the merchants themselves. The importance of this international trade[25] and the need for a body of practical rules governing trade led to the development of the

> **lex mercatoria:** 'law merchant'

---

21. Unfair Contract Terms Act 1977, Sch 1. In some cases, these contracts will be covered in relation to persons who deal as consumers.

22. Administration of Justice Act 1970, s 3(1). However, the origins of the court can be traced back to a Commercial List that was established in 1895.

23. See the Civil Procedure Rules 1998, Pt 58.

24. Judiciary of England and Wales, *Report of the Commercial Court and Admiralty Court 2005–06* (2006) 2.

25. The importance of international trade was recognized as far back as the Magna Carta 1215, with Art 41 stating that '[a]ll merchants shall have safe and secure exit from England, and entry to England, with the right to tarry there and to move about as well by land as by water, for buying and selling by the ancient and right customs'.

lex mercatoria, a body of laws that was based on those customs and practices of merchants that were common throughout Europe. Accordingly, the *lex mercatoria* was characterized by those features that were regarded as essential by merchants, namely it should be international in flavour, it should not be overly technical,[26] it should be applied based on the realities of commerce, and it should allow for the speedy resolution of disputes.

Not only were disputes resolved based upon the customs and practices of merchants, but the merchants themselves were involved in resolving the disputes. The *lex mercatoria* was applied via a series of specialist courts (such as the courts of the fairs and boroughs,[27] and the staple courts) that consisted of juries comprising equally of English and foreign merchants.[28] The *lex mercatoria* was commonly applied throughout most European countries and, by the fifteenth century, it was described as 'a law universal throughout the world'.[29] As Sealy and Hooley note:

> It was during this period that some of the most important features of modern commercial law were developed: the bill of exchange, the charterparty and the bill of lading, the concepts of assignability and negotiability, the acceptance of stoppage in transit and general average.[30]

The *lex mercatoria* and the common law

The precise relationship between the *lex mercatoria* and the common law is open to debate. Originally, the perception was that the *lex mercatoria* was a separate body of laws that developed independently of, and often differed from, the common law, but the more modern view appears to be that:

> [t]he medieval law merchant was not so much a corpus of mercantile practice or commercial law as an expeditious procedure especially adapted for the needs of men who could not tarry for the common law...Like the justice of the Chancery, it offered an exemption from, or a short circuit through, the delays of due process.[31]

The fifteenth century witnessed the beginning of a movement that would result in the abolition of the merchant courts and the incorporation of the *lex mercatoria* into the common law. By the fifteenth century, business in the merchant courts had dwindled and the majority of commercial law cases were heard in the Court of Admiralty. However, by the seventeenth century, the majority of commercial litigation would move from the Court of Admiralty to the common law courts, largely due to the work of Sir Edward Coke CJ. This was achieved by use of the action of

---

26. To avoid cases becoming overly technical, it was often the case that lawyers were not permitted in cases involving commercial law issues.

27. These courts were also knows as courts of piepowder, which derives from the French *pieds poudrés*, which means 'dusty feet', referring to the dusty feet of merchants as they travelled throughout Europe.

28. The equal rights given to foreign merchants derived from the *Carta Mercatoria* 1303, a charter granted by Edward I that provided foreign traders the right to free trade, protection of the law, and exemption from certain tolls and charges.

29. Yearbook 13 Edw IV 9 pl 5.

30. Len S Sealy and Richard JA Hooley, *Commercial Law: Text, Cases and Materials* (4th edn, OUP 2009) 14–15.

31. JH Baker, 'The Law Merchant and the Common Law' (1979) 38 CLJ 295, 301–2.

assumpsit and by partially incorporating the *lex mercatoria* into the common law. Although Coke CJ stated in 1628 that 'the lex mercatoria is part of the law of the realm',[32] it was only a partial incorporation, and the common law courts continued to apply common law principles, with occasional modifications that mirrored the *lex mercatoria*. A more complete incorporation of the *lex mercatoria* did not occur until the late seventeenth and early eighteenth centuries under Holt CJ and, in particular, Mansfield CJ. By the time he retired, Mansfield CJ had completed the task of fully incorporating the *lex mercatoria* into the common law—a task he performed so well that one commentator has stated:

> the reform which Lord Mansfield carried out…was ostensibly aimed at the simplification of commercial procedure but was, in fact, much more; its purpose was the creation of a body of substantive commercial law, logical, just, modern in character and at the same time in harmony with the principles of the common law. It was due to Lord Mansfield's genius that the harmonisation of commercial custom and the common law was carried out with an almost complete understanding of the requirements of the commercial community, and the fundamental principles of the old law and that marriage of ideas proved acceptable to both merchants and lawyers.[33]

→ *assumpsit*: a common law action that could be brought where an undertaking was breached

Codification[34]

By the nineteenth century, the *lex mercatoria* had been fully incorporated into the common law and a significant body of commercial law case law had been established. Unfortunately, this resulted in a mass of commercial law that was inaccessible and, in certain areas, lacked consistency. Accordingly, Parliament, following calls from the commercial community, decided to embark upon a programme of **codification**. Many European countries were also codifying their commercial law and, as most European countries had a civil law system, they established commercial codes that aimed to embrace all commercial law in one place. English law did not adopt an all-encompassing commercial code, but instead passed a series of Acts of Parliament, with each Act focusing on one particular area. This resulted in the passing of the Bills of Exchange Act 1882, the Factors Act 1889, the Partnership Act 1890, the Sale of Goods Act 1893, and the Marine Insurance Act 1906. It is a testament to the drafters of these Acts that all of these Acts are still in force today, with the exception of the Sale of Goods Act 1893 (which, in any case, was largely reproduced by the Sale of Goods Act 1979). That many other countries based their commercial codes on the provisions of these Acts[35] is further proof of the quality of their drafting.

→ codification: the process whereby the law is collected and restated in statute

Whilst the codification of commercial law doubtless made the law more accessible and consistent, it did have one negative side-effect. As noted, a key feature of the *lex mercatoria* was its cross-border consistency and the fact that it harmonized commercial law throughout many European countries. As countries established and

---

32. Sir Edward Coke, *The First Part of the Institutes of the Laws of England* (1628) folio 182.
33. Clive M Schmitthoff, 'International Business Law, A New Law Merchant' in RSJ Macdonald (ed), *Current Law and Social Problems* (University of Toronto Press 1961) 137.
34. For a detailed account, see Alan Rodger, 'The Codification of Commercial Law in Victorian Britain' (1992) 109 LQR 570.
35. For example, the Sale of Goods Act 1893 heavily influenced the USA's Uniform Sales Act.

amended their commercial codes and statutes, they began to focus increasingly on the commercial law issues that arose in their own countries. The result was that the harmonization of the *lex mercatoria* was lost and national laws began to diverge (although there are still areas of strong consistency).

Consumerism

The Industrial Revolution had a profound impact upon our system of commercial law. Production of consumer goods increased notably, as did the disposable income of the workforce. As trade in consumer goods increased, the provision of credit to consumers also rose sharply. These developments, along with the establishment of the welfare state post-World War II, had a notable effect on our system of commercial law. Specifically, it resulted in the courts recognizing that the traditional underpinnings of commercial law, notably the freedom and sanctity of contract discussed earlier, would not be appropriate in all cases. With the rise of consumerism, the courts could not assume that the parties to a contract were of equal bargaining power, and it was realized that weaker parties would require protection if the law were to remain just.

The result was the creation of a body of law that aimed to protect consumers. The principal common law contribution was the development of the law of negligence following *Donoghue v Stevenson*,[36] whilst Parliament passed a raft of consumer protection legislation. The past fifty years have been notable for the sheer mass of consumer legislation that has been passed, with notable examples being the Trade Descriptions Act 1968 (now largely repealed), the Fair Trading Act 1973 (also largely repealed), the Consumer Credit Act 1974, the Unfair Contract Terms Act 1977, and the Consumer Protection Act 1987. The process of consumer law protection is still going strong, as evidenced by more recent pieces of legislation, such as the Consumer Protection from Unfair Trading Regulations 2008.[37]

The result has been the recognition of consumer law as a distinct legal topic in its own right[38] (as opposed to being a form of commercial law that was applied in specific instances), but it does not follow from this that the two areas of law have developed separately. In some cases, the distinction between consumer and commercial transactions has been maintained (e.g. the Sale of Goods Act 1979 still distinguishes between consumer and non-consumer sales), but there is concern amongst many academics and businesses that consumer law is unduly influencing commercial law, which in turn has resulted in 'the steady degradation of English commercial law statutes'.[39] For example, Sealy and Hooley contend that:

> There must be some cause for concern as to how far consumer protection principles should be allowed to interfere in purely mercantile arrangements.

---

36. [1932] AC 562 (HL).   37. SI 2008/1277.

38. Although this text and its accompanying Online Resource Centre will cover certain consumer law topics (e.g. consumer credit, product liability), it will focus primarily on commercial law as it affects businesses. Students wishing to explore consumer law in more detail should consult a specialized consumer law text.

39. Michael Bridge, 'What is to be Done About Sale of Goods?' (2003) 119 LQR 173, 177.

The interventionist approach of consumer protection legislation appears to be at odds with the essential needs of the business community.[40]

International harmonization

As noted, the international nature of commercial law became eroded as the UK courts incorporated the *lex mercatoria* into national law and European countries created their own commercial law codes. However, beginning in the mid-nineteenth century, commercial law once again began to take on a more international flavour through the development of EU law and, in particular, transnational commercial law. These sources of international law are discussed later in this chapter. Here, the reasons behind the growth of transnational law and its purported benefits will be discussed.

🔗 The sources of international law are discussed at p 15

As noted, transnational commercial law originated in the mid-nineteenth century, but it was only in the latter half of the twentieth century that it actually became a reality. It arose following the realization that an 'international transaction cannot be treated the same way as a domestic one',[41] or, as Bradgate put it, 'international trade needs an international legal response'.[42] The following example demonstrates the problem.

Eg ComCorp Ltd

ComCorp Ltd enters into a contract with The Netherlands Trading Co (a company based in Amsterdam) to purchase a particular piece of machinery. Agents of the two companies sign the contract in France. A problem develops with the piece of machinery and ComCorp decides to terminate the contract and seek reimbursement of the purchase price. The Netherlands Trading Co refuses to refund the purchase price. ComCorp commences proceedings, alleging that English law governs the transaction. The Netherlands Trading Co states that Dutch law governs the transaction. Neither party is willing to allow French law to govern the contract.

Having a sound system of transnational law in place could avoid this situation arising. Indeed, increased harmonization of laws can bring about a number of potential advantages:[43]

- Divergent national laws can act as a barrier to cross-border commerce. Conversely, harmonized laws can help facilitate international trade.
- Harmonization can help fill the gaps in domestic law by providing laws in those areas where no domestic law exists.

---

40. Len S Sealy and Richard JA Hooley, *Commercial Law: Text, Cases and Materials* (4th edn, OUP 2009) 17.
41. Roy Goode, Herbert Kronke, and Ewan McKendrick, *Transnational Commercial Law: Text, Cases and Materials* (OUP 2007) 19.
42. Robert Bradgate, *Commercial Law* (3rd edn, OUP 2005) 14.
43. For a more detailed discussion of the advantages of harmonization of commercial law, see Loukas A Mistelis, 'Is Harmonization a Necessary Evil? The Future of Harmonization and New Sources of International Trade Law' in Ian F Fletcher, Loukas A Mistelis, and Marise Cremona (eds), *Foundations and Perspectives of International Trade Law* (Sweet & Maxwell 2001) 21.

- It can reduce the instances where a conflict of laws arises (as in the example given) and provide a neutral form of law with which to resolve a dispute.
- It can improve the clarity of the law by replacing a series of divergent national laws with a single set of transnational laws. This in turn can save time and expense and reduce the number of cases that are heard in the national courts (especially in those courts that are the preferred destination for 'forum shoppers').
- Transnational law can act as an impetus for domestic law reform as 'reforms can be more easily achieved once a provision has been adopted at international level'.[44]
- Transnational law is often translated into several languages, and so is more accessible than national law.

Nevertheless, the process towards harmonization of law has not been smooth and it has been resisted strongly.[45] Despite this, there exists a significant body of transnational commercial law that will be discussed later in the chapter. First, however, it is important to appreciate the domestic sources of commercial law.

Sources of commercial law

Having discussed the definition, history, and purposes of commercial law, the final part of this chapter moves on to look at the principal sources of commercial law, beginning with sources of domestic commercial law.

Contract

It has already been noted that party autonomy is a key feature of any system of commercial law. The principal means of providing parties with the autonomy they desire is by permitting them to negotiate and set the terms of the transaction themselves. It follows from this that the primary source of commercial law is the contract that exists between the parties. In essence, by agreeing the terms, obligations, and rights that will govern the transaction, that transaction is governed by law that has been largely created by the parties themselves. The role of the legal system is simply then to enforce the terms that the parties have freely entered into, or render unenforceable those terms deemed unfair or contrary to public policy.

It should, however, be noted that not all the terms of the contract will be freely and individually negotiated (largely because this would take too much time). The parties will usually negotiate certain key terms such as price and date of performance, but the remaining terms may be imposed by one party upon the other through the use of standard form contracts. In a commercial setting, this usually poses no issues and, in such cases, the courts will be reluctant to invalidate the terms of

---

44. ibid.
45. For a discussion of why harmonization has been resisted, see Roy Goode, 'Reflections on the Harmonization of Commercial Law' in Ross Cranston and Roy Goode, *Commercial and Consumer Law— National and International Dimensions* (Clarendon 1993) 24–7.

standard form contracts without good cause.[46] Conversely, where standard terms have been imposed by a business upon a consumer, then the law adopts a much more paternalistic approach.

Custom and usage

As Lord Lloyd has stated '[i]n the field of commercial law ... the custom of merchants has always been a fruitful source of law'.[47] Indeed, as has been discussed, the *lex mercatoria* was based largely on the customs of merchants. However, with the expansion of commercial law legislation (both transnational and domestic), does custom and usage still play an important role in commerce? The answer is undoubtedly yes.

The courts are responsive to the needs of commercial parties and can take into account any relevant customs or usages when interpreting commercial contracts and determining disputes. The most common way to give effect to a custom or usage is via the implication of a term into the contract, but in order for this to occur, the court will need to be satisfied that the relevant custom or usage is certain and reasonable.[48] Even if these conditions are satisfied, a term will not be implied if it would conflict with the express terms of the contract.[49] Accordingly, through careful drafting (e.g. through the inclusion in the contract of an **entire agreements clause**),[50] the parties can limit the ability of the courts to imply terms into the contract.

➡ entire agreements clause: a term of a contract which provides that the written terms provide the totality of the terms and that no further terms can be added

Domestic legislation

The process of commercial law codification that began in the nineteenth century has resulted in domestic legislation (both primary and subordinate) becoming an extremely important source of commercial law. However, the philosophy behind domestic commercial legislation has evolved over time. In the nineteenth and early twentieth centuries, Parliament, like the courts, prioritized the notions of freedom and sanctity of contract and so legislation adopted a laissez-faire approach that sought to give effect to the will of the parties involved.

Due to the influence of consumerism, much modern commercial legislation is not so liberal and adopts a strong interventionist function. There are many examples:

🔗 Consumerism is discussed at p 10

- The provision of credit to consumers is stringently regulated by the Consumer Credit Act 1974.
- Exclusion clauses and limitation clauses are strictly regulated by the Unfair Contract Terms Act 1977.
- Producers of defective goods can be held liable under the Consumer Protection Act 1987, even if they were not at fault for the defect.

---

46. Roy Goode and Ewan McKendrick, *Goode on Commercial Law* (4th edn, Penguin 2010) 12, state that certain standard form contracts are so widely used that they can be regarded as akin to 'non-parliamentary statutes'.

47. *Kleinwort Benson Ltd v Lincoln City Council* [1999] 2 AC 349 (HL) 394.

48. For a more detailed discussion of the implication of terms, see Edwin Peel, *Treitel on the Law of Contract* (13th edn, Sweet & Maxwell 2011) 222–35.

49. *Les Affréteurs Réunis Société Anonyme v Walford* [1919] AC 801 (HL).

50. See e.g. *Exxonmobil Sales and Supply Corporation v Texaco Limited (The Helene Knutsen)* [2003] EWHC 1964 (Comm), [2003] 2 Lloyd's Rep 686.

• The Unfair Terms in Consumer Contracts Regulations 1999 can render contractual terms unenforceable if they are deemed to be unfair.

Case law

The sources of law noted in the preceding pages would lack much of their force were it not for the courts. Contracts need to be upheld and enforced. Trade customs and usages need to be recognized, usually by implying terms into contracts. Legislation needs to be interpreted and applied. The courts perform all these roles and so case law forms an extremely important source of commercial law, and certain areas of the law are dominated by case law. For example, apart from the occasional piece of legislation, the law of agency is a creation of the courts and judges established virtually all the major principles of agency law. Despite this, case law as a source of commercial law is being constrained in certain areas by other sources of law. As Goode notes:

> In analysing commercial law cases, it is important constantly to bear in mind the diminishing role of the common law in defining contractual obligations and the growing impact of enacted law and of government intervention and EC directives and regulations.[51]

Equity

Lord Browne-Wilkinson once stated that 'wise judges have often warned against the wholesale importation into commercial law of equitable principles inconsistent with the certainty and speed which are essential requirements for the orderly conduct of business affairs'.[52] Lindley LJ was of the opinion that if the courts were to extend certain equitable doctrines to commercial law, then they would be 'doing infinite mischief and paralysing the trade of the country'.[53] From these statements, it is clear that, at least historically, the courts have been cautious in allowing equity to permeate too deeply into commercial law principles. For example, the courts are extremely reluctant to state that commercial parties owe fiduciary obligations towards one another on the ground that this would unduly interfere with the contract the parties have freely entered into.[54]

However, it has been argued that this caution is a thing of the past and that modern commercial law is much more willing to adopt equitable principles. As one academic has contended, 'Equity's place in the law of commerce, long resisted by commercial lawyers, can no longer be denied. What they once opposed through excessive caution, they now embrace with excessive enthusiasm.'[55] Equity's contribution to commercial law has manifested itself in several ways:

• As noted, contract is perhaps the primary source of commercial law, and equitable principles permeate the law of contract in several ways, including:

---

51. Roy Goode and Ewan McKendrick, *Goode on Commercial Law* (4th edn, Penguin 2010) 16.
52. *Westdeutsche Landesbank Girozentrale v Islington London Borough Council* [1996] AC 669 (HL) 704.
53. *Manchester Trust v Furness* [1895] 2 QB 539 (CA) 545.
54. See e.g. *Kelly v Cooper* [1993] AC 205 (PC).
55. Sir Peter Millett, 'Equity's Place in the Law of Commerce' (1998) 114 LQR 214, 214.

(i) equitable remedies such as liens, rescission, and specific performance are available in certain cases (e.g. rescission is usually available where a party has been induced into entering into a contract as a result of a misrepresentation);

(ii) the courts may be willing to provide a remedy to a party that has entered into a contract through duress, or where the bargain entered into is deemed unconscionable;

(iii) the courts may be willing to enforce certain promises via the doctrine of promissory estoppel.

- Whilst the courts may be reluctant to state that parties to a commercial contract occupy a fiduciary relationship, the courts will enforce fiduciary obligations if the parties expressly intended such obligations to arise.[56]

- Trusts are regularly used in certain areas of commercial law. For example, if a customer provides advance payment for goods or services and, before the goods or services are provided, the provider of the goods/services becomes insolvent, then the advance payments may be held on trust for the customer.[57] This is important as this will allow the customer to recover the monies advanced in priority to the other general creditors.

International commercial law

An understanding of the domestic sources of commercial law would not be complete without an understanding of the sources, and influence, of international commercial law.

European Union law

On 1 January 1973, the UK became a Member State of the European Community (or European Union as it is now known) and, in doing so, it agreed to recognize and enforce EU law.[58] This in turn has had a significant impact on English law in general, but aside from a few notable pieces of EU legislation (such as EC Directive 86/653[59] on commercial agents), the impact of the EU upon the private rights of commercial parties has been 'almost negligible'.[60] Instead, EU law in this area has focussed more on the rights of consumers, with Art 169 of the Treaty on the Functioning of the European Union providing that the Union shall 'promote the interests of consumers and ... ensure a high level of consumer protection'. Notable pieces of EU consumer legislation include:

EC Directive 86/653 is discussed at p 153

- Directive 85/374/EEC,[61] which led to the passing of Pt 1 of the Consumer Protection Act 1987;

---

56. See e.g. *Don King Productions Inc v Warren* [2000] Ch 291 (CA).

57. See e.g. *Re Kayford Ltd* [1975] 1 WLR 279 (Ch).   58. European Communities Act 1972, s 2(1).

59. Council Directive 86/653/EEC of 18 December 1986 on the coordination of the laws of the Member States relating to self-employed commercial agents [2006] OJ L382/17.

60. Roy Goode, *Commercial Law in the Next Millennium* (Sweet & Maxwell 1998) 88.

61. Council Directive 85/374/EEC of 25 July 1985 on the approximation of the laws, regulations and administrative provisions of the Member States concerning liability for defective products [1985] OJ 210/29.

- Directive 1993/13/EC,[62] which led to the passing of the Unfair Terms in Consumer Contracts Regulations 1994[63] (now repealed and replaced by the Unfair Terms in Consumer Contracts Regulations 1999);
- Directive 1999/44/EC,[64] which led to the passing of the Sale and Supply of Goods to Consumers Regulations 2002;[65]
- Directive 2005/29/EC,[66] which led to the passing of the Consumer Protection from Unfair Trading Regulations 2008;[67]
- Directive 2011/83/EU, which significantly enhances a number of consumer rights. Member States must implement this Directive by December 2013—at the time of writing, the UK has yet to implement the Directive.

International conventions and model laws

The EU is not the only international body that seeks to create, promulgate, and harmonize the law. Several other intergovernmental bodies exist, of which the two most notable are the United Nations Commission on International Trade Law (UNCITRAL)[68] and the International Institute for the Unification of Private Law (UNIDROIT).[69] The principal contribution of these bodies is the creation of international conventions and model laws.

Many of these Conventions are discussed in Part IV of the book, which focuses on international trade

A significant number of international conventions exist, with notable examples being (i) the 1980 Vienna Convention on Contracts for the International Sale of Goods; (ii) the 1983 Geneva Convention on Agency in the International Sale of Goods; (iii) the 1988 UN Convention on International Bills of Exchange and International Promissory Notes; (iv) the 1995 Convention on Independent Guarantees and Stand-By Letters of Credit, and; (v) the 2001 Convention on the Assignment of Receivables in International Trade. The important point to note regarding international conventions is that they bind no country, unless they are incorporated into domestic law by legislation. The UK was closely involved in the development of many of these conventions. It is therefore unfortunate that the UK fails to ratify many of these international conventions. For some, such as Lord Hobhouse, this is a cause for celebration, as he contends that:

> These conventions are inevitably and confessedly drafted as multi-cultural compromises between different schemes of law. Consequently they will normally have less merit than most of the individual legal systems from which they have been derived. They lack coherence and consistency. They create problems about their scope. They introduce uncertainty where no uncertainty existed

---

62. Council Directive 1993/13/EEC of 5 April 1993 on unfair terms in consumer contracts [1993] OJ L95/29.

63. SI 1994/3159.

64. Directive 1999/44/EC of 25 May 1999 on certain aspects of the sale of consumer goods and associated guarantees [1999] OJ L171/12.

65. SI 2002/3045.

66. Directive 2005/29/EC of 11 May 2005 concerning unfair business-to-consumer commercial practices in the internal market [2005] OJ L149/22.

67. SI 2008/1277.   68. For more information, see <www.uncitral.org>.

69. For more information, see <www.unidroit.org>.

before. They probably deprive the law of those very features which enable it to be an effective tool for the use of international commerce.[70]

For others, the UK's refusal to ratify is a cause for regret. For example, Goode states that '[w]e seem unable to organise our affairs so as to reap the fruits of our own arduous labours'.[71] An often-cited example is UNCITRAL's 1980 Vienna Convention on Contracts for the International Sale of Goods, which, at the time of writing, has been ratified by seventy-eight states (including the vast majority of the world's major trading states). The UK has not ratified it and is the most notable absence from the list of signatory states.

In addition to conventions, these bodies also create model laws that, as their name suggests, provides a set of laws that states can choose to adopt (in full or in part) if they so wish. An often-cited example is UNCITRAL's 1985 Model Law on International Commercial Arbitration, which significantly influenced the Arbitration Act 1996.

Mention should also be made of the International Chamber of Commerce (ICC)[72] which, unlike UNCITRAL and UNIDROIT, is not an intergovernmental body and so the uniform rules and trade terms that it creates are not aimed at governments, but are instead aimed at contracting parties. For example, the ICC's international commercial terms (or INCOTERMS as they are known) provides a set of model terms that can be used in international commercial transactions. These terms are updated regularly[73] and tend to reflect existing trade practice and the most commonly used trade terms.

⚲ INCOTERMS are discussed in detail on p 543

Transnational commercial law[74]

EU law, international conventions, model terms, and uniform trade rules constitute the formal framework of commercial law harmonization, but there are also more informal practices evolving, as the following quote indicates:

> The common practice of merchants may establish an uncodified international trade usage. The courts of one jurisdiction may decide to adopt a principle established in another or may reach the same point independently. In each case, the result is the same, the internationalization of what was at one time a purely local rule.[75]

The rules and principles that result from the combination of formal and informal harmonization efforts have been labelled as transnational commercial law, with a more precise definition of the term being '[t]hat set of private law principles and rules, from whatever source, which governs international commercial transactions and is common to legal systems generally or to a significant number of

---

70. Lord Hobhouse, 'International Conventions and Commercial Law: The Pursuit of Uniformity' (1990) 106 LQR 530, 533.

71. Roy Goode, *Commercial Law in the Next Millennium* (Sweet & Maxwell 1998) 94.

72. For more information, see <www.iccwbo.org>.

73. At the time of writing, the most recent update is INCOTERMS 2010, which constitutes the eighth update to the terms.

74. For more, see Roy Goode, Herbert Kronke, and Ewan McKendrick, *Transnational Commercial Law: Text, Cases and Materials* (OUP 2007).

75. Roy Goode and Ewan McKendrick, *Goode on Commercial Law* (4th edn, Penguin 2010) 19–20.

legal systems'.[76] With the growth of transnational commercial law, it has been argued that the historical regionalization of commercial law has been reversed and that transnational commercial law effectively constitutes a new *lex mercatoria*. Ultimately, this contention can be doubted on the ground as many of the rules and principles mentioned earlier can only be enforced if they are implemented by legislation or recognized through judicial decisions. Conversely, the *lex mercatoria* consists of a body of rules that are binding and, as Goode states, if a principle, usage, or custom requires external recognition to become binding, then 'it is not truly *lex*'.[77]

Conclusion

The chapters that follow will discuss the various specific areas of commercial law, but a full understanding of these specific areas is only possible if you appreciate the purposes of commercial law and the principles upon which commercial transactions are based. Accordingly, by discussing the aims and purposes of commercial law, you will better appreciate why these laws have come to be and whether or not they fulfil the aims discussed in this chapter.

Many commercial law transactions (especially those involving the sale of goods) concern the passing of property from one person to another. Accordingly, chapter 2 will discuss what property is and the concepts of ownership and possession.

Practice questions

1. 'Commercial law often has to balance competing aims. It is not possible to provide laws that are both certain and flexible and there is little doubt that English commercial law favours certainty over flexibility.'
   Discuss the validity of this statement.

2. 'Equity has no place in commercial law. Business persons require certainty in their dealings and the imposition of equitable principles upon commercial transactions will render the law unacceptably uncertain.'
   Do you agree with this statement? Provide reasons for your answers.

Further reading

Roy Goode, 'The Codification of Commercial Law' (1988) 14 Mon LR 135
   • Provides an excellent account of our commercial law system, focusing on whether or not UK commercial law should be codified. Also contains an excellent discussion on the purposes of an effective commercial law system.

---

76. Roy Goode, Herbert Kronke, and Ewan McKendrick, *Transnational Commercial Law: Text, Cases and Materials* (OUP 2007) 4.
77. Roy Goode, 'Rule, Practice and Pragmatism in Transnational Commercial Law' (2005) 54 ICLQ 539, 549.

Roy Goode, Herbert Kronke, and Ewan McKendrick, *Transnational Commercial Law: Text, Cases and Materials* (OUP 2007) ch 1

- Provides an account of the history and development of commercial law, focusing on the evolution and sources of transnational commercial law.

Sir Peter Millett, **'Equity's Place in the Law of Commerce'** (1998) 114 LQR 214

- Provides an excellent discussion of why and how equity has contributed to the development of commercial law.

Alan Rodger, **'The Codification of Commercial Law in Victorian Britain'** (1992) 109 LQR 570

- Provides a detailed account of the process of codification of commercial law that began in the nineteenth century.

Len S Sealy and Richard JA Hooley, *Commercial Law: Text, Cases and Materials* (4th edn, OUP 2009) ch 1

- Provides an accessible, but detailed, introduction to commercial law.

2 Personal property

- Basic concepts
- Ownership
- Possession

- Transferring possession
- Bailment
- Dealings in things in action

INTRODUCTION

This chapter is intended to provide an introduction to the concepts which underpin the law as it relates to property other than estates and interests in land. Accordingly, the chapter will focus on issues relating to property that must be appreciated in order to understand the discussion in the subsequent chapters. For example, (i) delivery and possession of goods, as well as the passing of title are discussed in Part III of this book; (ii) Chapter 25 deals with the granting of security over property; and (iii) Chapter 26 deals with business financing, which requires an understanding of the nature of business assets. Even such apparently mundane issues as the law relating to the transportation and storage of goods involve a good grasp of what the law treats as property and how it protects interests in property. Finally, agents often have possession of goods when acting on behalf of their principals and this may give rise to property issues.

That is not to say that this chapter is 'light' reading; the issues are complex and there remain numerous troublesome areas where the law is far from clear. The chapter starts by considering some basic principles by outlining the way in which English law categorizes property before moving on to consider how ownership is best thought of as a bundle of rights over something that the law recognizes as something which can be owned (i.e. property). English law recognizes only three types of proprietary claim to personal property, and the chapter then moves to consider two of these: ownership and possession.[1] After noting the key difference between personal and proprietary claims in relation to property, the nature of legal ownership, including co-ownership are discussed, along with the difference between legal and equitable ownership. The concept of possession is given a more extended treatment with focus on circumstances where ownership is separated from possession, so that the importance of possessory title to goods in English law can be appreciated.

---

1. The third proprietary interest, namely the charge, is a security interest only (i.e. it is an interest granted to a person called a 'chargee' in order to provide him with claims against the property if the owner fails to meet an obligation to the chargee—for example, paying a debt).

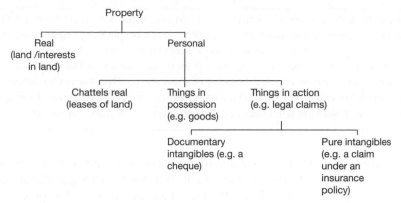

FIGURE 2.1 Types of property

The chapter ends with a brief discussion of how property which cannot be physically possessed can be transferred through assignment.

Basic concepts

Real and personal property

As Figure 2.1 demonstrates, English law draws a sharp distinction between (i) property which is land[2] or interests in land, known as 'real property'; and (ii) property which is not, known as personal property. Thus real property consists of property which the law treats as land, and personal property is simply a residual category consisting of all property which is not land. What is treated as real property extends beyond the physical structure of the land itself and includes things attached to it and to incorporeal[3] rights, such as rights of way, mortgages and charges over the land. We can see immediately that even in relation to land—that apparently most concrete of things—there exists property which cannot be touched, and indeed, as we shall see, probably the best way of understanding property, whether real or personal, is to treat it as something which the law recognizes can be owned and that ownership as simply a bundle of rights.

Eg **ComCorp Ltd**

Several years ago, Comcorp bought a piece of derelict land[4] from Victor, with the intention of building a factory upon it as soon as the cash became available. Before ComCorp completed

---

2. Or more accurately 'estates and interests' in land.
3. Literally this means something without a body—in other words something that has no three-dimensional existence. As we shall see, many things that can be owned do not have a three-dimensional existence.
4. Technically it bought a fee simple absolute estate in the land holding a tenure of free and common socage, otherwise known as 'freehold'.

> the purchase, its surveyor inspected the land and saw, inside a shed on the site, and a number of apparently dilapidated old cars, which Victor had bought many years before. Peter has land adjoining the site and decided that he would build a fence enclosing both his own and the derelict land. Peter had recognized that the old cars were in fact extremely valuable vintage vehicles, and he removed these from the site and now has them in his workshop, where he is in the process of restoring them. Comcorp has recently discovered what has happened and wishes to take physical possession of both the land and the vehicles.

However, there are substantial differences between real property and personal property, not least in relation to the remedy available for wrongful dispossession. Where a person takes possession of the land of another, then the law provides the title holder with a remedy to recover the land and eject the trespasser, along with recovering damages for any financial loss suffered. However, the position is different in relation to personal property. Assuming that a person wrongfully in possession of goods will not voluntarily surrender them, a person who has a right of immediate possession to them can sue in the **tort of conversion**. However, at common law the remedy in conversion was simply damages, leaving the wrongdoer in possession of the goods but with an obligation to pay compensation.[5]

➜ **tort of conversion:** interfering with goods in a manner inconsistent with another's right to possession

Types of personal property

As Figure 2.1 illustrates, English law divides personal property into three main categories: (i) **chattels** real; (ii) tangible property (known as 'things[6] in possession'); and (iii) intangible property (known as 'things in action'), which itself can be divided into documentary intangibles and pure intangibles. We will investigate these categories in more detail in this section.

➜ **chattel:** any tangible property other than freehold land

Chattels real (or leases of land)

Chattels real are leases of land which initially were simply regarded as personal arrangements between the landlord and tenant. By the sixteenth century (and probably before) it was established that leases of land had the characteristics of land, and consequently leases of land are the subject of works on real property and not of personal property, notwithstanding their classification as personal property.

Things in possession (or goods)

A thing in possession is a tangible object of property, that is to say a three-dimensional item which may range in size from a carbon tube with a diameter of a billionth of a metre to the ship the *Seawise Giant*, an ultra-large crude oil carrier, which, until it was scrapped, was nearly 500 metres long and weighed over 500,000 tonnes. Another word for things in possession is 'goods' or alternatively 'chattels'. In this chapter, the word 'goods' will be used, since typically elsewhere in the book, this word is used to designate things in possession.

---

5. By virtue of s 3 of the Torts (Interference with Goods) Act 1977, an award of specific recovery may be made on a discretionary basis. Normally the award is of damages, unless that provides an inadequate remedy. The right to recover land is as of right.

6. A thing (formerly known as a chose) is a legal term used to describe an asset other than land.

Things in action (or legal claims)

Things in action are intangible property, that is to say property which one cannot touch (and so cannot physically possess) and which consist of claims against another person. So, for example, a debt, a share in a company, a copyright, or a patent are all things in action, since they are all recognized in law as property but are incapable of physical possession. Nowadays,[7] things in action are typically treated as consisting of two separate sorts of property called 'documentary intangibles' and 'pure intangibles'.

Documentary intangibles are things in action where the documents with which they are associated are so identified with the underlying obligation that transfer of the document effects a transfer of the obligation. For example, in what are called 'documentary sales' of goods, the sale goods will be in the physical possession of a carrier in transit to the buyer and consequently inaccessible to either the buyer or the seller. Documents called bills of lading are used, which are regarded as documents of title to the goods identified in them, so that typically the seller has an obligation to tender a bill of lading to the buyer rather than the goods, and the buyer must meet his payment obligation by tendering the purchase price against receipt of the documents. Thus, if it is transferable (known a little misleadingly as 'negotiable'), a bill of lading can be bought and sold as if it were the goods themselves, since title to the document is recognized as title to the goods.[8]

While a bill of lading is an example (probably the only one) of a document of title to goods, the law also recognizes documents of title to the payment of money, for example cheques and other **bills of exchange**. Here, typically, the payment obligation of the acceptor to the drawer is transferred to the payee, and where the instrument is negotiable it will pass with the document to future lawful holders of the bill.[9]

Pure intangibles are simply pieces of intangible property which are not embodied in a document. Thus in our example involving a bill of exchange, we have assumed that the drawer and the acceptor have a relationship where the acceptor has a payment obligation to the drawer. That payment obligation—a debt—is a pure intangible but is capable of becoming a documentary intangible if a bill of exchange is drawn upon it. A share in a company, too, is a pure intangible, but does not become a documentary intangible even though there may be a document called a share certificate, which is issued by the company. Title to the share in the company does not generally pass on delivery of the share certificate,[10] but on entry into the share register of the company.

Ownership as a bundle of rights

When the word 'property' is used in normal language, we invariably mean to denote the thing which is owned. However, when we think about property in a legal

Documentary sales are discussed at p 487

Bills of lading are discussed further at p 484

➤ **bill of exchange:** a document signed by a person (called the 'drawer') requiring another person (called the 'acceptor') to make a payment to a third party (called the 'payee') and who is identified on the document (discussed at p 635)

---

7. Following the insightful classification of Roy Goode and Ewan McKendrick, *Goode on Commercial Law* (4th edn, Penguin 2010).

8. In fact this is only a possessory title, since the bill only embodies a right to possess the goods.

9. There are other forms of documentary intangibles. For example, title to some types of investment called 'bearer bonds' will pass with the bond document.

10. In other words, the share certificate is not a document of title.

context, we can see that this understanding of property raises two subsidiary questions, namely (i) 'what is ownership'; and (ii) 'what things can be owned'? Certainly the most influential analysis of what constitutes ownership in English law is that of Tony Honoré,[11] who argues that it is simply a collection of rights recognized by the legal system as corresponding to property rights and exercisable against a person in respect of a particular thing. Consequently, ownership simply consists of the ability to resist competing claims made by another person in respect of property by asserting your own. It is clear, therefore, that when we talk of competing claims we can see that ownership of personal property is relative and not absolute.

The concept of ownership is dealt with in more detail later in this chapter, but Honoré's understanding of ownership requires that the legal system recognizes the bundle of rights as being exercisable over something which can be owned. For example, I clearly have a range of rights in respect of my body, including, for example, the right not to be physically attacked by you; therefore, we might imagine that this bundle of rights might constitute property, yet it is not so. Traditionally in English law I do not own my own body.[12] A further example of the difficulty in determining what can be owned and what cannot is demonstrated by the Australian decision in *Victoria Park Racing and Recreation Grounds Co Ltd v Taylor*.[13] Here the owners of a racecourse sought to prevent the owners of a neighbouring piece of land that overlooked the racecourse from watching the horse races and broadcasting a radio commentary on them. By a majority of three to two, the High Court of Australia held that there could be no property rights in a spectacle because the racecourse owners had no physical means of excluding their neighbours from spectating. The minority, on the other hand, held that property rights had been infringed on the basis that the defendant had deprived the claimant of the right to commercially exploit the race meetings.[14] Whilst it would be dangerous to see this 'excludability' as being a sure way to separate 'property' from 'non-property', the importance the law places in the ability physically to exclude others from exercising control over goods can be appreciated in a number of the cases referred to in the remainder of this chapter.[15]

So what the law is prepared to treat as property is dependent not on some intrinsic character that distinguishes 'property' from 'non-property'.

---

11. Tony Honoré, 'Ownership' in AG Guest (ed), *Oxford Essays in Jurisprudence* (OUP 1961) 108. Honoré was himself heavily influenced by Hohfeld; see WN, Hohfeld, 'Some Fundamental Legal Conceptions as Applied in Judicial Reasoning' (1913) 23 Yale Law Journal 16.

12. However, the law in this area is developing. For example, whilst no one has property rights in a dead body nor in medical samples taken from a dead body (*Dobson v North Tyneside Health Authority and Newcastle Health Authority* [1997] 1 WLR 596 (CA)), property rights can be acquired in an anatomical skeleton prepared for use by medical students; and it has recently been accepted that products from a human body can be the subject of property rights (*Yearworth and Others v North Bristol NHS Trust* [2009] EWCA Civ 37, [2010] QB 1).

13. [1937] CLR 479 (High Court of Australia).

14. For a fascinating contextual insight into this case see Andrew Kenyon, Megan Richardson, and Sam Ricketson (eds), *Landmarks in Australia Intellectual Property Law* (Cambridge University Press 2009).

15. Kevin Gray, 'Property in Thin Air' (1991) 50 CLJ 252, points out that the ability to exclude others from enjoying a thing is a key factor in determining whether the thing can be the subject of property rights or not. For a further example of 'excludability' being indicative of the character of property, consider the issue of 'personality rights'; see G Scanlan and A McGee, 'Phantom Intellectual Property Rights' [2000] IPQ 264.

What types of property rights does English law recognize?

In addition to the security interest known as the 'charge', the proprietary rights recognized in respect of personal property are ownership and possession.[16] These rights are rights which are said to be *in* the asset itself, sometimes called '*jus in re*', and must be contrasted with personal rights exercisable by one person against another *over* a particular article of property because of an obligation in respect of it, a '*jus ad rem*'. Another way of putting this is to say that proprietary rights have the capability of 'going with the thing' because they are in or part of it, whilst personal rights in this context are rights as against an individual in respect of a thing. To understand this, consider the following example.

⊘ Charges and other security interests are discussed in Chapter 25 and will not be considered further in this chapter

---

Eg   ComCorp Ltd

Bastion Ltd agrees to sell 100 palettes to ComCorp. Before ownership of the palettes passes to ComCorp, CheckGoods Ltd wrongfully takes possession of the goods and refuses to supply them to ComCorp.

In such a case, ComCorp clearly has a claim in contract against Bastion for non-delivery. This is a personal right against Bastion in respect of the goods, but ComCorp does not have proprietary rights, since it does not have possession of the goods, nor is it their owner. Consequently, ComCorp does not have a right to make a proprietary claim against CheckGoods (for example, to sue CheckGoods in conversion for interference with ComCorp's right to possession).[17] However, if under the terms of the contract, ComCorp had become the owner of the goods, it would have a claim in conversion against CheckGoods,[18] as CheckGoods had interfered with ComCorp's proprietary rights.[19]

It might appear from this example that, whilst there is a difference between personal rights and proprietary rights, it does not really matter, because ComCorp did have some sort of claim against someone. However, suppose Bastion cannot be found, or suppose it is insolvent so that ComCorp's personal claim against it for breach of contract will probably not be met in full. The key characteristic of a proprietary right emerges, namely that it will survive the insolvency of a person who infringes it, whereas a merely personal claim in respect of goods will simply become a debt to be proved in the insolvency and will abate along with all the other claims of creditors who do not have proprietary rights. Consider the following example.

---

16. Roy Goode rightly points out that 'Real Rights' might be a preferable description for proprietary rights since a charge consists of rights *over* not *in* a thing. However, 'proprietary' is the commonly used name.

17. *Jarvis v Williams* [1955] 1 WLR 71 (CA) established that a mere contractual right to possession is insufficient; see Mark Simpson, Anthony Dugdale, and Michael Jones, *Clerk and Lindsel on Torts* (20th edn, Sweet & Maxwell 2010) 17–62.

18. Assuming ComCorp either had possession or an immediate right to possession of the goods.

19. *Pendragon plc v Walon Ltd* [2005] EWHC 1082 (QB).

The law on the transfer of property (ownership) in goods under the Sale of Goods Act 1979 is discussed at p 232

> ### Eg ComCorp Ltd
>
> Harvest Ltd agrees to sell 10,000 tonnes of wheat to ComCorp at $350 per tonne, with the wheat being currently loaded in an unidentified ship containing 20,000 tonnes of wheat. ComCorp pays the purchase price and under the terms of the contract and by virtue of s 20A of the Sale of Goods Act 1979, ownership of half of the cargo passes to ComCorp. Harvest Ltd becomes insolvent before ComCorp can take delivery, by which time the wheat is worth $400 per tonne.

As ComCorp has ownership of half the wheat, by virtue of s 283 of the Insolvency Act 1986, ownership of it will not vest in ComCorp's trustee in bankruptcy (though the $3.5million purchase price will). ComCorp will therefore be able to assert its proprietary right to the wheat as against Harvest and take possession of it. However, suppose Harvest became insolvent before ownership of the wheat passed to ComCorp. Ownership of the wheat will vest in Harvest's trustee in bankruptcy and ComCorp will be left with pursuing its personal claim for breach of contract along with all of Harvest's other creditors.[20]

Equities occupy the middle ground between personal rights and proprietary rights, examples being the right to rescind a contract for misrepresentation, or to have a transaction set aside for undue influence. In respect of the person making the misrepresentation or effecting the undue influence, the effect of an equity is purely personal—the contract is voidable at the instance of the innocent party, but this personal right does not 'go with the property'—so that the effect of the right to rescind will not affect a third party merely by virtue of their acquiring the relevant goods. However, if the third party acquired the goods with notice of the circumstances giving rise to the right to rescind, or was not a purchaser, then the equity will bind them also. Consequently, where the sale of goods has been induced by the tender of a dishonoured cheque, the 'rogue' will nevertheless be able to give good legal title to an honest purchaser of the goods from him, notwithstanding the fact that the seller, having discovered the misrepresentation, has avoided original contract of sale.

Having established that both ownership and possession create proprietary interests in goods, each of these concepts needs to be discussed in more detail.

Ownership

What is ownership?

Ownership is a remarkably difficult concept to define, but Honoré insists that it consists of the legal rights, being the 'standard incidents of ownership', that are left after specific rights have been granted to others.[21] Included amongst these 'standard incidents' Honoré lists the right to possess, the right to use, the right to income from the

---

20. This example is based on the facts of *Re Wait* [1927] 1Ch 606 (CA), which pre-dates s 20A of the Sale of Goods Act 1979.
21. See Tony Honoré, 'Ownership' in AG Guest (ed), *Oxford Essays in Jurisprudence* (OUP 1961) 126–8. The list of 'incidents' is at 113.

asset, and the right to transfer it. Yet, X might pass possession of some machinery to Y for ten years for Y to use in his business.[22] In this case X no longer has possession or use of the machinery, nor does he have an immediate right to possess, yet it would be correct to say that X remains the owner of it, as he still has the residual rights once we strip away those he has granted to Y. Indeed X will still be the owner, even if he does not have an indefeasible title to the goods, for example where he bought the machinery under a contract which for some reason can be rescinded.

The bundle of rights that make up 'ownership' and indeed the bundle of rights which make up 'possession' may properly be described as being interests in the object of those rights. To say that someone has an interest in goods is to denote the *sort* of rights they have over the object, for example the type of use to which they are entitled to put it and what rights they have to exclude others from exercising control over it.

Eg ComCorp Ltd

Returning to ComCorp's claim to the cars (as set out on p 21), it can now be said that in order to succeed in its claim against Peter, it would have to show that it had an *interest* in the cars which entitles it to possession. It could do this perhaps by showing that the contract of sale of the land from Victor also included a sale of the shed and its contents; that is to say, it has ownership of the cars. Since the right to possession is amongst the 'standard incidents of ownership', this is a right which ComCorp can assert against Peter.

Legal ownership of personal property is indivisible

In relation to personal property, it is not possible to create successive legal interests in the same thing. Suppose that X, the owner of a piece of machinery, leases it to Y. We have seen that X still remains the owner of it; he has simply parted with possession. Y also has an interest in the goods, not as owner, but by virtue of having possession of the machine. What X has done is to create an interest, not by carving it out of his own, but creating a new one derived from possession.[23] Consequently, in the case of the lease of goods, the lessee obtains simply a right to possess as against the lessor, which will not bind a purchaser of the machinery even with notice of the leasing contract unless the lessee is in possession of the goods.[24] In the absence of possession, the lessee is left with a personal claim in tort for damages against the purchaser for inducing a breach of contract.[25] Similarly a person can, in effect, only grant one legal

---

22. This would be a bailment, on which see later in this chapter. Leasing of goods is common.
23. The position is different in relation to land where a tenant has an estate in land which, subject to statute, will bind purchasers whether the tenant is in possession of the land or not.
24. Though see William Swadling, 'The Proprietary Effect of the Hire of Goods' in Norman Palmer and Ewan McKendrick (eds), *Interests in Goods* (2nd edn, Informa Law 1998), who argues that the lessee has no proprietary rights.
25. But see Roy Goode and Ewan McKendrick, *Goode on Commercial Law* (4th edn, Penguin 2010) 38, who argue that the lessee could alternatively formulate a claim in conversion, providing a possible remedy to recover the goods.

mortgage over goods, since a legal mortgage requires a transfer of legal title from mortgagor to mortgagee.[26]

Co-ownership of goods

A key issue with ownership of goods is that it is dependent on the ability to identify the goods owned. Consequently, for example, ownership of unidentified goods cannot pass under a sale of goods from the seller to the buyer. Similarly, where goods belonging to two different owners are mixed so that neither can distinguish his goods from the other's, then *prima facie* neither has ownership of the goods; neither can point to an item and claim, say, the right to possess it. This can be illustrated by considering the following case.

Indian Oil Corporation Ltd v Greenstone Shipping SA (Panama) (The Ypatianna) [1988] QB 345 (QB)

FACTS: Oil belonging to the claimant was pumped into a ship to be carried to India from Russia. It was mixed in the ship with oil belonging to the carrier, so that it could not be said which oil belonged to whom. The claimant argued that it was therefore entitled to all of the oil, as the carrier could not identify his oil so as to claim possession of it.[27]

HELD: Where goods become mixed so that they become indistinguishable from one another, the only sensible rule, at least where the person who mixed the goods was not motivated by fraud, was that the owners of the goods making up the mixture become co-owners in common of the mixture in proportion to their contributions to it.[28]

★ See Peter Stein, 'Roman Law in the Commercial Court' (1987) 46 CLJ 369

Co-ownership exists where two (or more) people contemporaneously have the right to possess the whole of some goods so that, by virtue of that relationship, neither can exclude possession of the other(s). Thus in *The Ypatianna* both the claimant and the carrier owned all of the oil and so collectively had a claim to it and individually were entitled to a share of the whole. Thus, since in co-ownership neither co-owner can exclude the possession of the other, a co-owner who destroys any part of the asset which they collectively own without the consent of all commits a tort.[29]

Two forms of co-ownership exist, namely ownership in common and joint ownership, and either can exist at law or in equity in relation to goods.[30] As we have seen

---

26. Of course, if possession of the goods was held by a person with possessory title, then both he and the owner could grant legal mortgages.

27. In reality a rather illogical claim since it, too, was in the same position, and in fact the carrier had possession of the mixture so that the claimant would have needed to have identified its goods in order to claim them from the carrier.

28. See also *Spence v Union Marine Insurance Co* (1868) LR 3 CP 427. The situation will be different where the separate goods of the parties have never been identifiable—see, for example, *Re London Wine (Shippers) Ltd* [1986] PCC 21 (QB).

29. Torts (Interference with Goods) Act 1977, s 10(1)(a).

30. Though probably there can be no legal ownership in common of things in action and a legal tenancy in common in land cannot be created after 1925 by virtue of the Law of Property Act 1925, s 34(1).

in ownership in common, each co-owner owns a share of the whole which as yet has not been divided (for this reason, ownership in common is often called 'ownership in undivided shares'). In joint ownership the co-owners also have collective ownership of the whole, but individually they own nothing. As a result, if a joint owner dies his interest ends and the whole of the asset falls into the hands of the survivor (this is known as 'the right of survivorship'). A joint owner may convert his collective ownership into ownership in common by giving notice of severance to the other, and any attempt by him to sell either the whole or any part of the asset will be treated as severance and operate only on his undivided share.[31]

Whether a state of co-ownership exists is normally dependent on the intention of the co-owners, but in cases like *Re Stapylton Fletcher*,[32] where a number of purchasers' cases of wine were stored together, but segregated from the seller's trading stock, and *Mercer v Craven Grain Storage Ltd*,[33] where farmers' grain became part of a fluctuating bulk, the courts were prepared to find a state of co-ownership so that ownership (and, in the case of *Mercer* at least, possession) was not lost by virtue of the inability of the owners to identify their own specific goods. However, in the case of a pre-paying buyer of goods held in bulk, it is only if the parties agree to the contrary that such a buyer does not become a co-owner by virtue of s 20A of the Sale of Goods Act 1979.[34]

Sections 20A and 20B of the Sale of Goods Act 1979 are discussed at p 253

Legal and equitable ownership

Prior to 1875 England had two parallel systems of law, one developed in the Court of Chancery (known as 'equity') and the other developed in the courts of common law. The administration of the two systems was combined in 1875, but the rules developed by each have, in the main, remained distinct.

The approach of the Court of Chancery to personal property differed in a number of ways from that of the Common Law Courts. First, it recognized trusts, so that where *A* transferred an asset to *X* to hold on trust for *B*, *B* was regarded as having proprietary rights (an equitable interest) as a beneficiary, though *X* still had legal title as a 'trustee'. Any variety of rights could exist under trusts, so that it was (and is) possible to have life, determinable, and other interests in assets held in trust. At common law, while similar results to life tenancies and so forth could sometimes be achieved, it was only by virtue of creating two titles, one deriving from ownership, the other from possession. The fact that it is possible for property to be owned at law by one person, but in equity by another, raises the question whether a person with an equitable proprietary right to possession which is recognized only as a contractual right at law can maintain an action in conversion. In *International Factors Ltd v Rodriguez*,[35] the Court of Appeal seemed to suggest that they could. Here a company agreed to

---

31. So far as possible, the common law avoided finding joint ownership in commercial situations, primarily because it is unlikely that the co-owners intended to be in effect gambling on who would die first. It might well be different in a family situation.

32. [1994] 1 WLR 1181 (Ch).

33. [1994] CLC 328 (HL), discussed further later in this chapter.

34. Section 20B makes provision for ensuring co-owners in such circumstances can withdraw their aliquot share without a potential tort claim from the other co-owners.

35. [1979] QB 351 (CA).

hold all cheques it received from customers on trust for the person to whom it had assigned debts owing to it by those customers. One of its directors was held liable in conversion when he paid some cheques into the company's bank account, since the assignee's title under the trust coupled with the right to immediate possession was sufficient. This analysis seems doubtful,[36] and Clerk and Lindsell treat this as a case where the assignee had possession through the agency of the company.[37] Similarly, the Court of Appeal in *MCC Proceeds Inc v Lehman Brothers International (Europe)*[38] held that a beneficiary under a trust could not sue a third party for conversion of bearer shares: the claim for the tort of conversion lay only with the legal owner, the trustee. Hobhouse LJ explained that the reason why a claim by a beneficiary must fail 'is not a quirk of history…Equitable rights are of a different character' from legal rights.[39]

Second, equity would treat an agreement to transfer an asset for value as equivalent to actually transferring it, once the consideration was paid, though with the one exception—sales of goods.[40] Thus by virtue of the maxim 'Equity looks on as done those things that ought to have been done', a specifically enforceable agreement to transfer a thing in action resulted in equitable title vesting in the intended transferee, though legal title remained in the intended transferor. Similarly, a contract to create a mortgage became an equitable mortgage, though it should be noted that equitable titles to interests may be defeated by the intervention of a bona fide purchaser of a legal interest in the asset.[41]

Possession

While English law has 'never worked out a completely logical and exhaustive definition of possession',[42] nevertheless it is clear that it requires two elements: (i) the exercise of control over the object, known as de facto possession; and (ii) an intention to possess the object, known as (amongst other things) *animus possidendi*. It is worth noting at the outset that possession is only possible in relation to tangible objects, so that what follows cannot apply to things in action.

➡ *animus possidendi:* 'the intention of possessing'

The exercise of control

Clearly it is quite possible to exercise control over goods without physically holding them in one's hands. If this were not so, then one could never possess a car, let alone an aircraft or a ship. What is required for possession to exist is the ability to control the access of others to the item. Thus, physical possession of a key to a warehouse

36. See *The Future Express* [1993] 2 Lloyd's Rep 542 (CA).
37. Mark Simpson, Anthony Dugdale, and Michael Jones, *Clerk and Lindsell on Torts* (20th edn, Sweet & Maxwell 2010) [17–62].
38. [1998] 4 All ER 675 (CA)
39. ibid 701. Though the Court of Appeal found no difficulty in allowing a claim in negligence by a beneficiary under a trust in *Shell UK Ltd v Total UK Ltd* [2010] EWCA Civ 180, [2011] 1 QB 86.
40. See *Re Wait* [1927] 1 Ch 606 (CA).
41. For more see Roy Goode 'Ownership and Obligations in Commercial Transactions' [1987] LQR 433.
42. *Dollfus Mieg et Cie SA v Bank of England* [1952] AC 582 (HL) 605 (Earl Jowett). See D Harris, 'The Concept of Possession in English Law' in AG Guest (ed), *Oxford Essays in Jurisprudence* (OUP 1963).

where goods are stored is treated as a form of possession, though clearly in this case possession is more symbolic than actual. The degree of control required will vary according to the nature of the goods, as the following case demonstrates.

 The Tubantia (No 2) [1924] P 78 (CA)

FACTS: A ship sank in over 100 feet of water and expert evidence was given that salvaging such a vessel would be very difficult. Major Sippe had marked the position of the wreck with buoys and lines and sent down divers to recover some of the cargo. Due to bad weather, they had to suspend diving operations and spent only around twenty-five days during the course of a year using divers on the wreck. Also, because of the depth the divers could only spend two hours per working day in the ship.

HELD: Major Sippe had possession of the wreck, bearing in mind its character.

COMMENT: The key to understanding this case, and indeed the whole idea of the mental element in possession is that Major Sippe was exercising as much control over the wreck as the circumstances would allow, and was also physically able to prevent the competitors from exercising control.

The Tubantia (No 2) also illustrates an important point, namely that once control has been exercised over goods along with the necessary intention to possess, the law resists arguments that possession has been abandoned without clear evidence of such an intent, primarily in order to avoid legitimizing a 'free-for-all' scramble for property.[43] A further demonstration of this point is provided by Pollock and Wright,[44] who insist that even where a careless banker leaves his doors and windows open, he still remains in possession of the cash and securities until the property is actually taken by a thief, notwithstanding the fact that this is the inevitable consequence of his action.[45]

The intention to possess

The intention to possess consists primarily of an intention to exclude others from possession, and this is a matter of fact, but it is important to note that this does not necessarily amount to an intention to own. Take, for example, the person who finds a valuable object, which he takes home and keeps safely. Clearly this person recognizes that he does not own the object, but, equally clearly, he intends to exclude others from exercising control over it, even though he recognizes that were the owner to assert rights over the property, he could not lawfully resist them, and indeed he may even take steps to find the owner. Nevertheless, he still has an intention to possess.

---

43. For an example of a case of such a free-for-all, see *Young v Hitchens* (1844) 6 QB 606, where on the facts the court held that a trawlerman was not in sufficient control of a shoal of fish in order to obtain possession until the net was completely closed around them.
44. Frederick Pollock and Robert Wright, *An Essay on Possession in the Common Law* (OUP 1888) [15]. Available at <http://free-law-books.troy.rollo.name/possession.pdf>.
45. Note, were the law to have been otherwise, the thief would not have committed larceny.

Even if he hands the item to the occupier of the area in which he found it, on the basis he should have it back if no one claims it, he still has an intention to possess.[46]

There are some instances where a person is said to have control over an object, but not possession of it, and this is typically explained because of the lack of the necessary intent to possess. Thus an employee may have control over his employer's goods, but so far as the law is concerned, possession is still in the employer. Similarly, a guest in a hotel or in the house of a friend may have control over the hotelier's/friend's goods in his room, but nevertheless is not legally in possession of them. In such cases, the employee/guest is said to have 'custody', but by virtue of the lack of the necessary intent does not have possession. Bridge[47] suggests that this analysis became necessary in order to prevent wrongdoers from avoiding convictions for larceny,[48] which required an unlawful deprivation of possession. If an employee had been held to have been in lawful possession of his employer's goods, his subsequent appropriation of them, for his own benefit, would not have amounted to larceny. Now under s 1 of the Theft Act 1968, the distinction between custody and possession is irrelevant for the purposes of the criminal law, but the distinction remains so far as the law of personal property is concerned. Thus, a hotel guest with custody of a bathrobe may be liable under the tort of conversion if he packs it in his suitcase.

Two illustrations of possession as a proprietary interest

Possession is a proprietary right, and thus is stronger than a personal right to call for delivery. A person with possession has a title to and interest in the goods. This, perhaps, can be illustrated by reference to two cases.

 Wilson v Lombank Ltd [1963] 1 WLR 1294

FACTS: Wilson bought a car from a person who turned out to be a rogue, and took it to a garage for repairs. After the repairs were completed, the car was left on the forecourt of the garage, but before Wilson could collect it, the garage permitted Lombank Ltd to remove the car. The car had been stolen and Lombank honestly believed that it owned the car. Subsequently, Lombank discovered that it did not own the car and so it delivered it to the true owner. Wilson sued Lombank for *trespass to goods*. Trespass to goods requires the claimant to have had possession of the goods and that the defendant interfered with that possession, so the issue was did Wilson have possession of the car?

HELD: When Wilson left the car with the garage, he still retained possession of the car, since the garage was holding it to his order at all times.[49] Consequently, Lombank was liable in trespass to Wilson for the full value of the car, together with the cost of the repairs.

➡ **trespass to goods:** Any direct physical interference with goods that are in the possession of another person, without the consent of the person in possession, unless there is lawful justification for the interference

---

46. *Parker v British Airways Board* [1982] QB 1004 (CA).
47. Michael Bridge, *Personal Property Law* (3rd edn, Clarendon Press 2002) 20–1.
48. Note that the crime of larceny has now been largely replaced by the crime of theft and theft-related offences under the Theft Act 1968.
49. Note that the garage did not have a lien on the car, since Wilson had a monthly credit account with it.

> **COMMENT:** This case illustrates two important points. First, Wilson was able to protect his right to possession against Lombank, even though there was someone who had a better title to the car than him. This reminds us that property rights are simply relative and a title which is less than absolute is still protected by the law. Second, the law may treat a person as being in possession even where the goods are physically controlled by someone else. In this case, Wilson had what is called 'constructive possession', something to which we shall return shortly (see p 37).

In *Wilson*, the person claiming to enforce his rights in relation to the property was entirely innocent. The same cannot be said for the claimant in the next case, but nevertheless the law protected his right to possession even though the goods had been stolen.

Costello v Chief Constable of Derbyshire [2001] EWCA Civ 381

FACTS: Derbyshire Constabulary seized a car that was in the possession of Costello. The police believed that the car was stolen and had evidence indicating that Costello actually knew that the car was stolen. The police were unable to locate the car's true owner, but refused to return the car to Costello. Costello commenced proceedings against the police force.

HELD: Although Costello knew that the car had been stolen, it was held that his rights as a person with possessory title were entitled to legal protection, even though that title had not been obtained by legal means, and that consequently the car must be returned to him after the police had completed their enquiries.

COMMENT: It is worth noting that the Court of Appeal did not believe that public policy grounds were sufficient to remove that protection, and that it would not have mattered if Wilson had stolen the car.

⭐ See Joshua Getzler, 'Unclean Hands and the Doctrine of Jus Tertii' (2001) 117 LQR 565

It is, however, important to note that in both of these cases the possessory title is fragile. In both *Costello* and *Wilson*, s 8 of the Torts (Interference with Goods) Act 1977 would have altered the situation had the defendant been able to identify a person with a better title, for example the true owner. Additionally, in *Wilson*, had the garage refused to return the car to Wilson before releasing it to Lombank, then Wilson would have had neither possession nor ownership when Lombank took the car and could not have sustained an action in negligence, conversion, or trespass against it.[50]

---

50. This is assuming that the case involved constructive possession, on which see p 37.

ComCorp Ltd

The previous ComCorp example (see p 21) illustrates how possessory title might assist ComCorp Ltd. Suppose that ComCorp did not acquire ownership of the cars along with title to the land from Victor. If ComCorp could show it had possession of the cars before Peter took them, then CompCorp would have a prior possessory title to them, so that as against Peter it has an immediate right to possess the goods. Consequently, ComCorp could protect this right by bringing an action for conversion against Peter. If, however, we suppose that ComCorp never had possession or ownership of the cars, then it has no claim, even though Peter had wrongfully taken the cars from the shed. In these circumstances only Victor (presumably the owner) has title to an interest which can successfully compete with Peter's possessory title.

Transferring possession

➡ transferee: a person to whom something is transferred

The most obvious way of transferring possession of goods is to physically hand them to the **transferee.** However, in some instances this is impossible or impractical, either because of the size of the object or its location. Similarly, in a contract of sale, it might be expedient that delivery of the goods takes place long before the buyer obtains physical possession. However, even if there is no physical delivery, the law provides mechanisms for what is called constructive and symbolic delivery. Thus transfer of possession can be effected symbolically, for example by passing over a key to a warehouse or perhaps transferring possession of a document of title,[51] while

🔗 Sale of Goods Act 1979, s 32(1) is discussed at p 234

s 32(1) of the Sale of Goods Act 1979 provides that delivery to a buyer's carrier effects delivery of possession.

However, a commercially important way in which possession of goods can be passed occurs when a third party who has physical possession of the goods on behalf of the transferor undertakes to hold them for another person. This process is called attornment and we will consider this in more detail later; but before this, it is important that we discuss the concept of bailment.

Bailment

What is bailment?

Bailment is a relationship under which a person (known as the bailor) transfers possession of goods to another person (known as the bailee). If you lend goods to a friend, you have both entered into a relationship of bailment, with you as the bailor and your friend as the bailee. Leaving goods with someone to be repaired is another example of a relationship of bailment. A typical commercial example is where a person, having agreed to sell and deliver goods to the buyer's premises, uses a carrier to

---

51. Possession of a document of title to goods is sometimes called 'constructive possession', though probably symbolic possession might be a preferable description.

transport them to the buyer. In this case, the seller is the bailor, the carrier the bailee. Other examples would include cases where possession of goods is transferred to the owner of a warehouse for safekeeping, or where the owner of a photocopier leases it to a business, while hire purchase also involves bailment. The essence of bailment is the transfer of possession where the bailee acquires only a limited possessory interest in the goods such that he must either redeliver the goods to, or effect delivery as instructed by, the bailor, though in cases such as leasing of goods, such obligations may be long postponed.

Whether possession has been transferred is always a matter of fact, depending on the degree of control transferred, as demonstrated by the following case.

 Ashby v Tolhurst [1937] 2 KB 242 (CA)

FACTS: The claimant parked his car in a car park operated by the defendant. An employee of the defendant allowed a thief to take the claimant's car, even though the thief could not produce a parking ticket and did not have the key to the car. Whether the defendant was liable for breach of contract depended upon whether the car had been bailed to the defendant.

HELD: The Court of Appeal held that possession of the car had not passed to the defendant; the relationship between them was therefore not that of bailor and bailee but of licensee and licensor.

COMMENT: Compare this case to *Mendelssohn v Normand Ltd.*[52] In *Mendelssohn*, the motorist handed the key of the car to the employee of the operator of the car park. The Court held that there was a bailment, since possession of the keys of the car gave control of the vehicle to the car park operator.

The need for the bailee to have only a limited possessory interest does not mean that a bailee cannot have rights to retain the chattel even as against the bailor. For example, where the goods are leased to the bailee or where, as is typical in cases of contracts of carriage of goods, warehousing, or for repair, the bailee retains a lien in respect of his charges. However, until the decision of the House of Lords in *Mercer v Craven Grain Storage Ltd,*[53] it was believed that for a bailment to exist, the bailee's duty of delivery had to relate to the chattel which had been bailed to him. In *Mercer*, a number of farmers deposited their grain in a grain store operated by the defendant. There was no segregation of each farmer's grain and the operator's duty was simply to return grain of equivalent weight and description from the fluctuating mass, yet the House of Lords held that the operator could be a bailee in these circumstances.[54]

---

52. [1970] 1 QB 177 (CA).   53. [1994] CLC 328 (HL).
54. This may be explained by treating the farmers as being co-owners in undivided shares of the mass, so that it was in their collective constructive possession while each owned a share in the whole. See Roy Goode and Ewan McKendrick, *Goode on Commercial Law* (4th edn, Penguin 2010) 241.

Bailee's duties to the bailor

Except as outlined later in this paragraph, a bailee owes the bailor a duty to take reasonable care of the chattel. Traditionally a distinction has been drawn between gratuitous bailments and bailments for reward, with a liability in the former case only lying for what was termed 'gross negligence'. However, in *Houghland v RR Low (Luxury Coaches) Ltd*,[55] the Court of Appeal rejected this approach and imposed in effect the common duty of care, though clearly it may be that what is reasonable in relation to a gratuitous bailment may not be reasonable where the bailee is being rewarded for his services. That said, the position is not entirely clear.[56] Once the bailor has shown that the bailee had possession of the chattel, it will be for the bailee to show he was not negligent if he cannot deliver up the goods[57] and presumably if they are damaged in his keeping. However, where the bailee is a 'common carrier'—that is a person who advertises to the public that he carries goods for a fee—strict liability is imposed, subject only to loss caused by a limited number of perils.

The same is true where there is a 'deviation' from the conduct of the bailment so that, for example, it has been held there is an absolute liability for mis-delivery by a bailee other than in the case of an **involuntary bailment**.[58] For example, in *Devereux v Barclay*,[59] a warehouseman was held liable for failure to deliver up barrels of oil to a purchaser, even though he had innocently delivered them to a third party who had bought apparently identical barrels of oil but of an inferior quality from the same vendor, who had also entrusted them to the defendant for safekeeping.

Typically, in a contractual bailment, the bailee will seek to limit liability. This ability is subject to restrictions both by statute and at common law. Thus deviation from the terms of the bailment, for example by not storing the chattel in accordance with the contractual agreement, where a carrier unreasonably deviates from an agreed route, or where there is an unauthorized sub-bailment, may result in the bailee losing the benefit of any contractual limitation clause, as the following case demonstrates.

➡ involuntary bailment: occurs when a person accidentally, leaves personal property in another's possession, for example, a vendor of a house leaving goods behind when he vacates it

---

 Gibaud v Great Eastern Rly Co [1921] 2 KB 426 (CA)

FACTS: Gibaud deposited his bicycle for safekeeping with the Great Eastern Railway Co at one of its stations. The company promised to store the bike in a cloakroom, but in fact left it in an area open to the general public, from where it was stolen. The contract contained a clause which stated that 'The company will not be in any way responsible in respect of any article deposited the value whereof exceeds £5 …' unless the passenger paid a higher fee. Gibaud commenced proceedings against the company.

---

55. [1962] 1 QB 694 (CA).
56. On this see A Bell, 'The Place of Bailment in the Modern Law of Obligations' in Norman Palmer and Ewan McKendrick (eds), *Interests in Goods* (2nd edn, Informa Law 1998). See also *Port Swettenham Authority v TG Wu & Co Sdn Bhd* [1979] AC 580 (PC).
57. *Houghland v RR Low (Luxury Coaches) Ltd* [1962] 1 QB 694 (CA).
58. *MB Pyramid Sound NV v Briese Schiffahrts GmbH & Co KG MS Sina, (The Ines) (No 2)* [1995] 2 Lloyd's Rep 144 (QB) 153.
59. (1819) 106 ER 521.

> **HELD:** The company could not rely on the exclusion clause but had committed no breach of the contract of bailment. It would have been different had the company agreed to store the bicycle in the cloakroom. As Scrutton LJ stated:
>
> > If you undertake to do a thing in a certain way, or to keep a thing in a certain place, with certain condition protecting it, and have broken the contract by not doing the thing contracted for, or not keeping the article in the place where you have contracted to keep it, you cannot rely on the conditions which were only intended to protect you if you carried out the contract in the way in which you had contracted to do it.[60]
>
> **COMMENT:** This observation by Scrutton LJ was recently applied in the High Court,[61] but to the extent that it suggests that failure to store goods as agreed automatically renders exclusion clauses void, it must be taken with caution. It was established in *Photo Production Ltd v Securicor Transport Ltd*[62] that it is a matter of construction of the relevant clause whether it covers the breach in question. However, drafting a clause which is intended to absolve a party from liability for carrying out his duties in a totally different way from that contracted for may prove difficult. See, for example, *Sze Hai Tong Bank Ltd v Rambler Cycle Co Ltd*,[63] a case of mis-delivery.[64] Perhaps a solution would be for the clause to ensure that improper storage or mis-delivery was not a breach of contract.[65]

Statute has also intervened to limit the capability of a bailee to limit his liability, particularly under the Carriage of Goods By Sea Act 1971, the Unfair Contract Terms Act 1977, and, where the bailor is a consumer, the Unfair Terms in Consumer Contracts Regulations 1999.

🔗 The Carriage of Goods By Sea Act 1971 is considered at p 558

Constructive possession

While a bailee remains in physical possession of a chattel and asserts no right of his own to retain it as against the bailor, the bailor is said to have 'constructive possession' by virtue of this bailment at will. In such circumstances, a bailor who is not himself the owner not only acquires a right to sue in negligence,[66] he also has a proprietary interest based on possession. Consequently, if a warehouseman becomes bankrupt, the bailor does not have to rely on his *personal* claim in contract against the warehouseman, which will become a money claim in the insolvency, but, on paying any claims in respect of which the warehouse may have a lien, he comes into constructive possession, which proprietary right is good as against the liquidator or trustee in bankruptcy.[67] However, if a bailee at will asserts rights as against the bailor

---

60. [1921] 2 KB 426 (CA) 435.
61. *Future Publishing Ltd v Edge Interactive Media Inc and Others* [2011] EWHC 1489 (Ch), [2011] ETMR 50.
62. [1980] AC 827 (HL).   63. [1959] 3 All ER 182 (PC).
64. See also Andrew Bell, *Modern Law of Personal Property in England and Ireland* (Butterworths 1989) 115–19.
65. See Rix J in *Motis Exports v Dampskibsselskabet AF* [1999] 1 Lloyd's Rep 837 (QB) 847.
66. *Leigh & Sillivan Ltd v Aliakmon Shipping Co Ltd, The Aliakmon* [1986] AC 785 (HL). Even if he is not in constructive possession of the goods, a bailor with a proprietary right to immediate possession has an action in conversion.
67. See Simon Mills (ed), *Goode on Property Rights in Insolvency and Sales* (3rd edn, Sweet & Maxwell 2009) 13–14.

(for example, he attempts an unauthorized sale of the asset), then constructive possession ends.

Attornment

⚭ In relation to the sale of goods, attornment is discussed at p 323

Attornment is a process whereby constructive possession can be passed from one person to another. A typical example occurs where a seller of goods which are in the possession of a third party effects delivery of them to the buyer by instructing the third party to hold them to the buyer's order. However, as established in the case of *Godts v Rose*,[68] the complete assent of all three parties in such a situation is necessary for the attornment and for constructive possession to pass. Attornment also effects a momentary transfer of possession to the purchaser/lessor in **sale and lease back** arrangements.[69]

➜ **sale and lease back:** the owner of goods sells them to a finance company but does not lose physical possession. In order to effect delivery the seller attorns that the chattel is now held to the order of the purchaser. The purchaser immediately leases the chattel back to the seller.

> ### 🔨 Godts v Rose (1855) 17 CB 229
>
> **FACTS:** Godts agreed to sell five tonnes of rape oil to Rose. The oil was stored in a warehouse and Godts sent an order to the warehouseman to hold the oil to the order of Rose. The warehouseman made out an order to this effect and gave it to Godts, who in turn tendered it to Rose in return for payment. Rose refused to pay, but wrongfully took possession of the order. Godts immediately instructed the warehouseman not to deliver the oil to Rose but the warehouseman did so. Godts sued Rose for interference with his (Godts') possession of the goods.
>
> **HELD:** The warehouseman, as attornor, had to give his undertaking to Rose as attornee on the instructions of Godts and Rose had to accept it. On the facts it was clear to Rose that when he took possession of the order, Godts did not consent to the attornor giving the undertaking.
>
> **COMMENT:** The court concluded that under the terms of the contract of sale, ownership of the goods would pass only once Godts had been paid. Perhaps it would not have mattered if *ownership* had passed, since the action which was a predecessor of conversion depended on interference with possession and, like conversion, could be maintained by a person with possessory title only.

Godts v Rose concerned the sale of unidentified goods out of bulk, since the seller had more than five tonnes of rape oil stored in the warehouse. It now seems clear that, in order to transfer constructive possession, the attornment must relate to specific goods and that where the goods are in bulk, the effect of a purported attornment is simply to give the 'attornee' a personal claim against the 'attornor'.[70] The effect

➜ **estop:** to deny the assertion of a right

of the purported attornment is to **estop** the 'attornor' from denying that he holds

---

68. (1855) 17 CB 229.   69. *Michael Gerson (Leasing) Ltd v Wilkinson* [2001] QB 514 (CA).
70. This situation has been labelled 'quasi attornment'; see Simon Mills (ed), *Goode on Property Rights in Insolvency and Sales* (3rd edn, Sweet & Maxwell 2009) 290 and Appendix.

property of that description for the order of the 'attornee',[71] but it does not give the 'attornee' proprietary rights in the goods which can be asserted in an insolvency.[72] It is unclear whether s 20A of the Sale of Goods Act 1979 affects this analysis where a bailee for a seller attorns in favour of a pre-paying buyer having an interest in common in the bulk, though the better view perhaps is that it does.[73]

✐ Section 20A of the Sale of Goods Act 1979 is discussed at p 253

Bailees, bailors, and third parties

On taking possession, the bailee obtains a possessory interest in the chattel, which is protected against interference by third parties. In *The Winkfield*,[74] a ship, the *Winkfield*, collided with another ship which was carrying mail, and some of the mail was lost. The case proceeded on the basis that the Postmaster General was the bailee of the letters and he successfully brought an action against the *Winkfield* in the tort of conversion for the full market value of the mail, even though he had no liability to the bailors for the loss.

By virtue of the decision in *The Winkfield*, although a successful claim by either bailor or bailee bars a claim by the other (as discussed later), circumstances can arise where a wrongdoer may potentially be faced with actions from two or more persons whose aggregate claims far exceed the value of the goods, for example where a finder of goods with possessory title and the owner each brings an action in conversion. This situation has been addressed by statute, and ss 7 and 8 of the Torts (Interference with Goods) Act 1977 now allow the wrongdoer to join all claimants into one action so that they can recover according to their actual loss. If the actions are not joined, s 7(3) imposes a duty on a claimant with possessory title to 'account over' to the other potential claimant 'to such extent as shall avoid double liability'. This seems partially to adopt the position at common law, as in *The Winkfield* the Court of Appeal held that the bailee must account to the bailors for the damages received over and above his own loss. It should be noted that account is a personal remedy—though it has been suggested that the successful claimant must hold any surplus on trust, which provides the bailor with a proprietary claim in the fund.[75] Finally, s 8 now permits a plea of *jus tertii*, so that, for example, a wrongdoer who is sued by a person with possessory title only (for example, a person in possession of stolen goods) can set up the superior title of the owner as a defence. However, it seems that he can do this only if the owner is joined as a party.[76]

➡ jus tertii: 'the right of a third person'

71. Rather surprisingly, this estopell does not require detrimental reliance: see *Maynegrain Ltd v Campafina Bank* [1982] 2 NSWLR 141 (NSWCA). Norman Palmer, *Bailment* (3rd edn, Sweet & Maxwell 2007) 16.80, note 9.

72. *Re London Wine (Shippers) Ltd* [1986] PCC 121 (QB). See also *Re Goldcorp Exchange* [1995] 1 AC 74 (PC).

73. For differing views see Len S Sealy and Richard JA Hooley, *Commercial Law Text Cases and Materials* (4th edn, OUP 2009) 75; Roy Goode and Ewan McKendrick, *Goode on Commercial Law* (4th edn, Penguin 2010) 290; Louise Gullifer 'Constructive Possession after the Sale of Goods (Amendment) Act 1995' [1999] LMCLQ 93.

74. [1902] P 42 (CA).

75. Norman Palmer, 'Possessory Title' in Norman Palmer and Ewan Mckendrick (eds), *Interests in Goods* (2nd edn, Sweet & Maxwell 1998) 67–8 by analogy with the position of a pledgee, who apparently holds the surplus proceeds of sale after his security has been satisfied on trust for the pledgor.

76. *De Franco v Commissioner of Police of the Metropolis The Times* 8 May 1987 (CA). See also Lightman J in *Costello v Chief Constable of Derbyshire* [2001] EWCA Civ 381, [2001] 1 WLR 1437 [15].

This right by a bailee to protect his right to possession appears to apply not only in cases of physical possession, but where the bailee simply has an immediate right to possession by way of a security interest, as the following case demonstrates.

Chabbra Corp PTE Ltd v Owners of the Jag Shakti (The Jag Shakti) [1986] AC 337 (PC)

FACTS: Chabbra Corp PTE Ltd (the seller) shipped a cargo of salt on board the *Jag Shakti* (a ship belonging to the defendants). The buyers of the cargo had pledged the bills of lading to Chabbra in order to finance the transaction. The buyers persuaded the defendants to release the goods to them, without presentation of the bills of lading, by providing them with an indemnity and then refused to redeem the **pledge** when the bills of lading were tendered to them by Chabbra. Chabbra sued the ship owners for conversion.

FACTS: Chabbra was entitled in principle to recover the full market value of the goods at unloading from the carrier, though owing to a lack of evidence as to that value, it must be content with the sum it had advanced to the buyers.

> ★ See Norman Palmer, 'Possessory Title' in Norman Palmer and Ewan McKendrick (eds), *Interests in the Goods* (2nd edn, Informa Press 1998) 68–71

> → **pledge:** a transfer of possession but not ownership of a chattel as security for the payment of a debt. Since a bill of lading is a document of title to the goods which are identified on it, pledging the bill of lading is treated as pledging the goods

By virtue of the existence of the concept of 'constructive possession', it is possible for both bailor and bailee to bring actions in tort to protect their possessory interests. It was held in *Nicolls v Bastard*[77] that full recovery by a bailee precluded a further action by the bailor and vice versa. This position was reaffirmed by the Court of Appeal in *O'Sullivan v Williams*,[78] where the owner of a car lent it to his girlfriend whilst he was on holiday. The defendant third party negligently damaged the car and the action with the owner was settled without prejudice to the claims of the girlfriend/bailee who failed in her subsequent claim for damages for among other things the inconvenience in not having the use of the car to get to work.

If the bailor does not have possession or an immediate right to possession, then he has no claim in either trespass or conversion. Generally, where goods are consigned to a carrier, the bailment will be terminable at will, subject perhaps to meeting the charge for freight and so, too, presumably where goods are stored in a warehouse. However, in the case of a lease of goods, the bailor is only entitled to possession either at the expiry of the term or if the bailee commits a breach which entitles the bailor to terminate the lease. The implications of this are well illustrated in the following case.

HSBC Rail (UK) Ltd v Network Rail Infrastructure Ltd [2005] EWCA Civ 1437

FACTS: HSBC Rail (UK) Ltd owned rolling stock, which it bailed to a train operating company (GNER). The rolling stock was damaged due to a derailment that was caused by a fault in the track owned by Network Rail Infrastructure Ltd. GNER claimed on its

---

77. (1835–42) All ER Rep 429.   78. [1992] 3 All ER 385 (CA).

insurance, repaired some of the damaged carriages, and paid sums to HSBC Rail in respect of those carriages which could not be repaired. The insurance company, acting in the name of HSBC Rail, then sought to recover from Network Rail the sums paid out to GNER.

HELD: The claim failed. Since HSBC Rail was neither in possession, nor did it have a right to immediate possession, of the rolling stock, it could only claim in tort for damage to its reversionary interest, and due to the actions of GNER, it had suffered no loss.

Passing possession through documents of title

Lawful possession of a document of title to goods carries with it constructive, or perhaps symbolic, possession of the goods. The only document of title to goods recognized at English law is probably the bill of lading,[79] though in mercantile practice a number of documents are treated as documents of title and may become so recognized in law in due course. The holder of a bill of lading who is either the shipper or has had the bill transferred to him either by endorsement (in the case of an 'Order Bill') or by delivery (in the case of a 'Bearer Bill'), has at least a possessory title to the goods and may obtain ownership of them if, as is often the case, the parties intended title to the goods to pass when the buyer pays against tender of the bill of lading by the seller.

Bills of lading are discussed in Chapter 19

It is not entirely clear how transfer of possession is effected through the bill of lading, but in the *Berge Sisar*,[80] it was suggested that the transfer of a bill of lading effected a transfer of the carrier's attornment to the shipper.

Indivisibility of possession

Since possession entails exercising physical control along with the intention to exclude others from control, it seems self-evident that possession cannot be shared even in the case of co-ownership, since possession in such a case is collective.[81] The problems appear to arise when we consider constructive possession. The key, however, is that in a case of constructive possession, the bailor and the bailee are not asserting competing claims. As has been discussed, constructive possession ceases if the bailee asserts rights in respect of the property against the bailor. In cases of competing claims to possession, the law will determine whose claim is paramount and, as the following case demonstrates, in difficult cases pragmatism may play a significant role.

---

79. *Official Assignee of Madras v Mercantile Bank of India* [1935] AC 53 (PC) 59 (Lord Wright).
80. *Borealis AB v Stargas Ltd and Others* [2001] UKHL 17, [2002] 2 AC 205 [18] (Lord Hobhouse). The matter is not settled. For a further discussion on this, see the judgment of Mance LJ in *East West Corporation v Dampskibsselskabet AF 1912* [2003] EWCA Civ 83, [2003] QB 1509.
81. At least while the co-owners are not in dispute with one another. Though see Michael Bridge, *Personal Property Law* (3rd edn, Clarendon Press 2002) 19.

Great Eastern Railway Company v Lord's Trustee [1909] AC 109 (HL)

FACTS: Great Eastern Railway Co (GER) extended credit to Lord for freight charges in respect of the carriage of Lord's coal. The parties agreed that GER had a lien upon Lord's coal stored on a yard belonging to GER and leased to Lord. GER had the keys to the yard gates and kept them locked out of business hours. When Lord defaulted on the credit agreement, GER locked the gates, and detained the coal. Lord was subsequently declared bankrupt and his trustee in bankruptcy commenced proceedings against GER, alleging, *inter alia*, that GER had no right to detain the goods.

HELD: The House of Lords concluded that, although Lord could enter the premises during normal business hours and remove as much coal as he liked without GER's permission, the goods were nevertheless in the possession and under the control of GER. Accordingly, GER could enforce its legal lien.

COMMENT: Without possession of the coal GER's lien would have taken effect as an equitable interest which would have been void for want of registration under the Bills of Sale Acts, which invalidity the majority of the House clearly wished to avoid. Although the outcome of the case may appear to be driven by policy considerations, the conclusion seems correct: the ultimate control over the coal was in GER, which had the key and could have locked the gates at any time. It is interesting to wonder, though, how it could be that Lord had a lease of the land (which carries with it the right of exclusive possession over the land) and yet not have exclusive possession as against the landlord of goods stored on the land. Perhaps a better question might be whether there can be a lease of land where the landlord can and does exclude the tenant from possession every night.

Dealings in things in action

As with goods, things in action can be dealt with, for example, on sale or by gift, or by way of security, and indeed a key form of business financing is through the sale of, or grant of security over, debts owed to a business known as 'receivable financing'. Consensual transfers of things in action are of two types: (i) those concerning pure intangibles; and (ii) those concerning documentary intangibles.

🔗 Receivable financing is discussed at p 712

Pure intangibles

Historically the common law did not recognize the transfer of the benefit of a contract or of a debt, though the Court of Chancery did and also recognized that a contract to assign effected an assignment. Now s 136 of the Law of Property Act 1925 enables the assignment at law of things in action whether by way of gift, sale, or mortgage. However, it does not apply to charges over things in action which do not operate by transferring a proprietary interest, and these can still only take effect in equity.

Under s 136 of the Law of Property Act 1925, a legal assignment must be in writing, signed by the assignor, and notice of the assignment must be given to the debtor or other obligee. So, for example, if a customer owes X a debt, X can assign this payment obligation to a financier. The financier will pay X the discounted value of the sum owing and will receive in return the right to pursue the claim against the customer.

An agreement to assign or an assignment that fails to meet the requirements of s 136 will nevertheless take effect as an equitable assignment, which has the same economic effect as a legal assignment, and it would appear that an assignment complying with s 136 has no legal advantage over an equitable assignment.[82]

Documentary intangibles

As has been noted, certain types of intangible property have been recognized by the law as being embodied in a document so that they may be transferred by transfer of the document rather than by assignment proper. As noted earlier, documents such as cheques and bills of exchange represent title to payment of money, while the bill of lading represents title to goods.[83]

If a thing in action is recognized as a documentary intangible, then delivery of the document, endorsed if necessary, will transfer legal title to the underlying rights which it embodies. Clearly the act of delivery must be accompanied by an intention to pass title and not, for example, be just for safe keeping; but just as the transferee obtains the rights, so the transferor loses them. Consequently, the obligor will obtain a good discharge if he pays the transferee, but not if he pays the transferor. Finally, the document itself is a chattel so that it can be pledged,[84] and the possessor of it may protect it through the normal tortious actions, for example trespass or conversion.[85]

Conclusion

English law has recognized only three proprietary interests in personal property: (i) ownership; (ii) possession; and (iii) the charge. This chapter has focussed on possession and ownership, and has shown that these interests are primarily protected through the tortious actions for conversion and trespass, both of which protect possession or a proprietary right to immediate possession. Consequently, these remedies are not available to a person who has ownership of a chattel without possession. On the other hand, even unlawful possession grants the possessor title to an interest which is protected from interference save by a person with a better title. The focus, therefore, in English personal property law is on possession, whether physical or constructive, so that bailment, the passing of possession without ownership, is both a key concept and a key way in which possession of goods can be transferred from sellers to buyers through attornment.

---

82. *E Pfeifer Weinkellerei-Weineinkauf GmbH & Co v Arbuthnot Factors Ltd* [1988] 1 WLR 150 (QB).

83. In fact, the bill of lading only transfers constructive possession to the goods, not their ownership.

84. As in *The Jag Shakti* [1986] AC 337 (PC)—a bill of lading.

85. As in *International Factors Ltd v Rodriguez* [1979] QB 351 (CA), which involved dealings in cheques to which the claimant only had equitable title.

Practice questions

1. Explain and give examples of the following terms:
   - thing in action;
   - possessory title;
   - bailment;
   - attornment;
   - equitable title;
   - assignment.

2. Explain why possession of goods is so important in English law.

3. Carol decided to set up business as a three-dimensional printer and wanted to acquire an RDX3 machine. These were normally made to order and consequently rare, but she located one and wanted to acquire it. She entered into an agreement with Lesley under which Lesley agreed to buy the machine from the manufacturers and to lease it to Carol for ten years, which was its expected working life. Lesley bought the machine but decided to sell it to Pete, who now has possession of it.

   Carol also sold one of her two-dimensional printers, an RDX2, to Jim and delivered it to him on the basis that Jim would hold the machine on trust for Carol until he paid for it. Jim has subsequently sold the RDX2 also to Pete.

   Carol agreed to buy 100 gallons of plastic polymer to use in the RDX3 from Andy. The polymer was stored in a warehouse belonging to Brenda, and Andy told Brenda to hold it to Carol's instructions. Pete persuaded Brenda to release the polymer to him and he now has possession of it.

   Andy, Brenda, Lesley, and Pete are all insolvent and Carol wants to know whether she can recover the RDX2, the RDX3, and the polymer from Pete.

Further reading

Michael Bridge, *Personal Property Law* (3rd edn, Clarendon Press 2002)
   - In the usual Clarendon Law series style, comparatively short but written by a recognized expert in the field.

Roy Goode 'Ownership and Obligations in Commercial Transactions' (1987) 103 LQR 433
   - Goode is at his insightful best in drawing our attention to the differences between proprietary and personal rights and how easily they can be confused.

Norman Palmer and Ewan McKendrick (eds), *Interests in Goods* (2nd edn, Informa Law 1998)
   - Although fifteen years old, the essays in this collection are all worth reading. For example, William Swadling is quite controversial in his chapter 'The Proprietary Effect of the Hire of Goods', when he argues that a lessee of a chattel acquire no proprietary rights, while Magnusson, in 'Proprietary Rights in Human Tissue', provides a fascinating example of how the law determines what is property.

Duncan Sheehan, *The Principles of Personal Property Law* (Hart Publishing 2011)
   - Comprehensive, scholarly, and up to date.

Sarah Worthington, *Personal Property Law: Text and Materials* (Hart Publishing 2000)
   - Although now a little out of date, has a wonderful selection of materials, while the text is both accessible and thought-provoking.

PART II

The law of agency

An introduction to the law of agency

- What is agency?
- Sources of agency law
- Types of agent

INTRODUCTION

As has been correctly stated, '[c]ommerce would literally grind to a halt if businessmen and merchants could not employ the services of factors, brokers, forwarding agents, estate agents, auctioneers and the like and were expected to do everything themselves'.[1] For many businesses, the use of agents is invaluable, and significant areas of commercial activity could not continue without the existence of agency. The law of agency is a complex, subtle, and often misunderstood subject, but an understanding of its operation is vital to all students, especially given the extent to which the law of agency can affect areas of the law, commercial or otherwise. It should also be noted that the law of agency is not only important in relation to business-to-business transactions, but can be of crucial importance in relation to consumer transactions, as consumers will often bargain and enter into contracts with agents.

Chapters 3 to 9 will provide students with a thorough understanding of the law of agency, with this chapter discussing several basic foundation issues relating to the law of agency, such as the sources of agency law and the various types of agent that exist. However, before any aspects of the law of agency can be discussed, it is vital that students understand exactly what the specific legal meaning of 'agency' is.

What is agency?

As Bowstead & Reynolds state '[i]t is customary to begin a systematic treatise with some sort of definition of its subject-matter'.[2] Unfortunately, whilst many definitions of agency exist, the concept is 'notoriously slippery and difficult to define'.[3] The words 'agent' and 'agency' are used in common parlance (e.g. estate agent, travel agent, recruitment agency, etc), but they have a specific legal meaning that is often at odds with their everyday usage. As Lord Herschell stated, '[n]o word is more

---

1. Basil S Markesinis and Roderick Munday, *An Outline of the Law of Agency* (4th edn, Butterworths 1998) 4.

2. Peter G Watts, *Bowstead & Reynolds on Agency* (19th edn, Sweet & Maxwell 2010) [1-002].

3. Roderick Munday, *Agency: Law and Principles* (OUP 2010) 1.

commonly and constantly abused than the word "agent".[4] The following two definitions provide clear and succinct accounts of the concept of agency:

> Agency is the fiduciary relationship that arises when one person (a 'principal') manifests assent to another person (an 'agent') that the agent shall act on the principal's behalf and subject to the principal's control, and the agent manifests assent or otherwise consents so to act.[5]

> Agency is the relationship arising where one person, the principal, ... appoints another, the agent, ... to bring about, modify, or terminate legal relations between the principal and one or more third parties.[6]

From these definitions, it can be seen that a typical agency relationship will involve three parties, namely:

1. the principal;
2. the agent; and
3. a third party (or third parties).

Figure 3.1 demonstrates the operation of a typical agency relationship.

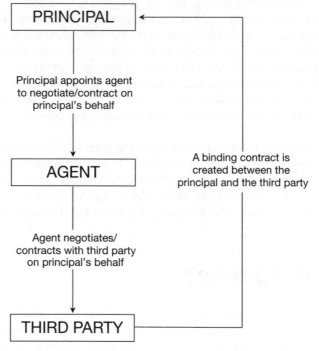

FIGURE 3.1 A typical agency relationship

4. *Kennedy v De Trafford* [1897] AC 180 (HL) 188.
5. American Law Institute, *Restatement of the Law—Agency* (American Law Institute 2006) § 1.01.
6. Roy Goode and Ewan McKendrick, *Goode on Commercial Law* (4th edn, Penguin 2010) 179.

In order to better understand the relationship between these three parties, consider the example of ComCorp.

Eg) ComCorp Ltd

In order to raise capital, the directors of ComCorp decide that a rare painting that belongs to ComCorp (the principal) will be sold at auction. The auctioneer, David (the agent), is instructed not to sell the painting for less than £50,000. David will receive commission of 2 per cent of the sale price. The highest bid is made by Tom (the third party), a local antique dealer, who bids £57,000. The hammer falls and the sale is made. David receives his commission of £1,140, and drops out of the transaction. A binding contract of sale exists between ComCorp and Tom.

This discussion indicates that a number of key characteristics will usually be present in a typical agency relationship:

- A relationship of agency will usually arise due to the express consent of the principal and agent, and the relationship will usually be a contractual one. However, as will be seen, implied and non-consensual agency relationships can exist, and it is not normally necessary for a contract to exist for a relationship of agency to arise. How a relationship of agency can be created is discussed in detail in Chapter 4.
- The agent will be appointed to act on behalf of his principal. The activities involved will differ from agent to agent.
- An agency relationship is a fiduciary one, meaning that the principal and agent will owe each other a number of duties and obligations. These duties and obligations are discussed in Chapter 6.
- The agent may have the ability to affect the legal position of his principal, usually by creating binding contracts between his principal and a third party.
- The agent's ability to affect the legal position of his principal will usually be limited in some way (in the ComCorp example, the reserve price attached to the painting constituted a limitation). This is known as the agent's authority and it is central to the agency relationship. The authority of an agent is discussed in detail in Chapter 5.
- Once the agent has completed his task, he will usually drop out of the transaction, leaving a binding agreement in place between his principal and the third party. The relationship between the principal and third party is discussed in Chapter 7.
- The agent will usually be remunerated for his services. The remuneration of an agent is discussed at p 137.
- Once the agent has performed the task for which he is appointed, the agency agreement will terminate, as will the agent's actual authority. The termination of the agency agreement and an agent's authority are discussed in Chapter 9.

It should be noted that the use of the word 'agent' in a person's job title or description will not necessarily mean that the person is an agent within the strict legal meaning of the term. Similarly, a person without the term 'agent' in his job description may still be an agent—for example, a company director will be an agent for the company for which he works, and a partner in a partnership will act as an agent for the firm.[7]

---

7. The Partnership Act 1890, s 5 provides that the partners are agents of the firm and agents of their fellow partners.

Sources of agency law

Historically, the law of agency was regarded (and taught) as a stand-alone legal topic. Today, it is usually taught as part of a larger commercial law course, but it is still deserving of recognition as a free-standing legal topic due to the prevalence of agents and the extent to which issues of agency can impact upon cases involving other areas of the law. It is therefore worth briefly explaining the various sources of agency law.

Domestic agency law is dominated by case law, with many of the fundamental principles established by the courts in the eighteenth and nineteenth centuries (which may explain why many students find agency cases difficult to understand). However, statute does have a role to play, with perhaps the most recent development of note being the enactment of the Commercial Agents (Council Directive) Regulations 1993,[8] which aims to provide protection to a specific type of agent, namely the commercial agent.

Commercial agents are discussed at p 52

The law of agency is also strongly affected by supranational laws and rules. The UK's membership of the EU means that it is obliged to enforce and implement EU laws relating to agents. For example, the 1993 Regulations mentioned earlier were enacted in order to implement an EC Directive that aimed to offer greater protection to self-employed agents.[9] Such laws will also result in a harmonization of agency law amongst EU Member States (indeed, the agency laws of many countries have notable similarities). In 1983, UNIDROIT[10] adopted the Convention on Agency in the International Sale of Goods, which aimed to harmonize the rules relating to agency contracts that involved the international sale of goods. At the time of writing, the Convention is not in force, as it does not have the required number of ratifications.[11] The UK has not ratified the Convention, so its provisions currently have no domestic force.

Finally, it should be noted that although the law of agency constitutes a legal topic in its own right, many other areas of the law also affect the activities of agents. As relationships of agency are commonly created via contract and the agent often has the power to contractually bind his principal to a third party, it follows that the law of contract has a strong role to play. An agent whose acts are negligent may find himself liable in tort. It may even be the case that the acts of an agent can result in criminal liability being imposed upon himself and his principal. An understanding of the law of agency can help in obtaining a more complete understanding of many other areas of the law.

---

8. SI 1993/3053.

9. Council Directive 86/653/EEC of 18 December 1986 on the coordination of the laws of the Member States relating to self-employed commercial agents [2006] OJ L382/17.

10. UNIDROIT (the International Institute for the Unification of Private Law) is an independent intergovernmental body that aims to study methods to modernize and harmonize private laws (notably commercial laws) between states and groups of states.

11. Ten states are required to ratify the Convention for it to come into effect. At the time of writing, only five states (France, Italy, Mexico, The Netherlands, and South Africa) have ratified it.

Types of agent

There are several special classes and classifications of agent that will be encountered in this text and in agency cases and statutes. It is therefore important to understand the function of these agents and their role within a commercial organization. It should be noted that several of these classes and classifications of agent have fallen out of usage and are no longer relevant to modern commercial agencies but, as they are referred to in many of the key agency cases, understanding their function is still useful.

General and special agents

A general agent is vested with authority to act for the principal in relation to the general business of the principal, or is vested with general authority to act on behalf of the principal in relation to certain trades or transactions. Conversely, a special agent's authority is usually narrower and is limited to a single subject matter or transaction. Although the distinction between general and special agents has lost much of its importance today, it has still been used occasionally to determine the scope of an agent's apparent authority.[12]

🔗 An agent's apparent authority is discussed at p 96

Factors and brokers

The term 'factor', which was used regularly in nineteenth-century legislation and case law, refers to an agent who is engaged to sell goods on behalf of his principal, with the crucial characteristic being that the factor would hold or control the goods in question and would often sell them in his own name without disclosing the name of his principal.[13] This non-disclosure meant that the factor was often invested with apparent authority to sell the goods, even if the sale had not been authorized by the principal. Today, the term 'factor' is rarely used in its original sense[14] and has been replaced by the broader term 'mercantile agent', which is defined as an 'agent having in the customary course of his business as such agent authority either to sell goods, or to consign goods for the purpose of sale, or to buy goods, or to raise money on the security of goods'.[15]

🔗 Sales of goods by mercantile agents are discussed in more detail on p 281

A broker is similar to a factor, in that he negotiates contracts for the sale of goods between his principal and third parties. The difference lies in the fact that the broker will not usually have control or possession of the goods (he is unlikely ever to see the goods) and he should not sell the goods in his own name.[16]

---

12. See e.g. *Armagas Ltd v Mundogas SA (The Ocean Frost)* [1986] AC 717 (HL).
13. *Baring v Corrie* (1818) 2 B & Ald 137. The factor will not cease to be a factor if he sells the goods in the name of his principal (*Stevens v Biller* (1884) 25 ChD 31 (CA)).
14. Indeed, today the term is used more commonly to describe the process by which a person or business (the 'factor') purchases receivables from another. Factoring is discussed in Chapter 26.
15. Factors Act 1889, s 1(1).
16. *Baring v Corrie* (1818) 2 B & Ald 137.

Del credere agents

➡ *del credere*: Italian for 'of belief' or 'of trust'

Like a factor or broker, a *del credere* agent will negotiate contracts between his principal and third parties. In addition, a *del credere* agent will, in return for increased commission/remuneration, also act as guarantor for the obligations of the third party. Thus, if a *del credere* agent negotiates a contract for the sale of goods between his principal and a third party, and the third party fails to pay for the goods (e.g. because it becomes insolvent), the *del credere* agent will become liable to pay the purchase price to the principal.

Confirming houses

🔗 International trade is discussed in Chapters 19–22

Confirming houses are of considerable importance in relation to international trade, where they can engage in a number of activities. A confirming house may act as agent for an overseas buyer who wishes to purchase goods in a country where the confirming house is based. In such a case, the confirming house may simply arrange for a contract of sale to be created between the overseas buyer and a domestic seller. Alternatively, the confirming house may buy the goods from the domestic seller and sell them on to its overseas principal.[17] Domestic sellers may often be reluctant to deal with overseas buyers, especially if they have never done business before, or little is known about the buyer. In such cases, the confirming house may act as agent for the overseas buyer, but will also enter into a separate and collateral contract with the seller, under which it guarantees (or 'confirms') that the buyer will perform its obligations. If the overseas buyer does not perform its obligations, the confirming house will become liable, which will usually involve it having to pay the seller the contractual price of the goods.

Commercial agents

Consider the following example:

Eg ComCorp Ltd

The directors of ComCorp Ltd are keen to expand the company's base. Accordingly, ComCorp (the principal) engages Charles (the agent) to locate potential new customers, introduce those customers to ComCorp, and help in creating contracts of sale between ComCorp and these new customers. In return, Charles will be paid commission for each sale made. Charles introduces the directors of ComCorp to a number of new potential customers (the third parties). ComCorp decides to terminate Charles's contract and deal directly with the potential customers, thereby avoiding the need to pay commission to Charles.

Commercial agents are often appointed to help develop and increase the customer base of the principal by locating new customers, introducing them to the

---

17. In such a case, the confirming house will still be acting as an agent for the overseas buyer (*Anglo-African Shipping Co of New York Inc v J Mortner Ltd* [1962] 1 Lloyd's Rep 610 (CA)).

principal, and/or helping in effecting transactions between them. The principal's revenue increases and, in return, the agent is paid commission for any transactions that take place. However, once the introduction has been made, the principal might feel that he no longer has a use for the agent and (as in the ComCorp example) may seek to bypass the agent and deal directly with the third parties, thereby avoiding the need to pay the agent the commission that he deserves. That agents may be vulnerable to exploitation by their principals has long been recognized by the courts. For example, Staughton LJ stated 'commercial agents are a down-trodden race, and need and should be afforded protection against their principals'.[18] Such protection was granted with the adoption of EC Directive 86/653,[19] which was implemented by the Commercial Agents (Council Directive) Regulations 1993.

Regulation 1(2) states that '[t]hese Regulations govern the relations between commercial agents and their principals'. It is therefore clear that the Regulations are concerned only with the principal/agent relationship, and are not concerned with the relationships that such persons might have with third parties. The basic effect of the Regulations is to provide certain protections to the commercial agent, although the Regulations do also impose obligations upon commercial agents. These protections and obligations (and how such protections and obligations differ from those of an ordinary agent) are discussed in Chapter 6. Here, the focus will be on the definition of a 'commercial agent', with reg 2(1) providing that a commercial agent is:

Commercial Agents (Council Directive) Regulations 1993, reg 2(1)

a self-employed intermediary who has continuing authority to negotiate the sale or purchase of goods on behalf of another person (the 'principal'), or to negotiate and conclude the sale or purchase of goods on behalf of and in the name of that principal . . .

This seemingly straightforward definition contains a number of key words and phrases that significantly restrict the scope of the Regulations.

'Self-employed'

In order to qualify as a commercial agent, the person must be 'self-employed' (usually referred to in case law as an 'independent contractor'). It follows from this that a person who is an agent by virtue of his employment will not be a commercial agent.

'Continuing authority'

A commercial agent must have *continuing* authority to negotiate on behalf of another person. This does not mean that a commercial agent's authority cannot be subject to any form of time limit, as regs 14 and 15 clearly envisage the possibility of fixed-term commercial agency contracts. However, as the *Poseidon* case demonstrates, the inclusion of the word 'continuing' would appear to indicate that an agent who is engaged

---

18. *Page v Combined Shipping and Trading Co Ltd* [1997] 3 All ER 656 (CA) 660.
19. Council Directive 86/653/EEC of 18 December 1986 on the coordination of the laws of the Member States relating to self-employed commercial agents [2006] OJ L382/17.

to effect a one-off transaction would not have continuing authority, and so would not constitute a commercial agent.

Case C-3/04 *Poseidon Chartering BV v Marianne Zeeschip VOF* [2007] Bus LR 446

FACTS: Poseidon Chartering BV ('Poseidon', the agent) was engaged by Marianne Zeeschip VOF ('Marianne', the principal) to negotiate the charter of a ship from a third party. Poseidon successfully negotiated a charterparty between Marianne and a third party, and received 2.5 per cent of the charter price as commission. From 1994 to 2000, Poseidon also acted as intermediary for the annual renewal of the charterparty and, upon each renewal, received commission. The parties fell out and Marianne terminated the contract between it and Poseidon. Poseidon initiated proceedings, claiming unpaid commission and damages that were owed to it as a commercial agent. Marianne contended that, as Poseidon had only negotiated one contract, it lacked continuing authority and so was not a commercial agent. A preliminary reference was sought from the European Court of Justice.

HELD: Advocate General Geelhaed, delivering the judgment of the Court, stated that:

> it is in my view important to distinguish between a situation in which an independent agent has been tasked by its principal to negotiate just one contract, and a situation in which such an agent has been tasked by its principal to negotiate a contract as well as numerous renewals of the contract. It is clear that the former situation cannot sensibly be interpreted as 'continuing authority'. If an agent responsible for the negotiation of a single contract were to fall within that concept, it would deprive the notion of 'continuing' of all meaning. In contrast, in my view the latter situation…must, as a matter of logic, fall within the concept. To my mind, the idea of 'continuing' authority requires simply that the agent be responsible either for negotiating more than one type of contract, or for (re-)negotiating the same contract on more than one occasion.[20]

'Sale or purchase of goods'

Regulation 2(1) specifies that an agent must have continuing authority to negotiate and/or conclude the sale or purchase of *goods* in order to qualify as a commercial agent. It follows that an agent whose function is to negotiate and/or conclude a contract of services will not be a commercial agent. However, where the agent's activities involve the provision of goods and services, then he may still qualify as a commercial agent, providing that the provision of goods is not considered to be a secondary activity.

What constitutes a secondary activity is discussed at p 58

The Regulations do not define what constitutes 'goods', but it is clear that the word is to be given a wide interpretation. In certain cases, the lack of a statutory definition has proved problematic, such as in cases involving contracts for the provision of software, where the approach adopted by the courts has been strongly criticized.

---

20. [2007] Bus LR 446, 452.

St Albans City and District Council v International Computers Ltd [1997] FSR 251 (CA)[21]

FACTS: St Albans City and District Council (St Albans) purchased from International Computers Ltd ('ICL') a software system that was designed to administer the collection of poll tax. The software incorrectly estimated the population of the local authority's area, with the result that the poll tax rate was set too low and St Albans received £484,000 less than it ought have. St Albans also had to pay an additional £685,000 in precept payments to Hertfordshire County Council. St Albans sought compensation from ICL.

HELD: The Court considered whether or not software amounted to goods in order to determine whether ICL had breached the implied term that goods should be reasonably fit for their purpose. Sir Iain Glidewell stated that, as discs were certainly goods, software that was delivered on a disc would also amount to goods. He also stated that a software program, in itself, does not amount to goods.

★ See Sarah Green and Djakhongir Saidov, 'Software as Goods' [2007] JBL 161

🔗 The implied term that goods should be reasonably fit for purpose is discussed at p 372

'Negotiate on behalf of the principal'

An agent who does not have authority to enter into contracts on behalf of his principal can still qualify as a commercial agent, as reg 2(1) covers those who have 'continuing authority to negotiate the sale or purchase of goods on behalf of another person (the "principal")'. Unfortunately, neither the Regulations nor the Directive define what type of activities amount to 'negotiation'. Bearing this in mind, consider this scenario.

Eg Comcorp Ltd

ComCorp engages an agent, Claire, to locate potential new customers and introduce them to ComCorp. ComCorp will then negotiate directly with these potential customers with a view to entering into contracts with them. A dispute arises and ComCorp terminates its contract with Claire. Claire contends that she is due commission as a commercial agent, but ComCorp contends that, as she did not have the authority to negotiate (merely to introduce), she is not a commercial agent.

Do agents who have authority merely to make introductions (usually known as canvassing or marketing agents) fall within the definition in reg 2(1), or does the agent need to have authority to engage in actual bargaining? The issue has not been conclusively settled. Early cases adopted a rather restrictive approach based on the dictionary definition of the word 'negotiate',[22] but more recent cases appear to favour the wider view that an agent need not have the authority to engage in actual bargaining in order to constitute a commercial agent.

---

21. It should be noted that this case related to the direct sale of goods under the Sale of Goods Act 1979 and not to contracts of sale effected through an agent. However, the principles established would also apply to cases involving the sale of goods effected through an agent.

22. See *Parks v Esso Petroleum Co Ltd* [2000] ECC 45 (CA).

PJ Pipe & Valve Co Ltd v Audco India Ltd [2005] EWHC 1904 (QB)²³

FACTS: Audco India Ltd ('AIL', the principal) engaged PJ Pipe & Valve Co Ltd ('PJV', the agent) (i) to promote AIL's capability and reputation as a valve manufacturer; (ii) to promote AIL to potential customers to ensure that AIL would be designated as an approved vendor; and (iii) to introduce potential customers to AIL and provide advice to AIL on the preparation of quotations. PJV did not have authority to agree prices or terms with any potential customers—potential customers would deal directly with AIL. A dispute arose and PJV sought commission owed under the 1993 Regulations. AIL argued that, as PJV could not bargain or agree terms, it did not have the authority to negotiate and so was not a commercial agent.

HELD: PJV was a commercial agent. Fulford J, referring to the Directive that was implemented by the 1993 Regulations, stated that:

> The purpose of the Directive...was to provide protection to agents by giving them a stake in the goodwill which they have generated for the principal, and as a result the courts should avoid a limited or restricted interpretation of the word 'negotiate' that would exclude agents who have been engaged to develop the principal's business in this way, and who successfully generated goodwill for the manufacturer, to the latter's benefit after the agency terminated. In the result, I conclude PJV acted as a commercial agent for the purposes of the Regulations, notwithstanding their lack of authority to progress agreement on commercial terms or prices.²⁴

COMMENT: The wider approach evidenced in *PJ Pipe* has been widely welcomed as giving effect to the purpose of the Directive. However, the lack of a uniform definition of 'negotiate' is still problematic. As one commentator has stated:

> the failure to define the term 'negotiate' in the Directive has led to divergences in the interpretation of Community law before the national courts. The courts have encountered difficulties when faced with different types of commercial arrangements to reach decisions on the scope of the Directive and implementing regulations. This has resulted in a degree of uncertainty in commercial practice which, it is submitted, could have been avoided had the Directive included a definition of the term.²⁵

Not only must the agent have authority to negotiate, but he must also negotiate on behalf of another person, namely the principal. It follows that if a person acts on his own behalf, he will not be a commercial agent, as the following case demonstrates.

---

23. See also *Tamarind International Ltd v Eastern Natural Gas (Retail) Ltd* [2000] CLC 1397 (QB); *Nigel Fryer Joinery Services Ltd v Ian Firth Hardware Ltd* [2008] EWHC 767 (Ch), [2008] 2 Lloyd's Rep 108; *Accentuate Ltd v Asigra Inc* [2009] EWHC 2655 (QB), [2009] 2 Lloyd's Rep 599.

24. [2005] EWHC 1904 (QB), [2006] EU LR 368 [155].

25. Caterina Gardiner, 'The EC (Commercial Agents) Directive: Twenty Years After its Introduction, Divergent Approaches Still Emerge From Irish and UK Courts' [2007] JBL 412, 420.

AMB Imballaggi Plastici SRL v Pacflex Ltd [1999] CLC 1391 (CA)

FACTS: AMB Imballaggi Plastici SRL ('AMB', the principal) manufactured products that were sold in England by Pacflex (the agent). Pacflex could have sold the products on a commission basis, but instead chose to purchase the products from AMB, mark them up, and sell them on. AMB issued proceedings against Pacflex for non-payment of goods and Pacflex counterclaimed that it was owed commission under the 1993 Regulations.

HELD: Pacflex was not a commercial agent under the 1993 Regulations, and so its counterclaim was dismissed. Waller LJ stated:

> If a person buys or sells himself as principal he is outside the ambit of the regulations. That is so because in negotiating that sale or purchase he is acting on his own behalf and not on behalf of another. All the regulations point in the direction of the words 'on behalf of' meaning what an English court would naturally construe them as meaning. The other person on whose behalf the intermediary has authority to negotiate the sale or purchase of goods is called the 'principal'; the duties are consistent with true agency and not with a buying and reselling; 'remuneration' is quite inconsistent with 'mark-up', particularly 'mark-up' within the total discretion of the reseller. Accordingly, as it seems to me, Pacflex never in fact acted as an agent negotiating on behalf of another at all.[26]

COMMENT: Where a person (such as a distributor) purchases goods from another, marks them up, and sells them on, he is unlikely to be acting as a commercial agent. However, the presence of a mark-up will not, in itself, deny the existence of a commercial agency relationship.[27]

'Negotiate and conclude on behalf of and in the name of the principal'

Regulation 2(1) differentiates between (i) an agent who is granted authority to negotiate on behalf of his principal, but not to enter into contracts; and (ii) an agent who has authority to 'negotiate and conclude the sale or purchase of goods on behalf of and in the name of that principal'. The issues concerning the terms 'negotiation' and 'on behalf of' discussed in the previous section will apply to both types of agents, but in relation to agents who have authority to negotiate and conclude contracts, a further requirement exists, namely that the agent must be acting 'in the name of' the principal. A person who has authority to negotiate and conclude contracts will not be a commercial agent if he does not do so in the name of his principal.

Where the agent acts on behalf of a principal whose existence and identity have been disclosed to the third party at or before the time of the transaction,[28] then no problem arises and the agent will most likely be acting in the name of his principal. Can the same be said of an agent who does not disclose the existence and/or identity of his principal? If an agent has not disclosed the existence of a principal,[29] then it

---

26. [1999] CLC 1391 (CA) 1394.
27. *Mercantile International Group plc v Chuan Soon Huat Industrial Group Ltd* [2002] EWCA Civ 288, [2002] CLC 913 [36]–[37].
28. Such a principal is usually known as a 'named principal'.
29. Such a principal is usually known as an 'undisclosed principal'.

cannot be said that the agent is acting in the principal's name. Difficulties arise when the agent has disclosed the existence of a principal, but has not disclosed the principal's identity.[30] No clear authoritative answer exists, but it has been suggested that, in such a case, the agent will be acting in the principal's name, providing that the agent has not undertaken personal liability on the contract.[31]

Exclusions

Regulation 2(1) specifies that three types of person will not be classified as a commercial agent. First, 'a person who, in his capacity as an officer of a company or association, is empowered to enter into commitments binding on that company or association' will not be a commercial agent. It follows that directors or company secretaries acting on behalf of their companies will not be acting as commercial agents, although the company itself can act as a commercial agent, providing that it is an independent contractor.[32] Second, 'a partner who is lawfully authorized to enter into commitments binding on his partners' will not be a commercial agent.[33] Third, 'a person who acts as an insolvency practitioner' will not be a commercial agent.

Even if a person is a commercial agent within the meaning of reg 2(1), he may still be excluded from the scope of the Regulations. For example, reg 2(2) provides that the Regulations will not apply to (i) commercial agents whose activities are unpaid; (ii) commercial agents when they operate on commodity exchanges, or in the commodity market; and (iii) the Crown Agents for Overseas Governments and Administrations.

Finally, reg 2(3) and (4) provide that the Regulations will not apply to persons 'whose activities as commercial agents are to be considered secondary'.[34] In order to understand whether a commercial agent's activities are secondary, recourse should be first had to Sch 1, para 2 of the Regulations, which describes an arrangement between principal and agent by reference to three criteria:

1. the business of the principal is the sale or purchase of goods of a particular kind, and;

2. the goods concerned are such that are (i) normally individually negotiated and concluded on a commercial basis, and (ii) procuring a transaction on one occasion is likely to lead to further transactions in those goods with that customer on future occasions, or to transactions in those goods with other customers in the same geographical area or among the same group of customers; and

3. accordingly, it is in the commercial interests of the principal in developing the market in those goods to appoint a representative to such customers with a view to the representative devoting effort, skill, and expenditure from his own resources to that end.

Where it can reasonably be taken that the primary purpose of the arrangement between the agent and principal does not fall within the description set out in Sch 1, para 2, then the activities of the commercial agent will be considered secondary and

---

30. Such a principal is usually known as an 'unnamed principal'.
31. Peter G Watts, *Bowstead & Reynolds on Agency* (19th edn, Sweet & Maxwell 2010) [11-019].
32. *Bell Electrical Ltd v Aweco Appliance Systems GmbH & Co KG* [2002] EWHC 872 (QB), [2002] CLC 1246.
33. Like a company, a partnership may act as a commercial agent, providing that it is an independent contractor.
34. Commercial Agents (Council Directive) Regulations 1993, reg 2(3). For a more detailed discussion on when activities are secondary, see Roderick Munday, *Agency: Laws and Principles* (OUP 2010) 27–33.

the Regulations will not apply.[35] Schedule 1, paras 3 and 4 then provide indicative factors that could indicate whether an arrangement falls within Sch 1, para 2, and Sch 2, para 5 provides a rebuttable presumption that certain persons (e.g. consumer credit agents) will not fall within the para 2.

Moore-Bick LJ provided a more accessible overview of the purpose of the paragraphs in Schs 1 and 2, namely to:

> distinguish between those persons falling within the definition of commercial agent in reg 2(1) who are engaged primarily to carry out the functions of a commercial agent, that is, generating customers, obtaining repeat orders, and creating and developing a market for their principal's goods, and those who are primarily engaged for some other purpose but who incidentally provide some or all of those services. In the latter case, their activities can properly be described as secondary.[36]

Conclusion

Despite its importance, the law of agency is an often-misunderstood subject and its importance is often not appreciated. Put simply, many areas of business would find it impossible to continue without the ability to engage agents, whilst commerce overall would become significantly more burdensome and inefficient. An understanding of commercial law cannot be complete without a firm appreciation and sound grasp of the law of agency.

There are many types of agents engaging in countless forms of activity, but, in recent years, one type of agent has acquired a new-found importance, namely the commercial agent. Commercial agents have long been recognized in continental Europe, and the UK's formal recognition of commercial agents through the Commercial Agents (Council Directive) Regulations 1993 was a significant development in the law of agency. As is discussed in subsequent chapters, the 1993 Regulations pervade many areas of the law of agency.

Having discussed what agency is and how a typical agency relationship might operate, Chapter 4 moves on to consider the various ways through which an agency relationship can be created.

Practice questions

1. Define the following terms:
    *   agency;
    *   principal;
    *   factor;
    *   broker;

---

35. ibid Sch 1, para 1.
36. *Edwards v International Connection (UK) Ltd* [2006] EWCA Civ 662 [17].

- *del credere* agent;
- canvassing agent.

2. 'Due to their restrictive scope, the Commercial Agents (Council Directive) Regulations 1993 fail to provide self-employed agents with the protection that they deserve.' Do you agree with this statement? Provide reasons for your answers.

Further reading

Caterina Gardiner, 'The EC (Commercial Agents) Directive: Twenty Years After Its Introduction, Divergent Approaches Still Emerge From the Irish and UK Courts' [2007] JBL 412
- The first half of this article discusses the definition of 'commercial agent' found in the 1993 Regulations, focussing on the case law surrounding the terms 'negotiate' and 'secondary activities'.

Roderick Munday, *Agency: Law and Principles* (OUP 2010) ch 1
- Provides a clear and accessible introduction to the concept of agency, as well as looking at the foundations of the agency relationship and the operation of the 1993 Regulations.

Séverine Saintier, *Commercial Agency Law: A Comparative Analysis* (Ashgate 2002)
- This text focuses on the Commercial Agents Directive and its implementation by the UK and France. Provides a detailed account of the background to the Directive and 1993 Regulations.

Peter G Watts, *Bowstead & Reynolds on Agency* (19th edn, Sweet & Maxwell 2010) chs 1 and 11
- The definitive text on the law of agency. Chapter 1 provides an excellent introduction to the law of agency, whereas chapter 11 discusses the 1993 Regulations.

4 The creation of the agency relationship

- Capacity
- Formality
- Agency by agreement

- Agency by ratification
- Agency by operation of law
- Agency arising due to estoppel

INTRODUCTION

Having discussed what agency is and the various types of agent that exist, this chapter moves on to consider the various methods by which a relationship of agency can be created, namely:

- agency by agreement;
- agency by ratification;
- agency by operation of law; and
- agency arising due to estoppel.

It is worth noting at the outset that the fact that the parties describe themselves as 'principal' and 'agent' will not conclusively establish that a relationship of agency exists, and the courts will disregard such labels if the realities of the relationship indicate that it is not one of agency. Similarly, an agency relationship might be held to exist, even though the parties (or one of the parties) do not wish for such a relationship to exist, or have expressly declared that such a relationship does not exist. Agency relationship can therefore be created consensually or non-consensually, as Table 4.1 indicates:

TABLE 4.1 Consensual and non-consensual agencies

Consensual agencies	Non-consensual agencies
• Agency by agreement (express and implied)	• Agency arising due to estoppel
• Agency by ratification	
• Agency by operation of the law	

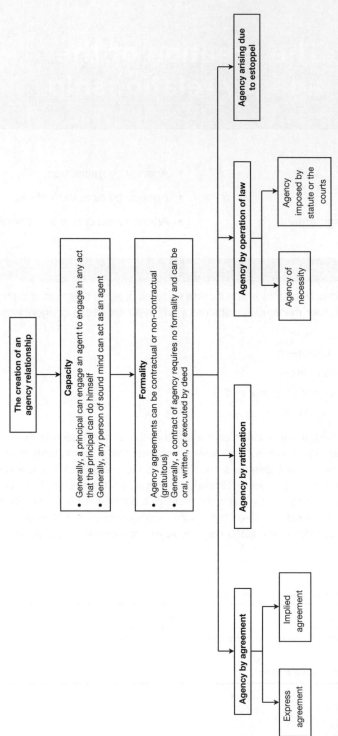

FIGURE 4.1 The creation of agency

All of these forms of agency are discussed in this chapter. However, before the methods of creation can be discussed, it is important to answer two preliminary questions:

1. How does the contractual capacity of the principal and/or agent affect the creation of an agency relationship?
2. What formalities are required in order to create an agency relationship?

Figure 4.1 provides an overview of all the major issues discussed in this chapter.

Capacity

In many cases, a relationship of agency will arise via contract and the agent will have the ability to affect the contractual position of his principal. In such cases, the contractual capacity of the principal and agent are of fundamental importance and, if either of the parties lacks capacity, any resulting contracts (including the contract of agency itself) may be void or voidable.

➡ contractual
capacity: the ability
and extent to which
a person can enter
into contractual
arrangements

Capacity of the principal

The general rule is that a principal can appoint an agent to engage in any act that the principal himself has capacity to engage in, or to put it more simply, 'whatever a party himself may do, he may do through the intermediary of an agent'.[1] It follows that an agent who lacks capacity to enter into a transaction in his own name may nevertheless enter into that transaction on behalf of his principal, providing that the principal has capacity to enter into that transaction. Bearing this in mind, consider the following example:

> **Eg** **ComCorp Ltd**
>
> ComCorp appoints an agent, Oliver, to negotiate and enter into a number of contracts on its behalf. Oliver carries out his instructions and creates a number of contracts between ComCorp and several third parties. ComCorp then discovers that Oliver is only 17 years old.

In this example, Oliver is a minor (i.e. a person under the age of 18).[2] A minor will lack the capacity to make many types of contract and can only enter into binding contracts in limited circumstances.[3] Where the minor lacks capacity, the contract will not normally be void, but will be voidable at the minor's instance. However, in cases of agency, a minor who is acting as agent can enter into binding contracts providing that his principal has capacity to enter into such contracts. Accordingly, in this example, Oliver's lack of capacity will not be an issue (although the contract of agency between ComCorp and Oliver might be voidable). The question that now arises is whether a minor can act as principal and, if so, the extent of his capacity. In such cases, the general rule regarding capacity already discussed will normally

---

1. Roderick Munday, *Agency: Law and Principles* (OUP 2010) 38.
2. Family Law Reform Act 1969, s 1.
3. Namely, where the contract is one for necessaries, or is a contract of service (e.g. employment or apprenticeship).

apply, namely that '[w]henever a minor can lawfully do an act for his own behalf, so as to bind himself, he can instead appoint an agent to do it for him'.[4] From this, it follows that:

- a contract that would bind a minor if he were to enter into it himself will also bind him if he enters into it via an agent;
- a contract that would not be binding on a person because he is a minor will not become binding simply because it is entered into by an adult agent acting on the minor's behalf.

Mental incapacity

Where the principal is mentally incapacitated, the issue is more complex. The law presumes that a person has mental capacity unless the contrary is established.[5] A person will lack mental capacity if 'at the material time he is unable to make a decision for himself in relation to a matter because of an impairment of, or a disturbance of the functioning of, the mind or brain'.[6] Even if a mentally incapacitated person does enter into a contract, general contract law provides that the contract will be binding unless the other party knew of the incapacity, in which case the contract will be voidable at the instance of the incapacitated person.[7] In relation to the contract of agency itself, it has been contended that this general contractual rule will apply,[8] but will it apply to any contracts entered into by the agent with third parties on the principal's behalf? Where the contract was entered into based upon the agent's actual authority, then it seems clear that the rule stated in the previous paragraph will not apply and the incapacitated principal will not be bound, irrespective of whether the third party knew of the incapacity.[9] In cases involving the agent's apparent authority, two contentions have been advanced:

1. Where the principal is mentally incapacitated at the time that he made the representation as to the agent's authority, then that principal will not be bound, irrespective of whether the third party knew of the incapacity.[10]

2. Where the principal becomes mentally incapacitated after the initial representation is made, then any contracts entered into by the agent on behalf of the principal will be binding on the principal, providing that the third party had no knowledge of the principal's incapacity.[11]

Capacity of the agent

As noted, an agent who lacks capacity to enter into a contract on his own behalf may nevertheless be able to enter into a contract on behalf of a principal who does have capacity to enter into such a contract. It follows that, in many cases, the capacity of the agent is irrelevant. The only general requirement that the law imposes is that the

---

4. *G(A) v G(T)* [1970] 2 QB 643 (CA) 652 (Lord Denning MR).
5. Mental Capacity Act 2005, s 1(2).   6. ibid s 2(1).
7. *Molton v Camroux* (1849) 4 Ex 17; *Imperial Loan Co Ltd v Stone* [1892] 1 QB 599 (CA).
8. Peter G Watts, *Bowstead & Reynolds on Agency* (19th edn, Sweet & Maxwell 2010) [2-009].
9. *Yonge v Toynbee* [1910] 1 KB 215 (CA). In such a case, the agent will be liable to the third party for breach of warranty of authority (discussed at p 176).
10. Peter G Watts, *Bowstead & Reynolds on Agency* (19th edn, Sweet & Maxwell 2010) [2-009].
11. *Drew v Nunn* (1878–79) LR 4 QBD 661 (CA).

agent be of sound mind and if, due to mental incapacity, a person cannot understand the nature of the acts he is required to undertake, then he will not be able to affect the legal position of the principal. The actual contract of agency between the principal and the agent would remain valid, unless the principal knew of the incapacity, in which case it would be voidable at the incapacitated person's instance.[12]

Formality

Generally, the law imposes no formalities upon those who wish to enter into an agency relationship. Thus, an agency relationship can be brought into existence orally, in writing, or by executing a deed. This lack of formality even extends to situations where the agent is appointed to enter into contracts on the principal's behalf that are required to be in writing, or evidenced in writing.[13] This principle is subject to exceptions, however, and, in certain cases, the law will impose stipulations as to formality, with examples including:

- if the agent is appointed to execute a deed on behalf of the principal, then generally the agent will need to be appointed via a deed;[14]
- If an agent is engaged to create or dispose of an interest in land, then he must be authorized to do so in writing.[15]

Agency by agreement

The vast majority of agency relationships are created through an agreement between the principal and agent (i.e. both parties consent to an agency relationship coming into existence). In many cases (especially in commercial agencies), the agreement will be established contractually, either orally, in writing, or via the execution of a deed. However, there is no requirement that a relationship of agency be contractual, and where no contract of agency exists or where a contract purports to exist but lacks validity,[16] then the agency is said to be 'gratuitous'. Agency by agreement is founded upon consent, not on the existence of a contract. As Colman J stated:

> Although in modern commercial transactions agencies are almost invariably founded upon a contract between the principal and agent, there is no necessity for such a contract to exist. It is sufficient if there is consent by the principal to

---

12. *Molton v Camroux* (1849) 4 Ex 17; *Imperial Loan Co Ltd v Stone* [1892] 1 QB 599 (CA).

13. *Heard v Pilley* (1869) LR 4 Ch App 548 (agent orally appointed to enter into contract that must be in writing).

14. *Berkeley v Hardy* (1826) 5 B & C 335. Note that this stipulation will not apply where the deed is signed at the direction of and in the presence of the principal, and two witnesses attest the signature (Law of Property (Miscellaneous Provisions) Act 1989, s 1(3)).

15. Law of Property Act 1925, s 53(1)(a).

16. For example, because sufficient consideration is not present, or because one/both of the parties lack the requisite contractual capacity.

the exercise by the agent of authority and consent by the agent to his exercising such authority on behalf of the principal.[17]

Whilst both contractual and gratuitous agencies are equally valid, there are two noteworthy differences between them:

1. Where an agency is gratuitous, the parties need not provide consideration for the agency agreement. Consideration must be present in the case of a contractual agency agreement.

2. Where the agency is contractual, the duties, rights and obligations of the principal and agent will be stated in the contract and can be defeated or enforced by either party via the normal laws of contract. In the case of gratuitous agencies, the duties, rights, and obligations of the parties are set out in law (although the law does also provide for certain rights and obligations in cases involving contractual agencies).

The duties, rights and obligations of the parties to a gratuitous agency are discussed in ch 6

Most agency agreements will be express, but the courts might also find an agreement can be implied based upon the conduct of the parties.

Express agreement

The paradigm method of creating an agency relationship occurs where the principal and agent expressly agree to enter into an agency relationship (i.e. the principal expressly appoints the agent, and the agent expressly agrees to act on the principal's behalf). This agreement will usually be contractual (either in writing or oral), but need not be.

Implied agreement

A relationship of agency might be implied based upon the words or conduct of the principal or agent. Bowstead and Reynolds state that an agency agreement between the principal and agent will be implied 'where one party has conducted himself towards another in such a way that it is reasonable from that other to infer from that conduct assent to an agency relationship',[18] and the Court of Appeal has confirmed that this is the correct test to apply when determining whether an agency agreement should be implied.[19] The use of the word 'reasonable' indicates that the courts are not concerned with the subjective intentions of the parties, but with what a reasonable person would infer based on the words and conduct of the other person. Implied agency agreements can be contractual or gratuitous.

The key requirement is mutual consent (or 'assent' as Bowstead & Reynolds state)—one party (*A*) acts in such a way towards another party (*B*), that it is reasonable for *B* to infer that *A* consents to an agency relationship arising between them. This could occur in numerous ways, including the following:

- The principal (*A*) might appoint the agent (*B*) to a position which would usually result in *B* having the authority to act on *A*'s behalf.[20] By being appointed to that position, *B* reasonably infers that he has *A*'s consent to act on *A*'s behalf.

17. *Yasuda Fire & Marine Insurance Co of Europe Ltd v Orion Marine Insurance Underwriting Agency Ltd* [1995] QB 174 (QB) 185.
18. Peter G Watts, *Bowstead & Reynolds on Agency* (19th edn, Sweet & Maxwell 2010) [2-030].
19. *Marine Blast Ltd v Targe Towing Ltd* [2004] EWCA Civ 346, [2004] 1 Lloyd's Rep 721 [21] (Mance LJ).
20. *Pole v Leask* (1863) 33 LJ Ch 155.

- The principal may acquiesce to another person acting as his agent. However, it should be noted that there will need to be an indication that the principal has acquiesced and acquiescence will not be presumed merely because the principal remained silent.[21]

- The agent (*B*) may act on behalf of the principal (*A*).[22] From this, *A* might reasonably infer that *B* has consented to act as his agent. However, it should be noted that merely carrying out the principal's instructions will not, in itself, result in the implication of an agency relationship, and that there must be some indication present that *B* was acting on *A*'s behalf.[23]

Agency by ratification

Consider the following example:

> ### Eg ComCorp Ltd
>
> ComCorp is looking to acquire several pieces of art to display in the lobby of their corporate headquarters. Daniella, an art dealer, purchases a number of paintings from an art gallery. She informs the gallery that she is purchasing the paintings on behalf of ComCorp, but this is not the case—she has not been appointed as ComCorp's agent and has no authority to act on ComCorp's behalf. Upon discovering this, the gallery seeks to repudiate the contracts of sale. ComCorp, however, upon discovering that Daniella has falsely been claiming to be its agent, wishes for the sale to go ahead and so ratifies Daniella's actions. The art gallery refuses to sell the paintings to ComCorp.

The question that arises is whether an agent must be imbued with authority before she acts, or whether ComCorp can retroactively authorize Daniella to act on its behalf, thereby holding the art gallery to the contracts of sale. Where an agent acts without any authority (as is the case in this example), or acts beyond the scope of his authority, then the principal can validate the agent's actions by a process known as 'ratification'. The basic effect of ratification is to authorize the agent to engage in the relevant acts retroactively. Where no relationship of agency exists, the effect is to create a relationship of agency and provide the agent with authority retroactively.

🔗 The effects of ratification are discussed in more detail on p 77

Requirements for ratification

As the effect of ratification is to alter retroactively the legal consequences of actions that have already taken place, it is a concept that must be watched closely. Accordingly, in order for a principal to effectively ratify the actions of his agent, a number of requirements will need to be satisfied.

---

21. *Burnside v Dayrell* (1849) 3 Ex 224.   22. *Roberts v Ogilby* (1821) 9 Price 269.
23. *Kennedy v De Trafford* [1897] AC 180 (HL).

Principal must exist at time of contract

In order for a principal to be able to effectively ratify the acts of the agent, the principal must exist at the time the agent undertook the act in question. This requirement arises primarily in relation to legal persons, notably bodies corporate such as companies and limited liability partnerships. Accordingly, if a company has not been fully incorporated at the time the agent's act was undertaken then, upon its incorporation, the company cannot ratify the act, as the following case demonstrates.

 Kelner v Baxter and Others (1866–67) LR 2 CP 174

FACTS: It was agreed that a company (the Gravesend Royal Alexandria Hotel Co Ltd) would be set up to run a hotel and Kelner (a wine merchant) would become one of its directors. On 27 January, Kelner agreed to sell a quantity of wine to the company, and this agreement was signed by the other directors 'on behalf of the Gravesend Royal Alexandria Hotel Co Ltd'. The company was incorporated on 20 February, but collapsed soon after, having not paid Kelner for the wine. Kelner initiated proceedings, claiming that, as the company did not exist at the time of the contract, the other directors were personally liable. The other directors contended that the company had ratified the contract upon its incorporation, and so it was liable for the price of the wine.

HELD: The company's purported ratification of the contract was ineffective, as it did not exist at the time of the contract. Erle CJ stated that 'where a contract is signed by one who professes to be signing "as agent," but who has no principal existing at the time, and the contract would be altogether inoperative unless binding upon the person who signed it, he is bound thereby'.[24] Accordingly, the directors who signed the contract were personally liable to compensate Kelner for the price of the wine.

COMMENT: The rule that the **promoters** of a company are personally liable for contracts entered into on behalf of a company that does not yet exist has been codified in s 51 of the Companies Act 2006.[25] The company cannot ratify the contract and take the benefit of it—if the company wishes to benefit from the contract, the original contract must be discharged and a new contract must be created with the company on the same terms.[26] It can be argued that this is commercially inconvenient, especially as the EC Directive that led to the enactment of s 51 did permit the company to 'assume the obligations' arising under the contract.[27]

➡ promoter:
a person who undertakes and enters into the process of setting up a company

Agent must purport to act for a disclosed principal

A principal can only ratify those acts that the agent purported to carry out on behalf of that principal. It follows that ratification cannot take place where the agent

---

24. (1866–67) LR 2 CP 174, 183.
25. Although not stated by s 51, it has been established that the promoter can also enforce the contract against the third party (*Braymist Ltd v Wise Finance Co Ltd* [2002] EWCA Civ 127, [2002] Ch 273). Section 51 is discussed in more detail on p 173.
26. *Howard v Patent Ivory Manufacturing Co* (1888) LR 38 ChD 156 (Ch).
27. First Council Directive 68/151/EEC of 9 March 1968 on co-ordination of safeguards which, for the protection of the interests of members and others, are required by Member States of companies within the meaning of the second paragraph of Article 58 of the Treaty, with a view to making such safeguards equivalent throughout the Community [1968] OJ L 65/8, Art 7.

purports to act on his own behalf, even if the agent is in fact acting on behalf of a principal.

Keighley, Maxsted & Co v Durant [1901] AC 240 (HL)

FACTS: Keighley, Maxsted & Co ('KM', the principal) instructed Roberts (the agent) to purchase a quantity of wheat at a certain price. Roberts could not obtain the wheat at this price and, in breach of his authority, agreed to purchase the wheat at a higher price from Durant. Although the wheat was actually being bought on behalf of KM and Roberts, Roberts did not disclose this, and so it appeared that he was buying it purely on his own account. KM then purported to ratify Roberts' actions, but KM and Roberts then failed to take delivery of the wheat, resulting in Durant having to sell it elsewhere at a loss. Durant initiated proceedings against KM and Roberts for the amount lost. At first instance, the court held that KM's ratification was invalid, and so only Roberts was liable. On appeal, it was held that KM's ratification was valid, and so it could be liable. KM appealed.

HELD: The appeal was allowed and the House held that KM's ratification was invalid because Roberts had not purported to act on behalf of a principal. Lord Macnaghten stated that it was 'a well-established principle in English law that civil obligations are not to be created by, or founded upon, undisclosed intentions'.[28] Accordingly, the decision at first instance was restored and Roberts held liable.

COMMENT: The result of this case is that an undisclosed principal can never ratify the unauthorized acts of his agent. This rule has been strongly criticized, with *Keighley* being described as a 'short-sighted decision'.[29] Roberts was already KM's agent, and he had merely exceeded his authority as regards the price of the wheat. KM then ratified his actions and Durant, in initiating proceedings, was merely trying to hold KM to its decision to ratify. Accordingly, it has been contended that 'a principal who ratifies should be liable in the situation where the person who is already an agent exceeds his authority'.[30]

The agent need only *purport* to act on behalf of another. From this, it follows that if an agent falsely purports to act on behalf of another person, that person can still ratify the acts of the agent, as the following case demonstrates.

Re Tiedemann and Ledermann Freres [1899] 2 QB 66 (DC)

FACTS: The principal authorized an agent to sell wheat on his behalf. The agent sold quantities of wheat to third parties, but, after seeing that the price of wheat began to rise, he purchased the wheat back from the third parties and re-sold it later that same day for a higher price, thereby making a profit. The agent was engaging in these sales on his own

---

28. [1901] AC 240 (HL) 247.
29. Ian Brown, 'The Significance of General and Special Authority in the Development of the Agent's External Authority in English Law' [2004] JBL 391, 394.
30. Peter G Watts, *Bowstead & Reynolds on Agency* (19th edn, Sweet & Maxwell 2010) [2-061].

behalf, but falsely claimed that he was doing so on behalf of the principal. The price of wheat began to fall and the third parties began to suspect that the agent was purchasing the wheat on his own account. Accordingly, they sought to repudiate the contracts of sale. The principal, unsurprisingly, sought to ratify the agent's unauthorized activities and recover the profits for himself.

HELD: The principal's ratification was valid. Channell J stated that 'the contracts could be validly ratified by the person in whose name they purported to be made, even although they were in fact made without his actual authority, and although [the agent] had in his mind some fraudulent intent'.[31] Channell J did state that if the principal was also acting fraudulently, then ratification would not have been permitted, but this was not the case here.

The final issue to discuss is whether the agent needs to identify the principal he is acting for, as opposed to merely disclosing his existence. The answer is no, but it would appear that the agent must do more than simply state that he is acting as an agent, as the statement of Willes J indicates:

> The law obviously requires that the person for whom the agent professes to act must be a person capable of being ascertained at the time. It is not necessary that he should be named; but there must be such a description of him as shall amount to a reasonable designation of the person intended to be bound by the contract.[32]

Principal must have competency at the time of the agent's act

The effect of ratification is to treat the agent's act as being authorized at the time it was undertaken (i.e. authority is granted retroactively). It follows from this that, in order for ratification to be effective, the law requires that 'at the time the act was done the agent must have had a competent principal'[33] (this is a corollary of the rule discussed at p 63, namely that a principal can, through an agent, undertake any act that he has competence to undertake personally). Where, at the time of the agent's act, the principal lacked competence to engage in such an act himself, then ratification cannot occur.

 Boston Deep Sea Fishing and Ice Co Ltd v Farnham (Inspector of Taxes) [1957] 1 WLR 1051 (Ch)

FACTS: In 1940, a trawler belonging to a French company named Pêcheries de la Morinie ('PM', the principal) was docked at an English harbour. Whilst at the harbour, France was occupied by German forces, resulting in PM becoming an alien enemy. Boston Deep Sea Fishing and Ice Co Ltd ('Boston', the agent), which owned 49 per cent of the shares in PM, took control of the trawler and continued to use it, despite the fact that PM had not granted it authority to do so. Once the hostilities had ended, PM purported to ratify the

---

31. [1899] 2 QB 66 (DC) 71.
32. *Watson v Swann* (1862) 11 CBNS 756, 771.
33. *Firth v Staines* [1897] 2 QB 70 (QB) 75 (Wright J).

acts of Boston. In order to correctly calculate the amount of tax owed by Boston as a result of profits gained through the use of the trawler, it became necessary to determine whether or not PM's ratification was valid.

HELD: Harman J stated that '[a]t the time the acts were done the French company was an alien enemy at common law. It was therefore not a competent principal because it could not have done the act itself.'[34] Accordingly, as PM lacked the competence to undertake the acts itself, it could not subsequently ratify those acts when undertaken by Boston.

Principal must have competency when purported ratification takes place

The law not only requires competence at the time of the agent's act, it also requires that 'at the time of the ratification the principal must have been legally capable of doing the act himself'.[35] So, to use an example similar to *Boston Deep Sea Fishing* discussed earlier, if an English company acted as agent for a principal based in a friendly state that subsequently became an enemy, then the principal could not ratify the acts of the English company until hostilities ceased.

It would appear that not only must the principal be legally capable of doing the act himself, he must also be actually capable of doing the act himself at the time of ratification.

 Grover & Grover Ltd v Mathews [1910] 2 KB 401 (KB)

FACTS: Grover & Grover Ltd ('Grover', the principal) instructed Mr Brows (the agent) to take out an insurance policy over the factory that it owned. Upon the expiration of the insurance policy, Brows contacted the insurers to renew the policy, although he was not authorized to do so by Grover. The insurers sent renewal details but, before the renewal premium could be paid, the factory burned down. Grover sought to ratify Brows' act (i.e. the renewal) by paying the premium, but the insurers refused to accept the premium, on the ground that it was sent after the loss had occurred.

HELD: Whilst Grover had capacity to enter into the contract of insurance, it could not actually do so in this case, as a contract of insurance cannot be entered into after the event causing the loss has occurred.[36] Accordingly, the purported ratification was invalid.

---

34. [1957] 1 WLR 1051 (Ch) 1058. It is a long-held common law principle that a person does not have capacity to contract with an enemy of the state, and an enemy cannot appoint an agent to engage in acts that might benefit that enemy (*Stevenson & Sons Ltd v Aktiengesellschaftfür Cartonnagen-Industrie* [1918] AC 239 (HL)). Further, s 1 of the Trading with the Enemy Act 1939 made it a criminal offence to trade with the enemy.

35. *Firth v Staines* [1897] 2 QB 70 (QB) 75 (Wright J).

36. It should be noted that this principle is not absolute. For example, s 86 of the Marine Insurance Act 1906 states that a contract of marine insurance can be ratified by a person who is aware of the loss.

Principal must have knowledge of material circumstances

Bowstead & Reynolds state:

> In order that a person may be held to have ratified an act done without his authority, it is necessary that, at the time of the ratification, he should have full knowledge of all the material circumstances in which the act was done, unless he intended to ratify the act and take the risk whatever the circumstances might have been.[37]

In *Suncorp Insurance and Finance v Milano Assicurazioni SpA*,[38] Waller J approved this passage and went on to state that the requirement of full knowledge existed in order to protect principals from being found to have ratified too early. Quite what amounts to 'full knowledge' is difficult to predict because it is 'necessarily dependent upon the specific circumstances of any case',[39] but where the principal is aware of 'the essentials of what happened as between the agent and the third party',[40] then the requirement of full knowledge will most likely be satisfied.

Limitations on ratification

The courts have stated that, in certain cases, ratification will not be effective, even if the requirements outlined in the previous section have been satisfied.

Acts which are void *ab initio*

Not all acts can be ratified. In the *Brook* case, the court drew a distinction between voidable acts and acts that are void *ab initio*, with only the former being capable of ratification.

 Brook v Hook (1870–71) LR 6 Ex 89

➡ promissory note: an unconditional promise by one person to pay another person a sum of money

FACTS: Jones (the agent) forged the signature of Hook (the principal) on a **promissory note**. In an attempt to prevent Jones from being prosecuted, Hook purported to ratify Jones' actions. However, the promissory note was not honoured and Brook (the third party in whose favour the note had been granted) initiated proceedings against Hook.

HELD: The ratification was ineffective. Kelly CB stated that 'although a voidable act may be ratified by matter subsequent, it is otherwise when an act is originally and in its inception void'.[41] The forged signature rendered the note a nullity and so Brook could not recover the proceeds of the note from Hook.

---

37. Peter G Watts, *Bowstead & Reynolds on Agency* (19th edn, Sweet & Maxwell 2010) [2-067].
38. [1993] 2 Lloyd's Rep 225 (QB).
39. *SEB Trygg Holding Aktiebolag v Manches* [2005] EWHC 35 (Comm), [2005] 2 Lloyd's Rep 129 [133] (Gloster J).
40. *ING Re (UK) Ltd v R&V Versicherung AG* [2006] EWHC 1544 (Comm), [2006] 2 All ER (Comm) 870 [153] (Toulson J).
41. (1870–71) LR 6 Ex 89, 99.

> **COMMENT:** The distinction drawn by Kelly CB between voidable acts (which can be ratified) and void acts (which cannot be ratified) has been described as 'unsatisfactory'[42] on the ground that unauthorized acts cannot properly be described as voidable and, if anything, are better described as being void. It has been argued that a better way of explaining the result in *Brook* is that an agent who forges his principal's signature is not in fact acting on his principal's behalf, and so the issue of ratification does not arise.[43]

Ratification must not unfairly prejudice a third party

Bowstead & Reynolds state that '[r]atification is not effective where to permit it would unfairly prejudice a third party'.[44] This principle has been judicially accepted,[45] but the case law in this area is extremely confusing and is rife with inconsistent interpretations. For example, consider the following case.

 Bird v Brown (1850) 4 Exch 786

FACTS: Bird (the agent), purportedly acting on behalf of Illins (the principal and consignor of goods), ordered the stoppage of those goods, after discovering that the consignee had become bankrupt. In fact, Bird had no authority to order such a stoppage. The goods eventually reached their destination where the consignee's trustee in bankruptcy made a formal demand for them. The goods were to be shipped to the consignee, but the shipmaster refused to deliver the goods on the basis they had been stopped in transit. Illins sought to ratify the stoppage in transit.

HELD: The ratification was ineffective.

COMMENT: The reasoning behind the decision has been a topic of considerable debate. In *Bird*, Rolfe B stated that 'the goods had already become the property of the [consignee], free from all rights of stoppage',[46] leading certain judges[47] to contend that the decision was based on the notion that ratification cannot occur where it would divest the vested proprietary rights of a third party. Other judges, however, contend that the *ratio* in *Bird* is that 'if a time is fixed for doing an act, whether by statute or by agreement, the doctrine of ratification cannot be allowed to apply if it would have the effect of extending that time'.[48] It has even been argued that *Bird* is not adequate authority for either of these views and

---

42. See e.g. Peter G Watts, *Bowstead & Reynolds on Agency* (19th edn, Sweet & Maxwell 2010) [2-057]; Len S Sealy and Richard JA Hooley, *Commercial Law: Text, Cases and Materials* (4th edn, OUP 2009) 144.

43. See Edwin Peel, *Treitel on the Law of Contract* (13th edn, Sweet & Maxwell 2011) [769], *Greenwood v Martins Bank Ltd* [1932] 1 KB 371 (CA) 378–9 (Scrutton LJ).

44. Peter G Watts, *Bowstead & Reynolds on Agency* (19th edn, Sweet & Maxwell 2010) [2-087].

45. *The Owners of the Ship 'Borvigilant' v The Owners of the Ship 'Romina G'* [2003] EWCA Civ 935, [2003] 2 All ER (Comm) 736, [70] (Clarke LJ).

46. (1850) 4 Exch 786, 800.

47. See e.g. Cotton LJ in *Bolton Partners v Lambert* (1899) LR 41 ChD 295 (CA) 307. This view was confirmed by Roch LJ in *Presentaciones Musicales SA v Secunda* [1994] Ch 271 (CA) 284.

48. *Presentaciones Musicales SA v Secunda* [1994] Ch 271 (CA) 279 (Dillon LJ). This view was confirmed by Clarke LJ in *The Owners of the Ship 'Borvigilant' v The Owners of the Ship 'Romina G'* [2003] EWCA Civ 935, [2003] 2 All ER (Comm) 736 [84].

⭐ See Tan
Cheng-Han, 'The
Principle in Bird v
Brown Revisited'
(2001) 117 LQR 626

'should no longer be regarded as the basis for determining cases where ratification takes place after property or contractual rights have vested, or cases where ratification takes place after a time limit provided for has been exceeded'.[49]

More recent cases have moved away from attempting to determine the precise reasoning behind *Bird* and instead state that these cases should be regarded as examples 'of the general rationale identified in *Bowstead & Reynolds'* Art 19, that is, unfair prejudice'.[50] It would therefore appear that the current approach of the courts, when determining whether to permit ratification, is to determine whether ratification would unfairly prejudice the third party, and not to place limitations on the instances when ratification may be rendered ineffective due to such unfair prejudice.

Ratification must take place within a reasonable time

In order for ratification to be effective, the principal must ratify the agent's act within a reasonable time, as established in the following case.

 Metropolitan Asylums Board v Kingham & Sons (1890) 6 TLR 217 (QB)

FACTS: Metropolitan Asylums Board ('MAB', the principal) invited suppliers to submit tenders for the supply of eggs, with supply due to begin on 30 September. Kingham & Sons ('Kingham') was notified on 22 September that its tender had been accepted by MAB's managers (the agents), but the acceptance was invalid as MAB's seal had not been affixed to the tender. On 24 September, Kingham informed the managers that the price stated in the tender was incorrect, and purported to withdraw the tender. On 6 October, MAB sought to ratify the acts of its managers by affixing the corporate seal to the tender, thereby holding Kingham to the tendered price. Kingham refused to perform, and so MAB commenced proceedings.

HELD: The purported ratification was ineffective, as it was too late. Fry LJ stated *obiter* that 'if ratification is to bind, it must be made within a reasonable time after acceptance by an unauthorised person. That reasonable time can never extend after the time at which the contract is to commence.'[51]

COMMENT: The requirement that ratification must take place within a reasonable time is a logical limitation designed to provide a measure of certainty, especially in cases where a third party has entered into agreements with an agent who lacks authority. In such a case, the third party will want to know quickly whether the agreement will continue or can be enforced. The second part of Fry LJ's *dictum* (namely that ratification cannot take place after the time when the contract was due to commence) has been doubted academically[52] and judicially[53] and so cannot be regarded as good law.

---

49. Tan Cheng-Han, 'The Principle in Bird v Brown Revisited' (2001) 117 LQR 626, 643–4.
50. *Smith v Henniker-Major & Co* [2002] EWCA Civ 762, [2003] Ch 182 [71] (Robert Walker LJ).
51. (1890) 6 TLR 217 (QB) 218.
52. See e.g. Peter G Watts, *Bowstead & Reynolds on Agency* (19th edn, Sweet & Maxwell 2010) [2-090].
53. See e.g. *Bedford Insurance Co Ltd v Instituto de Resseguros do Brasil* [1985] QB 966 (QB) 987.

Who can ratify?

Once the requirements for ratification have been met, the next issue to discuss is who has the ability to ratify the agent's acts. In *Jones v Hope*,[54] Brett LJ stated that 'nobody can ratify a contract purporting to be made by an agent except the party on whose behalf the agent purported to act.'[55] Accordingly, only the principal on whose behalf the agent purported to act can ratify. However, the principal need not personally ratify the agent's acts—he can authorize an agent to ratify the unauthorized acts on his behalf. In such a case, all the agent requires is the authority to ratify the act—he will not require authority to engage in the acts that are being ratified.[56]

Methods of ratification

In limited instances, the law will state that ratification must occur in a certain way. For example, an agent authorized to execute a deed must be appointed by deed, and it follows from this that the ratification of such an act must also be by deed.[57] Generally, however, the law does not specify the method by which ratification takes place. Ratification can be express or implied, and by words or by conduct. Express ratification occurs where the principal expressly manifests an intention to ratify the agent's act (e.g. by expressly stating that he intends to ratify). Implied ratification is less straightforward and occurs where:

> the conduct of the person in whose name or on whose behalf the act or transaction is done or entered into is such as to amount to clear evidence that he adopts or recognises such act or transaction: and may be implied from the mere acquiescence or inactivity of the principal.[58]

This formulation has, on numerous occasions, been confirmed by the courts as an accurate account of the law.[59] As stated, there will need to be 'clear evidence' that the purported principal ratifies the act or transaction—if the purported ratification is vague and could be interpreted to mean something else, it will be ineffective. Whether or not implied ratification has occurred is usually a question of fact based upon the circumstances of the case. The following case provides an example of the type of act that can amount to implied ratification.

---

54. (1880) 3 TLR 247.

55. ibid 251.

56. *Re Portuguese Consolidated Copper Mines Ltd* (1890) LR 45 ChD 16 (CA).

57. *Hunter v Parker* (1840) 7 M&W 322.

58. Peter G Watts, *Bowstead & Reynolds on Agency* (19th edn, Sweet & Maxwell 2010) [2-070].

59. See e.g. *Suncorp Insurance and Finance v Milano Assicurazioni SpA* [1993] 2 Lloyd's Rep 225 (QB) 234; *Sea Emerald SA v Prominvestbank—Joint Stockpoint Commercial Industrial & Investment Bank* [2008] EWHC 1979 (Comm) [102]–[103]; *Norwich Union Life & Pensions Ltd v Strand Street Properties Ltd* [2009] EWHC 1109 (Ch) [237].

Hogan and Others v London Irish Football Rugby Club Trading Ltd (QB, 20 December 1999)

FACTS: The principal, London Irish Football Rugby Club Trading Ltd ('the Club'), employed Anderson (the agent) as the director of rugby. His job was to coach the first fifteen and set up a recruitment programme to ensure the long-term success of the Club. The Club's board of directors expressly informed Anderson that he did not have the authority to enter into binding agreements with players. Despite this, he entered into negotiations with Hogan and three other players and offered each of them a two-year contract. These players attended training sessions, represented the Club, and were paid their contractual rate of remuneration. A few months later, these players were informed that their services were not required. They alleged that this amounted to a breach of their employment contracts, while the Club contended that the contracts were invalid, as Anderson had no authority to enter into binding contracts with players.

HELD: By allowing the players to attend training sessions and represent the Club, and by continuing to pay them their salaries, the Club had impliedly ratified Anderson's actions. Accordingly, the termination of the players' contracts amounted to a breach of contract, for which they were entitled to damages.

Acquiescence or inactivity

As Rowlatt J stated, '[r]atification is a unilateral act of the will'.[60] Accordingly, the principal is not required to communicate his intention to ratify to the agent or third party, providing that the intention to ratify is (expressly or impliedly) manifested in some way. From this, it follows that acquiescence or inactivity can amount to ratification, as stated by Moore-Bick J:

> [Ratification] does not…depend on communication with or representation to the third party…but since the intention to ratify must be manifested in some way it will in practice often be communicated to and relied upon by the other party to the transaction. Ratification can no doubt be inferred without difficulty from silence or inactivity in cases where the principal, by failing to disown the transaction, allows a state of affairs to come about which is inconsistent with treating the transaction as unauthorized.[61]

However, where the principal has not manifested an intention to ratify, then it is less likely that acquiescence or inactivity will amount to ratification and will instead be regarded as 'an unwillingness or inability on the part of the principal to commit himself'.[62]

Partial ratification

It is not possible for the principal to ratify part of the agent's actions and reject the rest or, as Robert Walker LJ stated '[a] party wishing to ratify a transaction must adopt it in its entirety'.[63] The rationale behind this limitation is that, if partial ratification

---

60. *Harrison & Crossfield Ltd v London & North-Western Railway Co* [1917] 2 KB 755 (KB) 758.
61. *Yona International Ltd v La Reunion Française SA* [1996] 2 Lloyd's Rep 84 (QB) 106.
62. ibid.
63. *Smith v Henniker-Major & Co* [2002] EWCA Civ 762, [2003] Ch 182 [56].

were permitted, a third party would be bound to the principal in a way that he did not intend. Accordingly, the general rule is that if the principal has not ratified the agent's act in its entirety, then ratification cannot be said to have occurred. However, the courts have also stated that, in certain cases, 'adoption of part of a transaction may be held to amount to ratification of the whole'.[64]

Can ratification, or a refusal to ratify, be revoked?

Once a principal has ratified the acts of his agent, he cannot then change his mind and revoke his ratification.[65] However, a principal who originally declined to ratify can change his mind and ratify the act,[66] providing that such ratification is made within a reasonable time,[67] and does not unfairly prejudice any third parties.[68]

Effects of ratification

Where a principal effectively ratifies an act of his agent, then the law will regard this ratification as being 'equivalent to antecedent authority'.[69] In other words, the law will regard the agent's actions as being authorized when they were undertaken, with the result that the contract between the principal and the third party will be enforceable by both parties. As the following controversial case demonstrates, this will even be the case where the third party purports to withdraw from the contract prior to ratification occurring.

 Bolton Partners Ltd v Lambert (1889) LR 41 ChD 295 (CA)

FACTS: Lambert offered to buy a factory that belonged to Bolton Partners Ltd ('Bolton', the principal). Lambert made the offer to Scratchley (the agent), who was Bolton's managing director. Scratchley purported to accept the offer, but he lacked the authority to do so. On 13 January, a dispute arose and Lambert purported to revoke his offer. On 17 January, Bolton commenced proceedings against Lambert for breach of contract, and sought specific performance to enforce the agreement. On 28 January, Bolton sought to ratify Scratchley's acceptance of Lambert's offer. Lambert contended that, as Scratchley's acceptance was invalid, he was free to revoke the offer and, as the offer had been revoked, Bolton could not ratify Scratchley's purported acceptance.

HELD: The ratification was valid, and the order for specific performance was granted. Cotton LJ stated that:

> The rule as to ratification by a principal of acts done by an assumed agent is that the ratification is thrown back to the date of the act done, and that the agent is put

---

64. ibid. For an example of this occurring, see *Re Mawcon Ltd* [1969] 1 WLR 78 (Ch).

65. *SEB Trygg Holding Aktiebolag v Manches* [2005] EWHC 35 (Comm), [2005] 2 Lloyd's Rep 129.

66. *Soames v Spencer* (1822) 1 D&R 32.

67. *Metropolitan Asylums Board v Kingham & Sons* (1890) 6 TLR 217 (QB). This case is discussed at p 74.

68. *McEvoy v Belfast Banking Co Ltd* [1935] AC 24 (HL).

69. *Koenigsblatt v Sweet* [1923] 2 Ch 314 (CA) 325 (Lord Sterndale MR).

> in the same position as if he had had authority to do the act at the time the act was
> done by him.[70]
>
> Applying this, Scratchley was authorized to accept Lambert's offer at the time he accepted
> it. It follows that a valid contract came into existence at that point, and so Lambert could
> not subsequently revoke his offer.

Unsurprisingly, the decision has been criticized for several reasons. First, the rule strongly favours the principal, but places the third party in an 'invidious position in that he cannot withdraw from the obligation before ratification, yet the principal may elect not to ratify without legal consequence'.[71] Second, it has been contended that, where a third party is trying to escape the contract prior to ratification occurring (as in *Bolton*), then ratification should be ineffective as 'until ratification takes place, there is no contract enforceable either by the agent or the principal'.[72] Third, many countries have moved away from *Bolton* and held ratification to be ineffective in such cases. As far back as 1920, one commentator stated '[w]here [the third party] did not know of the lack of authority…fairness…would allow him an option to withdraw…Most of the American courts have reached this decision in cases dealing with ratification. The English cases to the contrary must be wrong.'[73] The American Law Institute's *Restatement* also rejects the rule in *Bolton*,[74] and Article 15(2) of the Convention on Agency in the International Sale of Goods states that:

> [w]here, at the time of the agent's act, the third party neither knew nor ought to
> have known of the lack of authority, he shall not be liable to the principal if, at
> any time before ratification, he gives notice of his refusal to become bound by a
> ratification.

Despite the criticism, it has been argued that the decision in *Bolton* is justifiable for two reasons. First, it has been contended that 'if the principal ratifies the contract, the third party gets what he bargained for'.[75] From Lambert's perspective, a valid contract existed the moment the agent accepted his offer, and so any attempt at revocation would have predictably been regarded as a breach of contract on Lambert's part. Second, the rule in *Bolton* is not absolute and will not operate in many instances, as is demonstrated by the numerous requirements and limitations that exist upon a principal's ability to ratify.

In addition to providing antecedent authority, ratification may also entitle the agent to receive remuneration/commission,[76] or to be indemnified for any expenses incurred in the course of the ratified agency.[77]

🔗 An agent's right
to remuneration,
commission, or an
indemnity is discussed
at p 137

---

70. (1889) LR 41 ChD 295 (CA) 306.

71. Ian Brown, 'Ratification, Retroactivity and Reasonableness' (1994) 110 LQR 531, 531.

72. Tan Cheng-Han, 'The Principle in Bird v Brown Revisited' (2001) 117 LQR 626, 628–9.

73. WA Seavey, 'The Rationale of Agency' (1920) 29 Yale LJ 859, 891.

74. American Law Institute, *Restatement of the Law—Agency* (American Law Institute 2006) § 4.05.

75. Len S Sealy and Richard JA Hooley, *Commercial Law: Text, Cases and Materials* (4th edn, OUP 2009) 148.

76. *Keay v Fenwick* (1876) LR 1 CPC 745 (CA).

77. *Hartas v Ribbons* (1889) LR 22 QBD 254 (CA).

Agreements subject to ratification

Where a contract is entered into subject to ratification by the principal, then the rule in *Bolton* will not apply as, in such a case, the act of ratification creates the contract. In such a case, the third party is free to withdraw at any time before ratification, as demonstrated in the following case.

 Watson v Davies [1931] 1 Ch 455 (Ch)

FACTS: Davies offered to sell a piece of property to a charity. The charity (the principal) arranged for an inspection of the property to be carried out by several of its board members. The inspection team (the agents) told Davies that they had resolved to buy the property, and so accepted the offer subject to a formal meeting of the board (i.e. their acceptance was subject to ratification). The charity's secretary informed the board that the inspection team was inquorate and so had no authority to accept Davies' offer. A meeting of the full board was convened in order to ratify the inspection team's acceptance, but before the meeting took place, Davies withdrew the offer. Despite this, the board meeting went ahead, where it purported to ratify the acceptance of Davies' offer. Davies refused to proceed with the sale and Watson, the charity's managing director, sought an order for specific performance.

HELD: The court refused to grant specific performance. Maugham J stated that:

> [a]n acceptance by an agent subject in express terms to ratification by his principal is legally a nullity until ratification, and is no more binding on the other party than an unaccepted offer which can, of course, be withdrawn before acceptance.[78]

Accordingly, as Davies had withdrawn the offer prior to ratification, it could no longer be accepted.

Liability of the agent

The final issue to discuss is whether ratification exonerates the agent of all liability for breach of authority. Such liability can arise in two ways. First, the agent can be liable to the principal for exceeding his authority. If the principal ratifies the agent's act, does the principal also give up any right to sue the agent for exceeding his authority? In many cases, the principal will obtain an advantage from ratifying the agent's act, and so will not seek to commence proceedings against the agent (especially if he wishes to work with the agent again in the future). However, the courts have acknowledged that ratification will not automatically exonerate the agent of his breach of authority, and the issue should be considered in two stages:

> First, is there ratification of the contract which the agent purported to make. Second, has the principal waived the breach of duty if any vis-à-vis the agent. Often the facts will lead to ratification and exoneration, but not always.[79]

---

78. [1931] 1 Ch 455 (Ch) 469.
79. *Suncorp Insurance and Finance v Milano Assicurazioni SpA* [1993] 2 Lloyd's Rep 225 (QB) 234–5 (Waller J).

🔗 Breach of warranty of authority is discussed at p 176

Second, the agent can be liable to the third party for breach of warranty of authority, and the general rule is that ratification does not exonerate the agent's liability for such a breach. However, as the measure of damages for such a breach is based on the loss which the parties should reasonably have contemplated would result from the breach (i.e. the loss incurred as a result of the contract not coming into operation), and as the act of ratification will normally avoid such loss (by bringing the contract into operation), it follows that the agent will not normally be able to recover damages. If, however, the third party has incurred costs due to the unauthorized acts of the agent, then these may be recoverable.

Agency by operation of law

In several cases, an agency relationship may be imposed upon the parties by the operation of law. In such cases, the fact that the parties do not intend or wish for an agency relationship to arise is irrelevant. It does not follow, however, that the agency relationship is not consensual, as the law will deem that the parties consented, even if they did, in fact, not do so.

Agency of necessity

Consider the following example:

 ComCorp Ltd

ComCorp agrees to purchase a quantity of apples from a company based in Portugal. ComCorp enters into an agreement with FreightSafe Ltd to transport the apples by sea. The apples are loaded onto one of FreightSafe's ships but, due to poor weather conditions, the ship is forced remain in dock at a port in Portugal until the weather improves. Due to the delay, the apples begin to deteriorate and so the shipmaster decides to sell the goods on behalf of ComCorp, but, given their state, the price obtained is half what ComCorp paid for them. ComCorp states that the shipmaster had no legal right to sell the goods and initiates legal proceedings. The shipmaster contends that he was acting as ComCorp's agent.

The shipmaster was not appointed as ComCorp's agent (and even if he was, he was not authorized to sell the apples), nor did ComCorp ratify his actions, so on what basis can he claim to be an agent? The shipmaster would be likely to argue that the agency relationship arose through necessity. Agency of necessity usually arises where one person acts on behalf of another due to the existence of some form of emergency. Unlike agency by agreement or agency by ratification, agency of necessity is not based upon the consent of the parties, and usually arises in cases where a relationship of agency is not desired by the principal.

Where agency of necessity is established, the effect will usually be to increase the authority of an existing agent, but it can also create a relationship of agency where none previously existed. It is important to note that, in the following case, the House of Lords indicated that only certain types of case would amount to 'true' cases of agency of necessity.

 ### China-Pacific SA v Food Corporation of India (The Winson) [1982] AC 939 (HL)

FACTS: Food Corporation of India ('FCI') chartered a ship to transport a cargo of wheat from the USA to Bombay (now Mumbai). En route, the ship became stranded on a reef. The shipmaster entered into a contract with China Pacific SA ('CP'), a firm of professional salvors. CP managed to salvage 15,429 tonnes of wheat and, to protect it from deteriorating, stored it at its own expense. CP then sought to recover these storage expenses from FCI, but FCI refused to pay.

HELD: The House held that CP could recover the storage expenses from FCI.

➡ **salvor:** a person engaged in the salvaging of a ship, or of items lost at sea

⭐ See FD Rose, 'From Necessary to Restitution' (1982) 45 MLR 568

The decision in *The Winson* was not actually determined through agency principles, but was instead based on the law relating to salvage, bailment, and liens. However, as the case clearly involved a situation in which a relationship of agency might be found to exist, Lord Diplock decided to provide guidance regarding the scope of agency of necessity by distinguishing between two different types of case:

1. Cases where 'circumstances exist which in law have the effect of conferring on [a person] authority to create contractual rights and obligations between [another person] and a third party that are directly enforceable by each against the other';[80]

2. Cases where 'the only relevant question is whether a person who, without obtaining instructions from the owner of goods incurs expenses in taking steps that are reasonably necessary for their preservation is in law entitled to recover from the owner of the goods the reasonable expenses incurred by him in taking those steps'.[81]

In the second type of case, the ability of the 'agent' to legally bind his 'principal' to a third party is not a key issue—the only issue is whether the 'agent' can recover expenses for costs incurred, and so it could be argued that, strictly, no relationship of agency arises. Lord Diplock appeared to agree with this argument, and stated that only the first type of case provides a true example of agency of necessity, with the second type of case being more appropriately regarded as a form of restitution. Accordingly, this section will focus on the first type of case only.

Requirements for agency of necessity

In order for agency of necessity to arise, four requirements must be satisfied. It is worth noting that in *The Winson* (discussed earlier), Lord Diplock was of the opinion that these requirements might only apply to cases of true agency, and might not apply in their entirety to cases where the agent is simply seeking to recover his expenses.

---

80. [1982] AC 939 (HL) 958.
81. ibid.

The first requirement is that the actions of the agent must be necessary for the benefit of the principal. The test is an objective one, meaning that it does not matter whether the agent honestly believed that his actions were necessary—what matters is whether a reasonable person would regard the action taken as necessary.[82] The inevitable issue that arises is how is necessity to be determined. The courts have provided some specific guidance—for example, the Court of Appeal has stated that acting in order to avoid mere inconvenience will not be enough to establish necessity.[83] Overall, however, the scope of necessity is rather vague. Perhaps the best indication comes from Sir Montague Smith, who stated that the concept of necessity refers to:

> the force of circumstances which determine the course a man ought to take. Thus, when by the force of circumstances a man has the duty cast upon him of taking some action for another, and under that obligation, adopts the course which, to the judgment of a wise and prudent man, is apparently the best for the interest of the persons for whom he acts in a given emergency, it may properly be said of the course so taken, that it was, in a mercantile sense, necessary to take it.[84]

The second requirement is that it is not reasonably practicable for the agent to communicate with the principal. The exact scope of this test is unclear, as the following case demonstrates.

 Springer v Great Western Railway Co [1921] 1 KB 257 (CA)

FACTS: A quantity of tomatoes belonging to Springer was delivered to the Great Western Railway Co ('GWR'), who would then deliver them to Springer. The tomatoes were placed on a ship for delivery but, due to bad weather, their arrival was delayed. Upon arrival, GWR's dockworkers went on strike, further delaying the delivery of the tomatoes. By this time, the tomatoes had started to deteriorate and so GWR's traffic agent decided to sell the tomatoes locally, without first discussing this with Springer, which he could have done. Springer sought damages for breach of carriage, and GWR contended that the sale was justified because it was necessary.

HELD: GWR had 'time to communicate with [Springer] and it was commercially possible to do so and to ask him what he wished should be done with the tomatoes'.[85] The failure to do so meant that a relationship of agency based on necessity had not arisen and so Springer's action succeeded.

COMMENT: Debate arose as to how impracticable communication must be in order to satisfy this requirement. Scrutton LJ stated that communication had to be 'commercially impossible',[86] whereas Bankes LJ stated that communication had to be 'practically

82. *Tetley & Co v British Trade Corp* (1922) 10 Ll L Rep 678 (KB).
83. *Sachs v Miklos* [1948] 2 KB 23 (CA).
84. *The Australasian Steam Navigation Co v Morse* (1871–73) LR 4 PC 222 (PC) 230.
85. [1921] 1 KB 257 (CA) 268 (Scrutton LJ).
86. ibid 267.

impossible'.[87] McCardie J, in a different case, went further and stated that 'agency of necessity does not arise if the agent can communicate with his principal',[88] indicating that actual impossibility is required. It is contended that Scrutton LJ's less stringent formulation is preferable on the ground that it would include situations where communication was actually possible, but would not be commercially realistic (e.g. where an agent is acting on behalf of many principals simultaneously). In any event, with the advent of modern telecommunications, this requirement has become increasingly difficult to satisfy, resulting in a significant reduction in the number of actual cases of agency of necessity.

The third requirement is that the agent's actions were reasonable and prudent, and that he acted bona fide in the interests of the principal, with the following case providing an example of a situation where this requirement was not satisfied.

Prager v Blatspiel, Stamp and Heacock Ltd [1924] 1 KB 566 (KB)

FACTS: Blatspiel, Stamp and Heacock Ltd ('BSH', the agent), a London-based company, purchased fur skins on behalf of Prager (the principal), a Bucharest-based fur merchant, and was to despatch them to Romania. Prager paid for the skins, but, before they could be despatched, German forces occupied Romania and it became impossible for BSH to send the skins to, or contact, Prager. Subsequently, BSH sold the skins, by which time they had increased in value. When the war ended, Prager requested that BSH send the skins. When Prager discovered that the skins had been sold, he initiated proceedings against BSH. BSH contended that it was necessary to sell the skins quickly as they were getting 'stale', and so authority was granted to it via agency of necessity.

HELD: As the furs deteriorated very slowly and any loss in value caused by this was easily offset by the increase in the value of the furs, McCardie J emphatically rejected BSH's claim that the sale was necessary. He stated that 'I decide, without hesitation, that the defendants did not act bona fide...I hold that the defendants were not in fact agents of necessity, that the sales of the plaintiff's goods were not justified, and that the defendants acted dishonestly.'[89] Accordingly, BSH was ordered to compensate Prager for the price of the skins.

Little difficulty arises where, as in *Prager*, the agent has a single motive (namely to sell the skins and make a profit for itself). Problems can arise, however, where the agent acts for a variety of motives, some of which may be bona fide and others not so. The law has yet to provide an adequate solution to such instances. Lord Diplock has stated that 'it may well be that the court will look to the interest mainly served or to the dominant motive',[90] but which of these two tests is preferable is not clear.

The fourth, and final, requirement is that the principal was competent at the time of the agent's act. So, for example, if at the time of the agent's act, the principal was

---

87. ibid 266.

88. *Prager v Blatspiel, Stamp and Heacock Ltd* [1924] 1 KB 566 (KB) 571.

89. ibid 574.

90. *China-Pacific SA v Food Corporation of India (The Winson)* [1982] AC 939 (HL) 966.

an alien enemy,[91] or a company that had not been fully incorporated or had been dissolved,[92] then a relationship of agency by necessity will not arise.

Scope of agency of necessity

As can be seen from the cases discussed, virtually all of the cases in this area involve goods being transported by sea. The question that arises is whether agency of necessity is limited to maritime cases, or whether it can apply to any case involving some form of emergency. Unfortunately, the issue is unclear. Limiting the doctrine to maritime cases would appear illogical as 'an agent may be faced with the same necessity to act whether he finds himself on foreign waters or on land'.[93] Indeed, there have been a number of non-maritime cases involving perishable goods where the courts have found an agency of necessity to exist.[94] Despite this, the courts appear reluctant to extend the doctrine to non-maritime cases. For example, Bowen LJ, referring to the doctrine of agency of necessity stated that '[n]o similar doctrine applies to anything lost upon land, nor to anything except ships or goods in peril at sea'.[95]

Agency imposed by statute or the courts

An agency relationship may be imposed upon certain parties by statute. Examples include:

- Every partner in an ordinary partnership is an agent of the firm and of his fellow partners for the purposes of the business of the partnership.[96] Similarly, every member of a limited liability partnership is an agent of the limited liability partnership.[97]
- The administrator of a company is an agent of the company,[98] as is a receiver[99] and an administrative receiver.[100]
- In certain regulated consumer credit agreements, the person negotiating with the debtor will be deemed to be acting as an agent for the creditor.[101]

A relationship of agency may also, based upon the particular facts of the case, be imposed upon certain parties by the courts. For example, it is well established that while the directors of a company are agents of the company, they are not normally agents of the company's members.[102] However, in limited situations (e.g. where the

---

91. *Jebara v Ottoman Bank* [1927] 2 KB 254 (CA).

92. *Re Banque des Marchands de Moscou (No 1)* [1952] 1 All ER 1269 (Ch).

93. Samuel J Stoljar, *The Law of Agency* (Sweet & Maxwell 1961) 154.

94. See e.g. *Sims & Co v Midland Railway Co* [1913] 1 KB 103 (KB).

95. *Falcke v Scottish Imperial Insurance Co* (1887) LR 34 ChD 234 (CA) 249.

96. Partnership Act 1890, s 5.

97. Limited Liability Partnerships Act 2000, s 6(1).

98. Insolvency Act 1986, Sch B1, para 69.

99. ibid s 57(1). The receiver will only be an agent in relation to the property that is attached to the floating charge by which he was appointed.

100. ibid s 44(1)(a). Note that an administrative receiver will not be an agent of the company if the company is in liquidation.

101. Consumer Credit Act 1974, s 56(2).

102. *Gramophone and Typewriter Ltd v Stanley* [1908] 2 KB 89 (CA).

directors act for the members in selling their shares),[103] the courts have held that the directors can be acting as agents of the members.

Agency arising due to estoppel

An agent may be imbued with authority where his principal represents to a third party that the agent has authority to act in a particular way. In such a case, the agent may be imbued with apparent authority, and the principal may be estopped from denying that an agency relationship exists. The use of estoppel as the theoretical basis of apparent authority has been described as 'shaky'[104] and 'artificial',[105] principally on the ground that many cases of apparent authority do not fully satisfy the requirements for estoppel. Despite this, it is now generally accepted that estoppel does form the basis of apparent authority, albeit a form of estoppel 'with weak requirements, special to agency'.[106] Apparent authority and its basis in estoppel are discussed in detail in Chapter 5. All that need be noted here is that estoppel can serve to extend an agent's authority or to create a relationship of agency where none previously existed.

⚲ Apparent authority is discussed at p 96

Conclusion

Given that the actions of an agent can affect the legal position of the principal, it is vital for all parties involved to be confident that a relationship of agency does in fact exist, and so businesses should have a sound grasp of the methods by which a relationship of agency can be created. As discussed, it may even be the case that a relationship of agency may be imposed upon two parties who did not wish, or who had no desire, for such a relationship to arise. Such parties should be careful not to act in a manner that could lead the courts to rule that a relationship of agency does in fact exist.

Having discussed the various methods by which a relationship of agency can be created, Chapter 5 will discuss what is perhaps the most important and central concept within the law of agency, namely the authority of the agent.

Practice questions

1. Define the following terms:
    *   capacity;
    *   mental incapacity;
    *   gratuitous agency;
    *   ratification;

---

103. *Allen v Hyatt* (1914) 30 TLR 444 (PC).
104. Roderick Munday, *Agency: Law and Principles* (OUP 2010) 61.
105. Peter G Watts, *Bowstead & Reynolds on Agency* (19th edn, Sweet & Maxwell 2010) [8-029].
106. ibid [2-100].

- acquiescence;
- estoppel.

2. 'It is unjust to force a relationship of agency on parties who do not wish for such a relationship to arise. Accordingly, in order for a relationship of agency to arise, the consent of both parties should always be present.'

   Do you agree with this statement? Provide reasons for your answers.

3. James, an agent engaged by ComCorp, has been instructed to lease a piece of machinery that will be used in one of ComCorp's factories. His instructions state that the cost of leasing the machine should be no more than £1,500 per month, but he finds it extremely difficult to lease the machinery at this price. The directors of ComCorp contact James to let him know that ComCorp has obtained a lucrative contract, but that it will not be able to fulfil the contract unless it can obtain the piece of machinery in the next few days. James visits PlantHire Ltd and sees the piece of machinery he requires, but the monthly lease is £1,800. Despite this, James states, 'That is exactly what I need. I will lease it from you.' From this, Planthire believe that James is leasing it on his own account. When Planthire discover that James is in fact acting on behalf of ComCorp and he has breached his authority, they refuse to provide the machinery. ComCorp, however, is willing to pay the lease price of £1,800 per month, although, to recoup the extra £300 that it will have to pay, its directors consider commencing proceedings against James for breach of authority.

   Advise ComCorp's directors on

   (i) whether a binding contract exists between ComCorp and PlantHire; and

   (ii) whether ComCorp should sue James for breach of authority.

Further reading

Ian Brown, 'Authority and Necessity in the Law of Agency' (1992) 55 MLR 414
- Discusses several key cases relating to agency by necessity, and contends that the theoretical underpinnings of agency by necessity is murky and indistinct.

Ian Brown, 'Ratification, Retroactivity and Reasonableness' (1994) 110 LQR 531
- Discusses the rule established in *Bolton Partners v Lambert* and looks at the effects of subsequent cases on the rule.

Tan Cheng-Han, 'The Principle in *Bird v Brown* Revisited' (2001) 117 LQR 626
- Discusses the controversial case of *Bird v Brown* and contends that the principle established in that case has been over-extended to cover cases where it should not have been applied.

Roderick Munday, *Agency: Law and Principles* (OUP 2010) chs 2, 5, and 6
- Chapter 2 provides a clear general account of the creation of agency, whilst chapters 5 and 6 provide a detailed discussion of agency of necessity and agency by ratification, respectively.

Peter G Watts, *Bowstead & Reynolds on Agency* (19th edn, Sweet & Maxwell 2010) chs 2 and 4
- Chapter 2 provides a detailed exposition of the law relating to the creation of agency. Chapter 4 discusses in detail the law relating to agency by ratification.

The authority of an agent

- Actual authority
- Apparent authority
- Usual authority

INTRODUCTION

Throughout the previous chapters, repeated mention has been made of an agent's ability to enter into legally binding agreements on behalf of his principal. The general rationale behind holding such agreements as binding is that the principal has consented to the agent acting in such a way by bestowing authority upon the agent to act on his behalf. It follows that the authority of an agent is a central concept of the law of agency, with two principle types of authority being identifiable, namely actual authority and apparent authority. There is a third form of authority, known as usual authority, but, as will be seen, the reasoning behind the cases that established this form of authority is highly suspect. All three forms of authority will be discussed in this chapter, with Figure 5.1 highlighting the various forms of authority.

The principal may actually consent to the agent's actions (as is the case where the authority is actual, or where the agent's actions are ratified), or the law may deem the principal to have consented (e.g. where the agent acts due to necessity). However, the law also provides that a principal can be bound even where he does not consent to the agent's actions, namely where the agent acts based upon apparent authority.

Determining the existence and type of authority is vital as the legal consequences of an agent breaching his authority can be severe. The principal may not be bound by the agent's actions, and the agent may instead be personally liable (or both may be liable). In addition, the agent may lose the commission/remuneration to which he was entitled and may be found liable for breach of contract and/or breach of warranty of authority.

The consequences of an agent breaching his authority are discussed in Chapters 6 and 8

Actual authority

The classic definition of actual authority was provided by Diplock LJ, who stated that:

> An actual authority is a legal relationship between the principal and agent created by a consensual agreement to which they alone are parties. Its scope is to be ascertained by applying ordinary principles of construction of contracts,

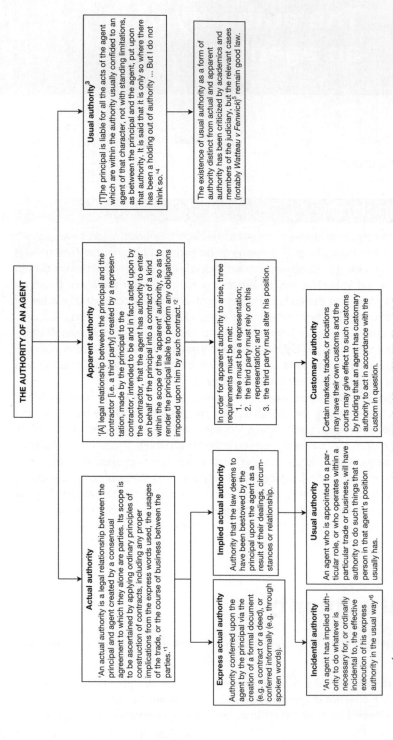

THE AUTHORITY OF AN AGENT

Actual authority

'An actual authority is a legal relationship between the principal and agent created by a consensual agreement to which they alone are parties. Its scope is to be ascertained by applying ordinary principles of construction of contracts, including any proper implications from the express words used, the usages of the trade, or the course of business between the parties.'[1]

Apparent authority

'[A] legal relationship between the principal and the contractor [i.e. a third party] created by a represen- tation, made by the principal to the contractor, intended to be and in fact acted upon by the contractor, that the agent has authority to enter on behalf of the principal into a contract of a kind within the scope of the 'apparent' authority, so as to render the principal liable to perform any obligations imposed upon him by such contract.'[2]

Usual authority[3]

'[T]he principal is liable for all the acts of the agent which are within the authority usually confided to an agent of that character, not with standing limitations, as between the principal and the agent, put upon that authority. It is said that it is only so where there has been a holding out of authority ... But I do not think so.'[4]

The existence of usual authority as a form of authority distinct from actual and apparent authority has been criticized by academics and members of the judiciary, but the relevant cases (notably *Watteau v Fenwick*)[5] remain good law.

Express actual authority

Authority conferred upon the agent by the principal via the creation of a formal document (e.g. a contract or a deed), or conferred informally (e.g. through spoken words).

Implied actual authority

Authority that the law deems to have been bestowed by the principal upon the agent as a result of their dealings, circum- stances or relationship.

In order for apparent authority to arise, three requirements must be met:
1. there must be a representation;
2. the third party must rely on this representation; and
3. the third party must alter his position.

Incidental authority

'An agent has implied auth- ority to do whatever is necessary for, or ordinarily incidental to, the effective execution of his express authority in the usual way'[6]

Usual authority

An agent who is appointed to a par- ticular role, or who operates within a particular trade or business, will have authority to do such things that a person in that agent's position usually has.

Customary authority

Certain markets, trades, or locations may have their own customs and the courts may give effect to such customs by holding that an agent has customary authority to act in accordance with the custom in question.

[1] *Freeman & Lockyer v Buckhurst Park Properties (Mangal) Ltd* [1964] 2 QB 480 (CA) 503 (Diplock LJ).
[2] ibid.
[3] Usual authority here refers to the form of usual authority that is independent from actual and apparent authority.
[4] *Watteau v Fenwick* [1893] 1 QB 346 (QB) 348–49 (Wills J).
[5] ibid.
[6] Peter G Watts, *Bowstead & Reynolds on Agency* (19th edn, Sweet & Maxwell 2010) [3-018].

FIGURE 5.1 The authority of an agent

including any proper implications from the express words used, the usages of the trade, or the course of business between the parties.[1]

This definition indicates that there are two types of actual authority:

1. express actual authority, which refers to the authority that the principal has expressly bestowed upon the agent, either orally or in writing;
2. implied actual authority, which refers to authority that the law deems to have been bestowed by the principal upon the agent as a result of their dealings, circumstances, or relationship.

Both forms of actual authority will now be discussed.

Express actual authority

Lord Denning MR defined express actual authority as 'authority given by express words, such as when a board of directors pass a resolution which authorises two of their number to sign cheques'.[2] Express actual authority is the most straightforward form of authority and refers to that authority that has been expressly conferred upon the agent by the principal. It arises most commonly where the agency relationship has been created by agreement and, in such a case, the agreement will delineate the express actual authority of the agent.

Agency by agreement is discussed at p 65

Express actual authority can be bestowed upon an agent through the creation of a formal document (such as a contract or a deed), or informally (e.g. through spoken words). It is important to know the method through which express actual authority has been conferred, as this can have a significant impact upon the construction of the agent's authority. In particular, the courts have adopted different approaches depending on whether or not the express actual authority was conferred upon the agent via a deed.

Authority granted by deed

Where the principal confers authority upon the agent by deed (e.g. via a power of attorney),[3] then, when determining the extent of the agent's express actual authority, the courts' approach is to construe the deed strictly and to limit the agent's powers to those found 'within the four corners of the instrument'.[4] The strictness of this approach can be seen in the following case.

Jacobs v Morris [1902] 1 Ch 816 (CA)

FACTS: Louis Jacobs (the principal) executed a power of attorney that conferred upon his brother, Leslie Jacobs (the agent), the power to purchase and make any contract for the purchase of any goods and, in connection with the principal's business, to make, draw, sign, accept or indorse bills of exchange or promissory notes. Leslie Jacobs, purporting to

---

1. *Freeman & Lockyer v Buckhurst Park Properties (Mangal) Ltd* [1964] 2 QB 480 (CA) 503.
2. *Hely-Hutchinson v Brayhead Ltd* [1968] 1 QB 549 (CA) 583.
3. The Powers of Attorney Act 1971, s 1(1) specifies that a power of attorney can be executed only via deed.
4. *Bryant, Powis and Bryant Ltd v La Banque du Peuple* [1893] AC 170 (PC) 177 (Lord MacNaghten).

> act under the power of attorney, borrowed £4,000 from Morris. Morris eventually sought to recover the sum from Louis Jacobs, who contended that his brother had no authority to borrow the money.
>
> **HELD:** The power of attorney conferred no express power upon the agent to borrow, and so the agent lacked the authority to borrow the £4,000. Further, as Morris had constructive notice that the agent had no authority to borrow the money[5] (and did so without his brother's knowledge), the Court held that Morris was estopped from recovering the £4,000 from Louis Jacobs.

Bowstead & Reynolds justify the strictness of this approach by noting that 'in the commercial sphere, powers of attorney tend to be drawn by lawyers and use technical wording which may be assumed to have been carefully chosen'.[6] They go on to note that such an approach is also justifiable in non-commercial cases (e.g. to protect an incapacitated principal who has executed a power of attorney to allow an agent to handle his financial affairs).

Authority not granted by deed

This strict approach to determining the scope of an agent's express actual authority does not apply where the authority is not conferred upon the agent by a deed (e.g. through a document not under seal, or orally). In such a case, a much more liberal approach is adopted under which the scope of the agent's express actual authority 'must be determined by inference from the whole circumstances',[7] as the following case demonstrates.

 Johnston v Kershaw (1866–67) LR 2 Ex 82

FACTS: Kershaw (the Liverpool-based principal) instructed Johnston (the agent, who was based in Pernambuco in Brazil) to purchase 100 bales of cotton. Johnston only purchased ninety-four bales, claiming that this was the maximum number that could be obtained at the time. Kershaw refused to pay for the bales on the ground that Johnston had not acted in accordance with the express authority conferred upon him (i.e. to purchase 100 bales). Johnston sued.

HELD: Johnston was acting within his express actual authority. The court was influenced heavily by the fact that 'the state of the market [in Pernambuco] was not such as to admit of the whole 100 bales being purchased at one and the same time'.[8] Taking this into account, it was within Johnston's express actual authority to 'buy as many bales as they could get, and make up the total number as soon as practicable'.[9]

---

5. This constructive notice arose due to the fact that, had Morris read the terms of the power of attorney, he would have known that the agent lacked the authority to borrow.

6. Peter G Watts, *Bowstead & Reynolds on Agency* (19th edn, Sweet & Maxwell 2010) [3-011].

7. *Ashford Shire Council v Dependable Motors Pty Ltd* [1961] AC 336 (PC) 349 (Lord Reid).

8. (1866–67) LR 2 Ex 82, 86 (Kelly CB).   9. ibid.

The operation of this liberal approach is demonstrated most clearly in cases where the authority bestowed upon the agent by the principal contains some form of ambiguity.

 Ireland v Livingston (1871–72) LR 5 HL 395 (HL)

FACTS: Livingston (the Liverpool-based principal) wrote to Ireland (his agent based in Mauritius), instructing him to purchase 500 tonnes of sugar in Mauritius and ship it to Britain. The instructions also stated an alternative amount could be shipped up to 50 tonnes more or less, and that Livingston would prefer the option of deciding whether the vessel sending the sugar should go to London, Liverpool, or the Clyde, but that if this was not possible, the sugar could be shipped to London or Liverpool. Ireland could only obtain just under 400 tonnes and arranged for this amount to be shipped to Liverpool in one vessel, which also contained goods belonging to other people. Upon arrival in Liverpool, Livingston refused to take delivery of the sugar and Ireland sued. Livingston contended that his instructions indicated that the vessel's destination should be determinable by Ireland but, by placing the sugar on a ship that contained other people's goods, Ireland would be unable to determine the vessel's destination. Ireland contended that the instruction indicating that the sugar could be shipped to London or Liverpool authorized him to ship the sugar on a single vessel containing cargo belonging to other people.

HELD: The House noted that Livingston's instructions were ambiguous and established the approach that should be adopted when confronted by an ambiguity in the agent's express actual authority:

> if a principal gives an order to an agent in such uncertain terms as to be susceptible of two different meanings, and the agent *bonâ fide* adopts one of them and acts upon it, it is not competent to the principal to repudiate the act as unauthorized because he meant the order to be read in the other sense of which it is equally capable. It is a fair answer to such an attempt to disown the agents' authority to tell the principal that the departure from his intention was occasioned by his own fault, and that he should have given his order in clear and unambiguous terms.[10]

Accordingly, as Ireland had acted based upon a bona fide interpretation of Livingston's instructions, his actions were within the scope of his express actual authority and his claim succeeded.

Ireland was decided prior to the telecommunications revolution and, today, it is likely the case that an agent cannot simply rely on his own interpretation of the principal's instructions. Speaking of the principle established in *Ireland*, Robert Goff LJ has stated that:

> there must be some limit to the operation of this principle. Obviously it cannot be open to every contracting party to act on a bona fide, but mistaken, interpretation of a contractual document prepared by the other, and to hold the other party to that interpretation … [A] party relying on his own interpretation of the relevant document must have acted reasonably in all the circumstances in

---

10. (1871–72) LR 5 HL 395 (HL) 416 (Lord Chelmsford).

so doing. If instructions are given to an agent, it is understandable that he should expect to act on those instructions without more; but if, for example, the ambiguity is patent on the face of the document it may well be right (especially with the facilities of modern communications available to him) to have his instructions clarified by his principal, if time permits, before acting on them.[11]

Implied actual authority

Consider the following example:

 ComCorp Ltd

ComCorp is looking to purchase a piece of machinery. OmniTech Ltd produces the machinery in question and enters into negotiations with Greg, one of ComCorp's directors. Greg tells the board of OmniTech that he acts as ComCorp's purchasing director and has full authority to enter into contracts of sale on behalf of ComCorp. In fact, Greg has never been appointed as the company's purchasing director, although he has undertaken this role on several occasions with the consent of ComCorp's board. A price is agreed for the purchase of the machinery and Greg signs the contract on behalf of ComCorp. However, the board of ComCorp believes that the purchase price is too high and refuses to honour the sale, contending that Greg lacked authority to enter into the contract on ComCorp's behalf.

Does Greg have actual authority to enter into the contract of sale with OmniTech? He almost certainly does not have express actual authority, but actual authority may also be implied based on the circumstances of the case and, as will be seen, it is likely that Greg does have implied actual authority to enter into contracts of sale on ComCorp's behalf. Where an agent has implied actual authority, this will usually serve to increase the agent's actual authority by operating alongside his existing express actual authority. However, the implication of actual authority can also result in the creation of an agency relationship where none previously existed.

Implied actual authority can arise in numerous ways, but there is no universally accepted categorization of implied actual authority. In this text, implied actual authority is divided into three types, namely:

1. incidental authority;
2. usual authority; and
3. customary authority.

Incidental authority

The first type of implied actual authority can be classified as incidental authority and provides that '[a]n agent has implied authority to do whatever is necessary for, or ordinarily incidental to, the effective execution of his express [actual] authority

---

11. *European Asian Bank AG v Punjab & Sind Bank (No 2)* [1983] 1 WLR 642 (CA) 656.

in the usual way'.[12] An agent who is expressly authorized to enter into a transaction on behalf of his principal might need to undertake several ancillary acts in order to enter into that transaction—the agent will have express authority to enter into the transaction and implied authority to undertake the relevant ancillary acts. Examples of incidental authority include the following:

- An agent engaged to purchase or sell goods on behalf of a principal has incidental authority to negotiate with third parties regarding the price for which the goods will be bought or sold.
- An agent engaged to act as a project manager for the development of a piece of land has incidental authority to appoint and agree remuneration for planning consultants and property managers.[13]
- An agent engaged to sell a piece of real estate has incidental authority to enter into a binding contract of sale and complete the formalities relating to the sale.[14]

It should, however, be noted that the concept of incidental authority is limited to those activities that are necessary and incidental to the execution of the agent's express actual authority. From this it follows that:

- an agent engaged to deliver goods to a third party does not have incidental authority to make warranties relating to the quality of those goods;[15]
- an estate agent engaged to locate a purchaser for a piece of land does not have incidental authority to enter into a contract for the sale of that piece of land;[16]
- an agent authorized to deliver goods to a specified person does not have incidental authority to sell those goods to someone else.[17]

Usual authority[18]

Often a person will be appointed to a particular role or occupation, or engaged within a particular trade or business, but his authority will not be specified in detail. In such cases, the concept of usual authority will be particularly important, as it will provide that an agent has authority to do such things that a person in that agent's position usually has. The leading case in this area provides a clear example of this type of implied actual authority in practice.

 Hely-Hutchinson v Brayhead Ltd [1968] 1 QB 549 (CA)

FACTS: Richards (the agent) was chairman of Brayhead Ltd (the principal) and, although he was not appointed formally as the managing director of the company, he acted as such with the board's acquiescence. Richards, purporting to act on behalf of Brayhead,

---

12. Peter G Watts, *Bowstead & Reynolds on Agency* (19th edn, Sweet & Maxwell 2010) [3-018].

13. *Norwich Union Life & Pensions Ltd v Strand Street Properties Ltd* [2009] EWHC 1109 (Ch), affirmed [2010] EWCA Civ 444.

14. *Rosenbaum v Belson* [1900] 2 Ch 267 (Ch).   15. *Woodin v Burford* (1834) 2 C&M 391.

16. *Hamer v Sharp* (1874–75) LR 19 Eq 108.   17. *Whittaker v Forshaw* [1919] 2 KB 419 (DC).

18. As is discussed on pp 101 and 105, usual authority can also refer to a form of apparent authority, and a type of authority in its own right.

agreed to indemnify Hely-Hutchinson[19] for any loss in relation to a company named Perdio Electronics Ltd. When Perdio went into liquidation, Hely-Hutchinson sought to enforce the indemnity against Brayhead but, unsurprisingly, it refused to honour the indemnity, contending that Richards had no authority to enter into the indemnity agreement with Hely-Hutchinson. Hely-Hutchinson commenced proceedings against Brayhead.

HELD: Lord Denning MR stated that:

> It is plain that…Richards had no express authority to enter into these … contracts on behalf of the company: nor had he any such authority implied from the nature of his office. He had been duly appointed chairman of the company but that office in itself did not carry with it authority to enter into these contracts without the sanction of the board. But I think he had authority implied from the conduct of the parties and the circumstances of the case.[20]

The conduct Lord Denning MR referred to was the fact that 'the board by their conduct over many months had acquiesced in [Richards] acting as their chief executive and committing Brayhead Ltd to contracts without the necessity of sanction from the board'.[21] Accordingly, the indemnity was valid and Hely-Hutchinson's claim succeeded.

★ See RS Nock, 'When is a Director, Not a Director?' (1967) 30 MLR 705

The task of the court is to determine whether or not the activities of the agent are usually incidental to the role, occupation, or trade being undertaken. This will be a question of fact in each case, with the following providing examples of when usual authority has been held to arise:

- The manager of a railway company has usual authority to bind the company to pay for medical assistance that is provided to an employee of the company following a workplace accident.[22]
- The master of a grounded ship has usual authority to enter into a contract for the salvage of the ship.[23]
- A ship's agent has usual authority to arrange for the stowage of cargo.[24]
- An auctioneer has usual authority to sell goods and to sign a contract of sale for both the seller and purchaser.[25]
- A horse dealer has usual authority to warrant as to the quality of a horse being sold.[26]

As is the case with incidental authority, the courts will not find usual authority to be conferred where it is not necessary or incidental to the agent's express actual authority. From this, it follows that usual authority will not be present where it would conflict with an express limitation or prohibition imposed by the principal.

---

19. In the case itself, Mr Hely-Hutchinson is referred to by his commonly known title, Viscount Suirdale.
20. [1968] 1 QB 549 (CA) 584.   21. ibid.
22. *Walker v The Great Western Railway Co* (1866–67) LR 2 Ex 228.
23. *The Unique Mariner* [1978] 1 Lloyd's Rep 438 (QB).
24. *Blandy Bros & Co v Nello Simoni* [1963] 2 Lloyd's Rep 393 (CA).
25. *Emmerson v Heelis* (1809) 2 Taunt 38.
26. *Howard v Sheward* (1866) LR 2 CP 148.

Customary authority

Certain markets, trades, or locations may have their own customs, and the courts may give effect to such customs by holding that an agent has customary authority to act in accordance with the custom in question, as occurred in the following case.

 Cropper v Cook (1867-68) LR 3 CP 194

FACTS: Cook (the Liverpool-based agent) was instructed to purchase wool by Hodgson, Mather & Co ('HMC', the principal). Cook did so, but purchased the wool in his own name and not in the name of HMC. HMC contended that, whilst it was the custom of the Liverpool wool-market that brokers were authorized to purchase wool either in their own name, or in the name of their principal, they could only purchase wool in their own name with the principal's consent, which had not been provided in this case. Accordingly, HMC refused to pay for the wool.

HELD: Cook was authorized to purchase the wool in his own name. Whilst Cook did not have express authority to do this, there was strong evidence provided indicating that it was a custom of the Liverpool wool-market that brokers were authorized to purchase wool either in their own name, or in the name of their principal, without providing the principal with notice of whether the purchase was made in the agent's name.

It should be noted at the outset that the usefulness of customary authority is limited, as it is difficult to establish the existence of customary authority (or as Devlin J stated, 'it is a bold task to endeavour to establish custom').[27] The requirements to establish customary authority were laid out by Ungoed-Thomas J, who stated that the custom:

> must be certain, in the sense that the practice is clearly established; it must be notorious, in the sense that it is so well known, in the market in which it is alleged to exist, that those who conduct business in the market contract with the usage as an implied term; and it must be reasonable.[28]

This passage indicates that the custom must be certain, notorious, and reasonable. Whether a custom is reasonable or not will depend heavily upon the circumstances of the case (although whether it is reasonable or not is ultimately a question of law), with the following case providing an example of a custom that was held to be unreasonable.

 Robinson v Mollett, Bull & Unsworth (1874–75) LR 7 HL 802 (HL)

FACTS: Robinson (the Liverpool-based principal) instructed Mollett, Bull & Unsworth ('MBU', the agent), a London-based broker, to purchase fifty tonnes of tallow from the London tallow market. MBU purchased several hundred tonnes of tallow in its own name,

---

27. *Stag Line Ltd v Board of Trade* (1949–50) 83 Ll L Rep 356 (KB) 360.
28. *Cunliffe-Owen v Teather & Greenwood* [1967] 1 WLR 1421 (Ch) 1438.

which was then parcelled out to fulfil the orders of numerous principals, including that of Robinson. Robinson discovered this and refused to accept the tallow. MBU resold it at a loss and commenced proceedings against Robinson to recover the shortfall.

HELD: It was clear that there was a custom in the London tallow trade that permitted brokers to make contracts in their own name for amounts of tallow greater than required by a single principal, and then to parcel the tallow out to numerous principals. However, the House held that the custom was unreasonable, as its effect was to convert the broker into a principal seller, who would then sell the tallow on for a profit. This would place the broker in a position that conflicted with that of his principal and would deprive the principal of what he bargained for, namely an agent who exerted effort solely on the principal's behalf. A custom that so radically altered the nature of an agency relationship could not be enforced, unless the principal had knowledge of the custom at the time he bestowed authority upon the agent. Accordingly, MBU's claim failed.

Two further requirements have subsequently been added, namely that (i) the custom must not be unlawful;[29] and (ii) it must not conflict with, or be excluded by, the terms of the contract between the parties. Providing that the various requirements have been satisfied, the custom will 'be considered as part of the agreement: and if the agreement be in writing, though the custom is not written it is to be treated exactly as if that unwritten clause had been written out at length'.[30] This will be so even if the principal was not aware of the custom.[31] However, as noted, an unreasonable custom will only form part of the agency agreement if the principal knew of it at the time when he bestowed authority upon the agent.

Apparent authority

Consider the following example.

 ComCorp Ltd

ComCorp is being sued for negligence by MultiTech Ltd. ComCorp engages a solicitor, Milly, to act on its behalf. The directors of ComCorp instruct Milly to make contact with MultiTech and sound them out about a possible settlement, and so Milly arranges a meeting with MultiTech's solicitor. During the meeting, the directors of ComCorp try to contact Milly to tell her that she should not agree to any settlement before ComCorp's board has discussed it. Unfortunately, Milly's phone is on silent and so she does not take the call. She proposes a settlement agreement, which is accepted by MultiTech's solicitor

---

29. Peter G Watts, *Bowstead & Reynolds on Agency* (19th edn, Sweet & Maxwell 2010) [3-035] states that older cases appear to indicate that an unlawful custom can be enforced providing that the principal has knowledge of it and assents to it, but it is contended by most commentators (including Bowstead & Reynolds themselves) that it is difficult to envisage the courts upholding an unlawful custom.
30. *Tucker v Linger* (1882–83) LR 8 App Cas 508 (HL) 511 (Lord Blackburn).
31. *Bayliffe v Butterworth* (1847) 17 LJ Ex 78.

> (MultiTech's solicitor is expressly authorized to accept any suitable offers of settlement). ComCorp contends that it is not bound by the terms of the settlement, as Milly had no authority to make it.

It is clear that Milly does not have express actual authority to settle on ComCorp's behalf, as she was instructed only to sound out MultiTech about the possibility of a settlement. Depending on the facts, it may be the case that she has implied actual authority to propose a settlement, but this is unlikely.[32] However, it would be unfair if principals were only bound to transactions entered into by agents who act within their actual authority, as third parties who deal with agents are unlikely to know what the agent is actually authorized to do. Accordingly, a second form of authority exists which is based on the authority that, from the third party's point of view, the agent appears to have, namely apparent authority (in older cases, apparent authority is also known as ostensible authority). Thus, in this example, Milly does not have actual authority to propose a settlement but, from the point of view of MultiTech's solicitor, what matters is the authority that she appears to have, and she does appear to have authority to make a settlement offer,[33] and so ComCorp will be bound by its terms. From this, it can be seen that '[a]pparent authority is really equivalent to the phrase "appearance of authority". There may be an appearance of authority whether in fact or not there is authority',[34] or, to put it more simply, 'apparent authority is the authority of an agent as it appears to others'.[35]

Apparent authority can serve to extend the scope of an agent's authority beyond that agreed to by the principal (as occurred in the ComCorp example), or it can even result in the creation of an agency relationship where none previously existed.

Actual authority, apparent authority, and estoppel

In the example just discussed, the agent (Milly) lacked actual authority, but did have apparent authority. In many cases, however, the actual authority and apparent authority of an agent will generally coincide and so the difference between the two forms of authority may not be important in practice.[36] Lord Denning MR provides an example of this:

> apparent authority...often coincides with actual authority. Thus, when the board appoints one of their number to be managing director, they invest him not only with implied [actual] authority, but also with ostensible authority to do all such things as fall within the usual scope of that office. Other people who

---

32. See *Waugh v HB Clifford & Sons Ltd* [1982] Ch 374 (CA) 387 (Brightman LJ).

33. ibid. It should, however, be noted that it is unlikely that a solicitor would enter into an agreement of this type without first consulting his principal.

34. James L Montrose, 'The Basis of the Power of the Agent in Cases of Actual and Apparent Authority' (1932) 16 Can Bar Rev 756, 764.

35. *Hely-Hutchinson v Brayhead Ltd* [1968] 1 QB 549 (CA) 583 (Lord Denning MR).

36. Indeed, as Peter G Watts, *Bowstead & Reynolds on Agency* (19th edn, Sweet & Maxwell 2010) [3-004] notes, '[i]n many nineteenth century cases, it is not possible to tell upon which doctrine the court bases its decision'.

see him acting as managing director are entitled to assume that he has the usual authority of a managing director.[37]

However, as Diplock LJ correctly noted, 'either may exist without the other and their respective scopes may be different'.[38] For example, a principal may terminate the agency agreement, in which case the agent's actual authority is also likely to be terminated, but the agent's apparent authority may continue. Even if both forms of authority co-exist, it may be the case that the agent's apparent authority exceeds his actual authority. Given this, it is vital to understand how actual and apparent authority differ and to be able to determine the scope of each.

Actual authority relates to the relationship between the principal and the agent, and is concerned with the authority that the principal has, expressly or impliedly, bestowed upon the agent. Conversely, according to Diplock LJ, apparent authority refers to:

> a legal relationship between the principal and the contractor [i.e. a third party] created by a representation, made by the principal to the contractor, intended to be and in fact acted upon by the contractor, that the agent has authority to enter on behalf of the principal into a contract of a kind within the scope of the 'apparent' authority, so as to render the principal liable to perform any obligations imposed upon him by such contract. To the relationship so created the agent is a stranger. He need not be (although he generally is) aware of the existence of the representation but he must not purport to make the agreement as principal himself. The representation, when acted upon by the contractor by entering into a contract with the agent, operates as an estoppel, preventing the principal from asserting that he is not bound by the contract. It is irrelevant whether the agent had actual authority to enter into the contract.[39]

When will apparent authority arise?

The quote of Diplock LJ in the previous paragraph indicates that, where an agent has apparent authority, then the principal will be estopped from denying that he is bound by the contract. This indicates a commonly stated premise, namely that the theoretical basis for apparent authority lies in the doctrine of estoppel. To quote Slade J 'apparent authority…is merely a form of estoppel, indeed, it has been termed agency by estoppel'.[40] It will be remembered that estoppel applies where a person (A) makes a promise to another (B), and B then relies on that promise. In such a case, it might then be inequitable to allow A to go back on his promise, and so he will be estopped from doing so. Accordingly, if the principal represents that an agent has authority to act in a certain way, and a third party relies on that representation, the principal can be estopped from denying the existence of such authority.

Whilst this basis for apparent authority is not universally accepted by academics,[41] it does appear to be generally accepted by the courts.[42] It follows that, in order for

---

37. *Hely-Hutchinson v Brayhead Ltd* [1968] 1 QB 549 (CA) 583.
38. *Freeman & Lockyer v Buckhurst Park (Mangal) Properties Ltd* [1964] 2 QB 480 (CA) 502.
39. ibid 503.
40. *Rama Corporation Ltd v Proved Tin and General Investments Ltd* [1952] 2 QB 147 (QB) 149.
41. See e.g. Peter G Watts, *Bowstead & Reynolds on Agency* (19th edn, Sweet & Maxwell 2010) [8-029].
42. See e.g. *Gurner v Beaton* [1993] 2 Lloyd's Rep 369 (CA) 379 (Neill LJ).

apparent authority to arise, the requirements for estoppel must also be present. Again, quoting Slade J, 'you cannot call in aid an estoppel unless you have three ingredients: (i) a representation, (ii) a reliance on the representation, and (iii) an alteration of your position resulting from such reliance'.[43]

Each of these three ingredients will now be discussed, but it should be noted that, in order to accommodate agency cases within the concept of estoppel, the courts have had to apply the law relating to estoppel in a somewhat liberal manner, leading to the conclusion that apparent authority is a form of estoppel 'with weak requirements, special to agency'.[44] This is especially noticeable in relation to the requirement for a representation, where the courts will accept a representation that is 'very general indeed',[45] and the requirement for an alteration of position, where the alteration need only be small.

Representation

It will be remembered that, in explaining how apparent authority differs from actual authority, Diplock LJ stated that apparent authority is 'a legal relationship between the principal and the contractor created by *a representation, made by the principal to the contractor*'.[46] From this, it follows that, in order for apparent authority to arise, there must be a representation. In order to fully understand this requirement, four issues need to be discussed:

1. What must this representation indicate?
2. From whom must this representation derive?
3. How must the representation be made?
4. When must the representation be made?

The first issue is unproblematic and requires little discussion. Again quoting Diplock LJ, the representation must indicate that:

> the agent has authority to enter on behalf of the principal into a contract of a kind within the scope of the 'apparent' authority, so as to render the principal liable to perform any obligations imposed upon him by such contract.[47]

In other words, the representation must indicate that the agent has the authority to act on behalf of the principal. Historically, the courts have stated that the representation had to be one of fact,[48] but this limitation should be reconsidered in light of recent case law, which has abolished the distinction between mistakes of fact and law[49] and of misrepresentations based on statement of fact and law.[50]

---

43. *Rama Corporation Ltd v Proved Tin and General Investments Ltd* [1952] 2 QB 147 (QB) 150.

44. Peter G Watts, *Bowstead & Reynolds on Agency* (19th edn, Sweet & Maxwell 2010) [2-100]. See also Roderick Munday, *Agency: Law and Principles* (OUP 2010) 61, who states that 'in the context of agency, estoppel wears a meaning different from its customary common-law usage'.

45. Peter G Watts, *Bowstead & Reynolds on Agency* (19th edn, Sweet & Maxwell 2010) [8-029].

46. *Freeman & Lockyer v Buckhurst Park (Mangal) Properties Ltd* [1964] 2 QB 480 (CA) 503 (emphasis added).

47. ibid.

48. *Chapleo v Brunswick Permanent Building Society (No 2)* (1880–81) LR 6 QBD 696 (CA).

49. *Kleinwort Benson Ltd v Lincoln CC* [1999] 2 AC 349 (HL).

50. *Pankhania v Hackney LBC* [2002] EWHC 2441 (Ch), [2002] NPC 123.

The second issue (namely from whom must the representation derive) is generally straightforward but, as we shall see, has been complicated in some unusual cases. As discussed, the basis for the apparent authority of an agent is that the agent appears to have authority to act on behalf of the principal because the principal has in some way acted to create that appearance. It follows from this that apparent authority will not generally be created where the representation comes from the agent himself—to allow otherwise would be to permit the agent to self-authorize or, as Lord Donaldson MR stated, 'to pull himself up by his own shoe laces'.[51] It does not follow, however, that the representation must come from the principal personally (although in the majority of cases concerning apparent authority, it will)—another agent authorized to act on behalf of the principal can also make the representation.[52]

However, a number of academics have contended that this rule cannot be absolute and that 'pragmatic exceptions eat into such an apparently clear principle'.[53] For example, Reynolds states that:

> [t]here may be cases where the agent only has authority in certain circumstances; only the agent knows whether they have arisen. The third party may be entitled to rely on the agent's statement, express or implied, that they have.[54]

But there are limits to this—in *Armagas Ltd v Mundogas SA (The Ocean Frost)*,[55] the House of Lords stated clearly that, where the third party knows that an agent lacks authority, a principal will not be bound where such an agent wrongly claims to have obtained such authority. However, the following case distinguished *The Ocean Frost* and held that apparent authority was present.

 First Energy (UK) Ltd v Hungarian International Bank Ltd [1993] BCC 533 (CA)

FACTS: First Energy (UK) Ltd sought to obtain credit facilities from Hungarian International Bank Ltd ('HIB', the principal), with the request being handled by Jamison (the agent), the senior manager of HIB's Manchester branch. First Energy had dealt with Jamison before and knew that he did not have actual authority to sanction a credit facility (indeed Jamison himself made this clear to First Energy), and that any letter offering such a facility would need to be signed by two of the bank's officials. Jamison wrote to First Energy informing it that HIB had approved the credit facility. The letter was not signed by two of the bank's officials and HIB had not approved the credit facility. Accordingly, HIB claimed that Jamison lacked the authority to offer the facility and that it was not therefore obliged to offer it to First Energy. HIB refused to offer the credit facility and First Energy commenced proceedings.

---

51. *United Bank of Kuwait v Hammoud* [1988] 1 WLR 1051 (CA) 1066.
52. *Attorney General of Ceylon v Silva* [1953] AC 461 (PC); *Armagas Ltd v Mundogas SA (The Ocean Frost)* [1986] AC 717 (HL).
53. Peter G Watts, *Bowstead & Reynolds on Agency* (19th edn, Sweet & Maxwell 2010) [8-023].
54. FMB Reynolds, 'The Ultimate Apparent Authority' (1994) 110 LQR 21, 23.
55. [1986] AC 717 (HL).

HELD: Jamison had apparent authority to inform First Energy that the facility had been approved. The Court distinguished *The Ocean Frost* on the ground that the agent in that case did not have authority to claim that he was authorized. Conversely, in *First Energy*, 'Jamison's position as senior manager in Manchester was such that he was clothed with ostensible authority to communicate that head office approval had been given for the facility'.[56] Accordingly, whilst Jamison lacked authority to sanction the credit facility, he did have authority to inform First Energy the his head office had authorized the facility, or, as Steyn LJ stated, 'the law recognises that in modern commerce an agent who has no apparent authority to conclude a particular transaction may sometimes be clothed with apparent authority to make representations of fact'.[57]

COMMENT: In upholding the agreement and finding for First Energy, it is clear that the Court's decision was 'heavily based on the desirability of third parties in commercial situations being able to rely on letters such as that written.'[58] Steyn LJ admitted this when stating that 'the principal moulding force of our law of contract . . . [is] . . . that the reasonable expectations of honest men must be protected'.[59] Despite the fact that the case does not fit easily with orthodox agency principles, it has been welcomed by a number of commentators[60] who agree with Evans LJ's conclusion that the decision is merely giving effect to 'the commercial realities of the situation'.[61] Despite this, the consensus does appear to be that the case is best 'regarded as exceptional on the facts',[62] but there can be no doubt that the principle established by Steyn LJ does have the potential to radically affect the doctrine of apparent authority should future courts decide to embrace it.

⭐ See Ian Brown, 'The Agent's Apparent Authority: Paradigm or Paradox?' [1995] JBL 360

The third issue (namely, how can the representation be made) can be problematic, as the courts have confirmed that the representation can be made in a number of different ways, some of which are not easy to identify in practice. The most straightforward form of representation is one made orally or in writing,[63] but the most common form of representation is one made by conduct. The most common form of representation by conduct occurs where the principal places the agent in a position that usually provides the agent with authority to engage in certain acts,[64] as the following case demonstrates.

56. [1993] BCC 533 (CA) 544 (Steyn LJ).   57. ibid 543.

58. FMB Reynolds, 'The Ultimate Apparent Authority' (1994) 110 LQR 21, 24.

59. [1993] BCC 533 (CA) 533. He went on to state (at p 544) that 'third parties who deal with companies in good faith ought to be protected'.

60. See e.g. Ian Brown, 'The Agent's Apparent Authority: Paradigm or Paradox?' [1995] JBL 360, 364–65.

61. [1993] BCC 533 (CA) 544.

62. FMB Reynolds, 'The Ultimate Apparent Authority' (1994) 110 LQR 21, 24.

63. *Trickett v Tomlinson* (1863) 13 CB (NS) 663.

64. Confusingly, this specific form of apparent authority is known as 'usual authority'. As is discussed on p 93, usual authority can also refer to a form of implied actual authority and, as discussed on p 105, it can also refer to a form of authority independent from actual and apparent authority.

Freeman & Lockyer v Buckhurst Park (Mangal) Properties Ltd [1964] 2 QB 480 (CA)

FACTS: Kapoor (the agent) and another person formed Buckhurst Park (Mangal) Properties Ltd ('Buckhurst', the principal), the purpose of which was to purchase and resell a large estate. Kapoor was a director of Buckhurst, along with a number of other persons. Kapoor acted as managing director with the board's acquiescence, although he had never been formally appointed to the role. He engaged a firm of architects (Freeman & Lockyer) on Buckhurst's behalf. The architects completed the work required of them and sought payment of their fees from Buckhurst. Buckhurst refused to pay, alleging that Kapoor lacked authority to engage the architects. The architects sued for payment.

HELD: The claim succeeded and Buckhurst was liable to pay the architects for the work they completed. Diplock LJ stated:

> The representation which creates 'apparent' authority may take a variety of forms of which the commonest is representation by conduct, that is, by permitting the agent to act in some way in the conduct of the principal's business with other persons. By so doing the principal represents to anyone who becomes aware that the agent is so acting that the agent has authority to enter on behalf of the principal into contracts with other persons of the kind which an agent so acting in the conduct of his principal's business has usually 'actual' authority to enter into.[65]

By acquiescing to Kapoor acting as managing director, Buckhurst had represented to the architects that Kapoor had the authority to engage in activities that a managing director would usually be authorized to undertake, including entering into contracts on behalf of the company.

 See JL Montrose, 'The Apparent Authority of an Agent of a Company' (1965) 7 Malaya L Rev 253

A representation can also be implied from a previous course of dealing, as occurred in the following case.

Summers v Solomon (1857) E&B 879

FACTS: Samuel Solomon ('SS', the principal) owned a jewellers shop and employed his nephew, Abraham Solomon ('AS', the agent), to manage it. SS had authorized AS to order jewellery for sale in the shop and, on this basis, AS had regularly ordered jewellery from Summers, which SS had then paid for. AS left SS's employment and moved to London, where he ordered goods from Summers and absconded with them. Summers commenced proceedings against SS for the cost of the jewellery. SS contended that AS no longer had authority to purchase jewellery on his behalf and so he was not liable.

HELD: Summers succeeded and SS was required to pay for the jewellery ordered by AS. Coleridge J stated:

> The question is, not what was the actual relation between the defendant and his nephew, but whether the defendant had not so conducted himself as to make the plaintiff suppose the nephew to be the defendant's general agent. What passes

> between the defendant and his nephew cannot limit the defendant's liability to the plaintiff.[66]
>
> Accordingly, the court held that the previous conduct of SS constituted a representation indicating that AS had apparent authority to order the jewellery. If SS wished to avoid liability, he should have informed Summers that AS's authority had been terminated.

The fourth and final issue to discuss is when the representation must be made. In the majority of cases, the representation will be made prior to the agent engaging in the act in question. However, the law does not require that this be the case and, as demonstrated in the following case, apparent authority can arise based on a subsequent representation.

 ### Spiro v Lintern [1973] 1 WLR 1002 (CA)

FACTS: John Lintern ('JL', the principal) wished to sell his house and instructed his wife, Gena Lintern ('GL', the agent), to put the house in the hands of an estate agent, but not to sell the property. The estate agent located a buyer (Spiro) and GL entered into a contract of sale. JL took no steps to articulate that his wife lacked authority to enter into the contract, even when Spiro visited him. JL also allowed Spiro to incur related expenses and to commence building work on the house without dispute. Before going abroad, JL executed a power of attorney empowering his wife to complete the sale. However, she instead transferred the property to a third party. Spiro sought to enforce the contract via an order for specific performance. JL argued that the contract was not valid, as his wife lacked the authority to enter into it on his behalf.

HELD: The Court held that JL's failure to disclose to Spiro that the wife lacked the authority to enter into the contract of sale constituted a representation that she did, in fact, have authority to sell the property. Accordingly, JL was estopped from denying that his wife lacked authority and the order for specific performance was granted.

Reliance

Reliance is a key component of estoppel and, as apparent authority is based upon the doctrine of estoppel, it follows that the third party must rely on the principal's representation in order for apparent authority to arise. Accordingly, apparent authority will not exist where the third party did not know of the principal's existence (i.e. the principal was undisclosed),[67] or did not know of the representation. As the following case demonstrates, apparent authority will also not arise where the third party knew, or ought to have known, that the agent lacked authority.

---

66. (1857) E&B 879, 884.   67. *AL Underwood Ltd v Bank of Liverpool* [1924] 1 KB 775 (CA).

Overbrooke Estates Ltd v Glencombe Properties Ltd [1974] 1 WLR 1335 (Ch)

FACTS: Overbrooke Estates Ltd (the principal) put up a piece of property for sale by auction. Prior to the auction, Glencombe Properties Ltd was sent a copy of the auctioneer's general conditions of sale, which stated that '[t]he vendors do not make or give and neither the auctioneers nor any person in the employment of the auctioneers has any authority to make or give any representation or warranty in relation to these properties'. At the auction, the auctioneer (the agent) told Glencombe that neither the local authority nor Greater London Council had plans for the property and were not interested in compulsorily purchasing it. Glencombe bought the property, but subsequently discovered from the local authority that the property was within an area that would be subject to a slum clearance programme. Upon discovering this, Glencombe stopped the payment and refused to honour the contract. Overbrooke sought specific performance, and Glencombe alleged that the auctioneer had apparent authority to make the statement and, given that it was inaccurate, it amounted to a misrepresentation, allowing Glencombe to rescind the contract of sale.

HELD: The court found for Overbrooke and ordered specific performance. Brightman J stated:

> It seems to me that it must be open to a principal to draw the attention of the public to the limits which he places upon the authority of his agent and that this must be so whether the agent is a person who has or has not any ostensible authority. If an agent has prima facie some ostensible authority, that authority is inevitably diminished to the extent of the publicised limits that are placed upon it.[68]

Applying this, the court held that Glencombe knew, or ought to have known, that the auctioneer lacked the authority to make the representation and, as such, could not have been said to have relied on the representation.

Determining whether or not a third party knew, or ought to have known that an agent lacks authority can be difficult in practice, but the courts have established certain presumptive indicators:

- Where a transaction is clearly not in the commercial interests of the principal, the third party will be put on notice that the agent is unlikely to have the requisite authority. In such a case, it will be 'very difficult for the [third party] to assert with any credibility that he believed the agent did have actual authority. Lack of such a belief would be fatal to a claim.'[69]
- Where an agent is engaged in a manner of business that an agent of that type would not normally engage in, then the third party will be put on notice that the agent may lack authority and the third party should ascertain whether or not the agent is authorized to conduct that business.[70]

---

68. [1974] 1 WLR 1335 (Ch) 1341.
69. *Criterion Properties plc v Stratford UK Properties LLC* [2004] UKHL 28, [2004] 1 WLR 1846 [31] (Lord Scott).
70. *Midland Bank Ltd v Reckitt* [1933] AC 1 (HL).

Bowstead & Reynolds[71] contend that the following *dictum*, made in relation to the imposition of a constructive trust, is relevant to determining whether or not a third party has notice of an agent's lack of authority:

> In deciding whether a person…had actual notice, (a) the court will apply an objective test and look at all the circumstances; (b) if by an objective test clear notice was given liability cannot be avoided by proof merely of the absence of actual knowledge; (c) a person will be deemed to have had notice of any fact to which it can be shown that he deliberately turned a blind eye…; (d) on the other hand, the court will not expect the recipient of goods to scrutinise commercial documents such as delivery notes with great care; (e) there is no general duty on the buyer of goods in an ordinary commercial transaction to make inquiries as to the right of the seller to dispose of the goods; (f) the question becomes, looking objectively at the circumstances which are alleged to constitute notice, do those circumstances constitute notice? This must be a matter of fact and degree to be determined in the particular circumstances of the case.[72]

Alteration of position

The third requirement laid down by Slade J is that the third party must have altered his position as a result of relying on the representation, but whether this is, in fact, enough is not entirely clear. In estoppel cases not involving the law of agency, not only must the person relying on the representation alter his position, he must do so to his detriment. In a number of agency cases, the courts have required that 'the person to whom the representation was made has suffered loss by acting upon it; or, to put it in another way, has altered his position to his detriment by acting on the representation'.[73] However, the majority of cases favour the view that a detriment is not required and all that need occur is that the third party altered his position as a result of the representation.[74] Further, this alteration of position need only amount to the third party entering into a contract with the principal,[75] which has resulted in several commentators questioning 'whether alteration of position in fact constitutes a separate requirement from reliance'.[76]

Usual authority

As has been discussed earlier in this chapter, the phrase 'usual authority' can refer to a specific form of implied actual authority, and a specific form of apparent authority. A small cluster of troublesome cases have established a third meaning, namely that

---

71. Peter G Watts, *Bowstead & Reynolds on Agency* (19th edn, Sweet & Maxwell 2010) [8-050].
72. *Feuer Leather Corp v Johnstone & Sons* [1981] Com LR 251 (QB) (Neill J).
73. *George Whitechurch Ltd v Cavanagh* [1902] AC 117 (HL) 135 (Lord Robertson).
74. See e.g. *Pickard v Sears* (1837) 6 A&E 469; *Freeman v Cooke* (1848) 2 Exch 654; *Rama Corporation Ltd v Proved Tin and General Investments Ltd* [1952] 2 QB 147 (QB); *Freeman & Lockyer v Buckhurst Park (Mangal) Properties Ltd* [1964] 2 QB 480 (CA).
75. See e.g. *Freeman & Lockyer v Buckhurst Park (Mangal) Properties Ltd* [1964] 2 QB 480 (CA); *Polish Steamship Co v AJ Williams Fuels (Overseas Sales) (The Suwalki)* [1989] 1 Lloyd's Rep 511 (QB); *Arctic Shipping Co Ltd v Mobilia AB (The Tatra)* [1990] 2 Lloyd's Rep 51 (QB).
76. Roderick Munday, *Agency: Law and Principles* (OUP 2010) 85.

usual authority also constitutes a type of authority distinct from actual and apparent authority. The leading case is *Watteau v Fenwick*, a seemingly straightforward case that is a little over a page long, which has nevertheless been described as 'the most difficult and controversial decision' in the law of agency.[77]

 Watteau v Fenwick [1893] 1 QB 346 (QB)

FACTS: Fenwick (the principal) appointed the former owner of a beerhouse, Humble (the agent), to act as the manager of that beerhouse. The liquor licence was taken out in Humble's name and his name appeared over the door of the beerhouse. Fenwick prohibited Humble from purchasing goods for the beerhouse, except bottled ales and water. In contravention of this, Humble purchased on credit a consignment of cigars and other items from Watteau, who mistakenly believed that Humble still owned the beerhouse. Upon discovering that Fenwick was the true owner of the beerhouse, Watteau issued proceedings against Fenwick for the price of the items that Humble had obtained on credit.

HELD: Watteau could recover from Fenwick the cost of the cigars. Humble had authority to purchase the cigars and so a binding contract existed between Fenwick and Watteau. Wills J stated that:

> the principal is liable for all the acts of the agent which are within the authority usually confided to an agent of that character, notwithstanding limitations, as between the principal and the agent, put upon that authority. It is said that it is only so where there has been a holding out of authority—which cannot be said of a case where the person supplying the goods knew nothing of the existence of a principal. But I do not think so.[78]

COMMENT: It is important to understand why this was not a case involving actual or apparent authority. Humble clearly lacked actual authority, as Fenwick had prohibited him from purchasing the goods in question. It is equally clear that Humble lacked apparent authority,[79] as Fenwick made no representation to Watteau (indeed, Watteau did not know of Fenwick's existence until after the goods had been supplied).

It has been contended that the result in *Watteau* is 'eminently just'[80] in that '[b]y placing [Humble] in a position where third parties would assume that [Humble] was the owner of the business, it is wholly appropriate that [Fenwick] can be held liable for purchases that typically would be made by someone managing his own business'.[81] The problem with this argument is that it ignores the fact that Fenwick could not enforce the contract against Watteau (because an undisclosed principal cannot ratify a contract). It is difficult to argue that, in such cases, a third

⚯ The law relating to the ratification of an agent's actions is discussed at p 67

---

77. GHL Fridman, 'The Demise of *Watteau v Fenwick*: *Sign-O-Lite Ltd v Metropolitan Life Insurance Co*' (1991) 70 Can Bar Rev 329, 329.
78. [1893] 1 QB 346 (QB) 348–49.
79. However, see AL Goodhart and CJ Hamson, 'Undisclosed Principals in Contract' [1931] CLJ 320, 336, who contend that Humble did indeed have apparent authority.
80. JG Collier 'Authority of an Agent—*Watteau v Fenwick* Revisited' (1985) 44 CLJ 363, 364.
81. Roderick Munday, *Agency: Law and Principles* (OUP 2010) 269.

party should be able to enforce the contract against the principal, but the principal cannot enforce the contract against the third party.

Irrespective of whether or not the result is just, the most significant problem that arises is that the court in *Watteau* failed to articulate a satisfactory rationale for the decision, with the result that the case has been almost universally criticized. Academics have branded it as 'dubious'[82] and have stated that Wills J's statement 'is supported neither by the previous cases nor by his own reasoning'.[83] The case has also garnered judicial criticism, with Bingham J describing *Watteau* as 'a somewhat puzzling case',[84] before going on to doubt whether it was correctly decided. Overseas judges have gone further, with one Canadian judge stating that he found it astonishing that 'an authority of such doubtful origin and of such unanimously unfavourable reputation should still be exhibiting signs of life and disturbing the peace of mind of trial judges'.[85]

Given these criticisms, the question to ask is to what extent *Watteau* remains good law. It is clear that the case has not spawned a body of authority—the case has been distinguished on numerous occasions and has been followed only once[86] (and that decision was reversed on appeal).[87] It does, however, remain good law, albeit law that appears unlikely to be followed in future cases. Even if a court were to wish to follow *Watteau*, it is clear that, in certain cases, the principle established by Wills J cannot be applied (e.g. where the third party knows, or ought reasonably to know, of the restriction on the agent's authority).[88]

Despite the criticism surrounding *Watteau* and the fact that it is unlikely to be followed, there does appear to be a tacit acknowledgement amongst a number of academics that *Watteau* might be a useful case if only a convincing justification can be found—this is evidenced by the numerous attempts to devise what the true basis of *Watteau* is. Many academics have tried to justify *Watteau* on agency principles, but none of these explanations have been sufficiently satisfactory. Accordingly, perhaps the most convincing argument is that the decision in *Watteau* is not actually based on the law of agency at all, but is instead an example of estoppel by conduct, as follows:

> By putting someone in charge of their business in such a way that he seemed to be the proprietor of it, [Fenwick] gave [Watteau] the impression that they, as owners of the hotel, were not a distinct legal entity from the person [Watteau] did business with…There is no doubt that this representation was relied on (since it is inconceivable that [Watteau] would have contracted with [Humble] personally had they known he was a mere manager). If so, [Fenwick] should not later have been allowed to resile from it and assert their separate identity, and hence were rightly held liable on the contract.[89]

82. Peter G Watts, *Bowstead & Reynolds on Agency* (19th edn, Sweet & Maxwell 2010) [3-005].
83. JA Hornby, 'The Usual Authority of an Agent' [1961] CLJ 239, 246.
84. *Rhodian River Shipping Co SA v Halla Maritime Corp (The Rhodian River and The Rhodian Sailor)* [1984] 1 Lloyd's Rep 373 (QB) 378.
85. *Sign-O-Lite Plastics Ltd v Metropolitan Life Insurance Co* (1990) 73 DLR (4th) 541, 548 (Wood JA).
86. *Kinahan & Co Ltd v Parry* [1910] 2 KB 389 (QB).
87. *Kinahan & Co Ltd v Parry* [1911] 1 KB 459 (CA). In this case, the Court stated that the principle in *Watteau* will not apply where the agent is acting on his own behalf, and not acting on behalf of his principal.
88. *Daun v Simmins* (1879) 41 LT 783 (CA).
89. Andrew Tennenborn, 'Agents, Business Owners and Estoppel' (1998) 57 CLJ 274, 279.

Conclusion

In many legal disputes, the rights, obligations, and liability of the parties can only be determined once the scope of the agent's authority has been determined. It is therefore fundamental to have a clear understating of the various forms of authority in order to understand the relationships that exist between the persons who are party to an agency agreement and the validity of any contracts that are created as a result of such an agreement. Having discussed the authority of an agent in this chapter, Chapters 6, 7, and 8 discuss the relationships that exist between the relevant parties, beginning with the relationship between the principal and the agent.

Practice questions

1. Commentating on the case of *First Energy (UK) Ltd v Hungarian International Bank Ltd*, Brown contends that the facts of the case are 'difficult to fit within … orthodox doctrine, but…it is suggested that the doctrine should expand in order to accommodate them'.

   Do you agree with this statement?

2. Discuss whether or not the agent had authority in the following situations:

   - Greg, a director of ComCorp, has been negotiating with SoftCorp for the purchase of a number of brand new personal computers. Although Greg is not expressly authorized to purchase such goods on behalf of ComCorp, he has done it before and the company has decided each time to keep the goods. Once the contract is concluded, the board of ComCorp discovers that Greg's wife is a director of SoftCorp and SoftCorp's board knew that Greg lacked express authority to purchase the computers from them. ComCorpes do not wish to purchase the computers from SoftCorp.

   - ComCorp's annual general meeting is approaching. Eric, the managing director of ComCorp, tells Susan, the company secretary, that it is important to keep the company's shareholders happy. A number of overseas investors plan to attend the AGM, and Susan arranges for limousines to collect the investors from the airport, and also books them into five-star hotel rooms. The board of ComCorpes chastizes Susan for such expenditure and states that she did not have the authority to spend such extravagant sums.

   - ComCorp is being sued by George, a disgruntled former employee of ComCorp, who claims that he was unfairly dismissed. Eric, the company's managing director, visits George and states that, if George drops his claim, the company will give him his old job back. George agrees and Eric provides him with a contract of employment, which George signs. The other board members discover this and are outraged. They believe George to be a well-known troublemaker and his claim for unfair dismissal was frivolous and was highly likely to fail. The board refuses to re-employ George on the ground that Eric was not authorized to offer him his old job back.

Further reading

Ian Brown, 'The Agent's Apparent Authority: Paradigm or Paradox?' [1995] JBL 360

- Discusses the case of *First Energy (UK) Ltd v Hungarian International Bank Ltd* and contends that orthodox agency principles should be expanded to support the principles established in the case.

GHL Fridman, 'The Demise of *Watteau v Fenwick*: *Sign-O-Lite Ltd v Metropolitan Life Insurance Co*' (1991) 70 Can Bar Rev 329

- Discusses the case of *Watteau v Fenwick* and contends that the English courts should follow their Canadian counterparts in declaring the case to be defunct.

Roderick Munday, *Agency: Law and Principles* (OUP 2010) chs 3 and 4

- Chapter 3 focuses on an agent's actual authority, whilst chapter 4 discusses the apparent authority of an agent.

FMB Reynolds, 'The Ultimate Apparent Authority' (1994) 110 LQR 21

- Discusses the relationship between *First Energy (UK) Ltd v Hungarian International Bank Ltd* and *Armagas Ltd v Mundogas SA (The Ocean Frost)*.

Peter G Watts, *Bowstead & Reynolds on Agency* (19th edn, Sweet & Maxwell 2010) chs 3 and 8

- Provides a detailed account of the law relating to actual and apparent authority.

- The duties of an agent
- The rights of an agent

INTRODUCTION

Having discussed how an agency relationship can be created and the authority of an agent in Chapters 4 and 5, Chapters 6, 7, and 8 examine the legal relationships that can exist between the three parties involved in a typical legal relationship, namely:

- the relationship between principal and agent;
- the relationship between principal and third party; and
- the relationship between agent and third party.

This chapter discusses the legal relationships that exists between the principal and agent and, in particular, focuses on the duties that each party owes the other, with Figure 6.1 providing an overview of the various duties. The precise scope and content of these duties will depend upon a number of factors, including:

i. whether the agency is contractual or gratuitous;

ii. whether the agent is acting within the scope of his authority;

iii. whether the agent is a specific type of agent upon whom extra duties are placed (e.g. a company director or a solicitor); and

iv. whether the agent is a commercial agent or not.

Accordingly, in order to fully understand the legal relationship between principal and agent, it is important to understand the issues discussed in Chapters 4 and 5. This chapter begins by discussing the duties that an agent owes to his principal.

The duties of an agent

In the case of *Armstrong v Jackson*,[1] McCardie J stated that '[t]he position of principal and agent gives rise to particular and onerous duties on the part of the agent, and the high standard of conduct required of him springs from the fiduciary relationship between his employer and himself'.[2] Although the fiduciary duties of an agent are

---

1. [1917] 2 KB 822 (KB).   2. ibid 826.

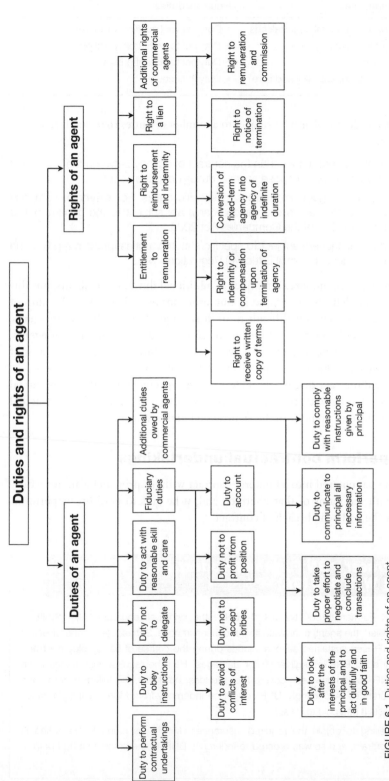

FIGURE 6.1 Duties and rights of an agent

TABLE 6.1 The duties of an agent

Duties of performance	Fiduciary duties
• Duty to perform contractual undertakings	• Duty to avoid conflicts of interest
• Duty to obey instructions	• Duty not to profit from position
• Duty not to delegate	• Duty not to accept bribes
• Duty to act with reasonable skill and care	• Duty to account

fundamental, an agent will also be subject to a number of duties that can derive from different sources:

- If the agency is contractual, then the contract of agency between the agent and principal will be likely to impose specific duties upon the agent.
- Certain types of agent are subject to specific duties. For example, company directors (who are agents of their company) are subject to the general duties found in ss 171–177 of the Companies Act 2006.
- Commercial agents are subject to specific statutory duties found in reg 3 of the Commercial Agents (Council Directive) Regulations 1993.

The law of agency also imposes a number of additional duties upon agents, but this gives rise to a problem. Agents come in numerous forms and the sheer breadth of agency relationships makes it difficult to draft specific duties applicable to agents. Accordingly, as will be seen, the duties imposed upon agents by the law of agency are couched in very general terms. The common law duties of agents can be split into two broad classifications, as demonstrated in Table 6.1.

All of these duties are discussed, along with the specific duties that commercial agents owe, beginning with perhaps the most fundamental duty of a contractual agent, namely the duty to perform his contractual undertakings.

Duty to perform contractual undertakings

An agent who has entered into a bilateral contract with his principal is under a duty to comply with the terms of that contract, and, if he fails to perform or performs inadequately, he will be in breach of contract.

 Fraser v BN Furman (Productions) Ltd [1967] 1 WLR 898 (CA)

FACTS: BN Furman (Productions) Ltd ('BNF', the principal) engaged Miller Smith & Partners ('Miller', the agent) to replace its various insurances. Subsequently, one of BNF's employees (Fraser) sustained serious injuries during the course of her employment and successfully sued BNF in negligence for damages. Had the required insurances been in place, BNF would have been covered for the loss, but Miller had failed to obtain the relevant insurances. Accordingly, BNF sought an indemnity from Miller for the damages and legal costs it had paid to Fraser.

HELD: In failing to obtain the required insurances, Miller was found to be acting in breach of contract, and so was ordered to indemnify BNF for the amounts it had paid to Fraser.

COMMENT: An interesting point arose in this case. It was accepted by BNF and Miller that if the insurances had been taken out, the relevant policy would contain a term stating that the principal would 'take reasonable precautions to prevent accidents and disease'. Miller argued that, as BNF had acted negligently, this term would have been breached, and the insurance company would not have paid out. Consequently, it was argued that BNF did not actually sustain a loss due to Miller's failure to perform. This argument failed because the court did not believe that the insurance company would have refused to pay out, but the court did not dismiss the idea that there had to be a causal connection between the failure to perform and the loss sustained by the principal.

The duty to perform contractual undertakings will also be breached if the agent exceeds his authority. Thus, a breach of duty occurred where a solicitor was instructed not to compromise a legal action, but did so anyway on the ground that it was in his client's interests to do so.[3]

As this duty is based upon the contractual obligations that exist between the principal and agent, it follows that the duty will not apply where the agency is gratuitous or where the contract of agency is unilateral. In both cases, the agent will not be under a duty to do anything at all, unless the agent assumes the responsibility to act, in which case liability could arise in tort.[4] If a gratuitous agent decides to perform, but performs inadequately, then liability can be imposed, as the following case demonstrates.

 ### Wilkinson v Coverdale (1793) 1 Esp 74

FACTS: Coverdale (the agent) had agreed to obtain, for no payment, insurance for Wilkinson's (the principal) premises (therefore, the agency was gratuitous). Coverdale purported to effect the insurance, but due to his negligence, he failed to comply with the relevant formalities, and so the insurance was invalid. The premises subsequently burned down and Wilkinson was precluded from claiming on the policy. Wilkinson commenced proceedings against Coverdale.

HELD: Where a gratuitous agent does not act at all, liability cannot be imposed upon him. However, where a gratuitous agent voluntarily chooses to act, but does so negligently, liability can be imposed. Accordingly, Wilkinson's action succeeded.

Duty to obey instructions

Consider the following example:

 ### ComCorp Ltd

ComCorp turns a healthy profit, and its directors are paid a hefty bonus. Lawrence, one of ComCorp's directors, decides to invest his bonus in the stock market and so instructs

---

3. *Fray v Voules* (1859) 1 E&E 839.   4. *Henderson v Merrett Syndicates Ltd* [1995] 2 AC 145 (HL).

> Andrew, a stockbroker, to purchase £10,000 worth of shares in OmniTech plc. Andrew
> considers this to be an extremely unwise decision, as OmniTech has not made a profit for
> several years, and is close to insolvency. Andrew, therefore, invests Lawrence's money
> in another company. Several days later, OmniTech enters insolvent liquidation and is
> dissolved.

The question that arises is whether Andrew has breached his duty as an agent. It is well established that an agent has to act in his principal's interests, but does this mean that an agent is free to disregard his principal's unwise instructions? To answer this question, the scope of the agent's duty to obey the instructions of his principal must be discussed, with the first important point to note being that the scope of this duty will depend upon whether the agency is contractual or gratuitous:

- Where the agency is gratuitous, then the agent is not under a duty to act at all (as discussed earlier), and so will not be under a duty to obey the principal's instructions.[5] However, if the agent does act on the principal's instructions, he can be liable if he exceeds his authority or if he acts in a negligent manner.

- Where the agency is contractual, then the agent is contractually obliged to obey his principal's instructions[6] and a failure to do so will amount to a breach of contract, thereby allowing the principal to obtain damages, as occurred in the following case.

 Turpin v Bilton (1843) 5 Man & G 455[7]

FACTS: Turpin (the principal) instructed an insurance broker, Bilton (the agent), to insure a ship against losses caused by 'the perils of the sea'. Bilton failed to obtain insurance. The uninsured ship, whilst in transit from Newcastle to Rio de Janeiro, encountered a storm and was lost. Turpin sued Bilton and claimed damages.

HELD: Bilton had failed to obey Turpin's instructions and was therefore in breach of the agency agreement. Bilton was ordered to pay damages to Turpin for the loss sustained.

The duty to obey the principal's instructions is strict, so a breach of duty cannot be avoided on the grounds that disobeying the principal's instructions was a reasonable course of action,[8] or that the instructions were disobeyed because they were improvident.[9] It follows that an agent will not be liable for losses caused as a result of obeying his principal's imprudent instructions.

---

5. *Coggs v Bernard* (1703) 2 Ld Raym 909.
6. Unless, as mentioned earlier, the agency contract is unilateral.
7. See also *Dufresne v Hutchinson* (1810) 3 Taunt 117.
8. *Fray v Voules* (1859) 1 E&E 839 (solicitor entered into compromise agreement, despite instructions to not do so).
9. *RH Deacon & Co Ltd v Varga* (1972) 20 DLR (3d) 653.

***Overend & Gurney Co v Gibb* (1871—72) LR 5 HL 480 (HL)**

FACTS: A company, Overend & Gurney Co (the principal), was formed for the express purpose of acquiring a particular partnership, and its directors (the agents) were granted express powers to acquire that partnership. The directors acquired the partnership on behalf of the company, even though the partnership was heavily in debt. The acquisition proved to be disastrous and the company sustained heavy losses. It issued proceedings against its directors for the losses sustained, alleging that in proceeding with the acquisition, the directors had acted negligently.

HELD: The claim failed, as the directors were merely carrying out their principal's instructions. The principal ought to have realized the imprudence of the acquisition or, as Lord Westbury put it, '[t]he vice that has occurred was in the very creation of the company, the evil that is complained of was the very thing for the purpose of accomplishing which the company was created and called into existence'.[10]

COMMENT: The *ratio* of *Overend* is that agents cannot be held liable for losses sustained as a result of following their principal's imprudent instructions, unless the imprudence is so great as to amount to gross negligence. However, certain agents (especially professionals) who feel that their principal's instructions lack prudence might need to warn their principals of this, lest they be in breach of the duty to act with skill and care.

The duty to act with skill and care is discussed at p 123

As the following case demonstrates, an agent will not be in breach of duty if he refuses to engage in acts that are illegal or would result in the creation of a void and unenforceable contract.

 ***Cohen v Kittell* (1889) 22 QBD 680 (QB)**[11]

FACTS: Cohen (the principal) instructed Kittell (the agent) to place bets on certain horses at Sandown Park and Newmarket races, even though such transactions were void under the Gaming Act 1845. Kittell did not place the bets and Cohen sued for the profits that he would have won had the bets been placed.

HELD: Cohen's action failed. Huddleston B stated:

> The contract of agency...is one by which the plaintiff employed the defendant to enter into contracts which, if made, would have been null and void, and the performance of which could not have been enforced by any legal proceeding taken by the defendant for the benefit of the plaintiff. The breach of such a contract by the agent can give no right of action to the principal.[12]

COMMENT: Would Cohen be entitled to the winnings if Kittell had placed the bets, and would Cohen be liable for the lost bets made on his behalf? Manisty J stated that the principal could recoup any winnings, and the Court of Appeal had previously held that the principal could not avoid paying out any lost bets.[13]

---

10. (1871–72) LR 5 HL 480 (HL) 503.

11. See also *Donovan v Invicta Airways Ltd* [1970] 1 Lloyd's Rep 486 (CA) and *Association of British Travel Agents Ltd v British Airways plc* [2000] 1 Lloyd's Rep 169 (QB).

12. (1889) 22 QBD 680 (QB) 682–3.

13. *Read v Anderson* (1883–84) 13 QBD 779 (CA).

Similarly, if the agent is a professional and the principal's instructions would require the agent to breach his profession's standards or rules of professional conduct, then no breach of duty will occur if the agent refuses to carry out the instructions.[14]

Ambiguous instructions

Where the principal's instructions are ambiguous (i.e. they are capable of being interpreted in multiple ways), then what should the agent do? The answer was provided for in the case of *Ireland v Livingston*,[15] where Lord Chelmsford stated:

The facts and decision of Ireland v Livingston are discussed at p 91

> if a principal gives an order to an agent in such uncertain terms as to be suscep-tible of two different meanings, and the agent *bonâ fide* adopts one of them and acts upon it, it is not competent to the principal to repudiate the act as unau-thorized because he meant the order to be read in the other sense of which it is equally capable.[16]

Accordingly, an agent will not breach the duty to obey instructions if the instruc-tions are capable of multiple interpretations, and the agent honestly and fairly acts in accordance with one of those interpretations. However, the agent will be expected to seek clarification before acting. As Robert Goff LJ stated:

> If instructions are given to an agent, it is understandable that he should expect to act on those instructions without more; but if, for example, the ambiguity is patent on the face of the document it may well be right (especially with the facilities of modern communications available to him) to have his instructions clarified by his principal, if time permits, before acting on them.[17]

Time limits

Not only must an agent obey the instructions of his principal, he must also obey them in a timely manner. Where the agency agreement specifies that performance must be completed within a specified period, then the agent must carry out his instructions within that period, but what if the agency agreement is silent regard-ing the time of performance? General contract law provides that where the con-tract is silent regarding the time for performance, then performance must occur within a reasonable time.[18] The same principle applies in relation to agency agree-ments so, if no period has been specified, then the agent must carry out his princi-pal's instructions within a reasonable time, having regard to the circumstances of the case.

---

14. *Hawkins v Pearse* (1903) 9 Com Cas 87 (stockbroker refused to follow instructions that violated stock exchange rules).

15. (1871–72) LR 5 HL 395 (HL).   16. ibid 416.

17. *European Asian Bank AG v Punjab & Sind Bank (No 2)* [1983] 1 WLR 642 (CA) 656.

18. *Pantland Hick v Raymond & Reid* [1893] AC 22 (HL). In certain circumstances, statute imposes a similar rule. For example, in relation to contracts for the sale of goods, s 29(3) of the Sale of Goods Act 1979 (dis-cussed at p 328) provides that where a seller is bound to send goods to the buyer, but no time is specified for the goods to be sent by, then the seller must send the goods within a reasonable time.

Barber v Taylor (1839) 5 M&W 527

FACTS: Taylor (the principal) instructed Barber (the agent) to purchase 150 bales of cotton on his behalf and to deliver them to Liverpool, and to forward to him the **bill of lading** (although no time limit was specified). Barber purchased 152 bales of cotton and shipped them to Liverpool, but did not forward the bill of lading to Taylor until four days after the goods had arrived at their destination.

HELD: The court held that Barber should have forwarded the bill of lading to Taylor within a reasonable time, which, having regard to the circumstances of the case, was within 24 hours of the goods' arrival in Liverpool. The failure to send the bill of lading within this period amounted to a breach of contract on Barber's part.

➡ **bill of lading:** a document signed and delivered by the master of a ship acknowledging receipt of goods to be delivered

Inability to carry out instructions

If an agent is unable to carry out his principal's instructions, or is unable to carry them out within the specified time (or within a reasonable time if no time is specified), then he may be in breach of duty if he does not inform the principal of this.

 Callander v Oelrichs (1838) 5 Bing NC 58

FACTS: Callander (the principal) instructed Oelrichs (the agent) to insure a cargo of wheat, with the insurance to be effected based upon certain special terms. Oelrichs could not obtain insurance on these special terms, and so obtained insurance on standard terms, but did not inform Callander of this. Due to poor weather, the wheat was damaged while in transit and, due to Oelrichs' inability to insure the wheat on the specified terms, Callander could not claim on the insurance policy. Callander sued Oelrichs.

HELD: Oelrichs was in breach of duty. Vaughan J stated that:

> there was no express stipulation for the Defendants to give notice in case they failed to effect the insurance: but it is a necessary inference, from the nature of the business in which they had engaged, that it was their duty to give that information.[19]

Duty not to delegate

Consider the following example:

 Eg ComCorp Ltd

ComCorp requires renovation work to be carried out on one of its factories and it engages QuickBuild Ltd to carry out the renovation work. The renovation work will require the factory's electrical wiring to be replaced, but QuickBuild lacks expertise in this area. Accordingly, QuickBuild engages Christoph, an electrical engineer, to carry out the rewiring

---

19. (1838) 5 Bing NC 58, 64–5.

> of the factory. The work is completed and the factory is reopened. Christoph invoices QuickBuild for the electrical work, and QuickBuild forwards the invoice to ComCorp, stating that it is liable to pay Christoph. ComCorp refuses to pay Christoph as it did not authorize QuickBuild to engage other persons to carry out the renovation work.

The issue that arises here is, where a principal authorizes an agent to perform a task, is that agent permitted to delegate that authority to another person (known as the sub-agent), and authorize that person to perform all, or part of, the task? In answering this question, the courts have adopted the Latin maxim *delegatus non potest delegare*, which translates as 'a delegate cannot delegate'. The result of this is that 'an agent cannot, without authority from his principal, devolve upon another obligations to the principal which he has himself undertaken to personally fulfil'.[20] There is a sound rationale for this—the principal will have chosen the agent to act on his behalf due to the characteristics of that agent, and so it is only right that that agent perform the required functions. Again quoting Thesiger LJ, 'confidence in the particular person employed is at the root of agency'.[21] Accordingly, if an agent wrongfully delegates his authority to a sub-agent, then several consequences can follow:

- There will be no privity of contract between the principal and sub-agent and so the actions of the sub-agent will not bind the principal.[22] However, the principal will be bound if he ratifies the agent's act of delegation,[23] and he may be bound if the agent has apparent authority to delegate.

- The agent will be acting in breach of duty and will be liable for all obligations arising under the transaction.[24]

- The principal will not be obliged to pay the sub-agent,[25] nor will the sub-agent have the right to a lien over the principal's goods.[26]

🔗 The agent's right to a lien is discussed at p 143

It is important to note that the rule that an agent cannot delegate is a general one only and, in a number of circumstances, an agent can validly delegate his authority. Again, Thesiger LJ provides the rationale behind validating delegation in certain cases:

> the exigencies of business do from time to time render necessary the carrying out of the instructions of a principal by a person other than the agent originally instructed for the purpose, and where that is the case, the reason of the thing requires that the rule should be relaxed, so as, on the one hand, to enable the agent to appoint what has been termed 'a sub-agent' or 'substitute'…and, on the other hand, to constitute, in the interests and for the protection of the principal, a direct privity of contract between him and such substitute.[27]

---

20. *De Bussche v Alt* (1878) LR 8 ChD 286 (CA) 310 (Thesiger LJ).   21. ibid.

22. *Caitlin v Bell* (1815) 4 Camp 183.   23. *Keay v Fenwick* (1876) 1 CPD 745.

24. *Caitlin v Bell* (1815) 4 Camp 183.   25. *John McCann & Co v Pow* [1974] 1 WLR 1643 (CA).

26. *Solly v Rathbone* (1814) 2 M&S 298.   27. *De Bussche v Alt* (1878) LR 8 ChD 286 (CA) 310.

When is delegation permissible?

Delegation will be effective where the principal expressly authorizes the agent to delegate (either beforehand or subsequently through ratification). Express authori-zation is quite commonplace, with Bradgate providing a notable example of express authorization:

> in corporate business structures, where authority to act on behalf of the company is vested in the board of directors, the directors will generally have authority to appoint sub-agents, such as senior executives, who in turn will generally have authority to appoint sub-sub-agents as employees of the business with some agency function.[28]

Delegation will also be valid where the principal impliedly authorizes it. Implied authorization can arise in several situations. The authority to delegate may be implied where the facts of the case indicate that delegation is necessary. For exam-ple, a body corporate (such as a company or limited liability partnership) can only act through human intermediaries and so delegation will be necessary.[29] It may be the case that an unforeseen circumstance arises that necessitates delegation.[30]

Authority to delegate may be implied where the act that is delegated is purely 'ministerial' and does not require the agent to exercise a discretion. Whether an act is ministerial or not will depend upon the facts of the case, with the following case providing an example of an act that was deemed ministerial.

 Allam & Co Ltd v Europa Poster Services Ltd [1968] 1 WLR 638 (Ch)

FACTS: Allam & Co Ltd, an outdoor advertising contractor, obtained licences from a number of site owners, allowing Allam to place advertisements on hoardings at those sites. Europa Poster Services Ltd (the agent), a rival outdoor advertising contractor, subsequently obtained from some of the same site owners (the principals) the exclusive right to place advertisements at the sites. Europa's solicitors (the sub-agents) wrote a letter to Allam, which purported to give notice of the termination of the relevant licences held by Allam. Allam sued Europa, claiming that the notices to terminate were not valid because, *inter alia*, Europa was not authorized to delegate authority to the solicitors.

HELD: The delegation was impliedly authorized and the notices of termination were valid. Buckley J stated:

> If the agent personally performs all that part of his function which involves any confidence conferred upon him or reposed in him by the principal, it is…immaterial that he employs another person to carry out some purely ministerial act on his behalf, in completing the transaction…[T]he substance of the letter itself…had been determined upon by the defendants, and that the firm of solicitors were in truth no more than an amanuensis of the defendants in transmitting the notice in written form.[31]

---

28. Robert Bradgate, *Commercial Law* (3rd edn, OUP 2000) 191.
29. In practice, delegation in such cases will almost always be express, usually through a provision within the company's articles (with art 3 of the Model Articles delegating managerial power to the board of directors).
30. The possibility of unforeseen circumstances resulting in implied authority to delegate was stated by Thesiger LJ in *De Bussche v Alt* (1878) LR 8 ChD 286 (CA) 311, but it should be noted that there appear to have been no cases as yet where this has been applied in practice.
31. [1968] 1 WLR 638 (Ch) 642–3.

Other circumstances where authority to delegate may be implied include:

- where, at the time the principal appointed the agent, he knew that, and agreed to, the agent delegating his authority;[32]
- where the particular circumstances surrounding the case, or the conduct of the parties, implies that delegation is permitted;[33]
- where it is usual practice within a trade or profession to delegate authority.[34]

Effects of authorized delegation

Consider the following example:

 ComCorp Ltd

The articles of ComCorp Ltd expressly confer authority upon the company's directors to delegate performance of their functions to other persons. The directors of ComCorp delegate certain managerial functions to several senior managers within the company, with these managers in turn being authorized to delegate certain functions.

In this example, ComCorp Ltd is the principal, its directors are agents, and the senior managers to whom the directors have delegated their managerial functions are sub-agents (if these managers delegate further, there will also be sub-sub-agents). There is no doubt that, as the delegation of authority is authorized, ComCorp will be liable for the acts of the sub-agents.[35] The question that arises is whether a contractual relationship exists between ComCorp and the sub-agents. The answer depends on whether there is privity of contract between the principal and the sub-agent, which will depend upon the intentions of the parties. The approach currently adopted by the courts was established in the following case.

 ***Calico Printers' Association Ltd v Barclays Bank Ltd* (1930) 36 Com Cas 71 (KB)**[36]

FACTS: Calico Printers' Association Ltd ('Calico', the principal) sold cotton to a consignee in Beirut and instructed Barclays Bank ('Barclays', the agent) to insure the goods. Barclays did not have an office in Beirut and so, with the knowledge of Calico, it appointed the Anglo-Palestine Bank (the sub-agent) to effect the insurance. The Anglo-Palestine Bank failed to effect the insurance and the cotton was subsequently destroyed in a fire. Calico

---

32. *Quebec & Richmond Rly Co v Quinn* (1858) 12 Moo PC 232.

33. *De Bussche v Alt* (1878) LR 8 ChD 286 (CA).

34. *Solley v Wood* (1852) 16 Beav 370 (customary practice for provincial solicitors to appoint London-based solicitors to represent them in the High Court).

35. Note that this is not because the sub-agent is regarded as the agent of the principal, but because the principal is bound by the authorized act of his agent.

36. The Court of Appeal upheld the decision ((1931) 145 LT 51 (CA)), but the relevant section of the High Court judgment relating to delegation of authority was not part of the appeal.

sued both banks, but Barclays avoided liability due to the presence of a valid exclusion clause. Accordingly, Calico sought damages from the Anglo-Palestine Bank.

HELD: The claim failed as there was no privity of contract between Calico and the Anglo-Palestine Bank. Wright J stated that the courts have generally:

applied the rule that even where the sub-agent is properly employed, there is still no privity between him and the principal; the latter is entitled to hold the agent liable for breach of the mandate, which he has accepted, and cannot in general claim against the sub-agent for negligence or breach of duty.[37]

The result is that, generally, there will be no privity of contract between the principal and the sub-agent, even where the principal has authorized the agent to appoint a sub-agent. Accordingly, if the sub-agent fails to perform, or performs inadequately, then the principal may sue the agent (the agent in turn may be able to sue the sub-agent) but, as the *Calico* case indicates, the principal cannot directly sue the sub-agent.[38] The benefit of such a rule is that it 'emphasises the importance of the contractual chain. It is natural for each agent in the chain to give credit to the party known to him, rather than to perhaps someone unknown.'[39] If the sub-agent has, or has had, any monies from the principal, then such monies can be recovered from the agent by the principal.[40] It should also be noted that, even if privity cannot be established between the principal and the sub-agent, the sub-agent may still owe fiduciary duties to the principal.[41]

The question that arises is when will privity of contract be established between a principal and sub-agent. Once again, the answer was provided by Wright J in *Calico*, who stated that:

To create privity it must be established not only that the principal contemplated that a sub-agent would form part of the contract, but also that the principal authorised the agent to create privity of contract between the principal and the sub-agent, which is a very different matter requiring precise proof.[42]

If a party can establish privity between the principal and sub-agent, then the sub-agent will be regarded as an agent of the principal with all the consequences of agency that ensue[43] (e.g. the sub-agent is subject to the rights and duties of an agent). In such a case, if the sub-agent fails to perform, or performs inadequately, then the

---

37. (1930) 36 Com Cas 71 (KB) 77.

38. The principal may be able to enforce a term of the contract against the sub-agent if he can bring himself within the exception to the privity rule found in s 1(1) of the Contracts (Rights of Third Parties) Act 1999. In order to do this, the principal will need to show that either (i) the contract expressly provided him with a right to enforce a term; or (ii) the term purported to confer a benefit on him and there is nothing in the contract indicating that the parties did not intend for the contract to be enforceable by a third party.

39. *Prentis Donegan & Partners Ltd v Leeds & Leeds Co Inc* [1998] 2 Lloyd's Rep 326 (QB) 334 (Rix J).

40. *Matthews v Haydon* (1786) 2 Esp 509.

41. *Powell & Thomas v Evan Jones & Co* [1905] 1 KB 11 (CA) (sub-agent made to account to principal for secret profit made).

42. (1930) 36 Com Cas 71 (KB) 78.

43. Given this, Peter G Watts, *Bowstead & Reynolds on Agency* (19th edn, Sweet & Maxwell 2010) [5-101] contends that the sub-agent is not actually a sub-agent, but is in fact a co-agent.

principal can sue the sub-agent, but he cannot sue the agent.[44] Finally, it should be noted that the fact that privity exists between the principal and the sub-agent will not automatically negate the existence of a contractual relationship between the agent and the sub-agent.[45]

Liability in tort

Even if a contractual relationship does not exist between the principal and the sub-agent, the sub-agent may still be liable to the principal in tort (notably under the tort of negligence) if it can be established that the sub-agent owed the principal a duty of care, as occurred in the following case.

 Henderson v Merrett Syndicates Ltd [1995] 2 AC 145 (HL)

FACTS: This case was one of many pieces of litigation that arose out of the collapse of the Lloyds insurance market. Investors known as 'Names' (the principals) had invested money in the Lloyds insurance market. These Names had engaged members' agents (the agents) and these members' agents had in turn engaged managing agents (the sub-agents). The various contracts expressly stated that the managing agents were to be regarded as agents of the members' agents, and so there was no direct contractual relationship between the managing agents and the Names. A major issue in the case was therefore whether, following the collapse of the market, the managing agents owed a tortious duty of care to the Names, and could therefore be held liable in negligence.

HELD: The managing agents did indeed owe a duty of care to the Names, as the criteria for a duty of care, as set out in *Hedley Byrne & Co Ltd v Heller & Partners Ltd*,[46] were met. Lord Goff stated:

> there is in my opinion plainly an assumption of responsibility in the relevant sense by the managing agents towards the Names in their syndicates...They obviously hold themselves out as possessing a special expertise to advise the Names on the suitability of risks to be underwritten...The Names, as the managing agents well knew, placed implicit reliance on that expertise, in that they gave authority to the managing agents to bind them to contracts of insurance and reinsurance and to the settlement of claims. I can see no escape from the conclusion that, in these circumstances, prima facie a duty of care is owed in tort by the managing agents to such Names.[47]

COMMENT: This case does not establish that a sub-agent will always owe a duty of care to the principal. In many cases, no duty of care will be owed, with Lord Goff noting that the situation that arose in *Henderson* was 'most unusual',[48] before going on to state that '[i]t cannot therefore be inferred from the present case that other sub-agents will be held directly liable to the agent's principal in tort'.[49]

⭐ See JD Heydon, 'The Negligent Fiduciary' (1995) 111 LQR 1

---

44. *Aiken v Stewart Wrightson Members Agency Ltd* [1995] 1 WLR 1281 (QB). As part of the duty to exercise skill and care, the agent will, however, be expected to exercise reasonable skill and care when appointing a sub-agent (*Thomas Cheshire & Co v Vaughan Bros & Co* [1920] 3 KB 240 (CA)).
45. *Prentis Donegan & Partners Ltd v Leeds & Leeds Co Inc* [1998] 2 Lloyd's Rep 326 (QB).
46. [1964] AC 465 (HL).   47. [1995] 2 AC 145 (HL) 182.   48. ibid 195.   49. ibid.

Duty to act with reasonable care and skill

All agents owe a duty of care to their principals to exercise reasonable care and skill in the carrying out of their agency. However, the source of this duty differs depending on whether the agency is contractual or gratuitous and so each will be considered separately.

Contractual agencies

Where the agency is contractual, then the common law will imply into the agency agreement a term requiring the agent to exercise reasonable care and skill. Where the agent is providing a service in the course of a business, then a similar term is implied by statute.[50] The agent will also owe a tortious duty of care and can therefore be liable in contract and tort if he fails to exercise reasonable care and skill.[51] The primary remedy will usually be to commence proceedings for breach of contract but, depending on the facts, it might be more advantageous to base the action in tort.[52] It should be noted that a contractual agent can exclude or limit liability for breach of duty through a disclaimer or exclusion clause, but clear words will need to be used if liability under tort is to be excluded or limited.[53] Such an exclusion clause would also be subject to the safeguards found in the Unfair Contract Terms Act 1977 and the Unfair Terms in Consumer Contracts Regulations 1999.

Irrespective of whether the action is brought in contract or tort, the standard of care expected is the same, namely the agent must exercise a standard of care that is reasonable in all the circumstances. Although the standard is objective, it will be largely dependent on the facts of the case. For example, if the agent was exercising any trade, profession, or calling, then 'he is required to exercise the degree of skill and diligence reasonably to be expected of a person exercising such trade, profession or calling, irrespective of the degree of skill he may possess'.[54] From this, it follows that a solicitor should act with a degree of skill that a member of the public would reasonably expect to see from a solicitor.[55] Certain circumstances may cause the standard expected of the agent to be raised (e.g. if the agent professes to have some form of special skill, which he fails to use).[56]

Gratuitous agencies

For obvious reasons, gratuitous agents do not owe a contractual duty of care to exercise due care and skill, but they do owe a tortious duty of care. The question that arises is whether the standard of care expected of a gratuitous agent differs from that of a contractual agent. Historically, there was little doubt that they did differ, with gratuitous agents being expected to display such care and skill as would be exercised

---

50. Supply of Goods and Services Act 1982, s 13.

51. *Henderson v Merrett Syndicates Ltd* [1995] 2 AC 145 (HL), *Esso Petroleum Co Ltd v Mardon* [1976] QB 801 (CA).

52. The key difference relates to the more generous limitation periods in tort cases. In contract cases, the limitation period commences as soon as the contract is breached, whereas in tort, the period does not commence until the damage is sustained.

53. *Henderson v Merrett Syndicates Ltd* [1995] 2 AC 145 (HL).

54. *Chaudhry v Prabhakar* [1989] 1 WLR 29 (CA) 34 (Stuart-Smith LJ).

55. *Simmons v Pennington* [1955] 1 WLR 183 (CA).

56. *Duchess of Argyll v Beusalinck* [1972] 2 Lloyd's Rep 172 (Ch).

in the conduct of their own affairs.[57] This highly subjective standard of care was clearly inconsistent with the more objective standards being adopted by the modern law of negligence and so, in the following seminal case, a more objective standard was established.

 Chaudhry v Prabhakar [1989] 1 WLR 29 (CA)

FACTS: Chaudhry (the principal) wished to purchase a car. Her knowledge of cars was lacking, so she asked Prabhakar (the agent), a friend of hers, to locate for her a second-hand car, stipulating that the car should not have been involved in any prior accidents. Prabhakar was not a mechanic, but he was a keen amateur enthusiast. He located a car and noticed that the bonnet had been repaired or replaced, but did not enquire as to whether the car had been involved in an accident. He recommended the car to Chaudhry and so she purchased it. Subsequently, it was discovered that the car had been involved in an accident and, due to the poor repair work undertaken, it was a valueless insurance write-off. Chaudhry sued Prabhakar, who contended that, as he was only a gratuitous agent, he only had to display the skill as would be exercised in the conduct of his own affairs. He claimed that he would have purchased the car himself and so had therefore not breached the standard of care.

HELD: The Court refused to accept Prabhakar's account of the standard of care and established a more objective standard, namely that a gratuitous agent has a duty to exercise such care and skill as may be reasonably expected of him in all the circumstances. As Prabhakar had failed to ask the seller whether the car had been involved in an accident, he had not exercised reasonable care and was therefore ordered to pay damages to Chaudhry.

COMMENT: Counsel for Prabhakar conceded that he was a gratuitous agent and therefore owed Chaudhry a duty of care, but it is arguable that Prabhakar was not actually an agent. May LJ stated that:

> I for my part respectfully doubt whether counsel's concession in the instant case was rightly made in law. I do not find the conclusion that one must impose upon a family friend looking out for a first car for a girl of 26 a Donoghue v Stevenson duty of care in and about his quest, enforceable with all the formalities of the law of tort, entirely attractive.[58]

 See Ian Brown, 'The Gratuitous Agent's Liability' (1989) 2 LMCLQ 148

Numerous academics have expressed support for May LJ's comment,[59] with several contending that liability should not have been imposed upon agency principles, but through finding that Prabhakar had provided negligent advice.[60]

The result of *Chaudhry* is that the standard of care for both paid agents and gratuitous agents is the same, namely to exercise such care as is reasonable in all the circumstances. However, the circumstances of the case will affect the standard of

---

57. *Coggs v Bernard* (1703) 2 Ld Raym 909.
58. [1989] 1 WLR 29 (CA) 38.
59. See e.g. Peter G Watts, *Bowstead & Reynolds on Agency* (19th edn, Sweet & Maxwell 2010) [6-030].
60. See e.g. NE Palmer [1992] SPTL Reporter 35, 36.

care expected, with Stuart-Smith LJ in *Chaudhry* stating that 'one of the relevant circumstances is whether or not the agent is paid'.[61] He went on to state:

> Where the agent is unpaid, any duty of care arises in tort. Relevant circumstances would be the actual skill and experience that the agent had, though, if he has represented such skill and experience to be greater than it in fact is and the principal has relied on such representation, it seems to me to be reasonable to expect him to show that standard of skill and experience which he claims he possesses. Moreover, the fact that principal and agent are friends does not in my judgment affect the existence of the duty of care, though conceivably it may be a relevant circumstance in considering the degree or standard of care.[62]

Fiduciary duties

In addition to the duties already discussed, and any duties imposed by the agency agreement, the agent is also subject to a number of duties that arise due to his position as a fiduciary. It is important to note at the outset that fiduciary duties arise due to equity, and exist independently of any agency agreement (although they can be incorporated into, or excluded by,[63] the agency agreement). Accordingly, both contractual and gratuitous agents are subject to these fiduciary duties.

Definitively defining what a fiduciary is can be difficult, but an often-cited definition is that offered by Millett LJ, who stated that '[a] fiduciary is someone who has undertaken to act for or on behalf of another in a particular matter in circumstances which give rise to a relationship of trust and confidence'.[64] From this simple definition alone, it is clear that, in the vast majority of cases,[65] an agent is to be regarded as a fiduciary, but identifying the agent as a fiduciary is only a starting point. As Frankfurter J stated, '[t]o say that a man is a fiduciary only begins analysis; it gives direction to further inquiry. To whom is he a fiduciary? What obligations does he owe as a fiduciary?'[66]

The answer to the first question is simple—the agent occupies a fiduciary position in relation to his principal. The second question is the important one, namely what fiduciary obligations will the agent owe towards the principal. Again, Millett LJ provides an often-quoted answer:

> The distinguishing obligation of a fiduciary is the obligation of loyalty. The principal is entitled to the single-minded loyalty of his fiduciary. This core liability has several facets. A fiduciary must act in good faith; he must not make a profit out of his trust; he must not place himself in a position where his duty and his interest may conflict; he may not act for his own benefit or the benefit of a

---

61. [1989] 1 WLR 29 (CA) 34.

62. ibid.

63. *Kelly v Cooper* [1993] AC 205 (PC). Contractual terms that aim to exclude the fiduciary obligations of the agent will be subject to strict common law and statutory safeguards, notably those found within the Unfair Contract Terms Act 1977 and the Unfair Terms in Consumer Contracts Regulations 1999.

64. *Bristol and West Building Society v Mothew* [1998] Ch 1 (CA) 18.

65. An agent may not always be a fiduciary, or may not be always acting in a fiduciary capacity. As FE Dowrick, 'The Relationship of Principal and Agent' (1954) 17 MLR 24 notes, if a principal engages an agent to carry out a task that does not involve placing any particular trust in the agent, then this will not give rise to a fiduciary relationship between the two parties.

66. *SEC v Chenery Corp* (1943) 318 US 80 (US Supreme Court) 85–6.

third person without the informed consent of his principal. This is not intended to be an exhaustive list, but it is sufficient to indicate the nature of fiduciary obligations.[67]

Four principal fiduciary duties can be identified, namely:

(i) the duty to avoid conflicts of interest;

(ii) the duty not to profit from the agent's position;

(iii) the duty not to accept bribes; and

(iv) the duty to account.

As Millett J indicated, this list cannot be regarded as exhaustive, and significant overlaps do exist between the duties (e.g. the duty not to accept bribes could be regarded as a specific aspect of the duty to avoid conflicts of interest).

Duty to avoid conflicts of interest

In *Aberdeen Railway Co v Blaikie Bros*,[68] Lord Cranworth LC stated:

> [n]o one having [fiduciary] duties to discharge, shall be allowed to enter into engagements in which he has, or can have, a personal interest conflicting, or which may possibly conflict, with the interests of those whom he is bound to protect.[69]

Accordingly, an agent cannot allow his interests to conflict with those of his principal, unless the principal has full knowledge of the conflict[70] and has consented to it.[71] Jacob LJ stated the rationale behind this rule:

> The law imposes on agents high standards...An agent's own personal interests come entirely second to the interest of his client. If you undertake to act for a man you must act 100% body and soul, for him. You must act as if you were him. You must not allow your own interest to get in the way without telling him.[72]

The no-conflict duty is a strict one—it therefore does not matter that the agent acted in good faith or had no dishonest motive. The duty can be breached providing that there is an actual conflict or 'a real sensible possibility of conflict'.[73] Where such a conflict is alleged, the burden of proof is placed upon the agent to prove that there was no conflict[74] or that the principal consented to the conflict. If the agent cannot do this, then the duty will be breached and the principal will be able to rescind the contract, as occurred in the following case.

---

67. *Bristol and West Building Society v Mothew* [1998] Ch 1 (CA) 18.

68. (1854) 1 Macq 461.   69. ibid 471.

70. *Fullwood v Hurley* [1928] 1 KB 498 (CA).

71. *Bray v Ford* [1896] AC 44 (HL). Disclosure and consent need not occur immediately, but must occur prior to the principal entering into binding commitments with the third party (*Harrods Ltd v Lemon* [1931] 2 KB 157 (CA)).

72. *Imageview Management Ltd v Jack* [2009] EWCA Civ 63, [2009] 1 Lloyd's Rep 436 [6].

73. *Boardman v Phipps* [1967] 2 AC 46 (HL) 124 (Lord Upjohn).

74. *Collins v Hare* (1828) 2 Bli (NS) 106.

***Armstrong v Jackson* [1917] 2 KB 822 (KB)**

FACTS: Armstrong (the principal) instructed a stockbroker, Jackson (the agent), to purchase 600 shares in a certain company. Jackson wrote to Armstrong and stated that his instructions had been complied with and the shares had been purchased. However, the shares that Armstrong bought were actually purchased from Jackson himself, and Jackson did not disclose this. Several years later, Armstrong discovered the truth and commenced proceedings against Jackson to have the transaction set aside.

HELD: Armstrong's claim succeeded and so Jackson was ordered to repay to Armstrong the amount paid for the shares. McCardie J stated:

> Now a broker who secretly sells his own shares is in a wholly false position. As vendor it is to his interest to sell his shares at the highest price. As broker it is his clear duty to the principal to buy at the lowest price and to give unbiased and independent advice...as to the time when and the price at which shares shall be bought, or whether they shall be bought at all. The law has ever required a high measure of good faith from an agent. He departs from good faith when he secretly sells his own property to the principal.[75]

Examples of instances where the courts have found a breach of the no-conflict rule to have occurred include the following:

- where an agent who is instructed to purchase property for the principal, sells to the principal his own property (as in the *Armstrong* case), or property in which he has an interest (e.g. a company director sells to his company products that are manufactured by another company, of which he is also a director);[76]
- where an agent is instructed to sell a piece of the principal's property, and the agent purchases the property himself,[77] or arranges for a third party to purchase it on the agent's behalf;[78]
- where an agent receives a secret commission from persons with whom he is entering into transactions on the principal's behalf;[79]
- where a third party agrees to provide an agent with business if the agent leaves the employment of the principal and sets up business on his own.[80]

These examples relate to situations where the interests of the agent directly conflict with the interests of the principal. However, a breach of the no-conflict duty can also arise where an agent is acting on behalf of a principal, and the agent puts himself in a position where he owes a duty to a third party which is inconsistent with his duty to his principal. This tends to arise where an agent is acting on behalf of multiple principals, and the courts have stated that an agent cannot act for both parties to a single transaction, unless both parties have consented to the agent acting in such a way. So, for example, an agent who is engaged to sell a hotel by the owner of the hotel and who also acts on behalf of the buyer that purchases that hotel, cannot claim commission from both the seller and buyer, unless they have consented to the agent

---

75. [1917] 2 KB 822 (KB) 824.   76. *Aberdeen Railway Co v Blaikie Bros* (1854) 1 Macq 461.
77. *McPherson v Watt* (1877) 3 App Cas 254.   78. ibid.
79. *Boston Deep Sea Fishing v Ansell* (1888) 39 ChD 339 (CA).   80. *Sanders v Parry* [1967] 1 WLR 753.

representing them both.[81] However, this principle is not absolute and in the controversial case of *Kelly v Cooper*, the Privy Council held that the duty not to compete could, depending upon the circumstances of the case, be impliedly excluded.

 Kelly v Cooper [1993] AC 205 (PC)

FACTS: Kelly (the first principal) instructed Coopers Associates (the agent), a firm of estate agents, to sell his house (the house was named 'Caliban'). Brant (the second principal), the owner of a nearby house (named 'Vertigo') also instructed Coopers to sell his house. Coopers showed both houses to Perot, who offered to purchase Vertigo. Brant accepted the offer and Coopers was paid commission for the sale. Shortly after the offer was accepted, Perot also offered to buy Caliban. Kelly accepted this offer, but he was unaware that Perot had also agreed to buy Vertigo. When Kelly found out that Perot had also agreed to purchase Vertigo, he refused to pay Coopers any commission. Kelly argued that it was clear that Perot wanted to buy both houses and, if Coopers had informed Kelly that Perot had already agreed to buy Vertigo, then Kelly could have negotiated a higher price for Caliban. Accordingly, he claimed that Coopers had placed itself in a position where its duties to the two principals conflicted. Kelly sued for damages for breach of duty, and Coopers counterclaimed for the commission owed.

HELD: Kelly's claim failed and Coopers' counterclaim succeeded. The Board agreed that the fact that Perot wanted to purchase both houses was a material fact that could have impacted upon the price of Caliban. The Board then went on to state that the scope of an agent's fiduciary duties will depend upon the express and implied terms of the agency agreement. Bearing this in mind, Lord Browne-Wilkinson stated:

> In the case of estate agents, it is their business to act for numerous principals: where properties are of a similar description, there will be a conflict of interest between the principals each of whom will be concerned to attract potential purchasers to their property rather than that of another. Yet, despite this conflict of interest, estate agents must be free to act for several competing principals otherwise they will be unable to perform their function . . . In the course of acting for each of their principals, estate agents will acquire information confidential to that principal. It cannot be sensibly suggested that an estate agent is contractually bound to disclose to any one of his principals information which is confidential to another of his principals.[82]

COMMENT: The decision and reasoning of the Board has proven controversial. Some critics have applauded the decision, stating that it helps 'refashion the law of fiduciary duties in a manner that takes greater account of modern commercial pressures and practice'.[83] Other commentators have been more critical, stating that the case 'seems to deny fiduciary obligations to all and to leave everything to express and even implied terms of the contract'.[84] What should an agent in such a difficult position do? Brown, in criticizing the decision in *Kelly*, provides a more acceptable and clear answer than that offered by the Board in *Kelly*:

> Once such a conflict arises between competing principals and the agent continues to act for both it must surely be with the certainty that he will breach his duties to

81. *Fullwood v Hurley* [1928] 1 KB 498 (CA).   82. [1993] AC 205 (PC) 214.
83. Richard C Nolan, 'Conflicts of Duty: Helping Hands From the Privy Council?' (1994) 15 Co Law 58, 58.
84. FMB Reynolds, 'Fiduciary Duties of Estate Agents' [1994] JBL 147, 149.

one or the other. An agent owes a duty to communicate facts to his principal with due diligence and the defendant's dilemma in *Kelly* should have been resolved by his seeking the consent of both principals to reveal Perot's interest to the other. In the absence of dual consent it is suggested that the defendant should have terminated both agencies, or at least one of them.[85]

Despite the academic criticism levelled at *Kelly*, it has been cited with approval by the Law Commission[86] and in several subsequent cases.[87] It should, however, be noted that the agent in *Kelly* was acting for two different principals in two different transactions. It is highly unlikely that the court would adopt the same view had the agent been working for two different principals in the same transaction (especially if the two principals were competitors).

 See Ian Brown, 'Divided Loyalties in the Law of Agency' (1993) 109 LQR 206

Duty not to profit from position

An agent is not permitted to profit from his position as agent, unless the principal knows of the profit and consents to the agent retaining it. The duty is applied extremely strictly, as the following case demonstrates.

Regal (Hastings) Ltd v Gulliver [1967] 2 AC 134 (HL)

FACTS: Regal (Hastings) Ltd ('RH', the principal) owned a cinema, and it decided to acquire two other nearby cinemas and sell all three cinemas as a going concern. In order to effect this, a subsidiary company, Hastings Amalgamated Cinemas Ltd (HAC), was created, with an issued share capital of £5,000. The landlord of the two cinemas would only let HAC acquire the cinemas if the company's paid-up share capital was £5,000. RH could only purchase £2,000 worth of shares in HAC, so it was decided that the directors of RH (the agents) would between them take up the remaining shares. Several weeks later, the entire scheme was abandoned and a new agreement was entered into whereby the directors would sell their shares in RH and HAC to the purchasers who were originally going to buy the cinemas. The shares in HAC had increased in value and so the directors made a profit of £2.80 per share. RH, now under the control of the new purchaser, commenced proceedings against the former directors to recover the profit made through the sale of the shares.

HELD: The House held that RH could recover the profit from its former directors, on the ground that the former directors had profited from their position as agents. The fact that the directors acted in good faith to help RH secure an opportunity that, due to its lack of funds, it could not undertake on its own was irrelevant. Lord Russell stated:

> The rule of equity which insists on those, who by use of a fiduciary position make a profit, being liable to account for that profit, in no way depends on fraud, or absence of bona fides...The liability arises from the mere fact of a profit having, in the stated circumstances, been made. The profiteer, however honest and well-intentioned, cannot escape the risk of being called upon to account.[88]

---

85. Ian Brown, 'Divided Loyalties in the Law of Agency' (1993) 109 LQR 206, 208.
86. Law Commission, *Fiduciary Duties and Regulatory Rules* (Law Com No 236, 1995).
87. See e.g. *Clark-Boyce v Mouat* [1994] 1 AC 428 (PC) 436, and *Henderson v Merrett Syndicates Ltd* [1995] 2 AC 145 (HL) 206.
88. [1967] 2 AC 134 (HL) 144–45.

In the Court of Appeal decision in *Boardman v Phipps*,[89] Lord Denning MR highlighted the three principal ways in which a breach of duty can arise. First, 'if [the agent] uses a position of authority, to which he has been appointed by his principal, so as to gain money for himself, then he is accountable to the principal for it'.[90] The following case demonstrates this type of breach.

 Industrial Development Consultants Ltd v Cooley [1972] 1 WLR 443

FACTS: Cooley (the agent) was managing director of Industrial Development Consultants Ltd (IDC, the principal). IDC had sought to acquire business from another company, EGB, but EGB refused to do business with IDC. The deputy chairman of EGB approached Cooley and indicated that EGB would be willing to contract with Cooley personally if he left the employment of IDC. Cooley then left the employment of IDC by falsely claiming that he was ill. Subsequently, Cooley entered into a contract with EGB. IDC commenced proceedings against Cooley.

HELD: IDC's action succeeded and it was able to claim from Cooley the profit that he received from the contract with EGB. Roskill J stated that Cooley was 'guilty of putting himself into the position in which his duty to his employers...and his own private interests conflicted and conflicted grievously'.[91]

★ See Harry Rajak, 'Fiduciary Duty of a Managing Director' (1972) 35 MLR 655

Second, the duty will be breached where 'the agent uses property, with which he has been entrusted by his principal, so as to make a profit for himself out of it, without his principal's consent'.[92]

 Shallcross v Oldham (1862) 2 Johns & H 609

FACTS: Oldham (the agent) was engaged as the master of a ship by the ship's owner, Shallcross (the principal). Oldham was instructed to employ the ship to the best advantage. Oldham could not procure freight for the ship, so he loaded it with his own cargo, sailed the ship to Hong Kong, and sold the cargo. Upon discovering this, Shallcross commenced proceedings against Oldham.

HELD: Oldham was ordered to pay to Shallcross the profit that he made through the sale of the cargo. Sir William Page-Wood VC stated that 'where a chattel is entrusted to an agent to be used for the owner's benefit, all the profits which the agent may make by using that chattel belong to the owner'.[93]

Third, an agent who acquires information or knowledge from the principal, and uses it for personal gain, will be in breach of duty.

---

89. [1965] Ch 992 (CA).   90. ibid 1018.   91. [1972] 1 WLR 443, 453.
92. *Boardman v Phipps* [1965] Ch 992 (CA) 1018 (Lord Denning MR).
93. (1862) 2 Johns & H 609, 616.

Lamb v Evans [1893] 1 Ch 218 (CA)

FACTS: Lamb (the principal) was the proprietor and publisher of a business directory. Lamb employed a number of canvassers (the agents) whose job was to obtain advertisements from businesses that would be placed within the directory. In return, the canvassers would earn commission. Lamb discovered that a number of the canvassers were proposing to canvass advertisements for a rival publication once their agreement with Lamb had ended. Lamb commenced proceedings.

HELD: Lamb's action succeeded and an injunction was granted preventing the canvassers from providing advertisements to the rival publication. Lindley LJ stated that 'an agent has no right to employ as against his principal materials which that agent has obtained only for his principal and in the course of his agency',[94] with the materials in this case being the information that was to be placed in the directory published by Lamb.

If an agent breaches the duty not to profit, then the principal may, depending on the facts, have access to several remedies:

- The principal can recover the profit from the agent. Where the profit was made through the use of the principal's property or through the use of confidential information, then the profit will be held on trust, with the advantage that the principal can recover any increase to the value of the profit (e.g. if the agent used the profit to purchase shares that have subsequently increased in value).
- The principal may be able to obtain an injunction, preventing the agent from profiting from his position (as in *Lamb v Evans*). This is especially useful if the agent has profited through the use of confidential information.
- If the agent's actions amount to a breach of contract, then the principal may be able to obtain damages.

Duty not to accept bribes

As Stone has stated, 'a bribed agent cannot be expected to put the interests of his or her principal first'[95] and so the agent's fiduciary position places him under a duty not to accept bribes. A bribe is simply 'a commission or other inducement which is given by a third party to an agent as such, which is secret from his principal'.[96] The courts take an extremely dim view of bribery, with Lord Templeman stating that '[b]ribery is an evil practice which threatens the foundations of any civilised society'.[97] Given the grave nature of bribery, the courts adopt a broad approach when determining whether a payment amounts to a bribe, as the following case demonstrates.

---

94. [1893] 1 Ch 218 (CA) 226.
95. Richard Stone, *Law of Agency* (Cavendish 1996) 65.
96. *Anangel Atlas Compania Naviera SA v Ishikawajima-Harima Heavy Industries Ltd* [1990] 1 Lloyd's Rep 167 (QB) 171 (Leggatt J).
97. *Attorney General for Hong Kong v Reid* [1994] 1 AC 324 (PC) 330.

Industries & General Mortgage Co Ltd v Lewis [1949] 2 All ER 573 (KB)

FACTS: Lewis (the principal) instructed Vermont (the agent) to find someone who could provide him with a loan. Vermont obtained, on Lewis's behalf, a loan from Industries & General Mortgage Co Ltd (IGM) and Lewis paid IGM a fee for providing the loan. However, unknown to Lewis, IGM had agreed to pay half of this fee to Vermont. IGM was unaware that Lewis did not know of this payment, and it was accepted that IGM had no dishonest intentions in making the payment.

HELD: Slade J stated that a payment amounts to a bribe if three elements are present, namely:

(i) that the person making the payment makes it to the agent of the other person with whom he is dealing; (ii) that he makes it to that person knowing that that person is acting as the agent of the other person with whom he is dealing; and (iii) that he fails to disclose to the other person with whom he is dealing that he has made that payment to the person whom he knows to be the other person's agent.[98]

Applying this, it was clear that the payment made by IGM to Vermont amounted to a bribe. The fact that IGM had no dishonest motive for making the payment was irrelevant, as 'proof of corruptness or corrupt motive is unnecessary in a civil action'[99] because 'once the bribe is established, there is an irrebuttable presumption that it was given with an intention to induce the agent to act favourably to the payer and, thereafter, unfavourably to the principal'.[100] Accordingly, Vermont had breached the duty not to accept a bribe and the amount of the bribe was recoverable by Lewis.

The agent becomes liable through the mere acceptance of, or agreeing to accept, the bribe—it is therefore not necessary to establish that the bribe actually influenced the agent.[101] It is also not necessary to show that the agent actively concealed the existence of the bribe[102]—the agent breaches his duty if he receives, or agrees to receive, a bribe that the principal is unaware of. It follows from this that the duty will not be breached where the principal knows of the payment and consents to it being given. That disclosure can legitimate a payment that would otherwise be a bribe is reflective of the view that 'the real evil is not the payment of money, but the secrecy attending it'.[103] The burden of proof for establishing disclosure is on the agent, who must disclose enough detail to enable the principal to fully understand the implications of the payment. If the disclosure is insufficient, then the duty not to accept bribes may still be breached or, depending on the extent of the disclosure, the agent may instead be found to have breached the duty to avoid a conflict of interest.[104]

---

98. [1949] 2 All ER 573 (KB) 575.   99. ibid.   100. ibid 576.

101. *Shipway v Broadwood* [1899] 1 QB 369 (CA).

102. *Temperley v Blackrod Mfg Co Ltd* (1907) 71 JP 341.

103. *Shipway v Broadwood* [1899] 1 QB 369 (CA) 373 (Chitty LJ).

104. *Hurstanger v Wilson* [2007] EWCA Civ 299, [2007] 2 All ER (Comm) 1037.

The grave nature of bribery is reflected in the wide-ranging civil remedies that are available to the principal:

- The principal can, without notice, terminate the contract of agency and dismiss the agent.[105]

- The agent will lose the right to any remuneration/commission that he was entitled to,[106] and will also lose the right to claim an indemnity.[107]

- The agent and the briber are jointly and severally liable under the tort of deceit for any loss suffered by the principal in respect of the transaction under which the bribe was taken.[108] Originally, the Court of Appeal held that the principal could recover the bribe and claim damages under the tort of deceit,[109] but the Privy Council has since stated that the principal must elect between the two remedies on the ground that to claim both would result in double recovery.[110] It has, however, been contended that there is no reason why the principal cannot recover the bribe and also be awarded damages in deceit for any excess loss sustained.[111]

- Where the bribe is made, any resultant contract entered into between the principal and third party is voidable and can be rescinded at the principal's instance.[112] Bowstead & Reynolds contend that where 'the bribed agent knows that the proposed contract is contrary to his principal's interests, or is reckless on that issue' then the contract will be void on the ground that the agent has acted without authority.[113]

- The principal can commence a restitutionary claim to recover the amount of the bribe from either the agent[114] or the briber[115] (i.e. the agent and the briber are jointly and severally liable). As noted previously, an agent who profits from his position will, in certain circumstances, hold that profit on trust for the principal, who can then recover that profit in full. Originally, however, the Court of Appeal in *Lister & Co v Stubbs*[116] stated that a principal's claim to recover the bribe was personal, and not proprietary, with the result that the bribe was not held on trust for the principal, and so the principal could not recover any profits made by the agent through the use of the bribe (e.g. if the agent invests the bribe money and makes a profit, or if bribe property increases in value). This view was criticized strongly,[117] and in the case of *Attorney General for Hong Kong v Reid*,[118] the Privy

---

105. *Bulfield v Foumier* (1895) 11 TLR 282.
106. *Andrews v Ramsay & Co* [1902] 2 KB 635 (KB). The principal can also recover commission already paid before the existence of the bribe was discovered.
107. *Stange & Co v Lowitz* (1898) 14 TLR 468.
108. *Fyffes Group Ltd v Templeman* [2000] 2 Lloyd's Rep 643 (QB).
109. *Salford Corp v Lever (No 2)* [1891] 1 QB 168 (CA).
110. *Mahesan S/O Thambiah v Malaysia Government Officers' Cooperative Housing Society* [1979] AC 374 (PC). For contrasting views on this case, see Andrew Tettenborn, 'Bribery, Corruption and Restitution: The Strange Case of Mr Mahesan' (1979) 95 LQR 68 and Caroline Needham, 'Recovering the Profits of Bribery (1979) 95 LQR 536.
111. Len S Sealy and Richard JA Hooley, *Commercial Law: Text, Cases and Materials* (4th edn, OUP 2009) 224.
112. *Taylor v Walker* [1958] 1 Lloyd's Rep 490 (QB). The right to rescind the contract is in addition to the other remedies discussed, so, for example, the principal may rescind the contract and recover the value of the bribe (*Logicrose Ltd v Southend United Football Club Ltd (No 2)* [1988] 1 WLR 1256 (Ch)).
113. Peter G Watts, *Bowstead & Reynolds on Agency* (19th edn, Sweet & Maxwell 2010) [6-087].
114. *Morison v Thompson* (1874) LR 9 QB 480.
115. *Mahesan S/O Thambiah v Malaysia Government Officers' Cooperative Housing Society* [1979] AC 374 (PC).
116. (1890) 45 ChD 1 (CA).
117. See e.g. Sir Peter Millett, 'Bribes and Secret Commissions' [1993] RLR 7.
118. [1994] 1 AC 324 (PC).

Council held that the bribe property was held on trust. However, the decision in *Reid* also attracted considerable academic[119] and judicial[120] criticism, largely based around the powerful remedy that it provided the principal.[121] Accordingly, in the following case, the Court of Appeal declined to follow *Reid* and followed its earlier decision in *Lister*.

 ### Sinclair Investments (UK) Ltd v Versailles Trade Finance Ltd [2011] EWCA Civ 347

FACTS: Investors had provided funding to TPL Ltd ('TPL') and, in return, the directors of the company promised high returns on the investment. Cushnie (the agent), a director of TPL, was also the principal shareholder in VGP (one of a series of companies referred to as the Versailles Group plc). Cushnie withdrew funds from TPL and moved it around the various companies within the Versailles Group. This gave the appearance of the Versailles Group's companies being much more profitable than they actually were, with the result that Cushnie's shares in VGP rocketed in value. He subsequently sold 5 per cent of his shares for £28.69 million, and used a portion of this money to purchase a house. The fraud was eventually discovered and Cushnie was found guilty of conspiracy to defraud and disqualified for fifteen years. Sinclair, one of the investors that provided funding to TPL, claimed that, following *Reid*, the proceeds of sale of the shares and the house purchased by Cushnie were held on trust.

HELD: Sinclair's contention was rejected and the Court held that Cushnie's actions did not give rise to a proprietary claim, but merely provided a personal claim. Lord Neuberger MR stated that the Court of Appeal could not follow *Reid* in preference to its own earlier decisions, unless those earlier decisions were **per incuriam** or unreliable for some other reason. He continued:

> previous decisions of this court establish that a claimant cannot claim proprietary ownership of an asset purchased by the defaulting fiduciary with funds which, although they could not have been obtained if he had not enjoyed his fiduciary status, were not beneficially owned by the claimant or derived from opportunities beneficially owned by the claimant. However, those cases also establish that, in such a case, a claimant does have a personal claim in equity to the funds.[122]

COMMENT: The decision in *Sinclair* has been described as 'welcome'[123] on the ground that it resolves the long-standing issue as to whether the principal's claim will be personal or proprietary. The decision will also benefit unsecured creditors of the agent, whose claims will no longer rank behind those of the principal. Others, however, have criticized the decision on the ground that the core duty of a fiduciary (i.e. the agent) is to act in

➡ *per incuriam*:
'through want of care'

---

119. See e.g. Keith Uff, 'The Remedies of the Defrauded Principal After *A-G for Hong Kong v Reid*' in David Feldman and Frank Meisel (eds), *Corporate and Commercial Law: Modern Developments* (Lloyds of London Press 1996) ch 13.

120. See e.g. the judgment of Lord Neuberger MR in *Sinclair Investments (UK) Ltd v Versailles Trade Finance Ltd* [2011] EWCA Civ 347, [2011] 3 WLR 1153.

121. For example, if the agent becomes insolvent, then the principal's claim to the proceeds of the bribe will rank ahead of the claims of any unsecured creditors.

122. [2011] EWCA Civ 347, [2011] 3 WLR 1153 [88].

123. See e.g. Graham Virgo, 'Profits Obtained in Breach of Fiduciary Duty: Personal or Proprietary Claim?' (2011) 70 CLJ 502, 503.

the best interests of his beneficiary (i.e. the principal), and that any breach of this duty 'requires that the law protects that beneficiary or principal and allows that beneficiary or principal proprietary claims over gains made as a result of the abuse of the position as a fiduciary'.[124]

⭐ See David Hayton, 'Proprietary Liability for Secret Profits' (2011) 127 LQR 487

The payment of a bribe can also result in criminal penalties being imposed under the common law (e.g. for conspiracy) and under statute, notably the Bribery Act 2010.[125] Prior to July 2011 (when the 2010 Act came into force), the law in this area was complex and inconsistent, with the various bribery offences being found in a mass of case law and several pieces of legislation.[126] The Law Commission[127] recommended that all bribery offences (both statutory and common law) be repealed and replaced by a number of general bribery offences. In implementing the Law Commission's recommendations, the Bribery Act 2010 provides for four general categories of offences:

1. Section 1 of the 2010 Act provides for two offences related to the paying of bribes, namely (a) where a person offers, promises, or gives a financial or other advantage to another person and intends the advantage to induce a person to perform improperly a relevant function or activity, or to reward a person for the improper performance of such a function or duty;[128] and (b) where a person offers, promises, or gives a financial or other advantage to another person and knows or believes that the acceptance of the advantage would itself constitute the improper performance of a relevant function or activity.[129]

2. Section 2 provides for several criminal offences relating to the taking of bribes (e.g. it is an offence to request, agree to receive, or accept a financial or other advantage intending that, in consequence, a relevant function or activity should be performed improperly).[130]

3. Section 6 provides that it is an offence to bribe a foreign official.

4. The offences in 1–3 are broadly similar to offences that existed before the enactment of the 2010 Act. The fourth offence, found in s 7, has no prior counterpart and is a brand new and potentially wide-ranging offence. Section 7(1) provides that a relevant commercial organization[131] commits an offence if a person associated with that organization bribes another person, intending to obtain or retain business for the organization, or to obtain or retain an advantage in the conduct of business for that organization.

---

124. Sukhninder Panesar, 'Commercial Fraud and Unauthorised Gains' (2012) 23 ICCLR 259, 264.

125. For a more detailed discussion of the 2010 Act, see G Sullivan, 'The Bribery Act 2010: Part 1: An Overview' (2001) 2 Crim LR 87 and Stephen Gentle, 'The Bribery Act 2010: Part 2: The Corporate Offence' (2011) 2 Crim LR 101.

126. Notably, the Public Bodies Corrupt Practices Act 1889, the Prevention of Corruption Act 1906, and the Prevention of Corruption Act 1916.

127. Law Commission, *Reforming Bribery* (Law Com No 313, 2008).

128. Bribery Act 2010, s 1(2).

129. ibid s 1(3).

130. ibid s 2(2).

131. Section 7(5) of the 2010 Act provides that relevant commercial organizations are bodies corporate and partnerships that are either (a) created in the UK and conduct business (whether in the UK or elsewhere); or (b) created outside the UK, but conduct business in the UK. It is clear that this is an extremely broad definition that will cover the vast majority of businesses that are created, or operate, within the UK.

Duty to account

The duty to account is the collective term for several obligations imposed upon the agent. First, the agent will be under a duty to keep the principal's money or property separate from his own and that of other persons.[132] If the agent breaches this duty and mixes the principal's money/property with his own, then the principal will be entitled to the whole mixed fund, unless the agent can establish which parts were his own property.[133] It should be noted that this duty arises only in relation to money/property that is beneficially owned by the principal and, in such a case, the agent is regarded as a trustee of such property.[134] Where the money/property is not beneficially owned by the principal, or where it can be shown that the principal has consented to the agent mixing his money/property with that of the principal, then the duty to account will not be a fiduciary one and the agent will be regarded as a simple debtor of the principal, and not as a trustee.[135]

Second, an agent who holds or receives money on behalf of his principal is under a duty to provide that money to the principal upon demand.[136] This duty applies even if the money in question is subject to a claim from a third party, or where the principal receives money in respect of a transaction that is void or illegal.[137]

Third, an agent must keep accurate accounts of all transactions entered into on behalf of his principal,[138] and must also be prepared to render those accounts to the principal upon demand.[139] This aspect of the duty can continue even after the contract between the principal and the agent has come to an end.[140]

If an agent breaches this duty, then the court will be 'compelled to . . . presume everything most unfavourable to him, which is consistent with the rest of the facts which are admitted or proved'.[141] Thus, if the agent contends that the accounts are not accurate (e.g. because they indicate the agent owes money to the principal, when the agent claims to have already paid the sum in question), the courts will be likely to uphold the information in the accounts, unless the agent can adduce evidence indicating the true state of affairs.[142]

Duties owed by commercial agents

Commercial agents are subject to additional duties as set out by reg 3 of the Commercial Agents (Council Directive) Regulations 1993, although it will be seen that these duties are rather similar to some of the common law duties discussed earlier.

---

132. *Gray v Haig* (1855) 20 Beav 219.   133. *Lupton v White* (1808) 15 Ves 432.
134. *Burdick v Garrick* (1870) LR 5 Ch App 233.   135. *Henry v Hammond* [1913] 2 KB 515 (KB).
136. *Edgell v Day* (1865–66) LR 1 CP 80.
137. *De Mattos v Benjamin* (1894) 63 LJ QB 248 (agent required to provide principal with winnings derived from illegal bets made on principal's behalf).
138. *Chedworth v Edwards* (1802) 8 Ves 46. Certain agents are also required by statute to maintain specific forms of accounts (see e.g. s 21A of the Estate Agents Act 1979).
139. *Pearse v Green* (1819) 1 J&W 135.
140. *Yasuda Fire & Marine Insurance Co of Europe Ltd v Orion Marine Insurance Underwriting Agency Ltd* [1995] QB 174 (QB). This case is discussed in more detail on p 201.
141. *Gray v Haig* (1855) 20 Beav 219, 226 (Romilly MR).
142. *Shaw v Dartnall* (1826) 6 B&C 56.

Regulation 3(1) sets out the general duty of a commercial agent, namely to 'look after the interests of his principal and act dutifully and in good faith'. Regulation 3(2) then goes on to establish three more specific duties:

1. A commercial agent must take proper effort to negotiate and, where appropriate, conclude the transactions he is instructed to take care of.

2. A commercial agent must communicate to his principal all the necessary information available to him. Whilst the common law requires agents to disclose conflicts of interest, secret commissions, and bribes, there is no general requirement placed upon an agent to disclose information to the principal. Accordingly, the disclosure obligations of commercial agents are more extensive than those of a general agent.

3. A commercial agent must comply with reasonable instructions given by his principal.

Whereas, the additional duties of a commercial agent strongly resemble the common law duties, there is a notable difference, namely that the common law duties can be contractually excluded or limited,[143] whereas the duties found in reg 3 cannot be derogated from.[144]

The rights of an agent

As the discussion thus far indicates, an agent owes a considerable number of duties to his principal. Conversely, the rights of an agent against his principal are much fewer in number. Bowstead & Reynolds contend that this is because 'English law ... has traditionally viewed the principal as the person requiring protection, against wrongful use of the agent's powers, and have paid little attention to the position of the agent.'[145] Despite this, the common law does provide agents with a number of important rights, with commercial agents being afforded further rights under the Commercial Agents (Council Directive) Regulations 1993.

Entitlement to remuneration

The common law does not provide agents with a right to be remunerated. Generally, an agent will only be entitled to remuneration if the agency agreement contains an express or implied term to that effect, or if the agent has the restitutionary right to claim a *quantum meruit*.

Where the agency agreement contains an express term providing for the agent to be remunerated, then the issue is largely straightforward and the agent will be entitled to remuneration in accordance with the express terms. Where no express term is present, the courts may be willing to imply a term, but, in practice, this occurs rarely. Lord Hoffmann stated the reason behind this:

> The question of implication arises when the instrument does not expressly provide for what is to happen when some event occurs. The most usual inference in

➜ *quantum meruit*: 'as much as he has deserved'—a reasonable sum based on services provided

---

143. *Kelly v Cooper* [1993] AC 205 (PC).
144. Commercial Agents (Council Directive) Regulations 1993, reg 5(1).
145. Peter G Watts, *Bowstead & Reynolds on Agency* (19th edn, Sweet & Maxwell 2010) [7-001].

such a case is that nothing is to happen. If the parties had intended something to happen, the instrument would have said so. Otherwise, the express provisions of the instrument are to continue to operate undisturbed.[146]

Whether or not a term providing for remuneration will be implied will depend upon the normal contractual rules relating to the implication of terms. Notably, the courts will not imply a term if such a term is inconsistent with the express terms of the contract.[147] Clearly, whether a term will be implied will be heavily dependent upon the facts of the case, but the courts have stated that it is highly likely that a term will be implied if it was obvious from the facts that the agent would be remunerated,[148] or where the agent was acting in a professional capacity.[149] Where a term is implied, then the agent will receive a reasonable sum.

 Way v Latilla [1937] 3 All ER 759 (HL)

FACTS: Way (the agent) agreed to send to Latilla (the principal) information relating to gold mines in South Africa, and, in return, Way would receive a concession in any gold mines that Latilla obtained. However, the agency agreement was silent in relation to the remuneration that Way would receive and Latilla denied offering Way a concession.

HELD: The House concluded that there was no completed contract between Way and Latilla providing for Way to be remunerated. There was, however, a contract of employment between the two parties 'under which Mr Way was engaged to do work for Mr Latilla in circumstances which clearly indicated that the work was not to be gratuitous'.[150] Accordingly, a term was implied into the contract, providing for Way to receive a *quantum meruit* of £5,000.

COMMENT: Compare the result in this case to that of *Kofi Sunkersette Obu v A Strauss & Co Ltd*,[151] in which the court distinguished *Way v Latilla* and refused to award a *quantum meruit* on the ground that the agency agreement contained an express term providing that the amount of commission paid would be determined by the principal.

Where the agency is gratuitous, then the agent may still be entitled to claim a *quantum meruit* if both principal and agent believed that a contract would come into being, but it ultimately did not.[152]

The decision of the following case is noteworthy, as the Court of Appeal aimed to provide guidance as to how to assess a *quantum meruit*.

146. *Attorney General of Belize v Belize Telecom Ltd* [2009] UKPC 10, [2009] 1 WLR 1988 [17].
147. *Broad v Thomas* (1830) 7 Bing 99.   148. *Way v Latilla* [1937] 3 All ER 759 (HL).
149. *Miller v Beal* (1879) 27 WR 403.   150. [1937] 3 All ER 759 (HL) 763 (Lord Atkin).
151. [1951] AC 243 (PC).
152. *William Lacey (Hounslow) Ltd v Davis* [1957] 1 WLR 932 (QB).

Benedetti v Sawiris [2010] EWCA Civ 1427

FACTS: An Italian energy company was looking to sell its stake in a wholly owned subsidiary. Benedetti (the agent) acted as a facilitator to enable a group of investors (of whom Sawiris (the principal) was one) to acquire the subsidiary. An agreement was drawn up which set out Benedetti's role in the acquisition. In the event, the acquisition proceeded in a way that was different to that set out in the agreement, and Benedetti's role was also different to that contemplated in the agreement. Following the acquisition, Benedetti sought his agreed fee of between €200 million and €300 million. Sawiris stated that, as Benedetti's role differed to that envisaged by the agreement, he was only entitled to €75 million. Benedetti sued, claiming a *quantum meruit*, and the High Court, in taking into account the amount offered by Sawiris, held that he was entitled to €75 million.[153] Both parties appealed.

HELD: The Court of Appeal reduced the value of the *quantum meruit* to €14.52 million. More importantly, it established a number of principles in relation to how a *quantum meruit* should be assessed:

- Etherton LJ stated that 'a quantum meruit claim is a restitutionary claim for unjust enrichment'.[154] Accordingly, it is 'the defendant's benefit which must be identified and valued',[155] as opposed to the loss of the claimant.

- Whilst the High Court was entitled to take into account the amount offered by Sawiris, it was wrong to take that offer 'into account to the extent of substituting it for the market value of the services provided. It gave Mr Benedetti a windfall: it was something he had not agreed, but which was in excess of market value as found by the judge.'[156]

- Benedetti contended that the original agreement should be used as a template for determining the *quantum meruit*. Whilst the court may take the original agreement into account, it will carry 'little, if any, weight if the parties have made it clear that it is no longer of any consequence in their dealings for any purpose or for that of determining the remuneration for services to be provided'.[157]

- Arden LJ stated that:

  if there is an agreement between the parties as to the way in which a party was to be remunerated, but that agreement was incomplete or for some other reason unenforceable so that the court is required to determine the amount of that remuneration on a claim for a quantum meruit, the exercise which the court must carry out is that of determining the reasonable value of the services rendered.[158]

COMMENT: Benedetti has been granted permission to appeal to the Supreme Court.

⭐ See Graham Virgo, 'Unjust Enrichment— Valuing Services' (2011) 70 CLJ 299

Effective cause

Often, an agency agreement will provide that an agent will only receive remuneration or commission if a particular event occurs or if he brings about a specified result. In such a case, the agent will not be entitled to remuneration or commission if that

---

153. *Benedetti v Sawiris* [2009] EWHC 1330 (Ch).
154. *Benedetti v Sawiris* [2010] EWCA Civ 1427 [140]. 155. ibid [142].
156. ibid [85] (Arden LJ). 157. ibid [63]. 158. ibid.

event or result does not occur, or, in other words, 'they get paid for results and not for effort'.[159] Further, unless the contract provides otherwise, the agent will only be entitled to remuneration or commission if he was the 'effective cause' of the relevant event or result.

Millar, Son & Co v Radford (1903) 19 TLR 575 (CA)

FACTS: Radford (the principal) instructed a firm of estate agents, Millar, Son & Co (the agents), to find a purchaser for his property or, if a purchaser could not be found, a tenant. Millar could not find a purchaser, but did find a tenant, who undertook a lease on the property. Fifteen months later, without the involvement of Millar, the tenant purchased the property from Radford. Millar claimed commission on the sale, but Radford refused to pay. Millar commenced proceedings.

HELD: Collins MR stated that 'the right to commission does not arise out of the mere fact that agents have introduced a tenant or purchaser. . . It is necessary to show that the introduction was an efficient cause in bringing about the letting or the sale.' As Millar clearly was not the effective cause, its claim failed.

Deprivation of opportunity to earn commission

In a number of cases, the courts have had to determine whether or not a principal is liable if he acts in a manner that prevents his agent from earning commission. The courts have repeatedly stated that a principal who prevents his agent from earning commission will only be liable if the agency agreement contains an express or implied term prohibiting the principal from acting in such a way. As the following case demonstrates, the courts are reluctant to imply such a term, especially where such a term would restrict the principal's ability to deal with his own property.

Luxor (Eastbourne) Ltd v Cooper [1941] AC 108 (HL)

FACTS: Two companies, Luxor and Regal (the principals), engaged Cooper (the agent) and instructed him to find a purchaser for their four cinemas. Luxor and Regal agreed to pay Cooper commission of £10,000 if he found them a purchaser who was willing to pay not less than £185,000 for the cinemas. Cooper found a purchaser who was willing to pay £185,000, and entered into negotiations with Luxor and Regal. However, Luxor and Regal

---

159. *Bentley's Estate Agents Ltd v Granix Ltd* [1989] 2 EGLR 21 (QB) 23 (Phillips J).

then pulled out of the negotiations and so Cooper could not earn the commission. Cooper sued, alleging that it was an implied term of the agency agreement that Luxor and Regal would not do anything to prevent him from earning commission.

HELD: Cooper's action failed and the House refused to imply a term preventing Luxor and Regal from withdrawing from the negotiations. Lord Wright stated:

> If the commission agent has a right to claim commission or damages if the vendor abandons the negotiations and does not complete the sale, his doing so is a breach of contract vis-à-vis the agent and it is immaterial to the agent how sensible or reasonable the vendor's conduct may be from his own point of view. Such a qualified implication seems to me too complicated and artificial. The parties cannot properly be supposed to have intended it, nor can it be taken to be necessary to give business efficacy to the transaction.[160]

Accordingly, a principal is free to prevent his agent from earning commission, unless there is an express or implied term in the agency agreement that provides that the principal will not act in such a way. In *Luxor*, the actions of the agent had not yet resulted in the creation of a contract between the principal and third party. The court may be more willing to imply a term prohibiting the principal from preventing the agent from earning commission where the agent has effected a binding contract between the principal and third party, especially if the principal is in breach of that contract.

Alpha Trading Ltd v Dunnshaw-Patten Ltd [1981] QB 290 (CA)

FACTS: Dunnshaw-Patten Ltd (the principal) instructed Alpha Trading Ltd (the agent) to locate a purchaser for a large quantity of cement, in return for which Alpha would receive commission based on the amount sold. Alpha located a purchaser and introduced it to Dunnshaw. A contract of sale to purchase 10,000 tonnes was entered into, but Dunnshaw failed to perform and so Alpha did not receive commission. Alpha commenced proceedings against Dunnshaw.

HELD: Alpha was entitled to the commission and was awarded damages of $25,000 plus interest. Brandon LJ stated that:

> The defendants did make a contract of sale with that buyer on the basis that, if the contract was performed, the agent would receive substantial remuneration. The only reason the contract was not performed was that the defendants were either unwilling or unable to perform it. It seems to me that, in a case of that kind, it is right for the court to imply a term that the defendants will not fail to perform their contract with the buyer so as to deprive the agent of the remuneration due to him under the agency contract.[161]

COMMENT: At first glance, it would appear that this decision is contrary to *Luxor*, but this is not the case, as Brandon and Templeman LJJ were strongly influenced by the following statement of Lord Wright in *Luxor*:

> if the negotiations between the vendor and the purchaser have been duly concluded and a binding executory agreement has been achieved, different considerations may

---

160. [1941] AC 108 (HL) 140.   161. [1981] QB 290 (CA) 304.

⭐ See JW Carter, 'The Life of an Agent in Commerce is a Precarious One' (1982) 45 MLR 220

arise. The vendor is then no longer free to dispose of his property...If he refuses to complete he would be guilty of a breach of agreement vis-à-vis the purchaser. I think...that it ought then to be held that he is also in breach of his contract with the commission agent, that is, of some term which can properly be implied.[162]

Loss of the right to remuneration/commission

An agent is not entitled to commission for transactions that occur after his agency agreement has come to an end, unless the agency agreement provides otherwise.[163] The agent will also lose the right to remuneration in several other situations, including:

- where the agent commits a serious breach of his duties, he may lose his right to commission;[164] however, any remuneration due at the date of the breach will still be payable;[165]
- the agent will not be entitled to remuneration in respect of transactions that are outside the scope of his authority,[166] unless the principal ratifies the unauthorized acts;
- an agent may not be able to recover remuneration in respect of transactions entered into for which he was unqualified or lacked capacity; so, for example, a person, purporting to act as a solicitor, could not recover remuneration for transactions entered into as a solicitor if he was not qualified under s 1 of the Solicitors Act 1974;
- an agent loses the right to remuneration if he knew, or ought to have known, that he was acting in an unlawful[167] or dishonest[168] manner.

Right to reimbursement and indemnity

Aside from several exceptions, which are discussed later in this section, every agent has the right to be reimbursed for any expenses, and to be indemnified for any losses or liabilities incurred by him during the execution of his agency. The source of this right, and its precise scope, will depend upon whether the agency is contractual or gratuitous.

Where the agency is contractual, there may be an express term providing the agent with the right to claim reimbursement and an indemnity. Where no express term is present, then the courts will imply such a term, unless it is clear from the contract that the implication of such a term has been excluded. A contractual agent can claim a full indemnity for all payments made, and losses and liabilities incurred,

---

162. *Luxor (Eastbourne) Ltd v Cooper* [1941] AC 108 (HL) 142.
163. *Crocker Horlock Ltd v B Lang & Co Ltd* [1949] 1 All ER 526 (KB).
164. *Salomons v Pender* (1865) 3 H&C 639.
165. *Boston Deep Sea Fishing v Ansell* (1888) 39 ChD 339 (CA).
166. *Mason v Clifton* (1863) 3 F&F 899.
167. *Josephs v Preber* (1825) 3 B&C 639.
168. *Kelly v Cooper* [1993] AC 205 (PC).

during the execution of the agency. This will not only include payments which the principal is legally bound to make, but also includes:

(i) payments which the principal is not legally bound to make, but which are binding upon the agent;[169]

(ii) payments which the agent is morally pressured to make; and[170]

(iii) payments which the agent has mistakenly made, but which are nonetheless reasonable.[171]

Where the agency is not contractual, then the right is clearly not based in contract, but is instead based in restitution. In this case, the scope of the right to reimbursement is narrower and the agent will only be entitled to recover those payments that:

(i) the agent was compelled to make;

(ii) the principal would ultimately be liable for; and

(iii) were for the principal's benefit.[172]

Loss of the right

The agent will lose the right to reimbursement and indemnity in certain circumstances:

- where the contract expressly excludes the agent from having such a right;
- where the agent had acted outside the scope of his express or implied actual authority;[173] the agent will regain the right if the principal subsequently ratifies the unauthorized acts;
- where the loss or liability incurred is due to the agent's own negligence, default, insolvency, or breach of duty;[174]
- where the agent knows, or ought to know, that the transaction he is undertaking is unlawful.[175]

Right to a lien

Consider the following example.

Eg ComCorp Ltd

ComCorp instructs an agent, Ben, to sell five pieces of machinery that the company no longer needs. Ben takes possession of the machinery. The agency agreement provides that Ben should claim for reasonable expenses as and when they occur, and that Ben will be reimbursed for these expenses within one week of him submitting a claim.

169. *Adams v Morgan & Co* [1924] 1 KB 751 (CA).

170. *Rhodes v Fielder, Jones and Harrison* (1919) 89 LJ KB 159 (KB).

171. *Pettman v Kebble* (1850) 9 CB 701.

172. *Brook's Wharf and Bull Wharf Ltd v Goodman Bros* [1937] 1 KB 534 (CA).

173. *Barron v Fitzgerald* (1840) 6 Bing NC 201.

174. *Thacker v Hardy* (1878) 4 QBD 685.

175. *Re Parker* (1882) 21 ChD 408. The agent may be able to obtain a contribution from the principal under s 1 of the Civil Liability (Contribution) Act 1978.

> Ben sells two of the pieces of machinery and submits a claim for the expenses he incurs. Two weeks later, Ben has still not been paid and ComCorp informs Ben that it will not be paying his expenses and that Ben should return the remaining three machines to ComCorp. Ben informs ComCorp that he will not return the remaining machines until his expenses have been reimbursed.

Is Ben entitled to retain possession of the machines? Generally, the answer is yes. If an agent or sub-agent[176] is not provided with the remuneration, reimbursement, or indemnity that he is entitled to, then the agent or sub-agent is granted a 'remedy of self-help'[177] in the form of a lien. A lien is simply a right to retain possession of the goods of another as security until that other person satisfies some debt or other obligation. Accordingly, if the principal refuses to provide an agent with the remuneration, reimbursement, or indemnity that he is entitled to, then the agent can retain possession of the principal's goods until the principal makes good on his obligations to the agent. It should be noted at the outset that there are two types of lien:

1. *General lien*: An agent entitled to a general lien can retain possession of any goods belonging to the principal until such time as the relevant obligation is met.
2. *Particular lien*: A person entitled to a particular lien can only retain possession of those goods of the principal to which the particular obligation relates.

Generally, the agent has only the right to a particular lien and the courts are very reluctant to provide an agent with a general lien.[178] However, the agent may acquire a general lien if the terms of the agency agreement provide for one, or the right to a general lien is recognized within a particular trade or custom.[179]

The agent's right to a lien is conditional upon four requirements being satisfied. First, the agent can only exercise a lien over goods that are already in his possession. Accordingly, a lien will not arise over goods that the agent does not possess.[180] Second, the agent must have acquired possession of the goods through lawful means, so, for example, if an agent, without the authorization of his principal, removes the principal's goods from a third party's premises, then no lien will lie over those goods, as they were acquired unlawfully by the agent.[181] Third, the agent must have acquired the goods in his capacity as an agent.[182] Fourth, a lien will only be effective if it is not excluded by the express or implied terms of the agency agreement.[183]

---

176. The sub-agent's right to a lien will only arise if the appointment of the sub-agent is authorized (*Solly v Rathbone* (1814) 2 M&S 298). If this is the case, then a sub-agent may have a lien over the principal's goods, even though the sub-agent's claim for remuneration, reimbursement, or indemnity is against the agent who appointed him.

177. *Compania Financiera 'Soleada' SA v Hamoor Tanker Corporation Inc (The Borag)* [1980] 1 Lloyd's Rep 111 (QB) 122 (Mustill J).

178. See Lord Campbell LC in *Bock v Gorrissen* (1860) 2 De G, F&J 434, 443, who stated that '[t]he law of England does not favour general liens'.

179. As a result of custom, general liens have been provided to specific agents, such as solicitors, stockbrokers, bankers, and marine insurance brokers.

180. *Shaw v Neale* (1858) 6 HL Cas 581 (HL).   181. *Taylor v Robinson* (1818) 8 Taunt 648.

182. *Muir v Fleming* (1822) Dow & Ry NP 29 (goods left with agent merely for safekeeping not deemed to be acquired by the agent in his capacity as an agent).

183. *Wolstenholm v Sheffield Union Banking Co* (1886) 54 LT 746.

Rights of commercial agents

Just as the Commercial Agents (Council Directive) Regulations 1993 impose duties upon commercial agents, so too do they provide them with certain rights. The principal must act dutifully and in good faith towards his commercial agent[184] and, in particular he must (i) provide his commercial agent with the necessary documentation relating to the goods concerned; and (ii) obtain for his commercial agent the information necessary for the performance of the agency contract.[185]

Other rights include the following:

- The commercial agent has the right to receive from the principal, on request, a signed written document setting out the terms of the agency contract, including any terms subsequently agreed.[186]

- An agency contract for a fixed period that continues to be performed by both parties after the period has expired shall be converted into an agency contract for an indefinite period.[187]

- If the principal wishes to terminate the agreement, then he must provide the commercial agent with notice as stipulated in reg 15.

- Upon the termination of the agency agreement, the commercial agent is entitled to an indemnity or compensation.[188]

The minimum notice periods set out in reg 15 are discussed at p 98

Remuneration

Part III of the 1993 Regulations provide the commercial agent with notable rights in relation to remuneration, with reg 6(1) providing that, where no agreement as to remuneration exists between the parties, then the commercial agent will be entitled to 'the remuneration that commercial agents appointed for the goods forming the subject of his agency contract are customarily allowed in the place where he carries on his activities'. If no such practice exists, the commercial agent will be entitled to 'reasonable remuneration taking into account all the aspects of the transaction'. It has been contended that the common law principles discussed in relation to standard agents could also operate within the scope of reg 6(1),[189] and so little needs to be said of reg 6(1) except to note that the presumption that the commercial agent will receive an amount of remuneration that is customary does not have a counterpart in relation to the general law of agency.

The noteworthy provisions (namely those found in regs 7–12) relate to a commercial agent's right to commission, with 'commission' referring to 'any part of the remuneration of a commercial agent which varies with the number or value of business transactions'.[190] To see why the provisions contained in regs 7–12 are so noteworthy, consider the following example.

---

184. Commercial Agents (Council Directive) Regulations 1993, reg 4(1).
185. ibid reg 4(2).   186. ibid reg 13(1).   187. ibid reg 14.   188. ibid reg 17.
189. Peter G Watts, *Bowstead & Reynolds on Agency* (19th edn, Sweet & Maxwell 2010) [11-025].
190. Commercial Agents (Council Directive) Regulations 1993, reg 2(1).

> ### Eg ComCorp Ltd
>
> ComCorp is looking to expand its customer base. Accordingly, it engages Marie (the commercial agent) and instructs her to locate potential customers and, if possible, to negotiate and enter into contracts of sale on ComCorp's behalf. The agency agreement is to last one year and commences in February 2013. In March 2013, Marie successfully negotiates a contract of sale on behalf of ComCorp with TechCorp plc. In May, ComCorp negotiates directly with TechCorp and enters into a contract of sale that is identical to the one entered into in March. Marie is seeking commission for both contracts, but ComCorp refuses to pay her commission for the second contract of sale, as it negotiated directly with TechCorp itself.

To what extent is Marie entitled to commission for the first contract and for future contracts that ComCorp enter into with TechCorp? The answer is found in reg 7(1).

> ### 🔑 Commercial Agents (Council Directive) Regulations 1993, reg 7(1)
>
> A commercial agent shall be entitled to commission on commercial transactions concluded during the period covered by the agency contract—
>
> (a) where the transaction has been concluded as a result of his action; or
>
> (b) where the transaction is concluded with a third party whom he has previously acquired as a customer for transactions of the same kind.

Regulation 7(1)(a) is straightforward and simply states that an agent is entitled to commission for any contracts that are concluded as a result of his action (such as the contract concluded by Marie in March in the ComCorp example). The phrase 'as a result of his action' is the 1993 Regulation's equivalent of the 'effective cause' requirement imposed upon standard agents, although the language used would appear to indicate a less strict standard.

 The effective cause requirement is discussed at p 139

Regulation 7(1)(b) is more noteworthy, and basically provides that an agent is entitled to commission for repeat orders, even if he is not involved in negotiating and concluding such orders. Accordingly, if an agent introduced a customer to the principal and a contract ensued, the agent would be entitled to commission under reg 7(1)(a)—if the principal subsequently deals directly with the customer without the agent's involvement and a contract ensues, the agent will be entitled to commission again under reg 7(1)(b). Therefore, in the ComCorp example, Marie would also be entitled to commission for the contract entered into in May.

It will be noted that reg 7 only applies to transactions that are concluded during the period of the agency agreement (accordingly, in the ComCorp example, reg 7 would not apply to transactions concluded after February 2014). Regulation 8 provides a commercial agent with the right to commission in relation to transactions that occur after that agency agreement has ended. However, this right will only arise if:

> (i) the transaction is mainly attributable to his efforts during the period covered by the agency contract and the transaction was entered into within a reasonable period after that contract terminated; or
>
> (ii) in accordance with the conditions mentioned in reg 7, the order of the third party reached the principal or the commercial agent before the agency contract terminated.

The provisions just discussed relate to whether commission is due. Regulation 10 relates to when commission is due and provides that commission will become due in one of three situations, namely:

> (i) where the principal has executed the transaction; or
>
> (ii) where the principal should, according to his agreement with the third party, have executed the transaction; or
>
> (iii) where the third party has executed the transaction.[191]

Conclusion

As this chapter has demonstrated, the legal relationship between principal and agent can be complex, with each party owing the other a number of vital duties (although, as has been noted, the agent owes considerably more duties to the principal than the principal owes the agent). Breach of duty can have significant effects upon the agency relationship, but it is important to note that the actions of the principal and agent can also affect the position of third parties. Accordingly, Chapters 7 and 8 look at position of third parties in relation to the principal and agent, with Chapter 7 discussing the relationship that exists between the principal and the third party.

Practice questions

1. 'The fiduciary duties placed upon agents are overly strict and fail to reflect the realities of modern commerce.'

   Do you agree with this statement? Provide reasons for your answer.

2. The machinery in one of ComCorp's factories is nearing the end of its operational lifespan and needs to be replaced. The machinery, if sold for scrap, would raise £5,000. Accordingly, ComCorp instructs Bruce, the manager of the factory, to sell the machinery for scrap and to 'make every effort to ensure that suitable replacement machinery is purchased and installed'. However, Bruce sells the machinery to MultiTech Ltd, a company of which his brother is the managing director. MultiTech pays £6,000 for the machinery and installs it into one of its factories. It also pays Bruce commission of £500.

   Bruce is not confident that he can purchase the correct replacement machinery and so he engages the services of an expert, Oliver, who he instructs to locate and

---

191. ibid reg 10(1).

purchase suitable machinery. Oliver locates and purchases the machinery and it is installed within the factory. However, the machinery is not suitable and, as a result, the factory's production rate is diminished considerably. ComCorp refuses to pay for the machinery. Accordingly, Oliver removes the machinery from the factory and states that it will not be returned until it is paid for.

Discuss whether or not any breaches of duty have occurred and, if a breach has occurred, discuss the likely remedies that will be available.

Further reading

Alan Berg, 'Bribery—Transaction Validity and Other Civil Law Implications' [2001] LMCLQ 27
* Discusses the remedies available to a principal in cases where his agent accepts a bribe.

FE Dowrick, 'The Relationship of Principal and Agent' (1954) 17 MLR 24
* Despite its age, this article still provides a useful and thorough discussion of the legal foundations that underpin the relationship between principal and agent.

Robert Flanagan, 'The (Fiduciary) Duty of Fidelity' (2008) 124 LQR 274
* Discusses certain judges' assertions regarding the existence of a duty of fidelity, and contends that such a duty demonstrates a failure to comprehend the relevant case law.

Joshua Getzler, 'Inconsistent Duties and Implied Content' (2006) 122 LQR 1
* Discusses several cases relating to whether implied consent can lessen the strictness of the fiduciary duties.

Roderick Munday, *Agency: Law and Principles* (OUP 2010) chs 8 and 9
* Chapter 8 focuses on the duties that an agent owes to his principal, whereas chapter 9 discusses the rights that an agent has against his principal.

Peter G Watts, 'Agents' Entitlement to Commission' [2009] JBL 268
* Discusses several cases in relation to the agent's entitlement to commission.

Peter G Watts, *Bowstead & Reynolds on Agency* (19th edn, Sweet & Maxwell 2010) chs 5, 6, and 7
* Chapter 5 examines the ability of an agent to delegate his functions. Chapter 6 focuses on the duties that an agent owes to his principal, whereas chapter 7 discusses the rights that an agent has against his principal.

Relations between principal and third party

- Contractual liability
- Tortious liability

INTRODUCTION

As noted in Chapter 3, the primary purpose of many agency agreements is to create a contractual relationship between the principal and third party. However, whether such a relationship actually comes into existence can depend on a number of factors. Problems may arise in the agency relationship, or the agent may act in an unauthorized manner. It may even be the case that the third party believes the agent to be the principal. Where issues arise, it is important to be able to determine the legal nature of the relationship between the principal and third party.

Accordingly, this chapter examines the relationship that exists between principal and third party and focuses, in particular, on the liability that exists between principal and third party and those instances when they can sue, and be sued by, the other. Liability principally arises in contract and tort (as Figure 7.1 indicates), and so these two areas of liability will be discussed, beginning with the contractual liability of the principal and third party.

Contractual liability

The contractual relationship between the principal and third party, and the extent to which one party can be liable to the other, can be complex and depends upon a number of variables, notably whether the principal is disclosed or undisclosed.

The distinction between a disclosed and undisclosed principal is discussed at pp 57–8

Disclosed principal

It will be remembered that, in a typical agency relationship, an agent will effect a contract between his principal and a third party, after which the agent will 'drop out' of the transaction. From this it follows that the general rule is that, where an agent makes a contract on behalf of a disclosed principal (named or unnamed), then the contract is between the principal and third party only, and either party can sue and be sued on it.

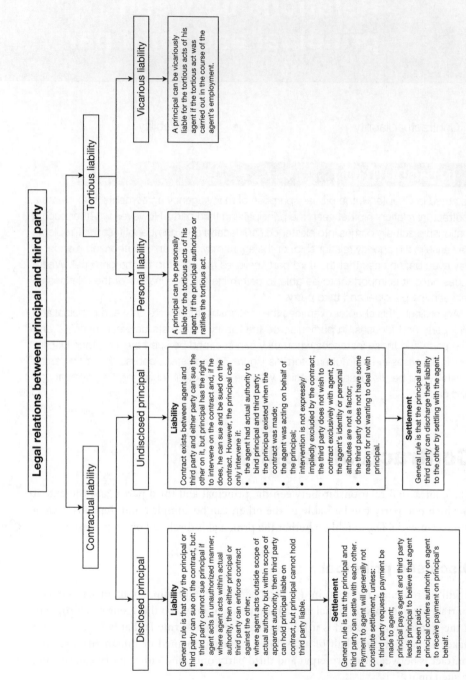

Legal relations between principal and third party

Contractual liability

Tortious liability

Disclosed principal

Undisclosed principal

Personal liability

Vicarious liability

Liability
General rule is that only the principal or third party can sue on the contract, but:
• third party cannot sue principal if agent acts in unauthorized manner;
• where agent acts within actual authority, then either principal or third party can enforce contract against the other;
• where agent acts outside scope of actual authority but within scope of apparent authority, then third party can hold principal liable on contract, but principal cannot hold third party liable.

Liability
Contract exists between agent and third party and either party can sue the other on it, but principal has the right to intervene on the contract and, if he does, he can sue and be sued on the contract. However, the principal can only intervene if:
• the agent had actual authority to bind principal and third party;
• the principal existed when the contract was made;
• the agent was acting on behalf of the principal;
• intervention is not expressly/impliedly excluded by the contract;
• the third party does not wish to contract exclusively with agent, or the agent's identity or personal attributes are not a factor;
• the third party does not have some reason for not wanting to deal with principal.

Personal liability
A principal can be personally liable for the tortious acts of his agent, if the principal authorizes or ratifies the tortious act.

Vicarious liability
A principal can be vicariously liable for the tortious acts of his agent if the tortious act was carried out in the course of the agent's employment.

Settlement
General rule is that the principal and third party can settle with each other. Payment to agent will generally not constitute settlement, unless:
• third party requests payment be made to agent;
• principal pays agent and third party leads principal to believe that agent has been paid;
• principal confers authority on agent to receive payment on principal's behalf.

Settlement
General rule is that the principal and third party can discharge their liability to the other by settling with the agent.

FIGURE 7.1 Legal relations between principal and third party

However, the ability of the principal and third party to sue on the contract will depend largely upon whether or not the agent has acted within the scope of his authority:

- Where the agent acts within the scope of his actual authority (express or implied), then if either the principal or third party breaches the contract, the innocent party can sue the party in breach.[1]
- Where the agent acts without authority, then the third party cannot sue the principal,[2] unless the principal ratifies the agent's unauthorized act.
- Where the agent acts outside the scope of his actual authority, but within the scope of his apparent authority, then the third party can hold the principal liable on the contract, but the principal cannot sue the third party on the contract unless he first ratifies the agent's actions. If, however, the third party knew that the agent lacked actual authority, then the principal will be able to rescind the contract, as the following case demonstrates.

 Jordan v Norton (1838) 4 M&W 155

FACTS: Norton (the principal) wrote to Jordan (the third party) and agreed to purchase a horse. In a subsequent letter, Norton stated that his son (the agent) would collect the horse from Jordan, but only if Jordan provided a warranty stating that the horse was 'sound and quiet in harness'. The son collected the horse, but received no warranty from Jordan. Two days later, Norton returned the horse on the ground that it was unsound. Jordan sued for payment.

HELD: The claim failed. Jordan knew that the son was not authorized to collect the horse without the required warranty, and so Norton was entitled to repudiate the contract and return the horse to Jordan.

In relation to deeds and negotiable instruments, the general rule does not apply and a disclosed principal will not be privy to a contract with a third party unless certain formalities are complied with:

- A principal cannot sue or be sued on a negotiable instrument (e.g. a bill of exchange, or a cheque), unless he has signed it,[3] or he has authorized another person to sign it and that person has signed it.[4]
- A principal cannot generally sue or be sued on a deed *inter partes* unless the deed describes him as being a party to it and it is executed in his name.[5] There are, however, exceptions to this rule (e.g. if the agent executing the deed does so as a trustee of the principal, then the principal can sue and be sued on the deed).[6]

It used to be the case that where an agent acted on behalf of a foreign principal, then it would be presumed that the agent did not have the right to establish privity of

---

1. See e.g. *Camillo Tank Steamship Co Ltd v Alexandria Engineering Works* (1921) 38 TLR 134 (HL).
2. See e.g. *Comerford v Britannic Assurance Co Ltd* (1908) 24 TLR 593 (KB).
3. Bills of Exchange Act 1882, s 23. In the case of a company, the corporate seal will act as a signature.
4. ibid s 91(1).
5. *Re International Contract Co, Pickering's Claim* (1871) 6 Ch App 525.
6. *Harmer v Armstrong* [1934] Ch 65 (CA).

This presumption and the reasons behind its abolition are discussed at p 174

contract between the principal and the third party, but this presumption was eventually abandoned.

Settlement with the agent

Consider the following example:

> ### Eg ComCorp Ltd
>
> ComCorp Ltd (the principal) instructs Ben (the agent) to purchase a piece of machinery from Heavy Plant Ltd (the third party) for £5,000. Ben enters into a contract of sale with Heavy Plant on ComCorp's behalf and the machinery is delivered to ComCorp. ComCorp believes that Ben has already paid for the machinery, so it pays Ben £5,000 plus his commission. In fact, Ben has not paid Heavy Plant Ltd and he is subsequently declared bankrupt. Heavy Plant invoices ComCorp for payment, but ComCorp states that it is not liable to pay as it has already provided the payment to Ben. Heavy Plant commences proceedings against ComCorp.

Is ComCorp liable to Heavy Plant or has ComCorp's payment to Ben settled the debt it owes to Heavy Plant? In many cases, it is possible for liability to be avoided if the parties reach a settlement. In the tri-partite agency relationship between principal, agent, and third party, it is important to determine who has the right to settle. Where the principal is disclosed, a binding contract will usually be created between the principal and the third party, to which the agent is not a party. From this, it follows that generally the principal can only be discharged from his obligation under the contract if he reaches a settlement with the third party, or vice versa. Consequently, a payment to the agent by the principal will not discharge the liability of the principal to the third party,[7] so, in the example given, ComCorp will likely be liable to Heavy Plant for the cost of the machinery.

This general rule is, however, subject to a number of exceptions:

- A principal can discharge his obligations to a third party if the third party requests that payment be made to the agent and such payment is made.[8]
- Where the principal has paid the agent and the third party leads the principal to believe that the agent has paid, then the principal's obligations to the third party will be discharged.[9]
- If the principal has conferred authority on the agent to receive payment on the principal's behalf, then the third party's liability to the principal will be discharged if he provides payment to the agent,[10] providing that the agent is authorized to receive payment in the form provided.[11]

---

7. *Irvine & Co v Watson & Sons* (1879–80) LR 5 QBD 414 (CA).

8. *Smyth v Anderson* (1949) 7 CB 21.   9. *Horsfall v Fauntleroy* (1830) 10 B&C 755.

10. *Butwick v Grant* [1924] 2 KB 483 (KB) 489–90 (Sankey J). If the agent is not authorized to receive payment on behalf of the principal, but receives such payment and passes it on to the principal, then the agent's actions will be deemed to be ratified and the third party's liability to the principal will be discharged.

11. *Hine Bros v Steamship Insurance Syndicate Ltd* (1895) 72 LT 79 (payment to agent by bill of exchange did not discharge third party's liability where agent was only authorized to accept payment in cash).

Undisclosed principal

Consider the following example:

> ### Eg ComCorp Ltd
>
> ComCorp (the principal) wishes to export goods overseas. It engages Jessica (the agent) to locate a suitable vessel and to charter it on ComCorp's behalf. She locates a vessel belonging to ShipHire Ltd (the third party), and charters it in her own name. At no point does she inform ShipHire that she is working on behalf of ComCorp. The chartermarket improves and ShipHire realizes that it could hire the ship to someone else for a higher rate. Accordingly, ShipHire contacts Jessica and tells her that it is cancelling the charterparty.

The question that arises is whether ComCorp can hold ShipHire liable on the charterparty. It could be argued that it would be most unfair to allow an undisclosed principal to hold a third party liable on a contract, as the third party will not know of the principal's existence; but in general, the law states that an undisclosed principal can sue and be sued on a contract made by his agent with a third party. What actually happens is that the law regards the contract as being between the agent and the third party,[12] but grants the principal the right to intervene and sue, and be sued, by the third party. This rule is extremely controversial, with Stone noting:

> The concept of the undisclosed principal clearly runs counter to the general contractual rule as to the necessity for privity of contract. The third party can find that they have rights against, and liabilities towards, a person with whom there was no intention to contract, and of whom the third party was in ignorance.[13]

Pollock notes that such a rule is rare amongst legal systems, stating that '[t]he right of one person to sue another on a contract not really made with the person suing is unknown to every other legal system except that of England and America'.[14] Given the controversy, what is the justification for allowing an undisclosed principal to enforce the contract? Numerous theories have been advanced by academics, the majority of which have been rejected by the courts. It has been argued that the undisclosed principal acquires the right to sue on the contract because the contract between the agent and third party is automatically assigned to the principal,[15] but the Privy Council has emphatically rejected this theory.[16] Diplock LJ stated, *obiter*, that:

> it matters not whether [the agent] discloses to the other party the identity of his principal, or even if he is contracting on behalf of a principal at all, if the other party is willing or leads the agent to believe that he is willing to treat as a party

---

12. *Sims v Bond* (1833) 5 B&A 389. The ability of the agent to sue, and be sued, when acting on behalf of an undisclosed principal is discussed on p 169.
13. Richard Stone, *Law of Agency* (Cavendish 1996) 94.
14. Sir Frederick Pollock (1887) 3 LQR 358, 359.
15. AL Goodhart and CJ Hamson, 'Undisclosed Principals in Contract' (1932) 4 CLJ 320.
16. *Siu Yin Kwan v Eastern Insurance Co Ltd* [1994] 2 AC 199 (PC) 210 (Lord Lloyd).

to the contract anyone on whose behalf the agent may have been authorised to contract.[17]

One commentator has used this *dictum* to contend that when a third party contracts with an agent, he is implicitly agreeing to contract with the agent and the agent's principal, should there be one.[18] However, it could be argued that the mere possibility that a principal might exist is not a sufficiently strong ground for implying a contract between the undisclosed principal and the third party. Munday[19] contends that, ultimately, the rule may simply be one of commercial convenience, citing the following passage of Lord Lindley:

> The explanation of the doctrine that an undisclosed principal can sue and be sued on a contract made in the name of another person with his authority is, that the contract is in truth, although not in form, that of the undisclosed principal himself. Both the principal and the authority exist when the contract is made; and the person who makes it for him is only the instrument by which the principal acts. In allowing him to sue and be sued upon it, effect is given, so far as he is concerned, to what is true in fact, although that truth may not have been known to the other contracting party.[20]

Intervention of the principal

Irrespective of the justification (or lack thereof) behind the rule, it has been upheld and applied numerous times by the court, and so the task is now to discuss the application of the rule. As noted, where an agent contracts with a third party on behalf of an undisclosed principal, a contract will exist between the agent and third party. The principal can intervene on this contract and consequently sue, and be sued by, the third party. The courts have recognized that the principal's intervention can cause unfairness to the third party, and so the principal's ability to intervene is subject to a number of limitations. The position has been neatly summarized by Lord Lloyd, who established five points, namely:

> (1) An undisclosed principal may sue and be sued on a contract made by an agent on his behalf, acting within the scope of his actual authority. (2) In entering into the contract, the agent must intend to act on the principal's behalf. (3) The agent of an undisclosed principal may also sue and be sued on the contract. (4) Any defence which the third party may have against the agent is available against his principal. (5) The terms of the contract may, expressly or by implication, exclude the principal's right to sue, and his liability to be sued. The contract itself, or the circumstances surrounding the contract, may show that the agent is the true and only principal.[21]

Each of these limitations will now be discussed, along with several limitations that have been subsequently established. First, the principal can only intervene if the agent had actual authority to bind the principal to the third party.[22] Ratification of

---

17. *Teheran-Europe Co Ltd v ST Belton (Tractors) Ltd* [1968] 2 QB 545 (CA) 555.
18. Tan Cheng-Han, 'Undisclosed Principals and Contract' (2004) 120 LQR 480, 502.
19. Roderick Munday, *Agency: Law and Principles* (OUP 2010) 240.
20. *Keighley, Maxsted & Co v Durant* [1901] AC 240 (HL) 261.
21. *Siu Yin Kwan v Eastern Insurance Co Ltd* [1994] 2 AC 199 (PC) 207.
22. *Keighley, Maxsted & Co v Durant* [1901] AC 240 (HL).

the agent's unauthorized acts will not subsequently permit the principal to intervene, because an undisclosed principal is incapable of ratifying the unauthorized actions of his agent. Second, the principal can only intervene if it existed at the time it was entered into—clearly, this requirement is primarily aimed at bodies corporate (such as companies and limited liability partnerships). Third, the principal can only intervene if the agent was acting on behalf of the undisclosed principal—this will be determined subjectively. Accordingly, if the agent was acting to benefit himself and not his principal, then the principal cannot intervene or be sued by the third party.[23] Fourth, a principal will not be permitted to intervene where such intervention is expressly excluded by the terms of the contract. This exclusion may be obvious (e.g. where the contract expressly states that the agent is the only party to it),[24] or it may be deduced from the facts, as in the following case.

 UK Mutual Steamship Assurance Association Ltd v Nevill (1887) 19 QBD 110 (CA)

FACTS: Tully (the agent) was the manager and part-owner of a ship. He became a member of the UK Mutual Steamship Assurance Association (the third party) and took out an insurance policy under the Association's rules. The Association's articles of association give it the power to require that members pay contributions, and Tully owed such contributions. Tully was declared bankrupt, and so the Association sought to recover the contributions from Nevill, another part-owner of the ship. The Association alleged that Nevill was an undisclosed principal and so could be liable. Nevill denied liability on the ground that he was not a member of the Association.

HELD: The Association's claim failed. It was a term of the articles of association that only members were liable to pay contributions and, as Nevill was not a member, making him liable to the Association would be inconsistent with the express terms of the articles.

Fifth, a principal will not be liable where, by implication, the contract excludes the intervention of the principal. The following case provides an example of such an exclusion.

 Humble v Hunter (1848) 12 QB 310

FACTS: Mrs Humble (the purported principal) owned a ship called *The Ann*. Her son, CJ Humble (the purported agent), chartered the ship to Hunter (the third party). The son signed the charterparty 'CJ Humble Esq, owner of the good ship or vessel called the Ann'. Mrs Humble sought to take over the contract from her son as an undisclosed principal.

---

23. *Rolls-Royce Power Engineering plc v Ricardo Consulting Engineers Ltd* [2003] EWHC 2871 (TCC), [2004] 2 All ER (Comm) 129.
24. *JH Rayner (Mincing Lane) Ltd v Department of Trade and Industry* [1990] 2 AC 418 (HL).

> **HELD:** She was not permitted to intervene and the court held that she was not in fact the principal. The description of the son as the 'owner' of the ship indicated that he was in fact the principal, which excluded the possibility of her intervening as principal.

However, in the following case, the effects of *Humble* were noticeably restricted, with Scott LJ in *Epps v Rothnie* contending that *Humble* 'can no longer be regarded as good law'.[25]

Fred Drughorn Ltd v Rederiaktiebolaget Transatlantic [1919] AC 203 (HL)

FACTS: Fred Drughorn Ltd ('FD', the third party) chartered a steamship to Lundgren (the purported agent), with the charterparty describing Lundgren as the 'charterer'. It transpired that Lundgren had in fact chartered the ship on behalf of Rederiaktiebolaget Transatlantic ('RT', the undisclosed principal), but FD did not know this. FD withdrew the services of the ship from Lundgren, on the ground that Lundgren had performed voyages not permitted under the charterparty. Lundgren commenced proceedings against FD, but before the case reached trial, Lundgren died. RT sought to intervene and substitute itself as claimant, on the ground that Lundgren was acting as its agent. The issue the House had to determine was whether evidence indicating that Lundgren was acting on behalf of RT was admissible.

HELD: The House held that the evidence indicating that Lundgren was acting on behalf of RT was admissible. In comparing *Humble* to the present case, Viscount Haldane stated that:

> the term 'charterer' is a very different term from the term 'owner' or the term 'proprietor.' A charterer may be and prima facie is merely entering into a contract. A charterparty is not a lease—it is a chattel that is being dealt with, a chattel that is essentially a mere subject of contract; and although rights of ownership or rights akin to ownership may be given under it prima facie it is a contract for the hiring or use of the vessel. Under these circumstances it is in accordance with ordinary business common-sense and custom that charterers should be able to contract as agents for undisclosed principals who may come in and take the benefit of the charterparty.[26]

COMMENT: Whilst Scott LJ's contention that *Fred Drughorn* has overruled *Humble v Hunter* cannot be regarded as correct, there is no doubt that the case has significantly restricted those instances where the intervention of a principal will be regarded as inconsistent with the contract. Munday suggests that, following this case, intervention of the principal may only be regarded as inconsistent with the contract 'where the agent has affected the clear role of owner of property which is the subject matter of the contract'.[27]

---

25. [1945] KB 562 (CA) 565.   26. [1919] AC 203 (HL) 207.
27. Roderick Munday, *Agency: Law and Principles* (OUP 2010) 249.

Sixth, the principal will not be permitted to intervene where the third party wishes to contract exclusively with the agent,[28] or where the identity or personal attributes of the agent are an important factor for the third party.

 Collins v Associated Greyhound Racecourses Ltd [1930] 1 Ch 1 (CA)

FACTS: Associated Greyhound Racecourses Ltd ('AGR', the third party) circulated a draft prospectus to a group of underwriters shortly before it was incorporated. An investment company agreed to purchase 1.16 million shares in AGR, or find persons who would subscribe for the shares. Two underwriters, Mason and Ovington (the agents), agreed to underwrite 12,000 shares addressed to the investment company, but they did not disclose that they were in fact acting on behalf of Collins (the undisclosed principal). Upon AGR's incorporation, the prospectus was issued to the public, where it was found to contain an innocent misrepresentation. Collins sought to intervene and rescind the underwriting agreement entered into by Mason and Ovington on his behalf.

HELD: Collins was not permitted to intervene. Lord Hanworth MR stated:

> the contract between the company and Mason and Ovington was one in which importance attached to the personality of the persons with whom the company were contracting. In such a case it is not right to treat the agents as necessarily interchangeable with their principal so as to enable the principal to come forward and seek to disaffirm the contract on the ground of a misrepresentation on which he alone had relied.[29]

★ See AL Goodhart and CJ Hamson, 'Undisclosed Principals in Contract' (1932) 4 CLJ 320

Finally, the courts have held that the principal will not be able to intervene where the third party has some reason for not wanting to deal with the undisclosed principal, but, as will be seen, the validity of this rule is open to question.

 Said v Butt [1920] 3 KB 497 (KB)

FACTS: Said (the undisclosed principal) was a theatre critic who wished to attend the first night performance of a play in the Palace Theatre (the third party). Said had made a number of serious and unfounded allegations against a number of the theatre staff, and therefore knew that his application for a ticket would be refused. Said therefore asked Pollock (the agent), a friend of his, to purchase a ticket for him. When Said turned up on the first night, Butt (the theatre manager) refused him admission. Said commenced proceedings against Butt.

HELD: Said's action failed. McCardie J stated:

> The personal element was here strikingly present. The plaintiff knew that the Palace Theatre would not contract with him for the sale of a seat … They had expressly refused to do so. He was well aware of their reasons. I hold that by the mere device

---

28. *Greer v Downs Supply Co* [1927] 2 KB 28 (CA).   29. [1930] 1 Ch 1 (CA) 33.

of utilizing the name and services of Mr. Pollock, the plaintiff could not constitute himself a contractor with the Palace Theatre against their knowledge, and contrary to their express refusal. He is disabled from asserting that he was the undisclosed principal of Mr. Pollock.[30]

COMMENT: The decision was ultimately based on the contention that there was a contract between Said and the theatre, and this contract was void on the ground of mistake as to identity. This reasoning has been strongly criticized, with Sealy and Hooley branding the case as 'wrongly decided'.[31] The criticism stems from the fact that, in cases involving an undisclosed principal, the contract is not between the principal and the third party, but is actually between the agent and the third party, with the principal acquiring a right to intervene in the contract. The subsequent case of *Dyster v Randall & Sons*,[32] the facts of which were very similar to *Said*, appears to have sought to limit the scope of *Said* by stating, *obiter*, that the principal will only be prevented from interfering if his identity was a 'material ingredient'.[33]

Settlement with the agent

A third party who deals with an agent acting for an undisclosed principal can discharge his liability if he reaches a settlement with the agent. If the principal subsequently seeks to enforce the contract against the third party, the settlement will provide the third party with a complete defence, as the following case demonstrates.

 Coates v Lewes (1808) 1 Camp 444

FACTS: Coates (the undisclosed principal) instructed an agent to sell a quantity of linseed oil. The agent, with the principal's authority, sold the linseed oil in his own name to Lewes (the third party). Lewes had no idea that the agent was acting on behalf of Coates, as Lewes paid the agent, who then paid Coates. Coates then sought to recover the purchase price from Lewes, and Lewes contended that the oil had already been paid for.

HELD: Coates' claim failed. The agent, with Coates' authority, acted as if he was principal, and therefore a third party who settles with such an agent will discharge his liability to the undisclosed principal.

Accordingly, a third party can discharge his obligations to an undisclosed principal if, prior to discovering the existence of the principal, he settles with the agent. The question that arises is whether the opposite is also true—can an undisclosed principal discharge his obligations to a third party by settling with the agent? As the following controversial case demonstrates, the answer appears to be yes.

30. [1920] 3 KB 497 (KB) 503.
31. Len S Sealy and Richard JA Hooley, *Commercial Law: Text, Cases and Materials* (4th edn, OUP 2009) 190.
32. [1926] Ch 932 (Ch).   33. ibid 938 (Lawrence J).

***Armstrong v Stokes* (1872) LR 7 QB 598 (QB)**

FACTS: J & O Ryder & Co ('R & Co', the agent) were commission agents who sometimes acted as agents on behalf of others, and sometimes acted on their own behalf. Armstrong (the third party) had dealt with R & Co on numerous occasions, but never enquired whether it was acting as an agent or on its own behalf. R & Co, acting on behalf of Stokes (the principal), purchased a number of shirts from Armstrong, but did not disclose that it was acting as Stokes's agent. Armstrong delivered the shirts to R & Co, who then passed them on to Stokes. Stokes paid R & Co for the shirts, but R & Co could not afford to pay Armstrong. Armstrong discovered that R & Co were acting on behalf of Stokes and so sued Stokes for the purchase price.

HELD: Armstrong's claim failed and the court held that the payment that Stokes made to R & Co discharged his liability to Armstrong. Blackburn J stated that to require an undisclosed principal to pay 'after they had fairly paid the price to those whom the vendor believed to be the principals, and to whom alone the vendor gave credit ... would produce intolerable hardship'.[34]

COMMENT: As discussed on p 152, the general rule is that a disclosed principal cannot discharge his obligations to a third party by settling with the agent. However, *Armstrong* states that an undisclosed principal can settle with an agent. The correctness of *Armstrong* has split academic commentators. Munday states:

> Given that the principal has either created this situation by choosing to remain concealed from the third party behind the cloak of the agent or has been aware that the agent proposed to act on his behalf in this way, it is...difficult to see why...the third party should suffer if the principal takes it into his head to settle with the agent.[35]

However, Reynolds argues in favour of *Armstrong*, stating:

> The principal has utilized the services of an intermediary who in the transaction into which he has entered has raised no expectation of the accountability of a principal. Surely the principal's duty is performed by keeping the intermediary in funds: if the third party loses, it is because of his misplaced trust in the intermediary. There is no need to make the principal the insurer.[36]

Tortious liability

Consider the following example:

 Eg ComCorp Ltd

ComCorp (the principal) wishes to expand its manufacturing capacity and so it instructs HomeBuild Ltd (the agent) to build two new factories. HomeBuild builds the factories as requested, but several months later, the roof falls in, injuring Rebecca, one of

---

34. (1872) LR 7 QB 598 (QB) 610.
35. Roderick Munday, *Agency: Law and Principles* (OUP 2010) 267.
36. FMB Reynolds, 'Practical Problems of the Undisclosed Principal Doctrine' (1983) 36 CLP 119, 134.

ComCorp's employees. It transpires that the roof was fitted in a negligent manner, but Rebecca cannot commence proceedings against HomeBuild as it is has since been dissolved.

The question that arises is can Rebecca sue ComCorp or, in other words, can the principal be held liable for the tortious acts of its agent? There is little doubt that where a principal authorizes his agent to engage in, or ratifies, a tortious act, then the principal can be liable to persons who sustain loss due to the agent's tort.

 Monaghan v Taylor (1886) 2 TLR 685 (DC)

FACTS: Taylor (the principal) was the proprietor of a music hall. He engaged a singer (the agent) who, on numerous occasions, sang a song that infringed the copyright of Monaghan (the third party). Monaghan sued Taylor on the ground that Taylor authorized the singer to sing the song. Taylor denied this.

HELD: The singer was hired to sing whatever songs she liked, and Taylor exercised no supervision or control over her. This was enough to establish that a relationship of agency existed and that Taylor had authorized the singer to sing the song complained of. Accordingly, Taylor was held liable for the copyright infringement and ordered to pay £2 for each occasion the song was sung.

→ tortfeasor: a person who commits a tort

Certain torts require the alleged **tortfeasor** to be in a certain state of mind before liability can be imposed. For example, the tort of deceit requires a false statement to be made knowingly, or without belief in its truth, or recklessly careless whether it be true or false.[37] Where the principal has the required state of mind, but the agent does not, then liability can be imposed on the principal, as the following case demonstrates.

 Cornfoot v Fowke (1840) 6 M&W 358

FACTS: Fowke (the third party) was looking for a house to rent for himself and his children to live in. He approached Clarke (the agent) and asked him if he knew of any houses to rent. Clarke stated that he knew of a suitable house, namely one that belonged to Cornfoot (the principal). Fowke asked Clarke whether there was anything objectionable about the house, to which Clarke answered no. Fowke agreed to rent the house and signed a lease agreement. A day later, Fowke discovered that the house was next door to a brothel. It transpired that Cornfoot knew of this, but Clarke did not. Fowke wrote to Cornfoot, informing him that he would not be taking up the lease. Cornfoot sued.

HELD: Rolfe B stated that:

> If the plaintiff, knowing of the nuisance, expressly authorized Clarke to state that it did not exist, or to make any statement of similar import; or if he purposely employed

---

37. *Derry v Peek* (1889) 14 App Cas 337 (HL).

an agent, ignorant of the truth, in order that such agent might innocently make a false statement believing it to be true, and might so deceive the party with whom he was dealing, in either of these cases he would be guilty of a fraud.[38]

COMMENT: In *Cornfoot*, liability was imposed upon a principal who knew that the statement made by his innocent agent was false. However, liability for deceit will not be imposed on a principal who innocently makes a false statement, which is repeated by the agent, even if the agent knew the statement to be false.[39]

Vicarious liability

If the agent of a principal is also his employee, then the principal can be vicariously liable for the tortious acts of his agent, providing that the acts were carried out in the course of the agent's employment.[40] The question that arises is whether an agent who acts in an unauthorized manner is acting within the scope of his employment. In other words, within the agency relationship, are the scope of employment and authority synonymous? In the following case, the House clearly stated that a principal will not be vicariously liable for the acts of an agent who is acting in an unauthorized manner.

 Armagas Ltd v Mundogas SA (The Ocean Frost) [1986] AC 717 (HL)

FACTS: Magelssen (the agent) was the vice-president and manager of Mundogas SA (the principal). Mundogas was trying to sell the ship *The Ocean Frost*. Armagas Ltd (the third party) was interested in purchasing the ship, but only if it could then charter it back to Mundogas for at least three years. Magelssen did not have the authority to agree such a deal, but told Armagas that he did. Armagas purchased the ship and Mundogas entered into a three-year charterparty. Magelssen's fraud came to light and Armagas sued Mundogas.

HELD: The claim failed. Lord Keith stated:

> At the end of the day the question is whether the circumstances under which a servant has made the fraudulent misrepresentation which has caused loss to an innocent party contracting with him are such as to make it just for the employer to bear the loss. Such circumstances exist where the employer by words or conduct has induced the injured party to believe that the servant was acting in the lawful course of the employer's business. They do not exist where such belief, although it is present, has been brought about through misguided reliance on the servant himself, when the servant is not authorised to do what he is purporting to do, when what he is purporting to do is not within the class of acts that an employee in his

---

38. (1840) 6 M&W 358, 370.   39. *Armstrong v Strain* (1952) 1 KB 232 (CA).

40. A discussion of what constitutes 'in the course of employment' is beyond the scope of this text, but will be covered by most tort textbooks (e.g. WVH Rogers, *Winfield & Jolowicz on Tort* (18th edn, Sweet & Maxwell 2010) 958–73.

position is usually authorised to do, and when the employer has done nothing to represent that he is authorised to do it.[41]

Accordingly, given that Magelssen was not acting within the scope of his actual or apparent authority, the House held that he was not acting within the scope of his employment and so Mundogas was not liable.

COMMENT: The House of Lords affirmed the decision of the Court of Appeal, but it is unclear as to the scope of the decision. The Court of Appeal decision was clearly stated as referring to all torts of representation, but, as Lord Keith's statement indicates, the decision of the House of Lords was couched solely in terms of fraudulent misrepresentation. As a result, Reynolds states that '[t]he question of how far this reasoning applies to other torts of representation remains therefore open to argument'.[42]

★ See David G Powles, 'Ship Sales and Frauds by Intermediaries' [1987] JBL 337

Conclusion

This chapter demonstrates that complications can arise which can prevent a contractual relationship being created between the principal and third party. Given that the primary purpose of many agency relationships is to effect contractual relations between a principal and a third party, it is of vital importance to be aware of those instances where this purpose might be prevented from coming to fruition.

Having discussed the relationship between the principal and agent, and between the principal and third party, Chapter 8 moves on to discuss the relationship between the agent and the third party. The chapter also discusses those instances where the third party will acquire a right to sue the principal and third party. Accordingly, there is a significant overlap between the discussion in this chapter and in Chapter 8.

Practice questions

1. 'The legal rules relating to a third party's liability to an undisclosed principal lacks a sufficiently clear justification and, as a result, the law in this area is confused and lacks fairness.'

   Discuss the validity of this statement.

2. Discuss whether or not a binding contract is created between the principal and third party in the following cases:

   • ComCorp wishes to purchase some authentic Chinese art, which it will hang on the walls of the lobby of its corporate headquarters. It locates an agent who acts on behalf of a number of Chinese art galleries, one of whom is willing to sell three paintings. A contract of sale is entered into, but the gallery then states that it does not intend to go ahead with the sale.

---

41. [1986] AC 717 (HL) 782–83.

42. FMB Reynolds, 'Apparent Authority; Principal's Liability for Fraud of Agent; Bribery of Agent' [1986] JBL 396, 397.

- ComCorp wishes to hire more office space and instructs an estate agent to locate a suitable property. The estate agent locates a suitable property for £2,500 per month, with six months rent payable up front. ComCorp agrees to rent the property and provides the estate agent with £18,000. The estate agent absconds with the money. The owner of the property demands payment from ComCorp, but ComCorp refuses to pay.
- ComCorp engages an agent to purchase, on its behalf, a heavy goods vehicle. ComCorp instructs the agent not to pay over £25,000 for the vehicle, but the agent cannot obtain a vehicle at this price. He does find a seller who will sell such a vehicle for £25,100 and so the agent enters into a contract of sale on the principal's behalf. ComCorp refuses to take delivery of the vehicle.
- ComCorp is conducting research on its competitors' products. It instructs an agent to purchase products manufactured by TechBuild Ltd, one of ComCorp's major competitors. The agent is told not to inform TechBuild that he is acting on behalf of ComCorp, and to purchase the goods on his own account, and then ComCorp will reimburse him. The agent enters into a contract of sale with TechBuild but, through the agent's carelessness, he divulges that he is acting on behalf of ComCorp. TechBuild refuse to sell ComCorp the goods, and ComCorp refuses to pay the agent for his services.

Further reading

Tan Cheng-Han, 'Undisclosed Principals and Contract' (2004) 120 LQR 480
- Discusses the rationale and operation of the law relating to undisclosed principals. Contends that the law in this area still contains many serious and unresolved problems.

AL Goodhart and CJ Hamson, 'Undisclosed Principals in Contract' (1932) 4 CLJ 320
- Provides a thorough discussion of the history and operation of the rules relating to undisclosed principals.

Roderick Munday, *Agency: Law and Principles* (OUP 2010) chs 8, 9, and pp 296–9
- Chapter 8 focuses on the duties that an agent owes to his principal, whereas chapter 9 discusses the rights that an agent has against his principal. Pages 296–9 discuss the tortious liability of a principal.

FMB Reynolds, 'Practical Problems of the Undisclosed Principal Doctrine' (1983) 36 CLP 11
- Provides a thorough analysis of the law relating to undisclosed principals. Contends that the rule allowing undisclosed principals to settle with their agents is a reasonable one.

Arnold Rochvarg, 'Ratification and Undisclosed Principals' (1989) 34 McGill LJ 286
- Discusses the various justifications advanced for the ability of an undisclosed principal to sue and be sued on a contract. Contends that undisclosed principals should be permitted to ratify the unauthorized actions of their agents.

Peter G Watts, *Bowstead & Reynolds on Agency* (19th edn, Sweet & Maxwell 2010) chs 5, 6, and 7.
- Chapter 5 examines the ability of an agent to delegate his functions. Chapter 6 focuses on the duties that an agent owes to his principal, whereas chapter 7 discusses the rights that an agent has against his principal.

8 Relations between agent and third party

- Contractual liability
- Tortious liability

INTRODUCTION

Having discussed the legal relations between the principal and agent and between the principal and third party in Chapters 6 and 7, it follows that this chapter moves on to consider the relations between the agent and third party. As discussed in Chapter 3, the typical function of an agent is to affect the legal position of his principal in relation to third parties. This is typically achieved by the agent effecting contractual relations between his principal and a third party (or third parties). To this contract, the agent is usually a stranger and it therefore follows that, providing all the parties perform their obligations, there will be no legal relations between the agent and third party, aside from any warranty of authority that might be deemed to exist.

The warranty of authority is discussed at p 176

However, this is not absolute and where the parties fail to properly perform their obligations, legal relations between the agent and third party may come into being which allow one party to sue, or be sued by, the other. This chapter discusses the general rule and also those situations where the agent and third party will acquire a cause of action against the other (as indicated by Figure 8.1). Such liability tends to arise in contract and/or tort, and so this chapter begins by discussing the contractual relationship between the agent and the third party.

Contractual liability

The contractual relationship between the agent and third party, and the extent to which one party can be liable to the other, is complex and depends upon a number of variables, such as:

- whether the principal is disclosed or undisclosed;
- whether or not the principal exists;
- whether or not there exists some custom or usage that would indicate that the agent and third party should be liable to one another;
- whether or not a collateral contract exists between the agent and third party;
- whether the agent is in breach of his warranty of authority.

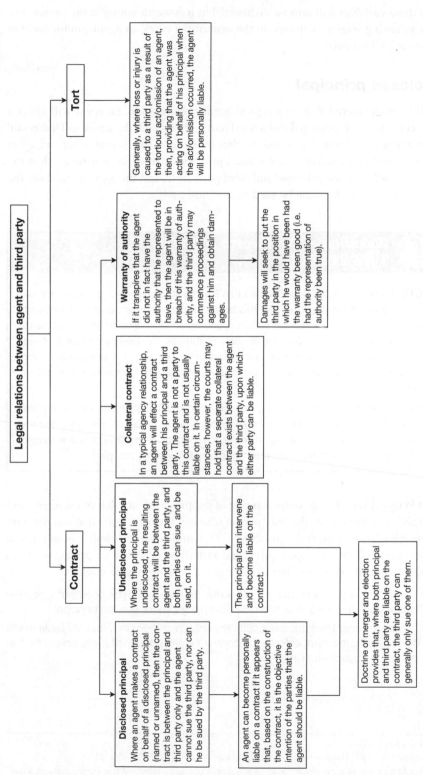

FIGURE 8.1 Legal relations between agent and third party

All of these variables will now be discussed, but it is worth noting at the outset that, as the following section indicates, in the majority of cases, an agent cannot sue, nor be sued by, a third party.

Disclosed principal

It will be remembered that, in a typical agency relationship, an agent will effect a contract between his principal and a third party, after which the agent will 'drop out' of the transaction. From this, it follows that the general rule is that, where an agent effects a contract on behalf of a disclosed principal (named or unnamed), then the contract is between the principal and third party only, and the agent cannot sue the third party, nor can the agent be sued by the third party.

 Wakefield v Duckworth & Co [1915] 1 KB 218 (KB)

FACTS: Duckworth worked for Duckworth & Co (the agent), a firm of solicitors. He was defending a client (the principal) who had been charged with manslaughter. Duckworth ordered a number of photographs from a photographer, Wakefield (the third party). These photographs would be used as part of the client's defence—a fact that was known to Wakefield. Wakefield sought to obtain the price of the photographs from Duckworth & Co. Duckworth & Co refused and so Wakefield commenced proceedings against the firm.

HELD: Wakefield's action failed. Lord Coleridge J stated that '[t]here is no question that the plaintiff knew that the defendants were solicitors acting on behalf of a client, and that being so … they were agents acting on behalf of a principal. *Prima facie* in such a contract the plaintiff would have to have recourse to the principal and not the agent.'[1]

As Wright J stated, 'the contract is that of the principal, not that of the agent, and *prima facie* at common law the only person who can sue is the principal and the only person who can be sued is the principal'.[2] This rule generally applies in full where the agent acts within the scope of his actual authority,[3] or where the principal ratifies the agent's unauthorized acts, but in other cases, the rule may be modified:

- Where the agent acts without authority, and the principal does not ratify the agent's unauthorized acts, then the third party cannot sue the principal.[4]
- Where the agent has apparent authority only, then the principal is still liable to the third party, but cannot enforce the contract against the third party, unless he first ratifies the agent's actions.

---

1. [1915] 1 KB 218 (KB) 220.
2. *Montgomerie v United Kingdom Mutual Steamship Association* [1891] 1 QB 370 (QB) 371.
3. It should be noted that exceptions do exist which will prevent a principal from being party to a contract, even if the agent is acting in an authorized manner—these exceptions are discussed on p 154.
4. *Comerford v Britannic Assurance Co Ltd* (1908) 24 TLR 593 (KB).

- Where the agent acts outside the scope of his actual authority, then he will be liable to the third party for breach of warranty of authority, unless the principal ratifies his unauthorized actions.

Breach of warranty of authority is discussed at p 176

It is worth noting that the application of the general rule to cases involving unnamed principals has been criticized. Several academics[5] have contended that English law should adopt the position found in the American *Restatement of the Law*, which provides that, where the agent acts for a disclosed principal but, at the time of the contract, the third party does not know of the principal's identity, then the agent should also be personally liable on the contract, unless otherwise agreed by the agent and third party.[6] The courts have not chosen to accept this recommendation, and the Court of Appeal has confirmed that the general rule discussed here applies in cases involving an unnamed principal.[7]

Agent party to the contract

Despite the general rule described in the previous section, an agent can become personally liable on a contract if it appears that, based on the construction of the contract, it is the objective intention of the parties that the agent should be liable.[8] The most obvious way in which this could occur is where the contract expressly states that the agent is to be a party to it, or if it states that the agent is to be liable on the contract, either alongside, or to the exclusion of, the principal.[9] However, an agent can still become party to a contract in the absence of an express provision. It should be noted that cases in this area provide general guidance only, and much turns on the construction of the contract in question and the circumstances surrounding it.

The most significant factor is the language used by the agent when signing the contract. As Rix LJ has stated, 'the way in which a party named in a contract signs that contract may be of particular strength in the overall question of whether he is a party to that contract with personal liability under it'.[10] The case law reveals the following general principles:

- An agent who signs a contract in his own name without any qualification will be a party to the contract,[11] unless other portions of the contract clearly indicate a contrary intention. Thus, where an agent signed a contract of sale in his own name, but the contract stated that the goods were being sold 'on account' of another, the court held that the agent was not a party to it.[12]
- The courts will not presume that an agent is not a party to the contract simply because he is described as an agent, manager, broker, or other similar description. Thus, no intention of avoiding liability will be presumed where the agent

---

5. See e.g. FMB Reynolds [1983] CLP 119; Peter G Watts, *Bowstead & Reynolds on Agency* (19th edn, Sweet & Maxwell 2010) [9-016].

6. American Law Institute, *Restatement of the Law—Agency* (American Law Institute 2006) § 6.02.

7. *N&J Vlassopulos Ltd v Ney Shipping Ltd (The Santa Carina)* [1977] 1 Lloyd's Rep 478 (CA).

8. *Bridges & Salmon Ltd v Owner of The Swan (The Swan)* [1968] 1 Lloyd's Rep 5.

9. *Montgomerie v United Kingdom Mutual Steamship Association* [1891] 1 QB 370 (QB).

10. *Internaut Shipping GmbH v Fercometal Sarl* [2003] EWCA Civ 812, [2003] 2 Lloyd's Rep 430 [46].

11. *Parker v Winslow* (1857) 7 E&B 942.

12. *Gadd v Houghton* (1876) 1 ExD 357.

signs the contract, but appends his signature with the words 'as solicitor'[13] or 'as director'.[14] Such words are likely to be regarded as merely descriptive, as opposed to indicating that the agent is acting in a representative capacity for another. However, as noted, the words used are merely one factor among many.

- Where the agent signs the contract and indicates that he is acting as an agent,[15] or where he indicates that he is acting on behalf of,[16] or on account of,[17] another person, then the presumption will be that he is not contracting personally, and so will not be a party to the contract, unless other portions of the contract clearly indicate a contrary intention.[18] Note, this will not apply to agents who execute deeds in their own name—such persons will still be liable even if they state within the deed that they are acting on behalf of another.[19]

Depending upon the construction of the contract, an agent may be party to a contract, and may be sued on it by a third party, but may not have the ability to sue the third party (i.e. he may be liable on the contract, but unable to himself enforce it). The opposite is not true—an agent who is not liable on a contract cannot enforce it against a third party.

Merger and election

As noted, where the agent is party to a contract, the third party may have the option of suing the principal or agent—an option that can be extremely useful, especially where either the principal or agent has become bankrupt/insolvent, or is protected by an exclusion clause. In such cases, the liability of the agent and principal is alternate, as indicated by Scrutton LJ:

> When an agent acts for a disclosed principal, it may be that the agent makes himself or herself personally liable as well as the principal. But in such a case the person with whom the contract is made may not get judgment against both. He may get judgment against the principal or he may get judgment against the agent.[20]

Accordingly, in order to prevent double recovery, the third party cannot sue both the principal and agent and must sue one or the other. In practice, this limitation arises in two ways:

1. If the third party has already obtained judgment against the principal, or the agent, then the third party is disbarred from obtaining judgment against the other (e.g. if judgment is obtained against the principal, the third party cannot then sue the agent),[21] even if the judgment is not satisfied. This is based on the doctrine of 'merger', which provides that multiple judgments may not arise out of a single obligation.

2. Where judgment has not already been obtained, the third party may elect to hold one party liable, which then releases the other party from liability (unsurprisingly,

13. *Burrell v Jones* (1819) 3 B&Ald 47.
14. *McCollin v Gilpin* (1881) 6 QBD 516.
15. *Redpath v Wigg* (1866) LR 1 Ex 335 (contract signed by the agent 'as agents').
16. *Universal Steam Navigation Co Ltd v J McKelvie & Co* [1923] AC 492 (HL).
17. *Gadd v Houghton* (1876) 1 ExD 357.
18. See e.g. *Young v Schuler* (1883) 11 QBD 651.
19. *Appleton v Binks* (1804) 4 East 148.
20. *Debenham's Ltd v Perkins* [1925] All ER Rep 234 (KB) 237.
21. *LGOC v Pope* (1922) 38 TLR 270.

this is known as 'election'). In order for election to arise, (i) the third party must clearly and unequivocally elect to sue one party; and (ii) the third party must have full knowledge of the facts, including knowing the identity of the principal.[22]

The doctrines of merger and election will not apply where (i) the claims against the principal and agent arise from separate causes of action; (ii) the principal and agent are jointly and severally liable on the contract; and (iii) where one party is not liable at all. It should be noted that the doctrines of merger and election apply not only to cases involving a disclosed principal, but also to cases where an agent and undisclosed principal are both liable, as is discussed next.

Undisclosed principal

Where the principal is undisclosed, then the third party will be under the impression that he is dealing solely with the agent. In such a case, the resulting contract will be between the agent and the third party, and both parties can sue, and be sued, on it.[23] It should be noted that, in cases involving an undisclosed principal, the principal can usually intervene and sue, and be sued, on the contract.[24] Where the principal does intervene, the agent will lose the ability to enforce the contract against the third party,[25] although the agent will still remain liable to the third party until such time as the third party elects whether to sue the agent or the principal.

An undisclosed principal's liability on a contract is discussed at p 153

Fictitious or non-existent principal

Special consideration must be given to two cases. The first is where the principal is fictitious, which usually occurs where the agent purports to act on behalf of another, but is in fact acting on his own behalf (i.e. the agent is the principal). The second case occurs where the agent purports to act on behalf of a principal that does not yet exist, which tends to occur where the promoter of a company acts on behalf of a company (or limited liability partnership) that has not yet been incorporated.

Agent acts as principal

As discussed, an agent who acts for a disclosed principal will not normally be liable on the contract, as a contract will exist between the principal and third party, between whom there will be privity. However, is this still the case where the agent purports to act on behalf of another, but is in fact acting on his own behalf? The general rule appears to be that a person who professes to be acting on behalf of another, but is in fact acting on his own behalf, will be personally liable on the contract and can be sued by a third party, as the following case demonstrates.

---

22. *Thomson v Davenport* (1829) 9 B&C 78.

23. *Sims v Bond* (1833) 5 B&A 389.

24. As both the agent and principal can be liable on the contract, the doctrine of election can also apply to a case involving an undisclosed principal.

25. *Atkinson v Cotesworth* (1825) 3 B&C 647.

Railton v Hodgson (1804) 4 Taunt 576n

FACTS: Hodgson, purporting to act on behalf of a firm, ordered goods from Railton. Hodgson had worked for the firm before, but no longer did so—he was in fact ordering the goods for himself, but used the firm's name in order to obtain the goods on credit. Railton delivered the goods to Hodgson and billed the firm for payment. However, the firm was insolvent and so Railton commenced proceedings against Hodgson.

HELD: Railton succeeded and Hodgson was held liable on the contract, and was therefore obliged to pay for the goods.

COMMENT: This case, and the principle it establishes, has been criticized. It has been argued that an agent who purports to act on behalf of another, but is in fact acting for himself, should not, unless he undertakes personal liability on the contract, be liable on the contract, as such a result is 'contrary to the principle of objective interpretation in contract to establish intentions unknown to the third party'.[26] In such cases, it would appear to be much more appropriate to hold the agent liable for breach of warranty of authority, or in tort.

Breach of warranty of authority is discussed at p 176, while liability in tort is discussed at p 181

Quite why the person incorrectly purporting to act on behalf of another should be liable on the contract is not entirely clear. No coherent justification has been forthcoming, and what justifications have been offered are rather vague, as evidenced by the following statement of Scrutton LJ:

> Why should not a man who contracts with another, thinking he is an agent, sue him when he finds out that he is the real principal? There seems to be no reason why he should not, provided the supposed agent has not expressly contracted as agent so as to exclude his liability as a principal party to that contract…I think it is the law. I am sure it is justice. It is probably the law for that reason.[27]

Despite the criticism levelled at *Railton* and cases like it,[28] it remains good law, and the general principle is that an agent who purports to act for another, but is in fact acting for himself, can be sued on the contract by a third party. The question that flows from this is whether or not the opposite is also true, namely can a third party be sued on the contract by the person who was purporting to be acting on behalf of another, but who was in fact acting for himself. It would be assumed that the answer would be no as, unless the contract indicates that an agent is party to the contract, the agent drops out of the transaction, leaving a contract between the principal and third party, between whom there is privity. One would assume that the person purporting to act as agent cannot subsequently enforce the contract as the *de facto* principal, or, as Lord Ellenborough stated, 'where a man assigns to himself the character of agent to another whom he names, I am not aware that the law will permit him to shift his situation, and to declare himself the principal, and the other to be a mere creature of straw'.[29] Despite this, the courts have held that, in a number of cases, the contract can be enforced against the third party, although it has been argued that such cases

---

26. Peter G Watts, *Bowstead & Reynolds on Agency* (19th edn, Sweet & Maxwell 2010) [9-091].
27. *Gardiner v Heading* [1928] 2 KB 284 (CA) 290.
28. See e.g. *Jenkins v Hutchinson* (1849) 13 QB 744; *Carr v Jackson* (1852) 7 Exch 382; *Gardiner v Heading* [1928] 2 KB 284 (CA).
29. *Bickerton v Burrell* (1816) 5 M&W 383, 386.

provide 'slender authority',[30] and making the third party liable on the contract is 'difficult to justify on principle'.[31]

The following case indicates that an agent who falsely claims to be acting on behalf of another can enforce the contract against the third party if the third party continues with the contract after becoming aware of the true situation.

 Rayner v Grote (1846) 15 M&W 359

FACTS: Rayner described himself as the agent of Messrs J & T Johnson, and contracted to sell fifty tonnes of soda ash to Grote on their behalf. In fact, the soda ash belonged to Rayner himself. Thirteen tonnes of the fifty were delivered to Grote, who accepted the goods and paid for them in part. Evidence indicated that, at the time Grote accepted the goods, he knew that the goods actually belonged to Rayner (i.e. he knew that Rayner was in fact the principal, and not an agent). Grote refused to accept the remaining thirty-seven tonnes and so Rayner sued.

HELD: The court held that Rayner could sue Grote for his non-acceptance and non-payment of the goods. Alderson B stated that:

> this contract has been in part performed, and that part performance accepted by the defendants with full knowledge that the plaintiff was not the agent, but the real principal … [W]e think that the plaintiff may, after that, very properly say that they cannot refuse to complete the contract by receiving the remainder of the goods and paying the stipulated price for them.[32]

COMMENT: The reasoning of the court is open to criticism. The simple fact is that Grote contracted to purchase goods from Messrs J & T Johnson and, to this contract, Rayner was not a party. No convincing justification has been advanced explaining why the agent should be able to enforce this contract to which he is not a party. It has been contended that the decision cannot be justified on orthodox agency principles and is better regarded as an example of a situation where, following the true situation coming to light, the contract is **novated** so that the agent becomes the seller.[33]

➡ **novation:** the act of substituting one contract for another

In *Rayner*, Alderson B was keen to point out that if the identity of the principal was a material factor, then the agent would not be permitted to take over the contract as principal and enforce it. He stated:

> In many cases, such as, for instance, the case of contracts in which the skill or solvency of the person who is named as the principal may reasonably be considered as a material ingredient to the contract, it is clear that the agent cannot then shew himself to be the real principal, and sue in his own name.[34]

---

30. Peter G Watts, *Bowstead & Reynolds on Agency* (19th edn, Sweet & Maxwell 2010) [9-089].
31. ibid.
32. (1846) 15 M&W 359, 365–6.
33. Peter G Watts, *Bowstead & Reynolds on Agency* (19th edn, Sweet & Maxwell 2010) [9-094].
34. *Rayner v Grote* (1846) 15 M&W 359, 365.

From this, it follows that the courts appear to be more willing to permit the agent to enforce the contract where the identity of the principal is not of importance (e.g. where the principal is unnamed).

Schmaltz v Avery (1851) 16 QB 655

→ freighter: a person or vessel that transports cargo and goods

FACTS: Schmaltz had entered a charterparty with Avery, the owner of a ship, under which the ship would be used to transport goods. The charterparty stated that Schmaltz was acting as agent for a **freighter**, but did not identify who the freighter was (i.e. the principal was disclosed, but unnamed). The charterparty contained a cesser clause, which provided that Schmaltz's liability would cease as soon as the cargo had shipped. It transpired that Schmaltz was not in fact acting on behalf of a freighter, and was in fact the freighter himself. Avery, upon discovering this, refused to take on board any cargo. Schmaltz sued to enforce the terms of the charterparty.

HELD: Schmaltz's action succeeded and he was permitted to enforce the charterparty. Patteson J stated:

> [t]here is no contradiction of the charterparty if the plaintiff can be considered as filling two characters, namely those of agent and principal...We see no absurdity in saying that he might fill both characters; that he might contract as agent for the freighter whoever that freighter might turn out to be, and might still adopt that character of freighter himself if he chose.[35]

The court was heavily influenced by the fact that the principal was unnamed and Avery did not seek to enquire who the principal was. Based upon this, the court concluded that Avery was not prejudiced by Schmaltz acting as principal and in fact, '[a]ny one who could prove himself to have been the real freighter and principal, whether solvent or not, might most unquestionably have sued on this charter party'.[36]

COMMENT: By allowing Schmaltz to enforce the charterparty, the court arguably acted in a manner that was inconsistent with the terms of the charterparty itself, given that the charterparty was between Avery and the freighter, and the agent signed the charterparty in such a way as to indicate clearly that he was not the freighter. The fact that the freighter was unnamed does not mean that Avery did not care who the freighter was. As Munday has correctly stated:

> the fact that a third party is indifferent to the party with whom he may have contracted does not necessarily entail that he is content to contract with the 'agent' who, by acting as agent, may have conveyed the impression that he was not in the running to assume the character of the principal.[37]

Despite the criticism levelled at *Schmaltz*, the courts have actually gone further and have held that an agent can enforce a contract against a third party, even where evidence exists which indicates that the third party would not have contracted had he known that the agent was in fact the principal.[38]

---

35. (1851) 16 QB 655, 663.   36. ibid 662 (Patteson J).
37. Roderick Munday, *Agency: Law and Principles* (OUP 2010) 321–2.
38. *Harper & Co v Vigers Bros* [1909] 2 KB 549 (KB).

Principal does not yet exist

An agent may purport to act on behalf of a principal that does not yet exist. This commonly occurs in the following situation:

> ### Eg ComCorp Ltd
>
> Lee, Eric, and Greg (the directors of ComCorp) decide to set up a subsidiary company. The subsidiary will be called Bastion Ltd and the application for incorporation is duly submitted to the Registrar of Companies. Before the certificate of incorporation is issued, all three promoters are busy preparing for the commencement of business. Lee rents office space, signing the rental agreement 'Lee, on behalf of Bastion Ltd'. Eric purchases office supplies, signing the contract of sale 'Eric, the agent of Bastion Ltd'. Greg hires a number of employees, signing the employment contracts as 'Bastion Ltd'.

The problem that arises is that Lee, Eric, and Greg (the agents) are all purporting to act, and enter into contracts, on behalf of Bastion Ltd (the principal), but the company does not yet exist and so it has no contractual capacity. Are such pre-incorporation contracts void or, because they are clearly for the benefit of the principal-to-be, are they regarded as valid and enforceable and, if so, who can enforce them? In other words, who is liable where an agent acts on behalf of a principal that does not yet exist? Historically, the common law provided the answer, but it was based on determining the intent of the parties, as revealed in the contract[39]—a process which proved to be notoriously difficult, which resulted in significant confusion in the law and a perception that cases in this area could turn based on complex and technical distinctions. For an example of the distinctions drawn, contrast the cases of *Kelner v Baxter*[40] and *Newborne v Sensolid (Great Britain) Ltd.*[41] In *Kelner*, the promoter signed the contact 'on behalf of' the unformed company (as Lee did in the ComCorp example), and it was held that a binding contract existed between the promoter and the third party.[42] In *Newborne*, the promoter signed the contract using the company's name and added his own signature underneath (as Greg did in the ComCorp example). It was held that the contract was between the promoter and the unformed company, and, as the company had no contractual capacity, no contract existed.

Fortunately, s 51(1) of the Companies Act 2006 has, in the majority of cases,[43] rendered this common law distinction redundant, by providing that:

---

39. *Phonogram Ltd v Lane* [1982] QB 938 (CA).

40. (1866) LR 2 CP 174.   41. [1954] 1 QB 45 (CA).

42. The court also held that a binding contract would exist where the promoter signed the contract as the company's agent (as Eric did in the ComCorp example).

43. The common law position will continue to apply to those cases where s 51(1) is inapplicable, such as where the company existed, but has since been dissolved (*Cotronic (UK) Ltd v Dezonie* [1991] BCC 200 (CA)).

Companies Act 2006, s 51(1)

A contract that purports to be made by or on behalf of a company at a time when the company has not been formed has effect, subject to any agreement to the contrary, as one made with the person purporting to act for the company or as agent for it, and he is personally liable on the contract accordingly.

Accordingly, where s 51(1) applies, an agent who makes a contract by or on behalf of a company that has not yet been incorporated, will be personally liable on that contract. Clearly, s 51(1) benefits third parties, who can now sue the agent, but can an agent sue a third party who refuses to honour a pre-incorporation contract? The wording is unclear, as the phrase 'and he is personally liable on the contract accordingly' appears to indicate that only the agent is liable on the contract. However, the preceding phrase indicates that the contract has effect as between the third party and the agent, which would allow both parties to enforce the contract, a position that has since been confirmed by the Court of Appeal.[44]

It is important to note that the company cannot ratify or adopt the contract once it has been fully incorporated.[45] The only way in which the company can take advantage of a pre-incorporation contract is for the parties to discharge the contract, and the company to then enter into the contract with the third party on the same terms.[46] It has been contended that companies will view this discharge procedure as an undue waste of time and effort, and that companies should be permitted to adopt pre-incorporation contracts.[47]

Foreign principal

Two notable problems can arise where an agent acts on behalf of a foreign principal, especially where contracts are effected between a foreign principal and a domestic third party. First, if a problem arises, the principal or third party may need to commence proceedings against the other but, as they are based in different countries, this can be a protracted, complex, and costly affair. Second, the principal and third party may have very little knowledge of each other and very little reason to trust each other. In order to remedy these problems, the courts developed a strong presumption of fact[48] that provided that where an agent acted on behalf of a foreign principal (disclosed or undisclosed), then only the agent could acquire rights and liabilities under the contract, and the agent did not have authority to establish privity of contract between the principal and a third party.[49] To quote Blackburn J:

---

44. *Braymist Ltd v Wise Finance Co Ltd* [2002] EWCA Civ 127, [2002] Ch 273.
45. Article 7 of the First EU Company Law Directive, which led to the passing of s 51(1), did allow the company to 'assume the obligations' of the pre-incorporation contract. As s 51(1) contains no such power, it could be argued that s 51(1) only partially implements Art 7.
46. *Howard v Patent Ivory Manufacturing Co* (1888) 38 ChD 156 (Ch).
47. See e.g. Robert R Pennington, 'The Validation of Pre-Incorporation Contracts' (2002) 23 Co Law 284.
48. In *Armstrong v Stokes* (1872) LR 7 QB 598, 605, Blackburn J stated that the presumption was so strong that 'we are justified in treating it as a matter of law'.
49. *Paterson v Gandasequi* (1812) 15 East 62; *Armstrong v Stokes* (1872) LR 7 QB 598; *Glover v Langford* (1892) 8 TLR 628.

the foreign constituent [the principal] has not authorized the merchants [the agent] to pledge his credit to the contract, to establish privity between him and the home supplier [the third party]. On the other hand, the home supplier, knowing that to be the usage, unless there is something in the bargain showing the intention to be otherwise, does not trust the foreigner, and so does not make the foreigner responsible to him, and does not make himself responsible to the foreigner.[50]

As this quote indicates, the presumption could be rebutted if there was clear evidence indicating that the principal and third party intended to have direct contractual relations. However, as the riskiness of international trade decreased, the presumption was eventually abandoned,[51] and a new approach established:

Trade has changed greatly and has increased enormously…British firms and companies do not hesitate to make contracts with foreign firms and companies, whether negotiated or not through British agents. British agents are loth to make themselves personally responsible for their foreign principals…In my opinion the true view is, whether the foreign principal is a buyer or a seller, that the fact that the principal is a foreigner and that the agent has not disclosed his name are…circumstances to be considered, and when the facts are doubtful or, in the case of a verbal contract, in dispute, or when there is a written contract the terms of which are ambiguous, they are of some importance; but when there is a written contract the terms of which are unambiguous they are of no importance, and it is not true to say that there is a presumption of fact or law that the agent for the foreign principal is personally liable.[52]

Custom

An agent may be held personally liable, or acquire the ability to sue, on a contract due to some form of custom or trade usage, as the following case demonstrates.

 Pike, Sons & Co v Ongley and Thornton (1887) LR 18 QBD 708 (CA)

FACTS: Ongley and Thornton (the agents) purported to sell 100 bales of hops to Pike, Sons & Co (the third party), with the contract stating that the sale was 'for and on account of the owner' (the principal). The hops were not delivered to Pike and so Pike sued Ongley and Thornton for non-delivery. Ongley and Thornton contended that they made the contract on behalf of their principal and so they were not personally liable. Pike pointed out that it was customary in the hop trade to impose personal liability on a broker if he did not disclose the identity of his principal at the time the contract was made.

HELD: Pike provided clear evidence of the custom within the hop trade, and so the Court enforced it, thereby making Ongley and Thornton personally liable.

---

50. *Die Elbinger AG Für Fabrication von Eisenbahn Materiel v Claye* (1873) LR 8 QB 313 (QB) 317.
51. *Teheran-Europe Co Ltd v ST Belton (Tractors) Ltd* [1968] 2 QB 545 (CA).
52. *Miller, Gibb & Co v Smith & Tyrer Ltd* [1917] 2 KB 141 (CA) 162–3 (Bray J).

> **COMMENT:** The Court imposed a notable limitation on the ability to give effect to a custom that sought to make an agent personally liable, namely 'whether such a custom contradicts the written contract.'[53] If a custom contradicts, or is inconsistent with, the terms of the contract, then the courts will not enforce it.[54]

Collateral contract

In a typical agency relationship, an agent will effect a contract between his principal and a third party. The agent is not a party to this contract and is not usually liable on it. In certain circumstances, however, the courts may hold that a separate collateral contract exists between the agent and the third party, upon which either party can be liable. The following example demonstrates how a collateral contract might arise.

Eg ComCorp Ltd

ComCorp wishes to purchase a used car, to be used by a newly appointed manager as a company car. Lee, one of ComCorp's directors, is authorized by the board to purchase a car at an upcoming auction. Lee attends the auction, makes the highest bid for a car, and purchases it on behalf of ComCorp.

A binding contract of sale will exist between the seller of the car (the principal) and ComCorp (the third party). The auctioneer (the agent) will not be a party to this contract and normally cannot be held liable on it.[55] However, a collateral contract will exist between the auctioneer and ComCorp, under which the auctioneer warrants that he has the authority to sell the car and that he has no knowledge of any defects in the seller's title.[56] If the auction is without reserve, then a collateral contract will exist between the auctioneer and the highest bidder, under which the auctioneer agrees to accept the highest bid that is made.[57] The collateral contract also provides that the auctioneer can sue ComCorp for price should it subsequently refuse to purchase the car.[58]

There are a number of examples of collateral contracts that exist in specific circumstances (such as where the agent is an auctioneer). There is, however, a general type of collateral contract that arises in many agency cases, namely a collateral contract containing a warranty of authority.

Breach of warranty of authority

Consider the following example:

---

53. (1887) LR 18 QBD 708 (CA) 713 (Fry LJ).
54. See e.g. *Barrow & Bros v Dyster, Nalder & Co* (1884) 13 QBD 635.
55. *Elder Smith Goldsbrough Mort Ltd v McBride* [1976] 2 NSWLR 631.
56. *Peto v Blades* (1814) 5 Taut 657.
57. *Barry v Heathcote Ball & Co (Commercial Actions) Ltd* [2001] 1 All ER 944 (CA).
58. *Williams v Millington* (1788) 1 H Bl 81.

> ### Eg ComCorp Ltd
>
> ComCorp wishes to obtain a piece of machinery that will be installed in one of its factories and used to fulfil a customer order. ComCorp has difficulty locating the machine, but is told by Christoph that he is an agent for MachineCorp Ltd, a company that owns the piece of machinery in question. Christoph also states that he has authority to lease the machinery to ComCorp. An agreement is drawn up between ComCorp and MachineCorp. It transpires that Christoph does not in fact have authority to lease MachineCorp's machinery. Further, MachineCorp has recently entered insolvent liquidation and the liquidator has sold the machine. ComCorp cannot locate a replacement and so is unable fulfil the customer order.

ComCorp cannot sue MachineCorp, as Christoph acted without authority and his actions have not been ratified. Even if ComCorp could sue MachineCorp, such an action would be pointless for two reasons. First, MachineCorp no longer has the machine, so specific performance would not be ordered; and second, as MachineCorp is insolvent, it is likely that it has no funds to pay any damages should the action succeed. Christoph is unlikely to be liable on the contract, as the principal was disclosed. However, ComCorp could seek to obtain damages from Christoph on the ground that he breached his warranty of authority.

An agent, through words or conduct, may represent that he has authority[59] to act on behalf of another person (as Christoph did in the ComCorp example). A third party may rely on this representation and act upon it (e.g. by entering into a contract with the agent's principal).[60] In such a case, the agent is deemed to have warranted that he has the level of authority that he represented to have—this is known as the agent's warranty of authority. If it transpires that the agent did not in fact have the authority that he represented to have, then the agent will be in breach of this warranty of authority, and the third party may commence proceedings against him and obtain damages, as occurred in the following case.

> ### Collen v Wright (1857) 8 E & B 647
>
> **FACTS:** Gardner (the principal) owned a farm. Wright (the agent) wrongly believed that he had authority to lease the farm to third parties, and so purported to lease the farm to Collen (the third party). Gardner refused to lease the farm to Collen, and so Collen attempted to obtain an order for specific performance requiring Gardner to lease the farm to him. When it was discovered that specific performance would not be granted, Collen commenced proceedings against Wright.

---

59. A breach of warranty of authority can also arise where an agent wrongly represents that another person has authority (*Chapleo v Brunswick Permanent Building Society* (1881) 6 QBD 696).

60. Note that a contract between the principal and third party need not arise in order for breach of warranty of authority to be established (*British Russian Gazette and Trade Outlook Ltd v Associated Newspapers Ltd* [1933] 2 KB 616 (CA)).

HELD: Collen's action succeeded and he could recover from Wright damages for the loss sustained due to the failed action against Gardner and the monies expended on the farm. Willes J stated that:

> I am of the opinion that a person, who induces another to contract with him as the agent of a third party by an unqualified assertion of his being authorised to act as such agent, is answerable to the person who so contracts for any damages which he may sustain by reason of the assertion of authority being untrue.[61]

COMMENT: Prior to *Collen*, it was not clear whether or not liability could be established for an innocent breach of warranty of authority—this case established that it could. Where, as in *Collen*, the agent acts in an entirely innocent manner, then a claim for breach of warranty of authority is the only claim that the third party can bring against the agent. Where the agent knows that he has no authority, then the third party can alternatively bring an action for deceit. Where the agent's statement claiming that he has authority is negligent, then the agent may be held liable under the principles established in *Hedley Byrne & Co Ltd v Heller & Partners Ltd*.[62] Actions in deceit are notoriously difficult to establish, and an action under *Hedley Byrne* would only succeed if the requisite special relationship existed. Accordingly, an action for breach of warranty of authority may be much easier to sustain.

The basis and nature of liability

For a time, the courts struggled to articulate a consistent basis for the imposition of liability for breach of warranty of authority, with some cases basing liability in contract, whilst others based it in tort. Whilst liability can be tortious where the agent's representation is fraudulent or negligent, liability for breach of warranty of authority is usually based in contract.[63] As Bramwell LJ stated:

> if a person requests and, by asserting that he is clothed with the necessary authority, induces another to enter into a negotiation with himself and a transaction with the person whose authority he represents that he has, in that case there is a contract by him that he has the authority of the person with whom he requests the other to enter into the transaction.[64]

In other words, by representing that he has authority, the agent brings into existence a unilateral[65] collateral contract between himself and the third party, under which he impliedly promises that the authority that he professes to have actually exists. By entering into the transaction with the agent, the third party provides consideration for the agent's promise.[66] Should the agent not have the requisite authority, he will be in breach of the collateral contract and will be liable to pay damages to the third party.

A consequence of liability being based in contract is that liability is strict (i.e. proof of fault is not required). An agent will breach his warranty of authority simply

---

61. (1857) 8 E & B 647, 657.   62. [1964] AC 465 (HL).
63. *Dickson v Reuter's Telegram Co Ltd (1877–78) LR 3 CPD 1 (CA); Allan & Anderson Ltd v AH Basse Rederi A/S (The Piraeus)* [1974] 2 Lloyd's Rep 266 (CA).
64. *Dickson v Reuter's Telegram Co Ltd* (1877–78) LR 3 CPD 1 (CA) 5.
65. The collateral contract is unilateral because it only imposes obligations upon the agent.
66. *Collen v Wright* (1857) 8 E&B 647, 658.

by representing a level of authority that does not in fact exist. Whether or not the agent acted innocently is completely irrelevant, as was stated by Willes J in *Collen v Wright* (discussed earlier):

> The fact that the professed agent honestly thinks that he has authority affects the moral character of his act; but his moral innocence, so far as the person whom he has induced to contract is concerned, in no way aids such person or alleviates the inconvenience and damage which he sustains.[67]

The imposition of strict liability can result in decisions that appear unduly harsh on the agent, as in the following case.

Yonge v Toynbee [1910] 1 KB 215 (CA)

FACTS: Yonge (the third party) claimed that Toynbee (the principal) had defamed him. Toynbee engaged a firm of solicitors (the agent) to defend the action. Before the action could commence, and unknown to the solicitors, Toynbee was certified as insane. The action proceeded and the solicitors delivered a defence in **interlocutory proceedings**. The solicitors and Yonge then discovered that Toynbee had been certified as insane, upon which Yonge applied to have the defence and all subsequent proceedings struck out. Yonge also contended that the solicitors should personally pay his costs as they had acted without authority.

HELD: It was clear that Toynbee's insanity had terminated the solicitors' authority and, as such, the solicitors had breached their warranty of authority and so were liable to pay damages to Yonge. Buckley LJ stated that liability for breach of warranty of authority 'arises from the fact that by professing to act as agent he impliedly contracts that he has authority, and it is immaterial whether he knew of the defect of his authority or not'.[68]

➡ **interlocutory proceedings:** proceedings that are incidental to the main object of the cause of action

🔗 The effect of the principal becoming incapacitated is discussed at p 64

In practice, the strict liability nature of the warranty of authority is mitigated by the fact that the courts have imposed numerous limitations concerning when the warranty will be implied, including the following:

- The warranty of authority will not be implied where the third party knew, or ought to have known, that the agent lacked authority[69] (e.g. where the agent warned the third party that he may lack authority,[70] or where a trade custom exists which should have put the third party on notice of the agent's lack of authority).[71]
- The agent will not be liable if he disclaims authority.[72]
- Bowstead & Reynolds contend that the law assumes that where the principal ratifies the unauthorized acts of the agent, then no loss arises. They then go on to to state that, in such a case, 'it may be more plausibly argued that there is no breach of warranty at all'.[73]

---

67. ibid 657.   68. [1910] 1 KB 215 (CA) 227.
69. *Beattie v Ebury* (1872) LR 7 Ch App 777.   70. *Yonge v Toynbee* [1910] 1 KB 215 (CA).
71. *Lilly, Wilson & Co v Smales, Eeles & Co* [1892] 1 QB 456 (QB).
72. *Halbot v Lens* [1901] 1 Ch 344 (Ch).
73. Peter G Watts, *Bowstead & Reynolds on Agency* (19th edn, Sweet & Maxwell 2010) [9-072].

- *Dicta* exist which indicate that the warranty of authority will not be implied where the agent has apparent authority.[74] However, the validity of these has been doubted,[75] and it appears that a breach of warranty of authority will occur but, as the third party can enforce the contract against the principal, it follows that no loss will be sustained and so only nominal damages can be claimed.
- Historically, the warranty of authority would not be implied in cases involving a representation of law[76]—the representation would need to be one of fact. However, given that this distinction has been abolished in other areas of contract law (e.g. misrepresentation, mistake), it remains to be seen whether this limitation will be upheld in future cases involving warranties of authority.

Measure of damages

As liability for breach of warranty of authority is based in contract, it follows that damages are usually assessed on a contractual basis, namely 'by considering the difference in the position [the third party] would have been in had the representation been true, and the position he is actually in, in consequence of its being untrue'.[77] In other words, damages will seek to put the third party 'in the position in which he would have been had the warranty been good *viz.* had the representation of authority been true'.[78] The following case demonstrates this in practice.

 Simons v Patchett (1857) 7 E&B 568

FACTS: Patchett (the agent) purchased a ship from Simons (the third party) for £6,000. Patchett claimed that he was purchasing the ship on behalf of Rostron & Co (the principal) and that he had authority to purchase the ship. It transpired that Patchett did not have authority to purchase the ship, and Rostron & Co refused to honour the sale. Simons sold the ship to another party for £5,500, and then brought an action against Patchett for breach of warranty of authority.

HELD: Simons' action succeeded. Had Patchett's warranty of authority not been breached (i.e. had his representation as to his authority been true), then Simons would have received £6,000. Accordingly, in order to put Simons in this position, Patchett was ordered to pay damages of £500.

In *Simons*, damages were assessed on the date of the breach, but the courts will abandon this rule where it is appropriate to do so, as occurred in the following case.

---

74. See e.g. *Rainbow v Howkins* [1904] 2 KB 322 (KB) 326 (Kennedy J). This view is also shared by Edwin Peel, *Treitel on the Law of Contract* (13th edn, Sweet & Maxwell 2011) 786–7.
75. See e.g. Peter G Watts, *Bowstead & Reynolds on Agency* (19th edn, Sweet & Maxwell 2010) [9-071]; Len S Sealy and Richard JA Hooley, *Commercial Law: Text, Cases and Materials* (4th edn, OUP 2009) 178.
76. *Rashdall v Ford* (1866) LR 2 Eq 750.
77. *Firbank's Executors v Humphreys* (1887) LR 18 QBD 54 (CA) 60 (Lord Esher MR).
78. Peter G Watts, *Bowstead & Reynolds on Agency* (19th edn, Sweet & Maxwell 2010) [9-078], approved by Dyson LJ in *Singh v Sardar Investments* [2002] EWCA Civ 1706, [2002] NPC 134 [50].

Habton Farms v Nimmo [2003] EWCA Civ 68

FACTS: Nimmo was a bloodstock agent (i.e. an agent who purchases and sells horses on behalf of others). He purchased a horse from Habton Farms (the third party) for £70,000, claiming that the purchase was on behalf of a racehorse owner named Williamson (the principal). Nimmo lacked the authority to purchase horses on Williamson's behalf, and so Williamson refused to take delivery of the horse. Habton Farms refused to sell the horse to anyone else and continued to demand payment. Around four weeks after the horse was supposed to be delivered to Williamson, it contracted peritonitis and had to be destroyed. Habton Farms commenced proceedings against Nimmo to recover the £70,000. Nimmo contended that, at the time of the breach of warranty of authority, the horse was still worth £70,000 and so Habton Farms had not sustained any loss, and so damages should be nominal.

HELD: The Court ordered that Nimmo pay damages of £70,000 to Habton Farms. Auld and Clarke LJJ acknowledged that, if damages were assessed in the usual way, then Habton Farms would only be entitled to nominal damages as, at the date of breach, the horse was still worth £70,000.[79] The majority decided that assessing damages at the date of breach was not appropriate in this case. Auld LJ stated that:

> [i]f the contract had proceeded, [Habton Farms] would have divested [itself] of the ownership, possession and risk of harm to the horse in return for the price some four weeks before the horse had to be put down. [Habton Farms] should not be in any worse position than it would have been if there had been a contract simply because it transpires that it is entitled to damages for Mr Nimmo's breach of warranty of authority and not to the notional sale price against Mr Williamson.[80]

COMMENT: The obvious question to ask is why the Court took a different approach to that evidenced in *Simons v Patchett*. Auld LJ stated that where a third party accepts the principal's repudiation and sells the goods to another party (as occurred in *Simons v Patchett*), then damages will be assessed on the usual basis. However, where the third party refuses to accept the principal's repudiation and continues to demand payment (as occurred in *Habton Farms*), then the usual method of assessment may not be appropriate.[81] The majority also stressed that Habton Farms' refusal to sell the racehorse to another buyer was caused by Nimmo's breach of warranty of authority.

⭐ See CA Hopkins, 'Damages for Breach of Warranty of Authority' (2003) 62 CLJ 559

Tortious liability[82]

Consider the following example:

---

79. [2003] EWCA Civ 68, [2004] QB 1 [61] (Clarke LJ).
80. ibid [127].
81. ibid.
82. Many ordinary principles of the law of torts apply to agents in the normal way. Students may therefore wish to consult a textbook on the law of torts for more information on the torts discussed in this section.

> ### Eg ComCorp Ltd
>
> ComCorp engages an agent, BuildQuick Ltd, to erect a building that will be used as office space for ComCorp's employees. The building is completed, but part of the ceiling falls in and injures Elen, an employee of ComCorp. It transpires that the relevant portion of the ceiling was not correctly fitted.

It is likely that BuildQuick, in failing to correctly fit the ceiling, has acted in a negligent manner. The question that arises is to what extent BuildQuick is liable. Where an agent commits a tort that causes loss to a third party, is the agent liable, or is the principal liable, or are both parties liable?

In many cases involving the tortious acts of agents (especially agents who are also employees), the principal will be vicariously liable for the tortious acts of the agent, but to what extent is the agent also personally liable? The general rule is that where loss or injury is caused to a third party as a result of the tortious act/omission of an agent, then, providing that the agent was acting on behalf of his principal when the act/omission occurred, the agent will be personally liable. This will be so irrespective of whether he was acting within or outside the scope of his authority—it is no defence for the agent to claim that he was acting under the authority of his principal or, as Lord Hoffmann put it '[n]o one can escape liability for his fraud by saying: "I wish to make it clear that I am committing this fraud on behalf of someone else and that I am not to be personally liable."'[83] However, this is not always the case and there are instances where an agent may avoid liability (e.g. where the principal ratifies the tortious act).[84]

The result is that, in many cases, both the principal and agent can be liable, and the third party has the option of suing either, or both. Accordingly, to use our ComCorp example, Elen could sue ComCorp and/or BuildQuick but, given that ComCorp employs her, she might prefer instead to sue BuildQuick alone. Alternatively, if one of the companies were to become insolvent, or was able to avoid liability via an exclusion clause, she would be able to sue the other and claim damages. However, in the case of certain torts, the issue is more complex and the third party's ability to sue the agent may be more difficult, or it may not even be possible.

The tort of deceit

It is well established that an agent can be liable to a third party if he engages in the tort of deceit. The classic definition of this tort was provided by Lord Herschell, who stated that:

> in order to sustain an action in deceit, there must be proof of fraud, and nothing short of that will suffice…[F]raud is proved when it is shown that a false representation has been made, (1) knowingly, or (2) without belief in its truth, or (3) recklessly careless whether it be true or false.[85]

---

83. *Standard Chartered Bank v Pakistan National Shipping Corp (No 2)* [2002] UKHL 43, [2003] 1 AC 959, [22].
84. See e.g. *Hull v Pickersgill* (1819) 1 B&B 282. Note that, clearly, not all tortious acts can be ratified.
85. *Derry v Peek* (1889) 14 App Cas 337 (HL) 374.

From this, it follows that an agent who deliberately or recklessly misrepresents his authority can be liable to a third party in deceit.[86] However, the courts are not quick to conclude that fraud has occurred and clear evidence of fraud will be required—'[f]raud is a serious allegation and therefore the cogency of evidence required to discharge the burden of proof must reflect the seriousness of the charge'.[87] It is also important to note that the principal's knowledge or recklessness will not be projected onto the agent. Accordingly, if an agent repeats a representation made by his principal, and the principal knows the representation to be untrue, but the agent does not, then the agent will not be liable in deceit.[88]

Negligent misrepresentation

It is also clear that an agent can be found liable if he negligently misrepresents his authority. It is important to distinguish between common law negligent misrepresentation (known as negligent misstatement) and statutory negligent misrepresentation under the Misrepresentation Act 1967.

Negligent misstatement

The leading case on negligent misstatement, namely *Hedley Byrne & Co Ltd v Heller & Partners Ltd,*[89] established that, in order for negligent misstatement to arise, a duty of care needed to exist. Lord Morris stated that 'if someone possessed of a special skill undertakes, quite irrespective of contract, to apply that skill for the assistance of another person who relies upon such skill, a duty of care will arise'.[90] It follows that an agent will only be liable if he owed a duty of care to the third party and, as Lord Morris' statement indicates and as future courts have made clear, this will depend upon whether the agent has assumed a responsibility towards the third party,[91] as occurred in the following case.

 Smith v Bush [1990] 1 AC 831 (HL)

FACTS: Smith (the third party) applied to a building society (the principal) for a mortgage to help her purchase a house. The building society engaged Bush (the agent) to survey the house and report on any issues that might affect its value. Bush failed to notice that the chimneys were not adequately supported and noted in his report that no essential repairs to the property were necessary. The building society provided Smith with a mortgage and she purchased the house. Subsequently, one of the chimneys collapsed and Smith sought damages from Bush.

---

86. *Polhill v Walter* (1832) 3 B&Ad 114.
87. *Maersk Sealand v Far East Trading Côte D'Ivoire* [2004] EWHC 2929 (Comm), [8] (Nigel Teare QC).
88. *Armstrong v Strain* [1952] 1 KB 232 (CA).
89. [1964] AC 465 (HL).
90. ibid 502–3.
91. See e.g. *Spring v Guardian Assurance plc* [1995] 2 AC 296 (HL), *Henderson v Merrett Syndicates Ltd (No 1)* [1995] 2 AC 145 (HL).

> **HELD:** The House held that Bush owed the claimant a duty of care, which he had breached, and so Bush was liable to pay damages to Smith. Lord Templeman stated:
>
> > by obtaining and disclosing a valuation, a mortgagee does not assume responsibility to the purchaser for that valuation. But in my opinion the valuer assumes responsibility to both mortgagee and purchaser by agreeing to carry out a valuation for mortgage purposes knowing that the valuation fee has been paid by the purchaser and knowing that the valuation will probably be relied upon by the purchaser in order to decide whether or not to enter into a contract to purchase the house.[92]

As the courts will have regard to all the circumstances of the case, it follows that determining and predicting whether or not an agent has assumed a responsibility towards a third party is not always an easy task. The courts have attempted to provide guidance by highlighting certain factors that should be taken into account, and these have been usefully collated by Sir Brian Neill in *BCCI (Overseas) Ltd v Price Waterhouse*.[93]

- The precise relationship between the adviser and advisee.
- The precise circumstances in which the advice or information or other material came into existence. Any contract or other relationship with a third party will be relevant.
- The precise circumstances in which the advice or information or other material was communicated to the advisee, and for what purpose or purposes, and whether the communication was made by the adviser or by a third party. It will be necessary to consider the purpose or purposes of the communication both as seen by the adviser and as seen by the advisee, and the degree of reliance which the adviser intended or should reasonably have anticipated would be placed on its accuracy by the advisee, and the reliance in fact placed on it.
- The presence or absence of other advisers on whom the advisee would or could rely.
- The opportunity, if any, given to the adviser to issue a disclaimer.

What is clear is that the courts are not quick to find that a duty of care exists between an agent and third party. As Nicholls VC stated:

> caution should be exercised before the law takes the step of concluding, in any particular context, that an agent acting within the scope of his authority on behalf of a known principal, himself owes to third parties a duty of care independent of the duty of care he owes to his principal. There will be cases where it is fair, just and reasonable that there should be such a duty. But, in general, in a case where the principal himself owes a duty of care to the third party, the existence of a further duty of care, owed by the agent to the third party, is not necessary for the reasonable protection of the latter. Good reason, therefore, should exist before the law imposes a duty when the agent already owes to his principal a duty which covers the same ground and the principal is responsible to the third party for his agent's shortcomings.[94]

---

92. [1990] 1 AC 831 (HL) 847.
93. [1998] BCC 617 (CA) 634–5.
94. *Gran Gelato Ltd v Richcliff (Group) Ltd* [1992] Ch 560 (Ch) 571.

Misrepresentation Act 1967

Statutory negligent misrepresentation derives from s 2(1) of the Misrepresentation Act 1967. However, s 2(1) only applies where 'a person has entered into a contract after a misrepresentation has been made to him by another party thereto', meaning that liability can only be imposed on the parties to the contract. In the majority of cases, the agent will not be a party to the contract and so no liability under s 2(1) will lie.[95] However, if the agent is a party to the contract, then liability under s 2(1) can be imposed.

Conversion

The tort of conversion occurs where a person intentionally[96] deals with goods in a manner that is inconsistent with another person's possession, or in a way that serves to deny another person's right to immediate possession of the goods. Accordingly, if an agent deals with goods belonging to a third party in a manner that is inconsistent with that third party's rights of possession, then the tort of conversion will have been committed, unless such dealing has been authorized by that third party. Examples of the types of activity that can amount to conversion include an agent selling goods without the true owner's consent,[97] or an agent refusing to provide goods to a person who has the right to immediate possession of the goods upon demand.[98]

As the following case demonstrates, conversion is a strict liability tort and so an agent can still be liable if he obtained the goods from the principal and reasonably believed that the principal was the true owner of the goods.

 Cochrane v Rymill (1879) 40 LT 744 (CA)

FACTS: Peggs (the principal) hired a number of cabs from Cochrane (the third party). Peggs instructed an auctioneer, Rymill (the agent), to sell the cabs at auction. Rymill was unaware that Peggs did not own the goods and had no right to sell them. Rymill took possession of the goods and sold them. He deducted his commission and expenses and gave the balance to Peggs. Cochrane discovered what had occurred and commenced proceedings against Rymill.

HELD: The Court held that Rymill had converted Cochrane's goods and so was ordered to pay damages. The fact that Rymill was unaware of Peggs' lack of title was irrelevant.

COMMENT: This case clearly demonstrates that liability for conversion is strict. However, Bramwell LJ was keen to point out that if Rymill had not held possession or control of the cabs, then conversion would not have occurred. He stated:

> Supposing a man were to come into an auctioneer's yard, holding a horse by the bridle and to say, 'I want to sell my horse: if you will find a purchaser I will

---

95. *Resolute Maritime Inc v Nippon Kaiji Kyokai* [1983] 1 WLR 857 (QB).
96. It should be noted that conversion requires an intentional act—it cannot be committed by omission (*Ashby v Tolhurst* [1937] 2 KB 242 (CA)).
97. *Consolidated Co v Curtis & Son* [1892] 1 QB 495 (QB).
98. *National Mercantile Bank v Rymill* (1881) 44 LT 767 (CA).

> pay commission.' And the auctioneer says: 'Here is a man who wants to sell a horse; will anyone buy him?' If he then and there finds him a purchaser and the seller himself hands over the horse, there could be no act on the part of the auctioneer which could render him liable to an action for conversion.[99]
>
> Subsequent cases have further mitigated the strictness of the tort. For example, an agent who, in good faith, receives or holds goods on behalf of the principal, but does not deal with them, will not have committed the tort of conversion.[100] Similarly, conversion will not occur where an agent, who holds goods belonging to another, refuses to hand over the goods until the legal position has been determined.[101]

Defamation

An agent who repeats or passes on a defamatory statement made by his principal will, along with the principal, be liable to the defamed person. For example, s 1(4) of the Defamation Act 1996 provides that '[e]mployees or agents of an author, editor or publisher are in the same position as their employer or principal to the extent that they are responsible for the content of the statement or the decision to publish it'. As defamation is a tort of strict liability, it matters not that the agent (or the principal) was not aware that the statement was defamatory.

The defences contained within the Defamation Acts of 1952 and 1996 are available to an agent.[102] Certain defences, notably qualified privilege, will not apply where the statement was made with malice.[103] However, providing that the agent did not act with malice, then these defences will be available to him notwithstanding that his principal did act maliciously.[104]

Conclusion

In a typical agency relationship, where the principal is disclosed and where all the parties involved perform their obligations, no legal relationship will generally exist between the agent and third party, save the relationship created by the agent's warranty of authority, which will be of no importance providing that the agent acts within his authority. However, as has been discussed, there are numerous situations where this typical situation is displaced and the agent and/or third party can become liable on the contract and can sue the other. For all parties involved, it is crucial to understand what circumstances can give rise to such liability, so that it can be avoided.

---

99. (1879) 40 LT 744 (CA) 746.

100. *Caxton Publishing Co v Sutherland Publishing Co* [1939] AC 178 (HL).

101. *Alexander v Southey* (1821) 5 B&A 247.

102. Additional defences may be available if the Defamation Bill that is, at the time of writing, making its way through Parliament, is enacted.

103. Defamation Act 1996, s 15(1) and Sch 1.

104. *Egger v Viscount Chelmsford* [1965] 1 QB 248 (CA).

Having discussed the legal relationships between the principal, agent, and third party, Chapter 9, the final chapter on the law of agency, moves on to discuss the various ways that a relationship of agency can be terminated, and the consequences of termination.

Practice questions

1. 'The courts have failed to devise a satisfactory justification for the imposition of liability of an agent who purports to act for another, but is in fact acting on his own behalf.' Discuss.

2. Discuss whether or not the agent can sue, or be sued, in the following cases:
   - Lee, a director of ComCorp, enters into a contract of sale under which goods are to be purchased from TechCorp plc. However, Lee does not disclose whether he is acting on behalf of another. He signs the contract 'Lee, a director and agent'. TechCorp discovers that Lee is a director of ComCorp and refuses to provide the goods, as it has had prior business dealings with ComCorp that have soured the relationship between the two companies.
   - ComCorp wish to rent some office space. It contracts with John, who tells them that he owns a building that would be suitable. It transpires that John does not own the building, and the building is in fact owned by a company, of which John is managing director. Further, John does not have express actual authority to lease out the building, although he has done so in the past with the board's acquiescence. After discovering this, ComCorp find an alternative building that is more suitable, and informs John that it does not consider itself bound by the contract, and will not be honouring it.
   - ComCorp wishes to purchase office furniture. It negotiates with Francoise, an agent based in London who is acting on behalf of OfficeMart SA, a French company that supplies office furniture. A contract of sale is finalized, which Francoise signs 'Francoise, on behalf of OfficeMart SA'. It transpires that Francoise used to act as agent for OfficeMart, but the company was dissolved three months before. Francoise bought up much of OfficeMart's stock and was planning on selling it to ComCorp, without informing them that the company no longer existed.

Further reading

Roderick Munday, *Agency: Law and Principles* (OUP 2010) chs 7, 12 and pp 287–96
   - Chapter 7 focuses on an agent's liability for breach of warranty of authority, whilst chapter 12 discusses the legal relationship between the agent and third parties. Pages 287–96 analyse to what extent an agent can be liable in tort.

FMB Reynolds, '**Election Distributed**' (1970) 86 LQR 318
   - Discusses the case law relating to the doctrine of election and contends that many of the relevant cases are not in fact cases concerning election at all, but are instead concerned with contract formation.

Robert Stevens, '**Why Do Agents "Drop Out?"**' [2005] LMCLQ 101
   - Discusses the various reasons why agents do not escape liability to third parties, focusing especially on contractual and tortious liability.

Christian Twigg-Flesner, 'Full Circle: Purported Agent's Right of Enforcement Under Section 36C of the Companies Act 1985' (2001) Co Law 274

- Discusses the effect of s 36C of the Companies Act 1985 (now reproduced as s 51(1) of the Companies Act 2006) and examines whether or not the provision has properly implemented the relevant EU Directive.

Peter G Watts, *Bowstead & Reynolds on Agency* (19th edn, Sweet & Maxwell 2010) ch 9

- Provides an extremely detailed exposition of the legal relations that exist between agents and third parties.

9 Termination of authority

- Termination by act of the parties
- Termination by operation of law
- Termination of commercial agencies
- The effects of termination

INTRODUCTION

In this final chapter on the law of agency, the various methods by which the authority of an agent can be terminated will be discussed. It is important to note at the outset that the termination of the agent's authority and the termination of the agency agreement are two separate issues and, as will be seen, the termination of one may not automatically result in the termination of the other (although in many cases, it will). Consequently, it is vital to understand the effects that can arise from a termination of the agent's authority, especially as, in certain cases, the right to terminate is not accompanied by the privilege to terminate, meaning that a wrongful termination (e.g. in breach of contract) may result in the non-terminating party being awarded a remedy. Where the agent is a commercial agent, additional rights, rules, and safeguards apply, notably the commercial agent's right to compensation or an indemnity.

Numerous methods exist by which the authority of an agent can be terminated, but they can be loosely organized into two distinct categories:

1. termination by an act of the parties; or
2. termination by operation of the law.

Figure 9.1 sets out the various methods of termination that can occur under these two categories.

Termination by act of the parties

An agent's authority may be terminated by the act of one or both of the parties. It should be noted that, whilst the acts discussed in this section will usually terminate the agent's actual authority, the facts of the case might lead the court to conclude that the agent still has apparent authority to act on behalf of the principal. Termination by an act of the parties can arise in a number of different ways.

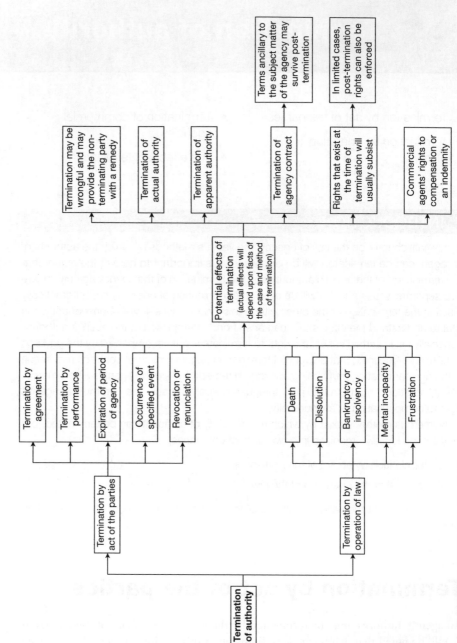

FIGURE 9.1 Termination of authority

Termination by agreement

Like any other contract, a contract of agency can be terminated upon the agreement of the principal and agent. Termination by agreement will also terminate the actual authority of the agent.

Termination by performance

The majority of terminations occur through performance. Once the agent fully performs the task he was appointed to undertake, the agency agreement and the agent's actual authority will terminate.[1]

Expiration of period of agency

The agency agreement might specify that the agent's appointment will be for a fixed period only. In such a case, the agency agreement and the agent's actual authority will terminate upon the expiration of the fixed period.[2] A notable exception to this occurs in the case of commercial agencies. Where a commercial agent is contractually appointed for a fixed period and the contract continues to be performed by both parties following the expiration of that period, then the agency contract shall not terminate and shall instead be converted into a contract of indefinite duration.[3] The significance of this will be seen when the notice periods required to terminate a commercial agency are discussed.

The notice periods required to terminate a commercial agency are discussed at p 198

In certain cases, a particular practice or trade custom might impose a particular expiry date on an agency agreement. In such cases, the expiration of that date will cause the agency agreement and the agent's actual authority to terminate, as the following case demonstrates.

Dickenson v Lilwal (1815) 1 Stark 128

FACTS: On 30 June, Lilwal (the principal) authorized a broker, Grainger (the agent), to sell a quantity of butter. On 6 July, Grainger, without any intermediate communication with Lilwal, sold a quantity of butter to Dickenson. Lilwal refused to go ahead with the sale, on the ground that Grainger was not authorized to make it. Dickenson sued Lilwal.

HELD: Lord Ellenborough stated that Lilwal was able to prove that 'according to the established practice and usage of the trade, the authority of the broker (as between himself and his principal) to sell, expires with the day on which the authority is given'.[4] Accordingly, the agency agreement and Grainger's actual authority terminated at the end of 30 June, and so Dickenson's action failed.

---

1. See e.g. *Blackburn v Scholes* (1810) 2 Camp 341; *Gillow & Co v Lord Aberdare* (1892) 9 TLR 12; *Bell v Balls* [1897] 1 Ch 663 (Ch).
2. *Danby v Coutts & Co* (1885) 29 ChD 550 (Ch).
3. Commercial Agents (Council Directive) Regulations 1993, reg 14.
4. (1815) 1 Stark 128, 130.

Occurrence of a specified event

The agency agreement might specify that, upon the occurrence of a particular event, the agency agreement will terminate. In such a case, the agreement and the agent's actual authority will terminate upon the specified event's occurrence. It has also been suggested that the agreement will also terminate upon the occurrence of an event that would lead the agent to 'reasonably infer that the principal does not or would not wish the authority to continue'.[5]

Revocation and renunciation

Consider the following example:

 ComCorp Ltd

> ComCorp engages Bruce to act as its agent. An agency agreement is drawn up which states that Bruce will act as ComCorp's agent for a period of one year, with both parties having an option to renew the agreement. After six months, Bruce's actions have significantly increased ComCorp's customer base, but Bruce informs ComCorp that, with immediate effect, he will no longer act as its agent. ComCorp states that Bruce must remain as its agent until the contract period expires and, if he refuses, ComCorp will obtain an order for specific performance requiring him to continue to act as ComCorp's agent.

As noted earlier, an agency agreement can be terminated upon the agreement of the principal and agent, but what if, as in the ComCorp example, only one party wishes to end the agreement? Can a principal or agent terminate an agency agreement without the other's consent? As a contract of agency is one for personal services, the courts have indicated that they will not compel performance via an order for specific performance.[6] It follows from this that, unless the agency is irrevocable (discussed later in this chapter), the principal may revoke the authority of the agent at any time, and the agent may renounce the authority granted to him by the principal at any time. The effect of revocation/renunciation is to terminate the agency agreement and the actual authority of the agent but, depending on the facts, the agent may continue to have apparent authority until such time as the third party has notice of the revocation/renunciation. However, whilst the parties may have the power to revoke/renounce the agent's authority, they 'may not have the liberty to exercise that power',[7] meaning that the revocation/renunciation may constitute a breach of contract (e.g. where a fixed-term contract of agency is revoked/renounced before the fixed period has expired, as occurred in the ComCorp example).

The revoking/renouncing party must provide the other party with notice of the revocation/renunciation.[8] If the agency contract does not specify a period of notice,

---

5. Peter G Watts, *Bowstead & Reynolds on Agency* (19th edn, Sweet & Maxwell 2010) [10-002].

6. *Chinnock v Sainsbury* (1860) 30 LJ Ch 409.

7. Francis Reynolds, 'When is an Agent's Authority Irrevocable?' in Ross Cranston (ed), *Making Commercial Law: Essays in Honour of Roy Goode* (Clarendon Press 1997) 259.

8. *Re Oriental Bank Corp, ex p Guillemin* (1885) LR 28 ChD 634 (Ch).

then reasonable notice must be provided, with the facts of the case determining what is reasonable. Where the agent is also an employee of the principal, then the minimum notice periods laid out by s 86(1) of the Employment Rights Act 1996 will apply. Where the agent is a commercial agent, the minimum notice periods established by reg 15(2) of the Commercial Agents (Council Directive) Regulations 1993 will apply.

Regulation 15(2) of the 1993 Regulations is discussed at p 198

Irrevocable agencies

The right to revoke is not absolute, as both case law and statute provide that certain relationships of agency are irrevocable. In such cases, the death,[9] dissolution, mental incapacity, bankruptcy, or insolvency[10] of the principal will not generally terminate the agent's authority. The principal will be unable to revoke the agent's authority, unless the agent consents to the revocation.[11] Where the agent does not provide such consent, then any attempt to terminate the agent's authority will be ineffective and will be likely to amount to a breach of contract.

Statute can provide that certain agencies are irrevocable, with two notable examples occurring in relation to the granting of powers of attorney:

1. Where a power of attorney is expressed to be irrevocable and is given to secure a proprietary interest of the donee of the power (the agent), or the performance of an obligation owed to the donee, then so long as the donee has that interest or the obligation remains unchanged, the power shall not be revoked by the donor (the principal) without the consent of the donee, or by the death, incapacity or bankruptcy of the donor or, if the donor is a body corporate, by its winding up or dissolution.[12]

2. Any lasting power of attorney created under the Mental Capacity Act 2005, and any enduring power of attorney created under the now repealed Enduring Powers of Attorney Act 1985, cannot be revoked due to the subsequent mental incapacity of the donor (the principal).[13]

The common law also provides for a number of irrevocable agencies. First, where the agent's authority is granted by deed, or for valuable consideration, for the purpose of securing or protecting an interest of the agent, then that authority cannot be revoked as long as the interest continues to exist, unless the agent consents to the revocation. It should be noted that the interest must be independent of the agency—it follows that protecting the agent's ability to earn remuneration or commission from the agency will not render that agency irrevocable. The following case provides an example of an agency agreement that is coupled with an interest that renders the agency irrevocable.

---

9. *Lepard v Vernon* (1813) 2 V&B 51.   10. *Alley v Hotson* (1815) 4 Camp 325.

11. Accordingly, it could be argued that to describe such agencies as 'irrevocable' is misleading, as the agency can be revoked providing that the agent consents.

12. Powers of Attorney Act 1971, s 4(1).

13. Mental Capacity Act 2005, s 13 and Sch 4, para 1.

Gaussen v Morton (1830) 10 B&C 731

FACTS: JL (the principal) owed Forster (the agent) £231. JL granted Forster a power of attorney, which allowed Forster to sell certain pieces of property owned by JL. Forster could then keep the proceeds of the sale to satisfy the debt owed by JL. Forster sold the property for £105 and received £20 from the purchaser by way of deposit. JL then purported to revoke the power of attorney.

HELD: The revocation was invalid as the agency was irrevocable. Lord Tenterden CJ stated that this case did not involve:

> a simple authority to sell and surrender the premises, but an authority coupled with an interest; for Forster was to apply the proceeds in liquidation of a debt due to himself...and there are several cases in which it has been held, that such an authority cannot be revoked.[14]

Second, where, in the course of an agency relationship, the agent becomes liable to a third party, and the principal is liable to indemnify the agent for such liability, then the principal cannot revoke the agent's authority without the agent's consent. If this were not the case, a principal could avoid indemnifying the agent by simply revoking the agent's authority. The following case provides an example of this form of irrevocable agency.

 Read v Anderson (1883–84) LR 13 QBD 779 (CA)

FACTS: Anderson (the principal) instructed Read (the agent) to place a number of bets on his behalf. Although the bets were placed on Anderson's behalf, Read was instructed to place them in his own name, which he did. The result was that, according to trade custom, Read became personally liable to the bookmakers for the bets placed. Read placed a number of losing bets on Anderson's behalf, and sought to obtain an indemnity from Anderson for the amounts wagered. Anderson refused to indemnify Read and stated that Read's authority had been revoked. Read initiated proceedings to recover the indemnity.

HELD: Read's claim succeeded and Anderson was required to indemnify Read for the bets placed. Bowen LJ stated that '[i]t will not be denied that if a principal employs an agent to do something which by law involves the agent in a legal liability, the principal cannot draw back and leave the agent to bear the liability at his own expense'.[15] Whilst Anderson was not liable in law to indemnify Read (because at the time gambling debts were not enforceable), the Court stated that Read would have suffered significant damage to his reputation if he did not make good on a lost bet. Accordingly, Read 'placed himself in a position of pecuniary difficulty at the defendant's request, who impliedly contracted...to indemnify him from the consequences which would ensue in the ordinary course of his business from the step which he had taken'.[16]

---

14. (1830) 10 B&C 731, 734.   15. (1883–84) LR 13 QBD 779 (CA) 783.   16. ibid.

> **COMMENT:** Although *Read v Anderson* and similar cases are discussed alongside cases of irrevocable authority, it has been argued that they are not really cases involving irrevocable authority as they do not concern the agent's authority to bind his principal to a third party. Instead, it has been argued that such cases are an example of the rule that the right to compensation or an indemnity does not extend to unauthorized acts of an agent[17]—a view that appears to have been judicially accepted.[18]

Termination by operation of law

Consider the following example:

 ComCorp Ltd

AgentCorp Ltd, a subsidiary of ComCorp, was created in order to run one of ComCorp's ancillary businesses. It was agreed that AgentCorp would act as ComCorp's agent when running these businesses.[19] Unfortunately, the management of AgentCorp is incompetent and AgentCorp soon becomes insolvent and is eventually liquidated and dissolved.

Unfortunate events may befall the principal or agent—one of them may die, or become mentally incapacitated or insolvent or, in the case of a body corporate, it may be dissolved. What effect do such events have upon the agent's authority? In such cases, the operation of law will usually terminate the agency agreement, irrespective of whether the parties desire the agreement to continue. Termination by operation of law can occur in several ways.

Death

The death of either the principal or agent will terminate the agency relationship, irrespective of whether the surviving party had notice of the other's death.[20] Where the principal dies, the actual authority of the agent will cease (unless it is irrevocable), and it is likely that his apparent authority will end too,[21] meaning that the agent may also be liable for breach of authority or breach of warranty of authority if he continues to act.[22] As the following case demonstrates, the agent will also lose

---

17. Peter G Watts, *Bowstead & Reynolds on Agency* (19th edn, Sweet & Maxwell 2010) [10-010].
18. See e.g. *Temple Legal Protection Ltd v QBE Insurance (Europe) Ltd* [2009] EWCA Civ 453, [2009] 1 CLC 553 [59] (Moore-Bick LJ).
19. It should be noted that, in the majority of cases, no agency relationship will exist between a parent company and its subsidiaries. This is a corollary of the rule that being a member is not enough per se to establish a relationship of agency (*Salomon v A Salomon and Co Ltd* [1897] AC 22 (HL)).
20. *Blades v Free* (1828) 2 B&C 167.   21. *Watson v King* (1815) 4 Camp 272.
22. *Yonge v Toynbee* [1910] 1 KB 215 (CA). It has been suggested (see e.g. Raphael Powell, *The Law of Agency* (2nd edn, Pitman 1961) 389) that such liability could be avoided via a term in the agency contract, but no case law authority exists for this view.

the right to any compensation or commission that he was entitled to for acts that occurred after the principal's death.

 Campanari v Woodburn (1854) 15 CB 400

FACTS: Campanari (the agent) agreed to sell a painting belonging to Woodburn (the principal), in return for which Campanari would receive £100. Woodburn died and the painting was subsequently sold, at a time when Campanari was not aware of Woodburn's death. The sale was confirmed by the administratrix of Woodburn's estate, but she refused to pay Campanari the £100. Campanari initiated proceedings.

HELD: The death of the principal terminated the contract of agency and '[t]he contract, after the death of the intestate, was not and could not be confirmed according to its terms'.[23] Accordingly, Campanari was not entitled to the £100.

Dissolution

The mere cessation of the agent's business will not, in itself, automatically result in the termination of a contract of agency.[24] Whether this also applies to cessation of the principal's business is unclear, although authorities indicate that the agency relationship will not be automatically terminated unless it renders the principal unable to perform its obligations.[25] What is clear is that, where the principal or agent is a partnership, limited liability partnership, or company, and it is wound up or dissolved, or where a sole proprietorship ceases to carry on business, the contract of agency will be terminated.[26] In order to recover damages, the agent will need to prove that either the principal's action in dissolving the business amounts to breach of an express term, or the contract contained an implied term providing that the principal would not deprive the agent of the opportunity to earn his commission. The courts are extremely reluctant to imply such a term.

The principal's ability to deprive his agent of the opportunity to earn commission is discussed at p 140

Bankruptcy and insolvency

Generally, the bankruptcy/insolvency of the principal terminates the agency relationship[27] (unless the agency is irrevocable) and revokes the agent's authority. The bankruptcy/insolvency of the agent does not terminate the relationship, unless it prevents him acting as an agent, or renders him unfit to perform his duties.[28]

---

23. (1854) 15 CB 400, 408 (Williams J).
24. *Triffit Nurseries v Salads Etcetera Ltd* [2000] BCC 98 (Ch), affirmed [2001] BCC 457 (CA).
25. ibid.   26. *Pacific and General Insurance Co Ltd v Hazell* [1997] BCC 400 (QB).
27. *Elliott v Turquand* (1881) 7 App Cas 79 (PC).
28. *McCall v Australian Meat Co Ltd* (1870) 19 WR 188.

Mental incapacity

In this context, a court will assess a person's mental capacity by asking was the person 'at the time the act was done of sufficient capacity to understand the nature of the act?'[29] Where the answer is no, the person will lack mental capacity. Where an agent becomes mentally incapacitated, then the agent's authority will be terminated on the ground of lack of competence.

Where a principal becomes mentally incapacitated, the agency agreement will be terminated, as will the actual authority of the agent (providing that the authority was not irrevocable),[30] irrespective of whether the agent knew of the incapacity.[31] Such a result could be extremely harsh on any third parties who contracted with the principal through an agent, but are unaware of the principal's subsequent incapacity. A measure of protection has been afforded to third parties in two ways. First, the principal can ratify the agreement if he reacquires mental capacity. Second, as the following case demonstrates, an agent's apparent authority may continue even after the principal becomes mentally incapacitated.

 Drew v Nunn (1879) 4 QBD 661 (CA)

FACTS: Nunn (the principal) had given his wife (the agent) authority to deal with Drew, and held her out as his agent. Nunn became insane and, whilst his insanity continued, the wife ordered goods from Drew. Drew was unaware of Nunn's insanity. Nunn reacquired his sanity, and refused to pay for the goods. Drew initiated proceedings and Nunn contended that his wife's authority automatically terminated when he became insane.

HELD: The Court held that the wife continued to have apparent authority to deal with Drew and so Drew was entitled to recover the cost of the goods. Brett LJ stated:

> The defendant became insane and was unable to withdraw the authority which he had conferred upon his wife: he may be an innocent sufferer by her conduct, but the plaintiff, who dealt with her bona fide, is also innocent, and where one of two persons both innocent must suffer by the wrongful act of a third person, that person making the representation which, as between the two, was the original cause of the mischief, must be the sufferer and must bear the loss. Here it does not lie in the defendant's mouth to say that the plaintiff shall be the sufferer.[32]

COMMENT: The decision has been criticized, principally on the ground that it seems to state that, in order for apparent authority to cease, the mentally incapacitated principal must inform any relevant third parties of the agent's lack of authority. Despite this, the rule that apparent authority can continue until such time as the third party becomes aware of the principal's mental incapacity remains good law. In *Drew*, it was even suggested *obiter* that the rule could apply to cases where the principal dies and the third party is unaware of the death.[33]

---

29. *Boughton v Knight* (1872–75) LR 3 P&D 64, 72 (Sir James Hannen).
30. *Drew v Nunn* (1879) 4 QBD 661 (CA).   31. *Yonge v Toynbee* [1910] 1 KB 215 (CA).
32. (1879) 4 QBD 661 (CA) 667–8.
33. ibid 668 (Brett LJ): 'Suppose that a person makes a representation which after his death is acted upon by another in ignorance that his death has happened: in my view the estate of the deceased will be bound to make good any loss, which may have occurred through acting upon that representation.'

Frustration

A contract of agency can be frustrated in the same manner as an ordinary contract. Thus, the agency relationship will be terminated where the subject matter of the agency was destroyed,[34] or where a subsequent event causes performance to become impossible, unlawful,[35] or radically different from what the parties originally contemplated.[36]

Termination of commercial agencies

The Commercial Agents (Council Directive) Regulations 1993 establish additional rules regarding the termination of commercial agency agreements.

Termination by notice

As noted earlier, either party can terminate the agency agreement by providing notice, and the 1993 Regulations preserve this rule in relation to commercial agency contracts that are concluded for an indefinite period.[37] The Regulations go further and provide for minimum periods of notice based on the length of the contract of agency, with reg 15(2) providing that:

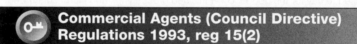

Commercial Agents (Council Directive) Regulations 1993, reg 15(2)

The period of notice shall be—

(a) 1 month for the first year of the contract;

(b) 2 months for the second year commenced;

(c) 3 months for the third year commenced and for subsequent years;

and the parties may not agree on any shorter period of notice.

As these are the minimum notice periods, it follows that the parties cannot agree on shorter notice periods, but can agree on longer notice periods if they so wish. Where the parties do agree on longer periods, then 'the period of notice to be observed by the principal must not be shorter than that to be observed by the commercial agent'.[38] Neither the Regulations nor the parent Directive specify the

---

34. *Rhodes v Forwood* (1876) LR 1 App Cas 256 (HL).   35. *Marshall v Glanvill* [1917] 2 KB 87 (KB).
36. *Davis Contractors Ltd v Fareham UDC* [1956] AC 696 (HL).
37. Commercial Agents (Council Directive) Regulations 1993, reg 15(1). Regulation 15(5) provides that this includes fixed term agency contracts that have been converted into agency contracts for an indefinite period by virtue of reg 14 (see p 191). It also provides that the earlier fixed period will also be taken into account when determining the notice period.
38. ibid reg 15(3).

appropriate remedy for breach of reg 15, and it is therefore likely that the courts will resort to domestic principles of law to determine the appropriate cause of action and remedies[39]—in practice, this will allow the innocent party to seek damages for breach of contract, but the termination will appear to remain valid.

Immediate termination

Where reg 16 applies, the minimum notice periods discussed earlier will not apply and either party will be able to terminate the agency agreement immediately. Regulation 16 states that:

 Commercial Agents (Council Directive) Regulations 1993, reg 16

These Regulations shall not affect the application of any enactment or rule of law which provides for the immediate termination of the agency contract—

(a) because of the failure of one party to carry out all or part of his obligations under that contract; or

(b) where exceptional circumstances arise.

Paragraph (a) is clearly referring to a breach of contract, although of course termination would only be valid if the breach was repudiatory.[40] It has been argued that paragraph (a) could also refer to the doctrine of frustration, but the more common belief is that frustration is covered by paragraph (b). The Regulations do not, unfortunately, provide any guidance as to what exceptional circumstances would give rise to the right to immediately terminate the agency agreement.

The effects of termination

The termination of an agent's authority can have a significant impact upon not only the agent, but also the principal and third parties. The effects of termination will depend upon the facts of the case, the type of agent, and the method of termination.

Effect on agent's authority

Generally, the termination of the agency relationship will also terminate the agent's actual authority. Where the principal revokes the agent's authority, then the agent's actual authority will not cease until such time as the agent receives notice of

---

39. See the Scottish case of *Roy v Mr Pearlman Ltd* 1999 SC 459 (Court of Session) 466 (Lord Hamilton).
40. In *Crane v Sky-In-Home Service Ltd* [2007] EWHC 66 (Ch), [2007] 2 All ER (Comm) 599 [84], Briggs J states that, as regards the 'enactment or rule of law' referred to by paragraph (a) of reg 16, '[t]he obvious candidate in English law is the doctrine of repudiatory breach'.

the revocation.[41] Even after the agent has received notice, he may still be able to act on behalf of his principal if he has apparent authority and the third party does not have notice of the revocation of the agent's actual authority.

 Trueman v Loder (1840) 11 Ad&E 589[42]

FACTS: Loder (the principal), who was based in St Petersburg, conducted business in London through Higginbotham (the agent), and this was well known amongst the business community. Loder informed Higginbotham that their relationship of agency was terminated. Subsequently, Higginbotham contracted with Trueman to sell a quantity of tallow, with the contract indicating that Higginbotham was acting on behalf of Loder (although this was an error and the agent intended to contract on his own account). Trueman never received the tallow and initiated proceedings against Loder for non-delivery of the goods.

HELD: As Trueman was unaware that the agent's authority had been revoked, Loder remained liable for Higginbotham's acts and so was liable for the non-delivery of the goods.

Where the agency ends due to the death, insolvency, bankruptcy, or mental incapacity of the principal, then the effects on the agent's authority will differ. Where the principal dies, the agency relationship and the agent's actual authority are terminated immediately (irrespective of whether the agent had notice of the principal's death),[43] and it is likely that the agent's apparent authority is also terminated.[44] It has been argued that similar reasoning should apply in cases where the principal becomes insolvent or bankrupt.[45] Where the principal becomes mentally incapacitated, the agency agreement will be immediately terminated, as will the actual authority of the agent, irrespective of whether the agent knew of the incapacity.[46] The agent's apparent authority may, however, continue following the principal's incapacity.[47]

Effect on contract of agency

Can certain terms within a contract of agency survive the termination of the agent's authority? As the following case demonstrates, the answer is yes.

---

41. *Re Oriental Bank Corp, ex p Guillemin* (1885) LR 28 ChD 634 (Ch).
42. See also *Curlewis v Birkbeck* (1863) 3 F&F 894.
43. *Blades v Free* (1828) 2 B&C 167.   44. *Watson v King* (1815) 4 Camp 272.
45. Peter G Watts, *Bowstead & Reynolds on Agency* (19th edn, Sweet & Maxwell 2010) [10-021].
46. *Yonge v Toynbee* [1910] 1 KB 215 (CA).   47. *Drew v Nunn* (1879) 4 QBD 661 (CA).

Yasuda Fire & Marine Insurance Co of Europe Ltd v Orion Marine Insurance Underwriting Agency Ltd [1995] QB 174 (QB)

FACTS: Orion acted as agent for Yasuda. A term of the agency contract stated that Yasuda had the right to inspect Orion's books and records. On several occasions, Yasuda sought to inspect the books, but was not permitted to do so on the ground that the books contained confidential information concerning other businesses that Orion was acting on behalf of. Yasuda contended that this amounted to a repudiatory breach and so it terminated the agency agreement. It then sought a declaration from the court granting it access to the records, as the books contained information relating to current business it had obtained through Orion's efforts. Orion contended that the term allowing access to the books ceased to have any effect when Yasuda terminated the agreement.

HELD: Colman J, referring to an earlier case[48] involving an arbitration clause, stated that:

> the survival of the arbitration clause in the face of an accepted repudiation is attributable to its having a contractual function ancillary to the subject matter of the contract, namely the resolution of disputes as to the parties' rights and obligations attributable to pre-existing events. There is, however, nothing in the speeches to suggest that an arbitration clause is the only kind of ancillary provision which could survive the acceptance of a repudiation.[49]

Relying on this, Colman J held that the obligation to inspect the books was ancillary to the subject matter of the agency agreement, and could therefore survive the termination of the agreement.

COMMENT: As discussed at p 136, this case also provides authority for the contention that certain duties of the agent can survive the termination of the agency agreement.

Right to remuneration, compensation, and commission

The general rule is that, upon the termination of the agent's authority, any rights that existed at the time of the termination will subsist. So, for example, if an agent is entitled to compensation, remuneration, or commission for acts undertaken prior to termination, then this entitlement will survive the termination of the agreement. Following the termination, no new rights can generally be vested, meaning that the agent cannot usually claim for future remuneration, compensation, or commission lost as a result of the termination, as the following case demonstrates.

---

48. *Heyman v Darwins Ltd* [1942] AC 356 (HL).   49. [1995] QB 174 (QB) 190.

Rhodes v Forwood (1876) LR 1 App Cas 256 (HL)

FACTS: Forwood (the agent) was appointed as the sole broker for the sale of coal from a colliery in Liverpool that belonged to Rhodes (the principal). The agreement provided that it would last for seven years, or as long as Rhodes continued to conduct business in Liverpool. After four years, Rhodes sold the colliery and the agreement was terminated. Forwood sought damages for the loss of future commission, arguing that there was an implied term that Rhodes would send coal to Liverpool to be sold by Forwood.

HELD: The action failed. Rhodes had not contracted, expressly or impliedly, to keep Forwood supplied with coal and therefore he was not liable to compensate Forwood for the commission lost due to the colliery's closure and the resulting termination of the agency agreement.

In the following case, however, the Court of Appeal distinguished *Rhodes* and held the principal liable to pay damages for commission lost due to the termination of the agency.

 Turner v Goldsmith [1891] 1 QB 544 (CA)

FACTS: A shirt manufacturer, Goldsmith (the principal), expressly agreed to employ a travelling salesman, Turner (the agent), for five years. After only two years, Goldsmith's factory was destroyed by fire and the business was not resumed. Turner commenced legal proceedings for loss of commission.

HELD: The Court distinguished *Rhodes* and awarded Turner substantial damages. In failing to send Turner a reasonable amount of clothing to sell, Goldsmith had breached the implied term not to deprive Turner of the opportunity to earn commission.

COMMENT: On what basis was *Rhodes* distinguished? In *Rhodes*, it was a term of the contract that the agent would be supplied with coal from the defendant's colliery. Conversely, in *Turner*, there was no term in the contract providing that the principal would supply the agent with clothing from the destroyed factory. The principal in *Turner* might have had other sources with which to supply the agent. Therefore, whether an agent can obtain compensation for monies lost due to the termination will depend very much on the construction of the contract—but one could question whether the distinction is significant enough to sustain such a different approach.

If the termination amounts to a breach of contract, then the innocent party may seek compensation for the breach. Where the agency is gratuitous, then damages for breach cannot be sought for obvious reasons, and the principal can terminate the agent's authority without facing any contractual liability, although the agent may be afforded a remedy under the law of restitution.

Where the agent is also an employee, he might also be entitled to compensation for wrongful or unfair dismissal. Where the agent is a commercial agent, then special rules apply which govern the agent's right to compensation or an indemnity, which are discussed next.

Effects of termination of commercial agencies

Additional safeguards and rights are provided in cases involving commercial agencies, with the most significant being the commercial agent's right to compensation or an indemnity.

Right to compensation or an indemnity

Regulation 17 provides commercial agents with the right to compensation or an indemnity for damage sustained due to the termination of the agency contract. It is worth noting at the outset the conflict that led to reg 17 covering both compensation and indemnities. When the Directive that led to the 1993 Regulations was being discussed, a significant conflict arose between the French and German approaches to the issue. France advocated that the agent should be able to obtain compensation, whereas the German approach was based on the agent obtaining an indemnity. This conflict was resolved by allowing Member States to choose whether to allow the agent to obtain compensation and/or an indemnity, and the UK decided to provide for both. As will be seen, when the calculation of compensation is discussed, the conflict inherent in reg 17 has also come to affect the development of domestic law.

Before the extent of this right is discussed, it is important to explain what forms of termination are covered by reg 17, but, unfortunately, the Regulations do not provide much guidance, aside from stating that the right to compensation or an indemnity will apply where the agency contract is terminated due to the death of the commercial agent.[50] Although not stated by the Regulations, it is clear that the termination by the principal of an agency contract of indefinite duration will constitute a termination for the purposes of reg 17 on the ground that the objective of the Regulations' parent Directive 'plainly requires it'.[51] Where the contract is for a fixed period, or the contract provides that it will terminate upon the agent reaching a certain age, it would be assumed that the right contained in reg 17 will not apply because 'the agent has taken on a fixed period contract and in doing so might be expected to have calculated whether or not he would receive adequate recompense for his outlay'.[52] However, this is not the case and in *Tigana Ltd v Decoro Ltd*,[53] Davis J stated that the word 'termination' simply meant 'the coming to an end'[54]—a view that has since been affirmed by the Court of Appeal.[55] Accordingly, the expiry of a fixed period agency contract will constitute a termination for the purposes of reg 17, unless it is subsequently renewed.[56]

To understand why the Regulations provide commercial agents with the right to compensation or an indemnity, consider the following example:

---

50. Commercial Agents (Council Directive) Regulations 1993, reg 17(8).
51. Peter G Watts, *Bowstead & Reynolds on Agency* (19th edn, Sweet & Maxwell 2010) [11-040].
52. ibid [11-041].   53. [2003] EWHC 23 (QB), [2003] ECC 23.   54. ibid [75].
55. *Light v Ty Europe Ltd* [2003] EWCA Civ 1238, [2004] 1 Lloyd's Rep 693.
56. *Moore v Piretta PTA Ltd* [1998] CLC 992 (QB).

ComCorp Ltd

ComCorp wishes to expand its customer sales base and engages Manjot (the agent) to canvass potential customers and provide their details to ComCorp. In return for this, Manjot will be paid commission for each sale made. Manjot provides ComCorp with a list of potential new customers, whereupon ComCorp terminates the agency agreement and negotiates directly with these potential customers, thereby purporting to deny Manjot the commission he claims to be entitled to.

To prevent principals taking advantage of their commercial agents in this way, the Regulations provide commercial agents with the right to compensation or an indemnity upon termination of the agency agreement. In effect, principals have to buy their way out of the agency agreement. Regulation 17(2) provides that the commercial agent shall be entitled to compensation rather than an indemnity, unless the agency contract states otherwise. Accordingly, the agent's right to compensation will be discussed first.

Regulation 17(6) provides that:

 Commercial Agents (Council Directive) Regulations 1993, reg 17(6)

… the commercial agent shall be entitled to compensation for the damage he suffers as a result of the termination of his relations with his principal.

In order to understand the operation of reg 17(6), two questions need to be answered. The first question is what types of 'damage' are compensatable under reg 17(6). A partial answer to this question can be found in reg 17(7), which states that:

> damage shall be deemed to occur particularly when the termination takes place in either or both of the following circumstances, namely circumstances which—
>
> (a) deprive the commercial agent of the commission which proper performance of the agency contract would have procured for him whilst providing his principal with substantial benefits linked to the activities of the commercial agent; or
> (b) have not enabled the commercial agent to amortize the costs and expenses that he had incurred in the performance of the agency contract on the advice of his principal.

The use of the word 'particularly' would indicate that reg 17(7) does not provide an exhaustive list of the types of damage that are compensatable, and the High Court has confirmed that reg 17(7) 'does not delimit the kind of loss for which compensation may be awarded'.[57] Accordingly, it appears that compensation will be available for other types of damage, providing that the commercial agent can establish a causal link between the termination and the damage sustained.

---

57. *Tigana Ltd v Decoro Ltd* [2003] EWHC 23 (QB), [2003] ECC 23 [96] (Davis J).

The second question is how compensation under reg 17 is calculated. As noted earlier, the concept of providing an agent with compensation upon termination of agency derived from French law. The question that arose was whether UK law should follow the French approach to calculating compensation, or whether it could devise its own approach. Earlier cases[58] adopted the French approach on the ground that 'the primary purpose of the Directive is the harmonisation of community law by requiring all member states to introduce rights and duties similar to those already subsisting in at least two of the member states of the Community'.[59]

Later cases[60] moved away from the French approach and stated that the UK was free to devise its own method of calculating compensation, a view that has since been confirmed by the Court of Justice when it stated:

> It must be observed that although the system established by article 17 of the Directive is mandatory and prescribes a framework…it does not give any detailed indications as regards the method of calculation of the indemnity for termination of contract…Therefore…within the framework prescribed by article 17(2) of the Directive, the Member States enjoy a margin of discretion which they may exercise.[61]

It has now been settled by the House of Lords that 'the method of calculation is a matter for each Member State to decide',[62] and so the UK is free to devise its own method of calculating compensation. Whilst such an approach will afford considerable flexibility, it has been argued that such an approach 'raises wider questions as to the effectiveness of this Directive as a tool for harmonisation of European private law.'[63] Nevertheless, that law is (for the time being) settled and so the question to ask is what method of calculation have the UK courts devised?

 Lonsdale (t/a Lonsdale Agencies) v Howard & Hallam Ltd [2007] UKHL 32

FACTS: Lonsdale acted as a commercial agent for Howard & Hallam Ltd ('H&H'). H&H manufactured shoes, which Lonsdale then sold to retailers on H&H's behalf. Sales declined sharply—in 1997/98, Lonsdale earned almost £17,000 in commission, but by 2002/03, this had fallen to £9,621. H&H ceased trading and terminated Lonsdale's agency by providing

---

58. See e.g. *King v T Tunnock Ltd* [2001] ECC 6 (Court of Session), *Ingmar GB Ltd v Eaton Leonard Inc* [2001] CLC 1825 (QB).

59. *Moore v Piretta PTA Ltd* [1998] CLC 992 (QB) 994 (John Mitting QC, sitting as Deputy High Court judge). The judge was referring to Germany (from where the indemnity provisions derived) and France (from where the compensation principles derived).

60. See e.g. *Barrett McKenzie & Co Ltd v Escada (UK) Ltd* [2001] EuLR 567 (QB); *Tigana Ltd v Decoro Ltd* [2003] EWHC 23 (QB), [2003] ECC 23,

61. Case C-465/04 *Honeyvem Informazioni Commerciali Srl v Mariella De Zotti* [2006] ECR I-02879, paras 34–36.

62. *Lonsdale (t/a Lonsdale Agencies) v Howard & Hallam Ltd* [2007] UKHL 32, [2007] 1 WLR 2055, [17] (Lord Hoffmann).

63. Séverine Saintier, 'Final Guidelines on Compensation of Commercial Agents' (2008) 124 LQR 31, 37. The European Commission's Action Plan on *A More Coherent European Contract Law* (Com (2003) 68 final) [18] also criticized the Directive for having 'two different legislative approaches in one and the same directive'.

reasonable notice. H&H paid Lonsdale £7,500 in compensation under reg 17(6), but Lonsdale contended that he was entitled to £19,670 (this figure being based on the French method of calculating compensation). Lonsdale initiated proceedings against H&H.

HELD: The House held that it was not bound to adopt the French approach (as discussed earlier), but could devise its own method of calculation. Lord Hoffmann stated that compensation should be calculated based on a valuation of the agency business, and approved Bowers J's statement that 'one is valuing the agency and its connections that have been established by the agent at the time at or immediately before termination, and it is really a question of compensating for the notional value of that agency in the open market'.[64] For this purpose, the courts would assume that the agency would continue and would therefore also need to value 'the income stream which the agency would have generated'.[65] Lord Hoffmann also stated that where a business is failing (as was the case here), the value of the agency and, consequently, the value of the compensation should be reduced. Accordingly, Lonsdale received £5,000 compensation.

COMMENT: The House's decision in *Lonsdale* has proven controversial and has been criticized on several grounds. First, it has been argued that the case will have significant cost implications, as expert evidence may be required to obtain an accurate valuation. In many cases, the claims involved might not justify the expense of obtaining a valuation. Lord Hoffmann himself expressed concern regarding such costs, but countered the criticism by stating that 'once it is firmly understood that the compensation is for the loss of the value of the agency, relatively few cases will go to court'.[66] Second, it has been argued that reducing compensation based on the failings of the business 'blurs the distinction between compensation and indemnity'[67] (as discussed in the next section, if a principal goes out of business, no indemnity will be payable) and that '[l]egal advisors on both sides may struggle to understand why aspects of indemnity now apply to compensation'.[68] Finally, it has been contended that the valuation method advocated by Lord Hoffmann is based on assumptions that are not accurate in practice, namely that a market for the buying and selling of commercial agencies exists, which can be used as the basis of a valuation. In fact, no such market exists because usually '[c]ommercial agencies are not assignable by the agent because they are by their nature personal to the agent'.[69] It follows that any valuation will be extremely speculative.

★ See Séverine Saintier, 'Final Guidelines on Compensation of Commercial Agents' (2008) 124 LQR 31

Where the agency contract provides that the commercial agent is entitled to an indemnity, then the key provision is reg 17(3), which provides that:

64. *Barrett McKenzie & Co Ltd v Escada* (UK) Ltd [2001] EuLR 567 (QB) 575, approved by Lord Hoffmann at [2007] UKHL 32, [2007] 1 WLR 2055 [28], although he did raise concern about the use of the word 'notional' and stated that '[a]ll that is notional is the assumption that the agency was available to be bought and sold at the relevant date'.

65. [2007] UKHL 32, [2007] 1 WLR 2055 [12] (Lord Hoffmann).

66. ibid [35] (Lord Hoffmann).

67. Séverine Saintier, 'Final Guidelines on Compensation of Commercial Agents' (2008) 124 LQR 31, 36.

68. Laura Macgregor, 'Compensation for Commercial Agents: An End to Plucking Figures from the Air?' (2008) 12 Edin LR 86, 92.

69. Andrew McGee, 'Termination of a Commercial Agency: The Agent's Rights' [2011] 8 JBL 782, 792.

Commercial Agents (Council Directive) Regulations 1993, reg 17(3)

… the commercial agent shall be entitled to an indemnity if and to the extent that—

(a) he has brought the principal new customers or has significantly increased the volume of business with existing customers and the principal continues to derive substantial benefits from the business with such customers; and

(b) the payment of this indemnity is equitable having regard to all the circumstances and, in particular, the commission lost by the commercial agent on the business transacted with such customers.

It is clear from reg 17(3)(a) that the primary purpose of the indemnity is to allow the agent to recover a sum in return for the increase of business that the principal enjoys (and may continue to enjoy) due the agent's efforts. It follows from this that 'if the principal went out of business and therefore derived no benefit from the customers introduced by the agent, no indemnity will be payable'.[70] Where an indemnity is payable, then the amount is limited to:

a figure equivalent to an indemnity for one year calculated from the commercial agent's average annual remuneration over the preceding five years and if the contract goes back less than five years the indemnity shall be calculated on the average for the period in question.[71]

The payment of an indemnity will not prevent the commercial agent from seeking damages.[72] So, for example, where, in breach of contract, the principal terminates the agency contract, then the agent could seek an indemnity for the business generated by his activities, and damages for the principal's breach of contract.

In four situations, the commercial agent's right to compensation or an indemnity will be lost:

1. If, within one year of the agency contract being terminated, the commercial agent has not notified the principal that he intends to pursue his entitlement to compensation or an indemnity, then the right to compensation or an indemnity will be lost.[73]

2. Where the principal has terminated the contract of agency because of an act attributable to the agent that would justify the immediate termination of the agency contract under reg 16, then the right to compensation or an indemnity will be lost.[74] In relation to this situation, the expiration of an agency contract due to the passing of time (e.g. where a fixed-term contract has expired) will not prevent the agent from obtaining compensation or an indemnity,[75] as the contract has not been terminated by the principal, nor was termination due to the act of the agent. Regulation 16 is discussed at p 199

---

70. *Lonsdale (t/a Lonsdale Agencies) v Howard & Hallam Ltd* [2007] UKHL 32, [2007] 1 WLR 2055 [20] (Lord Hoffmann).
71. Commercial Agents (Council Directive) Regulations 1993, reg 17(4).
72. ibid reg 17(5).   73. ibid reg 17(9).   74. ibid reg 18(a).
75. *Cooper v Pure Fishing (UK) Ltd* [2004] EWCA Civ 375, [2004] 2 Lloyd's Rep 518 [15] (Tuckey LJ).

3. Where the agency contract is terminated by the commercial agent, then the right to compensation or an indemnity will be lost, unless the termination is justified (a) by circumstances attributable to the principal; or (b) on the grounds of age, infirmity, or illness of the commercial agent in consequence of which he cannot reasonably be required to continue his activities.[76]

4. Where the commercial agent, with the agreement of his principal, assigns his rights and duties under the agency contract to another person, then the commercial agent's right to compensation or an indemnity will be lost.[77]

Finally, it should be noted that neither party can derogate from the provisions of regs 17 or 18 to the detriment of the commercial agent before the contract of agency expires.[78] From this, it follows that the parties can agree terms that are more favourable to the commercial agent if they so choose.

Restraint of trade

Where an agreement seeks to impose upon a commercial agent a restraint of trade clause, then it will be subject to a number of general contractual common law rules which are unaffected by the Regulations.[79] Regulation 20(1) imposes two additional requirements by providing that a restraint of trade clause will be valid only if and to the extent that:

(a) it is concluded in writing; and

(b) it relates to the geographical area or the group of customers and the geographical area entrusted to the commercial agent and to the kind of goods covered by his agency under the contract.

It is contended that reg 20(1) adds little to the common law. The requirement for the contract to be in writing is new but, in practice, restraint of trade clauses are almost always found in writing, usually within the terms of the agency contract itself. It has also been argued that the requirements found in (b) are 'broadly in accord with the common law rules'.[80] Further, it has been contended that the limitation imposed by reg 20(2), namely that a restraint of trade clause will not be valid for more than two years after the termination of the agency contract, may also be covered under the common law requirement of reasonableness.[81]

---

76. Commercial Agents (Council Directive) Regulations 1993, reg 18(b).
77. ibid reg 18(c).   78. ibid reg 19.   79. ibid reg 20(3).
80. Peter G Watts, *Bowstead & Reynolds on Agency* (19th edn, Sweet & Maxwell 2010) [11-056].
81. ibid.

Conclusion

The law relating to the termination of an agent's authority can be complex, due to the variety of methods of termination that exist. Some methods of termination are consensual, but many are not. Some methods will terminate the agency agreement and the agent's authority, while others will not. Some can be exercised without fear of legal reproach, but others will result in the terminating party committing some form of legal wrong. It is, however, vital that the parties to an agency agreement understand not only how the authority of an agent can be terminated, but also the potential effects that can arise from a termination.

This concludes the discussion of the law of agency. The next part of this text will focus on the law relating to the sale of goods, but there can be a significant overlap between the two areas of law, notably in cases where the principal appoints an agent to effect a contract of sale. In such a case, the validity of the agreement or the liability of the parties may be a matter for the law of agency and the law relating to the sale of goods.

Practice questions

1. Define the following terms:

   - irrevocable agency;
   - renunciation;
   - dissolution;
   - indemnity;
   - restraint of trade clause.

2. 'The decision of the House of Lords in *Lonsdale v Howard & Hallam Ltd* has had a detrimental impact upon the harmonisation of law in relation to commercial agents, and has blurred the distinction between compensation and an indemnity.'

   Do you agree with this quote? Provide reasons for your answers.

3. For each of the following situations, discuss where appropriate: (i) whether or not the authority of the agent and the agency agreement have been effectively terminated; and (ii) if termination has occurred, when did it occur and what will be the likely effects of termination:

   - John agrees to act as an agent for ComCorp. After 14 months have passed, ComCorp informs John that his authority will be terminated in one month's time. Five weeks later, John purports to enter into a contract on ComCorp's behalf.
   - Millie is an agent acting on behalf of ComCorp on a fixed-term contract. However, upon the expiration of the contract period, Millie continues to purport to act on behalf of ComCorp, including entering into a number of contracts purportedly on ComCorp's behalf.
   - ComCorp decides to sell a vacant office building that it owns. It engages an agent to sell the property on its behalf. A day later, the factory in question burns down and is destroyed.
   - ComCorp is experiencing severe financial difficulties and engages an agent to canvass new overseas customers. Whilst the agent is overseas, the directors of ComCorp decide to cease business and liquidate the company. The agent, who is unaware of the company's liquidation, subsequently enters into a number of contracts on behalf of ComCorp.

Further reading

Andrew McGee, 'Termination of a Commercial Agency: The Agent's Rights' [2011] 8
JBL 782
* Critically analyses the law in relation to a commercial agent's right to compensation or
an indemnity, with particular emphasis on the House of Lords decision in *Lonsdale v
Howard & Hallam Ltd*.

Roderick Munday, *Agency: Law and Principles* (OUP 2010) ch 13
* Provides a clear and accessible, yet detailed, account of the law relating to the
termination of agency.

Francis Reynolds, 'When is an Agent's Authority Irrevocable?' in Ross Cranston (ed),
Making Commercial Law: Essays in Honour of Roy Goode (Clarendon Press 1997) 259
* Discusses in detail those instances when the authority of an agent is deemed to be
irrevocable.

Séverine Saintier, *Commercial Agency Law: A Comparative Analysis* (Ashgate 2002) 242–60
* This text focuses on the Commercial Agents Directive and its implementation by the
UK and France, which is especially useful in relation to a commercial agent's right to
compensation or an indemnity. Pages 242–60 discuss the termination of commercial
agencies.

Séverine Saintier, 'Final Guidelines on Compensation of Commercial Agents' (2008) 124
LQR 31
* Critically evaluates the case of *Lonsdale v Howard & Hallam Ltd* and argues that the
approach adopted by the House of Lords raises questions about the effectiveness of
the EU's attempts to harmonize the law in this area.

Peter G Watts, *Bowstead & Reynolds on Agency* (19th edn, Sweet & Maxwell 2010) chs 10
and [11-035]–[11-056]
* The definitive text on the law of agency. Chapter 10 discusses the termination of
non-commercial agencies, whereas [11-035]–[11-056] discusses the termination of
commercial agencies.

PART III

The law relating to the domestic sale of goods

10 An introduction to the sale of goods

- Historical developments in sale of goods law

- Contract of sale of goods

- Distinguishing different kinds of transaction

- Sales and agreements to sell

- Specific goods and unascertained goods

- Existing goods and future goods

- The price

INTRODUCTION

The law relating to the sale of goods lies at the very heart of commercial law. Embracing both business and consumer contracts, it covers an almost endless range of transactions from the simple purchase of a bottle of milk costing less than £1 to a complex deal involving the purchase of a fleet of aircraft costing hundreds of millions of pounds. It regulates sales of different kinds from domestic retail to cross-border Internet transactions. Sale of goods law also lies at the heart of other aspects of commercial law, such as the law of agency (which is discussed in Chapters 3–9), where agents are often appointed solely for the purpose of selling their principal's goods. Contracts for finance and for insurance are further examples of transactions that often depend on the sale of goods for their entire purpose.

It is important not to lose sight of the fact that a contract of sale is a contract, albeit one with special features. Therefore, all elements of establishing the contract must be present; these being offer, acceptance, consideration,[1] certainty, and the intention to create legal relations. In certain situations, a relationship that has been created by legal compulsion is not contractual and therefore cannot amount to a contract of sale. Thus, for example, there is no contract of sale where a hospital dispenses medicine to an outpatient even where the patient pays the statutory prescription charge.[2] The relationship in such a case is a statutory one: the hospital is statutorily obliged to supply the medicine and the patient is similarly entitled to receive it.

---

1. Although, as we will shortly see, the consideration required for a contract of sale is fundamentally different to that at common law.

2. *Pfizer Corporation v Ministry of Health* [1965] AC 512 (HL).

Historical developments in sale of goods law

Prior to the original Sale of Goods Act 1893 (SGA 1893), contracts of sale were regulated by the common law. The purpose of the 1893 Act was to codify these common law principles and, following disquiet about the lack of a uniform law of sale throughout the UK, to assimilate Scottish law on the subject, which had until then had its roots in Roman law.

At one time, contracts of sale valued at £10 or higher had to be evidenced by 'a note or memorandum in writing',[3] and this requirement was only abolished in 1954.[4] The move to loosen the grip on the formality of these contracts continued into the Sale of Goods Act 1979 (SGA 1979), which, by s 4(1), provides that 'a contract of sale may be made in writing (either with or without seal), or by word of mouth, or partly in writing and partly by word of mouth, or may be implied from the conduct of the parties'.

The key piece of legislation regulating contracts of sale is now the SGA Act 1979, which consolidates (with some additional amendments) both the 1893 Act and amendments made to it prior to 1979. One such amendment is the Supply of Goods (Implied Terms) Act 1973, which regulates the rules relating to clauses purporting to exclude a seller's liability for the statutory implied terms contained in ss 12–15 of the 1893 Act. The SGA 1979 has itself been the subject of significant amendments by way of the Sale and Supply of Goods Act 1994, the Sale of Goods (Amendment) Acts 1994 and 1995, and more recently, in respect of consumer sales, by the Sale and Supply of Goods to Consumers Regulations 2002.[5] Other legislation relevant to contracts of sale, such as the Factors Act 1889, the Unfair Contract Terms Act 1977, and the Unfair Terms in Consumer Contracts Regulations 1999, will be discussed in the appropriate chapters.

Since the SGA 1893 is a codifying statute, the importance of previous case law is much less important, although by no means entirely irrelevant. In *Bank of England v Vagliano Brothers*,[6] Lord Herschell explained that the proper course for interpreting such a statute was:

> in the first instance to examine the language of the statute and to ask what is its natural meaning, uninfluenced by any considerations derived from the previous state of the law, and not to start with inquiring how the law previously stood, and then, assuming that it was probably intended to leave it unaltered, to see if the words of the enactment will bear an interpretation in conformity with this view. If a statute, intended to embody in a code a particular branch of the law, is to be treated in this fashion, it appears to me that its utility will be almost entirely destroyed, and the very object with which it was enacted will be frustrated. The purpose of such a statute surely was that on any point specifically

---

3. SGA 1893, s 4(1). It has been said that this requirement enabled a man to break a promise with impunity because it was not written down with sufficient formality (see the observations of Stephen J (1885) 1 LQR 1).

4. Law Reform (Enforcement of Contracts) Act 1954, s 2.

5. SI 2002/3045, implementing Directive 1999/44/EC. The amendments came into force on 31 March 2003.

6. [1891] AC 107 (HL).

dealt with by it, the law should be ascertained by interpreting the language used instead of, as before, by roaming over a vast number of authorities in order to discover what the law was, extracting it by a minute critical examination of the prior decisions.[7]

Lord Herschell was, of course, speaking only of the interpretation of a point that was dealt with by the statute. Where the point in question is not covered, then the previous decisions remain binding in the ordinary way. Lord Herschell qualified the statement for certain exceptional situations, for example, where the provisions are ambiguous or where a technical term had been used and, in such cases, resort to the previous cases would be legitimate. His Lordship explained:

> I am of course far from asserting that resort may never be had to the previous state of the law for the purpose of aiding in the construction of the provisions of the code. If, for example, a provision be of doubtful import, such resort would be perfectly legitimate. Or…if…words be found which have previously acquired a technical meaning, or been used in a sense other than their ordinary one … the same interpretation might well be put upon them in the code. I give these as examples merely; they, of course, do not exhaust the category. What, however, I am venturing to insist upon is, that the first step taken should be to interpret the language of the statute, and that an appeal to earlier decisions can only be justified on some special ground.[8]

Subsequent cases have not always adhered to Lord Herschell's *dictum*,[9] but even where they have,[10] it is submitted that disregarding the previous body of case law could lead to uncertainty and arbitrary decisions. For example, in *Rogers v Parish (Scarborough) Ltd*,[11] the Court of Appeal declined to consider the pre-Act authorities when considering whether or not a Range Rover was of merchantable quality. Although the SGA 1979 professed to 'define' merchantable quality, it did little more than to provide a structure[12] against which it might have been hoped the previous authorities might have been helpful.

The SGA 1979 codifies only the special rules of law pertaining to contracts of sale and expressly leaves intact the general principles of contract law which, by s 62(2), provide that:

> the rules of the common law, including the law merchant, except in so far as they are inconsistent with the provisions of this Act, and in particular the rules relating to the law of principal and agent and the effect of fraud, misrepresentation, duress or coercion, mistake, or other invalidating cause, apply to contracts for the sale of goods.

---

7. ibid 144.   8. ibid 145.

9. See, for example, the *dictum* of Lord Diplock in *Ashington Piggeries Ltd v Christopher Hill Ltd* [1972] AC 441 (HL) 501.

10. For example, in *Rogers v Parish (Scarborough) Ltd* [1987] QB 933 (CA).

11. [1987] QB 933 (CA).

12. Section 14(6) as originally enacted provided that 'Goods of any kind are of merchantable quality … if they are as fit for the purpose or purposes for which goods of that kind are commonly bought as it is reasonable to expect having regard to any description applied to them, the price (if relevant) and all the other relevant circumstances.'

Contract of sale of goods

The provisions of the SGA 1979 only apply to those transactions that fall within the Act's definition of a 'contract of sale of goods', which is defined by s 2(1).

 SGA 1979, s 2(1)

> A contract of sale of goods is a contract by which the seller transfers or agrees to transfer the property in goods to the buyer for a money consideration, called the price.

A contract of sale may take place between one part owner and another[13] and may be absolute or conditional.[14]

Property in goods

The 'property in goods' referred to in s 2(1) means, for these purposes, ownership. So, to transfer the property in goods simply means to transfer ownership in them.

Goods

'Goods' are defined in s 61(1) of the SGA 1979 as including 'all personal chattels other than things in action and money'. A 'personal chattel' is something physical such as a chair, television, or hat. Land and houses are not personal chattels but are 'real property'. Industrial growing crops and things attached to or forming part of the land which are agreed to be severed before sale or under the contract of sale are deemed to be goods. A 'thing in action' is an intangible right enforceable by legal action. It has no intrinsic value and its value derives from the right to sue in respect of it. Examples of things in action include cheques, shares in companies, patents, and copyrights. By way of illustration, a cheque for £100 has no intrinsic worth in the sense that the paper is not worth £100, but it gives the recipient the right to sue for the money if unpaid.

Computer software

Of particular importance in modern times is whether or not computer software constitutes 'goods' for the purpose of the SGA 1979.[15] Such items, of course, did not exist when the original SGA was passed in 1893, and even by 1979 computers and programs were much of a rarity. There is no reason to suppose that purchasers of computer software have any different expectations of fulfilment than purchasers of any other items (including the computers on which the software is installed), yet it remains somewhat uncertain whether or not 'goods' includes computer software and programs. Consequently, whereas the parties to a contract of sale of goods can state

---

13. SGA 1979, s 2(2).   14. ibid s 2(3).

15. For an excellent discussion on the subject, see Sarah Green and Djakhongir Saidov, 'Software as Goods' [2007] JBL 161.

with reasonable certainty their rights and obligations, parties to the sale of software are denied such certainty. The following case offers some guidance.

 St Albans City and District Council v International Computers Ltd [1996] 4 All ER 481 (CA)

FACTS: St Albans City and District Council ('St Albans') purchased from International Computers Ltd ('ICL') a software system that was designed to administer the collection of poll tax. The software incorrectly estimated the population of the local authority's area, with the result that the poll tax rate was set too low and St Albans received £484,000 less than it ought to have. St Albans also had to pay an additional £685,000 in precept payments to Hertfordshire County Council. St Albans sought compensation from ICL on the ground that the implied terms as to quality and fitness had been breached. Whether or not these implied terms applied depended on whether the software was 'goods' for the purpose of the SGA 1979.

HELD: Sir Iain Glidewell stated that it was necessary to distinguish between the program and the disk carrying the program. He stated, *obiter*, that although the disk clearly fell within the definition of goods, the program itself did not. A more difficult question is whether a disk will be deemed to be defective if the program encoded on it is defective so that the computer cannot perform its intended task. His Lordship provided the following example:

> Suppose I buy an instruction manual on the maintenance and repair of a particular make of car. The instructions are wrong in an important respect. Anybody who follows them is likely to cause serious damage to the engine of his car. In my view, the instructions are an integral part of the manual. The manual including the instructions, whether in a book or a video cassette, would in my opinion be 'goods' within the meaning of the 1979 Act, and the defective instructions would result in a breach of the implied terms [as to quality and fitness for purpose].[16]

He went on to explain that there was no logical reason why this should not also apply in relation to a computer disk onto which a program designed and intended to enable a computer to achieve particular functions has been encoded, so that if the disk was sold by the computer manufacturer, and the program was defective, there would *prima facie* be a breach of the terms as to quality and fitness for purpose implied by the SGA 1979. However, in this case, the defective program was neither sold nor hired. An employee of ICL went to the Council's premises where the computer was installed, taking with him a disk on which the new program had been encoded, and transferred the program onto the computer. As the program itself did not constitute 'goods' within the meaning of the SGA 1979, the transfer of the program in the way described did not constitute a transfer of goods. Consequently, there was no statutory implication of terms as to quality or fitness for purpose.

COMMENT: Based upon Sir Iain Glidewell's statement, software that was downloaded or transferred from one computer to another would not appear to qualify as goods. This approach has been criticized, with one commentator stating that Sir Iain Glidewell's statement:

★ See Sarah Green
and Djakhongir Saidov,
'Software as Goods'
[2007] JBL 161

leads to the conclusion that a disappointed consumer's rights in respect of defective software depend on the way the software is delivered—which would be rather like giving the purchasers of a washing-machine different rights depending on whether they had the machine delivered or took it home from the shop themselves, a bizarre result.[17]

Having held that the statutory implied terms as to quality and fitness for purpose did not apply to the contract, Sir Iain Glidewell went on to consider whether similar terms should be implied at common law into a contract for the transfer of a computer program absent the transfer of a disk or any other tangible thing on which the program is encoded. His Lordship observed that the terms implied by the SGA 1979 were originally developed by the courts of common law and have since, by analogy, been implied by the courts into other types of contract. The basis upon which a court is justified in implying a term into a contract in which it has not been expressed is strict and was summarized by the House of Lords in *Trollope & Colls Ltd v North West Metropolitan Regional Hospital Board*[18] in the following terms:

> An unexpressed term can be implied if and only if the court finds that the parties must have intended that term to form part of their contract; it is not enough for the court to find that such a term would have been adopted by the parties as reasonable men if it had been suggested to them; it must have been a term that went without saying, a term which, though tacit, formed part of the contract which the parties made for themselves.[19]

Consequently, Sir Iain Glidewell held that a contract for the transfer onto a computer of a program intended by both parties to enable the computer to achieve specified functions was, absent any express term as to quality or fitness for purpose, or of any term to the contrary, subject to an implied term at common law that the program will be capable of achieving the intended purpose. Similarly, in *Watford Electronics Ltd v Sanderson CFL Ltd*,[20] a case concerning the licensing rather than the sale of software,[21] the Court of Appeal held that, as no sale had taken place and the SGA 1979 did not therefore apply, so as to statutorily imply terms as to quality and fitness for purpose, similar terms would be implied at common law.

It is also necessary to consider the terms of the contract to identify precisely the nature of the transaction. Even in cases where the disk is sold, it does not necessarily follow that the software is also sold. In fact, in many cases the software is not sold, but merely licensed. In *Mayor & Burgesses of the London Borough of Southwark v IBM UK Ltd*,[22] the contract stipulated that title, copyright, and all other proprietary rights in the software remained vested in the manufacturer. The purchaser merely had a licence to use it. The Court held that there was no transfer of property in goods for the purpose of the SGA 1979, and as a consequence the Act did not apply to the contract. As Akenhead J explained:

---

17. Steve Hedley, 'Defective Software in the Court of Appeal' (1997) 56 CLJ 21, 23.

18. [1973] 1 WLR 601 (HL).   19. ibid 609 (Lord Pearson).

20. [2001] EWCA Civ 317, [2001] 1 All ER (Comm) 696.

21. Which is extremely common in software transactions.   22. [2011] EWHC 549 (TCC).

A preliminary question to consider is whether the…contract was a contract for the sale of goods at all. That involves a consideration first as to whether under section 2(1) there was to be a transfer' of 'property in goods' and secondly whether 'goods' were being sold. I have formed the view that there was here no 'transfer' of property in goods for the purposes of the 1979 Act. What was provided by IBM was in effect a licence…to use the software and, therefore, there is no transfer of property…[The contract] specifically talks about 'title, copyright and all other proprietary rights in the software' remaining vested in [the manufacturer]. Because copyright is identified as a specific right being retained, the use of the words 'title' and 'other proprietary rights' suggests strongly that ownership rights are retained.[23]

As Akenhead J found that there was no transfer of property, he did not need to consider whether computer software constituted 'goods' for the purpose of the SGA 1979. However, helpfully, he went on to consider this question, which will be important in cases where the arrangement between the parties does involve the transfer of property to the buyer. He stated *obiter* that, in principle, software could be 'goods' because:

(a) Although a CD with nothing on it is worth very little, there is no restriction in the SGA 1979 on any goods being excluded from the Act by reason of their low value. CDs are physical objects and there is no reason why they should not be considered as goods.

(b) The fact that a CD is impressed with electrons to add functions and values to it simply gives a CD a particular attribute. Thus, if a customer buys a music CD with a Beethoven symphony or a Mumford & Sons album on it, it must be 'goods' and it should, if new, be of satisfactory quality. There can be no difference if the CD contains software.

(c) The definition of 'goods' is expressed to be an inclusive rather than an exclusive one. Put another way, the Act is not excluding anything which might properly be considered as goods. It follows that 'goods' are not simply 'personal chattels', although a music or software CD may also fall into the category of being a personal chattel.[24]

Whether the software is supplied by way of tangible goods such as a disk or whether it is downloaded from the Internet is of secondary importance to the purchaser, who is more concerned with the qualities of the program rather than the method of its delivery or transfer. Yet, as has been discussed, the method used to transfer the program onto the computer could, insofar as the SGA 1979 is concerned, be of paramount importance. An approach that places greater emphasis on the physical medium rather than the qualities of the product transferred was criticized in the Scottish case of *Beta Computers (Europe) Ltd v Adobe Systems (Europe) Ltd.*[25] Here, Lord Penrose suggested that it was 'unattractive' to treat software as 'goods' just because it was supplied on physical medium such as a disk because:

it appears to emphasize the role of the physical medium, and to relate the transaction in the medium to sale or hire of goods. It would have the somewhat odd result that the dominant characteristic of the complex product, in terms of value

23. ibid [95].   24. ibid [96].   25. 1996 SLT 604.

or of the significant interests of parties, would be subordinate to the medium by which it was transmitted to the user in analysing the true nature and effect of the contract.[26]

Notwithstanding that the courts in the *St Albans* and *Watford* cases were prepared to imply, at common law, terms into the contracts that were not too dissimilar to those found in the SGA 1979, it would be wrong to conclude that it does not matter whether or not a contract is governed by the SGA 1979 (or other enactments containing similar implied terms). If the SGA 1979 (or any of these other enactments) do apply, then the terms including those as to satisfactory quality and fitness for purpose will usually *automatically* be implied by virtue of these Acts. In all other cases, it will be for the courts to decide whether or not to imply similar terms but, for three reasons, they will not be easily persuaded. First, the implication of terms is 'potentially so intrusive that the law imposes strict constraints on the exercise of this extraordinary power'.[27] Second, 'for a term to be implied, the following conditions (which may overlap) must be satisfied:

  (1) it must be reasonable and equitable;
  (2) it must be necessary to give business efficacy to the contract, so that no term will be implied if the contract is effective without it;
  (3) it must be so obvious that 'it goes without saying';
  (4) it must be capable of clear expression;
  (5) it must not contradict any express term of the contract.[28]

Third, as is discussed in Chapter 15, the opening words to the implied terms as to quality state that '[e]xcept as provided by this section ... and subject to any other enactment, there is no implied term about the quality or fitness for any particular purpose of goods supplied under a contract of sale'.[29]

Money consideration

English law usually requires something known as 'consideration' to render an agreement enforceable as a contract. Unlike an ordinary contract, where consideration may be satisfied by something of economic value, a contract of sale of goods requires consideration to be money. Payment by credit card is money for this purpose.[30] The following case demonstrates the need for money consideration.

---

26. ibid 608.
27. *Philips Electronique Grand Public SA v British Sky Broadcasting Ltd* [1995] EMLR 472 (CA) 481 (Sir Thomas Bingham MR).
28. ibid, approving the statement of Lord Simon in *BP Refinery (Westernport) Pty Ltd v the President, Councillors and Ratepayers of Shire of Hastings* (1978) 52 ALJR 20, 26 (PC).
29. SGA 1979, s 14(1).
30. See *Re Charge Card Services Ltd (No 2)* [1989] Ch 497 (CA).

Esso Petroleum Co Ltd v Customs & Excise Commissioners [1976] 1 WLR 1 (HL)

FACTS: Esso supplied its petrol stations with coins depicting World Cup soccer squad players to be distributed 'free' to customers who purchased four gallons of petrol. Customs & Excise contended that Esso were liable to purchase tax (the forerunner to Value Added Tax), as the coins were 'produced in quantity for general sale'.

HELD: The House of Lords held that the supply of the free gift did not constitute a contract of sale. The motorists' consideration in return for the gifts was not the payment of money but was the entering into of the separate (but linked) contract for the petrol.

★ See Roger Brownsword, 'Of Cups and Coins and Contracts' (1976) 27 NILQ 414

Distinguishing different kinds of transaction

Although a contract of sale is the typical way in which goods are supplied, it is by no means the only one. Certain legal consequences may depend on the way in which the supply of goods occurs.

Non-contractual supply

In the main, goods will be supplied pursuant to a contract of one kind or another, although the supply can arise without one. A typical example of a non-contractual supply of goods is a gift which, once handed to the recipient, becomes his property. The donor in such a case has little, if any, liability in respect of the condition of the gift, which immediately distinguishes it from a contract of sale. The donor might be liable if, for example, he knew the goods were dangerous but failed to warn the recipient of such danger, but would not be liable if they proved to be unsatisfactory in quality. Thus, if X gave his wife a food processor as a gift, X might be liable if he knew it was dangerous and she sustained injury from its use, but X would have no liability if it failed to process food satisfactorily. This example exposes the rather tortuous route that exists if a claim is to be brought. The retailer from whom X purchased the machine would doubtless be in breach of contract, but the contract was with X and X has suffered no loss. X's wife would not be entitled to sue the retailer for her loss as she has no contract with them (although had X given her the money and she bought the machine herself, she could then sue the retailer for breach of contract). She could bring a claim against the manufacturer in tort, but only if it could be established that the manufacturer was negligent in the manufacture of the machine.

It was discussed previously that in certain situations a relationship that has been created by legal compulsion will not be contractual and therefore cannot amount to a contract of sale. Thus, for example, there is no contract of sale where a hospital dispenses medicine to an outpatient even where the patient pays the statutory prescription charge.[31] The relationship in such a case is a statutory one: the hospital is statutorily obliged to supply the medicine and the patient is similarly entitled to receive it.

---

31. *Pfizer Corporation v Ministry of Health* [1965] AC 512 (HL).

Exchange or barter

A simple exchange where one person exchanges his goods for another person's goods can form the basis of a contract, but not one of sale of goods because of the absence of money consideration. However, if the exchange involves some money changing hands, for example, because one person's goods are worth more than the other's, then this may be deemed to constitute two contracts of sale.

 Aldridge v Johnson (1857) 7 E&B 885

FACTS: Aldridge agreed to purchase 100 quarters of barley (worth £215). Aldridge agreed to provide thirty-two bullocks (valued at £6 each or £192 for the lot) as part-payment. As the barley was worth more than the bullocks, Aldridge paid a sum of money to make up the difference.

HELD: The court held that this amounted to two contracts of sale of goods because the parties had given a price to both lots of goods and the consideration was satisfied in money.

COMMENT: Compare this case to *G J Dawson (Clapham) Ltd v H & G Dutfield*,[32] where the claimant sold to the defendant two second-hand lorries for £475, £250 of which was to be paid in cash, and £225 was to be credited by way of the part-exchange of two other lorries, provided that these were delivered within a month. The cash was paid, but the defendant failed to deliver the lorries in part-exchange. Hilbery J held that this was a single contract of sale for the two second-hand lorries for the price of £475. The arrangement for the part-exchange was a subsidiary agreement by which the defendant had the right to deduct £225 off the purchase price if he delivered the lorries within a month, but if he failed to do so the claimant was entitled to sue for the remainder of the purchase price as a debt due.

If the contract is one of exchange, terms will be implied by virtue of the Supply of Goods and Services Act 1982.

Work and materials

Many contracts of sale include, in addition to the sale of goods, the provision of a service. For example, if *X* buys a suit and asks the tailor to shorten the length of the trousers, this is still a contract of sale. However, if *X* takes his car for a service, and the garage tops up the oil and charges *X* for the oil used, the overall transaction is not a contract of sale but a contract for work and materials. At one time the classification of contract was important because, until its abolition in 1954,[33] contracts of sale of goods valued at £10 or higher had to be evidenced by a note or memorandum in writing, whereas there was no such requirement for contracts for work and materials. Although in the two examples just given the type of contract is obvious, in other cases, where the law draws the line is not always easy to determine and is not

---

32. [1936] 2 All ER 232 (KB).　　33. Law Reform (Enforcement of Contracts) Act 1954, s 2.

made any easier by the two leading cases reaching different conclusions. The test, however, is 'What is the substance of the contract?'

In *Lee v Griffin*,[34] the court held that a contract to make and fit a set of artificial teeth was a contract for the sale of goods. Blackburn J stated that:

> the contract was to deliver a thing which, when completed, would have resulted in the sale of a chattel; in other words, the substance of the contract was for goods sold and delivered. I do not think that the test to apply to these cases is whether the value of the work exceeds that of the materials used in its execution; for, if a sculptor were employed to execute a work of art, greatly as his skill and labour, supposing it to be of the highest description, might exceed the value of the marble on which he worked, the contract would, in my opinion, nevertheless be a contract for the sale of a chattel.[35]

In *Robinson v Graves*,[36] the Court of Appeal held that a contract to paint a portrait was one for work and materials. Referring to the earlier decision in *Lee v Griffin*, Greer LJ said:

> I treat that judgment as indicating that in the view of Blackburn J one has to look to the substance of the contract. If you find, as they did ... that the substance of the contract was the production of something to be sold by the dentist to the dentist's customer, then that is a sale of goods. But if the substance of the contract, on the other hand, is that skill and labour have to be exercised for the production of the article and that it is only ancillary to that that there will pass from the artist to his client or customer some materials in addition to the skill involved in the production of the portrait, that does not make any difference to the result, because the substance of the contract is the skill and experience of the artist in producing the picture. For these reasons I am of opinion that in this case the substance of the matter was an agreement for the exercise of skill and it was only incidental that some materials would have to pass from the artist to the gentleman who commissioned the portrait. For these reasons I think that this was not a contract for the sale of goods...but it was a contract for work and labour and materials.[37]

Work and materials contracts have been described as 'half the rendering of services and, in a sense, half the supply of goods'.[38] The law applies entirely different standards to these two 'halves' of the supplier's obligation:

(a) In respect of the supplier's obligation to carry out the work or service, where the supplier is acting in the course of a business, there is an implied term that he will carry out the service with reasonable care and skill.[39] Unlike the terms implied in the SGA 1979, which are classified as either conditions or warranties, this term is an innominate term to which the flexible (if uncertain) approach in *Hong Kong Fir Shipping Co Ltd v Kawasaki Kisen Kaisha Ltd*[40] will apply, and the consequences or seriousness of the breach will determine whether or not

---

34. (1861) 1 B&S 272.   35. ibid 278.   36. [1935] 1 KB 579 (CA).   37. ibid 587.
38. *Watson v Buckley Osborne Garrett & Co Ltd* [1940] 1 All ER 174 (Assizes) 180 (Stable J). This was a case concerning a hairdresser applying hair dye to a customer's hair, which caused the customer to contract dermatitis.
39. Supply of Goods and Services Act 1982, s 13. Prior to this enactment, there was no statutory duty placed on a supplier of a service to perform his work with any particular degree of care or skill.
40. [1962] 2 QB 26 (CA).

it takes effect as a condition or a warranty. In this way, if the consequences of the breach are so fundamental that the innocent party has been deprived of substantially the entire benefit of the contract, he will be entitled to treat the contract as repudiated and sue for damages. If, on the other hand, the effects of the breach do not cause such a deprivation, then, it will be treated as a breach of warranty restricting the innocent party to a claim in damages.

(b) As to his obligation to supply goods or materials pursuant to the work and materials contract, the supplier's obligation is one of strict liability in respect of the goods or materials having to be of satisfactory quality and reasonably fit for purpose.[41] Again, the supplier must be acting in the course of a business for this obligation to arise. The term here is a condition and is almost identical to a seller's obligation as to quality in a contract of sale. The reader is therefore directed to Chapter 15, where the statutory implied terms in contracts of sale are examined in detail.

The difference between these two implied terms is best illustrated by returning to the example given at the beginning of this section, where X takes his car for a service during which the garage tops up the oil. As the contract is one for work and materials, the garage's obligation as to the quality and fitness for purpose of the oil will be virtually identical to that in a case of a contract of sale. The oil will have to be of satisfactory quality and reasonably fit for purpose. This obligation is strict and does not depend on the negligence of the seller. Consequently, if the oil has an inherent manufacturing defect and causes damage to X's car, the garage will be liable even though they had no reason to suspect that it was defective. Insofar as the garage's obligation to service the car is concerned, the lower standard of 'reasonable care and skill' will be applied. In practice, this means that the supplier must perform his work in a careful manner.

Free issue of materials

With this type of contract, the customer provides the supplier with the materials which the supplier then uses to make the finished goods. It might be seen, for example, where the customer provides a roll of material to a dressmaker to make a dress. This kind of arrangement is not one of sale of goods because there is no transfer of ownership in the goods,[42] but is a contract for services to which the Supply of Goods and Services Act 1982 applies. This has already been discussed in relation to contracts for work and materials.

Hire purchase and hire

With these methods of possessing goods, ownership remains with the supplier. With hire purchase, the customer enters into an agreement to hire the goods for a period with an option at the end to purchase them. Even though most customers will exercise this option to purchase, and will therefore end up as owner, there is no obligation to do so. Accordingly, it is not a contract of sale. In *Helby*

---

41. Supply of Goods and Services Act 1982, s 4.
42. The goods belonged to the customer at all times.

v Matthews,[43] a case concerning the hire purchase of a piano, Lord Macnaghten observed:

> The contract…on the part of the dealer was a contract of hiring coupled with a conditional contract or undertaking to sell. On the part of the customer it was a contract of hiring only until the time came for making the last payment. It may be that at the inception of the transaction both parties expected that the agreement would run its full course, and that the piano would change hands in the end. But an expectation, however confident and however well-founded, does not amount to an agreement.[44]

In the case of a hire purchase contract, terms will be implied by virtue of the Supply of Goods (Implied Terms) Act 1973 and the Consumer Credit Act 1974. If the contract is one of hire, then the implied terms will be those contained in the Supply of Goods and Services Act 1982.

Table 10.1 summarizes the position of where the implied terms can be found in different kinds of contract.

Sales and agreements to sell

Both sales and agreements to sell may be contracts of sale of goods. The difference between these two types of transaction is that with a sale, the property in the goods is transferred from the seller to the buyer as soon as the contract is made,[15] whereas with an agreement to sell, the transfer of the property in the goods takes place at a future time or is subject to some condition later to be fulfilled.[46] An agreement to sell

TABLE 10.1 Implied terms in different kinds of contract

Type of transaction	Implied terms	If not SGA, why not?
Sale	Sale of Goods Act 1979, ss 12–15	N/A
Exchange or barter	Supply of Goods and Services Act 1982, ss 2–5	Consideration not 'money', as required by s 2(1) SGA, s 2(1)
Hire	Supply of Goods and Services Act 1982, ss 6–11	No transfer or agreement to transfer property in the goods as required by s 2(1) SGA
Hire-purchase	Supply of Goods (Implied Terms) Act 1973, ss 8–11; Consumer Credit Act 1974	No obligation by the hirer to purchase goods, hence no obligation to transfer property in them as required by s 2(1) SGA
Services—including where goods are also supplied (known as work and materials contracts)	Supply of Goods and Services Act 1982, ss 2–5 and 12–16	The substance of the contract is the provision of the overall service rather than the transfer of property in the goods as required by s 2(1) SGA

---

43. [1895] AC 471 (HL).   44. ibid 482.   45. SGA 1979, s 2(4).   46. ibid s 2(5).

becomes a sale when the time elapses or the condition is fulfilled subject to which the property in the goods is to be transferred.[47]

Specific goods and unascertained goods

At the time of making the contract the goods will either be specific or unascertained.

- Specific goods are goods that are identified and agreed upon at the time a contract of sale is made.[48] This means that both buyer and seller have identified and agreed upon precisely which goods will be sold under the contract.
- Unascertained goods are not defined in the SGA 1979, but are in effect all goods that are not specific.

The distinction between specific goods and unascertained goods relates only to the position at the time of making the contract. Consequently, subsequent events cannot turn unascertained goods into specific goods, although they will often make them ascertained. Goods may become ascertained as soon as they have been identified and agreed upon after the contract of sale is made.

The distinction between specific and unascertained goods is of particular importance in determining if and when property passes from seller to buyer. This is discussed in Chapter 11.

Existing goods and future goods

The goods which form the subject of a contract of sale may be either existing goods or future goods.

- Existing goods are goods that are either owned or possessed by the seller.[49]
- Future goods are goods to be manufactured or acquired by the seller after the making of the contract of sale.[50]

The price

The parties to a contract of sale will doubtless set their minds to many different terms and will reach agreement which then forms part of the contract. Other terms may be implied. Central to any contract of sale is the obligation of the seller to transfer ownership of the goods to the buyer and for the buyer to pay the price. It might be expected that the parties will have agreed the price in advance of the contract,

---

47. ibid s 2(6).   48. ibid s 61(1).   49. ibid s 5(1).   50. ibid ss 5(1) and 61(1).

but this is not always the case. The SGA 1979 sets out a number of rules regarding how price is to be ascertained.

Ascertaining the price

The key provision as regards ascertaining the price is s 8 of the SGA 1979.

SGA 1979, s 8

(1) The price in a contract of sale may be fixed by the contract, or may be left to be fixed in a manner agreed by the contract, or may be determined by the course of dealing between the parties.

(2) Where the price is not determined as mentioned in sub-section (1) above the buyer must pay a reasonable price.

(3) What is a reasonable price is a question of fact dependent on the circumstances of each particular case.

Provided that the parties have agreed to be bound and have agreed all of the main terms in the contract, the fact that further terms have yet to be negotiated will not prevent there from being a concluded and binding contract.[51] It is perfectly possible in law for parties to make an interim agreement for the sale of goods, which requires further negotiation to iron out the less important details of the transaction. It is ultimately a matter of degree whether or not a binding contract has been made.

***May & Butcher Ltd v The King* [1934] 2 KB 17n (HL)**

FACTS: May & Butcher Ltd ('May') agreed to buy tentage from the Crown at a price and date of payment that would be determined 'from time to time'. The relationship between the parties broke down and May sought to have the agreement enforced 'at a reasonable price' to be determined by the court.

HELD: The House of Lords held that there was no contract as the term regarding price was too uncertain. Had the agreement been silent about payment, then no doubt the price could have been fixed by the SGA 1893 on the basis of paying a reasonable price, but as the parties had shown that this was not their intention by providing that the price was to be determined by further agreement, the SGA 1893's provisions as to ascertaining the price were not applicable.

Consequently, s 8(2) will only apply in the absence of agreement as to price and not where the parties had provided a mechanism for determining price which had failed. Although *May & Butcher Ltd* has not been overruled, it has not always been followed and it has been said that 'the court is reluctant to hold void for uncertainty

---

any provision that was intended to have legal effect'.[52] This reluctance is evident from the decision of the Court of Appeal in the following case.

 Foley v Classique Coaches Ltd [1934] 2 KB 1 (CA)[53]

FACTS: Foley owned a petrol station with a piece of adjoining land. He agreed to sell this adjoining land to Classique Coaches Ltd ('Classique') on condition that it enter into a second agreement with him, whereby Foley would exclusively provide it with the petrol it required for its business. The parties agreed that this petrol would be bought at a price agreed by them 'from time to time'. For three years, this agreement continued, until Classique decided to repudiate the second agreement and source its petrol from elsewhere. Foley commenced proceedings and Classique argued that there was no agreement due to the uncertain price clause.

HELD: In holding that the second agreement was enforceable, the Court of Appeal distinguished *May & Butcher Ltd* and held that, in default of the parties reaching agreement for the price of the petrol, Classique must pay a reasonable price.

More recently, the lack of enthusiasm to follow *May & Butcher* can be seen in the Supreme Court's decision in *RTS Flexible Systems Ltd v Molkerei Alois Müller GmbH & Co KG*,[54] where Lord Clarke stated that:

> even if certain terms of economic or other significance to the parties have not been finalised, an objective appraisal of their words and conduct may lead to the conclusion that they did not intend agreement of such terms to be a precondition to a concluded and legally binding agreement.[55]

Subject to there being an enforceable agreement, and where the price cannot be determined by one of the methods set out in s 8(1), namely, to be fixed by the contract itself, left to be fixed in a manner agreed by the contract, or determined by a course of dealing between the parties, the buyer must pay a reasonable price.[56] What is a reasonable price is a question of fact dependent on the circumstances of each particular case.[57]

Price to be fixed by valuation

It will sometimes be the case that the parties agree that the price is to be fixed by the valuation of a third party. This is dealt with by s 9 of the SGA 1979.

---

52. *Brown v Gould and Others* [1972] Ch 53 (Ch) 56 (Megarry J).
53. Approved by the House of Lords in *Scammell & Nephew Ltd v Ouston* [1941] AC 251 (HL).
54. [2010] UKSC 14, [2010] 1 WLR 753.   55. ibid [45].   56. SGA 1979, s 8(2).
57. ibid s 8(3).

> ### 🔑 SGA 1979, s 9
>
> (1) Where there is an agreement to sell goods on the terms that the price is to be fixed by the valuation of a third party, and he cannot or does not make the valuation, the agreement is avoided; but if the goods or any part of them have been delivered to and appropriated by the buyer he must pay a reasonable price for them.
>
> (2) Where the third party is prevented from making the valuation by the fault of the seller or buyer, the party not at fault may maintain an action for damages against the party at fault.

Where the agreement is avoided by virtue of s 9(1), then the seller will be under no obligation to deliver the goods, and the buyer will be under no obligation to pay for the goods. However, if the goods have been delivered to the buyer and he has appropriated them, then he must pay a reasonable price for them. As s 9(2) notes, where the reason for the valuer not making the valuation is because of the fault of either of the parties, then the party who is not at fault may maintain an action for damages against the other.

Unless the valuer has acted fraudulently in making his valuation, such as where he has acted with the collusion of one of the parties, his valuation will be binding on them. Where fraud can be proved, then the valuation will have no effect. This is because 'fraud unravels everything'.[58] On the other hand, if the valuer arrives at his valuation honestly but negligently, it remains valid as between the parties, but the valuer will be liable in negligence to the injured party.[59] In such a situation, it will not be enough for the injured party to show that a different valuer would have arrived at a different figure; he must show that no reasonably competent valuer could have arrived at the valuation produced.

Contracts of substantial or indefinite duration

Consider the following example:

> ### Eg ComCorp Ltd
>
> ComCorp Ltd requires consignments of copper to be delivered to one of its factories every six months. ComCorp enters into an agreement with Aggregate Ltd to provide the copper. The agreement is to last for five years and provides that Aggregate Ltd will provide a fixed quantity of copper every six months at a fixed price of £15,000 per consignment. After the first consignment has been delivered and paid for, the market price of copper decreases and the same quantity of copper could be obtained for £9,000 per consignment. For obvious reasons, the board of ComCorp does not wish to be held to the agreement and seeks to renegotiate the price with Aggregate Ltd.

---

58. *Lazarus Estates Ltd v Beasley* [1956] 1 QB 702 (CA) 712. 'No court in this land will allow a person to keep an advantage which he has obtained by fraud. No judgment of a court, no order of a Minister, can be allowed to stand if it has been obtained by fraud. Fraud unravels everything' (Denning LJ).
59. *Arenson v Casson Beckman Rutley & Co* [1977] AC 405 (HL).

A different problem arises in cases such as in the above example, namely, where the contract of sale extends over a long period of time and the price is fixed at the date of contracting. It is, of course, perfectly possible for the parties to agree to renegotiate prices at given intervals or otherwise agree on a mechanism for price fluctuations, although it may be that they do not turn their minds to it or that it is not acceptable to one of them. A price which was agreed upon at the time of contracting may not be acceptable to one or more of the parties some years later. In general, the courts will not interfere with what might be (or might turn out to be) a bad bargain, although, in the following case, the Court did intervene.

Staffordshire Area Health Authority v South Staffordshire Waterworks Co [1978] 1 WLR 1387 (CA)

FACTS: In 1929, South Staffordshire Waterworks Co ('the water company') entered into an agreement with a hospital to supply 5,000 gallons of water per day free of charge and 'at all times hereafter' all the additional water it required at 7d per 1,000 gallons. In 1975, the water company gave notice to the hospital that, in six months' time, it would terminate the agreement and replace it with one whereby they would supply the hospital with 5,000 gallons of water per day free of charge, but any excess would be charged at the normal rate of 45p per 1,000 gallons. At first instance, it was held that by virtue of the words 'at all times hereafter', the original agreement had been made in perpetuity and that the water company was bound by it. The water company appealed.

HELD: The appeal was allowed and the first instance decision was reversed by the Court of Appeal. The Court stated that a power to terminate the agreement on reasonable notice should be inferred. Cumming-Bruce LJ held that the words 'at all times hereafter' must mean 'that the obligations granted and accepted by the agreement were only intended to persist during the continuance of the agreement; and the agreement ... was determinable on reasonable notice at any time'.[60]

COMMENT: This case turned on its facts, which are unlikely to arise often. The water company sought to terminate the original agreement some forty-six years after it was made and when the cost of water had increased by around fifteen times the original agreed price. Nevertheless, a contract to supply goods (or indeed services) at a price 'at all times hereafter' does not conclusively declare perpetuity, as the courts may well imply the meaning it did in the *Staffordshire* case.

★ See Demetrios H Hadjihambis, 'At All Times Hereafter' (1979) 30 NILQ 136

---

60. [1978] 1 WLR 1387 (CA) 1406.

Conclusion

Having now discussed the key developments and definitions found in contracts of sale and related contracts, the remaining chapters in this section expand upon this by examining the issues that arise.

Practice questions

1. What are the different ways in which goods can be acquired other than pursuant to a contract of sale?

2. I take my car for a service during which the garage tops up the oil. Due to an inherent fault with the oil, the engine seizes, causing thousands of pounds of damage. What type of contract is this? Why does the type of contract matter? What is the liability of the garage?

Further reading

Dame Mary Arden, 'Time for an English Commercial Code?' (1997) 56 CLJ 516
*   Discusses the original Sale of Goods Act 1893 which was intended simply to codify rather than alter the common law rules.

Paul Dobson, 'Sale of Goods or Contract for Services?' (1998) Student Law Review 24 (Sum)
*   Discusses the key differences between a contract for services and one of sale of goods.

Sarah Green and Djakhongir Saidov, 'Software as Goods Under the Sale of Goods Act' [2007] JBL Mar 161
*   Examines the legal treatment of software and discusses whether it should be classed as 'goods' under the SGA 1979.

George Gretton, 'Software: Binding the End-user' [1996] JBL 524
*   Discusses the decision in *Beta Computers (Europe) Ltd v Adobe Systems (Europe) Ltd* [1996] FSR 367 where Lord Penrose criticized the idea that software supplied on a permanent medium, such as a disk, would amount to a contract of sale of goods in the same way as, for example, the sale of a book.

Alan F Rodger, 'The Codification of Commercial Law in Victorian Britain' (1992) 108 LQR 570
*   Discusses the codification of the SGA, noting its application to Scotland in 1893 following disquiet about the need for a uniform law of sale.

11 The transfer of property and risk

- Transfer of property between seller and buyer
- Retention of title

- Passing of risk

INTRODUCTION

Both this chapter and Chapter 12 discuss the surprisingly difficult questions of ownership of the contract goods. Rather than referring to 'ownership' per se, the SGA 1979 uses the words 'property' and 'title'. The word 'property' is used when referring to the nature of the seller's obligations to the buyer in respect of the ownership of the goods and to the exact time when ownership is transferred to the buyer under a contract of sale. It is thus concerned with the transfer of property as between seller and buyer. On the other hand, the SGA 1979 uses the word 'title' when considering the various circumstances in which a buyer may become the owner of the goods, notwithstanding that the seller is neither the owner of them nor sold them with the owner's consent. This chapter deals with the transfer of property as between seller and buyer and Chapter 12 deals with the transfer of title.

This chapter will also consider the passing of risk. As discussed shortly, the general rule about risk is that unless the parties have otherwise agreed, risk passes with property (although the position is different when the buyer deals as consumer). This is one of the key reasons why it is important to know the precise moment that property passes. That is, however, not the only reason why it is important to know this. For example, with regards to payment, unless otherwise agreed, the seller may only sue the buyer for the price once property in the goods has passed,[1] and, if either the seller or the buyer becomes insolvent, then the rights of the other (non-insolvent) party may depend on whether or not property in the goods has passed to the buyer. Furthermore, although subject to a number of exceptions, as will be seen in Chapter 12, unless the buyer has acquired ownership in the goods, he cannot transfer that ownership to another party.

---

1. SGA 1979, s 49.

Transfer of property between seller and buyer

The transfer of property as between seller and buyer is dealt with in ss 16–19 of the SGA 1979. The first thing to appreciate is that these rules differ according to whether the contract of sale relates to specific or unascertained goods. The relevant time for determining whether the goods are specific or unascertained is when the contract is made.

 The distinction between specific and unascertained goods is discussed at p 226

Unascertained goods

Section 16 provides that, subject to s 20A, where there is a contract for the sale of unascertained goods, no property in them is transferred to the buyer unless and until the goods are ascertained. This is the position even if the parties agree otherwise, and is entirely logical, because until the parties have identified the precise goods to which the contract of sale relates, it will not be possible to say for which goods the property is intended to pass. As Lord Mustill stated in *Re Goldcorp Exchange Ltd,*[2] 'common sense dictates that the buyer cannot acquire title until it is known to what goods the title relates.'[3]

 Section 20A is discussed at p 253

Since property in the goods cannot be transferred to a buyer unless and until the goods are ascertained, it is, therefore, important to understand when goods will become ascertained. This was simply stated by the Court of Appeal in *Re Wait*[4] as when the goods are identified as *the* goods to be used in the performance of the contract. The following case demonstrates the application of this rule.

Re Blyth Shipbuilding and Dry Docks Company Ltd [1926] Ch 494 (CA)

FACTS: A contract for the building of a ship provided for payment by instalments, the first of which was to be paid when the parties signed the contract, followed by further payments due at various stages in the progress of the ship's construction. A clause in the contract provided that:

> from and after payment by the purchasers to the builders of the first instalment on account of the purchase price the vessel and all materials and things appropriated for her should thenceforth, subject to the lien of the builders for unpaid purchase money including extras, become and remain the absolute property of the purchasers.

After the purchaser made the first two instalments of the price and the vessel had been partly constructed, a receiver was appointed. Proceedings were commenced to determine the respective rights of the parties.

HELD: Property in the partly constructed ship had passed to the purchasers, but the property in the various materials that were intended to have been used in the ship's construction had not passed to them because, notwithstanding the intention of the

---

2. [1995] 1 AC 74 (PC).   3. ibid 90 (Lord Mustill).
4. [1927] 1 Ch 606 (CA).

shipbuilders to use these materials and which had been approved by the purchaser's surveyor, it had not been ascertained that those specific materials were to be used to the exclusion of any others such that it could be said that those materials had been unconditionally appropriated to the contract. As Pollock MR explained:

> What is meant by 'appropriated' in this sort of connection? Does it mean that once some goods have been appropriated and brought on to the site definitely to be used in the vessel, no others can be substituted for them; that if those particular goods were damaged or injured or found for some other reason unsuitable, no change could be made except at increased cost to the purchaser of the vessel? Does it mean that those goods and those only are the goods which are to be used and in respect of which, if any misfortune happens, it falls upon the shoulders of the purchaser? Unless such is found to be the case it does not appear that it would be right to say that the materials and things had been unconditionally appropriated.[5]

A further example of the rule that no property in unascertained goods can be transferred to the buyer unless and until they are ascertained can be seen in *McDougall v Aeromarine of Emsworth Ltd*.[6] Here, the shipbuilding contract provided that upon the payment by the purchasers of the first instalment, the ship together with all materials used in her construction will become the absolute property of the purchasers. Diplock J held that as the construction of the vessel had not yet commenced and there was nothing physically in existence, no materials intended for use had been identified and consequently no property in the goods passed on the payment of the first instalment.

Specific or ascertained goods

Where the contract is for the sale of specific or ascertained goods, the property in them is transferred to the buyer at such time as the parties to the contract intend it to be transferred.[7] For the purpose of ascertaining the intention of the parties, regard shall be had to the terms of the contract, the conduct of the parties, and the circumstances of the case.[8] Thus, where the terms of the contract expressly set out when property in the goods is to pass, the only argument is one of construction.[9]

Re Anchor Line (Henderson Brothers) Ltd [1937] Ch 1 (CA)

FACTS: The contract provided for the buyer to purchase a crane 'for a deferred purchase price' and with it having 'entire charge and responsibility' for the crane. The buyer was to make annual payments for interest and depreciation, with such sums to be deducted from the purchase price. Three years later, and before payment of the whole of the purchase price, the buyer became insolvent and the liquidator entered into a contract

---

5. [1926] Ch 494 (CA) 513.   6. [1958] 1 WLR 1126 (QB).   7. SGA 1979, s 17(1).
8. ibid s 17(2).   9. *Re Anchor Line (Henderson Brothers) Ltd* [1937] Ch 1 (CA).

for the sale of the assets to a new company. The seller argued that property in the crane had not passed to the buyer and that consequently it was not included in the assets that were sold to the new company. It was the seller's case that the liquidator must either accept the obligations arising under the initial contract and continue with the payments or alternatively return the crane to it. At first instance, Eve J held that property in the crane had passed to the new company on the making of the contract, in accordance with s 18, rule 1 of the SGA 1893.

Section 18, rule 1 is discussed at p 236

HELD: The Court of Appeal reversed the decision of Eve J, noting that s 18 applied only 'unless a different intention' appeared, and that, on a proper construction of the contract, a different intention did appear, in that property in the crane should not pass until the purchase was completed by payment of the entire price. Consequently, the liquidator was bound to pay the balance of the price due to the seller.

It is the intention of the parties at the time of making the contract that is important, and not their subsequent intention. Thus, where a buyer purchases goods at auction and pays for them by cheque, any document he signs at a later stage, such as one where he agrees that property in the goods will not pass to him until the cheque has cleared, will not be taken into account because this will be after the contract has already been concluded,[10] although conduct subsequent to the making of the contract may itself provide evidence of the parties' intention at the time of entering into the contract.[11]

The rules for ascertaining the intention of the parties

The rules for ascertaining the intention of the parties can be found in s 18 SGA 1979. It can be seen from the previous section that s 17 is the primary focus for the transferring of property in the goods. Section 18 is, therefore, secondary and its purpose is to fill any vacuum left by the parties in relation to the time of transfer. Of course, where the terms of the contract spell out when property is to pass, then the parties' intention prevails and the rules in s 18 do not arise.[12] It is only in cases where the parties fail to make clear their intentions as to when property in the goods will be transferred to the buyer (which in consumer cases is quite likely to be the norm, as these parties are unlikely even to direct their thoughts to this question) that it will be necessary to consider these rules.

Specific goods are governed by rules 1 to 4 (which are summarized in Table 11.1), with rules 1 to 3 being not only concerned with specific goods but also with the goods being in a deliverable state. Rule 4 is concerned with goods that have been provided to a buyer on approval or on a 'sale or return' or similar basis. Unascertained goods are governed by rule 5. The question of unidentified shares forming part of a bulk is dealt with separately in s 20A.

When goods are in a deliverable state is discussed at p 237

10. *Dennant v Skinner & Collom* [1948] 2 KB 164 (KB).
11. *Anonima Petroli Italiana SpA & Neste Oy v Marlucidez Armadora SA (The Filiatra Legacy)* [1991] 2 Lloyd's Rep 337 (CA).
12. See, e.g., *Weiner v Gill* [1906] 2 KB 574 (CA), discussed at p 244.

TABLE 11.1 Rules relating to specific goods

Rule	Circumstances when rule applies	Property in the goods passes to the buyer when ...
1	Where there is an unconditional contract for the sale of specific goods in a deliverable state.	The contract is made. This is irrespective of whether the time of payment or the time of delivery, or both, are postponed.
2	Where there is a contract for the sale of specific goods and the seller is bound to do something to the goods for the purpose of putting them into a deliverable state.	The thing is done and the buyer has notice that it has been done.
3	Where there is a contract for the sale of specific goods in a deliverable state but the seller is bound to weigh, measure, test, or do some other act or thing with reference to the goods for the purpose of ascertaining the price.	The act or thing is done and the buyer has notice that it has been done.
4	When goods are delivered to the buyer on approval or on sale or return or other similar terms.	(a) The buyer signifies his approval or acceptance to the seller or does any other act adopting the transaction. (b) If he does not signify his approval or acceptance to the seller but retains the goods without giving notice of rejection, then, if a time has been fixed for the return of the goods, on the expiration of that time, and, if no time has been fixed, on the expiration of a reasonable time.

Rule 1

Rule 1 is as follows:

> **⊶ SGA 1979, s 18, rule 1**
>
> Where there is an unconditional contract for the sale of specific goods in a deliverable state the property in the goods passes to the buyer when the contract is made, and it is immaterial whether the time of payment or the time of delivery, or both, be postponed.

The principle underlying rule 1 is that in the case of a contract of sale where the goods are identified and agreed upon and are in a state ready for delivery, the parties are deemed to have intended that the property in them should pass to the buyer immediately the contract is made, irrespective of whether or not the time of payment and/or the time of delivery are actually postponed to a later time. A typical example of when the time of payment is postponed is in relation to commercial contracts where the seller's trading terms permit payment to be made sometime after delivery, for example, within thirty days. In the context of a sale concluded at auction,[13] it has been stated that:

> A contract of sale is concluded at an auction sale on the fall of the hammer ...
> Accordingly, upon the fall of the hammer the property [in the goods] passed

---

13. Similar principles apply to any contract of sale.

to [the buyer] unless that prima facie rule is excluded from applying because of a different intention appearing or because there was some condition in the contract which prevented the rule from applying. In my view, this was clearly an unconditional contract of sale, and I can see nothing whatever to make a different intention appear. Passing of the property and right to possession are two different things: here the property had passed upon the fall of the hammer [even though the seller] had a right to retain possession of the goods until payment was made.[14]

Some of the terminology contained in rule 1 requires consideration. First, we must ask what is an 'unconditional contract' for the purpose of rule 1. It cannot refer to a contract without conditions, since it is hard to imagine a contract that does not contain terms that are so fundamental to a party's obligations that they are not contractual conditions of the contract. Further, with a contract of sale, the terms implied under ss 12 to 15 of the SGA 1979 contain conditions in any event. The words 'an unconditional contract' simply refer to a contract that contains nothing that either restricts when it might come into force or prevents the rule from applying (such as at the time of making the contract, the seller is not the owner of the contract goods and the buyer contracts with him with knowledge of this fact). In such a case, no ownership can pass to the buyer until the seller has himself acquired ownership. Thus, in *Varley v Whipp*,[15] where, at the time of making the contract to sell a second-hand reaping machine, the seller had not yet acquired ownership in it himself, Channell J held that this prevented the contract from being an unconditional contract of sale to which rule 1 could apply. Adopting similar reasoning, a term in a contract which prevents property in the goods passing to the buyer until payment has been made is similarly not an unconditional contract invoking rule 1. Such terms, known as 'retention of title' (or 'reservation of title') clauses, are instead subject to s 19 and are discussed later in this chapter.

 Retention of title clauses are discussed at p 255

Second, when will goods be in a deliverable state for the purpose of the SGA 1979? This will occur when the goods 'are in such a state that the buyer would under the contract be bound to take delivery of them'.[16] Goods will not be in a deliverable state where anything is needed to be done to them to make them comply with the contract of sale or to make them ready for delivery, as the following case demonstrates.

Underwood Ltd v Burgh Castle Brick & Cement Syndicate [1922] 1 KB 343 (CA)

FACTS: Underwood Ltd ('Underwood') agreed to sell a 30-tonne engine to Burgh Castle Brick & Cement Syndicate ('Burgh') to be delivered free on rail in London. Due to its weight, it was bolted to and embedded in a concrete flooring. Before it could be delivered onto the railway it had to be detached and dismantled by Underwood. Underwood detached it, but in loading it onto a truck, it was accidentally damaged, resulting in Burgh refusing to accept it. Underwood sued Burgh for the price, and Burgh pleaded that property in the engine had not at the date of the accident passed to them.

---

14. *Dennant v Skinner & Collom* [1948] 2 KB 164 (KB) 171 (Hallett J).
15. [1900] 1 QB 513 (QB).   16. SGA 1979, s 61(5).

HELD: The Court of Appeal held that rule 1 was not applicable and consequently the property in the engine had not passed to Burgh. Bankes, Scrutton, and Atkin LJJ held that this was so because Underwood was bound to do something, which it had not done, for the purpose of putting the engine into a deliverable state. Bankes and Atkin LJJ held that property had not passed on the further ground that the circumstances showed an intention that the property should not pass until the engine was placed in safety on rail in London. As Bankes LJ stated:

> Did the property in that engine pass on the contract of sale? No general rule can be laid down which will answer the question when the property passes in every contract of sale. In many sales of specific articles to be delivered, the property passes on the making of the contract. A man may select and agree to buy a hat and the shopman may agree to deliver it at the buyer's house. There notwithstanding the obligation to deliver the hat, the property passes at the time of the contract. But that is far from this case. Considering the risk and expense involved in dismantling and moving this engine, I have no hesitation in holding that the proper inference to be drawn is that the property was not to pass until the engine was safely placed on rail in London. In my view an elaborate discussion of the rules in s 18…is unnecessary. They only apply where a different intention does not appear, and in this case a different intention does appear, assuming for the moment that this machine was in a deliverable state when it was fixed in its position at Millwall…But was this engine in a deliverable state in its position at Millwall? The appellants contended that where a specific article is complete in itself, for example a complete engine or a complete cart—that is to say, where nothing more has to be done to make it an engine or a cart—it is then in a deliverable state within the meaning of s 18, r 1, and if the owner agrees to sell it the property passes to the buyer when the contract is made, and it is immaterial whether the time of payment or the time of delivery, or both, be postponed. I do not accept that test. A 'deliverable state' does not depend upon the mere completeness of the subject matter in all its parts. It depends on the actual state of the goods at the date of the contract and the state in which they are to be delivered by the terms of the contract. Where the vendors have to expend as much trouble and as much money as the appellants had to expend before this engine could be placed on rail, I cannot think that the subject matter can be said to be in a deliverable state.[17]

Similarly, in *Rugg v Minett*,[18] a term in the contract required the seller to top up the casks of turpentine prior to delivery. Before the seller was able to complete this task, the goods were destroyed by fire. It was held that the goods were not in a deliverable state and that property in them had not passed to the buyer.

The concluding words in rule 1, namely that 'it is immaterial whether the time of payment or the time of delivery, or both, be postponed' make it plain that ownership and possession of the contract goods are entirely different concepts. Thus, a buyer can become owner of the contract goods notwithstanding that he has not paid for them or that they remain in the custody of the seller. This was further explained by Hallett J in *Dennant v Skinner & Collom*,[19] where he stated:

> Passing of the property and right to possession are two different things: here the property had passed upon the fall of the hammer, but still Mr Dennant had a right to retain possession of the goods until payment was made.[20]

---

17. [1922] 1 KB 343 (CA) 344.   18. (1809) 11 East 210, 103 ER 985.
19. [1948] 2 KB 164 (KB).   20. ibid 172.

Rule 2

Rule 2 is as follows:

 SGA 1979, s 18, rule 2

> Where there is a contract for the sale of specific goods and the seller is bound to do something to the goods for the purpose of putting them into a deliverable state, the property does not pass until the thing is done and the buyer has notice that it has been done.

Unlike rule 1, which deals with an unconditional contract, rule 2 is concerned with a conditional contract. The condition, which is to be satisfied by the seller, is to put the contract goods into a deliverable state. This is not achieved merely by the specific article being complete in itself, but rather 'it depends on the actual state of the goods at the date of the contract and the state in which they are to be delivered by the terms of the contract'.[21] The seller must, of course, be 'bound' to take such steps and it will not be enough that he has been asked to do it. Once the seller has done this, and the buyer has notice that it has been done, then property in the goods passes to the buyer. Examples of the seller needing 'to do something to the goods for the purpose of putting them into a deliverable state' include the topping up of casks of turpentine,[22] unbolting and safely placing a 30-tonne engine on rail in London,[23] and the satisfactory laying of a carpet where such laying was a term of the contract.[24]

As already observed, once the seller has put the goods into a deliverable state, the property in the goods still does not pass until 'the buyer has notice that it has been done'. Precisely what constitutes 'notice' for this purpose and who needs to provide such notice is unclear. It seems only logical that 'notice' must mean effective notice so that if the seller posts a letter or sends an email to the buyer advising him that the goods are in a deliverable state but the letter or email are not received, then the buyer does not have notice for the purpose of the rule. The rule only states that the buyer must have notice that the goods have been put into a deliverable state; it does not say who needs to provide such notice. Applying the rules of statutory construction, as rule 5 spells out specifically which party needs to give 'assent' and to whom, and rule 2 is silent as to whether or not the seller must be the party that gives such notice to the buyer, it seems likely that it is unimportant who in fact gives such notice as long as the buyer has notice.

21. *Underwood Ltd v Burgh Castle Brick & Cement Syndicate* [1922] 1 KB 343 (CA) 345 (Bankes LJ).
22. *Rugg v Minett* (1809) 11 East 210.
23. *Underwood Ltd v Burgh Castle Brick & Cement Syndicate* [1922] 1 KB 343 (CA).
24. *Philip Head & Sons Ltd v Showfronts Ltd* [1970] 1 Lloyd's Rep 140 (QB).

Rule 3

Rule 3 is as follows:

 SGA 1979, s 18, rule 3

Where there is a contract for the sale of specific goods in a deliverable state but the seller is bound to weigh, measure, test, or do some other act or thing with reference to the goods for the purpose of ascertaining the price, the property does not pass until the act or thing is done and the buyer has notice that it has been done.

As with rule 2, rule 3 is concerned with a conditional contract with the condition to be met by the seller. It applies in cases where the passing of property is conditional upon the execution by the seller of an act in relation to the goods. In *Lord Eldon v Hedley Brothers*,[25] the seller sold a quantity of haystacks with delivery at the buyer's convenience and the price paid immediately although liable to adjustment once the haystacks were weighed on delivery. The Court of Appeal held that the property in the haystacks passed to the buyer when the contract was made. As the following case demonstrates, no one other than the seller may satisfy the condition and if anyone other than the seller weighs, measures, tests, etc. the goods for the purpose of ascertaining the price, then rule 3 will not apply.

 ***Nanka-Bruce v Commonwealth Trust Ltd* [1926] AC 77 (PC)**

FACTS: Nanka-Bruce arranged to consign a cargo of cocoa to Laing, at a rate of 59s per 60 lbs load. Laing would then resell the cocoa to Commonwealth Trust Ltd ('Commonwealth'), who would check the weights, thus enabling Laing to pay according to the weights so checked. Commonwealth bought and took delivery of the cocoa and credited Laing with the purchase price. Nanka-Bruce alleged that Commonwealth had converted the cocoa and so commenced proceedings. In order to resolve the dispute, the court had to determine who owned the cocoa.

HELD: The action failed. The Privy Council held that rule 3 did not apply as it was Commonwealth (and not Nanka-Bruce) who checked the weights. As property in the cocoa passed from Nanka-Bruce before Commonwealth had checked the weight, the cocoa had not been converted. The checking of the weights by Commonwealth was not a condition precedent to the passing of the property to the buyer.

COMMENT: Where the goods are weighed, measured, tested, etc. by a party other than the seller, even where that other party has some interest in the goods, property in the goods will not pass under rule 3, but will pass under rules 1 or 2 as appropriate unless it can be shown that the parties have agreed otherwise. As with the previous rule, the buyer must have notice that the act (of weighing, measuring, etc.) has been done.

25. [1935] 2 KB 1 (CA).

Rule 4

Rule 4 is as follows:

 SGA 1979, s 18, rule 4

When goods are delivered to the buyer on approval or on sale or return or other similar terms the property in the goods passes to the buyer:

(a) when he signifies his approval or acceptance to the seller or does any other act adopting the transaction

(b) if he does not signify his approval or acceptance to the seller but retains the goods without giving notice of rejection, then, if a time has been fixed for the return of the goods, on the expiration of that time, and, if no time has been fixed, on the expiration of a reasonable time.

It will be observed from the wording of rule 4 that there is no express reference to specific goods. Rule 4 is concerned with goods that 'are delivered to the buyer on approval or on sale or return or other similar terms'. Since a person who is in receipt of goods on approval or sale or return is under no obligation to purchase the goods, the use of the word 'buyer' in this rule might appear to be rather curious. It has also been queried whether a sale or return transaction is even a contract of sale at all or whether it is just 'an offer to sell, accompanied by delivery, which must actually be accepted before it becomes a contract of sale'.[26] If that is the case, then 'up to that point it is a mere bailment'.[27]

When will the buyer accept the transaction for the purposes of rule 4? The buyer signifying to the seller his approval or acceptance is straightforward enough, although what might amount to him doing 'any other act adopting the transaction' is more difficult and is not helped by the wording of the section being 'difficult to construe'.[28] The position of a person who has received goods on sale or return is that he has the *option* of becoming the buyer in three different ways. He may either (i) pay the price; or (ii) he may retain the goods beyond a reasonable time for their return; or (iii) he may do an act inconsistent with him being other than a buyer. For example, if the recipient of the goods retains them for an unreasonable period of time, or sells or pledges them, he does something inconsistent with the exercise of his option to return them and thereby adopts the transaction. In these situations, the property in the goods passes to him. The following case illustrates the position.

 Kirkham v Attenborough **[1897] 1 QB 201 (CA)**

FACTS: The claimant carried on business as a manufacturing jeweller and had delivered to a customer a large quantity of jewellery on sale or return, some of which was pledged with the defendant pawnbroker. The claimant claimed the return of the goods or their value.

---

26. See John N Adams and Hector MacQueen, *Atiyah's Sale of Goods* (12th edn, Pearson 2010) 318.

27. ibid.

28. *Kirkham v Attenborough* [1897] 1 QB 201 (CA) 204 (Lopes LJ).

HELD: The Court of Appeal held that where a person who has received goods on sale or return pledges them, he thereby does an act adopting the transaction within the meaning of rule 4(a) of the SGA 1893. As a result, the property in the goods passed to the customer and so the claimant, could not recover them from the defendant.

COMMENT: Lord Esher MR explained the position in the following way.

> By the Act the property is to pass to the buyer when 'he signifies his approval or acceptance to the seller or does any other act adopting the transaction'. The transaction mentioned cannot mean the delivery of the goods on sale or return, because that had been done already, and it must mean that part of the transaction which makes the buyer the purchaser of the goods—in other words, the transaction adopted is that the goods have been sold to and bought by the person who received them originally on sale or return. There must be some act which shews that he adopts the transaction; but any act which is consistent only with his being the purchaser is sufficient. The act done by [the customer], who was a possible purchaser under this contract, was that he pawned the goods. He could not get them back from the pawnbroker without repaying the sum advanced, and such a situation is inconsistent with his free power to return them. He ought not to have done this unless he meant to treat himself as purchaser, and by doing it he made himself purchaser; and the only right of the person who has entrusted him with the goods is to sue for the price of them.[29]

What amounts to a reasonable time for the purpose of the rule is a question of fact depending on all of the circumstances, which might include particular known trade fluctuations.[30] The following case provides an example of how the facts can influence what amounts to a reasonable time.

Poole v Smith's Car Sales (Balham) Ltd [1962] 1 WLR 744 (CA)

FACTS: The claimant and defendant were both car dealers. Poole was short of space in his premises and so, in August 1960, he arranged for Smith's Car Sales (Balham) Ltd ('Smith's') to keep a car at its premises on a sale or return basis. Poole authorized Smith's to sell the car if it could, provided that Poole received a minimum sum of £325 for it. In October and November 1960, Poole repeatedly asked Smith's to return the car to him, which it only did at the end of November. However, the car was returned in a badly damaged state and Poole refused to accept it. He sued Smith's for £325, this representing the price of the car sold and delivered to them.

HELD: The Court of Appeal held that in the absence of evidence of a contrary intention, the contract was one of delivery on sale or return within the meaning of rule 4 of the SGA 1893 and, accordingly, since there was no rejection of the property, it passed to Smith's after a reasonable time. In all the circumstances, including a seasonal decline in the second-hand car market, a reasonable time had elapsed and Smith's was liable.

★ See CF Parker, 'Sale or Return' (1962) 25 MLR 726

But what if the person who obtains the goods on sale or return then resells them to a third party again on the basis of sale or return? Is that an act in which 'he signifies his approval or acceptance to the seller or does any other act adopting the transaction' for the purpose of rule 4(a)?

 Genn v Winkel (1912) 17 Com Cas 323 (CA)

FACTS: On 4 January, Winkel (a diamond merchant) delivered a quantity of diamonds to Genn (a diamond broker) on sale or return. Later that day, Genn delivered the diamonds to a third person on sale or return, and this third person then transferred them to a fourth person. The fourth person then lost the diamonds. Winkel commenced proceedings against Genn for the price of the diamonds.

HELD: The claim succeeded and Winkel recovered the price of the diamonds from Genn. Buckley LJ stated:

> The fact that he lost them is immaterial, and also when he lost them. The question is: 'To whom did the goods belong at the moment when this happened?' It seems to me that on January 6, when the third person had parted with the goods to a fourth person, upon terms inconsistent with his obligation towards the defendant, the third person was buying, and, therefore, the defendant was buying, so that at that moment—namely, on January 6—the property passed from the plaintiff to the defendant.[31]

Fletcher Moulton LJ went on to discuss the rights of Genn against the other persons involved:

> The contract of sale or return appears to me clearly to be a contract whereby the person to whom the goods are delivered acquires a right to hold them for a reasonable time, during which he can make up his mind to keep the goods, in which case it becomes a sale on credit, and he is liable to pay the price, or he can return the goods. Under those circumstances a person who receives goods on sale or return and at once passes them on to someone else under a like contract is entitled to demand them from that third person just as soon as the original owner of the goods has the right to demand them from him, and, therefore, I do not see that he has lessened or impeded his power of returning the goods when the owner of the goods has a right to demand them back, but I am clear that, if he allows a period to elapse before he hands them to a third person on sale or return, he has done an act which limits and impedes his power of returning the goods as soon as the owner of the goods demands them. For instance, if fourteen days be a reasonable time in such a contract in this particular trade, and if he waits seven days before entrusting the goods to a third person on sale or return, that third person has a right to keep them as against him for fourteen days, whereas the original owner of the goods has a right to the return of them within seven days from that date, and I think that that is clearly an act inconsistent with anything but his having adopted the transaction. Therefore, I think that in that case it would be taken that the purchase was made.[32]

---

31. (1912) 17 Com Cas 323 (CA) 327.   32. ibid 325.

Where the person in receipt of the goods is unable to return them either within the period allowed or at all in circumstances that were beyond his control, then he cannot be said to have done an act which adopts the transaction,[33] nor can it be said that he has retained the goods without giving notice of rejection within the permitted time or any reasonable time,[34] both requiring some degree of voluntariness.

Re Ferrier (ex p Trustee v Donald) [1944] Ch 295 (Ch)

FACTS: Donald (an antique furniture dealer) delivered certain pieces of furniture to Ferrier on a sale or return basis, with a stipulated period of one week for returning the goods if unwanted. Two days after the delivery, the furniture was seized to pay Ferrier's creditors, which naturally prevented their return to Donald. Ferrier was subsequently declared bankrupt and Donald recovered possession of the furniture. Ferrier's trustee in bankruptcy claimed that the furniture had vested in Ferrier and so sought to recover the furniture from Donald.

HELD: Given the circumstances, Ferrier had not retained the goods within the meaning of rule 4(b) so they never became her property. Accordingly, Donald could retain the furniture.

As the following case demonstrates, where the terms of the contract spell out when property is to pass, then the parties' intention prevails and the rules in s 18 do not arise.

Weiner v Gill [1906] 2 KB 574 (CA)

FACTS: Weiner (a manufacturing jeweller) delivered some jewellery to Huhn, who traded as a retailer of such goods. The terms of the agreement stated that the goods were 'On approbation. On sale for cash only or return. Goods had on approbation or on sale or return remain the property of Weiner until such goods are settled for or charged.' Huhn then delivered the goods to Longman, after being told by Longman that Longman had a customer who might be interested in purchasing them. Huhn made this delivery to Longman on terms that he would either pay cash or would return them in a few days. In fact, Longman had no such customer and fraudulently pledged the goods with Gill, a pawnbroker. Weiner sought to recover the goods from Gill.

HELD: The Court of Appeal held that this was not a contract of sale or return within the meaning of rule 4 because the agreement made between Weiner and Huhn demonstrated that it was their intention that the property in the goods should not pass to Huhn until they were paid for. It followed that the property had not passed from Weiner and he was therefore entitled to recover the goods from Gill. The transaction was, therefore, not one to which s 18 applied, although it potentially fell under the remit of s 19 on reservation of title.

---

33. SGA 1979, s 18, rule 4(a).   34. ibid s 18, rule 4(b).

It will be remembered that rule 4 sets out what acts by the 'buyer' will cause the property in the goods to pass, although, apart from referring to a notice of rejection, it is silent as to what he must do if he wishes to return the goods. Clearly, returning them to the supplier will satisfy this requirement, although this might not always be practicable. In the following case, the Court of Appeal held that unless the terms of the agreement provide otherwise, any intimation between the parties that the 'buyer' does not wish to purchase the goods will suffice.

Atari Corporation (UK) Ltd v Electronics Boutique Stores (UK) Ltd [1998] QB 539 (CA)

FACTS: Electronics Boutique Stores (UK) Ltd ('EB') entered into a sale or return agreement with Atari Corporation (UK) Ltd ('Atari') for certain supplies of computer games and equipment. The agreement provided that payment should be made by November 1995, but allowed for the sale or return of the goods until the end of January 1996. On 19 January 1996, EB wrote to Atari advising it that it had withdrawn certain of the goods supplied and stated that once the unsold stock had been returned by the stores to its central warehouse, it would help with the handover and accounting. Atari replied that because EB had failed to pay the invoices by the due date, it was in breach of contract and had thereby lost the right to return the goods. At first instance, Hooper J found for Atari and held that, as the goods were not physically available for collection at that time, the 19 January letter was not a notice of rejection but was merely an indication that the goods would be returned at an unascertained date. EB appealed.

HELD: The Court of Appeal allowed EB's appeal and held that its 19 January letter did constitute effective notice sufficient to trigger their right to return the goods. Further, it was wrong to require that the goods be immediately available for collection at the time the notice was issued and that the goods only needed to be made available within a reasonable time.

COMMENT: This decision recognizes the commercial reality of this kind of transaction where goods are ordered by a central buying department for delivery into a warehouse for onward transmission to the buyer's stores. Decisions are often taken centrally and it would clearly be impractical for the goods to be available for collection at the same time as a rejection notice is given and often it will be impractical even to be in any position to advise the seller in precise terms which and how many of the goods are being rejected. Waller LJ pointed out that there was no requirement in rule 4 for the notice to be in writing and that it was unnecessary to set out in any detail the precise goods which were being rejected, provided the notice referred clearly to the goods in generic terms. He further pointed out that if a notice was given which did suggest that goods were available for immediate collection, then any failure to hand them over immediately would constitute a conversion of the goods by the 'buyer' but would not invalidate the notice. He went on to state that if it were permissible to serve a notice prior to the date by which the goods had to be returned to the supplier, giving reasonable notice of some future date for collection, he could see no reason why there should be a requirement to have the goods physically available at the time of the notice as opposed to the time of collection and, once again, a failure to have the goods available at the expiry of the reasonable notice would constitute a conversion but would not invalidate the notice. As to the commercial reality of the transaction, where the goods were spread out across various outlets throughout the country, it was open to the buyers to give notice exercising the right to reject with the sellers' entitlement to collect the goods arising only at a reasonable time after the notice.

⭐ See John N Adams, 'Sale or Return Contracts: Shedding a Little Light' (1998) 61 MLR 432

Rule 5 and unascertained goods

It has already been noted that, subject to the provisions contained in s 20A in relation to undivided shares in goods forming part of a bulk, s 16 explains that in the case of a contract for the sale of unascertained goods, no property in them can be transferred to the buyer unless and until the goods are ascertained. This provision is drafted in the negative: it does not explain when property in unascertained goods will be transferred to a buyer, but only when it cannot be transferred. Since property in the goods cannot be transferred to a buyer until the goods are ascertained, it is important to understand when goods will become ascertained. This was stated simply by the Court of Appeal in *Re Wait*[35] as when the goods are identified as *the* goods to be used in the performance of the contract. Consequently, where, after the making of the contract, the goods become ascertained, absent a contrary intention, property in them will not be transferred until they have been unconditionally appropriated to the contract by one of the parties with the assent of the other. This is set out by rule 5(1), which is as follows.

> **SGA 1979, s 18, rule 5(1)**
>
> Where there is a contract for the sale of unascertained or future goods by description, and goods of that description and in a deliverable state are unconditionally appropriated to the contract, either by the seller with the assent of the buyer or by the buyer with the assent of the seller, the property in the goods then passes to the buyer; and the assent may be express or implied, and may be given either before or after the appropriation is made.

 The requirement for goods to be in a deliverable state is discussed at p 237

It has already been seen that, in addition to the requirement that the goods need to be 'in a deliverable state', the goods must also be 'unconditionally appropriated to the contract'. To constitute an unconditional appropriation of the goods to the contract, the parties must have had, or be reasonably supposed to have had, an intention to attach the contract irrevocably to the goods, so that *those goods and no others* are the subject of the sale and become the property of the buyer.[36] This means, of course, that the seller will not be able to change his mind and supply any other goods, no matter how similar they are to those that have been allocated to the contract. Pearson J explained this principle in *Carlos Federspiel & Co SA v Charles Twigg & Co Ltd*:[37]

> A mere setting apart or selection by the seller of the goods which he expects to use in performance of the contract is not enough. If that is all, he can change his mind and use those goods in performance of some other contract and use some other goods in performance of this contract.[38]

The following example demonstrates the application of the principle in practice.

---

35. [1927] 1 Ch 606 (CA).
36. *Carlos Federspiel & Co SA v Charles Twigg & Co Ltd* [1957] 1 Lloyd's Rep 240 (QB).
37. [1957] 1 Lloyd's Rep 240 (QB).   38. ibid 255.

Eg ComCorp Ltd

ComCorp Ltd orders twenty bags of coal from a coal merchant to be delivered to its offices. The coal merchant agrees to deliver the coal when their driver is next in ComCorp's area so that he can make a number of deliveries on the same day. When the day comes around for delivery, the driver loads his van with 100 bags of coal, 20 of which are for ComCorp, which the driver moves towards the rear doors of his van so as to make the delivery to ComCorp easier. When he arrives at ComCorp's offices, the driver loads his trolley to its maximum load capacity of ten bags and wheels it to ComCorp's coal cellar where, after the cellar door has been unlocked by the manager, he empties the sacks, one at a time, before returning to his vehicle for the remaining ten bags, which he delivers in the same way.

The property in the coal cannot pass to ComCorp until it has been ascertained. It was certainly unascertained when the coal was loaded on the delivery vehicle, and it remained unascertained even when the driver moved the twenty bags towards the rear doors to ease delivery. It is irrelevant that those bags were intended for delivery to ComCorp. The reason for this can be seen from the judgment of Pearson J in the *Carlos Federspiel* case noted earlier. Merely setting aside the goods for delivery does not amount to an unconditional appropriation of them to the contract. The coal only became ascertained when it was unconditionally appropriated to the contract, and this occurred only when the driver emptied the sacks, one by one, in ComCorp's cellar. Rule 5(1) not only requires an unconditional appropriation of the goods to the contract, but also that this is done with the assent of the other party. This assent can be either express or implied and, in our example, it was implied when ComCorp's manager unlocked the cellar door. The sacks remaining on his trolley awaiting emptying, together with those he moved towards the van's rear doors, remained unascertained until he emptied them in the cellar. Unless there was a contrary intention, it was only at that stage that the property in the coal passed to ComCorp.

It will be noted from rule 5(1) that the unconditional appropriation may be by either the seller or the buyer, but must be with the other's assent. This assent may be express, but more likely it will be implied and may be given either before or after the appropriation is made. Where the assent is given after the unconditional appropriation is made, property in the goods passes when the other party's assent is given and not upon the appropriation of the goods.[39] Once the goods have been irrevocably appropriated to the contract then those goods, and no others, become the property of the buyer. This is the reason why the seller cannot then supply substitute goods in the purported performance of the contract. Once there has been an apparent intention to attach the goods irrevocably to the contract, then that is it. A good example of this can be seen in the following case.

39. *Pignataro v Gilroy* [1919] 1 KB 459 (KB).

Re London Wine Co (Shippers) Ltd
[1986] PCC 121 (QB)

FACTS: London Wine Co (Shippers) Ltd ('LWC') was a company dealing in wines. It ran a scheme whereby customers could purchase quantities of wine for investment. Customers bought wine, which remained stored in LWC's warehouse in bulk. The purchases would be entered in LWC's stock book and allocated an identification number. LWC provided the customers with documents of title confirming them to be the sole owners of the wine purchased. One customer bought LWC's entire stock of a particular wine. In other instances, a number of contracts were made with different buyers exhausting LWC's stock of a particular wine. In each case, LWC issued the customers with a document confirming that they were the sole owners of the wine they had purchased. LWC subsequently went into receivership. The question of ownership of the wine arose.

HELD: Oliver J held that in these cases there was no appropriation of the wines and therefore no property in the wine passed to the buyers. Consequently, the wine remained the property of LWC and thus formed an asset of LWC that the receiver was entitled to dispose of.

COMMENT: This case illustrates that no appropriation can take place unless there is an intention to attach specific goods irrevocably to the contract. As there were several purchasers of the same kind of wine, it was impossible to determine who owned which wine held by LWC. Even had there been just one customer, it was still impossible to attach specific bottles of wine to that customer's contract, and it was always open to LWC to have purchased further stocks for these customers. One of the categories of wines held by LWC for purchasers involved mortgages of the wines purchased by the purchaser, where the warehouseman holding such wines provided an acknowledgment to the mortgagee that the wine purchased by the mortgagor would be held to the mortgagee's order. As to these wines, it was held that the acknowledgments of the warehouseman given to the mortgagees might raise an estoppel in the purchaser's favour. An estoppel merely had the effect that LWC and the warehouseman could not deny that the purchaser had title to the quantity of wine in question held by the warehouseman, but did not create any actual title to the wine vested in the purchaser. The fact that LWC was estopped from denying that it had sold and appropriated to the contract a given quantity of wine of a particular description could not affect the rights of the receiver who, under the floating charge, acquired goods of that description.

Even where property has not been allocated to each individual customer, in a case where customers have paid for goods and left them with the seller for storage, on that seller's receivership the goods are to be regarded as being the property of the customer who has paid for them and not of the seller. The decision in *Re London Wine* was distinguished in *Re Stapylton Fletcher Ltd*,[40] where it was observed that, unlike the situation in *Re London Wine*, the reserve stocks were completely segregated from the trading stocks, the documentation was in good order, and the company did not regard the wine as still belonging to them, even to the extent of refraining from borrowing it.

---

40. [1994] 1 WLR 1181 (Ch).

Re Stapylton Fletcher Ltd [1994] 1 WLR 1181 (Ch)

FACTS: A wine merchant sold wine to customers who left it with him for storage, drawing it out at will. The wine merchant separated this wine from his general trading stock. On the wine merchant's receivership, the receiver applied to the court for directions as to who owned the wine. The customers argued that under s 16 of the SGA 1979, the goods had been ascertained by being set aside from the trading stock, and so belonged to them.

HELD: The wine was the property of the customers who had paid for it. The fact that the wine had been set aside in a bonded warehouse as non-trading stock was sufficient to show that the goods had been ascertained. Furthermore, a contract of sale did not create equitable rights, so no trust existed, nor any interest based on estoppel or specific performance.

COMMENT: See also *Customs & Excise Commissioners v Everwine Ltd.*[41] Here, E stored its wine in F's bonded warehouse. Each sale by E of wine was followed by a 'release note' to F specifying the goods sold. The Court of Appeal held that property had passed to the buyer only where the wine specified in the release notes represented the entire stock of wine of that particular description held by F on the day of the sale, because this amounted to an appropriation for the purposes of rule 5. However, in the cases where F held a larger quantity of stock of a particular wine to that sold, and there having been no physical separation of the sold wine, there was no appropriation of the wine to the contract and therefore no property passed to those buyers.

★ See NR Campbell, 'Passing of Property in Contracts for the Sale of Unascertained Goods [1996] JBL 199

Where the buyer has to collect the goods from a third party rather than from the seller himself, then the property (and risk) in the unascertained goods in the possession of that third party passes from the seller to the buyer when that third party acknowledges them as belonging to the buyer.

 Wardar's (Import & Export) Co Ltd v W Norwood & Sons Ltd [1968] 2 QB 663 (CA)

FACTS: W Norwood & Sons Ltd ('Norwood') sold to Wardar's (Import & Export) Co Ltd ('Wardar's') 600 cartons of frozen kidneys from a bulk of 1,500 cartons that were stored in a cold store belonging to an agent of Norwood. Wardar's carrier was sent to collect the goods, arriving at 8.00am, where he handed a delivery note to the agent, with such a note amounting to an authority from Norwood to the cold store to release the goods to him and directing the porters to load the kidneys onto the carrier's refrigerated van. By 8.00am, the agent had already set aside the 600 cartons for the carrier, by setting them on the pavement outside the cold store to await collection by the carrier. The loading commenced at 8.00am, but the carrier had not turned on the refrigerating machine in his vehicle, which required three hours operation to lower the temperature sufficiently. He only switched on the machine at 10.00am. Half of the cartons had been loaded by this time, when the carrier noticed that some of the kidneys still on the pavement were dripping. The loading was completed at 12 noon and the carrier signed a receipt for the kidneys with the qualification that he had received them 'in soft condition'. On arrival at their destination, the kidneys were found to be unfit for human consumption and were condemned. Wardar's refused to pay for the kidneys and commenced proceedings against Norwood. Norwood counterclaimed for the price of the kidneys.

HELD: The Court of Appeal held that property and risk in unascertained goods which were in the possession of a third party passed when that third party, having selected an appropriate part of the goods from the bulk for the buyer, acknowledged those goods as the buyer's, for there was then an unconditional appropriation of the goods to the contract. There was thus an unconditional appropriation of the goods to the contract when the delivery note was accepted and permission given to load the goods. Consequently, the risk of deterioration in the kidneys awaiting delivery on the pavement passed to Wardar's when the carrier handed over the delivery note to the cold store, for at that moment the cold store acknowledged that they belonged to Wardar's, and, since the damage occurred subsequently, the risk fell on Wardar's. Accordingly, Norwood's counterclaim succeeded and Wardar's was required to pay the purchase price.

The concept of unconditional appropriation is not unique to commercial law and, in the following case, it was applied in order to determine whether theft had been committed.

 Edwards v Ddin [1976] 1 WLR 942 (QB)

FACTS: Ddin drove into a garage and requested the attendant to fill up his tank with petrol and put oil in his engine. After the attendant had done so, Ddin drove off without paying. He was charged with theft, contrary to s 1 of the Theft Act 1968, which requires a dishonest appropriation of property *belonging to another* with the intention of permanently depriving the other of it. Edwards (the prosecutor) contended that the property in the goods had not passed to Ddin because the garage had reserved its rights of disposal over the goods under s 19(1) of the SGA 1893 until the condition of payment had been met, which meant that the goods still belonged to the garage and were therefore capable of being stolen from it.

HELD: Once the petrol and oil had mixed with the petrol and oil in Ddin's car, the garage could not be said to have reserved, as a term in the contract, the right of disposal under s 19, and that the delivery of the petrol and oil was an unconditional appropriation of the goods to the contract with the assent of both parties. This meant that under rules 5(1) and (2) of s 18 of the SGA 1893, the property passed to Ddin the moment it was placed in his car and, as it was then his property, he did not appropriate the goods of *another* (the owner of the garage) as was required to satisfy the offence of theft. Of course, the garage could have sued Ddin in the civil courts for the price of the fuel.

⭐ See Claire Miskin, 'Petrol Dishonesty Obtained Without Theft' (1977) 41 J Crim L 8

Rule 5(2) deals with appropriation by delivery to a carrier.

 SGA 1979, s 18, rule 5(2)

Where, in pursuance of the contract, the seller delivers the goods to the buyer or to a carrier or other bailee or custodier (whether named by the buyer or not) for the purpose of transmission to the buyer, and does not reserve the right of disposal, he is to be taken to have unconditionally appropriated the goods to the contract.

The act of delivering the goods is a clear example of appropriating the goods to the contract. Consequently, when the goods are delivered either to the buyer, or to a carrier for onward transmission to the buyer, this will usually amount to them being unconditionally appropriated to the contract. Rule 5(2) will not apply in cases where the seller reserves the right of disposal, as in such a case there is no unconditional appropriation of the goods, and, of course, no property in goods can pass where the goods are unascertained[42] and, as already observed, this necessitates an intention to attach specific goods irrevocably to the contract.

 The right of disposal is discussed at p 256

Healy v Howlett & Sons [1917] 1 KB 337 (KB)

FACTS: Healy (a fish exporter based in Ireland) contracted to sell twenty boxes of hard, bright mackerel to Howlett & Sons ('Howlett'). It was agreed that Healy was to send the fish to Howlett by rail. Later that day, Healy dispatched by rail 190 boxes of the fish and informed the railway company at Holyhead to deliver twenty of the 190 boxes to Howlett and to deliver the remaining 170 boxes to other buyers. Healy did not mark any of the boxes for any specific customer, leaving it to the railway company to allot the appropriate number of boxes to each order. Healy's invoice, which was sent by post after the fish had been loaded on the train, was endorsed with the words 'at sole risk of purchaser after putting fish on rail here'. Unfortunately, the train on which the mackerel had been loaded was delayed and arrived so late that the consignment of mackerel missed the connecting boat by which they ought to have been carried to Holyhead. When the consignment eventually arrived at Holyhead an official of the railway company, in accordance with Healy's instructions, picked out and earmarked twenty boxes for delivery to Howlett and did the same in respect of the fish for the other buyers. As a result of the delay, when the mackerel reached Howlett it was not in a merchantable condition and Howlett refused to accept delivery. Healy sued to recover the purchase price.

HELD: It was held that there had been no appropriation of the twenty boxes to Howlett until they had been set aside for it at Holyhead, by which time they had already deteriorated in quality. Consequently, Howlett was entitled to reject the mackerel, and Healy could not recover the price. The invoice containing the words 'at sole risk of purchaser after putting fish on rail here' was clearly a post-contractual document and, as there was no evidence of Howlett's assent to those words, it formed no part of it.

Rules 5(3) and 5(4) deal with ascertainment and appropriation 'by exhaustion', and state as follows.

---

42. SGA 1979, s 16.

SGA 1979, s 18, rules 5(3) and 5(4)

5(3) Where there is a contract for the sale of a specified quantity of unascertained goods in a deliverable state forming part of a bulk which is identified either in the contract or by subsequent agreement between the parties and the bulk is reduced to (or to less than) that quantity, then, if the buyer under that contract is the only buyer to whom goods are then due out of the bulk:

(a) the remaining goods are to be taken as appropriated to that contract at the time when the bulk is so reduced, and

(b) the property in those goods then passes to that buyer.

5(4) Paragraph (3) above applies also (with the necessary modifications) where a bulk is reduced to (or to less than) the aggregate of the quantities due to a single buyer under separate contracts relating to that bulk and he is the only buyer to whom goods are then due out of that bulk.

Rules 5(3) and 5(4) were added to s 18 by the Sale of Goods (Amendment) Act 1995 and place on a statutory footing the decision of Mustill J in the following case.

Karlshamns Oljefabriker A/B v Eastport Navigation Corp (The Elafi) [1981] 2 Lloyd's Rep 679 (QB)

FACTS: A cargo of 22,000 tonnes of copra was loaded onto a vessel (*The Elafi*) of which Karlshamns Oljefabriker A/B ('Karlshamns') purchased 6,000 tonnes in two separate contracts. Before Karlshamns received its part of the cargo, the vessel (which belonged to Eastport Navigation Corp) made deliveries in Rotterdam and Hamburg, where 16,000 tonnes of the copra were offloaded, leaving aboard only enough to satisfy Karlshamns' two contracts. Some of the cargo was damaged by water and a dispute arose as to who had the property (and risk) in the goods.

HELD: Mustill J held that Karlshamns' two orders could be aggregated and that the remaining quantity of copra on board the vessel had been ascertained by exhaustion. Consequently, the property in the remaining copra had passed to Karlshamns upon such ascertainment.

COMMENT: Before the 16,000 tonnes of the copra had been offloaded, Karlshamns' 6,000 tonnes were unascertained. They only became ascertained once the 16,000 tonnes had been offloaded because it was only then that there was any certainty that the remainder of the cargo was intended for Karlshamns. In this case, ascertainment and appropriation occurred at the same time.

⭐ See JWA Thornely, 'The Passing of Property on Sales of Parts of a Bulk' (1982) 41 CLJ 239

The following conditions must be met for rule 5(3) to apply:

- the goods must be in a deliverable state;
- the sale must be of a specified quantity of unascertained goods that form part of a bulk;
- the bulk referred to must have been identified by the contract or alternatively by subsequent agreement between the parties;
- the bulk must have been reduced to the amount of, or less than, the goods due to the buyer;
- the buyer is the only buyer remaining who is entitled to the goods from the bulk.

Where the rule does apply, the goods will be unconditionally ascertained by exhaustion and the property in them will be transferred to the buyer, as the following example demonstrates.

Eg ComCorp Ltd

ComCorp Ltd owns a fuel distribution business and uses a delivery tanker which holds 100,000 litres of fuel. The tanker is filled each day before it leaves the depot to make the deliveries. Taxi Services Ltd and Retail Delivery Ltd both agree to buy 40,000 litres each. Book Distributors plc agrees to buy the remaining 20,000 litres. At this stage, the fuel in the tanker is unascertained. ComCorp delivers the agreed amounts of fuel to Taxi Services and Retail Delivery, leaving 20,000 litres remaining in the tanker. As soon as these deliveries have been made, the fuel remaining in the tanker becomes ascertained by exhaustion, resulting in the property passing to Book Distributors under rule 5(3).

Table 11.2 explains the operation of the various aspects of rule 5.

TABLE 11.2 Rules relating to unascertained goods

Rule	Property in the goods passes to the buyer when ...
5(1)	goods that match the contract description and in a deliverable state are unconditionally appropriated to the contract. This can be by either the seller or the buyer, but must be with the other's assent, which may be express or implied and may be given either before or after the appropriation is made.
5(2)	the seller delivers the goods to the buyer or carrier for the purpose of transmission to the buyer, and does not reserve the right of disposal, he is to be taken to have unconditionally appropriated the goods to the contract.
5(3)	where there is a contract for the sale of a specified quantity of unascertained goods in a deliverable state forming part of a bulk which is identified either in the contract or by subsequent agreement between the parties and the bulk is reduced to (or to less than) that quantity, then, if the buyer under that contract is the only buyer to whom goods are then due out of the bulk: (a) the remaining goods are to be taken as appropriated to that contract at the time when the bulk is so reduced; and (b) the property in those goods then passes to that buyer.
5(4)	rule 5(3) applies also (with the necessary modifications) where a bulk is reduced to (or to less than) the aggregate of the quantities due to a single buyer under separate contracts relating to that bulk and he is the only buyer to whom goods are then due out of that bulk.

Undivided shares in goods forming part of a bulk

As noted previously, the rule in s 16 that no property in unascertained goods can be transferred to the buyer unless and until they are ascertained is subject to the exception in s 20A,[43] which is concerned with undivided shares in goods forming part of a bulk. Before considering s 20A in any detail, it might be helpful first to consider the judgment of the Court of Appeal in *Re Wait* so as to understand the kind of injustice that s 20A sought to remedy.

---

43. Added by the Sale of Goods (Amendment) Act 1995.

Re Wait [1927] 1 Ch 606 (CA)

FACTS: Wait purchased 1,000 tonnes of wheat, which was then loaded on a ship for delivery. The following day, he sold 500 tonnes of the bulk to a sub-purchaser, who paid Wait for the goods. However, by the date the ship docked, Wait had been declared bankrupt and his trustee in bankruptcy claimed the entire consignment of 1,000 tonnes.

HELD: The Court of Appeal held that Wait's trustee in bankruptcy was entitled to succeed and that the sub-purchaser was entitled to nothing, even though he had already paid Wait for his 500 tonnes of wheat. As the sub-purchaser's 500 tonnes had not been ascertained (i.e. separated from the 1,000 tonnes bulk and identified as *the* wheat to be used in the performance of the contract), property did not pass to him.

COMMENT: Following the enactment of s 20A, cases such as this would now be decided differently.

The effect of s 20A is to permit a buyer who has purchased a specified quantity of unascertained goods from an identified bulk to become co-owner of the bulk (together with other co-owners), provided that he has paid for some or all of the goods. In other words, such a buyer may obtain a share in the ownership of the bulk. The section does not, of course, alter the rule that property must be ascertained before it can pass to a buyer, but it provides some protection to a buyer who has paid for a specified quantity of otherwise unascertained goods from an identified bulk from the consequences of a seller becoming insolvent before the property is ascertained. For the purpose of s 20A, 'bulk' means 'a mass or collection of goods of the same kind which is contained in a defined space or area and is such that any goods in the bulk are interchangeable with any other goods therein of the same number or quantity'.[44]

The following conditions, set out in s 20A(1), must be met for s 20A to apply:

- The contract must be for the sale of a specified quantity of unascertained goods. This must be expressed in units of quantity (e.g. 50 litres or 1,000 tonnes) and not fractions or percentages (such as a quarter or 25 per cent).
- The goods (or some of them) must form part of a bulk that is identified either in the contract or by subsequent agreement between the parties.
- The buyer must have paid the price for some or all of the goods which are the subject of the contract and which form part of the bulk.

Provided that these conditions have been satisfied then, unless the parties agree otherwise, s 20A(2) states that:

- property in an undivided share in the bulk is transferred to the buyer; and
- the buyer becomes an owner in common of the bulk.

The parties may agree to oust the operation of s 20A, which will mean that the buyer will not get an undivided share in the bulk. Alternatively, they may agree that property in the undivided share will pass at some time after payment (although not before payment, as payment is a pre-condition to the application of the section).[45]

The undivided share of a buyer in a bulk at any time shall be 'such share as the quantity of goods paid for and due to the buyer out of the bulk bears to the quantity

---

44. SGA 1979, s 61.   45. ibid s 20A(1)(b).

of goods in the bulk at that time'.[46] To calculate the extent of a buyer's co-ownership at any time, it is necessary to divide the quantity of the goods paid for by the buyer and due to him by the quantity of goods in the bulk. Applying this to the facts in *Re Wait*, the sub-purchaser would have become a 50 per cent co-owner of the goods, with the remaining 50 per cent belonging to Wait's trustee in bankruptcy. Furthermore, where the aggregate of the undivided shares of buyers in a bulk determined under s 20A(3) would at any time exceed the whole of the bulk at that time, then the undivided share in the bulk of each buyer shall be reduced proportionately so that the aggregate of the undivided shares is equal to the whole bulk.[47]

Where a buyer has paid the price for only some of the goods due to him out of a bulk, any delivery to him out of the bulk will, for the purposes of s 20A, be ascribed in the first place to the goods in respect of which payment has been made,[48] and payment of part of the price for any goods will be treated as payment for a corresponding part of the goods.[49]

Deemed consent by co-owner to dealings in bulk goods

As discussed, the effect of s 20A is to create undivided shares in an identified bulk. This would create a problem because it would require *all* of the co-owners to be joined in order to transfer any part of the bulk. In some cases, this would also require the tracing of title to each part share. To overcome this problem, s 20B(1) provides that:

> a person who has become an owner in common of a bulk by virtue of s 20A shall be deemed to have consented to any delivery of goods out of the bulk to any other owner in common of the bulk, being goods which are due to him under his contract.

The practical effect of s 20(B)(1) is that a co-owner will not need the consent of the other co-owners in order to deal with his own share of the goods.

Retention of title

Consider the following example:

Eg ComCorp Ltd

ComCorp Ltd agrees to sell a quantity of goods to Buildquick Ltd, with Buildquick paying for the goods via twelve monthly instalments. Buildquick has, in the past, been close to insolvency, and the board of ComCorp is concerned that Buildquick might be liquidated before all the instalments have been paid. Accordingly, ComCorp includes a clause in the contract of sale which states that 'the goods shall remain the property of ComCorp Ltd until such time as the full purchase price has been paid'. After six instalments have been paid, Buildquick is liquidated and ComCorp seeks to recover the goods.

---

46. ibid s 20A(3).   47. ibid s 20A(4).   48. ibid s 20A(5).   49. ibid s 20A(6).

The question that arises is whether ComCorp is able to recover the goods from Buildquick. It has already been observed that, subject to the goods being ascertained, the parties are free to make whatever agreement they wish as to when property is to pass to the buyer. This means that the parties can, if they so wish, agree that property is to pass even if the goods have not been delivered and even if they have not been paid for. They can also agree that property in the goods is not to pass even after delivery and payment. Since many sellers sell their goods on credit terms to buyers who wish to pay only after they have resold the goods, the seller will wish to protect his position in the event his buyer is unable or unwilling to pay, possibly because of insolvency. The seller will want to know whether he has any rights over these goods entitling him to recover them, or their value, and, in the event of the buyer's insolvency, whether he has any priority over any of the other creditors. Since property passes when the parties intend it to pass, and for the purpose of ascertaining the intention of the parties regard shall be had to, amongst other things, the terms of the contract,[50] a properly advised seller will (as in the ComCorp example) incorporate into his contract a retention of title clause.[51] At its simplest, such a clause will provide that, notwithstanding the delivery of the goods, property does not pass until payment has been made. Since a retention of title clause has the effect of making property pass when the parties intend it to pass, it follows that the rules in s 18 will be inapplicable.

Where the goods are shipped and the bill of lading makes the goods deliverable to the order of the seller or his agent, then the seller is presumed to have reserved the right of disposal (i.e. ownership) in the goods.[52] Similarly, where the seller draws on the buyer for payment of the price and transmits the bill of exchange and bill of lading to the buyer together to secure either acceptance or payment of the bill of exchange, the buyer is bound to return the bill of lading if he does not honour the bill of exchange, and if he wrongfully retains the bill of lading the property in the goods does not pass to him.[53] Consequently, in this situation, property in the goods will remain with the seller.

As discussed shortly, some clauses go much further than the simple retention of title clause already noted, and the question that arises is whether these clauses are enforceable. Section 19 expressly permits a seller to 'reserve the right of disposal' of the goods until certain conditions have been fulfilled. Few conditions can be more important to sellers than being paid.

SGA 1979, s 19

(1) Where there is a contract for the sale of specific goods or where goods are subsequently appropriated to the contract, the seller may, by the terms of the contract or appropriation, reserve the right of disposal of the goods until certain conditions are fulfilled; and in such a case, notwithstanding the delivery of the goods to the buyer, or to a carrier or other bailee or custodier for the purpose of transmission to the buyer,

---

50. ibid s 17(2).

51. Retention of title clauses are also known as reservation of title clauses, or as *Romalpa* clauses (named after the leading case in this area, which is discussed on p 257).

52. SGA 1979, s 19(2).   53. ibid s 19(3).

the property in the goods does not pass to the buyer until the conditions imposed by the seller are fulfilled.

(2) Where goods are shipped, and by the bill of lading the goods are deliverable to the order of the seller or his agent, the seller is prima facie to be taken to reserve the right of disposal.

(3) Where the seller of goods draws on the buyer for the price, and transmits the bill of exchange and bill of lading to the buyer together to secure acceptance or payment of the bill of exchange, the buyer is bound to return the bill of lading if he does not honour the bill of exchange, and if he wrongfully retains the bill of lading the property in the goods does not pass to him.

Retention of title clauses will typically be invoked in the event of the buyer's insolvency where the buyer has yet to make full payment to the seller for goods bought (as in the ComCorp example discussed earlier). It is not, of course, necessary for the buyer to become insolvent before such a clause can be invoked: it can be invoked whenever the buyer owes money to the seller beyond the terms that were agreed in the contract. As with any contractual provision, a retention of title clause must be properly incorporated into the contract. If it has not been properly incorporated, then it will have no contractual force and will be unenforceable.

Simple retention of title clauses

In the simplest of cases, provided the clause has been properly incorporated into the contract of sale, an unpaid seller will be able to recover the goods sold. This is because the property in the goods will not have passed to the buyer, and the seller is merely recovering what belongs to him. This type of clause is often referred to as a 'simple retention of title' clause and permits the seller to recover unaltered goods sold but not paid for. It does not attempt to create any other kind of security.

More elaborate clauses

Difficulties often arise with retention of title clauses where the seller attempts to secure more extensive remedies against the buyer. A traditional starting point for discussion is the Court of Appeal's decision in the following case.

 Aluminium Industrie Vaassen BV v Romalpa Aluminium Ltd [1976] 1 WLR 676 (CA)

FACTS: Aluminium Industrie Vaasen BV ('AIV') sold aluminium foil to Romalpa Aluminium Ltd ('Romalpa'). The contract of sale contained an extensive retention of title clause, which included the following provisions:

- The ownership of the material to be delivered by AIV will only be transferred to the purchaser when he has met all that is owing to AIV no matter on what grounds.
- Until the date of payment, Romalpa, if AIV so desires, is required to store this material in such a way that it is clearly the property of AIV.

- AIV and Romalpa agree that, if Romalpa should make (a) new object(s) from the material, mix this material with (an)other object(s) or if this material in any way whatsoever becomes a constituent of (an)other object(s) AIV will be given the ownership of this (these) new object(s) as surety of the full payment of what Romalpa owes AIV.
- To this end AIV and Romalpa now agree that the ownership of the article(s) in question, whether finished or not, are to be transferred to AIV and that this transfer of ownership will be considered to have taken place through and at the moment of the single operation or event by which the material is converted into (a) new object(s), or is mixed with or becomes a constituent of (an)other object(s).
- Until the moment of full payment of what Romalpa owes AIV, Romalpa shall keep the object(s) in question for AIV in its capacity of fiduciary owner and, if required, shall store this (these) object(s) in such a way that it (they) can be recognized as such. Nevertheless, Romalpa will be entitled to sell these objects to a third party within the framework of the normal carrying on of his business and to deliver them on condition that, if AIV so requires, Romalpa, as long as it has not fully discharged its debt to AIV shall hand over to AIV the claims he has against his buyer emanating from this transaction.

Romalpa went into liquidation owing AIV more than £122,000. The receiver certified that aluminium foil to a value of more than £50,000 was being held by him. He also recovered more than £35,000 from Romalpa's customers, representing the price of finished goods made from the foil and sold to them, such money being in a separate bank account. AIV commenced proceedings, claiming it was entitled to a charge over the money held in the receiver's account.

HELD: The Court of Appeal upheld the retention of title clause and held that AIV was entitled to recover the foil and the £35,000. The obvious purpose of the clause was to secure for AIV so far as was possible, in the event of Romalpa's insolvency, against the risk of non-payment after it had parted with possession of but not the legal title to the goods, irrespective of whether or not that material retained its identity before payment was received. In order to give effect to that purpose, the Court was willing to imply, in addition to the power to sell the goods to sub-purchasers, an obligation on Romalpa to account in accordance with the normal fiduciary relationship of principal and agent, bailor and bailee, as expressly contemplated in the clause, and accordingly AIV was entitled to trace and recover the proceeds of the sub-sales.

COMMENT: The £50,000 worth of foil still belonged to AIV by virtue of the retention of title clause. That part of the claim was uncontroversial. However, the Court of Appeal also held that AIV was entitled to recover the £35,000 proceeds of sale on the ground that Romalpa were mere bailees of AIV's foil and which they had sold with the seller's implied authority and therefore had to account to them in equity. At first instance, Mocatta J held that no registrable charge arose in these circumstances and this was not further argued on appeal.

★ See Richard Prior, 'Reservation of Title' (1976) 39 MLR 585

The position without the retention of title clause would have been that both property and risk would have passed to Romalpa upon delivery. However, the retention of title clause provided otherwise. As Roskill LJ explained:

[The] sellers were to retain the property in the goods until all, and I underline '*all*', that was owing to them had been paid…It is obvious, to my mind, that the business purpose of the whole of this clause…was to secure [AIV], so far as possible, against the risks of non-payment after they had parted with possession of the goods delivered, whether or not those goods retained their identity after delivery…In the case of unmanufactured goods this was to be achieved by [AIV] retaining the property until all payments due had been made…In the case of mixed or manufactured goods…[AIV] were to be given the ownership of these mixed or manufactured goods as 'surety' for 'full payment'. 'Surety' I think in this context must mean…'security'…Further, the clause later provides that until 'full payment' is made, [Romalpa] shall keep the mixed goods for [AIV] as 'fiduciary owners'; not perhaps the happiest of phrases but one which suggests…that in relation to mixed or manufactured goods there was produced what…would be called a fiduciary relationship in this respect. The clause goes on to give to [Romalpa] an express power of sale of such goods, and the right to deliver them; and adds an obligation upon [Romalpa], if required by [AIV] so to do, to assign…to [AIV] the benefit of any claim against a sub-purchaser so long as [Romalpa] have not fully discharged all their indebtedness to [AIV].[54]

The sheer breadth of the retention of title clause in the *Romalpa* case is remarkable. That this obligation should continue until 'all that is owing' was paid to AIV was exceptionally onerous to Romalpa, because whenever Romalpa's customers paid it before Romalpa was due to pay AIV, Romalpa could not use those proceeds in its business for any purposes whatever save for paying AIV. This is because the clause required Romalpa always to retain those proceeds specifically for AIV's account and pay them over to it unless and until the *entirety* of outstanding indebtedness was discharged.[55] This would deprive Romalpa of all day-to-day finance and, so far from according with business efficacy, would produce precisely the opposite result, for it would cause acute cash-flow problems and make conduct of its business extremely difficult. Roskill LJ noted the force of this argument if one was to consider the matter solely from Romalpa's position, but held that the matter:

> has to be regarded in the light of the contractual provisions agreed upon by both parties, and the question of business efficacy, in relation to which there are here obvious competing business considerations, must be answered in the light of what both parties expressly agreed upon and therefore must be taken also impliedly to have agreed upon, and not unilaterally from the point of view of one party only.[56]

Therefore, in cases where there exists a regularity of trading, on credit terms, the buyer is likely to owe the seller some money at any given time, and this is the case even where the buyer pays his account on time. Consequently, the effect of an 'all that is owing' clause similar to that in the *Romalpa* case will mean that property in the goods will never pass to the buyer, even in respect of those goods paid for under a different contract. It seems strange that buyers would agree to such a provision, although, in practice, it is unlikely that the seller's continued ownership of the goods will present any real hardship to the buyer because a term would be likely to be

---

54. [1976] 1 WLR 676 (CA) 688.
55. Normally, a contractual term authorizing the buyer to resell the goods authorizes such sub-sales for his own account, but in *Romalpa*, the term meant that the sub-sales were made as agent for, and on account of, AIV and not for Romalpa's own account. See, further, *Pfeiffer Weinkellerei-Weineinkauf GmbH & Co v Arbuthnot Factors Ltd* [1988] 1 WLR 150 (QB).
56. [1976] 1 WLR 676 (CA) 689.

implied into such ownership preventing the seller from dealing with these goods in any way other than to discharge monies owing to him by the buyer.

The proposition in *Romalpa* that the seller may be entitled to the proceeds of sale has received significant criticism,[57] although the decision has been said to have turned on its own facts. It is certainly not without significance that the buyers in *Romalpa* conceded that they owed fiduciary obligations to the sellers. Although the proceeds of sale claim succeeded in *Romalpa*, such claims are unlikely to succeed again in the future for three reasons. First, as noted earlier, the buyers in *Romalpa* conceded that there was a fiduciary relationship between them and their supplier. This was followed by a further concession that the buyers held the goods manufactured from the foil as bailee for the supplier and that the supplier was a fiduciary owner of the goods. These concessions are unlikely to be made in future cases, and it is in any event doubtful that the relationship involved a bailment or even that a fiduciary relationship existed on the facts. Second, if all proceeds of sale are paid into a separate bank account (which should be the case if there was a fiduciary relationship between buyer and seller), then it would appear to frustrate the commercial reality of business. Any buyer is likely to need the money from the proceeds of their sales for their own business, and therefore paying such monies into a separate bank account would be unlikely to be the intention of the parties. Furthermore, if the buyers in *Romalpa* did hold the foil in a fiduciary capacity, they ought to have kept it entirely separate from their own goods. Third, the basis of a fiduciary relationship would mean that the seller would have been entitled to *all* the proceeds of sale, which might be more than he was in fact owed. On the other hand, if the seller was only entitled to recover the amount he was actually owed by the buyer from the proceeds of sale, then this would have required registering as a charge. But, is it really likely that either of the parties would have intended that the seller should receive a sum greater than he was actually owed?

All-liabilities clauses

The difference between a simple retention and an all-liabilities (or all-monies) clause is that simple retention involves reservation of ownership in goods which form the subject matter of one particular contract until the price and incidental charges under that contract have been paid. An 'all-liabilities' retention clause is fundamentally different in two material respects. First, it can apply to debts arising out of a contract other than the contract of sale which contains it.[58] Second, such debts need not even arise out of contracts of sale; any legal ground will suffice, even a claim for non-payment of an award of damages.[59] In *Armour v Thyssen Edelstahlwerke AG*,[60] the clause provided that 'all goods delivered by us remain our property (goods remaining

---

57. See e.g. *Re Weldtech Equipment Ltd* [1991] BCC 16 (Ch); *Compaq Computer Ltd v Abercorn Group Ltd* [1991] BCC 484 (Ch); and *Pfeiffer Weinkellerei-Weineinkauf GmbH & Co v Arbuthnot Factors Ltd* [1988] 1 WLR 150 (QB)). In these cases, the seller's claims to the proceeds of resale were held to be void as an unregistered charge. Phillips J went further in *Tatung (UK) Ltd v Galex Telesure Ltd* (1989) 5 BCC 325 (QB), suggesting that *Romalpa* was itself wrongly decided, as the seller's interest should have been held to be a charge.

58. If it was not for this difference there would be no point in the seller stipulating anything other than a simple retention provision.

59. *Armour v Thyssen Edelstahlwerke AG* [1991] 2 AC 339 (HL) 347 (Lord Keith).

60. [1991] 2 AC 339 (HL).

in our ownership) until all debts owed to us including any balances existing at relevant times—due to us on any legal grounds—are settled'. Thus an 'all-liabilities' clause means that a buyer will not get ownership until *all* monies or liabilities owed to the seller have been satisfied.

 Armour v Thyssen Edelstahlwerke AG [1991] 2 AC 339 (HL)

FACTS: Thyssen Edelstahlwerke AG ('Thyssen') was a manufacturer and supplier of steel. It sold steel to Carron Co Ltd ('Carron') for use in its manufacturing process. The contract of sale contained a condition that the steel remained the property of Thyssen after delivery until all debts were paid. The clause read 'all goods delivered by us remain our property (goods remaining in our ownership) until all debts owed to us including any balances existing at relevant times—due to us on any legal grounds—are settled'.

Receivers were appointed to Carron and a dispute arose as to the ownership of the steel. At first instance it was decided that property passed on delivery and this decision was affirmed on appeal by the Second Division of the Court of Session. Thyssen appealed to the House of Lords.

HELD: The House of Lords allowed Thyssen's appeal and held that a condition in a contract reserving title in the seller after delivery until all debts are paid is valid and enforceable, and that by virtue of ss 17 and 19(1) of the SGA 1979, property remained with the seller until the condition was complied with. A provision reserving title to the seller until payment of all debts due to it by the buyer does not amount to the creation by the buyer of a right of security in favour of the seller. Such a provision does in a sense give the seller security for the unpaid debts of the buyer, but it does so by way of a legitimate retention of title and not by virtue of any right over its own property conferred by the buyer.

★ See Robert Bradgate, 'Retention of Title in the House of Lords: Unanswered Questions' (1991) 54 MLR 726

In a straightforward contract of sale where the buyer retains the goods in an unaltered state, simple retention of title clauses work perfectly well and, in such cases, the arguments are limited to those of incorporation and construction. Problems arise in cases where the buyer either resells the goods, alters them, or uses them in the manufacture of finished goods and, as seen in the *Romalpa* case, clauses containing 'far-reaching and somewhat elaborate provisions'[61] have been devised to protect the interests of the seller in these situations. However, in seeking to protect sellers' interests, two different problems arise.

The goods sold have been mixed or incorporated into manufactured goods

Where the buyer uses the seller's goods in the manufacture of other products, there is nothing to prevent the parties from agreeing that property in the finished goods belongs to the seller until paid for. This is simply a matter of agreement. In this type of situation, the seller will have ownership of the finished goods because the parties have agreed that he does, and not as a result of a reservation of title. A party can

---

61. As they were described by Mocatta J in *Aluminium Industrie Vaassen BV v Romalpa Aluminium Ltd*, [1976] 1 WLR 676 (CA) 680.

only *reserve* title in goods where that party originally had title, as the following case demonstrates.

Re Peachdart Ltd [1984] Ch 131 (Ch)

FACTS: Freudenberg Leather Co Ltd ('Freudenberg') sold leather to Peachdart Ltd ('Peachdart'), who then used it in the manufacture of handbags. The contract provided that ownership of the leather and of any mixed goods using this leather would remain with Freudenberg until full payment had been received. Peachdart went into receivership owing money to Freudenberg for the leather bought.

HELD: It was held that although Freudenberg could reserve title over the leather it sold, it could not do so over the finished goods. The leather sold had changed its identity once it had been made into handbags and could no longer be said to be the same goods that were sold by Freudenberg and belonging to it.

COMMENT: Freudenberg sought to have ownership of the finished handbags. This created a charge which needed registering and will be discussed under the next subheading.

⭐ See JWA Thornely, 'Retention of Title: More Romalpa Repurcussions' (1984) 43 CLJ 35

Whether or not the goods sold have lost their identity is a question of fact. If they have, then, as in *Re Peachdart*, the goods sold will have lost their identity when they were made into finished products and therefore cease to be the property of the seller. Thus, the sale of man-made fibre used by the buyer in the manufacture of carpet,[62] the resin used by the buyer in the manufacture of chipboard,[63] and the sheets of cardboard which the buyer used to manufacture cardboard boxes[64] were all held to have lost their identity when used by the respective buyers in their manufacturing processes and thereby ceased to belong to the sellers.

As noted earlier, whether or not the goods sold have lost their identity is a question of fact. As the following case demonstrates, even where the goods have been incorporated into finished products, it does not necessarily mean that they have lost their identity.

Hendy Lennox (Industrial Engines) Ltd v Grahame Puttick Ltd [1984] 1 WLR 485 (QB)

FACTS: Hendy Lennox ('HL') sold a diesel engine to Grahame Puttick Ltd ('GP'), who used it in the manufacture of a generating set. HL had reserved title in the engine until it had been paid for. When GP went into receivership, HL sought to recover the engine. The receiver argued that property in the engine had passed to GP when it incorporated it into the generating set.

HELD: Staughton J held that the engine could be reclaimed by HL. This was because it had remained an engine throughout and could easily be identified by its serial number as

62. *Re Bond Worth Ltd* [1980] 1 Ch 228 (Ch).
63. *Borden (UK) Ltd v Scottish Timber Products Ltd* [1981] 1 Ch 25 (CA).
64. *Modelboard Ltd v Outer Box Ltd* [1993] BCLC 623 (Ch).

> belonging to HL and could be dismantled with relative ease from the finished generating set.
>
> **COMMENT:** If the goods sold have merely been incorporated by the buyer into other goods, then a seller with an appropriate retention of title clause will be entitled to recover the goods sold, provided they can still be identified and dismantled from the finished goods without damaging those goods.

The retention of title clause creates a registrable charge which will be void for non-registration

The question here is whether or not a retention of title clause creates a charge and, if so, whether that charge will be void if not registered. In *Clough Mill Ltd v Martin*,[65] the Court of Appeal confirmed that no registrable charge arises in the case of a simple retention of title clause where the seller merely seeks to reserve title in the goods sold until he is paid. This is because, with a simple retention of title clause, property in the goods does not pass to the buyer until he has paid for them. Consequently, until payment, the buyer does not own the goods and is simply unable to create a charge over the seller's own goods. As Oliver LJ put it in the *Clough Mill* case, 'a company can create a charge only on its own property and if it never acquires property in the goods…it cannot charge them'.[66] For reasons that are not too dissimilar, the House of Lords held in *Armour v Thyssen Edelstahlwerke AG*[67] that an all-monies clause did not create a charge either. As Lord Keith explained:

> I am…unable to regard a provision reserving title to the seller until payment of all debts due to him by the buyer as amounting to the creation by the buyer of a right of security in favour of the seller. Such a provision does in a sense give the seller security for the unpaid debts of the buyer. But it does so by way of a legitimate retention of title, not by virtue of any right over his own property conferred by the buyer.[68]

On the other hand, a charge will be created where there is a contract which, by way of security for the payment of a debt, confers an interest in property defeasible or destructible upon payment of such debt, or appropriates such property for the discharge of the debt.[69] Any charge created by a company is void if not registered. Even if registered, they face others[70] taking priority over them.

 Re Bond Worth Ltd [1980] 1 Ch 228 (Ch)

FACTS: Bond Worth Ltd ('Bond Worth'), a carpet manufacturing company, purchased man-made fibre from the seller, which it used in the manufacture of carpets. The conditions of sale included a retention of title clause. Bond Worth went into receivership

---

65. [1985] 1 WLR 111 (CA).   66. ibid 122.
67. [1991] 2 AC 339 (HL) (this case is discussed on p 261).
68. ibid 353.   69. *Re Bond Worth Ltd* [1980] Ch 228 (Ch) 248 (Slade J).
70. For example, factoring companies.

> when a large sum of money was owing to the seller under various contracts containing the retention of title clause.
>
> **HELD:** A retention of title clause, where property passes to the buyer only on payment and which refers to 'equitable and beneficial ownership', creates a floating equitable charge granted by the buyer in favour of the seller which, as such, was registrable and was void for non-registration.

Similarly, as will be recalled from the discussion in *Re Peachdart*,[71] the seller sought to have ownership in the finished handbags. This ownership was not *reserved* to them, but was *granted* to them by the buyer under the terms of the contract. It was held that the parties must be presumed to have intended that once the buyer had appropriated the leather so that it became unrecognizable as the goods sold, a charge over the finished goods or their proceeds would arise. In this case, such a charge arose in relation to the handbags and the proceeds of the handbags which had been sold, such charge being void for non-registration. Thus, where a retention of title clause seeks to protect not only the goods sold but, where the buyer uses these goods in the manufacture of finished goods which he then sells on, also an interest in the property of those finished goods, it is possible that a registrable charge is created in relation to the interests a seller might claim in those finished manufactured goods. Any charge created by a company is void if not registered. Consequently, retention of title clauses should be drafted in such a way as not to create a charge or, in cases where the seller needs to assert a continuing property interest in the goods, then those rights will need to be registered, failing which they will be invalid as against a liquidator or other creditors.

Passing of risk

Risk means the risk of theft, loss, or damage to the contract goods, but not the risk of non-payment, nor the risk that the goods will not conform to the contract of sale.[72] Risk involves one of the parties having to bear the loss and possibly having to pay contractual damages to the other party.

Different rules apply depending on whether or not the buyer deals as consumer.

Non-consumer cases

The general rule is set out in s 20(1) of the SGA 1979 and provides that unless the parties have otherwise agreed, risk passes with property. This is encapsulated in the
➡ *res perit domino:* maxim *res perit domino* and is one of the key reasons why it is important to know
'the thing is lost to the the precise moment that property passes.
owner'

---

71. [1984] Ch 131 (Ch).

72. Where the goods fail to conform to the contract of sale, the buyer may pursue the seller for breach of contract.

SGA 1979, s 20(1)

Unless otherwise agreed, the goods remain at the seller's risk until the property in them is transferred to the buyer, but when the property in them is transferred to the buyer the goods are at the buyer's risk whether delivery has been made or not.

The question to ask is whether or not property in the goods has passed to the buyer; actual possession being irrelevant. This can be seen from the following case.

 ***Pignataro v Gilroy* [1919] 1 KB 459 (KB)**

FACTS: Gilroy sold to Pignataro 140 bags of rice, with delivery to be taken in fourteen days. The sale was by sample, and the goods that were intended for Pignataro were at this stage unascertained. Gilroy notified Pignataro that 125 bags of the rice were available for collection at one address and fifteen bags at another address. Pignataro paid for the goods by cheque, but neglected to collect the fifteen bags for almost a month, during which time they were stolen. Pignataro sued for the cost of the missing fifteen bags of rice. At first instance, the judge held that the fifteen bags of rice had been stolen without any negligence on Gilroy's part, but entered judgment for Pignataro on the ground that the subject matter of the sale being unascertained goods and there being no evidence of appropriation by either party with the assent of the other, the property had not passed to Pignataro at the time of the loss. Gilroy appealed.

HELD: The appeal was allowed. Rowlatt J held that where, on a sale of unascertained goods by description, goods of that description and in a deliverable state are unconditionally appropriated to the contract by the seller, and the seller sends notice of that appropriation to the buyer, then in the event of the buyer neglecting to reply to that notice promptly, it must be inferred that he assents to the appropriation, and, on the expiry of a reasonable time after receipt of the notice, the property must be deemed to have passed. Consequently, as the property had passed to Pignataro before the goods were stolen, the risk also passed at this time and the loss lay on him.

As already observed, the rule in s 20(1) that risk passes with property is subject to the parties agreeing otherwise. This means that the parties may, if they so wish, agree that risk will pass either before or after property has passed. Retention of title clauses, for example, will often be drafted to enable the seller to retain property in the goods until paid for, but passing the risk to the buyer on possession. But any agreement to oust the presumption of the normal rule must, as with any contractual agreement, be made before or at the time of contracting.[73] Thus, in *Healy v Howlett & Sons*,[74] the words on the invoice 'at sole risk of purchaser after putting fish on rail here', which was only posted to the buyer after the contract had been made, were

Retention of title clauses are discussed at p 255

---

73. *Olley v Marlborough Court Ltd* [1949] 1 KB 532 (CA); *Grogan v Robin Meredith Plant Hire* [1996] CLC 1127 (CA).
74. [1917] 1 KB 337 (KB). For the facts, see p 251.

not construed as part of the contract. As Avory J explained, '[t]here is no evidence of the buyers' assent to those words, and they undoubtedly were placed on the invoice after the contract was made and in my opinion formed no part of it'.[75]

It has also been held that an agreement that the passing of property and the passing of risk will not occur simultaneously may be inferred from the circumstances.

 Sterns Ltd v Vickers Ltd [1923] 1 KB 78 (CA)

FACTS: The buyer contracted to buy 120,000 gallons of white spirit out of an undivided bulk of 200,000 gallons. The seller handed over a delivery warrant giving the buyer the right to immediate possession of the spirit it purchased. The buyer accepted the delivery warrant but decided to leave the spirit purchased with the seller. Before the buyer's 120,000 gallons had been separated from the bulk, the contents of the bulk storage tank deteriorated.

HELD: The Court of Appeal held that the parties were to be taken as having intended that the risk would pass to the buyer when it accepted the delivery warrant. The Court stated that, irrespective of whether or not the property in the undivided portion of the larger bulk had passed, upon the buyer's acceptance of the delivery warrant, the risk passed to it and it followed that the loss must be borne by it.

COMMENT: Property in the spirit could not have passed to the buyer because until its 120,000 gallons had been separated from the bulk, it remained unascertained and not appropriated to the contract. Nevertheless, the Court was prepared to hold that an agreement that the passing of property and the passing of risk were not to occur simultaneously was to be inferred from the circumstances of the case. Consequently, the risk (but not the property) transferred to the buyer in unascertained goods. This is troublesome. We have already seen that property in unascertained goods cannot pass to the buyer,[76] and this rule can clearly be supported on the ground that until the parties have identified the precise goods to which the contract of sale relates it will not be possible to say for which goods the property is intended to pass. Yet, following the same reasoning, it seems that risk can pass. But for which goods specifically was the buyer at risk? Although this could not be for more than 120,000 gallons of the spirit, it was clearly uncertain which 120,000 gallons were its .

Section 20A is discussed at p 253

Since 1995, under s 20A of the SGA 1979, such a buyer would become co-owner of the goods provided he had paid for some or all of them. Consequently, as an owner of the goods with a right to immediate possession, the risk would be transferred to the buyer unless the parties had agreed otherwise.

The rule in s 20(1) is also subject to the qualifications contained in s 20(2) and 20(3) in relation to fault.

---

75. ibid 345.   76. SGA 1979, s 16.

SGA 1979, s 20(2) and 20(3)

(2) But where delivery has been delayed through the fault of either buyer or seller the goods are at the risk of the party at fault as regards any loss which might not have occurred but for such fault.

(3) Nothing in this section affects the duties or liabilities of either seller or buyer as a bailee or custodier of the goods of the other party.

The following case demonstrates how s 20(2) operates in practice.

 Demby Hamilton & Co Ltd v Barden
[1949] 1 All ER 435 (KB)

FACTS: Demby Hamilton & Co Ltd ('DH') had prepared 30 tonnes of apple juice which Barden had ordered from it for supply at periodic intervals to third parties. Barden paid for and took delivery of part of the juice, but failed to give DH any delivery instructions for the balance because he had been unable to obtain them from the third parties. As a result, the juice became putrid and had to be destroyed. DH claimed the price of the destroyed juice.

HELD: Sellers J held that the risk that would ordinarily have rested with DH will pass to Barden, as he was at fault and he must therefore bear the loss. Accordingly, DH was able to claim for the price of the destroyed juice.

Section 20(3) is concerned with a party acting as 'bailee' or 'custodier' of the goods belonging to the other party. Parties are frequently bailees of goods owned by others. For example, a buyer who buys goods on a sale-or-return basis is merely a bailee of the goods until such a time as he either returns the goods or otherwise causes the property in them to pass to himself under s 18, rule 4. The effect of s 20(3) is simply to confirm that the section does not affect the normal duties or liabilities of either party when acting as bailee or custodian of the other's goods, and thereby ensures that the party who is in possession of goods owned by another party takes reasonable care of them and will bear the loss in the event of loss or destruction arising from his own negligence.

🔗 Section 18, rule 4 is discussed at p 241

Consumer cases

Section 20(1) to 20(3) no longer apply in consumer cases. The transfer of risk in consumer cases is now dealt with in s 20(4), which was added to the SGA 1979 by the Sale and Supply of Goods to Consumers Regulations 2002.

 SGA 1979, s 20(4)

In a case where the buyer deals as consumer ... subsections (1) to (3) above must be ignored and the goods remain at the seller's risk until they are delivered to the consumer.

Whereas in non-consumer cases, the default position is that risk passes with property, in cases where the buyer deals as consumer, the passage of property is irrelevant in determining whether or not the risk has passed to the buyer. Risk, in consumer cases, passes only with delivery. Thus, when the buyer deals as consumer, the goods remain at the seller's risk until they are delivered to the buyer and the maxim *res perit domino* does not apply.

Where the seller is authorized or required to send the goods to the buyer and he does so by carrier, then s 32(4) applies, which makes it plain that delivery means actual delivery to the buyer. Consequently, the goods will remain at the seller's risk until delivery has been made and the buyer has his goods.

 SGA 1979, s 32(4)

In a case where the buyer deals as consumer…if in pursuance of a contract of sale the seller is authorized or required to send the goods to the buyer, delivery of the goods to the carrier is not delivery of the goods to the buyer.

This not only reflects which party a typical consumer buyer would expect to be responsible for the goods until actual receipt, but also the commercial reality of a seller being in the better (or only) position to insure the goods until actual delivery has been made.

Conclusion

As the main purpose of a contract of sale is to transfer ownership in the goods from the seller to the buyer, it is important to know precisely when ownership is transferred. In the case of a contract for the sale of unascertained goods, no property in them can be transferred to the buyer unless and until the goods are ascertained. This rule is subject to the exception in s 20A in relation to undivided shares in goods forming part of a bulk. Where the contract is for the sale of specific or ascertained goods, the property in them is transferred to the buyer at such time as the parties to the contract intend it to be transferred. Where the parties fail to make clear their intentions in this regard, s 18 sets out a number of rules designed to ascertain their intentions, thus filling any vacuum left by them in relation to the time of transfer.

One of the main reasons why it is so important to know the precise moment that property passes is because, unless the parties have agreed otherwise, risk passes with property. This is different where the buyer deals as consumer and, in such cases, risk passes only with delivery. This means that when the buyer deals as consumer, the goods remain at the seller's risk until they are actually delivered to the buyer.

Practice questions

1. George sells 100,000 litres of milk each month to Dave's Bakeries Ltd, which uses it in the manufacture of bread and cakes, which it then sells through a number of retail shops. Dave's Bakeries Ltd also buys milk from several other suppliers. A clause in the contract between George and Dave's Bakeries Ltd provides:

   > Goods are supplied on the condition that the supplier shall retain legal and equitable ownership of them until full payment has been received by them for all sums owing. Any money from the sale of the goods shall be paid into a separate bank account noting on it the supplier's name. All goods shall be clearly labelled as belonging to the supplier until all sums owing have been paid.

   Dave's Bakeries Ltd has now gone into administration, owing £20,000 to George. In total, it owes in excess of £1million to other suppliers. It has 50,000 litres of milk stored in its cold stores and £10,000 worth of bread and cakes in its freezers. £5,000 is left in the company's general bank account and £1,000 in the specially designated account in accordance with the contract.
   Advise George.

2. Critically analyse the relationship between the transfer of property and the transfer of risk. Consider whether it was necessary for the draftsman of the SGA 1979 to fix risk with property.

Further reading

John N Adams, 'Sale or Return Contracts: Shedding a Little Light' (1998) 61 MLR 432
- Discusses the effect of s 18, rule 4 in the passing of property in relation to sale or return contracts.

G Battersby and A Preston, 'The Concepts of "Property", "Title" and "Owner" used in the Sale of Goods Act 1893' (1972) 35 MLR 268
- Considers the meaning of the words 'property', 'title', and 'owner' as they apply to contracts of sale.

James Crinion, 'All that Glitters. *Re Wait*, Section 16 and the Peril for the Pre-paying Buyer' (2005) 12 Commercial Law Practitioner 101
- Examines the rule in s 16 of the SGA 1979 which provides that the purchaser of unascertained goods has no proprietary rights to the goods until they are ascertained.

Iwan Davies, 'Continuing Dilemmas with Passing of Property in Part of a Bulk' [1991] JBL 111
- Discusses the Law Commission's Working Paper No 112 'Rights to goods in bulk' and the Court of Appeal's ruling in *Re Wait*.

Andrew Hicks, '*Romalpa* is Dead' (1992) 13 Co Law 217
- Discusses the entitlement of sellers to claim the proceeds of sale and asks whether the effects of *Romalpa* are dead in this regard.

Andrew Hicks, 'When Goods Sold Become a New Species' [1993] JBL 485
- Discusses the problems with retention of title clauses in cases where the buyer uses the contract goods in the manufacture of finished goods.

Hock Lai Ho, **'Some Reflections on "Property" and "Title" in the Sale of Goods Act'** (1997) 56 CLJ 571

- Discusses the uses and meanings of the distinct but related concepts of ownership, property, and title.

Nikki McKay, **'The Passing of Risk and s 20A Sale of Goods Act 1979'** (2010) 15 Cov LJ 17

- Considers the impact of s 20A SGA on the passing of risk.

Len S Sealy, **'Risk in the Law of Sale'** (1972) 31 CLJ 225

- Analyses the concept of the passing of risk in sale of goods transactions.

Duncan Webb, **'Title and Transformation: Who Owns Manufactured Goods?'** [2000] JBL 513

- Discusses the historical doctrines on the retention of title to manufactured goods when the manufacturer and owner of raw materials are different people. Discusses cases for transfer of ownership when raw materials have been transformed into finished goods.

12 The transfer of title

- *Nemo dat quod non habet*
- Exceptions to the *nemo dat* rule

INTRODUCTION

As noted in Chapter 11, 'property' and 'title' mean two entirely different things. Chapter 11 was concerned with the transfer of property in the goods as between seller and buyer, whereas this chapter will consider the various circumstances in which a buyer may become the owner of the goods, notwithstanding that the seller is neither the owner of them, nor sold them with the owner's consent. Disputes, in Chapter 11, were between seller and buyer, whereas in this chapter, they concern not the seller, but the owner of the goods and the buyer. The following case provides an example of the sort of problems that can arise.

The distinction between 'property' and 'title' is discussed at p 232

Greenwood v Bennett and Others [1973] QB 195 (CA)

FACTS: Bennett was the manager of a garage that owned a Jaguar car that was in need of repair. He left the car with Searle, who was going to repair it for an agreed price of £85. Rather than repair the car, Searle used it for his own purposes and severely damaged it in an accident. Without any authority to do so, Searle then sold the damaged car to Harper for £75, with Harper believing that Searle was the owner. Harper then spent £226 on repairing the car before selling it on to a finance company for £450. Prattle then acquired the car on hire purchase from the finance company. Searle was subsequently convicted of the theft of the car. The police commenced **interpleader proceedings** and so the court had to determine who was the true owner of the car.

HELD: The Court of Appeal held that Bennett was the true owner of the car. Searle did not have title and was thus unable to transfer title to Harper. Consequently, as Harper had no title, he was similarly unable to transfer title to the finance company.

COMMENT: Harper argued that as he had carried out the repairs in good faith, believing that he owned the car, the court should impose a condition of Bennett's repossession, which would entitle Harper to recover the £226 that he spent on making what was virtually a worthless car into one with a market value of £450. The Court agreed and held that as a condition of recovering the car, Bennett must compensate Harper for the amount he spent on repairing it. Unless such a condition was imposed, Bennett would have been unjustly enriched. Since this case was decided, the Torts (Interference with Goods) Act 1977 has been passed, which provides a statutory mechanism by which a person in the position of Harper can be compensated for monies spent in such circumstances.

interpleader proceedings: a process under which a third party can initiate proceedings to compel others to litigate to resolve a legal dispute

See Stuart Anderson, 'Unjust Enrichment and the Innocent Purchaser' (1973) 36 MLR 89

Nemo dat quod non habet

The Latin maxim *nemo dat quod non habet* (often abbreviated to *nemo dat*) translates as 'no one gives who possesses not' and broadly provides that a seller can only transfer to a buyer the ownership in the goods if he owns them or has the right to sell them at the time of sale. Thus, a seller who does not own the goods, and who is not authorized by the owner to sell them, cannot usually pass good title to an innocent buyer. The *nemo dat* rule protects the true owner of the goods at the expense of the innocent purchaser who loses out, unless one of the exceptions to the rule applies. These exceptions can be found in the SGA 1979, the Factors Act 1889 (FA 1889), and the Hire Purchase Act 1964 (HPA 1964), as well as in the common law. When any of these exceptions apply, the original owner of the goods loses his title in favour of the innocent purchaser.

A common theme in many of the cases is one of dishonesty, where the court will have to decide which of two innocent parties should suffer due to the dishonesty of another. This can arise in many different situations, such as where an innocent buyer buys goods from a seller who turns out to have stolen them; or where a person obtains goods on hire purchase and dishonestly sells them before they have been paid for; or where a seller sells goods for later collection but, before they have been collected, dishonestly resells them to another buyer; or where a person entrusts his goods to an agent for the purpose of obtaining offers for them, but the agent dishonestly sells them and disappears with the proceeds; or where a person takes his goods for repair but the repairer dishonestly sells them and disappears with the proceeds.

Although the application of the *nemo dat* rule (or one of its exceptions) will lead to one of the parties succeeding at the expense of the others, it was suggested in *Ingram v Little*[1] that a preferable solution might be to apportion the loss between the innocent victims. In his dissenting judgment, Devlin LJ explained:

> The true spirit of the common law is to override theoretical distinctions when they stand in the way of doing practical justice. For the doing of justice, the relevant question in this sort of case is…which of two innocent parties shall suffer for the fraud of a third.[2] The plain answer is that the loss should be divided between them in such proportion as is just in all the circumstances. If it be pure misfortune, the loss should be borne equally; if the fault or imprudence of either party has caused or contributed to the loss, it should be borne by that party in the whole or in the greater part.[3]

Notwithstanding the apparent fairness of such an approach, it does not represent the law. As already discussed, the law adopts an 'all or nothing' approach where the courts have to choose between upholding the rights of the original owner of the goods or protecting the interests of a purchaser who buys in good faith and for value. This was explained by Denning LJ in *Bishopgate Motor Finance Corporation Ltd v Transport Brakes Ltd*:[4]

> In the development of our law, two principles have striven for mastery. The first is for the protection of property: no one can give a better title than he himself

---

1. [1961] 1 QB 31 (CA).
2. This was the question originally posed by Ashurst J in *Lickbarrow v Mason* (1787) 2 TR 63.
3. [1961] 1 QB 31 (CA) 73.   4. [1949] 1 KB 322 (CA).

possesses. The second is for the protection of commercial transactions: the person who takes in good faith and for value without notice should get a good title. The first principle has held sway for a long time, but it has been modified by the common law itself and by statute so as to meet the needs of our own times.[5]

The first of Denning LJ's principles represents the general rule and is now enshrined in s 21(1) of the SGA 1979.

> ### o⟁ SGA 1979, s 21(1)
>
> Subject to this Act, where goods are sold by a person who is not their owner, and who does not sell them under the authority or with the consent of the owner, the buyer acquires no better title to the goods than the seller had, unless the owner of the goods is by his conduct precluded from denying the seller's authority to sell.

Two brief points need to be made about this section. First, it will be seen that it relates only to cases 'where goods are sold'. As will be discussed, in *Shaw v Commissioner of Police of the Metropolis*,[6] the Court of Appeal held that this means that the section therefore applies only in cases where there has been an actual sale and not where there is an uncompleted agreement to sell. Second, s 21(1) only applies where goods are sold by a person who is not their owner, whereas the *nemo dat* principle applies also to cases where, although the sale is made by the owner, he is unable to sell the goods free from any encumbrance or charge that exists in favour of a third party.

Exceptions to the *nemo dat* rule

The opening words of s 21(1) 'subject to this Act' indicate that it is subject to the provisions of the SGA 1979. This is where many of the exceptions to the rule can be found.

Sale by agent

Since s 21(1) talks about goods that are sold by a person who is not the owner and who does not sell them under the authority of the owner, a brief discussion is needed on the position of a sale by agent. No special problems arise where the agent sells the goods with the express authority of the owner, but it will be noted that the section goes on to refer to the 'consent' of the owner. As already noted, the opening words of the section indicate that it is subject to the provisions of the SGA 1979, s 62(2) of which preserves the common law rules pertaining to principal and agent. Therefore, a sale that is within the usual or apparent authority of an agent will bind the owner of the goods and thus pass good title to the buyer, even if the agent has exceeded his

⬈ The authority of an agent is discussed in Chapter 5

---

5. ibid 336.   6. [1987] 1 WLR 1332 (CA).

actual authority. Thus, where the owner has, by his conduct, held out the agent as having his authority to sell the goods, he will be precluded from denying the existence of such authority.

Consent of the owner

Earlier, it was noted that s 21(1) refers to the consent of the owner. This now requires a discussion of the principle contained in s 47(1) concerning the effect of a sub-sale by the buyer.

 SGA 1979, s 47(1)

Subject to this Act, the unpaid seller's right of lien or retention or stoppage in transit is not affected by any sale or other disposition of the goods which the buyer may have made, unless the seller has assented to it.

Where the buyer, who is not in possession of the goods, resells them with the seller's assent, the sub-buyer (i.e. the person buying the goods from the buyer) obtains good title free from the original seller's lien or retention or right of stoppage in transit. This clearly has all the hallmarks of an estoppel, although, as discussed later, with an estoppel the original seller must communicate his assent to the sub-buyer, whereas for the purpose of s 47(1), it will be enough that the original seller's assent has been communicated just to the buyer.

Estoppel

The concluding words in s 21(1) 'unless the owner of the goods is by his conduct precluded from denying the seller's authority to sell' set out this exception. Estoppel applies in cases where the owner of the goods acts in such a way that it appears that the seller has the right to sell the goods. As a consequence, the owner is then precluded (estopped) from denying the facts as he represented them to be or that the sale was unauthorized. Consequently, the unauthorized transaction proceeds as though it was authorized and the innocent third party purchaser then becomes the owner of the goods at the expense of the original owner. It should be observed that the doctrine of estoppel in relation to the transfer of ownership by a non-owner is almost identical to the apparent authority of an agent to transfer title in the goods in excess of his actual authority to do so.

This exception is little more than the application of the common law doctrine of estoppel. The section is silent as to when the owner is by his conduct precluded from denying the seller's authority to sell, although merely giving the third party possession of the goods will not amount to a representation that the third party is the owner or has the right to sell them.[7] As will become apparent from the cases, before the innocent purchaser can obtain title by estoppel, the original owner of the goods must have made a representation that the seller was authorized or entitled to sell the

---

7. *Jerome v Bentley & Co* [1952] 2 All ER 114 (QB).

goods, such representation being made either intentionally or negligently and upon which the innocent purchaser relied when buying the goods.

As already observed, s 21(1) relates only to cases 'where goods are sold'. The Court of Appeal held in the following case that this means that the section therefore applies only in cases where there has been an actual sale and not where there is an uncompleted agreement to sell.

Shaw v Commissioner of Police of the Metropolis [1987] 1 WLR 1332 (CA)

FACTS: Natalegawa was the owner of a Porsche that he advertised for sale. He was contacted by a swindler, London, who claimed to be interested in purchasing it on behalf of a client. Natalegawa allowed London to take delivery of the car. He also gave London a letter certifying that he had sold the car to him as well as a signed notification of sale and transfer slip. In fact, Natalegawa merely authorized London to sell it on his behalf. Shaw agreed to purchase the car from London and gave him a banker's draft as part payment but the bank refused to pay cash for the draft. London duly disappeared. None of the price was therefore paid. The police seized the vehicle. Shaw sought to recover it and commenced an action for the determination of the vehicle's ownership as between himself and Natalegawa.

HELD: The Court of Appeal held that Natalegawa's action in signing the letter and transfer slip amounted to conduct within the meaning of s 21(1) which would preclude him from denying London's authority to sell. For this reason, Shaw would have obtained good title to the vehicle provided London had sold it to him, which the Court found he had not. The subsection does not apply to a mere agreement to sell. Consequently, since Shaw had merely agreed to buy the vehicle on terms that the property in it was not to pass until the price was paid, Shaw had not acquired good title by virtue of s 21(1).

COMMENT: Although Shaw's action was wholly without merit, the reasoning of the Court of Appeal was rather unsatisfactory. It held that s 21(1) only applies to a party who has actually purchased goods and not to one who has merely agreed to do so. The reason why this was unsatisfactory is because s 21(1) appears to be a simple restatement of the common law principle of estoppel and, as such, ought to protect a party who, as a result of the representation made, has acted to his prejudice. On this basis, the Court of Appeal could simply have rejected Shaw's claim on the ground that he had not acted to his prejudice as he had not paid the price. It was also held that since London had neither bought nor agreed to buy the vehicle, ownership could not pass to Shaw under s 25.[8]

See JWA Thornely, 'Thieves, Rogues, Innocent Purchasers and Legislative Tangles' [1988] 47 CLJ 15

There are two distinct categories of estoppel to which s 21(1) applies: (i) estoppel by representation; and (ii) estoppel by negligence.

Estoppel by representation

An estoppel by representation might arise where the owner of the goods has, by his words or conduct, represented to the buyer that the seller is the true owner of the goods, or has his authority to sell the goods. This category of estoppel is, therefore,

---

8. Section 25 is another exception to the *nemo dat* rule (sale by a buyer in possession) and is discussed at p 297.

sometimes sub-divided into estoppel by words and estoppel by conduct. The *Farquharson* case is an early case that demonstrates the difficulties in establishing an estoppel, the principles from which can be seen in cases decided today.

 Farquharson Brothers & Co v King & Co [1902] AC 325 (HL)

FACTS: Farquharson Brothers & Co ('Farquharson') were timber merchants who stored the timber they imported with a dock company. Farquharson's clerk, Capon, was authorized to give delivery instructions to the dock company, which it acted upon. He was not, however, authorized to sell the timber save to a limited extent to known customers. He fraudulently transferred some of the timber to himself by using a false name and instructed the dock company to effect the transaction. He then sold this timber to King & Co ('King') using this false name and gave instructions to the dock company to deliver the goods accordingly. King knew nothing of Farquharson, nor that Capon was in truth Farquharson's clerk, and paid him for the goods in good faith. When Farquharson discovered Capon's fraud, it commenced an action for conversion.

HELD: The House of Lords held that Farquharson, not having held out Capon to King as its agent to sell to King, was not estopped from denying Capon's authority to sell the timber. As Capon had no title in the goods he sold nor any apparent authority to sell on behalf of Farquharson, he could not transfer to King any title in the goods. Consequently, Farquharson was entitled to recover from King the value of the timber.

COMMENT: This case also demonstrates that an estoppel can only be raised in cases where the representation caused the purchaser to be misled. As the statements made by Farquharson to the dock company had not come to King's attention, King could not possibly have been misled by them.

It is often difficult to know precisely what conduct by the original owner will amount to the necessary representation that the seller was authorized or entitled to sell the goods. A good example of the doctrine of estoppel succeeding can be seen in the following case.

 Eastern Distributors Ltd v Goldring [1957] 2 QB 600 (CA)[9]

FACTS: Murphy wanted to raise finance on a van that he owned in order to buy a car. He got together with a motor dealer, Coker, and they devised a scheme to deceive Eastern Distributors Ltd ('Eastern'), a finance company. They completed forms stating that Murphy's van was in fact owned by Coker, and Murphy wished to acquire it on hire purchase.[10] Eastern approved the hire purchase agreement, believing that the van was

---

9. It should be noted that this case has been overruled on another ground by the Court of Appeal in *Worcester Works Finance v Cooden Engineering Co* [1972] 1 QB 210 (CA).
10. Under this form of transaction, the finance company purchases the vehicle (in this case, the car) and then supplies it on hire purchase terms to the customer (Murphy).

owned by Coker. Murphy failed to make his hire purchase payments to Eastern, and sold the van to an innocent purchaser, Goldring. When the deception was discovered a dispute arose as to the ownership of the van, with Eastern commencing proceedings to recover the van from Goldring. Murphy was clearly the original owner and as such would be free to pass good title to Goldring unless he had lost his ownership because of the earlier deceit.

HELD: The Court of Appeal held that because of Murphy's intentional representation that the van was not owned by him but by Coker, he was estopped from asserting his ownership of it. Therefore, Murphy had lost his title to the van under the doctrine of estoppel and Eastern obtained good title when it purchased the van from Coker. Eastern's ownership of the van did not pass (back) to Murphy because, under a hire purchase agreement, ownership is not transferred until all instalments have been made. Thus, as Murphy no longer owned the van, he could not transfer ownership to Goldring. Accordingly, Eastern was entitled to recover the van from Goldring.

⭐ See Raphael Powell, 'Title to Goods Sold by Owner After Unauthorised Sale by Owner's Agent' (1957) 20 MLR 650

As already observed, before the innocent purchaser can obtain title by estoppel, the original owner of the goods must have made either an intentional or negligent representation that the seller was authorized or entitled to sell the goods. The representation made by the van's owner in *Eastern Distributors* was intentional, but in the following case, the representation was held to have been innocent and therefore no estoppel could be raised.

Mercantile Credit Co Ltd v Hamblin [1965] 2 QB 242 (CA)

FACTS: Hamblin wished to raise money on her car and approached a motor dealer with an impressive local reputation and with whom she had had previous dealings and trusted. The dealer told her that he could assist and got her to sign some blank forms, which she understood to be proposal forms for the loan secured on her car. The dealer gave her a blank cheque which he had signed, telling her that to save her from having to come back to his office, once he had ascertained the amount of the loan, he would telephone her and, provided she was happy with the figure, she could fill in the cheque. What Hamblin in fact signed was a proposal form to acquire the car on hire purchase, a delivery receipt with confirmation of insurance cover, and a banker's order. The dealer had told her to sign the forms blank, which he would then complete for her if the terms offered by the finance company (Mercantile Credit Co Ltd) were acceptable to her. The dealer filled out the forms and returned them to Mercantile without further reference to Hamblin and without her authority. The forms as completed by him stated, falsely, that he had absolute title in Hamblin's car and offered to sell it to Mercantile, which it accepted. The true facts emerged because Hamblin decided not to proceed with the loan, yet she received demands from Mercantile in respect of her 'missed payments'. Mercantile commenced proceedings against Hamblin, claiming it owned the car, but it could only succeed if Hamblin was estopped by her negligence or precluded by her conduct within the meaning of s 21(1).

HELD: The claim failed. The Court of Appeal accepted that Hamblin had not intended to make it appear that the car belonged to the dealer, and held that, on the facts of the case, it was not unreasonable for her to have placed her trust in the dealer and that she had not therefore been negligent in signing the forms before they had been completed. It followed that no estoppel could be raised against her and she retained title in the car.

⭐ See JWA Thornely, 'Sale of Goods-Transfer of Title by Estoppel-*Non Est Factum*' (1965) 21 CLJ 21

It has already been observed that where an owner merely gives a third party possession of the goods, this will not amount to a representation that the third party is himself the owner or has the right to sell the goods.[11] This is simply because the mere giving of possession does not amount to a representation that the third party has the right to sell the goods, as the following case demonstrates.

Central Newbury Car Auctions Ltd v Unity Finance Ltd [1957] 1 QB 371 (CA)

FACTS: A fraudster, claiming to be named Cullis, offered to take on hire purchase terms a Morris car from Central Newbury Car Auctions Ltd ('Newbury'). He left Newbury as part-exchange a Hillman car which, it later transpired, was not his, but which had also been acquired on hire purchase. The fraudster signed the necessary hire purchase documents and was given possession of the car and the car's registration book.[12] The finance company, realizing that Cullis was a fraudster, rejected the hire purchase proposal. By this time, Cullis had absconded with the car. A man, who was presumably Cullis, then sold the Morris car on to Mercury Motors, who sold it on to Unity Finance Ltd, who let it on hire purchase terms to Powell. When Newbury discovered this, it claimed to be entitled to recover the car from Powell. When Powell refused, Newbury commenced proceedings against Powell and Unity Finance Ltd.

HELD: The Court of Appeal held[13] that, on the facts of the case, no estoppel arose and Newbury was therefore entitled to recover the car. The mere handing over of a motor car together with its registration book does not, without more, constitute a representation that the person in receipt of the goods is entitled to deal with the car as owner, and if that person purports to sell the car, the true owner will not thereby be estopped from asserting his title. In the same way that an owner who gives to a third party possession of the goods does not thereby represent that the third party is himself the owner or has the right to sell the goods, neither will the giving to the third party the documents of title to the goods. The mere possession of such documents 'no more conveyed a representation that the merchants were entitled to dispose of the property than the actual possession of the goods themselves would have conveyed any such representation'.[14]

As the following case demonstrates, any representation by the owner must be voluntary and, if induced by threats, will be invalid.

Debs v Sibec Developments Ltd [1990] RTR 91 (QB)

FACTS: During the course of a violent armed robbery, Debs was forced at gunpoint to write out and sign a purported receipt for £46,000 in full and final settlement for his

---

11. *Jerome v Bentley & Co* [1952] 2 All ER 114 (QB).
12. A car's registration book (which is now known as a registration document) is not a document of title (*Joblin v Watkins & Roseveare (Motors) Ltd* [1949] 1 All ER 47 (KB)).
13. By a majority of Hodson and Morris LJJ; Denning LJ dissenting.
14. *Mercantile Bank of India Ltd v Central Bank of India Ltd* [1938] AC 287 (PC) 303 (Lord Wright).

Mercedes car, which was then taken by the robbers. The car's registration document was inside the car. As Debs had been threatened by the robbers, he did not report the robbery to the police for about a month. In the meantime, armed with the registration document in Debs' name and the 'receipt' signed by him, the robbers then sold the car, which was then resold to others before ending up in the possession of Sibec Developments Ltd ('Sibec'), who acquired it under a hire purchase agreement. When the police eventually recovered the car, Debs sued Sibec for damages for conversion. Sibec sought to rely on s 21(1), arguing that by signing the 'receipt' for the 'sale', Debs was thereby estopped from denying the seller's authority to sell.

HELD: Debs' claim succeeded. Simon Brown J held that the doctrine of estoppel by representation implied a representation voluntarily made. In this case, because Debs had been forced to sign the purported receipt at gunpoint, he was not estopped from denying the right to sell the car. The robbers, as sellers, could not pass good title to the buyer and that buyer could not pass good title to Sibec, nor to anyone else. As to the delay of a month before reporting the theft, the court held that Debs was under no duty of care to prospective future purchasers to report the theft to the police and, even if he had been under such a duty to the first innocent purchaser, the threats made to him justified his failure to report the loss earlier than he did report it. In any event, Sibec had suffered no loss because it had a complete remedy against the hire purchase company.

⭐ See Ian Brown, 'Involuntary Estoppel and Transfer of Title in the Sale of Goods' (1990) 41 NILQ 257

Estoppel by negligence

An estoppel by negligence arises where the owner of goods, by reason of his negligence or negligent failure to act, allows the seller of the goods to appear to the buyer as the true owner or as having the true owner's authority to sell the goods. For this reason, it has been said that this is, ultimately, an estoppel by representation, albeit under a different heading and one in which the representation arises through an omission.[15] Thus, a person who omits to correct a misrepresentation made by a third party where he has a duty to do so might in appropriate circumstances be held responsible for that representation. In *Saunders v Anglia Building Society*,[16] Lord Pearson went further and stated that the phrase 'estoppel by negligence' was misleading, not least because an estoppel does not arise from negligence but from a representation made by words or conduct.[17]

In any event, for this kind of estoppel to arise, it must first be shown that the owner of the goods had a duty to take care so as not to act negligently. Just as in the law of torts, there can be no question of negligence unless there is first established a duty of care,[18] and this requirement significantly limits the scope of this type of estoppel. This point can be seen from the following case, which considered both estoppel by representation and estoppel by negligence.

---

15. *Mayhew-Lewis v Westminster Scaffolding Group plc* (QB, 16 March 1999).
16. [1971] AC 1004 (HL).
17. ibid 1038. See, also, Professor Atiyah, *Essays on Contract* (Oxford University Press 1986) 316–19.
18. It should also be remembered that a person owes no duty to third parties to look after his own property.

Moorgate Mercantile Co Ltd v Twitchings
[1977] AC 890 (HL)

FACTS: Moorgate Mercantile Co Ltd ('Moorgate') was a finance company and supplied a car on hire purchase to McLorg. Moorgate failed to register the hire purchase transaction with HPI (an organization set up by finance companies to prevent fraud in connection with the supply of vehicles on hire purchase or where they have been stolen). Registering such a transaction with HPI was not compulsory, although the majority of hire purchase transactions were registered with it. McLorg then offered to sell the car to Twitchings (a motor dealer). As McLorg had not paid all the instalments, he did not own the car and therefore did not have the right to sell it. Twitchings contacted HPI to see if the car was registered with them (as having outstanding finance) and was told that it was not. Twitchings then bought the car from McLorg. When Moorgate discovered what had occurred, it commenced proceedings against Twitchings. Twitchings contended that Moorgate was estopped from asserting its title to the car, arguing that (i) there existed an estoppel by representation because HPI had represented that the car was not the subject of an outstanding hire purchase agreement and that this representation was given as agent of Moorgate; and (ii) there also existed an estoppel by negligence on the ground that Moorgate failed to register the hire purchase agreement with HPI.

HELD: By a majority, the House of Lords rejected both limbs of the doctrine and upheld Moorgate's claim. The House rejected the argument based on estoppel by representation because the statement made by HPI was in fact true. HPI did not say that there was no outstanding finance on the car, but only that nothing was registered with them. Furthermore, when responding to Moorgate's request for information, HPI was acting in its own capacity and not as agent for Moorgate. Estoppel by negligence was rejected (Lords Wilberforce and Lord Salmon dissenting) because the registering of hire purchase agreements with HPI by its members was not compulsory and therefore Moorgate, although careless, was under no duty to take reasonable care to register such agreements.

⭐ See Ian Fagelson, 'Wrongful Sale of Hire Purchase Cars' (1977) 40 MLR 64

The reasoning in *Moorgate* was followed and expanded upon in the following case which concerned, as in *Moorgate*, a hirer fraudulently selling hire goods to an innocent purchaser.

Cadogan Finance Ltd v Lavery & Fox
[1982] Com LR 248 (QB)

FACTS: Cadogan Finance Ltd ('Cadogan') supplied, on hire purchase terms, an aeroplane to Traders Delivery Services Ltd ('Traders'). Cadogan did not re-register the aeroplane in Traders' name, but instead left it to Traders to re-register the aeroplane. Traders re-registered the aeroplane, but registered the plane in its own name as owner (even though it was not). Traders' managing director and major shareholder, Lavery, acted as Traders' guarantor under the hire purchase agreement. Lavery, acting on Traders' behalf, purported to sell the aeroplane to Fox, who was completely unaware that it was subject to a hire purchase agreement and that Traders was not entitled to sell it. Traders eventually went into liquidation and Cadogan discovered the purported sale of the aeroplane to Fox. Cadogan sought to recover the aeroplane from Fox. Fox contended that Cadogan's failure to re-register the aeroplane itself amounted to estoppel by negligence.

> **HELD:** Cadogan could recover the aeroplane. Hobhouse J held that Cadogan was merely following usual practice and had no reason to believe that Traders was either unreliable or dishonest, and was unaware that Traders had failed to re-register the aircraft properly. In these circumstances, a reasonable person in the position of Cadogan would not foresee or contemplate that its decision not to deal with these matters personally would cause any loss to anyone. As a result, there was no relationship of proximity between Cadogan and Fox, and thus no duty of care arose between them. The real or proximate cause of Fox's loss was the fraud and not the failure to re-register. Consequently, Cadogan was not estopped from asserting its title to the aircraft.

Other forms of estoppel

In *Powell v Wiltshire and Others*,[19] the Court of Appeal considered a different form of estoppel, namely, 'estoppel by reason of privity' or 'estoppel by judgment'. With this form of estoppel, a party asserting its title to goods may be estopped from denying another's right to sell the goods if, in separate proceedings, a court has already held that that other party had better title to the goods. This form of estoppel operates by denying the party wishing to assert title from reopening a dispute as to ownership that has already been decided in another case. Even though the party seeking to assert title was not party to those other proceedings, the decision may be binding on him by way of an estoppel. Consequently, 'a person claiming title is privy to the interests of those through whom he claims that title for the purposes of the operation of the doctrine of estoppel *per rem judicatam*, but only if the title he claims was acquired after the date of the judgment'.[20] In *Powell*, the buyer had purchased the goods during the course of proceedings in another case, but before judgment had been given, such judgment declaring that the party selling the goods to him was not their owner. For this reason, the estoppel did not apply.

➡ *per rem judicatam*: 'in respect of the thing actually in dispute already adjudicated upon'

Sale by a mercantile agent

A mercantile agent is defined in s 1(1) of the FA 1889.[21]

 **FA 1889, s 1(1)**

> The expression 'mercantile agent' shall mean a mercantile agent having in the customary course of his business as such agent authority either to sell goods, or to consign goods for the purpose of sale, or to buy goods, or to raise money on the security of goods.

---

19. [2005] QB 117 (CA).   20. ibid 126 (Latham LJ).

21. It will be noted that, although there are obvious similarities between a mercantile agency and a common law agency, they are not the same. A mercantile agent will also be an agent under common law, but an agent under common law will not necessarily be a mercantile agent. This is because, although a common law agent need not necessarily act in the course of a business, acting in the course of business is a requirement of a mercantile agent.

This exception to the *nemo dat* rule naturally applies only to a person who is acting as a mercantile agent. Whether an agent will be considered in law to be a mercantile agent is not dependent on him being labelled such in the contract, but will be a matter of substance.[22] However, if this person (whether a mercantile agent or not) has actual or apparent authority to sell the goods, then ownership will pass to the buyer under common law agency rules and it will be unnecessary to consider the rules of mercantile agency. Thus, at common law, a third party would usually be protected where he purchases goods from a dealer acting in the ordinary course of business where those goods were entrusted to the dealer by their true owner. The problem with this, however, was that the common law offered no protection to a party who lent money on the security of the goods, as the factor in such a case was deemed to have been acting outside the normal course of business. This was because 'though a factor has power to sell, and thereby bind his principal, he cannot bind or affect the property of the goods by pledging them as a security for his own debt'.[23] This limitation was unnecessarily restrictive where goods were imported, because the import merchant's commercial agents would frequently pledge to bankers the goods or their documents of title so as to enable them to raise money until the arrival of the goods when they could be resold. As a result, a series of Factors Acts were passed, the current one being the FA 1889, s 2 of which[24] sets out the powers of the mercantile agent regarding the disposition of the owner's goods. Notwithstanding the original purpose behind the passing of the Factors Acts, as we will shortly see, the provisions of the FA 1889 are nowadays normally seen in cases where a motor vehicle has been entrusted to a dealer for the purpose of sale or obtaining offers for a sale.

⊙ FA 1889, s 2

(1) Where a mercantile agent is, with the consent of the owner, in possession of goods or of the documents of title to goods, any sale, pledge, or other disposition of the goods, made by him when acting in the ordinary course of business of a mercantile agent, shall, subject to the provisions of this Act, be as valid as if he were expressly authorised by the owner of the goods to make the same; provided that the person taking under the disposition acts in good faith, and has not at the time of the disposition notice that the person making the disposition has not authority to make the same.

(2) Where a mercantile agent has, with the consent of the owner, been in possession of goods or of the documents of title to goods, any sale, pledge, or other disposition, which would have been valid if the consent had continued, shall be valid notwithstanding the determination of the consent: provided that the person taking under the disposition has not at the time thereof notice that the consent has been determined.

---

22. *Weiner v Harris* [1910] 1 KB 285 (CA).
23. *Paterson v Tash* (1742) 2 Strange 1178 (Lee CJ).
24. Which is expressly preserved by s 21(2) of the SGA 1979, subsection (a) of which provides: 'Nothing in this Act affects the provisions of the Factors Acts or any enactment enabling the apparent owner of goods to dispose of them as if he were their true owner.'

> (3) Where a mercantile agent has obtained possession of any documents of title to goods by reason of his being or having been, with the consent of the owner, in possession of the goods represented thereby, or of any other documents of title to the goods, his possession of the first-mentioned documents shall, for the purposes of this Act, be deemed to be with the consent of the owner.
>
> (4) For the purposes of this Act the consent of the owner shall be presumed in the absence of evidence to the contrary.

Before an unauthorized sale by a mercantile agent can confer good title to an innocent buyer, a number of requirements must be satisfied.

The seller must be a mercantile agent

This requirement is self-evident and reference should be made to the definition in s 1(1) of the FA 1889 considered at the beginning of this section. The mercantile agent must be independent from his principal. This rules out a person who is the principal's employee or mere servant, but not someone who is acting for a single principal,[25] providing he acts as agent in the customary course of business. There is no need for him regularly to be engaged as a mercantile agent, it being sufficient that he acted as such during the particular transaction in dispute. The question as to whether or not the person is a mercantile agent is to be considered at the time he obtains possession of the goods. This means that if he subsequently falls within the meaning of mercantile agent whilst still in possession of the goods, he will not be deemed to be a mercantile agent for the purpose of the transaction.[26] Thus:

> a man who at the time is not carrying on any business, or acting in any business capacity, asks the owner of a car to lend it to him to drive to a place where he has an urgent mission to fulfil, and says that he will bring it back in half an hour. He gets the car by cheating the owner out of the possession of it. The fact that he afterwards becomes a dealer and sells it as a mercantile agent does not bring the case within the section, because the owner in that case did not put it into the power of a mercantile agent to sell and make an apparently good title to the chattel.[27]

The Act will not apply if the agent sells the goods on his own behalf as owner because the essence of agency will be missing. Nor will it apply where a person agrees to find a buyer for another's goods out of pure friendship, as there will be no business characteristic in such an arrangement. Neither will it apply in any case where he is not authorized to deal with the goods in his own name without disclosing the name of his principal. This latter point was considered in *Rolls Razor Ltd v Cox*,[28] a case where the defendant was a door-to-door salesman selling washing machines and engaged by a company that supplied him with a van and stock. Lord Denning MR explained:

> Now I am quite clear that these salesmen were not factors. The usual characteristics of a factor are these: He is an agent entrusted with the possession of goods of

---

25. *Lowther v Harris* [1927] 1 KB 393 (KB).
26. *Heap v Motorists' Advisory Agency Ltd* [1923] 1 KB 577 (KB).
27. ibid 588 (Lush J). This was the example advanced by Lush J during the course of argument.
28. [1967] 1 QB 552 (CA).

several principals, or sometimes only one principal, for the purpose of sale in his own name without disclosing the name of his principal, and he is remunerated by a commission…These salesmen lacked one of these characteristics. They did not sell in their own names, but in the name and on behalf of their principals, Rolls Razor Ltd. They were agents pure and simple, and not factors.[29]

The mercantile agent must be in possession of the goods or documents of title to the goods when he sells, pledges, or disposes of the goods

Unless the mercantile agent is in possession of the goods or of the documents of title to the goods at the time he sells, pledges, or otherwise disposes of the goods, the buyer will not be protected by the Act.

Beverley Acceptances Ltd v Oakley [1982] RTR 417 (CA)

FACTS: Oakley borrowed £25,000 from Green in order to buy two Rolls Royce cars. He signed a form in which he pledged the cars to Green as security for the loan and giving Green power to sell them to cover the amount owing. Oakley left the cars in Green's compound, together with their keys and the registration document for one of them. Oakley also entered into negotiations with Beverley Acceptances Ltd ('Beverley'), a finance company, to obtain a further loan of £25,000 on the security of the same two cars. Oakley deceived Green into giving him the keys to the compound, the keys to the two cars, and the registration document of one of them by telling him he needed them for insurance purposes, but in fact he wanted them in order to show them to Beverley's representatives. Oakley returned the cars to Green's compound. Beverley advanced the further money to Oakley. Oakley executed two bills of sale in Beverley's favour. When Beverley discovered that Green was in possession of the two cars and that he claimed to be a pledgee to secure his loan to Oakley, it commenced proceedings against Oakley and Green.

HELD: The Court of Appeal held that for the purposes of the FA 1889, the registration document was not a document of title, since it stated that the registered keeper might not be the legal owner and therefore could not provide proof of ownership. In order for Beverley to rely on possession by a mercantile agent under s 2(1), possession had to be simultaneous with the disposition. In the present case, Oakley had not been in possession at the time of the execution of the bills of sale, and Beverley, as buyer, was therefore not protected by the Act.

COMMENT: This case demonstrates that it is not enough for the mercantile agent to have been in possession of the goods etc.; he must be in possession of the goods or documents of title to the goods when he sells, pledges, or disposes of the goods.

The mercantile agent must be in possession of the goods or documents of title with the owner's consent

There is a rebuttable presumption that the owner has consented to the mercantile agent having possession of the goods or documents of title, although this may be

---

29. ibid 568.

displaced if there is evidence to the contrary.[30] As Denning LJ pointed out in *Pearson v Rose & Young*,[31] for the owner's consent to be valid, it must be given in such a way as to clothe the mercantile agent with apparent authority to sell his goods. This is because:

 Apparent authority is discussed at p 96

> Parliament has not protected the true owner, if he has himself consented to a mercantile agent having possession of them: because, by leaving them in the agent's possession, he has clothed the agent with apparent authority to sell them; and he should not therefore be allowed to claim them back from an innocent purchaser.[32]

With the sale of a second-hand motor vehicle, the owner must consent to the mercantile agent having possession of the vehicle, the registration document, and the keys. Without possession of all of these things, as will be discussed later, a sale will not amount to a sale in the ordinary course of business of a mercantile agent and will therefore be outside the protection afforded by the FA 1889.

As the following cases illustrate, the key issue is the owner's consent, and it matters not if that consent has been obtained by fraud, provided the consent has in fact been given.

Pearson v Rose & Young [1951] 1 KB 275 (CA)

FACTS: Pearson wished to sell his car and so he left it with a motor dealer, Reliance Motor Haulage Contractors Ltd ('Reliance'). Pearson instructed Hunt, a mercantile agent for Reliance, not to sell the car, but to see what offers he could obtain. Hunt asked Pearson to show him the car's registration document, which he did. Whilst Hunt was holding the registration document, he induced Pearson to leave by pretending that he had to accompany his wife to hospital urgently. Pearson left, forgetting that Hunt still held the car's registration documents. Hunt then sold the car to a third party and handed him the registration document. The car was eventually sold to Rose & Young. Pearson demanded that Rose & Young return the car, but it refused, so Pearson commenced proceedings. Hunt was subsequently convicted of fraud.

HELD: The Court of Appeal held that this was not a transaction under which the FA 1889 would provide protection so as to give good title to the party who purchased the car from the dealer. Although Pearson had consented to Hunt having possession of his car as a mercantile agent, he did not consent to him having possession of the registration document. Denning LJ observed that Pearson 'no more consented to Hunt having possession of the registration book than if Hunt had stolen it from his pocket'.[33] The Court noted that Hunt could have sold the car without the registration document but, in so doing, it would not have amounted to a sale in the ordinary course of business of a mercantile agent and any such sale would therefore have been outwith the protection afforded by the FA 1889.

COMMENT: As to whether a mercantile agent's fraud negates the owner's consent, Denning LJ explained:

---

30. FA 1889, s 2(4).   31. [1951] 1 KB 275 (CA).   32. ibid 286.   33. ibid 290.

> If the true owner was induced to part with the goods by some fraud on the part of the mercantile agent, does that mean that he did not consent to the mercantile agent having possession of them? Again the answer at first sight seems obvious: A consent obtained by fraud is no consent at all, because fraud negatives consent. The effect of fraud, however, in this, as in other parts of the law, is as a rule only to make the transaction voidable, and not void; and if therefore an innocent purchaser has bought the goods before the transaction is avoided, the true owner cannot claim them back. For instance, if a mercantile agent should induce the owner to pass the property to him by some false pretence, as by giving him a worthless cheque; or should induce the owner to entrust the property to him for display purposes, by falsely pretending that he was in a large way of business when he was not, then the owner cannot claim the goods back from an innocent purchaser who has bought them in good faith from the mercantile agent. The agent's offence may in some cases be obtaining goods by false pretences, or in other cases larceny by a trick … but in each case, whether the owner intended to pass the property or not, at any rate he consented to the agent having possession. Though consent may have been obtained by fraud but, until avoided, it is a consent which enables the Factors Act 1889 to operate.[34]

As already noted, if an owner leaves his car with a mercantile agent without the keys or registration document (or locks the registration document in the glove compartment), then any sale by the agent will not be in the ordinary course of his business and will not therefore give good title under the FA 1889.

 Stadium Finance Ltd v Robbins
[1962] 2 QB 664 (CA)

FACTS: Robbins left his car with Palmer, a motor dealer, to put in his showroom on the understanding that any enquiries would be referred to him and that he would make the decision whether or not to sell. Robbins inadvertently left the registration document in the locked glove compartment and took the keys with him. Palmer obtained another key, located the registration document, and sold the car to Stadium Finance Ltd ('Stadium'), which let it on hire purchase to one of Palmer's own salesmen, who later defaulted on the hire purchase agreement. Stadium wished to take possession of the car but Robbins had already done so. Stadium commenced proceedings against Robbins.

HELD: The Court of Appeal held that the sale of the car, without the registration document and the ignition key, was not a sale in the ordinary course of business of a mercantile agent within the meaning of s 2(1) of the FA 1889, and the presumption of the owner's consent raised by s 2(4) was rebutted by the circumstances. For these reasons, Stadium's claim failed and Robbins retained the car.

See JA Hornby, 'Mercantile Agents Car Registration Books' (1962) 25 MLR 719

Since *Pearson*, it is clear that, provided the owner intentionally gives possession to the mercantile agent, it is irrelevant that his consent was obtained by fraud. For the same reason, neither should it matter for these purposes that the contract itself is illegal, although there is some troubling *dicta* in *Belvoir Finance Co Ltd v Harold Cole*

---

34. ibid 287.

& Co Ltd,[35] where Donaldson J suggested that, in a case where a mercantile agent is in possession of the owner's goods under an illegal hire purchase agreement, the illegality of that agreement prevents a purchaser from establishing the owner's consent for the purposes of s 2(1) of the FA 1889.[36] If this is correct, it would mean that an owner could rely on his own illegality to defeat the rights of a bona fide purchaser, although it is submitted that this cannot have been Donaldson J's intention.

Section 2(1) talks about the consent of the 'owner'. In the following case, the Court of Appeal considered a situation in which the right of ownership existed in more than one party. In such a case, the parties together will be the 'owner' for the purpose of s 2(1).

 Lloyds Bank Ltd v Bank of America National Trust and Savings Association [1938] 2 KB 147 (CA)

FACTS: The case concerned the dealings in documents of title. Strauss & Co Ltd ('Strauss') pledged bills of lading with Lloyds Bank, who released them back to Strauss under a trust receipt so it could sell them, as its trustee, with the proceeds of sale to be used to discharge its loan. Instead of effecting a sale, and without Lloyds Bank's authority, Strauss fraudulently pledged them with Bank of America (which was unaware of Strauss' fraud). Lloyds Bank commenced proceedings against the Bank of America for the return of the documents.

HELD: The Court of Appeal held that in a case where two or more parties have ownership of the goods or documents of title, then together they will be 'owner' for the purpose of s 2(1). Strauss was therefore in possession of the documents of title with the consent of Lloyds Bank. Consequently, as the requirements of the section were met, Bank of America took its title free of any interest of Lloyds Bank, who thereby lost its security. Sir Wilfrid Greene MR explained that:

> … it happens very frequently that the incidents and rights of ownership are divided among two or more hands. One person may have the right to possession, which is one of the rights incident to ownership, and another person may have all the other rights incident to ownership. Nevertheless it is only the two of them who can confer on a third party the ownership of the property in question. It is only by their combining in an assignment that they can confer a good title. I am quite unable to read the word 'owner' in this section as excluding such a case. It seems to me that, where the right of ownership has become divided among two or more persons in such a way that the acts which the section is contemplating could never be authorized save by both or all of them, these persons together constitute the owner. If it is with the consent of those persons that the mercantile agent is in possession of the documents, then he is in possession of them with the consent of the owner within the meaning of the section.[37]

---

35. [1969] 1 WLR 1877 (QB).
36. In *Belvoir*, the finance company was able to establish title by founding its claim on its earlier purchases of the cars without having to refer to the illegal agreements.
37. [1938] 2 KB 147 (CA) 162.

The mercantile agent must be in possession of the goods or documents of title in his capacity as mercantile agent

The necessary consent to enable the operation of the FA 1889 must be consent to the possession by a mercantile agent acting as a mercantile agent. This was explained by Denning LJ in *Pearson v Rose & Young*.[38]

> That means that the owner must consent to the agent having them for a purpose which is in some way or other connected with his business as a mercantile agent. It may not actually be for sale. It may be for display or to get offers, or merely to put in his showroom; but there must be a consent to something of that kind before the owner can be deprived of his goods.[39]

It follows, therefore, that possession of the goods by a mercantile agent for the purpose of, for example, repairing them would not satisfy this requirement and, as the following case demonstrates, neither would possession as hirer.

 Staffs Motor Guarantee Ltd v British Wagon Co Ltd [1934] 2 KB 305 (KB)

FACTS: Heap was a mercantile agent and had in his possession a lorry that he used to own before selling it to British Wagon Co Ltd and then taking it back on hire purchase. He then fraudulently sold it to Staffs Motor Guarantee Ltd ('Staffs'), who was unaware of the hire purchase arrangements. He failed to maintain the hire purchase payments and the lorry was repossessed by British Wagon. Staffs argued that it was protected by s 2(1) of the FA 1889, as it took possession of the vehicle with Heap's consent and that he was a mercantile agent.

HELD: MacKinnon J held that Heap was not in possession of the lorry as a mercantile agent within the meaning of s 2(1) of the FA 1889, but as a mere bailee. Consequently, the sale of the lorry by Heap to Staffs did not provide protection to it under the section.

COMMENT: MacKinnon J also held that similar reasoning also applied to a claim brought under another of the exceptions, namely s 25(1) of the SGA 1893 (now s 24 of the SGA 1979), although this part of the judgment has since been overruled.

The dealing in the goods by the mercantile agent must be in the ordinary course of business of mercantile agents generally

The mercantile agent only needs to be acting in the ordinary course of business of mercantile agents generally and not of his own particular business or trade. This requirement was explained by the Court of Appeal in *Oppenheimer v Attenborough & Son*[40] as:

> acting in such a way as a mercantile agent acting in the ordinary course of business of a mercantile agent would act; that is to say, within business hours, at a proper place of business, and in other respects in the ordinary way in which a mercantile agent would act, so that there is nothing to lead the pledgee to

---

38. [1951] 1 KB 275 (CA). This case is discussed on p 285.   39. ibid 288.
40. [1908] 1 KB 221 (CA).

suppose that anything wrong is being done, or to give him notice that the disposition is one which the mercantile agent had no authority to make.[41]

This requires an objective approach looking at mercantile agents generally, rather than the particular agent under scrutiny in any particular case. Consequently, the authority given by s 2 of the FA 1889 to a mercantile agent, who is in possession of goods with the consent of the owner, to pledge the goods when acting in the ordinary course of business of a mercantile agent, is a general authority given to every mercantile agent, and is not restricted by the existence in any particular trade of a custom that a mercantile agent employed in that trade to sell goods has no authority to pledge them. It will be a question of fact in each case whether or not a mercantile agent has acted in the ordinary way in which a mercantile agent would act.[42] These propositions can be seen from the *Oppenheimer* case itself, where the mercantile agent was a diamond broker. He pledged diamonds that had been entrusted to him without the authority of the owner. Although it is not usual for diamond brokers to have the authority to pledge, the Court of Appeal held that the mercantile agent had acted in the ordinary course of business of mercantile agents generally, the result being that the pledgee obtained good title to the diamonds pledged.

The third party must acquire the goods in good faith and without notice that the mercantile agent lacked the authority

Section 2(1) of the FA 1889 has the following proviso: 'provided that the person taking under the disposition acts in good faith, and has not at the time of the disposition notice that the person making the disposition has not authority to make the same'. This has two distinct parts. The first requires that the person taking under the disposition acts in good faith; and the second that that person has not notice that the person making the disposition has not authority to make it. It was held by Lush J in *Heap v Motorists Advisory Agency Ltd*[43] that the burden of proof in this regard rests with the third party buyer. The test of good faith is subjective and is satisfied when it is done honestly, irrespective as to whether it is done negligently.[44]

Finally, it should be noted that a mercantile agent is only able to pass that title which the person who consented to him having the goods or documents of title had in the first place. If that person was not in fact the owner of the goods (for example, because he had stolen them), then no title will be passed by the mercantile agent to the buyer.

Sale in market overt

This was dealt with in s 22 of the SGA 1979 and was the oldest of the exceptions to the *nemo dat* rule, the leading case having been established in 1595.[45] A sale in market overt occurred when goods were sold in an open, public, and legally constituted market[46] between the hours of sunrise and sunset.[47] The rationale for this rule was that a dishonest person would be unlikely to sell stolen goods or goods that he did not own in such a market, and seems to reflect the high degree of supervision that was

---

41. ibid 230 (Buckley LJ).   42. *Biggs v Evans* [1894] 1 QB 88 (QB).
43. [1923] 1 KB 577 (KB) 589.   44. SGA 1979, s 61(3).
45. *The Case of Market Overt* (1595) 5 Coke Rep 83 180.
46. *Lee v Bayes* (1856) 18 CB 599, 601 (Jervis CJ).
47. *Reid v Commissioner of Metropolitan Police* [1973] QB 551 (CA).

seen in established markets in the Middle Ages. The rule did not apply in Scotland or Wales, nor to privately owned markets (which accounted for more than half the livestock markets in England and Wales), and did not affect the law relating to the sale of horses. It was clearly an outdated rule and was described by the Law Reform Committee[48] as capricious in its operation. The Committee recommended that it should either be abolished or extended to cover all retail sales at trade premises and sales by auction. A similar proposal was made in a 1994 Department of Trade and Industry (DTI) consultation document.[49] The rule was finally abolished by s 1 of the Sale of Goods (Amendment) Act 1994 for contracts made after 3 January 2005. No modern-day equivalent was enacted in its place.

Sale under a voidable title

The key provision here is s 23 of the SGA 1979.

 SGA 1979, s 23

When the seller of goods has a voidable title to them, but his title has not been avoided at the time of the sale, the buyer acquires a good title to the goods, provided he buys them in good faith and without notice of the seller's defect of title.

It will be observed from the section that a buyer can acquire a good title to the goods, notwithstanding that the seller only has a voidable title to them, although, as will be discussed shortly, where the seller's title is void, then the buyer gets no title at all.[50] It is, therefore, of the utmost importance to appreciate the difference between a void contract and one that is merely voidable, since s 23 will only operate in the case of the latter. Where a contract is declared void *ab initio*, it means that there was never a contract at all and therefore no party can enforce the agreement. A voidable contract, on the other hand (such as might arise in the case of misrepresentation) is one that can be set aside if the innocent party so chooses. In other words, the innocent party has the option of avoiding the contract and rendering it void. If he chooses not to set aside the contract, then the agreement takes effect in the normal way. But is it fair that the rights of the parties should depend on the technicality of whether the contract is void or voidable? The harshness of the rule can be seen in the following case.

➡ void *ab initio*: 'invalid from the beginning'

 ***Ingram v Little* [1961] 1 QB 31 (CA)**

FACTS: The three claimants, elderly ladies who were joint owners of a car, advertised it for sale. A rogue, introducing himself as Hutchinson, offered to buy it with a cheque.

---

48. Law Reform Committee, *Twelfth Report: Transfer of Title to Chattels* (Cmnd 2958, HMSO 1966).
49. DTI, *Transfer of Title: Sections 21 to 26 of the Sale of Goods Act 1979* (DTI 1994).
50. The section only applies in cases where the seller has a voidable title and where the goods are then sold to a buyer; a mere agreement to sell is not enough. For a case where the party with the voidable title pledges the goods with an innocent pledgee, see *Whitehorn Bros v Davison* [1911] 1 KB 463 (CA).

The claimants told him that they were not prepared to accept payment by cheque. The rogue replied that he was PGM Hutchinson, a reputable businessman, living at an address he gave in Caterham. One of the claimants decided to go to the local post office, where she ascertained from the telephone directory that there was such a person as PGM Hutchinson and that he lived at the address given by the rogue. As a result of this information, the claimants believed that the rogue was this gentleman and decided to let him have the car in exchange for his cheque. The rogue's cheque was dishonoured on presentation, but in the meantime he had sold the car to Little, who bought it in good faith. The claimants claimed against Little for the return of the car or alternatively damages for its conversion.

HELD: By a majority, the Court of Appeal held (Devlin LJ dissenting) that where a person physically present and negotiating to buy a chattel fraudulently assumed the identity of another person, the test to determine to whom the offer was made was how the promisee ought to have interpreted the promise. Applying that test to the facts of the case (and treating the claimants as the offerors), the offer was made solely to the real PGM Hutchinson and the rogue was incapable of accepting it. Consequently, the claimants' mistake prevented the formation of a contract with the rogue, resulting in the claimants' claim succeeding at the expense of Little.

COMMENT: This case has been severely criticized and subsequently doubted by the courts[51] to such an extent that it can possibly be regarded as wrongly decided. It has been argued that it is 'difficult to escape the conclusion that the court allowed its sympathy for the ladies to cloud its judgment of the issues'.[52]

Had the Court of Appeal declared the contract voidable rather than void,[53] then the innocent purchaser might have been protected by s 23, although this would have been at the expense of the original owners. The Law Reform Committee[54] recommended that, in the case of a sale to a fraudster, his title should always be treated as voidable, thus favouring the innocent purchaser over the original owner. Although this recommendation has never been enacted, subsequent cases have produced a similar result. The following case bears all the similarities of *Ingram v Little*, but the Court of Appeal took a different approach.

 Lewis v Averay (No 1) [1972] 1 QB 198 (CA)

FACTS: Lewis was the owner of an Austin Cooper car, which he decided to sell. He was contacted by a rogue, who, after test-driving the car, offered to buy it. The rogue told Lewis that he was Richard Green and spoke about the film world, leading Lewis to believe that he was in fact the well-known film actor, Richard Greene, who played Robin Hood in the series of that name. The rogue wrote out a cheque and signed it 'R A Green'. He wanted

51. See e.g. *Shogun Finance Ltd v Hudson* [2003] UKHL 62, [2004] 1 AC 919 [87] (Lord Millett).
52. Laurence Koffman and Elizabeth MacDonald, *The Law of Contract* (7th edn, OUP 2010) 290-1.
53. Which is now the position since the House of Lords decision in *Shogun Finance Ltd v Hudson* [2003] UKHL 62, [2004] 1 AC 919, discussed in further detail at p 302.
54. Law Reform Committee, *Twelfth Report: Transfer of Title to Chattels* (Cmnd 2958, HMSO 1966).

to take the car straight away, but Lewis was not willing for him to have it until the cheque had cleared. To hold him off, Lewis told him there were one or two small jobs he would like to do on the car before letting him have it, and that would give time for the cheque to be cleared. The rogue insisted he took the car straight away and told Lewis he was not concerned about these small jobs. To prove his identity, the rogue showed Lewis a pass from Pinewood Studios bearing the name Richard A Green and showing a photograph of the rogue. As a result, Lewis let the rogue take the car. A few days later, Lewis was told the cheque was worthless. By this time, the rogue, giving his name as Lewis, had sold the car to Averay, an innocent purchaser who took possession of it together with its logbook, which was still in Lewis's name. The rogue disappeared and (the real) Lewis brought an action against Averay, asserting that the car was still his.

HELD: Lord Denning MR explained that the real question is whether there was a contract of sale under which the property in the car passed from Lewis to the rogue. If there was such a contract then, even though it was voidable for fraud, nevertheless Averay would get a good title to the car. But if there was no contract of sale by Lewis to the rogue, either because there was no agreement between the parties, or because any apparent agreement was a nullity and thus void *ab initio* for mistake, then no property would pass from Lewis to the rogue and Averay would not get a title because the rogue had no property to pass to him. His Lordship then explained the dilemma and the principles which should be followed:

> As I listened to the argument in this case, I felt it wrong that an innocent purchaser (who knew nothing of what passed between the seller and the rogue) should have his title depend on such refinements. After all, he has acted with complete circumspection and in entire good faith: whereas it was the seller who let the rogue have the goods and thus enabled him to commit the fraud. I do not, therefore, accept the theory that a mistake as to identity renders a contract void. I think the true principle is ... this: When two parties have come to a contract—or rather what appears, on the face of it, to be a contract—the fact that one party is mistaken as to the identity of the other does not mean that there is no contract, or that the contract is a nullity and void from the beginning. It only means that the contract is voidable, that is, liable to be set aside at the instance of the mistaken person, so long as he does so before third parties have in good faith acquired rights under it...When a dealing is had between a seller like Lewis and a person who is actually there present before him, then the presumption in law is that there is a contract, even though there is a fraudulent impersonation by the buyer representing himself as a different man than he is. There is a contract made with the very person there, who is present in person. It is liable no doubt to be avoided for fraud, but it is still a good contract under which title will pass unless and until it is avoided...In this case Lewis made a contract of sale with the very man, the rogue, who came to the flat. I say that he 'made a contract' because in this regard we do not look into his intentions, or into his mind to know what he was thinking or into the mind of the rogue. We look to the outward appearances. On the face of the dealing, Lewis made a contract under which he sold the car to the rogue, delivered the car and the logbook to him, and took a cheque in return. The contract...was, of course, induced by fraud...But it was still a contract, though voidable for fraud. It was a contract under which this property passed to the rogue, and in due course passed from the rogue to Averay, before the contract was avoided. Though I very much regret that either of these good and reliable gentlemen should suffer, in my judgment it is Lewis who should do so.[55]

⭐ See CC Turpin, 'Mistake of Identity' (1972) 30 CLJ 19

---

55. [1972] 1 QB 198 (CA) 207.

The result in *Lewis v Averay* makes it clear that where a seller intends to, and does, contract with a person physically present, albeit a rogue, title to goods passes to the rogue, and unless the contract has been avoided in the meantime, title will pass to a subsequent innocent buyer. Such a contract is voidable, and not void. A voidable contract is perfectly valid unless and until the innocent party takes steps to rescind it. In certain circumstances, the innocent party may not be able to rescind the contract and, for present purposes, this is where such an action will interfere with the rights of the third party. Where the third party has acquired rights under a voidable contract, it will then be too late for the innocent owner to rescind it. Timing is thus critical and can be summarized thus:

- Where the party with a voidable title to the goods resells them to an innocent third party, then that third party will gain good title provided that the original contract has not by then been avoided.
- Conversely, where the party with the voidable title resells the goods to an innocent third party after the contract has been avoided, then there will no longer be any title in the goods which would be capable of being passed to the third party.

Where the parties do not deal face to face (e.g. by post), then different considerations apply, as the following case demonstrates.

 Cundy v Lindsay (1878) 3 App Cas 459 (HL)

FACTS: A rogue, Alfred Blenkarn, sent a letter to Lindsay ordering a large quantity of goods. Blenkarn used the address '37 Wood Street, Cheapside' and signed the letter in such a way that it appeared to be 'Blenkiron & Co'. There was a respectable firm of that name who traded from 123 Wood Street, Cheapside. Lyndsay dispatched the goods to 'Messrs Blenkiron & Co, 37 Wood Street, Cheapside'. The goods were received by Blenkarn at that address, whereupon, without paying Lindsay for them, he sold them to Cundy, who was entirely ignorant of the fraud. Lindsay commenced proceedings to recover the goods.

HELD: The claim succeeded. The House of Lords held that the contract between the rogue and Lindsay was void. As a result, no property in the goods ever passed to the rogue, meaning that it was quite impossible for the rogue to transfer title to Cundy. Accordingly, Lindsay was able to recover the goods.

The different approaches taken by the courts vis-à-vis whether a contract is void or voidable has now been clarified by the House of Lords in *Shogun Finance Ltd v Hudson*,[56] where it was held that it is necessary to distinguish between contracts made face-to-face and those made at a distance. With the former, unless the specific identity of the party is of some particular significance, the innocent party can be presumed to have intended to deal with the person in front of them, so that any fraud as to their identity merely renders the contract voidable.[57] On the other hand, with a contract concluded at a distance, especially one in writing, which by necessity identifies specifically who the contracting parties are, the contract can be taken to have been intended between

---

56. [2003] UKHL 62, [2004] 1 AC 919, discussed in further detail at p 302.
57. Disapproving the majority decision in *Ingram v Little* [1961] 1 QB 31 (CA).

those parties alone, so that where a fraudster forges the signature of one of the parties the result is that the contract is void. This distinction has been severely criticized by some judges, with Lord Denning describing it as 'a distinction without a difference',[58] adding that such distinctions 'do no good to the law'.[59] Academics have also doubted the correctness of *Shogun*, with one commentator stating the case to be 'a huge disappointment in terms of clarifying the applicable principles'.[60]

Avoiding a voidable contract

Section 23 applies only where the title is voidable. The most obvious way of avoiding a voidable contract in this type of situation is for the innocent party to inform the other party that the contract is no longer binding, or by evincing an intention to do so and by taking all possible steps, such as notifying the police in cases of fraud.[61]

Car & Universal Finance Co Ltd v Caldwell [1965] 1 QB 525 (CA)

FACTS: A rogue bought a car and fraudulently induced the seller (Caldwell) to part with it in return for a cheque, which later proved worthless. As soon as Caldwell was aware of this fraud, he informed the police and the Automobile Association. Before the car or the rogue could be traced, the rogue sold the car to an innocent third party, who then sold it onto Car & Universal Finance Co Ltd ('CUFC').

HELD: The Court of Appeal held that informing the police and the motoring organization was enough to avoid the (voidable) contract. As Caldwell had avoided the contract prior to the car being resold by the rogue,[62] CUFC acquired no title under s 23.

COMMENT: The decision in *Car & Universal Finance* is not without its difficulties and is certainly rather harsh on the innocent third-party purchaser (such as CUFC). It is also rather arbitrary in its application, as the innocent party's claim to the goods bought in good faith will depend on the speed that the original owner takes in avoiding the contract and the speed taken by the rogue in reselling the goods. It is certainly curious that the original owner should be able to avoid the contract by communicating his intention to do so to a complete stranger to the contract (i.e. to the police or motoring organizations). The decision in *Car & Universal Finance* was also criticized by the Law Reform Committee[63] as detracting substantially from the operation of s 23 and recommended that it should be reversed. In the almost factually identical Scottish case of *McLeod v Kerr*,[64] the Court of Session held that 'by no stretch of imagination' could such a seller's conduct amount to rescission of the contract.[65]

★ See WR Cornish, 'Rescission Without Notice' (1964) 27 MLR 472

---

58. *Lewis v Averay (No 1)* [1972] 1 QB 198 (CA) 206. See also the dissenting speeches of Lord Millett and Lord Nicholls in *Shogun Finance* itself.

59. ibid.

60. Jill Poole, *Textbook on Contract Law* (10th edn, OUP 2010) 117.

61. *Car & Universal Finance Co Ltd v Caldwell* [1965] 1 QB 525 (CA).

62. In such cases, the onus is on the innocent purchaser to show that the purchase was concluded before the original owner avoided the contract (*Thomas v Heelas* (CA, 27 November 1986).

63. Law Reform Committee, *Twelfth Report: Transfer of Title to Chattels* (Cmnd 2958, HMSO 1966) paras 15 and 40(3).

64. 1965 SC 253 (Court of Session).   65. ibid 257 (Lord Clyde LP).

In any event, since the Court of Appeal's ruling in *Newtons of Wembley Ltd v Williams*,[66] the harshness of the decision in *Car & Universal Finance* in relation to the innocent buyer has been mitigated. As will be discussed shortly, in *Newtons of Wembley v Williams*, it was held that for the purpose of the exception to the *nemo dat* rule contained in s 25 of the SGA 1979 (namely buyer in possession after sale), a good title may be transferred to an innocent buyer, even though the original owner had managed to avoid the rogue's title before the sale. Any case with facts similar to those in *Car & Universal Finance* is likely also to fall within the scope of s 25, which means that its importance as an authority is now somewhat diminished.

Good faith and without notice

Just like the other exceptions to the *nemo dat* rule, the buyer must act in good faith and without notice of the seller's defect in title when he buys the goods. But, with s 23, the burden of proof is different, favouring the buyer. With s 23, it is incumbent on the original owner to show that the third party purchaser did not act in good faith and bought with notice of the seller's defective title,[67] whereas with the other exceptions it is for the third party purchaser to show that he did act in good faith and without notice.[68] For these purposes, 'a thing is deemed to be done in good faith when it is in fact done honestly, whether it is done negligently or not'.[69]

Sale by a seller in possession after sale

This exception is stated in s 8 of the FA 1889 and in s 24 of the SGA 1979, both of which represent the current law.[70] The text shown in italics in the key provision box below are those words that were omitted from the original SGA in 1893,[71] and remained omitted when s 24 of the 1979 Act was enacted. Other than simple error,[72] there appears to be no logical reason for this omission, although the result appears to be that s 8 of the FA 1889 is slightly wider in scope than s 24 of the SGA 1979.

 FA 1889, s 8

Where a person having sold goods continues or is in possession of the goods or of the documents of title to the goods the delivery or transfer by that person or by a mercantile

---

66. [1965] 1 QB 560 (CA).

67. *Whitehorn Bros v Davison* [1911] 1 KB 463 (CA).

68. The different burdens of proof were criticized by the Law Reform Committee, which recommended that the burden of establishing good faith and lack of notice should always rest with the third party purchaser, irrespective of which exception is under scrutiny: Law Reform Committee, *Twelfth Report: Transfer of Title to Chattels* (Cmnd 2958, HMSO 1966) paras 25 and 40(13).

69. SGA 1979, s 61(3).

70. As noted, s 21(2)(a) of the SGA 1979 expressly preserves the FA 1899: 'Nothing in this Act affects the provisions of the Factors Acts or any enactment enabling the apparent owner of goods to dispose of them as if he were their true owner.'

71. Which was s 25(1) in that Act.

72. It seems that the draftsman of the Sale of Goods Bill 1893 proceeded on the basis that it was intended to repeal ss 8 and 9 of the FA 1889 and subsequently overlooked its retention.

> agent acting for him of the goods or documents of title under any sale, pledge, or other disposition thereof *or under any agreement for sale, pledge, or other disposition thereof* to any person receiving the same in good faith and without notice of the previous sale shall have the same effect as if the person making the delivery or transfer were expressly authorised by the owner of the goods to make the same.

This exception to the *nemo dat* rule allows a seller, who after a sale remains in possession of the goods or of the documents of title to them, to pass good title to a second buyer. Provided the requirements are satisfied, the effect shall be 'as if the person making the delivery or transfer were expressly authorised by the owner of the goods to make the same'.

The following example demonstrates how s 8 FA 1889/s 24 SGA 1979 operate in practice.

Eg ComCorp Ltd

ComCorp sells ten computers to Smiths Ltd. They are of a precise specification and no more are available. It was a sale of specific goods in a deliverable state and property that passed to Smiths the moment the contract was made. As Smiths now owns the computers, ComCorp no longer has any interest in them and cannot pass title to anyone else. But, let us assume that ComCorp keeps possession of the computers for a few days until Smiths is able to collect them, and during this time ComCorp (wrongly) resells them to Jones Ltd. Even though ComCorp no longer owns the computers and would not ordinarily be in any position to transfer title to any other party, as it is a seller in possession after sale, Jones obtains good title to the goods at the expense of Smiths. Smiths could, of course, sue ComCorp for non-delivery of the goods but this does not affect Jones's ownership.

Although the seller must be in possession of the goods, this can be satisfied if they were, with the seller's consent, in the possession of another party who was holding them on the seller's behalf.[73] It was once thought that the capacity of the seller was important and therefore, before a third party could succeed under this exception, he had to show that the seller was in possession of the goods qua seller and not in some other capacity.[74] However, the Privy Council in *Pacific Motor Auctions Pty Ltd v Motor Credits Ltd*[75] held that those earlier decisions had been wrongly decided and that the words 'continues or is in possession'[76] referred only to the continuity of actual possession, rather than the capacity in which the seller had the goods in his possession. Being a decision of the Privy Council, it is of persuasive authority only in the English courts, although it has since been followed by the Court of Appeal in *Worcester Works Finance Ltd v Cooden Engineering Co Ltd*,[77] which held that the correct

---

73. *City Fur Manufacturing Co Ltd v Fureenbond (Brokers) London Ltd* [1937] 1 All ER 799 (KB).

74. *Staffs Motor Guarantee Ltd v British Wagon Co Ltd* [1934] 2 KB 305 (KB); *Eastern Distributors v Goldring* [1957] 2 QB 600 (CA).

75. [1965] AC 867 (PC).

76. Under s 28(1) of the Sale of Goods Act 1923, which is the New South Wales equivalent to s 24 of the SGA 1979.

77. [1972] 1 QB 210 (CA).

approach is one of continuity of possession, rather than examining whether the seller was in possession of the goods 'as seller' or in some other capacity, such as bailee. Thus, provided the seller remained, without interruption, in physical possession of the goods, then the innocent second buyer gets good title under this exception to the *nemo dat* rule.

The seller must dispose of the goods to the subsequent buyer under a 'sale, pledge or other disposition'. In *Worcester Works Finance*, Lord Denning MR stated that 'disposition' being 'a very wide word' extends 'to all acts by which a new interest (legal or equitable) in the property is effectually created',[78] although not where mere possession of the goods is given to the subsequent buyer. Thus, a disposition must involve a transfer of *property* in the goods, as contrasted with a mere transfer of *possession*. Furthermore, a seller in possession can give good title to the goods even if his possession is without the consent of the buyer.[79]

Although a subsequent buyer must take delivery of the goods or of the documents of title to them, it was held by the Court of Appeal in *Michael Gerson (Leasing) Ltd v Wilkinson*[80] that in respect of a sale and leaseback agreement where the goods do not actually leave the premises, a constructive delivery of the goods will suffice. This is simply for pragmatic reasons: although the goods never leave the seller's premises, they should nevertheless be regarded as having been constructively delivered by the seller to the finance company which bought them, since the finance company could not otherwise lease them back to the seller.

It is also important to consider the effects of s 48(2) of the SGA 1979, which provides that where an unpaid seller who has exercised his right of lien, retention, or stoppage in transit, resells the goods, the buyer acquires a good title to them as against the original buyer. This is considered in further detail in Chapter 16.

Sale by a buyer in possession after sale

This exception is the converse of the previous one. In the majority of situations, a buyer in possession of the goods will own them, and, as owner, he can pass good title to whomsoever he wishes without any question of *nemo dat* arising. The exception stated in s 9 of the FA 1889 and s 25(1) of the SGA 1979 is concerned with situations in which the buyer is in possession of the goods but does not in fact own them. As with the previous exception, both sections represent current law, and once again the text shown in italics are the words that have been omitted from the SGA 1979. Again, for the reasons already discussed, s 9 of the FA 1889 is slightly wider in scope than its SGA 1979 counterpart.

FA 1889, s 9

Where a person having bought or agreed to buy goods obtains with the consent of the seller possession of the goods or the documents of title to the goods the delivery or

---

78. ibid 218.   79. ibid 220.   80. [2001] QB 514 (CA).

> transfer by that person or by a mercantile agent acting for him of the goods or documents of title under any sale, pledge, or other disposition thereof *or under any agreement for sale, pledge, or other disposition thereof* to any person receiving the same in good faith and without notice of any lien or other right of the original seller in respect of the goods, shall have the same effect as if the person making the delivery or transfer were a mercantile agent in possession of the goods or documents of title with the consent of the owner.

This exception allows a person in possession of the goods and who has either bought or agreed to buy them to pass good title to a third party, even though he has no such title to pass. As there is a requirement for the person in possession to have either bought or agreed to buy, this necessarily rules out a person who has acquired the goods under a hire purchase or conditional sale agreement.

 Helby v Matthews [1895] AC 471 (HL)

FACTS: Helby owned a piano, which he let to Brewster on hire purchase terms. A term of the hire purchase agreement provided that, at the end of the period of hire, provided Brewster had met all of the instalments, he would own the piano absolutely. Before the end of the hire period, Brewster pledged the piano with Matthews, a pawnbroker, as security for a loan.

HELD: The House of Lords held that, as Brewster was not under any legal obligation to purchase the piano but merely had an option to do so, he could not be said to have 'agreed to buy goods' within the meaning of s 9. Consequently, the pawnbroker acquired no title by virtue of the section, and Helby was therefore entitled to recover the piano from him.

The following example illustrates the simplest operation of the rule.

 ComCorp Ltd

ComCorp sells ten computers to Smiths Ltd, who is a dealer in computers. It was a sale of specific goods in a deliverable state, and property would have passed to Smiths the moment the contract was made had it not been for ComCorp's retention of title clause in its contract of sale, reserving to itself title in the goods until paid for. Smiths gave ComCorp a cheque for the computers and ComCorp allowed Smiths to take possession of them. Smiths' cheque was dishonoured, but before ComCorp could take any steps to recover the computers, Smiths sold them to Jones Ltd. This sale was in the ordinary course of business of computer dealers. Jones obtains good title to the computers even though Smiths had no such title itself.

A number of conditions need to be satisfied before this exception can operate so as to protect the sub-buyer. As the opening words to the section provide, its operation depends on a person buying or agreeing to buy goods. It will not, therefore, operate if he merely acquires the goods on hire purchase,[81] or even buys them under a sale or return contract.[82] This is because in either situation the person who obtains goods on hire purchase or sale or return does not necessarily buy or agree to buy them. A buyer under a conditional sale agreement is not a person who has bought or agreed to buy goods.[83]

The protection afforded to a sub-buyer is only available if the goods or documents of title were in the possession of the buyer with the consent of the seller. The section talks in terms of the buyer who 'obtains' possession of the goods or the documents of title to the goods with the consent of the seller. It is therefore immaterial whether such consent was afterwards withdrawn.[84] The section is silent as to the timing of such possession, although it has been held that it does not matter whether he had possession before he contracted with the sub-buyer provided he had possession before transfer or delivery of the goods or documents of title to him.[85] Although there must be delivery or transfer of the goods or documents of title to the sub-buyer under a sale, pledge, or other disposition, constructive delivery will suffice.[86] When selling or otherwise disposing of the goods, the buyer must act in the way a mercantile agent acting in the ordinary course of business of a mercantile agent would act. This is so even where the buyer is not a mercantile agent: the section only says he must act in this way, not that he must be one. This was confirmed by the Court of Appeal in *Newtons of Wembley Ltd v Williams*,[87] (discussed below) where Pearson LJ held that where there is a disposition by a buyer who is not a mercantile agent, it will be deemed to have been made in the ordinary course of his business of a mercantile agent if the buyer was acting in a way in which a mercantile agent would normally be expected to act.[88]

It will be recalled that in connection with s 23 of the SGA 1979, where a party with a voidable title resells the goods to an innocent third party, then that third party will obtain good title provided that the original contract has not by then been avoided. Where such a transaction also falls within the scope of s 9 of the FA 1889 or s 25(1) of the SGA 1979, then a good title may be transferred to the innocent buyer even though the original owner had managed to avoid the rogue's title before the sale.

 Newtons of Wembley Ltd v Williams
[1965] 1 QB 560 (CA)

FACTS: Newtons of Wembley Ltd ('Newtons') sold a car to Andrew, with Andrew paying by cheque. Andrew drove the car away but, shortly after, his cheque was dishonoured.

---

81. *Helby v Matthews* [1895] AC 471 (HL).
82. *Edwards (Percy) Ltd v Vaughan* (1910) 26 TLR 545 (CA).
83. FA 1889, s 9(1); SGA 1979, s 25(2)(a).
84. *Cahn & Mayer v Pockett's Bristol Channel Steam Packet Co Ltd* [1899] 1 QB 643 (CA).
85. ibid.
86. *Michael Gerson (Leasing) Ltd v Wilkinson* [2001] QB 514 (CA).
87. [1965] 1 QB 560 (CA).   88. ibid 580.

Newtons notified the Hire Purchase Information Bureau. Newtons also tried to trace Andrew, but could not locate him. As a result, Newtons was deemed to have avoided the contract with Andrew. The following month, Andrew sold the car to Biss for cash in Warren Street in London. Biss then sold the car to Williams. Williams, who took the car in good faith and without notice of any defect in Andrew's title, then offered the car for sale, whereupon the Hire Purchase Information Bureau was informed, with the result that Newtons attempted unsuccessfully to seize the car.

HELD: The Court of Appeal held that Newtons, having taken all available steps to recover the car and disaffirm the contract of sale as soon as it realized Andrew's cheque had been dishonoured, had thereby avoided the contract with him even though it was unable to communicate notice of rescission to Andrew. Accordingly, at common law, title to the car vested in Newtons. However, since Andrew had bought the car and since he had initially obtained possession of it with Newtons' consent, he was to be treated by virtue of s 9 of the FA 1889 as if he were a mercantile agent in possession of it with Newtons' consent, which consent was by virtue of s 2(2) of the Act to be deemed to continue, notwithstanding that it had been revoked by Newtons' rescission of the contract. But, s 9 could not be invoked unless it could be shown, not only that the person taking under the relevant disposition took in good faith and without notice of the original seller's rights, but also that the disposition was made in the ordinary course of business of a mercantile agent. Where there is a disposition by a buyer who is not a mercantile agent, it will be deemed to have been made in the ordinary course of his business of a mercantile agent if the buyer was acting in a way in which a mercantile agent would normally be expected to act. Applying the points made previously to the facts of the case, Biss had bought the car from Andrew in Warren Street in good faith and without notice of Newtons' rights, and in view of the established street market in London's Warren Street for cash sales of second-hand cars, the sub-sale by Andrew to Biss was made in the ordinary course of business of a mercantile agent. Consequently, it was effective to pass a good title to Biss and then to Williams under ss 2 and 9 of the FA 1889. Newtons' claim therefore failed and Williams acquired good title.

 See JWA Thornely, 'Sales by Persons with Voidable Titles and Buyers in Possession' [1965] CLJ 24

As has been discussed, s 9 of the FA 1889 (and, similarly, s 25(1) of the SGA 1979) provides protection 'where a person having bought or agreed to buy goods obtains with the consent of the seller...' But, what if the owner's goods have been stolen and the thief sells them to *X*, who then sells them to *Y*? Does *Y* acquire title? On a literal reading of the section, one might be forgiven for concluding that, since *X* took possession of the goods with the consent of the seller (who just so happens to be the thief), *X*'s sale to *Y* takes effect as if *X* was in possession with the consent of the owner. Such an interpretation was rejected by the House of Lords in the following case.

National Employers' Mutual General Insurance Association Ltd v Jones [1990] 1 AC 24 (HL)

FACTS: Hopkin's car was stolen by thieves, who sold it to Lacey. Lacey then sold it to Thomas, who sold it to Autochoice (Bridgend) Ltd ('Autochoice'), who sold it to Mid Glamorgan Motors Ltd ('MGM'), who then sold it to Jones. Autochoice, MGM, and Jones all bought the car in good faith and without notice of Hopkin's title. Hopkin's insurers, National Employers' Mutual General Insurance Association Ltd ('the insurance company'), asked

Jones to return the car, but Jones refused. The insurance company then commenced proceedings against Jones, claiming, *inter alia*, delivery up of the car or, alternatively, its value. Jones defended the claim on the ground that he had acquired good title to the car by virtue of s 9 of the FA 1889.

HELD: The House of Lords held that the purpose and scope of the FA 1889 was to protect those dealing in good faith with mercantile agents to whom goods or documents of title had been entrusted by the true owner to the extent that their rights overrode those of the true owner. The Act was not, however, intended to enable a bona fide purchaser to override the true owner's title where the agent had been entrusted with the documents or goods by a thief or even a purchaser from a thief. As a result, Jones had not acquired title to the car under s 9 and the insurance company was therefore entitled to recover the value of the car from Jones.

COMMENT: Lord Goff explained that the words at the end of s 9 'with the consent of the owner' must be taken as meaning that the delivery or transfer given by the intermediate transferor shall have the same effect as if he was a mercantile agent in possession of the goods or documents of title with the consent of the owner *who entrusted them to him*.[89] Since an owner does not entrust his goods to a thief, the section will not apply in the example shown. The same construction must also be placed on s 25(1) of the SGA 1979.

⭐ See Graham Battersby, 'The Sale of Stolen Goods: A Dilemma for the Law' (1991) 54 MLR 752

Sale of a vehicle acquired on hire purchase

As already discussed, s 9 of the FA 1889 and s 25(1) of the SGA 1979 apply only to transactions where the first buyer actually buys or agrees to buy the goods, and not to a person who acquires them on hire purchase or under a conditional sale agreement. It follows, therefore, that a person who acquires goods by one of these methods and sells them before he pays the final instalment will pass no title to the buyer. The problem was highlighted by Devlin J in *Eastern Distributors Ltd v Goldring*,[90] who stated that '[i]t is very hard on the defendant…but his fate is, unfortunately, a common one where hire-purchase agreements are concerned and is now one of the regular ways in which unsuspecting buyers are deceived by what they take to be ownership'.[91]

As a result of these problems, Pt III of the Hire Purchase Act 1964 (HPA 1964)[92] makes an exception to the problem noted here, but only in certain cases of a motor vehicle sold by a person who had acquired it on hire purchase.[93]

🔑 HPA 1964, s 27

(1) This section applies where a motor vehicle has been bailed or (in Scotland) hired under a hire-purchase agreement, or has been agreed to be sold under a conditional

---

89. [1990] 1 AC 24 (HL) 63.   90. [1957] 2 QB 600 (CA). This case is discussed on p 276.

91. ibid 614.

92. The majority of the HPA 1964 has been repealed. Pt III remains in force, although as re-enacted by the Consumer Credit Act 1974.

93. The DTI did suggest in its 1994 consultation paper that Pt III of the HPA 1964 should be extended to include all goods purchased on hire purchase or conditional sale agreements. This proposal was never enacted.

sale agreement, and before the property in the vehicle has become vested in the debtor, he disposes of the vehicle to another person.

(2) Where the disposition referred to in subsection (1) above is to a private purchaser, and he is a purchaser of the motor vehicle in good faith without notice of the hire-purchase or conditional sale agreement (the 'relevant agreement') that disposition shall have effect as if the creditor's title to the vehicle has been vested in the debtor immediately before that disposition.

(3) Where the person to whom the disposition referred to in subsection (1) above is made (the 'original purchaser') is a trade or finance purchaser, then if the person who is the first private purchaser of the motor vehicle after that disposition (the 'first private purchaser') is a purchaser of the vehicle in good faith without notice of the relevant agreement, the disposition of the vehicle to the first private purchaser shall have effect as if the title of the creditor to the vehicle had been vested in the debtor immediately before he disposed of it to the original purchaser.

In broad terms, s 27 provides that a bona fide private purchaser of a motor vehicle from a person in possession under a hire purchase agreement or conditional sale agreement obtains title to the vehicle even though the seller has no title himself. The section refers to 'the creditor's title', which limits any title passing under s 27 to the title of the creditor as described in the agreement as having let the vehicle. Thus, if a thief sells a car to *A*, who supplies it on hire purchase to *B*, who sells it to *C* (a private purchaser), *C* can only acquire the title which was vested by the thief in *A*, which being none, *C* acquires no title. The sale of anything other than a motor vehicle is not covered under this exception. So, if *X* acquires a car and a piano on hire purchase and sells them both to *Y*, a private purchaser, before *X* has paid the final instalment then, provided the requirements of s 27 are satisfied, *Y* will obtain good title to the car but not to the piano.[94]

The requirements under s 27

A purchaser will acquire good title to a motor vehicle provided the requirements of s 27 are satisfied. These requirements can be summarized as follows:

(a) The section applies only to a 'motor vehicle', which for these purposes is a 'mechanically propelled vehicle intended or adapted for use on roads to which the public has access'.[95] Thus, the sale of bicycles, caravans (unless motorized), boats and the like, not being motor vehicles, are therefore not protected.

(b) The seller must be in possession of the motor vehicle either as hirer under a hire purchase agreement or purchaser under a conditional sale agreement. In *Shogun Finance Ltd v Hudson*,[96] a rogue took possession of a vehicle under a hire purchase agreement by using a stolen driving licence as evidence of his name and address. He then resold the vehicle to Hudson (a private purchaser) and disappeared. When the finance company found out about the fraud, it sued Hudson in conversion. The House of Lords held the agreement to be void for mistake, as the finance company clearly intended to deal with the person

---

94. The pledge in *Helby v Matthews* [1895] AC 471 (HL) (discussed on p 298) was of a piano which was subject to a hire purchase agreement.
95. HPA 1964, s 29(1)(b).   96. [2003] UKHL 62, [2004] 1 AC 919.

actually named on the agreement, rather than the rogue. As the rogue was therefore not a seller in possession of the vehicle under a hire purchase agreement, Hudson could not rely on s 27 to acquire title.

(c) As the section makes plain, there needs to be a disposition. The timing of the disposition is important, as the following case demonstrates.

Kulkarni v Manor Credit (Davenham) Ltd [2010] EWCA Civ 69

FACTS: A motor dealer acquired a car from Manor Credit (Davenham) Ltd under a hire purchase agreement and, in breach of that agreement, sold and delivered it to Kulkarni later that same day. Three days earlier, the dealer had given Kulkarni the car's registration number to enable him to insure it. When Manor Credit discovered the dealer's fraud, it repossessed the car. Kulkarni brought a claim against Manor Credit in conversion, asserting title to the vehicle on the ground that, as he was a private purchaser of a motor car from a person in possession under a hire purchase agreement, he was protected by s 27 of the HPA 1964. The key issue was whether there had been a disposition of the car at a time when the dealer was hirer. It was Kulkarni's case that there had been no transfer of the property in the car until delivery, because the car had not been in a deliverable state until its registration plates had been attached and these were only attached on the day of delivery.

HELD: The Court of Appeal held that, as there was no evidence that the registration plates had been attached to the car prior to delivery, the goods were not in a deliverable state under s18, rule 5(1) of the SGA 1979, and Kulkarni would not have been bound to take delivery of it. When Kulkarni took possession, the dealer was already hirer under a hire purchase agreement and Kulkarni was a purchaser under a disposition that first took place upon delivery. Consequently, Kulkarni acquired ownership under s 27, thus defeating Manor Credit's title.

Section 18, rule 5(1) is discussed at p 246

See Louise Merrett, 'Is Possession Nine Tenths of the Law in the Sale of Goods?' (2010) 69 CLJ 236

COMMENT: Section 27 does not apply to a case where the seller sells the vehicle to an innocent purchaser before becoming hirer under a hire purchase agreement.

(d) Section 27 only applies to pass title to a 'private purchaser', which for these purposes is a purchaser other than a trade or finance purchaser.[97] A person will be a trade purchaser even though he had no dealings with the trade other than the one in question. Thus, where a person bought motor vehicles in circumstances where he had not taken any formal steps to set himself up as a motor dealer, purchasing them as a business venture with a view to selling them at a profit made him a trade purchaser for the purposes of the Act.[98] A person who trades as a motor dealer, even part-time, is also a trade purchaser, even if he buys the car for his own personal use.[99] A party is not a private purchaser if it purchases a vehicle with the intention of resale in the event of default by the borrower under the loan agreement.[100]

---

97. HPA 1964, s 29(2).
98. *GE Capital Bank Ltd v Rushton* [2005] EWCA Civ 1556, [2006] 1 WLR 899.
99. *Stevenson v Beverley Bentinck Ltd* [1976] 1 WLR 483 (CA).
100. *Welcome Financial Services Ltd v Nine Regions Ltd (t/a Log Book Loans)* [2010] 2 Lloyd's Rep 426 (QB).

(e) The private purchaser must be the first private purchaser who buys the vehicle in good faith without notice[101] of the hire purchase or conditional sale agreement.[102] Thus, if X acquires a motor vehicle on hire purchase and before making the last payment sells it to Y, a motor dealer, who then resells it to Z, a private purchaser, who buys it in good faith and without notice of the hire purchase arrangement and is therefore unaware of the defect in both X's and Y's title, Z acquires good title to the vehicle, notwithstanding that he has purchased it from Y rather than from X and even though Y did not acquire any title himself. In this example, s 27 does not pass ownership to Y because Y is not a private purchaser. Z is the first private purchaser and, as such, acquires good title to the vehicle. Z can then pass title in the ordinary way to a subsequent purchaser as he now owns the vehicle. The first private purchaser must either purchase the motor vehicle or acquire it on hire purchase.[103]

Finally, even where a private purchaser acquires title under s 27, it does not exonerate the seller from either civil or criminal liability for making the sale.[104]

Special powers of sale

The relevant provision is s 21(2)(b) of the SGA 1979.

 SGA 1979, s 21(2)(b)

Nothing in this Act affects...the validity of any contract of sale under any special common law or statutory power of sale or under the order of a court of competent jurisdiction.

Section 21(2)(b) covers miscellaneous situations in which a non-owner of goods may nevertheless pass good title to a purchaser. These situations include common law powers of sale, for example, those of a pawnbroker selling the goods of the pledgor when the loan remains unpaid, as well as statutory powers of sale, such as the powers given to law enforcement officers to sell goods seized under a writ of execution. In such a case, it gives a good title to the purchaser of the goods sold by a bailiff which have been taken by the bailiff out of the possession of the execution debtor, irrespective of whether or not the purchaser had notice that the goods in question were not the property of the execution debtor.[105] The subsection also covers other statutory provisions. So, where a person who purchased a vehicle from a local authority exercising its power of sale under the Road Traffic Regulation Act 1984, he acquired good title to the vehicle, notwithstanding that it had been stolen before coming into the hands of the local authority seller.[106]

---

101. Notice means actual notice (*Barker v Bell* [1971] 1 WLR 983 (CA)).

102. It was held by the Court of Appeal in *Dodds v Yorkshire Bank Finance Ltd* [1992] CCLR 92 (CA) that the test of bona fides is a subjective one of honesty, so that where a purchaser's initial suspicion that the vehicle might have been subject to a hire purchase agreement had been laid to rest by the seller's assurances to the contrary, she was to be treated as a purchaser acting in good faith without notice of such an agreement.

103. HPA 1964, s 27(4).   104. ibid s 27(6); *Barber v NWS Bank plc* [1996] 1 WLR 641 (CA).

105. *Dyal Singh v Kenyan Insurance Ltd* [1954] AC 287 (PC).

106. *Bulbruin Ltd v Romanyszyn* [1994] RTR 273 (CA).

A purchaser can also acquire good title to the goods where the sale was made pursuant to a court order, irrespective of any objections by the original owner. This was said to be based not on any consideration of the right of sale of one party or another, but is directed to the injustice which might result if perishable goods perished and became of no value while the dispute between the parties as to their ownership was being decided at law.[107]

Conclusion

The law relating to the transfer of title by a non-owner is utterly bizarre and has been the subject of a significant amount of criticism. Notwithstanding the laudable, but seemingly impractical,[108] attempt made by Devlin LJ in *Ingram v Little*[109] to apportion the loss between the innocent owner and the equally innocent buyer:

> [the] statutory protection for the bona fide purchaser has developed in a piecemeal and haphazard fashion; and some of the relevant provisions have been so drafted and interpreted as to make their application depend not on principles of equity or justice but on fine technicalities which have little rhyme and less reason.[110]

Significant recommendations made by the Law Reform Committee[111] have never been enacted. These include, for these purposes, removing the strict distinction between contracts void for mistake and those merely voidable for fraud; reversing the decision in *Car & Universal Finance Co Ltd v Caldwell*,[112] thus requiring direct communication to the other party before a voidable contract can be rescinded; and amending s 9 of the FA 1889 and s 25(1) of the SGA 1979 to remove there being any need for the buyer in possession to act as a mercantile agent before being able to pass good title. This would have the effect of reversing the *dictum* of Pearson LJ in *Newtons of Wembley Ltd v Williams*[113] in this regard. The Committee also described the market overt rule as capricious in its operation and, along with the recommendations made in the 1994 consultation document of the DTI,[114] it was recommended that its scope be either abolished or extended to cover all retail sales at trade premises and sales by auction. Amongst the other recommendations made in the DTI consultation paper was that Pt III of the HPA 1964 should be extended to cover all goods purchased on hire purchase or conditional sale agreements and not just motor vehicles. However, notwithstanding the many calls for reform, it has only been the repeal of the market overt rule in 1995 that has made any attempt to bring this area of the law into line with modern commercial practices.

---

107. *Larner v Fawcett* [1950] 2 All ER 727 (CA).

108. Largely because of the problems caused when the goods pass through several parties. See the Law Reform Committee, *Twelfth Report: Transfer of Title to Chattels* (Cmnd 2958, HMSO 1966).

109. [1961] 1 QB 31 (CA). This case is discussed on p 290.

110. *The Report of the Crowther Committee on Consumer Credit* (Cmnd 4596, HMSO 1971) para 4.2.8.

111. Law Reform Committee, *Twelfth Report: Transfer of Title to Chattels* (Cmnd 2958, HMSO 1966).

112. [1965] 1 QB 525 (CA).   113. [1965] 1 QB 560 (CA).

114. DTI, *Transfer of Title: Sections 21 to 26 of the Sale of Goods Act 1979* (HMSO 1994).

Practice questions

1. Do you consider that the principles of *nemo dat* strike an acceptable balance between the original owner of the goods and the innocent purchaser?

2. ComCorp opens a new office and needs to purchase some computers. It purchases six computers from Chris, who advertises himself as a local computer salesman. In fact, Chris is a rogue and has stolen the computers from his employer, Computer Sales plc. Chris delivers and installs the computers in ComCorp's offices and ComCorp pays him for the goods. Six months later, as a result of the recession, ComCorp closes its office and sell the computers to Tom, who has just set up a new publishing business. Tom pays ComCorp for these computers and collects them from its offices. When Computer Sales plc finds out what has happened it dismisses Chris, who promptly disappears. Computer Sales plc writes to ComCorp demanding the return of the computers. ComCorp explains that it paid for them in good faith, but that in any event it has now sold them to Tom. Tom also refuses to hand them over to Computer Sales plc, claiming ownership as he, too, has paid for them and had no idea they were originally stolen.

    Who has title in the computers? Would your advice be different if, instead of the subject matter being computers, they were motor vehicles?

Further reading

Adrian Chandler and James Devenney, 'Mistake as to Identity and the Threads of Objectivity' (2004) 3 Journal of Obligation and Remedies 7
- Discusses the problems associated with identity in sale contracts and considers the different approaches of the judges in *Shogun Finance Ltd v Hudson*.

Brian Davenport, 'Consultation—How Not to Do it' (1994) 110 LQR 165
- Critiques the DTI's consultation paper on transfer of title and the innocent purchase of goods belonging to a third party.

Iwan Davies, 'Wrongful Disposition of Motor Vehicles—A Legal Quagmire' [1995] JBL 47
- Discusses the distinction between void and voidable hire purchase agreements insofar as the passing of title is concerned.

Catherine Elliott, 'No Justice for Innocent Purchasers of Dishonestly Obtained Goods' [2004] JBL 381
- Discusses the injustice resulting from the House of Lords decision in *Shogun Finance Ltd v Hudson* on an innocent purchaser of a motor vehicle as it removes from the scope of s 27 a transaction where a rogue impersonates another person in order to acquire a vehicle either on hire purchase terms or under a conditional sale agreement.

Angela Foster, 'Sale by a Non-owner: Striking a Fair Balance between the Rights of the True Owner and a Buyer in Good Faith' (2004) 9 Cov LJ 1
- Examines how the law seeks to balance the rights of the true owner of property and an innocent third party who bought it in good faith where the purchase was transacted by an unauthorized seller.

Louise Merrett, 'The Importance of Delivery and Possession in the Passing of Title' (2008) 67 CLJ 376

- Evaluates the operation of statutory exceptions to the *nemo dat* rule. Reviews the exceptions in ss 24 and 25 of the SGA 1979 in relation to sales by a seller or buyer in possession of goods, and discusses, with reference to case law, the meaning of 'continues in possession', the practical problems caused by the need for continuous physical possession, and the importance of 'delivery' and 'possession' having consistent meanings throughout the Act.

Louise Merrett, 'Is Possession Nine Tenths of the Law in the Sale of Goods?' (2010) 69 CLJ 236

- Considers the question of possession and title in relation to *nemo dat*.

——'Issues as to Title: Consumers and the Hire Purchase Act' (2010) Consumer Law Today 1

- Considers the Court of Appeal's judgment in *Kulkarni v Manor Credit (Davenham) Ltd* on whether a disposition of a car fulfilling the requirements of s 18 of the SGA 1979 had occurred either when the registration details of the car were provided to a prospective purchaser so that he could insure it, or three days later when the number plates were attached to the car and the car was delivered to the purchaser. Notes the relevance of the answer to the availability to the purchaser of protection under Pt III of the Hire Purchase Act 1964.

- Goods perishing before the contract is made
- Goods perishing after the contract is made
- *Force majeure* clauses

INTRODUCTION

This chapter considers the effect on the parties' contract of sale in the event that the goods perish. Before doing so, it is necessary to consider briefly the position of non-existent goods. It might be considered sensible to think that where the seller sells specific goods, a condition would be implied that the goods existed at the time of the making of the contract and that the seller would be liable to the buyer if he sold goods that did not exist. After all, the seller does warrant that he has the right to sell the goods[1] and, where he sells the goods in the course of a business, also warrants that they are of satisfactory quality and fit for purpose.[2] However, such a seller is generally not liable.

The position at common law prior to the Sale of Goods Act 1893 (SGA 1893) was that in the case of a contract of sale, if, unbeknown to the parties, the goods did not exist at the time the contract was made, there will be no liability to pay the price. This can be seen from the following case.

 Couturier v Hastie (1856) 5 HL Cas 673 (HL)

FACTS: A contract was entered into for the sale of a cargo of corn. At the time of making the contract, both seller and buyer believed that the cargo existed. However, unbeknown to both parties, the ship's captain had, the previous month, sold the corn to a third party as it was starting to ferment. When the buyer discovered that the corn had been sold to someone else, he repudiated the contract. The seller brought an action against the buyer for the price.

HELD: The House of Lords held that as the contract had contemplated the existence of the corn which, unbeknown to the parties, had ceased to exist because of the earlier sale, the buyer was not liable to pay for the goods because they were not in existence at the time the contract was made.

---

1. SGA 1979, s 12(1).
2. ibid s 14(2) and (3).

The position under statute will now be discussed, beginning with the situation where the goods perish prior to the contract being made.

Goods perishing before the contract is made

Section 6 of the Sale of Goods Act 1979 (SGA 1979) provides that:

 SGA 1979, s 6

Where there is a contract for the sale of specific goods, and the goods without the knowledge of the seller have perished at the time when the contract is made, the contract is void.

When will the goods be deemed to have perished?

Although the cargo of corn in *Couturier v Hastie* had not in fact perished, it was treated as such and certainly as a commercial entity it had ceased to exist. Section 6 is generally understood to represent the legislature's view of the effect of *Couturier v Hastie*.[3]

Although the word 'perish' is not defined in the SGA 1979, it is clear that it covers a number of different situations beyond the actual physical destruction of the goods, and includes perishing in a commercial sense. Where there has been total physical destruction of the goods then there can be little doubt that they have perished within the meaning of the Act. Beyond total destruction, the courts have also held that goods will be deemed to have perished if they become significantly altered so that, for commercial purposes, they can no longer be said to be the same goods that were the subject of the contract,[4] or where the goods become so damaged that they are deemed to be different from those the parties had contracted for.[5] Goods that have been irretrievably lost due to theft have also been said to have perished.[6]

---

3. The basis for the decision in *Couturier v Hastie* has been disputed. At one time it was thought that it was decided on the basis that the contract was void for mistake; indeed, this appears to be the interpretation placed on it by the drafters of the SGA 1893, even though the Lord Chancellor did not declare the contract void, nor even refer to the word 'mistake' in his speech. However, it is now generally understood that the decision turned on the construction of the contract, in particular, that a buyer is not generally obliged to pay the price if the seller is unable to deliver the goods. This principle can now be seen in s 28 of the SGA 1979.

4. *Asfar & Co v Blundell* [1896] 1 QB 123 (CA).

5. *Oldfield Asphalts Ltd v Grovedale Coolstores (1994) Ltd* [1998] 3 NZLR 479. The questions in this case concerned whether or not a building came within definition of specific goods under the New Zealand equivalent of s 6 and whether, as a result of fire, the building had perished, thereby entitling the buyer to treat the contract as void. The Court rejected the argument that s 6 was confined to perishable goods such as food.

6. *Barrow, Lane & Ballard Ltd v Phillip Phillips & Co Ltd* [1929] 1 KB 574 (KB) (this case is discussed on p 311).

Asfar & Co v Blundell [1896] 1 QB 123 (CA)[7]

FACTS: A ship carrying a shipment of dates sank during the course of the voyage and was subsequently salvaged. On arrival at the port, it was found that, although the dates still retained the appearance of dates, and although they were of value for the purpose of distillation into spirit (as evidenced by the fact that they were eventually sold for such a purpose), they were so impregnated with sewage and in such a condition of fermentation as to be declared unfit for consumption by the sanitary authority, which refused them to be landed in London.

HELD: It was held by the Court of Appeal that the dates had perished because, for commercial purposes, they were so altered that they were no longer the same goods that were the subject of the contract. Lord Esher MR stated:

> The first point taken on behalf of the defendants...is that there has been no total loss of the dates...The ingenuity of the argument might commend itself to a body of chemists, but not to businessmen. We are dealing with dates as a subject-matter of commerce; and it is contended that, although these dates were under water for two days, and when brought up were simply a mass of pulpy matter impregnated with sewage and in a state of fermentation, there had been no change in their nature, and they still were dates. There is a perfectly well known test which has for many years been applied to such cases as the present—that test is whether, as a matter of business, the nature of the thing has been altered. The nature of a thing is not necessarily altered because the thing itself has been damaged; wheat or rice may be damaged, but may still remain the things dealt with as wheat or rice in business. But if the nature of the thing is altered, and it becomes for business purposes something else, so that it is not dealt with by business people as the thing which it originally was, the question...is whether the thing...has become a total loss. If it is so changed in its nature by the perils of the sea as to become an unmerchantable thing, which no buyer would buy and no honest seller would sell, then there is a total loss.[8]

A different approach, however, was taken by Morris J in the following case.

 Horn v Minister of Food [1948] 2 All ER 1036 (KB)

FACTS: Horn entered into a contract with the Minister of Food, under which the Minister purchased 33 tonnes of Majestic ware potatoes in a certain **clamp**. When the clamp was opened the potatoes were found to be rotten. The delivery was cancelled and Horn commenced proceedings for the cost of the 33 tonnes of potatoes.

HELD: Morris J held that, as the potatoes had not ceased to exist and were still in a form that would permit their being called potatoes, the potatoes had not perished[9] even though they were worthless.[10] Accordingly, Horn could recover the price of the potatoes.

➡ **clamp:** a heap of potatoes or other root vegetables, stored under straw or earth

---

7. A case not decided under s 6.   8. [1896] 1 QB 123 (CA) 127.
9. Within the meaning of s 7 of the SGA 1893.
10. This view was clearly *obiter* because Morris J held that, as the risk in the goods had already passed to the buyer, the section had no application.

> **COMMENT:** The decision in *Horn* is certainly harsh and is out of line with the other authorities on the matter. What is clear, however, is that if the goods have only suffered slight damage or deterioration, but insufficient to render them commercially different in character than that bargained for, they will not be deemed to have perished within the meaning of the section.

Partial loss

What if there has only been a partial loss of the goods sold? Will they still be deemed to have perished?

 Barrow, Lane & Ballard Ltd v Phillip Phillips & Co Ltd [1929] 1 KB 574 (KB)

FACTS: Barrow, Lane & Ballard Ltd ('Barrow') agreed to sell a specific lot of 700 bags of ground nuts to Phillip Phillips & Co Ltd ('Phillip'). Unknown to either party, before the contract of sale had been made, 109 of the 700 bags had disappeared (it was believed that they had been stolen). One hundred and fifty bags were delivered to Phillip, at which time it was discovered that no more of the 700 bags remained. Barrow sued Phillip for the price of all 700 bags.

HELD: The claim failed. Wright J found that there was no prospect of the goods being recovered and held that s 6 of the SGA 1893 applied where even part of the goods had perished at the time the contract was made and that the contract was therefore void.

COMMENT: This case clearly turned on its facts. The sale was for a specific indivisible lot of 700 bags of nuts. Had the contract been severable (i.e. for the sale of separate lots, with each lot being invoiced and paid for separately) then it would seem that only the contract(s) representing the missing goods would have been held to be void.

It has been suggested that in a case where only part of the goods have perished, then the seller might be required to make the remaining (unperished) goods available to the buyer, although the buyer in such a case will not be under any obligation to accept them.

 HR & S Sainsbury Ltd v Street [1972] 1 WLR 834 (QB)[11]

FACTS: Street agreed to sell 275 tonnes of barley to HR & S Sainsbury Ltd ('Sainsbury'), this barley being grown on Street's farm. Due to a poor harvest and without any fault on Street's part, the crop only came to 140 tonnes. As a result, Street acted on the basis that the contract was frustrated and he sold the available crop to a third party. Sainsbury claimed

---

11. This case was decided under common law, although it is likely that a case on similar facts falling within s 6 would be decided the same way.

damages from Street and conceded that, in the event of Street's failure through no fault of his own to produce a crop of 275 tonnes, Street was under no obligation to make good the difference, but asserted that Street was in those circumstances under an obligation to deliver the quantity that was actually harvested.

HELD: MacKenna J held that where a buyer contracts with a seller to purchase a specific portion of a crop, and performance becomes impossible owing to a failure of the crop without any default on the part of the seller, then the seller is not liable to the buyer in damages, although he is obliged to deliver the actual amount that has been harvested. His Lordship confirmed the rule in *Howell v Coupland*,[12] but held that that did not affect Street's obligation to deliver the quantity actually produced. He arrived at this decision on the basis that there was no implied term in the parties' contract that the seller need not deliver to the buyer the actual quantity harvested in the event of the seller's inability through no fault of his own to produce the whole contracted amount.

Given the broad meaning attributed to 'perish', it is important that the operation of the section is sufficiently flexible and treated more as a rule of construction in appropriate cases. Otherwise, a seller might too easily be able to protect himself under s 6 in a case where the implied conditions as to quality in s 14 would render him liable to the buyer. This is because a seller who delivers goods which are of unsatisfactory quality or unfit for purpose will generally be liable to the buyer irrespective of whether the defect arose before or after the making of the contract, unless he can avail himself of s 6, in which case he avoids all liability to the seller as the contract will be void. The following case from New Zealand demonstrates the position.

 Rendell v Turnbull & Co (1908) 27 NZLR 106[7]

FACTS: The seller contracted to sell a quantity of 'table potatoes'. At the time of making the contract, the potatoes were in such a poor state that they could not properly be described as 'table potatoes'. The buyer sued for damages on the ground that the seller had breached the implied term as to description.

HELD: The court rejected the buyer's claim and instead held that the contract was void by virtue of s 6, as the potatoes had perished.

COMMENT: This produces the rather curious result that a seller will be in a better position if the goods deteriorate so badly that they can no longer be described as the same goods under the contract, thus availing him of the provisions of s 6, although it is submitted that the result reflects the fact that neither party would have contemplated such an event and that it would therefore not be just for the risk of its occurrence to rest with either one of the parties at the expense of the other.

Goods will not be held to have perished where the seller is himself responsible for their non-existence. Thus, where the seller agrees to sell goods to *X*, but then sells

---

12. (1875–76) LR 1 QBD 258 (CA).

and delivers those goods to *Y*, he will be liable to *X* for non-delivery[13] and cannot assert that the goods have perished.

Unascertained goods

It has already been seen that s 6 applies only to contracts for the sale of specific goods. In addition to the provisions contained in s 6, the common law might also declare void a contract for the sale of unascertained goods where the goods either do not exist or have perished at the time of the making of the contract, thereby making it impossible from the outset for the contract to be performed. In order to understand what will make performance impossible, the distinction between purely generic unascertained goods and unascertained goods from an identified bulk is critical.

- Where a seller has agreed to sell purely generic unascertained goods (e.g. 50,000 tonnes of wheat), then, if those goods which the seller was to supply have perished at the time of making the contract, he can still fulfil the contract by supplying the goods from another source. For this reason, it is not impossible for him to perform the contract and the contract will not be void.

- Where the seller is obliged to supply a specified, but unidentified, quantity of unascertained goods from an identified bulk or a specific source (e.g. 500 tonnes of steel from the 1,000 tonnes stored at the London warehouse of Steelworks Ltd) and that source has ceased to exist at the time of making the contract, then, because the seller was obliged to supply the goods from that (and no other) source, it will be impossible for him to fulfil the contract and it will be void at common law.

The following example demonstrates these principles in practice.

> ### Eg ComCorp Ltd
>
> ComCorp is the owner of a ship, *The Josephine Butler*. Its cargo, also owned by ComCorp, consists of 100,000 tonnes of wheat. ComCorp sells 5,000 tonnes of this particular wheat to Hampshire Bakers Ltd. Unfortunately, at the time of entering into the contract, *The Josephine Butler* had sunk and the wheat was lost.

This is a contract for the sale of a specified quantity of unascertained goods from an identified bulk. The goods are unascertained because ComCorp could fulfil the contract by supplying *any* 5,000 tonnes of the wheat on board *The Josephine Butler*, rather than a *specific* 5,000 tonnes. The contract is for the sale of unascertained goods from an identified bulk, because ComCorp must supply the 5,000 tonnes out of the 100,000 tonnes on board *The Josephine Butler* and not from any other source. As the wheat from which the supply be made is lost, it is impossible for ComCorp to fulfil the contract. The contract is void at common law. Section 6 does not apply because the goods are not specific.

However, had the contract been simply to supply 5,000 tonnes of wheat (without specifying its source), then the fact that *The Josephine Butler* had sunk with its cargo of wheat would not make it impossible for ComCorp to fulfil the order, and it would have

---

13. *Goodey & Southwold Trawlers Ltd v Garriock, Mason & Millgate* [1972] 2 Lloyd's Rep 369 (QB).

to do so from another source. This would be the case even if ComCorp had in mind to supply the wheat from *The Josephine Butler*. The contract in that case would not be void.

Contrary agreement

Section 6 is likely to be applied only in the absence of an agreement made by the parties to the contrary.[14] Any such agreement will typically be found in the contract. The court will look at its terms to determine whether or not the parties intended it to remain valid in circumstances where, at the time of making the contract, its subject matter was non-existent or had perished. For example, the parties might agree that the buyer acquires no more than a mere expectation or chance in a venture, hoping that the goods do in fact exist. If they do, then the buyer acquires title in them. This is known as 'a *spes*' and the buyer takes the risk of the venture turning to nothing but agrees to pay the price in any event. Therefore, in such circumstances, the contract remains valid even if the anticipated goods turn out not to exist.[15]

On the other hand, it may be that the seller must accept the risk that the goods might not exist. This will be the likely outcome where the seller warrants the existence of the goods, as occurred in the following Australian case.

 ## McRae v Commonwealth Disposals Commission (1951) 84 CLR 377

FACTS: The Commonwealth Disposals Commission ('the Commission') invited tenders for the purchase of the salvage rights of a shipwrecked oil tanker, located at Jourmaund Reef off the coast of Papua. McRae's tender was accepted by the Commission, and he spent considerable sums preparing for the salvage expedition. When McRae arrived at the location provided by the Commission, no tanker was found. It transpired that neither the tanker nor the reef existed. McRae sued for damages, and the Commission contended that the contract was void.

HELD: The High Court of Australia held that because the Commission had impliedly warranted that the wreck existed, the contract was not void. The Commission was therefore liable to McRae in damages for breach of contract for the price paid for the wreck and his wasted expedition costs.[16] The Court held that s 11 of the Victorian Goods Act 1928,[17] which was equivalent to s 6, applied only to cases where the goods had once

---

14. SGA 1979, s 55(1). Although note should be taken of the fact that, whereas several other sections of the Act expressly state that they are subject to contrary agreement, there is no such provision in s 6. Professor Atiyah has argued that s 6 merely lays down a rule of construction which may be ousted by the contrary intention of the parties: see Patrick S Atiyah, '*Couturier v Hastie* and the Sale of Non-Existent Goods' (1957) 73 LQR 340.
15. The House of Lords in *Couturier v Hastie* (1856) 5 HL Cas 673 (HL) held that the buyer in that case had not agreed to buy a *spes*.
16. Although the Court did not make an award to compensate McRae for the profit he might have made had the wreck existed and the salvage exercise been successful. This was 'not because what was promised was valueless but because it is impossible to value a non-existent thing' ((1951) 84 CLR 377, 414 (Dixon and Fullagar JJ)).
17. Section 11 of the Victorian Goods Act 1928 provides: 'where there is a contract for the sale of specific goods, and the goods without the knowledge of the seller have perished at the time when the contract is made the contract is void'.

existed but had since perished. The section therefore had no application to the facts of the case because the goods never existed at all and the Commission ought to have known that that was the case.

Whether an English court would decide a similar case in this way is open to debate. On the one hand, it could be said that s 6 is no more than a partial statement of the position at common law and that the common law rules apply equally to cases where the goods have perished, as well as to those cases where they had never existed at all. Thus, a contract for the sale of goods that have never existed would be declared void. In such a case, the innocent buyer might be able to bring a claim against the seller for misrepresentation. However, s 6 does appear to contemplate the position only where the goods did at one time exist: goods that have never existed cannot be said to have perished. This was certainly the view of MacKenna J in *HR & S Sainsbury Ltd v Street*, where he said that both ss 6 and 7 only deal with goods that once existed.[18]

Goods perishing after the contract is made

Having considered the position of goods that have perished before the contract was made, this section is concerned with the position where there is an agreement to sell specific goods which subsequently perish before the risk passes to the buyer. This is dealt with in s 7 of the SGA 1979.

 SGA 1979, s 7

Where there is an agreement to sell specific goods and subsequently the goods, without any fault on the part of the seller or buyer, perish before the risk passes to the buyer, the agreement is avoided.

The section makes plain that once the risk has passed to the buyer it will not be possible to avoid the agreement. Neither will the agreement be avoided if, when the goods perish, property has already passed to the buyer.[19] This is because s 7 applies only to agreements to sell and not to sales. When property in the goods passes to the buyer an agreement to sell becomes a sale, thus ousting the section. Unlike s 6, which renders the contract void, under s 7 the agreement is avoided.

Although s 7 provides a statement of the common law doctrine of frustration, it is more limited in its scope for three reasons. First, the section is limited to an agreement to sell specific goods[20] that perish before the risk has passed to the

---

18. [1972] 1 WLR 834 (QB) 837.

19. See e.g. *Horn v Minister of Food* [1948] 2 All ER 1036 (KB).

20. Quasi-specific goods are not covered.

buyer.[21] Second, it does not apply to goods that become ascertained after the contract is made.[22] Third, only agreements to sell (specific goods) are covered, and not immediate sales.

It can be seen from the wording of s 7 that its application is excluded where either the seller or the buyer is at fault. This is also the case with frustration at common law.[23] 'Fault' means a 'wrongful act or default'.[24]

Frustration, for the purpose of s 7, can arise (as the section says) when the goods subsequently[25] perish before the risk passes to the buyer. As with s 6, s 7 may be excluded by agreement between the parties.

Perishing of future goods

 The meaning of 'perish' under s 6 is discussed at p 309

The meaning of 'perish' in s 7 is the same as for s 6. Section 7 will not apply to contracts for the sale of future goods, so that if such goods fail to materialize, the contract will not be avoided by the section. Such a contract may, as the following case demonstrates, be frustrated at common law.

Howell v Coupland (1875-76) LR 1 QBD 258 (CA)

FACTS: Coupland agreed to sell to Howell 200 tonnes of regent potatoes to be grown on a specific piece of land. The land in question ought not to have had any problems in producing this quantity, although, due to the fault of neither party, the crop failed and only 80 tonnes were harvested, which Howell accepted and then sued Coupland for non-delivery of the remaining 120 tonnes.

HELD: The Court of Appeal held that Coupland was not liable to Howell for non-delivery because the unforeseen potato blight made further delivery impossible, the effect of which frustrated the contract and released Coupland from his obligation to deliver any more than could reasonably have been harvested.

COMMENT: The Court implied a term into the contract to the effect that each party should be free of further performance if the crop perished. The position would, of course, have been otherwise had the contract not specified a particular crop because the seller could then have supplied regent potatoes from another source.

Unascertained goods

Section 7 (as with s 6) applies only to contracts for the sale of specific goods, although as discussed in *Howell v Coupland*, a contract may be frustrated at common law. It is important to distinguish between purely generic unascertained goods

---

21. Once the risk has passed to the buyer, the buyer then bears the loss and must pay the price.
22. It is somewhat curious why the section should draw a distinction between specific and ascertained goods.
23. *Bank Line Ltd v Arthur Capel & Co* [1919] AC 435 (HL) 452 (Lord Sumner).
24. SGA 1979, s 61(1).
25. In a case where the goods have already perished by the time the contract is made, s 6 should then be considered.

and unascertained goods from an identified bulk. As Blackburn J explained at first instance in *Howell v Coupland*:

> Had the contract been simply for so many tons of potatoes of a particular quality, then, although each party might have had in his mind when he made the contract this particular crop of potatoes, if they had all perished, the defendant would still have been bound to deliver the quantity contracted for; for it would not have been within the rule of a contract as to a specific thing. But the contract was for 200 tons of a particular crop in particular fields, and therefore there was an implied term in the contract that each party should be free if the crop perished. The property and risk had clearly not been transferred under the terms of this contract, so that the consequence of the failure of the crop is, that the bargain is off so far as the 120 tons are concerned.[26]

The distinction between purely generic unascertained goods and ascertained goods from an identified bulk is discussed at p 313

Undivided shares in goods forming part of a bulk

In Chapter 11, it was noted that the effect of s 20A of the SGA 1979 is to permit a buyer who has purchased and paid for a specified quantity of unascertained goods from an identified bulk to become co-owner of the bulk, pending delivery to him of his entitlement to the goods pursuant to the contract. In other words, such a buyer obtains a share in the ownership of the bulk.

Section 20A of the SGA 1979 is discussed at p 253

The question here is which party bears the loss in the event of the destruction of the goods? Perhaps surprisingly, the SGA 1979 is almost silent on this point. Section 20, which deals with the passing of risk, does not assist because this section concerns itself only in the passing of risk in goods that are to be transferred to the buyer under the contract and not the buyer's temporary interest in the bulk that is created by s 20A. Similarly, the definition of 'goods' in s 61(1) that includes[27] 'an undivided share in goods' is also only concerned with the goods that are to be transferred. The problem is not solved either by reference to the older cases, where buyers had not acquired any proprietary interest in the goods.[28] On the contrary, s 20A makes the prepaying buyer an owner in common of the bulk. It is necessary, therefore, to consider the extent of the loss.

Total loss

Where there has been a total loss of the bulk, and provided the seller has retained no interest in the goods, then by analogy with the principles in s 20(1), the *res perit domino*[29] rule can be applied and the loss rests with the buyer.

The res perit domino rule is discussed at p 264

Partial loss

Where the loss relates only to part of the bulk, then, again provided the seller has retained no interest in the goods, the destruction will be taken as first destroying the seller's share of the bulk. This result reflects the position that the seller is obliged

---

26. (1873–74) LR 9 QB 462 (QB) 466, confirmed by (1875-76) LR 1 QBD 258 (CA).
27. Added by the Sale of Goods (Amendment) Act 1995.
28. See e.g. *Sterns Ltd v Vickers Ltd* [1923] 1 KB 78 (CA), where the buyer merely had control over its contractual entitlement but no proprietary interest of any kind.
29. It will be remembered that this rule states that when a thing is lost or destroyed it is lost to the person who was the owner of it at the time.

to supply all of the buyers from the bulk in accordance with their contractual entitlement.[30] For this reason, therefore, it would not be appropriate to adopt the usual presumption that the loss should be borne rateably by all co-owners including the seller. If there remains a shortfall, the loss is then borne rateably by the buyers in accordance with their share in the bulk. This result accords with s 20A(4), which considers the co-ownership interests remaining in the (reduced) bulk, referring only to the 'aggregate of the undivided shares of buyers' without any reference to the interest of the sellers so that 'the undivided share in the bulk of each buyer shall be reduced proportionately'.[31]

The relationship between s 7 and the doctrine of frustration

As has been discussed, in the case of an agreement to sell specific goods which, without any fault on the part of the seller or buyer, perish before the risk passes to the buyer, the agreement is avoided by s 7. In other situations, the contract may become frustrated at common law. Although s 7 has many similarities to the common law rules of frustration,[32] the Law Reform (Frustrated Contracts) Act 1943 (which applies to common law frustration by setting out the legal consequences of a contract that has been held to have been frustrated) has no application to contracts avoided by s 7 of the SGA 1979.[33]

Where the risk in the goods has not yet passed to the buyer, and s 7 has no application, then the common law rules of frustration might apply. These rules are not limited to the circumstances set out in s 7 and might therefore apply even where the goods have not perished. Although it is impossible to provide an exhaustive list of potentially frustrating events,[34] a contract will become frustrated at common law where its main purpose has become impossible properly to achieve.[35] Thus, the courts have held a contract to be frustrated where, after the contract was made, an event occurred which either rendered performance impossible,[36] illegal,[37] or radically different from that which the parties originally contemplated, thus frustrating the common purpose of both parties.[38] In such cases, the parties may be relieved from any further obligations under the contract and may also be entitled, for example, to

---

30. See, further, Law Commission Report, *Sale of Goods Forming Part of a Bulk*, (Law Com No 215, 1993) para 4.14.

31. In respect of goods in transit, see SGA 1979, ss 32 and 33.

32. Which in any event are preserved by the SGA 1979, s 62(2).

33. Law Reform (Frustrated Contracts) Act 1943, s 2(5)(c).

34. For a more comprehensive discussion of types of event that can cause a contract to become frustrated, readers are advised to consult a text on the law of contract.

35. *Herne Bay Steam Boat Co v Hutton* [1903] 2 KB 683 (CA).

36. See e.g. *Taylor v Caldwell* (1863) 3 B&S 826 (KB) (destruction of the subject matter).

37. See e.g. *Denny, Mott & Dickson Ltd v James Fraser & Co Ltd* [1944] AC 265 (HL) (supervening illegality by virtue of subsequent legislation) and *Avery v Bowden* (1855) 26 LJ QB 3 (QB) (subsequent illegality due to outbreak of war).

38. See e.g. *Krell v Henry* [1903] 2 KB 740 (CA) (contract to hire rooms to watch coronation procession of King Edward VII was frustrated when procession was postponed due to the King's illness) and *Herne Bay Steam Boat Company v Hutton* [1903] 2 KB 683 (CA) (contract to hire steamship to view naval review and to cruise around the fleet was not frustrated when the review, but not the fleet, was cancelled because of King Edward VII's illness).

recover monies that had already been transferred under the contract. As with s 7, neither party may be at fault if the common law rules are to apply.

If, before the agreement is avoided or frustrated, the buyer has paid some money to the seller, then, if the agreement is avoided under s 7, the buyer is entitled to recover advance monies paid provided there has been a total failure of consideration.[39] A total failure of consideration will occur where the buyer has received nothing and has therefore had no benefit under the agreement. In the unlikely event[40] that the buyer has received any benefit for the advance monies paid, then he will not be entitled to the return of any of his money.

However, where the contract is frustrated at common law, then the position is governed by the Law Reform (Frustrated Contracts) Act 1943,[41] s 1(2) of which provides that all sums paid or payable in pursuance of the contract before the time when the parties were discharged shall, in the case of sums paid, be recoverable from him and, in the case of sums payable, shall cease to be payable, provided that, if the party to whom the sums were paid or payable incurred expenses before the time of discharge in or for the purpose of the performance of the contract, then the court may, if it considers it just to do so, having regard to all the circumstances of the case, allow him to retain (or recover) the whole or any part of the sums paid or payable, provided that this is not in excess of the expenses actually incurred. Unlike the position under s 7, it is unnecessary to show a total failure of consideration for s 1(2) to operate.

Force majeure clauses

Due partly to the rather narrow scope of the common law doctrine of frustration, parties frequently provide for unexpected events by incorporating into their contracts of sale a *force majeure* provision. A *force majeure* clause is simply a clause that provides for a certain outcome in the event of certain unfortunate or unexpected events occurring. These contractual clauses are usually wider in effect than the unexpected events that would give rise to the contract being frustrated at common law and might include events such as industrial action, bad weather, and so on. A *force majeure* clause will typically require the party seeking to rely on such an event to give prompt notice to the other party of the occurrence of such an event.

➡ *force majeure*: 'superior force', referring to an event or cause that cannot be prevented

A significant practical difference between frustration and *force majeure* is that with the former all obligations under the contract are automatically terminated irrespective of the wishes of the parties,[42] whereas the parties are free to decide for themselves what happens if a *force majeure* event materializes. For example, in the case of industrial action, a *force majeure* clause might allow for extra time for the performance of an obligation, such as the delivery of the goods, although preserving the right to excuse the seller altogether if the interruption is sufficiently lengthy.

---

39. *Fibrosa Spolka Akcyjna v Fairbairn Lawson Combe Barbour Ltd* [1943] AC 32 (HL).
40. Unlikely because in normal circumstances once the goods have been delivered to the buyer the risk in the goods is then his and s 7 only applies in cases where the goods perish before the risk passes to the buyer.
41. Which, as already noted, does not apply to agreements avoided under s 7.
42. *Hirji Mulji and Others v Cheong Yue Steamship Company Ltd* [1926] AC 497 (PC).

Conclusion

A contract for the sale of specific goods which, without the knowledge of either party, have perished at the time when the contract is made, is void.

Where the agreement is either avoided under s 7 or frustrated at common law, then the parties are excused from further performance. In practical terms, this means that the seller is excused from delivering the goods and the buyer is excused from paying for them. These provisions do little more than give effect to the presumed intentions of the parties, which, if expressed in the contract, take effect instead in the usual way. Where a relevant event occurs that has already been provided for in the contract, such as the goods perishing or a *force majeure* event, then the result is what the parties have agreed. In such a case it is not accurate to talk, for example, of the contract being frustrated or avoided, as these terms relate only to cases where there is an absence of agreement by the parties.

Practice questions

1. Why is it important to distinguish the events that caused the contract goods to perish both from the position before the contract was made from those events that arose after the contract came into existence?

2. If a case similar to the facts in *Howell v Coupland* were to arise today, would the buyer be obliged to accept the crop that had in fact been harvested even if this was less than the contract amount?

Further reading

Patrick S Atiyah, '*Couturier v Hastie* and the Sale of Non-Existent Goods' (1957) 73 LQR 340
- Argues that section 6 of the SGA 1979 merely lays down a rule of construction which may be ousted by the contrary intention of the parties.

Celia Battersby, 'Frustration: A Limited Future' (1990) 134 SJ 354
- Discusses the strict limits of the application of the doctrine of frustration.

Ewan McKendrick, 'The Construction of Force Majeure Clauses and Self-Induced Frustration' [1990] 2 LMCLQ 153
- Discusses the interaction between frustration and *force majeure* clauses in contracts.

Gerard McMeel, 'Interpretation and Mistake in Contract Law: "The Fox Knows Many Things..."' [2006] 1 LMCLQ 49
- Discusses the development of common-law principles for the interpretation of contracts and consideration of intentions in assessing whether there has been mistake in the negotiation or formation of contracts.

Hannah Roberts, 'Room with a View' (2011) L Ex Jul 27
- Considers the issues raised in cases of frustration at common law and discusses how the doctrine operates.

——'On the Perishing of Goods' (1997) 19 Buyer 7
- Discusses the meaning of 'perished' and 'specific goods' in relation to the SGA 1979.

Delivery and payment

- The duties of seller and buyer
- Delivery
- Acceptance
- Payment

INTRODUCTION

This chapter will consider the duty of the seller to deliver the goods and the duty of the buyer to accept the goods and to pay the price. The parties to the contract can make whatever agreement they want in respect of delivery and payment and, in practice, they will often do so in relation to the time, place, and manner of the delivery and the payment. Where the parties have not agreed on these matters, the Sale of Goods Act 1979 (SGA 1979) lays down certain rules.

The duties of seller and buyer

The duties of the seller and buyer in relation to delivery are set out in s 27 of the SGA 1979.

SGA 1979, s 27

It is the duty of the seller to deliver the goods, and of the buyer to accept and pay for them, in accordance with the terms of the contract of sale.

Unless the parties otherwise agree, delivery of the goods and payment of the price are concurrent conditions, as the following provision makes clear.

SGA 1979, s 28

Unless otherwise agreed, delivery of the goods and payment of the price are concurrent conditions, that is to say, the seller must be ready and willing to give possession of the goods to the buyer in exchange for the price and the buyer must be ready and willing to pay the price in exchange for possession of the goods.

Section 28 only requires the seller to be 'ready and willing' to give possession of the goods to the buyer and the buyer to be 'ready and willing' to pay the price in exchange for possession. The section imposes no requirement for the seller actually to tender delivery before he becomes entitled to sue the buyer for the price or for damages, provided he can show that the buyer would have refused to accept the goods if delivery had been tendered. All the seller needs to do in such circumstances is to show that he was ready and willing to give possession of the goods in question.[1]

Delivery

As s 27 makes clear, the seller is under a duty to deliver the goods. The word 'delivery' has a very specific legal meaning, which is wholly different from its colloquial meaning (e.g. when the supermarket delivers the goods ordered by its customer). The definition of 'delivery' can be found in s 61(1) of the SGA 1979.

 SGA 1979, s 61(1)

'Delivery' means voluntary transfer of possession from one person to another.[2]

For such a simple word, the concept of 'delivery' is rather confusing, not least because it does not in fact require the seller to hand over the goods to the buyer,[3] and, as s 29 makes clear, unless otherwise agreed, it is not the seller's responsibility to convey the goods to the buyer, but it is for the buyer to collect them.

Actual delivery

Where the seller does transfer physical possession of the goods to the buyer (or his agent) this is known as actual (or physical) delivery. This is the common form of delivery in consumer transactions.

Constructive delivery

In the absence of actual delivery of the goods, the 'voluntary transfer of possession', and hence delivery, may be satisfied by constructive delivery. Constructive delivery occurs where the seller who does not have physical possession of the goods transfers control (or the right to possession) of those goods to the buyer. Constructive delivery may occur in the following ways.

---

1. *Levey & Co v Goldberg* [1922] 1 KB 688 (KB).
2. Except that in relation to ss 20A and 20B it includes such appropriation of goods to the contract as results in property in the goods being transferred to the buyer. This exception was added by the Sale of Goods (Amendment) Act 1995.
3. Although, in many cases, this is precisely what happens.

Where the buyer continues in possession of the goods although in his own right

This type of constructive delivery can be seen in hire-purchase transactions. Here, the buyer will already have possession of the goods at the time he exercises his option to purchase at the end of the term of hire. The reason 'delivery' is satisfied in such a case is because of the different capacity in which the buyer then possesses the goods. Initially, during the period of hire purchase, he possessed the goods in the capacity of bailee (hirer), but when he exercises his option to purchase, he possesses them as owner.

Where there is delivery of something that provides physical control of the goods

An example of this type of constructive delivery is where the seller hands over control of the goods, for example, by handing over the keys to the premises where they are held, or the keys of a car. In this example, although actual delivery does not occur, control of the goods is transferred to the buyer, thereby satisfying the definition of delivery. Although this is regarded as a type of constructive delivery, it is, in practical terms, rather close to actual delivery.[4]

Where the seller transfers to the buyer the document of title to the goods

Where the seller holds a document of title[5] to the goods, the transfer to the buyer of such document gives the buyer legal control over the goods and thus (constructive) delivery is established, provided this was the intention of the transferor.[6] The transfer will only be deemed effective if the buyer is given possession of the document noting that the buyer's possession of it is authorized. Such authorization may be demonstrated by the document bearing the name of the bearer or indorsed by the person named on it.

Attornment

This relates to the situation where the goods are in the possession of a third party. An attornment in respect of goods occurs where the party in possession of the goods acknowledges to the buyer that he holds them on his behalf.

 SGA 1979, s 29(4)

Where the goods at the time of sale are in the possession of a third person, there is no delivery by seller to buyer unless and until the third person acknowledges to the buyer that

---

4. Although Len S Sealy and Richard JA Hooley, *Commercial Law: Text, Cases and Materials* (4th edn, OUP 2009) 424, term this as an example of 'symbolic' delivery (i.e. handing over something that symbolizes the goods).

5. 'Document of title' includes any bill of lading, dock warrant, warehouse-keeper's certificate, and warrant or order for the delivery of goods and any other document used in the ordinary course of business as proof of the possession or control of goods or authorizing or purporting to authorize either by endorsement or by delivery the possessor of the document to transfer or receive goods thereby represented (Factors Act 1889, s 1(4)).

6. See e.g. the judgment of His Honour Judge Diamond QC in *The Future Express* [1992] 2 Lloyd's Rep 79 (QB) 95–96 (confirmed by [1993] 2 Lloyd's Rep 542 (CA)).

> he holds the goods on his behalf; but nothing in this section affects the operation of the issue or transfer of any document of title to goods.

The acknowledgment referred to in s 29(4) is known as 'attornment'. This is where a third party attorns to the buyer by acknowledging to the buyer that the third party now holds the goods on the buyer's behalf.

An example can be seen in cases where the goods are held to the order of the seller, by a third party, such as a warehouseperson. In this example, the seller gives the buyer a delivery order or warrant for the goods that are held in a warehouse. Before possession or property can be transferred to the buyer, the warehouseperson must 'attorn' by accepting the delivery order or warrant.[7] The goods in question must also be physically segregated or otherwise ascertained, although the fact of attornment itself may be sufficient to raise an estoppel against the warehouseperson.[8]

Sale and leaseback arrangements, where the goods remain in the seller's possession throughout, also give rise to an attornment (albeit notionally), and thus constructive delivery, notwithstanding that the buyer is quite unable to give directions to the seller in respect of the goods.[9] In this type of situation, the seller attorns by acknowledging the fact that he holds the goods as the buyer's bailee.

Delivery to a carrier

Delivery of the goods to a carrier is *prima facie* deemed to be a delivery to the buyer pursuant to s 32(1) of the SGA 1979.

 SGA 1979, s 32(1)

> Where, in pursuance of a contract of sale, the seller is authorised or required to send the goods to the buyer, delivery of the goods to a carrier (whether named by the buyer or not) for the purpose of transmission to the buyer is prima facie deemed to be a delivery of the goods to the buyer.

The section is concerned specifically about delivery 'to a carrier' which, unlike other sections in the Act[10] where delivery to a bailee for the purpose of onward transmission to the buyer might suffice, s 32(1) is strictly confined to delivery to a carrier. Delivery of the goods to a carrier who is an agent or servant of the seller will not constitute delivery to the buyer because of the connection between seller and carrier.[11]

Section 32(1) does not apply in cases where the buyer deals as consumer,[12] with the obvious result that delivery to a carrier in such a case is not deemed to be

---

7. *Sterns Ltd v Vickers Ltd* [1923] 1 KB 78 (CA); *Wardar's (Import & Export) Co Ltd v W Norwood & Sons Ltd* [1968] 2 QB 663 (CA).

8. *Re London Wine Co (Shippers) Ltd* [1986] PCC 121 (QB).

9. See *Michael Gerson (Leasing) Ltd v Wilkinson & Anr* [2001] QB 514 (CA).

10. Namely ss 18 rule 5(2), 19(1), 45, and 46.

11. *Galbraith & Grant Ltd v Block* [1922] 2 KB 155 (KB).

12. SGA 1979, s 32(4).

delivery to the buyer and the risk will not be transferred to the consumer buyer. The justification for s 32(1) being disapplied in consumer cases was explained by Rix LJ in *Scottish & Newcastle International Ltd v Othon Ghalanos Ltd*[13] as:

> [reflecting] a feeling that a consumer would not expect the goods to be at his risk until physical delivery had been effected…[and] highlights the difference between what one might call a layperson's view of delivery as being something essentially physical, and a merchant's or lawyer's view of it as being more conceptual.[14]

Place of delivery

An obvious question in relation to delivery is where should delivery be made? Section 29 makes it clear that unless the parties have otherwise agreed, it is not the seller's responsibility to convey the goods to the buyer, but it is for the buyer to collect them.

SGA 1979, s 29

(1) Whether it is for the buyer to take possession of the goods or for the seller to send them to the buyer is a question depending in each case on the contract, express or implied, between the parties.

(2) Apart from any such contract, express or implied, the place of delivery is the seller's place of business if he has one, and if not, his residence; except that, if the contract is for the sale of specific goods, which to the knowledge of the parties when the contract is made are in some other place, then that place is the place of delivery.

Unless the parties have agreed otherwise, the expenses of, and incidental to, putting the goods into a deliverable state must be borne by the seller.[15]

The place of delivery is that which the parties have agreed. In the absence of any such agreement, then the place of delivery is the seller's place of business if he has one, or otherwise his place of residence. If the contract is for specific goods which, when the contract was made, were known by the parties to be in some other place, then that other place is the place of delivery. Given that, in the absence of agreement, the default place of delivery is that of the seller, he is perfectly entitled to levy a charge for delivering the goods to his customer. Delivery charges are frequently set out in the parties' contract of sale, or implied from the previous course of dealing, although given that the seller will be providing a service beyond his legal obligation, he will be entitled to make such a charge in any event.

If the seller agrees to deliver the goods at his own risk at a place other than that where they were when sold, then, unless the parties agree otherwise, the buyer remains liable for any deterioration in the goods necessarily incident to the course of transit.[16]

---

13. [2006] EWCA Civ 1750, [2007] 2 Lloyd's Rep 341.   14. ibid [22].   15. SGA 1979, s 29(6).
16. ibid s 33.

No general liability for delivering the goods to a rogue

The seller will have complied with his duty of delivery if, on arrival at the agreed destination, he hands them to a person whom he reasonably believes is authorized to accept them. In other words, the seller's duty on physically delivering the goods to the buyer's premises is limited to handing them over to someone who appears to have the authority to receive them, although he ought to take reasonable care to ensure that no unauthorized person receives them. Once the seller has delivered the goods to such a person, he will not be liable if that person has gained access to the buyer's premises and later misappropriates the goods, as the following cases demonstrate.

 Galbraith & Grant Ltd v Block [1922] 2 KB 155 (KB)

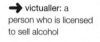 **victualler:** a person who is licensed to sell alcohol

FACTS: A wine merchant, Galbraith & Grant Ltd ('Galbraith'), engaged a carrier to deliver a case of champagne to the premises of Block (who was a **victualler**). The delivery driver said that he delivered the goods to a man at a side entrance of Block's premises, and that someone on the premises signed the delivery note in Block's name. Block argued that his premises were closed at the time this delivery was meant to have occurred, that he had never received the goods, and that the signature was not his nor had he authorized anyone to sign it. Block refused to pay for the champagne and Galbraith commenced proceedings.

HELD: Galbraith's claim succeeded and he recovered the purchase price. The court held that a seller who is told to deliver goods at the buyer's premises discharges his obligations if he delivers them there without negligence to a person apparently having authority to receive them. He cannot know what authority the actual recipient has. His duty is to deliver the goods at the proper place and to take all proper care to see that no unauthorized person receives them. He is under no obligation to do more. If the buyer has been unfortunate enough to have had access to his premises obtained by some apparently respectable person who takes his goods and signs for them in his absence, the loss must fall on him, and not on the innocent carrier or seller.

 Computer 2000 Distribution Ltd v ICM Computer Solutions plc [2004] EWCA Civ 1634

FACTS: A rogue, purportedly acting on behalf of a reputable company, ordered a substantial quantity of electronic goods from ICM Computer Solutions plc ('ICM'). ICM acted on the orders and in turn placed orders with its suppliers for the goods. In accordance with the rogue's instructions, ICM requested that the suppliers deliver the goods to a Mr Richard Cole at a given business address. A security guard at the business address signed for the goods. The goods were later collected by a man who purported to be Richard Cole (presumably the rogue), who absconded with the goods. ICM refused to pay its suppliers for the goods as it never received them. The suppliers commenced proceedings against ICM.

HELD: The Court of Appeal held that, as the goods had been delivered in accordance with the contract, ICM was liable to pay for them. The terms of the contract showed that the goods were to be delivered to the named individual. As the goods had been collected by that named individual, it followed that the suppliers had delivered the goods in accordance with the terms of ICM's contract. The fact that they had been signed for by the security guard did not matter. It was found that the security guard had authority to receive goods on behalf of persons carrying on business at the business address and there was no reason for the carrier to suspect that the named individual and the reputable company were not carrying on business at the business address.

Time of delivery

In consumer contracts, time for delivery will not be of the essence unless a date for delivery has been agreed and is construed as a condition of the contract. Conversely, in ordinary commercial contracts for the sale of goods, the rule is that time is *prima facie* of the essence with respect to delivery.[17] Therefore, a seller who has failed to deliver the goods within the stipulated period cannot *prima facie* call upon the buyer to accept delivery after that period has expired. This is because the seller 'has himself failed to fulfil the bargain and the buyer can plead the seller's default and assert that he was not ready and willing to carry out his contract'.[18] In *Bunge Corporation v Tradax Export SA*,[19] Lord Lowry explained that it was important for the term as to time to be regarded as a condition (and hence of the essence) because of:

> [the] enormous practical advantages in certainty, not least in regard to string contracts where today's buyer may be tomorrow's seller. Most members of the string will have many ongoing contracts simultaneously and they must be able to do business with confidence in the legal results of their actions.[20]

Explaining why such terms should not be held to be innominate terms, his Lordship said that 'decisions would be too difficult if the term were innominate; litigation would be rife and years might elapse before the results were known [and] the difficulty of assessing damages is an indication in favour of condition'.[21]

Where the time of delivery is not met, the buyer is entitled to sue for non-delivery and, if he wishes, to treat the contract as repudiated. The buyer may, of course, be content to accept late delivery of the goods (i.e. affirm the seller's breach). If he does so, then it must follow that he waives his right to treat the contract as repudiated and reject the goods, but he will still have the right to sue for damages.[22] If the buyer chooses not to repudiate the contract, but instead allows an additional specified time for delivery and the goods are still not ready when this additional time has elapsed, he may then treat the contract as repudiated. In effect, by allowing the further specified time for delivery by the giving of reasonable notice, he has attached a condition to his waiver which revives his right to treat the contract as repudiated if the goods are still not ready.

---

17. *Hartley v Hymans* [1920] 3 KB 475 (KB); *Bunge Corporation v Tradax Export SA* [1981] 1 WLR 711 (HL).
18. *Hartley v Hymans* [1920] 3 KB 475 (KB) 484 (McCardie J).
19. [1981] 1 WLR 711 (HL).   20. ibid 720.   21. ibid.   22. SGA 1979, s 11(4).

**Charles Rickards Ltd v Oppenheim
[1950] 1 KB 616 (CA)**

FACTS: In August 1947, Oppenheim placed an order with Charles Rickards Ltd ('CR') to build a body onto the chassis of a car. It was understood that CR could obtain it within six or seven months at the latest. From March 1948, Oppenheim pressed for delivery. In June 1948, Oppenheim wrote to CR telling it that he would not accept delivery after 25 July 1948. When Oppenheim was informed by CR that the body of the car would not be ready by that date, Oppenheim cancelled the order. CR completed the car in October 1948, but Oppenheim refused to accept delivery. CR sued for the price.

HELD: The Court of Appeal held that although the initial stipulation making time of the essence was waived by Oppenheim's requests for delivery after March 1948, this did not disentitle him from giving, at a later time, a reasonable notice making time for delivery of the essence. Oppenheim's June 1948 letter constituted reasonable notice and was, therefore, valid so as to make time of the essence of the contract, the result being Oppenheim was entitled to repudiate the contract and so CR's claim failed.

Where the buyer is to collect the goods and no time for delivery has been stipulated in the contract, then the seller must be ready to hand them over in return for payment on demand by the buyer at any time after the contract is made. However, the seller may treat any such demand as ineffectual unless it is made at a reasonable hour; and what is a reasonable hour is a question of fact.[23] If, following such a reasonable demand, the seller fails to hand over the goods, he will be in breach of a condition, which the buyer may treat as a repudiation of the contract and sue for non-delivery. In cases where the seller is bound to send the goods to the buyer, but no time for sending them has been agreed, the seller is bound to send them within a reasonable time.[24]

Delivery and quantity

The contract will usually provide for the quantity of goods to be delivered. Section 30 of the SGA 1979 sets out the position where the seller delivers the wrong quantity of goods to the buyer. Before considering s 30, it is important to note that s 30(5) explains that s 30 is 'subject to any usage of trade, special agreement, or course of dealing between the parties'. This means that s 30(1) and 30(2) (which relates to deliveries for less or more than contracted for) may be modified, typically by express agreement made by the parties or implied, for example, by trade usage, where a certain tolerance of either short or over deliveries is considered normal, or alternatively by previous course of dealing between the parties.

The seller delivers less than he contracted to sell

Where the seller delivers a quantity of goods that is less than that which he agreed to sell, then the key provision will be s 30(1) of the SGA 1979.

---

23. ibid s 29(5).   24. ibid s 29(3).

SGA 1979, s 30(1)

> Where the seller delivers to the buyer a quantity of goods less than he contracted to sell, the buyer may reject them, but if the buyer accepts the goods so delivered he must pay for them at the contract rate.

The buyer is entitled to sue for non-delivery in respect of the goods that ought to have been delivered, but were not in fact delivered. The reason for the short delivery is of little concern to the buyer and may even be due to the buyer himself rejecting part of the goods on the ground that they are not in conformity with the contract of sale.

The buyer's entitlement to sue for non-delivery is subject to three caveats. First, any shortfall that is merely a 'microscopic deviation' of the contract quantity is likely to be disregarded by the courts under the *de minimis non curat lex* principle.[25] This principle is now encapsulated in s 30(2D)(a) of the SGA 1979, which provides that where the seller delivers a quantity of goods less than he contracted to sell, the buyer will not be entitled to reject the goods unless the shortfall 'is material'. Second, even in cases where the breach is not *de minimis*, a buyer who does not deal as consumer may nevertheless not be entitled to reject in cases where the shortfall is so slight that it would be unreasonable for him to do so.[26] This provision is quite similar to the different remedies available to consumer and non-consumer buyers found in s 15A of the SGA 1979 in relation to the statutory implied terms. Third, certain shipments of goods are prone to shortages, such as fuel, which could result in wastage through evaporation. In such cases, this kind of shortage falls within a degree of tolerance either specified in the contract of sale itself or otherwise implied by custom. A buyer would not be entitled to reject for short delivery in this last example, but would simply pay a lesser price to cover the goods actually delivered.

➡️ *de minimis non curat lex*: 'the law does not concern itself with trifles'—damages will generally not be awarded for trifling breaches

🔗 Section 15A of the SGA 1979 is discussed at p 443

As will shortly be discussed, a buyer is not bound to accept delivery by instalments.[27] Therefore, if a buyer chooses to accept a short delivery, the seller will not be able to compel him to accept the remainder of the contract goods at a later date, although the buyer may, if he so wishes, choose to do so. If the buyer chooses not to take the shortfall at a later date, he will be entitled to recover the price paid for such shortfall on the basis of total failure of consideration in respect of such shortfall, as well as damages for non-delivery in respect of any loss he has suffered for not having the missing goods at the agreed time. The buyer is, of course, under a duty to mitigate his loss, which might mean that although he is within his rights to refuse to take the shortfall at a later date, such refusal might amount to a failure to mitigate resulting in the non-recovery or reduction of any claim.

The seller delivers more than he contracted to sell

Where the seller delivers a quantity of goods that is greater than that which he agreed to sell, then the key provision will be s 30(2) of the SGA 1979.

---

25. *Arcos Ltd v EA Ronaasen & Son* [1933] AC 470 (HL) 480 (Lord Atkin).
26. SGA 1979, s 30(2A)(a).   27. ibid s 31(1).

SGA 1979, s 30(2)

Where the seller delivers to the buyer a quantity of goods larger than he contracted to sell, the buyer may accept the goods included in the contract and reject the rest, or he may reject the whole.

The buyer may choose either to accept the correct quantity of the goods and reject the surplus, or he may reject the whole. Where the buyer chooses to accept the whole of the goods so delivered, he must pay for them at the contract rate.[28] In such a case, the buyer waives any remedy for such breach. This is because the seller in such a situation is deemed to have offered the buyer a new contract of sale that the buyer has accepted.[29]

Similar to the position considered earlier in respect of a seller making a short delivery, any trifling excess in quantity will be disregarded under the *de minimis* principle.

 Shipton, Anderson & Co v Weil Bros & Co[1912] 1 KB 574 (KB)

FACTS: Weil Bros & Co ('WB') agreed to purchase 10 per cent more or less than 4,500 tonnes of wheat from Shipton, Anderson & Co ('Shipton'). Shipton delivered a cargo of wheat that weighed 55 lbs more than 4,950 tonnes (i.e. 55 lbs more than the maximum contractual amount). Shipton did not claim payment for the extra 55 lbs (which was only worth about 4 shillings), but WB rejected the whole cargo on the ground that it was in excess of the amount stated in the contract. Shipton sold the cargo at a loss, and claimed the difference from WB.

HELD: Shipton's claim succeeded and it recovered the value of the loss from WB. Given that the quantity of the excess was trifling and Shipton had not claimed payment for this excess, it could be said that Shipton had substantially performed its obligations under the contract and WB was not entitled to reject the cargo under s 30(2).

The principle in *Shipton* is now encapsulated in s 30(2D)(b) of the SGA 1979, which provides that where the seller delivers a quantity of goods larger than that contracted for, the buyer may not reject all of the goods unless the excess 'is material'. The buyer is, of course, perfectly entitled to reject the quantity in excess of the contract quantity and just keep and pay for the quantity actually contracted for.[30] Where the seller delivers a quantity of goods larger than he contracted to sell, a buyer who does not deal as consumer may not reject the whole under s 30(2) if the excess is so slight that it would be unreasonable for him to do so.[31] Again, the similarity between this provision and the different remedies available to consumer and

---

28. ibid s 30(3).
29. *Gabriel, Wade & English Ltd v Arcos Ltd* (1929) 34 Ll L Rep 306 (KB) (Acton J).
30. SGA 1979, s 30(2).   31. ibid 30(2A)(b).

non-consumer buyers found in s 15A of the SGA 1979 in relation to the statutory implied terms is clear to see.

It is interesting to note that in respect of both short and excess deliveries, s 30(2A) is expressed only in terms of when the buyer does not deal as consumer. There is no corresponding provision explaining what happens in the case of a buyer who does deal as consumer, although it seems reasonable to conclude that it implies that a buyer who does deal as consumer will be entitled to reject the goods in the circumstances set out therein.

Delivery by instalments

Delivery by instalments typically arises in the commercial context, and is not so common in consumer transactions. Unless otherwise agreed, the buyer of goods is not bound to accept delivery by instalments.[32] Thus, where the seller delivers short, he will not be entitled to make up the shortfall at a later stage unless the buyer agrees. Where only part of the contract goods have been delivered and accepted, the buyer will be entitled to refuse to accept later deliveries of the balance of the goods and will only be liable to pay pro rata for the goods accepted.

 Behrend & Co Ltd v Produce Brokers Co Ltd [1920] 3 KB 530 (KB)

FACTS: Under two similar contracts, Behrend & Co Ltd ('Behrend') agreed to sell a quantity of cotton seed to Produce Brokers Co Ltd ('PB'). The contracts provided that the cotton seed would be shipped from Alexandria and delivered to London. On the arrival of the ship in London, PB paid for the goods. It was then discovered that only a portion of the seed had been delivered. The ship then left with the remainder of the seed on board in order to discharge other cargo. The ship returned to London two weeks later and the balance of the seed was tendered to PB but it refused to accept it. PB retained the portion that had been delivered and claimed repayment of the price paid for the rejected portion.

HELD: When the delivery had begun, PB was entitled to receive the whole quantity that it had ordered before the ship left the port. Given that this had not occurred at that time, PB was entitled to keep the part actually delivered and to reject the balance, and it was entitled to recover the price paid for the portion it rejected.

Where there is a contract for the sale of goods to be delivered by stated instalments, which are to be separately paid for, and the seller makes defective deliveries in respect of one or more instalments, or the buyer neglects or refuses to take delivery of or pay for one or more instalments, it is a question in each case depending on the terms of the contract and the circumstances of the case whether the breach of contract is a repudiation of the whole contract or whether it is a severable breach giving rise to a claim for compensation, but not to a right to treat the whole contract as repudiated.[33]

---

32. ibid s 31(1).
33. ibid s 31(2).

Where the contract of sale is severable, and the buyer has accepted one or more of the instalments, he is not prevented from rejecting later instalments for breach of condition, as the following case demonstrates.

 Jackson v Rotax Motor and Cycle Company [1910] 2 KB 937 (CA)

FACTS: The buyer purchased a large number of motor horns of different descriptions and prices with delivery to be made 'as required'. The horns were delivered in several instalments. After accepting the first instalment, the buyer rejected the later instalments on the ground that they were not of (what was then referred to as) merchantable quality. At first instance, it was found that a large proportion of the horns were dented and badly polished owing to defective packing and careless workmanship, but that they could easily and cheaply have been made merchantable. As a result, the court refused to hold that the consignment as a whole was unmerchantable but made an allowance to the buyer in respect of the defective goods. The buyer appealed.

HELD: The appeal was allowed and the Court of Appeal held that, on the true construction of the contract, acceptance of the first instalment of the goods did not preclude the buyer from rejecting the later instalments, and that on the facts of the case the buyer was justified in rejecting the later instalments as they were not of merchantable quality.

In *Jackson*, the first instalment of goods was in breach of contract. Is a buyer entitled to treat the entire contract as repudiated and reject all instalments where it is just the later instalments that give rise to the breach of condition? This situation is provided for in s 31(2) of the SGA 1979.

 SGA 1979, s 31(2)

Where there is a contract for the sale of goods to be delivered by stated instalments, which are to be separately paid for, and the seller makes defective deliveries in respect of one or more instalments, or the buyer neglects or refuses to take delivery of or pay for one or more instalments, it is a question in each case depending on the terms of the contract and the circumstances of the case whether the breach of contract is a repudiation of the whole contract or whether it is a severable breach giving rise to a claim for compensation but not to a right to treat the whole contract as repudiated.

This issue arose for determination in the following case, in which Lord Hewart CJ established two tests that should be applied by the courts.

 Maple Flock Co Ltd v Universal Furniture Products (Wembley) Ltd [1934] 1 KB 148 (CA)

FACTS: Maple Flock Co Ltd ('Maple Flock') entered into a severable contract with Universal Furniture Products (Wembley) Ltd ('UFP'), under which UFP agreed to buy from Maple

Flock 100 tonnes of rag flock to be delivered by instalments. The first fifteen instalments of the flock were satisfactory, but the sixteenth was defective as it was found to be in breach of the relevant government standard. This was followed by four more satisfactory instalments. UFP purported to rescind the entire contract. Further deliveries were then made which were satisfactory, but UFP maintained its entitlement to rescind the entire contract and refused to accept any further deliveries. Maple Flock claimed that this was a breach of contract and commenced proceedings.

HELD: Maple Flock's claim succeeded and the Court of Appeal held that UFP was not entitled to repudiate the contract. Where there is a sale of goods under a severable contract and only some of the instalments are defective, whether the buyer will be entitled to reject the entirety of the goods and regard the entire contract as repudiated will turn on the true meaning of s 31(2), with the main tests to be considered being (i) the quantitative ratio which the breach bears to the contract as a whole; and (ii) the degree of probability that such a breach will be repeated. As to the ratio quantitatively which the breach bore to the contract as a whole, Lord Hewart CJ said that the delivery complained of amounted to no more than 1½ tonnes out of a contract for 100 tonnes, and the likelihood of the breach being repeated was practically negligible. It was for this reason that the Court of Appeal held that UFP was not entitled to regard the entire contract as repudiated.

Where delivery is to be made by instalments, parties will often contract on the basis that 'each instalment is to be considered as a separate contract'. In this type of case, the courts are likely to hold that there is only one contract, although severable. This means that if there is a breach that is sufficiently serious, the entire contract might be repudiated.[34]

Delivery to a carrier

Delivery of the goods to a carrier is dealt with in s 32(1) of the SGA 1979.

 SGA 1979, s 32(1)

Where, in pursuance of a contract of sale, the seller is authorised or required to send the goods to the buyer, delivery of the goods to a carrier (whether named by the buyer or not) for the purpose of transmission to the buyer is prima facie deemed to be a delivery of the goods to the buyer.

Where the buyer deals as consumer, s 32(1) will not apply, and delivery of the goods to a carrier will not amount to delivery to the buyer.[35]

Unless otherwise authorized by the buyer, the seller must make such contract with the carrier on behalf of the buyer as may be reasonable, having regard to the nature of the goods and the other circumstances of the case. If the seller fails to do so, and the goods are lost or damaged in course of transit, the buyer may decline to treat the delivery to the carrier as a delivery to himself or may hold the seller responsible in damages.[36] Whether or not the seller has made the contract with the

34. *Smyth & Co Ltd v TD Bailey Son & Co* [1940] 3 All ER 60 (HL).   35. SGA 1979, s 32(4).
36. ibid s 32(2).

carrier on reasonable terms for the buyer's benefit will be a matter of fact, but it was held in the following case that the seller will not have satisfied this requirement where he contracts with the carrier at the owner's risk where the same carrier would have contracted to deliver the goods at his own risk for the same price.

Thomas Young & Sons v Hobson & Partner (1949) 65 TLR 365 (CA)

FACTS: The seller sold seven electric engines to the buyer. It was a term of the contract that the engines should be delivered by rail. The seller sent the engines at the buyer's risk. The seller loaded the engines onto the rail in box wagons, but failed adequately to secure them, which resulted in them arriving in a damaged condition. The buyer refused to accept them from the railway. It was found that there was no difference in the freight costs as between 'owner's risk' and 'company's risk'.

HELD: The Court of Appeal held that the seller had failed in its duty under s 32(2) of the SGA 1893 to make such contract with the carrier on behalf of the buyer as was reasonable, having regard to the nature of the goods and the other circumstances of the case, and that the buyer was accordingly entitled to refuse to treat the delivery to the railway company as delivery to himself and was accordingly entitled to reject the goods.

Carriage by sea

➔ **FOB contract:** A free on board contract, under which the buyer arranges for the shipment and insurance of the goods. With such a contract, as soon as the goods are loaded onto the vessel, the seller's responsibility for them comes to an end (discussed at p 516)

Where the goods are being carried by sea, the risk is likely to be with the buyer, especially in the case of a **FOB contract**. Where the goods are sent by the seller to the buyer by a route involving sea transit, under circumstances in which it is usual to insure the goods, the seller must give such notice to the buyer so as to enable him to insure them during their sea transit. If the seller fails to do so, the goods are at his risk during such sea transit, although the parties may agree otherwise.[37]

Acceptance

It will be recalled that s 27 provides that it is the duty of the seller to deliver the goods, and of the buyer to accept and pay for them, in accordance with the terms of the contract of sale. In this regard, the buyer's duty to accept the goods amounts to little more than an obligation to refrain from any conduct signifying their rejection. Therefore, a buyer who takes delivery of the goods does not, without more, signify his acceptance of them[38] in the sense of signifying his willingness to retain the goods because he is satisfied with them.

The duties of the seller to deliver the goods and of the buyer to accept them are reciprocal. Thus, provided the seller tenders goods that are in conformity with the contract, the buyer is obliged to accept them. If, in breach of this duty, where the seller is ready and willing to deliver the goods in conformity with the contract and requests the buyer to take delivery of them, and the buyer does not take delivery of

---

37. ibid s 32(3).
38. Although the taking of delivery is typically the buyer's first step towards acceptance under s 35 of the SGA 1979. Acceptance under s 35 is discussed on p 434.

the goods within a reasonable time after such a request, he will be liable to the seller for any loss occasioned by his neglect or refusal to take delivery, and also for a reasonable charge for the care and custody of the goods.[39] What is a reasonable time is a question of fact.[40] The buyer's delay in taking delivery of the goods could be so great as to evince an intention to repudiate the contract, in which case it will be as though he has wrongly refused to accept delivery.[41] In such a case, the seller may maintain an action against the buyer for damages for non-acceptance.[42]

If the seller tenders goods that do not conform to the contract of sale, the buyer is not obliged to accept delivery of them and may bring an action against the seller for non-delivery. In such a case, s 36 of the SGA 1979 provides that the buyer is not bound to return them to the seller.

 SGA 1979, s 36

Unless otherwise agreed, where goods are delivered to the buyer, and he refuses to accept them, having the right to do so, he is not bound to return them to the seller, but it is sufficient if he intimates to the seller that he refuses to accept them.

Section 36 confirms the old common law position stated in *Grimoldby v Wells*,[43] where Brett J held that, although a buyer may return or offer to return the goods, it would be sufficient and more usual 'to signify his rejection of them by stating that the goods are not according to contract and they are at the vendor's risk. No particular form is essential; it is sufficient if he does any unequivocal act shewing that he rejects them.'[44] In the same case, Lord Coleridge CJ explained the reason behind this policy in the following terms:

> By the supposition the vendor has not complied with the contract, and has sent goods which as against the purchaser he had no right to send; why should he be entitled to impose upon the purchaser, who never bargained for such goods, and who has a right to reject them, the burden of sending them back, possibly for a considerable distance, at a considerable expense?[45]

Where goods are delivered to the buyer which are not in accordance with the contract of sale, so that the buyer has a right to reject them, the seller upon receipt of notice of rejection is entitled to have the goods placed at his disposal so as to allow him to resume possession forthwith. If the buyer does any act that prevents the seller from so resuming possession, that act will be inconsistent with the seller's right. It is not enough that the buyer should be in a position to give the seller possession at some later date, as he must be able to do so at the time of the rejection.[46]

Where the buyer refuses to accept delivery of the goods in the circumstances envisaged, he is a mere bailee of the goods (albeit an involuntary and gratuitous one), and he holds them at the seller's risk, in whom the property in the goods remains.

39. SGA 1979, s 37(1).   40. ibid s 59.   41. ibid s 37(2).   42. ibid s 50(1).
43. (1874–75) LR 10 CP 391.   44. ibid 395.   45. ibid 394.
46. *Hardy & Co v Hillerns & Fowler* [1923] 2 KB 490 (CA) 496 (Bankes LJ).

Payment

It was noted at the beginning of this chapter that s 28 provides that, in the absence of agreement to the contrary, delivery of the goods and payment of the price are concurrent conditions. This means that, unless otherwise agreed, the buyer does not need to make payment until delivery is made. It also means that, unless otherwise agreed, a buyer is not entitled to defer payment by way of credit. Unless the parties have agreed otherwise, the starting point is that the seller is entitled to be paid in cash, but it should be noted that, in many cases, the parties do agree otherwise. Payment made by cheque is only a conditional discharge of the buyer's liability, with total discharge taking place once the cheque has been honoured. The position is slightly more complicated when payment is made by banker's draft or credit card. In *ED & F Man Ltd v Nigerian Sweets & Confectionery Co*,[47] Ackner J held that letters of credit were given as conditional and not absolute payment, and that the buyer's debt had not been discharged when the bank became insolvent before it made payment to the seller. Accordingly, the buyer remained liable to pay the seller, notwithstanding that he had already paid the bank. However, in *Re Charge Card Services Ltd (No 2)*,[48] the Court of Appeal held that where a customer's payment by credit card has been accepted by the seller, he is absolutely discharged, even where the credit card company becomes insolvent and fails to make payment to the seller. Therefore, in such a case, the seller cannot then pursue the customer for its money. This is because requiring the customer in such circumstances to pay twice 'is a result which no one could have intended in the context of a credit card transaction'.[49]

Where the buyer has paid the price and the seller has not delivered the goods, then the buyer will be entitled to recover the price paid plus interest. This is because the consideration for his payment will have failed.[50] However, where the goods have been destroyed at a time when they were at the buyer's risk, then the buyer remains under a duty to pay the price and he will not be able to escape payment by arguing that delivery in these circumstances will be impossible. The same is the position if the goods were stolen when they were at the buyer's risk.

The risk of the parties is discussed in Chapter 11

It is, of course, the buyer's duty to pay for the goods in accordance with the terms of the contract. Unless a different intention appears from the terms of the contract, stipulations as to time of payment are not of the essence.[51] Therefore, late payment of the price will constitute a breach of warranty only and will not entitle the seller to treat the contract as repudiated.[52] This appears to reflect the position that the seller's loss is only a loss of interest on the money he ought to have received at an earlier time. Where a seller intends to put the money to some specific use and makes this known to the buyer before the contract is made, time of payment might then be of the essence on those facts and, provided the loss is not too remote, the seller will be entitled to recover special damages in respect of the loss suffered by him as a result of the failure by his buyer to pay sums due to him under the contract.[53] It is, of course, open to the parties to agree that the time for payment of the price is of the essence of the contract, denoting that timely payment is a condition. In such a case,

---

47. [1977] 2 Lloyd's Rep 50 (QB).   48. [1989] Ch 497 (CA).
49. ibid 516 (Browne-Wilkinson VC).   50. SGA 1979, s 54.   51. ibid s 10(1).
52. *Payzu Ltd v Saunders* [1919] 2 KB 581 (CA).   53. *Wadsworth v Lydall* [1981] 1 WLR 598 (CA).

late payment will amount to a repudiatory breach of the contract.[54] Even though stipulations as to time of payment are not ordinarily of the essence in a contract of sale, significant delays in payment may be such that it constitutes an intention to repudiate the contract.

Section 28 creates something that might at first appear to be something of a statutory impasse. The section makes delivery of the goods and payment of the price concurrent conditions, yet with the former, at least in a commercial contract, time for delivery is of the essence, thereby elevating the obligation of delivery into a condition, the breach of which entitles the buyer to terminate the contract. However, although the obligation to pay the price is stated to be a condition concurrent with delivery, the time for payment is not usually of the essence, making late payment only a breach of warranty without any corresponding entitlement to terminate. This so-called impasse is partly resolved by reading further on in the section, where it clarifies that these conditions are satisfied provided each of the parties is 'ready and willing' to perform his obligation before the other party performs his. This problem is also eased if one reads the word 'condition' in s 28 not in the sense of a contractual promise, but rather as a **condition precedent**. There is no doubt, however, that when s 10(1) talks about stipulations as to time of payment not being of the essence of a contract of sale, this does relate to the time of payment as not being a condition of the contract but merely a warranty, and this is certainly how the courts have treated it.[55] Equally without doubt is that, in ordinary commercial contracts for the sale of goods, time is *prima facie* of the essence with respect to delivery and is therefore a condition of the contract.[56] This would mean that a commercial buyer could treat as repudiated a contract where the seller fails to deliver the goods on time, whereas a seller will only be entitled to claim damages if his buyer does not pay on time. The unpaid seller does, of course, have a range of other remedies available to him, such as retaining possession of the goods until paid for.

Finally, it will be remembered that the parties are perfectly entitled to oust the presumption in s 28 as to payment and delivery being concurrent conditions, and instead insist that one party performs his obligations first, be that delivery or payment.

➡ **condition precedent:** a condition that must be complied with before an offer can be accepted, or before a contract becomes operational

🔗 The remedies available to an unpaid seller are discussed in Chapter 16

Payment in advance of delivery

Where the parties agree that payment should be made in advance of delivery and the buyer wrongfully neglects or refuses to pay the price, the seller may bring a claim against the buyer without tendering delivery of the goods.[57] All the seller needs to do in this situation is to show that he intended to continue with the contract and that, but for the non-payment, he would have delivered the goods. A consumer buyer may be able to avoid any risk in the seller failing to deliver the goods after payment has been made by paying at least some of the price by credit card. In such a case, he will be protected by s 75 of the Consumer Credit Act 1974.

Payment in advance of delivery is often required in international sales where the buyer is required to pay by a banker's letter of credit, thus ensuring payment to the

🔗 Section 75 of the Consumer Credit Act 1974 is discussed in the online chapter entitled 'Aspects of Consumer Credit'

---

54. *Lombard North Central plc v Butterworth* [1987] QB 527 (CA).

55. See e.g. *Payzu Ltd v Saunders* [1919] 2 KB 581 (CA).

56. *Hartley v Hymans* [1920] 3 KB 475 (KB); *Bunge Corporation v Tradax Export SA* [1981] 1 WLR 711 (HL).

57. SGA 1979, s 49(2).

seller. With letters of credit, the seller's obligation to deliver the goods will be conditional on the buyer having in place the required letter of credit complying with the terms of the contract of sale.[58]

Delivery in advance of payment

In commercial transactions, it is often the case that the seller will extend credit terms to the buyer (e.g. payment to be made thirty days after delivery). With this sort of agreement, the seller is obliged to deliver the goods in advance of payment. As with any contract, such terms can only be varied by agreement. Therefore, even though this might prove unpalatable to sellers, after the contract is made, the seller cannot insist on prior payment even if he believes that the buyer may not be able to pay for the goods. Where such a seller is concerned about payment, having already entered into a contract with his buyer on credit terms he must weigh up whether his losses might be greater by supplying goods and not getting paid for them or risking a claim his buyer might make for non-delivery. The seller is, of course, perfectly entitled to amend his terms for payment for subsequent contracts. This is precisely what the seller did in *Total Oil Great Britain Ltd v Thompson Garages (Biggin Hill) Ltd*,[59] where a garage entered into a contract with a petrol supplier for deliveries of fuel, on terms that payment would be made by cheque when the fuel was delivered. After two of the garage's cheques were dishonoured the petrol supplier sought to amend its terms, demanding payment by banker's draft prior to future delivery. Lord Denning MR held this new stipulation to be a repudiation of the contract on the ground that the new terms 'evinced an intention no longer to be bound by the agreement'.[60]

Where the parties agree that delivery should be made before payment and the seller wrongfully neglects or refuses to deliver the goods to the buyer, the buyer may maintain an action against the seller for damages for non-delivery[61] and need not in these circumstances tender the price. Such a buyer may alternatively be able to maintain an action against the seller in conversion, since the buyer will *prima facie* be entitled to immediate possession of the goods. However, this remedy will not be available to a buyer who is insolvent, as in such circumstances the unpaid seller will be entitled to exercise a lien on the goods and will thereby be entitled to retain possession of them until the seller pays or tenders the price.[62]

58. *WJ Alan & Co Ltd v El Nasr Export and Import Co* [1972] 2 QB 189 (CA).
59. [1972] 1 QB 318 (CA).
60. ibid 322.
61. SGA 1979, s 51(1).
62. ibid s 41(1)(c).

Conclusion

Payment and delivery are concurrent conditions in a contract of sale. This means that the seller must be ready and willing to deliver the goods and the buyer must be ready and willing to pay for them in accordance with the terms of the contract.

The meaning of 'delivery' (defined in s 61(1) of the SGA 1979 as the 'voluntary transfer of possession from one person to another') is far from straightforward. Not only is there no requirement for the seller to hand over the goods to the buyer, but s 29 makes clear that, unless otherwise agreed, it is not even the seller's responsibility to convey the goods to the buyer but it is for the buyer to collect them. Delivery can range from the actual physical delivery of the goods to several methods of constructive delivery, such as where the seller hands over control of the goods, for example, by handing over the keys to the premises where they are held, or where the seller transfers to the buyer the document of title to the goods, thus giving the buyer legal control over them.

Practice questions

1. Section 27 of the SGA 1979 imposes on the seller a duty to deliver the goods.Critically evaluate this duty.

2. What is meant by the 'concurrent conditions' in s 28 of the SGA 1979 in respect of payment of the price and delivery?

Further reading

Paul Dobson, **'Late Payment of Instalments by Hirers'** [1987] JBL 147
- Discusses the Court of Appeal's judgment in *Lombard North Central Plc v Butterworth* on whether late payment will amount to a repudiatory breach of the contract.

Paul Dobson, **'Sale of Goods—Delivery'** (2005) 45 SL Rev 12
- Considers the Court of Appeal's judgment in *Computer 2000 Distribution Ltd v ICM Computer Solutions Plc* on whether the defendant was liable to pay the cost of goods it had ordered from three suppliers, which had been correctly delivered according to its instructions to an individual who was found to be a fraudster, or whether it was relieved of this liability by the fact that it had never received the goods.

EP Ellinger, **'Does an Irrevocable Credit Constitute Payment?'** (1977) 40 MLR 91
- Discusses whether a court should ordinarily infer an intention on the part of a seller to accept a letter of credit as an absolute payment for the goods sold.

Roy Goode, **'Twentieth Century Developments in Commercial Law'** (1983) 3 Legal Studies 283
- Discusses why the term as to time of delivery in *Bunge Corporation v Tradax Export SA* needed to be classified as a condition, rather than as an innominate term.

Simon Pedley and Claire Stewart, **'Delivery of Goods: Fraudsters and Obligations'** (2005) 7 ECL&P 12
- Comments on the Court of Appeal's decision in *Computer 2000 Distribution Ltd v ICM Computer Solutions Plc* on whether the responsibility for checking the credentials of an

end customer placing an order for computer equipment, and of the delivery address he gave, lay with the seller of the computers or the supplier it engaged to deliver them. Considers whether the supplier was in breach of contract for delivering the computers to a security guard at the address rather than to the end customer in person. Examines the implications of the judgment for online retailers.

Jeremy Thomas, 'Great Escapes: Terminating a Contract for Breach' (2006) 17 Practical Law Companies 33

- Discusses recent case law concerning the circumstances in which parties are entitled to terminate commercial contracts for breach. Examines the termination of contracts for any breach, repeated breaches, material breach, and substantial breach. Highlights drafting considerations. Includes a specimen termination clause.

15 The statutory implied terms

- Status of the implied terms
- Section 12—the right to sell, encumbrances, and quiet possession
- Section 13—correspondence with description
- Section 14(2)—satisfactory quality
- Section 14(3)—fitness for purpose
- Section 15—sale by sample
- Exclusion of the statutory implied terms

INTRODUCTION

At one time, the common law rule of ***caveat emptor*** was the key principle underpinning contracts of sale, although this had been largely eroded by the time of the original Sale of Goods Act 1893 (SGA 1893), which introduced the statutory implied terms of quality and fitness for purpose. To a large extent, the principle of *caveat emptor* is still alive and well in relation to purely private sales, and this is because the terms implied by the Sale of Goods Act 1979 (SGA 1979) in s 14(2) and 14(3) in relation to the quality and fitness for purpose of the goods only apply to sales made in the course of a business.[1] Section 14(1) of the SGA 1979 states the following.

 caveat emptor: 'let the buyer beware'

SGA 1979, s 14(1)

Except as provided by this section and section 15 . . . and subject to any other enactment, there is no implied term about the quality or fitness for any particular purpose of goods supplied under a contract of sale.

It can be seen, therefore, that sale of goods contracts are still to some extent governed by the principle of *caveat emptor*, although (as s 14(1) makes clear) this is subject to other enactments. This is an important qualifier, as statute, and in particular ss 12–15 of the SGA 1979, have significantly eroded the principle of *caveat emptor* by implying into contracts for the sale of goods a number of terms that favour the

---

1. Other implied terms found in ss 12, 13, and 15 apply irrespective of the status of the seller.

purchaser of goods. In fact, it could be argued that the terms implied by the SGA 1979 go so far that, in practice, the governing principle is now *caveat venditor*.

➡ *caveat venditor*: 'let the seller beware'

Sections 12 to 15 of the SGA 1979 imply seven terms into contracts for the sale of goods:

1. Section 12(1)—the right to sell the goods.
2. Section 12(2)(a)—goods will be free from charges and encumbrances.
3. Section 12(2)(b)—the buyer will enjoy quiet possession of the goods.
4. Section 13—goods will correspond with their description.
5. Section 14(2)—goods will be of satisfactory quality.
6. Section 14(3)—goods will be fit for purpose.
7. Section 15—goods will correspond with sample.

However, before the implied terms themselves are examined, it is important to understand the status of these terms.

Status of the implied terms

English law classifies contractual terms either as conditions, warranties, or innominate terms. The terms implied by the SGA 1979 are expressly classified by the Act,[2] as illustrated in Table 15.1.

It can be seen that the terms implied by the SGA 1979 are classified as either conditions or warranties. There appears to be no way, therefore, that these terms can be considered as innominate. The relevance of whether a term is a condition or warranty lies in the remedy for breach:

- If the term breached is a condition, the buyer can usually treat the contract as repudiated, reject the goods, and claim damages.
- If the term breached is a warranty, the buyer cannot repudiate the contract, nor can he reject the goods, but he can claim damages.

These consequences are subject to two notable qualifications. First, if the seller breaches a condition of a contract of sale, the buyer may waive the condition, or

TABLE 15.1 Status of the implied terms

Section	Implies term that...	Status of term
12(1)	the seller has the right to sell the goods	Condition
12(2)(a)	the goods are free of any charge or encumbrance	Warranty
12(2)(b)	the buyer will enjoy quiet possession of the goods	Warranty
13	the goods will correspond with their description	Condition
14(2)	the goods will be of satisfactory quality	Condition
14(3)	the goods will be fit for purpose	Condition
15	the bulk will correspond with the sample	Condition

2. It should be noted that the SGA 1979's express classifications only apply to England, Wales, and Northern Ireland, and not to Scotland. This text will focus on the English law position.

may elect to treat the breach of the condition as a breach of warranty and not as a ground for treating the contract as repudiated.[3] Second, a buyer who does not deal as consumer and who would otherwise have the right to reject the goods following a breach of the terms implied by ss 13 to 15 will not be permitted to do so if the breach is so slight that it would be unreasonable for him to reject them.[4] In such a case, the breach may instead be treated as a breach of warranty, allowing the non-consumer buyer to claim damages only.

Section 12—the right to sell, encumbrances, and quiet possession

Consider the following example.

> ## Eg ComCorp Ltd
>
> ComCorp Ltd purchased a number of tablet computers from Better Computing plc, a computer manufacturer. As a result of reports in the press, ComCorp discovered that these computers had been manufactured using a microprocessor that infringes a patent granted to Noble plc. When it brought this to the attention of Better Computing, Better Computing stated that it bought these microprocessors from a bona fide source, has sold many thousands of these computers, and that there is nothing to worry about. It said that in any event any claim that Noble might bring would be against it and not its customers.

The question that arises is whether or not Better Computing plc has the right to sell the computers. The answer can be found in s 12 of the SGA 1979, which implies three terms into contracts of sale, which can be found in s 12(1), 12(2)(a), and 12(2)(b), as illustrated in Table 15.2. Each of these terms will now be examined in more detail.

TABLE 15.2 The terms implied by s 12

Section	Implies term that ...	Status of term	Possible remedies
12(1)	the seller has the right to sell the goods	Condition	Repudiation of contract and damages
12(2)(a)	the goods are free of any charge or encumbrance	Warranty	Damages only
12(2)(b)	the buyer will enjoy quiet possession of the goods	Warranty	Damages only

---

3. SGA 1979, s 11(2).
4. ibid s 15A(1). It should be noted that s 15A(2) goes on to say that s 15A(1) will not apply if a contrary intention appears in, or is to be implied from, the contract.

The right to sell the goods

The first, and arguably most important, term implied by s 12 can be found in s 12(1).

 SGA 1979, s 12(1)

In a contract of sale ... there is an implied term on the part of the seller that in the case of a sale he has a right to sell the goods, and in the case of an agreement to sell he will have such a right at the time when the property is to pass.

The wording of the subsection clearly indicates that, in order for the seller to comply with the term implied by s 12(1), two questions must be affirmatively answered, namely:

1. Has the seller ever had the right to sell the goods?
2. If so, did the seller have the right to sell the goods at the relevant time?

The right to sell

It might be thought that the term implied by s 12(1) requires the seller to be the owner or to have good title to the goods being sold, or to be able to transfer good title to the buyer, but this is not the case.[5] Ownership of the goods and the right to sell them are two different concepts and must not be confused. The term implied by s 12(1) merely provides that the seller has the 'right to sell the goods'. Initially, one might conclude that the seller would lack the right to sell the goods if he himself does not hold title to them, but this is not necessarily the case, as a seller can effect a contract of sale on behalf of another person who does have title to the goods, providing that this other person so consents (e.g. where, with the principal's consent, an agent sells goods that belong to his principal). This is why s 12(1) does not require the seller to have title to the goods, nor does it require the seller to be able to transfer good title. Of course, if the seller does have title to the goods, then he will usually have the right to sell the goods, but, as the following case demonstrates, this is not always so.

 ***Niblett Ltd v Confectioners' Materials Co Ltd* [1921] 3 KB 387 (CA)**

FACTS: The seller contracted to sell 3,000 cases of condensed milk to the buyer, with the buyer stipulating that the milk should be of three brands; namely 'Freedom', 'Tuscan', or 'Nissly'. Two thousand cases of 'Freedom' brand were delivered and 1,000 of 'Nissly'. The buyer paid for the goods, but the 1,000 'Nissly' brand cases were seized by customs officials on the ground that use of the 'Nissly' label breached a trade mark belonging to Nestlé Co. Nestlé stated that the buyer could only sell on the 1,000 'Nissly' cases if it first removed the labels on the tins, which would significantly reduce the value of the goods. The buyer alleged, *inter alia*, that the seller had no right to sell the goods and sought damages.

---

5. See e.g. *Karlshamns Oljefabriker A/B v Eastport Navigation Corp (The Elafi)* [1981] 2 Lloyd's Rep 679 (QB).

> **HELD:** The claim succeeded. The Court of Appeal stated that, although the seller had title to the goods, and transferred title in the goods to the buyer, the presence of the trade mark infringement meant that the seller did not have the right to sell the goods. Scrutton LJ stated '[i]f a vendor can be stopped by process of law from selling, he has not the right to sell'.[6] Accordingly, the term implied by s 12(1) had been breached, entitling the buyer to damages.

Niblett clearly demonstrates that a seller who holds valid title to goods, or who can transfer valid title in the goods to another, will not automatically have the right to sell those goods. It should be noted that cases such as *Niblett* are relatively rare and, in the majority of cases, a seller who holds or can transfer valid title will also have the right to sell the goods.

As the term implied by s 12(1) is one of strict liability, it follows that it is irrelevant whether or not the seller knew, or ought to have known, that he did not have the right to sell the goods.

➜ strict liability: liability without fault

When must the right to sell exist?

In order for a seller to comply with the term implied by s 12(1), he will need to demonstrate that, not only did he have the right to sell the goods, but also that he had the right to sell the goods at the relevant time. What constitutes the relevant time will depend upon whether the contract purported to effect a 'sale' (i.e. a present transfer of property in the goods) or purported to effect an 'agreement to sell' (i.e. where the transfer of property in the goods will not take place until a future date, or upon the fulfilment of some condition). It is also important to distinguish between a contract for the sale of specific goods and one for the sale of unascertained goods:

- Where the contract purports to effect a sale of specific goods, then the seller must have the right to sell the goods at the time the contract is made.[7]
- Where the contract purports to effect a sale of unascertained goods, then the seller must have the right to sell the goods at the time that property in the goods would be transferred to the buyer under s 18, rule 5 of the SGA 1979.
- Where the contract purports to effect an agreement to sell, then the seller need not have the right to sell the goods at the time the contract was made, but must have the right to sell the goods at the time when the property is to pass to the buyer.[8] The following example demonstrates this.

🔗 Section 18, rule 5 of the SGA 1979 is discussed at p 246

Eg ComCorp Ltd

In January 2013, ComCorp Ltd enters into an agreement with VanMart Ltd for the purchase of a van. The agreement provides that ComCorp will pay for the van in twelve

---

6. [1921] 3 KB 387 (CA) 398.

7. SGA 1979, s 18, rule 1 (discussed on p 236). Note that this section only applies to unconditional sales of specific goods—it will therefore not apply where a condition as to transfer of title exists (e.g. where the contract provides that no transfer of title will occur until payment has been received).

8. *Kulkarni v Manor Credit (Davenham) Ltd* [2010] EWCA Civ 69, [2010] 2 All ER (Comm) 1017 [9] (Rix LJ).

monthly instalments and that ownership will only be transferred once the final payment has been made. At the time of the agreement, VanMart does not actually have the right to sell the van, and only acquires this right in November 2013. However, as VanMart has the right to sell the goods at the time the property in the van is transferred (i.e. when the final instalment is paid in December 2013), no breach of s 12(1) has occurred.

Remedies

The term implied by s 12(1) is a condition.[9] Accordingly, breach of this term will usually entitle the buyer to reject the goods, repudiate the contract, and recover damages. As the following case establishes, where a breach of the term implied by s 12(1) occurs, the buyer will *prima facie* be able to recover the full purchase price on the ground that there has been a total failure of consideration.

 Rowland v Divall [1923] 2 KB 500 (CA)

FACTS: Divall purchased a car from an individual who, unbeknown to him, had stolen it. Divall subsequently sold the car to Rowland (a motor dealer) for £334. Rowland painted the car and kept it in his showroom for two months, after which time it was purchased by a customer for £400. Two months later, upon discovering that the car was stolen, the car was repossessed by the police and returned to the original owner. The customer recovered from Rowland the £400 he paid for the car and, in turn, Rowland sought to recover the £334 that he paid to Divall on the ground that there had been a total failure of consideration. At first instance, Bray J refused to allow Rowland to recover the full purchase price on the ground that there had been several months' use of the car and so there had not been a total failure of consideration. Rowland appealed.

HELD: The Court of Appeal allowed Rowland's appeal and held that he was entitled to recover the £334 from Divall. Rowland had not contracted for the use of the car, but rather had contracted to obtain valid title in the car. As he had not obtained valid title to the car, there was a total failure of consideration and he could therefore recover the whole of the purchase price paid.

Rowland has been criticized on the ground that it allows a buyer to recover the full purchase price, even though he may have enjoyed use of the goods for a considerable period. The practical effect of *Rowland* was to provide the buyer with free use of the car for several months. Consider the following example.

 ComCorp Ltd

ComCorp Ltd has had a very profitable year and purchases for its directors a case of fine champagne from Kate's Wines Ltd. ComCorp's directors drink all the champagne before ComCorp discover that Kate's Wines had unwittingly bought the champagne from a thief. In these circumstances, could it really be said that ComCorp has suffered a total failure of

---

9. SGA 1979, s 12(5A).

consideration? According to the decision in *Rowland v Divall* it has so suffered because ComCorp could never own the champagne, even though its directors have consumed it and therefore would be entitled to the return of the price it paid to Kate's Wines. The true owner of the champagne could sue ComCorp or Kate's Wines (or, if they could find him, the thief) for damages in the tort of conversion. If the true owner sues Kate's Wines it will mean that Kate's Wines will be liable to him for the value of the champagne, as well as having to return to ComCorp the price ComCorp originally paid, whereas ComCorp will have benefited by having had the champagne for nothing.

The following case provides a further example of how a breach of s 12(1) can result in the buyer obtaining a significant and arguably unjustifiable benefit.

 Butterworth v Kingsway Motors Ltd [1954] 1 WLR 1286 (Assizes)

FACTS: Bowmaker Ltd entered into a hire-purchase agreement with Rudolph, under which Rudolph took possession of a car on hire-purchase terms. Rudolph began paying the instalments but, prior to paying all the instalments and exercising the option to purchase, she sold the car to Kennedy, who in turn sold it to Hayton. Hayton sold the car to Kingsway Motors Ltd ('Kingsway'), who then sold it to Butterworth. As Rudolph had not paid all the instalments (although she was continuing to pay them) and had not exercised the option to purchase, she did not have the right to sell the car and so all of the sellers were in breach of s 12(1) to their respective buyers. Nearly a year later, Butterworth received a letter from Bowmaker informing him that, as Rudolph had not exercised the option to purchase, he did not own the car and it should be returned to Bowmaker, who were still the legal owners. Butterworth wrote to Kingsway, claiming recovery of the purchase price. A week later, Rudolph finished paying off the instalments and exercised the option to purchase. Kingsway argued that the effect of this was to vest valid title in all of the sellers and so Butterworth would not be entitled to recovery of the purchase price, as he had obtained valid title and therefore there was no total failure of consideration.

HELD: At the time Butterworth wrote to Kingsway, Kingsway was in breach of s 12(1). The exercising of the option to purchase conferred valid title on Rudolph, who could then feed valid title to the subsequent purchasers. However, this feeding would stop at Butterworth as, prior to Kingsway obtaining title, Butterworth had written to Kingsway, and the letter was held to amount to a repudiation of the contract. Accordingly, Butterworth was entitled to recover the full purchase price.

COMMENT: Kennedy, Hayton, and Kingsway all acquired valid title and therefore could not recover the full purchase price as there had not been a total failure of consideration and they had accepted the goods. They could, however, recover damages from their respective sellers based on the difference in value of the car between the time when ownership should have passed and the time when ownership actually did pass.

It should be noted that *Butterworth* was decided prior to the enactment of the Hire Purchase Act 1964, s 27 of which permits persons in Rudolph's position to vest title in the first bona fide private purchaser. *Rowland* and *Butterworth* have been strongly criticized, principally on the ground that such cases allow a seller to recover more than

Section 27 of the Hire Purchase Act 1964 is discussed at p 301

he has actually lost. Speaking of *Rowland*, one commentator has stated that 'there is not a single word in any of the judgments which attempts to correlate the result with the actual loss suffered by the plaintiff'.[10]

In 1966, the Law Reform Committee recommended that s 12 should be amended to state that no buyer should be able to recover more than his actual loss, giving credit for any benefit he might have obtained through having the goods in his possession—a recommendation that was accepted by the Law Commission on several occasions.[11] The recommendation has, however, been criticized[12] and was never implemented, nor did the government show any signs of doing so. After further consultation, in 1987 the Law Commission reversed its position and stated that, for two reasons, the buyer should be able to recover the full purchase price:

1. quantifying the benefit obtained through possession of the goods would be difficult and uncertain; and

2. reducing the damages awarded based on the benefit obtained through possession of the goods would, in effect, be requiring the buyer to pay the seller for the use of someone else's goods.[13]

Despite this, a number of prominent commentators[14] have contended that the principle derived from *Rowland* should be revisited and that the damages awarded to the buyer should take into account any benefits received through his possession of the goods.

In addition to rejecting the goods and recovering the purchase price, the buyer can also recover a sum for any consequential losses sustained that were naturally and directly caused by the breach of the implied term (e.g. money spent repairing the goods).[15]

The remedies available to the buyer, including the additional remedies afforded to consumer buyers, are discussed in more detail in Chapter 17

Freedom from charges or encumbrances

The second term implied by s 12 can be found in s 12(2)(a), which provides that:

SGA 1979, s 12(2)(a)

the goods are free, and will remain free until the time when the property is to pass, from any charge or encumbrance not disclosed or known to the buyer before the contract is made.

---

10. Gunther H Treitel, 'Some Problems of Breach of Contract' (1967) 30 MLR 139, 146.

11. Law Commission, *Exemption Clauses in Contracts* (Law Com No 24, 1969) paras 11–19; Law Commission, *Law of Contract: Pecuniary Restitution on Breach of Contract* (Law Com No 121, 1983) para 1.9–1.12.

12. See e.g. Gunther H Treitel, 'Some Problems of Breach of Contract' (1967) 30 MLR 139, 148. For a scathing criticism, see Patrick S Atiyah, 'Law Reform Committee: Twelfth Report' (1966) 29 MLR 541, 541, who describes the Law Reform Committee's report as 'a depressing illustration of the extreme amateurism which seems to characterize all attempts at law reform in this country'.

13. Law Commission, *Sale and Supply of Goods* (Law Com No 160, 1987) para 6.4.

14. See e.g. Michael G Bridge, *Benjamin's Sale of Goods* (8th edn, Sweet & Maxwell 2010) [4-006].

15. *Mason v Burningham* [1949] 2 KB 545 (CA).

Four points should be noted. First, the phrase 'charge or encumbrance' refers only to a proprietary or possessory right, and not to a mere contractual right.[16] Second, in order to avoid a breach of the term implied by s 12(2)(a), the goods must be free from charges or encumbrances at the time that the agreement was entered into, and must continue to remain free until such time as property in the goods passes to the buyer. Third, the term implied by s 12(2)(a) will not be implied where the existence of the charge or encumbrance is disclosed or made known to the buyer prior to the contract being entered into. Fourth, a breach of the term implied by s 12(2)(a) is not dependent on the charge or encumbrance being enforced or asserted: the mere existence of a charge or encumbrance is enough to establish a breach.

In practice, it has been argued that the term implied by s 12(2)(a) is of 'little practical significance',[17] as the implied term relating to quiet possession (discussed later in this chapter) is wide enough to encompass breaches of s 12(2)(a).

Remedies

The term implied by s 12(2)(a) is a warranty,[18] meaning that a breach will not entitle the buyer to repudiate the contract and reject the goods. The buyer will only be entitled to claim damages, but how such damages are quantified can be uncertain and complex. Where the person who benefits from the charge or encumbrance asserts or enforces the charge or encumbrance, then the quantum of damages will depend on whether the buyer loses possession of the goods:

- If the buyer loses possession of the goods, he can claim damages based on the value of the goods at the time of dispossession.[19]
- If the buyer is not dispossessed of the goods, the *prima facie*[20] measure of damages will be the difference in value between the goods when they were delivered and the value that the goods would have had if the contract had been complied with[21] (i.e. if the goods were not subject to the charge or encumbrance).
- Irrespective of whether the buyer loses possession, he can claim from the seller reasonable costs incurred in avoiding the charge or encumbrance,[22] including legal costs and any damages awarded against the buyer.[23]

Where the person who benefits from the charge or encumbrance does not assert or enforce the charge or encumbrance, then it could be argued that the buyer has sustained no loss and so should only be able to recover nominal damages. However, in such a case, it is likely that the buyer can recover damages based on the diminution in the value of the goods,[24] or based on the amount that the buyer would have to spend to remove the charge or encumbrance.

---

16. *Athens Cape Naviera SA v Deutsche Dampfschiffahrtsgesellschaft Hansa Aktiengesellschaft (The Barenbels)* [1985] 1 Lloyd's Rep 528 (CA).

17. Roy Goode and Ewan McKendrick, *Goode on Commercial Law* (4th edn, Penguin 2010) 314.

18. SGA 1979, s 12(5A).　　19. *Jenkins v Jones* (1881–82) LR 9 QBD 128 (CA).

20. As this is a *prima facie* measure of damages only, it can be displaced. See e.g. *Bence Graphics International Ltd v Fasson UK Ltd* [1998] QB 87 (CA).

21. SGA 1979, s 53(3); *Louis Dreyfus Trading Ltd v Reliance Trading Ltd* [2004] EWHC 525 (Comm), [2004] 2 Lloyd's Rep 243.　　22. *Niblett Ltd v Confectioners' Materials Co Ltd* [1921] 3 KB 387 (CA).

23. *Lloyds and Scottish Finance Ltd v Modern Cars and Caravans (Kingston) Ltd* [1966] 1 QB 764 (QB).

24. SGA 1979, s 53; *Turner v Moon* [1901] 2 Ch 825 (Ch).

Right to enjoy quiet possession

The third term implied by s 12 can be found in s 12(2)(b), which provides that:

SGA 1979, s 12(2)(b)

...the buyer will enjoy quiet possession of the goods except so far as it may be disturbed by the owner or other person entitled to the benefit of any charge or encumbrance so disclosed or known.

In many cases, a breach of the term implied by s 12(1) will also amount to a breach of the term implied by s 12(2)(b).[25] However, it is important to note a crucial difference between the various terms. The terms implied by s 12(1) and (2)(a) only impose obligations up until the point when property passes. Conversely, as s 12(2)(b) states that the buyer *will* enjoy quiet possession of the goods, it follows that the implied term is a continuous one that will continue to apply even after property has passed to the buyer. Consequently, the term implied by s 12(2)(b) can be breached even after title has been transferred to the buyer, as the following case demonstrates.

Rubicon Computer Systems Ltd v United Paints Ltd (2000) TCLR 453 (CA)

FACTS: Rubicon Computer Systems Ltd ('Rubicon') sold a computer system to United Paints Ltd ('UP'). The system was delivered and installed in December 1988. A dispute arose and UP withheld part of the contract price. In response, in June 1989, Rubicon activated a time lock, which prevented UP from accessing the computer system. A stand-off ensued, which lasted until March 1994, at which point Rubicon deactivated the time lock. By this time, the computer system was obsolete. Rubicon commenced proceedings to recover the outstanding balance of the contract price. UP counterclaimed for recovery of the price and damages on the ground that Rubicon, in activating the time lock, had breached the term implied by s 12(2)(b) entitling UP to enjoy quiet possession of the goods. At first instance, UP's counterclaim succeeded. Rubicon appealed.

HELD: The appeal was dismissed and UP's counterclaim was upheld. The Court of Appeal held that, although Rubicon had transferred valid title to UP, the duty implied by s 12(2)(b) was a continuous one that had been breached by activating the time lock. UP was therefore allowed to recover the purchase price and damages.

In *Rubicon*, it was the seller's interference that caused the breach of s 12(2)(b) to occur, but this need not be the case. As the following case demonstrates, a breach of s 12(2)(b) can also occur where a third party interferes with the buyer's quiet possession of the goods.

---

25. See e.g. *Niblett Ltd v Confectioners' Materials Co Ltd* [1921] 3 KB 387 (CA) (discussed at p 344).

Microbeads AG v Vinhurst Road Markings Ltd [1975] 1 WLR 218 (CA)

FACTS: In 1970, Microbeads AG ('Microbeads') sold to Vinhurst Road Markings Ltd ('Vinhurst') three road-marking machines. Vinhurst was not satisfied with the performance of the machines and refused to pay the full contract price. Unknown to Vinhurst, in 1966 an unconnected third party had applied for a patent regarding such machines, which was finally granted in 1972. The result of this was that the machines infringed the third party's patent and the third party sought an injunction preventing Vinhurst from using the machines. Microbeads commenced proceedings to recover the outstanding balance of the contract price and was successful at first instance. Vinhurst appealed, alleging that Microbeads had breached the terms implied by s 12(1) and s 12(2)(b).

HELD: The appeal was allowed. The Court of Appeal held that, as Microbeads had the right to sell the goods at the time the contract was entered into, the term implied by s 12(1) had not been breached. However, by obtaining the patent and seeking an injunction, the third party had interrupted Vinhurst's enjoyment of the machines. Accordingly, the term implied by s 12(2)(b) had been breached and Vinhurst could obtain damages from Microbeads.

⭐ See Brian Elkan, 'Sale of Goods and Patent Infringement' (1975) 34 CLJ 199

To understand the operation of the term implied by s 12(2)(b), three important questions need to be answered. The first question is at what point in time will the term implied by s 12(2)(b) actually come into effect. Will the term become effective once the contract is entered into, or will it only become effective once title is transferred? Although there appears to be no direct authority on the point, it has been argued that, based on the wording of s 12(2)(b), the answer is neither and that the term will only come into effect once the goods are delivered to the buyer, irrespective of whether he also acquires title at this point.[26]

The second question is what sort of conduct is required in order to breach the term implied by s 12(2)(b). There is no doubt that the term will not protect a buyer against every possible form of interference that might arise, but the scope of the term is unclear. However, the case law to date does provide the following guidance:

- Where the interference is caused by the seller's breach of contract or tortious conduct, then the term implied by s 12(2)(b) will almost certainly be breached.[27]
- Where the interference is caused by the lawful conduct of a third party, then the term implied by s 12(2)(b) will usually be breached,[28] unless the interference is in no way due to the fault of the seller.
- Where the interference is caused by the unlawful conduct of a third party, then the term implied by s 12(2)(b) will not be breached,[29] unless the seller was involved in some way with the unlawful conduct and it was connected sufficiently to the contract of sale.

---

26. Michael G Bridge, *Benjamin's Sale of Goods* (8th edn, Sweet & Maxwell 2010) [4-025]. The author also argues that interference with the buyer's right to possession would also probably suffice.
27. *Niblett Ltd v Confectioners' Materials Co Ltd* [1921] 3 KB 387 (CA); *Rubicon Computer Systems Ltd v United Paints Ltd* (2000) TCLR 453 (CA).
28. *Microbeads AG v Vinhurst Road Markings Ltd* [1975] 1 WLR 218 (CA).
29. *Malzy v Eichholz* [1916] 2 KB 308 (CA).

The third question is for how long following the delivery of the goods will the term implied by s 12(2)(b) continue to operate. There is no doubt that certain forms of conduct will cause the term to no longer operate, for example, consuming or selling the goods.[30] In the absence of such conduct, it is unclear how long the term will continue to operate. The cases to date[31] indicate that the term can continue to operate for several years following the delivery of the goods to the buyer. However, some judges have expressed the opinion that the operation of the term should be limited.[32]

Remedies

The term implied by s 12(2)(b) is a warranty,[33] meaning that a breach will not entitle the buyer to repudiate the contract and reject the goods. The buyer will only be entitled to claim damages. Where the buyer loses possession of the goods due to the breach, then damages will be assessed based on the value of the goods at the time he was dispossessed of them. In other words, the measure of damages for breach of warranty is the estimated loss directly and naturally resulting, in the ordinary course of events, from the breach of warranty.[34] Where the buyer is not dispossessed, then the rebuttable presumption is that damages will be assessed on the basis of the difference in value between the goods at the time of delivery and the value the goods would have had if the term implied by s 12(2)(b) had not been breached.[35] The buyer can also usually recover legal costs and consequential losses, providing they are not too remote.

Transfer of a limited title

The three terms implied by s 12(1) and (2) will not be implied into a contract of sale where 'there appears from the contract or is to be inferred from its circumstances an intention that the seller should transfer only such title as he or a third person may have'.[36] Section 12(3) applies to those situations where the seller's (or third person's) title to the goods is in some way impaired or limited, or the seller is unaware as to the full extent of his title. In such cases, s 12(3) provides that the seller or third party will transfer only the title that he actually has. A contract of sale may come within the scope of s 12(3) if it contains an express provision stating that the seller intends to transfer only the title that he actually has, or alternatively, such an intention may be implied based upon the circumstances surrounding the contract. The following case demonstrates the operation of s 12(3) and provides an example of when an implied intention to transfer limited title may arise.

---

30. *Ocean Chemical Transport Inc v Exnor Craggs Ltd* [2000] 1 Lloyd's Rep 446 (CA).
31. See e.g. *Microbeads AG v Vinhurst Road Markings Ltd* [1975] 1 WLR 218 (CA); *Empresa Exportadora de Azucar v Industria Azucarera Nacional SA (The Playa Larga and The Marble Islands)* [1983] 2 Lloyd's Rep 171 (CA).
32. See e.g. Ackner LJ in *Empresa Exportadora de Azucar v Industria Azucarera Nacional SA (The Playa Larga and The Marble Islands)* [1983] 2 Lloyd's Rep 171 (CA).
33. SGA 1979, s 12(5A).
34. ibid, s 53(2); *Lloyds and Scottish Finance Ltd v Modern Cars and Caravans (Kingston) Ltd* [1966] 1 QB 764 (QB).
35. *Louis Dreyfus Trading Ltd v Reliance Trading Ltd* [2004] EWHC 525 (Comm), [2004] 2 Lloyd's Rep 243.
36. SGA 1979, s 12(3).

Chapman v Speller (1850) 14 QB 621 (KB)

FACTS: A sheriff seized goods from a judgment debtor and intended to sell them at auction to satisfy the debtor's debt. The goods were bought at auction by Speller, and later sold to Chapman. It was then discovered that the goods were not the property of the judgment debtor, and so Chapman had to return the goods to the true owner. Chapman sought the return of the price paid to Speller, on the ground that Speller did not have the right to sell the goods.

HELD: The claim failed. The sheriff could not know that the debtor's title was defective. Accordingly, it was inferred that Speller intended to transfer only the title that he actually had. Patteson J explained that the true consideration was the assignment of the right, whatever it was, that Speller had acquired by his purchase at the sheriff's sale and that this consideration had not failed. The money paid by Chapman was therefore not for the goods but merely for this right Speller had acquired.

The effect of s 12(3) differs depending on which of the three terms implied by s 12(1) or (2) are involved:

- Section 12(1): *Chapman*[37] demonstrates that the likely effect of s 12(3) is to completely disapply the term implied by s 12(1).

- Section 12(2)(a): where s 12(3) applies, the term in s 12(2)(a) will not be implied. Instead a more limited term will be implied which provides that 'all charges or encumbrances known to the seller and not known to the buyer have been disclosed to the buyer before the contract is made'.[38]

- Section 12(2)(b): where s 12(3) applies, the term in s 12(2)(b) will not be implied, but a more limited term will be implied which provides that the buyer's quiet possession of the goods will not be disturbed by (a) the seller; (b) a third person, in cases where the parties to the contract intend that the seller should transfer only such title as that third person may have; or (c) anyone claiming through or under the seller or that third person otherwise than under a charge or encumbrance disclosed or known to the buyer before the contract is made.[39]

Table 15.3 summarizes the effect of s 12(3) on the terms implied by s 12(1) and (2).

Section 13—correspondence with description

Consider the following example.

ComCorp Ltd

ComCorp Ltd purchases from iDevice Ltd a number of tablet devices for use by its directors. iDevice's website states that the tablets will have 32 GB of memory and a battery

---

37. Although pre-dating the SGA 1893.   38. SGA 1979, s 12(4).   39. ibid s 12(5).

> life of 8–10 hours. Upon receiving the devices, the directors discover that the tablets only have 16 GB of memory and require recharging every 4–6 hours.

TABLE 15.3 The effect of s 12(3) on the terms implied by ss 12(1) and (2)

Implied term	Effect of contract of sale coming within s 12(3)	Replacement implied term
12(1)—Right to sell	The term will not be implied	No replacement term will be implied
12(2)(a)—Freedom from charges or encumbrances	The term will not be implied, but a more limited term will be implied by s 12(4)	12(4)—All charges or encumbrances known to the seller and not known to the buyer have been disclosed to the buyer before the contract is made
12(2)(b)—Right to enjoy quiet possession	The term will not be implied, but a more limited term will be implied by s 12(5)	12(5)—The buyer's quiet possession of the goods will not be disturbed by (a) the seller; (b) a third person, in cases where the parties to the contract intend that the seller should transfer only such title as that third person may have; or (c) anyone claiming through or under the seller or that third person otherwise than under a charge or encumbrance disclosed or known to the buyer before the contract is made

The question that arises is whether ComCorp can obtain replacement devices from iDevice Ltd, or whether it can return the tablets and obtain a refund. The answer can be found in s 13(1), which provides the following.

🔑 SGA 1979, s 13(1)

Where there is a contract for the sale of goods by description, there is an implied term that the goods will correspond with the description.

It is clear that the courts will not adopt an overly technical or restrictive definition of the word 'description'. As Lord Diplock stated:

> 'Description'…is an ordinary English word. The Act contains no definition of what it means when it speaks…of a contract for the sale of goods being a sale 'by description'. One must look to the contract as a whole to identify the kind of goods that the seller was agreeing to sell and the buyer to buy.[40]

What is a 'contract for the sale of goods by description?'

The term implied by s 13(1) will only be implied into contracts for the 'sale of goods by description'. Accordingly, it is crucial that such contracts can be identified.

---

40. *Berger & Co Inc v Gill & Duffus SA* [1984] AC 382 (HL) 394.

Unfortunately, as noted earlier, the SGA 1979 provides no definition of this and identifying a contract for the sale of goods by description is not always an easy matter. In *Grant v Australian Knitting Mills Ltd*,[41] Lord Wright explained 'there is a sale by description even though the buyer is buying something displayed before him on the counter: a thing is sold by description, though it is specific, so long as it is sold not merely as the specific thing but as a thing corresponding to a description'.[42]

In *Joseph Travers & Sons Ltd v Longel Ltd*,[43] Sellers J approved the definition found in Benjamin's *Sale of Personal Property*,[44] which stated that contracts for the sale of goods by description could be of two types, namely:

1. unascertained or future goods, as being of a certain kind or class, or to which otherwise a description in the contract is applied; or
2. specific goods, bought by the buyer in reliance, at least in part, upon the description given, or to be tacitly inferred from the circumstances, and which identifies the goods.

The first type is straightforward. The courts have stated on numerous occasions that a contract will be one by description where the buyer is purchasing goods that he has not seen, as he will be relying on the description alone. However, historically, the sale of specific goods (the second type) was not regarded as a sale by description, as the act of selecting the goods meant that the buyer could inspect the goods himself and determine whether or not they corresponded with the seller's description. This is no longer the case, and the second type of contract for the sale of goods by description relates solely to specific goods. It is, however, a relatively complex definition and imposes two limitations, namely (i) the description must identify the goods; and (ii) the buyer must rely on the description. In addition, a third limitation has been added, namely, that only descriptive words that form terms of the contract will form part of the sale by description. These three limitations will now be discussed.

Identification of the goods

Not every descriptive word or phrase concerning the goods will be regarded as part of the goods' description for the purposes of s 13. The definition given indicates that, in relation to specific goods, only those descriptive words that identify the goods will form part of the sale by description. Therefore, the question arises as to how the courts will determine which words identify the goods. The courts distinguish between descriptive words that relate to the goods' identity and descriptive words that relate to the goods' attributes (e.g. quality, fitness for purpose, etc.), with only the former coming within the scope of s 13. Accordingly, the fact that goods are of sufficient quality or fit for purpose will not usually be relevant in determining whether the goods correspond with their description, as such factors do not identify the goods but merely describe their attributes. The following case demonstrates how the distinction between the goods' identity and attributes is relevant in determining whether the term implied by s 13(1) has been breached.

41. [1936] AC 85 (PC).   42. ibid 100 (Lord Wright).   43. (1948) 64 TLR 150 (KB).
44. JP Benjamin, *Benjamin's Treatise on the Sale of Personal Property* (7th edn, Bowen-Merrell 1899) 641.

Ashington Piggeries Ltd v Christopher Hill Ltd [1972] AC 441 (HL)

FACTS: A mink-breeder, Christopher Hill Ltd ('CH'), contracted to purchase from Ashington Piggeries Ltd ('Ashington') a consignment of 'Norwegian herring meal fair average quality of the season', with which to feed its mink. Ashington added a preservative to the food, which reacted with the herring to form a chemical (DMNA) that was harmless to most animals, but fatal to mink. As a result, thousands of CH's mink died. CH refused to pay for the food and Ashington sued for the contract price. CH counterclaimed, alleging that the terms implied by ss 13(1), 14(2), and 14(3) had been breached.

HELD: The House of Lords held that the implied terms as to satisfactory quality (s 14(2)) and fitness for purpose (s 14(3)) had been breached. However, the term implied by s 13(1) had not. Lord Guest stated 'the fact that the herring meal was contaminated by DMNA did not result in a different substance from the herring meal in the description. There was no loss of identity. In my opinion, no breach of section 13 by [Ashington] occurred.'[45]

Lord Diplock agreed, stating 'the occurrence of this reaction may affect the quality of the meal. It does not alter its identity as "herring meal".'[46]

 See Ingrid Patient, 'Ruminating on Mink Food' (1971) 34 MLR 557

In *Ashington Piggeries*, the descriptive words 'Norwegian herring meal' identified the goods, while the descriptive words 'fair average quality of the season' merely described an attribute of the goods, namely their quality. The goods sold were indeed Norwegian herring meal and so the words that identified the goods corresponded with their description. Accordingly, there was no breach of s 13(1).

Reliance

The mere presence of descriptive words will not, without more, make the contract one for the sale of goods by description. It is also necessary to show that the buyer relied on the descriptive words, as the following case demonstrates.

Harlingdon & Leinster Enterprises Ltd v Christopher Hull Fine Art Ltd [1991] 1 QB 564 (CA)

FACTS: Both parties carried on business as art dealers. Christopher Hull Fine Art Ltd ('CH') acquired two paintings that it believed were painted by Gabrielle Münter, a German expressionist painter. It contacted Harlingdon & Leinster Enterprises Ltd ('Harlingdon') and asked if Harlingdon would be interested in purchasing the paintings. An employee of Harlingdon examined the paintings and, during the examination, was informed that CH knew nothing of Gabrielle Münter. Conversely, Harlingdon and its employees were experts in German expressionist paintings. Harlingdon purchased one of the paintings for £6,000. It transpired that the paintings were forgeries and Harlingdon rejected the painting, claiming that CH had breached the term implied by s 13(1).

HELD: Nourse LJ stated that 'the description must have a sufficient influence in the sale to become an essential term of the contract and the correlative of influence is reliance'.[47]

---

45. [1972] AC 441 (HL) 473. 46. ibid 504. 47. [1991] 1 QB 564 (CA) 574.

Harlingdon had not relied on CH's description, but had instead relied on the expertise of its own employee. Accordingly, the sale was not one by description, there was no breach of the term implied by s 13(1), and Harlingdon could not reject the painting.

COMMENT: The emphasis on reliance has been criticized. One commentator has argued that the requirement of reliance has significantly tipped the balance of power in favour of the seller and that 'the buyer now, is put "on guard" and should be extremely wary of what the seller says or does. In other words, *caveat emptor*! Not only does this undermine the spirit of the legislation, it also pays little regard to the realities of the market place.'[48] Furthermore, Nourse LJ pointed out 'in theory it is no doubt possible for a description of goods which is not relied on by the buyer to become an essential term of a contract for their sale. But in practice it is very difficult, and perhaps impossible, to think of facts where that would be so.'[49]

 See LA Lawrenson, 'The Sale of Goods by Description–A Return to Caveat Emptor?" (1991) 54 MLR 122

In practice, it should not be difficult for the buyer to establish that he relied on the descriptive words. In *Varley v Whipp*,[50] Channell J stated that 'the term "sale of goods by description" must apply to all cases where the purchaser has not seen the goods, but is relying on the description alone'.[51] Accordingly, in cases involving the sale of unascertained and future goods, reliance will be especially easy to establish; indeed, in cases involving such goods, it will be almost certain that the sale will be one by description. The same is true of specific goods unseen at the time the contract is entered into.[52] Even in cases where the buyer has seen the goods, reliance will still usually be easy to establish. For example, goods in shops will be seen by the buyer, yet the buyer will often rely entirely on descriptions found on the goods' packaging. Indeed, s 13(3) provides that 'a sale of goods is not prevented from being a sale by description by reason only that, being exposed for sale or hire, they are selected by the buyer'. The following case demonstrates this.

Beale v Taylor [1991] 1 QB 564 (CA)

FACTS: Taylor advertised his car for sale, which he believed to be a 1961 Triumph Herald 1200. The advertisement read 'Herald convertible, white, 1961, twin carbs, £190...' Beale bought the car and shortly afterwards found that it was in fact made up of two cars, welded together. The rear portion consisted of a 1961 Triumph Herald 1200 model, but the front portion consisted of an earlier 1948 model.

HELD: The Court of Appeal held that there could be a sale by description of a specific chattel, even where the chattel was displayed and inspected by the buyer, so long as it was sold not merely as the specific thing but as a thing corresponding to a description so that the buyer relied at least in part on a description. When Beale made his offer for the car, he relied on the description given in the advertisement and on the badge showing that it was a 1961 Triumph Herald 1200. It was therefore a sale by description. Since the car

---

48. LA Lawrenson, 'The Sale of Goods by Description—A Return to Caveat Emptor?' (1991) 54 MLR 122, 124.

49. [1991] 1 QB 564 (CA) 574.   50. [1900] 1 QB 513 (QB).   51. ibid 516.

52. Although Michael G Bridge, *Benjamin's Sale of Goods* (8th edn, Sweet & Maxwell 2010) [11-008] argues that this was contrary to the intentions of the Act's draftsman.

> did not correspond with its description, Beale was entitled to damages for breach of the condition implied by s 13.

In *Beale*, the entire car was not what the description claimed it to be. However, *Beale* should be contrasted with the following case, where the car was accurately described as being vintage, but some of its components were not.

 Brewer v Mann [2012] EWCA Civ 246

FACTS: Mann advertised for sale a '1930 Bentley Speed Six' motorcar. Brewer obtained the car on hire purchase terms.[53] Brewer later argued that the car did not conform to this description because the engine was not an original Bentley engine but a Bentley engine that had been modified to Speed Six specifications. Brewer further argued that the bodywork had been altered.

HELD: The Court of Appeal held that the description of the car in the hire purchase contract did not require it to be an original 1930 Bentley Speed Six. Consequently, alterations to its engine and bodywork did not constitute a breach of its description. The identity of a vintage car was to be ascertained by the normal customs of the vintage car trade and, on the evidence of both experts, the car did correspond with its description as a '1930 Bentley Speed Six'.

★ See James Wilson, 'Battle of the Bentley' (2012) 162 NLJ 510

The description must constitute a term of the contract

Even if a description does identify the goods, and the buyer relies on that description, it will still be necessary to establish that the description constitutes a term of the contract, as opposed to a mere representation or puff.[54] If the descriptive statement is a mere representation or puff, the contract will not be one for the sale of goods by description, as the following case demonstrates.[55]

 T&J Harrison v Knowles & Foster [1918] 1 KB 608 (CA)

FACTS: Knowles & Foster ('Knowles') wished to sell two steamships to T&J Harrison. They provided them with particulars of the ships, which stated that the deadweight capacity of each ship was 460 tonnes. T&J Harrison, relying upon these particulars, agreed to purchase the ships and a contract was drawn up. However, the contract made no mention of the ships' deadweight capacity. The ships were delivered to T&J Harrison, whereupon it

---

53. The implied term as to description, therefore, is to be found in s 9 of the Supply of Goods (Implied Terms) Act 1973, which provides: '(1) Where under a hire-purchase agreement goods are bailed or (in Scotland) hired by description, there is an implied term that the goods will correspond with the description … (2) Goods shall not be prevented from being bailed or hired by description by reason only that, being exposed for sale, bailment or hire, they are selected by the person to whom they are bailed or hired.'
54. *Heilbut, Symons & Co v Buckleton* [1913] AC 30 (HL).
55. See also *Oscar Chess Ltd v Williams* [1957] 1 WLR 370 (CA).

discovered that the deadweight capacity of each ship was only 360 tonnes. T&J Harrison sought damages for breach of contract.

HELD: The Court of Appeal rejected the claim. Pickford LJ stated 'the particulars merely contained a representation made innocently as to the deadweight capacity of the ships, which may have induced [T&J Harrison] to enter into the contract, but which afforded no ground for a claim for damages for breach of contract'.[56]

COMMENT: Compare this case to *Howard Marine and Dredging Co Ltd v A Ogden & Sons (Excavations) Ltd*,[57] where a similar mistake as to the deadweight capacity of two barges resulted in the claimant obtaining damages under s 2(1) of the Misrepresentation Act 1967.

The requirement that the descriptive statement must amount to a term of the contract has been described as 'highly artificial'[58] and that its imposition performs the 'somewhat odd (and redundant) function of declaring that it is an implied term that the seller must comply with an express term of the contract'.[59] Nevertheless, the requirement remains and, if the descriptive words amount to no more than a representation, no liability will lie under s 13(1) and the buyer will need to seek a remedy elsewhere (usually by basing his claim on misrepresentation). If the descriptive words amount to a mere puff, the buyer will have no remedy at all.

What extent of correspondence is required?

Once it has been determined that the contract is one for the sale of goods by description, the next step is to determine whether the goods correspond with the description. But what extent of correspondence is required? To a degree, this will depend upon the terms of the contract—if the contract provides a detailed list of descriptive qualities that the seller should comply with, then it will be likely that an extremely close correspondence between the description and the goods will be required. Even where a detailed contract does not exist, the courts tend to apply an extremely strict standard, so that even minor deviations from the description can result in the term implied by s 13(1) being breached, as the following two cases demonstrate.

 Arcos Ltd v EA Ronaasen & Son [1933] AC 470 (HL)

FACTS: Ronaasen & Son ('Ronaasen') contracted to purchase from Arcos Ltd a number of timber staves to be used in the making of barrels. The contract stated that the staves should be of an inch thick. Upon delivery, it was discovered that many of the staves were nine-sixteenths of an inch thick. The one-sixteenth increase in thickness made no difference at all to Ronaasen's ability to use the staves to make barrels, but it rejected the staves and terminated the contract on the ground that the goods did not correspond with their description.

---

56. [1918] 1 KB 608 (CA) 609.   57. [1978] QB 574 (CA).
58. Roy Goode and Ewan McKendrick, *Goode on Commercial Law* (4th edn, Penguin 2010) 318.
59. Patrick S Atiyah, John N Adams, and Hector MacQueen, *Atiyah's Sale of Goods* (12th edn, Pearson 2010) 143.

HELD: The House of Lords held that, as the majority of the staves had not complied with the description, the term implied by s 13(1) was breached and Ronaasen's termination of the contract was valid, even though it suffered no actual loss and the staves were perfectly usable. Lord Atkin justified the decision by stating 'if the written contract specifies conditions of weight, measurement and the like, those conditions must be complied with. A ton does not mean about a ton, or a yard about a yard.'[60]

Moore & Co Ltd v Landauer & Co [1921] 2 KB 519 (CA)

FACTS: Moore & Co Ltd ('Moore') contracted to sell a quantity of tinned fruit to Landauer & Co ('Landauer'), with a term of the contract providing that the fruit would be packaged in cases each containing thirty tins. The overall correct quantity was delivered but some of the tins were packed in cases containing twenty-four tins. Landauer refused to take delivery of the goods. There was no difference in the market value of the goods, whether packed twenty-four or thirty tins to a case.

HELD: The Court of Appeal held that this was a sale of goods by description and that the statement in the contract that the goods were to be packed thirty tins to a case was part of the description. As some of the goods tendered did not correspond with that description, Landauer was entitled to reject the entire consignment.

These cases emphasize a point already made, namely that the quality of the goods will usually have no effect upon whether the goods correspond with their description. *Arcos* and *Moore* have, however, attracted considerable criticism and the question to ask is whether the inflexible position evidenced in these cases is justifiable. It has been argued that, in the commercial context, the decisions are entirely justifiable on the ground that 'merchants put a high premium on certainty: a firm rule means they know where they stand, whereas much delay would be caused if every case had to go to court in order to ascertain whether the deviation from the contract was significant'.[61]

Whilst this justification is entirely valid, the House of Lords' subsequent acknowledgement that these decisions were 'excessively technical and due for fresh examination'[62] was welcome and, in the following case, the House of Lords demonstrated a much more flexible approach that is much more in line with commercial reality.

---

60. [1933] AC 470 (HL) 479.

61. Len S Sealy and Richard JA Hooley, *Commercial Law: Text, Cases and Materials* (4th edn, OUP 2009) 400.

62. *Reardon Smith Line Ltd v Yngvar Hansen Tangen* [1976] 1 WLR 989 (HL) 998 (Lord Wilberforce).

Reardon Smith Line Ltd v Hansen Tangen
[1976] 1 WLR 989 (HL)[63]

FACTS: In order to help finance the construction of a tanker, it was chartered before work on its construction had even begun. The charterers sub-chartered the tanker to the claimant. The tanker did not yet have a name, so the charterparty referred to it by reference to the shipyard at which it was to be built, namely 'Yard No 354 at Osaka'. It transpired that the tanker was too large to be built at Osaka, so it was built at another shipyard in Oshima. By the time the tanker had been completed, the charter market had fallen due to an oil crisis, meaning that such tankers could be chartered for much less than the claimant had agreed to pay in the charterparty. The claimant therefore terminated the charterparty on the ground that the tanker was not built at the shipyard specified in the charterparty, and therefore it did not correspond with its description.

HELD: The House of Lords held that the claimant's termination of the charterparty was unlawful. The shipyard number did not form part of the description. Lord Wilberforce, Lord Simon, and Lord Kilbrandon held that even if a strict and technical view had to be taken as regards the description of unascertained future goods as to which each detail of the description must be assumed to be vital, it was right to treat contracts of sale of goods in a similar manner to other contracts generally so as to ask whether a particular item in a description constituted a 'substantial ingredient of the identity of the thing sold' and, only if it did, to treat it as a condition. In the present case, it was plain that the hull or yard number of the vessel 'was obviously immaterial to the parties'[64] so as not to raise it to a matter of fundamental obligation and thereby a condition of the contract.

The words 'Yard No 354 at Osaka' were not and were never intended to be part of the contract description of the vessel, but only a means of identifying it. The vessel tendered was the vessel that was contracted for. The House of Lords avoided an unsatisfactory outcome by holding that the words in question did not form part of the description; an outcome that the courts have used on several occasions to avoid the inflexible position evidenced in cases such as *Moore* and *Arcos*. Despite this, it is still the case that, in relation to words that do form part of the description, an extremely rigid approach is still adopted and the description must be strictly complied with in order to avoid breaching the term implied by s 13(1). The application of the *de minimis* rule to s 13(1) cases would appear to provide the only exception to this, so that 'microscopic deviations' from the description will not result in the term implied by s 13(1) being breached.[65]

Remedies

The term implied by s 13(1) is a condition.[66] Accordingly, breach of the term implied by s 13(1) will usually entitle the buyer to reject the goods, repudiate the contract, and recover damages.

---

63. This was not a sale of goods case, as the claimant had not contracted to purchase the tanker but to charter it. The claimant therefore pressed the House of Lords to apply by analogy the terms that would have been implied had it been a contract of sale.
64. [1976] 1 WLR 989 (HL) 1001 (Lord Simon).
65. *Arcos Ltd v EA Ronaasen & Son* [1933] AC 470 (HL) 479 (Lord Atkin).   66. SGA 1979, s 13(1A).

Section 14(2)—satisfactory quality

Consider the following example.

 ComCorp Ltd

ComCorp Ltd purchases laptop computers for several of its managers. One of the managers, Tom, who uses the laptop for business and personal use, notices that the laptop screen contains a small crack in the lower left corner and that the laptop housing is scuffed. The laptops were manufactured and sold by Mobile Hardware plc. ComCorp, disillusioned with the quality of Mobile Hardware's goods, wishes to reject Tom's laptop and obtain a refund, but Mobile Hardware states that, while it will repair any faulty goods, it will not provide a refund.

The question that arises is whether ComCorp can return the defective laptops and recover the purchase price. The answer can be found in what is perhaps the most important term implied by the SGA 1979, namely the term implied by s 14(2).

 SGA 1979, s 14(2)

Where the seller sells goods in the course of a business, there is an implied term that the goods supplied under the contract are of satisfactory quality.

Even before the enactment of the SGA 1893, the common law demanded that goods should meet a certain standard. For example, in *Gardiner v Gray*,[67] Lord Ellenborough stated that the contract goods must be 'saleable in the market' and that 'the purchaser cannot be supposed to buy goods to lay them on a dunghill'; this *dictum* being the precursor to the requirement of merchantable quality in the SGA 1893.

From 'merchantable' to 'satisfactory' quality

The term as to satisfactory quality implied by s 14(2) is of relatively recent origin—the original implied term required goods to be of 'merchantable' quality.[68] As one commentator stated, the expression 'merchantable quality ... always has been a commercial man's notion',[69] and, for a time, this was perfectly acceptable, as the Act primarily regulated dealings between commercial parties, and cases under the Act tended to involve goods that were not bought by consumers.[70] However, as time

---

67. (1815) 4 Campbell 144.   68. SGA 1893, s 14(2) (now repealed).

69. AG Guest, *Benjamin's Sale of Goods* (2nd edn, Sweet & Maxwell 1981) [808].

70. See e.g. *Henry Kendall & Sons v William Lillico & Sons Ltd* [1969] 2 AC 31 (HL) (Brazilian groundnut extractions); *Cehave NV v Bremer Handels GmbH (The Hansa Nord)* [1976] QB 44 (CA) (citrus pulp pellets).

progressed, the suitability of 'merchantable quality' as a standard came under question. The word 'merchantable' derived from Victorian case law and basically asked 'Were the goods of such quality that one merchant buying them from another, would have regarded them as suitable?'[71] A merchant who purchases goods that are unsatisfactory for one purpose can often sell them on for another purpose, thereby rendering them merchantable.[72] This led the courts to adopt a usability test, the narrowness of which can be seen in the following case.

 Henry Kendall & Sons v William Lillico & Sons Ltd [1969] 2 AC 31 (HL)

FACTS: The buyer purchased from the seller a quantity of animal feed for feeding to pheasants, partridges, and their chicks. Many of the birds died or were rendered unfit for breeding due to contaminant contained in some Brazilian groundnut extraction, which made up a proportion of the feed. It was discovered that the feed was not fit for certain birds, but could be safely fed to many other animals, such as cattle. The buyer recovered damages from the seller, and the seller then claimed an indemnity from the supplier of the feed, alleging, *inter alia*, that the term implied by s 14(2) had been breached.

HELD: It was held that the term implied by s 14(2) had not been breached. Lord Reid stated that goods would only be deemed unmerchantable if they 'were of no use for *any* purpose for which goods which complied with the description under which these goods were sold would normally be used'.[73] The feed was multi-purpose in that it could be fed to different types of animal. Accordingly, as it was still of use for one of its purposes, the goods were held to be merchantable.

COMMENT: It should be noted that the House of Lords held that the term as to fitness for purpose had been breached, enabling the seller to recover an indemnity from its supplier.

Under the usability test, providing that the goods were fit for one of the purposes for which those goods are commonly purchased, they would not be unmerchantable. However, this standard was clearly inappropriate in consumer sales. For example, a consumer who purchased a brand new car and, upon delivery, discovered a deep scratch in its bodywork, would not have succeeded were he to have alleged a breach of s 14(2), as the car was still usable. The courts eventually recognized the unsuitability of the usability test, and moved over to a test based on whether the goods were acceptable. The following case demonstrates how this broader test is much more suitable, especially in cases involving consumer sales.

---

71. Law Commission, *Sale and Supply of Goods* (Law Com No 160, 1987) para 3.7.
72. See Lord Reid in *Henry Kendall & Sons v William Lillico & Sons Ltd* [1969] 2 AC 31 (HL) 75, who stated that 'merchantable can only mean commercially saleable'.
73. [1969] 2 AC 31 (HL) 77 (emphasis added).

Rogers v Parish (Scarborough) Ltd [1987] QB 933 (CA)

FACTS: Rogers purchased a new Range Rover from Parish (Scarborough) Ltd ('Parish'). The car was defective and was replaced. The replacement car had several gearbox, engine, and bodywork defects, although it was still driveable. After several failed attempts by Parish to repair the car, Rogers rejected it, alleging, *inter alia*, that the term implied by s 14(2) had been breached. At first instance, the judge, applying the usability test, held that no breach had occurred as the vehicle was not unroadworthy and was still driveable. Rogers appealed.

HELD: The appeal was allowed. The Court of Appeal held that the term implied by s 14(2) had been breached. Mustill LJ stated that roadworthiness was not the only purpose of having such a vehicle and that other purposes would include 'not merely the buyer's purpose of driving the car from one place to another but of doing so with the appropriate degree of comfort, ease of handling and reliability and, one might add, of pride in the vehicle's outward and interior appearance'.[74] Accordingly, whilst the car was usable, it was certainly not acceptable and so Rogers was permitted to repudiate the contract.

★ See Ian Brown, 'The Meaning of Merchantable Quality in Sales of Goods: Quality or Fitness for Purpose?' [1987] LMCLQ 400

The increase in consumer sales and the move from usability to acceptability led the Law Commission to state that the concept of 'merchantable quality' was 'outmoded…and inappropriate in the context of a consumer transaction'.[75] It also added that the term 'concentrates too exclusively on fitness for purpose and does not make sufficiently clear that other aspects of quality, such as appearance and finish, and freedom from minor defects may also be important'.[76]

Accordingly, it was decided that the standard of 'merchantable quality' needed to be replaced with a more modern and appropriate standard. The Law Commission decided to recommend that the acceptability test form the basis for the new standard, under which goods would be required to be 'fully acceptable to a reasonable person, bearing in mind the description of the goods, their price, and all the other circumstances'.[77] However, when s 14(2) was eventually amended by the Sale and Supply of Goods Act 1994, the Law Commission's standard was not adopted and s 14(2) was amended to imply a term of 'satisfactory quality'. The government did, however, accept the Law Commission's recommendation[78] that a list of aspects of quality should be added to broaden the scope of the term and avoid the overemphasis on fitness for purpose that had hitherto existed. Before these aspects are discussed, it is important to understand the scope of the term implied by s 14(2).

Scope

Section 14(2) contains a number of important phrases that significantly impact upon the breadth of its scope.

---

74. [1987] QB 933 (CA) 944.
75. Law Commission, *Sale and Supply of Goods* (Law Com No 160, 1987) paras 2.9–2.10.
76. ibid para 2.9.   77. ibid para 3.19.   78. ibid paras 3.28–3.66.

'In the course of a business'

Goods sold privately are not required to be of 'satisfactory quality', as the term implied by s 14(2) is only implied into contracts where the goods are sold 'in the course of a business'. The status of the seller is therefore of crucial importance. Conversely, in terms of the *scope* of s 14(2), the buyer's identity is irrelevant,[79] as s 14(2) protects both business and consumer purchasers. The SGA 1979 does not in fact define the word 'business', but it does state that it will include 'a profession and the activities of any government department or local or public authority'.[80]

The phrase 'in the course of a business' is a wide one and will cover sales that are integral to the business, incidental sales that are regularly carried out, and one-off sales. Further, as the phrase '*a* business' is used, the sale need not relate to the *actual* business that is engaged in. The courts' liberal and purposive interpretation of the phrase can be seen in the following case.

 Stevenson v Rogers [1999] QB 1028 (CA)

FACTS: For over twenty years, Rogers had engaged in business as a fisherman. In 1983, he purchased a second fishing boat, the *Jelle* and, in 1986, he sold his first fishing boat, the *Dolly Mopp*. In 1988, after deciding to have a new custom-made boat built, he sold the *Jelle* to Stevenson. Stevenson contended that the boat was not of satisfactory quality. Rogers countered that the boat was not sold in the course of a business and therefore did not need to be. At first instance, the judge held that the sale was not in the course of a business as it was not an integral part of his business as a fisherman. Stevenson appealed.

HELD: The appeal was allowed. The Court of Appeal held that the sale was in the course of a business. Potter LJ stated that the words in s 14(2) should be construed 'at their wide face value'[81] and that there was no reason to 'reintroduce some implied qualification ... in order to narrow what appears to be the wide scope and apparent purpose of the words, which is to distinguish between a sale made in the course of a seller's business and a purely private sale of goods'.[82]

COMMENT: The decision in *Stevenson* has proven controversial. It certainly increases the scope of protection offered by s 14(2), as a sale will almost always be in the course of a business unless it is a purely private sale outside the confines of a business carried on by the seller. However, the case also creates two notable problems. First, the decision produces inflexibility insomuch as the regularity of the sale or how integral it is to the business is irrelevant. Second, as discussed later in this chapter, the phrase 'in the course of a business' is also used in the Unfair Contract Terms Act 1977 and, in relation to that Act, the courts have taken a more restrictive approach. The result is that a seller may be acting in the course of a business under s 14(2), but not acting in the course of a business under the 1977 Act. This lack of uniformity renders the law more complex than perhaps it need be. However, notwithstanding these criticisms, the law is now clear: for the purpose of the SGA 1979, a sale by a business is a sale in the course of a business.

★ See Len S Sealy, 'When is a Sale Made in the Course of a Business?' (1999) 58 CLJ 276

---

79. In terms of excluding liability for breach of the term implied by s 14(2), however, the buyer's status may be crucial—see p 382.
80. SGA 1979, s 61(1).   81. [1999] QB 1028 (CA) 1039.   82. ibid.

'Goods supplied under the contract'

The term is implied only in relation to goods 'supplied under the contract'.[83] This phrase makes clear what the courts had already held,[84] namely that the term does not simply apply to the goods that are sold, but can extend to other items, such as the containers in which the goods are supplied. In many cases, the goods sold will constitute the goods supplied under the contract but, as the following case demonstrates, this need not be the case.

 Wilson v Rickett Cockerell & Co Ltd [1954] 1 QB 598 (CA)

FACTS: The Wilsons, a husband and wife, purchased a tonne of Coalite from Rickett Cockerell & Co Ltd ('Rickett'). Mrs Wilson used the Coalite to make a fire, and an explosion occurred due to a piece of explosive material that had been inadvertently delivered with the Coalite. The Wilsons sought damages on the ground that the goods breached the term implied by s 14(2). At first instance, the claim failed, as the judge held that the explosive material did not form part of the goods. The Wilsons appealed.

HELD: The appeal was allowed and the Wilsons obtained damages. Denning LJ stated that s 14(2) 'applies to all goods so delivered, whether they conform to the contract or not: that is, in this case, to the whole consignment, including the offending piece, and not merely to the Coalite alone'.[85]

Situations expressly outside the scope of s 14(2)

Section 14 itself provides that the term implied by s 14(2) will not be implied in four situations:

1. The term will not extend to any matters making the goods unsatisfactory that were specifically drawn to the buyer's attention before the contract is made.[86] It has been argued that the burden of establishing this exception is on the seller, although there is no requirement that the seller must be the person to draw the buyer's attention to the defect.[87]

2. Where the contract is one for sale by sample, the term implied by s 14(2) will not extend to matters making the goods unsatisfactory, which would have been apparent on a reasonable examination of the sample.[88] This makes clear that, in the event of a conflict between s 14(2) and s 15(2)(c), the latter provision prevails.

3. The term will not be implied where the sale is effected through an agent who is acting for a principal who is not selling in the course of a business and either the buyer knows this, or reasonable steps have been taken to bring this to the buyer's attention.[89]

4. The term will not extend to any matter making the quality of the goods unsatisfactory where the buyer examines the goods before the contract is made, which

Contracts for the sale of goods by sample are discussed at p 379

---

83. SGA 1979, s 14(2).   84. *Geddling v Marsh* [1920] 1 KB 668 (KB).   85. [1954] 1 QB 598 (CA) 607.
86. SGA 1979, s 14(2C)(a).
87. Michael G Bridge, *Benjamin's Sale of Goods* (8th edn, Sweet & Maxwell 2010) [11-041].
88. SGA 1979, s 14(2C)(c).
89. ibid s 14(5). In such a case, the term implied by s 14(3) will also not be implied.

that examination ought to reveal.[90] For this exception to arise, the buyer must actually examine the goods in question, although he is under no obligation to do so. It might appear rather odd that a buyer who does not examine the goods before agreeing to buy them should be in a stronger position than a buyer who does examine them, but that is the effect of s 14(2C)(b). For this reason, a buyer would be well advised either not to examine the goods at all or to ensure that his examination is as thorough as reasonably possible. Of course, a buyer might not be expected to notice every defect and the rule in s 14(2C)(b) may depend on the nature of the examination. For example, a buyer who examines the body-work of a car he is looking to buy is likely to be expected to notice any defects in the bodywork, but unless he examines the car mechanically, it might not be reasonable to expect mechanical defects to be revealed. The effect of s 14(2C)(b) can be seen in the following case.

 ***Bramhill v Edwards* [2004] EWCA Civ 403**

FACTS: The Bramhills (a husband and wife) purchased a motor-home from Edwards. It was 102 inches wide, which was 2 inches wider than that permitted under the relevant road regulations. The Bramhills had inspected, but not measured, the vehicle before purchase. It was only after they had used the vehicle for about six or seven months that they measured it and found it to be 102 inches wide. It was then some months later that they formally complained about its width. The main issues for the Court were whether, because it was too wide to be driven legally on the roads in the UK, it was of satisfactory quality and, if not, whether s 14(2C)(b) disentitled the Bramhills from relying on any such breach that might be found on the ground that they examined it before purchase and that their examination should have revealed its unlawfully excessive width. Edwards accepted that the vehicle was in excess of the maximum permitted width and therefore could not be driven lawfully on the roads in the UK. However, he said that the relevant authorities turned a blind eye to such minor infringements of the Regulations.

HELD: The Court of Appeal confirmed the decision of the trial judge, who held that the vehicle was of satisfactory quality. Although the test is objective, the reasonable person referred to in s 14(2A) must be one who is in the position of the buyer with knowledge of all relevant background facts. The Bramhills were knowledgeable about motor homes and were aware that the authorities turned a blind eye to the illegality and this was a common occurrence. The Court also considered (*obiter*, because of the finding that the vehicle was of satisfactory quality) that s 14(2C)(b) would have disentitled the Bramhills from relying on any breach that might have been found because they had examined the vehicle before purchase and their examination, had they gone on to measure it, should have revealed its unlawfully excessive width.

★ See Christian Twigg-Flesner, 'Examination Prior to Purchase: A Cautionary Note' (2005) 121 LQR 205

When will goods be of 'satisfactory quality'?

The SGA 1893 did not provide a definition of the phrase 'merchantable quality'. On this, the Law Commission stated that 'it is not satisfactory for an Act which purports to codify a whole branch of the law to use a technical term, the meaning of which

---

90. ibid s 14(2C)(b).

is far from self-evident and becomes meaningful only when the case law is looked at'.[91] The Law Commission therefore recommended that a statutory definition be introduced, which can today be found in s 14(2A), which provides that 'goods are of satisfactory quality if they meet the standard that a reasonable person would regard as satisfactory, taking account of any description of the goods, the price (if relevant) and all the other relevant circumstances'.

This definition establishes a largely objective standard, so it will be irrelevant whether or not the seller or buyer believed the goods to be satisfactory. However, the Court of Appeal has stated that, although the test is objective, it would be inappropriate to base it on a reasonable person with no knowledge of the facts of the case: instead the 'reasonable person must be one who is in the position of the buyer, with his knowledge'.[92]

The s 14(2A) definition also identifies two specific factors to take into account. The first is the description of the goods.[93] Clearly, the description of the goods will be a significant factor in determining their quality, especially given that many purchasers rely solely on descriptions attached to the goods. The following case demonstrates how the description was a significant factor in determining whether the goods were of merchantable quality.

BS Brown & Son Ltd v Craiks Ltd [1970] 1 WLR 752 (HL)

FACTS: BS Brown & Son Ltd ('Brown') purchased from Craiks Ltd a consignment of cloth, but there was a misunderstanding as to the use Brown was to make of the cloth. Brown intended to resell the cloth to dressmakers, whereas Craiks believed the cloth would be for industrial use. The cloth complied with the contractual description but, while it was fit for industrial use, it was not suitable for dressmaking. Accordingly, Brown rejected the goods, alleging that the term implied by s 14(2) had been breached.

HELD: The House of Lords held that the cloth was of merchantable quality. The goods complied with the contract description and, as Brown had not informed Craiks that the cloth would be used to make dresses, there were no grounds to hold that the goods were not of merchantable quality. The real question was whether or not the goods were of use for any purpose for which goods complying with the description under which they were sold would normally be used.

The second factor is the price of the goods.[94] Clearly, whether or not goods are satisfactory can depend on their price. One would expect premium goods sold at a

---

91. Law Commission, *Exemption Clauses in Contracts. First Report: Amendments to the Sale of Goods Act 1893* (Law Com No 24, 1973) para 42. Similar criticism can be levelled at the current standard of 'satisfactory quality'.
92. *Brambill v Edwards* [2004] EWCA Civ 403, [2004] 2 Lloyd's Rep 653 [39] (Auld LJ), approving AG Guest, *Benjamin's Sale of Goods* (6th edn, Sweet & Maxwell 2003) [11-049].
93. There is debate as to whether the word 'description' under s 14(2) is given a wider definition than under s 13. See the contrasting opinions of Stuart-Smith and Slade LJJ in *Harlingdon and Leinster Enterprises Ltd v Christopher Hull Fine Art Ltd* [1991] 1 QB 564 (CA) 583, 586.
94. For a more detailed discussion on the relevance of price, see Patrick S Atiyah, John N Adams, and Hector Macqueen, *Atiyah's Sale of Goods* (12th edn, Pearson 2010) 183–6.

high price to be of a higher quality than low-cost, bargain goods. However, price will not always be a consideration, which is why s 14(2A) states that price should only be taken into account 'if relevant'. It is, however, likely that the price of the goods will often be relevant, especially in cases that involve high-[95] or low-priced goods, or second-hand goods.

Thain v Anniesland Trade Centre
1997 SLT (Sh Ct) 102

FACTS: Thain purchased a second-hand Renault car from Anniesland Trade Centre ('Anniesland') for £2,995. The car was around five years old and had 80,000 miles on the odometer. Two weeks later, it developed a gearbox fault. Thain insisted that the gearbox be replaced but, given the value of the car, Anniesland stated that this was not economical. Accordingly, Thain rejected the car and sought recovery of the purchase price on the ground that it was not of satisfactory quality.

HELD: The court held that the term implied by s 14(2) had not been breached. The Sheriff Principal stated:

> people who buy second-hand cars get them at less than the original price in large part because second-hand cars have attached to them increased risk of expensive repairs. The price of the Renault, £2,995, was considered reasonable because there was the risk of expensive repair attached to the Renault. In choosing to buy the Renault the pursuer accepted the risk of expensive repair inevitably attaching to a car that was between five and six years old and which had over 80,000 miles on the clock. [Thain] might have insulated herself from that risk for three months had she been prepared to pay [Anniesland's] price for a warranty, but she preferred not to pay for a warranty. She accordingly assumed the risk of expensive repair.[96]

⭐ See Jennifer Hamilton, 'Thain v Anniesland Trade Centre' (1999) 4 SLPQ 58

In 2002, the SGA 1979 was amended by the Sale and Supply of Goods to Consumers Regulations 2002,[97] and a new s 14(2D) was inserted which provides that, where the buyer deals as a consumer, the relevant circumstances mentioned in s 14(2A) include 'any public statements on the specific characteristics of the goods made about them by the seller, the producer or his representative, particularly in advertising or on labelling'. However, such a statement will not amount to a relevant circumstance if the seller can show that:

- at the time the contract was made, he was not, and could not reasonably have been, aware of the statement;[98] or
- before the contract was made, the statement had been withdrawn in public or, to the extent that it contained anything which was incorrect or misleading, it had been corrected in public;[99] or

95. See *Clegg v Olle Andersson T/A Nordic Marine* [2003] EWCA Civ 320, [2003] 2 Lloyd's Rep 32 [72], where Hale LJ stated that 'in some cases, such as a high priced quality product, the customer may be entitled to expect that it is free from even minor defects, in other words perfect or nearly so'.
96. 1997 SLT (Sh Ct) 102, 106 (N D Macleod QC).   97. SI 2002/3045.
98. SGA 1979, s 14(2E)(a).   99. ibid s 14(2E)(b).

- the decision to buy the goods could not have been influenced by the statement.[100]

Aspects of quality

As already noted, the Law Commission was concerned that, when determining whether goods were of merchantable quality, the courts were overemphasizing fitness for purpose as the only criterion for determining quality. Accordingly, the Law Commission recommended that a list of aspects of quality be introduced into the SGA 1979 that would, if relevant, be taken into account by the courts. Section 14(2B) now provides a non-exhaustive list of five aspects of quality that are, in appropriate cases, to be taken into account when determining the quality of the goods. At this stage, three points should be noted:

1. Section 14(2B) begins by stating that the quality of the goods includes their 'state and condition'. This could lead the courts to conclude that the labelling and packaging of the goods are also covered by s 14(2), as they can impact upon the state or condition of the goods.[101]

2. By the time s 14(2B) was inserted into the SGA 1979, the courts had already come to recognize the validity of many of the aspects listed within it. Accordingly, with one notable exception, s 14(2B) does not significantly alter the law.

3. The aspects listed in s 14(2B) will only apply 'in appropriate cases'. Accordingly, goods do not need to satisfy all the aspects and there may be cases when some (or all) of the aspects listed will not be relevant.

The first aspect is 'fitness for all the purposes for which goods of the kind in question are commonly supplied'.[102] As noted, this aspect had, in many cases, been regarded as the sole criterion for determining the quality of the goods. By placing it amongst four other aspects, the Law Commission intended to 'demote' fitness for purpose and indicate strongly that quality should not be determined solely by reference to usability.[103] Accordingly, it represents a notable departure from previous law, which stated that goods would be merchantable if they were fit for any of their purposes for which goods of that type were commonly bought.[104] Now, where this aspect of quality is relevant, in order for goods to be of satisfactory quality, they will need to be fit for *all* of their normal purposes (goods bought for abnormal purposes are covered by the term implied by s 14(3), which is discussed later).

The second aspect is 'appearance and finish'.[105] The courts[106] had already recognized that buyers of goods (especially consumers) purchased goods, not just for their functionality, but also for their aesthetic qualities. The importance of this aspect will depend upon the facts of the case. For example, scratches in the bodywork of a new car would be likely to render the goods unsatisfactory. Conversely, one might expect to find scratches in the bodywork of a second-hand car.

---

100. ibid s 14(2E)(c).   101. *Niblett v Confectioners' Materials Co Ltd* [1921] 3 KB 387 (CA).
102. SGA 1979, s 14(2B)(a).
103. Law Commission, *Sale and Supply of Goods* (Law Com No 160, 1987) para 3.31.
104. *M/S Aswan Engineering Establishment Co v Lupdine Ltd* [1987] 1 WLR 1 (CA).
105. SGA 1979, s 14(2B)(b).
106. Notably Mustill LJ in *Rogers v Parish (Scarborough) Ltd* [1987] QB 933 (CA) (this case is discussed on p 364).

The third aspect is 'freedom from minor defects'.[107] Originally, the Law Commission recommended that 'appearance, finish and freedom from minor defects' should be regarded as one aspect of quality.[108] However, the Law Commission became concerned that this could be interpreted to mean that the minor defect was one that must relate to appearance or finish, and so it instead recommended that the two matters be separated.[109] As already discussed, under the old law, the courts adopted a usability test, under which goods that remained usable would not be regarded as unmerchantable, even if they contained minor (or, in some cases, not so minor) defects. Section 14(2B)(c) makes it clear that this is no longer the case and goods may be unsatisfactory if minor defects are present. That these minor defects can be quickly or easily remedied will not be enough to render the goods satisfactory.[110]

The fourth aspect is 'safety'.[111] In a series of cases (most of which involved motor vehicles), the courts acknowledged that unsafe goods would, depending on the circumstances, almost certainly be unmerchantable.[112] Despite this, the Law Commission felt that 'safety' should be included within the list of aspects of quality because, given its importance, its omission was odd, especially given that safety has become an increasingly important factor in consumer goods, particularly in relation to goods such as electronics and vehicles.[113] The requirement as to safety will extend not only to the goods themselves, but also to their packaging and instructions. Instructions will be of particular importance for goods that are safe only if used in a certain way.

The fifth and final aspect is 'durability'.[114] Prior to the introduction of s 14(2B), the higher courts had long held that goods that became defective following purchase might, depending on the facts, not be of merchantable or satisfactory quality.[115] The Act, however, made no mention of durability and the Law Commission was concerned that, outside the higher courts, it may not be clear that goods should be reasonably durable.[116] Although it was suggested that durability should be the subject of its own implied term, the Law Commission wisely decided that it should form part of the implied term as to satisfactory quality. It should be noted that s 14(2B)(e) does not require the goods to remain of the same standard (i.e. satisfactory quality) as when they were first purchased, as many goods will deteriorate in quality through use or the passage of time. The obvious issue that arises is for how long following purchase does the durability requirement continue? The Law Commission decided not to specify a maximum length of time, but instead stated that goods would be

---

107. SGA 1979 s 14(2B)(c).

108. Law Commission, *Sale and Supply of Goods* (Working Paper No 58, 1983) para 4.15.

109. Law Commission, *Sale and Supply of Goods* (Law Com No 160, 1987) paras 3.38–3.39.

110. See e.g. *Jackson v Rotax Motor and Cycle Co Ltd* [1910] 2 KB 937 (CA) 943–44 (Cozens-Hardy MR); *Rogers v Parish (Scarborough) Ltd* [1987] QB 933 (CA) 944 (Mustill LJ).

111. SGA 1979, s 14(2B)(d).

112. See e.g. *Lee v York Coach & Marine* [1977] RTR 35 (CA); *Bernstein v Pamson Motors (Golders Green) Ltd* [1987] 2 All ER 220 (QB).

113. Law Commission, *Sale and Supply of Goods* (Law Com No 160, 1987) paras 3.44–3.46.

114. SGA 1979, s 14(2B)(e).

115. See e.g. *Beer v Walker* (1877) 46 LJQB 677; *Mash and Murrell v Joseph I Emmanuel* [1961] 1 All ER 485 (QB); *Crowther v Shannon* [1975] 1 WLR 30 (CA); *Lambert v Lewis* [1982] AC 225 (HL).

116. Law Commission, *Sale and Supply of Goods* (Law Com No 160, 1987) para 2.15.

required to last for a reasonable time.[117] This is logical, as it would be impossible to provide a definitive period of time, given the numerous factors that may be relevant (e.g. price; how the goods have been looked after; what the normal life expectancy is of the goods; the description of the goods, etc.). Accordingly, whether goods are sufficiently durable will depend upon the facts of the case. Whilst this does make the courts' task more difficult and does create a measure of uncertainty, the Law Commission felt that this was 'unavoidable'.[118]

Remedies

The term implied by s 14(2) is a condition.[119] Accordingly, breach of the term implied by s 14(2) will usually entitle the buyer to reject the goods, repudiate the contract, and recover damages.

Section 14(3)—fitness for purpose

Consider the following example.

 ComCorp Ltd

ComCorp Ltd launches a new product, and to enable it effectively to target the potential market for that product, it engages a software engineer, MarkeTech Ltd, to create a piece of software that could, based on criteria provided by ComCorp, create a list of geographical areas where the product would be likely to sell well. The disk containing the software is delivered to ComCorp. However, the software program contains an error and, as a result, the product is marketed to areas that do not fit with ComCorp's criteria. The product sells poorly and ComCorp alleges that it is due to the error contained in the software.

The issue that arises is whether ComCorp can recover the price paid for the software and obtain damages from MarkeTech for the loss of business. The answer lies in s 14(3), which provides that:

 SGA 1979, s 14(3)

Where the seller sells goods in the course of a business and the buyer, expressly or by implication, makes known—
   (a) to the seller, or
   (b) where the purchase price or part of it is payable by instalments and the goods were previously sold by a credit-broker to the seller, to that credit-broker

---

117. ibid para 3.51.   118. ibid para 3.49.   119. SGA 1979, s 14(6).

> any particular purpose for which the goods are being bought, there is an implied term that the goods supplied under the contract are reasonably fit for that purpose, whether or not that is a purpose for which such goods are commonly supplied, except where the circumstances show that the buyer does not rely, or that it is unreasonable for him to rely, on the skill or judgment of the seller or credit-broker.

Like s 14(2), the term implied by s 14(3) will only be implied where the goods are sold 'in the course of a business' and will be implied in relation to 'goods supplied under the contract'. These phrases are to be given the same meaning as under s 14(2).

Communication of particular purpose(s)

Where the purpose for which the goods are bought is obvious (i.e. because they have only one common use), or where the goods will be used for one of several common purposes, then the seller will be taken to have such knowledge and the buyer will not need to make the purpose expressly known. Thus, where the buyer broke his tooth whilst eating a bun that contained a stone, the seller was taken to know the purpose for which the buyer purchased the bun (i.e. to eat it).[120]

However, where the buyer requires the goods for a non-common or abnormal purpose, then the term implied by s 14(3) will only be implied if the buyer communicates that purpose to the seller, as the following case demonstrates.

Griffiths v Peter Conway Ltd [1939] 1 All ER 685 (CA)[121]

FACTS: Griffiths purchased a Harris tweed coat from Peter Conway Ltd. Shortly thereafter, she developed dermatitis, which was found to have been caused by the coat. It transpired that Griffiths had abnormally sensitive skin, and that the coat would not have caused a person with normal skin to develop dermatitis. Griffiths commenced proceedings, alleging that the coat was not fit for purpose.

HELD: The claim failed. Griffiths required the coat for a particular purpose (i.e. that it should not adversely affect her abnormally sensitive skin) and, as she had not made this particular purpose known to Peter Conway Ltd, the term implied by s 14(3) did not apply.

Reasonably fit for purpose

The standard required is that goods are reasonably fit for purpose, thereby clearly indicating that goods need not be perfect in this regard. What is reasonable will depend upon the circumstances of the case, bearing in mind the characteristics of the goods such as age, price, and so on. Second-hand goods may not need to reach the same standard as new ones, as the following case demonstrates.

---

120. *Chaproinière v Mason* (1905) 21 TLR 633 (CA).
121. See also *Slater v Finning Ltd* [1997] AC 473 (HL).

Bartlett v Sidney Marcus Ltd [1965] 1 WLR 1013 (CA)

FACTS: Bartlett purchased a second-hand Jaguar car from Sidney Marcus Ltd ('SM'), a motor dealer. SM informed Bartlett that the clutch was defective, but a minor repair could remedy the defect. On the understanding that Bartlett would repair the clutch, the price was discounted by £25 to £950. Bartlett drove the car for several hundred miles before taking it to a garage for repair, where it was discovered that, in order to repair the clutch, the engine would need to be dismantled, at a cost of £84. Bartlett alleged, *inter alia*, that the car was not reasonably fit for purpose. The trial judge agreed and ordered SM to pay £45 in damages. SM appealed.

HELD: The appeal was allowed. The Court of Appeal held that the car was fit for purpose. Lord Denning MR stated:

> the car was far from perfect. It required a good deal of work to be done on it. But so do many second-hand cars. A buyer should realise that when he buys a second-hand car defects may appear sooner or later ... Even when he buys from a dealer the most he can require is that it should be reasonably fit for the purpose of being driven along the road. This car came up to that requirement.[122]

Other factors may also be relevant:

- *Durability*: it is likely that case law concerning durability of goods under s 14(2) will also apply to s 14(3), so that goods that become defective or malfunction within a reasonable time following delivery may not be fit for purpose.[123] Although the goods must be reasonably fit for purpose at the time of delivery, they must continue to be so for a reasonable period afterwards.[124]

- *The buyer's use of the goods*: if the buyer misuses the goods, even if those goods are unsatisfactory or unfit for purpose, but the loss sustained is in fact caused by the buyer's misuse, then it may be the case that the term implied by s 14(3) will not be breached.[125]

- *The goods' packaging and labelling*: goods which, in themselves, could be fit for purpose might nevertheless become unfit if not packaged correctly or accompanied by suitable warnings/instructions. This is particularly likely in the case of potentially dangerous goods that need to be handled, stored, or used in a certain way.[126]

Section 14(3) imposes an objective, strict liability standard. Accordingly, it is no defence for the seller to show that he did not know of the defect or that he could not have known of it. As Lord Reid has stated, s 14(3) 'covers not only defects which the seller ought to have detected but also defects which are latent in the sense that even the utmost skill and judgment on the part of the seller would not have detected them'.[127] The following case demonstrates this.

---

122. [1965] 1 WLR 1013 (CA) 1017.   123. See e.g. *Crowther v Shannon Motor Co* [1975] 1 WLR 30 (CA).
124. *Lambert v Lewis* [1982] AC 225 (HL).   125. ibid.
126. See e.g. *Vacwell Engineering Co Ltd v BDH Chemicals Ltd* [1971] 1 QB 88 (QB) (chemicals that were not stored correctly, which exploded).
127. *Henry Kendall & Sons v William Lillico & Sons Ltd* [1969] 2 AC 31 (HL) 84.

Frost v Aylesbury Dairy Co Ltd [1905] 1 KB 608 (CA)

FACTS: Frost purchased milk from Aylesbury Dairy Co Ltd ('Aylesbury'), which was then consumed by himself and his wife. The milk was infected with typhoid, which the wife contracted, and from which she later died. Frost alleged that the milk was not fit for purpose. Aylesbury argued that Frost had not relied on the seller's skill and judgment, as no amount of skill or judgment could have enabled it to discover the defect in the milk.

HELD: The milk was not fit for purpose. The fact that Aylesbury could not have discovered the typhoid was irrelevant, as it matters not whether the defect was discoverable, patent, or latent.

The final point to note is that it is for the purchaser of the goods to prove on the balance of probabilities that the goods sold were not fit for their purpose.[128]

Reliance

The term implied by s 14(3) will not be implied 'where the circumstances show that the buyer does not rely, or that it is unreasonable for him to rely, on the skill or judgment of the seller or credit-broker'. Initially, all that the buyer need do is establish that the seller knew of the purpose for which the buyer purchased the goods, and the courts will then presume that the buyer relied on the seller's skill and judgment by purchasing the goods that the seller supplied as fit for that purpose.[129] As Lord Wright explained in *Grant v Australian Knitting Mills Ltd*,[130] 'the reliance will be in general inferred from the fact that a buyer goes to the shop in confidence that the tradesman has selected his stock with skill and judgment'.[131] However, where the buyer requests the goods by their trade name in circumstances that exclude any discussion about their suitability, then he will not be relying on the skill or judgment of the seller.[132]

The seller may be able to rebut the presumption by demonstrating that the buyer did not rely on the seller's skill and judgment. For example, in the following case, the presumption was rebutted because it was clear that the buyer relied upon his own skill and judgment, and not that of the seller.

Teheran-Europe Co Ltd v ST Belton (Tractors) Ltd [1968] 2 QB 545 (CA)

FACTS: Teheran-Europe Co Ltd ('Teheran-Europe') was a Persian (Iranian) company that carried on business in Tehran as an importer of machinery. Its managing director visited London to inspect a type of mobile air compressor being sold by ST Belton (Tractors) Ltd ('Belton'). Teheran-Europe ordered twelve of the compressors and informed Belton that they were required for resale in Persia. It transpired that the compressors were not suitable

---

128. *Leicester Circuits Ltd v Coates Brothers plc* [2003] EWCA Civ 290.
129. *Henry Kendall & Sons v William Lillico & Sons Ltd* [1969] 2 AC 31 (HL) 80 (Lord Reid).
130. [1936] AC 85 (PC).   131. ibid 99.   132. *Baldry v Marshall* [1925] 1 KB 260 (CA).

for resale under Persian law and Teheran-Europe therefore alleged, *inter alia*, that the term implied by s 14(3) had been breached.

HELD: The Court of Appeal held that the term implied by s 14(3) had not been breached. Lord Denning MR explained the position in the following way:

> The particular purpose must be made known 'so as to show that the buyer relies on the seller's skill or judgment.' That means that the buyer makes the particular purpose known to the seller in such a way that the seller knows that he is being relied upon. That cannot be said here. The sellers here did not know they were being relied on for resale in Persia. They knew nothing of conditions in Persia. The buyers knew all about those conditions. The buyers saw the machine here. They read its description. They relied upon their own skill and judgment to see that it was suitable for resale in Persia, and not on the seller's. At all events, they did not make the purpose known to the seller in such circumstances as to show him that they relied on the seller's skill and judgment. So I do not think there was an implied term that they should be fit for the purpose of being resold in Persia.[133]

 See AH Hudson, 'Privity and the Foreign Principal' (1969) 32 MLR 207

Even if reliance is present, the term implied by s 14(3) will not be implied if the seller can demonstrate that such reliance was unreasonable.

Partial reliance

In many cases, the buyer will rely on a mixture of his own knowledge and experience, and that of the seller. Where such partial reliance exists, the courts will seek to determine whether the unsuitability of the goods lay within the area of expertise of the buyer or of the seller. If the goods are not fit for purpose due to an issue that lies within the buyer's own area of expertise, then the term implied by s 14(3) will not be breached. Conversely, if the issue was within the seller's area of expertise, then the term will be breached, as occurred in the following case.

Cammell Laird & Co Ltd v Manganese Bronze & Brass Co Ltd [1934] AC 402 (HL)

FACTS: Cammell Laird & Co Ltd ('Cammell Laird'), a firm of shipbuilders, had agreed to build two ships for a third party. Cammell Laird sub-contracted the construction of the propellers to Manganese Bronze & Brass Co Ltd ('Manganese'). Cammell Laird provided Manganese with the broad specifications of the propellers, but the exact details of the propellers (e.g. thickness of the blades) would be a matter for Manganese's skill and judgment. The propellers were defective as they were too thin. Accordingly, Cammell Laird sought damages on the ground that the propellers were not fit for purpose.

HELD: Cammell Laird's action succeeded. Lord Warrington stated:

> reliance need not be exclusive. Here there was a substantial area outside the specification, which was not covered by its directions and was therefore necessarily left to the skill and judgment of the seller. Without attempting to express an opinion on the actual cause of the trouble, I think it is clear that it arose from some defect in the seller's area.[134]

---

133. [1968] 2 QB 545 (CA) 554.   134. [1934] AC 402 (HL) 414.

Many of the above principles were relevant in the following case, which also usefully set out the questions the courts should consider when faced with a possible breach of the term implied by s 14(3).

 BSS Group plc v Makers (UK) Ltd (t/a Allied Services) [2011] EWCA Civ 809

FACTS: BSS Group plc ('BSS') had supplied Makers (UK) Ltd ('Makers') with materials, including piping, adaptors, and valves, for the installation of a new plumbing system in a public house. A particular part, 'Uponor', was used for the project. Makers requested further materials from BSS, specifically identifying that they were to be used in the same project. BSS supplied a different type of valve that was incompatible with the adaptor. A connection became insecure under pressure, resulting in substantial flooding of the public house. Since BSS had known that Makers was using an Uponor system, having previously supplied Uponor components for the same project, it was an irresistible inference from Makers' enquiry regarding further parts that it was making known to BSS its intention to use the valves as a device intended to regulate or control the flow of water in pipes used in the project. It was also an obvious inference that it was making known to BSS that it intended to use such valves in conjunction with the Uponor plastic piping that BSS was aware it was using. At the very least, it ought to have been apparent to BSS that Makers was likely to so use the valves and Makers had therefore made known a particular purpose for which the valves were intended to be used. The trial judge, in holding that the goods were not fit for purpose, stated that Makers had expressly, or at least impliedly, made it known to BSS that the valves were to be used with Uponor piping and had relied on BSS's skill and judgment as to the compatibility of the parts. BSS appealed.

HELD: The Court of Appeal held that the relevant questions for assessing a claim for a breach of s 14(3) were those identified by Clarke LJ in *Jewson Ltd v Boyhan*:[135]

(a) whether the buyer, expressly or by implication, had made known to the seller the purpose for which the goods were being bought;
(b) if so, whether they were reasonably fit for that purpose;
(c) if they were not reasonably fit for that purpose, whether the seller had shown that the buyer had not relied upon its skill and judgment or, if it had, that it had been unreasonable to do so.

Applying the above, the Court dismissed the appeal and upheld the trial judge's decision for the reasons he originally stated.

Relationship between s 14(2) and (3)

From the cases discussed, it can be seen that goods deemed not fit for purpose could also be regarded as of unsatisfactory quality and, indeed, it is common to plead a breach of both implied terms. However, there are two crucial differences between them. First, the term implied by s 14(3) relates to 'any particular purpose for which the goods are being bought', whereas s 14(2) is more concerned with 'fitness for all

---

135. [2003] EWCA Civ 1030, [2004] 1 Lloyd's Rep 505 [54]–[58].

the purposes for which goods of the kind in question are commonly supplied'. The practical difference between particular and common purposes was discussed in the following case.

 Jewson Ltd v Boyhan [2003] EWCA Civ 1030

FACTS: Boyhan, a property developer, acquired a building that he intended to convert into flats, which were then to be sold. Individual heating boilers needed to be installed in the flats, but it would have been prohibitively expensive to install gas boilers. Boyhan contacted Jewson Ltd, a builders' merchants, who recommended a particular type of electric boiler. Relying on this, Boyhan purchased a number of boilers from Jewson, and they appeared to work well. However, it transpired that the boilers reduced the SAP rating[136] of the flats to an unacceptable level, which made the flats less attractive to potential buyers. Boyhan therefore refused to pay for the boilers, alleging that they breached the terms implied by s 14(2) and (3). Jewson sued to recover the cost of the boilers.

HELD: The claim succeeded. As the boilers functioned perfectly well as boilers, there was no breach of the term implied by s 14(2). Boyhan had not communicated to Jewson the need to have a low SAP rating, so there was also no breach of the term implied by s 14(3). As to the relationship between the two subsections, Clarke LJ stated:

> the function of section 14(2), by contrast with section 14(3), is to establish a general standard of quality which goods are required to reach. It is not designed to ensure that goods are fit for a particular purpose made known to the seller. That is the function of section 14(3).[137]

★ See Christian Twigg-Flesner, 'The Relationship Between Satisfactory Quality and Fitness for Purpose' (2004) 63 CLJ 22

Second, each term is subject to limitations that the other is not subject to, for example:

- the term implied by s 14(3) will not be implied where the buyer does not rely on the seller's skill and judgment, or where it would be unreasonable to rely on such judgment. The term implied by s 14(2) is not subject to these limitations;
- the express limitations on the term implied by s 14(2) found in s 14(2C) do not apply to the term implied by s 14(3).

Remedies

The term implied by s 14(3) is a condition.[138] Accordingly, breach of this term will usually entitle the buyer to reject the goods, repudiate the contract, and recover damages.

---

136. The Standard Assessment Procedure (SAP) rating is used to measure energy efficiency. A low rating renders the dwellings less attractive financially and could also make it more difficult for would-be buyers to obtain a mortgage.

137. [2003] EWCA Civ 1030, [2004] 1 Lloyd's Rep 505 [68].   138. SGA 1979, s 14(6).

Section 15—sale by sample

Consider the following example.

Eg **ComCorp Ltd**

A number of ComCorp's employees claim that their uncomfortable office chairs are causing them back pain. ComCorp decides to provide all office workers with ergonomically designed chairs and adjustable footrests. Office Supplies Ltd provides ComCorp with a sample office chair and footrest and, after testing the products, ComCorp purchases 150 of these chairs and footrests. Of the 150 footrests purchased, around 60 of them could not be adjusted due to a manufacturing defect that was not present in the sample. Subsequently, all the chairs (including chairs sent out as samples) were found to contain a design defect that caused them to become unstable after a minimal amount of use.

The question that arises is whether ComCorp can return the chairs and footrests and recover the purchase price. The answer can be found in s 15(2), which provides that:

SGA 1979, s 15(2)

In the case of a contract for sale by sample there is an implied term—

(a) that the bulk will correspond with the sample in quality;
(b) [repealed]
(c) that the goods will be free from defect making their quality unsatisfactory, which would not be apparent on reasonable examination of the sample.

Section 15 implies one two-part term into contracts of sale, but for ease of exposition, each part will be regarded as a separate term. It is important to note that the terms implied by s 15(2) are implied only into contracts for 'sale by sample'. Unfortunately, the Act's definition of 'sale by sample' has been described as 'not at all helpful',[139] and merely provides that '[a] contract of sale is a contract for sale by sample where there is an express or implied term to that effect in the contract'.[140] Accordingly, the mere fact that the seller has exhibited a sample of the goods to the buyer (for example, by displaying them in a shop window) will not usually, in itself, make the sale one by sample.[141] A seller may produce samples merely to indicate the nature of the goods and may not intend the sample to be compared to the bulk. In order for a sale to be one by sample, it will need to be shown that, objectively, the parties intended the sale to be one by sample, or that the sample was intended to

---

139. Michael G Bridge, *Benjamin's Sale of Goods* (8th edn, Sweet & Maxwell 2010) [11-074].
140. SGA 1979, s 15(1).
141. *Gardiner v Gray* (1815) 4 Campbell 144 (Assizes).

form a basis of comparison for the bulk. This could occur in several ways, including the following:

- The contract may contain an express term stating that the sale is one by sample, or stating that the bulk must correspond to the sample.[142] In such a case, the contract will almost certainly be a sale by sample.
- No express term may be present, but it may be the case that a particular trade or custom indicates that sales by sample are normal practice.[143]

An important consideration in determining whether or not a sale is by sample is an understanding of what a sample is supposed to achieve. In *James Drummond & Sons v EH Van Ingen & Co Ltd*,[144] Lord Macnaghten explained:

> the office of a sample is to present to the eye the real meaning and intention of the parties with regard to the subject matter of the contract which, owing to the imperfection of language, it may be difficult or impossible to express in words. The sample speaks for itself.[145]

Bulk must correspond with sample in quality

The first term implied by s 15 can be found in s 15(2)(a), which provides that the quality of the bulk will correspond with the quality of the sample. However, as Lord Macnaghten pointed out in *James Drummond*,[146] this does not mean that the bulk must correspond with the sample in every way:

> The sample speaks for itself. But it cannot be treated as saying more than such a sample would tell a merchant of the class to which the buyer belongs, using due care and diligence, and appealing to it in the ordinary way and with the knowledge possessed by merchants of that class at the time. No doubt the sample might be made to say a great deal more. Pulled to pieces and examined by unusual tests which curiosity or suspicion might suggest, it would doubtless reveal every secret of its construction. But that is not the way in which business is done in this country.[147]

In other words, the extent to which the sample corresponds with the bulk will depend upon the level of examination that the sample receives. A visual examination may reveal no differences, but a detailed examination may reveal significant, material differences. The question that arises is what type of examination should be used to determine whether the bulk corresponds with the sample. Lord Macnaghten's statement indicates that, generally, the seller only guarantees that the sample will correspond to the bulk as regards those qualities that can be discerned by a reasonable or ordinary examination of the goods. What amounts to a reasonable examination was addressed by the Earl of Selborne when he stated that the quality of the sample 'ought to be restricted to those qualities which were patent, or

---

142. See e.g. *Re Walkers, Winser & Hamm and Shaw, Son & Co* [1904] 2 KB 152 (KB), where the contract expressly provided that the quality of a shipment of barley should be 'as per sample'.
143. See e.g. *Syers v Jonas* (1848) 154 ER 426, where the sale of a shipment of tobacco was held to be a sale by sample on the ground that it was universally acknowledged by the tobacco trade that sales of tobacco were always sales by sample.
144. (1887) LR 12 App Cas 284 (HL).   145. ibid 297.   146. (1887) LR 12 App Cas 284 (HL).
147. ibid.

were discoverable from such examination…as, under the circumstances, the [buyer] might be expected to make'.[148] This acknowledges that what amounts to a reasonable examination is likely to differ from trade to trade. For example, in some trades, a mere visual examination of the sample may be standard practice, and in such cases, no breach of s 15(2)(a) will occur if the sample and bulk do not correspond due to a defect that could not have been discovered based upon a visual examination.[149] Conversely, in other trades, more rigorous or scientific examinations may be the norm and, if such examinations reveal differences between the sample and the bulk, then a breach of s 15(2)(a) may have occurred.

It will be no defence for the seller to show that the bulk could be made to correspond with the sample easily or inexpensively. For example, in *E&S Ruben Ltd v Faire Bros & Co Ltd*,[150] a breach of s 15(2)(a) occurred even though the goods in question could have been made to correspond with the sample by simply warming them up.

Freedom from defects

Despite the utility of s 15(2)(a), it is subject to two notable limitations. First, if both the sample and the bulk contain the same defect in quality, there will be no breach of the term implied by s 15(2)(a), as the quality of the sample and the bulk will match (albeit in a manner unsatisfactory to the buyer). Second, s 15(2)(a) will not generally be breached where the bulk does not correspond with the sample due to a latent defect that could not have been discovered on reasonable examination.

To remedy these limitations, s 15(2)(c) expands upon s 15(2)(a) by providing that 'the goods will be free from any defect, making their quality unsatisfactory, which would not be apparent on reasonable examination of the sample'. It follows from this that if the defect could have been discovered by engaging in a reasonable examination of the sample, then s 15(2)(c) will not apply. It will be remembered that the term implied by s 14(2) is subject to a similar exception (found in s 14(2C)(c)), but there is a key difference. Section 14(2C)(c) will only apply if an examination actually takes place, whereas s 15(2)(c) applies irrespective of whether an examination has taken place or not. The relationship between these various implied terms can be seen in the following case.

 Godley v Perry [1960] 1 WLR 9 (QB)

FACTS: Godley, a six-year-old child, bought a toy catapult from a shop owned by Perry. The catapult broke whilst being fired, and struck Godley, causing him to suffer an injury to his left eye, which resulted in the eye being removed. Perry's wife had tested a sample of the catapults before buying them from Burton & Sons (Bermondsey) Ltd ('Burton'), and Burton had tested a sample before purchasing them from Graham Bros. Godley commenced proceedings against Perry on the ground that the terms implied by ss 14 and 15 had been breached. Perry denied liability and brought in Burton & Sons, alleging

---

148. ibid 288.   149. See e.g. *Steels & Busks Ltd v Bleecker Bik & Co Ltd* [1956] 1 Lloyd's Rep 228 (QB). 150. [1949] 1 KB 254 (KB).

that Burton had breached the terms implied by ss 14 and 15(2)(c). Burton, in turn, brought in Graham Bros, alleging that Graham Bros had breached the terms implied by ss 14 and 15(2)(c).

HELD: The catapult was not of merchantable quality, so Perry had breached the term implied by s 14(2). The sales by Burton to Perry, and by Graham Bros to Burton, were sales by sample, and, as the defect was not apparent on a reasonable examination of the sample, it was held that Burton and Graham Bros had breached the term implied by s 15(2)(c).

 See Aubrey L Diamond, 'The Case of the Unmerchantable Catapult' (1960) 23 MLR 200

Remedies

The terms implied by s 15 are conditions.[151] Accordingly, breach of either term will usually entitle the buyer to reject the goods, repudiate the contract, and recover damages.

Exclusion of the statutory implied terms

Consider the following example.

> ## Eg ComCorp Ltd
>
> Greg, the chief executive of ComCorp Ltd, has always wanted a Ferrari. After receiving a healthy bonus from ComCorp, he purchases a new Ferrari from Flash Motors Ltd. Two weeks later, the car suffers from a massive gearbox failure. However, Flash Motors refuses to pay for the cost of a new gearbox, and draws Greg's attention to a clause in the contract of sale, which states that 'Flash Motors Ltd accepts no liability for any malfunctions or defects that arise more than one week after the vehicle is purchased.'

Having discussed the statutory implied terms, the question that now arises is to what extent these terms can be excluded or restricted by a contractual term seeking to exclude or restrict them (as Flash Motors Ltd are attempting to do in the example above). In relation to non-consumer sales, the answer can be found in s 55(1) of the SGA 1979.

> ## O— SGA 1979, s 55(1)
>
> Where a right, duty or liability would arise under a contract of sale of goods by implication of law, it may (subject to the Unfair Contract Terms Act 1977) be negatived or varied by express agreement, or by the course of dealing between the parties, or by such usage as binds both parties to the contract.

---

151. SGA 1979, s 15(3).

Accordingly, the SGA 1979 itself permits the parties to expressly exclude or vary the impact of the implied terms. However, as will become apparent, the ability to exclude or vary the terms implied by the SGA 1979 is highly limited. The key provision is s 6 of the Unfair Contract Terms Act 1977 (UCTA 1977), which provides:

1. The terms implied by s 12 of the SGA 1979 cannot be excluded or restricted by reference to any contractual term.[152]

2. As against a person dealing as consumer, the terms implied by ss 13 to 15 of the SGA 1979 cannot be excluded or restricted by reference to any contractual term.[153]

3. As against a person dealing otherwise than as consumer, the terms implied by ss 13 to 15 of the SGA 1979 can be excluded or restricted by reference to a contractual term, but only in so far as the term satisfies the requirement of reasonableness.[154]

As can be seen, s 6 of the UCTA 1977 distinguishes between consumer and non-consumer sales. It is therefore very important to be able to distinguish between the two types of sale. Although s 12 of the UCTA 1977 defines when a person will be dealing as a consumer, this has been described as 'appallingly drafted',[155] and does not provide a clear delineation between consumer and non-consumer sales.

Consumer sales

Section 6(2) of the UCTA 1977 provides that liability for breach of the terms implied by ss 13 to 15 of the SGA 1979 cannot be excluded against a person dealing as consumer. It will be noted that s 6(2) applies to the exclusion or restriction of *liability* for breach. From this, it would appear to follow that if the seller can, via a contractual term, exclude himself from the *scope* of ss 13 to 15 of the SGA 1979, then this may not amount to an exclusion clause to which s 6(2) would apply. For example, it was seen previously that the term implied by s 13(1) will only be implied where the contract is for the sale of goods by description. If the seller includes a term in the contract of sale providing that any descriptive terms used should not be relied on by the buyer and that the buyer should seek to assure himself that the goods match the description used, this may be enough to take the contract outside the scope of s 13. In such a case, the term in s 13(1) will not be implied and so s 6(2) of the UCTA 1977 will not apply. Clearly, this constitutes an important limitation on the scope of s 6(2) and is one that should be closely watched by the courts.[156]

The UCTA 1977 expressly states that, in certain circumstances, a buyer will never be regarded as dealing as a consumer (e.g. where he is not an individual and the goods are sold by auction or by competitive tender).[157] In all other cases, the relevant test can be found in s 12(1) of the UCTA 1977, which provides that a buyer deals as a consumer if three requirements are satisfied:

---

152. UCTA 1977, s 6(1).   153. ibid s 6(2).   154. ibid s 6(3).

155. Len S Sealy and Richard JA Hooley, *Commercial Law: Text, Cases and Materials* (4th edn, OUP 2009) 420.

156. For an excellent discussion of the relationship between the UCTA 1977, s 6(2) and the inherent restrictions contained within the SGA 1979, ss 13–15, see Patrick S Atiyah, John N Adams, and Hector Macqueen, *Atiyah's Sale of Goods* (12th edn, Pearson 2010) 230–3.

157. UCTA 1977, s 12(2)(b).

1. the buyer does not make the contract in the course of a business, nor hold himself out as doing so; and

2. the other party does make the contract in the course of a business; and

3. goods are of a type ordinarily supplied for private use or consumption.

Each requirement will now be discussed.

The buyer does not make the contract in the course of a business, nor hold himself out as doing so

The first requirement is that the buyer does not make the contract in the course of a business, nor does he hold himself out as doing so.[158] Section 14 of the UCTA 1977 states that the term 'business' includes 'a profession and the activities of any government department or local or public authority'. However, the word 'includes' makes it clear that this is not an exhaustive definition and so the task of defining when a person is dealing as a consumer has been largely left to the courts.

Problems arise in cases where goods are bought for both business and personal use. This arises most often where a business purchases goods, but the goods are not used exclusively for the purpose of the business. In such a case, is the business dealing as a consumer? One would assume that, based on a literal interpretation of the word 'business', a business structure (e.g. sole proprietorship, ordinary partnership, LLP, or company) could never be regarded as dealing as a consumer. However, in the following somewhat controversial case, the Court of Appeal held that this was not so and that a business can indeed deal as a consumer.

 R & B Customs Brokers Co Ltd v United Dominions Trust Ltd [1988] 1 WLR 321 (CA)

FACTS: R & B Customs Brokers Co Ltd ('R & B') was a freight forwarding and shipping agent. It purchased from United Dominions Trust Ltd ('UDT') a car for one of its directors, which was used for both business and private purposes, this being the second or third time that R & B had done this. The roof leaked and UDT failed to repair the defect. Accordingly, R & B sought to reject the car, alleging that the term implied by s 14(3) of the SGA 1979 had been breached. UDT sought to rely on an exclusion clause that excluded liability for the breach of s 14(3). As s 14(3) cannot be excluded against a person dealing as a consumer, the court had to determine whether or not R & B was dealing as a consumer.

HELD: Dillon LJ stated that where a transaction was only incidental to the carrying on of the relevant business, a degree of regularity was required before it could be said that the transaction was an integral part of the business. Here, the purchase of the car was clearly not an integral part of R & B's business, nor was it regular enough to become integral. Accordingly, R & B was held to be dealing as a consumer and the term implied by s 14(3) could not be excluded. R & B was thus entitled to reject the car.

★ See Diane R Price, 'When is a Consumer Not a Consumer?' (1989) 52 MLR 245

Under *R & B Customs Brokers*, a party will only be acting in the course of a business if the transaction is integral to the business, or is regular enough for it to

---

158. ibid s 12(1)(a).

become integral. This allows for a greater number of persons to come within the protection afforded by s 6 of the UCTA 1977 but, unsurprisingly, the notion that a business may not be acting in the course of a business has proven controversial and *R & B Customs Brokers* has been criticized.[159] In *Stevenson v Rogers*,[160] the Court of Appeal held that the test established in *R & B Customs Brokers* was limited to cases involving s 12 of the UCTA 1977 and that in cases involving the sale of goods, a sale would be in the course of a business unless it was a purely private sale. Although *Stevenson* has its critics,[161] many academics[162] preferred its approach and hoped that when the issue was litigated upon again, the approach advanced in *Stevenson* would be adopted. However, in *Feldarol Foundry plc v Hermes Leasing (London) Ltd*,[163] the Court of Appeal confirmed that the correct meaning of the words 'in the course of a business' will depend on whether they appear in the SGA 1979 or in the UCTA 1977. For the purpose of s 14 of the SGA 1979, they should be interpreted as they were in *Stevenson*, while a similar expression for the purpose of s 12 of the UCTA 1977 should be interpreted as per *R & B Customs Brokers*.[164] Consequently, the meaning given to 'in the course of a business' can now be stated as per Table 15.4.

The tension between *R & B Customs Brokers* and *Stevenson* was also considered when the Law Commission recommended that a new comprehensive regime should be created that would apply to 'consumer contracts',[165] which would be defined as a contract between an individual (the consumer) who enters into it wholly or mainly for purposes unrelated to a business of his, and a person (the business) who enters into it wholly or mainly for purposes related to his business.[166] The use of the word 'individual' would mean that only natural persons could be regarded as consumers and, accordingly, it is clear that the approach in *Stevenson* was favoured over that found in *R & B Customs Brokers*. The enactment of the Law Commission's bill would provide much-needed clarity to this area of the law. Unfortunately, whilst

TABLE 15.4 In the course of a business

Section	Meaning	Case
UCTA, s 12(1)	The purchase must be an integral part of the business, or, if the goods are bought as a one-off purchase, they must have been bought with the intention of selling them on for a profit, or if the goods purchased are of a kind which the business has bought with some degree of regularity	*R & B Customs Brokers Ltd v United Dominions Trust Ltd* [1988] 1 WLR 321 (CA)
SGA, s 14	A sale by a business is a sale in the course of a business	*Stevenson v Rogers* [1999] QB 1028 (CA)

159. See e.g. Ian Brown, 'Business and Consumer Contracts' [1988] JBL 386; Elizabeth Macdonald, '"In the Course of a Business": A Fresh Examination' [1999] 3 Web JCLI 1.
160. [1999] QB 1028 (CA). This case is discussed on p 365.
161. See e.g. Ian Brown, 'Sales of Goods in the Course of a Business' (1999) 115 LQR 384.
162. See e.g. John de Lacy, 'Selling in the Course of a Business Under the Sale of Goods Act 1979' (1999) 62 MLR 776.
163. [2004] EWCA Civ 747, (2004) 101 LSG 32.   164. ibid [15]–[16].
165. Law Commission, *Unfair Terms in Contracts* (Law Com No 292, 2005).
166. Draft Unfair Contract Terms Bill, cl 26.

the Government did indicate in 2006 that it was ready to go forward with the Law Commission's recommendations, no progress has been made since.

The other party does make the contract in the course of a business

The second requirement is that the other party does make the contract in the course of a business.[167] Consequently, purely private sales are not covered. It will be noted that the other party must make the contract in the course of *a* business, not *the* business. It follows from this that the other party need not make the contract in the course of its normal business and, providing that the contract is made in the course of any business, the condition will be satisfied.

Goods are of a type ordinarily supplied for private use or consumption

The third, and final, requirement is that the goods passing under, or in pursuance to, the contract are of a type ordinarily supplied for private use or consumption.[168] It follows that, if the goods are of the type ordinarily supplied in the course of a business (e.g. steel girders, heavy digging equipment, etc.), then the buyer will not be dealing as a consumer, even if the goods are bought in a private capacity. However, if the buyer is an individual (e.g. not a LLP or company), then this third condition will not apply and the status of the goods will therefore be irrelevant.[169] The Law Commission has recommended that this condition be abolished in all cases,[170] but this recommendation has yet to be acted upon.

Non-consumer sales

Where the buyer does not deal as a consumer, then the terms implied by ss 13 to 15 of the SGA 1979 may be excluded or restricted by reference to a contractual term, but only in so far as the term satisfies the requirement of reasonableness.[171] The burden of proof is placed upon the person who is claiming that the excluding or restricting term is reasonable (usually the seller) to prove that it is.[172]

The requirement of reasonableness

The requirement of reasonableness lies at the heart of the UCTA 1977. To aid the courts, the UCTA 1977 itself provides three sources of limited guidance. First, s 11(1) provides that a term will be reasonable if it is a fair and reasonable one to be included, having regard to the circumstances that were or ought reasonably to have been known to or in the contemplation of the parties when the contract was made. From this, it can be seen that the courts should determine reasonableness based on the circumstances when the contract was made and not at the time when the dispute arose or the case is heard. From an evidential perspective, this could cause problems, especially where there is a considerable period of time between the act complained of and the case being heard.

---

167. UCTA 1977, s 12(1)(b).   168. ibid s 12(1)(c).   169. ibid s 12(1A).
170. Law Commission, *Unfair Terms in Contracts* (Law Com No 292, 2005) paras 3.30–3.31.
171. UCTA 1977, s 6(3).   172. ibid s 11(5).

Second, s 11(2) provides that, in cases involving s 6, the court is to have regard in particular to those matters specified in Schedule 2. The use of the words 'in particular' indicates that the list of matters in Schedule 2 is not exhaustive.[173] The matters listed in Schedule 2 are:

(a) the strength of the bargaining positions of the parties relative to each other, taking into account (among other things) alternative means by which the customer's requirements could have been met;

(b) whether the customer received an inducement to agree to the term, or, in accepting it, had an opportunity to enter into a similar contract with other persons, but without having a similar term;

(c) whether the customer knew or ought reasonably to have known of the existence and the extent of the term (having regard, among other things, to any custom of the trade and any previous course of dealing between the parties);

(d) where the term excludes or restricts any relevant liability if some condition was not complied with, whether it was reasonable at the time of the contract to expect that compliance with that condition would be practicable;

(e) whether the goods were manufactured, processed, or adapted to the special order of the customer.

The third source of guidance can be found in s 11(4) and applies solely to clauses seeking to restrict liability to a specified sum of money (i.e. s 11(4) does not apply to clauses that exclude liability altogether). In such cases, the court should have regard in particular to:

(a) the resources which he could expect to be available to him for the purpose of meeting the liability should it arise; and

(b) how far it was open to him to cover himself by insurance.

It cannot be overemphasized that, in all cases, it is the clause as a whole that must be reasonable in relation to the particular contract; the question is not whether its particular application in the particular case is reasonable. If a clause is drawn so widely as to be capable of applying in unreasonable circumstances, it will be deemed unreasonable, even though in the actual situation that has arisen, its application is reasonable.[174] A clause may well have various parts to it but, because the whole clause must be subjected to the test of reasonableness, it is not permissible to look only at that part of it that the party seeking to exclude or restrict their liability wishes to rely on.[175] A court may be particularly unwilling to find a clause reasonable if it purports to exclude all potential liability.[176]

Where a term is found to be unreasonable, it cannot be relied on to exclude or restrict liability. In such a case, the contract continues as normal, but without reference to the offending clause.

---

173. See e.g. *George Mitchell (Chesterhall) Ltd v Finney Lock Seeds Ltd* [1983] 2 AC 803 (HL), where the House of Lords thought that the availability of insurance was also a relevant matter.

174. *Walker v Boyle* [1982] 1 WLR 495 (Ch).

175. *Stewart Gill Ltd v Horatio Myer & Co Ltd* [1992] QB 600 (CA).

176. *Lease Management Services Ltd v Purnell Secretarial Services Ltd* [1994] CCLR 127 (CA).

The doctrine of fundamental breach

At one time, it was held that some breaches of contract were so serious that no exclusion clauses could ever excuse them.[177] Thus, if a seller contracted to sell a computer but instead supplied a printer, it would not appear sensible to allow him to rely on a term in his contract that permitted him to substitute the goods ordered for some other goods. The promise to supply a computer was a fundamental term of the contract and such a significant breach of it would provide the buyer with a remedy, irrespective of any exclusion clause in the seller's contract. However, the so-called doctrine of fundamental breach was rejected by the House of Lords in *Suisse Atlantique Société d'Armement SA v NV Rotterdamsche Kolen Centrale*,[178] where their Lordships stated *obiter* that there was no rule of substantive law that a fundamental breach of a contract nullifies an exemption clause and that it is a matter of construction whether the clause was intended to apply to such a breach as has occurred. If a breach by one party entitles the other to repudiate the contract, but he affirms it, the exemption clause continues in force unless, on its construction, it was not intended to operate in those circumstances. The decision in *Suisse Atlantique* was confirmed by the House of Lords in the following case.

Photo Production Ltd v Securicor Transport Ltd [1980] AC 827 (HL)

FACTS: Securicor Transport Ltd contracted with Photo Production Ltd to provide a night patrol service at a factory. The contract excluded Securicor's liability for any injurious act or default of any of its employees unless such act or default could have been foreseen and avoided by the exercise of due diligence on the part of the employer. The contract further provided that Securicor shall not be responsible for any loss suffered through fire or any other cause except in so far as is solely attributable to the negligence of the company's employees acting within the course of their employment. One of Securicor's employees deliberately started a fire in the factory, which was destroyed by it.

HELD: The House of Lords held that whether an exclusion clause was capable of excluding or limiting liability was a matter of construction of the contract and that, generally, parties to a contract, when they bargained on equal terms, should be free to apportion liability in the contract as they see fit. Their Lordships confirmed that there was no rule of law that a fundamental breach of the contract prevented an exclusion clause from being effective. As a result, it was held that the wording of the exclusion clause was adequate to exclude liability for what occurred.

COMMENT: The decision in *Photo Production* also serves as a strong affirmation of the freedom-to-contract approach to commercial contracting, as opposed to the interventionist approach seen in some of the earlier cases such as *Karsales*. Furthermore, since these earlier cases were decided, we now have the UCTA 1977, which prevents exemption clauses from being used freely in consumer contracts. The problem is not as serious in commercial transactions because many parties are likely to be of similar bargaining power

⭐ See Len S Sealy, 'Contract—Farewell to the Doctrine of Fundamental Breach' (1980) 39 CLJ 252

---

177. See e.g. *Karsales (Harrow) Ltd v Wallis* [1956] 1 WLR 936 (CA).
178. [1967] 1 AC 361 (HL).

and/or more able to negotiate their own contracts, as well as being more able to protect their own risks by insurance.

Conclusion

The terms implied by ss 12 to 15 of the SGA 1979 are of fundamental importance to the parties and go a long way to eroding the principle of *caveat emptor*. It has been observed throughout this chapter that significant obligations have been imposed on sellers by virtue of the statutory implied terms, most notably upon sellers who sell in the course of a business. The SGA 1979 also sets out the remedies available to the seller and to the buyer in the event of a breach of the contract of sale. These remedies are discussed in Chapters 16 and 17.

Practice questions

1. 'Given the breadth of the term implied by s 14(2) of the SGA 1979, it can be argued that the term implied by s 14(3) is no longer needed.'

   Do you agree with this assertion? Give reasons for your answer.

2. ComCorp Ltd purchases twenty pine office cabinets from Homeware Ltd, after viewing a sample cabinet in Homeware's factory. Upon delivery of the goods, Lee, a director of ComCorp, notices some minor scratches on the rear of one of the cabinets. It is also discovered that the cabinets are made from oak, not pine, although this makes no practical difference to ComCorp or to the users of the cabinets.

   Lee also purchases a new washing machine from his local branch of ElectroMart Ltd, who agree to deliver it to Lee's home. On the way home, Lee stops at his local branch of BuyPhone Ltd and purchases a new mobile phone. Upon returning home, Lee removes his phone from the box in order to charge it up. He notices that the glass screen of the phone contains a number of small scratches, but the phone functions perfectly. ElectroMart deliver and install the washing machine as promised. Lee uses the machine to wash a batch of assorted clothing, including an antique sixteenth-century tablecloth. The washing machine contains a defective drum, which causes the machine to shake violently and leak, flooding Lee's kitchen and severely scratching the cabinets surrounding it. It also transpires that the antique tablecloth has been damaged during the wash. No other clothing was damaged.

   Discuss to what extent the terms implied by ss 12 to 15 of the SGA 1979 have been breached and what possible remedies might be available.

Further reading

Ian Brown, 'Forgery, Fine Art and the Sale of Goods' (1990) 106 LQR 561

- Discusses the Court of Appeal's decision in *Harlingdon & Leinster Enterprises Ltd v Christopher Hull Fine Art Ltd* and the recurrent difficulties of scope and interrelation of the implied terms contained in ss 13 and 14(2) of the SGA 1979.

Ian Brown, 'The Meaning of Merchantable Quality in Sales of Goods: Quality or Fitness for Purpose?' [1987] LMCLQ 400

- Discusses the meaning of merchantable quality against the decisions of the Court of Appeal in *Rogers v Parish (Scarborough) Ltd* and *Aswan Engineering Establishment Co v Lupdine Ltd*.

Ian Brown, 'Sales of Goods in the Course of a Business' (1999) 115 LQR 384

- Discusses whether the implied condition of merchantability applied to the sale of a fishing boat where the vendor, who had established a business as a fisherman, only occasionally sold on boats he had previously used in his business.

W Cowan Ervine, 'Satisfactory Quality: What Does it Mean?' [2004] JBL 68

- Considers the term implied in contracts of sale under s 14(2) of the SGA 1979 that goods should be of satisfactory quality. Discusses the background to the Act and the section. Examines case law in which the satisfactory quality term and related issues have been considered by the courts, including the relationship between fitness for a particular purpose and satisfactory quality, the relevance of the description applied to goods in assessing the standard of quality that could be expected, and the factors that may be taken into account in determining satisfactory quality.

Brian Elkan, 'Sale of Goods and Patent Infringement' (1975) 34 CLJ 199

- Discusses the Court of Appeal's judgment in *Microbeads AG v Vinhurst Road Markings Ltd* in relation to a breach of s 12(1) and (2) of the SGA 1979, when the goods sold were affected by a patent that was applied for before but only granted after the sale.

Ingrid Patient, 'Ruminating on Mink Food' (1971) 34 MLR 557

- Discusses the missed opportunity of the House of Lords when reversing the Court of Appeal's judgment in *Ashington Piggeries v Christopher Hill*, especially in relation to settling a number of difficulties relating to ss 13 and 14 of the SGA 1893.

Diane Price, 'When is a Consumer Not a Consumer?' (1989) 52 MLR 245

- Examines the meaning of 'consumer' as it applies to contracts of sale of goods.

Christian Twigg-Flesner, 'The Relationship Between Satisfactory Quality and Fitness for Purpose (2004) 63 CLJ 22

- Examines the Court of Appeal's ruling in *Jewson v Boyhan* in which the defendant claimed that the boilers supplied by the sellers were sold in breach of s 14(2) and (3) of the Sale of Goods Act 1979 as they did not reach the acceptable Standard Assessment Procedure ratings for energy efficiency for residential dwellings. Discusses the relationship and distinction between these two subsections.

James Wilson, 'Battle of the Bentley' (2012) 162 NLJ 510

- Discusses the Court of Appeal's ruling in *Brewer v Mann* that a Bentley dealer did not breach a collateral warranty that the car sold would be a genuine 1930 'Speed Six' containing an authentic engine. Notes the distinction drawn between an authentic and continuous documentary history, and an item's description.

16

The remedies of the seller

- When is the seller unpaid?
- Real remedies
- Personal remedies

INTRODUCTION

A seller is principally concerned with getting paid by the buyer. This chapter will consider the remedies available to a seller if the buyer fails to pay for the goods pursuant to a contract of sale. It should be noted at the outset that the term 'seller' also includes 'any person who is in the position of a seller, such as an agent of the seller to whom a bill of lading has been indorsed, or a consignor or agent who has himself paid (or is directly responsible for) the price'.[1] This is of particular assistance to an agent who, having paid the price to the seller with the intention of recovering the money from the buyer, will have the same protection afforded to unpaid sellers as if he were the seller directly.

The unpaid seller has two different types of remedy: real remedies and personal remedies. A real remedy is a remedy against the goods, such as a lien, whereas a personal remedy is one against the buyer personally, such as an action for the price.

When is the seller unpaid?

Section 38(1) of the SGA 1979 envisages two situations where the seller will be unpaid.

○— SGA 1979, s 38(1)

(a) when the whole of the price has not been paid or tendered; or

(b) when a bill of exchange or other negotiable instrument has been received as conditional payment, and the condition on which it was received has not been fulfilled by reason of the dishonour of the instrument or otherwise.

---

1. SGA 1979, s 38(2).

The situation set out in s 38(1)(a) is straightforward. Section 38(1)(b) covers the situation where the buyer tenders a bill of exchange, cheque, or other negotiable instrument in payment for the goods, but that bill of exchange, cheque, or negotiable instrument is then dishonoured. The tendering of the bill of exchange or other negotiable instrument is treated as a conditional payment and until it has been honoured the seller is an unpaid seller. The position with payment made by credit card is different and is treated as an absolute, and not conditional, payment even if the credit card company fails to pay the seller.[2]

The remedies available to an unpaid seller can be found in Pts V and VI of the Sale of Goods Act 1979 (SGA 1979). Part V sets out the real remedies of the unpaid seller, while Pt VI sets out his personal remedies. Our discussion begins with the real remedies of the unpaid seller.

Real remedies

Section 39 of the SGA 1979 sets out the real remedies that are available to the unpaid seller. In effect, these remedies use the goods themselves as a form of security in the event of the buyer's non-payment. These remedies differ depending on whether or not the property in the goods has passed to the buyer.

🔑 SGA 1979, s 39

(1) Subject to this and any other Act, notwithstanding that the property in the goods may have passed to the buyer, the unpaid seller of goods, as such, has by implication of law:

    (a) a lien on the goods or right to retain them for the price while he is in possession of them;

    (b) in case of the insolvency of the buyer, a right of stopping the goods in transit after he has parted with the possession of them;

    (c) a right of re-sale as limited by this Act.

(2) Where the property in goods has not passed to the buyer, the unpaid seller has (in addition to his other remedies) a right of withholding delivery similar to and co-extensive with his rights of lien or retention and stoppage in transit where the property has passed to the buyer.

Where the property in the goods has passed to the buyer, then s 39(1) provides the unpaid seller with three rights exercisable against the goods:

➡ **lien:** the right to hold the property of another until an obligation is satisfied

(a) the unpaid seller will have a **lien**, over the goods, or, alternatively, a right to retain them whilst he is in possession of them;

➡ **stoppage in transit:** the right of an unpaid seller to stop, whilst in transit, the delivery of goods to the buyer and to retain possession of them until the price is paid

(b) if the buyer is insolvent, and if the unpaid seller has already despatched the goods, then the unpaid seller will have the right of **stopping the goods in transit**;

(c) the unpaid seller may re-sell the goods, as provided for in the SGA 1979.

---

2. *Re Charge Card Services Ltd (No 2)* [1989] Ch 497 (CA).

Where the property in the goods has not passed to the buyer, then s 39(2) provides that, in addition to the three rights provided for in s 39(1), the unpaid seller also has the right to withhold delivery of the goods. These remedies will now be discussed.

The unpaid seller's lien

Section 41(1) sets out the circumstances in which the unpaid seller is entitled to retain possession of the contract goods.

 SGA 1979, s 41(1)

Subject to this Act, the unpaid seller of goods who is in possession of them is entitled to retain possession of them until payment or tender of the price in the following cases:

(a) where the goods have been sold without any stipulation as to credit;

(b) where the goods have been sold on credit but the term of credit has expired;

(c) where the buyer becomes insolvent.

Although commonly referred to as the seller's lien, and indeed the section itself uses this term, the remedy is, strictly speaking, only a lien if the property in the goods has already passed to the buyer, whereas, if the property in the goods is still with the seller, it is a right of retention.[3]

Section 41(1) needs to be read alongside s 28, which provides that, unless the parties have agreed otherwise, payment and delivery are concurrent conditions in a contract of sale. Where the goods are sold on credit terms, the parties will have agreed otherwise, and, in such a case, the seller will not be entitled to refuse delivery until the term of credit has expired[4] or the buyer becomes insolvent.[5] The relationship between ss 41(1)(b) and 41(1)(c) is of considerable practical importance in the event the buyer becomes insolvent. The effect of s 41(1)(b) is that the seller is not entitled to retain possession of the goods during the term of credit, although where credit has been granted, it is usual for delivery to be made before payment becomes due. The seller in such circumstances is thus deprived of his lien because, as will shortly be discussed, his lien or right of retention are rights in possession. This means that they will automatically terminate the moment the seller ceases to have possession of the contract goods. Section 41(1)(c) is therefore an important exception to the rule in s 41(1)(b) and means that, notwithstanding the fact that credit has been granted to the buyer, if the buyer becomes insolvent, the seller will have a lien provided he has not relinquished possession of the goods. The seller can only invoke s 41(1)(c) if the buyer is insolvent; it will not be sufficient that the buyer has merely failed to pay. A person is deemed to be insolvent within the meaning of the SGA 1979 if he has either ceased to pay his debts in the ordinary course of business or he cannot pay his debts as they become due.[6]

In the case of delivery made in instalments, and where the unpaid seller has already made a part-delivery of the goods, he may still exercise his lien or right of

> Section 28 of the SGA 1979 is discussed at p 321

---

3. SGA 1979, s 39(2).   4. ibid s 41(1)(b).   5. ibid s 41(1)(c).   6. ibid s 61(4).

retention on the remainder, unless such part-delivery has been made under such circumstances as to show an agreement to waive such lien or right of retention.[7] This means that in a typical case the unpaid seller need not deliver the remainder of the goods whilst the buyer still owes money for the goods, but this will depend on whether or not the contract is severable, such as where delivery is made in instalments with the instalments paid for separately.[8] Contracts may be severable in other situations, such as where the contract specifies 'deliveries as required'[9] or where delivery is to be made in instalments, with the number and size of each instalment left to the seller's own discretion,[10] or where the goods are to be delivered in instalments with the price to be paid on a monthly account rather than against each instalment.[11] With a severable contract, the unpaid seller will not be entitled to a lien over one of the instalments to compel the buyer to pay for other instalments, although if the buyer's failure to pay is such as to give rise to a repudiatory breach of the contract, then the seller is thereby excused from further performance of his contractual obligations, including making further deliveries, and in such a case the question of lien will not arise.

The unpaid seller is only entitled to exercise his lien in relation to the price. Previous debts or disputes are not relevant. Likewise, a seller will not be entitled to exercise a lien in respect of a claim in damages under s 37 where the buyer fails to take delivery of the goods.

Termination of lien or right of retention

The unpaid seller's lien or right of retention are, of course, rights in possession and exist even if he is in possession of the goods as agent, bailee, or custodier for the buyer.[12] As they are rights in possession, it means that any lien or right of retention will automatically terminate the moment the seller ceases to have possession of the goods. Section 43(1) sets out the three situations where the unpaid seller will lose his lien or right of retention:

(a) when he delivers the goods to a carrier or other bailee or custodier for the purpose of transmission to the buyer without reserving the right of disposal of the goods;[13]

(b) when the buyer or his agent lawfully obtains possession of the goods;

(c) by waiver of the lien or right of retention.

Where the unpaid seller loses his lien or right of retention under s 43(1)(a), he may still be able to exercise his right of stoppage in transit under s 44 (discussed later in this chapter) and thereby recover the contract goods. If the buyer or his agent obtains possession of the goods otherwise than lawfully, then the seller will not lose his lien or right or retention, as in such a case s 43(1)(b) will not be triggered.

Additionally, the unpaid seller's lien or right of retention will be lost the moment he ceases to be an unpaid seller, which will arise if the buyer pays or tenders the

---

7. ibid s 42.　　8. ibid s 31(2).　　9. *Jackson v Rotax Motor & Cycle Co Ltd* [1910] 2 KB 937 (CA).
10. *Regent OHG Aisestadt & Barig v Francesco of Jermyn Street Ltd* [1981] 3 All ER 327 (QB).
11. *Longtottom & Co Ltd v Bass Walker & Co Ltd* (1922) 12 Ll L Rep 192 (CA).
12. SGA 1979, s 41(2).
13. It is usual for contracts of sale to contain retention of title clauses. These are discussed at p 255.

price.[14] Similarly, in the unlikely event that the unpaid seller's buyer disposes of the contract goods in such a way as to invoke one of the exceptions to the *nemo dat* prin-ciple, the innocent third-party sub-buyer will acquire good title to the goods unfet-tered by the unpaid seller's lien. The innocent third-party sub-buyer will then be in a position to require the unpaid seller to hand possession of the goods to him, leav-ing the unpaid seller to pursue a personal remedy against his buyer. However, since most of the *nemo dat* exceptions require the seller to be in possession of the goods, the question of the unpaid seller's lien or right of retention would not usually arise.[15] The seller can also lose his lien where the buyer has possession, not of the contract goods, but of the documents of title.[16]

 Nemo dat is discussed at p 272

Where the buyer has resold the goods

It is important to read s 43(1) in conjunction with s 47 under which an innocent sub-buyer may acquire title to the goods free of the unpaid seller's lien. Thus, s 47 sets out other situations where an unpaid seller may lose his right of lien, retention, or stoppage in transit. The first provision to note is s 47(1).

 SGA 1979, s 47(1)

Subject to this Act, the unpaid seller's right of lien or retention or stoppage in transit is not affected by any sale or other disposition of the goods which the buyer may have made, unless the seller has assented to it.

It can be seen from s 47(1) that the unpaid seller's right of lien, retention, or stoppage in transit is not affected by any sale or other disposition of the goods which the buyer may have made, unless the seller has assented to it. The question of what amounts to 'assent' for the purpose of the subsection was considered in the following case.

Mordaunt Brothers v British Oil and Cake Mills Ltd [1910] 2 KB 502 (KB)

FACTS: British Oil and Cake Mills Ltd contracted to sell a quantity of boiled linseed oil to Crichton Brothers, who then resold it to Mordaunt Brothers. Possession of the oil sold remained with British Oil who had not been paid by Crichton Brothers, even though Mordaunt had paid Crichton Brothers for its purchase. Crichton Brothers had sent delivery orders to British Oil requiring the oil be delivered to Mordaunt, and these orders were acknowledged by British Oil and entered in its records. Crichton Brothers fell into arrears and British Oil exercised its right of lien as an unpaid seller and refused to make any further deliveries. Mordaunt sued, claiming that British Oil had assented to the sale of the oil by

---

14. SGA 1979, s 38(1).
15. ibid s 43(1)(b). Note the word 'lawfully' in the subsection. The position will be otherwise if the buyer or his agent obtains possession of the goods unlawfully.
16. See e.g. s 9 of the FA 1889 or s 25 of the SGA 1979 'buyer in possession after sale'. These provisions are discussed in Chapter 12.

Crichton Brothers to Mordaunt, and so, under s 47(1), British Oil had precluded itself from exercising the unpaid seller's right to a lien or retention.

HELD: Mordaunt's claim failed. Pickford J held that the acts of acknowledging the orders and entering them in its ledgers did not amount to the necessary 'assent' by British Oil to the resale for the purpose of s 47. The mere assent by the unpaid seller to a sale by his buyer was not the 'assent' contemplated by s 47 as affecting the unpaid seller's right of lien. In order to affect his right of lien, the assent must be given in such circumstances as to show an intention on the part of the unpaid seller to renounce his rights against the goods. It was not enough to show that the fact of a subcontract had been brought to his notice and that he has assented to it merely in the sense of acknowledging the information. His assent to the subcontract in that sense would simply mean that he acknowledged the right of the purchaser under the subcontract to have the goods subject to his own paramount right under the contract with his original purchaser to hold the goods until paid for. Such an assent would imply no intention of making delivery to a sub-purchaser until payment was made under the original contract. The assent contemplated by s 47 meant something more than that. That section contemplated an assent given in such circumstances as show that the unpaid seller intended that the subcontract was to be carried out irrespective of the terms of the original contract.

In *Mordaunt*, British Oil had at no time any reason to doubt Crichton Brothers' ability to pay and in any event was not informed of the sub-sale to Mordaunt until after the sale had been effected. Those were important reasons that led Pickford J to conclude that British Oil in that case had not assented to the sub-sale merely in the sense that it acknowledged its existence and the right of Mordaunt to have the goods subject to its own paramount rights under the contract with Crichton Brothers to hold the goods until it paid the purchase price.

The position is different where the seller is anxious to sell, perhaps because of a falling market, and where he is aware that his buyer will only be able to pay him out of the money he obtains from reselling the goods to his own customers, which would only come about against delivery orders in favour of those customers. An unpaid seller will not be deemed to assent to a resale by the buyer and thereby lose his lien unless he intends to renounce his rights against the goods and take the risk of the buyer's honesty or that he will pay. This can be seen in the following case.

DF Mount Ltd v Jay & Jay (Provisions) Co Ltd [1960] 1 QB 159 (QB)

FACTS: Jay & Jay (Provisions) Co Ltd ('Jay') sold part of a consignment of canned peaches to Merrick for resale to two of his customers, agreeing that the purchase price would be paid by Merrick from the money he would eventually receive from his customers. Jay made out delivery orders in favour of Merrick, which he indorsed with the words 'please transfer to our sub-order', and forwarded them to the wharf where the goods were stored. Merrick then sold the goods to DF Mount and at the same time agreed to repurchase them a week later at a price that would return a profit for DF Mount. Merrick made out a fresh delivery order in the same form as those made out by Jay in his favour, save that it was in favour of DF Mount and signed by him, and sent it to

DF Mount, receiving in return its cheque for the purchase price. A week later, DF Mount sent that delivery order to the wharf and, in pursuance of its agreement with Merrick, sent him a delivery order in respect of the goods made out in his favour, receiving from Merrick a cheque for the higher price of the goods. Merrick's cheque was dishonoured, whereupon DF Mount cancelled the delivery order in his favour. Meanwhile, Jay, who had not been paid for the goods, cancelled its contract with Merrick and requested the wharf to cancel the delivery orders made out in his favour. Merrick was subsequently convicted of obtaining money by fraud from DF Mount. Both Jay and DF Mount claimed they were entitled to the goods.

HELD: Salmon J gave a judgment in favour of DF Mount and held that Jay had assented to Merrick reselling the goods within the meaning s 47 in the sense that it intended to renounce its rights against the goods and to take the risk of Merrick's honesty. He stated:

> In the present case [Jay] were anxious to get rid of the goods on a falling market. They knew that Merrick could only pay for them out of the money he obtained from his customers, and that he could only obtain the money from his customers against delivery orders in favour of those customers. In my view, the true inference is that [Jay] assented to Merrick reselling the goods, in the sense that they intended to renounce their rights against the goods and to take the risk of Merrick's honesty. [Jay] are reputable merchants and I am sure that it was not their intention to get rid of their goods on a falling market through Merrick on the basis that, if he defaulted, they could hold the goods against the customers from whom he obtained the money out of which they were to be paid.[17]

COMMENT: Salmon J also held that DF Mount was additionally entitled to succeed under a different section of the Act, namely s 25(2).[18] He explained that:

> the object of [s 25(2)] is to protect an innocent person in his dealings with a buyer who appears to have the right to deal with the goods in that he has been allowed by the seller to be in possession of the goods or documents of title relating to them. In such a case the subsection provides that any transfer of the goods or documents of title by the buyer to a person acting in good faith and without notice of any want of authority on the part of the buyer shall be as valid as if expressly authorised by the seller. In the present case [Jay] sent the documents of title to Merrick with the intention that they should enable him to obtain money from his customers. With the help of these documents, which he sent to the wharf so that [they] would give a reassuring reply to any inquiry that [DF Mount] might make, or at least not query any delivery order they received from [DF Mount], Merrick managed to obtain a substantial sum of money from [DF Mount]. In my view, the transfer by Merrick of the delivery order ... was, by virtue of s 25 (2), as valid as if expressly authorised by [Jay].[19]

See TC Thomas, 'Sale of Goods–Seller's Lien–Resale' [1960] CLJ 34

---

17. [1960] 1 QB 159 (QB) 167.
18. SGA 1893, s 25 (2): 'Where a person having bought or agreed to buy goods obtains, with the consent of the seller, possession of the goods or the documents of title to the goods, the delivery or transfer by that person, or by a mercantile agent acting for him, of the goods or documents of title, under any sale, pledge, or other disposition thereof, to any person receiving the same in good faith and without notice of any lien or other right of the original seller in respect of the goods, shall have the same effect as if the person making the delivery or transfer were a mercantile agent in possession of the goods or documents of title with the consent of the owner.' The *nemo dat* exceptions are discussed in Chapter 12.
19. [1960] 1 QB 159 (QB) 169.

The second provision to note is s 47(2).

 SGA 1979, s 47(2)

Where a document of title to goods has been lawfully transferred to any person as buyer or owner of the goods, and that person transfers the document to a person who takes it in good faith and for valuable consideration, then:

(a) if the last-mentioned transfer was by way of sale the unpaid seller's right of lien or retention or stoppage in transit is defeated; and

(b) if the last-mentioned transfer was made by way of pledge or other disposition for value, the unpaid seller's right of lien or retention or stoppage in transit can only be exercised subject to the rights of the transferee.

The effect of s 47(2) can be seen in the following case.

 Ant Jurgens Margarinefabrieken v Louis Dreyfus & Co Ltd [1914] 3 KB 40 (KB)

FACTS: Finkler purchased a quantity of seeds from Louis Dreyfus & Co Ltd. Finkler paid for the goods by cheque and was given by Louis Dreyfus a delivery order that was indorsed by Finkler before being transferred to Ant Jurgens, a sub-buyer. When Finkler's cheque was dishonoured, Louis Dreyfus refused to make delivery, asserting a lien over the goods that were still in its possession. Ant Jurgens commenced proceedings.

HELD: Pickford J held that the delivery order was a document of title to the goods that had been transferred to Ant Jurgens, who took it in good faith and for valuable consideration. Louis Dreyfus' right of lien was therefore defeated by virtue of s 47[20] and Ant Jurgens' claim succeeded.

COMMENT: Since a buyer is able to confer on a sub-buyer a title better than that which he himself had, s 47(2) provides further exceptions to the *nemo dat* principle.

Where the seller has delivered or transferred to the buyer a document of title to goods

Where a document of title to goods has been lawfully transferred to any person as buyer or owner of the goods, and that person transfers the document to a person who takes it in good faith and for valuable consideration, then if the last-mentioned transfer was by way of sale, the unpaid seller's lien, right of retention, or stoppage in transit is defeated. Further, if the last-mentioned transfer was made by way of pledge or other disposition for value, then the unpaid seller's right of lien, retention, or stoppage in transit can only be exercised subject to the rights of the transferee.[21]

---

20. Section 47 of the Sale of Goods Act 1893 was not divided into subsections, as now appears in the 1979 Act. What is now s 47(2) of the 1979 Act was then included as a proviso to the general rule that now appears as s 47(1).

21. SGA 1979, s 47(2).

It should be appreciated from s 47(2) that two different transfers are needed in order for this subsection to apply: first, the transfer of the document of title to a person as buyer or owner of the goods; and second, that person must then transfer the same document of title to another person in the circumstances stated in the subsection. This can be contrasted with the *nemo dat* exception in s 25(2), where there is no requirement that the same document of title be transferred.[22]

It is important to appreciate that the unpaid seller's lien is a right to retain possession of the contract goods. It has already been observed that once the seller has parted with possession of the goods, the right of lien no longer applies. As the following case demonstrates, this is so even if the seller subsequently regains possession of the goods.

Valpy v Gibson (1847) 4 CB 837

FACTS: Gibson sold a consignment of cloth to Brown, a merchant based in Birmingham. Gibson dispatched the cloth in four cases via shipping agents, requesting them to put them on board ship to Brown's direction. After the goods had been loaded on the vessel, Brown's agent ordered them to be off-loaded and returned to Gibson so they could be repacked into smaller cases. Gibson was in possession of the cloth when Brown was declared bankrupt. Gibson had not been paid for the goods. Brown's assignees (of which Valpy was one) commenced proceedings, claiming that Gibson had converted the goods, but Gibson contended that he had an unpaid seller's lien.

HELD: Wilde CJ held that Gibson did not have an unpaid seller's lien. He stated:

> The right which it was contended the defendants had, as vendors in the actual and lawful possession of the goods, on the insolvency of the vendee, cannot, we think, be sustained. The goods being sold on credit, and the complete property and possession having vested in Brown, they became his absolutely, without any lien or right of the vendors attaching to them, any more than on any other property of Brown; and their delivery to the defendants to be repacked, could not have the effect of creating a lien for the price, without an agreement to that effect.[23]

With international sales, the seller's right of lien is likely to be of very limited application because, unless he has sold the goods **ex works**, the seller is likely to have handed possession of the goods to a carrier in accordance with the contract of sale.

Ultimately, of course, an unpaid seller wants his money rather than the right to keep hold of the goods sold. He is, therefore, entitled to sue the buyer for the price and this entitlement co-exists with any lien or right of retention he might have over the goods. Thus, s 43(2) of the SGA 1979 provides that the unpaid seller who has a lien or right of retention will not lose his lien or right of retention by reason only that he has obtained judgment against the buyer for the price of the goods. Section 43(2) can prove especially valuable in cases where, notwithstanding that the unpaid

➡ **ex works:** where goods are sold ex works, then all the seller need do is to make the goods available to the buyer at the seller's premises

---

22. See e.g. the judgment of Salmon J in *DF Mount Ltd v Jay & Jay (Provisions) Co Ltd* [1960] 1 QB 159 (QB) 169.

23. (1847) 4 CB 837, 865.

seller has sued the buyer and obtained judgment, the buyer still fails to pay, possibly because he is insolvent.

Stoppage in transit[24]

As already discussed, s 43(1)(a) provides that an unpaid seller will lose his lien or right of retention when he delivers the goods to a carrier or other bailee or custodier for the purpose of transmission to the buyer without reserving the right of disposal of the goods. Where applicable, the seller's right of stoppage in transit will enable him to resume possession of the contract goods at any time during the period of transit. The right of stoppage, therefore, can be seen as similar in effect to the seller's right of lien.

Although more limited than a lien, this remedy will be of considerable benefit to an unpaid seller where the buyer becomes insolvent after the seller has already parted with possession of the goods. Indeed, the buyer must be insolvent; it will not be sufficient that he has merely failed to pay. Thus, the unpaid seller will not be entitled to stop the goods that are already in transit merely because he is unpaid A person is deemed to be insolvent within the meaning of the SGA 1979 if he has either ceased to pay his debts in the ordinary course of business or he cannot pay his debts as they become due.[25]

The right of stoppage in transit is provided for in s 44 of the SGA 1979 and is available to the unpaid seller irrespective of whether or not the property in the goods has passed to the buyer.[26]

 SGA 1979, s 44

Subject to this Act, when the buyer of goods becomes insolvent the unpaid seller who has parted with the possession of the goods has the right of stopping them in transit, that is to say, he may resume possession of the goods as long as they are in course of transit, and may retain them until payment or tender of the price.

The seller will only have parted with the possession of the goods if he passes possession of them to a carrier independent of himself.[27] Where the seller employs his own deliveryman or where the deliveryman is the seller's agent, then it cannot be said that he has parted with the possession of the goods as required by s 44. If the seller has not parted with the possession of the goods as required by s 44, then they cannot be said to be in transit within the meaning of s 44 and the right of stoppage will not apply. Rather, in such a case, the unpaid seller can simply recall the goods

24. In the SGA 1893 and in cases decided under that Act, this remedy was referred to by its Latin phrase 'stoppage *in transitu*'.
25. SGA 1979, s 61(4).   26. ibid s 39(2).
27. For these purposes, 'carrier' might involve any or all of the following means of transporting the goods: road, air, sea, or rail. The House of Lords has held that the Post Office was the buyer's agent and so could amount to a carrier (*Badische Anilin Und Soda Fabrik v Basle Chemical Works, Bindschedler* [1898] AC 200 (HL)), but it has been contended that this is no longer an acceptable view (see e.g. PS Atiyah, John N Adams, and Hector Macqueen, *Atiyah's Sale of Goods* (12th edn, Pearson 2010) 331).

from his deliveryman should the need arise and instead exercise his right of lien over the goods.

The unpaid seller may only stop the goods in transit and thus resume possession of them provided he does so during the course of transit. Goods are deemed to be in the course of transit from the time they are delivered to a carrier (or other bailee or custodier) for the purpose of transmission to the buyer, until the time the buyer or his agent takes delivery of them from the carrier (or other bailee or custodier).[28]

If the buyer or his agent obtains delivery of the goods before their arrival at the appointed destination, then the transit is at an end.[29] The transit is also at an end if, after the arrival of the goods at their appointed destination, the carrier (or other bailee or custodier) acknowledges to the buyer or his agent that he holds the goods on his behalf and continues in possession of them as bailee or custodier for the buyer or his agent.[30] This is to reflect that in this situation, the seller is no longer in control of the goods. It will be immaterial that a further destination for the goods may have been indicated by the buyer.[31] The transit will also be deemed to be at an end in cases where the carrier (or other bailee or custodier) wrongfully refuses to deliver the goods to the buyer or his agent.[32] However, the transit will not be deemed to be at an end just because the goods are rejected by the buyer and, as a consequence, the carrier (or other bailee or custodier) continues in possession of them; this is the case even if the seller refuses to take them back.[33] Where part-delivery of the goods has been made to the buyer or his agent, the remainder of the goods may be stopped in transit, unless such part-delivery has been made under such circumstances as to show an agreement to give up possession of the whole of the goods.[34] In cases involving carriage by sea, when the goods are delivered to a ship that has been chartered by the buyer it is a question of fact, depending on the circumstances of the particular case, whether they are in the possession of the master as an independent carrier or as agent of the buyer.[35] The capacity in which the master has possession will determine whether or not the goods are still in transit or whether delivery has taken place whilst they remain on the vessel.

As the goods will already be in transit to the buyer, the seller must act quickly if he is to stop them in transit and thus prevent delivery from being made. Section 46(1) of the SGA 1979 sets out how the seller may exercise his right of stoppage in transit, which is either by taking actual possession of the goods or by giving notice of his claim to the carrier or other bailee or custodier in whose possession the goods are. Any such notice may be given either to the person in actual possession of the goods (i.e. the delivery driver) or to his principal.[36] Giving notice to the person who is in actual possession of the goods is likely to be more straightforward but, if given to the principal, the notice will not be effective unless given at such time and under such circumstances that the principal, by the exercise of reasonable diligence, may communicate it to his servant or agent in time to prevent actual delivery of the goods to the buyer.[37] When notice of stoppage in transit is given by the seller to the carrier, he must redeliver the goods to, or according to the directions of, the seller. The expenses of the redelivery will be borne by the seller.[38]

---

28. SGA 1979, s 45(1).   29. ibid s 45(2).   30. ibid s 45(3).   31. ibid s 45(3).
32. ibid s 45(6).   33. ibid s 45(4).   34. ibid s 45(7).   35. ibid s 45(5).
36. ibid s 46(2).   37. ibid s 46(3).   38. ibid s 46(4).

Liability between carrier and seller

It is important to consider the question of liability as between the carrier and the seller. The seller who wishes to stop the goods in transit is under a duty to provide clear instructions to the carrier in respect of the disposal or return of the goods in question, and the carrier must act on such a notice served by the seller to stop the goods whilst in transit. If the seller fails to give such clear instructions to the carrier, the carrier will not be liable to the seller for the consequences.[39] Where such notice has been wrongly served because the seller had no right to stop the goods, the carrier will be protected, as the buyer's remedy will be against the seller alone.[40] However, a carrier to whom a notice of stoppage has been given and who goes on (wrongly) to deliver the goods to the buyer will have committed the tort of conversion, for which he will be liable to the seller.

The carrier has himself a right of lien over the goods for the cost of freight charges properly due, and this right takes priority over the seller's right of stoppage. In practice, this means that, unless the seller is willing to pay the carrier for the cost of freight, the carrier will be entitled to refuse to redeliver the goods to him.

Right of resale

The right of the unpaid seller to resell the goods is set out in s 48 of the SGA 1979.

 SGA 1979, s 48

(1) Subject to this section, a contract of sale is not rescinded by the mere exercise by an unpaid seller of his right of lien or retention or stoppage in transit.
(2) Where an unpaid seller who has exercised his right of lien or retention or stoppage in transit resells the goods, the buyer acquires a good title to them as against the original buyer.
(3) Where the goods are of a perishable nature, or where the unpaid seller gives notice to the buyer of his intention to resell, and the buyer does not within a reasonable time pay or tender the price, the unpaid seller may resell the goods and recover from the original buyer damages for any loss occasioned by his breach of contract.
(4) Where the seller expressly reserves the right of resale in case the buyer should make default, and on the buyer making default resells the goods, the original contract of sale is rescinded but without prejudice to any claim the seller may have for damages.

It can be seen from s 48(1) that any exercise by the unpaid seller of his right of lien, retention, or stoppage in transit, does not, in itself, rescind the contract of sale and his obligations under the terms of the contract of sale remain. This means that the seller must deliver the goods if the buyer pays the price. Accordingly, it can be seen that the seller's right to resell the contract goods, although quite generous, is not unlimited.

---

39. *Booth Steamship Co Ltd v Cargo Fleet Iron Co Ltd* [1916] 2 KB 570 (CA).
40. *The Tigress* (1863) Brown & Lush 38.

Under s 48(2), where the unpaid seller who has exercised his right of lien, retention, or stoppage in transit resells the goods, the buyer acquires a good title to them as against the original buyer. There is no requirement for this new buyer to act in good faith and without notice of the previous sale.[41]

Section 48(3) makes clear that, in a case where the goods are of a perishable nature or where the unpaid seller gives notice to the buyer of his intention to resell, and the buyer does not within a reasonable time pay or tender the price, the unpaid seller may then resell the goods and recover from the original buyer damages for any loss occasioned by his breach of contract.

Section 48(4) provides that if the seller has expressly reserved the right of resale to protect his position in case the buyer fails to pay for the goods, and if the buyer then does fail to pay for the goods and the seller goes on to resell them, the original contract of sale is then rescinded. This is without prejudice to any claim the seller may have in damages against the defaulting buyer. The practical effect of rescission is that if property in the goods has already passed to the buyer, then it reverts to the seller. This means that when the seller exercises his right to resell the goods, he does so as owner. As he resells as owner, he will be entitled to keep any profit he makes should he resell at a price higher than he agreed to sell to the first buyer, as well as any deposit he received from the first buyer. If, instead of making a profit on the resale, the seller makes a loss, then he is entitled to recover such loss from the first buyer in addition to any other loss he may have suffered as a result of the first buyer's failure to pay, as the following case demonstrates.

 Ward Ltd v Bignall [1967] 1 QB 534 (CA)

FACTS: Ward Ltd contracted to sell to Bignall two motor cars for a total price of £850. Bignall paid a deposit of £25 but refused to pay the balance or take delivery of the vehicles. Ward gave him notice that unless he paid the balance, it would dispose of the vehicles. Ward subsequently sold one of the vehicles for £350, but the other remained unsold. Ward sued Bignall for the balance of the contract price plus certain advertising expenses, less the £350 it had received on the sale of one of the vehicles.

HELD: The Court of Appeal held that when Ward resold one of the vehicles, the original contract of sale was rescinded. Thus, Bignall was no longer the owner as ownership had reverted to Ward on the resale. Ward's only claim was for damages for non-acceptance of the goods rather than for the price, because the resale served to rescind the contract. This meant that the market value of the unsold vehicle, which remained Ward's own property, had to be taken into account. Diplock LJ explained the position thus:

> By making the act of resale one which the unpaid seller is entitled to perform, the subsection empowers the seller by his conduct in doing that act to exercise his right to treat the contract as repudiated by the buyer, that is, as rescinded, with the consequence that the buyer is discharged from any further liability to perform his primary obligation to pay the purchase price, and becomes subject to the secondary obligation to pay damages for non-acceptance of the goods.[42]

---

41. Unlike the situation under FA 1889, s 8/SGA 1979, s 24 (*nemo dat* exception 'sale by a seller in possession'), where the buyer must act in good faith and without knowledge of the previous sale. *Nemo dat* and its exceptions are discussed in Chapter 12.
42. [1967] 1 QB 534 (CA) 550.

★ See JWA Thornely, 'Effects of Resale by Unpaid Sellers of Goods' (1967) CLJ 168

> **COMMENT:** The Court of Appeal in *Ward* overruled *Gallagher v Shilcock*,[43] where Finnemore J had held that when a seller resells the goods, he does so not in the capacity of owner but rather in a capacity analogous to that of a pledgee, with the result that any profit made by the seller as a result of his own efforts in reselling the goods had to be paid to the defaulting buyer.

There is often no practical reason to prevent an unpaid seller from reselling the goods in circumstances where he has no right to do so. As already observed, s 48(2) provides that the buyer will acquire good title to the goods as against the original buyer. Likewise, provided one of the exceptions to the *nemo dat* principle applies, the seller will confer good title on the new purchaser. The obvious exception is that contained in FA 1889, s 8/SGA 1979, s 24. It follows that if the seller does resell the goods, thus conferring good title upon the new purchaser in circumstances where he had no right to do so, then the original buyer will be entitled to bring an action against him for non-delivery of the goods under s 51(1).

Interrelationship with FA 1889, s 8/SGA 1979, s 24

As we have already seen, where an unpaid seller who has exercised his right of lien, retention, or stoppage in transit resells the goods, the buyer acquires a good title to them as against the original buyer.[44] In order for the unpaid seller to be in a position to resell the goods under s 48(2) he must, of course, be in possession of them. This presents a degree of overlap with the *nemo dat* exception set out in FA 1889, s 8/SGA 1979, s 24, although the two provisions are by no means identical. The differences are shown in Table 16.1.

🔗 Section 8 of the FA 1889 and s 24 of the SGA 1979 are discussed at p 295

TABLE 16.1 Sale by a seller in possession

SGA 1979, s 48(2)	FA 1889, s 8/SGA 1979, s 24
Applies only where the seller is unpaid	Applies whether the seller is paid or unpaid
Applies only where the unpaid seller has exercised his right of lien, retention, or stoppage in transit	Applies where the seller continues or is in possession of the goods or of the documents of title to the goods
Applies irrespective of whether or not the new purchaser acts in good faith and without knowledge of the previous sale	Only applies to protect a bona fide purchaser who takes the goods or documents of title to the goods without notice of the previous sale
Applies whether or not the goods are delivered to the second buyer	Only applies where the goods or documents of title to the goods are delivered to the second buyer
Applies only in cases of a resale of the goods	Operates for the benefit of a sub-buyer as well as someone who takes under a pledge or other disposition of the goods

---

43. [1949] 2 KB 765 (KB).   44. SGA 1979, s 48(2).

Personal remedies

The unpaid seller's remedies against the buyer for breach of the contract of sale are set out in ss 49 and 50 of the SGA 1979. Under these sections, the seller can sue for the price or for damages for non-acceptance of the goods. Although these remedies are in addition to the seller's rights over the goods themselves, they are, in many cases, likely to be less attractive than a seller's real remedies simply because, as already observed, those remedies use the goods themselves as a form of security for the buyer's debt and will prove invaluable in cases where the buyer is insolvent. On the other hand, provided the buyer is not insolvent, most sellers simply want their money for the goods sold.

Action for the price

Section 49 deals with an action for the price and applies only in the two situations specified in the section, with the first being found in s 49(1).

 SGA 1979, s 49(1)

Where, under a contract of sale, the property in the goods has passed to the buyer and he wrongfully neglects or refuses to pay for the goods according to the terms of the contract, the seller may maintain an action against him for the price of the goods.

Section 49(1) applies where the property in the goods has passed to the buyer. The seller will only be entitled to sue under this subsection if the buyer wrongfully neglects or refuses to pay for the contract goods. Failure to pay is not in itself wrongful and will not be wrongful unless the price is due under the terms of the contract. It will not be due, for example, where the seller has extended credit to the buyer. Neither will a failure to pay be wrongful if the seller himself is in breach of his obligations (for example, if the seller is not ready and willing to give possession of the goods to the buyer in exchange for the price). Likewise, if the goods fail to conform to the contract of sale, the buyer may have a legitimate reason for refusing to make payment and such refusal will therefore not be wrongful.

The concurrent obligations of delivery and payment are discussed at p 321

The second situation where s 49 applies can be found in s 49(2).

 SGA 1979, s 49(2)

Where, under a contract of sale, the price is payable on a day certain irrespective of delivery and the buyer wrongfully neglects or refuses to pay such price, the seller may maintain an action for the price, although the property in the goods has not passed and the goods have not been appropriated to the contract.

Section 49(2) sets out the rather exceptional situation where the seller may sue for the price before the property in the goods has passed to the buyer and the goods have not been appropriated to the contract. It applies in cases where the parties have agreed that payment will be made upon the occurrence of a specific event rather than on a particular date. This is known as a payment on a 'day certain'. The event might be something like the completion of the manufacturing stage of the goods or some other stage in the process that the parties have agreed should be the day certain for the purpose of payment.[45] Where the price is payable on a day certain irrespective of delivery and the buyer wrongfully neglects or refuses to pay such price, the seller may maintain an action for the price, although the property in the goods has not passed and the goods have not been appropriated to the contract. As with an action under s 49(1), the buyer must have wrongfully neglected or refused to pay the price.

Where the contract provides that the price is to be paid in instalments, each payable on a day certain, the seller may bring a claim in respect of each instalment as it falls due for payment.[46] Being able to bring such a claim could prove especially invaluable to a seller in a case where he manufactures high-value goods to be paid for by the buyer in instalments which the buyer fails to meet. In such a case, the seller is entitled to sue for agreed instalments of the price at the time the buyer fails to pay them, rather than having to wait and commence a general claim in damages.

Section 49(2) does not cover the situation where the price is payable upon delivery of the goods even if the parties have agreed the date for delivery. This is simply because this would not be a case where the price is payable on a day certain irrespective of delivery as required by the subsection, even if it was the buyer's own wrongful act that had prevented the price from becoming due and payable.[47] In such cases, the sellers will only have a claim in damages for non-acceptance of the goods under s 50 and will not be entitled to the price.[48] Even in cases where delivery has occurred before the 'day certain', the seller will still not be entitled to claim payment until the 'day certain' arrives.

Damages for non-acceptance of the goods

Section 50(1) provides that a seller can maintain an action against a buyer for non-acceptance where the buyer wrongfully neglects or refuses to accept and pay for the goods. As before, the buyer's conduct must be wrongful, and it will not be wrongful for a buyer to refuse to accept goods that fail to conform to the contract of sale.

The general rule for measuring damages

The general rule for the measure of damages for a breach of s 50(1) is set out in s 50(2).

---

45. See e.g. *Workman Clark & Co Ltd v Lloyd Brazileno* [1908] 1 KB 968 (CA).   46. ibid.
47. *Stein, Forbes & Co v County Tailoring Co* (1916) 86 LJ KB 448 (KB); *Colley v Overseas Exporters (1919) Ltd* [1921] 3 KB 302 (KB).
48. ibid.

SGA 1979, s 50(2)

The measure of damages is the estimated loss directly and naturally resulting, in the ordinary course of events, from the buyer's breach of contract.

The damages recoverable will depend on whether or not the seller had already procured or manufactured the goods in question at the time of the buyer's breach. If he has, then the *prima facie* measure of damages will be the difference between the contract price and the value of the goods to the seller at the date of the buyer's breach. This can be seen in the following case.

 Harlow & Jones Ltd v Panex (International) Ltd **[1967] 2 Lloyd's Rep 509 (QB)**

FACTS: Panex agreed to buy 10,000 tonnes of steel from Harlow. The goods were to be delivered **FOB** during August or September at Harlow's option. Harlow notified Panex in July that the goods would be ready at the beginning of August and requested that it arrange a vessel. Panex failed to reply, but on 1 August notified Harlow that it would be calling forward half the goods in mid-August, with the remainder to be loaded by the end of August. On 3 August, Panex told Harlow that, due to non-confirmation, the mid-August vessel had been missed and that as a consequence Panex could not now ship in August. On 11 August, Panex demanded a reply within 24 hours as to whether Harlow could guarantee all the goods ready for loading between 20 and 27 August. On 22 August, Panex informed Harlow that it accepted Harlow's conduct as repudiation of the contract. Harlow commenced proceedings against Panex, alleging wrongful failure to accept the goods on or before 30 September.

HELD: Roskill J held that Panex was liable. The only term that was necessary to imply was that Harlow would notify Panex when Harlow expected to load, and then Panex would be under the normal duty under a FOB contract to provide the vessel at the correct time. Harlow's only obligation was to give the notice it had given, but which Panex had ignored. As there was no available market in the steel, the measure of damages was, according to s 50(2), the difference on 30 September between the contract price of the goods and the then value of them to Harlow. Harlow had taken back 1,500 tonnes of the steel and the measure of damage would be the loss of profit equal to the difference between the price at which Harlow bought and the price it would have got from Panex.

→ FOB: 'free on board'—typically used in international contracts for the sale of goods in which the seller's duty can be discharged by placing the goods on board a ship for onward transmission to the buyer

🔗 FOB is discussed in more detail on p 516

In cases like *Harlow & Jones*, where there is no available market, the seller will often encounter practical difficulties in being able to calculate the value of the goods at the date of the buyer's breach. If he has manufactured the goods specifically for the contract and they are unique to the specific buyer, it is quite possible that the goods will have no value to any other party, in which case his loss will be the entire sale price. Of course, such a seller will be under a general duty to mitigate his loss, which might mean him having to modify the goods so as to make them marketable to another buyer.

In cases where, at the time of the buyer's breach, the seller had not yet procured or manufactured the goods then, *prima facie*, his measure of damages will be the profit he would have made on the contract but for the breach.

Where there is an available market for the goods in question

Where there is an available market for the goods in question, then the relevant provision is s 50(3).

SGA 1979, s 50(3)

Where there is an available market for the goods in question the measure of damages is prima facie to be ascertained by the difference between the contract price and the market or current price at the time or times when the goods ought to have been accepted or (if no time was fixed for acceptance) at the time of the refusal to accept.

The question that arises is what is an 'available market'. At one time, an available market was said to refer to something akin to a Corn Exchange or Cotton Exchange where 'there was a fair market where they could have found [another] purchaser'.[49] Several decades later, Upjohn J stated in *Thompson Ltd v Robinson (Gunmakers) Ltd*[50] that, had the matter been *res integra*, he would have found that an available market merely meant that the situation in the particular trade in the particular area was such that the particular goods could freely be sold, and that there was a demand sufficient to absorb readily all the goods that were thrust on it, so that if a purchaser defaulted, the goods in question could readily be disposed of.

➔ *res integra*: 'an entire thing'—a point not governed by an earlier decision or by a rule of law

It should be remembered that s 50(3) merely lays down a *prima facie* rule for the measure of damages for cases where there exists an available market for the goods in question. In some circumstances, the application of this rule could result in an incorrect or unfair assessment of damages. For this reason, the *prima facie* rule can be displaced where there is no means of readily disposing of the goods that were contracted to be sold or otherwise where it would be unjust to apply the rule to ascertain the measure of damages to be awarded.

Thompson Ltd v Robinson (Gunmakers) Ltd [1955] Ch 177 (Ch)

FACTS: Robinson contracted to buy from Thompson a brand new Standard Vanguard motor car, but wrongfully failed to take delivery when it was available. The price of the car had been fixed by the manufacturers. Thompson mitigated its loss by persuading its supplier to take the car back without penalty. Thompson then brought a claim against Robinson for the loss of profit, which amounted to £61. Robinson argued that, as there was no difference between the market price of the car and the selling price, Thompson was only entitled to nominal damages. Robinson's case was that s 50(3) applied because

---

49. *Dunkirk Colliery Co v Lever* (1878) LR 9 Ch D 20 (CA) 25 (James LJ).   50. [1955] Ch 177 (Ch).

there was an available market for that particular car and that the price for the car had been fixed by the manufacturer. Thompson had mitigated its loss and therefore had suffered no loss.

HELD: The court rejected Robinson's argument. Upjohn J held that the meaning of 'available market' in s 50(3) is not limited to a market such as the Cotton Exchange or Baltic or Stock Exchange, but merely means that the situation in the trade in the particular area is such that the goods can freely be sold if a purchaser defaults. If there is not a demand which can readily absorb all the goods available for sale, so that if a purchaser defaults the sale is lost, there will not be an available market within the meaning of the subsection. In such a case the seller's loss is the loss of his bargain, and he will be entitled, by way of damages, to the profit that he would have made but for the buyer's wrongful failure to take delivery. Upjohn J stated that, even if there had been an available market, s 50(3) provided only a *prima facie* rule and, if it was unjust to apply it, it was not to be applied. The measure of damages was therefore Thompson's loss of profit. Robinson was ordered to pay damages of £61.

The decision in *Thompson* can be contrasted with the following case where, because the seller could easily sell the goods elsewhere, the Court only awarded nominal damages.

 ### Charter v Sullivan [1957] 2 QB 117 (CA)

FACTS: Sullivan failed to accept delivery of a Hillman Minx car, which he had contracted to buy from Charter. Shortly after Sullivan's breach, Charter resold the car for the same price to another purchaser, the retail price having been fixed by the manufacturer. Charter claimed from Sullivan the loss of profit on the repudiated sale. Demand for Hillman Minxes exceeded the supply Charter was able to obtain. In other words, the number of sales of Minxes that Charter could make was limited by the number of the cars he could obtain. He did not, therefore, lose a sale or any profit.

HELD: The Court of Appeal held that on the facts of the case, Charter had failed to prove any loss arising from Sullivan's breach. The case was one to which s 50(2) should be applied in preference to s 50(3). Section 50(2) explains that the measure of damages is the estimated loss directly and naturally resulting, in the ordinary course of events, from the buyer's breach of contract. Charter was entitled to recover only nominal damages to represent the fact of Sullivan's breach. Sellers LJ explained that where a seller can prove that profit has been irretrievably lost on a sale of goods by the buyer's default, it would be recoverable as damages in accordance with s 50(2). However, where there was a resale of the goods, the seller has the burden of proving a loss of profit beyond that which, on the face of it, has been recouped by the resale.

Unique goods

The available market rule in s 50(3) does not apply to sales of unique or one-off goods. This is because with these types of goods, the seller will only be in a position to sell them once and the Court will not permit him to make a double recovery. As the following case demonstrates, the sale of second-hand cars has been held to fall into the unique goods rule where no available market within the meaning of s 50(3) exists and the damages recoverable will be limited to the particular loss sustained, if any, on the particular transaction.

Lazenby Garages Ltd v Wright [1976] 1 WLR 459 (CA)

FACTS: Lazenby Garages Ltd ('Lazenby') bought a second-hand BMW car in February 1974 for £1,325. A few days later, Wright agreed to buy it from Lazenby for £1,670 and to take delivery on 1 March. He then told Lazenby that he did not wish to proceed with the purchase and refused to accept delivery. About six weeks later, Lazenby sold the same car to another buyer for £1,770. Despite that more profitable sale, Lazenby claimed damages from Wright for what it described as its 'loss of profit' of £345, being the difference between the £1,325 it had paid and the £1,670 purchase price agreed with Wright. Wright's defence was that Lazenby had not suffered any loss by his refusal to accept delivery.

HELD: The Court of Appeal held that where the subject matter of a repudiated sale was a unique article (like a second-hand car) for which there was no available market within the meaning of s 50(3), then the seller could recover as damages only the particular loss sustained on the transaction, and nothing more. In this case, as Lazenby had resold the very car at a higher price, it had not suffered any loss and therefore was not entitled to recover any damages.

Section 50(3) refers to 'the time or times when the goods ought to have been accepted'. This means no more than the time or times when the buyer ought to have taken delivery of the contract goods and not to the buyer's unequivocal act of acceptance in the sense of him retaining the goods for such a period of time or in such circumstances as to result in him losing any right he might have had to reject them.[51]

Seller's additional claim for interest or special damages and for losses from buyer's failure to take delivery of the goods

In addition to his right to sue the buyer for the price or for damages for non-acceptance of the goods, the seller may also be entitled, under s 54, to recover interest or claim special damages based on the loss arising from any special circumstances of which the parties were aware at the time the contract was made. The seller also has available to him a claim under s 37 in respect of any loss he has sustained following the buyer's failure or refusal to take delivery of the goods.

SGA 1979, s 37

(1) When the seller is ready and willing to deliver the goods, and requests the buyer to take delivery, and the buyer does not within a reasonable time after such request take

---

51. Acceptance in this latter sense is dealt with in Chapter 17.

delivery of the goods, he is liable to the seller for any loss occasioned by his neglect or refusal to take delivery, and also for a reasonable charge for the care and custody of the goods.

(2) Nothing in this section affects the rights of the seller where the neglect or refusal of the buyer to take delivery amounts to a repudiation of the contract.

It is important to distinguish a buyer's non-acceptance of the goods from his mere failure or refusal to take delivery of them. With the former, the buyer is rejecting the goods, whereas with a failure or refusal to take delivery, although possibly signifying his intention to reject, it might equally just be an indication that he is not quite ready to take delivery. A buyer who wrongfully neglects or refuses to accept the goods will thereby wrongly reject them, which will amount to repudiation either of the entire contract or to that part of it which relates to the goods in question.[52] However, because time of taking delivery of the contract goods will not always be of the essence, it follows that it will not necessarily be repudiatory conduct for a buyer to fail or refuse to take delivery of the goods when they are tendered, although where a buyer's failure or refusal to take delivery does signify an intention to reject the goods, the seller is then entitled to exercise his remedies for non-acceptance.

The assessment (but not the basis) of the seller's recoverable loss and expense will be influenced by the timing of the buyer's wrongful refusal to accept the contract goods. If the buyer intimates his refusal to accept the goods before tender of delivery, then the seller is likely to be in a position to avoid the expense of what would amount to an abortive tender. Where the buyer only intimates his refusal at the time of, or after, tender of delivery, then the seller will be entitled to recover his expenses not only in making the tender but also in having to return the refused contract goods to where they came.

Conclusion

Although the main priority for the seller is getting paid for the goods sold, there are other remedies available to him. As we have seen in this chapter, the unpaid seller has available to him both real remedies (i.e. against the goods) and personal remedies (against the buyer personally). His choice of remedy will often be determined by the nature of the buyer's breach and whether or not the buyer is insolvent.

Practice questions

1. In *DF Mount Ltd v Jay & Jay (Provisions) Co Ltd* [1960] 1 QB 159, Salmon J stated:

   It seems to me that the language of [s 25(2) of the Sale of Goods Act 1893] is less rigorous than that of the proviso to s 47 and does not compel me to hold that the subsection applies only in those cases where the buyer transfers the same document as that of which he is in possession with the consent of the seller.

---

52. SGA 1979, s 50(1), discussed at p 406.

Consider whether such a different construction was the intention of the draftsman of the 1893 Act or is indeed correct.

2. Under s 48(2) of the SGA 1979, where the unpaid seller who has exercised his right of lien, retention, or stoppage in transit resells the goods, the buyer acquires a good title to them as against the original buyer. There is no requirement for this new buyer to act in good faith and without notice of the previous sale. This can be contrasted with FA 1889, s 8/SGA 1979, s 24, where the buyer must act in good faith and without knowledge of the previous sale.

Critically evaluate this statement.

Further reading

John Adams, 'Damages in Sale of Goods: A Critique of the Provisions of the Sale of Goods Act' [2002] JBL 553
- Discusses and compares buyers' and sellers' remedies, including differential between contract and market, place of tender, late delivery, sub-sales, lost volume sellers, price and anticipatory breach, and specific performance.

Gordon Goldberg, 'Resale: Performance or Rescission' [1995] LMCLQ 470
- Discusses whether a contract of sale of goods remains in existence after a seller has exercised his right of resale or whether it is rescinded.

Vanessa Mak, 'The Seller's Right to Cure Defective Performance—A Reappraisal' [2007] LMCLQ 409
- Discusses whether English law lends support to a right to cure for the seller in case of defective performance in sale contracts.

John Thornely, 'The Legal Characteristics of Plastic Money' (1989) 48 CLJ 24
- Discusses the decision in *Re Charge Card Services Ltd* and considers the legal characteristics and differences between credit cards and payments by cheque.

David Tiplady, 'Supply of Goods and Charge Cards' [1989] 1 LMCLQ 22
- Considers whether the presumption that a buyer of goods is personally liable applies in credit card transactions so that a supplier has recourse to the buyer if the credit company fails to pay.

——'Damages and the Available Market' (2004/5) Buyer 1
- Examines the definition of an available market within the meaning of s 50(3) of the SGA 1979 and assesses how the appropriate level of damages might be calculated where the market price of the goods is inapplicable.

——'Liability for Loss of Goods' (2008/9) Buyer 1
- Considers whether the burden of proof in a loss-of-profits claim was on the seller to show that it could not have obtained a re-order from the buyer or on the third party to show that the seller could have done so.

- Non-delivery of the goods

- Specific performance

- Damages for breach of warranty

- The buyer's right to reject the goods

- Circumstances where the buyer will not be entitled to reject the goods

- Additional rights of buyers in consumer cases

INTRODUCTION

This chapter sets out the remedies available to the buyer under a contract of sale. Until the implementation of the Sale and Supply of Goods to Consumers Regulations 2002[1] (which came into force on 31 March 2003), the buyer's remedies against the seller were relatively straightforward and can be found in ss 51–53 of the Sale of Goods Act 1979 (SGA 1979). These remedies are damages for non-delivery of the contract goods,[2] specific performance,[3] and damages for breach of warranty.[4] Additionally, in respect of a breach of condition, the buyer generally has the right to reject the goods and repudiate the contract. Since many of the terms implied by ss 12–15 of the SGA 1979 are conditions, this will be the buyer's primary remedy for breach of these implied terms. Where the term is a warranty, such as appears in ss 12(2)(a) and 12(2)(b), then the buyer's remedy is a claim in damages.

Since the implementation of the 2002 Regulations, a buyer who deals as consumer has additional remedies of repair, replacement, reduction in price, or rescission. These additional consumer remedies will be discussed towards the end of the chapter, but first, this chapter will consider the remedies that are available to all buyers, including consumers, beginning with those remedies granted to a buyer where the seller fails to deliver the goods, or fails to deliver the goods on time.

Non-delivery of the goods

In ordinary commercial contracts for the sale of goods the rule is that time is *prima facie* 'of the essence' with respect to delivery.[5] In consumer contracts, time for delivery

---

1. SI 2002/3045, implementing Directive 1999/44/EC.   2. SGA 1979, s 51.
3. ibid s 52.   4. ibid s 53.
5. *Hartley v Hymans* [1920] 3 KB 475 (KB); *Bunge Corporation v Tradax Export SA* [1981] 1 WLR 711 (HL).

will not be of the essence unless a date for delivery has been agreed and is construed as a condition of the contract. In *Bunge Corporation v Tradax Export SA*,[6] Lord Lowry explained that it was important for the term as to time in a commercial contract to be regarded as of the essence (and hence classified as a condition) because of:

> [the] enormous practical advantages in certainty, not least in regard to string contracts where today's buyer may be tomorrow's seller. Most members of the string will have many ongoing contracts simultaneously and they must be able to do business with confidence in the legal results of their actions.[7]

Where the time of delivery is not met, the buyer is entitled to sue for non-delivery and, if he wishes, to treat the contract as repudiated. The buyer may, of course, be content to accept late delivery of the goods. If he does so, then it must follow that he waives his right to treat the contract as repudiated and reject the goods, but he will still have the right to sue for damages.[8] Where, prior to the contractual delivery date, the seller informs the buyer that he will not deliver the contract goods, then he commits an anticipatory breach of the contract, entitling the buyer to accept such breach as bringing the contract to an end and to buy alternative goods without having to await the agreed delivery date.

Section 50 of the Sale of Goods Act 1979 is discussed at p 406

In Chapter 16 it was noted that s 50 of the SGA 1979 deals with damages for non-acceptance of the goods and arises where a buyer wrongfully neglects or refuses to accept and pay for the goods. Just as a seller can sue a buyer for non-acceptance of the goods, a buyer can sue a seller for damages for breach of contract for non-delivery under s 51. This section applies where a seller wrongfully neglects or refuses to deliver the goods to the buyer.

SGA 1979, s 51

(1) Where the seller wrongfully neglects or refuses to deliver the goods to the buyer, the buyer may maintain an action against the seller for damages for non-delivery.
(2) The measure of damages is the estimated loss directly and naturally resulting, in the ordinary course of events, from the seller's breach of contract.
(3) Where there is an available market for the goods in question the measure of damages is prima facie to be ascertained by the difference between the contract price and the market or current price of the goods at the time or times when they ought to have been delivered or (if no time was fixed) at the time of the refusal to deliver.

The buyer will only be entitled to sue for non-delivery if the seller's refusal to deliver is wrongful. In Chapter 14 it was noted that the seller's duty to deliver and the buyer's duty to pay are concurrent conditions.[9] Thus, a seller would be perfectly entitled to refuse delivery if the buyer indicates that he will not pay. In such a case, as the refusal to deliver will not be wrongful, a claim under s 51 will not succeed.

Since a claim under s 51 arises where the seller wrongfully neglects or refuses to deliver 'the goods' to the buyer, it follows that where the seller delivers goods that are not in accordance with the contract, he has not delivered 'the goods' demanded

---

6. [1981] 1 WLR 711 (HL).   7. ibid 720.   8. SGA 1979, s 11(4).   9. ibid s 28.

under the contract. Consequently, where the buyer lawfully rejects such goods, a claim for damages for non-delivery under s 51 can arise. This is in addition to reclaiming the price paid.

Section 51(2) and (3) deal with the measure of damages. It follows that if the buyer is able to buy for the same price goods similar to those that the seller wrongfully refused to deliver, then his measure of damages will be nominal. If he has to pay more for the goods. Then the *prima facie* measure of damages is the difference between the contract price and the market price he ultimately had to pay for the goods from another source.

The relevant market price is that pertaining at the date of the breach. It was held in *Pagnan & Fratelli v Corbisa Industrial Agropacuaria Limitada*[10] that, although the innocent buyer is not bound to go on the market and buy at the date of the breach or bound to gamble on the market changing in his favour, if he waits and the market turns against him, this cannot increase the liability of the seller. Similarly, if the market turns in his favour, the seller's liability is not diminished. This is because 'if the innocent party goes on to the market and buys or sells after the date of the breach, this is **res inter alios acta** so far as the party in default is concerned' and the subsequent purchase will be an independent and disconnected transaction.[11] Given that an innocent party is under a duty to take all reasonable steps to mitigate his loss, the rule in *Pagnan* is not beyond criticism on the ground that a party at fault should be entitled to any benefit deriving from such mitigation.

➡ *res inter alios acta alteri nocere non debet*: 'a transaction between others does not prejudice a person who was not a party to it'

The subsequent purchase in *Pagnan* was not an independent and disconnected transaction and the buyer did not suffer any loss or damage. In such a case, the *prima facie* rule in s 51(3) will be displaced.

🔨 *Pagnan & Fratelli v Corbisa Industrial Agropacuaria Limitada* [1970] 1 WLR 1306 (CA)

FACTS: Corbisa contracted to supply maize to Pagnan to be delivered to an Italian port. It was agreed that Pagnan would be entitled to reject the maize if it was not satisfied with its condition on arrival. When the ship arrived on 19 October 1965, part of the cargo was damaged and Pagnan rejected the whole. Corbisa admitted that it was in breach of contract. Pagnan obtained a sequestration order entitling it to detain the cargo against payment of damages. On 13 November 1965, Pagnan then contracted to purchase the same goods from Corbisa at a greatly reduced price. Pagnan then sued Corbisa under the first contract for the difference between the contract price and the market price as at the date of Corbisa's breach. The tribunal found that the November purchase was part of a continuous course of dealing between the same parties for the exact same goods, and by such purchase Pagnan had diminished and mitigated its loss and so was not entitled to damages.

HELD: The Court of Appeal held that the *prima facie* rule for measuring damages in s 51(3) would not apply because the second contract was not independent and disconnected from the first contract and Pagnan had suffered no loss or damage.

---

10. [1970] 1 WLR 1306 (CA).   11. ibid 1315 (Salmon LJ).

Late delivery

The SGA 1979 does not provide any specific rules for late delivery of the contract goods. Where the buyer lawfully rejects a late tender of the goods, the case is dealt with in the same way as for non-delivery under s 51. Consequently, damages for late delivery will only arise where the buyer either elects to accept the late tender or is obliged to do so. The measure of damages for late delivery will be similar to that which is applicable for breach of warranty,[12] and will be assessed under ordinary contractual principles by applying the rule in *Hadley v Baxendale*.[13] Where the buyer accepts the late tender of the goods, his damages for late delivery will differ, depending on whether the goods were bought for his own use or for the purpose of resale.

The rule in Hadley v Baxendale is discussed at p 423

Goods bought for buyer's own use

Where the buyer purchases the goods for his own use, then the measure of damages will be the loss, if any, he has suffered as a result of the late delivery. The usual measure of damages will be the market value of the goods on the date the goods should have been delivered less the market price, if lower, on the date they were actually delivered. Of course, if the market value of the goods is higher on the date of actual delivery then the buyer has suffered no loss in this regard. In addition, the buyer ought to be able to claim damages to compensate him for any losses sustained as a result of him being deprived of the goods during the period of delay. He is, of course, under a duty to mitigate his loss, and this might require him, where reasonably practicable, to hire similar goods until the arrival of the delayed goods. If he does hire goods during this period, he ought to be able to recover the reasonable cost of the hire.

Goods bought for the purpose of resale

Where the buyer purchases the goods for the purpose of resale, and their market value has decreased by the time they were eventually delivered compared to their value when they ought to have been delivered, then the buyer is entitled to be compensated for this loss. The general rule is that the buyer's entitlement to damages is calculated as the difference between the market price of the goods at the time they should have been delivered and their market price at the time they were in fact delivered.[14] The contract price is thus irrelevant. The rule is predicated on the assumption that the buyer will resell the goods immediately he has possession of them, in which case his loss caused by the seller's delay will be any fall in the market price between the two dates just noted.

However, in *Wertheim v Chicoutimi Pulp Co*,[15] the Privy Council held that the buyer was entitled only to the difference between the market price at the time the goods ought to have been delivered and the price at which the buyer managed to resell the goods which, in this case, was considerably less than the measure of damages noted earlier as being the general rule. This resulted in the original buyer receiving a much lesser sum than he would have been awarded had the general rule been adopted.

---

12. And is thus different to the measure of damages for non-delivery, which are assessed as for breach of condition.

13. (1854) 9 Ex 341.

14. See *Koufos v Czarnikow Ltd ('The Heron II)* [1969] 1 AC 350 (HL).   15. [1911] AC 301 (PC).

Wertheim v Chicoutimi Pulp Co [1911] AC 301 (PC)

FACTS: Chicoutimi Pulp Co contracted to deliver 3,000 tonnes of moist wood pulp to Wertheim between 1 September and 1 November 1900. The contract price of the goods was 25s per tonne. Wertheim had agreed to resell the goods for 65s per tonne. The market price of the goods when delivery should have been made was 70s per tonne but had dropped to 42s 6d by the time delivery had actually been made. Wertheim claimed 27s 6d a tonne, which was the difference between the market price at the due date of delivery (70s) and the market price at the date of actual delivery (42s 6d).

HELD: The Privy Council held that since Wertheim had already agreed to resell the goods at 65s per tonne, his loss was only 5s per tonne, which was all he was entitled to recover. The general intention of the law in awarding damages for breach of contract is that a claimant should be placed in the same position he would have been in if the contract had been performed. In the case of late delivery, the measure of damages will typically be the difference between the market price at the respective dates of due and actual delivery. However, in cases where the purchaser has resold the goods at a price in excess of that prevailing at the date of actual delivery (as occurred here), then he must give credit for that excess when estimating his losses.

COMMENT: The Privy Council's decision is certainly controversial and has been the subject of much criticism on the ground that it flies in the face of the general principle that, unless specifically contemplated by the parties, the fact that the buyer has chosen to resell the goods should be ignored.[16]

Was there an available market for the goods?

Where there is an available market for the goods in question, s 51(3) provides that the measure of damages is *prima facie* to be ascertained by the difference between the contract price and the market or current price of the goods at the time the goods ought to have been delivered, or (if no time was fixed) at the time of the refusal to deliver. As the following example illustrates, this enables the buyer to recover as damages any difference in the market value of the goods.

 ComCorp Ltd

ComCorp Ltd agrees to purchase 100 office desks at a total price of £10,000, with delivery to be made on 1 March. At 1 March, the market price of these desks had increased to £12,000. The seller fails to deliver. ComCorp's measure of damages under s 51(3) is £2,000. On the other hand, if the market price as at 1 March had fallen to £8,000, then although the seller is still in breach of contract, ComCorp has suffered no financial loss. It will not be open to the seller to claim this difference from ComCorp, as it is he himself who is in breach.

Where there is no available market for the goods, then the damages are calculated in accordance with s 51(2). This means that the damages will be assessed under

---

16. See e.g. the decision of the Court of Appeal in *Slater v Hoyle & Smith Ltd* [1920] 2 KB 11 (CA), discussed at p 426.

common law in accordance with the first limb in *Hadley v Baxendale*.[17] This provides that the damages that the buyer ought to receive in respect of the breach of contract should be the loss which would arise naturally 'according to the usual course of things',[18] from the breach. The buyer is, of course, under a duty to take reasonable steps to mitigate his loss, and will only be entitled to recover damages for the loss actually suffered as a result of the seller's breach.

The relevance of the buyer's sub-contract

In cases where the market rule applies, the buyer will not generally be entitled to additional damages to compensate him for the profit he expected to make from reselling the contract goods, and this is so even where the seller knew, or ought reasonably to have foreseen when making the contract, that the purpose of the buyer's purchase was the reselling of the goods. This is because where an available market exists for the purchase of equivalent goods from another source, then such market must exist equally for the buyer to obtain such equivalent goods to satisfy his sub-contract. The buyer will be required to seek such an alternative source for the goods in order to discharge his duty to mitigate his loss, and he ought to do this irrespective of whether the market price has increased or decreased since making the contract with the seller.

 Williams Brothers v E T Agius Ltd [1914] AC 510 (HL)

FACTS: Williams Brothers agreed to buy from ET Agius Ltd a cargo of 4,500 tonnes of coal at the price of 16s 3d per tonne. Williams then agreed to sell to Ghiron a cargo of coal of the same amount and description at 19s per tonne. Ghiron then sold to Agius the cargo he had bought from Williams at 20s per tonne, and ceded to Agius all his rights and liabilities under his contract with Williams. Agius failed to deliver the cargo. At the date of Agius's breach of contract, the market price of the coal was 23s 6d per tonne. The question arose as to whether the measure of damages in respect of the non-delivery was the difference between the contract price and the market price at the time of the breach, or whether it was the difference between the contract price and the price at which Williams sold the goods to Ghiron.

HELD: The House of Lords held that the correct measure of damages was the difference between the contract price and the market price at the time of the breach. The fact of the buyer's sub-sale is ignored and therefore cannot reduce the amount of damages, even in cases where the sale is made below the market price. Lord Moulton explained that this is because:

> it is immaterial what the buyer is intending to do with the purchased goods. He is entitled to recover the expense of putting himself into the position of having those goods, and this he can do by going into the market and purchasing them at the market price. To do so he must pay a sum which is larger than that which he would have had to pay under the contract by the difference between the two prices. This difference is, therefore, the true measure of his loss from the breach, for it is that which it will cost him to put himself in the same position as if the contract had been fulfilled.[19]

---

17. (1854) 9 Ex 341.   18. ibid 355 (Alderson B).   19. [1914] AC 510 (HL) 530.

It can be seen, therefore, that the fact that the buyer bought the goods for the purpose of resale is generally ignored for the purpose of calculating damages for non-delivery, and the *prima facie* rule noted earlier prevails. However, in *R&H Hall Ltd v WH Pim Junior & Co Ltd*,[20] the House of Lords set out a number of conditions which, provided all are present, will displace the *prima facie* rule and the court will instead take account of the buyer's resale of the goods, and any loss which the buyer sustains in connection with the resale will be recoverable:

- The parties to the first contract must have contemplated that the buyer was going to resell the goods. Consequently, the first seller will have known that his buyer would sustain loss in the event of non-delivery.

- The resale contract must have been made before the delivery due date on the first contract.

- The resale contract must be for the exact same (not just similar) goods as were to be supplied under the first contract.

- The resale contract must be in accordance with the market and not be an extravagant or unusual bargain.

Where the seller could not reasonably have contemplated that his buyer intended to use the exact same goods to satisfy the sub-sale, then he is entitled to assume that his buyer will be able to obtain alternative goods to satisfy his sub-sale and, unless the buyer has committed himself such that he is obliged to resell the exact same goods that his seller has failed to deliver, then he should satisfy the sub-contract by buying goods of a similar nature in the market.[21] The question is one of what was reasonably contemplated. Merely by selling goods to a merchant (who by definition intends to resell them) does not, without more, mean that the seller reasonably contemplates that he intends to resell the exact same goods. All the seller contemplates in such a situation 'is that the merchant buys for re-sale, [and] if the goods are not delivered to him he will go out into the market and buy similar goods and honour his contract in that way'.[22] On the other hand, provided the seller ought reasonably to have contemplated the sub-sale of the exact same goods that he was contracted to, but failed to supply, then he will not be allowed to assert that his buyer had an available market in which to replace the goods. This is precisely why, for the rule to exist, the sub-sale must be for the exact same goods and not merely goods of an equivalent nature. The buyer's claim in such a case will be either one of loss of profit on the sub-sale,[23] or alternatively for an indemnity in respect of his liability to the sub-buyer.[24]

Specific performance

The usual remedy for breach of a contract of sale is rejection of the contract goods and/or an award of damages. There are, however, occasions where a monetary award

---

20. [1928] All ER Rep 763 (HL).
21. *Kwei Tek Chao v British Traders & Shippers Ltd* [1954] 2 QB 459 (QB).
22. ibid 489 (Devlin J).   23. *R&H Hall Ltd v WH Pim Junior & Co Ltd* [1928] All ER Rep 763 (HL).
24. *Bence Graphics International Ltd v Fasson UK Ltd* [1998] QB 87 (CA).

will not provide the buyer with an adequate remedy. This gap is filled by an order of specific performance, which is provided for in s 52 of the SGA 1979.

 SGA 1979, s 52

(1) In any action for breach of contract to deliver specific or ascertained goods the court may, if it thinks fit, on the [claimant's] application, by its judgment or decree direct that the contract shall be performed specifically, without giving the defendant the option of retaining the goods on payment of damages.

(2) The [claimant's] application may be made at any time before judgment or decree.

(3) The judgment or decree may be unconditional, or on such terms and conditions as to damages, payment of the price and otherwise as seem just to the court.

Where appropriate, the court will make an order that the contract is to be specifically performed. As this entails the seller actually delivering the goods to the buyer, he will therefore not have the option of retaining the goods and instead paying damages to the buyer. Specific performance compels the seller to complete his obligations under the contract. A typical case where such an order may be made is where substitute performance is unavailable, for example, where the subject matter of the contract is unique (such as with the sale of a valuable painting, family heirloom, or an antique) and where an award of damages will clearly not compensate the buyer appropriately: it will not be ordered when an award of damages will be an adequate remedy for non-delivery or in the case of ordinary goods which the buyer purchases for the purpose of resale. Thus, in *Cohen v Roche*,[25] McCardie J refused to grant an order for specific performance of eight Hepplewhite chairs because they were 'ordinary articles of commerce and of no special value or interest'[26] and which the buyer intended to resell for profit. There were thus no grounds to order the seller specifically to perform the contract, and the buyer's judgment was limited to damages for breach of contract.

In many cases, it will be obvious whether or not substitute goods are in fact available, although, as the following case demonstrates, the courts appear willing to consider the question of availability rather widely and apply a degree of commercial reality to the issue.

Sky Petroleum Ltd v VIP Petroleum Ltd [1974] 1 WLR 576 (Ch)

FACTS: Sky Petroleum Ltd ('Sky') owned a number of petrol stations. It agreed to buy all of its fuel products from VIP Petroleum Ltd ('VIP') at fixed prices for at least ten years. Due to worldwide shortages of fuel, VIP purported to **determine** the agreement. As this would have left Sky without any realistic prospects of obtaining its fuel from alternative suppliers, it sought an interlocutory injunction to prevent VIP from terminating the contract.

➡ **determine:** to bring to an end or extinguish; to terminate

---

25. [1927] 1 KB 169 (KB).   26. ibid 181.

> **HELD:** The injunction was granted, even though this meant that the contract would thereby be specifically enforced. Goulding J accepted that there was nothing unique about fuel products but, in the specific circumstances of the case, damages would not have been an adequate remedy because for all practical purposes no alternative supply was readily available and VIP was the sole means of keeping Sky's business operational.
>
> **COMMENT:** It will be observed from s 52(1) that an order for specific performance will be available 'in any action for breach of contract to deliver specific or ascertained goods'. The fuel products in this contract were neither. Goulding J explained why, in this case, it did not much matter:
>
> > Now I come to the most serious hurdle in the way of the plaintiffs which is the well known doctrine that the court refuses specific performance of a contract to sell and purchase chattels not specific or ascertained. That is a well-established and salutary rule, and I am entirely unconvinced [by the argument] that an injunction in the form sought…would not be specific enforcement at all. The matter is one of substance and not of form, and it is, in my judgment, quite plain that I am, for the time being, specifically enforcing the contract if I grant an injunction. However, the ratio behind the rule is, as I believe, that under the ordinary contract for the sale of non-specific goods, damages are a sufficient remedy. That, to my mind, is lacking in the circumstances of the present case. The evidence suggests, and indeed it is common knowledge that the petroleum market is in an unusual state in which a would-be buyer cannot go out into the market and contract with another seller, possibly at some sacrifice as to price. Here, the defendants appear for practical purposes to be the plaintiff's sole means of keeping their business going, and I am prepared so far to depart from the general rule as to try to preserve the position under the contract until a later date. I therefore propose to grant an injunction.[27]

Specific performance is only available to a buyer and is at the discretion of the court.[28] It will be observed from s 52(1) that the remedy is available only in respect of a breach of contract to deliver specific or ascertained goods.[29] In *Re Wait*,[30] Lord Hanworth MR explained that it applies 'to all cases where the goods are specific or ascertained, whether the property has passed to the buyer or not'.[31] Thus, even where the property in the goods (but not possession) has already passed to the buyer, an order for specific performance can be made. The court will not make an order for specific performance if the contract is for the sale of unascertained goods that have not been appropriated to the contract.[32] Although Lord Hanworth MR made it plain in *Re Wait* that specific performance applies whether or not the property in the goods had passed to the buyer, it seems that the courts are more likely to make an order for specific performance to protect a party that actually owns the goods, rather than a party who merely has a contractual right in them. This can be seen from *Redler Grain Silos Ltd v BICC Ltd*,[33] where the property in the goods had passed to the buyer, but

---

27. [1974] 1 WLR 576 (Ch) 578.

28. Since an order for specific performance is an equitable remedy, it is therefore discretionary, and the usual equitable maxims apply: 'he who comes to equity must come with clean hands'; 'he who seeks equity must do equity', etc. These maxims simply mean that the remedy will not be available if the party seeking it (in this case, the buyer) has not behaved fairly or properly, as it is a general rule that equity does not aid a party at fault.

29. *Sky Petroleum Ltd v VIP Petroleum Ltd* [1974] 1 WLR 576 (Ch).   30. [1927] 1 Ch 606 (CA).

31. ibid 617.   32. ibid.   33. [1982] 1 Lloyd's Rep 435 (CA).

TABLE 17.1 Examples of specific performance

Case	Goods	Decision
Behnke v Bede Shipping Company Ltd [1927] 1 KB 649 (KB)	A ship having 'peculiar and practically unique value' and whose boilers had to, and did, satisfy the German authorities	Granted
Hasham v Zenab [1960] AC 316 (PC)	A plot of land	Granted (even before the date of performance had arrived because the seller had repudiated the contract within minutes of making it and was therefore in repudiatory breach of the contract)
Sky Petroleum Ltd v VIP Petroleum Ltd [1974] 1 WLR 576 (Ch)	Fuel for the purpose of resale	Granted. Although not unique, damages would not have been an adequate remedy because no alternative supply was available in time to prevent the buyer going out of business
CN Marine Inc v Stena Line A/B (The Stena Nautica) (No 2) [1982] 2 Lloyd's Rep 336 (CA)	A ship	Refused. Damages were held to be an adequate remedy
Société des Industries Metallurgiques SA v Bronx Engineering Co Ltd [1975] 1 Lloyd's Rep 465 (CA)	Machinery, weighing more than 220 tonnes	Refused. Damages were held to be an adequate remedy
Patel v Ali [1984] Ch 283 (Ch)	A house	Refused. Specific performance will be refused where it would be unfair to a defendant or result in significant hardship
Cohen v Roche [1927] 1 KB 169 (KB)	Eight Hepplewhite chairs, which the buyer intended to resell for profit	Refused. The goods were 'ordinary articles of commerce and of no special value or interest'

the seller wrongfully retained possession of them to sell to another party, apparently content to pay damages in lieu of delivering them to the original buyer. The Court of Appeal confirmed that an injunction to prevent the sale to the other party was the correct remedy, and it was irrelevant to inquire whether damages would have been an adequate remedy. Although arriving at the question of the performance of the contact in a different way, the result still meant that the seller delivered the goods to the original buyer as intended under the terms of the contract.

Table 17.1 sets out some examples where the question of whether or not specific performance should be granted was examined. It will be observed that some of the decisions are difficult to reconcile.

Damages for breach of warranty

Where there is a breach of warranty by the seller, or where the buyer elects (or is compelled) to treat the seller's breach of condition as a breach of warranty, the buyer is not, by reason only of such breach of warranty, entitled to reject the goods.[34] A buyer in such circumstances may instead either:

(a) set up against the seller the breach of warranty in diminution or extinction of the price;[35] or

(b) maintain an action against the seller for damages for the breach of warranty.[36]

Subject to the provisions contained in s 35A in relation to partial rejection, where the contract is not severable and the buyer has accepted the goods in whole or in part, the breach of condition can only be treated as a breach of warranty, and not as a ground for rejecting the goods and treating the contract as repudiated, unless there is an express or implied term of the contract to that effect.[37]

Partial rejection is discussed at p 441

Just because the buyer has set up the breach of warranty in diminution or extinction of the price, it does not prevent him from maintaining an action for the same breach of warranty if he has suffered further damage.[38]

A claim for breach of warranty is, of course, a claim for breach of contract, and general contractual principles therefore apply. The measure of damages 'is the estimated loss directly and naturally resulting, in the ordinary course of events, from the breach of warranty'.[39] As with any breach of contract, there must be a causal link between the breach and the loss sustained. Even then, the party in breach will not be liable for all losses sustained by the innocent party. He will only be liable for those losses that can be said to have been within the contemplation of the parties at the time they made the contract[40] as the probable result of its breach. Any other losses will be irrecoverable as being too remote and therefore not considered to be within the scope of the parties' contractual obligations. The remoteness rule was explained by Alderson B in *Hadley v Baxendale*:[41]

> Where two parties have made a contract which one of them has broken, the damages which the other party ought to receive in respect of such breach of contract should be such as may fairly and reasonably be considered either arising naturally, i.e., according to the usual course of things, from such breach of contract itself, or such as may reasonably be supposed to have been in the contemplation of both parties, at the time they made the contract, as the probable result of the breach of it.[42]

The rule in *Hadley v Baxendale* consists of two limbs:

1. Damage 'such as may fairly and reasonably be considered either arising naturally, i.e., according to the usual course of things, from such breach of contract'. This limb of the rule, which is now embodied in s 53(2), relates to damage that is an inevitable consequence of the breach of contract and which the party in breach ought to have contemplated as arising from the breach.[43]

---

34. SGA 1979, s 53(1).   35. ibid s 53(1)(a).   36. ibid s 53(1)(b).   37. ibid s 11(4).
38. ibid s 53(4).   39. ibid s 53(2).
40. In *Jackson v Royal Bank of Scotland plc* [2005] UKHL 3, [2005] 1 WLR 377, the House of Lords confirmed that the test for remoteness is based on the contemplations or knowledge of the parties at the time they entered into the contract and not at the date of its breach.
41. (1854) 9 Ex 341.   42. ibid 355.
43. In *H Parsons (Livestock) Ltd v Uttley Ingham & Co Ltd* [1978] QB 791 (CA), the Court of Appeal rejected the idea that the strict duty owed by virtue of the implied terms in the SGA 1979 excluded the operation of *Hadley v Baxendale*.

2. Damage 'such as may reasonably be supposed to have been in the contemplation of both parties, at the time they made the contract, as the probable result of the breach of it'. This second limb relates to those special or abnormal losses that would not ordinarily be in the contemplation of the party in breach as being likely to result from a breach of the contract and would be recoverable only if the parties had actual knowledge of those consequences at the time of entering into the contract.

The rule in *Hadley v Baxendale* was subsequently applied by the Court of Appeal in the following case.

 Victoria Laundry (Windsor) Ltd v Newman Industries Ltd [1949] 2 KB 528 (CA)

FACTS: Victoria Laundry (Windsor) Ltd ('VL') traded as launderers and dyers. It wished to expand its business and had the opportunity of winning lucrative government dyeing contracts. In order to fulfil these contracts, it needed a larger boiler, which it bought second-hand from Newman Industries Ltd ('Newman'). While the boiler was being dismantled by a third party that had been engaged by Newman, it sustained damage, resulting in delivery to VL being some 22 weeks late. Newman was aware of the nature of VL's business and were also aware that VL intended to use the boiler as soon as possible. However, VL had not told Newman about the government contracts. VL sued Newman for breach of contract and claimed damages of:

- £16 for every week that it had operated without the boiler, which represented the profit that VL would have made had the boiler been delivered on time; and
- a further £262, which represented the cost of a government contract that VL could no longer fulfil due to the boiler arriving late.

HELD: VL could recover the £16 per week, but could not recover the £262 for the lost government contract. The Court of Appeal held that as Newman had knowledge of the nature of VL's business, and having promised delivery of the boiler by a particular date, it could not reasonably assert that it could not foresee that loss of profit would result if there was a significant delay in making delivery. This loss clearly fell within the first limb of the rule in *Hadley v Baxendale*. However, VL could not recover damages in respect of its loss of profits from the anticipated government dyeing contracts because Newman had no knowledge of them and they were accordingly irrecoverable under the second limb as special or abnormal losses, which would be recoverable only if Newman had actual knowledge of the possibility that such losses might arise at the time of entering into the contract with VL.

The *prima facie* rules set out in the SGA 1979 in relation to the assessment of damages mirror these general contractual principles.

Breach of warranty of quality

In the case of breach of warranty of quality, s 53(3) provides that the loss is *prima facie* the difference between the value of the goods at the time of delivery to the buyer and the value they would have had if they had conformed to the contract. This rule is designed simply to compensate the buyer for the lower value in the goods as a result of the defects. Apart from showing the value that the goods ought to have had, the market price itself is therefore irrelevant to the determination of damages, although not necessarily irrelevant to the buyer, who may wish (provided he is so entitled) to reject the defective goods if the market price has fallen, thereby shifting the loss caused by such a fall onto the buyer. The law will not protect the seller in such circumstances, and provided the buyer is entitled to reject the goods, the fact that he might have been motivated to do so by a fall in the market is not relevant.

The different values are to be measured as at the contractual date for delivery,[44] although where the seller knew or ought reasonably to have known that the goods sold were likely to be resold without being examined by the buyer, then the date for valuation will be when the goods have been delivered to the sub-buyer.[45] Furthermore, in the case of a resale, where any defect would not be discovered until after the buyer had resold the goods to his own customer, damages should be assessed on the basis of the buyer's liability to his ultimate customer and not under the *prima facie* rule in s 53(3).[46] In any event, as the measure of loss in s 53(3) is only a *prima facie* rule, it may be displaced if there is evidence that the buyer has suffered loss greater or less than the difference in these values.

 Bence Graphics International Ltd v Fasson UK Ltd [1998] QB 87 (CA)

FACTS: Fasson manufactured and sold to Bence some vinyl film. Bence then printed identification markings on it before selling it on to end-users, for use in labelling bulk containers. A condition of the contract between Fasson and Bence provided that the film and markings should remain in good condition for a period of five years. As a result of a defect in the film, it soon degraded to such an extent that the markings became illegible. Bence sought to recover from Fasson the whole of the purchase price, or alternatively an indemnity against claims from end-users. The trial judge assessed damages under s 53(3), holding that the appropriate measure of damages was the difference between the value of the goods on delivery and their value if the warranty had been fulfilled. Fasson appealed.

HELD: The Court of Appeal allowed Fasson's appeal and held that the *prima facie* measure of damages for breach of warranty of quality under s 53(3) would be displaced where it had been in the contemplation of the parties at the time the warranty was given that the goods would be resold and that, in the circumstances of the case, where Fasson would have known that any defect would not be discovered until after Bence had resold the goods, it was appropriate that damages should be assessed on the basis of Bence's actual liability to the ultimate buyer and not under the *prima facie* rule in s 53(3).

COMMENT: On the assumption that the film, when it was delivered in its defective state, had no market value, the *prima facie* measure of damages under s 53(3) (namely, the difference between their value on delivery and the value they would have had but for the breach) was the entire contract price of more than £564,000. As a result of Fasson's breach, Bence was also exposed to the risk of end-users claiming damages, which would have resulted in this *prima facie* sum being exceeded. However, as it turned out, only a few

---

44. *Argos Distributors Ltd v Advertising Advice Bureau* [1996] CLY 5285 (County Court).
45. *Van den Hurk v Martens & Co Ltd (In Liquidation)* [1920] 1 KB 850 (KB).
46. *Bence Graphics International Ltd v Fasson UK Ltd* [1998] QB 87 (CA).

★ See GH Treitel, 'Damages for Breach of Warranty of Quality' (1997) 113 LQR 188

complaints were ever made by end-users, so that Bence's actual loss was considerably less than the *prima facie* sum. This is a classic case where the *prima facie* rule in s 53(3) should be displaced, and by displacing it, the Court of Appeal in effect applied the principles in *Hadley v Baxendale* so that only the actual losses could be recovered.

In *Argos Distributors Ltd v Advertising Advice Bureau,*[47] the goods supplied were so defective that their value was nil. The county court extinguished the contract price in its entirety, holding that the seller was not entitled to any payment on the basis of a total failure of consideration.

Damages are not confined to those calculated under s 53(3). For example, in *Godley v Perry,*[48] Edmund Davies J held that damages for personal injury or death could be recovered in a case where a defective catapult broke and injured a six-year old boy and was therefore not of merchantable quality nor fit for purpose, as required by the SGA 1893. Damages can also be awarded to recover monies that the buyer has to pay out to his sub-buyer arising from the breach,[49] provided the seller knew or ought to have known that the goods were to be resold. In the *Argos* case, the court also awarded the buyers damages in respect of the profit they lost on the sale, as well as a further sum as damages for future profits on expected repeat orders.[50]

Sub-sales

As already observed, the fact that the buyer has bought the goods for the purpose of resale is generally ignored when assessing his measure of damages. Although this can lead to a windfall profit, the principle can be justified.

 Slater v Hoyle & Smith Ltd [1920] 2 KB 11 (CA)

FACTS: Hoyle & Smith Ltd ('Hoyle') bought, from Slater, 3,000 pieces of cloth of a specified quality. Slater delivered 1,625 pieces of cloth, but it was of a quality poorer than that specified in the contract. Hoyle paid for the inferior quality cloth, but refused to accept any further deliveries. Hoyle resold some of this poorer quality cloth under a separate contract he had made with a customer (the sub-buyer), which specified the higher-quality material and for which Hoyle received payment in full. Hoyle therefore made no loss on this transaction. Slater sued Hoyle for non-acceptance of the goods and Hoyle counterclaimed for Slater's breach of contract.

HELD: The Court of Appeal held that the sub-sale was irrelevant insofar as his measure of damages were concerned and that Hoyle was entitled to receive as damages the difference between the value of the goods contracted for and the value of the goods which were actually delivered. In considering the obvious objection to allowing Hoyle to benefit in this way, Scrutton LJ stated:

> It was said that as the sub-buyer … had made no claim on the buyers, the buyers should not recover anything for the inferiority in the goods they redelivered to him; for, as the sub-buyer had paid the buyers their full contract price, to allow them to recover

47. [1996] CLY 5285.
48. [1960] 1 WLR 9 (QB). This case is discussed on p 381.
49. ibid.
50. *Argos Distributors Ltd v Advertising Advice Bureau* [1996] CLY 5285.

> in addition something for the inferiority would be to give them more if the goods were inferior than they would have got if they were sound and were to be delivered... [T]he buyers had two contracts with the sub-buyer, the first below the market price, the second above it. Neither sub-contract formed the basis of the original contract; the buyers were under no obligation to deliver the goods of the original contract to the sub-buyer, and in fact they delivered under the first sub-contract a large quantity of goods not obtained from the sellers. Further, the [trial] judge has refused to make the sellers pay the profits which the buyers might have made by supplying sound goods from this contract under their second sub-contract, but the sellers, though freed from liability for the higher price of the second sub-contract, desire to take advantage of the lower price of the first subcontract. Can they do so?[51]

It is a well-established principle that, where there is a market price, damages do not include the loss of any particular contract unless *that* contract had been in the contemplation of the parties to the original contract. Buyers are, of course, perfectly at liberty to satisfy any sub-contracts by buying alternative goods in the market.

In the result, Scrutton LJ held:

> Either the sub-sale was of the identical article which was the subject of the principal sale or it was not. If it was not, it is absurd to suppose that a contract with a third party as to something else, just because it is the same kind of thing, can reduce the damages which the unsatisfied buyer is entitled to recover under the original contract. If, on the other hand, the sub-sale is of the self-same thing or things as is or are the subject of the principal sale, then ex-hypothesi the default of the seller in the original sale is going to bring about an enforced default on the part of the original buyer and subsequent seller. And how can it ever be known that the damages recoverable under that contract will be calculable in precisely the same way as in the original contract? All that will depend upon what the sub-buyer will be able to make out. The only safe plan is, therefore, in the original contract, to take the difference of market price as the measure of damages and to leave the sub-contract and the breach thereof to be worked out by those whom it directly concerns.[52]

Consequential losses

Any consequential losses for breach of warranty will be assessed under ordinary contractual principles. In *Parsons (Livestock) Ltd v Uttley Ingham & Co Ltd*,[53] the Court of Appeal held that where parties contemplate the type of consequence that may follow from a breach of contract, they will be liable for specific damage of that type, even where such specific damage was itself not foreseeable. However, where the buyer has failed to take reasonable precautions, then the seller may not be liable for the resulting consequences of his breach, as such failure by the buyer may constitute a *novus actus interveniens:*.

➡ *novus actus interveniens:* 'a new intervening act'—an act or event that breaks the chain of causation between a wrong committed by a defendant and the loss sustained by the claimant

 ### Lambert v Lewis [1982] AC 225 (HL)

FACTS: Lewis, a farmer, bought a trailer coupling from Lexmead (Basingstoke) Ltd ('Lexmead'). The coupling was defective, but Lewis allowed his employees to continue to use it without having it repaired or taking any steps to ascertain whether it was safe to continue to use it, even though he was or ought to have been aware that it was dangerous. In the event, the coupling gave way, causing the trailer to become detached and career across the road into the path of a car. In the resulting accident, the driver of the car (Lambert) and his son were killed and others were injured.

HELD: The House of Lords held that, although Lexmead was in breach of the implied terms as to fitness for purpose and merchantable quality, once it became apparent to Lewis that the locking mechanism of the towing hitch was broken, and consequently was no longer in the same state as when it was delivered, there was no longer any warranty by Lexmead of its continued safety in use on which Lewis was entitled to rely. In those circumstances, Lewis' claim against Lexmead failed and he could not succeed in claiming an indemnity from Lexmead in respect of his own liability to the injured parties. Lexmead would only have been liable to indemnify Lewis if it had expressly contracted with him on terms that he need not take the very precaution for which he had been held liable.

★ See Michael G Bridge, 'Defective Products, Contributory Negligence, Apportionment of Loss, and the Distribution Chain: Lambert v Lewis' (1982) 6 Can Bus LJ 184

The buyer's right to reject the goods

The buyer may reject the goods in a number of circumstances, many of which are straightforward, including:

- where the contract of sale expressly gives the buyer the right to reject the goods for a specific event, then upon the occurrence of that event the buyer may reject the goods;
- where the seller breaches a condition of the contract of sale (such as a breach of the terms implied by s 14(2) or 14(3) requiring the goods to be of satisfactory quality or fit for purpose), the buyer may reject the goods. This is in addition to his right to a claim in damages. If delivery has not yet occurred, then the buyer can simply refuse to take delivery or, in any event, he may inform the seller that he rejects the goods;
- where the seller commits a repudiatory breach of the contract of sale, the buyer may accept such breach as bringing the contract to an end.

Other instances where the buyer has the right to reject are more complex and require further discussion.

Breach of an innominate term

Where the seller has breached an innominate term which results in the buyer being deprived of substantially the entire benefit of the contract, then the buyer will be entitled to reject the goods. If the breach does not have this effect, then the buyer will only be entitled to succeed in damages, as the following case demonstrates.

 Cehave NV v Bremer Handelsgesellschaft mbH (The Hansa Nord) **[1976] QB 44 (CA)**

FACTS: Cehave agreed to purchase from Bremer a quantity of citrus pulp pellets for use as animal feed. The contract price was £100,000, which Cehave paid. A trade-standard term of the contract required 'shipment to be made in good condition'. When the shipment arrived at Rotterdam some of the goods were damaged. Further, the market price had fallen. Cehave rejected the entire shipment on the ground that shipment was not made in good condition, and sought to recover the £100,000 paid. Bremer rejected the claim. Bremer was able to sell the entire shipment to an importer for £30,000, who then resold it later the same day for the same sum to Cehave, who went on to use it for animal feed by using smaller percentages in its compound feeds than would have been normal had the goods been sound.

HELD: The Court of Appeal held that, since the contract of sale stipulated that the pellets were being bought for use in cattle feed and the whole cargo was in fact used for that purpose, Cehave's only remedy was a claim in damages. This was because the goods were of merchantable quality as required by s 14(2) and the term requiring 'shipment to be made in good condition' was not a condition such that any breach would entitle the buyer to reject the goods, but rather an innominate term, which gave no right to reject unless the breach went to the root of the contract so as to deprive the buyer of substantially the entire benefit of the contract. Since the whole cargo was used for its intended purpose as animal feed, the breach did not go to the root of the contract and Cehave, though entitled to damages, was not entitled to reject.

Where the seller delivers the wrong quantity of goods

The contract will typically set out the quantity of goods to be delivered. Section 30 of the SGA 1979 explains the position where the seller delivers the wrong quantity of the goods. However, before considering s 30, it is important to note that s 30(5) explains that s 30 is 'subject to any usage of trade, special agreement, or course of dealing between the parties'. This means that s 30(1) and (2), which relates to deliveries for less or more than contracted for, may be modified, typically by express agreement made by the parties, or implied, for example, by trade usage where a certain tolerance of either short or over deliveries is considered normal or alternatively by previous course of dealing between the parties.

Where the seller delivers less than he contracted to sell

Where the seller delivers less than the amount stipulated in the contract, then the relevant provision is s 30(1).

 SGA 1979, s 30(1)

Where the seller delivers to the buyer a quantity of goods less than he contracted to sell, the buyer may reject them, but if the buyer accepts the goods so delivered he must pay for them at the contract rate.

The buyer is entitled to sue for non-delivery in respect of the goods that ought to have been delivered but were not in fact delivered. The reason for the short delivery is of little concern to the buyer and may even be due to the buyer himself rejecting part of the goods on the ground they are not in conformity with the contract of sale.

The buyer's entitlement to sue for non-delivery is subject to three caveats. First, any shortfall that is merely a 'microscopic deviation' of the contract quantity is likely

The *de minimis* principle is discussed at p 329

to be disregarded by the courts under the *de minimis* principle.[54] This principle is now encapsulated in s 30(2D)(a) of the SGA 1979, which provides that where the seller delivers a quantity of goods less than he contracted to sell, the buyer will not be entitled to reject the goods unless the shortfall 'is material'. Second, even in cases where the breach is not *de minimis*, a buyer who does not deal as consumer is nevertheless not entitled to reject in cases where the shortfall is so slight that it would be unreasonable for him to do so.[55] This provision is quite similar to the different remedies available to consumer and non-consumer buyers found in s 15A of the SGA 1979 in relation to the statutory implied terms. Third, certain shipments of goods are prone to shortages, such as fuel, which could result in wastage through evaporation. In such cases, this kind of shortage falls within a degree of tolerance either specified in the contract of sale itself or otherwise implied by custom. A buyer would not be entitled to reject for short delivery in this last example, but would simply pay a lesser price to cover the goods actually delivered.

Section 15A of the Sale of Goods Act 1979 is discussed at p 443

Section 31(1) makes plain that, unless otherwise agreed, a buyer is not bound to accept delivery by instalments. Therefore, if a buyer chooses to accept a short delivery, the seller will not be able to compel him to accept the remainder of the contract goods at a later date, although the buyer may, if he so wishes, choose to do so. If the buyer chooses not to take the shortfall at a later date, he will be entitled to recover the price paid for such shortfall on the basis of total failure of consideration in respect of such shortfall, as well as damages for non-delivery in respect of any loss he has suffered for not having the missing goods at the agreed time. He is, of course, under a duty to mitigate his loss, which might mean that although he is within his rights to refuse to take the shortfall at a later date, such refusal might amount to a failure to mitigate, resulting in the non-recovery of any loss.

Where the seller delivers more than he contracted to sell

Where the seller delivers more than the amount stipulated in the contract, then the relevant provision is s 30(2).

 SGA 1979, s 30(2)

> Where the seller delivers to the buyer a quantity of goods larger than he contracted to sell, the buyer may accept the goods included in the contract and reject the rest, or he may reject the whole.

The buyer may choose either to (i) accept the correct quantity of the goods and reject the rest; or (ii) he may reject the whole. Where the buyer chooses to accept the whole of the goods so delivered, he must pay for them at the contract rate.[56] In such a case, the buyer also waives any remedy for such breach. This is because the seller in such a situation is deemed to have offered the buyer a new contract of sale, which the buyer has accepted.[57]

---

54. *Arcos Ltd v EA Ronaasen & Son* [1933] AC 470 (HL) 480 (Lord Atkin).
55. SGA 1979, s 30(2A)(a).   56. ibid s 30(3).
57. *Gabriel, Wade & English Ltd v Arcos Ltd* (1929) 34 Ll L Rep 306 (KB).

Similar to the position considered earlier regarding a seller making a short delivery, any trifling excess in quantity will be disregarded under the *de minimis* principle. Thus, in *Shipton, Anderson & Co v Weil Brothers & Co*,[58] Lush J held that as the quantity in excess of that contracted for was so trifling and the sellers had not in any event claimed the price for the excess, the sellers had substantially performed the contract and the buyers were not entitled to reject the entire cargo under s 30(2) of the SGA 1893.[59] The principle in *Shipton* is now encapsulated in s 30(2D)(b) of the SGA 1979, which provides that where the seller delivers a quantity of goods larger than that contracted for, the buyer may not reject all of the goods unless the excess 'is material'. The buyer is, of course, perfectly entitled to reject the quantity in excess of the contract quantity and just keep and pay for the quantity actually contracted for.[60] Where the seller delivers a quantity of goods larger than he contracted to sell, a buyer who does not deal as consumer may not reject the whole under s 30(2) if the excess is so slight that it would be unreasonable for him to do so.[61] Again, one will see the similarity between this provision and the different remedies available to consumer and non-consumer buyers found in s 15A of the SGA 1979 in relation to the statutory implied terms.

 Shipton is discussed in more detail on p 330

It can be seen that in respect of both short and excess deliveries, s 30(2A) is expressed only in terms of when the buyer does not deal as consumer. There is no corresponding provision explaining what happens in the case of a buyer who does deal as consumer, although it seems reasonable to conclude that it implies that a buyer who does deal as consumer will be entitled to reject the goods in the circumstances set out therein.

Delivery by instalments

Deliveries by instalments typically arise in the commercial context, being somewhat uncommon in consumer transactions. Unless otherwise agreed, the buyer of goods is not bound to accept delivery by instalments.[62] Thus, where the seller delivers short, he will not be entitled to make up the shortfall at a later stage unless the buyer agrees. Where only part of the contract goods have been delivered and accepted, the buyers will be entitled to refuse to accept later deliveries of the balance of the goods and will only be liable to pay pro rata for the goods accepted.

Behrend & Co Ltd v Produce Brokers Co Ltd [1920] 3 KB 530 (KB)

FACTS: Under two similar contracts, Behrend & Co Ltd ('Behrend') agreed to sell a quantity of cotton seed to Produce Brokers Co Ltd ('PB'). The contracts provided that the cotton seed would be shipped from Alexandria and delivered to London. On the arrival of the ship in London, PB paid for the goods. It was then discovered that only a portion of the seed had been delivered. The ship then left with the remainder of the seed on

---

58. [1912] 1 KB 574 (KB).
59. Which provides that, 'where the seller delivers to the buyer a quantity of goods larger than he contracted to sell, the buyer … may reject the whole'.
60. SGA 1979, s 30(2).   61. ibid s 30(2A)(b).   62. ibid s 31(1).

> board in order to discharge other cargo. The ship returned to London two weeks later and the balance of the seed was tendered to PB, but it refused to accept it. PB retained the portion that had been delivered and claimed repayment of the price paid for the rejected portion.
>
> **HELD:** When the delivery had begun, PB was entitled to receive the whole quantity that it had ordered before the ship left the port. Given that this had not occurred at that time, PB was entitled to keep the part actually delivered and to reject the balance, and it was entitled to recover the price paid for the portion it rejected.

Where there is a contract for the sale of goods to be delivered by stated instalments, which are to be separately paid for, and the seller makes defective deliveries in respect of one or more instalments, or the buyer neglects or refuses to take delivery of or pay for one or more instalments, it is a question in each case, depending on the terms of the contract and the circumstances of the case, whether the breach of contract is a repudiation of the whole contract or whether it is a severable breach giving rise to a claim for compensation but not to a right to treat the whole contract as repudiated.[63]

Where the contract of sale is severable, and the buyer has accepted one or more of the instalments, he is not prevented from rejecting later instalments for breach of condition.

Jackson v Rotax Motor and Cycle Company [1910] 2 KB 937 (CA)

FACTS: The buyer purchased a large number of motor horns of different descriptions and prices with delivery to be made 'as required'. The horns were delivered in several instalments. After accepting the first instalment the buyer rejected the later instalments on the ground that they were not of merchantable quality. At first instance, it was found that a large proportion of the horns were dented and badly polished owing to defective packing and careless workmanship, but that they could easily and cheaply have been made merchantable. As a result, the court refused to hold that the consignment as a whole was unmerchantable, but made an allowance to the buyer in respect of the defective goods. The buyer appealed.

HELD: The appeal was allowed and the Court of Appeal held that on the true construction of the contract, acceptance of the first instalment of the goods did not preclude the buyer from rejecting the later instalments and that on the facts of this case the buyer was justified in rejecting the later instalments as they were not of merchantable quality.

In *Jackson*, the first instalment of goods was in breach of contract. Is a buyer entitled to treat the entire contract as repudiated and reject all instalments where it is just the later instalments that give rise to the breach of condition? This situation is provided for in s 31(2) of the SGA 1979.

---

63. SGA 1979, s 31(2).

SGA 1979, s 31(2)

Where there is a contract for the sale of goods to be delivered by stated instalments, which are to be separately paid for, and the seller makes defective deliveries in respect of one or more instalments, or the buyer neglects or refuses to take delivery of or pay for one or more instalments, it is a question in each case depending on the terms of the contract and the circumstances of the case whether the breach of contract is a repudiation of the whole contract or whether it is a severable breach giving rise to a claim for compensation but not to a right to treat the whole contract as repudiated.

This issue arose for determination in the following case, in which Lord Hewart CJ established two tests that should be applied by the courts.

 ***Maple Flock Co Ltd v Universal Furniture Products (Wembley) Ltd* [1934] 1 KB 148 (CA)**

FACTS: Maple Flock Co Ltd ('Maple Flock') entered into a severable contract with Universal Furniture Products (Wembley) Ltd ('UFP'), under which UFP agreed to buy from Maple Flock 100 tonnes of rag flock to be delivered by instalments. The first fifteen instalments of the flock were satisfactory, but the sixteenth was defective as it was found to be in breach of the relevant government standard. This was followed by four more satisfactory instalments. UFP purported to rescind the entire contract. Further deliveries were then made which were satisfactory, but UFP maintained its entitlement to rescind the entire contract and refused to accept any further deliveries. Maple Flock claimed that this was a breach of contract and commenced proceedings.

HELD: Maple Flock's claim succeeded and the Court of Appeal held that UFP was not entitled to repudiate the contract. Where there is a sale of goods under a severable contract and only some of the instalments are defective, whether the buyer will be entitled to reject the entirety of the goods and regard the entire contract as repudiated will turn on the true meaning of s 31(2), with the main tests to be considered being (i) the quantitative ratio which the breach bears to the contract as a whole; and (ii) the degree of probability that such a breach will be repeated. As to the ratio quantitatively which the breach bore to the contract as a whole, Lord Hewart CJ said that the delivery complained of amounted to no more than 1½ tonnes out of a contract for 100 tonnes, and the likelihood of the breach being repeated was practically negligible. It was for this reason that the Court of Appeal held that UFP was not entitled to regard the entire contract as repudiated.

Where delivery is to be made by instalments, parties will often contract on the basis that 'each instalment is to be considered as a separate contract'. In this type of case, the courts are likely to hold that there is only one contract, although severable. This means that if there is a breach that is sufficiently serious, the entire contract might be repudiated.[64]

---

64. *Smyth & Co Ltd v TD Bailey Son & Co* [1940] 3 All ER 60 (HL).

The buyer is not bound to return rejected goods

Unless otherwise agreed, where goods are delivered to the buyer, and he refuses to accept them, having the right to do so, he is not bound to return them to the seller, but it is sufficient if he intimates to the seller that he refuses to accept them.[65] If the seller wants them back, then he must collect them. Furthermore, in *Kolfor Plant Ltd v Tilbury Plant Ltd*,[66] the Divisional Court held that the buyer, having been entitled to reject the goods, was also entitled to damages in respect of the cost of transporting them to a safe place and storing them until the seller collected them. The buyer succeeded on the ground that the loss arose from the seller's breach of contract and ought therefore to have been foreseen by him. Where the seller requests the return of the rejected goods, then the buyer must comply, even if the seller has not returned his purchase money or if the cheque intended as a refund is dishonoured.[67] This is because a buyer who has rejected the goods after paying the price is not in the same position as an unpaid seller under ss 38 and 39 of the SGA 1979 and therefore has no lien upon the goods and consequently is not entitled to retain possession of them until the money paid has been returned.[68] Such a buyer should instead commence an action against the seller to recover the price paid on the ground of there having been a total failure of consideration.

Circumstances where the buyer will not be entitled to reject the goods

The buyer will not be entitled to reject the goods in the following circumstances.

Acceptance

The buyer will lose his right to reject the goods if he has accepted them, although the right to reject after acceptance remains available for a breach of s 12(1) of the SGA 1979. In *Kwei Tek Chao v British Traders & Shippers Ltd*,[69] Devlin J confirmed that, provided the buyer has not accepted the goods within the meaning of s 35, he may exercise his right of rejection even after the property has passed to him.

 Partial rejection is discussed at p 441

As already observed, subject to the provisions contained in s 35A in relation to partial rejection, where the contract is not severable and the buyer has accepted the goods in whole or in part, the breach of condition can only be treated as a breach of warranty and not as a ground for rejecting the goods and treating the contract as repudiated, unless there is an express or implied term of the contract to that effect.[70]

The mere act of taking delivery is not in itself acceptance. Acceptance is dealt with in s 35 of the SGA 1979.

---

65. SGA 1979, s 36.   66. (1977) 121 Sol Jo 390 (DC).
67. *J L Lyons & Co Ltd v May & Baker Ltd* [1923] 1 KB 685 (KB).
68. ibid 688 (Shearman J).   69. [1954] 2 QB 459 (QB).   70. SGA 1979, s 11(4).

SGA 1979, s 35

(1) The buyer is deemed to have accepted the goods subject to subsection (2) below:

    (a) when he intimates to the seller that he has accepted them, or

    (b) when the goods have been delivered to him and he does any act in relation to them which is inconsistent with the ownership of the seller.

(2) Where goods are delivered to the buyer, and he has not previously examined them, he is not deemed to have accepted them under subsection (1) above until he has had a reasonable opportunity of examining them for the purpose:

    (a) of ascertaining whether they are in conformity with the contract, and

    (b) in the case of a contract for sale by sample, of comparing the bulk with the sample.

(3) Where the buyer deals as consumer or (in Scotland) the contract of sale is a consumer contract, the buyer cannot lose his right to rely on subsection (2) above by agreement, waiver or otherwise.

(4) The buyer is also deemed to have accepted the goods when after the lapse of a reasonable time he retains the goods without intimating to the seller that he has rejected them.

(5) The questions that are material in determining for the purposes of subsection (4) above whether a reasonable time has elapsed include whether the buyer has had a reasonable opportunity of examining the goods for the purpose mentioned in subsection (2) above.

(6) The buyer is not by virtue of this section deemed to have accepted the goods merely because:

    (a) he asks for, or agrees to, their repair by or under an arrangement with the seller, or

    (b) the goods are delivered to another under a sub-sale or other disposition.

At its most basic level, a buyer is deemed to have accepted the goods if he intimates acceptance to the seller,[71] although in practice this would rarely happen. It is more likely that a buyer will be deemed to have accepted the goods when, following delivery to him, he does any act in relation to them which is inconsistent with the ownership of the seller.[72] The question that arises is what amounts to such an act.

Asking for, or agreeing to, repair of the goods

Prior to the introduction of s 35(6) in 1994,[73] a buyer was deemed to have accepted the goods if he asked for, or agreed to, their repair. Asking for, or agreeing to, a repair was deemed to constitute acceptance under s 35(1)(b) because it was inconsistent with the ownership of the seller. Section 35(6)(a) makes it plain that asking for, or agreeing to, goods being repaired is not to be treated as deemed acceptance of the goods, and therefore will not in itself prevent a buyer from exercising his right to reject.

Further, although s 35(6)(a) does not operate to 'stop the clock' for the purpose of determining what is a reasonable time for the purpose of s 35(4), the courts are more likely to treat it that way where the buyer has acted reasonably, and especially where he is awaiting information from the seller as to the problem and the likelihood of remedying the same.

---

71. ibid s 35(1)(a).   72. ibid 2 35(1)(b).

73. As a result of the Sale and Supply of Goods Act 1994.

J & H Ritchie Ltd v Lloyd Ltd [2007] UKHL 9

FACTS: J & H Ritchie Ltd ('Ritchie') bought some farming equipment from Lloyd Ltd ('Lloyd'). Upon its first use, the equipment was found to be faulty. Ritchie returned the equipment to Lloyd for inspection and possible repair. After a few weeks, Lloyd informed Ritchie that the equipment had been repaired and was ready for collection. However, Lloyd would not tell Ritchie what had been done, but insisted that the equipment was now to 'factory-gate specification'. Ritchie wanted to know what had been done to the equipment and was concerned because it was unable to test it properly until the following season. As a result of its concern, Ritchie rejected the equipment and demanded the return of the price paid. Lloyd refused and so Ritchie commenced proceedings.

HELD: The House of Lords observed that prior to the introduction of s 35(6)(a), it was questionable whether asking the seller to repair defective goods might amount to an implied intimation of acceptance by the buyer or to an inconsistent act that would prevent him from rejecting the goods. Parties will often attempt to have defective goods remedied, but the very informality of these kinds of arrangement gives rise to a problem in identifying the legal situation with regard to the right of rejection. When Ritchie took the goods to Lloyd for inspection and repair, the parties entered into a separate 'inspection and repair' agreement. Their Lordships, therefore, felt it appropriate to imply a term into that agreement that, so long as Lloyd was performing his obligations under this agreement, Ritchie was not entitled to exercise his right to rescind the contract of sale. Although the right to reject is lost when a buyer decides to accept the goods or is deemed to have accepted them, such election could not reasonably be expected to be made until the buyer had received the necessary information to enable him to make an informed decision, and the seller could not refuse to provide this information. Accordingly, Lloyd was under an implied obligation to provide Ritchie with the necessary information requested and, in the absence of this information, Ritchie was entitled to reject the goods even though they had, in fact, been repaired to a satisfactory standard. Lloyd's refusal to supply the information amounted to a material breach of the inspection and repair agreement, which entitled Ritchie to rescind it and to refuse to collect the repaired equipment. Once Ritchie had rescinded the inspection and repair agreement, there was nothing to prevent it from exercising its right to rescind the sale contract and reclaim the purchase price of the contract goods.

⭐ See Michael G Bridge, 'Sale of Goods in Scotland—A Second Tender: J&H Ritchie Ltd v Lloyd Ltd' [2007] JBL 814

Complaining about the goods and rejecting them are, of course, two entirely different things, and no amount of complaining will equate to rejection, as the following case demonstrates.

Lee v York Coach & Marine [1977] RTR 35 (CA)

FACTS: In March 1974, Lee purchased from York Coach & Marine ('York') a seven-year-old car for £355. The car came with a new MOT certificate. In the two weeks following purchase, Lee twice returned the car for repairs, using it only for the purpose of driving her children to school and for one 40-mile journey. When York refused to carry out any further repairs, Lee had the car examined, and it was found to be in such a poor condition that it should not have been given an MOT certificate. In the expert's opinion, the car was in a dangerous state, especially in respect of its braking system and of corrosion to its sub-frame. Lee commenced proceedings in order to recover the purchase price of the car on the ground that she was entitled to rescind the contract of sale. York contended that at no time prior to the issue of proceedings in September 1974 did Lee expressly reject the car and that it was now too late to do so.

HELD: The Court of Appeal held that the car was neither of merchantable quality nor fit for its intended purpose, since although it had in fact been driven on the road, there was clear evidence that it was not in a condition where it could safely be so driven. However, since Lee held onto the car for more than a reasonable period of time before rejecting it, she had lost her right to reject, and her remedy lay only in damages.

In the following Scottish case, the court had to consider whether acceptance or rejection occurs where a buyer is awaiting the receipt of information to enable him to decide whether or not to have the goods repaired.

 Fiat Auto Financial Services v Connelly (2007) SLT (Sh Ct) 111 (Sheriff Court)

FACTS: Connelly purchased a new car for use by him as a private-hire taxicab. The purchase was made with a loan provided by Fiat Auto Financial Services ('Fiat'). Shortly after delivery, the vehicle manifested a number of faults, which were investigated by the supplying dealer, although never properly diagnosed, resulting in the faults persisting. Specifically, the vehicle broke down within days following delivery and there was a serious fault with the vehicle's engine management system, which the seller attempted but failed to repair. The vehicle suddenly lost power on a number of occasions and there was a defect in the steering. After nine months and having driven in excess of 40,000 miles in the vehicle, Connelly sought to reject it. Fiat accepted that the vehicle was not of satisfactory quality nor fit for purpose, but sought to enforce the finance agreement on two grounds. First, it argued that as Connelly had used it for the purpose of a private-hire taxicab from September 2003 until at least July 2004, during which time it had travelled in excess of 40,000 miles, he had lost his right to reject by virtue of s 35(1)(b) because such use was inconsistent with the ownership of the seller. Second, it argued that Connelly failed to intimate rejection of the vehicle within a reasonable time as required by s 35(4).

HELD: The Sheriff Court rejected both of Fiat's arguments. First, Connelly's continued use of the vehicle as a private-hire taxicab did not necessarily amount to an act that was inconsistent with the ownership of Fiat, because throughout his period of possession he was communicating regularly with the seller about his concerns about the vehicle's quality and fitness for purpose. Second, any right to reject is not lost during a period where a purchaser is awaiting information so as to be in a position to make an informed judgement as to whether or not to accept the goods or alternatively to seek a repair. For these reasons, therefore, Connelly had rejected the vehicle within a reasonable time. The clock stopped running against the time for rejection after the initial failed attempt to repair the engine management system and when Connelly first sought to reject the vehicle, and it did not then restart because the period thereafter was taken up with Connelly requesting and the seller agreeing to carry out the necessary repairs. The court pointed out that Connelly's right of rejection was not lost by virtue of the fact that the vehicle was not returned to the seller until some time after he formally rejected it or by the mileage covered by the vehicle.

> The Sheriff in *Fiat* emphasized the word 'merely' in s 35(6),[74] and cited with approval the statement of Morritt LJ in *Clegg v Olle Andersson (t/a Nordic Marine)*:[75]
>
>> [Section 35(5)] provides that whether or not the buyer has had a reasonable time to inspect the goods is only one of the questions to be answered in ascertaining whether there has been acceptance in accordance with [s 35(4)]. [Section 35(6)(a)] shows that the time taken merely in requesting or agreeing to repairs, and ... for carrying them out, is not to be counted. In these circumstances I consider that time taken to ascertain what would be required to effect modification or repair is to be taken into account in resolving the question of fact which arises under [s 35(4)].[76]
>
> The Sheriff thus held that this passage was authority for the proposition that the right to reject is not lost during any period where the purchaser is waiting for information to make an informed judgement as to whether to accept or reject the goods or to seek a repair.[77]

★ See Paul Dobson, 'Sale of Goods–Acceptance & Rejection' (2008) 53 SL Rev 11

If, as appears to be the case, the policy behind the rules of acceptance (and consequently rejection) in s 35 is to provide finality to sale transactions,[78] the decisions in *Clegg* and *Fiat* could leave sellers exposed to buyers rejecting the contract goods considerably after the time of delivery in cases where there has been a lengthy period of unsatisfactory repairs.

Delivery of the contract goods to another person under a sub-sale or other disposition

At one time, a buyer who resold or delivered the contract goods to a sub-buyer lost the right to reject them. For example, in *Hardy & Co v Hillerns & Fowler*,[79] the Court of Appeal held that the mere act of reselling the contract goods and dispatching them to a sub-buyer was an act that was inconsistent with the ownership of the seller, thus denying the original buyer any right to reject the goods, as he was deemed to have accepted them. The decision in *Hardy* was seen as grossly unfair to certain buyers, for example, those who bought goods in sealed containers with the sole aim of reselling them. In such a case, there would be no opportunity of examining the goods until they were received by the ultimate buyer, by which time rejection was impossible. Via two provisions in the SGA 1979, this unfairness is now remedied. First, s 35(1) must now be read subject to s 35(2), which states that a buyer who has not previously examined the goods is not deemed to have accepted them until he has had a reasonable opportunity of examining them for the purpose either of ascertaining whether they are in conformity with the contract or, in the case of a contract for sale by sample, of comparing the bulk with the sample. Second, s 35(6)(b) expressly states that the buyer is not deemed to have accepted the goods merely because the goods are delivered to another under a sub-sale or other disposition. Where the buyer buys the goods for the purpose of resale, it will often be the case that a defect will only be discovered once the goods have been resold. It was held by HHJ Jack QC in *Truk (UK) Ltd v Tokmakidis GmbH*[80] that in the case of a resale, a reasonable time in which

---

74. 'The buyer is not by virtue of this section deemed to have accepted the goods *merely* because: (a) he asks for, or agrees to, their repair by or under an arrangement with the seller ...' (emphasis added).
75. [2003] EWCA Civ 320, [2003] 2 Lloyd's Rep 32.   76. ibid [63]–[64].
77. (2007) SLT (Sh Ct) 111 (Sheriff Court) 115.   78. ibid.
79. [1923] 2 KB 490 (CA). See also *Perkins v Bell* [1893] 1 QB 193 (CA).
80. [2000] 2 All ER (Comm) 594 (QB).

to intimate rejection for the purpose of s 35(4) will usually be the time taken to resell the goods, together with a further period of time during which the ultimate purchaser would have the opportunity to test the goods and determine their conformity to the contract of sale. HHJ Jack QC explained the position thus:

> Where goods such as machines of one kind or another are sold for the purposes of resale, and they turn out to be defective, it often happens—I would suggest more often than not—that the defect is discovered only when the sub-buyer comes to use the goods. He then rejects them and causes the buyer in turn to reject them. That is an everyday event in both consumer and non-consumer transactions. Section 35 refers to it in sub-section (6)(b), where it is provided that acceptance shall not be deemed to have occurred merely by reason of delivery under a sub-sale. This leads to the conclusion that, where goods are sold for resale, a reasonable time in which to intimate rejection should usually be the time actually taken to resell the goods together with an additional period in which they can be inspected and tried out by the sub-purchaser. As an example, consider the position of a trader who has bought for stock an item of electrical equipment which may be sold in a week or in several months. Certainly it would usually be right in such cases at least to take account of the period likely to be required for resale.[81]

The judge also held that where the parties have agreed that the price is not to be paid until after delivery, the reasonable period of time will usually be at least until the date for payment, which in the *Truk* case, was held to be whichever was the earlier of the date of resale or six months from the date of delivery, as that reflected the reasonable interests of both the buyer and the seller and took account of the terms of the contract itself.[82]

Retaining the goods for more than a reasonable length of time

The buyer is also deemed to have accepted the goods when, after the lapse of a reasonable time, he retains the goods without intimating to the seller that he has rejected them.[83] What amounts to a reasonable time is a question of fact,[84] and the questions that are material in determining whether a reasonable time has elapsed include whether the buyer has had a reasonable opportunity of examining the goods.[85] As Table 17.2 illustrates, it is very difficult to predict from the cases what period of time will be held to be reasonable, as most turn on their own specific facts, some of which have already been discussed. This was acknowledged by Rougier J in *Bernstein v Pamson Motors (Golders Green) Ltd*,[86] when he pointed out that 'the complexity of the intended function of the goods is clearly of prime consideration here. What is a reasonable time in relation to a bicycle would hardly suffice for a nuclear submarine.'[87]

When does this reasonable time begin to run? Does it only start after the buyer has discovered the defect or from an earlier date? It is submitted that any suggestion that the time for rejecting goods only starts once the buyer has discovered a defect is unreasonable, since this could enable him to recover the full purchase price months or even years after the date of acquisition and after he has had substantial use of the

---

81. ibid 605.   82. ibid .   83. SGA 1979, s 35(4).   84. ibid s 59.   85. ibid s 35(5).
86. [1987] 2 All ER 220 (QB). This case is discussed in more detail on p 440.   .87. ibid 230.

TABLE 17.2 What is a reasonable time?

Case	Time before rejecting goods
Lee v York Coach & Marine [1977] RTR 35 (CA)	Six months was held to be too long before rejecting a second-hand car which was neither of merchantable quality nor fit for purpose because of defective brakes and a corroded sub-frame
Bernstein v Pamson Motors (Golders Green) Ltd [1987] 2 All ER 220 (QB)	Three weeks was held to be too long before rejecting a new car that had been driven just 140 miles
Clegg v Andersson (t/a Nordic Marine) [2003] EWCA Civ 320	A delay of seven months was not too long to wait before rejecting a yacht
Jones v Callagher [2004] EWCA Civ 10	Seventeen months was held to be too long before rejecting kitchen units
Fiat Auto Financial Services v Connelly (2007) SLT (Sh Ct) 111 (Sheriff Court)	Nine months and 40,000 miles was not too long to wait before rejecting a taxicab
Douglas v Glenvarigill Co Ltd [2010] CSOH 14; 2010 SLT 634 (Court of Session-Outer House)	A period of fifteen months was held to be too late to reject the vehicle without previous complaint

goods. In *Bernstein v Pamson Motors (Golders Green) Ltd*,[88] Rougier J held that a reasonable time for the purpose of s 35(1) was a reasonable time 'to examine and try out the goods in general terms',[89] with the result that three weeks was deemed to be too long before rejecting a new car that had been driven just 140 miles. It is perhaps a pity that this decision did not receive the scrutiny of an appeal,[90] but, in any event, since *Bernstein*, s 35 has been amended,[91] and s 35(1) must now be read subject to the provisions of s 35(2), which states that a buyer who has not previously examined the goods is not deemed to have accepted them until he has had a reasonable opportunity of examining them for the purpose of ascertaining whether they are in conformity with the contract or, in the case of a contract for sale by sample, of comparing the bulk with the sample. As a result of the changes to s 35, the Court of Appeal in *Clegg v Andersson (t/a Nordic Marine)*[92] held that even if *Bernstein* had been correctly decided, it was no longer good law.

 Clegg v Andersson (t/a Nordic Marine) [2003] EWCA Civ 320

FACTS: Clegg purchased, from Andersson, a yacht under a contract that provided that the shoal draught keel would comply with the manufacturer's specification. When the yacht was delivered in August, Clegg noticed that the keel was too heavy. He registered and insured the yacht and requested from Andersson information to enable him to decide whether or not repair was appropriate. Andersson did not provide this information until

---

88. [1987] 2 All ER 220 (QB).   89. ibid.
90. The appeal was settled by the parties on the basis that the right to reject the vehicle had not been lost and with the buyer being compensated in full by the manufacturer (see (1987) 137 NLJ 962).
91. By the Sale and Supply of Goods Act 1994.   92. [2003] EWCA Civ 320, [2003] 2 Lloyd's Rep 32.

the following February, and, three weeks later, Clegg purported to reject the yacht and claimed the return of the purchase price and damages for breach of contract.

HELD: The Court of Appeal held that Clegg was entitled to reject the yacht. The fact that Clegg registered and insured the yacht were not acts inconsistent with Andersson's ownership, and the correspondence between the parties did not amount to an intimation of acceptance by Clegg. Furthermore, the time Clegg had possession of the yacht did not amount to acceptance for the purposes of the reasonable time rule.

★ See FMB Reynolds, 'Loss of the Right to Reject' (2003) 119 LQR 544

Acceptance by signing delivery note

It is quite common for a seller to require a buyer to sign a delivery or acceptance note confirming that the goods delivered are in satisfactory condition and are accepted by the buyer. In the case of a consumer buyer, s 35(3) makes it plain that a buyer cannot lose his right to rely on s 35(2) by agreement, waiver, or otherwise. Section 35(3) therefore protects the consumer buyer in such cases, and these buyers will not be deemed to have accepted the goods by express intimation under s 35(1)(a). Business buyers, on the other hand, can exclude s 35 by agreement, although this will be subject to the test of reasonableness under the Unfair Contract Terms Act 1977.

Latent defects

In the case of a latent defect, it was held in *Douglas v Glenvarigill Co Ltd*[93] that although time will begin to run for the purpose of s 35(4) as soon as the goods are delivered, some degree of delay in rejecting the goods might be reasonable if the defect is not immediately apparent, although the buyer must bring the defect to the seller's attention as soon as possible. Lord Drummond Young in *Douglas* observed that if it had been intended that the period should run from the appearance of a defect, then that would have been expressly provided. Further, rejection was a relatively drastic remedy, and at a certain stage commercial closure was required to permit the parties to arrange their affairs on the basis that the goods had been effectively sold. Damages remained as an alternative and adequate remedy, thus a buyer was not left without recourse against the seller.

Right of partial rejection

It was formerly the case that a buyer who had accepted all or part of the contract goods was precluded from rejecting any of them. This rule did not apply to a contract that was severable or to a case where the seller delivered more than the contract quantity. In addition to these two exceptions, which still apply today, unless a contrary intention appears in, or is to be implied from the contract, s 35A of the SGA 1979[94] now gives a buyer a right of partial rejection.

---

93. [2010] CSOH 14; 2010 SLT 634 (Court of Session—Outer House). It was held that it was too late to reject the vehicle after a period of fifteen months without previous complaint.
94. Added by the Sale and Supply of Goods Act 1994.

SGA 1979, s 35A

(1) If the buyer—
  (a) has the right to reject the goods by reason of a breach on the part of the seller that affects some or all of them, but
  (b) accepts some of the goods, including, where there are any goods unaffected by the breach, all such goods, he does not by accepting them lose his right to reject the rest.
(2) In the case of a buyer having the right to reject an instalment of goods, subsection (1) above applies as if references to the goods were references to the goods comprised in the instalment.

Section 35A applies to cases where the seller delivers a consignment of goods where only some of them are defective or where some of the goods delivered were not contracted for. The section applies, unless there is a contrary intention,[95] to cases where a buyer has the right to reject the goods by reason of a breach on the part of the seller that affects some or all of the goods. In such a case, where he accepts some of the goods, he does not, by accepting them, lose his right to reject the remainder that do not conform to the contract.

For a buyer to rely on s 35A he must first satisfy the two preconditions contained in s 35A(1)(a) and s 35A(1)(b), namely, that he has the right to reject the goods, for example, because the seller has breached a condition of the contract and that he accepts the remainder of the goods that do conform to the contract.

Where the goods represent a 'commercial unit', then regard also needs to be had to s 35(7).

SGA 1979, s 35(7)

Where the contract is for the sale of goods making one or more commercial units, a buyer accepting any goods included in a unit is deemed to have accepted all the goods making the unit, and in this subsection 'commercial unit' means a unit division of which would materially impair the value of the goods or the character of the unit.

It can be seen from s 35(7) that a commercial unit means a unit, division of which would materially impair the value of the goods or the character of the unit. Examples of what might constitute a 'commercial unit' for the purpose of s 35(7) would include items of furniture or a set of encyclopaedias. If one part of the commercial unit is defective but the remainder is not, s 35(7) makes plain that it is not possible for the buyer to accept one part and reject the other(s). If the buyer in such a case accepts the part of the commercial unit that conforms to the contract, then he is deemed to have accepted all the goods in the unit, as the following example demonstrates.

---

95. SGA 1979, s 35A(4). This intention can be express or implied.

> ### Eg ComCorp Ltd
>
> ComCorp purchases a twenty-four-volume set of encyclopaedias for its new library that is nearing completion. It also purchases thirty bags of plaster needed by the builder to finish the walls of the library. ComCorp stamps the first page of encyclopaedia volume 1 with its company stamp and opens one bag of plaster in readiness for the plastering to commence.
>
> By marking volume 1 in this way, ComCorp will be deemed to have accepted it within the meaning of s 35, and, as the encyclopaedias represent a commercial unit for the purpose of s 35(7), ComCorp is bound to accept all the volumes in the commercial unit. On the other hand, as the bags of plaster do not constitute a commercial unit, ComCorp will not be deemed to have accepted them all just because it has opened one of them.

Waiver or election

Where the buyer has either waived the condition or elected to treat the breach of condition as a breach of warranty and not as a ground for treating the contract as repudiated, he will not then be entitled to reject the goods.[96] It is likely to amount to a waiver if the seller is in breach of condition prior to the delivery of the goods and the buyer nevertheless accepts them with full knowledge of the breach. Denning LJ explained this principle in *Charles Rickards Ltd v Oppenheim*:[97]

> Whether it be called waiver or forbearance on his part, or an agreed variation or substituted performance, does not matter. It is a kind of estoppel. By his conduct he evinced an intention to affect their legal relations. He made, in effect, a promise not to insist on his strict legal rights. That promise was intended to be acted on, and was in fact acted on. He cannot afterwards go back on it.[98]

Where the breach is slight and the buyer does not deal as consumer

Section 15A provides that where the buyer would have had the right to reject goods by reason of a breach on the part of the seller of a term implied by ss 13, 14, or 15,[99] but the breach is so slight that it would be unreasonable for him to reject the goods, then, if the buyer does not deal as consumer, the breach is not to be treated as a breach of condition but may be treated as a breach of warranty. This will be the case unless a contrary intention appears in, or is to be implied from, the contract.[100] It is for the seller to show that the breach is so slight that it would be unreasonable for the buyer to reject the goods.[101]

The following example demonstrates how s 15A operates in practice.

---

96. ibid s 11(2).   97. [1950] 1 KB 616 (CA).   98. ibid 623.
99. The term implied by s 12(1) is not subject to s 15A. Therefore, any buyer (whether or not he is dealing as consumer) will be entitled to treat the seller's breach of the s 12(1) condition as a repudiation of the contract. Section 15A is irrelevant insofar as s 12(2)(a) or 12(2)(b) are concerned because these imply warranties only.   100. SGA 1979, s 15A(2).   101. ibid s 15A(3).

ComCorp Ltd

ComCorp purchases the entire stock of computers from Computer Wholesalers plc and sells them to the public. One of the computers purchased is defective but the defect is so slight that it would be unreasonable for ComCorp to reject it. ComCorp then sells this computer to Wally who does not inspect it before purchase, but notices the defect a short time later. The same breach occurs in both contracts but the remedies may be very different. As Wally has dealt as consumer, he may be entitled to reject the computer and treat the contract as repudiated. However, the result of s 15A is that, because ComCorp did not deal as consumer when purchasing the computer from Computer Wholesalers plc, it will not be entitled to treat its contract with Computer Wholesalers plc as repudiated and may only bring a claim against it in damages for breach of warranty.

In *Moore & Co Ltd v Landauer & Co*,[102] the seller contracted to sell a quantity of tinned fruit, which was to be packaged in cases each containing thirty tins. The overall correct quantity was delivered, but some of the tins were packed in cases containing twenty-four tins. The buyer refused to take delivery of the goods. There was no difference in the market value of the goods whether packed twenty-four or thirty tins to the case. This was a sale of goods by description, which the seller breached by failing to tender some of the goods so as to correspond with the description. As a result, and notwithstanding the minor effect of the breach, the Court of Appeal held that the buyer was entitled to reject the entire consignment. At that time, there was no statutory equivalent of s 15A, although it seems likely that had s 15A been in force at that time, the court would have held that the breach was so slight that, provided the buyer did not deal as consumer, it would have been unreasonable for it to have rejected the goods.

The curing of a defective tender

Provided the seller is able to do so within the time permitted by the contract, a seller usually has the right to cure a defective tender of goods if doing so is not inconsistent with the terms of the contract.

 ***Borrowman, Phillips & Co v Free & Hollis* (1878–79) LR 4 QBD 500 (CA)**[103]

FACTS: The buyer agreed to purchase from the seller a cargo of maize on the *Charles Platt*. When the seller tendered delivery of the cargo, the buyer refused to accept it on the ground that there were no shipping documents with it. The seller insisted that the tender was valid. The dispute was referred to arbitration, which decided that it was not valid without the documents. The seller then offered a second cargo on the *Maria D*, still within the time permitted by the contract, but the buyer refused to accept it on the ground that

---

102. [1921] 2 KB 519 (CA).
103. Approved by the House of Lords in *Motor Oil Hellas (Corinth) Refineries SA v Shipping Corp of India (The Kanchenjunga)* [1990] 1 Lloyd's Rep 391 (HL).

they were not bound to accept any cargo in substitution for that of the *Charles Platt*, which had already been declared invalid. As a result, the seller had to sell the cargo of maize at a loss and sued the buyer for damages for non-acceptance of the goods. At first instance, Denman J held that the buyer was not obliged to accept the second tender once the seller had appropriated the first cargo to the contract. The seller appealed.

HELD: The appeal was allowed. The Court of Appeal held that the buyer was obliged to accept the second cargo and were therefore liable in any claim made by the seller in damages in respect of any loss which they sustained following their refusal to accept.

Repudiation of the contract

Where the buyer is entitled to reject the goods, he may also be entitled to treat the contract as repudiated. In many cases, the buyer will exercise both remedies at the same time. The buyer may, of course, reject the goods without treating the contract as repudiated, in which case the seller is perfectly entitled to retender the goods so as to comply with the contract. If the seller does exercise his right to retender the goods, then the buyer will be obliged to pay the price. In practice, if the buyer is happy to allow the seller another opportunity to retender goods that conform to the contract of sale, then he will merely reject the defective tender without treating the contract as repudiated.

A buyer may, in fact, treat the contract as repudiated by the seller without rejecting the goods. For example, where the breach is either the seller's failure to deliver the goods by the agreed date or where the seller informs the buyer that he will not do so, the buyer may, if he so chooses, accept such breach as a repudiation by the seller of the contract, in which case he will be entitled to damages for non-delivery under s 51 of the SGA 1979. To accept conduct as a repudiation, the innocent party must unequivocally communicate that he accepts the breach as bringing the contract to an end.[104] Such communication requires no particular form, it being sufficient that the communication or conduct clearly and unequivocally conveys to the repudiating party that that aggrieved party is treating the contract as at an end. In exceptional cases, it might be enough for the innocent party simply to fail to perform.[105]

Sometimes, especially if not legally advised or represented, a contracting party will seek to terminate the contract without giving any reason or, if a reason is given, that reason might be a poor one. In such a case, the repudiation will not be wrongful, provided that a valid reason did exist at the time of the repudiation. This is because 'it is a long established rule of law that a contracting party who, after he has become entitled to refuse performance of his contractual obligations, gives a wrong reason for his refusal, does not thereby deprive himself of a justification which in fact existed, whether he was aware of it or not'.[106] This rule is subject to three exceptions:

1. It will not apply if the point not taken is one which, had it been taken, could have been put right by the other contracting party.[107]

---

104. *Vitol SA v Norelf Ltd (The Santa Clara)* [1996] AC 800 (HL).

105. ibid 811. Lord Steyn postulates a case where a contractor is told by his employer not to turn up for work the next day. The contractor's failure to return the following day might, in the absence of any other explanation, convey a decision to treat the contract as at an end.

106. *Glencore Grain Rotterdam BV v Lebanese Organisation for International Commerce (The Lorico)* [1997] CLC 1274 (CA) 1285 (Evans LJ), approving the so-called 'basic rule' in *Taylor v Oakes Roncoroni & Co* (1922) 127 LT 267.

107. *Heisler v Anglo-Dal Ltd* [1954] 1 WLR 1273 (CA) 1278.

2. It will not apply where the party is estopped from relying on the valid reason because of his earlier representation.[108]

3. It will obviously not apply where the buyer has already accepted the goods within the meaning of s 35.

Additional rights of buyers in consumer cases

The Sale and Supply of Goods to Consumers Regulations 2002[109] came into force on 31 March 2003. The Regulations made amendments to the existing sale of goods legislation by inserting, as a new Pt 5A, six new sections, ss 48A–F, into the SGA 1979, and providing additional remedies to a buyer who 'deals as consumer'.[110] The remedies contained in these new sections coexist with and are in addition to the pre-existing regime of remedies contained in the SGA 1979 which are available to all buyers, irrespective of their status, and which have already been discussed in this chapter.

Member states were expressly permitted by Directive 1999/44/EC[111] to 'adopt or maintain in force more stringent provisions…to ensure a higher level of consumer protection'.[112] Consequently, a consumer buyer may choose to enforce one of the new remedies added by Pt 5A or, provided the seller has committed an actionable breach of condition, he may alternatively choose to reject the goods under the pre-amended parts of the SGA 1979.

Who is a consumer?

For the purposes of the Regulations, a consumer is 'any natural person who … is acting for purposes which are outside his trade, business or profession'.[113] Clearly, a body corporate (such as a company or LLP) cannot be a consumer, as it is not a natural person. In most cases, it will be fairly obvious whether or not this definition has been satisfied, the focus being on whether the predominant purpose for the purchase was private or otherwise. Some cases will be more difficult to determine: for example, a sole trader who purchases goods such as a computer for his work and private use.

When do the additional remedies apply?

Provided the buyer deals as consumer, the additional remedies will apply if 'the goods do not conform to the contract of sale at the time of delivery'.[114] Goods will not

---

108. *Glencore Grain Rotterdam BV v Lebanese Organisation for International Commerce (The Lorico)* [1997] CLC 1274 (CA) 1286 (Evans LJ).   109. SI 2002/3045.

110. As the 2002 Regulations amend the SGA 1979, it is the SGA 1979 and not the Regulations that should be pleaded.

111. European Parliament and Council Directive of 25 May 1999 on certain aspects of the sale of consumer goods and associated guarantees [1999] OJ L171/12.   112. ibid Art 8.

113. Sale and Supply of Goods to Consumers Regulations 2002, reg 2.   114. SGA 1979, s 48A(1).

conform to the contract if there is, in relation to them, a breach of an express term of the contract or a term implied by ss 13, 14, or 15 of the SGA 1979.[115] If the breach relates to a different implied undertaking, for example, the implied term as to title in s 12(1) of the SGA 1979, then these additional remedies will not apply. Although s 48F refers to a breach of an express term of the contract, it is silent as to the nature of such an express term. It seems, therefore, that even a breach of a minor express term will enable a consumer buyer to have recourse to these additional remedies which (as we will shortly observe) includes rescission of the contract, something which the pre-amended SGA 1979 does not usually allow.

Reverse burden of proof

It was observed previously that provided the buyer deals as consumer, the additional remedies will apply if the goods do not conform to the contract of sale at the time of delivery.[116] As it will often be difficult for the buyer to prove that the goods did not conform to the contract at this date, s 48A(3) greatly assists him by reversing the burden of proof in relation to these remedies by providing that goods which do not conform to the contract at any time within six months from the date of delivery will be presumed not to have conformed at the date of actual delivery,[117] unless:

(a) it is established that the goods did so conform at that date; or
(b) the presumption is incompatible with the nature of the goods or the nature of the lack of conformity.[118]

The presumption will be incompatible with the nature of the goods if the goods are not intended to survive six months, such as with perishable foodstuffs. The nature of the lack of conformity relates to the circumstances which show that the lack of conformity is inconsistent with the application of the six-month presumption, because it is more likely that the thing complained about was caused by the consumer. This would occur if, for example, the consumer complained about a dent in the goods after, say, five months of ownership.

The additional remedies

Where the additional remedies apply, the buyer may have the right to one of the following remedies:

- require the seller to repair the goods;[119]
- require him to replace the goods;[120]
- require him to reduce the purchase price of the goods by an appropriate amount;[121]
- rescind the contract.[122]

Each remedy will now be discussed.

---

115. ibid s 48F.   116. ibid s 48A(1).
117. The reverse burden of proof does not apply to the pre-amended remedies of damages and rejection.
118. SGA 1979, s 48A(4).   119. ibid s 48B(1)(a).   120. ibid s 48B(1)(b).
121. ibid s 48C(1)(a).   122. ibid s 48C(1)(b).

Repair or replacement of the goods

In cases where there is a lack of conformity in the goods for the purpose of s 48F, 'repair' means to bring the goods into conformity with the contract.[123] Where the buyer requires the seller to repair or replace the goods, which under the additional remedies he must do in the first place, the seller must repair or replace them within a reasonable time without causing significant inconvenience to the buyer.[124] The decision as to whether to elect for repair or replacement is one for the consumer and not the seller. The seller must also bear any necessary costs incurred in doing so, including the cost of any labour, materials, or postage.[125] Any question as to what is a reasonable time or significant inconvenience is to be determined by reference to the nature of the goods[126] and the purpose for which the goods were acquired.[127] This means that goods that are time-sensitive, such as a wedding dress, will need to be repaired or replaced more speedily than, for example, a dress purchased for a holiday to be taken in six months time. No doubt, in due course, the courts will rule on what amounts to 'significant inconvenience', although it seems that sellers will often be in a good position to prevent it. For example, a seller of a motor car may well avoid causing significant inconvenience to his buyer by providing him with a courtesy car whilst his is in for repair pursuant to a request under s 48B(1)(a).

The buyer will not be entitled to the repair or replacement remedies if such remedies are either impossible to perform[128] or are disproportionate in comparison to the other of those remedies,[129] or disproportionate in comparison to an appropriate reduction in the purchase price or rescission of the contract.[130]

One remedy will be disproportionate in comparison to the other if the one imposes costs on the seller which, in comparison to those imposed on him by the other, are unreasonable, taking into account the value the goods would have if they conformed to the contract of sale,[131] the significance of the lack of conformity,[132] and whether the other remedy could be effected without significant inconvenience to the buyer.[133]

If the buyer requires the seller to repair or replace the goods then, until he has given the seller a reasonable time in which to repair or replace them, he will not be able to reject the goods and terminate the contract for breach of condition nor choose a different remedy, for example, requiring the seller to replace the goods when he first required him to repair them.[134]

Where the buyer has requested either of the repair or replacement remedies and the seller fails to comply, then, on the application of the buyer, the court may make an order requiring specific performance by the seller of his obligation to repair or replace the goods.[135] The seller's failure can also trigger the abatement and rescission remedies under s 48C.

---

123. ibid s 61(1).   124. ibid s 48B(2)(a).   125. ibid s 48B(2)(b).   126. ibid s 48B(5)(a).
127. ibid s 48B(5)(b).   128. ibid s 48B(3)(a).   129. ibid s 48B(3)(b).   130. ibid s 48B(3)(c).
131. ibid s 48B(4)(a).   132. ibid s 48B(4)(b).   133. ibid s 48B(4)(c).   134. ibid s 48D.
135. ibid s 48E(2). The courts' discretion may be more limited than it would be in respect of its powers to make an order for specific performance otherwise than under this subsection (see D Harris, 'Specific Performance—A Regular Remedy for Consumers?' (2003) 119 LQR 541).

Price reduction and rescission

The buyer will be entitled to avail himself of the abatement and rescission remedies under s 48C only if either of the two conditions set out in s 48C(2) have been satisfied. These are that:

(a) he has not required the seller to repair or replace the goods because either of these remedies would either be impossible, disproportionate in comparison to the other of those remedies, or disproportionate in comparison to an appropriate reduction in the purchase price or rescission of the contract; or

(b) he has required the seller to repair or replace the goods, but the seller has not done so within a reasonable time and without significant inconvenience to the buyer.

Where the consumer buyer has successfully rescinded the contract, the seller may reduce the amount of the price reimbursed 'to take account of the use he has had of the goods since they were delivered to him'.[136]

Which set of remedies should the consumer buyer seek to enforce?

As already discussed, the consumer buyer has the choice of seeking to enforce either the pre-amended remedies or those that were added by the 2002 Regulations. The differences are important. The pre-amended parts of the SGA 1979 do not require the buyer to allow the seller the opportunity of repairing or replacing the goods (although, in practice, this is what many sellers will offer). This means that where there is a breach of condition by the seller and the buyer has decided that he wants no more to do with the goods, he is best advised (provided he is entitled to do so) to reject the goods under the pre-amended parts of the SGA 1979. Due to the hierarchical manner of the newer remedies, it is not possible for the buyer to do this immediately under s 48A. As discussed, the buyer only has a short time in which to reject the goods for a breach of condition and there is great uncertainty about the length of time he has before his right to reject is lost. Therefore, the additional right of rescission under s 48C will, in appropriate cases, provide the buyer with a final chance of 'rejecting' the goods where the repair and replacement route has either failed, taken too long, or caused significant inconvenience to him.

The effect of s 48C(3) is also an important consideration for consumer buyers when deciding which of the regimes to follow. It was seen earlier that where the buyer rescinds the contract, any reimbursement of the price may be reduced to take account of the use he has had of the goods since they were delivered to him. Thus, s 48C(3) makes it plain that a full refund will not be forthcoming in every case, especially where the buyer has had some use of the goods. On the other hand, provided he has not accepted the goods within the meaning of s 35, the buyer may reject them for breach of condition and thereby reclaim the whole of the purchase price.

---

136. ibid s 48C(3).

Conclusion

The remedies available to a buyer in the event the seller is in breach of the contract of sale will depend on a number of factors, including whether the term breached is a condition or a warranty and whether the buyer is dealing as consumer.

A buyer's statutory remedies can be found in ss 51 to 53 of the SGA 1979 and encompass damages for non-delivery of the contract goods, specific performance, and damages for breach of warranty. Where the seller breaches a condition of the contract, the buyer generally has the right to reject the goods and repudiate the contract. Since many of the terms implied by ss 12 to 15 of the SGA 1979 are conditions, this will be the buyer's primary remedy for breach of these implied terms. Where the term is a warranty, such as appears in s 12(2)(a) and (b), or where the buyer has either waived the condition or elected to treat the breach of condition as a breach of warranty and not as a ground for treating the contract as repudiated, then the buyer's remedy is a claim in damages. Since 31 March 2003, when the Sale and Supply of Goods to Consumers Regulations 2002 came into force, a buyer who deals as consumer has available to him the additional remedies of repair, replacement, reduction in price, or rescission.

Practice questions

1. Consider whether the remedies available to a buyer afford adequate protection in the event the seller is in breach of the contract of sale.

2. Bob enters into a contract with Bill in June to sell him 1,000 tonnes of coal at £100 per tonne, with delivery to be made on 1 August. Bob fails to deliver. On 1 August the market price for coal is £120 per tonne but Bill waits until 1 September, at which time he buys the coal and pays just £90 per tonne.
   Advise Bill.

Further reading

Florian Faust, '*Hadley v Baxendale*—An Understandable Miscarriage of Justice' (1994) 15 Journal of Legal History 41
* Reassesses the case of *Hadley v Baxendale*, which introduced the rule of foreseeability into the common law of contract.

D Harris, 'Specific Performance—A Regular Remedy for Consumers?' (2003) 119 LQR 541
* Considers the amendments to the SGA 1979 made by the Sale and Supply of Goods to Consumers Regulations 2002, which provide the consumer buyer with four remedies where goods fail to conform to the contract of sale at the time of delivery, including specific performance. Examines the power and discretion of the court under s 48E(2) to make an order requiring specific performance. Discusses the scope of the power and the use of specific performance to compel the seller to repair the contract goods.

Martin Hogg, 'The Consumer's Right to Rescind under the Sale of Goods Act: A Tale of Two Remedies' (2003) 36 Scots Law Times 277
* Following the implementation of reforms, the Sale of Goods Act 1979 now provides for two routes for a consumer to rescind a sale of goods contract for material breach. This

article argues that this dual approach is confusing and that only a single remedial route should be provided.

Vanessa Mak, 'The Seller's Right to Cure Defective Performance—A Reappraisal' [2007] 3 LMCLQ 409

- Reviews the case law on whether a purchaser has the right to reject defective goods or should allow the vendor the opportunity to deliver a satisfactory substitute. Considers the Court of Appeal's ruling in *Clegg v Andersson* [2003] EWCA Civ 320.

Janet O'Sullivan, 'Rescission as a Self-help Remedy: A Critical Analysis' (2000) 59 CLJ 509

- Discusses the extent to which inconsistencies in case law and amongst commentators over the operation of the remedy of rescission as a self-help remedy reflect a historical misinterpretation and highlight the need to abolish such a notion.

Chris Willett, Martin Morgan-Taylor, and Andre Naidoo, 'The Sale and Supply of Goods to Consumers Regulations' [2004] JBL 94

- Discusses the Sale and Supply of Goods to Consumers Regulations 2002 and considers the implications of taking into account public statements in assessing satisfactory quality; the conformity with Council Directive 1999/44; amendments to the rules on risk; remedies including repair, replacement, price reduction, and rescission.

18

Product liability

- Product liability in negligence
- Product liability under statute

INTRODUCTION

Product liability is concerned with circumstances where a product has been supplied and which causes damage by virtue of some characteristic that might be described as a defect. Clearly the primary source of law in this area lies in relation to contracts for the sale of goods, especially breaches of duties to supply goods of satisfactory quality corresponding with any contractual description. In such circumstances, the relationship between a buyer and a seller will be regulated by their contractual arrangements, including any valid exclusion clauses. In most instances, the claim by a buyer against the seller will relate simply to the lack of quality or conformity in the product itself, but it is clear that the heads of damage in actions for breach of contract also include consequential damage, including personal injury.[1]

Problems arise however, even in relation to actions by buyers against sellers where the seller is, for example insolvent or untraceable, or perhaps where he is protected from contractual liability by an exclusion clause.[2] Further, the defective goods may not only injure the buyer, and the contract is unlikely to provide a remedy for potential claimants who are not party to the contract of supply, since it must be comparatively rare for such a person to derive any benefit from the Contracts (Rights of Third Parties) Act 1999. In such circumstances a claimant, whether buyer or not, will be forced to rely on the law of tort or on statute for a remedy.

Product liability in negligence

Until the case of *Donoghue v Stevenson*,[3] there appeared to be no general duty in tort concerning the safety of goods, though the supply of goods which were intrinsically or were known to be dangerous did carry a duty in tort to some classes of third party at least. In *Donoghue*, the House of Lords, by a bare majority, held that a manufacturer

---

1. As a good example, see *Grant v Australian Knitting Mills* [1936] AC 85 (PC), where the seller of the goods (underwear) was liable to the purchaser not only for the value of the underwear, but also for the appalling dermatitis which they caused.
2. Similarly, it may be unattractive for a buyer to pursue a claim against a seller who is domiciled or resident in a foreign jurisdiction where, at the very least, enforcement of a judgment might be difficult.
3. [1932] AC 562 (HL).

of foodstuffs owed a duty of care to consumers of those goods. Previously, the approach of the courts to cases of negligence was to extend circumstances where duties arose on a piecemeal basis by analogy to earlier decisions, but in *Donoghue* Lord Atkin formulated what has become known as the 'neighbour principle', providing a generalized statement of when a duty of care to third parties arises. Thus, for Lord Atkin, the duty of a manufacturer in respect of a product is simply an example of how a person owes a duty to others whom he can reasonably foresee might be injured by a lack of care:

 Donoghue v Stevenson [1932] AC 562 (HL)

FACTS: Donoghue drank a bottle of ginger beer that had been purchased for her by a friend. After drinking some of the ginger beer, the remains of a decomposed snail fell out of the bottle. Donoghue claimed that she suffered from shock at the sight of the snail and later suffered from gastroenteritis as a result of consuming the contaminated ginger beer. Donoghue therefore commenced proceeding against Stevenson, the manufacturer of the ginger beer.

HELD: Lord Atkin, Lord Macmillan, and Lord Wright held that the manufacturer of the ginger beer owed a duty of care to take reasonable care to prevent its contamination. Lord Alkin stated:

> [A] manufacturer of products, which he sells in such a form as to show that he intends them to reach the ultimate consumer in the form in which they left him with no reasonable possibility of intermediate examination, and with the knowledge that the absence of reasonable care in the preparation or putting up of the products will result in an injury to the consumer's life or property, owes a duty to the consumer to take that reasonable care.[4]

COMMENT: The minority (Lord Buckmaster and Lord Tomlin) held that there was no liability on the basis that, in principle, if the manufacturer of foodstuffs was liable to a consumer, then so should the manufacturer of any article be liable to any person who suffers injury by virtue of a defect in the product, and that this was undesirable since it created a liability to a potentially unlimited number of persons. Lord Wright confined liability to the manufacturer of foodstuffs, and all three of the judges in the majority found it important that the bottle in which the ginger beer was supplied was opaque, so that it was impossible for the consumer to have examined the product prior to its consumption. The decision in *Donoghue* is important for two reasons. First, because Lord Atkin's 'neighbour principle', became recognized as the unifying factor in determining the incidence of an obligation to take care, and second, because the scope of that duty to manufacture safe products was extended far beyond the manufacturer–consumer relationship.

Initially it was uncertain whether the principles enunciated by Lord Atkin in *Donoghue* would be adopted, but after *Grant v Australian Knitting Mills*,[5] it became clear that they would, and indeed in succeeding cases the duty was extended to include a whole range of relationships far beyond that of manufacturer–consumer. Each of the key words in Lord Atkin's formulation have come under scrutiny, and in each

---

4. ibid 599.   5. [1936] AC 85 (PC).

instance the scope of the duty has been extended beyond that envisaged in *Donoghue*. Each of these key words will now be considered in turn.

Who is a 'manufacturer'?

The term 'manufacturer' now encompasses anyone in the supply chain who has a role in relation to quality control and not solely the person who made the product. Persons who negligently erect a product,[6] repair a product,[7] or assemble a product[8] are now treated as manufacturers. In general, however, liability does not extend to suppliers of products (for example, intermediate sellers and distributors in the supply chain who are unaware of the defect and have done nothing to create or exacerbate it). The rationale would seem to be that suppliers could not reasonably have foreseen that there was a risk of damage to a third party; but there are circumstances in which a person performing such a distributive role will take on a function which imposes upon them a duty to examine the product to determine its safety.

 Andrews v Hopkinson [1957] 1 QB 229 (QB)

FACTS: Hopkinson, a car salesman, told Andrews that a car was 'a good little bus. I would stake my life on it. You will have no trouble with it.'[9] Andrews wanted to buy the car on hire purchase, so Hopkinson sold the car to a finance company, which hired it to Andrews. The car had a major mechanical defect, which would have been readily appreciated had Hopkinson inspected it. Due to this defect, the car was involved in a collision with another vehicle a week later. Andrews commenced proceedings against Hopkinson to obtain damages for the injuries he sustained in the crash.

HELD: There was no direct contract of sale between Andrews and Hopkinson. Despite this, Hopkinson was nevertheless held liable for negligence, since he had a duty in relation to the safety of the cars he supplied.

★ See Aubrey L Diamond, 'The Hire Purchase Dealer's Liability' (1958) 21 MLR 177

This duty of inspection and testing is imposed on an intermediate distributor and has been held to apply even where the initial supplier is an unknown quantity, as occurred in the following case.

 Watson v Buckley, Osborne, Garrett & Co Ltd [1940] 1 All ER 174 (KB)

FACTS: An importer of hair dye represented that the dye contained 4 per cent acid, when in fact it contained 10 per cent acid. The dye was obtained from the importer

---

6. *Brown v Cotterill* (1934) 51 TLR 21 (KB) (negligent erection of a tombstone).

7. *Haseldine v Daw* [1941] 2KB 243 (CA) (failure to repair a faulty lift).

8. *Howard v Furness-Houlder Argentine Lines Ltd* [1936] 2 All ER 296 (KB) (a safety valve had been fitted upside down).

9. In fact, the court also held that, by using this term, the seller had warranted its fitness to the buyer in a contract which was collateral to the contract for the sale of goods between the hire purchase company and the seller and so, additionally, had contractual liability.

and distributed by a distributor to a number of hair salons. A hair salon used the dye on Watson's hair, in accordance with the distributor's instructions, and, as a result, Watson contracted dermatitis. The importer had since become insolvent and so Watson commenced proceedings, *inter alia*, against the distributor for the injuries she sustained.

HELD: The court held that the distributor should have tested the product, because (i) it had no experience of the reliability of the importer; (ii) special care was needed in respect of the product, since even at 4 per cent acid concentration it was potentially dangerous; and (iii) in its advertising material, the distributor described the product as absolutely harmless and requiring no testing by the end user. Accordingly, the distributor was held liable in tort for Watson's injuries.

What is a 'product'?

In *Grant v Australian Knitting Mills*,[10] the Privy Council rejected a range of arguments on behalf of the defendant that the principle in *Donoghue* applied only to a limited range of goods, in particular foodstuffs. In *Grant* itself, underwear was held to fall under the *Donoghue* principle, and it has been applied to such things as the supply of tombstones,[11] hair dye,[12] cars,[13] industrial chemicals,[14] and pharmaceuticals,[15] much as the minority in *Donoghue* suspected it would. There is no logical reason to limit the principle by reference to the subject matter of the thing supplied, though the application of the principle to computer software would appear to have to be by way of analogy, though loss caused by defective software storage media would fall clearly within it.[16]

Grant v Australian Knitting Mills Ltd [1936] AC 85 (PC)

FACTS: Grant bought two pairs of woollen pants from a shop, which had been supplied by Australian Knitting Mills Ltd ('AKM'). Grant suffered from very severe dermatitis when he wore the clothing, caused, the court held, because chemicals used in the manufacturing process had not been removed from the garments before sale. Grant sought damages from AKM.

HELD: AKM was liable to pay damages to Grant under the *Donoghue* principle. AKM intended that the product be supplied to consumers and therefore owed them a duty of care to supply a safe product.

COMMENT: Lord Wright rejected arguments advanced by AKM that the *Donoghue* principle applied only to goods which caused internal harm, or were to be consumed,

---

10. [1936] AC 85 (PC).   11. *Brown v Cotterill* (1934) 51 TLR 21(KB).
12. *Watson v Buckley, Osborne, Garrett & Co* [1940] 1 All ER 174 (KB).
13. *Andrews v Hopkinson* [1957] 1 QB 229 (QB).
14. *Vacwell Engineering Co Ltd v BDH Chemicals Ltd* [1971] 1 QB 88 (CA).
15. *Distillers Co (Biochemicals) v Thompson* [1971] AC 458 (PC).
16. *St Albans City and District Council v International Computers Ltd* [1996] 4 All ER 481 (CA). This case is discussed on p 217.

> or confined to food, or supplied in sealed containers. He concluded that liability did not concern the nature of the product, though clearly greater care might be required in order to meet the duty of care in respect of some types of product than others.

Packaging itself has been held to be within the principle,[17] and defective packaging can cause an otherwise appropriate product to be defective.[18]

Need the defendant be a 'seller'?

While in Lord Atkin's formulation the 'manufacturer' must 'sell' the product, there is no obvious reason why this need necessarily be so,[19] and the gratuitous provision of goods by way of commerce, for example, by circulating free samples,[20] would seem to fall within the principle.[21]

Need the claimant be a 'consumer'?

Although, in most instances, the most likely person to be injured by a product is a user of it, as can be appreciated by consideration of almost all of the cases cited in this chapter so far, the principle extends to include any person who might foreseeably be injured by it. For example, in *Stennet v Hancock and Peters*,[22] the defendant was held liable when he negligently repaired the wheel of a lorry which sheared off at speed and hit the claimant who was a passer-by, while in *Brown v Cotterill*,[23] monumental masons were held liable when a tombstone they had negligently erected fell and hit the infant claimant.

The effect of an intermediate examination

In *Donoghue*, the fact that there was no possibility for Donoghue to have examined the product before it was consumed seemed to be essential to liability, though it is clear that the mere possibility of the product being examined is not enough to avoid liability, as the following case demonstrates.

Herschtal v Stewart & Ardern Ltd [1940] 1 KB 155 (KB)

FACTS: Stewart & Ardern Ltd ('Stewart') supplied a defective car to Herschtal. The next day, Hersctal drove the car and, whilst turning a corner, a rear tyre came off and Herschtal

---

17. *Hill v James Crowe (Cases) Ltd* [1978] 1 All ER 812 (QB).

18. *Aswan Engineering Establishment Co v Lupdine Ltd and Another (Thurgar Bolle Ltd, third party)* [1987] 1 All ER 135 (CA).

19. John Murphy and Christian Whitting, *Street on Torts* (13th edn, OUP 2012).

20. *Hawkins v Coulsdon and Purley Urban District Council* [1954] 1 QB 319 (CA) 333 (Denning LJ).

21. The provision of drugs by the NHS, though not a 'seller', is clearly covered. See also Case C-203/99 *Veedfald v Arhus Amtskommune* [2001] CCR I-3569, where a not-for-profit organization was a 'producer'.

22. [1939] 2 All ER 5 78 (KB).   23. (1934) 51 TLR 21(KB).

sustained a nervous shock. It was established that the tyre came off due to negligent fitting by an employee of Stewart. Herschtal commenced proceedings against Stewart. Stewart contended that it was not liable, as Herschtal had the opportunity to examine the car.

HELD: Herschtal's claim succeeded. The court found that, since Stewart knew that Herschtal needed the car for immediate use, the fact that Herschtal had the opportunity to examine the car was not enough to avoid liability; such examination must have been reasonably anticipated to have taken place and that the examination would have disclosed the fault.

Cases like *Herschtal* suggest that the absence of a likelihood of an intermediate examination is essential in order for a duty of care to arise, so that, for example, in *Farr v Butters*,[24] it was held that the supplier of a defective crane had no duty to the crane operator who had discovered the defects while erecting it. The alternative view is that it is a matter that is relevant to the issues of causation,[25] forseeability of loss, and determining the degree of care needed by the defendant, increasing it where there is no likelihood of intermediate examination so that it is not determinative of the outcome. Although it is not clear which is the correct understanding, Lord Lloyd has expressed a view in favour of the latter.[26]

Labelling instructions and warnings

Normally any attempt by the supplier of goods to exclude liability for negligence will be ineffective by virtue of the Unfair Contract Terms Act 1977. However, such a supplier might seek to discharge his duty of care by providing suitable labelling, warnings, or instructions, as occurred in *Hurley v Dyke*,[27] where a motor trader was held not liable for injury to a passenger in a defective car he had sold at auction 'as seen and with all its faults and without warranty'. The House of Lords held that this was a sufficient warning to the purchaser, and although it was conceded by the claimant that the defendant's duty was met once he had given sufficient warning, the House appeared to believe that this concession had been rightly made. Indeed, Viscount Dilhorne and Lord Scarman indicated that the defendant would not necessarily have been liable even if he had known of the defect.

The fact that a warning has been given will not necessarily absolve the defendant from liability, so that warning that a defect exists without making clear the implications of that defect may not be sufficient. Thus in *Haseldine v Daw*,[28] Goddard CJ suggested that where a lift repairer indicated to the landlord of property that, although he had attempted to repair a defect in a lift mechanism, the lift was still unsafe, such a warning would meet the repairer's duty of care, but simply warning of a defect was not sufficient.

There is a particular difficulty in relation to warnings given to patients in respect of prescription drugs by pharmaceutical companies. Normally a warning about use or side-effects will relieve the manufacturer from liability, but in North America, only disclosure to the patient's medical practitioner will suffice, and then only if

---

24. [1932] 2 KB 606 (KB).   25. Going to the issue of contributory negligence.
26. *Aswan Engineering Establishment Co v Lupdine Ltd* [1987] 1 All ER 135 (CA) 153–4.
27. [1979] RTR 265 (HL).   28. [1941] 2 KB 343 (KB) 380.

accurate and full.[29] This is sometimes known as the 'learned intermediary rule',[30] but, as *Buchan v Ortho Pharmaceuticals*[31] demonstrates, a high duty of disclosure is imposed on the supplier, and this is a continuing duty, so that once the supplier becomes aware of additional information, failure to disseminate it may itself form a ground of liability.[32]

Though the presence of a warning may enable a defendant to show that he has met his duty, the absence of a suitable warning or instructions may provide evidence of a breach of duty, and this may be demonstrated by a comparison between two pairs of cases. In *Holmes v Ashford*,[33] the supplier of a hair dye was held not liable by virtue of the inclusion of a warning in the instructions for use that the dye should be tested before it was generally applied to the customer's hair, while in *Watson v Buckley*,[34] a statement that the dye was 'absolutely safe' rendered the supplier liable. Similarly, in *Vacwell Engineering Co Ltd v BDH Chemicals*,[35] the absence of a warning that an industrial chemical was explosive when mixed with water demonstrated a breach of duty by the supplier, while in *Kubach v Hollands*,[36] a warning by the manufacturer to the retailer that a chemical which he had mis-labelled should be tested before use ensured that the manufacturer's duty had been met, even though the retailer did not pass on this warning to the purchaser, a teacher, whose pupil was injured when the chemical exploded.

Breach of duty and proof of causation

The claimant must not only prove that the manufacturer owes a duty of care to him, but that this duty has been broken; in other words, he must prove that the manufacturer failed to take reasonable care. In *Donoghue v Stevenson*,[37] Lord McMillan said:

> The burden of proof must always be upon the injured party to establish that the defect which caused the injury was present in the article when it left the hands of the…[defendant]…There is no presumption of negligence in such a case as the present, nor is there any justification for applying the maxim, *res ipsa loquitur*. Negligence must be…proved.[38]

→ *res ipsa loquitur*: 'the thing speaks for itself'—an occurrence which proves negligence unless the defendant can prove otherwise

However in many instances where the claim is that the defect arose in the manufacturing process, in practice once the defect is proved the manufacturer must explain it in some way to avoid liability.

---

29. *Buchan v Ortho Pharmaceuticals (Canada) Ltd* (1986) 25 DLR (4th) 658 (Ontario Court of Appeal), where the supplier of oral contraceptive pills was held liable, as the warning leaflet was less comprehensive than those used by the supplier in other parts of the world.

30. See Pamela Ferguson, 'Liability for Pharmaceutical Products: A Critique of the Learned Intermediary Rule' (1992) 12 OJLS 59.

31. (1986) 25 DLR (4th) 658 (Ontario Court of Appeal).

32. *Hollis v Dow Corning* (1995) 129 DLR 609, where a supplier of silicon breast implants was held liable to a patient for failure to circulate data which indicated that in 0.1% of cases the implants could burst.

33. [1950] 2 All ER 76 (CA).   34. [1940] 1 All ER 174 (KB). This case is discussed on p 454.

35. *Vacwell Engineering Co Ltd v BDH Chemicals Ltd* [1971] 1 QB 88 (CA).

36. [1937] 3 All ER 907 (KB).   37. [1932] AC 562 (HL).   38. ibid 623.

Allegations of defective construction—the non-standard product

Where the allegation is that the loss was caused as a result of something going wrong in the manufacturing process, it would be almost impossible for a claimant to show by positive evidence precisely how the manufacturer broke his duty, a matter recognized by Lord Wright in *Grant v Australian Knitting Mills Ltd*,[39] who said in relation to the excess chemicals included in the garment purchased:

> [I]f excess sulphites were left in the garment that could only be because someone was at fault. The appellant is not required to lay his finger on the exact person in all the chain who was responsible or to specify what he did wrong. Negligence is found as a matter of inference from the existence of the defects taken in connection with all the known circumstances.[40]

Typically, this would be done by the claimant demonstrating that the goods were substandard, that is to say that there was a defect and that, on the balance of probabilities, it did not arise by virtue of what happened after the product left the control of the manufacturer. However, where on the facts the defect may plausibly have arisen from other causes, for example the action of a third party or simply an accident during normal use, the claimant may have considerable difficulty in establishing that the defect probably occurred during the manufacturing process, as demonstrated in the following case.

Evans v Triplex Safety Glass Co Ltd [1936] 1 All ER 283 (KB)

FACTS: Evans purchased a Vauxhall car, the windscreen of which was manufactured by Triplex Safety Glass Co Ltd ('Triplex'). About a year after the purchase, the windscreen shattered for no apparent reason, whilst Evans was driving, injuring both him and his passengers. Evans sued Triplex.

HELD: Whilst Evans did not have to eliminate every possible cause of the damage, he did have to eliminate every probable cause and he had failed to do this. The glass may have been damaged when it was installed in the car by Vauxhall, or it may have been damaged during the period of over one year during which he owned the car.

COMMENT: In this case, Triplex brought evidence to show that the glass was not prone to shattering, in other words, that there was not a defect in its design, which left Evans having to show defect in manufacture. Clearly in the case of products such as glass, the possibility of its having been damaged by an intermediate cause, particularly as it had been on the vehicle for such a long time, would have been very difficult for Evans to disprove. However, this case can be compared with perhaps a more typical case like *Donoghue* itself, where the likelihood of an intermediate cause was very low.

In many cases, the proof of the defect is effected by comparing evidence of the actual product against evidence of the manufacturer's specification or against other

---

39. [1936] AC 85 (PC).   40. ibid 101.

non-substandard products produced by the manufacturer. This would certainly been the way the claimant would have proceeded in *Donoghue*,[41] but in *Grant* there was no compelling direct evidence that there were excess sulphites in the underwear, nor that sulphites caused the damage. However, both problems are solved by an interesting though circular form of reasoning adopted by Lord Wright, who accepted that 'the garments must have caused the dermatitis because they contained excess sulphites, and must have contained excess sulphites because they caused the disease'.[42] However, as Lord Wright explains, this is against a background of evidence that sulphites were used in the manufacture of the pants and could cause the harm complained of.

The non-standard product and the defence of appropriate system

A key element in *Donoghue* was the allegation that the manufacturer lacked an appropriate system to avoid contamination of the ginger beer by snails,[43] so that it would have been open to the manufacturer to demonstrate that he had not broken his duty by proof of an appropriate system of quality control. This indeed was one of the defences in *Grant*, where the manufacturer had supplied nearly half a million pairs of pants without a problem. But as Lord Wright pointed out, however good the system, human error by an employee[44] was always a possibility. The following case illustrates how difficult it is for a manufacturer to plead appropriate system as a defence against this sort of background.

 Hill v James Crowe (Cases) Ltd [1978] 1 All ER 812 (KB)

FACTS: Hill had been injured when a packing case on which he was standing collapsed, through, he alleged, poor manufacture. He commenced proceedings against the manufacturer (James Crowe (Cases) Ltd). The manufacturer explained that all its packing cases were carefully made, had never failed before in the company's fourteen-year history, and could easily take the weight of four men.

HELD: Hill's claim succeeded. Mackenna J seemed to infer that the manufacturer's explanation regarding the quality of its goods was all the more evidence that an error had occurred, for which the manufacturer was liable.

Allegations of defective design or nature—the defective standard product

The claimant will have greater difficulty where the allegation is not that there was a defect in the construction of the product, but in its design or nature, so that all

---

41. Only a preliminary issue, namely whether defendant owed the claimant a duty of care, was settled in *Donoghue v Stevenson*. The case proceeded on the basis of an assumption that the claimant's evidence was true.
42. [1936] AC 85 (PC) 96.
43. See in particular [1932] AC 562 (HL) 602 (Lord Thankerton).
44. For which the employer would be vicariously liable.

products of this type carry a risk, the most obvious examples being sharp-bladed tools. In *Evans*, for example, the manufacturer accepted that its glass was not perfect—it could shatter—and that every variety of windscreen had advantages and disadvantages, including price, but this did not mean that there was an actionable defect in the specification of the glass. The fact that manufacturers commonly have to compromise in design and specification, even when made wholly or partially on financial grounds, is a matter which in general the courts treat sympathetically.[45] Similarly, because of the variety of side-effects that can be caused by prescription drugs, it may not be possible for a pharmaceutical company to predict the reactions of all patients, so that the occurrence of an adverse reaction may not be particularly probative. Similarly, some drugs, though particularly beneficial for almost all patients, may give rise to known side-effects for patients who react abnormally. In such instances, these unavoidable side-effects may be regarded as being acceptable when measured against the benefits they give to the vast majority of patients. It is therefore not particularly surprising that there is no reported case in this country in which a drug manufacturer has been held liable.[46] The question here seems to involve asking whether it was reasonable for the defendant to market the product weighing the risks and benefits, and instructions and warnings may be a key constituent in the process.

What sort of damage?

Liability extends loss caused by personal injury and loss to property including consequential loss but not to **pure economic loss**, which in general is irrecoverable in tort.[47] Thus the loss suffered by a retailer or an intermediate distributor who has to compensate his customer because of a defective product cannot be recovered in tort from a person above him in the distribution chain. Similarly, loss which arises because the defective product is less valuable than a perfect one is not recoverable, and nor are costs associated with putting the defect right or additional costs of working incurred by virtue of the defect.

➡ **pure economic loss:** loss which arises without damage to the claimant's person or property

---

Eg ComCorp Ltd

Comcorp Ltd decided to provide its director, Greg, with a new car. It purchased the car from CheapCars Ltd. The car was delivered to ComCorp's office car park, but, as he was driving across the car park, Greg hit another of ComCorp's vehicles used by Lee because the brakes on the new car failed. Greg suffered a whiplash injury to his neck and was off work for weeks. CheapCars has since gone into insolvent liquidation, so any contractual claims against it are worthless.

Assuming ComCorp can prove the loss was caused by the manufacturer's negligence, it has a claim in respect of the crash damage to Lee's car. Greg has a claim for the whiplash injury and his loss of wages, since although the latter is economic loss, it is

---

45. On conscious design compromises, see Christopher Newdick, 'The Future of Negligence in Product Liability' (1987) 103 LQR 288, 300–4.

46. For a review of the difficulties facing the claimant against a pharmaceutical company, see Pamela Ferguson, 'Pharmaceutical Products of Liability: 30 Years of Law Reform?' [1992] JR 226.

47. See *Spartan Steel v Martin & Co Ltd* [1973] 1 QB 27 (CA).

> not 'pure'—Greg has been physically injured. However, assuming the defective brakes are
> not regarded as separate items of property, ComCorp cannot make a tortious claim for
> the cost of repairing Greg's car, whether the cost of putting the brakes right or repairing
> the crash damage; both are pure economic loss. However, ComCorp may have warranty
> claims against the manufacturer in contract.

This principle extends to damage caused by the defect to the product itself, which is also irrecoverable as pure economic loss (namely the reduction in value of the product); only physical damage to property of the claimant other than the defective product can be recovered.[48] This may be illustrated by considering the following case.

 Muirhead v Industrial Tank Specialities Ltd [1986] QB 507 (CA)

FACTS: A manufacturer sold electric pumps to a supplier which he knew were to be used in the United Kingdom. The supplier sold them to an installer who installed them in Muirhead's premises in order to pump seawater through Muirhead's lobster storage tanks. The pumps kept cutting out because they were not suitable for running on UK voltages, and Muirhead regularly had to pay an electrician to start them again. Ultimately, the motors failed completely and all of the lobsters died.

HELD: The Court of Appeal held that the manufacturer was liable in negligence to Muirhead for the retail value of the lobsters (physical damage), but not the value of the motors themselves, nor the costs associated with trying to make them work, as these losses were forms of pure economic loss.

⭐ See Simon
Whittaker, 'Defective
Products and
Economic Loss' (1986)
49 MLR 369

Whilst in *Muirhead* the division between the defective goods themselves and other property belonging to the claimant was clear, this is not always the case. Returning for a moment to our example of ComCorp and the damaged car, could it not be argued that the brakes and the car body are separate pieces of property so that a defect in one causes direct physical loss to the other, especially as the brakes and the body would have been manufactured by different companies? According to Lloyd LJ in the following case, the answer may be yes.

 Aswan Engineering Establishment Co v Lupdine Ltd [1987] 1 WLR 1 (CA)

FACTS: Lupdine Ltd manufactured a liquid waterproofing compound called Lupguard. Lupdine purchased plastic drums from Thurgar Bolle as containers for the product, which it exported around the world, including to Saudi Arabia. Aswan purchased a quantity of Lupguard, which would be delivered to it in the plastic drums manufactured by Thurgar Bolle. The plastic drums containing the Lupguard were unloaded from a ship and left for

---

48. *Murphy v Brentwood District Council* [1990] 2 All ER 908 (HL).

several days stacked six high on the dockside in temperatures of over 50°C. The plastic drums collapsed and their contents were lost. Aswan commenced proceedings. The principal legal issues raised in this case concerned the term implied by s 14(3) of the Sale of Goods Act 1979 as to fitness for purpose, but the question arose whether, if the plastic drums were defective,[49] they should be regarded as forming one product along with Lupguard, so that all loss to Aswan was purely economic, or whether they could be regarded as a separate product, so that the defect in the drums injured other property (the Lupguard) belonging to Aswan.

HELD: Lord Lloyd provisionally held that the defective drums caused physical damage to the Lupguard, which would (on the assumption there was a defect) be recoverable.

COMMENT: Lord Lloyd pointed out that had Aswan bought the plastic drums separately from the Lupguard, then, clearly, if the drums were defective, damage was caused to other property of Aswan (namely the Lupguard). Here, however, title to both the drums and the Lupguard passed simultaneously to Aswan. However, Lord Lloyd indicated that this was not conclusive, nor was the fact that it was rather artificial to think of the property in the drums passing at all, since both of these facts would also be true of a car supplied with a defective tyre, yet he was of the opinion that the tyre and the car were separate property. However, Nicholls LJ would not have found the manufacturers of the drums liable, not on the ground of whether there were two or one pieces of property, but because it would be unreasonable to impose liability.

🔗 The term implied by s 14(3) of the Sale of Goods Act 1979 is discussed at p 372

⭐ See Paul Dobson, 'Merchantable Quality and Negligence' [1987] JBL 145

The issues involved in determining what might constitute 'other property' damaged by the defective product have been considered primarily in relation to buildings, where there is considerable resistance to finding a general tortious liability for builders for defective premises. However, in *Murphy v Brentwood*,[50] Lord Bridge raised the possibility that in a 'complex structure' including a chattel, a defect in one part of the structure might properly be regarded as having caused damage to other property comprised in the remainder of the structure. The outcome of the reasoning is rather inconclusive since, as Lord Bridge has himself accepted,[51] it is often artificial to treat two parts of the same structure as separate, though in *D & F Estates*[52] some at least in the House of Lords were prepared to treat ancillary parts of a building, such as the central heating boiler or even the electrical system, as 'other property', and this approach might find a place in relation to chattels as well.

Product liability under statute

Fault-based liability in negligence was abandoned in the United States in the mid-1960s in favour of a strict liability system,[53] while in Britain, following the thalidomide tragedy,[54] there was public pressure for change in the law, with both the Law Commission[55] and the Pearson Commission[56] recommending the adoption of

---

49. In fact, the Court held that the drums were not defective.
50. [1991] 1 AC 398 (HL).   51. *D & F Estates Ltd v Church Commissioners for England* [1989] AC 177 (HL).
52. ibid.   53. *Greenman v Yuba Power Products, Inc* (1963) 27 Cal Rptr 697.
54. Thalidomide was a drug that was prescribed to thousands of pregnant women in the 1950s and 1960s to help alleviate morning sickness. An unforeseen side effect of the drug resulted in thousands of these women giving birth to babies with severe deformities.
55. Law Commission, *Liability for Defective Products: Report of the Two Commissions* (Law Com No 82, 1977).
56. Royal Commission on Civil Liability and Compensation for Personal Injury (TSO 1978).

non-fault liability in respect of defective products.[57] However, it was not until the European Economic Community (now the European Union) accepted the need for a change in the law in Europe by passing the Product Liability Directive[58] that the change to strict liability arrived. The Directive was implemented in the UK by Pt I of the Consumer Protection Act 1987 (CPA 1987), which came into force on 1 March 1988. Although the European Court of Justice (ECJ) has held that the Directive is of 'maximal' effect,[59] Art 13 allows fault-based or contractual obligations to co-exist with the Directive, so that product liability under the common law both in contract and negligence exist in parallel with liability derived from the Directive.

Who can be liable?

Section 2 of the CPA 1987 imposes liability on four types of person: producers, 'own branders', importers into the EU, and, in certain circumstances, suppliers.

Consumer Protection Act 1987, s 2(1) and (2)

(1) Subject to the following provisions of this Part, where any damage is caused wholly or partly by a defect in a product, every person to whom subsection (2) below applies shall be liable for the damage.

(2) This subsection applies to—
   (a) the producer of the product;
   (b) any person who, by putting his name on the product or using a trade mark or other distinguishing mark in relation to the product, has held himself out to be the producer of the product;
   (c) any person who has imported the product into a member State from a place outside the member States in order, in the course of any business of his, to supply it to another.

Producers

Producers of a product are defined in s 1(2) as:

   (a) the person who manufactured it;
   (b) in the case of a substance which has not been manufactured but has been won or abstracted, the person who won or abstracted it;
   (c) in the case of a product which has not been manufactured, won, or abstracted, but essential characteristics of which are attributable to an industrial or other process having been carried out (for example, in relation to agricultural produce), the person who carried out that process.

The typical example of a person falling within paragraph (b) would be a person who has mined the product from the soil, for example coal or iron. Paragraph (c) is a

---

57. For an outline of the arguments in favour of imposing strict liability, see Law Commission, *Liability for Defective Products: Report of the Two Commissions* (Law Com No 82, 1977) 38.
58. Council Directive 85/374/EEC of of 25 July 1985 on the approximation of the laws, regulations and administrative provisions of the Member States concerning liability for defective products [1985] OJ L210/29.
59. Case C-183/00 *Gonzalez Sanchez v Medicina Asturiana SA* [2002] ECR I-3901.

catch-all paragraph and seems to envisage a person who processes a product, but the degree of processing required in order to give rise to its 'essential characteristics' is unclear. Presumably, a farmer who simply harvests peas and bags them does not fall within this paragraph, but would do so if he froze them, though one is forced to ask what the 'essential characteristics' of frozen peas are—is it that they are peas, that they are frozen, or perhaps that both are essential characteristics?

Own branders

Consider the following example:

 Eg ComCorp Ltd

ComCorp Ltd decided to become a wholesale supplier of car fuel pumps. It sources the fuel pumps from Pumpo plc, which imports them in bulk into the UK from the manufacturer in Korea, which sources the electrical components from a company in China and the mechanical components from another company in Thailand. Pumpo plc then packs each fuel pump into boxes supplied to it by ComCorp Ltd which bear the name 'CoCo Brand', the brand name under which ComCorp Ltd trades. ComCorp then supplies the fuel pumps to a range of retailers including Reg. Reg sells a fuel pump to Bernie, who is injured when the electric motor driving the fuel pump on his car bursts into flames.

Is ComCorp liable to Bernie under the CPA 1987?

In a case where, for example, a retailer purchases goods from a manufacturer who puts the retailer's name on the goods so that it appears to a purchaser that the retailer also manufactured goods, then it would seem the retailer has attracted liability for defects in the goods under this head. Matters become more complex where either a retailer or an intermediate distributor uses a proprietary brand. The obvious solution for a person in such a situation to avoid liability would be to label the goods as 'Made for …' or 'Imported into the UK for…' As with 'holding out' in other areas of law, for example the law relating to the apparent authority of agents, the issue is determined as a matter of fact by considering the impression given to the relevant third party.

> The liability of a principal for holding out an agent as having authority is considered at p 96

Importers

In order to avoid consumers having to pursue claims against manufacturers in foreign jurisdictions, the Directive and consequently the Act imposes liability on the importer of a defective product into the EU. By virtue of Art 5 of Council Regulation 44/2001 (Brussels I), the consumer will be able to pursue an action against the importer (or indeed any other person domiciled in the EU) in the courts of the state where damage took place, and any judgment obtained in a court of the EU can be enforced with minimal difficulty throughout the EU.

Suppliers

Generally, suppliers are not liable under the Act, but by virtue of s 2(3), liability is imposed on a supplier who fails to respond within a reasonable time to a request from a claimant (or potential claimant) to identify either:

- the person who supplied him with the product;
- or its producer, own brander, or importer.

Additionally it must not be reasonably practicable for the claimant to identify all of these persons, and the request must be made within a reasonable period after the damage has occurred.

In this way, a claimant or potential claimant can follow goods back along the distribution chain until he can identify someone with liability under s 2(2), or, if he cannot, he can pursue a claim against a supplier who cannot himself identify either his own supplier or someone else identified in s 2(2).

What is a product?

Section 1(2) of the CPA 1987 defines what constitutes a 'product', with s 45(1) defining what amounts to 'goods' (which is a key term used in the s 1(2) definition).

 Consumer Protection Act 1987, ss 1(2) and 45(1)

Section 1(2): 'product' means any goods or electricity and (subject to subsection (3) below) includes a product which is comprised in another product, whether by virtue of being a component part or raw material or otherwise;.

Section 45(1): 'goods' includes substances, growing crops and things comprised in land by virtue of being attached to it and any ship, aircraft or vehicle.

Since the definition of 'product' includes component parts, the definition of 'manufacturer' in s 2(2) would include both the manufacturers of components and the person who assembles these components to create the whole product. Returning for a moment to the ComCorp example earlier, all three of the Korean, Chinese, and Thai companies would therefore be manufacturers for the purposes of the Act, and the Chinese and Korean manufacturers have each produced a defective product.

Although it seems unlikely that a whole building is a product, since it is not 'goods', the component parts of a building, even though regarded as part of the land through permanent attachment to it, would be 'products' so that the producers of defective bricks or other building materials would potentially have liability under the Act.[60] Until 2000, agricultural produce was excluded from the definition of 'product' unless it had undergone an industrial process. This exclusion has now been removed, but it is difficult to see how a farmer will be a 'producer' as defined by s 1(2) unless he has effected some processing, though it is clear that Parliament did intend to extend liability to farmers.

Information does not seem to fall within the scope of the Act, so that provision of faulty software in itself cannot found liability. This, however, leaves open the problem where faulty software causes the hardware with which it is supplied to malfunction.[61]

---

60. Subject to the issue of whether any damage is pure economic loss. See p 461.
61. See Simon Whittaker, 'European Product Liability and Intellectual Products' (1989) 105 LQR 125. See also *St Albans City and District Council v International Computers Ltd* [1996] 4 All ER 481 (CA).

What is a defect?

In order to succeed, the claimant will need to demonstrate that any damage has been caused by a defect in the product. Section 3(1) stipulates that 'there is a defect in the product ... if the safety of the product is not such as persons are generally entitled to expect', thus products which are unsatisfactory without being unsafe are not defective. However, unlike at common law, there is no defence for a producer who demonstrates that he has taken all reasonable care—in that sense, therefore, the Act imposes 'strict' liability subject to the availability of certain defences.

The key question, therefore, is, 'What are persons generally entitled to expect by way of safety?' It is important to note that the issue is not what they actually expect, so that in *Richardson v LRC Products Ltd*,[62] it was held that whilst consumers might expect condoms not to fail, the manufacturers did not claim 100 per cent effectiveness, and the court accepted evidence that condoms did burst on occasion for no discernible reason, so that the public was not entitled to an expectation of perfection. On the other hand, it may be that general public expectation is low, but nevertheless the court might determine the public was entitled to more than it anticipated.[63]

In determining the issue of public expectation, s 3(2) provides that all circumstances must be taken into account, including:

(a) the manner in which, and purposes for which, the product has been marketed, its get-up, the use of any mark in relation to the product and any instructions for, or warnings with respect to, doing or refraining from doing anything with or in relation to the product;

(b) what might reasonably be expected to be done with or in relation to the product; and

(c) the time when the product was supplied by its producer to another.

A good example, which illustrates how the Act operates, is found in the following case.

 Iman Abouzaid v Mothercare (UK) Ltd [2000] All ER (D) 2436 (CA)

FACTS: Abouzaid (a 12-year-old child) was helping his mother to strap his brother into a pushchair, which had been purchased from Mothercare. The pushchair had a buckle secured by an elastic strap, which sprang from Abouzaid's fingers and severely damaged his eye. Abouzaid commenced proceedings.

HELD: The Court of Appeal held that Mothercare was not liable at common law, since the possible danger was not known to Mothercare as there had been no previous comparable accidents. Nevertheless, under the CPA 1987, it was irrelevant whether the hazard that caused the damage was known or could have been known to the producer; the public had a right to expect a high degree of safety in a childcare product. Consequently the pushchair had a defect for which Mothercare was liable.

---

62. [2000] Lloyd's Rep Med 280 (QB).
63. *A v The National Blood Authority* [2001] 3 All ER 289 (QB).

Section 3(2)(c) makes it clear that the safety of a product is to be judged by reference to public expectations at the time of its production and not with the benefit of hindsight. It was therefore important in *Iman Abouzaid* that there was no evidence that public expectations of safety had changed between date of the sale of the product and the trial date where there was evidence that the public could at least expect warnings of any dangers. However, public expectations of the standards of safety may change over time, perhaps as a result of technological advances in design. Clearly, a car manufactured to the safety standards applicable in 1980 would probably be defective if manufactured today.[64]

Standard and non-standard products

Although liability is strict, it is not absolute, and the claimant must prove that the product has a defect. As at common law, this may be easier in the case of a substandard product than where every product produced carries the risk.[65] The following case, however, demonstrates that distinguishing between standard and non-standard products is not necessarily easy.

A v The National Blood Authority [2001] 3 All ER 289 (QB)

FACTS: The claimants (of which there were 114) were infected with Hepatitis C through contaminated blood transfusions supplied by the National Blood Authority (NBA). Although the risk of transmission of Hepatitis C by blood transfusion was known at the time, so that one bag in 100 contained infected blood, there was no means of either preventing the contamination or testing for it. The NBA argued that the fact that the danger was unavoidable should be taken into account in determining whether the product was defective; every bag of blood carried the risk of contamination, consequently, infected blood should not be regarded as 'substandard'. Similarly, since the risk was unavoidable the public was not entitled to expect 100 per cent safety.

HELD: Both arguments were rejected. Burton J concluded that the infected bags were substandard in that they were 'different from the norm which the producer intended for use by the public'. He characterized the argument that all the blood products were equally defective because each carried the risk as 'very philosophical' and one which, if accepted, would apply to every case, since there is a risk of a manufacturing flaw in any product. Burton J also concluded that the public was entitled to expect 100 per cent safety in relation to blood products and not to be exposed to 'Russian roulette'.

COMMENT: Is it clear that an infected bag of blood was not what the NBA intended to produce? It might argue that what it wanted to produce was bags of blood—which is exactly what it did produce.

---

64. But what about one manufactured to 2000 safety standards? There are some difficult factual matters here, for example, when does a desirable safety feature become essential and to what extent is the price of the car relevant?

65. Per Burton J in *A v The National Blood Authority* [2001] 3 All ER 289 (QB) [38] (Burton J). But see *Iman Abouzaid v Mothercare (UK) Ltd* [2000] All ER (D) 2436 (CA), where the fact that a standard product caused an injury seemed to be treated as clear evidence of a defect, at least where public expectations of safety were high.

Apart, perhaps, from the difference in the consequences of failure of the product, this case is difficult to reconcile with *Richardson*, where the public was also exposed to a form of Russian roulette. Burton J envisaged the public being so exposed only when the risks were known to and accepted by society, which required 'publicity and probably express warnings'. Yet *Richardson* seemed to proceed on the basis that the public did not know the risks of failure with condoms.

Richardson v LRC Products Ltd is discussed at p 467

⭐ See Christopher Hodges, 'Compensating Patients' (2001) 117 LQR 528

As noted earlier when considering the common law position, certain products have inherent dangers which cannot be avoided, while other products are sold which could be made safer, but only by imposing further expense on the consumer, for example by installing on-board computer systems in cars which significantly reduce the possibility of collisions. It is unclear whether the typical common law approach to such problems of weighing risks and benefits, taking into account the obviousness of the risk to the public and the impact of any instructions or warnings provided with or in respect of the product, will be adopted under the Act. For example, the social desirability of the provision of blood transfusions would have been an important factor in determining liability at common law, but it does not weigh heavily in Burton J's judgment in *A v The National Blood Authority*. Instead, his focus was on the state of the public's expectation of safety. It remains to be seen how the social desirability of the existence of a product might be regarded as affecting public expectation.

Improper use, warnings, and instructions

Section 3(2)(a) and (b) draws our attention to the fact that products may become unsafe if used in a manner which is inappropriate, and the way in which the product has been marketed, any instructions or warnings given with it, and reasonable expectation in respect of the uses to which it might be put by the consumer, are all relevant matters in determining public expectations of safety. The issues raised earlier in relation to the position at common law on such matters are relevant here, and both *A v The National Blood Authority* and *Iman Abouzaid* are instructive. In *Iman Abouzaid*, the Court made it clear that appropriate warnings of the danger might have been sufficient to temper public safety expectations, while in the *National Blood Authority* case, although Burton J seemed to be prepared to treat blood products as if they were a drug, so that full disclosure of the risks would normally be sufficient, some hesitancy on his part can be detected.

Damage

A claimant can only recover compensation under the Act if a defect in the product wholly or partially causes 'damage'. Section 5 (1) defines 'damage' as 'death or personal injury or any loss of or damage to any property (including land)'. Damage to the product itself or to the whole or any part of a product with which it has been supplied is excluded,[66]

---

66. CPA 1987, s 5(2). Consequently, there is no ambiguity like that witnessed in *Aswan Engineering* over whether there is one piece of property or two; the supplier of the drums in *Aswan* would have avoided liability under the Act even if the property injured had been intended for private use.

and no liability arises unless the damages, before interest, at least equal £275. Finally, by virtue of s 5(3), there is no liability in respect of damage to property unless it is of a description ordinarily intended for private use and is mainly so intended by the claimant. Consequently, damage to business property is excluded, so that the Act would not apply to cases such as *Aswan* or *Muirhead*.

The Act makes no reference to recovery for financial loss which is consequential on property damage or personal injury, though the general view is that such loss is recoverable.[67]

Defences

By virtue of s 7, it is not open to a defendant to limit or exclude liability 'by any contract term, by any notice or by any other provision'. The defendant who has produced a defective product is therefore left with the statutory defences. It should be noted, however, that s 7 does not prevent instructions or warnings as to use from being relevant in determining whether a product is defective or not.

The six statutory defences are set out in s 4, with the first four being relatively simple and straightforward:

- A defendant can avoid liability if he can show that 'the defect is attributable to compliance with any requirement imposed by or under any enactment or with any EU obligation'.[68] The application of this defence is obvious where the requirement is compulsory, but what is the situation where it is permissive? If legislation were to permit the inclusion of a chemical in a product at a level which was known to cause harm, it would seem unlikely that the 'compliance' defence would apply.[69]

- It is a defence for the defendant to show that he 'did not at any time supply the product to another'.[70] Consequently, a producer, own brander, or importer must also supply the product if they are to be made liable, so that where the product that causes the damage has, for example, been stolen from such a person then this provision provides them with a defence. Section 46 defines 'supply' widely and includes gifts, while the European Court of Justice (ECJ) in *Veedfald v Arhus Amtskommune*[71] has held that a product manufactured in one part of an organization can be supplied for use by another part of the same organization, even though it never leaves the organization's premises.

- A defendant can avoid liability if he can show that the supply of the product was not in the course of the defendant's business.[72] In *Veedfald*,[73] the defendant manufactured products as part of its provision of medical services, which were provided entirely free to the claimant, being funded publicly. Nevertheless, the ECJ held that the exemption from liability did not apply in such circumstances.

- It will be a defence to show that the defect did not exist in the product at the relevant time,[74] with the relevant time being the time when the product was supplied, unless the supplier is sought to be made liable by virtue of s 2(3), in which

---

67. See e.g. Mark Simpson, Anthony Dugdale, and Michael Jones, *Clerk and Lindsel on Torts* (20th edn, Sweet & Maxwell 2010) [11-81].

68. CPA 1987, s 4(1)(a).

69. This example is based on *Alberry and Budden v BP Oil* [1980] JPL 586 (CA), when the Court refused to find liability for negligence at common law in these circumstances.

70. CPA 1987, s 4(1)(b).   71. Case C-203/99, *Veedfald v Arhus Amtskommune* [2001] CCR I-3569.

72. CPA 1987, s 4(1)(c).   73. Case C-203/99, *Veedfald v Arhus Amtskommune* [2001] CCR I-3569.

74. CPA 1987, s 4(1)(d).

case the claimant must show the defect arose after the last supply by a producer, importer, or own brander.[75] This defence makes it clear that a liability falls on producers of defective products and not on producers of products that later become defective. However, as the commentary under the defence in section 4 makes clear, the producer of a perfectly sound product which, when incorporated into another product, makes that product defective, may be liable.

The fifth and sixth defences deserve more discussion. The fifth defence is the most controversial. It is known as the 'development risks' defence (or the 'state of the art' defence) and was included in s 4(1)(e) of the CPA 1987 as a result of Art 7 of the Product Liability Directive.

Consumer Protection Act 1987, s 4(1)(e) and Directive on Liability for Defective Products 1985, Art 7(e)

Section 4(1)

it shall be a defence for [the defendant] to show …

(e) That the state of scientific and technical knowledge at the relevant time was not such that a producer of products of the same description as the product in question might be expected to have discovered the defect if it had existed in his products while they were under his control.

Article 7

The producer shall not be liable if he proves …

(e) … that the state of scientific and technical knowledge at the time when [the producer] put the product into circulation was not such as to enable the existence of the defect to be discovered.

This defence has proved controversial on two grounds. First, the Directive does not make its inclusion in national law compulsory and both the Law Commission and the Pearson Commission had recommended that no such defence should be included in English law. As Pearson commented, 'it provides a gap through which another thalidomide disaster might easily slip',[76] and indeed it seems likely that the pharmaceutical industry will potentially be a major beneficiary of the defence.

Second, Art 7(e) of the Directive defines the defence in terms of the state of scientific and technical knowledge—that is, 'knowledge in the scientific community'—while the Act defines it in terms of what a hypothetical producer might be *expected* to have discovered—that is, 'knowledge expected of the industrial community'. Obviously, a producer would find it easier to prove that no producer of similar products could have been expected to discover a defect, than that no one could have discovered the defect, bearing in mind the scientific and technical knowledge at the

---

75. ibid s 4(2)(b).

76. *Royal Commission on Civil Liability and Compensation for Personal Injury* (TSO 1978) Vol 1 [1259].

time. In *European Commission v UK*,[77] the ECJ pointed out that scientific knowledge which was not, in practice, accessible could be disregarded, and accepted that the Act did not irremediably fail to comply with the Directive, leaving the UK courts to interpret the Act in the light of the wording of the Directive. This, of course, leaves open the question of exactly when a hypothesis, which is published in an obscure scientific journal but which later proves to be correct, becomes 'knowledge'.

In *A v National Blood Authority*,[78] whilst it was known that a percentage of the products produced would contain the hepatitis C virus, it was not scientifically feasible to identify which products had been contaminated. Literally, therefore, in relation to any one bag of blood, scientific knowledge did not enable the existence of the defect to be discovered. However, Burton J held that the defence was not intended to operate in this way; once a generic risk in relation to this type of product was known, then the producer supplies at his own risk. In other words, s 4(1)(e) provides protection against a risk that an innovative product *might* cause damage—a ' development risk'—but not once that risk is known to have materialized.

The sixth, and final, defence applies where the defect constituted a defect in a product (the subsequent product) in which the product in question had been comprised, and the defect was wholly attributable to the design of the subsequent product or to compliance by the producer of the product in question with instructions given by the producer of the subsequent product.[79] This defence typically arises where a component supplier is being sued, and the defect in a finished product was wholly attributable either to the design of that product or failure by its producer to comply with instructions given by the component supplier, as the following example demonstrates.

Eg ComCorp Ltd

ComCorp Ltd obtained a contract to supply a kit car manufacturer with fuel pumps. ComCorp Ltd's specification sheet indicates that the fuel pump must not be installed within 30 cm of the exhaust manifold, but the car's design places the pump much closer than this. Peter buys a kit car, follows the design and is seriously injured when the car catches fire. The assumption in s 4(1)(f) is that the fuel pump is itself defective, and this is questionable, but even assuming that is the case, ComCorp Ltd has a defence under the section. It would appear *prima facie* that ComCorp Ltd would continue to have such a defence even if it had known of the details of the car's design, though perhaps its failure to refuse to supply a clearly unsuitable part means that the defect in the car was not wholly attributable to its design.

Limitation period

By virtue of s 11A(4) of the Limitation Act 1980, a claimant has three years within which to bring an action under the Act from the later of the date when the damage

---

77. Case C-300/95 *EC Commission v United Kingdom* [1997] ECR I-2649. For further discussion of this case, see Christopher Hodges, 'Development Risks: Unanswered Questions' (1998) 61 MLR 560 and Mark Mildred and Geraint Howells, 'Comment on Development Risks: Unanswered Questions' 61 (1998) MLR 570.
78. [2001] 3 All ER 289 (QB).   79. CPA 1987, s 4(1)(f).

occurred and the date on which he knew of the relevant facts, including that the damage was significant, the fact that it was caused by the defect, and the identity of the defendant. No action can be brought under the Act after the expiration of a period of ten years from the date when the product was put into circulation by the defendant;[80] this is an absolute bar so that even deliberate concealment will not prevail, so that the claimant must therefore rely on his claim, if any, in negligence.

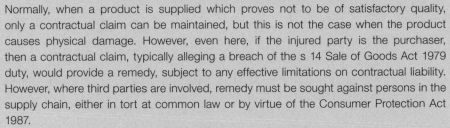

Conclusion

Normally, when a product is supplied which proves not to be of satisfactory quality, only a contractual claim can be maintained, but this is not the case when the product causes physical damage. However, even here, if the injured party is the purchaser, then a contractual claim, typically alleging a breach of the s 14 Sale of Goods Act 1979 duty, would provide a remedy, subject to any effective limitations on contractual liability. However, where third parties are involved, remedy must be sought against persons in the supply chain, either in tort at common law or by virtue of the Consumer Protection Act 1987.

As we have seen, while common law liability is fault-based, when the damage is caused by a 'non-standard product', fault is not necessarily difficult to prove. Although theoretically the fault in the product does not give rise to the doctrine of *res ipsa loquitor* as such, nevertheless the manufacturer will need to account for the defect in a way which shows he was not negligent. He might seek to do this either by showing he employed an appropriate quality control system, though commonly even this will not be sufficient, or by bringing evidence that the defect may have occurred after it left his hands. Proof of fault is more problematic in the case of a product which left the manufacturer in perfect condition but which nevertheless caused damage because by its nature it was capable of causing damage—the so-called defective standard product. Here the common law requires that it was reasonable for the product to be distributed, weighing the risks and benefits, and instructions and warnings may be a key constituent in the assessment process. Were this not so, then the manufacture of almost any article might be inhibited by fear of liability, a matter which may well have influenced the minority in *Donoghue v Stephenson*[81] to resist the imposition of any generally applicable liability on manufacturers.

Whilst the courts readily extended liability at common law well beyond manufacturers to a whole range of suppliers, it was clear following the thalidomide tragedy that fault-based liability was inadequate, especially in the case of damage caused by a defective standard product.

The Consumer Protection Act 1987 now imposes strict liability on participants in the supply chain for damage to person or property caused by 'defective products' subject to limited defences. However, the definition of 'defective' in the statute makes it clear that liability lies not only in respect of defective standard products, like the ginger beer in *Donoghue*, since a defective product is one the safety of which 'is not such as persons are generally entitled to expect'[82] and, as *Iman Abouzaid* demonstrates, public expectation may be very high in respect of some types of product. However, there remains an issue of how far public expectation can be affected by notices and warnings so as to render a

---

80. Limitation Act 1980, s 11A(3).   81. [1932] AC 562 (HL).   82. CPA 1987, s 3(1).

supplier free from liability for an otherwise defective product which has caused damage, particularly in relation to pharmaceuticals.

Finally, although the Consumer Protection Act 1987 removed the need to show fault on the part of participants in the supply chain, the common law nevertheless remains important, particularly since the Act only applies to consumer products and in particular instances may have a shorter limitation period than actions based on the common law.

Practice questions

1. Define the following terms:
   - the neighbour principle;
   - pure economic loss;
   - defective product;
   - the 'state of the art' defence.

2. 'Since the Consumer Protection Act 1987 there is no need to apply the *Donoghue* principle in English law'.

   Discuss.

3. Mobilico manufactures two types of equipment—the Mobo Standard and the Mobo De-Luxe—which were originally designed as mobility aids for disabled people. Both types of equipment are very effective, but the Mobo Standard can cause disorientation for the very occasional user, often resulting in that person falling. The company will give a refund where a user has this problem. The Mobo De-Luxe does not cause this problem but is three times the price. Mobilico supplies its equipment to two types of purchaser: Reg, who is a specialist retailer of mobility equipment; and Compo, who adapts the Mobo De-Luxe and installs it in the cabs of heavy industrial machinery for the driver to sit in.

   Reg sells a Mobo Standard to Consuella, who becomes disorientated, falls, and is very severely injured. Mobilico supplies an instruction booklet with the equipment in English, which Consuella finds hard to understand and does not read. Compo sells an industrial machine to Bigg, but a year after delivery the machine goes out of control when the driver's seat malfunctions. The machine itself is destroyed and this means Bigg's factory is put out of action for six weeks, with consequent loss of production. Don the driver is also injured. The Mobo De-Luxe has never malfunctioned before, but the malfunction may be as a result of a programming error in one of the computer-controlled welding machines Mobilico has installed.

   Discuss Mobilico's liability in tort to Conseuella, Bigg, and Don.

Further reading

Pamela Ferguson: 'Liability for Pharmaceutical Products: A Critique of the Learned Intermediary Rule' (1992) 12 OJLS 59
- Outlines the learned intermediary rule and argues that whilst warnings to the consumer in relation to non-prescription drugs may be appropriate, only full disclosure to the patient's medical practitioner is adequate for prescription drugs.

Richard Goldberg, 'Paying for Bad Blood: Strict Product Liability after the Hepatitis C Litigation' (2002) Med LR 165

- Looks in detail at *A v National Blood Authority* and engages with the reasoning of Burton J.

Mark Mildred, 'Pitfalls in Product Liability' [2007] JBL 141

- Looks at the history of product liability litigation in England, suggesting that evidential problems in relation to causation and the existence of a defect are at the root, even where liability is strict.

Christopher Newdick, 'The Future of Negligence in Product Liability' (1987) 103 LQR 288

- Provides background material on the EU Directive on Product Liability and outlines its provisions, though his prediction that it might open practitioners' eyes to the possibilities of litigation appears to be misplaced—though perhaps almost all cases settle.

Peter Shears, 'The EU Product Liability Directive—Twenty Years On' [2007] JBL 884

- Provides a fascinating survey of a range of English and European decisions on the effect of the Product Liability Directive.

Simon Whittaker, 'European Product Liability and Intellectual Products.' (1989) 105 LQR 125

- Examines the concept of a 'product' with especial reference to intellectual property referring to both European and American sources.

PART IV

The law relating to the international sale of goods

19

An introduction to international sales and documentation

- The character of international trade

- Increased risk in international sales

- The bill of lading and the development of documentary sales

- The bill of lading in Cif and other documentary sales contracts

- The characteristics of the bill of lading

- Transfer of contractual rights

- Alterations to bills/reissuing bills

INTRODUCTION

This chapter is the first of four dealing with the law of international sales of goods. In addition, Chapter 25 is also relevant, since it deals with two of the more common mechanisms for payment in international sales contracts.

After identifying what amounts to an international sale for our purposes, the ways in which the nature of the law of international sales of goods differs from domestic sales are discussed, before exploring how documents are used to deal with some of the legal risks associated with contracts involving international deliveries. The chapter then looks at a typical international sale in outline, before focussing in detail on how the bill of lading, perhaps the most characteristic document used in international sales, operates.

The character of international trade

What is an 'international' sale?

What characterizes an international sale of goods for the purposes of this chapter is that the parties to the contract are businesses, usually substantial ones, located in different states, and the goods are to be transported (carried) from one state to another, though not necessarily to the buyer's state of residence. As is discussed, physical separation of buyer and seller and the process of transportation raises particular risk issues which require particular responses from traders and their legal advisers—issues which are absent, or at least less acute in purely 'domestic' sales, where the parties and the goods are in the same state and probably in closer proximity to one another. Perhaps, therefore, it is better to describe these 'international' contracts as 'export sales'.[1] However, although our paradigm contract involves separation of parties and international transportation of goods, some of the cases involve only one or the other of these characteristics. Finally, it should be noted that the focus is almost exclusively on contracts where goods are to be carried by sea, since it was in relation to this mode of transport that the law of international sales originated, and almost all of the types of problem that arise in international sales can arise in this context, so that, suitably adapted, the legal principles applying there can apply elsewhere.

Law and the commercial reality of international trade

Without doubt there is a special culture or spirit in international trade founded on a recognition that the parties to such a contract should be able to 'look after themselves', with an expectation, not always realized, that the law will adapt to support accepted business practice. A good example of this attitude is demonstrated in *Brown Jenkinson v Percy Dalton*,[2] where the transporter (called a 'carrier') of barrels of orange juice agreed, in return for an indemnity, that he would describe the barrels, which were leaking slightly, as being in 'apparent good condition' on a document he knew the owner would give to a third party buyer of the juice. If he had described the goods accurately, he knew that the buyer would have rejected the document and refused to pay the purchase price. He also knew this mis-description could expose him to liability to the third party buyer. However, it was common practice to describe slightly defective goods in this way because it facilitated trade, and neither he nor the **shipper** thought they were doing anything wrong, since the defect was minor and the shipper/seller would compensate the buyer for the reduction in value in the goods. In fact, the buyer successfully claimed against the carrier instead of seeking compensation under the sales contract, and the carrier in turn sued on the indemnity. Looked at dispassionately, it is clear that the carrier has committed the tort of deceit, but few in international trade would have thought what the carrier had done was wrong, so when the Court of Appeal held that the indemnity was unenforceable, thus relieving the seller who had initiated the mis-description from any liability, there was substantial criticism of the decision on the basis that it disappointed the reasonable expectations of the parties. A similar reaction greeted the decision in *The Galatia*,[3] where market views on what made a document commercially unacceptable seemed to be subordinated to a strictly legal analysis.

Brown Jenkinson illustrates another cultural peculiarity of international sales, namely the recognition that normally certainty is more important than 'fairness'. See, for example, the following case, which established that, normally, stipulations as to the time for doing something (other than payment of the price) are conditions of a contract entitling the innocent party to treat the contract as being at an end.

➡ **shipper:** the person who contracts with the carrier for the transport of the goods under a contract of carriage

---

1. This is the term used in Roy Goode and Ewan McKendrick, *Goode on Commercial Law* (4th edn, Penguin 2010) 941.

2. [1957] 2 QB 621 (CA).

3. *M Golodetz & Co Inc v Czarnikow-Rionda Co Inc (The Galatia)* [1980] 1 WLR 495 (CA).

> ### Bunge Corporation v Tradax Export SA [1981] 1 WLR 711 (HL)
>
> **FACTS:** The buyer of goods had to give the seller fifteen days' notice of the arrival of the ship onto which the goods were to be loaded. The buyer gave the notice five days late and the seller terminated the contract for breach of a condition, even though, on the facts, it was not inconvenienced in any way by the delay.
>
> **HELD:** The House of Lords held that since it was the understanding of merchants that such a delay permitted termination, the five-day delay in providing notice constituted a breach of a condition, which permitted the seller to terminate the contract.

Similarly, some contracts involve a chain of buyers and sellers so that a buyer may already have sold the goods to another person at the time of the breach. In contracts like these,[4] it was important for a party to know he had no further obligations under the broken contract, thus freeing him to source the goods elsewhere. Consequently a simple rule was essential. In fact, breaches of time clauses are often used by unscrupulous buyers to extract themselves from contracts where the market price of the goods has declined below that stipulated in the agreement enabling them to buy more cheaply elsewhere. Nevertheless this unfairness is seen as preferable to a rule on termination of contract which depends on a less certain concept such as one requiring the innocent party unforeseeably to be substantially deprived of what he was entitled to expect under the contract.[5] Merchants would certainly subscribe to the *dictum* of Lord Mansfield when he said '[i]n all mercantile transactions the great object should be certainty: and therefore it is of more consequence that a rule should be certain than whether the rule is established one way or the other. Because speculators in trade then know what ground to go upon.'[6] This view seems to be shared by Parliament so that, for example, the provisions of the Unfair Contract Terms Act 1977, which in effect require exclusion or limitation of liability clauses to be 'fair', do not apply to international supply contracts.[7]

This desire for certainty also seems to be an important force in standards of documentation. Rather surprisingly, very substantial transactions, involving many millions of pounds, are commonly entered into by merchants on standard form contracts published by their trade association completely unamended, or, even worse, amended without any legal assistance in a way that apparently contradicts the standard form. Similarly, changes in terminology used in agreements relevant

---

4. Known as 'string' contracts because there is a string of buyers and sellers. There was a string in *Bunge v Tradax*, though only a short one, and there seemed no obvious reason why the seller decided to terminate the contract.

5. This is the formulation adopted in Arts 25 and 49 of the Convention on the International Sale of Goods.

6. *Vallejo v Wheeler* (1774) 1 Cowp 143, 153.

7. Unfair Contract Terms Act 1977, s 26. The definition of an international supply contract is wider than the working definition we have adopted for 'international sales'. In fact, s 2(1)—no exclusion for personal injury or death—does apply to contracts for the carriage of goods by sea by virtue of Sch 1.

to international trade are resisted on the basis that at least the wording of the old contracts were understood[8] and new wordings could introduce unwanted ambiguity. Thus, for example, the 'SG' (ships and goods) insurance policy, which had first been adopted in 1779 and was itself a revised version of earlier forms, continued in use in London, the principal marine insurance market in the world, until it was finally withdrawn on 31 March 1982.

In conclusion, there is a tension between the attitude of market participants and the law. Certainly, judges will often seek to create a simple, though recognizably 'broad brush' rule, rather than one which accords more with logical nuanced legal analysis,[9] and, as has been discussed, can expect market criticism where a decision fails to accord with mercantile practice and belief. However, as Schmitthoff points out, English law, at least as applied in international sales, is governed more by the principles of party autonomy and that agreements are binding than by detailed rules,[10] and this approach accords well with the sensibilities of the trading community,[11] which may explain why English law is commonly chosen as the governing law of contracts even where there is very little, if any, connection with England itself.

Increased risk in international sales

The fact that the seller, the buyer, and the goods are physically separated from one another poses specific problems, which are to a great extent the product of changes in the way that international trade was conducted in the nineteenth century. Until the establishment of regular shipping lines, with ships timetabled to make voyages from specific places at specific times[12] and 'modern' telegraphic, radio, and postal services, the only effective method for international sales involved a buyer taking his ship to a foreign port, perhaps selling some goods he has on board, buying others, and going on to the next port, where the process could be repeated. Consequently, buyer and seller would contract face to face and each could examine the goods being traded. However, once it became possible for buyers and sellers to communicate readily at long distances, contracts could be made and goods despatched without the parties having ever met, with the buyer seeing the goods for the first time only after they were discharged from the ship, possibly months later. Also the carrier will almost certainly be a third party with whom either the buyer or the seller

---

8. Often because they had been regularly litigated—so much for certainty.

9. See e.g. Lord Mance in *Scottish & Newcastle International Ltd v Othon Ghalanos Ltd* [2008] UKHL 2, All ER 768 [52], where he held that for the sake of certainty and simplicity, goods are delivered on shipment in Fob contracts, notwithstanding the fact there are variants of Fob where this is a rather strange conclusion.

10. Clive Schmitthoff, *Select Essays on International Trade Law* (Kluwer Academic Publishers 1988) 256.

11. See on this Patrick Devlin, 'Relation Between Commercial Law and Commercial Practice' (1951) 14 MLR 247.

12. Known as 'liner trade', but of course not confined to passenger liners, which is now the normal meaning of the word 'liner'.

will have to form a separate contract for the carriage of the goods, posing privity problems.

This method of trading causes concerns for both parties. The concern for the seller is that he will not be paid for the goods, especially since it will be more difficult to establish the financial standing of the buyer. Once the goods have been shipped (that is to say, loaded into the ship), he has lost physical possession of them and, if shipment is by or on behalf of the buyer, probably constructive possession too,[13] subject to contractual terms to the contrary. Similarly, subject to contrary intention, where the buyer is the shipper, property in the goods will pass by virtue of s 18, rule 5(2) of the Sale of Goods Act 1979 (SGA 1979). Even where the seller retains constructive possession of the goods, he has the practical problems associated with storage and disposal of the goods at the port of discharge if he has to recover physical possession should the seller default in payment. Whatever the situation in relation to title to the goods, taking legal action potentially in a foreign jurisdiction against a buyer who may have disappeared or be bankrupt is not attractive. The seller therefore would like payment in advance of shipment.

On the other hand, the buyer does not want to pay in advance, partly for cash flow reasons and partly because he does not know that the goods match the description, or that they have been shipped or even exist at all. Also, where the buyer wishes to sell the goods while they are at sea, the problems are compounded because his purchaser has even less connection with the goods than the buyer. Finally, it is possible that either party may need to sue the carrier if the goods are damaged while at sea. The seller will need to be able to sue the carrier if the buyer defaults or rejects the goods, while the buyer will need to sue if he has accepted the damaged goods.

The parties might be prepared to compromise, since if the seller were to obtain a promise that he will be paid from someone whom he can trust, for example the buyer's bank, then he would have no reason not to despatch the goods. He might not be actually paid for some time, but this is less of a problem, because he can probably borrow from his own bank on the strength of the promise by the buyer's bank to pay. However, he does not want to have to wait for payment until the goods actually arrive. He will also want the buyer's bank to pay, even if there is some real or imaginary dispute over quality raised by the buyer. The seller does not want to wait for payment until this is resolved. Thus the buyer's bank must be committed to pay, regardless of the quality of the goods. This also means that it will pay before the buyer has had the chance to benefit from the goods. Consequently, the bank will probably have to finance the transaction by lending to the buyer, and so would like to have some claim over the goods in case the buyer does not reimburse it. But the goods are probably thousands of miles away, in a ship. While this mechanism satisfies many of the issues for both seller and buyer, there remains the problem of how the buyer can be sure the goods he has agreed to buy have been loaded onto the ship.

Constructive possession of goods is discussed at p 37

Section 18, rule 5 of the SGA 1979 is discussed at p 246

---

13. See *Cowas-Jee v Thompson* (1845) 18 ER 560.

What is needed is something which is tangible and easily transportable which in a sense symbolizes the goods while they are unavailable to either buyer or seller and which fulfils the following functions:

- giving constructive possession in the goods as against the carrier and third parties which can be delivered to the buyer or his bank passing property in the goods if this is the intention of the parties—in other words, being transferable and operating as a document of title to the goods;
- identifying the goods and evidencing that the carrier has received and loaded them—in other words a receipt for the goods;
- establishing the apparent condition of the goods;
- transferring the benefits of the contract of carriage.

A document, called a bill of lading, gradually assumed these functions. Ideally, this document would also have provided some protection against dishonesty by one or other of the parties, but market participants adopted practices that positively lent themselves to the perpetration of fraud, and the courts have recognized that the key issue appears to be protection against the bankruptcy, not the fraud of, a counterparty.[14]

The bill of lading and the development of documentary sales

A bill of lading is a document, traditionally two-sided, produced by the carrier of the goods, which is normally given to the shipper once the goods have been loaded onto the ship. On one side, amongst other things, it gives a description of the goods, when they were loaded, and to whom the goods are to be delivered (the 'consignee') once they arrive in the port of discharge. On the other side, it will normally detail the terms of the contract of carriage. A key term of this contract is that the carrier promises the shipper that it will only release the goods identified on the bill to a person who tenders the bill of lading to them. Bills of lading are normally transferable, so that the right to claim possession of the goods from the carrier will pass with possession of the bill. In this way, the bill operates as a 'key to the floating warehouse',[15] which is what the ship has in effect become.

In a slightly simplified form, the face of a typical bill of lading is set out in Figure 19.1.

---

14. See e.g. the practice of issuing three original bills of lading, which enabled the fraud in *Glyn Mills Currie & Co v East and West India Dock Co* (1882) 7 App Cas 591 (HL), and of carriers releasing goods without the production of bills of lading, which enabled the fraud in *The Future Express* [1993] 2 Lloyd's Rep 542 (CA).

15. A term coined by Bowen LJ in *Burdick v Sewell and Nephew* (1884) 13 QBD 159 (CA) 174.

Shipper ComCorp Ltd International Trade Road Portsmouth UK		Bill of lading Original		[Carrier's logo here]
Consigned to the order of Billy Buyers Factory Road Willy Willy NSW Australia				
Notify address Big Bank Big St Sydney NSW Australia				
Vessel The Annika N	**Port of loading** Portsmouth UK	**Port of discharge** Sydney NSW		**Place of origin of goods** UK
Marks and numbers GDO 271/53/60	**Description of goods** 1 off 40' Standard—Agricultural machinery Shipped on board 17 February 2012	**Weight** 30.500 kg		**Measurement**
SHIPPED on board in apparent good order and condition, weight, measure, marks, numbers, quality, quantity, content, and value unknown, for carriage to the port of discharge or as near thereunto as the vessel may safely get and lie always afloat, to be delivered there in like good order and condition. In accepting this Bill of Lading the Merchant expressly accepts and agrees to all provisions on both pages, whether written, printed, stamped, or otherwise incorporated, as fully as if they were all signed by the Merchant. One original Bill of Lading must be surrendered duly endorsed in exchange for the goods or delivery order. In witness whereof, the number of original Bills of Lading stated herein has been signed, one of which being accomplished, the other (s) to stand void.				
Freight To be paid at port of discharge	**Declaration of value** (see Clause X)	**Number of originals** Three	**Place and date of issue** Portsmouth UK 17 February 2012	**Signature** *I M A Skipper* **For Carver Carriers plc**

FIGURE 19.1 A simplified face of a bill of lading

How a bill of lading might be used in a typical transaction—the facts

What follows is primarily an outline description, somewhat simplified for the purpose of exposition, of a type of contract which developed after the mid-nineteenth century in order to optimize the advantages that the bill of lading brings to international sales. This type of contract is called 'Cif', which stands for 'cost, insurance, freight'.

Cif and other standard trade terms are discussed at Chapter 20

A typical Cif contract, the 'back story' to the simplified bill of lading, might operate as indicated in the following example.

Eg ComCorp Ltd

ComCorp Ltd (in the UK) agrees to sell agricultural machinery to Billy Buyers, who lives in New South Wales, for whom the most convenient port is Sydney. It agrees that ComCorp will pay the cost of transport to Sydney and insure the goods against loss or damage during the voyage. Billy Buyers has agreed to borrow money from Big Bank to fund the purchase of the goods and it is agreed between him and ComCorp that ComCorp will be paid by the bank at Big Bank's Portsmouth branch on being given a bill of lading for the goods plus a suitable insurance policy.[16] Once it has paid ComCorp, Big Bank will debit Billy's account.

ComCorp then arranges and pays for the contract of carriage and a contract of marine cargo insurance, and transports the goods to the carrier's ship. Typically, the carrier will give the shipper (ComCorp) a receipt for the goods (commonly called a 'mate's receipt'), normally prepared from information the shipper has supplied to the carrier, including a description of the goods. After the goods have been loaded, the carrier will then prepare, and the captain of the ship will date and sign, a bill of lading based on the data in the mate's receipt.[17] ComCorp Ltd can then tender the bill of lading and insurance policy at Big Bank's Portsmouth branch and, assuming the documents conform to the contract of sale, ComCorp will be paid. The documents will be sent by Big Bank to its head office in Sydney to await the arrival of the goods. The carrier, Carver Carriers plc, will notify Big Bank once the goods arrive in Sydney. There is one further advantage to the use of a bill of lading. Suppose Billy Buyers agrees to sell the goods only a few days after the ship has sailed from Portsmouth to On Sale Pty Ltd, also Cif. Billy can complete this sale by arranging for On Sale Pty Ltd to pay him at Big Bank Sydney against a tender of the documents by Billy or his bank.

How a bill of lading might be used in a typical transaction—the law

In the ComCorp example, the bill of lading symbolizes the goods. In return for handing custody of the goods to the carrier, ComCorp has received a document which in law gives it control over the goods, as the carrier has agreed to deliver the goods to whoever has the bill of lading. Lawful possession of the bill is treated as lawful possession of the goods. In delivering the bill of lading as instructed by the buyer to Big Bank, ComCorp passes not just the right to possession of the goods but property in them too, and in return it gets paid.[18] When Big Bank pays ComCorp, it is exposed to a risk that Billy will not repay them, but it now has possession of the bill of lading, which means it can have a security interest known as a pledge over the goods. If Billy does not pay, then the bank can sell the goods as pledgee to reimburse itself.

 Pledges are discussed at p 685

---

16. This can be described as: 'Cif Sydney cash against documents at Big Bank Portsmouth UK Branch'.

17. For an interesting though slightly dated description of the shipping process, see Devlin J in *Heskell v Continental Express* Ltd [1950] 1 All ER 1033 (KB) 1037. A bill of lading should never be dated earlier than the date on which the whole or last of the cargo that it covers was loaded (*Mendala III Transport v Total Transport Corp* (*The Wilomi Tanana* [1993] 2 Lloyd's Rep 41 (QB) 45 (Hobhouse J)).

18. In the absence of evidence to the contrary, the intention of the parties in a contract like this would be that property in the goods would pass with the bill of lading.

In fact, Billy has already sold the goods, and On Sale Pty Ltd will want the bill of lading because it cannot take physical delivery of the goods from the carrier without it. Big Bank is happy to release the bill and so lose control over the goods, but only if On Sale Pty Ltd credits Billy's account with the bank. To complete the story, the holder of a bill of lading has transferred to him all of the rights under the contract of carriage, so that first Billy, then On Sale Pty Ltd, had the right to sue the carrier if the carrier broke its duty under the contract of carriage.

In this example, Big Bank is mainly acting as Billy's agent in completing the purchase, while of course looking after its own financial interests. However, ComCorp is taking a risk that after the goods have been despatched, Billy will instruct the bank not to complete, leaving ComCorp to sue Billy with the goods 10,000 miles away. In order to give ComCorp protection against this, it could have required Billy to procure Big Bank to enter into a separate arrangement under the terms of which the bank would be personally liable to ComCorp to pay against stipulated documents. Although complicating matters, this additional protection is easily accommodated within a Cif contract; indeed, in our example, the processes for receiving payment would not change at all. The contract of sale would require Billy Byers to cause Big Bank to issue a **letter of credit**, obliging Big Bank to pay ComCorp when they tender the bill of lading and the insurance policy to the bank.

➜ letter of credit: in this context an irrevocable undertaking by a bank to effect payment on being presented with a number of stipulated documents

🔗 Letters of credit are discussed at p 656

In sales like Cif, it is almost as if it is the documents which are being bought and sold, and as a result they are often called 'documentary sales', with the key documents—the bill of lading, the policy of marine cargo insurance, and the letter of credit—forming the 'Cif documentary triangle'. Although Cif contracts are the most common exemplar of documentary sales, other types of contract can have this characteristic, typically certain types of what are called **Fob** contracts, in which the seller agrees to arrange for the goods to be loaded on the ship free of charge to the buyer, but the buyer agrees to pay the cost of transportation. Often the parties will agree that the seller will arrange for the contract of carriage, since it is easier for him to do this, being 'on the spot' and for him to receive the bill of lading from the carrier. It is therefore sensible that payment for the goods should be in return for tender of the documents.

➜ Fob: free on board

The bill of lading in Cif and other documentary sales contracts

We have seen how the Cif contract developed in order to give some security to the parties to an international contract for the sale of goods and although it may be that the 'pure' Cif is a rarity,[19] since the parties will normally supplement it in some way,[20] nevertheless there are certain characteristics of the documentation which will apply to Cif contracts and documentary forms of Fob unless the parties expressly or impliedly agree to the contrary. As Fob is such a flexible contract format, it is

🔗 The flexibility of the Fob format is discussed at p 526

---

19. See Roskill LJ in *The Albazero, Owners of Cargo Laden on Board the Albacruz v Owners of the Albazero* [1975] 3 WLR (CA) 523.
20. For example, perhaps adopting INCOTERMS, on which see p 543.

impossible to be as dogmatic about the characteristics of the documentation, but where under the terms of a Fob contract the seller has a duty to tender a bill of lading, it would almost certainly have to have the characteristics set out in the sections that follow.

The need for a shipped transferable bill of lading

For contractual tender in a Cif contract, the bill of lading must be a 'shipped bill'. 'Shipped' means that the bill acknowledges that the goods have actually been loaded onto the ship, as opposed to a 'received for shipment' bill or other document, which states that the goods have been received ready for loading. In Cif, since the contract calls for a document of title to the goods, and 'received for shipment' bills of lading would appear not to be documents of title,[21] then the parties will have to expressly agree that tender of an alternative to a shipped bill of lading is acceptable. Although the nature of a Fob contract, unlike Cif, does not require a transferable document of title, where a bill of lading is stipulated in a Fob contract, the courts will require very strong evidence of a custom as to what is acceptable tender in a particular trade or in a particular port before concluding that tender of a shipped bill of lading is not required by the contract.[22]

Just as the agreement of the parties is needed for the requirement that a shipped bill of lading must be tendered, so too, unless the parties agree otherwise, the document must be freely transferable. In fact in some trades, contrary agreement is commonplace, especially where the ships are fast and the routes short, since delays in the arrival of bills of lading pose problems and the need for a sale of the goods while afloat is less pressing, thus removing the need for a transferable document. In such cases documents such as 'sea waybills' or ships delivery orders may be stipulated in the contract of sale of the goods. A sea waybill is a receipt for goods incorporating the terms of the contract of carriage in a non-transferable document which stipulates delivery of the goods to a named consignee[23] and which does not have to be produced in order to induce delivery. A ship's delivery order is a document issued by the carrier,[24] under which the carrier undertakes to a person identified in the document to deliver the goods to which the document relates to that person. Ship's delivery orders are typically issued long after loading, often in response to a shipper to whom a single bill of lading or sea waybill has been issued who wishes to split a bulk cargo for sale to a number of buyers while the goods are still afloat.

The need for a 'clean' bill

A clean bill of lading is one that states that the goods were loaded on board in 'apparent good order and condition'. In addition, the bill must not be 'claused'; that is to say, the initial statement must not be qualified by any notation as to the goods'

---

21. See *Diamond Alkali Export Corporation v Fl Bourgeois* [1921] 3 KB 443 (KB) and Michael G Bridge, *Benjamin's Sale of Goods* (18th edn, Sweet & Maxwell 2010) [18-06].
22. *Yelo v S M Machado & Co Ltd* [1952] 1 Lloyd's Rep 181 (QB).   23. Carriage of Goods by Sea Act 1992, s 1(3).
24. Or attorned by him so that he undertakes to act as bailee in favour of the person named in the order. An instruction or agreement by a warehouseman to deliver goods is not a ships delivery order; see *Colin & Sheilds v W Weddel & Co Ltd* [1952] 2 All ER 337 (CA).

condition on loading. However, as the following case demonstrates, qualifications in relation to occurrences after loading do not amount to 'clausing'.

M Golodetz & Co Inc v Czarnikow-Rionda Co Inc (The Galatia) [1980] 1 WLR 495 (CA)

FACTS: In 1975, Golodetz agreed to sell 13,000 tonnes of sugar **c&f** to Czarnikow, with Czarnikow agreeing to insure the goods. The port of loading was Kandla and 200 tonnes were loaded but were then damaged as a result of a fire and unloaded again. The remainder of the sugar was loaded safely and two bills of lading issued, one for the undamaged sugar and one for 200 tonnes which had typed on it 'Cargo . . . discharged Kandla . . . damaged by fire and/or water used to extinguish fire . . .'. Czarnikow argued that it was entitled to reject the bill of lading relating to the 200 tonnes of damaged sugar.

HELD: The bill was clean and should have been accepted by Czarnikow, since the notation clearly related to damage that happened after loading.

COMMENT: The bill had been rejected by two banks when presented for payment under letters of credit under the then applicable standard banking terms,[25] which were ambiguous as to whether a qualification indicating damage after loading amounted to clausing. Donaldson J suggested that any ambiguity ought to be resolved in favour of 'general maritime and commercial law'.[26] He concluded that the crucial time for a bill of lading is on loading, since this is the vital time, both as between shipper and carrier (the carrier's duty is to deliver the goods in the condition they were at shipment), and between seller and buyer in Cif and Fob contracts, since this is when risk passes.

The decision that the meaning of 'clean' should depend on the law is not without objection. It was by no means clear what the law on this issue was, and in fact the tenor of Lord Sumner's judgment in *Hansson v Hamel and Horley Ltd*[27] was that the law ought to reflect commercial practice. However, the current UCP wording seems to be materially the same as that in 1975 when it states '[a] bank will only accept a clean transport document. A clean transport document is one bearing no clause or notation expressly declaring a defective condition of the goods or their packaging.' Consequently the terminology has not been revised to reverse the conclusion in *The Galatia*.

➜ c&f: cost and freight—similar to Cif, except the seller need not insure the goods.

🔗 The passing of risk in Fob and Cif contracts is dealt with in Chapter 20

Because of the importance between seller and buyer that the bill of lading is clean, carriers come under some pressure to issue clean bills in respect of clearly suspect cargo, a matter dealt with in more detail later.

Commercial acceptability

As the function of the Cif contract is to permit negotiability, the courts have insisted that, since bills of lading 'have to be taken up or rejected promptly and without the

---

25. Known as the 'UCP'. 'UCP' stands for Uniform Customs and Practice, the standard set of rules utilized, in effect, by all banks when dealing with the payment mechanism known as letters of credit. Issued by the International Chamber of Commerce, the UCP determines, among other things, what documents a bank will accept as a conforming tender in order to induce payment. For more, see Chapter 24.
26. [1980] 1 WLR 495 (CA) 509.   27. [1922] 2 AC 36 (HL) 46.

opportunity for prolonged inquiry'[28] and because 'they have to be such as can be re-tendered to sub purchasers', it is essential that they be of such form and content as to be commercially acceptable to traders and their bankers.[29]

However, this formulation raises an important question. Should the determination of what documents are acceptable in commercial practice be determined by the law, or should commercial practice determine what is acceptable under the law? *The Galatia*[30] makes clear that, while a 'tender of documents which, properly read and understood call for further inquiry or are such as to invite litigation is clearly a bad tender', the key words are 'properly read and understood'; in other words, it is the law which determines commercial practice and not vice versa.

It should be noted that the requirement of commercial acceptability applies not only to bills of lading but to other documents required under a Cif or Fob contract.

The number and time for delivery of bills of lading

Bills of lading are often issued in sets of three originals, and the case of *Sanders v MacLean*[31] raises the issue of when or indeed whether all three bills must be delivered to a purchaser under a Cif contract, since any delay in receipt of the 'key to the floating warehouse' would involve a buyer in additional cost. It was held in *Sanders* that unless agreed to the contrary, only one of the three bills needed to be delivered, and that the Cif seller owed a duty to despatch the bill promptly to a buyer, but that there was no duty to ensure that it arrived before the goods themselves.

 Sanders Bros v MacLean & Co (1883) 11 QBD 327 (CA)

FACTS: A quantity of scrap iron was shipped by Mollivo in Sebastopol and sold to Sanders, Cif Philadelphia. Mollivo received three original bills of lading; he forwarded two of these to Sanders in London, who had sold the goods on to MacLean. Sanders tendered the two bills, but they were rejected by MacLean, who claimed that it was entitled to all three of the bills. Sanders contacted Mollivo, who forwarded the final bill to Sanders, who then tendered all three to MacLean, who again rejected them, as there was insufficient time for them to arrive in Philadelphia before the goods were discharged there. This would mean that the carrier would discharge the goods into a warehouse whose charges would have to be paid by the person taking delivery of the iron. Sanders argued that MacLean had wrongfully rejected the bills of lading.

HELD: MacLean committed a breach of condition in rejecting the first tender since, on the authority of the House of Lords decision in *Glyn Mills & Currie*,[32] only one bill of lading was needed to obtain possession of the goods from the carrier. Thus property in the goods and the right to possession of them would pass on receipt of only one bill of lading under

---

28. *Hansson v Hamel and Horley Ltd* [1922] 2 AC 36 (HL) 46 (Lord Sumner).   29. ibid.

30. *M Golodetz & Co Inc v Czarnikow-Rionda Co Inc (The Galatia)* [1980] 1 WLR 495 (CA), adopting the views of Donaldson J, also reported at [1980] 1 WLR 495.

31. (1883) 11 QBD 327 (CA).

32. *Glyn Mills Currie & Co v East and West India Dock Co* (1882) 7 App Cas 591 (HL).

a Cif contract. A requirement to tender all three in a set ought not to be implied simply because, as *Glyn Mills & Currie* illustrates, there is scope for fraud unless a buyer obtains all three.

Even if MacLean had lawfully rejected the first tender, it had no right to reject the second. Although the seller of goods Cif should make every reasonable effort to forward the bills of lading to the buyer as soon as possible after the shipment, there is no implied condition that the bills of lading will be available at the port of discharge before the arrival of the goods or before storage charges are incurred.

COMMENT: The requirement that all originals must be tendered is a common term in Cif contracts because of the fraud problem, and essential where payment is to be by documentary credit, since Arts 20(a)iv and 21(a)iv of UCP 600 stipulate that the bank will only accept all of the shipping documents in a set.[33]

The absence of an implied duty to ensure that the bills arrive before the goods makes complete sense in a case like *Sanders*, where there was a string (though a short one) of contracts where delays in transmission of the bill as it passes from hand to hand are inevitable. However, as the editor of *Benjamin* suggests, a seller who fails to forward the documents by air would 'probably be in breach of his obligation to tender them with the required degree of promptness'.[34]

It should be noted that the duty of prompt despatch may be displaced expressly by the contract or by implication. Thus in *Toepfer (Hamburg) v Lenersan-Poortman NV (Rotterdam)*,[35] the contract stated: 'Payment: net cash against documents . . . not later than 20 days after date of bill of lading. . .'. The ship was delayed through going aground and the shipping documents were tendered some months after the date of loading. The Court of Appeal held that the seller's express obligation was to tender documents in time for the purchaser to accept and pay for them within twenty days of the date of the bill of lading. The Court also held that failure to do so was a breach of condition entitling the purchaser to treat the contract as being at an end, since it is inappropriate to distinguish between the duty to despatch goods promptly (breach of which certainly is a breach of condition) and the similar duty in respect of documents.

The characteristics of the bill of lading

As has been discussed, the bill of lading is intended to fulfil three roles and each will be considered in turn.

---

33. The International Chamber of Commerce has drafted a uniform set of trade terms known as Incoterms, which can be adopted by contracting parties if they so wish. INCOTERMS 2010 expressly state that all originals must be tendered. For more on INCOTERMS, see Chapter 20.
34. Michael G Bridge, *Benjamin's Sale of Goods* (8th edn, Sweet & Maxwell 2010) [19-067].
35. [1980] 1 Lloyd's Rep 143 (CA).

It is a receipt

As a receipt, the bill acts as evidence as against the carrier as to its contents.

Statements as to quantity

The Hague Visby Rules are discussed at p 558

The Carriage of Goods by Sea Act 1971 implements the Hague Visby Rules, which stipulate the minimum duties of a carrier. Article III(3) of the Rules requires a carrier, on demand from the shipper, to issue a bill of lading which contains the leading marks necessary for identification of the goods, either the number of packages or pieces, or the quantity, or weight, and the apparent order and condition of the goods.[36] In favour of the shipper the bill is *prima facie* evidence, but is conclusive in favour of a bona fide transferee by virtue of Art III(4). It is important to note that the duty only applies if the information is demanded by the shipper, so that the typical caveat on bills of lading, 'weight, measure, marks, numbers, quality, quantity, content and value unknown', does not constitute a breach of the carrier's Art III(3) duty unless an unequivocal statement of such matters is expressly or impliedly required by the shipper.[37] As on the simplified bill of lading in Figure 19.1, it is common for a weight to be given on a bill of lading which also states 'weight unknown'. It is presumed that this given weight will not be 'wildly at odds' with the quantity actually loaded.[38]

On whether the common law or the Hague Visby Rules apply to a bill of lading, see p 559

Actual authority is discussed at p 87, and apparent authority is discussed at p 96

If the common law applies to the bill, a statement as to the quantity of the goods is *prima facie* evidence that goods in that quantity were loaded, leaving the carrier to prove short shipment.[39] However, by virtue of the rule in *Grant v Norway*[40] that the master of a ship has no authority to sign a bill of lading for goods which have never been shipped, at common law a bill of lading remains only *prima facie* evidence, even in favour of a subsequent bona fide holder. However, s 4 of the Carriage of Goods by Sea Act 1992 provides that statements in a bill of lading, signed by the master or a person with actual or apparent authority, representing that goods have been received for shipment or actually shipped, 'shall, in favour of a person who has become the lawful holder of the bill, be conclusive evidence against the carrier'. Two issues arise. First, the words 'who has become the lawful holder' seem to preserve the common law position in respect of the shipper. Second, the definition of a bill of lading for the purposes of the Carriage of Goods by Sea Act 1992 (COGSA 1992) does not include a straight bill,[41] so that the common law position would appear to apply to the consignee unless the shipper and carrier contract to the contrary.[42]

---

36. See if you can find each of these on the simplified bill of lading in Figure 19.1. Note also that, just after the representation that the goods were loaded in apparent good order and condition, the bill states 'weight, measure, marks, numbers, quality, quantity, content and value unknown'.

37. *Agrosin PTE Ltd v Highway Shipping Co Ltd (The Mata K)* [1998] 2 Lloyd's Rep 614 (QB). For the impact of such a statement, see Longmore J in *Noble Resources Ltd v Cavalier Shipping Corp (The Atlas)* [1996] 1 Lloyd's Rep 642 (QB) 646.

38. *Conoco (UK) v Limai Maritime Co (The Sirina)* [1988] 2 Lloyd's Rep 613 (QB) 615 (Phillips J).

39. *Henry Smith & Co v Bedouin Steam Navigation Co Ltd* [1896] AC 70 (HL).

40. (1851) 10 CB 665.

41. *J I MacWilliam Co Inc v Mediterranean Shipping Co SA (The Rafaela S)* [2005] UKHL 1, [2005] 2 AC 423.

42. The rule in *Grant v Norway* has been the subject of substantial criticism. The law of agency has moved on since 1851, in particular in relation to apparent authority after *Freeman & Lockyear v Buckhurst Park Properties (Mangal) Ltd* [1964] 2 QB 480 (CA); and see especially *Lloyd v Grace Smith & Co* [1912] AC 716 (HL) in relation to an agent doing wrongfully that which he was employed to do correctly.

Where the representation is made fraudulently or negligently then, *prima facie*, there seems no reason why an action in tort for deceit or negligent misstatement might not lie against the carrier. However, if it is beyond the authority of a master to make misstatements as to quantity, then it seems to follow that such statements must be outside the course of his employment,[43] rendering the carrier immune to a vicarious liability claim.[44] An action for breach of warranty of authority would be available against the signatory personally.[45]

🔗 Breach of warranty of authority is discussed at p 176

Before considering other statements on a bill of lading it is necessary to consider their effects generally.

The legal effect of statements other than statements as to quantity

The courts have refused to extend *Grant v Norway* so that, for example, a statement in a bill of lading that the goods were stowed in a hold and not on deck was held to bind the carrier.[46] However, there remains the issue of the legal effect of such statements.

It was decided in *Compania Naviera Vasconzada v Churchill & Sim*[47] that words in a bill of lading describing the condition of the goods in a bill of lading are not contractual so as to give rise to an obligation to discharge goods in such a condition, but instead are a representation of fact which may create an estoppel in favour of a purchaser. Consequently the claimant must not only have a separate cause of action in contract or tort against the carrier, but he must also rely on the words in the bill of lading and act on them. In *Silver v Ocean Steamship Co*,[48] the Court of Appeal held that reliance can be presumed in the case of a transferee, but it is clear the presumption is rebuttable so that in *The Skarp*,[49] where the terms of the contract of sale required the buyer to accept the bill, Langton J concluded that there was no reliance on the representation—had the bill contained an accurate description, the buyer would still have accepted it. Similarly, in a rising market a buyer might be expected to accept a bill recording defects,[50] where, even with the flaws, the goods would be worth more than the purchase price. However, in *The Dona Mari*,[51] with similar facts to *The Skarp*, Kerr J argued that, since the carrier was not a party to the contract of sale, its terms ought to be irrelevant to the issue of his liability. With respect, this seems incorrect, since these terms are clearly relevant to the issue of whether the claimant relied on the representation in the bill or would in any event have taken up the bill regardless of its content.

Finally, in relation *Churchill & Sim*, the extent of the applicability of the rule is unclear. First, it may apply solely to the representation that the goods were loaded in apparent good order and condition—in other words confined to its own situation. Second, the reasoning may be based on the construction of the words on the bill,

---

43. *Armagas Ltd v Mundogas SA, The Ocean Frost* [1986] AC 717 (HL) is authority for this proposition, at least in relation to fraud.

44. *Blue Nile Co Ltd v Emery Customs Brokers (S) Pte Ltd* [1990] 2 MLJ 385 (High Court of Singapore).

45. *V/O Rasnoimport v Guthrie & Co Ltd* [1996] 1 Lloyd's Rep (QB).

46. *The Nea Tyhi* [1982] 1 Lloyd's Rep 606 (QB).   47. [1906] 1 KB 237(KB).

48. [1930] 1 KB 416 (CA).   49. [1935] P 134 (PDA).

50. Known as a 'claused bill'. For more on claused bills, see p 488.

51. *Peter Cremer GmbH v General Carriers SA (The Dona Mari)* [1974] 1 WLR 341 (QB).

which have the character of a statement of fact not an undertaking.[52] On this basis, the decision will extend to the issues of description, inaccurate leading marks,[53] or quantities.[54] Finally, it may be founded on the reasoning that, since the description of the goods came from the shipper, it should not be presumed that the carrier would warrant the accuracy of a statement to the person who provided it and, though the bill is in the hands of a transferee, that cannot change the terms of the contract.[55] On this basis, *Churchill & Sim* would apply to the description, marks, and apparent quality, but not to quantity, since it is said the shipper will only state the quantity delivered to the carrier but not the quantity shipped.[56] It should be noted that the statement 'freight prepaid' on a bill has been held not to be a contractual term, but a statement of fact.[57]

Statements as to condition

Statements in a bill of lading as to the apparent condition of the goods on loading, although *prima facie* evidence in favour of the shipper, are conclusive in favour of a bona fide transferee, at least where the Hague Visby Rules apply, and almost certainly at common law,[58] though of course, as noted earlier, although conclusive, they only operate as statements of fact, not as contractual warranties.

It should be noted that the statement simply relates to the apparent condition of the goods, so that only defects externally visible on a reasonable examination are covered.[59]

Statements as to leading marks

Where the Hague Visby Rules apply, any statement as to leading marks is conclusive evidence in favour of a transferee of the bill. However, at common law it was held in *Parsons v New Zealand Shipping Co*[60] that, unless the marks are material to the identity of the goods, for example to distinguish them from goods belonging to third parties, the carrier is not estopped from claiming the goods he has a duty to deliver were shipped under different marks to those stated in the bill of lading.

Statements as to date

Except in relation to a 'received for shipment' bill of lading, bills of lading should not be issued until all of the cargo described in it has been shipped on board.[61]

---

52. But the same could be said of the phrase that the goods are 'shipped under deck', yet it was held in *The Nea Tyhi* [1982] 1 Lloyd's Rep 606 (QB) that storage of the goods in a hold was a term of the contract.

53. Statements of marks were held to raise an estoppel in *Parsons v New Zealand Shipping Co* [1901] 1 QB 548 (QB).

54. See to the contrary Mocatta J in *V/O Rasnoimport v Guthrie & Co Ltd* [1996] 1 Lloyd's Rep (QB), who would extend *Churchill v Simms* to cover quantity.

55. Though in fact *LeDuc & Co v Ward* (1888) 20 QBD 475 (CA) demonstrates this is not always so.

56. Of course, the same argument would apply to statements as to quality—the shipper will only state the quality of the goods delivered to the carrier, but not their quality when shipped.

57. *Cho Yang Shipping Co Ltd v Coral (UK) Ltd* [1997] 2 Lloyd's Rep 641 (CA).

58. Applying by analogy the reasoning in *LeDuc & Co v Ward* (1888) 20 QBD 475 (CA).

59. For an example of apparent and non-apparent defects, see Scrutton LJ in *Silver v Ocean Steamship Co Ltd* [1930] 1KB 416 (CA) 427, which included insufficiency of packing amongst the issues relating to good order and condition.

60. [1901] 1 QB 548 (QB).

61. *Mendala III Transport v Total Transport Corp (The Wilomi Tanana)* [1993] 2 Lloyd's Rep 41 (QB) 45 (Hobhouse J).

The bill of lading will state the date on which the goods were loaded and this may be of vital importance: first, because the buyer and seller may have contracted that the goods be shipped during a specific period of time known as the 'shipping period' and shipment outside this period will permit the buyer to reject the bill or the goods,[62] which he would probably do if the goods are worth less than the contract price;[63] and second, because the price of the goods may be determined by reference to the date of shipment.[64] A holder of a misdated bill of lading may therefore have accepted it because of the misdating when he would otherwise have rejected it, or have paid a higher price for goods than he would otherwise would have done. In this case, he may have a claim against the seller, but this may be unattractive; for example, the seller may be insolvent, or enforcement of a judgment against him may be difficult. Therefore a claim against the carrier may have to be considered. In cases where the price of the goods is date-dependent, whether the effect of the statement is a warranty or merely gives rise to an estoppel, a contractual claim would seem to be likely to succeed. However, in relation to a misdating causing a loss of the right to reject, this is more doubtful—what loss does the holder suffer because the goods were shipped a few days late, unless the whole of the reduction in the value of the goods can be attributed to the delay in sailing? It therefore appears that the holder will need to rely on claims in tort. Where the misdating is through fraud of the carrier, then an action for fraudulent misrepresentation will lie.[65] Although there is no authority directly on point, it would appear that a negligent misstatement of the date would give rise to liability under the *Hedley Byrne* principle.[66]

The issues between buyer and seller in relation to misdated bills of lading are discussed at p 541

Disputes between carrier and shipper over the content of bills of lading

Since the bill of lading operates as a receipt, it is clear from what has been said, that if the cargo or its packaging is not in good condition, where there is a clear difference between the shipper's figure and the actual quantity of cargo loaded, or indeed any other discrepancy between the statements on the bill of lading and reality, these matters ought to be reflected on the bill, since failure to do so will expose the carrier to claims from the person taking delivery of the goods. However, because of the importance of a clean bill of lading to shippers intending to effect sub-sales, or a bill of lading conforming to a letter of credit, the carrier may be offered an indemnity against liability in order to induce him to issue an inaccurate bill, as in *Brown Jenkinson v Percy Dalton*.[67] Here the carrier signed clean bills of lading for barrels of orange juice, which were clearly leaking, against an indemnity for liability offered by the shippers. The carrier was successfully sued by the consignee, being estopped from denying that the goods were in good condition on loading, but failed in their claim on the indemnity, because it was held to be unenforceable as an illegal

---

62. *Bowes v Shand* (1876–77) 2 App Cas 455 (HL).

63. See e.g. *Kwei Tek Chao v British Shippers & Traders Ltd* [1954] 2 QB 459 (QB).

64. See e.g. *Mendala III Transport v Total Transport Corp (The Wilomi Tanana)* [1993] 2 Lloyd's Rep 41 (QB).

65. *The Saudi Crown* [1986] 1 Lloyd's Rep 261 (QB). Presumably an action based on deceit.

66. In *Heskell v Continental Express* Ltd [1950] 1 All ER 1033 (QB), Devlin J held that a carrier was not liable for negligence when a bill of lading was issued though no goods were ever loaded. However, fourteen years later, as Lord Devlin, he cast doubt on that decision in *Hedley Byrne v Heller & Partners* [1964] AC 465 (HL) 532. But see *Caparo Industies plc v Dickman* [1990] 2 AC 605 (HL).

67. *Brown Jenkinson & Co Ltd v Percy Dalton (London) Ltd* [1957] 2 QB 621 (CA).

contract because it was a fraud on the buyer. The fact that giving such indemnities was common did not assist the carrier. It was accepted in this case that some indemnities would be unobjectionable where there is a bona fide dispute between shipper and carrier over whether some matter ought to be amended or the bill ought to be claused.[68] However, it appears to continue to be common practice for indemnities to be accepted to induce the carrier to make statements they know to be false.[69]

Under the terms of the contract of carriage, the shipper will warrant to the carrier that the information he has provided as to quantity, quality, condition, and so forth of the goods is accurate.[70] However, such a clause will not permit a contractual claim where the bill has been signed without clausing through the carrier's negligence, since this acts as a *novus actus interveniens*, breaking the chain of causation between the breach of contract by the shipper in providing inaccurate information and the loss suffered by the carrier.[71]

The decision whether to clause or not is made by the master of the ship, and liability will arise if he incorrectly determines to clause a bill, since a shipper is entitled to a clean bill unless there is a good reason to clause. This raises the issue of how to determine whether a bill ought to have been claused. In *The David Agmashenebeli*,[72] the master claused the bills of lading with the words 'Cargo discoloured also foreign materials…'. The court accepted that, whilst the master might take expert advice on the condition of the cargo, he would not normally be criticized for not doing so. His duty was to honestly exercise his own judgment on the appearance of the cargo. If he decided that it was not in apparent good order and condition, and this was a view that could properly be held by a reasonably observant master, then he was entitled to clause the bill, even though other masters might not have reached the same conclusion.

It is evidence of the contract of carriage

As already noted, a bill of lading will typically have the terms on which the carrier operates either printed on the back, as in the case of our simplified bill of lading in Figure 19.1, or will incorporate such terms by reference. When the bill is held by the shipper, these provisions are only 'excellent evidence' of the terms of the contract.[73]

---

68. The captain has the right to delay signing the bills until any dispute as to the true position has been determined—see *Boukadoura Maritime Corp v Marocaine de l'Industrie et du Raffinage SA (The Boukadoura)* [1989] 1 Lloyd's Rep 393 (QB)—so the shipper may need to break any deadlock in order to meet contractual obligations to deliver a clean bill to a third party purchaser or a bank.

69. The basis of the case is not that the carriers intended or believed the consignee would be defrauded (they not unreasonably assumed he would be financially compensated by the seller), but that they made statements knowing them to be false, thus committing the tort of deceit. The position may be different under Art 17(3)–(4) of the Hamburg Rules, which requires proof of intention to defraud a subsequent holder of the bill of lading.

70. Even if not expressly included in the contract, such indemnities arise in contracts to which the Hague Visby Rules apply by virtue of Art 3(5).

71. *Naviera Mogor SA v Société Metallurgique de Normandie (The Nogar Marin)* [1988] 1 Lloyd's Rep 412 (CA).

72. *The David Agmashenebeli (Cargo Owners) v The David Agmashenebeli (Owners) (The David Agmashenebeli)* [2002] 2 All ER (Comm) 806 (QB).

73. *SS Ardennes (Cargo Owners) v SS Ardennes (Owners)* [1951] 1 KB 55 (KB) 59 (Goddard CJ). See also *Cho Yang Shipping Co Ltd v Coral (UK) Ltd* [1997] CLC 1100 (CA), though here the issue (a statement that freight had been pre-paid) did not relate to a contractual term because of the rule in *Churchill & Sim*.

Necessarily the parties must have concluded a contract before the goods were loaded, and it is loading which triggers the issue of the bill of lading. Consequently, it is on these initial terms that the parties contract.

SS Ardennes, (Cargo Owners) v SS Ardennes (Owners) [1951] 1 KB 55 (KB)

FACTS: The Cargo Owners' agent orally agreed with the agent for the owners of the *Ardennes* that the goods—oranges—would be carried directly to London. The bill of lading allowed for deviation and the ship went via Antwerp, arriving in London later than would have been the case had she used a direct route.

HELD: It was held that the carrier had no contractual right to deviate, since the bill did not accurately incorporate the actual contract of carriage, and so the carrier was liable for the reduction in value of the oranges caused by their late arrival and for an increase in import duty which would have been avoided.

However, were this rule to apply between the carrier and a subsequent holder, it would undermine one of the functions of the bill of lading, since such a holder could never be sure of the terms of carriage. Thus in *LeDuc v Ward*,[74] the carrier sought to introduce oral evidence which, had it been accepted, would have benefited the carrier; but it was held that, as between the carrier and a transferee the bill of lading is conclusive evidence of the terms of carriage, though because of the rule in *Grant v Norway*, this is not the case in respect of goods not received by the carrier.[75]

It is a document of title

The purpose of a document of title to goods is to enable the holder to deal in them, particularly by sale or pledge, even though physical possession is with a bailee. This was accepted in *Lickbarrow v Mason*,[76] recognizing the custom of merchants that a 'shipped' bill of lading[77] is a document of title to the goods it identifies, thus enabling goods to be sold or pledged whilst afloat. Thus banks could be granted security over goods through possession of a document, rather than of the goods themselves, while the goods might be sold many times over whilst at sea simply by delivery (suitably indorsed) of a document.

---

74. (1888) 20 QBD 475 (CA).

75. *LeDuc* does not proceed on the basis of estoppel, but because of the parol evidence rule; but were the oral agreement to favour the holder, estoppel may be a preferable basis for the decision.

76. (1787) 2 TR 63. For a full description of *Lickbarrow v Mason*, see Michael Bools, *The Bill of Lading a Document of Title to Goods* (LLP 1997) Ch 1.

77. 'Shipped' means that the bill acknowledges that the goods have actually been *loaded* on to the ship, as opposed to a 'mate's receipt', which states that the goods have been *received* ready for loading. Received for shipment bills of lading would appear not to be documents of title. See *Diamond Alkali Export Corporation v Fl Bourgeois* [1921] 3 KB 443 (KB) and Michael G Bridge, *Benjamin's Sale of Goods* (8th edn, 2010 Sweet & Maxwell) [18-06].

What does this characteristic mean?

Although there is some disagreement amongst commentators as to the precise meaning of this characteristic,[78] certain things are clear:

🔗 For bills of exchange, see p 635

1. Unlike instruments which relate to property consisting of payment obligations, for example bills of exchange,[79] title to the underlying property does not pass with the delivery of a suitably indorsed transferable bill of lading. Title to identifiable goods will pass with a bill of lading only if both that is the intention of the parties[80] and the transferor himself has title. In other words, a bill of lading, may be transferable, but unlike a bill of exchange is not in a strict sense negotiable; an honest purchaser without notice of any defect in title can acquire no better title to the underlying property than his transferor.[81]

🔗 For bailment and constructive possession see Chapter 2

2. The carrier as bailee has physical possession of the goods but the shipper[82] has constructive possession. Transfer of a transferrable bill of lading transfers constructive possession of identifiable underlying goods,[83] if the parties so intend.[84] The bill is therefore a symbol for the goods which are at sea and incapable of physical delivery; delivery of the bill is symbolic delivery of the goods, so that the holder can demand physical delivery of the goods from the carrier on their discharge from the ship.[85]

3. As with instruments, title to a bill of lading (suitably indorsed as necessary) passes by delivery accompanied by the requisite intention to pass title, so that there is no need for a separate assignment or notice to be given to the obligor.

Whether a bill of lading is transferable or not and how transfer is effected depends on the way the bill is made out, and, in the normal case, specifically how the 'Consignee' box is completed on the face of the bill. In the simplified bill of lading set out in Figure 19.1, the Consignee box contains the notation: 'Consigned to the order of Billy Buyers'. By analogy with bills of exchange, which developed before the modern form of the bill of lading, this notation indicates that the bill is to be transferable through indorsement and delivery by the named consignee. Had the consignee box simply read 'Consigned to Billy Buyers' then only he can recover possession from the carrier so that the bill is not transferable—known as a 'straight' or 'straight consigned' bill. Conversely, had the box read 'Consigned to bearer', 'Consigned to holder', or even 'Consigned to' (and then left blank) then transfer is by delivery

---

78. See for a review, Charles De Battista, *Bills of Lading in Export Trade* (Tottel Publishing 2008) [2-03-4].

79. By which we mean ownership, not just a possessory title. For more details, see p 26.

80. SGA 1979, s 17. This is true also of instruments.

81. See e.g. Lord Campbell in *Gurney v Behrend* (1854) 3 E&B 262, 272. Of course, the transferee will obtain better title, as with any other property where an exception to the *nemo dat* rule applies, e.g. where ss 2, 3, or 9 of the Factors Act 1889 or ss 24 or 25 of the Sale of Goods Act 1979 apply.

82. In fact, the contract of carriage may give constructive possession to a third party, but this complicating factor is ignored for the purpose of exposition.

83. Technically the constructive possession arises because the carrier as bailee has no right to retain possession of the goods as against the shipper, and somehow this relationship is transferred with the bill of lading, but it is not entirely clear how this is effected. In *Borealis AB v Stargas Ltd (The Berge Sisar)* [2002] EWCA Civ 757, [2002] 2 AC 205, it was suggested that the transfer of a bill of lading effected a transfer of the carrier's attornment to the shipper, but this answer simply raises a further question—how? On attornment, see p 38.

84. *The Future Express* [1992] 2 Lloyd's Rep 79 (QB) 94, affirmed [1993] 2 Lloyd's Rep 542 (CA).

85. See Bowen LJ in *Sanders Bros v McLean & Co* (1883) 11 QBD 327 (CA) 341, adopting terminology and concepts first introduced in *Barber v Meyerstein* (1866) LR 2 CP 38.

without the need for indorsement. As with bills of exchange, a bill of lading can be indorsed in favour of a named transferee (in which case that transferee must indorse it in order to effect a further transfer) or indorsed in blank (in which case it can be transferred by delivery without indorsement).

The bill of lading and the right to delivery

A carrier may refuse delivery of the goods to an owner of them without the delivery to it of the bill of lading relating to them, a point now recognized by the Court of Appeal in *The Houda*.[86] Thus, even if the bill of lading names *X* as consignee, the carrier is neither obliged nor entitled to deliver the cargo to *X* without his producing a bill of lading. The shipper, while in possession of the bill of lading, retains the right to direct the carrier to whom the goods should be delivered,[87] and that instruction is to deliver against a bill of lading, not an instruction to deliver to *X*.

Similarly, the carrier is under a duty to release the goods on production of a bill of lading, presuming its charges for freight have been paid, unless it has notice that someone other than the holder has better title. As a corollary to this, the carrier is protected from claims in contract or in the tort of conversion if it delivers the goods against the production of an original bill of lading, even if the holder does not have title to the goods or a right to immediately possess them, unless it has notice of a better title.[88] This immunity from suit, since it arises from the obligation to deliver under the bill of lading, would appear not to apply where the person with better title has no connection with the bill, for example where the goods were stolen prior to shipment.

Sets of bills and the position of the carrier

Where only one bill of lading has been issued, there are unlikely to be problems arising from the rights, duties, and immunities of the carrier. However, it remains customary for a set of three originals to be issued, even though the practice dates from the days when voyages were hazardous and was intended to guard against the loss at sea of a single bill. Since delivery of any one bill of lading to the carrier entitles the holder to delivery of the goods, the practice offers clear opportunities for fraud, as *Glyn Mills Currie & Co v East and West India Dock Co*[89] illustrates.

 Glyn Mills Currie & Co v East and West India Dock Co (1882) 7 App Cas 591 (HL)

FACTS: Goods were shipped and three original transferable bills of lading were issued, each stating that three bills had been issued and 'the one of which bills being accomplished

---

86. *Kuwait Petroleum Corp v I & D Oil Carriers Ltd (The Houda)* [1994] 2 Lloyd's Rep 541 (CA), a case involving charterparty bills. Authorities outside charterparties include *The Stettin* (1889) 14 PD 142 (PDA) and *Barclays Bank Ltd v Commissioners of Customs & Excise* [1963] 1 Lloyd's Rep 81 (QB).

87. *Elder Dempster Lines v Zaki Ishag (The Lycaon)* [1983] 2 Lloyd's Rep 548 (QB).

88. *Glyn Mills Currie & Co v East and West India Dock Co* (1881–2) 7 App Cas 591 (HL). See also Millett LJ in *Kuwait Petroleum Corp v I & D Oil Carriers Ltd (The Houda)* [1994] 2 Lloyd's Rep 541 (CA).

89. (1882) 7 App Cas 591 (HL).

the others to stand void'.[90] The bills were clearly numbered first, second, and third. The shipper indorsed and delivered the bills to the consignees, who indorsed and delivered the 'first' bill to their bank, Glyn Mills as security for a loan.[91] On discharge of the goods, the consignees sold the goods to a third party and delivered the second bill, unindorsed to the warehouseman East and West, who delivered the goods as ordered by the consignees to a third party buyer. The consignees were insolvent and the bank sued the warehouseman in conversion.

HELD: The warehouseman was not liable in conversion. The words 'the one of which bills being accomplished the others to stand void' meant that once the goods had been delivered in accordance with the contract of carriage, in the absence of notice of the competing right to possess, no claims in contract or tort could be made against the carrier in relation to mis-delivery.

COMMENT: Apart from anything else this is a pragmatic decision, since were a carrier to be liable in circumstances such as *Glyn Mills*, he would have to investigate the title of every claimant for delivery of the goods who held a bill of lading—an impossible task. The case also illustrates the fact that in general the courts have concluded that it is for the buyer and seller (and their banks) to take the risk of fraud, not the carrier.

Finally Lord O'Hagan pointed out[92] that there was nothing to prevent the bank pursuing its claim against the third party purchaser. The rule in *Barber v Meyerstein*,[93] that the person who first obtains lawful possession of a bill of lading though only one of a set of three also obtains the property which it represents, and any subsequent dealings with the others of the set are subordinate to the rights passed by that one, would therefore seem to give the bank in *Glyn Mills* a claim against the third party.

Delivery of goods without delivery of a bill of lading

It was noted in *The Houda* that it is common practice in some trades for goods to be released without the production of a bill of lading against an indemnity by a seller of the goods (or more usually its bank) holding the carrier harmless.[94] That this practice is commonplace is not surprising, not least because the use of fast ships and delays in the issue of bills of lading regularly result in the goods arriving before the documents on short voyages. However, since the carrier is under a duty not to deliver the goods except against delivery of a bill of lading, he loses the protection afforded by *Glyn Mills* if he delivers against an indemnity. However, the cause for the non-production of bills of lading is not always innocent, as the following case demonstrates.

---

90. The corresponding wording in materially the same form to that in *Glyn Mills* is still used today. See e.g. the simplified bill of lading in Figure 19.1.

91. This was a pledge giving the bank 'special property' in the goods.

92. (1882) 7 App Cas 591 (HL) 603–4.   93. (1869–70) 4 HL 317 (HL).

94. However, as *The Houda* establishes, this practice does not, in the absence of an agreement to the contrary, require the carrier to accept the indemnity and release the goods without a bill of lading.

Sze Hai Tong Bank Ltd v Rambler Cycle Co Ltd [1959] AC 576 (PC)

FACTS: Rambler agreed to sell bicycles to Southern for delivery in Singapore, payment against documents. In accordance with a common practice at the time in Singapore, the carrier delivered the goods to Southern, the consignee, without production of a bill of lading, having been given an indemnity against loss by the Southern's bank, Sze Hai Tong. Southern never paid for the goods and Rambler sued the carrier in contract and in conversion.

HELD: Not surprisingly, the Privy Council held a carrier who delivers the goods without production of the bill of lading does so at his peril, and the carrier was liable for breach of contract and for conversion.[95]

COMMENT: In *Sze Hai Tong*, the carrier knew that the person entitled to delivery was the shipper, and consequently it was acting wrongfully, but this knowledge of fault is not essential to liability; delivery to a person entitled to possession but without a bill of lading or to a person with a forged bill of lading[96] will not attract the *Glyn Mills* immunity. Although there have been suggestions that the carrier may retain immunity when delivering to the person entitled to possession in the absence of a bill of lading, for example where the bill(s) have been lost or stolen,[97] these were doubted in *The Houda* and appear to be wrong.[98]

★ See KW Wedderburn, 'Contract–Exceptions Clause–Fundamental Breach–Agents' [1960] CLJ 11

One way to avoid delivering the goods without a bill of lading is for one of the set of bills to be sent by the carrier on the ship along with the goods and given to the consignee on arrival at the port of discharge, even though there is a distinct possibility that in the meantime the shipper has sold the other two. However, it is open to question whether the *Glyn Mills* immunity would apply here; the carrier must have notice of the possibility of third party rights and since an indemnity is normally taken from the consignee against delivery, the carrier seems to be recognizing fault.

There remains the issue of terms being included in the contract of carriage excluding liability of the carrier for mis-delivery. In *Sze Hai Tong*, the bill of lading provided that 'the responsibility of the carrier . . . shall be deemed . . . to cease absolutely after the goods are discharged'. The Privy Council construed this clause so that it did not exempt the carrier from liability for deliberately disregarding the primary function of the contract of carriage—to deliver the goods safely against production of the bill of lading. However, Lord Denning appeared to acknowledge

---

95. In *Sze Hai Tong*, the bank admitted liability on the indemnity, but the principle in *Brown Jenkinson & Co Ltd v Percy Dalton (London) Ltd* [1957] 2 Lloyd's Rep 1(CA) would apply as much to indemnities like this as to indemnities given to procure clean bills of lading—see p 495.

96. *Motis Exports Ltd v Dampskibsselskabet AF 1912* [2000] 1 All ER (Comm) 91(CA). See Paul Todd's casenote on *Motis Exports* 'Delivery against Forged Bills of Lading' [1999] LMCLQ 449.

97. See Clarke J in *Sucre Export SA v Northern River Shipping Ltd, The Sormovskiy* [1994] 2 Lloyd's Rep 266 (QB) and Diplock J in *Barclays Bank Ltd v Commissioners of Customs and Excise* [1963] 1 Lloyd's Rep 81 (QB).

98. See Rix J in *Motis Exports Ltd v Dampskibsselskabet AF 1912* [1999] 1 Lloyd's Rep 837 (QB), where he accepted that, following *The Houda*, there were no exceptions to the general rule against delivery without a bill of lading in the absence of an effective exemption clause. The decision was upheld on appeal in *Motis Exports Ltd v Dampskibsselskabet AF 1912* [2000] 1 All ER (Comm) 91 (CA).

the possibility that an effective clause might be drafted,[99] as did Millett LJ in *The Houda*,[100] though a very clear clause would be needed.[101]

Finally, it should be noted that in order to maintain an action against the carrier for mis-delivery, the claimant must have some claim against the carrier in contract or tort. A transferee of a stale bill will acquire no contractual claim nor obtain a right to immediate possession[102] unless the exceptions in s 2(2) of the Carriage of Goods by Sea Act 1992 apply.

Stale bills are discussed at p 503

Transfer of contractual rights

In documentary sales, the buyer will not necessarily be a party to the contract of carriage, and consequently at common law cannot sue[103] or be sued on the contract in such a case. However, assuming the bill of lading and the other contractual documents conform, the buyer must accept them and pay the contract price, while risk in the goods will have passed on shipment. Consequently it is the buyer[104] or the buyer's bank, not the seller, who is normally interested in ensuring the carrier meets its obligations, so that the privity rule is a clear obstacle to the control of legal risk in international sales. The Bills of Lading Act 1855 dealt with the issue by stipulating that the rights and obligations under the contract of carriage passed under the Act with property in the goods. Although a material improvement on the common law position, the Act had a number of defects, not least that 'property' did not include the 'special property' of a pledgee,[105] so that there were problems for banks claiming security over the goods. Also, since at the time property in undivided bulk shipments could not pass,[106] the Act had limited application in the bulk-carrying trade. The 1855 Act was repealed and replaced by the COGSA 1992 in response to a Law Commission report.[107]

Scheme of the Carriage of Goods by Sea Act 1992[108]

Documentation

The 1855 Act applied only to shipped transferable bills of lading but the COGSA 1992 applies to any 'bill of lading', any 'sea waybill', and any 'ship's delivery

---

99. *Sze Hai Tong Bank Ltd v Rambler Cycle Co Ltd* 1959] AC 576 (PC) 586.

100. [1994] 2 Lloyd's Rep 541 (CA).

101. For an example, see *Glebe Island Terminals Pty v Continental Seagram Pty (The Antwerpen)* [1994] 1 Lloyd's Rep 213 (NSW CA). See also John Wilson, 'The Presentation Rule Revisited' [1995] LMCLQ 289.

102. See *The Future Express* [1993] 2 Lloyd's Rep 79 (CA).

103. *Thompson v Dominy* (1845) 14 M&W 403.

104. Or the buyer's insurance company if subrogated to the buyer's rights through having met an insurance claim for loss or damage to the goods whilst in the carrier's possession.

105. *Sewell v Burdick & Nephew* (1884) 10 App Cas 74 (HL).

106. *Aramis (Cargo Owners) v Aramis (Owners) (The Aramis)* [1989] 1 Lloyd's Rep 212 (CA). The position is different now if s 20A of the SGA 1979 applies.

107. Law Commission, *Rights of Suit in Respect of Carriage of Goods by Sea* (Law Com No 196, 1991).

108. For good surveys of the Act and further background to the issues which plagued the 1855 Act, see FMB Reynolds, 'The Carriage of Goods by Sea Act 1992' [1993] LMCLQ 436; J Beatson and JJT

order'.[109] Section 1(2) makes it clear that the bill must be transferable either by indorsement or by delivery,[110] but may be a 'received for shipment' bill.[111] In the case of sea waybills or ship's delivery orders, the named consignee or his agent takes delivery through proof of identity and authority, as required.

Transfer and extinction of rights

Section 2(1) of the COGSA 1992 effects an assignment of all rights of suit under the contract of carriage to a lawful holder of a bill of lading or (as appropriate) to the person to whom delivery is to be made under a sea waybill or ship's delivery order.

Carriage of Goods by Sea Act 1992, s 2(1)

(1) Subject to the following provisions of this section, a person who becomes—

  (a) the lawful holder of a bill of lading;

  (b) the person who (without being an original party to the contract of carriage) is the person to whom delivery of the goods to which a sea waybill relates is to be made by the carrier in accordance with that contract; or

  (c) the person to whom delivery of the goods to which a ship's delivery order relates is to be made in accordance with the undertaking contained in the order,

shall (by virtue of becoming the holder of the bill or, as the case may be, the person to whom delivery is to be made) have transferred to and vested in him all rights of suit under the contract of carriage as if he had been a party to that contract.

'A 'holder' as defined in s 5(2) of the COGSA 1992 includes a person in possession of the bill who is either named as the consignee in it or who has possession as a result of a transfer of the bill to him. It should be noted that, unlike the 1855 Act, there is no requirement for property in the underlying goods to pass in order for the 1992 Act to operate.

Under the 1855 Act, rights were not transferred in respect of bills of lading, known as 'stale' or 'spent' bills, where delivery of the goods had been made in accordance with the terms of the contract.[112] Consequently, because of delays in the transmission of the bill, a buyer might receive it after the goods had been discharged to him, but would acquire no contractual rights against the carrier. However, if all stale bills transferred rights against the carrier, the possibility of trading in such bills as naked causes of action emerges, thus avoiding the law against **champerty**. Consequently, COGSA 1992 retains the general bar on the transmission of contractual rights under

➡ **champerty:** formerly a tort and a crime, champerty occurs where one person finances the legal proceedings of another person in return for a share in any monetary award ordered by the court

---

Cooper, 'Rights of Suit in Respect of Carriage of Goods by Sea' [1991] LMCLQ 196; Robert Bradgate and Fidelma White, 'The Carriage of Goods by Sea Act 1992' (1993) 56 MLR 188.
109. COGSA 1992, s 1(1).   110. ibid s 1(2)(a).   111. ibid s 1(2)(b).
112. See *Barber v Meyerstein* (1870) LR 4 HL 317 (HL) 330; *Enichem Anic SpA v Ampelos Shipping Co Ltd (The Delfini)* [1990] 1 Lloyd's Rep 252 (CA) 269.

stale bills subject to two exceptions. Under s 2(2) a stale bill transfers rights to sue if the holder acquires the bill either by virtue of:

- s 2(2)(a), a transaction effected in pursuance of any contractual or other arrangements made before the bill became stale; or
- s 2(2)(b), the rejection of goods or documents delivered to another person under arrangements made before the bill became stale.

Thus if, for example, goods are delivered to a buyer against a letter of indemnity before he receives the bill of lading, s 2(2)(a) will nevertheless vest the right to sue the carrier in him once the bill of lading is delivered to him. Similarly, if goods are sold by a shipper and delivered by the carrier against a letter of indemnity to a buyer who then rejects the goods as against the seller for breach of condition, then s 2(2)(b) will re-vest the right to sue the carrier in the shipper/seller, even though the bill is stale. It should be noted that s 2(2)(b) may operate many times up a string of contracts until the bill returns to the shipper, but the rights pass with the bill not the property in the goods, as was the case under the 1855 Act. Therefore where a buyer has surrendered the bill in order to induce delivery, only for the goods to be rejected for breach of a condition, the seller will need to secure an assignment of the buyer's rights under the contract of carriage for him to be able to claim in contract against the carrier.

East West Corporation v DKBS 1912 [2003] EWCA Civ 83

FACTS: East West sold goods cash on delivery to a company in Chile and DKBS agreed with East West to transport the goods. Bills of lading were issued naming East West as shippers and a Chilean bank as consignee. The bank was to act as East West's agent for the collection of the purchase price and the bills of lading were sent by East West to the bank for this purpose. Property in the goods remained with East West and the bank held no security interest. DKBS delivered the goods to one of the buyers without presentation of the bills of lading. The buyer did not pay and the bank redelivered the bills of lading to East West without indorsing them in their favour. East West sued DKBS *(inter alia)* in contract and bailment.

Bailment is dealt with on p 34

HELD: The Court reached several conclusions. First, in relation to the contractual claim, the bank was a holder by virtue of s 5(2) of the COGSA 1992 and consequently East West's rights had passed to them by virtue of the operation of s 2(1). This had extinguished East West's contractual rights by virtue of s 2(5)(a), a principal acting as East West had done does not retain the right to sue in his own name.

Second, since the bills had not procured possession they were not stale, so that s 2(2) did not apply. Consequently, in order for East West to obtain the right to sue DKBS in contract, the bank would have had to indorse the bills in their favour.

Third, COGSA 1992 operated solely on contractual rights. Rights arising from a bailment (or in tort) remain unaffected by the Act.

Fourth, bailment arises through the bailee voluntarily taking custody of another's goods. Since bailment to a carrier is revocable at will, the shipper/bailor retains an immediate right to the possession of the goods. Where that right to claim immediate possession is passed to an agent whose agency can be terminated at will, the principal still retains the right to immediate possession for these purposes. Thus in this case there remained a relationship of bailment between the carrier, BKBS, and the shipper, East West, such that the carrier had a duty to take reasonable care of the goods, a duty which it had broken.

COMMENT: Several comments can be made. First, this case is important in the law of bailment as it specifically recognizes that a bailee's duties can be owed not solely to the bailor (the bank after the bills had been received by it), but simultaneously to a third party owner with an immediate right to possession of the goods, of whom the bailee was aware. In other words, even where the bailment is contractual in origin it can exist independently of that contract.

Second, Mance LJ mentions the possibility that a bearer bill of lading or one not specifically indorsed which is in the physical possession of an agent for the purposes of taking delivery of the goods, might not be in the constructive possession of the principal. Mance LJ leaves the question open, concluding that, since the bank was named as consignee, this is analogous to a specific indorsement in its favour. But possession is a flexible concept in English law and it is not obvious why even a specifically indorsed bill delivered to an agent should not be regarded as being in the constructive possession of the principal who presumably would then be a 'holder' for the purposes of COGSA 1992.

Third, this decision certainly undermines the scheme of COGSA 1992.[113]

★ See Simon Baughen, 'Misdelivery and the Boundaries of Contract and Tort' [2003] 4 LMCLQ 413

Extinguishment of rights

In order to avoid a multiplicity of actions, s 2(5) of the COGSA 1992 provides that the transfer of rights under the Act extinguishes the rights of the shipper under a bill of lading (but not a sea waybill) and the rights of anyone who has previously acquired rights by virtue of the Act. The assumption is that under Cif and Fob contracts, risk in the goods will pass to the buyer/holder on shipment, and that thus there is no need for the shipper to retain rights to sue the carrier except where the purchaser rejects the goods for breach of condition and consequently returns the documents, a matter covered by s 2(2)(b). However, the buyer may not reject the goods but sue the seller for damages instead. In such a case the seller must take an assignment back of the buyer's rights under the contract of carriage if he is to sue the carrier in contract.

Imposition and transfer of burdens under the contract

The scheme of the COGSA 1992 is such that a person who wishes to take advantage of the rights transferred to him by virtue of s 2 by taking or demanding delivery from the carrier of any of the goods, or claiming against the carrier in respect of the goods, becomes subject to the same liabilities under that contract as if he had been a party to it.[114] So, too, if he took or demanded delivery before the s 2 rights were vested in him. Under the principle of mutuality which seems to underpin COGSA 1992, the House of Lords held *obiter* in *The Berge Sisar*[115] that once an intermediate holder has ceased to have any interest in the goods, it ceases to have obligations under the

---

113. See Norman Palmer, *Palmer on Bailment* (3rd edn, Sweet & Maxwell 2009) [20.030].

114. COGSA, s 3(1).

115. *Borealis AB v Stargas Ltd (The Berge Sisar)* [2002] EWCA Civ 757, [2002] 2 AC 205.

contract also. It should be noted that s 3(3) of the COGSA 1992 provides that the shipper as an original party remains liable regardless of what liabilities have been imposed on intermediate holders by virtue of s 3.

Borealis AB v Stargas Ltd (The Berge Sisar) [2002] EWCA Civ 757

FACTS: Borealis agreed to buy a quantity of propane from Stargas on condition it did not contain more than a certain percentage of hydrogen sulphide, a corrosive chemical. The propane was shipped from Saudi Arabia to Sweden under five bills of lading. The ship arrived at the port of discharge before the documents, but Borealis allowed the ship to berth at its jetty and took samples of the cargo. However, the samples showed that the gas contained excess hydrogen sulphide and Borealis instructed the ship to leave the jetty and sold the gas, indorsing the bills of lading when they arrived some while later in favour of the purchaser. The carrier sued Borealis for losses it incurred because the corrosive cargo had damaged the ship, arguing that Borealis as lawful holders of the bills of lading had demanded or requested delivery of the cargo, and so had became subject to liabilities under the contract of carriage. There were two main questions:

1. Did Borealis ever become liable to the carrier under s 3 of the COGSA 1992 when it received the indorsed bills of lading from Stargas?
2. If so, did Borealis' liability end when it indorsed the bills of lading to the purchaser?

HELD: Lord Hobhouse, with whom the reminder of the House agreed, held that when Borealis took possession of the bills of lading, it became lawful holder of them and so took the benefits of the contract of carriage by virtue of s 2(1). Consequently, if it had made a claim under the contract or had taken or demanded delivery of the goods, it would become subject to the burdens of the contract of carriage by virtue of s 3. However, although the words 'claim' or 'demand' had a range of meanings, because of the likelihood of large and potentially uninsured liabilities arising under a contract of carriage, demanding delivery for the purposes of the Act requires a formal demand made to the carrier for delivery of the goods to him. Similarly, making a claim requires a formal claim against the carrier asserting the legal liability of the carrier to the holder. Consequently, Borealis' acts were very far from a formal demand for delivery or a formal contractual claim.

As a result of this decision, no answer was needed to the second question, but the House held *obiter* that the transfer of the bill of lading would have terminated any obligations which Borealis had acquired by virtue of s 3(1)(c).

COMMENT: Normally a modern statute, following a Law Commission report, would be expected to deal specifically with crucial matters such as whether the transfer of a bill of lading terminates liabilities under the contract of carriage. If Parliament intended liabilities to terminate, then surely Parliament would have said so.[116] However, Lord Hobhouse concluded that the statute and indeed the Law Commission had not considered the possibility of there being a s 3(1) transfer after a dispute had arisen. That said, the structure of the Act was founded on mutuality, and therefore a transfer which causes the transferee to lose the contractual benefits conferred on him by the Act must also cause the loss of the

---

116. The conclusion (*obiter*) of Thomas J in *Aegean Sea Traders Corp v Repsol Petroleo SA (The Aegean Sea)* [1998] 2 Lloyd's Rep 39 (QB).

contractual burdens. This reasoning may be important in determining whether the liabilities pass with the bill (as Lord Hobhouse intimates) or only when the transferee seeks to take advantage of his s 2 rights by making demands or taking delivery under the contract. Lord Hobhouse also noted that the wording of both ss 2 and 3 of the 1992 Act adopt that of the 1855 Act under which it had been decided that transfer of the bill of lading did divest the transferror of liabilities.[117]

Under the 1855 Act, holders incurred liability for obligations incurred before they became holders in addition to the original party,[118] a situation which the 1992 Act appears to preserve.[119]

Alterations to bills/reissuing bills

There may be a perfectly good reason why a bill of lading needs to be amended after issue. For example, it may contain an innocent misstatement as to the date of loading, or the shipper may request a change in the port of discharge. However, the parties to the bill must agree. Thus in *The Wiloma Tanana*,[120] the carrier signed bills of lading which innocently misstated the date of loading by one day. The error was realized soon after shipment and the carrier applied to the court to determine whether it could amend the bill or issue fresh bills. It was held that the consent of the current holder (who was the shipper) had to be obtained, though not the consent of the purchasers from the shipper, who had no rights under the contract of carriage since they were not yet in possession of the bills. This was so even though the amount the sub-purchasers would pay for the goods was dependent on the date on the bill of lading. However in *SIAT v Tradax*,[121] bills of lading stating the port of discharge as either Ravenna/Venice were rejected under a contract 'cif Venice', whereupon the master amended the bills to read 'cif Venice'. It was held that the buyer was entitled to reject these also, since amendments could not cure pre-existing contractual problems. It was also noted in the case that amended bills would generally not be regarded as good tender in commercial circles, so that an amendment is unlikely to be agreed to by a current holder contemplating an onward documentary sale, though it may be that correction of minor clerical errors would be acceptable.[122]

The alternative to amendment, namely issuing a substitute bill of lading, is potentially equally problematic, unless all originals are surrendered first.[123] If the difference between the original and the substitutes (known as 'switch bills') is material, there is a significant risk that the carrier will be liable in the tort of deceit. In addition, in documentary sales, buyers may be entitled to reject switch bills on the basis

---

117. *Smurthwaite v Wilkins* (1862) 11 CB (NS) 842.

118. *Effort Shipping Co Ltd v Linden Management SA (The Gianis NK)* [1998] 2 WLR 206 (HL).

119. ibid 214–15 (Lord Lloyd).   120. [1993] 2 Lloyd's Rep 41 (QB).

121. *SIAT di del Ferro v Tradax Overseas SA* [1980] 1 Lloyd's Rep 53 (QB).

122. *Soules Caf v PT Transap (Indonesia)* [1999] 1 Lloyd's Rep 917 (QB).

123. *Ishag v Allied Bank International* [1981] 1 Lloyd's Rep 92 (QB) and *Elder Dempster Lines v Ishag* [1983] 2 Lloyd's Rep 548.

of *dicta* in *Hansson v Hamel and Horley*[124] that bills of lading must be issued within a short time of shipment. Finally, as *The Atlas*[125] illustrates, switch bills of lading issued in a different port from the original may alter the duties of the carrier by causing a different international convention on carrier liability to apply.[126]

Clearly the carrier will require a suitable indemnity to be given before it would consider issuing switch bills, but this may not be enforceable under the *Brown Jenkinson v Percy Dalton* principle.[127]

Conclusion

This chapter has introduced an important concept in relation to international trade, the documentary sale, under which the mechanics of the completion of the sale is effected by delivery of documents both by the seller, with documents relating to the goods, and by the buyer, with documents representing payment. Particular forms of trading terms favour a documentary approach to completion, so much so that with Cif contracts the whole basis is that the seller must tender a bill of lading and a policy of insurance covering goods, and unless the parties agree otherwise, will then be entitled to payment often through the buyer (or more likely his bank) paying, by use of a document, a bill of exchange with or without the mechanism of a letter of credit.

Later chapters deal with these other key documents in the 'Cif triangle', but in this chapter the focus was on the bill of lading, a document of title to goods such that, subject to the intention of the parties, delivery of the bill of lading constitutes symbolic delivery of possession of the goods it covers. The bill of lading performs at least two other functions in addition to the passage of possession. It is a receipt for the goods, so that the carrier who issues it is *prima facie* at least under an obligation to physically deliver the goods to the holder in the quantity and condition and of the description set out in the bill. Similarly, it now has the role in transferring rights of suit against the carrier to persons with possession of it.

One matter has not been considered—the attempts to replace the physical bill of lading with an electronic alternative. This has been deliberate. Whilst the use of bills of lading has declined in some parts of the shipping industry, particularly in favour of sea waybills, it remains important in bulk carrying where the ability to sell goods in transit can be a fundamental part of a business's trading strategy, and efforts to replace it have met resistance and difficulties. Additionally, the complexities of the legal and commercial issues involved warrant detailed consideration in order to do them justice, and space has not permitted this sort of extended treatment. Instead, this chapter has sought to explain how this unique document operates and to provide a platform on which to build an understanding of the international sale of goods.

---

124. [1922] 2 AC 36 (HL).
125. *Noble Resources Ltd v Cavalier Shipping Corp (The Atlas)* [1996] 1 Lloyd's Rep 642 (QB).
126. In this case, the original bills were issued in Russia and so were covered by the Hague Rules, whereas the switch bills were issued in Hong Kong and so were subject to the Hague Visby Rules, which are more generous to the cargo owner.
127. *Brown Jenkinson & Co Ltd v Percy Dalton (London) Ltd* [1957] 2 QB 621 (CA).

Practice questions

1. Explain how the bill of lading is:
   - a receipt for the goods;
   - a document of title to the goods;
   - a contract of carriage.

2. 'The use of bills of lading promotes both protection against the insolvency of counterparties and the perpetration of fraud by them.'
   Discuss.

3. You have been consulted twice in relation to a number of transactions in relation to some goods. Fletcher was the shipper of goods and was issued with three original bills of lading. He agreed to sell the goods on Cif terms to Godber on 1 February and tendered one bill of lading. Godber consulted you and asked whether she had to accept one bill of lading. You were busy and said that it was her duty to do so.
   She has indicated that she may sue you for negligence if she loses financially on the deal.
   Was your advice accurate?
   Godber accepted the bill of lading on 2 February. However, when she presented the bill of lading to the carrier, she was told that the goods had been delivered to Baraclough on 2 February. Fletcher had called the carrier saying the bills of lading had been lost and told it that he had sold the goods to Baraclough and the carrier should deliver the goods to her. The carrier had demanded an indemnity from 'Indemnity Bank', and once Fletcher had arranged for this, they had issued a ship's delivery order in Baraclough's favour and delivered the goods against it.
   Godber consults you and asks whether she has a claim against the carrier. She also wonders whether the carrier will be happy to pay anyway, because it always has the indemnity. She also asks whether she has a claim against Baraclough. You look at the bill of lading and see that it was issued in a state which is not a party to any convention on the liability of carriers and it contains a clause which states that 'all duties of the carrier shall cease once the goods have been stored in its warehouse at the port of discharge and all risk of loss or damage to the goods shall be in the owner'.
   Has Godber got a claim against the carrier? Is the indemnity enforceable against Indemnity Bank? Has Godber got a claim against Baraclough?

Further reading

Robert Bradgate and Fidelma White, 'The Carriage of Goods by Sea Act 1992' (1993) 56 MLR 188
  - Reviews the Carriage of Goods by Sea Act 1992 against the background of the 'old law' and the Law Commission Report that led to the legislation. In the surprisingly few cases which have involved detailed investigation of the Act, it seems clear that both the Law Commission report and the defects in the old law are being used to guide an interpretation of the Act, and this article is a good entry point into both.

WP Bennett, *The History and Present Position of the Bill of Lading as a Document of Title to Goods* (Cambridge University Press 1914)
- Although a book, this is really a long article and is available again as a reprint. A fascinating survey and analysis of the bill of lading as symbolic of the goods it describes and, apart from being interesting in itself, is a perfect means of understanding the strange way in which a bill of lading is a document of title.

Diana Faber, 'Electronic Bills of Lading' [1996] LMCLQ 232.
- A good introduction to the problems and the attempts to overcome them in relation to the creation of electronic substitutes for bills of lading, which have not been covered in this chapter. It outlines both the problems and proposes solutions.

Andrew Higgs and Gordon Humphreys, 'Waybills: A Case of Common Law Laissez Faire in European Commerce' [1992] JBL 453
- Reviews the use of waybills in the context of the Carriage of Goods by Sea Act 1992, whether all of the problems have been overcome, and the alternative approach taken in French law.

Paul Todd, 'Casenote on *The Sormovskiy* 3068' (1994) 8 OGLTR D91
- A short casenote on *Sucre Export SA v Northern River Shipping Ltd (The Sormovskiy)* canvassing the idea that there are some circumstances where the carrier has to deliver without production of a bill of lading, for example when it/they have been lost. Perhaps a good place to start before reading Wilson's much longer casenote on the same case.

Paul Todd, 'Non-genuine Shipping Documents and Nullities' [2008] LMCLQ 547
- When is a bill of lading a nullity? There is a surprising lack of material on this and Todd draws parallels with the law on nullity in relation to letters of credit and bills of exchange and provides suggestions when a bill of lading might be rejected because it is a nullity.

John Wilson, 'The Presentation Rule Revisited' [1995] LMCLQ 289
- Although involving consideration of charterparty bills of lading, which have not been covered in this chapter, this is an extended case note on *The Houda*[128] and *Sucre Export SA v Northern River Shipping Ltd (The Sormovskiy 3068)*,[129] considering the problems for carriers in delivering goods in the absence of bills of exchange.

---

128. *Kuwait Petroleum Corp v I & D Oil Carriers Ltd (The Houda)* [1994] 2 Lloyd's Rep 541 (CA).
129. [1994] 2 Lloyd's Rep 266.

20 International trade terms

- Introduction to trade terms
- Free alongside ship (Fas)
- Free on board (Fob)
- Cost, insurance, freight (Cif)
- Incoterms 2010

INTRODUCTION

In Chapter 19, it can be seen that buyers and sellers of goods conclude contracts which, in the case of domestic sales, will typically deal with a range of issues, including, for example, passing of property, passing of risk, insurance of the goods in transit, and place and time for delivery of the goods. It is no different in international sales, but as also seen in Chapter 19, the performance of contractual duties is materially complicated by the international dimension. Consequently, it becomes essential that the buyer and seller reach a positive agreement in relation to such matters. The cost of loading, transporting, unloading, and insuring a cargo from Shanghai to Rotterdam may represent a significant percentage of the price of the goods, so knowing whether carriage and insurance are included in the contract price is vital for both parties.

A range of trade terms, appropriate for, but not necessarily specific to, international sales have been developed through mercantile custom, in order to meet the need of traders for certainty in matters in relation to risk, ancillary costs, and documentation, and these terms are available for incorporation by the parties into their contract.[1] The fact that these trade terms are ubiquitous has led to the use of abbreviations to indicate which term applies, consisting of three characters such as Fas (free alongside ship), Fob (free on board), and Cif (cost, insurance, freight), followed by the name of the place where the duties of the seller end.

In this chapter, after an introduction to trade terms, Fas, Fob, and Cif, contracts at common law will be discussed in some detail, focussing specifically on the passing of property and risk in the goods, concluding with a look at the attempts by the International Chamber of Commerce to standardize and clarify the meaning of these terms.

---

1. In fact, whilst the terms were developed primarily in the international trade context, many are suitable for domestic sales as well, which is now reflected in the 2010 edition of Incoterms.

Introduction to trade terms

Consider the following example.

> ### Eg ComCorp Ltd
>
> ComCorp wishes to purchase machinery from Barking Inc, a company in British Columbia, Canada. Barking has agreed it will transport the goods to Vancouver, pay for loading the goods onto a ship and the cost of transporting the goods to Southampton, and that it will insure the goods against being lost or damaged in transit, but when the draft contract arrives all it says about such matters is 'Cif Southampton'. ComCorp wants to know whether Barking is trying to trick it.
>
> Barking has also quoted a lower price for the goods 'FOB Vancouver Incoterms 2010'. ComCorp wants to understand why Barking is prepared to offer a lower price on these FOB terms.

The different trade terms encapsulate the seller's duties so far as delivery of the goods to the buyer is concerned. For example:

- The parties might agree that the goods will be sold 'Exw' Portsmouth. This stands for 'ex-works' and means that the seller will deliver the goods to the buyer at the seller's place of business in Portsmouth, but has no duties in relation to the cost of transport or insurance of the goods to the buyer's place of business. In other words 'come and get it'.

- The parties might agree to buy and sell goods 'Fob Portmouth'. 'Free on board' means, among other things, that the seller will, at his own cost, have the goods transported to Portsmouth and loaded into a ship, but will not pay the cost of carriage on the ship.

- The parties might agree a contract 'Cif Santander'. 'Cost insurance freight' means, among other things, that the seller will pay the cost of transporting and loading the goods onto a ship and will pay the cost of carriage to Santander.

However, as with all customary mercantile law, the same term may not mean precisely the same thing in different places or in particular trades, or indeed may be modified by the practice of the parties. To minimize the risk of a misunderstanding arising for this reason, there have been attempts to create standard contract terms. These would then apply to international trade contracts into which they have become incorporated, regardless of the nationality, location, or other characteristic of the parties or trade custom. Without doubt the most successful body in promoting such harmonization is the International Chamber of Commerce (ICC) through its sponsorship and publication of 'Incoterms'.[2]

The most common trade terms used in international trade (whether incorporating Incoterms or not) are 'free alongside ship' (Fas), 'free on board' (Fob), and 'cost, insurance, freight' (Cif). It is possible that the balance may change through a

---

2. For an alternative known as Intraterms, see AH Hermann, *International Trade Terms, Standard Terms for Contracts for the International Sale of Goods* (Kluwer Law International 1994).

combination of the increase in container traffic, the decline in break bulk cargoes,[3] and the increasing use of waybills rather than bills of lading. Similarly, the clearer classification of Incoterms, which signals to practitioners that these terms are to be used exclusively where the goods are carried by sea and so not suitable for intermodal forms of transport,[4] may change the balance. However, these three terms illustrate elements common to all of the international trade terms, and once these have been understood so, too, can all of the others. When referring to a common law trade term, this text will, in accordance with common practice, capitalize the initial letter of the term and then use lower case for the remainder of the term. Incoterms always use capital letters.

Bills of lading and waybills are discussed at p 484

Free alongside ship (Fas)

Outline of seller's and buyer's duties

As with all trade terms, the acronym will be followed by a location, in this case the name of the port of shipment. Under contracts 'Fas', the seller delivers the goods to the buyer when they are 'delivered alongside' the ship, which is a term of art meaning 'placed in the possession of the carrier in the manner contemplated by the parties'.[5] The buyer will have nominated the particular vessel, and arranging loading and its cost is the buyer's responsibility. It should be noted that where a ship is berthed at a dockside, the goods will be placed alongside the vessel or its loading berth if it has not yet arrived. Where the vessel is berthed away from the shore, then the seller must arrange and pay for **lighterage**.

→ **lighterage:** the cost of loading and transporting the goods to the nominated vessel in suitable craft

The common law implies a duty on the seller to tender appropriate delivery documents, in this instance at least a commercial invoice, since this will be required to clear customs in the country of import. Under Incoterms, the seller is under an express duty to provide proof of delivery, but it seems likely that no such duty arises under the common law.[6] However, there may be a duty at common law for the seller to obtain an export licence,[7] and under Incoterms the seller is under a duty to 'clear the goods for export'. Additionally, it is common for the parties to expressly agree to the provision of other documentation, for example specifying the documents evidencing delivery, or requiring **certificates of conformity**, and consequently the seller must meet these obligations.

→ **certificate of conformity:** a document from an expert certifying that the quality of the goods matches the contract specification

Finally, there are also certain issues relating to the Sale of Goods Act 1979 (SGA 1979) which the seller must address in order to avoid a breach of duty. It goes without saying that the seller must deliver goods which conform to the contract of sale, in particular meeting the requirements of ss 12 to 15 of SGA 1979.

Sections 12 to 15 of the SGA 1979 are discussed in Chapter 15

---

3. Break bulk are goods which are not in containers, nor bulk cargos (like oil or grain), but consist of individual items, perhaps in sacks or barrels.

4. Intermodal transport occurs where a number of transportation methods are used, e.g. road and/or rail, sea, and then road and/or rail again. 'Multimodal' has the same meaning.

5. *Nippon Yusen Kaisha v Ramjiban Serowgee* [1938] AC 429 (PC) 444.

6. See Carole Murray, David Holloway, and Daren Timson-Hunt, *Schmitthoff Export Trade: The Law and Practice of International Trade* (11th edn, Sweet & Maxwell 2007) 19 ff, 20.

7. *W Hardy & Co Inc v AV Pound & Co Ltd* [1956] AC 588 (HL) by parity of reasoning with Fob authorities.

Since the seller must deliver to a vessel, or at least to a specific location, the buyer is under a duty to nominate the vessel or identify the place, giving the seller sufficient time to arrange transport to enable loading within any loading period agreed by the parties. The buyer is also, of course, under a duty to pay the seller in accordance with the terms of the contract.

 More details may be obtained on p 521, since the issues here are common to Fob contracts

Delivery and passing of property and risk in the goods

Delivery of the goods is presumed to occur on their delivery to the carrier by virtue of s 32(1) of the SGA 1979, though this presumption can be displaced by contrary agreement.

SGA 1979, s 32(1)

Where, in pursuance of a contract of sale, the seller is authorized or required to send the goods to the buyer, delivery of the goods to a carrier (whether named by the buyer or not) for the purpose of transmission to the buyer is prima facie deemed to be a delivery of the goods to the buyer.

 Reference should be made to Ch 11 for detailed guidance on the passing of property

The SGA 1979 stipulates the circumstances when property passes in ss 16 to 20, but for present purposes, it is sufficient to be aware that by virtue of s 17 the passing of title to specific or ascertained goods depends on the intention of the parties, and that *prima facie* the intention in Fas contracts is that property passes on 'delivery alongside'.[8] Although generally, at the date of the sale agreement, goods sold under a Fas contract will not be specific, so that by virtue of s 16 property cannot pass, by the time of delivery alongside, they will normally have been appropriated to the contract. Consequently, property and, by virtue of s 20(1) of the SGA 1979, also risk will be presumed to pass from seller to buyer.

However, even though goods may have been appropriated to the contract, s 19(1) of the SGA 1979 makes it clear that the seller may reserve a right of disposal, in which event the appropriation of the goods to the contract will not be unconditional, so that property will not pass until all conditions have been met. Further, it has been held that s 19(2) of the SGA 1979 applies to Fas contracts by parity of reasoning with Fob cases.[9]

SGA 1979, s 19(2)

Where goods are shipped, and, by the bill of lading, the goods are deliverable to the order of the seller or his agent, the seller is prima facie to be taken to reserve the right of disposal.

---

8. *Nippon Yusen Kaisha v Ramjiban Serowgee* [1938] AC 429 (PC) 444. This conclusion arises in any event by virtue of the operation of rules 5(1) and 5(2) of s 18 of the SGA 1979 (discussed on pp 246 and 251).
9. *Transpacific Eternity SA v Kanematsu Corp (The Antares III)* [2002] 1 Lloyd's Rep 233 (QB). Arguments had been advanced in earlier editions of *Carver on Charterparties* that the seller had a duty to pass property on delivery under a Fob and, by extension, Fas contracts.

Consequently in *The Antares III*,[10] where the bill of lading had been issued in the name of the seller[11] and to its order, and there being no evidence to the contrary (there was little reliable evidence in the case), the presumption set out in s 19(1) that the seller intended to reserve a right of disposal applied, and thus property did not pass on delivery but only when the right of disposal determined.

There remains the issue of whether a similar presumption applies where there is no bill of lading, especially as typically in Fas cases where the buyer is the shipper, documentation will be in the buyer's, not the seller's, name. This was the issue in the *Nippon Yusen Kaisha v Ramjiban Serowgee*.[12]

Nippon Yusen Kaisha v Ramjiban Serowgee [1938] AC 429 (PC)

FACTS: Ramjiban agreed to buy cloth from the manufacturer 'Fas Calcutta, payment against mate's receipt' and immediately resold on the same terms to IEC. IEC entered into a contract of carriage from Calcutta to Japan with the carrier Nippon Yusen. The manufacturer delivered the goods alongside the vessels nominated by IEC and received mate's receipts naming IEC as shipper. Ramjiban paid the manufacturer, and in return received the mate's receipts, which he then tendered to IEC. IEC could not pay, being insolvent. Ramjiban discovered that Nippon Yusen had issued bills of lading to IEC, and that IEC had used them to sell the goods to another party. At the port of discharge, Nippon Yusen delivered the cloth to the other party against the bills of lading. Ramjiban sued Nippon Yusen for damages, claiming that:

Mate's receipts are discussed at p 486

1. in issuing bills of lading without receiving the mate's receipts, Nippon Yusen wronged the holders of these receipts, because it was a term of the contract of carriage that bills of lading would only be issued by the carrier once it had received the mate's receipts; and/or

2. property in the goods did not pass to IEC and consequently not to the persons to whom the carrier released the goods in Japan. Therefore Nippon Yusen committed the tort of conversion in wrongfully releasing the goods.

HELD: Nippon Yusen was entitled to waive the term relating to issue of bills of lading, especially as this was a common practice in Calcutta and the term was for its protection, not Ramjiban's. (In fact both parties to the contract of carriage had agreed to vary the term and Ramjiban was not a party to the contract of carriage.) Property normally passes on delivery to the buyer's carrier in Fas contracts, but a term for payment against mate's receipt would generally indicate that the buyer was reserving a right of disposal; consequently property would not pass until payment was received.

COMMENT: In fact, the Board held that property had passed, as another term in the contract of sale imposed a lien over the goods in favour of Ramjiban until payment in full by IEC and this showed that property must pass IEC before payment, since one cannot have a lien over one's own property.

---

10. *Transpacific Eternity SA v Kanematsu Corp (The Antares III)* [2002] 1 Lloyd's Rep 233 (QB).

11. The Fas seller was named as shipper and consignee, though the mate's receipt had named the buyer as consignee only.

12. [1938] AC 429 (PC).

There remains the issue of the passing of risk in such a case. Unless the parties agree otherwise, s 20 of the SGA 1979 provides that risk passes with property. It seems clear that such a contrary agreement is normally to be implied into Fob and Cif contracts where risk normally passes on delivery, and there seems no reason in principle why Fas contracts should not be similarly construed.[13] Consequently, risk of loss is in the buyer before property in the goods themselves has passed to him.

Free on board (Fob)

Consider the following example.

 ComCorp Ltd

ComCorp is about to enter into a contract with Barkers 'Fob Vancouver shipment April/May 2012'. The directors of ComCorp want to know what this means, whether there are any other terms which might be important to include in relation to the transportation of the goods, and what their duties might be.

In the simplest form of Fob contract (called 'strict' Fob by some judges and commentators) the seller's duties in outline are to ship[14] the goods, onto a vessel identified (called 'nominated') by the buyer, who arranges carriage (and insurance if he so decides). Thus the place that appears after the acronym 'Fob' indicates the port of loading, as with Fas contracts. The parties will almost certainly agree when the goods are to be shipped by the seller, normally expressed as a length of time known as the 'shipping period'. However, once 'unpacked' the terms of a typical strict Fob contract are much more extensive, some provisions being automatically included simply by using the word 'Fob', others which may need agreeing specifically.

Thus in a typical strict Fob contract, the duties of the seller may be summarized as duties to:

- ship goods of the appropriate quality and description;
- produce a commercial invoice;
- deliver the goods on board at the named port of loading within the shipping period;
- pay loading charges;
- obtain export licences;.
- give proof to the buyer that the goods have been delivered and loaded;
- provide the buyer with enough information to enable him to insure the cargo if he wishes.

---

13. See Michael G Bridge, *Benjamin's Sale of Goods* (8th edn, Sweet & Maxwell 2010) [21-011].
14. To ship in this instance means to arrange for goods to be taken on board a ship.

The buyer's duties will include duties to:

- enter into a **contract of carriage** for the goods;
- nominate an 'efficient' vessel (i.e. one which is suitable to carry the goods, which can load them inside the shipping period);
- take delivery of documents and goods and pay in accordance with the contractual terms.

➡ **contract of carriage:** a contract entered into between a person requiring goods to be transported (a shipper) and a person who has the capacity to transport them (a carrier)

So far as Incoterms 2010 is concerned, FOB is classified with terms which can only apply to contracts where the carriage is solely by sea, proposing the more general FCA (free carrier) as more appropriate for other modes of transport. However, in trade usage FOB (and Fob) is commonly employed for any method of carriage, or even multimodal transport. It is also particularly flexible, with a range of variants and adaptations being commonly used. Consequently, while the basic structure of the contract is clear with delivery, and along with it risk and theoretically property in the goods passing when the goods (to use the age-worn phrase) 'pass over the ship's rail', this is only a starting point when describing the term. The trade term 'Fob' has been in use for almost 200 years and was perfectly adapted to a trading practice where ship owners (or charterers) take a ship from port to port, buying and selling goods. When the ship was full, it would probably then sail to its home port for the cargo to be sold. This is no longer the only (or even the typical) trading model, but it explains how the Fob contract arose.[15]

Construction of the contract

There are two fundamental issues that can arise in relation to the construction of Fob contracts. First, the fact that the parties designate the contract as Fob does not necessarily make it so. It is possible to imagine circumstances where the duties of the sellers are such that the terms of the contract are inimical to the essence of Fob so as to make the contract Cif, for example. In such a case, the designation Fob is simply a term relating to a base price, with the final sale price increasing to reflect any additional costs the seller might incur in carrying out duties beyond those for which he has quoted. In other words, 'Fob' in such an instance is a price, but not a delivery term, a possibility which may affect the construction of any contract employing trade terms.[16]

The second issue relates to the degree of precision required to identify the place of shipment. In *Boyd & Co Ltd v Louca*,[17] the expression 'fob stowed good Danish Port' was held to give the buyer a right (and imposed a duty) to identify a port matching this description, giving the seller enough time to make appropriate delivery arrangements to enable shipping within the shipping period. However, it seems clear that there were alternative constructions that may have been put on this terminology, and this is best illustrated by an example.

---

15. See DM Sassoon, 'The Origin of Fob and Cif Terms and the Factors Influencing their Choice' [1967] JBL 32.
16. For an example of a Cif designation being construed as, in effect, a DAP (delivery port of *discharge*), see *Comptoir d'Achat et de Vente du Boerenbond Belge S/A v Luis de Ridder Limitada (The Julia)* [1949] AC 293 (HL). This may be the effect of certain types of contract called 'cif delivered': see p 539.
17. [1973] 1 Lloyd's Rep 209 (QB).

Suppose a buyer agrees to buy a quantity of cider from a seller 'Fob any UK port'. How might this be construed? Clearly the agreement must be construed as a whole—there may be indications of which port was actually intended. Any previous dealings between the parties might also assist, as might the customs of the particular trade. However, assuming there is no other evidence, then there are three possible outcomes:

1. The contract is void for uncertainty. In general, courts will seek to avoid this conclusion, trying to give effect where possible to commercial arrangements. But, for example, in *Cumming & Co Ltd v Hasell*,[18] the High Court of Australia held void a contract 'Fob' where no port of loading was indicated.

2. The seller decides the port of loading. Especially where the parties have agreed that the seller arrange carriage as agent for the buyer (an extended form of Fob), this might be a reasonable inference. However, if the buyer is to arrange carriage, the seller might nominate a port that has no links with the buyer's intended port of discharge or no capability to load cider, making this construction highly inconvenient and consequently implausible.

3. The buyer retains the right to nominate the port, the conclusion reached in *Boyd & Co Ltd v Louca*[19]—the convenient construction in strict Fob where the buyer must arrange carriage.

Consequently, construing contracts incorporating trade terms is not necessarily obvious, and the mechanics of how the transport needs to be arranged can be crucial, in the absence of more direct evidence.[20]

Seller's duties in strict Fob

Duties in relation to goods

⊘ Issues relating to goods Fob are similar to those concerning Cif contracts, see p 531

As noted previously, the primary duty in relation to the goods, in addition to the duties in relation to identity, quality, and quantity agreed or implied into the contract of sale, is to arrange both for their transport to the port of loading and their loading onto the nominated vessel. All costs incurred up to this point are for the seller; all costs after loading are for the buyer. This, for example, includes the costs of stowing the goods once loaded, that is moving and securing them inside the ship so as to optimize the space, or levelling bulk goods (e.g. grain or beans), known as trimming. The parties may agree that these additional costs shall be borne by the seller, in which case the trade term will be expressed as Fobs, Fobt, or Fobst respectively, though there remains the question whether these additional provisions are price terms only, or alter the point of delivery and when risk in the goods passes.[21]

---

18. (1920) 28 CLR 508 (Aus HC).   19. [1973] 1 Lloyd's Rep 209 (QB).

20. For a good example in construing an apparently similar term to Fob, Fot (free on truck, a term used typically in carriage by road), see *Bulk Trading Corporation Ltd v Zenziper Grains & Feedstuffs* [2001] 1 Lloyd's Rep 357 (CA).

21. 'Fob in' is another way of expressing Fobst. See Barney Reynolds, 'Stowing, Trimming and Their Effects in Delivery Risk Property in "FOBS", "FOBT" and "FOBST"' [1994] LMCLQ 119.

Place and timing of delivery

It is normally a condition of the contract, not an innominate term, that loading takes place at the nominated port.[22] Consequently the seller may avoid the contract if the buyer can only make the vessel available for loading at another location (even if it is more convenient for the seller).[23] However, it may be that, save where the seller would suffer some detriment, the buyer can require the seller to 'deliver short' of the vessel, for example if the buyer asks that the goods be left at the dockside, in effect waiving his right for the goods to be loaded.[24]

Similarly, the timing of delivery is normally a condition of the contract. Consequently, it is normally a condition that the goods are loaded within the loading period agreed by the parties.[25] Problems with the timing of delivery typically involve the seller delivering the goods alongside, leaving insufficient time to load within the agreed shipping period, but the same right of rejection applies where the goods are loaded too early, as in *Bowes v Shand*,[26] where loading was almost completed before the commencement of the shipping period.

However, the terms of the contract may be such as to rebut the normal presumption. For example, in *ERG Raffinerie Mediterranee SpA v Chevron USA Inc*,[27] the contract contained two time clauses, a shipping period and a nomination period; that is to say, the time during which the buyer had to nominate the ship onto which the goods had to be loaded. The nomination period permitted the buyer to nominate a ship which might be ready to load so near the end of the shipping period that the seller would have insufficient time to load within the shipping period. Consequently, the time of loading could not have been essential to the parties and so was a warranty.

Documentation

Typically the parties will agree what documentation the seller must provide to the buyer, but regardless of agreement, it is the seller's duty to provide the buyer with the documentation needed in order to obtain possession of the goods. In strict Fob, since it is the buyer who arranges the contract of carriage, the seller will receive only a mate's receipt or document with like effect from the carrier, and it is this that must be tendered to the buyer in order for him to obtain a bill of lading, while at the same time providing notice to the buyer that the seller has delivered the goods to the carrier. Matters are more complex when the seller arranges the carriage, and these are discussed later in this chapter.

There is a range of documentation which, depending on the nature of the goods, may be required before they can be exported, for example a commercial invoice, certificate of origin, dangerous goods note, or an export licence. Under Incoterms 2010, the seller has a duty to provide a commercial invoice and obtain an export licence at his own cost. At common law, there is said to be no general rule concerning these matters,[28] but typically the buyer will specify the requisite documentation and commonly payment will be due on presentation of the documentation.

22. *Petrograde Inc v Stinnes GmbH* [1995] 1 Lloyd's Rep 142 (QB).   23. ibid.
24. On this, see Michael G Bridge, *Benjamin's Sale of Goods* (8th edn, Sweet & Maxwell 2010) [20-018].
25. *All Russian Co-Operative Society Ltd v Benjamin Smith & Sons* (1923) 14 Ll L Rep 351 (CA).
26. (1877) 2 App Cas 455 (HL). It should be noted that this was not a Fob contract, but nothing seems to hang on this issue.
27. [2007] EWCA Civ 494, [2007] 2 All ER (Comm).
28. *AV Pound & Co Ltd v M W Hardy & Co Inc* [1956] AC 588 (HL).

However, if the contract is silent in relation to the documentation, the seller must provide, the position, especially in relation to export licences, remains unclear.

In *HO Brandt & Co v HN Morris*,[29] the Court of Appeal held that normally in Fob contracts the duty to obtain an export licence is on the buyer because it is the buyer's duty to nominate a vessel capable of exporting the goods, and this is impossible without an export licence. However, in *AV Pound & Co Ltd v MW Hardy & Co Inc*,[30] it was impossible on the facts for the buyer to obtain the necessary licence. Therefore the House held that it was not possible to lay down a general rule; each case must depend on its facts, and here the duty was on the seller.

Brandt and *Pound* are readily distinguishable. In *Brandt*, both buyer and seller were in the UK and it was the buyer who wanted to export the goods, making it easier to conclude that the parties intended the buyer to have this obligation; whilst in *Pound*, the seller was to be the exporter. Similarly, in *Brandt* it was easier for the buyer to supply all of the necessary details to the authorities (since their client was the ultimate purchaser), whilst in *Pound* only the seller's suppliers, whose identity was kept secret from the buyer, could make an application for the licence. Consequently, 'convenience' may well be an important factor in determining upon whom the duty to supply export-related documentation falls. This being so, since a commercial (as opposed to a pro forma) invoice will be required by the buyer in order to import the goods at their destination, and only the seller can provide this, there seems to be a strong argument that there is at common law an implied duty to supply such an invoice.[31]

Generally, whoever has the duty in relation to export licences, that duty is one to use 'best endeavours' and is not an absolute warranty that the licence will be obtained.[32] But this is not always so. In *Peter Cassidy Seed Co Ltd v Osuustukkuk-Auppa IL*,[33] a Fob contract for the sale and purchase of 3,000 kilograms of Finnish ant eggs was made on terms: 'Delivery: prompt, as soon as export licence granted'. Devlin J concluded that this term imposed an absolute duty on the Finnish sellers to obtain a licence on the basis that they had thought that getting one was a formality, and, had they intended to make the duty to deliver conditional, they could have done so using routine commercial terminology: 'delivery subject to export licence'. Normally where the party having a 'best endeavours duty' fails to obtain an export licence, the contract is frustrated, but failure to use such endeavours is a breach of contract, and this duty can be quite onerous. So, for example, in *Brauer & Co (Great Britain Ltd v James Clark (Brush Materials) Ltd*,[34] the sellers could only obtain an export licence on paying a sum equal to 20 per cent of the contract price to their suppliers. The Court of Appeal held that they had not used their best endeavours to obtain the licence when they failed to make the payment.

---

29. [1917] 2 KB 784 (CA).   30. [1956] AC 588 (HL), which involved a sale 'Fas'.

31. A pro forma invoice is often a preliminary invoice indicating to the buyer his financial commitment, but it is not a demand for payment. A commercial invoice is a finalized demand for payment. Although the legal position on commercial invoices is not completely clear, there is an important financial incentive for the seller to invoice his customer for payment.

32. *Re Anglo-Russian Merchant Traders Ltd* [1917] 2KB 679 (CA).   33. [1957] 1 WLR (QB).

34. [1952] 2 All ER 497 (HL).

Buyer's duties in strict Fob

Duty to nominate the ship and timing

In 'strict' Fob, the buyer is the shipper and, apart from the payment obligation, his primary duty is to give effective instructions to the seller to enable him to carry out his duties, in that it must be possible and lawful for the seller to comply with them.[35] The most obvious example of the buyer's duties is the duty to nominate an 'efficient' vessel. By this is meant a vessel that can load the goods at the agreed port of loading during the shipping period. This duty is a condition, a breach of which, for example because the nominated vessel does not arrive in time or does not have the gear necessary to load the goods, entitles the buyer to avoid the contract. Commonly, the parties will agree the notice period that the seller must give to the buyer of the ship's 'readiness to load', but otherwise the buyer must give the seller reasonable notice, providing enough time in which to transport the goods to the vessel and effect loading. As with all 'time clauses', these periods are generally construed as conditions of the contract, as the following case demonstrates.

Bunge Corporation v Tradax Export SA [1981] 1 WLR 711 (HL)

FACTS: This case illustrates a common trade practice—the 'string' contract. The contract was for 15,000 tonnes of soya bean meal 'Fob one US Gulf port' nominated by the sellers, Tradax. The buyer, Bunge, had to nominate the ship and give Tradax fifteen days' notice of its anticipated arrival in the Gulf of Mexico. Tradax then had to nominate the port of loading. The parties were involved in a string of contracts, with the goods being bought and sold by a series of traders many times, even before the goods were loaded. The notice of the ship's arrival in the Gulf was given five days late. Tradax avoided the contract for breach of a condition and sold the goods elsewhere, but at a lower price, and sued Bunge for damages for the difference.

HELD: The notice clause was a condition of the contract.

⭐ See JW Carter, 'Classification of Contractual Terms: The New Orthodoxy (1981) 40 CLJ 219

Until *Bunge v Tradax*, on some views, English law was aligning itself with the position then only recently adopted in the CISG,[36] which allows the innocent party to avoid the contract if the breach was such as 'substantially to deprive him of what he is entitled to expect under the contract'.[37] In *Bunge*, the House of Lords rejected the argument that whether a term is a condition or a warranty depended primarily on the consequences of a breach, concluding that it depended on the intention of the parties express or implied and that normally clauses stipulating time for

---

35. *Soufflet Nagoce v Bunge SA* [2009] EWHC 2454 (Comm), [2010] 1 All ER 1023; *Agricultores Federados Argentinos v Ampro SA* [1965] 2 Lloyd's Rep 157 (QB).

36. The CISG is the United Nations Convention on Contracts for the International Sale of Goods. The objective of the convention is to provide a standard international law of contract. Currently around sixty nations, including most nations in the EU, but excluding the UK, have adopted the CISG standard.

37. This is the effect of Arts 25 and 49 of the CISG, interpreted through para 29 of the Explanatory Notes.

performance will be conditions in mercantile contracts.[38] Three primary reasons support this view:

1. This was the general understanding of merchants.

2. Certainty is important, especially where (as here) there was a string of contracts. The sellers were in a falling market and did not know whether the buyers would default; consequently, they had to decide quickly whether to wait and see whether the buyers would perform or mitigate any potential losses by selling to a third party, confident that the original buyers had no claim upon them.

3. Lord Roskill, with whom all the House agreed, stated that:

   [T]he most important single factor... is that until the requirement of the 15 consecutive days' notice was fulfilled the respondents could not nominate the 'one Gulf port'... [and] in a mercantile contract when a term has to be performed by one party as a condition precedent to the ability of the other party to perform another term... the term as to time for the performance of the former obligation will in general fall to be treated as a condition.

If the parties do not want 'time to be of the essence' they will make express provision, and this is the only certain way of ensuring that a 'time' clause is a warranty or innominate term, though such a conclusion may arise by virtue of other terms of the contract.[39]

Unless agreed otherwise, the duty of the buyer to nominate a vessel to enable loading during the shipping period does not imply readiness to load throughout the period. Consequently, the parties may agree not only that the buyer must nominate a vessel, but also give notice to the seller of the time during the shipping period when the ship will be ready to load the goods.

 J & J Cunningham Ltd v Robert A Munro Ltd (1922) 28 Com Cas 42 (KB)

FACTS: The seller Cunningham sold 200 tonnes of Dutch bran for shipment during October 1920 fob Rotterdam. Munro the buyer nominated a ship and Cunningham transported the bran to the port and loaded it into small vessels (lighters) to be taken to the ship before it had received notice of readiness to load. The ship could not load for fourteen days, during which time the bran became mouldy in the lighters.

HELD: Munro was entitled to reject the goods on delivery to the ship for breach of the s 14(2) SGA 1979 implied condition as to quality. Hewart LCJ accepted *obiter* that the position would have been different had Cunningham transported the goods having been notified by Munro of the ship's readiness to load, only for loading to be delayed. In such a case, risk of deterioration in the quality of the goods would pass to Munro on the date notified through some form of estoppel.

---

38. Except in relation to the payment obligation. See SGA 1979, s 10(1).
39. See e.g. *ERG Raffinerie Mediterranee SpA v Chevron USA Inc* [2007] EWCA Civ 494, [2007] 2 All ER (Comm).

> **COMMENT:** It is probably true that the *dictum* concerning the hypothetical case of delays in readiness to load is better understood as one where the buyer warrants that the ship will load at a certain time and the seller sues for breach of that warranty. Otherwise, the 'estoppel' would seem to provide a cause of action in itself.

The potential problems for sellers illustrated in *J & J Cunningham* can become even more acute because, unless the parties agree otherwise, the buyer may cancel the first[40] nomination and substitute another, making anticipating a likely date of loading potentially financially hazardous for the seller. Clearly, the substitute vessel must be 'efficient'—for example allowing the buyer enough time to ship the goods within the loading period—but equally clearly this substitute nomination may involve the buyer in additional warehousing or loading costs.

Agricultores Federados Argentinos v Ampro SA [1965] 2 Lloyd's Rep 157 (QB)

FACTS: Maize was to be shipped between 20 and 29 September. The buyer, Ampro, nominated a ship but she was delayed. On 29 September, Ampro nominated a second vessel which could load that day, but only if the seller Agricultores, paid overtime rates to the stevedores. Agricultores refused to accept the second nomination and avoided the contract.

HELD: The second ship was an efficient vessel, it was possible and lawful for the maize to be loaded within the shipping period, but by parity of reasoning with J & J *Cunningham v Munro*, any additional cost of loading would have been at Ampro's expense. Consequently Agricultores unlawfully repudiated the contract.

COMMENT: Although there is a good deal of 'common sense' justice about the way in which the court dealt with the allocation of risk in this case, it is in fact very difficult to see on what legal basis the additional costs of loading were for the buyer to meet, other than to conclude that the duty of a buyer in strict Fob is to nominate a vessel which can be loaded at normal loading rates within the shipping period.

It is clear that in circumstances like this the seller can be left with difficult decisions. Suppose the buyer makes a late nomination such that the seller concludes that it is unlikely that loading could be completed within the loading period. Should the seller treat this as a repudiatory breach and terminate the contract, leaving itself open to the argument that it had been possible to load in time, or should it proceed to load with the risk it has waived its right to terminate if timely loading proves impossible? This was the issue in the following case.

---

40. Or subsequent nominations, unless only one substitution is provided for in the contract.

> ### ⚖ Bunge & Co v Tradax England Ltd [1975] 2 Lloyd's Rep 235 (QB)
>
> **FACTS:** The contract for 1,000 tonnes of barley Fob had a loading period of 1 to 20 Jan 1973. The buyer, Bunge, nominated a vessel but she was delayed and so Bunge substituted a second vessel, expected to be ready to load on 19 January 1973. Tradax said there would be insufficient time to load the cargo within the shipping period but nevertheless proceeded to load. Only 110 tonnes of barley were loaded within the shipping period and the seller refused to load any more.
>
> **HELD:** Tradax had not accepted the breach and, in any event, even if it had, it had no duty to continue loading outside the shipping period.

Buyer's payment obligation

🔗 Section 28 of the Sale of Goods Act 1979 is discussed in more detail on p 321

Section 28 of the SGA 1979 provides that, in the absence of agreement to the contrary, the duty to pay arises when possession of the goods passes to the buyer and, since delivery of goods to the carrier is *prima facie* deemed to be delivery to the buyer,[41] it appears that once the goods have passed over the ship's rail, the duty to pay arises.[42] However, it is highly unlikely that the parties will not have made express arrangements for the payment of the price. As noted previously, the seller must provide the buyer with any documentation required to enable the buyer to obtain possession from the carrier, and the buyer will require a commercial invoice at the least in order to enable the goods to be imported at their destination. The buyer, too, will probably want some evidence that the goods have been loaded, while the seller is unlikely to pass possession of the goods to the carrier without some form of receipt.

Consequently, even strict Fob lends itself to a documentary sale, so that if the parties adopt this format, the payment obligation will arise (at the earliest) on tender of an agreed list of documents by the buyer. The documents to be tendered depend on the arrangements made in respect of the contract of carriage. For example, there is no reason why, even though the buyer is the shipper, the buyer and seller might not agree that the carrier be required by the buyer to deliver a bill of lading to the seller, in return for the mate's receipt the seller received on passing possession of the goods to the carrier. Payment could then be made against the bill of lading, clearly a more secure form of arrangement than that used in *Nippon Yusen Kaisha v Ramjiban Serowgee*.[43] In such a case, analysis of the payment obligation is identical to that in Cif contracts. That said, it is open to the parties to specify what documents are required and, indeed, when payment is due, since the seller may not be prepared to ship goods before payment, or conversely may be prepared to extend a lengthy credit period to the buyer.

---

41. SGA 1979, s 32(1).
42. Though see Jason Chuah, *Law of International Trade* (4th edn, Sweet & Maxwell 2009) 49 to the contrary. Article 58(1) of the CISG stipulates that, unless otherwise agreed, the buyer's duty to pay arises 'when the seller places either the goods or the documents controlling their disposition at the buyer's disposal'. Though see Art 58(3), which provides that the buyer is not bound to pay the price 'until he has had an opportunity to examine the goods', unlikely in a Fob contract.
43. [1938] AC 429 (PC).

Delivery and the passing of property and risk in strict Fob

Delivery

Delivery in a strict Fob contract takes place when the goods are 'over the ship's rail' by virtue of s 32(1) of the SGA 1979, since the buyer is the shipper having entered into the contract of carriage directly.

Passing of property

Property in specific or ascertained goods passes when the parties intend,[44] and the presumption in Fob is that they intend this on delivery of the goods.[45] Similarly, by virtue of s 18, rule 5 of the SGA 1979, property in previously unascertained goods passes when conforming goods are unconditionally appropriated to the contract and *prima facie* this appropriation will be on delivery.[46] This leaves the seller exposed to the insolvency of the buyer until payment is received, and consequently the seller may seek to minimize that risk by expressly retaining title in the goods to himself until payment is made.

 On retention of title generally, see p 255

Similarly, as we have seen, the parties may arrange a documentary sale and may expressly agree that property passes with the specified documents, which the seller will only release on payment.

Passing of risk

Risk *prima facie* passes with property,[47] but this presumption will normally be rebutted in Fob contracts, with risk passing on delivery over the ship's rail under the common law.[48]

⚖ *Inglis v Stock* (1885) 10 App Cas 263 (HL)

FACTS: Drake sold 200 tonnes of sugar, 'average minimum quality of 90% saccharine content' 'f.o.b. Hamburg; payment by cash in London in exchange for bill of lading', to Beloe, who resold it to Inglis on materially the same terms. Drake also sold another 200 tonnes on similar terms to Inglis directly. Drake shipped the sugar for both contracts in separately identified bags, each containing sugar of slightly different quality, but there was no indication which bags were allocated to which contract; the bags would be segregated on arrival by Drake, who retained the bills of lading. The goods were insured under Inglis' 'floating' insurance policy.[49] The ship carrying the sugar sank. Drake then appropriated

---

44. SGA 1979, s 17.

45. *Colonial Insurance Company of New Zealand v Adelaide Marine Insurance Company* (1887) LR 12 App Cas 128 (PC).

46. *Carlos Federspiel & C) SA v Charles Twigg & Co* Ltd [1957] 1 Lloyd's Rep 240 (QB). *Stock v Inglis* 1840 12 QBD 564 (CA) shows why this is not always the case.

47. SGA 1979, s 20.

48. *Inglis v Stock* (1885) 10 App Cas 263 (HL). But see Devlin J in *Pyrene Co Ltd v Scindia Navigation Ltd* [1954] 2 QB 402 (QB) 419.

49. In a floating policy, a trader agrees a sum insured with the insurer being the estimated value of all shipments he will make during a period. The trader reports the value of each shipment when he has the

some bags to Beloe's contract and some to Inglis'. Beloe and Inglis paid Drake on tender of the relevant bills of lading, even though the sugar quality was slightly below the agreed level. Inglis claimed on his policy of insurance, but the insurer resisted the claim, arguing that property in the goods had not passed to Inglis until after the goods were lost and this meant that he had no insurable interest.

🔗 Insurable interest is discussed at p 583

HELD: In the case of specific goods, risk clearly passed in Fob contracts on delivery, whether title to the goods had then passed or not, and there was no reason why in a Fob contract for goods in bulk the same should not be true. Consequently, since risk had passed to Inglis, he had an insurable interest.

COMMENT: Note that it was Drake who shipped the goods and that Beloe fulfilled his Fob contract with Inglis without himself shipping the goods. Note that the buyers could have rejected the goods for non-conformity with the contractual description under s 13 of the SGA 1979. Note also that (excluding the non-conformity point) the buyers still had to pay, even though the goods were destroyed; risk had passed on shipment.

Clearly, in *Inglis v Stock*, property in the goods could not pass to the buyers since the goods were neither specific nor appropriated to the respective contracts. In any event, retention of the bills of lading by the seller and the arrangement as to payment indicated that this was a documentary sale where property passed on delivery of the documents against payment. Thus, although property did not pass on delivery of the goods over the ship's rail, risk did.

Variants of Fob

In strict Fob, the contract of carriage is arranged directly by the buyer, but often it is easier if the seller undertakes these and additional duties. In *Scottish & Newcastle International Ltd v Othon Ghalanos Ltd,*[50] Lord Mance recognized that the term 'Fob' can be used by parties when the seller has agreed to do far more than just ship conforming goods.

> It embraces (a) cases where the buyer arranges and nominates the ship, but the seller ships and takes the bill of lading in his own name as consignor, (b) cases where the seller arranges shipment and takes the bill in his own name as consignor and (c) cases where the buyer arranges and nominates the ship, and the seller ships but the buyer is named in the bill as consignor...Further, in cases (a) and (b), the seller may be either the only party to the bill of lading or acting as agent for the buyer as a (more or less undisclosed) principal: In either of cases (a) and (b) the seller may of course prepay the freight, and recoup himself by invoicing the buyer.[51]

🔗 The *Pyrene* case is discussed in more detail on p 559

The origin of this type of division is the judgment of Devlin J in *Pyrene Co Ltd v Scindia Navigation Ltd,*[52] and *Pyrene* is itself an example of type (c), i.e. 'strict' Fob, while terms like 'classic Fob' have been used to describe cases like *Wimble v Rosenberg,*[53] and

---

information and the insurer deducts that value reported from the insured sum until it is exhausted. The trader then takes out a new floating policy.

50. [2008] UKHL 2, [2008] All ER 768.   51. ibid [34].   52. [1954] 2 QB 402 (QB).

53. [1913] 3 KB 743(CA), where the seller nominated the ship and arranged and paid for carriage as agent for the buyer.

'extended Fob' to describe cases where the seller arranges carriage, taking the bill of lading in his own name. However, the original reason for the classification was in relation to the rights and obligations of the seller vis à vis the carrier, and it is unhelpful to focus too closely on the categories after all: in *Wimble* the seller nominated the vessel but it is often seen as characteristic of the 'classic' type that the *buyer* nominate the ship. That said, where the seller has undertaken 'additional duties' beyond shipment, these duties may impact issues of the passing of property and risk.

Delivery, property, and risk in Fob where the seller has additional duties

Delivery

It was held in *Scottish & Newcastle International Ltd v Othon Ghalanos Ltd*[54] that it would be unhelpful for the point of delivery in Fob contracts to vary depending on the category of Fob contract involved, and that consequently, unless agreed otherwise by the parties, the point of delivery in Fob was on shipment. This is clearly the case where, as in *Scottish & Newcastle*, the only duty of the seller in relation to the contract of carriage is to receive and forward bills of lading made out in the buyer's name, since the carrier is acting for the buyer so that s 32(1) of the SGA 1979 will apply. It is less easy to see why this should be so where the seller is the shipper and acting as principal vis à vis the carrier and the buyer is not an undisclosed principal, a situation envisaged by Lord Mance as possible in a Fob contract. In such a case, any delivery to the seller is illusory, since he has neither physical nor constructive possession of the property. The position is identical in Cif contracts and is discussed later in this chapter.

Property

The passing of property has already been discussed in relation to strict Fob, and the comments there apply with equal force where the seller has extended duties. However, there remains one further consideration concerning the effect of the shipping documents where no express agreement has been reached with regards to the passing of property, but where the seller retains possession of them or has them made out in his name. It was noted that *prima facie* by so doing the seller intends to retain a right of disposal, and so only conditionally appropriates goods to the contract on loading so that property in them will not pass. But this is not the only construction that might be put on such actions. Notwithstanding his control over the documents, the seller might still intend to unconditionally appropriate the goods to the contract and simply want to retain constructive possession of them, thus facilitating exercise of rights of lien[55] and/or his retaking physical possession through his rights of stoppage in transit.[56]

---

54. [2008] UKHL 2, [2008] All ER 768 [52] (Lord Mance).   55. SGA 1979, s 39.

56. ibid, s 44. Roy Goode and Ewan McKendrick, *Goode on Commercial Law* (4th edn, Penguin 2010) 1039 suggest a further possibility, namely that even though the appropriation was unconditional, the seller still intended to retain ownership. In documentary sales this may be the appropriate finding.

Where the shipping document in question is a bill of lading, it was held in *The Ciudad de Pasto*[57] that s 19(2) of the SGA 1979 applies to Fob, and the presumption raised by s 19(1) in favour of the retention of a right of disposal by a seller to whom the bill of lading is made out will not readily be rebutted.

 SGA 1979, s 19

(1) Where there is a contract for the sale of specific goods or where goods are subsequently appropriated to the contract, the seller may, by the terms of the contract or appropriation, reserve the right of disposal of the goods until certain conditions are fulfilled; and in such a case, notwithstanding the delivery of the goods to the buyer, or to a carrier or other bailee or custodier for the purpose of transmission to the buyer, the property in the goods does not pass to the buyer until the conditions imposed by the seller are fulfilled.

(2) Where goods are shipped, and by the bill of lading the goods are deliverable to the order of the seller or his agent, the seller is prima facie to be taken to reserve the right of disposal.

The facts of *The Ciudad del Pasto* demonstrate the application of s 19 (especially s 19(2)) in practice.

 Mitsui & Co Ltd and Another v Flota Mercante Grancolombiana SA (The Ciudad de Pasto) [1989] 1 All ER 951 (CA)

Letters of credit are discussed at p 656

FACTS: The only valid bill of lading was made out in the name of the seller, Vikingos, which had received payment of 80 per cent of the purchase price before shipment, and a letter of credit[58] had been opened in his favour for the balance. The goods were damaged while being carried from Cartagena to Yokahama before the final payment had been received by Vikingos.

HELD: It was held that the s 19(2) presumption was not rebutted, the seller had not received the full price in cleared funds at the date of the damage, and so he retained title. Thus, by virtue of the decision in *The Aliakmon*,[59] the buyer, Mitsui, had no cause of action in tort against the carrier, Flota Mercante.

Similarly, where the seller retains the bill of lading for delivery against payment, even though it is made out to the order of the buyer and thus outside the s

---

57. *Mitsui & Co Ltd and Another v Flota Mercante Grancolombiana SA (The Ciudad de Pasto)* [1989] 1 All ER 951 (CA).

58. A letter of credit is an undertaking by a bank to make a payment, often against tender of stipulated documents.

59. *Leigh & Sillivan Ltd v Aliakmon Shipping Co Ltd (The Aliakmon)* [1986] AC 785 (HL). It was held that the fact that risk had passed to the claimant was not enough; negligence protects person or property, so the claimant must have some title, whether full or only possessory to the goods to succeed.

19(2) presumption, there is still a presumption in favour of a reservation of a right of disposal until payment.

The matter seems less clear where a bill of lading is not involved, but in *Nippon Yusen Kaisha v Ramjiban Serowgee*,[60] the Privy Council seemed to take it as self-evident that having a mate's receipt made out in the name of the sellers would indicate that property was not intended to pass on delivery, but held that the terms of the contract indicated that property was intended to pass before tender of the document. The case well illustrates that the issue whether property passes is a matter of the intention of the parties and so is case-specific.

Risk

It seems established that risk passes on shipment, regardless of documentary or other additional services to be performed by the seller. After all, in *Stock v Inglis*,[61] the bills of lading were made out in the seller's name and the seller had yet to perform duties in relation to the goods. It may be that in Fobs, Fobt, and Fobst contracts, risk may pass when the goods have been loaded and not on passing the ship's rail.

Finally, there is a further statutory provision which affects the passage of risk where the seller is involved in arranging the contract of carriage. Section 32(3) of the SGA 1979 states that risk in goods sent by sea by a seller will not pass to the buyer until the seller has given sufficient information to the buyer to enable him to insure them.

Perhaps surprisingly, s 32(3) has been held to apply to Fob contracts even though the goods are delivered to the buyer on loading, but it is believed that it may have little practical impact, since the duty to notify may be deemed met if the buyer has the information necessary for him to insure the goods.[62] It would seem that failure to give notice is not a breach of contract (unless it is an express or implied term). Section 32(2) simply relates to risk; it does not give rise to a right to damages or repudiation of the contract.

 Wimble v Rosenberg [1913] 3 KB 743 (CA)

FACTS: Wimble sold 200 bags of rice 'f.o.b. Antwerp . . . cash against bill of lading'. Rosenberg, the buyer, asked Wimble to arrange for the goods to be carried to Odessa on their behalf, Wimble selecting the ship, concluding the contract of carriage and paying the costs of carriage as Rosenberg's agents. The ship sank less than a day into the voyage. Rosenberg's practice was to insure the goods on being notified of the name of the vessel, but in this case they did not receive notification until after the ship sank and were unsurprisingly subsequently refused insurance. Wimble presented the bills of lading for payment, but Rosenberg refused to pay, arguing risk remained in Wimble by virtue of s 32(3) of the Sale of Goods Act 1893—now 1979.

HELD: The majority, Vaughan Williams and Buckley LJJ, held that s 32(3) did apply: the section uses 'sent' not 'delivered' and literally the despatch of the goods to the buyer involves sea transit. However, the Court held Rosenberg in breach by refusing to pay.

---

60. [1938] AC 429 (PC)—involving a Fas contract. 61. (1885) 10 App Cas 263 (HL).
62. *Wimble v Rosenberg* [1913] 3 KB 743 (CA).

Buckley LJ concluded that the duty of notification was fulfilled if in fact the buyers did have enough information in order to insure the goods, while Hamilton LJ held s 32(3) had no application to Fob contracts.

COMMENT: It is possible to insure goods in marine transit without knowing the name of the ship as, for example, in *Stock v Inglis*, or where it is effected on the basis that the identity of the vessel will be provided later.

Cost, insurance, freight (Cif)

Consider the following example.

 ComCorp Ltd

ComCorp has agreed to purchase 'One Turbomatic Combination Grinder Cif Hull shipment April/May 2012 cash against documents'. ComCorp wants to know what it needs to do next to get the machine to its premises in Brentford.

In outline, the typical duties of the parties in a Cif contract are summarized as follows. The duties of the seller are:

- either to ship or to buy afloat goods which match the contractual description;
- to enter into, at his own expense, a contract of carriage by sea for physical delivery of the goods to the contractual port of discharge, or to acquire the benefit of such a contract;
- to obtain a bill of lading matching the contractual requirements;
- to acquire a policy insuring the goods against marine perils;
- to tender the bill of lading, the insurance policy, a commercial invoice, and any other documents required by the contract to the buyer.[63]

The duties of the buyer are:

- to accept the documents tendered if they conform to the contract;
- to accept the goods on arrival if they conform to the contract;
- to pay the contract price as required by the contract. In a documentary sale, this will be against delivery of the documents, unless otherwise agreed.

It can be seen that most of the seller's duties relate to documents. Additionally, many Cif contracts involve 'payment against shipping documents', so that in many respects the comment by Scrutton J, in *Arnhold Karberg & Co v Blythe Green Jourdain & Co*[64] that they are not so much sales of goods as sales of documents, has some merit.[65] However, the seller's duties in relation to goods, though separate, are just as

---

63. Adapted from Lord Atkinson's *dictum* in *Johnson v Taylor Bros & Co Ltd* [1920] AC 144 (HL) 155.
64. [1915] 2 KB 379 (KB).
65. Bankes LJ disapproved of this comment on appeal, *Arnhold Karberg & Co v Blythe Green Jourdain & Co* [1916] 1 KB 495 (CA) 510, as did Warrington LJ at 514.

important as those relating to documents and the interplay between the two poses interesting problems. Consequently, it is perhaps more accurate to think of the contract as one 'for the sale of goods to be performed by the delivery of documents'.[66] Nevertheless, it is clear that in a Cif contract the buyer must accept and pay for documents, even if they relate to goods which no longer exist, and that the seller's duties do not extend to effecting physical delivery of the goods at the port of discharge, but delivery of conforming documents, which are taken as the equivalent of the goods.[67]

Seller's duties under a Cif contract—goods

Reference should be made to Chapter 15, which concerns a seller's duties generally in relation to goods. This section simply highlights issues which are specifically relevant to international sales. Typically in international trade, sales will be by description, so that s 13 of the SGA 1979; will apply, implying a condition that the goods correspond to the contractual description, which may include provisions as to packaging,[68] the date of shipment,[69] or the identity of the ship.

The term implied by s 13 of the Sale of Goods Act 1979 is discussed at p 353

 Manbre Saccharine Co v Corn Products Ltd [1919] 1KB 189 (KB)

FACTS: The contract was for '4,000 280 lb. bags American pearl starch' Cif London, including war risks insurance. Corn Products Ltd, the seller, shipped the correct quantity of starch, but some was packed in 140 lb bags. Corn Products also effected insurance policies which covered the contract goods and other goods on the same ship. The ship sank and Corn Products, knowing this, tendered the bills of lading relating to the goods and a letter saying that it held Manbre, the buyer, covered under insurance policies it had purchased. Manbre refused to pay on the ground that the ship had sunk before the documents were tendered. At trial, Manbre also argued that the documents were defective, as no policy of insurance had been tendered, and that the goods did not correspond to description because of the packaging.

HELD: McArdle J stated that the obligation of the seller in a Cif contract is to deliver documents rather than goods—to transfer symbols rather than the physical property represented thereby. If the seller fulfils his contract by shipping the appropriate goods in the appropriate manner under a proper contract of carriage, and if he also obtains the proper documents for tender to the buyer, the rights or duties of either party are unaffected by the loss of ship or goods.

However, the Cif buyer was entitled (in the absence of agreement to the contrary) to receive the actual policy of insurance relating to his goods alone and the packaging was part of the contractual description of the goods—why specify it otherwise? Thus Manbre could reject the documents for non-conformity and could have rejected the goods.

---

66. *Arnhold Karberg & Co v Blythe Green Jourdain & Co* [1916] 1 KB 495 (CA) 510 (Bankes LJ). See also Ademuni Odeke, 'The Nature of Cif Contracts: Is it a Sale of Documents or Sale of Goods?' [1992] JCL.
67. Lord Wright in *Smyth & Co Ltd v Bailey Son & Co Ltd* [1940] 3 All ER 60 (HL) 70. See *Manbre Sacharine Co v Corn Products* [1919] 1 KB 189 (KB) as an example.
68. *Manbre Sacharine Co v Corn Products Ltd* [1919] 1 KB 189 (KB).
69. Lord Cairns in *Bowes v Shand* [1887] 2 AC 433 (HL) 467.

> **COMMENT:** Note that Manbre added to the ground on which it succeeded during the course of the dispute. Manbre's original objection, that the goods no longer existed failed.[70] Note also that this case (as is common) involved both the right to avoid the contract and a claim for damages for the difference between the contract price and the market price of the starch, had it been delivered. Finally, note that today, in relation to the breach caused by the incorrect packaging, s 15A of the SGA 1979 would need to be considered.

Section 15A of the Sale of Goods Act 1979 is discussed at p 443

Thus, in *Bowes v Shand*,[71] where the goods were described as '600 tons Madras rice, to be shipped at Madras…during the months of March and/or April, 1874, *per Rajah of Cochin*', the buyer was held to be entitled to treat the contract as repudiated by the sellers, as almost all of the rice had been loaded during February. In the main, the courts have resisted arguments that merchants introduce words which serve no contractual purpose, even where, as in *Bowes*, the rice loaded in February would have been identical in quality to that which would have been loaded in March, or, as in *Manbre Saccharine*, where there was no evidence adduced that the size of the bags was important to the buyers.[72]

Not only must the description of the goods correspond with the contract, the goods must also meet the s 14(2) SGA 1979 requirement for them to be of satisfactory quality (assuming no fault on the part of the seller) at the point when risk in the goods passes to the buyer.[73] Even before the re-formulation of the s 14(2) duty with the explicit reference to durability, it had been held that perishable goods at least should remain of satisfactory quality from the time of shipment, throughout normal transit to the destination, and for a reasonable time thereafter to allow for disposal of the goods.[74] That aspect of the implied term, however, will be displaced where, as in *The Mercini Lady*,[75] there is a requirement for a conclusive certificate of quality to be issued on loading. Similarly, since packaging is part of the goods themselves, it would appear that the packaging must be such as to protect the goods in transit against normal incidents of the voyage, if only by virtue of the durability aspect of s 14.

In *Bowes v Shand*, the bills of lading related to non-conforming goods, but in *Hindley & Co Ltd v East India Produce Co Ltd*,[76] the sellers bought goods afloat from a fraudster and sold these in good faith Cif. Only on arrival of the ship was it discovered that no goods matching the bills of lading had been shipped. The seller's argument that their duty related solely to the tender of conforming documents failed, the court holding

---

70. See on this point *Boston Deep Sea Fishing and Ice Co v Ansell* (1888) 39 ChD 339 (CA) 352,
71. ibid.
72. It is open to question whether similar decisions to those in *Bowes v Shand* or *Manbre Sacharine* in relation to s 13 would be made today in the light of the apparent reconsideration of the section suggested by *Reardon-Smith Line Ltd v Hansen Tangen* [1976] 3 All ER 570 (HL).
73. Notwithstanding *Viskase Ltd v Paul Kiefel GmbH* [1999] 1 All ER (Comm) 641. See Michael G Bridge, *Benjamin's Sale of Goods* (8th edn, Sweet & Maxwell 2010) [11-049].
74. *Mash & Murrell Ltd v Joseph I Emmanuel Ltd* [1962] 1 WLR (QB), reversed on the facts on appeal. The goods here were (fittingly) potatoes!
75. *KG Bominflot Bunkergesellschaft fur Mineraloele mbh & Co KG v Petroplus Marketing AG (The Mercini Lady)* [2010] EWCA Civ 1145, [2011] 2 All ER 522. This was a Fob contract and the court doubted whether, where the seller did not know the destination of the goods, a requirement like that suggested in *Mash* could have application.
76. [1973] 2 Lloyd's Rep 515 (QB).

that a Cif contract is for the sale of goods and here there were no goods conforming to the contractual description.

Seller's duties under a Cif contract—documents

The documents must conform

The seller must tender documents strictly in conformity with the contract. Thus, for example, in *Manbre Saccharine,* the buyer was entitled to reject the documents partly because the bill of lading's description of the goods did not correspond with the contractual description. It seems that such a rejection would have been valid, even if in fact the goods shipped had been in accordance with the contract, but the bill of lading described the packaging incorrectly.[77] Similarly, the date on the bill of lading must evidence shipment within the shipping period; thus had *Bowes v Shand* involved a Cif contract (the contract was probably 'ex quay'), the buyer could have rejected bills of lading showing a February shipment.

The duty of strict conformity extends beyond the bill of lading to any other documentary requirements agreed by the seller and buyer but, as *Gill & Duffus SA v Berger & Co Inc*[78] demonstrates, termination of a contract for wrongful refusal to accept shipping documents relieves the seller of a duty to deliver other documents which can only be acquired after unloading.

 Gill & Duffus SA v Berger & Co Inc [1984] AC 382 (HL)

FACTS: The contract was for 500 tonnes 'Argentine bolita beans—1974 crop c.i.f. Le Havre' payment against documents. This was a sale by sample and a certificate of quality at port of discharge was to be conclusive as to conformity of the goods. The goods arrived in Le Havre, but only 445 tonnes were discharged. Berger, the seller, presented documents for payment but these were rejected. It re-presented the documents, this time including a certificate of quality in respect of the 445 tonnes, but Gill & Duffus again rejected them. The seller treated this as a breach of condition. Berger sued Gill & Duffus for the contract price of the beans; Gill & Duffus counter-claimed for damages for non-delivery.

HELD: A certificate of quality issued at the port of discharge cannot be required for tender before payment in a normal Cif contract, since normally documents would be tendered to the buyer before the goods arrived at the port of discharge. The parties had not varied the normal position. Consequently the certificate of quality was not one of the documents the seller had a duty to tender to the buyer in order to receive payment. Further 'a refusal by the buyer to accept the tender of shipping documents which on the face of them conform to the requirements of a c.i.f. contract and upon such acceptance to pay the contract price amounts to a breach of condition'.[79]

Consequently, Gill & Duffus wrongfully repudiated the contract and when Beger treated the contract as terminated, its obligation to deliver any goods and certificates of quality relating to all of the goods ended and it was entitled to sue for damages.

---

77. On the need for documentation to be accurate, see *Finlay v Kwik Hoo Tong* [1929] 1 KB 400 (CA).
78. [1984] AC 382 (HL).   79. ibid 391 (Lord Diplock).

★ See Malcolm
Clarke 'Papering Over
Cracked Goods—Cif
Contracts' (1984) 43
CLJ 433

> **COMMENT:** Had the House concluded that the certificate of quality was a shipping document, then even the second tender would have been defective as it did not cover the all of the contract goods.

This case illustrates that the right to reject the goods and the right to reject the documents are separate; if this were not so, then the certificate of quality could have had no function in this case. However, although the absence of the certificate of quality did not allow rejection of the documents, its content was vital to determining whether there would have been a right to reject the goods had the seller not treated the contract as terminated. Had the goods not conformed, the buyer could have rejected the goods, even if they had accepted the shipping documents.

The invoice

The duty to tender a commercial invoice (as opposed to a pro forma invoice) has been recognized as a requirement of Cif contracts for at least 150 years,[80] and indeed a commercial invoice is essential to the international buyer, since this will be required to clear customs in the country of importation. Where the price of the freight is payable to the carrier on arrival (freight collect), the buyer will need to pay this before the goods will be released by the carrier. The seller will reflect this in the invoice by deducting the cost of freight from the contract price.

The bill of lading

🔗 Bills of lading and
alternative documents
in Cif contracts are
discussed at p 488

We have already considered some of the characteristics of bills of lading in relation to Cif contracts, but in outline the requirements are as follows:

- The bill must be shipped, clean, and freely transferrable.
- It must be effective as a document of title, that is to say, it must relate only to the contract goods and no others,[81] a matter complicated where the goods remain part of a bulk after shipment.
- It must remain an effective contract of carriage in the sense that it will transfer all rights under the contract of carriage to the buyer.

Each of these characteristics is subject to the contrary intentions of the parties, and whilst using the term 'Cif' imports the requirement for a bill of lading, the parties often agree on an alternative document, for example a ship's delivery order or sea waybill. It is also common for goods sold Cif to remain in bulk until discharge. In such a case, the parties would have to agree that the shipping documents do not have to identify specific goods.

There are two problems, specific to the Cif contract, and some forms of Fob, which need further consideration. First, the documents must provide continuous coverage, that is to say they must cover the whole sea transit from port of loading to port of discharge. Thus the bill or bills of lading tendered must be capable of providing a claim against the carrier or carriers in respect of the whole period of marine transportation. There is no obvious problem where carriage is accomplished

---

80. See e.g. *Ireland v Livingston* (1872) LR 5 HL 395 (HL) 406.
81. *Comptoir d'Achat et de Vente de Boerenbond Belge SA v Luis de Ridder Ltd ('The Julia)* [1949] AC 293 (HL) 309 (Lord Porter).

in one voyage; however, there may be no direct route between the two ports so that the goods have to be transhipped at some intermediate location. The potential for problems is well illustrated in *Hansson v Hammel & Horley Ltd*[82] and *Landauer & Co v Craven & Speeding Bros*,[83] where the fact that the insurance policy covered the whole voyage was held not to be sufficient to cure the gap in the coverage by bills of lading. The matter is made more acute by the UCP 600,[84] which provides that bills of lading suggesting transhipment are not acceptable for payment under letters of credit, unless there is one bill of lading covering the whole sea transit, and then only if the goods are containerized or similar,[85] limiting even further the acceptability of anything other than through bills of lading.

The UCP 600 is discussed at p 656

Hansson v Hammel & Horley Ltd [1922] 2 AC 36 (HL)

FACTS: The contract was for 950 tonnes of bagged cod guano 'Cif Kobe or Yokahama'. The goods were in Braatvag Norway and the buyer, Hammel & Horley Ltd, knew there was no ship that sailed directly from Braatvag to Japan. The goods were shipped Braatvag to Hamburg on a bill of lading dated 21 April, transhipped in Hamburg to another carrier's vessel, where a clean bill of lading dated 5 May, was issued, with Hamburg as port of shipment, but noting that the bags were 'Shipped from Braatvag according to Bill of Lading on the 22nd April, 1920' in apparent good order and condition. Hammel rejected the seller's tender of the 5 May bill of lading and refused to pay. The guano arrived undamaged.

HELD: Since this bill of lading would not have provided the buyer with any claim against the carrier from Norway to Hamburg had that carrier damaged the goods, it was not good tender. A 'through bill of lading' was required, where the carrier accepted responsibility for the entire sea transit.

COMMENT: Lord Sumner raises another important issue:

> When documents are to be taken up the buyer is entitled to documents which substantially confer protective rights throughout. He is not buying a litigation . . . These documents have to be handled by banks, they have to be taken up or rejected promptly and without any opportunity for prolonged inquiry, they have to be such as can be re-tendered to sub-purchasers, and it is essential that they should so conform to the accustomed shipping documents as to be reasonably and readily fit to pass current in commerce. I am quite sure that, under the circumstances of this case, this ocean bill of lading does not satisfy these conditions. It bears notice of its insufficiency and ambiguity on its face.[86]

The editor of *Benjamin's Sale of Goods*[87] suggests that had the seller tendered both bills, that would have been good tender, but presumably not if the parties had agreed, or it was trade practice that a through bill of lading (i.e. one bill from port of loading to port of discharge) was necessary. What might the effect of UCP 600, Art 20 have today on this situation?

---

82. [1922] 2 AC 36 (HL).　　83. [1912] 2 KB 94 (KB).

84. The UCP 600 is a standard set of terms on which banks issue letters of credit—an important mechanism in ensuring payment in international sales.

85. UCP 600, Art 20(b) and (c).　　86. [1922] 2 AC 36 (HL) 46.

87. Michael G Bridge, *Benjamin's Sale of Goods* (8th edn, Sweet & Maxwell 2010) [19-027].

The second problem is that the bill of lading must be procured 'on shipment'[88] and 'issued in the port of shipment'.[89] Consequently, Lord Sumner seems to suggest that even had the Hamburg bill actually covered the earlier leg of the journey, it would have been defective, since shipment was thirteen days earlier in a different country. That said, practices in many trades differ dramatically from this presumption of timeliness, and local practices may also displace it.[90]

The insurance policy

In the absence of agreement to the contrary, the seller must tender an 'effective' policy of insurance; a note indicating he may hold it in trust, or may have assigned some of the rights under it to the buyer is not enough,[91] even a certificate of insurance[92] issued by or on behalf of the insurer is insufficient.[93] Thus in *Diamond Alkali Export Corp v Fl Bourgeois*,[94] the court held that even though the certificate, if assigned, would on its terms transfer the rights under the policy to the buyer, the rights could not pass by endorsement, as would be the case with a policy of insurance under s 50(3) of the Marine Insurance Act 1906, and in any event all of the terms of the policy may not appear on the certificate, so that the holder will not necessarily know the extent of the cover. However, the parties may agree to the use of certificates,[95] and Art 28 of the UCP 600 contemplates their use, though not the use of cover notes.[96]

Marine cargo insurance is discussed in Chapter 22

The policy must be effective not in the sense that it actually covers the eventuality which causes the loss,[97] but that it provides a valid claim against the insurers in respect of the perils insured. Consequently, a policy which is voidable by the insurer for non-disclosure or misrepresentation[98] is insufficient. In addition, the policy must only cover the goods sold to the buyer and not those of any other person,[99] and must provide for continuous cover, including transit to any port of transhipment.[100]

Unless the parties agree to the contrary, the policy must be on terms which are current in the trade in question and for the route to be used. In *C Groom Ltd v Barber*,[101] it was accepted that at the time of the contract, which was also the time the insurance was acquired, it was not normal to effect 'war risks' cover; consequently it was not necessary to effect such cover even though at the date of tender of the documents, war risks cover had become normal in the trade on that route. Commonly, the contract of sale will stipulate the value of the insurance to be effected, but otherwise

---

88. *Hansson v Hammel & Horley Ltd* [1922] 2 AC 36 (HL) 47 (Lord Sumner). He indicates that this should not be taken literally, so he probably means 'without undue delay'.

89. ibid 48.   90. See *Arnold Otto Meyer N V v Aune* [1939] 3 All ER 168 (KB).

91. See *Manbre Saccharine Co v Corn Products* [1919] 1KB 189 (KB).

92. A certificate of insurance is a document issued by an insurer stating that a certain risk is covered, that the cover is subject to the full terms of the policy, and sometimes full or part of the policy terms are included.

93. *Diamond Alkali Export Corp v Fl Bourgeois* [1921] 3 KB 443 (KB).   94. ibid.

95. See e.g. *Burstall & Co v Grimsdale & Sons* (1906) 11 Comm Cas 280 (KB).

96. A cover note is simply evidence that a policy exists.

97. *C Groom Ltd v Barber* [1915] 1 KB 316 (KB).

98. However innocent, see *Cantiere Meccanico Brindisino v Janson* (1912) 17 Comm Cas 182 (KB).

99. See *Manbre Saccharine*. See also *Hickox v Adams* (1876) 34 LT 404 (CA) and *Comptoir d'Achat et de Vente de Boerenbond Belge SA v Luis de Ridder Ltd (The Julia)* [1949] AC 293 (HL).

100. *Belgian Grain & Produce v Cox* (1919) 1Ll LRep 256 (CA).   101. [1915] 1 KB 316 (KB).

the seller must insure for a 'reasonable amount', but how this might be assessed is not necessarily that easy, particularly if the market price is fluctuating dramatically. For example, in *Manbre Saccharine*, the contract price for the goods was about 73p per cwt; at shipment the market price was £1.75 per cwt; the seller insured for £2; and the market price when the goods were lost was £2.10.

Other documentation

Clearly, the parties may agree to the tendering of any number of other documents. However, in the absence of any such agreement, the seller must obtain any documentation necessary for the exportation of the goods, since he is the exporter, whilst the duty of obtaining an import licence is on the buyer.[102]

Whether the duty on the seller to obtain any export clearances is absolute or simply to use best endeavours raises similar issues to those applying to Fob contracts.

Time and place of tender of the documents

The seller, once he has received the shipping documents, must tender them to the buyer within a reasonable time. There is no duty, in the absence of agreement to the contrary, to tender them before the arrival of the goods at the port of discharge.[103] Needless to say, any agreement about the timing of tender will be a condition of the contract.[104]

In the absence of any agreement, the place of delivery of the documents is at the buyer's place of business or residence.[105]

Duties of the buyer

The buyer is under a duty to accept conforming documents and goods, and to pay in accordance with the terms of the contract. The duty to pay is against documents in the absence of a contrary intention,[106] and such a duty survives non-delivery[107] or destruction of the cargo.[108] Where the parties agree a different payment obligation (e.g. to pay ninety days after arrival),[109] the seller meets his obligations on tender of conforming documents, and the buyer must accept tender and pay on the due date, unless by then he has shown the goods were non-conforming and he has terminated the contract. The obligation to accept conforming documents is a condition of the contract, as demonstrated in *Gill & Duffus SA v Berger & Co Inc.*[110]

---

102. *Mitchell Cotts & Co (Middle East) Ltd v Hairco Ltd* [1943] 2 All ER 552 (CA), though this case turns on the terms of wartime regulations.

103. *Sanders v McLean* (1883) 11 QB 327(CA). For further discussion see p 490.

104. *Toepfer (Hamburg) v Lenersan-Poortman NV (Rotterdam)* [1980] 1 Lloyd's Rep 143 (CA).

105. *Owners of Cargo Laden on Board the Albacruz v Owners of the Albazero (The Albazero)* [1974] 2 All ER 906 (QB) 928 (Brandon J).

106. *Biddell Brothers v E Clemens Horst Co* [1912] AC 18 (HL).

107. *Gill & Duffus SA v Berger & Co Inc* [1984] AC 382 (HL).

108. *Manbre Saccharine v Saccharine Products* [1919] 1 KB 189 (KB); see also *Biddell Bros v E Clemens Horst Co* [1911] 1 KB 934 (CA) 960 (Kennedy LJ), approved on appeal.

109. As in *Scottish & Newcastle International Ltd v Othon Ghalanos Ltd* [2008] UKHL 2, [2008] All ER 768 (eventually construed as a Fob contract). These parties had a long trading relationship and so trusted one another. Typically where ninety days credit was being offered, the buyer would need to tender a bill of exchange accepted by his bank payable in ninety days in return for the shipping documents.

110. [1984] AC 382 (HL).

Delivery and passing of property and risk in the goods

Delivery

It was established in *Biddell Brothers v E Clemens Horst Co*[111] that, in a normal Cif contract, the parties agree that delivery of the goods should take place when they pass over the ship's rail on loading, and that the delivery obligations of the seller are completed once he delivers the shipping documents. At that point, the delivery obligations under the contract are complete and unless agreed otherwise, the seller is then entitled to payment by virtue of s 28 of the SGA 1979. However, s 61 of the SGA 1979 defines 'delivery' of goods as the voluntary passing of possession, and in Cif, and likewise in Fob, where the seller retains the bill of lading, the buyer has no control over the goods until he has the bill of lading. This would suggest that delivery of the goods occurs with delivery of the documents. However, s 32 of the SGA 1979 states that, *prima facie*, delivery of the goods to a carrier is deemed to be delivery to the buyer, recognizing that actual delivery in the s 61 sense will only occur later.[112]

Passing of property

The point at which ascertained property passes is dependent on the intention of the parties, and in Cif that is unlikely to be at shipment, since s 32(1) of the SGA 1979 can have no application. In Cif contracts the seller is the shipper, the bill of lading will almost always be made to his order, and, unlike in some Fob contracts, it is difficult to see why in effecting the contract of carriage he would be acting as the buyer's agent, save in very unusual circumstances.[113] Thus the primary presumption will be that the seller will have retained a right of disposal on shipment, so that any appropriation of the property to the contract at this point will be conditional only.[114] Thus, for example, in *Smyth & Co v Bailey & Co Ltd*,[115] although the seller was required to give a notice of appropriation of goods to the contract that notice was not 'unconditional' as required by s 18, rule 5, the s 19(2) presumption continued to apply.

The presumption is that in a Cif contract, the parties intend property to pass with the documents, whether against payment or where the seller has agreed to give credit. This is a presumption which is not easily rebutted, so that, for example, even in *Cheetham & Co Ltd v Thornham Spinning Co*,[116] where the goods had been unloaded, were stored in the buyer's warehouse, and some of which had been sold by the buyers, the seller was still held to have retained ownership through retaining possession of the bill of lading. Even where the whole of the purchase price has been paid, there may be occasions where retention of the bills of lading evidences a right of disposal, where perhaps the seller has expressly agreed to retain the risk of total loss.[117] Only rarely has it been held that property passes before the buyer receives the shipping

---

111. [1912] AC 18 (HL).

112. Though see Lord Rodger in *Scottish & Newcastle International Ltd v Othon Ghalanos Ltd* [2008] UKHL 2, [2008] All ER 768 [18]–[21].

113. As the *Scottish & Newcastle* case shows, having the bills made to the order of the buyer suggests the contract may not actually be Cif.

114. SGA 1979, s 19(2).   115. [1940] 3 All ER 60 (HL).

116. [1964] 2 Lloyd's Rep 17 (QB).   117. *The Gabbiano* [1940] P 166 (PDA).

documents, and then in unusual circumstances, for example, in *The Albazero*,[118] where in a sale which was not truly at 'arm's length' between sister companies, the property passed on the posting of the bill of lading to the buyers.

All of this discussion has assumed that the goods are ascertained, but prior to the Sale of Goods Amendment Act 1995, by virtue of s 16 of the SGA 1979, property in bulk goods could not pass even on delivery of the shipping documents and payment by the buyer.[119] As a result of s 20A of the SGA 1979, a buyer acquires, on payment, a tenancy in common in goods in an identified bulk, subject to contrary intention, thus reversing the decision in *Re Wait*.[120]

The effect of s 20A is discussed at p 253

Passing of risk

In a Cif contract, the seller's duties in respect of the goods end on shipment; thereafter his duties relate to the documents representing those goods. It is therefore clear that risk in the goods must pass on shipment, and it has been held that a clause such that risk passes on delivery at the port of discharge is repugnant to a Cif contract and therefore void.[121] However, what are called 'Cif delivered' clauses are common, especially in the bulk oil trade. Here, the contract requires delivery at the port of discharge between two dates, and obviously, if the goods are lost, this delivery condition will not be met, so that risk seems to pass only on discharge, not loading. If the clause is inimical to a Cif designation, the court must decide either that the parties intended a Cif contact, in which case the delivery clause is void, or that the parties in effect intended a Dap (delivered at place) contract so that the delivery clause would be valid and non-delivery would permit repudiation of the contract.[122]

Remedies for breach of documentary duties in documentary sales[123]

The basic situation is best understood by considering the following example.

See Chapter 17 for remedies in relation to alleged breaches relating to the goods

---

Eg ComCorp Ltd

ComCorp Ltd agrees to buy some raw materials from Barking plc 'Cif cash against documents'. Barking tenders a mate's receipt instead of a bill of lading. ComCorp Ltd wishes to know what its options are.

---

118. *Owners of Cargo Laden on Board the Albacruz v Owners of the Albazero (The Albazero)* [1974] 2 All ER 906 (QB).

119. *Re Wait* (1927) 136 LT 552 (CA).   120. ibid.

121. *Law & Bonar Ltd v British American Tobacco Ltd* [1916] 2 KB 605 (KB). Though see *The Gabbiano* [1940] P 166 (PDA).

122. See *Comptoir D'Achat et de Vente du Broerenbond Belge SA v Louis de Ridder Limitada (The Julia)* [1949] AC 293 (HL) and *CEP Interagra SA v Select Energy Trading GMBH (The Jambur)* LMLN 289 (QB). Noted by Paul Todd in [1991] 5 OGLR 58.

123. It should be noted that the principles in this section, suitably adjusted, can be applied to Fob contracts where the seller has documentary duties.

Where a seller tenders documents which do not conform to the contract, the buyer has two options: either to accept the tender and pay the contract price (i.e. waive the breach); or to reject the documents and sue the seller for damages for non-delivery. By virtue of s 51(3) of the SGA 1979, *prima facie* the damages for non-delivery of goods will be the difference between the contract price and market price when they ought to have been delivered. In Cif contracts for these purposes, delivery of the goods is effected by tender of documents, not on loading; consequently, damages will be calculated by reference to prices on the date when the documents ought to have been delivered. There is no issue of the buyer rejecting the goods, title to them, even if it has passed (which is unlikely), will re-vest in the seller,[124] and the buyer need not take delivery of them, even if they conform in every respect with the terms of the contract.

Eg ComCorp Ltd

On being tendered the mate's receipt, ComCorp rejects it and refuses to pay. Barking's lawyers advise it that the contract with ComCorp permits the tender of a mate's receipt and Barking notifies ComCorp of this. ComCorp now wants to know what options Barking has.

Where, in a Cif contract, the buyer wrongfully refuses to accept the documents tendered, the seller has two options. First, he can accept the rejection as a repudiatory breach, terminate the contract, and sue the buyer for damages for breach of contract. In such a case the seller will retain the documents and consequently, as part of his task of minimizing his loss, will seek to sell the goods to a third party, his damages being measured in part by reference to the difference between the original contract price and the price ultimately obtained.

Alternatively, if s 49(1) or (2) of the SGA 1979 applies, the seller can sue for the price.

SGA 1979, s 49

(1) Where, under a contract of sale, the property in the goods has passed to the buyer and he wrongfully neglects or refuses to pay for the goods according to the terms of the contract, the seller may maintain an action against him for the price of the goods.

(2) Where, under a contract of sale, the price is payable on a day certain irrespective of delivery and the buyer wrongfully neglects or refuses to pay such price, the seller may maintain an action for the price, although the property in the goods has not passed and the goods have not been appropriated to the contract.

---

124. *Kwei Tek Chao v British Traders and Shippers Ltd* [1954] 2 QB 459 (QB).

Normally property passes with the documents in Cif and the seller cannot argue that, by refusing tender of the documents, it is the buyer's fault property has not passed,[125] so that s 49(1) will only rarely apply to Cif contracts. So, too, setting a specific date for payment (thus triggering s 49(2)) will also be unusual in such contracts. However, in a contested claim, where the seller insists that the contract remains in force and sues for the price, practical difficulties arise where the goods are in the physical possession of the carrier, since storage costs until trial of the issue will be substantial. Consequently, the parties will typically agree on a without prejudice basis to dispose of the goods to a third party. In this event, the proceeds of sale are taken into account as part of any judgment.

From this discussion, it can be seen that the seller has two parallel sets of duties, one in relation to documents, the other in relation to the goods. It is equally clear that, in consequence, the buyer has two separate rights of rejection for non-conformity. Returning to *Gill & Duffus SA v Berger & Co Inc*,[126] the House held that the degree of separation between the duties in relation to documentation and those in relation to the goods is so great that, even had the goods not conformed to the contract, this would not have made the rejection of the documents lawful. This appears contrary to the general proposition that a party who gives an invalid ground for repudiating a contract normally can later advance a separate valid justification.[127] This aspect of the case has been criticized, since it is as if there are two contracts, one for goods, the other for documents; the buyer, in rejecting the documents, is repudiating the whole contract, and if the goods do not conform he was not wrong to do so. That said, if in *Gill & Duffus*, the buyer had been able to prove non-conformity in the goods, then this would surely have resulted in the seller receiving nominal damages for wrongful rejection of the documents.

 The case of *Gill & Duffus* is discussed at p 533

It follows from this duality of rights of rejection that acceptance of the documents does not generally affect the buyer's right to reject non-conforming goods.[128] However, deciding whether to reject non-conforming goods, having accepted the shipping documents, poses a problem for the buyer who will probably already have paid the price, since if he rejects them he will have neither goods, nor the purchase price, leaving him solely with a claim in damages for any loss. This was the dilemma the buyer faced in the following case, which raises an interesting problem over the calculation of damages where the non-conformity of both goods and documents is one of form, rather than substance.

Kwei Tek Chao v British Traders and Shippers [1954] 2 QB 459 (QBD)

FACTS: Traders and Shippers agreed to sell Cif Hong Kong, 20 tonnes of Rongalite, with 31 October 1951 as the last day of shipment. It tendered bills of lading showing that the goods had been shipped within the shipping period and received payment. In fact, the

---

125. *Colley v Overseas Exporters (1919) Ltd* [1921] 3 KB 302 (KB).   126. [1984] AC 382 (HL).
127. See *Boston Deep Sea Fishing and Ice Co v Ansell (*1888) 39 ChD 339 (CA) 354. For an example involving international sales, see *Manbre Saccharine Co Ltd v Corn Products Ltd* [1919] 1 KB 189 (KB). See further Hugh Beale (ed), *Chitty on Contracts* (31st edn, Sweet & Maxwell 2012) [24-014].
128. *Kwei Tek Chao v British Traders and Shippers Ltd* [1954] 2 QB 459 (QB).

goods had been shipped on 3 November and the dates on the bills of lading had been changed without the knowledge of Traders and Shippers. The buyer, Kwei Tek, could not have known this when it accepted the tender of the documents and paid. By the time the goods reached Hong Kong, Kwei Tek knew of the deception, but nevertheless it accepted the goods. The price of Rongalite had declined to almost zero by the time of delivery. The buyer sued the seller.

HELD: Shippers and Traders had shipped non-conforming goods, but the buyer, having accepted the goods, lost the right of rejection, leaving only a claim for nominal damages. Shippers and Traders had tendered non-conforming documents, as shipping documents must be accurate, but the buyer had accepted them and was left with a remedy in damages. Had Shippers and Traders tendered accurate documents, as it should, the buyer would have rejected them and terminated the contract. The breach in relation to accuracy of the documents had deprived the buyer of this right. Had the buyer been able to repudiate the contract, it would not have paid the purchase price. The loss caused by the non-conformity of the documents was therefore the price the buyer paid to the seller.

★ See LCB Gower, 'Sale of Goods—C.I.F. Contracts' (1954) 17 MLR 260

The starting point for the assessment of the quantum of damages is the difference in value between conforming and non-conforming goods,[129] and where, as in *Kwei Tek*, the non-conformity was simply the date of shipment (see *Bowes v Shand*[130]), damages will generally be nominal in respect of the breach. However, the court awarded substantial damages for the breach of the implied term to tender accurate documents established in *Finlay v Kwik Hoo Tong*.[131]

Kwei Tek was distinguished in *Proctor & Gamble Philippine Manufacturing Corp v Kurt A Becher GmbH*,[132] where, although the bill of lading incorrectly stated the shipping date, shipment took place within the shipping period. Consequently, if the bill had been dated correctly, the buyer could not have rejected it, since it would still have matched the contractual description. It therefore lost nothing because of the breach of the implied term as to accuracy.

That is not to say that a buyer who accepts non-conforming documents may always reject non-conforming goods. In *Panchaud Freres SA v Etablissements General Grain Co*,[133] the contract required shipment June/July and, while the bill of lading was dated 31 July,[134] other documents tendered suggested loading somewhat later. The Court of Appeal held, though the precise grounds are not clear, that by accepting documents, which on their face indicate a non-conformity in the goods, the buyer is precluded from rejecting the goods for that non-conformity.

129. See *Taylor & Sons Ltd v Bank of Athens* (1922) 27 Com Cas 142 (KB).

130. (1877) 2 App Cas 455 (HL).

131. *James Finlay & Co Ltd v NV Kwik Hoo Tung Handel Maatschappij* [1929] 1 KB 400 (CA), approving the decision of Wright J at first instance, who held that in relation to Cif contracts: 'it is an implied condition of the contract that the bill of lading so to be tendered shall be a true and accurate document and correctly state the date of shipment'.

132. [1988] 2 Lloyd's Rep 21 (CA).

133. [1970] 1 Lloyd's Rep 53 (CA). See JW Carter, 'Panchaud Freres Explained' (1999) 14 JCL 239.

134. Documents dated on the last day of a shipping period are rightly viewed with suspicion, at least by the legal profession.

The right to cure[135]

It is unclear whether, if a seller tenders non-conforming documents, he has a 'right to cure', that is a right to re-tender conforming documents within the time permitted for tender by the contract. In *Borrrowman, Phillips & Co v Free & Hollis*,[136] the Court of Appeal permitted a re-tender of conforming goods when the original tender (probably wrongly) was rejected, but that may be by virtue of the special facts of the case. But if *Borrowman* does indicate that there is a right of re-tender in relation to goods, there seems no good reason why it should not apply equally to re-tender of documents. Nevertheless (assuming the right actually exists), the right to re-tender ends if the seller repudiates the contract, perhaps by multiple non-conforming tenders. Wrongful rejection of documents by the buyer does not end the right unless the sellers accept the repudiation as terminating the contract. This can be seen in *Borrowman* itself, where the seller insisted on the original tender and only retendered when it was clear the buyer would not accept it, and so demonstrably had not accepted the rejection as a repudiation. Similarly, in *Gill & Duffus SA v Berger & Co Inc*,[137] the buyer wrongfully rejected the initial tender of documents, but no issue was taken by the House of Lords to the seller re-tendering.[138]

Incoterms 2010

Incoterms were first published in 1936, with subsequent revised editions following in 1953, 1967, 1976, 1980, 1990, and 2000. The latest edition, Incoterms 2010, took effect on 1 January 2011, but the parties may choose any edition to incorporate into their contract by using the recommended format, for example 'CIF INCOTERMS 2000'. In some jurisdictions Incoterms have statutory force, whereas in others they have been treated as customary, so that there is no necessity to stipulate that it is the Incoterm definition of the agreed term that applies. This is not so in England, where omitting reference to Incoterms will normally result in an application of the common law interpretation which may differ from the corresponding Incoterm.[139] That said, it may be that in particular trades or between particular parties, Incoterms have become customary and the English courts would then take this into account in determining whether parties contracted on the common law or the Incoterms basis.

---

135. See primarily in relation to re-tender of conforming goods: WCH Ervine, 'Cure and Retender Revisited' [2006] JBL 799 and V Mak 'The Seller's Right to Cure Defective Performance' [2007] LMCLQ 409. An express right to cure is included in the CISG, Arts 34 (documents) and 37 (goods).

136. (1878) 4 QBD 500 (CA).

137. [1984] AC 382 (HL). The re-tendering of documents following a rejection of an initial tender is the norm where payment is by a bank under a letter of credit under UCP 600. On this see Chapter 24.

138. It should be noted that where a letter of credit is involved, much more often than not the initial tender of documents is rejected and the seller re-tenders the documents, presumably without demur by the bank.

139. Subject to agreement to the contrary, Art 9(2)6 of the CISG incorporates into international trade contracts a usage of which the parties knew or ought to have known. Consequently, failure to stipulate 'Incoterms' may be or become irrelevant in practice in states which have ratified the Vienna Convention. But see Michael G Bridge, *Benjamin's Sale of Goods* (8th edn, Sweet & Maxwell 2008) [18-004], where the editor queries whether (in this instance in relation to English Law) that adoption of Incoterms might exclude the operation of CISG as permitted under Arts 6 and 12 of the Vienna Convention were England to ratify the Convention.

What do Incoterms deal with?

Incoterms expressly deal with four issues:

1. Price—what is included in the quoted price; for example, does it include insurance against loss in transit, or the cost of loading or unloading the goods?
2. Duties of the parties in relation to arranging carriage of the goods, including duties in relation to documentation in certain instances.
3. Delivery—where will delivery of the goods take place?
4. Risk—when does risk in the goods pass from seller to buyer?

The ICC publishes a useful wall chart, which illustrates the material pictorially, and an Internet search will also reveal similar diagrams. However, it is essential to remember that these are only some of the issues that are relevant to the parties. They do not, for example, deal with when property in the goods passes (which will be governed by the SGA 1979), how payment is to be made, nor any terms relating to the consequences of breach of contract and the many other matters that a properly drawn contract of sale might deal with. Thus, while the use of trade term is very convenient, it does not address all of the issues, and consequently the buyer or seller might insist on the use of their own standard terms, which may or may not incorporate Incoterms, or they might use one of the standard form contracts provided by their trade association.[140] So Incoterms support, rather than supplant the engagement of the parties in the contract-making process.

By using Incoterms, the parties make express agreement about a range of issues, but using the equivalent common law term does not necessarily import the same range of agreement, and even where it does, the terms of the agreement may be different, so care is always needed. The bulk of this chapter has focussed on the common law interpretation of three key trade terms, but reference should constantly be made to the Incoterm equivalent for a comparison.

The structure of Incoterms 2010

Incoterms adopt the three-character abbreviation convention (though they are always capitalized and do not use '&'), and under Incoterms 2000 there were thirteen terms divided into four groups, depending on the initial letter, with no obvious distinction between those which are only suitable for carriage by sea. The use by contracting parties of terms which were unsuitable for the mode of transport employed requires some ingenuity on the part of the courts to determine what the parties actually intended. The 2010 terms adopt a different structure to earlier editions, in having eleven terms in two groups The first group contains terms applicable only to carriage by sea or inland waterway; the second contains terms which can be used by any mode of transport or with multi-modal transport. In this way, the ICC hopes that the re-classification of Incoterms will reduce the incidence of such 'nonsense' as 'Cif Gatwick'.[141]

---

140. For example, there are more than eighty standard form contracts provided by the Grain & Feed Trade Association (Gafta). For more information go to <http://www.gafta.com/contracts>.
141. See Gbenga Oduntan, '"C.I.F. Gatwick" and Other Such Nonsense Upon Stilts' [2010] ICCLR 6.

Summary of Incoterms 2010

The terms in their groups are listed here in order of the increasing duties of the seller. The revised terms emphasize that the parties should attempt to be as precise as possible about where delivery is to be and what costs are covered in the quoted price.

Terms for sea and inland waterway transport only

- **FAS** Free Alongside Ship: the goods are delivered and risk passes to buyer once the goods are delivered alongside the nominated vessel at the stated port, or nowadays more likely at a named terminal at the port of loading. The seller arranges export clearance but the buyer pays all other costs after delivery including the cost of loading.

- **FOB** Free On Board: the goods are delivered and risk passes to buyer once the goods pass the ship's rail of the nominated vessel at the stated port of loading or, nowadays, more likely at a named terminal at the port of loading. The seller arranges export clearance and pays the cost of loading, but all other costs after delivery are for the buyer.

- **CFR** Cost and Freight: the goods are delivered and risk passes to buyer once the goods pass the ship's rail. The seller arranges and pays for the cost of carriage to the named port of discharge. All other costs after delivery, including arranging import and associated costs, is for the buyer. Note this term is the Incoterms equivalent of the common law term 'c&f'; Incoterms does not use '&'.

- **CIF** Cost, Insurance, and Freight: the goods are delivered and risk passes to buyer once the goods pass the ship's rail. The seller arranges and pays for the cost of carriage and insurance of the goods to the named port of discharge. All other costs after delivery, including arranging import and associated costs, is for the buyer.

Terms for any mode or modes of transportation

- **EXW** Ex Works: the goods are delivered and risk passes when the seller puts the goods at disposal of buyer at seller's premises. All costs after delivery, including loading on the first mode of transport, is for the buyer. The seller must, if asked and at the buyer's expense, render assistance to the buyer in obtaining export clearance.

- **FCA** Free Carrier: the goods are delivered and risk passes when the seller delivers the goods to the carrier at the named place of loading. The cost of loading is for the seller, who must also obtain at his own cost any export licence and otherwise clear the goods for export.

- **CPT** Carriage Paid To: the goods are delivered and risk passes when the seller delivers the goods to the carrier for transport to the named place. The cost of loading and carriage is for the seller, who must also obtain at his own cost any export licence and otherwise clear the goods for export.

- **CIP** Carriage and Insurance Paid To: the goods are delivered and risk passes when the seller delivers the goods to the carrier for transport to the named place. The cost of loading carriage and insurance is for the seller, who must also obtain at his own cost any export licence and otherwise clear the goods for export.

- **DAT** Delivered at Terminal: the goods are delivered and risk passes when the goods are unloaded at the quay, warehouse, yard, or terminal at the named place. All costs up to delivery, including the cost of clearing the goods for export, are on the seller, but the buyer pays for and arranges import. DAT replaces DEQ, (delivered ex-quay) and DES (delivered ex ship) in the old Incoterms.

- **DAP** Delivered at Place: the goods are delivered and risk passes when the seller makes them available to the buyer at the named place of destination. All costs up to delivery, including the cost of clearing the goods for export, are on the seller, but the buyer pays for and arranges import. DAP replaces DAF (delivered at frontier) and DDU (delivered duty unpaid) in the old Incoterms.

- **DDP** Delivered Duty Paid: the goods are delivered and risk passes when the seller places them at the buyer's disposal at the named place of destination. The buyer is responsible for unloading. All costs up to delivery, including the cost of clearing the goods for export and import, are on the seller.

Conclusion

Trade terms provide a mechanism whereby buyers and sellers of goods can conveniently express their intentions. So far as they are concerned, the key issue is the allocation of the cost of transportation of the goods from the seller to the buyer, but to the lawyer more important are the issues of when risk and property in the goods pass, and when delivery is made. While there remains some uncertainty about such matters in respect of certain situations at common law, the difficulties emerge not so much from the terms themselves but the interplay between the trade term and other express or implied terms in the contract of sale. Extremely large transactions are typically undertaken using standard form contracts 'tweaked' by the traders to suit what they have agreed, without any consideration by a lawyer or other document specialist, and seemingly without considering whether the contract as a whole is internally consistent. It is therefore surprising that there are not more disputes, since the sums involved can be eye-watering.

In this chapter, we have focussed almost exclusively on three trade terms which can only apply to carriage of goods by sea: Fas, Fob, and Cif. For lawyers, the most interesting is Cif, since it is the term most associated with documentary sales, though, as we have seen, variants of Fob lend themselves to such sales, and indeed Fas can be adapted to meet this form. The key documents for Cif are the bill of lading and the policy of marine insurance, and a good deal of material relevant to this chapter is therefore dealt with in Chapters 19 (bill of lading) and 22 (policy of insurance). However, in Chapter 21 we turn to look at the contract which generates the bill of lading, the contract of carriage for the goods.

Practice questions

1. (a) When does risk and property pass in:
   - a Fas contract;
   - a Fob contract;
   - a Cif contract?

   (b) When does the seller make delivery in:
   - a Fas contract;
   - a Fob contract;
   - a Cif contract?

   (c) What are Incoterms?

2. Is it true to say that Cif is a contract for the sale of documents?

3. Stanley and Bernie entered into three contracts. The first was for 100 tonnes of Spudulite, an explosive substance; a price was agreed, but the only other term was 'Fob'.

Yesterday Bernie nominated a ship and a port and date for loading, but he has discovered that the ship cannot load on that date and he has just called Stanley and said that this did not matter, Stanley should just transport the goods to the port and leave them at Bernie's warehouse. Stanley has discovered that an export licence has not been obtained and in any event would like to avoid the contract, because he only has a limited supply of Spudulite and can sell it for a higher price to someone else.

The second contract is one for a chemical called Xalite 'Cif loading Shoreham 27—31 January delivered Bremen between 1 and 4 February. Cash 5 days after delivery'. The goods were loaded on 31 January but arrived in Bremen on 5 February because the ship was unavoidably detained. Bernie accepted the documents on 3 February but refused to pay for the goods.

The third contract was identical to the first, but was for a chemical called Yalite. The goods were loaded in a different ship on 31 January and unloaded in Bremen on 4 February. Bernie accepted the bill of lading, which stated the date of loading as 30 January and paid Stanley on 9 February.

Stanley commenced proceedings in the High Court against Bernie, claiming the price of the Xalite. Bernie has applied to have the action struck out, as English courts do not have jurisdiction. Both parties agree that the English courts only have jurisdiction if the goods were delivered in England. Bernie has also indicated that if his strike out application fails, he will counterclaim for the price he paid for the Yalite, as he has discovered the error on the bill of lading.

Advise Stanley whether he can 'get out' of the contract for Spudalite and on his prospects in relation to the other two contracts.

Further reading

LCB Gower, 'FOB Contracts' (1956) 19 MLR 417
- An insightful case note on *AV Pound & Co Ltd v MW Hardy & Co Inc* and the obligations of Fob seller to obtain export licences.

Daniel Murray, 'Risk at Loss of Goods in Transit; A Comparison of the 1990 Incoterms with Terms from Other Voices' (1991) 23 University of Miami Inter American Law Review 93
- Although referring to a previous edition of Incoterms, this is a good source of comparative material—especially American. Pages 101 to 121 deal with the three terms we covered in this chapter, and these Incoterms have not changed radically since 1990 in relation to the passing of risk.

Ademuni Odeke, 'The Nature of C.i.f. Contracts: Is it a Sale of Documents or Sale of Goods?' [1992] Journal of Contract Law
- A really good source of ideas on this issue, engaging with the issues which would arise were documentary sales to be regarded as sales of documents.

Barney Reynolds, 'Stowing, Trimming and their Effects on Delivery, Risk and Property in Sales 'f.o.b.s.', 'f.o.b.t.' and f.o.b.s.t.'. [1994] LMCLQ 119

- Provides good background material on the key issues of delivery and the passing of risk and property in 'normal' Fob contracts, as well as those imposing a duty on the seller to pay for stowing and trimming.

David Sassoon, **'The Origin of Fob and Cif Terms and the Factors Influencing their Choice'** [1967] JBL 32

- A classic article from a real expert in the field. As well as being of fascinating historical interest, it explains how the modern legal understanding of these two terms arose against commercial imperatives which were changing the way international trade was being done.

Gunther Treitel, **'Rights of Rejection under Cif Sales'** [1984] LMCLQ 565 and **'Damages for Breach of a Cif Contract'** [1988] LMCLQ 457

- This pair of case notes provide an insightful review of *Gill & Duffus SA v Berger & Co Inc* in relation to rights of rejection and *Procter & Gamble Phillipine Manufacturing Corp v Becher* in relation to the claim for damages for tender of mis-dated bills of lading.

21 Contracts of carriage of goods by sea

- The carriers' duties at common law
- Common law exceptions
- Contracting out of obligations
- Carriers' duties under the Hague Visby Rules

- Limitation on the carrier's liability under the Hague Visby Rules
- Non-contractual claims by the shipper

INTRODUCTION

If X has a cargo to transport by sea, then there are three ways in which X might arrange this. First, X may own its own ships, in which case, X will not need to enter into a contract for the carriage of the goods. X is, in a sense, its own carrier. Alternatively, where X has a large cargo, X might enter into a contract with a shipowner under the terms of which a whole vessel or a substantial part of it is 'hired' to X, either solely for this one cargo or for a period of time during which X may transport many cargoes. These contracts are called charterparties, the first type, being a 'voyage charterparty' and the second a 'time charterparty'. Typically, the shipowner will not part with possession and control of the ship, so that the use of the word 'hire' is not strictly accurate. Consequently time and voyage charterparties of this type are contracts for the carriage of goods and do not create property rights in the ship.[1] In fact, additionally there are comparatively rare 'demise' or 'bareboat' charters, where the charterer takes possession and complete control of the ship, which operates in effect as a lease of the vessel.

This chapter does not deal with charterparties, though the principles, if not the details in relation to the liability of the carrier, are similar. Instead, the situation where the shipper will only form a contract to book space on a ship will be discussed. In such a case, the person requiring the goods to be carried, called the 'shipper', enters into a contract of carriage of the goods with the person having possession and control of the ship, the 'carrier'. Of course, the carrier need not have title to an absolute interest in the ship; he may be a charterer having at most only possessory title, and the shipper may well pass his rights in the goods along with his rights against the carrier to a third party. Consequently, while throughout this chapter, the words 'shipper' and 'carrier' will be

---

1. Though see *De Mattos v Gibson* (1859) 45 ER 108, where the purchaser of a ship from the owner was held bound by a charterparty, of which he knew.

used, in reality often the parties concerned would more accurately be described as the 'cargo interests' and the 'ship interests'.

This chapter will first consider the situation where the parties to the contract of carriage are subject to the common law and discover that, typically, the carrier will seek to exclude substantially all liability to the shipper. It will then consider how international agreements have provided for a minimum, non-excludable, series of obligations on the carrier, in particular under what are called the Hague and the Hague Visby Rules.

The carrier's duties at common law

→ **common carrier:** a person who advertises to the public that he is available to transport goods for a fee

At common law, a **common carrier** had strict liability to carry the cargo safely, subject only in respect of loss caused by limited exceptions, namely act of God, action of public enemies, and inherent vice, and even then the carrier remained liable if his negligence had contributed to the loss. All carriers were not necessarily common carriers,[2] in which case they had an implied duty to take reasonable care of the goods;[3] but the obvious dangers of being designated a common carrier led to the introduction of a whole range of exceptions into contracts for the carriage of goods by sea. Before these contractual exceptions are discussed, it is important to consider in more detail the carrier's common law duties to the shipper.

Availability

On normal contractual principles, where a shipper has booked space on a ship, the carrier commits a breach of contract if he refuses to load the cargo without good cause, for example simply because there is insufficient space available in the vessel. However, the terms of any contract will typically provide that the carrier may 'shut out' the goods subject to his returning any prepaid freight charges.

Implied duty to take reasonable care

In *The Xantho*,[4] it was held that even where the contract excluded the liability of a common carrier there was an implied term in a contract of carriage that the carrier must 'use due care and skill in navigating the vessel and carrying the goods'. Thus, for example, in *Notara v Henderson*,[5] the carrier was held liable for failing to take reasonable measures to protect a cargo of beans from suffering further damage from decomposition after they had been wetted in a collision for which the carrier was not responsible.

Implied duty of seaworthiness

Lord Blackburn explained the situation succinctly in *Steel v State Line Steamship Co.*[6]

---

2. *Nugent v Smith* (1876) 1 CPD 423 (CA).
3. See *Coggs v Bernard*, 92 ER 107—a case on gratuitous carriage on land.
4. *Wilson Son & Co v Owners of Cargo per 'Xantho'* (1887) 12 App Cas 503 (HL).
5. (1872) LR 7 QB 225.   6. [1877] 3 AC 72 (HL).

where there is a contract to carry goods in the ship…There is a duty on the part of the person who furnishes or supplies that ship…(u)nless something is stipulated which prevents it, that the ship shall be fit for its purposes. That is generally expressed by saying it shall be seaworthy.[7]

This duty has two limbs. First, the ship must be of suitable design and construction and suitably equipped to enable it to encounter the normal perils of the contemplated voyage. Clearly this is in part dependent on both the route and the anticipated meteorological and other conditions. Similarly, the master and the crew must be competent so that, for example, if the captain is insufficiently experienced to be able to deal with the types of difficulties which might be expected to be encountered by the ship during the contemplated voyage, then the ship may be held to be unseaworthy, though this is always a matter of fact, so that the expertise of another officer might compensate for such a deficiency. Second, the ship must also be cargo worthy, that is to say it must be fit to carry the contractual cargo, and where the cargo requires particular conditions for its safe passage, the ship must be appropriately designed or adapted to provide those conditions.

It would appear that the ship must be fit for the voyage and appropriately crewed at the time of sailing;[8] that is to say, when the ship leaves her moorings with no intention of returning.[9] However, the ship must be fit to carry the cargo safely at the point of loading.[10] Consequently, if goods are loaded into a ship but are crushed as other goods are loaded on top of them, there is no breach of the warranty of seaworthiness; the damage is caused through poor stowing, since at the point when the first goods were loaded they were completely safe, even though it was inevitable that damage would occur when the carrier continued loading in accordance with its stowage plan.[11]

The duty to provide a seaworthy ship is, without an effective exclusion clause,[12] an absolute obligation, leaving the carrier liable even where he has taken all reasonable care and this duty is personal, so that delegation to apparently competent subcontractors will not relieve the carrier of this duty. However, the duty is not to provide a ship that can withstand all conceivable hazards.[13] Although there have been a number of attempts to suggest a test for seaworthiness, perhaps the most satisfactory is that in *McFadden v Blue Star Line*,[14] namely that a ship is unseaworthy if there are defects which, had he been aware of them, a prudent owner would have remedied before sending the ship to sea.

The burden of proof of unseaworthiness falls on the party alleging it, though some incidents may raise the presumption that the ship was unseaworthy, particularly the presence of seawater in the cargo holds, though it is always open to the carrier to provide an alternative explanation in such circumstances.[15] Similarly, the shipper must also show that the loss he suffers was caused by the breach of the seaworthiness duty.

---

7. ibid 86.   8. *Stanton v Richardson* (1874) 9 CP 390 (HL).
9. *The Rona* (1884) 51 LT 28 (PDA).   10. *McFadden v Blue Star Line* [1905] 1 KB 697 (KB).
11. *Elder, Dempster & Co Ltd v Paterson, Zochonis & Co* [1924] AC 522 (HL).
12. The drafting of which might prove tricky. Though see *Mitsubishi Corp v Eastwind Transport Ltd* [2004] EWHC 2924 (Comm), [2005] 1 All ER (Comm) 328—which concerned 'cargoworthiness'.
13. *President of India v The West Coast Steamship Co* [1963] 2 Lloyd's Rep 278 (QB).
14. [1905] 1 KB 697 (KB) 706.
15. *International Packers London Ltd v Ocean Steamship Co Ltd* [1955] 2 Lloyd's Rep 218 (QB).

International Packers London Ltd v Ocean Steamship Co Ltd [1955] 2 Lloyd's Rep 218 (QB)

FACTS: Cases of tinned corned beef were shipped from Brisbane for Glasgow via Freemantle. During the voyage, seawater entered the hold and damaged some of the goods because tarpaulins which were covering hatches to the hold were washed away in a severe storm. On the advice of an expert surveyor, the captain discharged and sold some of the cases in Freemantle and sailed for Glasgow with the remainder of the tins, since the surveyor had advised these cases would not be harmed. On arrival it was discovered that the tins had been damaged through dampness in the hold and the effect of other cargo stored above them. The shipper, International Packers, claimed:

1. the ship was unseaworthy because the hatches ought to have been watertight; or

2. the carrier, Ocean Steamship, had a duty to protect goods from circumstances caused by an earlier danger, even if it was not liable in respect of those circumstances; and

3. the surveyor had been negligent in his advice and Ocean Steamship was responsible for the loss on the corned beef that had been discharged in Glasgow.

HELD: The ship was seaworthy; the ship had been appropriately equipped and the presence of the water in the hold was explained by the negligence of the crew in securing the tarpaulins. However, on discovering the problem, the carrier had a duty to take steps to preserve the remaining cargo. The surveyor had been negligent and, since the duty of seaworthiness was personal to the carrier, the carrier was responsible for the loss caused by the negligent advice.

🔗 The Hague Rules, along with successor provisions, are discussed at p 558

COMMENT: The contract was covered by a regime called the Hague Rules, which exempts carriers from vicarious liability for negligent management of the ship by the crew. Clearly, the tarpaulins were for the protection of both the ship and the cargo, and consequently the carrier was not liable for loss caused by the negligence of the crew in failing to secure them, only for later negligence in relation to protecting the cargo from damage.

Implied duty in relation to deviation

Subject to any effective contractual terms to the contrary, the carrier has a duty, at common law, to use all reasonable care to deliver the goods to the agreed place of delivery within a reasonable time. The carrier is under a duty to carry the goods by the most direct route between the port of loading and the port of discharge, but it is open to the carrier to show that the route taken, even if not the most direct, was normal and customary,[16] and where there is more than one usual route then the carrier may choose any such route at its option. The carrier may only depart from the route for the purposes of saving human life and for the prosecution of the voyage or the safety of the adventure.

---

16. *Reardon Smith Line Ltd v Black Sea and Baltic General Insurance Co Ltd* (1939) AC 562 (HL).

Skaramanga & Co v Stamp (1880) 5 CPD 295 (CA)

FACTS: Stamp's ship, *The Olympias*, agreed at a fee of £1,000 to tow another ship which was in distress. Clearly the primary purpose of this deviation was to preserve property, since the seamen aboard could easily have been taken off and the stricken ship abandoned; but equally clearly, in the process of preserving the property the lives of the seamen aboard were saved. While towing the other ship *The Olympias* was stranded and the cargo belonging to Skaramanga was lost.

HELD: This was not a justifiable deviation. It was only where the preservation of property was a secondary objective and necessary in order to save human life that the exception applied; consequently, the carrier was liable for the loss of the cargo and could not rely on a clause in the contract excluding liability for 'perils of the sea', which include standing.

Additionally, the master of a ship is permitted to take all necessary steps in order to protect the ship and or its cargo from undue risks. Thus, deviating from the settled route in order to put into port to effect repairs is permissible even when the repairs are necessary because the ship was unseaworthy at the commencement of the voyage.[17]

Deviation is also sometimes used to describe other deliberate acts of the carrier which depart from the contract of carriage, in particular in relation to the way goods are to be carried. Thus where a contract stipulates that the goods are to be carried in a cargo hold but they are actually carried on deck, then this would be regarded as a 'deviation', but in this case in relation to an express duty.

Implied duty of reasonable dispatch

The contract of carriage may specify a timetable for the carrier to perform the loading operation, the voyage, and discharge of the goods, but in the absence of specified times, the carrier has a duty to perform his duties within a reasonable time and this duty will not be breached even in the case of protracted delay, so long as the delay is beyond the control of a carrier who has acted reasonably and carefully.[18]

The effect of breach

In *Hong Kong Fir Shipping Co Ltd v Kawasaki Kisen Kaisha Ltd (The Hong Kong Fir)*,[19] the Court of Appeal held that the carrier's duty to provide a seaworthy ship was, in the absence of express agreement, an innominate term, so that the legal effect of the breach was dependent upon its severity. Thus a breach of the duty which deprives the innocent party of substantially the whole of the benefit of the contract will be treated as breach of a condition entitling the innocent party not only to sue for damages but also to treat the contract as being at an end. Any other breach simply permits an action in damages. It would appear that breach of the duty of reasonable dispatch is also an innominate term, but deviation from route in breach of contract has always been taken as a fundamental breach of contract, which frees the innocent

Hong Kong Fir and the innominate term is discussed at p 223

---

17. *Kish v Taylor* [1928 2 KB 424 (HL).   18. *Hick v Raymond* [1893] AC 22 (HL).
19. [1962] 2 QB 26 (CA).

party not only from his obligations under the contract, but enables him to sue for damages freed from any exceptions and all limitations of liability contained in the contract of carriage. This analysis must be read in the light of *Photo Productions Ltd v Securicor Transport Ltd*,[20] where the theory that a 'fundamental breach' of contract deprived the guilty party of the benefit of exclusion clauses or clauses restricting implied common law duties was discredited, though in that case Lord Wilberforce suggested that perhaps deviation from the agreed route in the case of a carrier might be considered as a special case for historical reasons.[21] Consequently, at least in theory, a suitably drafted clause, perhaps, for example, defining the duty of the carrier in relation to deviation as one not to wilfully expose the goods to additional known hazards, might be sufficient.

 Photo Productions Ltd and the doctrine of fundamental breach are discussed at p 388

Common law exceptions

Act of God

A carrier is not liable for loss due to natural causes without any human intervention.

Nugent v Smith (1876) 1 CPD 423 (CA)

FACTS: The defendant was sued as a representative of a firm of carriers of goods by sea which had agreed to carry Nugent's horse. A violent storm caused the death of the horse while at sea bound for Aberdeen. It was established that the carrier was not negligent, but, as a common carrier could escape liability only if he could demonstrate that the death was caused by an act of God. Brett J, at first instance, suggested that acts of God were confined to very limited circumstances when he defined them as 'such a direct and violent and sudden and irresistible act of nature as the defendant could not by any amount of ability foresee would happen, or, if he could foresee that it would happen, could not by any amount of care and skill resist, so as to prevent its effect',[22] and consequently the carrier was held liable.

HELD: On appeal Cockburn CJ, however, concluded an act of God included acts of nature which, although conceivably preventable by extraordinary measures, could not 'be guarded against by ordinary exertions of human skill and prudence'.[23]

COMMENT: *Nugent* certainly reduces the severity of the rule that a common carrier has 'no fault liability' since, where the loss or damage is from natural causes, he has a defence '[i]f he uses all the known means to which prudent and experienced carriers ordinarily have recourse'.[24]

---

20. [1980] AC 827 (HL).

21. Though see *Kenya Railways v Antares Co Pte Ltd (The Antares) (No 1)* [1987] 1 Lloyd's Rep 424 (CA) 430 (Lord Lloyd). On the way in which the law on deviation may be changing, see C Mills, 'The Future of Deviation in the Law of Contracts for the Carriage of Goods' [1983] LMCLQ 587 and Charles Debattista 'Fundamental Breach and Deviation in the Carriage of Goods by Sea' [1989] JBL 22.

22. (1876) 1 CPD 19 (CPD) 34.   23. (1876) 1 CPD 423 (CA) 437.

24. ibid (438).

Act of the Queen's enemies

This exception relates to losses caused by acts committed by states or their subjects with whom the country is at war[25] and covers not only seizures of goods but also losses arising where the ship deviates in order to avoid capture.[26] It does not, however, apply to losses arising from armed robbery.[27]

Inherent vice

This exception is dealt with at p 557.

Contracting out of obligations

In addition to exclusions of liability implied by the common law, the contract of carriage will typically include a long list of exemption clauses which relieve the carrier from liability for loss occasioned by specified causes, subject to any statutory provision which restricts the capability of the parties to contract freely.[28] The judicial approach to these exemptions, and this includes the common law exceptions, is that they only 'exempt the carrier from the absolute duty of a common carrier and not from the want of reasonable skill, diligence and care',[29] but, as noted earlier, it may be possible, by specific drafting, to exclude liability for negligence. Thus in *Mitsubishi Corp v Eastwind Transport Ltd*,[30] the contract of carriage stated that:

> the carrier shall not be responsible for loss or damage to or in connection with the Goods of any kind whatsoever (including deterioration, delay or loss of market) however caused (whether by unseaworthiness or unfitness of the vessel...or by faults, errors or negligence, or otherwise howsoever).

It was alleged that the refrigeration unit was faulty when the ship sailed, and the claimant argued that this exclusion clause was void, since it exempted the carrier from all liabilities, which was inimical to any contract. It was held that if clause operated as the claimant argued, it would indeed have been void, but it was insufficient to exclude liability for dishonesty and consequently effectively excluded liability for negligence.[31]

The various typical contractual exemptions will now be discussed.

---

25. *Spence v Chodwick* (1847) 10 QB 517.

26. *Duncan v Köster* (*The Teutonia*) [1872] LR 4 CP 171 (PC). 27. *Forward v Pittard* (1775) 1 TR 27.

28. In particular in England the Carriage of Goods by Sea Act 1971, which gives the Hague Visby Rules the force of law. On this see p 558. Section 2(2) of the Unfair Contract Terms Act 1977 does not apply, except where the shipper is a consumer.

29. *Notara v Henderson* (1872) LR QB 225, 235.

30. [2004] EWHC 2924 (Comm), [2005] 1 All ER(Comm) 328.

31. Note that the Hague Visby Rules did not apply, since the case involved a voyage from Brazil—a non-signatory to the Brussels Convention or Protocol.

Loss caused by perils of the sea

 For consideration of marine insurance, see Chapter 22

Typically, the shipper will have the benefit of a contract of marine insurance, which will provide cover in respect of, amongst other things, a range of 'perils of the sea'. Consequently, it may seem unexceptionable that the carrier should exclude liability for such losses.[32] This appears all the more true because it would appear that the meaning of 'perils of the sea' in that context is identical when used in a contract of carriage of goods by sea.[33] In a policy of insurance, loss caused by perils of the sea comprises damage caused by any perils which are peculiar to the sea or to ships at sea. However, as Wiles J remarked, such perils do not include the 'natural and inevitable action of the wind and waves, which result in what might be described as wear and tear. There must be some casualty, something which could not be foreseen as one of the 'necessary incidents of the adventure',[34] though it was held in the following case that such perils do extend to consequential loss caused by perils of the sea.

Canada Rice Mills Ltd v Union Marine and General Insurance Co Ltd [1941] AC 55 (PC)

FACTS: This case involved an insurance claim where a cargo of rice was damaged through 'sweating' when the ventilation system had to be closed in order to prevent seawater entering the hold during a storm which, though violent, was to be expected on this route.

HELD: The Privy Council held that perils of the sea need not be occasioned by extraordinary violence of the wind or waves,[35] but that whenever:

> there is an accidental incursion of seawater into a vessel at a part of the vessel, and in a manner, where seawater is not expected to enter in the ordinary course of things, and there is consequent damage to the thing insured, there is prima facie a loss by perils of the seas.[36]

COMMENT: Lord Wright then concluded that damage to cargo resulting from actions which are taken as part of routine seamanship in order to avoid a peril of the sea is also caused by perils of the sea. This case involved a deliberate act designed to protect both cargo and ship, but there is some dispute whether if, for example, a member of the ship's crew negligently opened a valve, the resulting incursion of seawater would amount to the peril of the sea. Lord Wright (clearly *obiter*) held in *Canada Rice Mills* that it would, though he may have been confining his comments to contracts of insurance. Both Wilson[37] and Carr[38] insist that perils of the sea do not include losses that could have been avoided by the exercise of reasonable care. Chuah[39] points out that in the United States perils of the sea do not extend to cover negligent acts leading to the damage.

---

32. In fact, unless the shipper has what is called 'All Risks' cover, the typical marine insurance contract will not cover all perils of the sea and indeed the term has not been used in such policies since 1982. Thus the shipper may not have a claim against the carrier, nor against his insurer in some circumstances.
33. *Hamilton, Fraser & Co v Pandorf & Co* (1887) 12 App Cas 518 (HL).
34. *Wilson, Son & Co v Owners of Cargo per 'Xantho'* (1887) 12 App Cas 503 (HL) 515.
35. *Hamilton, Fraser & Co v Pandorf & Co* (1887) 12 App Cas 518 (HL) (Lord Bramwell).
36. [1941] AC 55 (PC) 177 (Lord Wright).
37. John F Wilson, *Carriage of Goods by Sea* (7th edn, Pearson 2010) 266.
38. Indira Carr, *International Trade Law* (4th edn, Routledge 2009) 219.
39. Jason Chuah, *Law of International Trade* (4th edn, Sweet & Maxwell 2009).

Loss caused by the arrest or restraint of princes

This clause is intended to cover threats of or actual intervention by a state authority in a time of peace that interferes with the performance of the carrier of his duties. It has been held to exempt the carrier from losses arising from seizure of the goods by government authorities, blockades, searches of vessels, quarantines, and where a German ship complied with an order of the German government and discharged the cargo at a neutral port and not the contractual port of discharge.[40]

Loss caused by inherent vice and/or defective packaging

Inherent vice denotes a characteristic of the cargo which makes it in effect 'damage itself', and is particularly relevant in the case of perishable goods. Where this susceptibility to damage is well known, the carrier is required 'to adopt a system which is sound in the light of all the knowledge which the carrier has, or ought to have about the nature of the goods'.[41] The defective packaging clause is intended to cover circumstances when the goods have not been packed in such a way that they will withstand the normal occurrences to be expected on the contractual voyage. Whilst it is been held that the carrier's duty to take care of the goods is not increased, even where the goods are insufficiently packed to the knowledge of the carrier,[42] nevertheless a carrier who issues a clean bill of lading cannot plead this exception as against a person who is not a party to the contract of carriage, such as a consignee[43] and possibly not even the shipper.

Loss caused by strikes or lockouts

A strike was defined by Sankey J as 'a general concerted refusal by workmen to work in consequence of an alleged grievance',[44] and this has been extended to include sympathetic strikes where the strikers have no dispute with their own employer, but withdraw their labour in support of fellow workers. A strike also includes a 'go slow' or other withdrawal of cooperation with an employer with a view to improving working conditions.[45]

Loss caused by errors in navigation

A simple clause excluding loss caused by 'errors in navigation ' will not without more exclude liability for negligent loss[46] on the basis that clauses seeking to exclude liability should be construed against the person who drafted them and who seeks their benefit. Since it is possible to draft a clause that specifically addresses liability

---

40. *Rickards v Forestal Land, Timber and Railways Co Ltd* [1942] AC 50 (HL).

41. *Albacora SRL v Wescott & Laurance Line Ltd* [1966] 2 Lloyd's Rep 53 (HL) 58 (Lord Reid).

42. *Gould v South East & Central Railway* [1920] 2 KB 186 (KB).

43. *Silver v Ocean Steamship Corp* [1930] 1 KB 416 (CA).

44. *Williams Brothers (Hull) Ltd v Naamlooze Venootschap* (1915) 21 Com Cas 253 (KB) 257.

45. *Tramp Shipping Corp v Greenwich Marine Inc (The New Horizon)* [1975] 2 Lloyd's Rep 314 (CA).

46. *Seven Seas Transportation Ltd v Pacifico Union Marina Corp (The Oceanic Amity)* [1984] 2 All ER 140 (CA).

for negligent errors, it must be assumed that the draughtsman did not intend to cover them.

Carriers' duties under the Hague Visby Rules

As has been discussed, the carrier may be held strictly liable at common law for the safe transportation of goods, but equally under the common law the carrier is free to limit liability by the insertion of suitable clauses in the contract of carriage. Historically, the carrier has been the stronger contracting party and consequently contracts of carriage of goods by sea almost inevitably contained widely drawn clauses ensuring that the goods were carried at the shipper's risk. This, however, was not the position in other legal systems. For example, in the United States exclusion clauses were read very restrictively and legislation followed, restricting the ability of the carrier to limit his liability.[47] Clearly, however, by its very nature, regulation of the carriage of goods by sea has to be an international process, and the International Convention for the Unification of Certain Rules Relating to Bills of Lading, Brussels, 1924, known as the 'Hague Rules', set a minimum level of liability for carriers; for example they did not permit carriers to exclude liability for lack of care, nor below certain monetary limits.[48] The Hague Rules were amended by the Brussels Protocol in 1968, giving rise to the Hague Visby Rules, which were introduced into the law of the United Kingdom by the Carriage of Goods by Sea Act 1971. Not all signatories of the Hague Rules implemented the Hague Visby Rules, a major example being the US.

Either the Hague Rules or the Hague Visby Rules have been adopted by almost 100 states, but it is important to recognize that the interpretation of the rules may vary between states, since there is no international court in order to provide a uniform understanding of their terms, nor is there a term in the convention requiring courts of signatory states to take account of the need to promote uniformity in the application. Nevertheless, in general, English courts seek to interpret the Hague Visby Rules in accordance with the law of other states adhering to the Convention, but this is not always possible, not least because of the problems of accessing decisions made in other contracting states.[49]

The basic structure of both the Hague Rules and the Hague Visby Rules is to establish that the carrier owes a duty to take reasonable care in carrying out a series of stipulated duties, and removes the capability of the carrier to exclude or limit liability for breach of these duties by providing that any provision in the contract

---

47. The legislation was known as the Harter Act.
48. Introduced into English law by the Carriage of Goods by Sea Act 1924.
49. See e.g. *Jindal Iron & Steel Co Ltd v Islamic Solidarity Shipping Co Jordan Inc* [2004] UKHL 49, [2005] 1 WLR 1363,where the House of Lords was unable to determine a common international view on whether Hague Visby Rules, Art III makes the carrier responsible for damage caused to goods during loading or unloading where the shipper is effecting such operations. American decisions had made no reference to earlier English decisions. The problem of accessing decisions of other countries may be reduced now the Comité Maritime International has created a useful database of cases involving a number of maritime treaties, including the Hague Visby Rules. See <http://comitemaritime.org>.

of carriage which reduces the liability of the carrier below the minimum provided for in the Rules is ineffective. To this effect, Art III(8) of the Hague Visby Rules states:

> Any clause, covenant or agreement in a contract of carriage relieving the carrier or the ship from liability for loss or damage to or in connection with goods arising from negligence, fault or failure in the duties and obligations provided in this Article or lessening such liability otherwise than as provided in these Rules, shall be null and void and of no effect.

The Carriage of Goods by Sea Act 1971 ensures that the Hague Visby Rules 'have the force of law', so that where, by virtue of that Act, the Rules apply, the parties cannot contract out of the effect of the Rules.

When do the Hague Visby Rules apply?

By virtue of the operation of Art I(b), the contract of carriage must be 'covered by a bill of lading or similar document of title'.

Pyrene Co Ltd v Scindia Navigation Co Ltd [1954] 2 QB 402 (QB)

FACTS: Pyrene agreed to sell a number of fire engines to the Indian Government 'Fob London'. The buyer made all arrangements for the contract of carriage with Scindia Navigation. Through Scindia's negligence, one of the fire engines was dropped and damaged in the course of loading before it crossed over the ship's rail, so that property in the fire engine did not pass to the buyer. A bill of lading was prepared, but it did not include the damaged fire engine. Pyrene sued Scindia for negligence. Scindia claimed that the Hague Rules limited its liability to £200. Pyrene argued first, that it was not bound by the contract of carriage, since it was not party to it; and second, that since the contract of carriage in respect of the damaged fire engine was never issued, the Hague Rules could not apply.

HELD: Devlin J held that the shipper (the buyer) must be taken to have entered into the contract of carriage as agent for the seller, Pyrene, at least to the extent that it was related to the process of loading, since under an Fob contract the seller has a duty to have their goods loaded onto the ship. Devlin J also held that when the contract of carriage was agreed, it was contemplated that a bill of lading would be issued and therefore the contract was 'covered' by a bill of lading within Art 1(b).

On the traditional view, the words 'or similar document of title' have no particular meaning, since bills of lading are the only shipping documents which are also documents of title. It was held in the *Rafaela S*[50] that the Hague Visby rules to apply to a straight, consigned bill of lading either because, according to Lord Rodger it is a bill of lading notwithstanding the fact that it is not transferable, or, according to Lords Steyn and Bingham, because it is 'a similar document title'. Lord Steyn held that the

---

50. *MacWilliam Co Inc v Mediterranean Shipping Co SA (The Rafaela S)* [2005] UKHL 11, [2005] 2 AC 423.

words, 'a similar document of title' 'postulate a wide rather than a narrow meaning',[51] while Lord Rodger suggested that the Act simply requires a document that 'entitles the holder to have the goods carried by sea—and obviously, to have them delivered to the appropriate person at the end of the voyage'.[52] This has led some writers[53] to speculate whether the Hague Visby rules may be held to be applicable to contracts covered by non-negotiable sea waybills or multi-modal transport documentation, but it must be accepted that the only safe practice is to expressly make contracts using such documents subject to the Hague Visby Rules if this is desired.

By virtue of Art X, either the bill of lading must be issued in a contracting state, or the carriage must be from a port in a contracting state. Alternatively, the parties may agree that the Rules are to govern the contract. While the Hague Visby Rules themselves require the carriage to be between two different states, s 1(3) of the Carriage of Goods by Sea Act 1971 extends the scope in English law to include shipments inside the United Kingdom. By virtue of s 1(6), the Act also extends the scope of the Convention by providing that the parties may agree to incorporate the Hague Visby Rules into a bill of lading to which the Rules would not otherwise apply, and even into a non-negotiable receipt (for example, a sea waybill) which expressly provides that the Rules are to govern the contract 'as if the receipt were a bill of lading'.[54]

The incorporation of the Rules into contracts of carriage is commonplace, but it is vital to determine whether any such incorporation has purely contractual effect or whether it engages s 1(6), since in the latter case the Rules will have 'the force of law', so that any provisions in the contract of carriage which are inconsistent with the Rules will be void.[55] Thus in *The European Enterprise*,[56] the parties agreed that the Hague Visby Rules should apply to a sea waybill, but did not use the words 'as if the receipt were a bill of lading'. Steyn J held that, as a result, whilst the parties had incorporated the Rules into the contract, they had not done so by virtue of the statute so that the Rules were simply a contractual term permitting the parties to depart from their terms. It should be noted, however, that even if the incorporation is purely contractual, the form of incorporation may make it clear that the Rules shall have precedence over any other inconsistent terms in the contract. In each case it is a matter for the construction of the contract to determine what the parties intended, but in many instances what is called a 'clause paramount' is included, in which case the effect will almost certainly be as described by Lord Denning MR:

> When a paramount clause is incorporated into a contract, the purpose is to give the Hague Rules contractual force; so that, although the bill of lading may contain very wide exceptions, the Rules are paramount and make the shipowners liable for want of due diligence to make the ship seaworthy and so forth.[57]

---

51. ibid [44].   52. ibid [75].

53. See e.g. Roy Goode and Ewan McKendrick, *Goode on Commercial Law* (4th edn, Penguin 2010) 114.

54. Carriage of Goods by Sea Act 1971, s 1(6)(b).

55. By virtue of Art III(8). But see *Browner International Transport Ltd v Monarch SS Co Ltd (The European Enterprise)* [1989] 2 Lloyd's Rep 185 (QB)191, where Steyn J suggested that a voluntary partial incorporation of the Rules by virtue of s 1(6)(b) of the Carriage of Goods by Sea Act 1971 was permissible.

56. [1989] 2 Lloyd's Rep 185 (QB).

57. *Adamastos Shipping Co Ltd v Anglo-Saxon Petroleum Co Ltd* [1957] 2 QB 233 (CA) 266—a case involving a charterparty.

The contract of carriage must be for 'goods', which, by virtue of Art I(c), includes 'goods, wares, merchandise, and articles of every kind whatsoever except live animals and cargo which by the contract of carriage is stated as being carried on deck and is so carried'. The rationale for these exclusions appears to be the increased risk that damage will occur to the goods, in the first instance because of increased mortality or morbidity of animals during a sea voyage, and in the second instance because of the exposed location of the cargo. In such instances, the parties are free to contract on such terms as they see fit, which may well significantly modify the duties of the carrier that would otherwise apply under the Rules. It should be noted that exclusions of liability (save for liability for death or personal injury resulting from negligence) need not meet the test of 'reasonableness' as required by s 2 of the Unfair Contract Terms Act 1977, except in favour of a person dealing as a consumer.[58]

Three further issues should be noted. First, if the parties have incorporated the Hague Visby Rules into the contract pursuant to s1(6) of the Carriage of Goods by Sea Act 1971, then by virtue of s 1(7) the 'live animals' and 'deck cargo' exceptions do not apply, so that in effect the Rules apply to all of the shipper's goods. It has been held that such incorporation can be partial,[59] so that if, for example, a sea waybill contains a clause incorporating the Rules, it would remain open to the carrier to expressly exclude the effect of s 1(7).

Second, in order to take advantage of the 'deck cargo' exclusion, the cargo must actually be stowed on deck and the fact that this is so must be clearly stated on the bill of lading. However, on many occasions a carrier will be unable to tell at the time the contract is made whether goods will actually be carried in the holds of the ship or on deck, and so will require some flexibility in order to load the ship as efficiently as possible, the final location of any particular piece of cargo being dependent perhaps more on chance than on any conscious decision by the carrier. Consequently, the contract of carriage may contain a clause giving the carrier the right to stow the goods where he sees fit.

Svenska Traktor AB v Maritime Agencies (Southampton) Ltd [1953] 2 QB 295 (QB)

FACTS: The contract of carriage concerned a consignment of fifty tractors. The bill of lading issued by the carrier Maritime stated that the carrier 'has liberty to carry goods on deck and shipowners will not be responsible for any loss, damage or claim arising therefrom'. A tractor carried on deck was washed overboard. Maritime argued that the effect of this clause gave it the right to carry the goods on deck and, since the Rules did not apply to deck cargo, it was free to limit its liability for loss.

HELD: It was held that the Hague Rules applied. It was only if the contract made it clear that the goods would be carried on deck and actually were carried on deck that the exception in Art 1(c) operated. A statement that the goods would be carried on deck was a warning to the shipper and to any future owners of the goods that the Rules did not apply

---

58. UCTA 1977, Sch 1, para 2.

59. *Browner International Transport Ltd v Monarch SS Co Ltd (The European Enterprise)* [1989] 2 Lloyd's Rep 185 (QB).

and that warning had to be clear. Consequently, the exclusion clause was invalid by virtue of what is now Art III(8) of the Hague Visby rules.

The need to enable consignees or assignees of the bill of lading to know whether the goods were being carried on deck is also the basis of the decision in the US case of *Encyclopaedia Britannica v Hong Kong Producer*,[60] where it was held that that the Hague Rules continued to apply, even where the bill stated that the goods would be carried on deck, unless the shipper informs the carrier in writing before the delivery of goods to the carrier that he requires under-deck stowage, since persons deriving title from the shipper could not know from the bill whether the shipper had required under-deck stowage. It appears that the same rule applies to contracts of carriage of containerized cargo or goods like timber, where it is customary for carriage to be on deck.

Third, by virtue of Art VI if the parties so agree, the Rules do not apply to contracts of carriage of 'particular goods', that is to say 'shipments where the character or condition of the property to be carried or the circumstances, terms and conditions under which the carriage is to be performed are such as reasonably to justify a special agreement'.[61] In such circumstances, the parties may freely negotiate the terms of the contract of carriage and may, if they wish, completely exclude the operation of the Rules. The fact that Art VI only applies in extraordinary circumstances is emphasized in a final proviso, which states that the article 'shall not apply to ordinary commercial shipments made in the ordinary course of trade'. Article VI only applies where 'no bill of lading has been or shall be issued and that the terms agreed shall be embodied in a receipt which shall be a non-negotiable document and shall be marked as such',[62] and in this way ensures that the contract cannot be transferred by the shipper to a person who is unaware that advantage has been taken of Art VI.

Scope of the activities covered by the Hague Visby Rules

Under the Hague Visby Rules the contract of carriage covers the period from the time when the goods are loaded to the time they are discharged from the ship,[63] which, taken literally, would suggest that they can have no application to the process of loading and unloading. However, Art III rule 2 states that 'the carrier shall properly and carefully load, handle, stow, carry, keep, care for and discharge the goods carried', and in *Pyrene Co Ltd v Scindia Navigation Co Ltd*,[64] Devlin J held that the Rules applied not to a *period of time* but to a *contract* which would include loading and unloading. This interpretation accords well with s 1(3) of the Carriage of Goods by Sea Act, which provides that the Hague Visby Rules apply to contracts 'in relation to and in connection with the carriage of goods by sea'. Consequently, the Rules will apply 'tackle to tackle'; that is, from the time when the ship's lifting gear engages with the cargo to the point when it disengages at the port of discharge. The question

---

60. [1969] 2 Lloyd's Rep 536. 61. Hague Visby Rules, Art VI. 62. ibid.
63. ibid Art 1(e). 64. [1954] 2 QB 402 (QB).

arose in *The Jordan II*,[65] whether the parties could agree that, where loading was to be effected by the shipper, the carrier should have no liability in view of the fact that by Art III, any provision limiting the liability of the carrier was void. The House of Lords held Art III does not impose a liability on the carrier to perform loading and unloading operations, merely that if they do so they will perform them properly and carefully.

Jindal Iron & Steel Co Ltd v Islamic Solidarity Shipping Co Jordan Inc (The Jordan II) [2004] UKHL 49

FACTS: Jindal, the shipper, alleged that the goods had been damaged by rough handling during loading or unloading operations, which were carried out by its agents. The contract of carriage excluded liability of the carrier, Islamic Solidarity for loss in relation to such operations. Jindal argued that Art III r 2 imposed upon the carrier the duty to load, stow, and discharge the cargo, and so the agreement transferring such responsibility was therefore invalidated by Art III r 8.

HELD: It is for the parties to agree who is to take responsibility for loading stowing and unloading the goods.

COMMENT: As the House pointed out, it would be quite strange if the Rules imposed a liability on the carrier for work which it did not carry out and did not have a duty to carry out. However, any transfer of liability must be clearly expressed, and the fact that the shipper agrees to perform the loading and discharge operations 'free of expense to the carrier' does not raise the presumption that the carrier has no liability for their proper performance. Under the terms of such a contract, the carrier would still have the personal duty to effect loading and cannot evade liability by subcontracting performance.

See Sarah Derrington, 'The Hague Rules–A Lost Opportunity' (2005) 121 LQR 209

Jindal suggests that any contract transferring responsibility for damage caused by negligent loading must be clear in this regard; nevertheless, it has been held that a contract transferring responsibility for loading and stowing cargo to the shipper[66] 'at their expense under the supervision of the Captain' was sufficiently clear to transfer liability for damage caused on loading to the shipper, since the captain owed no duty to the shipper to supervise; the clause simply gave him the option to do so in order to protect the carrier's interests, thus indicating that the carrier did not have the duty under the contract to load the goods. Indeed, Lord Atkin has held that the carrier has both the right and the duty to supervise such loading activities, even in the absence of express contractual provisions.[67]

Whilst it now seems clear that, subject to contrary agreement by the parties, the Rules will apply to 'tackle to tackle' where only one voyage is involved, it is less clear whether they will apply when there is transhipment.

---

65. *Jindal Iron & Steel Co Ltd v Islamic Solidarity Shipping Co Jordan Inc (The Jordan II)* [2004] UKHL 49, [2005] 1 WLR 1363.

66. *CompaniaSud American Vapores v MS ER Hamburg Schiffahrtsgesellschaft* [2006] 2 Lloyd's Rep 66 (QB)—a case involving a charterparty.

67. *Court Line Ltd v Canadian Transport Co Ltd* [1940] AC 924 (HL).

> ### Mayhew Foods v Overseas Containers Ltd [1984] 1 Lloyd's Rep 317 (QB)
>
> **FACTS:** The contract of carriage involved transporting a consignment of frozen chickens by road to a port on the south coast of England and thence by ship to the port of Jeddah. The contract permitted the carrier to effect part of the sea transit in one ship and then transfer the goods to another for the remainder of the voyage, a process which is called transhipment. Originally, it was not envisaged that the goods would have to be transhipped, but owing to a change of plans, the carrier transported the goods from Shoreham in Sussex to Le Havre, where they were unloaded and stored before being loaded on another ship for the 'ocean leg' of the voyage. The chickens were rotten when they arrived in Jeddah, caused by an error which had taken place whilst the goods were being stored in Le Havre awaiting transhipment, and the question arose whether the Hague Visby Rules applied whilst the goods were being stored, since if they did not, the carrier had successfully limited his liability for this loss.
>
> **HELD:** Bingham J held that the Hague Visby Rules did apply since the discharge, storing, and transhipment of the goods was nevertheless 'in relation to and in connection with the carriage of goods by sea' and consequently within the scope of the Rules.

In *Mayhew*, whilst the Hague Visby Rules applied 'tackle to tackle', they did not apply to the road transport leg of the contract, a matter which is made clear by Art VII, which frees the parties to make any arrangement in relation to activities preceding loading onto or following unloading from the ship. Nevertheless, parties are free if they so choose to extend the scope of the Hague Visby Rules to cover activities that would not attract the compulsory application of the Rules. However, it was held in *The MSC Amsterdam*[68] that any such voluntary extension must be clearly expressed. Article V also makes it clear that the carrier may accept increased duties or liabilities than those in the Rules if incorporated into the bill of lading.

Duties of the carrier under the Hague Visby Rules

As to the ship

Article III r 1 stipulates that the carrier has a duty:

> [B]efore and at the beginning of the voyage, to exercise due diligence to (*a*) make the ship seaworthy; (*b*) properly man, equip and supply the ship; (*c*) make the holds, refrigerating and cool chambers, and all other parts of the ship in which goods are carried, fit and safe for their reception, carriage and preservation.

This duty, unlike at common law, is not absolute, but one to exercise due diligence, a point reinforced by s 3 of the Carriage of Goods by Sea Act 1971. It has been held that this duty of due diligence, which, according to Lord Devlin, is almost

---

68. *Mediterranean Shipping Co SA v Trafigura Beheer BV (The MSC Amsterdam)* [2007] EWCA Civ 79, [2008] 1 All ER (Comm) 385.

synonymous with the duty of care in negligence,[69] arises at least from the beginning of loading until the ship starts on her voyage.[70]

Maxine Footwear Co Ltd v Canadian Government Merchant Marine Ltd [1959] AC 589 (PC)

FACTS: After the cargo had been loaded but before the ship set sail, an attempt was made to thaw some frozen drainpipes with an oxyacetylene torch under the supervision of one of the ship's officers. The pipes were insulated with cork, which was set alight, and the fire spread so rapidly that the ship had to be sunk, destroying cargo belonging to Maxine Footwear Ltd. The carrier, Canadian, argued first, that the obligation of cargoworthiness under Art III r 1 had to be met (as at common law) at the point of loading. Second, that by virtue of Art IV r 2(b), they were only liable for fire damage caused by its actual fault, i.e. it was not vicariously liable for the negligence of its employees.

The immunities granted by Art IV are discussed at p 569

HELD: It was clear that the phrase 'before and at the beginning of the voyage' in Art III changed the common law and applied to both limbs of the duty to provide a seaworthy ship. Consequently, the ship had to be seaworthy in both senses at the commencement of loading until the commencement of the voyage. Consequently, the carrier owed a duty to the shipper to exercise due diligence that the ship remained seaworthy throughout that period, and since the ship had caught fire through a failure by the carrier to adopt a safe working practice, the carrier had broken this duty.

See ER Hardy-Ivamy, 'The Carriage of Goods by Sea Act 1924 and the Doctrine of "Stages"' (1960) 23 MLR 198

COMMENT: The Board also held that the duty to use due diligence to provide a seaworthy ship is an overriding obligation, so that where it is broken, the carrier will lose the benefit of the immunities granted to him by Art IV r 2.

Assuming that the ship was seaworthy before and at the beginning of the voyage, subsequent defects will not cause the carrier to be in default of its obligations under Art III r 1. It should be noted, though, that 'the beginning of the voyage' in Art III r 1 is at the initial port of loading. It may well be that the ship will sail to the port of discharge in a number of stages, calling at intermediate ports on the way, but the ship need not be seaworthy at each stage.[71] However, where faults manifest themselves during a voyage which are attributable to the ship being in an unseaworthy state prior to sailing, then the carrier will be liable for any lack of due diligence. For example, in *The Subro Valour*,[72] while the ship was at sea, a fire in the engine room was started by electrical wiring which had been exposed by shelving rubbing against it. There was no evidence to suggest that anything unusual had occurred during the voyage so that the court concluded that the wiring must have been vulnerable to damage when the ship set sail, thus rendering the ship unseaworthy.

We noted previously that the duty to exercise due diligence has been equated with the duty of care in the tort of negligence, and this is broadly true with one important difference. Whereas in an action for negligence, the defendant will have a defence if he has employed a competent or reputable subcontractor to carry out

---

69. *The Amstelot* [1963] 1 Lloyd's Rep 223 (HL) 235.

70. *Maxine Footwear Co Ltd v Canadian Government Merchant Marine* [1959] AC 589 (PC) 603.

71. *Leesh River Tea Co v British India Steam Navigation Co* [1966] 2 Lloyd's Rep 193 (CA).

72. [1995] 1 Lloyd's Rep 509 (QB).

work which subsequently proves to be negligently performed, this defence is not available in relation to the duty of 'due diligence' under the Hague Visby Rules.[73] Consequently, the carrier remains liable to the shipper, however reputable or apparently competent the subcontractor, for example even when he has procured a certificate from a Lloyds registered shipping surveyor where the survey was negligently conducted.[74]

Riverstone Meat Co Pty Ltd v Lancashire Shipping Co Ltd (The Muncaster Castle) [1961] AC 807 (HL)

FACTS: Lancashire Shipping engaged a reputable firm of ship repairers and surveyors to carry out work on the ship. An employee of the repairers failed to refit covers to storm valves, which let seawater into the hold and which damaged a cargo of tinned ox tongues belonging to Riverstone on the voyage from Sydney to London. Riverstone sued the carrier for failure to use due diligence to provide a seaworthy ship. Lancashire Shipping argued that by using a reputable firm of ship repairers, he had exercised due diligence and that it had no capability for checking the experts' work.

HELD: The duty to provide a seaworthy ship was a personal obligation of the carrier under the Rules as at common law and consequently cannot be delegated; as Viscount Simonds said, 'the shipowner's obligation of due diligence demands due diligence in the work of repair by whomsoever it may be done'.[75]

The allocation of the burden of proof in relation to unseaworthiness has proved problematic. There are two issues involved, one relating to proof that the ship was seaworthy at the relevant time and the second relating to whether due diligence has been exercised. Article IV r 1 provides that '[w]henever loss or damage has resulted from unseaworthiness, the burden of proving the exercise due diligence shall be on the carrier'. Read literally, the Article may suggest that the burden of proof of unseaworthinesslies is on the shipper, and this has been the approach of English courts.

The Hellenic Dolphin [1978] 2 Lloyd's Rep 336 (QB)

FACTS: Water entered the ship through a four-foot-long gash in the ship's side, of which the carrier was unaware. The water destroyed the cargo of asbestos, but there was no direct evidence whether the damage to the ship's hull had occurred before or after loading. The carrier claimed the defence of 'perils of the sea' under Art IV r 2(c), which would not be available to him were the ship unseaworthy through his lack of due diligence.[76]

HELD: The court held that the carrier was entitled to this defence unless the shipper could prove that the loss resulted from the ship being unseaworthy before or at the beginning

---

73. *Riverstone Meat Co Pty Ltd v Lancashire Shipping Co Ltd (The Muncaster Castle)* [1961] AC 807 (HL).
74. *Union of India v NV Reederij Amsterdam* [1963] 2 Lloyd's Rep 223 (HL). In this case, the survey was competently conducted so the carrier could demonstrate it had acted with due diligence.
75. *Riverstone Meat Co Pty Ltd v Lancashire Shipping Co Ltd (The Muncaster Castle)* [1961] AC 807 (HL) 844.
76. *Maxine Footwear Co Ltd v Canadian Government Merchant Marine* [1959] AC 589 (PC).

of the voyage. It would therefore seem that the initial burden is on the shipper to prove unseaworthiness, which, once proved, passes the burden to the carrier to demonstrate the exercise of due diligence.

Tetley,[77] amongst others, argues that because it is normally far easier for the carrier to establish the facts and extremely difficult for the shipper to discharge the burden of proving unseaworthiness, the burden of proof should be on the carrier, both in relation to proof of the exercise due diligence and that the ship was seaworthy at the relevant time.

As to cargo management

Article III r 2 requires the carrier to 'properly and carefully load, handle, stow, carry, keep, care for and discharge the goods carried'. In *Albacora SRL v Westcott and Laurance Line Ltd*,[78] it was argued by the shipper that the word 'properly' extended the carrier's duties beyond acting carefully where the only proper way of carrying that particular cargo was in refrigerated holds, even though this was unknown to the carrier. In the House of Lords, Lord Reid rejected the carrier's argument that the word 'properly' was tautologous, but concluded that it denotes the obligation to adopt a sound system in the light of all of the knowledge that the carrier either had or ought to have had.[79] Lord Pearce agreed, stating that '[a] sound system does not mean a system suited to all the weaknesses and idiosyncrasies of particular cargo but a sound system under all the circumstances in relation to the general practice of carriage of goods by sea'.[80]

Consequently, the duty corresponds with the normal duty of care in negligence except, as with the duty in relation to seaworthiness, the obligation in relation to cargo management is personal to the carrier, so that he cannot rely simply on having delegated the duty to an apparently competent third party.[81]

As with issues concerning seaworthiness under Art III r 1, there is some dispute over the burden of proof in cases alleging a breach of duty concerning cargo management under Art III r 2. This duty is subject to a list of exceptions set out in Art IV, but the carrier cannot take advantage of these exceptions where the damage to the goods could have been avoided by due diligence. Clearly, the shipper must prove that the goods were damaged in transit, but will readily do this, probably by the production of a clean bill of lading, along with proof either that the goods have not been delivered or have been delivered in a damaged condition. In *Gosse Millard Ltd v Canadian Government Merchant Marine Ltd*,[82] Wright J held that once the shipper has proved the loss or damage of the goods in transit, the carrier must prove that he exercised due diligence before he can take advantage of the Art IV exceptions. However, in *Albacora SRL v Westcott and Laurance Line Ltd*,[83] Lord Pearce doubted this proposition, so that the law appears to be that, once loss or damage to the goods in transit is proved by the shipper, the carrier must prove that this is caused by one of

---

77. William Tetley, *Marine Cargo Claims* (4th edn, Sweet & Maxwell 2008) 889.
78. [1966] 2 Lloyd's Rep 53 (HL).   79. ibid 58.   80. ibid 62.
81. *International Packers Ltd v Ocean SS Co Ltd* [1955] 2 Lloyd's Rep 218 (QB).
82. [1927] 2 KB 432 (KB).   83. [1966] 2 Lloyd's Rep 53 (HL) 64.

the exceptions, which, once proved, leaves the shipper to prove lack of due diligence on the part of the carrier. However, as Lord Pearson observed:

> There is no express provision, and in my opinion there is no implied provision in the Hague Rules that the shipowner is debarred as a matter of law from relying on an exception unless he proves absence of negligence on his part. But he does have to prove that the damage was caused by an excepted peril or excepted cause, and in order to do that he may in a particular case have to give evidence excluding causation by his negligence.

As to documents

Article III r 3 provides that after receiving the goods, the carrier:

> shall on demand of the shipper, issue to the shipper a bill of lading showing among other things (a) The leading marks necessary for the identification of the goods'…(b) Either the number of packages or pieces or, the quantity or weight…(c) The apparent order and condition of the goods.

According to the Article, the leading marks and the number quantity or weight of the goods to be included on the bill of lading are those supplied in writing by the shipper, provided that the carrier is not bound to include on the bill of lading any marks, number, quantity, or weight which he has reasonable ground for suspecting do not accurately represent the goods or which cannot reasonably be checked.

This proviso, coupled with the fact that the duty to provide a bill of lading complying with the Art III r 3 specifications is not absolute,[84] commonly results in bills of lading containing provisions such as 'weight and condition unknown' or the like. Similarly, where goods are containerized, it is common to see descriptions such as '20 container said to contain…', followed by a description provided by the shipper. The effect of such reservations is to remove much of the benefit that would otherwise be provided by Art III r 4. This Article provides that statements made on a bill of lading are regarded as *prima facie* evidence of the receipt by the carrier of the goods as described, but that 'proof to the contrary shall not be admissible when the bill of lading has been transferred to a third party acting in good faith'. Thus in *The Mata K*,[85] the bill of lading stated that the weight of the goods was 11,000 metric tonnes, but on the face of the bill of lading were also included the words 'weight, measure, quantity, quality, condition, content and value unknown'. On discharge of the goods, a shortage in the weight was discovered. It was held that the endorsement clearly indicated that the presumption did not apply. The effect of such notations were explained in a later case by Longmore J as follows:

> [I]f the bills provide 'weight…Number…Quantity unknown', it cannot be said that the bills 'show' that number or weight. They 'show' nothing at all because the shipowner is not prepared to say what the number or weight is. He can of course be required to show it under Art III (3) but, unless and until he does so, the provisions of Art III (4) as to prima facie evidence cannot come into effect.[86]

---

84. Since it depends on the 'demand of the shipper'.
85. *Agrosin Pte Ltd v Highway Shipping Co Ltd (The Mata K)* [1998] 2 Lloyd's Rep 614 (QB).
86. *Noble Resources Ltd v Cavalier Shipping Corp (The Atlas)* [1996] 1 Lloyd's Rep 642 (QB) 646.

Clearly, where the bill of lading is not subjected to such reservations, the carrier is exposed to liability for non-delivery by virtue of misdescriptions of the goods by the shipper. Article III r 5 therefore provides the carrier with an indemnity against the shipper for such liability arising because of inaccuracy in the marks, number, quantity, or weight of the goods, while making it clear that this does not absolve the carrier from any liability to a third party.

Article III r 3(c) requires that the bill of lading shall state the apparent order and condition of the goods, which requires only a reasonable external inspection. This statement is simply one of opinion and is not a warranty of the actual condition of the goods to purchasers of them; an honest though mistaken belief will not render the carrier liable if it is a belief that could properly be held by a reasonably observant master, even if most masters might not have agreed with him.[87]

Where the master is not satisfied as to the apparent condition of the cargo, he may 'clause' the bill of lading, and there is a strong incentive to do so where there is apparent damage, since the carrier must deliver the goods in the same condition as they were received,[88] and the bill of lading is *prima facie* evidence of what it states as against the shipper and conclusive evidence as against subsequent holders of the bill.

The 'clausing' of bills of lading is discussed at p 488

Excluded causes of loss

Article IV r 2 contains a list of causes of damage or loss to goods for which the carrier is not responsible, the most important of which correspond to typical express exclusions at common law.

🔒 Hague Visby Rules, Art IV r 2

Neither the carrier nor the ship shall be responsible for loss or damage arising or resulting from:

(a) Act, neglect, or default of the master, mariner, pilot, or the servants of the carrier in the navigation or in the management of the ship.

(b) Fire, unless caused by the actual fault or privity of the carrier.

(c) Perils, dangers and accidents of the sea or other navigable waters.

(d) Act of God.

(e) Act of war.

(f) Act of public enemies.

(g) Arrest or restraint of princes, rulers or people, or seizure under legal process.

(h) Quarantine restrictions.

(i) Act or omission of the shipper or owner of the goods, his agent or representative.

---

87. *The David Agmashenebeli* [2003] 1 Lloyd's Rep 92 (QB) 104 (Colman J).
88. Subject to any applicable defences or exceptions.

(j) Strikes or lockouts or stoppage or restraint of labour from whatever cause, whether partial or general.

(k) Riots and civil commotions.

(l) Saving or attempting to save life or property at sea.

(m) Wastage in bulk of weight or any other loss or damage arising from inherent defect, quality or vice of the goods.

(n) Insufficiency of packing.

(o) Insufficiency or inadequacy of marks.

(p) Latent defects not discoverable by due diligence.

(q) Any other cause arising without the actual fault or privity of the carrier, or without the fault or neglect of the agents or servants of the carrier, but the burden of proof shall be on the person claiming the benefit of this exception to show that neither the actual fault or privity of the carrier nor the fault or neglect of the agents or servants of the carrier contributed to the loss or damage.

Many of these causes are self-explanatory, but four merit further discussion.

Default in management of the ship

Article IV r 2(a) provides that the carrier shall not be liable for loss or damage arising or resulting from the 'act, neglect, or default of the master, mariner, pilot or the servants of the carrier in the navigation or in the management of the ship'. There are some instances where the application of the exception is clear, for example where goods are damaged because a ship collides with another or runs aground through the negligence of the captain. But what amounts to a default in navigation[89] and also what amounts to a default in the management of the ship[90] have both been the subject of disputes in the courts, as the following two cases demonstrate.

 Whistler International Ltd v Kawasaki Kisen Kaisha Ltd (The Hill Harmony) [2000] 1 AC 638 (HL)

FACTS: Under the terms of the contract (a time charterparty) the carrier was under an express duty to follow the shortest route. Instead, the captain followed a longer route because he had experienced bad weather on the previous voyage on the contractual route. The shipper argued that the carrier was liable for failure to prosecute the journey without utmost dispatch. The carrier claimed the benefit of Art IV r 2(a). The High Court and the Court of Appeal found for the carrier on the basis that the choice of the appropriate route was a matter of navigation.

HELD: It was incorrect to state that all questions of what route to follow were questions of navigation. Where compliance with the contractual route exposed the ship to a risk which the carrier had not agreed to bear, the captain might as a matter of seamanship (which

89. *Whistler International Ltd v Kawasaki Kisen Kaisha Ltd (The Hill Harmony)* [2000] 1 AC 638 (HL).
90. *Gosse Millard Ltd v Canadian Government Merchant Marine Ltd* [1929] AC 223 (HL); contrast with *International Packers Ltd v Ocean Steamship Co Ltd* [1955] 2 Lloyd's Rep 218 (QB).

the House equated with navigation) take another route, but here the carrier had failed to prove that that was the case. In any event, there had been no error in navigation, and the ship had proceeded safely on the route intended by the captain; the captain's error was in misinterpreting what was permitted under the contract.

⭐ See Simon Baughen, 'Navigation or Employment?' [2001] 2 LMCLQ 177

Gosse Millard Ltd v Canadian Government Merchant Marine Ltd [1929] AC 223 (HL)

FACTS: The ship, which was carrying a cargo of tin plate from South Wales to Canada, was damaged and needed repair in a dry dock in Liverpool. While being repaired, the hatches were left open so that rainwater entered the hold and caused the tinplate to rust. The carrier claimed the benefit of Art IV r 2(a).

HELD: The carrier had broken its duty under Art III r 2 to properly and carefully load, handle, stow, carry, keep, care for, and discharge the goods. 'Management of the ship' in Art IV r (2)(a) concerned acts done for the safety of the ship and not primarily in connection with the cargo. Here the primary purpose of covering the hatches would have been to protect the cargo and consequently the Art IV r 2(a) exception did not apply.

COMMENT: This case must be compared with *International Packers*, where, in similar circumstances, Art IV r (2)(a) did apply because water entered the hold through negligent acts by the crew in seeking the safety of the ship.

🔗 The *International Packers* case is discussed at p 552

Saving or attempting to save life or property

As has been discussed, at common law, the carrier is under a duty to carry the goods by the most direct or usual safe route between the port of loading and the port of discharge or otherwise in accordance with the contract subject to two exceptions. Article IV r 4 preserves the common law exception permitting deviation in saving or attempting to save life, but adds further exceptions possibly permitting deviation solely to save property at sea and any reasonable deviation, stating that such deviations 'shall not be deemed to be an infringement or breach of these Rules or of the contract of carriage, and the carrier shall not be liable for any loss or damage resulting therefrom'.

The inclusion of the right to deviate in order solely to save property, if it exists, may pose serious problems for the shipper. Salvage operations can be extremely lucrative for the salvor, but such actions may inevitably result in damage to the cargo, for example if it is perishable and the salvage operations are protracted, which has led some writers to doubt whether deviation solely in order to save property is mandated by the Hague Visby Rules.[91]

What amounts to a 'reasonable deviation' was considered in the following case.

---

91. See Indira Carr, *International Trade Law* (4th edn, Routledge 2010) 243–4.

Stag Line Ltd v Foscolo, Mango and Co Ltd [1932] AC 328 (HL)

FACTS: Two engineers were working on a fuel-saving device in the ship owned by Stag Line Ltd when she set sail. The ship deviated from its normal route in order to set the engineers ashore when they had completed their work, but instead of returning to the usual route as quickly as possible, the ship continued to sail close to the shore, ran aground, and the cargo belonging to Foscolo, Mango and Co Ltd was lost.

HELD: It was held in the House of Lords that the deviation to set the engineers ashore was not unreasonable, but continuing the voyage without attempting to resume the original route as soon as possible was. A range of opinions were expressed in the House, but Lord Atkin in the fullest judgment concluded that a deviation may be reasonable regardless of whether it was made solely in the interests of the shipper or of the carrier or of neither of them:

> The true test seems to be what departure from the contract voyage might a prudent person controlling the voyage at the time make and maintain, having in mind all the relevant circumstances existing at the time, including the terms of the contract and the interests of all parties concerned, but without obligation to consider the interests of anyone as conclusive.[92]

While the detail of what amounts to a 'reasonable deviation' remains uncertain, it is clear that the courts take a restrictive approach limiting successful invocations to cases where the deviation is either to protect the ship or the cargo. Until *Photo Productions Ltd v Securicor Transport*,[93] unjustified deviation was regarded as a fundamental breach of contract, which deprived the guilty party of the benefit of any contractual exclusions. The justification for this conclusion derives at least in part from the fact that at the time when the doctrine was developed, cargo insurance cover would be lost in the event of a deviation, since cover was provided only in respect of the contract voyage,[94] so that in effect the carrier replaced the insurer in providing an indemnity. However, the standard Institute Cargo Clauses now extends insurance to cover deviations, and, following *Photo Productions v Securicor*, it may well be that appropriately drafted exclusion clauses may survive unjustified deviations.[95]

The Institute Cargo Clauses are considered further at p 590

Finally, it is common practice to include express 'liberty to deviate' clauses into contracts of carriage, and the question arises, if a deviation apparently permitted by such a clause were nevertheless held to be unreasonable under Art IV r 4, would the deviation clause survive Art III r 8.[96] It now seems generally accepted that the effect of such a clause is simply to define the nature and scope of the voyage and not limit or exclude the duties or liability of the carrier whilst engaged in it.

---

92. [1932] AC 328 (HL) 343–4.   93. [1980] AC 827 (HL).

94. Marine Insurance Act 1906, s 46(1).

95. See Lloyd LJ in *Kenya Railways v Antares Co Pte Ltd (The Antares) (No 1)* [1987] 1 Lloyd's Rep 424 (CA) and in *State Trading Corporation of India Ltd v M Golodetz Ltd* [1989] 2 Lloyd's Rep 277. See also Charles Debattista, 'Fundamental Breach and Deviation in the Carriage of Goods by Sea' [1989] JBL 22.

96. Which renders void any provision which reduces the carrier's duty to below the Hague Visby minima.

Latent defect

Article IV r 2(q) provides a defence for the carrier where the loss is caused by 'latent defect', which means a hidden defect in the ship which could not be discovered by exercising 'due diligence'. It is by no means clear what this defence adds to Art IV r 1, since the carrier only owes a duty to exercise due diligence in relation to the seaworthiness of the vessel before and at the commencement of the voyage; in other words, it is not an absolute duty. The carrier cannot be liable under Art IV r 1 simply by failing to carefully inspect the ship prior to setting sail; there must also be a cause of loss which such an inspection would have revealed, so that it would appear that the 'latent defect' defence is superfluous.

Any other cause arising without actual fault

Article IV r 2(q) provides a catch-all defence, but rarely needs to be used, partially by virtue of the breadth of the other excepted clauses, and this can be illustrated by consideration of the following case.

Leesh River Tea Co v British India Steam Navigation Co [1967] 2 QB 250 (HL)

FACTS: The stevedores employed by British India, the carrier, to unload part of the ship stole a small brass cover plate over a storm valve. The loss of this plate was not discoverable by British India, but its absence permitted water to enter the cargo hold and damage Leesh River's goods.

HELD: The Court of Appeal held that since the carrier was not responsible for the actions of the stevedores when stealing the plate, Art IV r 2(q) provided a defence so long as the carrier could show that it was not otherwise in default. However, since the carrier was not responsible for the loss of the plate, the entry of the water was a peril of the sea and so Art IV r 2(c) applied as well.

COMMENT: Similarly, whilst Art IV r 2(q) was held to apply when a crate broke open whilst being unloaded, since the carrier could show that the lid had been insecurely fastened before loading, it is difficult to see why Art IV r 2(n) was not equally applicable.[97] In both of these instances, the carrier was able to identify the actual cause of loss, but read literally the exception may suggest that even where the cause cannot be pinpointed, the carrier can nevertheless escape liability under Art IV r 2(q) by showing a sound working system, but the authorities conflict on this matter.[98]

---

97. *Goodwin Ferreira & Co Ltd v Lamport & Holt Ltd* (1929) 34 Ll LR 192 (KB).

98. See *Pendle & Rivett Ltd v Ellerman Lines Ltd* (1928) 29 Ll LR 133 (QB) 136; compare this to the American decision, *The Vermont* [1942] AMC 1407, where the cause of the contamination of a cargo of coconut oil was never established, but the carrier avoided liability by showing careful cargo management and cleaning and testing of the tanks.

Limitation on the carrier's liability under the Hague Visby Rules

Time

Article III r 6 sets out two main conditions that the claimant must meet if he is to make a claim against the carrier. The first is that written notice of loss or damage must be given to the carrier where the loss or damage is apparent before the goods enter into the custody of the consignee, or within three days of their entering his custody if the loss or damage is not apparent. Failure to do so does not bar an action, but means that the delivery to the consignee is *prima facie* evidence the delivery was in accordance with the contract.

The second condition is contained in Art III r 6(d), which requires the action to be started within one year of the date of delivery or the date it ought to have been delivered subject to extension as agreed by the parties. Delivery here appears to mean the passing of physical or at least constructive possession to the consignee,[99] but whether delivery has taken place under a contract of carriage may not be obvious, especially where, by virtue of a contractual dispute, the parties decide to change the port of discharge. The question is, 'Did the parties vary the original contract and substitute a new destination or did they enter into a new contract leaving the original port as the place where the goods ought to have been delivered.'

Trafigura Beheer BV v Golden Stavraetos Maritime Inc (The Sonia) [2003] EWCA Civ 664

FACTS: This was a contract for carriage of goods where aircraft fuel was to be discharged at Lagos, but Trafigura, which owned the goods, refused to take delivery from the carrier, GSM, on the ground that the cargo had been contaminated in the ship. After a long dispute, the parties agreed that the fuel should be discharged in Greece. It was held at first instance that Lagos was the place where the goods were to be delivered, so time ran from the due date of discharge there; the voyage to Greece was under a separate contract of carriage.

HELD: The Court of Appeal disagreed; since the fuel remained in the ship throughout and was delivered by the same carrier to the order of the same consignee, delivery in Greece had been made under a variation of the original contract.

★ See Tim Stephenson, 'Differing Views on "Delivery:" The Sonia' (2003) 4 S & TLI 18

Finally, it has been held that the Hague Visby time limit differs slightly to limitation under the Limitation Act 1980. The Act serves to bar an action for recovery, but does not extinguish the claim, so that, for example, money liability under a time-barred claim may nevertheless set off by a claim by the other party to a contract. However, in *The Aries*,[100] the House of Lords held that a claim in relation to short

---

99. *Grimaldi Compagnia di Navigazione SpA v Sekihyo Lines Ltd (The Seki Rolette)* [1998] 2 Lloyd's Rep 638 (QB).
100. *Aries Tanker Corp v Total Transport Ltd (The Aries)* [1977] 1 All ER 398 (HL).

delivery that was timebarred under Art III r 6 was extinguished and could not be set off against a claim for freight by the carrier.

Financial limits

Article IV r 5 states that unless the value of the goods has been declared to the carrier before shipment and included in the bill of lading, the maximum liability of the carrier in relation to goods is the higher of 666.67 units of account per package or two units of account per kilogramme of the gross weight of the goods lost or damaged.

The effect of the wording appears to be that the total claim is limited, even if there is little or no physical loss to the goods carried but substantial consequential loss.[101]

➜ unit of account: the SDR as defined by the International Monetary Fund—at 1 January 2013 it was worth 95p

Non-contractual claims by the shipper

Tortious claims primarily in negligence or conversion may be made against the carrier or others, and such claims exist whether shipping documents have been issued or not. Additionally, in appropriate cases they can provide a means of evading the limitations set out in the contract of carriage, though it should be noted that Art IV bis r 1 provides that the defences and limits of liability provided for in the Rules apply equally to tortious claims. Nevertheless, where the goods are damaged by the negligence of the carrier or a third party, for example a stevedoring company, then the owner of the damaged goods or the person in possession of them when the damage occurred may bring an action.[102] Negligence actions against third parties are likely to be subject to the same contractual limitations and exclusions as those protecting the carrier, notwithstanding the fact that the defendant is not an obvious party to the contract. First, Art IV bis r 2 provides that contractual protections of the carrier apply equally to their servants or agents (not being independent sub-contractors), while typically the contract of carriage will include a clause extending such protections to sub-contractors—a so-called 'Himalaya' clause. Although in *Scruttons Ltd v Midland Silicones Ltd*,[103] the House of Lords held that the rules of privity and the requirement for consideration apply to such clauses, thus *prima facie* preventing a third party from benefiting from them, a means of meeting such objections was found by the Privy Council in *The Eurymedon*.[104] Here it was accepted that the carriers entered into the contract not only for themselves, but as agents for the third parties, and that the contract thus created between the shipper and the third party was one where, in consideration of the third party unloading the goods, they should enjoy the benefits of the limitations set out in the contract of carriage.

---

101. *Serena Navigation Ltd v Dera Commercial Establishment (The Limnos)* [2008] EWHC 1036 (Comm), [2008] 2 All ER (Comm) 1005.
102. *Leigh & Sillivan Ltd v Aliakmon Shipping Co Ltd (The Aliakmon)* [1986] AC 785 (HL). An entitlement to immediate possession is also likely to be sufficient.
103. [1962] AC 446 (HL).
104. *New Zealand Shipping Co Ltd v AM Satterthwaite & Co Ltd* [1975] AC 154 (PC).

Additionally, where, for example, the goods have been released by the carrier to a third party, a person with an immediate right to possess them may be able to bring an action in conversion against the third party, even though that party acted honestly and with no notice of the claimant's rights.[105]

Conclusion

In English law there are two possible sets of principles which affect the contractual relationships between a carrier and the shipper. At common law the carrier may well in theory be strictly liable for loss, but will seek to limit this liability by excluding liability caused by a list of excepted perils, and indeed may seek to exclude liability for any loss except caused through his own fraud. To counter this practice, the Carriage of Goods by Sea Act 1971 implements the Hague Visby Rules, which provide that the carrier owes a duty to exercise due diligence, both that the ship is seaworthy and in his care of the goods. In addition, the carrier cannot contract out of these duties. However, there are other sets of rules governing the carriage of goods by sea which apply in other jurisdictions, in particular the Hamburg Rules and the Rotterdam Rules, and a table of comparisons between the Hague Visby and these rules is included in the online resources.

Practice questions

1. Describe the principal features of the following;
    *   seaworthiness;
    *   perils of the sea;
    *   deviation;
    *   the Hague Visby Rules;
    *   default in management of the ship.

2. 'In the history of contracts of carriage of goods by sea the law has swung from a position which was too favourable to the shipper to one which is too favourable to the carrier.'
    Discuss.

3. Carrie runs a small shipping line and Shipton enters negotiation with her to carry some of his goods from Portsmouth to Santander Spain. First, he wants to transport a crate containing spare parts. Carrie agrees and issues him with a document headed 'Sea waybill'. As with all of Carrie's shipping documents, it contains a clause which states that Carrie is not liable for any loss howsoever caused. Second, he wants to transport a container of very valuable antique furniture. They agree that the container will be carried in the hold of the ship. Finally, he wants to transport two crates, each containing 1,000 cartons of leather goods. The first crate is stored in number 1 hold and the second in number 2 hold. The ship sails and arrives at Santander on 1 April 2013.

---

105. See e.g. Earl Cairns in *Glyn Mills Currie & Co v The East and West India Dock Company* (1881–82) LR 7 App Cas 591 (HL) 602.

When the ship arrives at Santander, the crate of spare parts is dropped on the quayside and the goods are damaged, while the container of antiques which had been carried on deck had been washed overboard by a freak wave and lost. The cartons of leather goods in number 1 hold are damaged because water enters the hold as a hatch cover has not sealed the opening. The cartons in number 2 hold also have water damage, though there seems to be no obvious explanation as to how this happened.

Shipton has no insurance and he tries to persuade Carrie to compensate him for his loss. She is very charming, but after protracted negotiations she says she will not pay. It is now March 2014. Advise Shipton on his claims against Carrie.

Further reading

Anthony Diamond, 'The Next Sea Carriage Convention?' [2008] LMCLQ 135
- Contains a discussion of the legal issues raised by the draft text of the Rotterdam Rules and provides an interesting comparison with the position under the Hague Visby Rules.

Chinyere Ezeoke, 'Allocating Onus of Proof in Cargo Claims: The Contest of Conflicting Principles' [2001] LMCLQ 261
- Reviews the ways in which the courts have applied differing burdens of proof in relation to the duty of care and defences of excepted perils depending on the circumstances.

HL Morgan Jr, 'Unreasonable Deviation under COGSA' (1977–78) 9 JMLC 481
- Although the 'COGSA' in question is the US statute concerning the Hague Rules, this short article nevertheless contains an interesting survey of both English and US decisions on deviations both geographical and others amounting to 'fundamental breach'.

W Tetley, 'The Hamburg Rules—A Commentary' [1979] LMCLQ 1
- Probably the best short review of the provisions of the Hamburg Rules.

John Wilson, *Carriage of Goods by Sea* (7th edn, Pearson 2010)
- A leading student text on the area and also used as a ready source by professionals involved in international trade.

22

Marine cargo insurance and other risk control mechanisms in international sales

- Tools of risk management
- Elements of marine cargo insurance: contract
- Elements of marine cargo insurance: causation
- Elements of marine cargo insurance: claims
- The Institute Cargo Clauses

INTRODUCTION

The primary focus of this chapter is to look at one context, in which risk in a commercial transaction can be transferred. In all sales of goods, other than when conducted face to face, there is a risk that the goods will be damaged or lost in transit from seller to buyer. The parties may seek to control this risk in a number of ways, but typically will transfer its financial impact to a third party through insurance. In the international sales of goods, particularly where the goods are transported by sea, not only are the physical risks increased when compared with a domestic sale, but the logistics are such that determining the cause of the loss may be difficult and attributing liability problematic, not least because of linguistic and geographical separation of the parties. Consequently, it is preferable to have the security of a claim against an identifiable financially secure party in the event of loss.

🔗 Documentary sales are discussed at p 487

In documentary sales and their terrestrial equivalents, where the goods are symbolically embodied in documentation, the buyer is induced to make payment or at least to accept risk of loss or damage to the goods only because that risk is insured and because he obtains the benefits of that insurance through delivery of the relevant document. Consequently, contracts of marine cargo insurance have an essential role to play in such sales, and it is to this form of insurance that this chapter is primarily devoted. In so doing, the key elements of insurance, the nature of the contract, the concepts of risk coverage, causation, and claims are introduced and given a specific context, thus equipping the reader to apply these elements to other insurances. Thus this chapter deals with one of the trio of documents that make up the 'Cif triangle', namely:

1. the bill of lading;
2. the letter of credit; and
3. the policy of insurance.

In addition, contract, causation, and claims are given an extended treatment in the Online Resource Centre along with further examples of commercial insurances. However, the chapter starts with a brief overview of the tools the parties to an international sale of goods might use in order to control the commercial risks.

Tools of risk management

A buyer and a seller may use a range of techniques for controlling their risks when involved in an international contract of sale. The risks involved are many and various, and this section simply takes one example and examines very briefly how that type of risk might be managed, looked at primarily from a legal perspective. Political risks (for example that the goods might be seized by a foreign government), commercial risks (for example that the value of the goods might go down in the period between contract and delivery), currency risk and so forth are all important, perhaps more important than the risks we will look at, and they all can be controlled. However, this section is simply to give a 'flavour' of the risk control process.

Identification and quantification

Often the key to risk management is to identify and then if possible measure the risk. For example, there is a risk that the goods in transit may be damaged while in the custody of the sea carrier. Once this has been identified, then a part of that risk can be legally quantified by reviewing the contract of carriage and determining the financial limits on the liability of the carrier, and determining whether, if the goods were damaged, these limits would result in a part of the loss falling on one of the parties. Quantification of the likelihood of damage occurring in the first place is also important, but that is not susceptible to legal analysis.[1]

Then there is the solvency risk involved—how likely it is that the carrier will pay what it owes in the event of damage. There may be a currency risk, in that if the carrier has, at least under the Hague Rules/Hague Visby Rules, a liability expressed other than in sterling, there may be a risk that any legal action against the carrier would have to be conducted in a foreign court and so forth. Some of these matters can be identified by looking at the contract, others by consulting rating agencies, but at least they have been identified.

The Hague Rules and Hague Visby Rules are discussed at p 558

Assuming the likelihood of any of these risks materializing and the size of their financial impact is beyond the capabilities of most traders, but whole sections of the financial services market is devoted to doing just that, and providing products by means of which a trader may transfer that risk to a third party—but at a price!

What has been discussed here is just one of the sources of risk related to the carrier. But what happens if the carrier does not complete the contract of carriage and just leaves the goods in a port on the far side of the world? What happens if he becomes insolvent and the goods are seized in a foreign country to pay his debts? What happens if the carrier is a crook, sells the goods, sinks the ship, and disappears? There are many more possibilities and, of course, risk does not simply emanate from the carrier, so identification of risk is complex.

---

1. Though it will be expressed in the premium charged by an insurer taking on this risk calculated by an actuarial process.

Allocation through documentation

Simply knowing who will be responsible if things go wrong is a form of risk control—it helps in the identification process and helps to minimize the chance that a problem becomes a dispute. A key tool in this process is appropriate documentation that allocates responsibilities. Good documentation does not remove risk; there is always the risk of litigation arising, no matter how carefully documents are drafted—after all, there was still litigation right up until it was withdrawn in 1982 on the meaning of the standard form marine insurance policy used throughout the world for over 200 years.[2] However, if the parties have a clear view of who will bear the financial burden should a particular risk eventuate, then we have at least minimized the legal risk of litigation. Similarly, a clause determining the **proper law of the contract** and the countries of which court should have jurisdiction[3] in the event of dispute will also reduce uncertainty in relation to potential litigation.

➡ **proper law of a contract:** determines which country's laws are used to determine the contract's legal effect

Control

Some types of risk can be controlled. For example, the danger identified earlier of damage to goods in transit is more likely to be realized by the effect of inadequate packaging than by the negligence of the carrier. This risk can therefore be controlled to an extent by employing specialists to pack goods ready for export, while containerization will also reduce the chance both of damage and of pilferage.[4] Similarly, proper loading and handling instructions to the carrier will reduce the likelihood of damage.

Price

One form of risk management is to include in the price an element to cover the risks the business has identified. Thus counterparty insolvency risk (in our case, will the buyer/seller/carrier/**freight forwarder**/bank/insurance company etc be solvent if a claim has to be made) might be quantified[5] and the price of goods adjusted to reflect this. This in itself does not reduce the risk of counterparty default, but at least the business has either been rewarded for taking the risk, or it may use the increase in gross profit generated by the adjustment to pay for a transfer of the risk.

➡ **freight forwarder:** a business which specializes in arranging the logistics of transportation of goods

---

2. See *Shell Petroleum International Ltd v Gibbs (The Salem)* [1983] 1 All ER 745 (HL), where the meaning of 'perils of the sea', the cornerstone of the main insuring clause in the policy, had to be considered by the House of Lords a year after the 200-year-old policy form had been withdrawn.

3. The parties might choose instead to arbitrate rather than litigate. Proper law and jurisdiction/arbitration clauses may reduce risk but will not eliminate it. See the *West Tankers* litigation saga, Case C-185/07 *West Tankers Inc v Riunione Adriatica di Sicurtà SpA (The Front Comor)* [2009] 1 AC 1138; *West Tankers Inc v Allianz SPA & Generali Assicurazione Generali SPA* [2012] EWCA Civ 27, [2012] 2 All ER (Comm) 113; *West Tankers Inc v Allianz SpA & anr* [2012] EWHC 854 (Comm), [2012] 2 All ER. (Comm) 395.

4. Though see *NSW Leather Co Pty Ltd v Vanguard Insurance Co Ltd* (1991) 105 FLR 381, where containers were broken into, the contents removed, replaced by scrap material of the same weight, and false seals affixed, so that it was not until delivery that the loss was discovered.

5. Typically by the providers of financial instruments who sell 'insurance' against a counterparty default.

Transfer and hedging

Risk transfer is one of the most obvious means of risk management. If a risk can be transferred either to a counterparty in the sale or preferably to a financial institution, then the risk has been minimized.[6] The whole structure of documentary sales is to effect risk transfer in relation to damage or loss to the goods through insurance and payment default through letters of credit or bank guarantees; a similar result can be obtained in respect of a regular major trading partner through the use of credit default swaps. A range of other financial risks can be transferred: for example currency risk, where the price of goods is in one currency but the seller's costs are in another, can be hedged by the use of currency futures. Similarly, a seller always has a risk that goods he has despatched will be rejected on arrival, or the buyer may refuse to pay, so that the seller has to recover possession of the goods, and these risks can also be insured.

Conclusion

Perhaps the important message from this discussion is that the lawyer can have a vital role in the risk management process in relation to international sales of goods. Good documentation leads to more ready risk identification and appropriately worded risk transfer instruments, whether insurance policies, currency future contracts, credit default swaps, or whatever can significantly reduce the financial risks borne by an exporter or importer.

The focus of the remainder of this chapter is on one means of risk transfer and the legal principles that underpin marine cargo insurance.

Elements of marine cargo insurance: contract

At its most basic, under an insurance contract one person (the insurer) agrees to pay a sum of money and/or provide other benefits to another person (the assured[7]) on the occurrence of an event during the period of the insurance, but sometimes only if it arises from a particular cause. In fact, a range of contracts might meet this general description, from a 'flutter on the horses' to a contract of guarantee or a financial derivative contract, but what characterizes an insurance contract is that it is normally intended to provide compensation for an adverse event. So whilst X might enter into a bet whether a parcel will arrive, even if it is not X's parcel, an insurer will insure X against its non-arrival only if X will suffer financial loss if it does not arrive. This is described as the need to have an 'insurable interest'. Equally, whilst the bet might be for any sum of money, the insurance will only pay X the amount of X's loss. A contract of insurance like this is a contract of indemnity. Finally, X's counterparty in the bet would be under no duty before the bet is made to tell X, for example, that he's

---

6. Though not eliminated, financial institutions do become insolvent.

7. 'Insured' means the same thing—'assured' is used in this chapter because this is the word used in the Marine Insurance Act 1906.

seen the parcel in the back of the carrier's van marked for delivery today, while in an insurance contract, both parties are under strict duties of disclosure in relation to material facts affecting the insurance. Insurance is a contract of utmost good faith.

These concepts of indemnity, insurable interest, and utmost good faith were worked out at common law, but they and other principles governing the insurance of 'marine adventures' were codified in the Marine Insurance Act 1906. Although the Act only applies directly to insurance of 'maritime perils', it is accepted as encapsulating elements of insurance generally. Consequently, the 1906 Act is commonly referred to in insurance cases even in matters entirely unrelated to the sea.

Insurance as a contract of indemnity

Indemnification

Section 1 of the Marine Insurance Act 1906 defines a contract of marine insurance as one 'whereby the insurer undertakes to indemnify the assured ... against marine losses'. Consequently, in a policy written on an indemnity basis, the assured can recover no more from the assured than his pecuniary loss. Although life insurance is not normally written on an indemnity basis, almost all other insurance is, though the indemnity may be imperfect.[8] This is particularly so in the case of 'valued' policies, where the parties at the outset place a value on the property insured. In such cases, except where there is gross overvaluation such that the good faith of the assured is impugned, the fixed sum is conclusive as to the loss sustained where the property is lost or damaged.[9]

Where the property is insured in respect of the same risk under two separate policies—double insurance[10]—the insurers will pay claims in proportion to the amount otherwise payable under each,[11] and an insurer may be required to return a like proportion of the premium to the assured to reflect the fact that he was exposed only to a percentage of the risk, while he charged a premium in respect of the whole of it.[12]

Subrogation

➡ subrogation: the ability to take on the legal rights of others

The principle of indemnity underpins the concept of **subrogation**. Often the insured loss may have been caused by a third party against whom the assured may have a claim: for example, a carrier may negligently damage the goods of a shipper, giving the shipper a contractual claim for compensation. Normally the shipper will pursue an insurance claim if he has one,[13] but once he has been indemnified in respect of the damage, then the insured goods and the benefit of any other rights and remedies he might have are transferred to the insurer, who is subrogated to his claims[14] and has an equitable lien or charge over any sums the assured might recover.[15]

🔗 Equitable liens and charges are discussed in Chapter 25

8. *British and Foreign Insurance Co Ltd v Wilson Shipping Co Ltd* [1921] 1 AC 188 (HL) 241 (Lord Sumner).
9. *Irving v Manning* (1847) 1 HLC 287 (HL).   10. Marine Insurance Act 1906, s 32.
11. ibid s 80.   12. ibid s 84(3)(f).
13. Since typically the recovery will be more generous than under the financial limitations on the liability of carriers under the Hague Visby Rules. See Chapter 21.
14. Marine Insurance Act 1906, s 79(1) (total loss) and 79(2) (partial loss).
15. *Napier and Ettrick v Hunter* [1993] AC 713 (HL). Lord Templeman and Lord Goff both concluded *obiter* that the charge would attach to any right to sue in respect of a loss which has been indemnified.

Insurable interest[16]

The concept of insurable interest is complex, but, put simply, it means that the assured must suffer a measurable loss of the type which the insurance covers if the risk insured against occurs. Producing one all-embracing definition of insurable interest has proved elusive,[17] though s 5 of the Marine Insurance Act 1906 is a statutory formulation of the law so far as marine insurance is concerned. Under s 5, a person has an insurable interest if he has a relation to property subject to a marine risk 'in consequence of which he may benefit by the safety or due arrival of insurable property, or may be prejudiced by its loss ... damage [or] detention ... or may incur liability in respect [of it]'.

What may amount to a sufficient relationship to property to found an interest is therefore potentially very wide—extensive use rights may suffice,[18] as well as the more obvious loss if the property is damaged and one owns the property, or where risk in it has passed in a contract for sale. However, while all of these relationships to the property create an interest, it is not necessarily one which the policy in question protects. The interest might be insurable but not actually be insured.

When must the assured have an insurable interest?

Section 6 of the Marine Insurance Act 1906 requires the assured to have an insurable interest normally at the time of the loss, though not necessarily at the time when the insurance is effected.[19]

 Marine Insurance Act 1906, s 6

(1) The assured must be interested in the subject-matter insured at the time of the loss though he need not be interested when the insurance is effected:

Provided that where the subject-matter is insured 'lost or not lost', the assured may recover although he may not have acquired his interest until after the loss, unless at the time of effecting the contract of insurance the assured was aware of the loss, and the insurer was not.

(2) Where the assured has no interest at the time of the loss, he cannot acquire interest by any act or election after he is aware of the loss.

Thus in *Anderson v Morice*,[20] a purchaser of a cargo of rice who had neither property nor risk in it when it was destroyed could not claim on a policy of insurance through lack of insurable interest, even though the policy was acquired before the accident and property in the goods passed to him before the insurance claim was made.

---

16. For a more detailed treatment of insurable interest, see the Online Resource Centre chapter entitled 'Principles of insurance law'.

17. *Feasey v Sun Life Assurance Company of Canada* [2003] EWCA Civ 885, [2003] 2 All ER (Comm) 587 [71] (Waller LJ).

18. *Sharp v Sphere Drake Insurance* [1992] 2 Ll Rep 501.

19. This requirement is repeated in Institute Cargo Clauses, cl 11(1).

20. (1876) 3 Asp MLC 290 (HL).

This rule is modified where the policy is on a 'lost or not lost' basis. Where neither insurer nor assured knows whether a risk has eventuated, cover under a policy can in effect be backdated. For example, a purchaser of goods may insure them immediately before they are loaded on a ship, but the insurance may cover them throughout their transit from the seller's factories, which may have started weeks before.[21] An unusual example of the operation of such a clause can be seen in the following case.

NSW Leather Co Pty Ltd v Vanguard Insurance Co Ltd (1991) FLR 381

FACTS: Under a Fob contract, leather, packed in containers, was insured 'warehouse to warehouse'. Under such a policy the goods become insured once they leave the seller's warehouse on their way to be loaded in the ship. The goods were stolen in transit from the warehouse, that is before risk and property in the goods had passed to the buyer. Vanguard, the insurer, refused to pay on the basis that the assured buyer, NSW Leather, did not have an insurable interest in the goods when the loss occurred.

HELD: The Supreme Court of New South Wales held that although the buyer acquired title to the stolen goods when he paid for them,[22] the 'lost or not lost' basis of the insurance meant that once he had either risk or property in the goods he could claim for losses occurring before he bought the policy,[23] so long as the loss occurred during a period covered by the policy. On this basis, NSW Leather could make a claim under the policy.

A commonly used policy—the Institute Cargo Clauses (ICC)[24]—is written on this basis. Clause 11(2) reads:

> [T]he Assured shall be entitled to recover for insured loss occurring during the period covered by this insurance, notwithstanding that the loss occurred before the contract of insurance was concluded, unless the Assured were aware of the loss and the insurers were not.

What type of loss covered by a marine cargo insurance?

Whilst the concept of interest is very wide, it is clear that the type of loss the assured suffers must be covered by the policy.[25] Consequently, a range of potential interests, though real enough, will not be covered by a marine cargo policy that only covers

---

21. See e.g. *Wünsche Handelsgesellschaft International mbH v Tai Ping Insurance Co Ltd* [1998] 2 Lloyd's Rep 8 (CA).

22. Though note that he had no duty to do so, since the goods were never delivered to him—delivery in a Fob contract is when the goods are loaded in the ship.

23. It would have been different if the goods had been stolen from the warehouse before they started their transit; here the policy would not have been attached to the goods at the time of the loss. See *Fuerst Day Lawson Ltd v Orion Insurance Co Ltd* [1980] 1 Lloyd's Rep 656 (QB).

24. The ICC is the most commonly used policy wording for marine cargo insurance in London, which has around a 20 per cent share of the world marine insurance market. For an explanation of the ICC, see p 590.

25. See the detailed analysis of this issue by Waller LJ in *Feasey v Sun Life Assurance Company of Canada* [2003] EWCA Civ 885, [2003] 2 All ER (Comm) 587.

loss or damage to property. For example, a selling agent will lose commission on the sale of property if the property is destroyed, but this purely financial interest is not insured under a policy that insures loss of or damage to property.[26] Likewise in *NSW Leather v Vanguard Insurance*[27] (discussed earlier), when the empty containers were delivered to the purchaser, he had to determine whether to terminate the contract of sale against the seller for non-delivery of the stolen goods. The Court held that even without the 'lost or not lost' clause, he did have a number of interests in the safe delivery of the leather—for example loss of anticipated profits and financial risk in the seller meeting its obligation—but these were not the types of interest marine cargo insurance covers.[28] The same issues also arose in *Anderson v Morice*,[29] where the purchaser's anticipated profit on resale was certainly recognized by the House of Lords as an interest, but not one protected under a property insurance.

A purchaser who has risk in the goods but not property in them has an insurable interest which is covered by a standard marine insurance policy,[30] as is a purchaser to whom title has passed but whose interest is contingent, for example, on his not rejecting the goods for breach of a condition in the contract of sale.[31] Likewise a purchaser's interest may be defeasible if the seller terminates the contract.[32] Similar issues arise for an unpaid seller who has passed property and possession, and who either recalls the property or has it rejected by the purchaser. This contingent title would found an interest covered under a marine cargo insurance policy if the seller has the benefit of one.[33] If he has not, he may have purchased a separate seller's contingency insurance.

Utmost good faith[34]

What are the duties?

In 1766 in *Carter v Boehm*,[35] Mansfield CJ introduced into the law of insurance an obligation that the parties owe one another a duty of good faith, and this duty is now codified in s 17 of the Marine Insurance Act 1906. The duty principally involves the assured disclosing to the insurer all circumstances which are material to the contract and not misrepresenting any material circumstances. These requirements are now to be found in ss 18 and 20 of the Marine Insurance Act 1906. Section 18(2) states that a circumstance is material and so must be disclosed (or not misrepresented) if it would 'influence the judgment of a prudent insurer in fixing the premium, or determining whether he will take the risk'. It is now established that this involves a

---

26. *Lucena v Craufurd* (1808) 127 ER 858 (HL).

27. *NSW Leather Co Pty Ltd v Vanguard Insurance Co Ltd* (1991) 105 FLR 381.

28. Policies are available to cover such risks. Thus the financial risk involved when one pays for goods before physical delivery can be covered by a performance guarantee.

29. (1876) 1 App Cas 713 (HL).   30. *Inglis v Stock* (1885) 10 App Cas 263 (HL).

31. Marine Insurance Act 1906, s 7.   32. ibid.

33. In a Cif contract, the seller will recover the insurance policy along with the other documents if the seller terminates the contract. In a Fob contract, the purchaser will have taken out the insurance, but the terms of the contract may require the purchaser to take out insurance for both parties' benefit.

34. For a more detailed treatment of utmost good faith, see the Online Resource Centre chapter entitled 'Principles of insurance law'.

35. (1766) 3 Burr 1905.

two-part test.[36] First, looked at objectively, would the hypothetical prudent insurer have taken the circumstance into account in assessing the risk though he need not have thought it decisive? Second, but subjectively this time, was the insurer actually induced to enter into the contract on the terms agreed by the non/mis-disclosure?

This duty of disclosure applies whether the insurer has asked about the circumstance or not. It is a positive duty to volunteer all of the material circumstances, though the insurer may waive his rights to information, for example by being told that certain information is available and not asking to see it.[37] It also does not matter that the material non/mis-disclosure was irrelevant to the cause of the loss for which a claim was being made.[38]

 Marine Insurance Act 1906, ss 17, 18 and 20

Section 17

A contract of marine insurance is a contract based upon the utmost good faith, and, if the utmost good faith be not observed by either party, the contract may be avoided by the other party.

Section 18(1) and (2)

(1) Subject to the provisions of this section, the assured must disclose to the insurer, before the contract is concluded, every material circumstance which is known to the assured, and the assured is deemed to know every circumstance which, in the ordinary course of business, ought to be known by him. If the assured fails to make such disclosure, the insurer may avoid the contract.

(2) Every circumstance is material which would influence the judgment of a prudent insurer in fixing the premium, or determining whether he will take the risk.

Section 20(1), (2) and (3)

(1) Every material representation made by the assured or his agent to the insurer during the negotiations for the contract, and before the contract is concluded, must be true. If it be untrue the insurer may avoid the contract.

(2) A representation is material which would influence the judgment of a prudent insurer in fixing the premium, or determining whether he will take the risk.

(3) A representation may be either a representation as to a matter of fact, or as to a matter of expectation or belief.

---

36. *Pan Atlantic Insurance Co Ltd v Pine Top Insurance Ltd* [1995] 1 AC 501 (HL).

37. ibid. In personal and small business insurance, insurers have voluntarily agreed not to treat as non-disclosure any circumstances about which they have not asked a question on the proposal form.

38. Thus in *Banque Financiere de la Cite SA v Westgate Insurance Co Ltd* [1990] 2 Lloyd's Rep 377 (HL), no point was taken that the fraud that the insured's employee had committed and which the insurers had not disclosed to the insured had nothing to do with the cause of the loss. The case also illustrates that the duty of disclosure is mutual by virtue of s 17.

Though it is clear that the s 18 and s 20 duties do not extend beyond the pre-contractual period, there is some debate[39] on the issue whether and in what form the s 17 duty of good faith might so extend. Some decisions proceed on the basis that the principles involving material circumstances do apply, suitably adapted, especially at 'decision points' where the insurer has to decide, for example, whether to charge more for cover because the assured has changed the destination of goods in transit.[40]

It is clear, however, that making a dishonest claim, for example claiming for a loss which has never happened or exaggerating the size of a loss,[41] or by faking evidence,[42] even if the claim is perfectly valid, in order to improve your chances of getting a good settlement, will invalidate the claim.[43]

What needs to be disclosed?

The types of circumstance which a prudent underwriter will take into account fall into two main classes: physical and moral hazards. Mance J described it thus:

> It is important to realize what is embraced by 'risk'. It is not simply the peril or possibility of loss or damage occurring within the scope of the policy. It embraces other matters which would, if known, be likely to influence a prudent underwriter's decision. It includes what is known as 'moral hazard', which may merely increase the likelihood of it being made to appear (falsely) that loss or damage has occurred falling within the scope of the policy.[44]

Physical hazards therefore involve not only the description of the goods, whether they are deck cargo and whether they were containerized or not,[45] but also how many claims the assured has brought in the past under previous policies. Moral hazard usually involves matters about the assured. Thus insurers will regard as material that insurance has been declined by another insurer,[46] or that the assured has been the subject of serious and plausible allegations of fraud, even if they turn out to be false.[47]

---

39. See e.g. *Manifest Shipping Co Ltd v Uni-Polaris Shipping Co Ltd (The Star Sea)* [2001] UKHL 1, [2003] 1 AC 469. Compare this with *Black King Shipping Corporation v Massie, 'Litsion Pride'* [1985] 1 Lloyd's Rep 437 (QB).

40. *Fraser Shipping Ltd v Colson* [1997] 1 Lloyd's Rep 360 (CA). See especially Potter LJ at 370.

41. *Goulstone v Royal Insurance Company* (1858) 1 F&F 276.

42. But see *K/S Merc-Scandia XXXXII v Lloyd's Underwriters (The Mercandian Continent)* [2001] EWCA Civ 1275, [2001] 2 Lloyd's Rep 563, where the Court of Appeal held that the fraud would have to be such as to amount to a repudiatory breach such that the insurer would have been entitled to terminate the contract on normal contractual principles quite apart from the issue of utmost good faith.

43. *Agapitos v Agnew* [2002] EWCA Civ 247 [2003] QB 556 (CA).

44. *Insurance Corp of the Channel Islands v Royal Hotel Ltd* [1998] Lloyd's Rep IR 151 (QB) 156.

45. See *Wünsche Handelsgesellschaft International mbH v Tai Ping Insurance Co Ltd* [1998] 2 Lloyd's Rep 8 (CA), where the Court concluded that the description of the goods at loading as containerized did not imply in the circumstances of the case (the insurance attached at the commencement of transit from inland factories) that they would be containerized throughout the insured transit.

46. *Container Transport International Inc v Oceanus Mutual Underwriting Association (Bermuda)* [1984] 1 Lloyd's Rep 476 (CA). Though see *Glasgow Assurance Corp Ltd v Symondson & Co* (1911) 104 LT (KB).

47. *Brotherton v Aseguradora Colseguros SA* [2003] 2 All ER (Comm) 298 (CA). *North Star Shipping Ltd and Others v Sphere Drake Insurance plc* [2006] EWCA Civ 378, [2006] 2 All ER (Comm) 65.

What is the effect of material non-disclosure?

Section 17 of the Marine Insurance Act 1906 makes it clear that the remedy for pre-contractual material non-disclosure is avoidance of the policy *ab initio*, and it has been held that there is no alternative such as a claim for damages either in contract or in tort for the breach of the duty of good faith.[48] Under a void policy, the premium must be returned to the assured, so too any claims previously paid under the insurance must be returned to the insurer. In relation to post-contract non-disclosure at 'decision points', it seems likely that it is merely the variation in the policy that the non/mis-disclosure induced which is avoided *ab initio*, though the whole policy can be terminated on normal contractual principles if the assured's actions amount to a breach of a condition.[49]

A dishonest claim will be avoided and the policy terminated, but it is not avoided *ab initio*.[50] Consequently, under the insurance 'fraudulent claims' rule, only the fraudulent claim itself will be lost. Mance LJ in *Gottlieb*[51] left open the issue whether honest claims being pursued in parallel to the dishonest one but which were not actually paid at the date of the fraud will also be lost on the basis that the insurer has terminated the contract for breach of a condition. However, it is clear that any payments already made in respect of honest claims may be retained by the assured.[52]

Elements of marine cargo insurance: causation[53]

Consider the following example.

 ComCorp Ltd

ComCorp has an insurance policy which insures it against losses to goods caused by 'collision or contact of the ship with any external object' but not against losses from seizure or attempted seizure by pirates nor for 'entry of sea water into the ship'. The ship is pursued by pirates and hits a rock, water enters the ship, and damages the goods. ComCorp wants to know whether it can claim on the insurance.

Marine cargo insurance provides indemnity for losses caused by an insured risk. This seems straightforward enough, but a brief consideration of this ComCorp scenario demonstrates that it is not. The water was the direct cause of the damage but it

---

48. *Banque Financière de la Cite SA v Westgate Insurance Co Ltd* [1990] 2 Lloyd's Rep 377 (HL).

49. See Longmore LJ in *K/S Merc-Scandia XXXXII v Lloyd's Underwriters (The Mercandian Continent)* [2001] EWCA Civ 1275, [2001] 2 Lloyd's Rep 563.

50. *Manifest Shipping Co Ltd v Uni-Polaris Shipping Co Ltd (The Star Sea)* [2001] UKHL 1, [2003] 1 AC 469.

51. *Axa General Insurance Ltd v Gottlieb* [2005] EWCA Civ 112, [2005] 1 All ER (Comm) 445.

52. ibid.

53. For a more detailed treatment of causation, see the Online Resource Centre chapter entitled 'Principles of insurance law'.

entered the ship because of hitting the rock, but the ship hit the rock because of the pirates. What the court looks for is the 'proximate cause' of the loss, but until the end of the nineteenth century this was normally treated as the last cause operating in time—the water in our example—so that on this basis, ComCorp's claim would have failed. However, it was finally accepted by the House of Lords in *Leyland Shipping v Norwich Union Fire Insurance Society Ltd*[54] that, while from Aristotle[55] onwards, philosophers had argued about what might cause an event, for legal purposes the proximate cause is not necessarily the closest in time to the loss, but is the 'real cause', the 'predominant' cause, or the 'effective' cause.[56] But are we much further forward with this formulation, in particular by what criteria is the reality predominance or efficiency of the causes to be assessed?

In *Noten v Harding*,[57] in the process of deciding whether the damage to goods was caused by the goods themselves or by an external cause Bingham LJ asked: '[W]hat was the real or dominant cause of that damage? Unchallenged and unchallengeable authority shows that this is a question to be answered applying the common sense of a business or seafaring man.' [58] But as he then remarked 'the parties to the appeal put different answers into the mouth of this hypothetical oracle'. The Court decided unanimously that the proximate cause was the moisture in the gloves—they had damaged themselves—but exactly the opposite conclusion had been reached in an almost identical case sixty years earlier.[59]

In what follows in this chapter the word 'cause' is used many times, and it is important to note that this refers to the 'proximate cause' .

Elements of marine cargo insurance: claims

Burden of proof

The issue of the burden of proof in a claim can be complex. Many of the problems that used to arise were in the context of proving that the loss was caused by 'perils of the sea', fortunately a term no longer used in the industry standard insurance policy—the ICC. However, unless the ICC policy is issued on an all risks basis, the assured will have to prove that the loss was caused on the balance of probabilities[60] by an insured peril, that is to say a cause of loss which is covered by the policy. Typically, this will be done by establishing a *prima facie* case, leaving it to the insurer to disprove it (i.e. by showing a more likely (and uninsured) cause of the loss, or by

---

54. [1918] AC 350 (HL).

55. See William Charlton, *Aristotle Physics Books I and II* (Clarendon Press 1983) 193.

56. *Leyland Shipping v Norwich Union Fire Insurance Society Ltd* [1918] AC 350 (HL) 369 (Lord Shaw).

57. *TM Noten BV v Harding* [1990] Lloyd's Rep 283 (CA).

58. ibid 288. For a more detailed consideration of the issues, see p 599.

59. *CT Bowring & Co Ltd v Amsterdam London Insurance Co* (1930) 36 Ll LR 309.

60. *Rhesa Shipping Co SA v Edmunds ('The Popi M')* [1985] 2 Lloyd's Rep 1 (HL).

demonstrating that any of the exceptions contained in the policy apply). However, proving a likely cause for accidents at sea can be difficult.[61]

Where the insurance covers loss or damage to goods from any cause, however, the assured may find his task comparatively easy; he need only give evidence plausibly, showing that the loss was due to an accident; he does not need to show exactly how his loss was caused.[62] The insurer must then prove (on the balance) that what caused the loss was excluded under the policy.

A number of further issues relating to the burden of proof are dealt with later in this chapter.

Title to the policy

A claimant under a policy must have title to that policy either because he was the original assured or because the benefit of the contract has passed to him, for example through assignment. He must also, of course, have an insurable interest in the policy. Section 15 of the Marine Insurance Act 1906 states that simply selling or otherwise parting with an interest in the goods does not automatically transfer the rights under a policy insuring those goods. Consequently, there must be an assignment of the benefit of the policy, in the absence of which, unless the seller of the goods has become a trustee of the policy for the purchaser of the goods, neither seller nor buyer can claim under the policy in respect of losses occurring after risk and property in the goods have passed to the buyer.[63] However, by virtue of s 50(3), a policy may be 'assigned by indorsement thereon or in other customary manner' so that in a documentary sale like Cif, the custom is that simple delivery of the policy is sufficient to assign it to a purchaser of the goods to which it relates. Section 50(2) makes it clear that the assignee gets no better title than the assignor had and is subject to the same defences as might have been raised against the original assured.

🔗 See p 598 for an example of the problems that s 50(2) can cause to an innocent assignee

Finally, although normally the assured must have an insurable interest under the policy at the time of the loss, this does not apply where he acquires title to the policy after the loss, so long as a predecessor in title had such an interest at the relevant time.[64] Were this not so, then a purchaser of goods afloat under a Cif contract would be unable to claim in respect of losses occurring before the assignment.

The Institute Cargo Clauses

As noted earlier, an insurance policy indemnifies the assured against loss caused by an insured risk. What risks an insurer is prepared to cover in a policy depends on the insurer, but to a great extent insurance practice throughout the world as to

---

61. See *Compania Martiartu v Royal Exchange Assurance Corporation (The Arnus)* [1923] 1 KB (CA) for an example where the courts relied on 'unknown perils of the sea' as a cause. This is an advantage to an assured where the policy specifically covers perils of the sea, but where it lists causes without using this generic term, then the assured will also have to prove that his loss was not inexplicable. See *The Popi M* [1985] 2 Lloyd's Rep 1 (HL).
62. See Lord Sumner in *British and Foreign Marine Insurance Company Limited v Gaunt* [1921] 2 AC 41 (HL).
63. *Powles v Innes* (1843) 11 M&W 10. The seller has no insurable interests and the buyer no right to sue.
64. Marine Insurance Act 1906, s 50.

coverage has been heavily influenced by London practice, particularly that of the Lloyds underwriting market. The influence of Lloyds is so great that the schedule to the Marine Insurance Act 1906 includes the standard Lloyds of London insurance market policy, current in 1906 for loss to ships and goods in respect of 'marine perils'. Known as the 'SG' (ships and goods) policy, it had first been adopted in 1779 and was itself a revised version of earlier forms. The Institute of London Underwriters formulated its replacement, the Lloyds Marine Policy, and the SG policy was finally withdrawn on 31 March 1982.

The Lloyds Marine Policy consists of a schedule identifying the matters specific to the particular insurance, for example the identity of the assured and of the subject matter of the insurance, the sum insured, the premium and so forth, to which standard clauses and indorsements are added. Those relevant to cargo insurance are the Institute Cargo Clauses A, B, and C (ICC(A), ICC(B), and ICC(C), respectively), which were revised with effect from January 2009 primarily in order effect an updating in terminology, though the effect of some of the terms has changed slightly from the 1982 edition. Each set of clauses covers different risks, from the narrowest coverage (ICC(C)) to the widest (ICC(A)), and these differences are reflected in the price payable (called the 'premium')—the fewer risks that the insurer accepts, the lower the premium. Each of the clauses is subject to a set of common exceptions.[65]

Whilst the forms of policy adopted by Lloyds are not always used by other providers of marine insurance, these forms are typical and provide a sound basis for understanding the coverage provided by a policy of marine cargo insurance. Consequently, the remainder of this chapter will be dedicated to dealing with the Institute Cargo Clauses. The coverage of each clause will be dealt with in turn, starting from the narrowest level of cover and building up, followed by consideration of the exclusions and the other terms of the insurance which are common to all three clauses.

Institute Cargo Clause C: cover

The 'SG' policy, covered loss caused by 'maritime perils', defined in s 3 of the Marine Insurance Act 1906 as:

> the perils consequent on, or incidental to, the navigation of the sea, that is to say, perils of the seas, fire, war perils, pirates, rovers, thieves, captures, seisures, restraints, and detainments of princes and peoples, jettisons, barratry, and any other perils, either of the like kind or which may be designated by the policy.

There is a wealth of authority relating to the meaning of 'perils of the seas' and 'maritime perils', but neither term is used in the ICC. Instead, coverage extends to 'loss of or damage to the subject-matter insured reasonably attributable to' a list of specific perils. Incidentally, all of the risks covered by ICC(C) are also covered in ICC(B), so that in this section references to ICC(C) also apply to ICC(B).

Each of the listed risks are now considered in turn.

---

65. In fact, ICC(B) and (C) have an exception which does not apply to ICC(A)—deliberate damage or destruction of the goods—ICC 4.7.

Fire or explosion[66]

In fact, fire was never regarded as a peril of the sea;[67] after all, a fire can as well start on land as on a ship, but it was always a named peril in cargo insurance. Loss or damage caused by fire extends to loss or damage by smoke[68] or heating if it emanates from a fire and to loss caused by preventative measures, for example from water used to put out a fire, or by goods being thrown into the sea in order to create a fire break.[69] It should be noted that in neither *The Diamond* nor *Symington* were any of the goods burnt; the immediate cause of the loss was smoke, water, or jettison. The cover extends to loss even where the fire is started deliberately.[70]

It should be remembered here, as with all of the other risks discussed in this chapter, that the risk must not simply be involved in the loss, but must be its proximate cause if any claim is to be made. In relation to claims for loss caused by fire, the facts of *The Knights of St Michael*[71] are instructive. Here, a cargo of coal bound for Chile began to heat and would have spontaneously combusted had the captain not unloaded it in Sydney. Although *prima facie* the shipper could have claimed on his cargo insurance for the extra costs he would incur in transporting the goods from Australia to Chile, which risk is covered by ICC cl 12, he would have almost certainly have been met by the defence that the loss was proximately caused by the natural propensity of the coal to self-combust, known as inherent vice, and not by fire per se.[72]

🔗 On inherent vice see p 599

Stranding, grounding, sinking, or capsize of the ship[73]

'Stranding' means running aground; merely striking a rock and remaining stuck for a little over a minute is not a stranding.[74] A stranding necessarily involves an accident; grounding need not as, where a ship is moored so that as it falls with the tide, it rests on the sea or river bed and *prima facie* only loss reasonably attributable to fortuitous grounding is covered.[75] However, in *The Lapwing*,[76] it was held that where the vessel came to rest on the bottom through the negligence of the captain, this was a stranding, so the issue of fortuity may in practice be unimportant. Although not true under the SG policy, under ICC(C) there must be a causal link between the stranding of the vessel and the loss.[77]

There is little authority on the meaning of sinking and capsize, and it would appear that the terms are to be given their normal dictionary definitions.[78] Thus in *Bryant and May v London Assurance*[79] the ship was so low in the water on arrival that, although floating, sea water was washing over the decks. In a case like this, the cargo

---

66. ICC(B) and (C), cl 1.1.1.

67. See e.g. *Schiffshypothekenbank Zu Luebeck AG v Norman Philip Compton (The Alexion Hope)* [1988] 1 Lloyd's Rep 311 (CA) 316 (Lord Lloyd).

68. *The Diamond* [1906] P 282 (PDA).

69. *Symington & Co v Union Insurance Society of Canton Ltd* [1928] All ER Rep 346 (CA).

70. *Gordon v Rimmington* (1807) 1 Camp 123.   71. [1898] P 30 (PDA).

72. ICC cl 12 is also subject to a defence that the loss was caused by the insured's fault and not notifying the carrier of the characteristics of the quality of coal carried may well amount to fault.

73. ICC(B) and (C), cl 1.1.2.

74. *M'Dougle v Royal Exchange Assurance Co* (1816) 4 Camp 283.

75. *Magnus v Buttemer* (1852) 11 CB 876.   76. [1940] P 112 (PDA).

77. Cl 1.1 requires that the loss be 'reasonably attributable' to the insured risk.

78. *Bryant and May v London Assurance Corporation* (1866) 2 TLR 591.   79. ibid.

owner could not have relied on sinking as a cause and would probably have failed to recover under an ICC(C) policy.

Overturning or derailment of land conveyance[80]

Clause 8 of the policy extends cover 'warehouse to warehouse', so that loss arising from insured risks while in transit on land to a ship from a warehouse or vice versa is also covered.

Collision or contact of vessel craft or conveyance with any external object other than water[81]

The normal situation is where the exterior of the ship (or, for example, lorry since it is a 'conveyance') collides with the object; however, the word 'contact' has a wider meaning and extends beyond physical contact; for example, it includes a magnetic or acoustic contact with a mine.[82]

Discharge of cargo at a port of distress[83]

If a ship is damaged while at sea and has to be repaired or to have its cargo re-stowed because the cargo has shifted before it can safely proceed, it will put into a port of distress (or refuge). Additional costs which the shipper suffers because of this are covered.[84] Typically, these will relate to general average, but loss from this cause is specifically covered in cl 4.5.

General average sacrifice[85] and general average contribution[86]

In a sea voyage three interests may be at risk: the shipper's interest in the cargo; the shipowner's interest in the ship; and, if different, the carrier's interest in freight charges. In consequence, they are in a sense involved in a 'common marine adventure'. Suppose that the ship encounters a storm and in order to save it (along with its cargo), some of the cargo is sacrificed by being thrown overboard and the carrier incurs expenditure in engaging a tug to tow the ship to safety. Clearly, there has been a loss and expenditure which was for the good of all the parties and the law requires all the benefited parties to contribute.[87]

Under s 66(2) of the Marine Insurance Act 1906, for the sacrifice or expenditure to attract general average, they must have been extraordinary, voluntarily, and reasonably made, and in a time of danger for the purpose of preserving the property of at least two parties. This definition is also used in the York Antwerp[88] Rules on

---

80. ICC(B) and (C), cl 1.1.3.   81. ibid cl 1.1.4.

82. *Costain-Blankevoort (UK) Dredging Co Ltd v Davenport (Inspector of Taxes) (The Nassau Bay)* [1979] 1 Lloyd's Rep 395 (QB), though such a cause would be excluded by ICC(B) and (C), cl 6(3) unless Institute War Clauses (Cargo) 1/1/09 applied.

83. ICC(B) and (C), cl 1.1.5.

84. But not loss caused by delay, ICC(B) and (C), cl 4(5) save in connection with expenses incurred in general average.

85. ICC(B) and (C), cl 1.2.1.   86. ibid cl 2.

87. Calculation is notoriously lengthy and complicated, but the general principles are set out in the York Antwerp Rules, Rule XVII.

88. The York Antwerp Rules actually use 'intentionally', not 'voluntarily', but there is no difference in meaning. Technically the costs of salvage, which are also shared, are not part of 'general average' under the Marine Insurance Act 1906, but the distinction becomes unimportant if the York Antwerp Rules have been incorporated into the contract of carriage.

general average, which will typically be incorporated into a contract of carriage of goods by sea and which will therefore require the shipper to make a contribution to the carrier or to a fellow cargo owner.

Clause 1.2.2 of the ICC(C) covers the loss through general average sacrifice (that is, where the assured's goods have been sacrificed), while cl 2 covers loss for general average contribution where the assured is required to contribute to the other's sacrifice or expenditure as required either by the contract or the applicable law. Clause 2 does not cover general average contributions in respect of risks specifically excluded by the policy, other than for loss through delay.[89]

Under s 66(4) of the Marine Insurance Act 1906, in the case of a general average sacrifice, the assured may 'recover in respect of the whole loss without having enforced his right of contribution from the other parties liable to contribute'.

Jettison[90]

Jettison is the intentional casting of property into the sea for good reason. This may be through general average sacrifice in order to save the ship and the remainder of its cargo, or, as in *Taylor v Dunbar*,[91] because the goods (in this case unrefrigerated meat) had become putrid. In *Taylor*, the assured failed to recover under his SG policy, because the court held that the cause of the loss was delay—the same would be true under any of the ICC clauses.

Institute Cargo Clause B: cover

ICC(B) covers all of the causes of loss included in ICC(C) but also covers the additional risks outlined in the paragraphs that follow.

Washing overboard[92]

Although this requires no particular explanation, it is clearly important to have the benefit of such cover where cargo may or will be carried on deck.

Entry of sea lake or river water into vessel craft hold conveyance container or place of storage[93]

First, it should be noted that there is no cover for loss caused by rainwater entry, so that, for example, the cargo owners in *The Canadian Highlander*[94] could have made no claim under a policy in the form of ICC(B). Second, this clause makes provision for recovery under the policy even if it happens on land, so long as the insurance has attached to the goods. Finally, the loss may not be confined to the wetted goods themselves but to other goods which may be affected where that wetting has caused damage.[95]

---

89. ICC(B) and (C), cl 4.5.   90. ICC(B) and (C), cl 1.2.2.   91. (1869) LR 4 CP 206.
92. ICC(B), cl 1.2.2.   93. ICC(B), cl 1.2.3.
94. *Gosse Millard Limited v Canadian Government Merchant Marine Limited (The Canadian Highlander)* [1929] AC 223 (HL) discussed on p 571.
95. *Montoya v London Assurance Co* [1851] 6 Exch 451 (wetted hides gave off a rancid smell, which damaged the flavour of tobacco stored in the hold).

Total loss of any package lost overboard or dropped whilst loading or unloading the ship[96]

It should be noted that this cover extends only to loading and unloading the ship, and does not cover **constructive total loss**. The clause would, for example, have covered the loss in *The Stranna*,[97] where, due to negligent loading of a deck cargo of timber, the ship suddenly heeled over, the wood fell into the water, and floated away, thus causing a total loss.

→ constructive total loss: occurs when insured property is so damaged or positioned that the cost of repair or recovery exceeds the goods' value once repaired or recovered

Institute Cargo Clause A: cover

ICC(A) is an 'all risks policy'—this does not mean it covers all losses, but loss and damage to the goods from all causes. It is therefore unlikely that an all risks policy would cover the loss in *Cator*,[98] where the goods were physically undamaged but lost value because water had entered the ship, causing fear amongst potential purchasers that there was damage to the goods.

British and Foreign Marine Insurance Co Ltd v Gaunt [1921] 2 AC 41 (HL)

FACTS: Gaunt, the assured, bought some wool Fob and insured it for loss under an all risks policy from 'the sheep's back' to his mill in Yorkshire. The wool was damaged by water while being stored and then transported on the decks of small ships for final shipment at a major port, where it arrived wet.

HELD: 'All risks' did not cover all damage, but covered all losses by any accidental cause of any kind occurring during the transit, i.e. a loss not caused by the natural behaviour of the goods. The burden of proof to show there was an accidental cause and one not arising because of the nature of the goods was on the assured. But in an all risks policy the assured does not need to prove the exact nature of the accident which caused the loss, simply that the damage would not be expected to occur in the course of a normal transit. In this case, he had shown that the loss must have been due to some accident and therefore could claim on the policy.

COMMENT: Some of the terminology used by the House in this case is concerned with ensuring that 'all risks' did not cover loss caused by what is called 'inherent vice' or otherwise only covered things that were not inevitable to happen. These issues have recently been reconsidered by the Supreme Court (see 'Clause 4(4): Loss damage or expense caused by inherent vice or nature of the subject matter insured' on p 599). The ICC expressly exclude inherent vice and a number of other risks, raising the question whether, in proving the loss is covered by the policy by elimination, as was suggested in *Gaunt*, the assured needs to eliminate the likelihood of loss from these exempted causes. It is clear that there could have been no claim under ICC(C) and a real problem under ICC(B), because there was no evidence whether the wetting was from fresh or seawater. The case is also an interesting illustration of rule 17 of the rules for construction of insurance policies

---

96. ICC(B), cl 1.3.
97. [1938] 1 All ER 458 (CA).
98. *Cator v Great Western Insurance Co of New York* (1873) 8 LR 8 CP 552.

> in the Schedule to the Marine Insurance Act 1906, which states that unless there is a usage to the contrary, the assured must declare to the insurer that goods will be carried on deck. In *Gaunt,* the House decided that the 'usage' in question was the usage in the particular trade, and since here carriage on deck was normal, the insurer should have been aware of it and so could not rely on non-disclosure of the fact, though normally this would be a material circumstance.

As *Gaunt* demonstrates, all risks insurance, as with other property insurance, does not cover inevitable loss, commonly expressed as the rule that insurance covers risk, not certainty. Consequently, if the assured cannot prove the likely cause of the loss, then he must eliminate inevitable loss. For example, in *Fuerst Day Lawson Ltd v Orion Insurance Co Ltd,*[99] the assured agreed to buy barrels of 'essential oils', risk and title to the barrels passing on loading. On arrival in England it was discovered the oil in the barrels had been removed and replaced with water. The assured could not prove that the substitution took place after title or risk passed. Consequently, although the cause of loss (theft) was covered by the policy, on the likely facts, the actual loss was inevitable.[100] Similarly, in *Coven SPA v Hong Kong Chinese Insurance,*[101] a cargo of 2,800 tonnes of beans was insured against 'All Risks…including shortage in weight'. By accident, only 2,400 tonnes were loaded. The Court of Appeal held that there must be a loss of or damage to the goods: 'all risks property insurance does not insure against a "paper loss" like this'.[102]

The issue of insurance covering risk of loss, not certainty of loss, is reflected in many of the exclusions under the ICC, which are covered in the next section.

Exclusions

There is a set of excluded causes of loss which is common to ICC(A), (B), and (C). As has been discussed, in order to make a successful claim, the burden of proof is on the assured to show that the loss was proximately caused by an insured risk. Once this has been done, the insurer must pay unless he can show that the loss was caused by one of the excluded risks. Suppose, for example, that the shipper wishes to send delicate goods by sea. The goods arrive damaged because of the movement of the ship in a storm. If the shipper has either cover on an ICC(B) or (C) basis, the cause of the loss is not an insured risk, but ICC(A) insures all risks, so *prima facie* the loss is covered by the policy. However, cl 4.3 of the ICC(A) excludes loss caused by insufficiency of packaging. The shipper can show the damage was a fortuity—an accident caused by the storm—so under *Gaunt* he will be successful unless the insurer can show the cause of the loss was insufficient packing.

The main exclusions are dealt with in the following sections.

---

99. [1980] 1 Lloyd's Rep 656 (QB).
100. This case can also be explained by the fact the insured property—the oil—probably never started on the journey from the warehouse (where cover commenced) to England, therefore at no time was the oil insured under the policy so there was no attachment of the policy. See ICC 8 at p **607**.
101. [1999] Lloyd's Rep IR 565 (QB).
102. But see *NSW Leather Co Pty v Vanguard Insurance Co Ltd* (1991) 105 FLR 381 (discussed on p 584).

Clause 4(1): Loss damage or expense attributable to wilful misconduct of the assured

This exclusion repeats s 55(2) of the Marine Insurance Act 1906 and in fact can be regarded as an example of the 'risk not certainty' rule,[103] and, more obviously, that a person cannot benefit from his own wrongful act. It should be noted that the wrongful act is in making the insurance claim, not the wilful default itself. Thus setting to sea in an unseaworthy ship is not necessarily wrongful, but making a claim based on a loss caused by that unseaworthiness is.[104]

The mental state to found a defence of wilful misconduct is something far beyond even gross negligence.[105] It requires a person intentionally or with reckless carelessness or indifference, doing or persisting in doing something which he appreciates will probably cause loss. A person acts with reckless carelessness if he is aware of a risk that goods may be lost or damaged, but deliberately goes ahead and takes the risk, knowing that it is unreasonable for him to do so.[106] The insurance cases on wilful misconduct in the main involve wilful misconduct of a shipowner claiming on hull and machinery insurance, and the obvious examples where a cargo owner might be guilty of wilful misconduct, such as deliberately not packing the goods adequately or sending them on a ship which he knows to be unseaworthy, are dealt with by specific exclusions. Nevertheless, some appreciation of the issues can be gleaned from some of the shipowner cases.

A key issue is that, although the insurer must show that the assured either procured the loss or was recklessly indifferent whether it occurred and then presented an insurance claim, he does not need to show that the loss was incurred in order to make a claim.[107] The fact that a voyage may be risky is not enough to prove wilful default,[108] but setting out on the basis that any loss insured may be evidence of such a state of mind.[109]

 Wood v Associated National Insurance Co Ltd [1984] 1 Qd R 297

FACTS: The insured vessel needed repair and was moored in a dangerous location for the anticipated weather conditions. The crew was very inexperienced, though the skipper was competent. The boat was repaired and the skipper, Wood, who was also the owner and the assured, went ashore and increased the insurance on her, as the repairs had increased her value. He did not return, though he could have done, and two days later a storm which had been forecast sank the boat; the young crew members were

103. See *Wood v Associated National Insurance Co Ltd* [1985] 1 Qd R 297, 305 (McPherson J).

104. *Thompson v Hopper* (1856) 6 E&B 937.

105. *National Oil Well (UK) Ltd v Davy Offshore Ltd* [1993] 2 Lloyd's Rep 582 (QB).

106. See Creswell J in *Thomas Cook Group Ltd v Air Malta Co Ltd* [1997] 2 Lloyd's Rep 399 (QB)—a case involving road carrier's liability. The formulation in the text is based on Lord Alverstone's definition in *Forder v Great Western Railway Co* [1905] KB 532 (KB) 535, involving a railway carrier's liability.

107. *National Oil Well (UK) Ltd v Davy Offshore Ltd* [1993] 2 Lloyd's Rep 582 (QB).

108. *Papadimitriou v Henderson* [1939] 3 All ER 908 (KB).

109. *Wood v Associated National Insurance Co Ltd* [1984] 1 Qd R 297.

> nearly drowned. The insurer refused to pay on the grounds that the cause of the loss was Wood's wilful misconduct.
>
> **HELD:** The Queensland Court of Appeal held that Wood's acts amounted to wilful misconduct by the vessel's owners; he had exposed the vessel to danger knowing she was in no condition to encounter them and indifferent to the risk that she would not survive them.
>
> **COMMENT:** The Court both at first instance and on appeal found evidence of reckless indifference to loss on the basis that this was a not a risk that an uninsured owner would have run. Certainly, this is a point of distinction between *Wood*[110] and *Papadimitriou*,[111] where the Court (in early 1939) clearly did not want to dissuade vessels from entering potential war zones by voiding their insurance claims. The impact of insurance on the mind of the assured as a factor the court may take into account in assessing wilful misconduct has a long pedigree. Thus in *Thompson v Hopper*,[112] Wiles J (in the minority) found for the assured partially on the basis that '[t]here is not a tittle of evidence that the vessel was sent out with any sinister intention, or that the risk to which she was exposed was not one which a shipowner uninsured might run in good faith to expedite a profitable enterprise'.[113]

Consequently, adapting *Wood*, we might imagine a case involving cargo insurance where the shipper, knowing of all of the circumstances, causes the skipper not to return to his vessel. In such a case, he may well be guilty of wilful misconduct.

While it seems entirely correct that where a loss has been caused by the reckless indifference or worse of the assured, the position is less obvious when the claimant on the policy was not the original assured. Again, we must rely on material from insurances on ships rather than on cargo. In *The Ionna*,[114] a ship was insured by the owner, who then mortgaged it and the insurance policy to the claimant, who had lent him the money to buy the ship. The ship was **scuttled** by the owner and the insurers successfully resisted the claim on the grounds of wilful misconduct of the assured. Technically this is correct—mortgages of policies are effected by assignment and an assignee can have no better claim than the assignor and, though harsh, this would appear to apply equally where a cargo policy is assigned by way of sale along with the goods as in a Cif contract.

➡ scuttling: the deliberate and wrongful sinking of a ship with or without the connivance of the owner

Clause 4(2): Loss caused by ordinary leakage, loss in weight or volume, or wear and tear to the goods[115]

This exception is an amplified and amended version of s 55(2) of the Marine Insurance Act 1906, and is also another example of the fact that only losses which are fortuities, not certainties, are insured. Examples of losses excluded by this exception include losses in the weight of cargoes caused by sweating, where there is a loss of water content through evaporation. Similarly, changes in temperature

---

110. ibid.   111. *Papadimitriou v Henderson* [1939] 3 All ER 908 (KB).
112. (1856) 6 E&B 937.   113. ibid 1049–50.
114. *Graham Joint Stock Shipping Co Ltd v Merchants' Marine Insurance Co ('The 'Ionna')* [1924] AC 294 (HL). For a more recent example, see *Continental Illinois National Bank & Trust Co of Chicago v Alliance Assurance Co Ltd ('The Captain Panagos DP')* [1989] 1 Lloyd's Rep 33 (CA).
115. Note that damage to goods from leakage from other goods is not covered under either ICC(B) or (C), but is covered under ICC(A).

may significantly reduce volumes,[116] while settlement of bulk grain cargoes, even after trimming, can have the same effect. Finally, a proportion of oil and fats that are transported in tanks may stick to the walls or to the pipelines and can never be recovered. Leakage is less of an issue nowadays than when liquid cargo was transported in wooden barrels, but the exclusion would apply to any ordinary seepage of liquid through the walls of its container.

Each of these examples concern losses which arise without any accident occurring and which are consequently uninsured. However, the exclusion does not extend beyond the 'ordinary', that is to say that which would be anticipated in the nature of things. As Lord Mance said in *The Cendor Mopu*,[117] 'ordinary wear and tear and ordinary leakage and breakage would thus cover loss or damage resulting from the normal vicissitudes…of handling and carriage…without any fortuitous external accident or casualty'.[118]

Clause 4(3): Loss damage or expense caused by insufficiency or unsuitability of packing

Using the terminology of the clause, the packing and preparation of the goods must be such as to enable them to 'withstand the ordinary incidents of the insured transit'—yet again another example of exclusion of loss which is an inevitable result of the transit.

Damage or loss to the goods is an obvious result of insufficient packing, but as in *Berk & Co v Style*,[119] the cost of repacking inadequately bagged goods would also be irrecoverable. However, the clause only excepts loss where the packing is carried out by the assured or his employees (not sub-contractors) or before attachment of the insurance. Attachment occurs when the goods become subject to the insurance. So in a 'warehouse to warehouse' insurance, the policy attaches once the goods leave the warehouse on their way to the ship.

Clause 4(4): Loss damage or expense caused by inherent vice or nature of the subject matter insured

This exclusion, too, is an example of 'risk not certainty' and derives from s 55(2)(c) of the Marine Insurance Act 1906. The classic definition of inherent vice was given by Lord Diplock in *Soya v White*,[120] where he said: '[i]t means the risk of deterioration of the goods shipped as a result of their natural behaviour in the ordinary course of the contemplated voyage without the intervention of any fortuitous external accident or casualty.'[121] In that case the cargo—soya beans—'sweated' because by their nature internal biological processes took place which caused heat to build up and evaporate moisture in the beans, a clear example of inherent vice. That the cause of the loss must not be an 'external' to the goods was considered in the following case.

---

116. An unsuccessful defence in *De Monchy v Phoenix Insurance Co of Hartford* (1929) 34 Ll L Rep 201 (HL).

117. *Global Process Systems Inc v Syarikat Takaful Malaysia Bhd (The Cendor Mopu)* [2011] UKSC 5, [2011] 1 All ER 869.

118. ibid [81].   119. [1955] 1 QB (QB).

120. *Soya GmbH Mainz Kommanditgesellschaft v White* [1983] 1 Lloyd's Rep 122 (HL)

121. ibid 126. In fact, the insurance excluded sweating from the exclusion.

TM Noten BV v Harding [1992] 2 Lloyd's Rep 283 (CA)

FACTS: Leather gloves were loaded in the moisture-laden atmosphere of Calcutta and during the voyage to Rotterdam gave off moisture which condensed on the roof of the container they were stored in and 'rained' on the gloves, ruining them.

HELD: The Court of Appeal held that the proximate cause of the loss was the gloves themselves and was not an external cause, that is from inherent vice. In the process the Court cast doubt on a first instance decision to the contrary, *Bowring v Amsterdam*,[122] which focussed on the fact that the 'rain' was external to the goods, though it emanated from them.

COMMENT: *Bowring v Amsterdam* may be distinguishable on the ground that in that case the goods were not containerized, so it was not inevitable that, if they gave off moisture that condensed, it would fall on them.[123]

★ See PT Muchlinski, 'The Loss of Goods Due to Inherent Vice' [1991] LMCLQ 162

It had been suggested in *Mayban v Alstom*[124] that if it was inevitable that the goods would not have survived a normal voyage undamaged, then this demonstrated inherent vice. Here the evidence was that the goods, a 350-tonne generator, was damaged on an otherwise normal though stormy voyage from the UK to Malaysia, and the court inferred that the loss was caused by the inability of the transformer to withstand the ordinary conditions of the voyage, thus proving (or perhaps tending to prove) inherent vice. This test was rejected in the Supreme Court in *The Cendor Mopu*,[125] a case involving an oil production rig. Here Lord Mance[126] suggested inherent vice would only cover inherent characteristics of or defects in a hull or cargo leading to it 'causing loss or damage to itself … without any fortuitous external accident or casualty'. Thus 'anything that would otherwise count as a fortuitous external accident or casualty will suffice to prevent the loss being attributed to inherent vice'.[127] In this case, although the structure of the rig was weakened before commencing on the voyage, a commonsensical answer by a business or seafaring man to the question 'What caused the loss?' would have been a 'leg-breaking wave', not that the rig caused the damaged to itself.

 Global Process Systems Inc v Syarikat Takaful Malaysia Bhd (The Cendor Mopu) [2011] UKSC 5

FACTS: The cargo, insured under ICC(A), was an oil production rig consisting of a platform and three 100m legs, 12m in diameter, being transported upside down on a barge from

---

122. *CT Bowring & Co Ltd v Amsterdam London Insurance Co* (1930) 36 Ll LR 309.
123. Though this would have required finding that the proximate cause of loss was that condensation took place immediately over the goods.
124. *Mayban General Insurance BHD v Alstom Power Plants* Ltd [2004] EWHC 1038 (Comm), [2004] 2 Lloyd's Rep 609.
125. *Global Process Systems Inc v Syarikat Takaful Malaysia Bhd (The Cendor Mopu)* [2011] UKSC 5, [2011] 1 All ER 869.
126. ibid [82].   127. ibid [80].

Texas to the Far East via the Cape of Good Hope in winter. The rig was almost thirty years old and was known to both the owner and the insurer to have metal fatigue. While off the Cape, it was hit by a wave and one of the legs fell off, which caused vibrations so that over the next few days the other two legs also fell off. The weather, though bad, was normal for the route and time of year. The judge at first instance found that it was not inevitable, just highly probable that at some point during the voyage the legs would have sheered and that the immediate cause of the loss was an otherwise ordinary wave which hit the first leg with just the right force at just the wrong moment—a leg-breaking wave. The question was whether the loss of the legs was through a fortuitous external accident or casualty or inherent vice of the rig.

HELD: The Supreme Court held, unanimously, that the proximate cause was not inherent vice but the leg-breaking wave, and that therefore the assured owner, GPS, could claim under the policy.

COMMENT: The Court rejected the test that inability to withstand the normal vicissitudes of the insured voyage proved inherent vice. Both Lord Saville and Lord Mance accepted that were such a test to be adopted, losses which occurred in otherwise uneventful voyages would not be covered, and this would frustrate the purpose of all risks insurance. Also, it would in effect introduce a **promissory warranty** that the goods were 'cargoworthy'; that is, capable of undertaking the voyage without damage, a warranty excluded by s 40(1) of the Marine Insurance Act 1906, subject to agreement to the contrary. In any event, cl 5.3 of the ICC(A) expressly excludes any such warranty. Lord Mance found it difficult to decide whether the cause was the wave, not the weak nature of the structure. The fact that it was essential to make this determination is important because it demonstrates that Lord Mance seems to believe that if the loss were inevitable the insurance claim would fail. In the context of this particular case this seems surprising. It can be argued that the whole nature of the insurance was whether or not the rig was so weak it could never make the journey. The assured did not promise it could (no warranty of cargoworthiness) and did not disguise the weakness of the rig; the insurer promised indemnity if the rig was too weak. For inevitable loss to have provided a defence to the claim seems to attack the very risk the insurer had undertaken.

➡ promissory warranties: in insurance, terms which, if broken, permit the innocent party to terminate the contract

🔗 For seaworthiness, of which cargoworthiness is a type, see p 550

⭐ See 'Cargo Insurance: All Risks Cover' (2011) 17 JIML 10

It should be noted that the exclusion is for inherent vice in the goods themselves and not in other goods. Thus if, say, timber is stowed on a ship containing other goods which spontaneously combust and destroy the timber, then the exclusion will not apply to the timber; the cause of the loss would be fire, an insured risk under ICC(A), (B), and (C).

Clause 4(5): Loss damage or expense caused by delay

This exclusion repeats s 55(2)(b) of the Marine Insurance Act 1906 and applies even if the cause of the delay is an insured risk. Thus the failed claim in *Taylor v Dunbar*,[128] where damage to the goods was caused when bad weather delayed the ship, would also fail under ICC(A).[129] Similarly, were the facts of one of the earliest cases on all risks insurance, *Schloss Bros v Stevens*,[130] to be repeated, the claim would fail today, since it was delay which caused the loss as the goods were exposed to a hot and wet

---

128. (1869) LR 4 CP 206.
129. Note bad weather as such is not an insured risk under ICC(B) or (C).
130. [1906] 2 KB 665 (KB).

climate to which they were unsuited, even though the delay was caused by a political revolution, a risk covered under ICC(A).[131]

The only exception occurs where delay causes a general average contribution recoverable under cl 2 of the ICC.

Clause 4(7): Deliberate damage or deliberate destruction[132]

This exception only applies to ICC(B) and (C). The damage or destruction must be wrongful, so that loss through jettison would not be excluded. But suppose that the shipowner scuttles the ship; it may be that the destruction of the goods would not be covered on the grounds that the loss is not 'fortuitous', but even if scuttling is covered *prima facie*, cl 4(7) may well exclude it. The issue is whether or not 'deliberate damage' in the policy exclusion includes damage caused by a deliberate act directed at another end—namely the sinking of the ship so that the damage to the cargo is simply an unintended but nevertheless inevitable result. Certainly, neither scuttling by or with the connivance of the shipowner nor **barratrous** scuttling are 'perils of the sea'[133] and ICC(B) and (C) are policies which cover only a specified list of such perils so that it might be expected that they do not offer cover for such acts. On this basis, loss or damage caused by deliberately set fires or where water is deliberately let into the ship would also be excluded from cover.

➡ barratry: an act done by a ship's crew contrary to the interests of the owner

Cover in respect of deliberate damage can be obtained by adding the Institute Malicious Damage Clause to the policy—at an additional cost of course.

Clause 5: Unseaworthiness of ship with the privity of the assured

Under s 40(2) of the Marine Insurance Act 1906, there is an implied warranty in an insurance on cargo that, 'at the commencement of the voyage, the ship is not only seaworthy as a ship, but also that she is reasonably fit to carry the goods or other moveables to the destination contemplated by the policy'. Clause 5(3) of the ICC removes this warranty and cl 5(1) instead excludes from cover loss or expense caused because the ship was unfit to make the contemplated voyage safely or was unable to carry the goods safely (unseaworthy). But the assured must be 'privy' to the unseaworthiness at the time of loading.

Seaworthiness is defined in s 39(4) of the Marine Insurance Act 1906, as being '[r]easonably fit in all respects to encounter the ordinary perils of the sea of the adventure insured' at the commencement of the voyage. The insurer might meet the burden of proof to show unseaworthiness either by direct evidence or by inference if problems emerge soon after sailing in the absence of another explanation,[134] but the primary issue is proving privity of the assured.

Here again, the principal cases involve an identical expression used in hull and machinery policies, but the issues are the same in cargo insurance. In *The*

---

131. Loss caused by revolution is an excluded loss but can be obtained at extra cost under Institute War Clauses (Cargo) 09.
132. ICC(B) and (C), cl 4.7.
133. *P Samuel & Co Ltd v Dumas* [1924] AC 431 (HL).
134. See Brett LJ in *Pickup v Thames and Mersey Marine Insurance Co Ltd* (1877–78) LR 3 QBD 594. In *Anderson v Morice* (1876) 1 App Cas 713 (HL), for example, the ship was loading in port and there was no satisfactory explanation for the loss raising an inference of unseaworthiness. This was rebutted by evidence that the ship was well maintained and well run.

Eurythenes,[135] Lord Denning held that privity requires the assured to have knowledge not only of the facts constituting the unseaworthiness, but also that those facts made the ship unseaworthy. However, knowledge meant not only actual knowledge, but also 'Nelsonian blindness',[136] that is 'turning a blind eye' to the truth, and deliberately not making inquires in order to avoid learning a truth he would prefer not to know. The knowledge must also be the knowledge of the assured personally, or, in the case of a company, its 'controlling mind'.[137] If it can be shown that a reasonably prudent person in his place would have known the facts and have realized that the ship was unseaworthy, then this might raise an inference of privity, but it would still be open to the shipper to bring evidence to the contrary. However, negligence, not even to a 'very high degree' on its own is enough.[138]

 ## Manifest Shipping Co Ltd v Uni-Polaris Shipping Co Ltd (The Star Sea) [2001] UKHL 1

FACTS: The insured shipowner renewed an insurance of its fleet of more than thirty ships, including the *Star Sea*, against damage by fire, amongst other things. Two ships in the fleet had been lost through engine room fires in the previous year, believed to have been caused by the Liberian captains not knowing how to operate the fire extinguishing equipment, and the insurers had paid the claims. The fleet was managed by a separate company run by the owner of the fleet and the technical director, Mr Nicholaidis. Mr Nicholaidis had been given an expert's report on one of the fires, which stated that the fire was not extinguished partly because the system which sealed off the engine room in the case of a fire (the 'dampers') was faulty. An engine room fire started in the *Star Sea* and she was lost because the captain and crew did not know how to operate the fire extinguishing system and the engine room dampers were faulty. The insurers refused to pay the claim on the ground that there was a breach of s 39(5) of the Marine Insurance Act 1906 warranty (namely that the *Star Sea* was unseaworthy with the privity of the assured) and the assured commenced legal action.

HELD: While the assured had taken a completely inadequate response to the earlier fires, the judge had not made a finding that any of the relevant individuals had suspected or believed that the *Star Sea* herself might be unseaworthy because of defects in the dampers or the incompetence of the captain. To be privy to unseaworthiness, the assured must either know or deliberately ignore the existence of facts which he did not want to know.

COMMENT: Here it is clear Mr Nicholaidis (who was treated as part of the assured's controlling mind) had information which, had he thought about it, might have caused him to conclude that the ship might be unseaworthy, but on the facts he did not draw that conclusion. Also the assured, in response to the earlier fires, had employed all

---

135. *Compania Maritima San Basilio SA v Oceanus Mutual Underwriting Association (Bermuda) Ltd (The Eurythenes)* [1976] 3 All ER 243 (CA) 252.

136. So called after Admiral Lord Nelson, who, at the battle of Copenhagen 1801, on being told of an order to withdraw but believing victory was in sight, reputedly put a telescope to his blind eye so as not to see the signal. Needless to say, he was victorious—had he not been he might have suffered the fate of Admiral Byng, executed for failure to defeat the French, according to Voltaire *'pour encourager les autres'.*

137. See *Tesco Supermarkets Ltd v Nattrass* [1972] AC 153 (HL).

138. *Manifest Shipping Co Ltd v Uni-Polaris Shipping Co Ltd* [2001] 1 All ER 743 (HL) [34] (Lord Hobhouse).

⭐ See Norma J Hird, 'The Star Sea—The Continuing Saga of Utmost Good Faith' [2001] JBL 311

Greek officers but had not bothered to check whether they knew how to operate the fire extinguishing equipment any better than the previous Liberians. But the House concluded that there was no point in appointing new officers if the assured was turning a blind eye to incompetence; if having incompetent officers was the plan, why not remain with the previous group whom they could be sure were incompetent.[139]

➜ stuffing: putting goods into a container

In the case of a shipper who books space on a ship, it is in fact unlikely that the shipper will be privy to unseaworthiness; he probably knows nothing about the ship and equally probably will never see it. Privity is far more likely where the carriage of goods is under a charterparty. However, cl 5(2) of the ICC extends the exception to circumstances where the container in which the goods are **stuffed** is unfit and was packed, either before the policy attached to the goods or was packed by the assured or his employees who were privy to the unfitness. Where the assured or his employees are involved in stuffing the container, it is possible that he or they would become aware of defects in it, such that, for example, it might collapse when stacked with other containers, or that the refrigeration unit in a refrigerated container (a reefer) was in poor condition.

Unlike under the exception in cl 4.1 (wilful default of the assured) where an innocent assignee is denied cover, cl 5.2 protects an innocent transferee of the policy who is also a purchaser in good faith of the insured goods. Thus, if, for example, a seller stuffs a container knowing that it has a weakened structure, he will be denied cover for loss caused by the container collapsing in transit, but a Cif purchaser in good faith from him can make a claim. Interestingly, if instead of the container being inadequate, loss is caused by inadequate packaging of the goods, the good faith purchaser will be denied cover by virtue of cl 4.3, where there is no saving clause for bona fide purchasers.

Clause 6: War, seizure, and detainment[140]

Clause 6 extends to a range of belligerent activities, including civil war, revolution, rebellion, insurrection, civil strife, and hostile acts by a belligerent power. It extends to some results of the aftermath of war, namely loss or damage caused by derelict mines, torpedoes, bombs, or other derelict weapons of war, and to actual or attempted capture, seizure, arrest, restraint, or detainment.

Loss or damage caused through seizure or detainment would cover piracy and cl 6 in ICC(A) removes piracy from the exclusion so that it is covered. However, for ICC(B) and (C) loss caused by piracy is excluded. It is common nowadays that, rather than making off with the ship and/or its cargo, pirates demand a ransom to release them.[141] Payment of the ransom by the ship owner will attract a general average contribution from carrier and shipper which, by virtue of a combination of cl 2 and cl 6, will not be covered for ICC(B) or (C) policies. Incidentally, the term 'piracy'

---

139. Such comments should not be construed as suggesting that all Liberian masters are incompetent; in reality, many ships are commanded by highly competent Liberian officers and men.

140. ICC, cl 6.

141. In 2008, thirty vessels were seized off Somalia alone and ransomed at a total cost of $60 million—see *Masefield AG v Amlin Corporate Member Ltd* [2011] EWCA Civ 24; [2011] 1 WLR 2012 [7]. It was accepted (by Rix LJ at [74]) that it is not illegal or contrary to public policy to pay a ransom to Somali pirates.

includes acts of 'passengers who mutiny and rioters who attack the ship from the shore'.[142]

If the insurer is prepared to offer it, it is possible to 'buy back' cover excluded under cl 6 by including the Institute War Clauses (Cargo) wording in the policy, though if piracy is also to be covered the assured will also require the malicious damage clause.

Clause 7: Strikes, riots, civil commotions, and terrorism[143]

What constitutes a strike has been widely interpreted by the courts,[144] and the clause itself is apparently sufficiently widely drafted to include all forms of industrial action. A riot involves twelve or more persons present together who use or threaten unlawful violence for a common purpose,[145] while terrorism is an act of any person acting for or in connection with an organization seeking by force to overthrow or influence any government.[146] The clause also includes any politically, ideologically, or religiously motivated loss or damage.

If the insurer is prepared to offer it, it is possible to 'buy back' cover excluded under cl 7 by including the Institute Strikes Clauses (Cargo) wording in the policy. However, the typical cause of loss through strikes or terrorism is delay, and this is not covered by strikes clauses.

Attachment and duration of the insurance

Clause 8: Commencement of cover

By virtue of cl 8, cover under the ICC policy commences when the goods to which it relates are first moved in the warehouse or other place of storage named in the insurance for the purpose of immediate loading onto the carrying vehicle for the commencement of the transit. At this point, the insurance is said to 'attach' to the goods. The place of storage may be a warehouse at the port of loading, it may be in a stack of containers at the port, but the ICC wording also permits nomination of a place many miles from the port, so that it can provide some cover in respect of road or rail transport to the port of loading.[147] For example, in the following case, the insurance attached to goods in factories up to 1,000 miles from the port of loading and covered transport by road, rail, and canal barge, as well as by the ocean-going ship.

Wünsche Handelsgesellschaft International mbH v Tai Ping Insurance Co Ltd [1998] CLC 851 (CA)

FACTS: Wünsche Handelsgesellschaft International mbH (WHI) bought tinned vegetables from China. The tins were transported in boxes from many canning factories in China to

---

142. Rule 8 of the Rules for Construction of Policies in the Schedule to the Marine Insurance Act 1906.
143. ICC, cl 7.
144. *Tramp Shipping Corp v Greenwich Maritime Inc (The New Horizon)* [1975] ICR 261 (CA).
145. Public Order Act 1986, s 10(2).   146. ICC, cl 7.
147. As ICC(B) and (C), cls 1.1.3 and 1.1.4 specifically recognize.

a warehouse in Shenzhen, where the boxes were put into containers and then transported by road to Hong Kong and loaded on a ship for Hamburg. The insurance policy covered the goods in specific containers and was issued just before the containers were loaded on the ship in Hong Kong, but stated it covered the goods 'ex factory in PR of China to warehouse Hamburg'. Some of the goods were damaged before reaching the warehouse in Shenzhen.

HELD: The words 'including ex factory in PR of China' meant that the inland transport was covered; the policy was intended to apply to the goods to which it attached from the time they left the canning factories. Clearly, the policy could not attach to the boxes of tinned vegetables until it was issued, but from that moment it attached to the goods in the specified container and the cover was retroactive, commencing when the goods began their journey from the factories.

COMMENT: The policy in this case was not in the ICC form, which contemplates either coverage from the final warehouse (or other place of storage) before loading or from a named place, not as here, where there was a generic description of places of origin. In *Wünsche*, the loss occurred before the policy was issued, but, as we have seen, policies which cover this sort of loss are common; indeed, ICC is in this 'lost or not lost' form. A claim was advanced for boxes stolen in the canning factories, but this was rejected as this was an insurance for goods in transit and it did not attach until the insured journey commenced. It is also worth noting that the policy in this case was 'warehouse to warehouse'; cover continued until the goods arrived in the warehouse in Hamburg and did not end when the goods were discharged from the ship.

However, what if the goods never leave the warehouse bound for their intended destination? Clearly, the policy does not attach to goods inside the warehouse, so loss or damage there is not covered. Nor does the policy attach if the goods leave the warehouse not bound for the ship; for example, if they have been stolen.[148] Section 44 of the Marine Insurance Act 1906 states: 'Where the destination is specified in the policy, and the ship, instead of sailing for that destination, sails for any other destination, the risk does not attach.' The application of s 44 can be seen in the following case.

Nima Sarl v Deves Insurance Public Co Ltd (The Prestrioka) [2002] EWCA Civ 1132

FACTS: The policy in the 1982 ICC(A) form insured the cargo of rice 'warehouse to warehouse Kohsichang, Thailand to Dakar port, Senegal'. The cargo was loaded in Thailand but the ship did not set sail for Senegal; it was always intended by the owner to sail somewhere else and sell the cargo to criminals. The assured, Nima, argued that the policy attached to the goods at the point they left the warehouse, and could not become unattached (by operation of s 44 of the Act) upon the vessel sailing for another destination.

HELD: Section 44 meant there was no attachment at all if, at the moment of sailing, the intended destination was not Dakar. Consequently, if hypothetically the goods had been stolen on their way to the ship, the *prima facie* attachment of the policy on leaving the warehouse would have been illusory because of the intention of the shipowner or master.

⭐ See 'Phantom Ships and English Marine Insurance Law' (2001) 2 STL 1

---

148. See e.g. see the claim for losses before leaving the warehouse in *Wünsche Handelsgesellschaft International mbH v Tai Ping Insurance Co Ltd* [1998] 2 Lloyd's Rep 8 (CA). See also *Fuerst Day Lawson Ltd v Orion Insurance Co Ltd* [1980] 1 Lloyd's Rep 656 (QB).

Clause 10.2 of the ICC(A), although not totally felicitously worded, is intended to reverse this decision; attachment in such a case will occur on leaving the warehouse, but of course the cause of the loss must be covered under the policy for a successful claim. In *The Prestrioka*, for example, the cause of loss was theft, which is not covered under ICC(B) or (C).

Clauses 8 and 9: Termination of cover

Consider the following example.

Eg ComCorp Ltd

Comcorp buys some goods in five containers Cif.[149] The policy of insurance it is given incorporates the ICC and states the cover is from 'Assured's warehouse Lille (France) to ComCorp's warehouse Liverpool (England)'. The route for the goods in five container lorries is by road from Lille to Cherbourg, by ferry across the English Channel, and by road again to the warehouse in Liverpool. The first container lorry pulls into the Liverpool warehouse for unloading when the driver is coshed, and the lorry and its container stolen. ComCorp has a depot in Portsmouth, and container lorries bound for Liverpool often stay there overnight. On hearing about the robbery, ComCorp decides to unload the second lorry at the Portsmouth depot, putting the goods into smaller vans for delivery to sub-purchasers. One of the vans is stolen that night. The third lorry arrives at the Portsmouth depot and one of ComCorp's employees decides to unhitch the trailer and leave the goods in the container, as both the Portsmouth and Liverpool warehouses are full. The container is destroyed by fire that night. The fourth lorry is still on the boat when ComCorp decides to send it to Immingham (Humberside). As the lorry exits the docks, the trailer overturns on a roundabout and some of the goods inside the container are damaged. Customs detain the fifth container, which is temporarily stored in a stack of other containers in Portsmouth docks. The problems are still unresolved three months later, when the container is crushed by the weight of the other containers on top of it and the goods are badly damaged.

Comcorp wonders whether its ICC policy will cover these losses.

From the point of attachment, the insurance 'continues during the ordinary course of transit' until the insured transit comes to an end. In the simple case of pure carriage of goods by sea, it would be easy to define the termination—when the goods are unloaded from the ship at the port of discharge. Where the policy covers 'warehouse to warehouse', the transit insured is anticipated to end not on a dockside at an inland final destination,[150] though of course the goods may be temporarily unloaded and/or stored elsewhere awaiting onward transmission to this final destination. Clause 8 tackles the issues by identifying five termination events, the earliest of which to occur marks the termination of cover. The events are as follows:

1. The most obvious is completion of unloading at the final destination; that is, the place of termination named in the policy.

---

149. Note that this contract is probably not under Incoterms—but had it been CIF (Incoterms 2010) then, since this is multi-modal transport, the parties should have used DAP (delivered at place) Liverpool.
150. Called in the ICC the 'final warehouse or other place of storage'.

2. The assured or his employees unload elsewhere and decide either to store the goods there other than as a 'staging post' for onward transit to the final destination or to separate them into smaller units for allocation to sub purchasers or otherwise for distribution. In effect, the assured decides to treat this as the final destination. In this case, the insurance terminates once unloading is complete at this place.[151]

3. The assured or his employees might decide that, rather than unload the goods, they will use the lorry, railway wagon, or container in which the goods have been transported as a place of storage,[152] again, in effect treating this as the final destination. The insurance terminates when this decision is made.

4. If, after being finally unloaded from the ship, the goods are to be sent to a different destination from that named in the policy, the insurance terminates as soon as the journey to this new destinations starts.[153]

5. Cover ends sixty days after discharge of the goods from the ship at the final port of discharge.[154] Although not confined to this situation, a typical problem is where the goods cannot clear customs for some reason. If it appears that the goods will remain impounded for longer than sixty days, the assured will have time to make alternative insurance arrangements.

Clause 9 deals with cases where the transit ends short of the final destination for reasons beyond the control of the assured. For example, the carrier may decide to terminate the sea leg of the transit at a completely different port than that originally intended, or decide that a container lorry will detach the container at a place other than as agreed. The insurance will terminate on the termination of the contract of carriage, though under cl 12 the insurer will reimburse the assured for any extra charges he incurs for unloading, storing, and forwarding the goods to the final destination. Of course, the losses incurred on the journey from this 'distress location' to the final destination will not insured—the insurance has terminated—but on giving prompt notice to the insurers of the change in the insured transit, the assured can request continuation of cover either to the final destination originally agreed or to a new agreed final destination. Cover will then continue until arrival at their destination or until possession of them has been delivered to a purchaser on sale, in any event subject to a maximum of sixty days cover from the date of arrival at the distress location. The insurers may charge an additional premium for this cover.

Clause 10: Change of voyage, deviations, and delay

Section 45 of the Marine Insurance Act 1906 defines a change of voyage as a voluntary change of destination of the ship from that contemplated by the policy. It goes on to state that once that decision has been 'manifested', whether by the ship changing course or not, the insurer is 'discharged from liability'. Clause 10 of the ICC modifies the effect of this termination event in two ways: first, by requiring that the termination event only occurs if the change of destination was made by the assured; and second, by stating that cover can be maintained 'at rates and terms to be agreed'. The assured must notify the insurers promptly of the change, and until the new terms are agreed there is no insurance cover. However, ICC 10 stipulates that if a loss occurs prior to agreement being reached, cover may be provided, but only if

---

151. ICC(A), cl 8.1.2.   152. ibid cl 8.1.3.   153. ibid cl 8.2.   154. ibid cl 8.1.4.

it 'would have been available at a reasonable commercial market rate on reasonable market terms'.

Clearly, this clause is unlikely to apply where the shipper has booked space on the carrier's ship; it is directed principally at charterparties. It should be noted that this is not the standard 'held covered' clause which appears in hull and machinery clauses, and was incorporated into the 1982 edition of the ICC where, pending agreement on terms, cover is maintained. As *The Litsion Pride*[155] illustrates, there is a positive incentive to delay notification of a change of voyage with a 'held covered' wording, while under the new wording there is a disincentive to late notification, since there is no cover until agreement is reached.

It should be noted that s 46(1) of the Marine Insurance Act 1906 has an identical effect to s 45, but in relation to 'deviations' where the ship temporarily diverts from the insured route, intending to regain it. Similarly, under s 48 of the Marine Insurance Act 1906, unreasonable delay in prosecuting the insured voyage is a termination event. However, cl 8.3 of the ICC stipulates that subject to the express termination events in cls 8.1 and 9, the insurance remains in force notwithstanding any deviations, delay beyond the control of the assured, and a range of other events which might be regarded as varying the insured voyage and thus otherwise terminating the insurance.

Conclusion

Insurance is a valuable risk transfer mechanism whereby buyers and sellers can protect themselves from the financial consequences of loss or damage to goods in transit. Where a person has either title to or risk in goods to which marine cargo insurance has attached, that person has an insurable interest under the policy, and if they have title to the policy, they may claim in respect of loss or damage to the goods proximately caused by an insured risk. Unless the policy is issued on a 'lost or not lost basis', the insurable interest must arise before the insured event occurs, though an assured may still claim even though he acquires title to the policy after the goods have been lost or damaged, so long as his predecessor(s) in title had a valid claim under it. Subject to terms in the policy to the contrary, any defences the insurer may have had against his predecessors in title will be available against an assignee of it.

Insurance policies will either list the maritime risks in respect of which an indemnity is offered, like ICC(B) and (C), or cover 'all risks', as with ICC(A). However, there will always be exceptions to the cover offered, though in the case of the ICC many of these exceptions consist of inevitabilities, not risks. Under the ICC policy, risk attaches to the goods once they commence their transit to the ship for loading and cover terminates once the goods have reached their final destination, whether that originally envisaged, as substituted by the carrier, or short of that location.

---

155. *Black King Shipping Corporation v Massie (Litsion Pride)* [1985] 1 Lloyd's Rep 437 (QB).

Practice questions

1. Explain and give examples of the following expressions:
   - the duty of utmost good faith;
   - material non-disclosure;
   - insurance is a contract of indemnity;
   - insurance covers loss caused by an insured risk;
   - attachment of risk.

2. The doctrine of utmost good faith provides insurers with an opportunity to unfairly reject claims they ought to pay.

   Do you agree with this statement?

3. Shippam had two containers of goods he wanted to transport by sea. He contacted Carrie Cont Ltd, a sea carrier which he knew would offer a cheap rate for carriage, because a number of containers of goods carried by them had disappeared over the last few months and Carrie Cont had 'a bit of a reputation' as a result.

   Carrie Cont issued a warehouse receipt to Shippam stating the two containers had been received by Carrie Cont at their dockside warehouse and were ready for loading on board the ship. Shippam insured both containers of goods with Marinsco. While the ship was at sea, Shippam sold the goods to Bayer, passing over the receipt and insurance policy in return for the price.

   The first container of goods was not unloaded at the port of discharge and, owing to a computer malfunction, Carrie Cont does not know whether it was loaded onto the ship or not.

   When the second container was unloaded, staining was discovered on the goods, so they were ruined. There were three theories how this might have happened: first, since the container was carried on deck, sea water entered it; second, the goods had 'sweated' during the voyage, causing condensation which had condensed on the roof of the container and rained on the goods; and third, water in high pressure hoses used by Carrie Cont to wash down the container in the warehouse, as required by the port health authorities, had penetrated the container, which was in a poor condition.

   Bayer claimed on the policy for both losses. In respect of the first claim Marinsco asked for proof of the cause of loss. Bayer argued that it was obvious that he had a claim, but the insurer persisted. Bayer contacted Shippam, and Shippam, in order to help Bayer, forged a letter from Carrie Cont stating that the goods had been loaded on the ship and must be presumed to have been off-loaded at the wrong port and had since been lost. Shippam forwarded this letter to the Marinsco, but it took no notice of it, as it had decided to pay the claim by this time and had already despatched a cheque in full settlement.

   Marinsco has now discovered all of the facts—though no-one knows what caused the staining in the second container. It wants to know whether it can recover the money it paid to Bayer in respect of the first container and resist his claim in respect of the second container.

   Advise Marinsco.

Further reading

Malcolm Clarke, **'Insurance: The Proximate Cause in English Law'** (1981) 40 CLJ 284
- An article by the writer of the major practitioner's work on insurance law, where, after reviewing a range of authorities, he argues that the proximate cause of a loss is the event, which, in all the circumstances prevailing at the time of the event, led inevitably to the kind of loss in question.

John Dunt, *Marine Cargo Insurance* (Informa Press, 2009)
- A practitioner's work, which examines the recently revised Institute Cargo Clauses in detail. The author played a key role in the 2009 revision and this is a work of authority well set out and well indexed, and can be relied on as a reference source.

Angelo Forte, **'The Materiality Test in Insurance'** [1993] LMCLQ 557
- A review by a leading Scots academic lawyer of judicial decisions on the issue of materiality in disclosure under the obligation of utmost good faith. His chapter 'Good Faith and Utmost Good Faith ' in Forte (ed) *Good Faith in Contract and Property Law* (Hart Publishing 1999) provides an interesting contrast between the Scots and English legal positions on the issue of good faith.

Susan Hodges, *Cases and Materials on Marine Insurance Law* (Routledge Cavendish 1999)
- Although now sadly slightly out of date, this is an excellent collection of the leading cases on marine insurance, accompanied by an often insightful commentary. There is a text by the same author, *The Law of Marine Insurance* (Cavendish 1996), also highly recommended to an interested student.

Peter Musthill, **'Fault and Marine Losses'** [1988] LMCLQ 310
- An influential article on the meaning of inherent vice dealing with the issues raised in *The Miss Jay Jay*,[156] in which the author was also the judge. Here the vessel was poorly designed and constructed, but was held not to have sunk through inherent vice.

Beth Richards-Bray, **'Global Process Systems Inc v Syarikat Takaful Malaysia Bhd (The Cendor Mopu)'** (2011) 16 Cov LJ 75
- A short and accessible case commentary on *The Cendor Mopu* which succinctly identifies the problems involved in concluding that inevitable loss proves that the insured property must have been damaged though inherent vice.

HY Yeo, **'Post Contractual Good Faith. A Change of Judicial Attitude'** (2003) 66 MLR 425
- A substantial case comment on *The Star Sea*,[157] tracing the origins of the idea of a continuing duty of disclosure, and concluding that statutory reform of the doctrine is called for, since currently s 17 of the Marine Insurance Act 1906 provides an opportunity for insurers to avoid contracts on grounds unrelated to the cause of an otherwise insured loss.

---

156. *Lloyd (J J) Instruments Ltd v Northern Star Insurance Co Ltd (The Miss Jay Jay)* [1987] 1 Lloyd's Rep 32(QB).

157. *Manifest Shipping Co Ltd v Uni-Polaris Shipping Co Ltd, (The Star Sea)* [2001] UKHL 1, [2003] 1 AC 469.

PART V

Methods of payment, security, and finance

- What is money?
- What is payment?

INTRODUCTION

Ultimately, almost all commercial transactions will involve an obligation to make a payment in money by one party or another. The payment obligation and the meaning of money are therefore central to commercial law, and in this short chapter, these two ideas will be discussed.

The chapter has four objectives. First, it introduces the idea of money, which in modern commerce will take one of two forms—either physical cash, notes and coins typical of small retail transactions—and money payments that ultimately result in fund transfers involving the debiting and crediting of the parties' bank accounts. Second, it considers the legal nature of physical cash, identifying it as a special type of personal property and providing an indirect link with Chapter 2.[1] Third, it considers what is involved in the meeting a payment obligation, looking briefly at how performance of the obligation is effected. Finally, it sets out the basic nature of a bank account to enable consideration of the electronic payment mechanisms through funds transfers. This material also provides a foundation for Chapter 24, which is devoted to bills of exchange and documentary credits.

What is money?

Introduction

Aristotle, writing in the fourth century BCE, sought to examine how the worth of disparate things might be measured against one another, and concluded that one way, amongst others, was through expressing their value in a common medium, namely money. Money therefore forms a measure of value. Thus X can, in a sense, add sheep to cows to goats by expressing each in monetary terms and reaching a sum of those values. In the same way, X can more readily 'swap' cows for sheep, since X does not need to find a person with sheep who wants a cow; all X need do is find a person who wants his cow and will give him its value expressed in money, and then find another who is prepared to sell X his sheep. Thus money forms a means of

---

1. This discussion also provides a sound basis for topics outside the scope of this book, in particular the subject of 'tracing', normally covered in courses on equity and trusts.

exchange, a means of meeting a payment obligation. Similarly, money is a convenient store of value, something to be retained and used to exchange for other things.[2] Money as a store of value is itself a piece of property, whether in the form of cash or in the form of a credit balance in the books of account of a bank, and where, as a result of a transaction, a payment obligation is created, that obligation will *prima facie* have to be discharged by a money payment.

Physical money

This section considers the position in English law of English currency in the form of cash. Cash in the sense of notes and coins is obviously tangible, so that if *X* were to steal *Y*'s £50 Bank of England banknote, *Y* could maintain an action against *X* for damages for the tort of conversion (a tort which deals with interference with the possession of goods), because *X* has 'converted' the paper on which the note is written. However, currency is also a thing in action, title to which passes on delivery of a document, or in other words a documentary intangible. The note simply says that the Bank of England will pay the bearer on demand £50, in other words perform the payment obligation the note embodies by tendering another note or notes and/or coins. Thus the value of the currency is simply its stated value as a unit of account—it is the means whereby we determine how much one person owes to another.[3]

Documentary intangibles are discussed at p 43

Although both a chattel and a thing in action, cash has two important characteristics which deserve brief discussion. First, it is fully negotiable, that is to say title to cash passes with delivery to a person who gives value for it, even where the payer himself merely had possession as an exception to the *nemo dat* rule. Authority for this proposition can be found in the following case.

The nemo dat rule is discussed at p 272

Miller v Race (1758) 1 Burr 452

FACTS: A banknote was stolen from the owner and came into Miller's hands as payment for an hotel bill. When Miller presented the note for payment, the bank refused to pay and the chief cashier of the bank, Race, refused to return it to him, so he sued Race for the eighteenth-century version of modern day tort of conversion.

HELD: The Court of Kings Bench held that the Miller obtained title to the note, since he had acted honestly, not suspecting theft, and had given valuable consideration; were it not so then no one could safely accept cash in payment. Consequently, the bank committed a tort in not returning the note and had to meet its obligation under the note to pay the holder Miller.[4]

---

2. The analysis of money found in William Charlton, *Aristotle Physics Books I and II* (Clarendon Press 1983) Chap 9 remains a starting point for economic analyses of money even today. For a very brief but fascinating discussion of the function of money in economic/political discourse see Alistair Hudson, *The Law of Finance* (Sweet & Maxwell 2009) 41–6.

3. Until 1931, Bank of England notes were repayable in gold. The US continued to redeem US$ in gold at a set rate of $35 per oz until 1971.

4. But see *Lipkin Gorman v Karpnale Ltd* [1991] 2 AC 548 (HL): where payment was made under an unenforceable gambling contract, title to the notes did not pass to the casino. Gambling contracts are now enforceable by virtue of s 335 of the Gambling Act 2005.

The second characteristic is that cash is fungible (i.e. replaceable by an identical item). Fungibility is best illustrated by an example. If *X* agrees to sell *Y* a spade, then unless the contract concerns a specific spade, *X* meets his obligation to *Y* by delivering a spade matching the contractual description. In other words, in this example the spade is a fungible—any one spade of the right description can be substituted for any other like spade. However, normally where *X* lends *Y* a spade, the spade is not fungible—*Y*'s obligation is to return the spade *X* lent him and not an identical one.[5] But, when money is lent there is no obligation to return the very notes and coins which were borrowed; indeed, were this not so the function of the loan would disappear. The borrower must be able to pass title to the cash in order to derive value from it.

What is payment?

The concept of payment[6]

Consider the following example.

Eg ComCorp Ltd

ComCorp Ltd has used the services of a computer contractor under an informal contract. The contractor has done the work but seems to have disappeared. The only express terms in the contract as to payment were the amount due and that ComCorp was to pay at the end of the month. ComCorp is anxious not to breach the terms as to payment and wonders what its obligations are in relation to where and how to make the payment. In particular, it wonders whether the contractor can demand cash.

Payment in a legal commercial sense involves the meeting of a performance obligation expressed in money terms. Typically in the commercial world, the payment obligation will arise under contract or under a statutory obligation, but payment may also be required to satisfy a judgment or indeed any other debt, however arising. Thus in the case of a sale of goods there must be a money consideration,[7] so the buyer's duties include a payment obligation. Similarly, contracts of employment, agency, or for the provision of banking, insurance, or other financial services, such as an agreement for loan of money, will normally involve performance of a payment obligation.[8] For the sake of simplicity, the assumption in this chapter is that the payment obligation is consensual and the paradigm transaction generating the payment obligation is either sale of goods, provision of services, or a loan of money.

The nature of the money obligation found in s 2(1) of the SGA 1979 is discussed at p 216

---

5. Though see *Mercer v Craven Grain Storage Ltd* [1994] CLC 328 (HL), considered further at p 35.
6. The best analysis of payment and money is Charles Proctor (ed), *Goode on Payment Obligations in Commercial and Financial Transactions* (2nd edn, Sweet & Maxwell 2009).
7. Sale of Goods Act 1979 (SGA 1979), s 2(1).
8. In the case of an employment contract, it must involve a payment obligation.

Terms for payment

The basis on which payment is to be made is for the parties to determine, in terms of place, time, and mode of performance. In accordance with normal contractual principles, there is a requirement for strict performance with contractual terms, so that determining the terms for payment may be become important in determining whether, when, and by whom a breach has been committed, particularly where breach may trigger remedies beyond an action for recovery of a debt, for example forfeiture of a lease or making a power of sale exercisable under a charge or mortgage.

Place of payment

In professionally drawn contracts, the place and time, and, increasingly commonly, mode of performance will be set out, though in practice the parties may not adhere to the express terms and either vary them or waive strict compliance.[9] For example, some insurance policies, even today, provide for the payment of claims at the insurer's head office on production of the policy and proof of claim. In claims for domestic contents insurance policies, under which the insurer may at its option either pay in cash or replace the damaged goods with new ones, this might be more than a little inconvenient for both parties.

> **payee:** a person to whom money is paid, or is to be paid

Where no express or implied place for payment is specified, the normal inference is for payment to be made at the **payee's** place of business, if in England,[10] and where the payee's place of business is abroad, then the court is likely to construe the contract as requiring payment abroad, especially where there is no obvious alternative and the contract's only connection with England is the place of performance by the payee.[11] Similarly, the place of payment may be obvious from the circumstances surrounding the contract; for example, where it is known to the payee at the time of the contract that the payer makes similar payments in a particular way.

Time of payment

The terms of the agreement will determine when payment is to be made, though sometimes construction may be a matter of some difficulty.[12] The requirement for strict compliance needs to be borne in mind. Thus, commonly, loan agreements provide for repayment on demand, failing which the lender is entitled to look to any security it may have taken. This places an onerous obligation on the borrower, who is permitted only the time it would take him to acquire funds from a convenient source, '[f]or instance, he might require time to get it from his desk, or to go across the street, or to his bankers for it'.[13] Thus in *Cripps v Wickenden*,[14] appointing a receiver one hour after the notice to repay was delivered was held to be entirely appropriate, particularly as the debtor had no means of payment immediately available. This rule

---

9. See e.g. *Gyles v Hall* (1726) 2 P Wms 378.
10. *Robey & Cov Snaefell Mining Co Ltd* (1887) 20 QBD 152.
11. *The Eider* [1893] P 119 (CA).
12. As in *Mardorf Peach & Co Ltd v Attica Sea Carriers Corp of Liberia (The Laconia)* [1977] AC 850 (HL), where the contractual date for payment was a Sunday—should payment be made on the preceding Friday or the succeeding Monday?
13. *Toms v Wilson* (1862) 122 ER 524, 453 (Cockburn CJ).
14. *Cripps (Pharmaceuticals) Ltd v Wickenden* [1973] 2 All ER 606 (QB).

is, if anything, more stringent today than in the time of *Cripps*, since although the mechanics for payment are a little more complex than a walk across the street, the means of making payment are almost instantaneous.[15] Commonwealth courts have adopted an apparently more relaxed approach in permitting a delay which is 'reasonable in all the circumstances',[16] but this approach was rejected by Walton J in *Bank of Baroda v Panessar*[17] and doubted by the Court of Appeal in *Lloyds Bank plc v Lampert*.[18]

Section 41 of the Law of Property Act 1925 imports the approach of equity in determining whether a failure to meet a time stipulation in a contract is a breach of a condition. Thus unless the time of payment is expressly or by necessary implication made 'of the essence of the contract', or where there is an unreasonable delay in payment and time has been made of the essence by the service of a notice to this effect by the payee, then failure to pay on time does not enable the payee to terminate the contract.[19] Subject to contrary intention, time for payment is not 'of the essence' in contracts for the sale of goods,[20] and this will typically be the case in other contracts.[21] However, even where time is not of the essence, persistent and calculated late payments may be sufficiently serious to justify the innocent party in bringing the contract to an end.[22]

Mode of payment

As with other aspects of payment, it is for the parties to determine the mode of payment, for example by cash or by funds transfer, and payment by a different mode need not be accepted as payment by the creditor.[23] Thus in a contract where payment is to be made by crediting a specific bank account, crediting a different one, even if owned by the creditor at the same bank, is not payment. Where there is no agreed method of payment, then the creditor must determine whether to accept payment by that mode.

On the other hand, any act accepted by the creditor as meeting the performance obligation will amount to performance, but normally payment will be made in one of the following ways:

- payment in part exchange;
- novation;
- set off/net off;
- cash; or
- funds transfer to creditor's bank account.

---

15. *Bank of Baroda v Panessar* [1987] Ch 335 (Ch).

16. See the cases cited in *Bank of Baroda v Panessar* [1987] Ch 335 (Ch) 349 and Walton J's critique of them.

17. [1987] Ch 335 (Ch).   18. [1999] 1 All ER (Comm) 161 (CA).

19. *United Scientific Holdings Ltd v Burnley BC* [1978] AC 904 (HL).   20. SGA 1979, s 10.

21. See e.g. *Decro-Wall International SA v Practitioners in Marketing Ltd* [1971] 1 WLR 361(CA) (regular late payments not sufficient); *Simmers v Innes* [2008] UKHL 24, [2008] SC (HL Sc) 137 (delay in completing buyout of fellow shareholder's interest in a company). However, time for payment of a deposit on a sale of a ship (*Portaria Shipping Co v Gulf Pacific Navigation Co Ltd* [1981] 2 Lloyd's Rep 180 (QB)) or of a house (*Samarenko v Dawn Hill House Ltd* [2011] EWCA Civ 1445, [2012] 3 WLR 638) generally will be a breach of a condition.

22. *Alan Auld Associates Ltd v Rick Pollard Associates* [2008] EWCA Civ 655, [2008] BLR 419.

23. *Re Charge Card Services Ltd (No 2)* [1989] Ch 497 (CA).

⊘ Bills of exchange and documentary credits are discussed in Chapter 24

Payment may also be made through the medium of some form of financial instrument, such as a cheque or bill of exchange, or a documentary or other credit, but these will also ultimately result in either a cash payment or funds transfer.

Payment by cash and funds transfer will be discussed later, but a little needs also to be said of payment through part exchange, novation, and set off/net off.

Part exchange is a payment rather than part of a barter, because the parties place a monetary value on the goods exchanged.[24]

Payment by novation occurs when one loan agreement, typically between a bank and its customer, is replaced by another, the proceeds of the successor loan being used to repay the first. The terms of the second loan may or may not differ from the first, but often it will be secured with a floating charge, whilst the first may not have been. The reason for using novation rather than simply granting a charge to secure the first loan is to counteract the vulnerability of floating charges granted other than to secure 'new value'.[25] The bank will simply debit the new loan account and credit the old one, leaving a nil balance; nothing physical passes between the parties.

⊘ Floating charges are discussed at p 702

Set off/net off involves a contractual agreement where there are mutual dealings between parties under which all sums otherwise due for payment by a party are aggregated and set off against sums due for payment to that party, and the net balance settled periodically in the form of a running account. Consequently, making the payment mandated by the netting process discharges the separate payment obligations which the mutual dealings would otherwise have generated. This process, known as settlement netting, may involve more than two parties and will be considered further in the discussion of funds transfers.

Payment in cash

The fact that a contract requires payment in cash may indeed mean precisely that; the debtor must offer notes or coins to the creditor. However, the court may conclude that such was not the actual intention of the parties or that the terms of contract have been varied where the creditor has previously accepted an alternative mode of payment.

A/S Awilco v Fulvia SpA di Navigazione (The Chikuma) [1981] 1 All ER 652 (HL)

FACTS: The contract provided for a series of payments in cash in US dollars by Fulvia into a named account at Awilco's bank. The 83rd payment, like the others, was by funds transfer, and the transfer was received on the due date for payment. Clearly, the parties had varied the contract so far as mode of payment was concerned, but in any event this was a standard form contract where previous decisions had established that 'cash' meant 'cash or its equivalent'.[26] Here the payment from Fulvia's bank could not be recalled, but would earn no interest for three days after receipt, and could not be used Awilco without penalty during that time.

---

24. *Aldridge v Johnson (1857)* 7 E & B 885; *Dawson (G J) (Clapham) Ltd v Dutfield* [1936] 2 All ER 232 (KB).
25. Insolvency Act 1986, s 245.
26. *Tenax Steamship Co Ltd v Reinante Transoceanica Navigation SA (The Brimnes)* [1975] 1 QB 929 (CA).

> **HELD:** The House of Lords held that the transfer had to have the financial effect of cash; here it did not and so payment was late.

In the absence of a course of dealings and any contractual term as to payment, then refusal by the creditor of notes and coins which constitute legal tender would apparently be a breach of contract, because any payment obligation is performed *prima facie* by legal tender.[27] However, were the creditor to refuse such tender, the payment obligation would remain unperformed, as, according to Hobhouse J, in a face-to-face meeting where the debtor seeks to hand legal tender to the creditor, 'the physical act of delivery (in the absence of some misrepresentation or mistake) will not be achieved without the concurrence of the [creditor]'.[28] Where the creditor does refuse payment, the debtor can avoid any costs associated in an action for recovery of the sum due by making a payment into court, and lawful tender will provide a defence to any action by the creditor for non-performance.

Payment by funds transfer

Consider the following example.

 ComCorp Ltd

ComCorp Ltd has a factory where in the past all wages have been paid in cash every Thursday. ComCorp Ltd's insurer has now refused to provide insurance against theft of the cash before it is paid and the employees have all agreed to be paid directly into their bank accounts, as a number of them have been mugged coming home from work on Thursday afternoons. ComCorp Ltd wants to know how such direct payments might be made into the employees' accounts.

Although payments in cash are numerous, so are the disadvantages, especially when dealing with large and/or regular transactions. Consequently, the value of cashless transactions far exceeds those payments made in cash.[29] Apart from payment by part exchange, novation, or set off/net off, cashless payments are made by funds transfers from one bank account to another.

The nature of a bank account

The nature of a bank account needs to be explained briefly.[30] The banker/customer relationship in relation to bank accounts[31] is contractual and not proprietary;[32] thus

---

27. *Halsbury's Laws* (5th edn, 2010) vol 9(1), para 943.

28. *TSB Bank of Scotland plc v Welwyn Hatfield DC* (1993) 2 Bank LR 267 (QB) 272.

29. For example, over 90 per cent of the UK's workforce is paid by direct crediting into their bank accounts.

30. For a full description, see more specialist treatments such as Peter Ellinger, Eva Lomnicka, and Christopher Hare, *Ellinger's Modern Banking Law* (5th edn, OUP 2010) ch 4.

31. Banks perform other services, for example holding valuables for safe keeping, where the relationship is one of bailor/bailee, and fund management which, *inter alia*, involves agency and custodianship.

32. *Foley v Hill* (1848) 2 HLC 28 (HL).

when a customer deposits cash or where funds are transferred into the account, the bank has the right to use the money as it sees fit and in return agrees to return an amount equal to that paid in. This repayment obligation may be on demand,[33] on giving notice, or at a set date in the future,[34] and there may be a duty to pay interest dependent on the terms of the agreement between the bank and the customer, but there is no duty to return the money *in specie*. Consequently, a bank account is a thing in action, and where a customer's account is in credit, the customer lends money to the bank,[35] when overdrawn the bank lends money to the customer. A bank account is therefore a debt, the value of which is determined by the credit or debit balance. Consequently, a bank customer may demand payment of the debt and it has been held that, unless agreed to the contrary, payment can be demanded in cash.[36]

 Foley v Hill (1848) 2 HLC 28 (HL)

FACTS: The claimant deposited over £6,000 with the bank in an interest-bearing account in 1829. Interest was credited until December 1831. The claimant commenced his action for account in 1838 and, amongst other things, the bank claimed it was not liable, since the claim was statute barred as there had been no acknowledgement of the debt for over six years.[37] The claimant argued that the bank was either a trustee of the money or his agent, in which case the Statute of Limitations would not have applied.

HELD: Money, when paid into a bank, ceases to be the money of the customer; it is the money of the bank to deal with and make profit from it. The bank is simply responsible to repay to the customer a sum equivalent to that he received.

COMMENT: Lord Brougham pointed out that the nature of banking (or at least that of deposit taking) was the taking in of money and using it to make a profit, returning an equal amount with or without interest as and when agreed between the parties. That business could not be carried on if the bank was either agent or trustee of the depositor. Lord Brougham went on to consider the case where a bank took deposit of an investment and undertook to collect the income on it from the issuer—a common function of banks. He left open the nature of the relationship, as it, too, would depend on the terms of the contract, but it clearly is capable of being one either of trusteeship or agency.

---

33. In which case a demand must actually be made (*Joachimson v Swiss Bank Corporation* [1921] 3 KB 110 (CA)), unless the bank is being wound up (*Re Russian Commercial and Industrial Bank* [1955] 1 Ch 148 (Ch)).

34. In which case the bank must initiate repayment (*Bank of America National Trust and Savings Association v Herman Iskandar* [1998] 2 SLR 265 (Sing CA) 284–5).

35. See *Joachimson v Swiss Bank Corporation* [1921] 3 KB 110 (CA) 127 (Lord Atkin).

36. In *Libyan Arab Foreign Bank v Bankers Trust Co* [1989] QB 728 (QB), it was held that in principle a customer could demand the whole of his credit balance, $292 million, in cash on giving reasonable notice, so that the requisite foreign currency could be acquired from the US. If the sterling equivalent were demanded, the ready availability of English currency in London would possibly suggest same-day delivery of the cash was required.

37. It is now established that the six-year limitation period runs from the date when the debt became payable, and unless the deposit is for a fixed period, that date is when there is a demand for payment. Where an account has been dormant for fifteen years or more, the Bank may apply the balance under the Dormant Bank and Building Society Accounts Act 2008 to a fund for charitable and similar purposes, and the customer then has a claim only against that fund.

> Finally, it should be noted that such was the state of delay in the Court of Chancery at the time that this very simple case had taken almost ten years to make its way to the House of Lords.

The structure of funds transfers

Although there is a range of mechanisms for originating a funds transfer, structurally all funds transfers are the same: they simply involve the adjustment of balances in bank accounts held by a payer and a payee with corresponding adjustments for the payer's and the payee's banks. The following example demonstrates this.

Eg ComCorp Ltd

ComCorp Ltd has to pay £3,000 to one of its suppliers, Ben. The most likely method of payment is that ComCorp will pay the money from its bank account into the bank account of Ben. ComCorp will send a payment instruction to its bank (Black Bank plc), and Black Bank will then debit ComCorp's account with £3,000, and send a payment instruction, on ComCorp's behalf, to Ben's bank (White Bank plc). White Bank will then credit Ben's account with £3,000.

In this example, there is no transfer of property between payer (ComCorp) and payee (Ben),[38] simply alterations in book entries in the books of account maintained by the parties' bankers. As Lord Millett said in *Foskett v McKeown*:[39]

> We speak of money at the bank, and of money passing into and out of a bank account. But of course the account holder has no money at the bank. Money paid into a bank account belongs legally and beneficially to the bank and not to the account holder … No money passes from paying bank to receiving bank or through the clearing system (where the money flows may be in the opposite direction). There is simply a series of debits and credits which are causally and transactionally linked.

What has happened is that the value of ComCorp's thing in action against Black Bank has reduced, while that of Ben against White Bank has increased. In our example, the banks appear simply as conduits for payment instructions and book keepers of their customers' accounts. However, were things to be left with ComCorp's account being debited £3,000 and Ben's account being credited with £3,000, Black Bank will be £3,000 better off and White Bank £3,000 worse off as a result of the transaction. There therefore needs to be some adjustment between the financial situations of the two banks; Black Bank needs to pay White Bank £3,000. Lord Millett refers to this in the quotation when he mentions the 'clearing system', which is the means whereby the banks calculate their mutual obligations with a view to

---

38. *R v Preddy* [1996] AC 815 (HL). In our example, ComCorp does not assign a thing in action (the debt owed by Black Bank to it) to Ben—it simply authorizes Black Bank to reduce the value of that thing in action if it arranges for the value of Ben's thing in action against White Bank to be increased. See Staughton J in *Libyan Arab Foreign Bank v Banker's Trust Co* [1989] QB 728 (QB) 750.
39. [2001] 1 AC 102 (HL) 127.

settlement, and then effect this settlement[40] through book entries either relating to accounts which the banks have with each other,[41] or with a third party[42] with whom they both have accounts.[43]

These messages to adjust the debtor–creditor relationship which pass between the banks are now primarily electronic and the two domestic electronic payment clearing systems for commercial payments are BACS (Bankers Automated Clearing Services) and CHAPS (Clearing House Automated Payment System). Electronic payment systems which are consumer activated[44]—automated teller machines and credit/debit cards—are not discussed in this chapter, and nor are the clearing systems for paper-based payments using cheques or bills of exchange.

CHAPS and BACS as examples of payment systems

CHAPS, which has seventeen participants, each of which is a bank, is a good illustration of an electronic clearing system. A funds transfer through CHAPS operates as demonstrated by the following example.

Eg ComCorp Ltd

ComCorp Ltd notifies its bank (Black Bank plc) that it wishes to make a CHAPS transfer to Marie via her bank (White Bank plc). If agreed, Black Bank will debit ComCorp's account and initiate a payment. An electronic message is sent from Black Bank to the Bank of England, which debits Black Bank's Bank of England settlement account and credits White Bank's settlement account. The Bank of England electronically confirms this has been done to Black Bank, which automatically sends a payment message to White Bank. White Bank may then initiate a checking process and, when complete, it sends what is called a 'logical acknowledgement message' to Black Bank. Once this message is sent, under CHAPS rules which also form part of the banker's contract with his customer,[45] White Bank must give same-day value to Marie by crediting her account with White Bank subject to provisions in the CHAPS rules allowing for return, for example for wrongly delivered payments, payments sent in error, or where Marie's bank account identification is incorrect.

CHAPS is also an example of gross settlement, that is to say the inter-bank payment obligation generated each time there is a CHAPS transfer is settled separately, as we have seen, by debits and credits at the participating banks' accounts at the Bank of England. Of course, there will be many thousands of similar transactions

---

40. See Benjamin Geva, 'The Clearing House Arrangement' (1991) 19 Can BLJ 138.

41. When they are called 'correspondent' banks, each having a bank account with the other and agreeing to give effect to payment orders from the other.

42. Where the banks are members of the same central clearing system, this will be with the Bank of England; if not, then with another bank (a correspondent bank which they have in common) with which they both have accounts.

43. Or with whom both of their clearing agents have an account.

44. See e.g. the Faster Payments System, which provides a two-hour processing time for Internet and telephone banking and standing orders.

45. *Tayeb v HSBC Bank plc* [2004] EWHC 1529 (Comm), [2004] 4 All ER 1024 .

during the course of a day between customers of the two banks (e.g. some where Black Bank is the payer and some where White Bank is the payer), but each transaction is settled separately, even though they are financially self-cancelling to a great extent. Until 1996, CHAPS operated on a net settlement basis, whereby these debits and credits generated throughout the banking day between the two banks would be set off against one another to determine their net financial position, which would then be settled at the end of the day.[46] Thus, CHAPS prior to 1996, was an example of bi-lateral netting: each participant's debtor or creditor status was determined as against each other participant's separately without reference to other parties in the clearing system.

A significant charge is made for a CHAPS transfer, and so although well suited to high-value payments; where there is a need for high-volume payments, the BACS clearing system is more appropriate. Thus, BACS is used for making bulk direct credits like the payment of wages and salaries and direct debits for regular bill payments. BACS is owned and operated by sixteen UK banks and building societies, and in 2011 almost 5.7 billion UK payments were made through BACS, with a total value of £4.3 trillion.[47]

Details of the debit and credit transfers transmitted to BACS electronically either directly or through the medium of tape or disc by 9pm on any clearing day (Day 1) will be processed by BACS overnight. The payees' bank will receive files relating to its customers who are to be paid by 6pm the next clearing day (Day 2) and will credit the payees at the opening of business on the following day (Day 3).

As well as providing an illustration of a payment system, BACS also exemplifies multi-lateral settlement netting. In a multi-lateral settlement process, at the end of each clearing period (in BACS this is at the end of each clearing day) each participant's financial position is established as against all of the other participants as a whole, rather than against each counterparty in turn. Each participant is therefore either a net creditor or a net debtor as against the other participants, and meeting this net net[48] payment obligation discharges the bank's obligations against each of the other participants. Consequently, it is this net net debit or credit that entered in the participant's account at the Bank of England at the end of the netting period. The danger with such a system is that one of the participants who is a net net debtor at the end of the clearing period becomes insolvent during a banking day. In *Re BCCI No 8*,[49] it was held that multi-lateral netting was ineffective, being contrary to the *pari passu* rule in insolvency. However, multi-lateral netting arrangements remain effective on 'designated systems' like BACS and CHAPS in respect of transfers

> *pari passu* rule: 'with equal step'—on an equal footing, each creditor shares proportionately in the loss

---

46. In fact, for administrative ease, the actual payment process through adjustments on the participating banks' accounts with the Bank of England was done on a multilateral basis, i.e. one adjustment on each bank's position with the Bank of England corresponding to the net net position, but contractually each bank's payment obligation was calculated on a bi-lateral net basis.

47. By contrast, in 2011 there were 35 million CHAPS transactions transferring £60 trillion.

48. The expression 'net net' is used to indicate that each of the bilateral net positions is itself netted off against all similar net positions.

49. *Morris v Rayners Enterprises Incorporated (In re BCCI No 8)* [1998] AC 214 (HL), following *British Eagle International Airlines Ltd v Compagnie Nationale Air France* [1975] 2 All ER 390 (HL). The relevant netting rules were amended slightly and have been held not to contravene the *pari passu* rule: see *International Air Transport Association v Ansett Australia Holdings Ltd* (2008) 242 ALR 47 (Australian High Court).

entered onto the system before the insolvency commenced, so that only the net net debit will need to be pursued in the participant's insolvency.[50]

When is a payment made in a funds transfer to the payee?

A payment to a payee is made through a funds transfer when the payee's bank unconditionally accepts the payee as its creditor in respect of the sum due and the funds are at the payee's disposal.[51] There is no need for the account of the payee's bank account to actually be credited.[52] How (or whether) the banks settle their obligations arising from the transaction is also immaterial. Consequently, whether the payee's bank is prepared to unconditionally credit the payee depends on its own view of the risk it runs that it will not itself receive full value from the payer's bank. Typically, for example, where the payee's bank and the payer's bank are correspondent banks, the payee's bank will probably not insist on settlement of its running account before unconditionally crediting the payee. Alternatively, it may insist on having its account with another bank credited before unconditionally committing to pay the payee. Consequently, where the payer wishes to make a payment which will be at the disposal of the payee on the same day, then the use of a system like CHAPS, which allows for almost instantaneous communication between the payee's bank and the payer's bank, is usually necessary. With a BACS payment, the payee's bank will have been paid by the payer's bank at the end of banking day (Day 2) before it unconditionally accepts the payee as its creditor in respect of the amount of the payment and credits the payee on Day 3.

Similarly, the payee's bank may receive a payment instruction which it cannot or does not wish to action, even though it has received payment from the payer's bank. For example, in *Tayeb v HSBC*,[53] the payee's bank received a CHAPS transfer instruction and returned the 'logical acknowledgement message' to the payer's bank and credited the payee, only to (wrongly) reverse the credit and return the transfer, later suspecting money laundering. In this instance, the suspicion of money laundering was unfounded, but the case illustrates issues other than credit risk which might prompt the payee's bank to delay the decision to credit the payee; other examples might be a suspicion that the payee is not entitled to the payment, or if the payee's bank wishes to check with the payee whether the payee wishes to receive payment.

➜ **money laundering**: a process whereby the origins of money (typically criminal) are obscured, often by passing it through multiple bank accounts

---

50. Financial Markets and Insolvency (Settlement Finality) Regulations 1999, SI 1999/2979. The effect of *Re BCCI No 8* had been that an insolvent participant could recover balances due to it from participating members, while participating members to which it owed money must pursue these claims in the insolvency, thus giving effect to bilateral set off only.

51. *Tayeb v HSBC Bank plc* [2004] EWHC 1529 (Comm), [2004] 4 All ER 1024; *A/S Awilco v Fulvia SpA di Navigazione (The Chikuma)* [1981] 1 All ER 652 (HL). But the beneficiary need not accept payment: see *Mardorf Peach & Co Ltd v Attica Sea Carriers Corporation of Liberia (The Laconia)* [1977] AC 850 (HL).

52. *Astro Amo Compania Naviera SA v Elf Union SA and First National City Bank (The Zographia M)* [1976] 2 Lloyd's Rep 382 (QB). See also *Momm v Barclay's Bank International Ltd* [1977] QB 790 (QB). This case involved an in-house transfer, but the principle seems to apply generally.

53. *Tayeb v HSBC Bank plc* [2004] EWHC 1529 (Comm), [2004] 4 All ER 1024.

Tayeb v HSBC Bank plc [2004] EWHC 1529 (Comm)

FACTS: Tayeb had sold an asset and was owed around £1 million, which the buyer sought to pay by a CHAPS transfer. HSBC, Tayeb's bank, received notification to credit his account with £1 million and the 'logical acknowledgement message' was automatically transmitted to the payer's bank. Because of the size of the transfer, Tayeb's account was not automatically credited, but the instruction was manually verified and entered into HSBC's computer system, the effect being that Tayeb's account had been credited. HSBC became suspicious that the £1 million was the proceeds of crime and two hours later placed a stop on the account, preventing withdrawals, and next day debited the account and returned the transfer to the payer's bank. Thus the buyer was re-credited with the £1 million and although Tayeb asked the buyer to retransmit the money when HSBC became satisfied there was no money laundering involved, they refused. Tayeb sued HSBC for £1 million, claiming that by unconditionally crediting the account HSBC had acknowledged him as its creditor.

HELD: The bank was liable. The CHAPS rules allow for the return of a transfer where the transfer cannot be applied to the payee's account or where the transfer has been made in error; the rules do not grant a right, nor is one to be implied, which gives the receiving bank a discretion to reverse a transfer on suspicions of money laundering. A customer's contract with the bank contains an implied term that the bank will operate an account which can receive a CHAPS transfer in accordance with the CHAPS rules. Consequently, the bank was in debt to the claimant for £1 million.

COMMENT: Coleman J recognized that for CHAPS to work, transfers must proceed on the basis that once a transfer has been accepted it is safe for the beneficiary to treat the funds as irrevocably his own. He pointed out that if the seller of a house in a chain of buyer and sellers could not rely on this assumption, then it would be necessary for conveyancing to return to the system of physical completion. Similarly, many financial transactions have to rely on irrevocability of payment; any uncertainty about the matter would cause serious commercial concern. The CHAPS Rules permit a reversal in cases of mistaken transfers—for example where a transfer has been made twice or where the wrong payee has been identified—but typically the receiving bank will check with the payee first. HSBC had argued that there was a banking practice which entitled a receiving bank to refuse a CHAPS transfer order to credit an account (or to reverse a credit) in order to enable it to avoid liability under anti-money laundering legislation. This legislation makes it an offence to be concerned in an arrangement for laundering money suspected of being criminal property.[54] The court held that there was insufficient evidence of such a banking practice. Coleman J did, however, suggest two instances where a CHAPS transfer might be reversed: first, in the case of fraud by the recipient by analogy with documentary credits; and second, where the payment was illegal.

The rights of a bank not to pay in a case of fraud under a documentary credits are discussed at p 672

See EP Ellinger, 'Irrevocability of CHAPS Money Transfer' (2005) 121 LQR 48

Can payment orders be recalled?

In principle, since the payer's bank is the agent of the payer for the purposes of carrying out the payment instruction, the payer may recall the instruction until the transaction is complete,[55] at least until he has incurred liabilities to a third party.[56]

---

54. In *Tayeb,* the relevant statute was Criminal Justice Act 1988, s 93A, now Proceeds of Crime Act 2002, ss 327 and 328.

55. *Gibson v Minet* (1824) 130 ER 206.

56. *Campanari v Woodburn* (1854) 15 CB 400; *Warlow v Harrison* (1859) 1 E & E 309 (neither case involves banking).

However, the mandate of the payer's bank to act on the payer's instructions will not be dependent on principles of agency as such, but on the terms of contract the payer has with his bank, which itself may depend on the terms of any clearing system through which the payment must go and on banking practice.[57] In a CHAPS transfer, unless it involves a mistaken payment as defined in the CHAPS rules, the order is irrevocable once it is entered into CHAPS, since in the ordinary course of events, the payee's bank will credit the payee, thus triggering the payer's bank's obligation to reimburse it.[58] BACS rules provide for recall by communication from the paying bank to the receiving bank by 3.30pm on Day 2, in other words the last point before the payee is credited at the opening of business on Day 3.

Where there is no clearing involved—that is where both the payee and the payer have the same bank—then the payee is paid and the transfer beyond recall when the bank unconditionally recognizes the payee as its creditor in respect of the sum transferred, whether or not the respective accounts have been debited and credited.[59]

 Momm v Barclays Bank International Ltd [1977] QB 790 (QB)

FACTS: Herstatt Bank had an account with the London Branch of Barclays and ordered Barclays to transfer £120,000 from that account to Momm's account at the same branch. Barclays entered the transaction into its computer system, even though Herstatt's account was already overdrawn. Later that day Herstatt, was declared insolvent: the transfer was processed on Barclay's computer overnight, but the next day it reversed the transfer. The transfer and re-transfer did not appear on Momm's account, who only discovered what had happened later.

HELD: The payment was made as soon as the decision was made to credit Momm's account unconditionally. This was evidenced by the initiation of the computer process. Kerr J also held that in accordance with banking practice, a payment is made if the payee's account is credited with the payment at the close of business on the day on which the payee has free use of the funds (the 'value date'), at least if the credit was made intentionally and in good faith and not by error or fraud.

COMMENT: Clearly, where the payer and payee bank are at the same branch, the value date would be the date of transfer, since there are few matters which might make the transfer conditional, but the balance on the payer's account is only up to date as at the close of business on the previous day. Consequently, the payee might well be credited on condition that there were sufficient funds.[60] It has been suggested that where it is difficult to determine whether a credit is conditional, payment is made at the moment when the payee would be told on inquiry to his bank that the account was to be credited.[61]

---

57. Though see Roy Goode and Ewan McKendrick, *Goode on Commercial Law* (4th edn, Penguin 2010) 507, who argues that the banking contract, clearing rules, and banking practice are separate issues.
58. This is the implication of *Tayeb v HSBC Bank plc* [2004] EWHC 1529 (Comm), [2004] 4 All ER 1024 [60] and [92].
59. *Tenax Steamship Co Ltd v Reinante Transoceanica Navigation SA (The Brimnes)* [1975] 1 QB 929 (CA).
60. See *Sutherland v Royal Bank of Scotland plc* [1997] SLT 329.
61. Benjamin Geva, 'Payment into a Bank Account' (1990) 3 JIBL 108, 112–15.

Conclusion

Although most commercial transactions will involve a payment obligation, what amounts to payment is not as self-evident as it might appear. Ideally the parties will agree when, where, and how the payment obligation their arrangement has created will be met. In a consumer retail situation, it might be obvious that the payment obligation is to be met immediately and in cash, or alternatively the retailer may indicate he will accept a funds transfer through the mechanism of a payment, credit, or debit card. However, in a business-to-business transaction, the time when the payment obligation arises will need to be agreed, and although the parties may stipulate cash settlement, almost certainly they will not actually envisage payment with a suitcase of £50 notes, but some form of funds transfer, which they will treat as being cash or its equivalent.

The nature of money, even in the form of cash, is again not self-evident. Although a tangible asset and thus a chattel, cash is also a debt owed by the Bank of England[62] to the lawful holder and thus a thing in action. A bank account is also a thing in action; it is simply a right to make a claim to be paid money against the bank's payment obligation arising under the banker customer agreement.

The nature of tangible personal property is discussed in Chapter 2

Funds transfers, unlike cash transactions, do not involve the passing of property from payer to payee. The payer's bank account is debited and the payee's bank account credited with the relevant amount with a consequent settlement at some point between their respective bankers. However, the time when a bank's customer is treated as having received a funds transfer depends on the confidence that his bank has that the payer's bank will settle the interbank indebtedness created. However, although the value of money transferred through domestic electronic funds transfer systems like BACS and CHAPS is staggering,[63] and the security mechanisms complex, the interbank settlement process at its heart is simple, ultimately a matter of book entries in the accounts of the participating banks at the Bank of England. Putting it another way, it is a process whereby an obligation by the central bank to pay is substituted for a payment obligation by a commercial bank to pay another commercial bank. In both BACS and CHAPS, the payee's bank knows that the payer's bank has settled the interbank indebtedness before the payee's account is credited, but until settlement has occurred, a bank unconditionally accepting its customer as having been paid through a funds transfer takes a risk that it will never be paid by its other counterparty, the payer's bank.

Because both cash and bank accounts are both promises to pay, put crudely, money in contemporary commerce is simply a promise to pay something which itself is a promise to pay.

Practice questions

1. Explain the following terms and expressions:

   - money;
   - gross settlement, net settlement;
   - bi-lateral netting;
   - multi-lateral netting;

---

62. This is true in England but some Scottish and Northern Irish banks also issue bank notes.
63. Though Fedwire in the US handles around ten times the value annually.

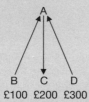 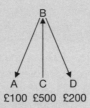 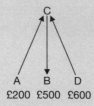 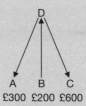

FIGURE 23.1 The financial positions of the banks

- a bank account and a bank note are both 'things in action';
- repayment on demand.

2. Antimony Bank (A in Figure 23.1), Borax Bank (B in Figure 23.1), Chlorine Bank (C in Figure 23.1), and Deuterium Bank (D in Figure 23.1) are the only participants involved in a bi-lateral net clearing system. At the end of a clearing period, their obligations are shown in Figure 23.1.

Antimony Bank's customers have received £100 more from customers of Borax Bank than customers of Borax Bank have received from customers of Antimony Bank. The net position between the two banks is therefore that Borax Bank must pay £100 to Antimony Bank. However, Antimony Bank's customers have received £200 less from Chlorine Bank's customers than customers of Chlorine Bank have received from customers of Antimony Bank. The net position between these two banks is that Antimony Bank must pay £200 to Chlorine Bank. Finally, Antimony Bank's customers have received £300 more from Deuterium Bank's customer than Deuterium Bank's customers have received from Antimony Bank's customers. Overall, therefore, Antimony Bank will make one payment (to Chlorine Bank) and receive two payments (from Borax Bank and Deuterium Bank). In a similar fashion, the net positions of the other participants can be determined from Figure 23.1. However, Deuterium Bank becomes insolvent before any settlement occurs and will pay its creditors only 10 per cent of what they are owed.

What is the effect of this insolvency on the other clearing participants?

Since Antimony Bank and Chlorine Bank will lose money through Deuterium Bank's default, can Antimony Bank and Chlorine Bank reverse the entries in their books of account with their customers who have received payments from Deuterium Bank's customers during the day?

What would the situation be if instead of this being a bi-lateral clearing system, it had been a multilateral clearing system?

Further reading

Michael Brindle and Raymond Cox (eds), *Law of Bank Payments* (4th edn, Sweet & Maxwell 2010)
- Although a practitioner's text covering the whole range of payment mechanisms, Chapter 3, dealing with funds transfers, is particularly relevant for our purposes, with good explanations of settlement and of bi-lateral and multi-lateral netting.

Peter Ellinger, Eva Lomnicka, and Christopher Hare, *Ellinger's Modern Banking Law*
(5th edn, OUP 2010)

- Originally a student text on banking law, it has become an invaluable tool to practitioners. It covers banking law comprehensively, but Chapter 13 is particularly relevant since it deals with funds transfers.

Benjamin Geva, **'Payment into a Bank Account'** (1990) 3 JIBL 108

- In addition to containing a useful analysis on the timing when payment is actually made and discussion of the value date in banking, this article suggests that as a rule of thumb a payment is made into a bank account at the earliest moment the account holder would be told that the funds had been credited.

Charles Proctor (ed), *Goode on Payment Obligations in Commercial and Financial Transactions* (2nd edn, Sweet & Maxwell 2009)

- The most comprehensive monograph on the legal nature of the payment obligation. It covers the mode, place, and timing of payment and defences claim for payment. The coverage of funds transfers is up to date and foreign payments are also dealt with.

- The nature of an instrument
- Bills of exchange
- Letters of credit
- The key characteristics of credits

INTRODUCTION

This chapter falls into two main parts. First, it aims to provide an introduction to the concept of an important piece of property called an instrument, principally by focussing on one specific example: the bill of exchange. Bills of exchange, of which cheques are a particular type, although declining in importance in domestic sales, remain important in international sales, especially in conjunction with a bank payment mechanism called letters of credit, and consideration of letters of credit constitutes the second part of this chapter. While bills of exchange are not the only instruments, and letters of credit are not the only mechanism supporting the financing of international trade, by focussing on these two important commercial documents it is possible to obtain a good understanding of the types of legal issues involved in documentary payments. In addition, they form part of the 'documentary triangle' in international documentary sales, alongside bills of lading and policies of marine cargo insurance.

Bills of lading are discussed in Chapter 19, where the idea of the 'documentary triangle' is introduced at p 487. Marine cargo insurance is discussed in Chapter 22

The nature of an instrument

Chapter 2, which was concerned with personal property, dealt primarily with tangible property, but mention was made of intangible property, called things in action, such as the right to claim money from a debtor. Normally, passing legal title to such a thing in action requires a written assignment signed by the assignor and for notice to be given to the debtor as required by s 136 of the Law of Property Act 1925. In addition, the assignee has no better claim against the debtor than the assignor, so that where, for example, the assigned debt arises under a contract of sale of goods, defences available under the contract against the seller will be equally available against the assignee.

Receivables financing, which relies on the assignment of debts, is discussed at p 712

> ### Eg ComCorp Ltd
>
> ComCorp Ltd has sold goods to David for delivery in two years' time for £100,000. David, who cannot pay immediately, has tendered a document which he has signed, stating 'I

> promise to pay to ComCorp Ltd or its order £100,000 on 1st June 2015'. Bill, who is looking for investment opportunities, has offered £80,000 to ComCorp Ltd for the document. If ComCorp Ltd were to sell the document to Bill, would he be able to claim the £100,000 from David on the due date?

However, possession of certain documents of title to money, known as instruments,[1] carry with them the right to claim the money comprised in the debt, and these documents are treated as the embodiment of the payment obligation they represent. With an instrument, unlike an ordinary debt, the payment obligation embodied in it is separate from the relationship that led to its creation. Consequently, the embodied payment obligation is insulated from certain types of dispute arising out of the underlying contract once value has been given for it. Similarly, there is insulation from defects in title to the instrument, for example where it was procured or transferred through fraud or duress. Consequently, the holder of an instrument is entitled to summary judgment under Pt 24 of the Civil Procedure Rules, except in exceptional circumstances, by virtue of these characteristics known as the autonomy of the payment.[2] The extent of the insulation from defences and defects is considered in more detail later in this chapter, but suppose in our ComCorp example, ComCorp sells the document signed by David to Bill, but David lawfully rejects the goods when they are delivered, so that there is total failure of consideration under the sales contract. Bill would still be entitled to summary judgment against David for the £100,000, assuming he acted in good faith and without notice of the issues giving rise to the right to reject. On the other hand, if Bill had simply taken an assignment of the benefit of the sales contract, which superficially looks very similar to taking an assignment of the instrument, he would have been vulnerable to any defence David has against a claim for the purchase price by ComCorp Ltd.

Whether a document is treated as an instrument is determined by commercial practice and statute, and consequently the list of instruments is not closed; new species of instruments may be created through the ingenuity and practice of market participants.[3] Currently all instruments are in the form either of a promise to pay, or an order to a third party to pay a sum of money. Thus, a document like the one in the ComCorp example in which one person promises to pay another an ascertainable sum of money at a fixed date will constitute an instrument called a promissory note if that is what is intended,[4] while a cheque, which is an order to a bank to pay money to the payee, is also an instrument—a bill of exchange.

 Claydon v Bradley **[1987] 1 WLR 521 (CA)**

FACTS: The claimant lent money to a company in which the defendant was the major shareholder. The defendant signed a document headed with the company's name and address as follows:

---

1. Instruments are not confined to debts as such, but all embody either an obligation to pay money or an order to someone to pay.
2. *Cebora SNC v SIP (Industrial Products) Ltd* [1976] 1 Lloyd's Rep 271 (CA).
3. See *Goodwin v Robarts* (1876) 1 App Cas 476 (HL). The judgment in the Court of Exchequer (1874–75) LR 10 Ex 76 by Cockburn CJ is a *tour de force* on the history of negotiability in the law merchant.
4. *Claydon v Bradley* [1987] 1 WLR 521 (CA).

> Received from Mr. and Mrs. T. Claydon The Sum of £10,000 (Ten Thousand Pounds) as a loan to be paid back in full by 1st. July 1983 with an interest rate of 20% (Twenty Percent) per annum. Yours faithfully, P.M. Bradley.'

The company went into liquidation and could not repay the debt in full, so the claimant sued the defendant, since the signatory of a dishonoured bill of exchange or promissory note is personally liable on it unless he 'adds words to his signature, indicating that he signs for or on behalf of a principal, or in a representative character',[5] and Mrs Bradley had not done that. Section 83(1) of the Bills of Exchange Act 1883 defines a promissory note as:

> an unconditional promise in writing made by one person to another … engaging to pay on demand or at a fixed or determinable future time, a sum certain in money, to, or to the order of, a specified person or to bearer.

So, was the document a promissory note?

HELD: The document was not a promissory note so that the drawer was not personally liable on it. First, it contemplated repayment on *or before* 1 July, which is not a fixed time. Second, the document was primarily a receipt for money. Though it did record the terms of the loan, it was not intended to be capable of being enforced by someone other than the lender.

COMMENT: In reaching their decision on the function of the note, the court was heavily influenced by the Privy Council decision in *Akbar Khan v Attar Singh*,[6] where Lord Atkin explained that negotiable instruments 'must come into existence for the purpose only of recording an agreement to pay money and nothing more, though … they may state the consideration' and, referring to a document similar to that in *Bradley*, continued:

> Receipts and agreements generally are not intended to be negotiable, and serious embarrassment would be caused in commerce if the negotiable[7] net were cast too wide. This document plainly is a receipt for money containing the terms on which it is to be repaid … Being primarily a receipt even if coupled with a promise to pay it is not a promissory note.

Note how influenced the court was that it was not in the contemplation of the parties that anyone other than the Bradleys should enforce the debt. However, it should be noted that it seems only minor changes in the terminology in *Bradley* might have resulted in a different outcome.

Instruments may be negotiable or not negotiable. 'Negotiable' means 'transferable'—usually as a result of being sold. Where the instrument is 'negotiable', two incidents flow from this.

First, the instrument may be transferred either by delivery alone or by delivery and indorsement (signing on the back), depending on its form. The result is that a transfer of a negotiable instrument will (subject to the intention of the parties) pass legal title to the rights embodied in it without any other process of assignment or for

---

5. Bills of Exchange Act 1882, s 26(1). A bank note is a promissory note. Look at one and see how the Chief Cashier avoids personal liability to pay the holders of Bank of England notes.

6. [1936] 2 All ER 545 (PC).

7. In context, it seems likely Lord Atkin was only referring to transferability of the document when he referred to negotiability, though of course, if an instrument is not transferable, its second characteristic of curing the transferor's defects in title becomes irrelevant.

notice of the assignment to be given to the debtor, providing an exception to the rule of privity of contract. However, the fact that a document is freely transferable does not make it an instrument so that, for example, whilst title to a contract of marine insurance passes at law without meeting the s 136 requirements,[8] the insurer can raise defences to claims by a bona fide assignee in respect of breaches committed by a predecessor in title; in other words the policy document does not create a separate payment obligation apart from the underlying contract of insurance.

Second, an honest transferee for value of a negotiable instrument (known as a holder in due course in relation to bills of exchange) takes free from defects in the title of the transferor,[9] thus good title to a negotiable instrument may be passed by a thief[10] or fraudster—providing an example of an exception to the *nemo dat* rule.[11]

Although promissory notes (including banknotes), bearer bonds and debentures, share warrants, bankers' drafts, and bills of exchange are all negotiable instruments,[12] only detailed consideration will be given to bills of exchange.

Bills of exchange

Bills of exchange are defined by s 3 of the Bills of Exchange Act 1882 and are unconditional orders given by one person to another to pay money, the most common example of which being a cheque, where the order is directed to a bank and is payable on demand, that is to say immediately the holder of the cheque presents it to the bank for payment.[13]

In order to understand how bills of exchange function, it is necessary to examine their form, the parties to them, and the statutory definition.

A sample three-party bill of exchange

Consider the following example.

Eg ComCorp Ltd

ComCorp Ltd has agreed to buy some new equipment from Candy & Holly Ltd for £500,000 and has been given six months to pay. ComCorp wants to pay from its account

---

8. At common law it passed by indorsement or in some instances delivery only and this position is preserved in the Marine Insurance Act 1906, s 50(3).

9. The two aspects of negotiability are contrasted in *Crouch v The Credit Foncier of England Ltd* (1872–73) LR 8 QB 374 (QB), where mercantile custom accepted, and the parties had agreed, that title to the document and the right to claim on it passed on delivery and so was negotiable in the first sense, but the court held that it failed to meet the legal requirements to constitute negotiability in the second.

10. *Miller v Race* (1758) 97 ER 398, but only if the thief has not had to indorse it in order to purport to pass title.

11. *London Joint Stock Bank v Simmons* [1892] AC 201 (HL).

12. Examples of non-negotiable instruments include postal orders.

13. Bills of Exchange Act 1882, s 73. If you have a cheque book, look at the form of the cheques and identify the statutory requirements.

> with Banco Rico. Candy & Holly Ltd wants a bill of exchange drawn on a reputable bank for the amount owing. What might such a bill of exchange look like?

Although not intended to suggest the typical image of a bill of exchange, Figure 24.1 contains the essential elements. The bracketed letters in italics are for ease of reference to the text, and are not part of the bill. Refer to the statutory definition in s 3 of the Bills of Exchange Act 1882 to identify the operative parts of this sample bill of exchange.

The parties to the sample bill of exchange

Texts and cases on bills of exchange use a range of terms to identify the parties. Listed here are the parties to the sample bill of exchange in Figure 24.1.

(a) The drawer—the person signing the bill and giving the order to pay (in our example ComCorp Ltd).

(b) The drawee—the person to whom the instruction is given (in our example, Banco Rico). The assumption in this chapter is that the drawee will be a bank, but there is no requirement that this is so.

(c) The acceptor—a person who has accepted the obligation to pay (again, in our example, Banco Rico). As will be discussed, there may be more than one acceptor.

(d) The payee—the person to whom the drawee/acceptor is ordered to make payment and the person whom the drawer wants to pay (in our example Candy & Holly Ltd).

Understanding the sample bill of exchange

In our example, Banco Rico has accepted the obligation to pay £500,000 at what is called the 'maturity date' of the bill, 7 October 2013. When Banco Rico pays on the bill of exchange it will debit ComCorp's account with £500,000, which means Candy & Holly Ltd has given six month's credit to ComCorp Ltd. Notice that the obligation is to pay 'Candy & Holly Ltd or order'. This means that the bill is 'negotiable'; that is, it can be transferred by Candy & Holly Ltd to another person and, since it is an instrument, with the document will pass the right to claim the payment from Banco Rico. So Candy & Holly Ltd could sell ('negotiate') the bill, perhaps to

	London 7th April 2013
Accepted	To Banco Rico (b)
Payable at London Head Office or Sydney Branch	Six months after the date above please pay to Candy & Holly Ltd (d) or order the sum of GBP 500,000 (Five Hundred Thousand Pounds Sterling), for value received.
	ComCorp Ltd (a)
Rio Bueno For and on behalf of Banco Rico (c)	*Per pro G. D. Osborne – director.*

Figure 24.1 A sample bill of exchange

its own bank, in return for immediate payment. The purchaser of a bill will only give a discounted and not face value for it, but Candy & Holly Ltd will receive payment immediately and not have to wait six months. A non-negotiable bill would have said simply 'pay to Candy & Holly Ltd only'. In order to transfer the bill, Candy & Holly Ltd simply has to sign the back ('indorse'), which is its order to pay someone else and deliver the bill to the purchaser/transferee. Although an 'order bill' like this requires indorsement in order to transfer it, title to a 'bearer bill'—that is one made out to 'bearer' rather than a named person—simply passes on delivery of the document.

At maturity, whoever is the holder of the bill at the time will present it to Banco Rico for payment and, subject to some limited defences, the bank must pay even if its customer, ComCorp Ltd, is insolvent and will never reimburse it.

✐ These defences are discussed at p 652

The statutory requirements of a bill of exchange

The definition of a bill of exchange is given in s 3 of the Bills of Exchange Act 1882.

🔑 Bills of Exchange Act 1882, s 3

(1) A bill of exchange is an unconditional order in writing, addressed by one person to another, signed by the person giving it, requiring the person to whom it is addressed to pay on demand or at a fixed or determinable future time a sum certain in money to or to the order of a specified person, or to bearer.
(2) An instrument which does not comply with these conditions, or which orders any act to be done in addition to the payment of money, is not a bill of exchange.

Taking each of the statutory requirements in turn and, where relevant, referring to the sample bill of exchange:

'Unconditional'

It should be noted that the requirement of unconditionality applies only in relation to the instruction to the bank; the drawer may impose conditions on the payee without the bill becoming conditional.[14] If the bank is required to pay out of a specified fund, then the order is not unconditional, it is dependent on the fund being adequate. However, as s 3(3) of the Bills of Exchange Act 1882 makes clear, an order which is otherwise unqualified remains unconditional, even if it indicates a particular fund or account out of which the bank is to reimburse itself,[15] or if it contains a statement of the transaction which gives rise to the bill.[16] It remains unclear whether an instruction to a bank to pay 'against documents' (in other words, only if the holder presents specific shipping documents, a common requirement in international sales of goods) is unconditional.[17]

---

14. *Roberts & Co v Marsh* [1915] 1 KB 42 (CA).
15. Thus a cheque drawn on a particular account is treated as an unconditional order to pay with an authority to the bank to reimburse itself by debiting the account.
16. Commonly a bank issuing a letter of credit will require that bills drawn under the credit identify the transaction to which they relate.
17. There is indirect Australian authority to suggest it is not unconditional—*Lister v Schulte* [1915] VLR 374. See also *Rosenhain v Commonwealth Bank of Australia* (1922) 31 CLR 46, 52–3.

'Order'

The sample bill, although polite, is nevertheless an order by the drawer to the bank to pay the payee. However, where the bank is not instructed but merely authorized to pay, then it is not a bill of exchange.[18]

'In writing'

In the sample bill, the document has been drafted for a particular transaction, but typically bills will be at least partly pre-printed by the bank. Although in theory any surface which may be written on may be used as a bill of exchange, in practice in relation to cheques at least, the contractual terms on which banks agree to offer services to their customers will require the use of pre-printed cheque forms.[19]

The requirement for writing, however, poses a serious limitation to the development of the bill of exchange. Although parties to a contract may form it instantaneously through electronic communication and make payment instantaneously though funds transfers, such transfers cannot be bills of exchange. Even were the Secretary of State to exercise his power under s 8 of the Electronic Communications Act 2000 to amend the 1882 Act in order to facilitate the use of electronic communication, it seems improbable that this would be sufficient to permit bills of exchange, which are a physical embodiment of a payment obligation, to have incorporeal form.[20]

'Addressed by one person to another'

There is no reason why the drawer of a bill should not also be the payee; indeed in the years before automatic teller machines, the normal way to withdraw cash from one's own bank account was by drawing a cheque payable to 'Self'. However, a bill cannot be addressed to the drawer (it would be an order to oneself), but the holder of a document in this form can treat it either as a bill of exchange or a promissory note.[21]

'Signed by the person giving it'

What amounts to 'signing' is not defined in the Act, though the affixing of a rubber-stamped facsimile by the signatory has (in a totally different context) been held to be sufficient,[22] and facsimile signatures are commonly used on cheques. Until the minister exercises his power under s 8 of the Electronic Communications Act 2000, the consensus is that an electronic signature is insufficient.[23] The signature may be effected by an agent,[24] who will become personally liable on the bill if it is dishonoured

---

18. *Hamilton v Spottiswoode* (1849) 4 Ex 200.
19. AP Herbert's fictitious case of *Haddock v Board of Inland Revenue*, in which a cheque for £57 in back tax was written on the side of a cow, has spawned numerous imitators and has even received judicial recognition in the Court of Appeals for Maryland in *Messing v Bank of America*, 143 Md App 1, 15–16, 792 A2d 312, 320–1 (2002).
20. See Law Commission, *Electronic Commerce: Formal Requirements in Commercial Transactions Advice from the Law Commission* (2001) paras 9.4–9.7. See also Hugh Beale and Lowri Griffiths, 'Electronic Commerce: Formal Requirements in Commercial Transactions' [2002] LMCLQ 467.
21. Bills of Exchange Act 1882, s 5(2).
22. *Goodman v J Eban* Ltd [1954] 1 QB 550 (CA) (bill of costs from solicitor required to be signed by virtue of s 65(2)(i) of the Solicitors Act 1932; see now s 69 of the Solicitors Act 1974).
23. See Hugh Beale and Lowri Griffiths, 'Electronic Commerce: Formal Requirements in Commercial Transactions' [2002] LMCLQ 467, 483.
24. Bills of Exchange Act 1882, s 91.

unless the bill shows that he signed as agent, but 'the mere addition to his signature of words describing him as an agent, or as filling a representative character, does not exempt him from personal liability'.[25] Thus in our sample bill, the signature was 'GD Osborne per pro ComCorp Ltd',[26] a common means of indicating agency status, but signing simply 'GD Osborne director' or 'GD Osborne agent' would be insufficient.

A forged or unauthorized signature is of no effect; the document is not a bill of exchange.[27]

Payable 'on demand or at a fixed or determinable future time'

Section 10 of the Bills of Exchange Act 1882 provides that bills made payable 'on demand', 'at sight' (meaning on presentation to the bank for payment), 'on presentation', or where no time for payment is expressed, are all 'payable on demand'. These are commonly all called (slightly incorrectly) 'sight' bills. Where the bill is not payable on demand, the date for payment must be capable of being determined through its being payable either:

- at a fixed period after its date (as in the sample bill above) or at a fixed period after sight; or
- on or at a fixed period after the occurrence of a specified event which is certain to happen, though the time of happening may be uncertain.[28]

But as *Claydon v Bradley* illustrates, a note payable 'on or before' a given date does not provide a fixed period,[29] and similarly an obligation payable ninety days after the date of acceptance is not a bill of exchange because the contingency—acceptance— may never happen since the bank might not accept the bill.[30]

However, there is a balance to be struck between requiring bills to be free from ambiguity and giving them the legal effect the parties intended. On the one hand their essence is negotiability and a future holder will not have been privy to circumstances that can resolve such ambiguity, while on the other it is clearly inappropriate to permit technicalities to destroy the validity of a document which is clearly intended to operate as a bill of exchange. In the following case, the Court of Appeal seemed to decide that the balance should favour validity.

 Hong Kong and Shanghai Banking Corp Ltd v GD Trade Co Ltd [1998] CLC 238 (CA)

FACTS: GD Trade bought a number of consignments of floppy discs from Prime, which it was agreed should be paid for using bills of exchange. Prime, the drawers, used printed forms of bills of exchange supplied by HKS Bank. The maturity date was printed on the

---

25. ibid s 26.

26. This formulation also protects the drawer from liability if the signatory exceeds his authority in signing. See p 655.

27. Bills of Exchange Act 1882, s 24. For further consideration of unauthorized or forged signatures, see p 654.

28. Bills of Exchange Act 1882, s 11. Thus e.g. in *Colehan v Cooke* (1792) Willes 793, a payment obligation six weeks after the death of the drawer's father was ascertainable.

29. Though see the case note on *Williamson v Rider* [1962] All ER 268 (CA) by AH Hudson (1962) 25 MLR 593.

30. *Korea Exchange Bank v Debenhams (Central Buying) Ltd* [1979] 1 Lloyd's Rep 548 (CA).

form as 'At ... sight of [description of documents]', permitting the drawer to insert suitable words in the gap. Prime, using a manual typewriter, typed the words '90 days after acceptance' in the blank space between the words 'At' and 'sight' which, because the font was too large, partially obscured the words 'sight of', though they could still be read. The documents ordered GD Trade to pay the HKS Bank who were Prime's bank. GD Trade accepted the documents.

It was argued that, following *Korea Exchange Bank v Debenhams (Central Buying) Ltd*,[31] this meant that the maturity date was subject to a contingency (acceptance) which might not happen.

HELD: It was clear from each document that the drawer had not intended to delete the words 'sight of'. Properly construed, the documents were payable 'at 90 days after acceptance/sight'. Since 'sight' means presentation for acceptance, whether the bill is actually accepted or not, a term for payment at a fixed period after sight therefore ensures certainty as to the date of maturity whether the bill is accepted or refused. Therefore this was a bill of exchange.

COMMENT: The Court, had it wished, could have accepted the argument that the maturity date of the documents was sufficiently ambiguous to warrant their not being treated as bills of exchange. But while mindful of the need for bills to be sufficiently certain to be commercially negotiated, the court pointed out that a bill:

> is a document in use in hundreds of commercial transactions and, in the case of an instrument which has been drawn as a bill with the plain intention that it should take effect as such, the court should lean in favour of a construction which upholds its validity as a bill where that is reasonably possible.

In this case the bills had been accepted, and the acceptance actually stated the date on which the bill matured. The Court of Appeal did not have to consider an argument advanced at first instance that acceptance estopped the acceptor from denying the validity of the bill, but did suggest that such an acceptance, at least if made before the bill was negotiated, could cure the lack of certainty notwithstanding s 11(2), which states, 'An instrument expressed to be payable on a contingency is not a bill, and the happening of the event does not cure the defect.'[32]

⭐ See Christopher Forsyth, 'When is a Bill of Exchange Not a Bill of Exchange? The Effect of an Inadvertent Deletion' (1999) 58 CLJ 58

It should be noted that a bill does not need to be dated in order to be valid,[33] but where, as in the sample bill, the maturity date is calculated by reference to the date of the bill, then the bill must be dated in order to meet the requirements of s 11 of the Bills of Exchange Act 1882. Similarly, a bill payable at a fixed period after 'sight'[34] must include the date of acceptance.

---

31. [1979]1 Lloyd's Rep 548 (CA).
32. The same view concerning acceptances which cure ambiguity was taken in *Novaknit Hellas v Kumar Bros International Ltd and Others* [1998] Lloyd's Rep Bank 287 (CA), where it was also held that acceptance in this form turned the instrument into a promissory note.
33. Bills of Exchange Act 1882, s 34(a).
34. Which is either the date of the acceptance if the bill be accepted, and the date of noting or protest if not.

'A sum certain in money'

The amount payable may be expressed in sterling or a foreign currency, and the payment obligation may be in instalments with or without an **acceleration clause** and with or without interest.[35]

'To or to the order of a specified person, or to bearer'

The payee may be described on a bill of exchange as 'bearer'—that is to say, the person in possession of the bill[36]—but in other cases the payee must be named or otherwise indicated with reasonable certainty.[37] Thus an instrument payable to 'Cash' or 'Wages' is not a bill of exchange, but nevertheless is a valid order to pay the bearer.[38]

➜ **acceleration clause:** in the event of a default under an agreement providing for payment in instalments, an acceleration clause makes all sums due immediately

Curing formal defects—incomplete bills

By virtue of s 20(1) of the Bills of Exchange Act 1882, when a bill omits a statutory requirement, the person in possession of it has a *prima facie* authority to rectify any omission as he thinks fit. A person who was a party to such an 'inchoate' instrument before its rectification will be liable only if it is completed within a reasonable time and strictly in accordance with the authority given,[39] but no such limitations apply as against a transferee who acquires the bill in good faith and for valuable consideration after it has been completed (i.e. a holder in due course).

Transfer of bills of exchange

One of the advantages of a bill of exchange is that it can be made payable in the future, thus providing a credit mechanism for the person whose payment obligation the bill is intended to satisfy, as is the case with our sample bill in Figure 24.1. The corresponding disadvantage to the payee can be ameliorated through the mechanism of negotiability; that is to say, the payee can sell the bill (usually at a discount) for cash, passing title to it to the purchaser without notice to the person(s) liable on it and free from any defects in title. It should be noted that the Bills of Exchange Act uses the word 'negotiability' to refer to transferability, but a bill may be transferred without perfecting the title of a subsequent holder. Thus a cheque marked 'not negotiable' can still be transferred, but a transferee obtains no better title than the transferor.[40]

Not all bills of exchange can be transferred. Bills of exchange (not being cheques) marked 'not transferable' or 'not negotiable', or those made payable to payee only, can only be enforced by the named payee.[41] Similarly, cheques crossed 'account payee' or 'account payee only' are not transferable.[42]

---

35. Bills of Exchange Act 1882, s 9.   36. ibid s 2.   37. ibid s 7(1).

38. *North and South Insurance Corporation, Limited v National Provincial Bank Ltd* [1936] 1 KB 328 (KB). Because 'Cash' or 'Wages' is not a person so s 7(3) of the Bills of Exchange Act 1882, which provides that if the payee is a fictitious or non-existing person the bill may be treated as payable to bearer, cannot apply.

39. Bills of Exchange Act 1882, s 20(2).

40. ibid s 81. The same is true for an order bill which is delivered to a transferee but not indorsed—Bills of Exchange Act 1882, s 31(4).

41. ibid s 8(1). See *Hibernian Bank Ltd v Gysin and Hason* [1939] 1 KB 483 (CA).

42. ibid s 81A(1).

Transfer of bearer bills

Bearer bills are transferred by passing possession, whether actual or constructive, to the transferee, i.e. title to them passes by delivery.[43] Bearer bills are bills where either:

- the payment order is expressed as 'Pay Bearer';[44]
- the last (or only) indorsement is in blank;[45] or
- the payee[46] or the last or only indorsee[47] is a fictitious or non-existent person.

An indorsement involves the holder of a bill signing it on the back and is required to transfer title to an order bill. Indorsements can either be 'special', where the indorser specifies the person to whom, or to whose order, the bill is to be payable, or 'in blank' where the indorsement specifies no indorsee. To illustrate how the law operates consider our sample bill of exchange in Figure 24.1. This was originally made payable to 'Candy & Holly Ltd or order' and so is not a bearer bill. However, suppose an authorized signatory of the payee indorsed the bill 'Pay Holly Johnson or order'. This is a special indorsement, since it specifies an indorsee, so the bill is still an order and not a bearer bill. Finally, suppose Holly Johnson simply signs the back of the bill, this is an indorsement in blank, and now the bill is a bearer bill, title to it will pass on delivery, unless there is a further special indorsement. The back of the bill would look something like Figure 24.2.

Section 7(3) of the Bills of Exchange Act 1882 provides that a bill made payable to a fictitious or non-existent person can take effect as a bearer bill. The operation of s 7(3) is well illustrated by the following case.

Pay Holly Johnson or order

Holly Johnson

Authorised signatory for and on behalf of Candy & Holly Ltd.

Holly Johnson

Figure 24.2 Reverse side of sample bill of exchange

Clutton v Attenborough & Son [1897] AC 90 (HL)

FACTS: An employee deceived his employer into signing a cheque payable to 'George Brett or order' on the basis that a person called Brett needed paying for work he had done for the firm. No such person had ever done work for the firm; Brett was a figment of the employee's imagination. The employee then took the cheque ostensibly to give to the payee, but indorsed it in Brett's name and sold it to the defendant. Clearly, if this were an

---

43. ibid s 31(2).   44. ibid s 8(3).

45. ibid s 8(3). The inference is that a special indorsement will convert a bearer bill into an order bill. See also Bills of Exchange Act 1882, s 34(4). But since the signature of a holder is irrelevant to the transfer of a bearer bill, can it be an indorsement at all? See Sheppard J in *Miller Associates (Australia) Pty Ltd v Bennington Pty Ltd* (1975) 7 ALR 144 (Supreme Court of New South Wales) 149 and Roy Goode and Ewan McKendrick, *Goode on Commercial Law* (4th edn, Penguin 2010) 529. For an alternative view, see Peter Ellinger, Eva Lomnicka, and Christopher Hare, *Ellinger's Modern Banking Law* (5th edn, OUP 2011) 440.

46. Bills of Exchange Act 1882, s 7(3).   47. ibid s 34(3).

order bill, the defendant could not obtain title to it—the indorsement was fictitious—but they would have title if s 7(3) rendered it a bearer bill since they had possession of it.

HELD: Although undoubtedly there were any number of people called 'George Brett' in the world, the House of Lords had no doubts that this George Brett was a non-existent person; this was therefore a bearer bill.

Section 7(3) goes further than the obvious case, as in the following case where it was held that where the payee does exist, but the drawer never intends him to benefit, the payee is also a non-existent or fictitious person.

 Bank of England v Vagliano [1891] AC 107 (HL)

FACTS: Vagliano Bros was a firm of merchants and bankers and regularly received bills drawn on them by Vucina, made payable to Petridi & Co, a merchant in Russia. Vagliano Bros would accept these bills for payment at their banker—The Bank of England. A clerk in Vagliano Bros' London office forged Vucina's signature as drawer of a number bills in this form, had them accepted in the ordinary way by his employer, and then forged Petridi and Co's indorsement in favour of a fictitious person. He then collected payment from the Bank of England by purporting to be that fictitious person.

The question was whether the Bank of England was entitled to debit Vagliano's account with the sums paid to the clerk.

HELD: The bank was so entitled. Lord Herschell and Lord MacNaughton held that the drawer and the payee were 'fictitious persons' for the purposes of s 7(3) so that they were payable to the bearer, Lord Macnaughten explaining that 'fictitious' does not solely mean 'imaginary' but 'feigned' or 'counterfeit'. Lord Halsbury LC, Lord Watson, and Lord Morris agreed, though only as an additional ground. Their primary argument was that Vagliano Bros had misled the Bank of England into making the payments.

COMMENT: The only genuine signature on these documents was that of the acceptor, Vagliano Bros; consequently, they were not bills of exchange since s 3 requires the signature of the drawer and consequently *prima facie* s 7(3) cannot apply. Lord Halsbury concluded that Vagliano Bros being in a position to determine whether the transaction with Vucina was genuine was estopped from denying the validity of the document as a valid bill, and Lords Herschell and Morris seem to agree.

However, the focus in this case centres on the intentions of the person who drew the document, in this case the fraudster. Ellinger points out that surely the state of mind of the main obligor (in this case the acceptor) ought to be paramount.[48]

⭐ See JR Adams 'The Vagliano Case' (1891) LQR 295

Vagliano seems to insist that the state of mind of the drawer of the bill is key in determining the status of the payee for the purposes of the section. Thus in *Clutton*, where the drawer clearly intended to pay a non-existent person, s 7(3) applied, while in the superficially similar case of *Vinden v Hughes*,[49] where the only difference was that the employee deceived his employer into signing a cheque payable to favour

---

48. Peter Elinger, Eva Lomnicka, and Christopher Hare, *Ellinger's Modern Banking Law* (5th edn, OUP 2011) 405, fn 34.
49. [1905] 1 KB 795 (KB).

of a genuine customer, it did not. In each of these cases the court must determine who of a number of more or less innocent parties bears the loss, and it perhaps seems peculiar that the answer to this question may depend on such an apparently unimportant issue as whether the fraudster was imaginative or not.[50] Similarly, in each of the cases, the fraudster was an employee who took advantage of a weak system of internal control, yet, while some of the judges commented on this fact, it was not a determinative factor in the outcomes.[51]

Transfer of 'order bills'

Order bills are transferred by indorsement and delivery whether actual or constructive.[52] Order bills are bills where either:

- the payment order is to a specific payee. Thus looking at our sample bill, an order 'Pay Candy & Holly Ltd or order' is an order bill, as is 'Pay Candy & Holly Ltd', so long as the bill does not 'contain words prohibiting transfer or indicating an intention that it should not be transferable';[53] or

- the only or last indorsement is in blank and the holder inserts a special indorsement above it.[54] We can illustrate this by returning to our sample bill of exchange, where the last indorsement was in blank by Holly Johnson, making it a bearer bill. Suppose Holly delivers possession of the bill to Lewis Reed. Lewis can turn it back into an order bill by inserting the words 'Pay Lewis Reed' (or indeed any one else's name) above Holly's signature.

Finally, in relation to order bills, suppose Lewis then delivers possession of the bill to Little Joe Bank. This is now an order bill which requires Lewis' indorsement, but suppose he fails to sign the back. Section 31(4) of the Bills of Exchange Act 1882 provides that Little Joe Bank obtains no better title to the bill than Lewis had, but also gives it the right to require Lewis to indorse it. Thus, if Lewis had caused Holly to transfer the bill to him by fraud, Little Joe Bank will take, subject to Holly's rights if it receives notice of them before it obtains Lewis' indorsement, even though the bank gave valuable consideration to Lewis for the bill.[55]

Who can claim on a bill of exchange?

The holder of a bill is the person with possession of it and who in the case of an order bill is either the payee or (if indorsed) the indorsee. It is the holder who can make a claim on a bill of exchange.

---

50. Clearly, if the bill or cheque were drawn in the name of a person who was clearly fictitious, then the drawer cannot have intended a real person. Lord Esher MR in the Court of Appeal in *Bank of England v Vagliano* (1889) 23 QBD 243 (CA) 253 suggests 'Roland Græme' (a character in Walter Scott's 1820 novel *The Abbot*) as an example. Perhaps today Lord Voldemort as a payee might fill the bill.

51. On this issue, see the strong dissenting judgments of La Forrest and McLachlin JJ in *Boma Manufacturing Ltd v Canadian Imperial Bank of Commerce* (1997) 140 DLR (4th) 463 (Supreme Court of Canada) 495–6.

52. Bills of Exchange Act 1882, s 31(3).

53. ibid s 8(4). Such a bill can be converted into a bearer bill through an indorsement in blank.

54. ibid s 34(4).

55. *Whistler v Forster* (1863) 143 ER 441. The transfer, until indorsement, takes effect in equity only, the bank in our example is only safe once it receives legal title as a bona fide purchaser.

The rights of all holders

The rights of a holder can be summarized as follows:

- He can transfer title to the bill to a new holder.[56]
- He can present the bill for acceptance[57] or payment.[58]
- He can sue on it in his own name in the case of dishonour.[59]
- He can give good discharge to a drawee or acceptor in due course,[60] even where the holder has no title; for example, he is a thief of a bearer bill.[61]
- He can 'cure' inchoate bills in accordance with s 20(1) of the Bills of Exchange Act 1882 and insert a date in accordance with s 12 of the Bills of Exchange Act 1882.
- He can effect indorsements, whether special or in blank.[62]
- He can require the drawer to supply a duplicate bill if the original has been lost.[63]

These rights apply to all holders, but liability on a bill of exchange is primarily contractual, and the degree to which the autonomy of payment on a bill insulates a holder from defences depends on the status of the holder. The Bills of Exchange Act 1882 recognizes three possible statuses: the mere holder; the holder for value; and the holder in due course.

Who is a mere holder?

A mere holder is a person who is neither a 'holder for value' nor a 'holder in due course'. He will neither have given value for the bill nor derive title from someone who has and consequently any presentment he makes for payment can be met by the defence of lack of consideration

Who is a holder for value?

Every person whose signature appears on a bill of exchange is presumed to have given value,[64] leaving it to the claimant to prove otherwise. Section 27 of the Bills of Exchange Act 1882 provides that a holder may give value in one of three ways.

1. Section 27(1)(a)—any consideration sufficient to support a simple contract is sufficient to give value.[65] Consequently, if the current holder purchased the bill for cash, for example, then he is a holder for value.
2. Section 27(1)(b)—an antecedent debt or liability.[66] The obvious example is where A owes B money and B accepts a bill of exchange from A in discharge[67] of the debt, though perhaps this would meet the requirements of paragraph 1 anyway.[68] However, there is no such uncertainty where B accepts a bill of

---

56. Bills of Exchange Act 1882, s 31 (3).   57. ibid s 41(1)(a).   58. ibid s 45(3).

59. ibid s 38(1).   60. ibid ss 59(1) and 38(3).

61. Note that a thief of a stolen order bill is not a holder, being neither the payee nor an indorsee of the bill.

62. Bills of Exchange Act 1882, s 34(4).   63. ibid s 69.   64. ibid s 30(1).   65. ibid s 27(1)(a).

66. ibid s 27(1)(b).

67. Almost inevitably this is a conditional discharge only; in other words, the bill is taken as payment for the debt on the condition that the cheque is not dishonoured. If this condition is not met the debt remains on foot.

68. See *Currie v Misa* (1875) LR 10 Exch 153.

exchange as security for an existing debt; then, absent any forbearance to sue, he has given no consideration for the bill but nevertheless gives value for the purposes of s 27 of the Bills of Exchange Act 1882.[69] But what if *X* owes *Y* money and *Y* receives a bill drawn, accepted, or negotiated by a third party, as in *Oliver v Davis*?[70] Here the debtor procured his fiancée's sister to draw a cheque in favour of the creditor, who, as holder of it, sued the drawer. The Court of Appeal unanimously held that a debt where the debtor is a stranger to the bill is not sufficient to provide value given by the holder for the purposes of s 27(1)(b). Section 27(1)(b), according to Evershed MR, is simply intended to get over the fact that at common law the giving of a cheque for an existing debt imports no consideration, since the consideration from the creditor has already been given—it is 'past consideration'.[71] The Court concluded that in circumstances like *Oliver*, if *Y* is to provide value for the bill, some consideration must pass from *Y*, satisfying the requirements either of s 27(1)(a) or 27(2).

3. By virtue of s 27(2), where value has at any time been given for a bill, the holder is deemed to be a holder for value as regards the acceptor and all parties to the bill who became parties prior to such time. The most obvious example of the operation of the section is where the current holder was given the bill by the previous holder,[72] who received it as payment for a debt. By virtue of s 27(2), the current holder can claim on the bill as against the drawer or acceptor, even though he personally gave no consideration for it. However, it was held in *Churchill and Sim v Goddard*[73] that, whilst a volunteer can make a claim against a remote party, that is someone with whom he has not dealt directly, as between immediate parties the claimant must have provided value. Consequently, in our example, the current holder could make no claim against a person who gratuitously indorsed it in his favour, but he could make a claim against the acceptor who is a 'remote party', since the holder has had no dealings with him. Similarly, in *AEG (UK) Ltd v Lewis*, where a daughter drew a cheque in favour of a contractor who had repaired a gas installation at the home of her parents, it was held that the contractor could not claim against the daughter when she stopped the bank from paying the cheque. The contractor was an immediate party to the cheque and had given no value for it, since he had completed the work before receiving it. However, had the contractor negotiated the cheque for value to *X*, who in turn had given it to *Y*, *Y* would have a claim against the daughter on the cheque by virtue of s 27(2).[74]

---

69. See Roy Goode and Ewan McKendrick, *Goode on Commercial Law* (4th edn, Penguin 2010) 531–2.

70. [1949] 2 KB 727 (CA). In this case, there was no evidence that *B* had agreed with *C* not to enforce the debt against *A*; if he had, then this forbearance to sue would have provided consideration sufficient for s 27(1)(a).

71. *Oliver v Davis* [1949] 2 KB 727 (CA) 735. But note that in *Currie v Misa* the conditional discharge of an existing debt *was* held to provide consideration for the transfer of a bill of exchange, so perhaps s 27(1)(b) has a wider application than was envisaged in *Oliver*. However, see *AEG (UK) Ltd v Lewis* (1993) 2 Bank LR 119 (CA), and *MK International Development Co Ltd v Housing Bank* (1991) 1 Bank LR 74 (CA) 78–9, which insist that the antecedent debt cannot be that of a stranger to the bill.

72. But not a holder in due course—if he were, then s 29(3) would make the holder a holder in due course also.

73. [1937] 1 KB 92 (CA) 110 (Scott LJ).

74. Note that the Court of Appeal had decided on the facts that the contractor had not released the debt owed by the parents, which release would have constituted the giving of value, as the gas fitter who had accepted the cheque from the daughter did not have authority from his employer to release the debt. But surely at least by the time the cheque was presented for payment, the contractor showed it had adopted the act of the employee in releasing the debt, which adoption related back to the acceptance of the cheque by the employee.

However, there is some question whether the value can be provided by a stranger to the bill. In *Diamond v Graham*,[75] Diamond would lend money to Herman only if Graham drew a bill in his (Diamond's) favour as security for Herman's payment obligation. The Court of Appeal held that value need not pass from the holder to another party to the bill, since the terminology of the section did not require this, and consequently Diamond succeeded, since he had certainly given value for the cheque by lending the money to Herman. In this respect the decision is unexceptionable. However, Dankwerts LJ held that further consideration had been provided for Graham's bill, this time by Herman, who had drawn a cheque in Graham's favour. In other words, a stranger to the disputed bill can provide value for the purposes of the sub-section. This suggestion appears incorrect, at least so far as immediate parties are concerned.[76]

In summary, on the issue of value under s 27, although not beyond dispute, it seems that whilst value can be provided by a holder *to* a stranger to the bill, value cannot be provided *by* a stranger.

Who is a holder in due course?

A holder in due course in relation to a bill of exchange is in effect the equivalent of a bona fide purchaser for value without notice in relation to goods, and every holder of a bill is presumed to be a holder in due course,[77] leaving it to the defendant to prove that the requirements set out in s 29 of the Bills of Exchange Act 1882, which define such a holder, have not been satisfied. However, the burden of proof is shifted if the bill was drawn, accepted, or negotiated as a result of fraud, duress, illegality, force, or fear, unless the holder can prove that value in good faith has been given for the bill after the vitiating event. The statutory requirements in s 29 of the Bills of Exchange Act 1882 require consideration of six issues.

Bills of Exchange Act 1882, s 29

(1) A holder in due course is a holder who has taken a bill, complete and regular on the face of it, under the following conditions; namely,

(a) That he became the holder of it before it was overdue, and without notice that it had been previously dishonoured, if such was the fact:

(b) That he took the bill in good faith and for value, and that at the time the bill was negotiated to him he had no notice of any defect in the title of the person who negotiated it.

First, the claimant must be a holder of the bill, a matter considered previously, but it has been held that a payee cannot be a holder in due course.[78] That said, it

---

75. [1968] 2 All ER 909 (CA).
76. See *Churchill and Sim v Goddard* [1937] 1 KB 92 (CA) 110 (Scott LJ); *Pollway Ltd v Abdullah* [1974] 1 WLR 493 (CA) 497 (Roskill LJ); *Hasan v Wilson* [1977] 1 Lloyd's Rep 432 (QB) 442 (Robert Goff J).
77. Bills of Exchange Act 1882, s 30(2).
78. *Jones Ltd v Waring and Gillow Ltd* [1926] AC 670 (HL).

would seem that a payee-holder may nevertheless have similar rights to a holder in due course.[79]

Jones Ltd v Waring and Gillow Ltd [1926] AC 670 (HL)

FACTS: Bodenham bought some furniture worth £14,000 from the defendant by hire-purchase agreement, which required a £5,000 initial deposit. Bodenham persuaded the claimant to draw a cheque payable to the defendant by fraudulently claiming he was an agent for the defendant. The claimant thought it was placing an order for 500 cars from the defendant and that the cheque represented a deposit for this order. Bodenham gave the cheque to the defendant who delivered the furniture to him. On discovering the truth, the claimant sought to recover the £5,000 from the defendant. The defendant claimed it was a holder in due course and so immune from defects in title.

HELD: The claimant was entitled to recover the £5,000 as money paid under a mistake of fact, since a holder in due course did not include the original payee of a cheque, and therefore the defendant could not avail itself of the benefit of s 38(2) of the Bills of Exchange Act 1882.

COMMENT: *Prima facie* this decision is a little surprising, especially since s 2 of the Bills of Exchange Act 1882 defines 'holder' as 'the payee or indorsee of a bill or note.' Prior to the Bills of Exchange Act 1882, it was clear that a payee was as privileged as an indorsee of a bill and, as Moulton LJ pointed out in *Lloyds Bank, Ltd v Cooke*,[80] one would have expected such a radical change to be made explicitly, particularly as there seems no principled reason why such a distinction should be drawn.

That said, it does appear from the Act that it effected a change in the law, as Viscount Cave LC said:

> it appears from s 29(1) that a 'holder in due course' is a person to whom a bill has been 'negotiated', and from s 31 that a bill is negotiated by being transferred from one person to another … In view of these definitions it is difficult to see how the original payee of a cheque can be a 'holder in due course' within the meaning of the Act.[81]

Finally, it should be noted that the lack of due diligence on the part of the claimant who paid £5,000 in 1919, worth perhaps £500,000 today, to a man whom it barely knew without checking his story did not bar the claimant from success.

⭐ See 'Money Paid Under a Mistake of Fact' (1927–29) 3 CLJ 83

Second, the bill must be complete and regular on its face, and 'face' also includes the back of the bill.[82] A bill is irregular if it contains a feature which would put a reasonable holder on inquiry, in other words it is an issue about appearances. Thus

---

79. See *Talbot v Von Boris* [1911] 1 KB 854 (CA), where a payee-holder was held not to be affected by duress which induced signature of the bill since he had no notice of it—duress would be a defence against all but a holder in due course. *Hasan v Wilson* [1977] 1 Lloyd's Rep 431 (QB) is to like effect in a case of a bill drawn by reason of fraud. Both of these cases were approved in *Dextra Bank & Trust Co Ltd v Bank of Jamaica* [2002] 1 All ER (Comm) 193 (PC) [22].
80. [1907] 1 KB 794 (CA) 806.   81. [1926] AC 670 (HL) 680.
82. *Arab Bank Ltd v Ross* [1952] 2 QB 216 (CA).

in *Arab Bank Ltd v Ross*,[83] the payee was described on the bill as 'Fathi and Fathi sal Nabulsy Company', but the word 'Company' was omitted on the indorsement by one of the partners in favour of the claimant bank. It was held that the bank were not holders in due course, since bankers would not normally accept an indorsement which did not correspond with the name of the person negotiating an order bill.[84]

It is unclear whether a person who receives an incomplete bill (and so can only be a holder for value) can by virtue of his power under s 20 of the Bills of Exchange Act 1882 to perfect inchoate bills, convert himself into a holder in due course; s 29(1) of the Bills of Exchange Act 1882 requires a holder who has taken a complete bill, but there are authorities to the contrary.[85]

Third, the bill must not be overdue for payment. Where the bill is payable on a particular day, it is overdue if not presented for payment on that day. In the case of a bill payable on demand, it is overdue if it appears to have been in circulation for an unreasonable length of time.[86]

Fourth, the holder must have no notice of previous dishonour, either non-payment or non-acceptance.

Fifth, the holder must have taken the bill without notice. The doctrine of constructive notice does not apply to bills of exchange—honest negligence is not bad faith,[87] but 'Nelsonian blindness' is, as illustrated in the following case.

 Jones v Graham (1877) 2 App Cas 616 (HL)

FACTS: Here, bills which had been drawn and accepted with a view to defrauding creditors, were purchased by Jones at just over 10 per cent of their face value. Jones knew the acceptor, Graham, was in financial difficulties, but did not contact people from whom he knew he could obtain information.

HELD: While emphasizing that a holder might not ask obvious questions through 'honest blundering and carelessness', Lord Blackburn pointed out that the facts of this case supported a finding that he must have had a suspicion that there was something wrong and did not ask questions in order to avoid discovering a truth he would prefer not to know. In the circumstances, the House of Lords held unanimously that Jones took with notice of the fraud.

Sixth, the holder must take the bill in 'good faith and for value',[88] a formulation which seems to suggest that the good faith and the giving of value must coincide, causing commentators to conclude that a holder in due course must himself actually give consideration rather than being deemed to do so by virtue of s 27(2).[89] However, Musthill LJ, *obiter* in *MK Development Co Ltd v The Housing Bank*,[90] suggested to the

---

83. [1952] 2 QB 216 (CA).
84. Nevertheless the bank could still enforce the bill as a holder for value since no defect in title to the bill had been proved, the indorsement was valid though not regular.
85. See e.g. *Glenie v Bruce Smith* [1908] 1 KB 263 (CA) 268–9.
86. Bills of Exchange Act 1882, s 36(3).   87. ibid s 90.   88. ibid s 29(1)(b).
89. See e.g. Roy Goode and Ewan McKendrick, *Goode on Commercial Law* (4th edn, Penguin 2010) 535–6; Benjamin Geva, 'Absence of Consideration in the Law of Bills and Notes' (1980) 39 CLJ 360, 364.
90. (1991) 1 Bank LR 74 (CA) 80.

contrary, and in *Clifford Chance v Silver*,[91] the Court of Appeal concluded that the claimant firm of solicitors who held a bill as stakeholder (and so had not personally given value for it) were holders in due course because they were deemed to be holders for value through s 27(2) and otherwise met the requirements of s 29.[92]

Section 29(3) provides that any holder deriving title from a holder in due course and who is not himself a party to any fraud or illegality affecting it, has all the rights of that holder in due course. As McKendrick points out,[93] this simply appears to be an example of the common law rule that a transferee from a person who has obtained an overriding title through an exception to the *nemo dat* rule can shelter behind that title, even if giving no value for it and even if aware of (though not a party to) any defect in that title.[94] Rather surprisingly, in *Jade International Steel Stahl und Eisen GmbH & Co KG v Robert Nicholas (Steels) Ltd*,[95] it was held that a drawer/payee obtained derivative holder in due course status under s 29(3) when the bill was negotiated and then renegotiated back to him.[96] This decision seems doubtful, since s 37 of the Bills of Exchange Act 1882 seems to confine the rights of a person who has regained possession of a bill of exchange to either re-issuing the bill or re-negotiating it, but the section does not expressly prohibit his making a claim against the drawer or acceptor.

Who is liable on a bill of exchange?

Consider the following example.

Eg ComCorp Ltd

Taking our sample bill in Figure 24.1 as an example, the last things that happened were that Holly Johnson had indorsed the bill in blank, thus making it a bearer bill, and negotiated it to Lewis Reed, who had negotiated it to Little Joe Bank, indorsing it before the bank discovered that Lewis had defrauded Holly in order to obtain the bill. ComCorp Ltd has just discovered these things because when Little Joe Bank presented the bill for payment at Banco Rico, Banco Rico refused to pay, being insolvent, and ComCorp has just received a notice from Little Joe Bank of the dishonour of the bill and is concerned what this means for it.

Only signatories to the bill can be liable on it;[97] consequently, the drawee is not liable on the bill until he has accepted it.[98] Liability is hierarchical. The primary

---

91. [1992] NPC 103 (CA).

92. See in support LP Hitchens, 'Holders for Value and their Status: *Clifford Chance v Silver*' [1993] JBL 571. See also Mark Sneddon, 'Deemed Holder for Value of Cheque or Bill of Exchange as Holder in Due Course' (1989) 17 ABLR 400.

93. Roy Goode and Ewan McKendrick, *Goode on Commercial Law* (4th edn, Penguin 2010) 537.

94. *May v Chapman* (1834) 16 M&W 355.   95. [1978] QB 917 (CA).

96. For a critical approach to this decision, see JWA Thornley, 'Reverse Negotiation of Bills of Exchange' (1978) 37 CLJ 236.

97. Bills of Exchange Act 1882, s 23.

98. *Credit Lyonnais Bank (Nederland) NV v Export Credit Guarantee Department* [1998] 1 Lloyd's Rep 19 (CA) 39 (Hobhouse LJ). This position is expressly stated by s 53(1) of the Bills of Exchange Act 1882.

obligor is the acceptor,[99] below him the drawer, and below him in order of signing are any indorsers, and at the bottom the holder. At maturity, the holder presents the bill for payment to the acceptor and, assuming payment is made in accordance with the terms of the bill, it is discharged.[100] However, if the bill is dishonoured,[101] the holder will send a notice of dishonour to the persons above him in the liability hierarchy,[102] who will then be liable to compensate him. The holder can choose to claim compensation against any or all of these persons, who in turn have a claim for compensation against anyone above them in the hierarchy. The chapter will now examine why this is so.

The liability of the acceptor

By virtue of s 54 of the Bills of Exchange Act 1882, the acceptor promises to pay on the bill according to its terms and is estopped from denying certain matters in relation to the drawer and the payee. The section is self-explanatory and is set out here.

Bills of Exchange Act 1882, s 54

The acceptor of a bill, by accepting it—
(1) Engages that he will pay it according to the tenor of his acceptance:
(2) Is precluded from denying to a holder in due course:
    (a) The existence of the drawer, the genuineness of his signature, and his capacity and authority to draw the bill;
    (b) In the case of a bill payable to drawer's order, the then capacity of the drawer to indorse, but not the genuineness or validity of his indorsement;
    (c) In the case of a bill payable to the order of a third person, the existence of the payee and his then capacity to indorse, but not the genuineness or validity of his indorsement.

The liability of the drawer

By virtue of s 55(1) of the Bills of Exchange Act 1882, the drawer of a bill of exchange promises that it will be paid in accordance with its terms and, if dishonoured, he will compensate the holder. Also, since an indorser can also be liable on the bill, the drawer promises to compensate any indorser if it is forced to pay. The drawer also is estopped from denying to a holder in due course the existence of the payee and the payee's capacity at the time the drawer signs to indorse the bill.

Consequently, returning to ComCorp Ltd, the company is liable to Little Joe Bank on the bill of exchange as it was the drawer of it; that is, unless it can raise some defence against the claimant based on, for example, some defect in the bank's title, a

---

99. Except in the case of an accommodation bill where, in the words of s 28 of the Bills of Exchange Act 1882, 'a person has signed a bill as drawer, acceptor, or indorser, without receiving value therefor'. It is done typically by the signatory to enable a friend to raise money, using the signatory's financial reputation. Accommodation bills are not considered further in this chapter.
100. Bills of Exchange Act 1882, s 59 (see p 656).
101. See ss 43 and 47 of the 1882 Act for how dishonour may occur.
102. Bills of Exchange Act 1882, s 48.

matter which is dealt with later in this chapter. So, too, if Little Joe Bank chooses to pursue Candy and Holly Ltd, ComCorp Ltd must compensate it.

The liability of an indorser

By virtue of s 55(2) of the Bills of Exchange Act 1882, an indorser promises that the bill will be paid in accordance with its terms and, if dishonoured, will compensate the holder or subsequent indorsers, who are compelled to pay. An indorser is estopped from denying to a holder in due course the genuineness and regularity of the drawer's and all previous indorsers' signatures. He is also estopped from denying to the immediate prior and all subsequent indorsers (whether holders for value or not) that when he indorsed the bill, the bill was valid and he had a good title to it.

Liabilities on bearer bills

Title to a bearer bill passes on delivery without the need for indorsement. Where a transferor of a bearer bill chooses to indorse, then he is liable as an indorser; if he does not, then he is not liable as an indorser.[103] However, he may be liable under s 58(3) of the Bills of Exchange Act 1882, since he 'warrants to his immediate transferee being a holder for value that the bill is what it purports to be, that he has a right to transfer it, and that at the time of transfer he is not aware of any fact which renders it valueless'.

Exclusion of liability

A drawer or indorser can exclude liability by expressly stating that the bill is without recourse to himself.[104]

Types of defences to claims under bills of exchange

Whether a defence is available to a defendant on a bill of exchange is dependent partially on the type of defence and partially on the status of the claimant. The types of defence fall into three categories.

Personal defences

Personal defences arise either out of the underlying contract which gave rise to the payment obligation embodied in the bill, or out of the negotiation of the bill between the defendant and the claimant. Thus total or partial failure of consideration arising through lawful rejection of goods for which the bill was drawn or accepted, or where that contract is avoided for misrepresentation, are personal defences, as are rights of set off. Similarly, if *A* negotiates the bill to *B*, a defence by *A* arising out of that transaction against a claim by *B* will be a personal defence.

Defects in title

A holder has a defect in title where the bill or its acceptance has been obtained 'by fraud, duress, or force and fear, or other unlawful means, or an illegal consideration', or negotiated 'in breach of faith, or under such circumstances as amount to a fraud'.[105]

---

103. ibid s 58(2).   104. ibid s 16(1).   105. ibid s 29(2).

Real claims based on nullity[106]

The following all amount to nullity claims and will be subjected to more detailed discussion later in the chapter:

- where the liability of the defendant or the title of the claimant depends on a forgery or an act in excess of capacity or authority of a signatory;
- where there is a material alteration of the bill;
- where the bill is discharged;
- where fraud/illegality renders the bill void (not voidable).

The impact of defences on holders

Mere holders

A mere holder is open to any of the types of defence listed in the previous section, particularly lack of consideration.

Holders for value

The position of a holder for value is not specifically set out in the Bills of Exchange Act 1882. Consequently, unless also a holder in due course, a holder for value will, it seems, take subject to personal defences, defects in title and real defences based on nullity, since he does not have the protection of s 38(2) of the Bills of Exchange Act 1882. His only advantage seems to be that where consideration has at some time been given for the bill, by virtue of s 27(2) (the absence of consideration passing to the acceptor as in *Diamond v Graham*[107]), does not provide a defence for the acceptor or prior parties to the bill.[108] There is, however, some dispute over this. The editors of *Ellinger*, for example, argue that s 27(2) of the Bills of Exchange Act 1882 requires that total failure of consideration between prior parties cannot be raised against a holder for value,[109] and suggest the same is true of a quantified (liquidated) claim for partial failure of consideration,[110] pointing out that a holder for value has given consideration for the bill so that the failure of consideration by remote parties seems irrelevant. However, it is clear that in relation to immediate parties at least, total failure or a partial failure of consideration involving a liquidated amount is a good defence,[111] but not where the dispute relates to a matter sounding in unliquidated damages.

---

106. Sometimes called 'real defence' because of the invalidity of the *res* (i.e. the bill) itself. See Roy Goode and Ewan McKendrick, *Goode on Commercial Law* (4th edn, Penguin 2010) 553.

107. [1968] 2 All ER 909 (CA).

108. See Roy Goode and Ewan McKendrick, *Goode on Commercial Law* (4th edn, Penguin 2010) 553–4. See also Benjamin Geza, 'Equities as to Liability on Bills and Notes: Rights of a Holder not in Due Course' (1980) 5 Can Bus LJ 53 and 'Absence of Consideration in the Law of Bills and Notes' (1980) 39 CLJ 360.

109. Peter Ellinger, Eva Lomnica, and Christopher Hare (eds), *Ellinger's Modern Banking Law* (5th edn, OUP 2011) 703–4. See *Watson v Russell* (1864) 5 B & S 968, approved in *Dextra Bank & Trust Co Ltd v Bank of Jamaica* [2002] 1 All ER (Comm) 193 (PC) [22]. See to similar effect AG Guest (ed), *Chalmers and Guest on Bills of Exchange and Cheques* (17th edn, Sweet & Maxwell 2009).

110. Citing *Archer v Bamford* (1822) 3 Stark 175 and noting that in *Harris (Oscar) Son & Co v Vallarman & Co* [1940] 1 All ER 185 (CA), the issue was regarded not settled.

111. *Forman v Wright* (1851) 11 CB 481; *Thoni GmbH & Co KG v RTP Equipment* [1979] 2 Lloyd's Rep 282 (CA).

Holders in due course

As against immediate parties, personal remedies such as total failure of consideration or a partial failure of consideration giving rise to a liquidated loss provides a defence, even against a holder in due course. However, by virtue of s 38(2) of the Bills of Exchange Act 1882, a holder in due course can enforce the bill, notwithstanding defects in title of previous holders and free from personal defences which may have been available to previous parties. Consequently, it is only in exceptional circumstances that the court will not award summary judgment in favour of a holder in due course.

 ### Cebora SNC v SIP (Industrial Products) Ltd [1976] 1 Lloyds Rep 271 (CA)

FACTS: SIP granted the Cebora the sole right to distribute its products in the UK. Cebora bought products from SIP and drew five bills of exchange in SIP's favour, but later Cebora gave instructions to its bank that the bills should be dishonoured. A dispute had broken out between the parties and SIP had started distributing the products through a subsidiary. SIP applied for summary judgment under what is now Pt 24 of the Civil Procedure Rules and Cebora counterclaimed for damages for late delivery, non-delivery, and other breaches of the distribution agreement.

HELD: Since the dispute gave rise to an unliquidated claim, SIP was entitled to summary judgment, leaving Cebora to pursue a separate action for damages. In other words, SIP had to pay up on the bill of exchange and then pursue its claims. This looks like a nil sum game but it is not. As a result of this summary judgment, it is the distributors, not the manufacturers, who are 'out of the money', putting the manufacturers in a superior bargaining position in relation to the dispute, as well as in a better cash flow situation.

COMMENT: The rationale for this decision is the autonomy of payment principle. Merchants and their bankers operate on the basis that it is only in exceptional circumstances that a holder in due course cannot treat a bill of exchange as the equivalent of cash on the bill's maturity. The basis of negotiability depends on insulating the bill from underlying disputes. Were it otherwise, even between the parties, a seller might just as well give credit to a buyer as accept a time bill if he cannot be confident that the bill will be paid at maturity, regardless of contractual disputes.

Of the exceptional circumstances, the most important concerns defences based on nullity, which will now be considered.[112]

Defences based on nullity

Forged and unauthorized signatures

A document cannot be a bill of exchange unless signed by the drawer,[113] and so literally it could be that the document in *Bank of England v Vagliano*[114] was not a bill

---

112. There are two others: (i) where the holder is suing in a representative capacity for another party when defences or set off available against that party are available against the holder; and (ii) failure to enforce the bill in accordance with its terms.

113. Bills of Exchange Act 1882, s 3(1).   114. [1891] AC 107 (HL).

of exchange,[115] though once we accept that it is, an acceptor (like Vagliano) is precluded from raising forgery of the drawer's signature or the capacity or authority of the drawer to sign.[116]

As noted earlier, only signatories to the bill can be liable on it,[117] and by virtue of s 24 of the Bills of Exchange Act 1882 no title can be obtained through a forged or unauthorized signature. Thus where an indorsee's signature is forged or unauthorized, not only is he not liable,[118] but no subsequent party can enforce the bill against parties signing prior to the forgery, since the forgery creates a defect in title—a defence against even a holder in due course. However, an indorsee who becomes a party after the forgery is liable on the bill, being estopped from denying the validity of the bill as against a holder in due course.[119]

Similarly, as we noted earlier, payment to a thief on a bearer bill discharges the payer subject to his acting in good faith, and without notice of the defect in title, a thief is a holder. However, a thief of a bill requiring indorsement cannot pass title, since necessarily his indorsement will be a forgery.

It should be noted that where a signature is effected by an agent but without actual authority, the principal will nevertheless be bound if the agent had apparent or usual authority, unless s 25 of the Bills of Exchange Act 1882 applies. Section 25 deals with the situation where there is a signature 'by procuration'. This gives notice that the agent has limited authority and the principal is bound only within the actual limits of his authority. What amounts to signature by procuration is unclear. In the sample bill, Greg Osborne signed 'per pro', short for the latin phrase *'per procurationem'*, meaning 'through the agency of', and this clearly would fall within s 25, as would the abbreviation 'pp', though in typical use the agent (incorrectly) signs and then puts 'pp [name of principal]' underneath the signature, literally the opposite of what has been effected. On the other hand, Rio Bueno has signed 'for and on behalf of' Banco Rico, which is in modern English treated (erroneously) as being synonymous with 'per pro'. It is unclear whether that would fall inside s 25.

The authority of agents is discussed in Chapter 5

A person whose signature has been forged, although he cannot ratify it,[120] can be estopped from raising the forgery where he makes a representation which is relied on to the detriment of the other party, as the following case demonstrates.

 Greenwood v Martins Bank Ltd [1933] AC 51 (HL)

FACTS: Mrs Greenwood forged a cheque drawn on her husband's bank account, but the husband did not inform the bank (Martins Bank Ltd), believing the money would be returned to him. When eventually he told his wife he would be informing the bank, she shot and killed herself. Mr Greenwood then sought to recover the sums paid out under the forged cheque.

HELD: The House of Lords held that not telling the bank immediately he discovered the truth amounted to a representation that the cheque was not a forgery. Had Mr Greenwood done so, the bank would have been able to sue Mrs Greenwood in tort for whose tort

---

115. However, probably the better analysis is that the drawer was the fraudulent employee using someone else's name for the purposes of the fraud.
116. Bills of Exchange Act 1882, s 54(2)(a).   117. ibid s 23.   118. *Roberts v Tucker* (1851) 16 QB 560.
119. Bills of Exchange Act 1882, s 55(2)(b) and (c).   120. ibid s 24.

> the husband was liable at the time.[121] Consequently, Mr Greenwood was estopped from claiming the cheques were forged. However, for the estoppel to apply, the bank must suffer loss as a result of the silence, which, in the case of a one-off forgery, is unlikely nowadays.[122]

Lack of capacity

A person who lacks capacity to form a contract cannot be liable on a bill of exchange,[123] but this does not affect the liability of any other party.[124]

Material alteration

Section 64 of the Bills of Exchange Act 1882 renders void a bill of exchange which has been materially altered without the assent of all persons liable on it except:

- in favour of any holder as against a person who made the alteration or assented to it or against a subsequent indorser; and
- generally in favour of a holder for value if the alteration is not apparent.

A material alteration would include altering the date, the sum payable, or the time or place for payment.[125]

Discharge of the bill

A discharged bill is one which has no further legal effect, so that no party can be liable on it. Bills can become discharged in the following ways:

- payment in due course by or on behalf of the drawee or acceptor—payment in due course means 'payment made at or after the maturity of the bill to the holder thereof in good faith and without notice that his title to the bill is defective';[126]
- the acceptor becomes the holder of the bill in his own right at or after maturity;[127]
- the holder at or after its maturity renounces his rights against the acceptor either in writing or by delivering the bill to the acceptor;
- by a cancellation of the bill by the holder which is apparent on its face;[128]
- material alteration under s 64.

Letters of credit

Until now, this chapter has focussed on a particular instrument—the bill of exchange—which continues to be used in both domestic and international

---

121. The forgeries were committed before the abolition of a husband's liability for his wife's torts by the Law Reform (Married Women and Tortfeasors) Act 1935.

122. One might imagine a situation where the forgery was committed by an employee forging his employer's signature in circumstances where the employer would be vicariously liable for his employee's act under the rule in *Lloyd v Grace Smith & Co* [1912] AC 716 (HL). The employer does not tell the bank, which loses its opportunity to pursue the employee in tort.

123. Bills of Exchange Act 1882, s 22(1).   124. ibid s 22(2).   125. ibid s 64(2).

126. ibid s 59(1).   127. ibid s 61.   128. ibid s 63.

transactions. However, it is to its use in international trade, in conjunction with another financial undertaking, that we must now turn. Chapter 19 introduced the concept of the documentary sale, the practice of completing the international sale of goods by the seller tendering a document symbolizing the goods rather than the goods themselves (since they are in transit to the buyer in a ship and so inaccessible, thus preventing physical delivery), possibly accompanied by a policy insuring the goods against loss or damage whilst at sea and other shipping documents. This process plus the loading of the goods onto the ship effects the delivery obligation of the seller, but it remains for the buyer to meet his primary obligation, the duty to pay.

Eg ComCorp Ltd

Comcorp Ltd is negotiating the sale of a very expensive machine to a new customer for delivery to Mumbai. The parties have agreed that this is to be a Cif sale, but the buyer wishes to pay ninety days after receipt of the shipping documents. ComCorp's sales department is keen to proceed with the contract, but its finance director is concerned because ComCorp's cashflow is such that it needs to receive payment as soon as possible. The finance director wishes to know how both parties' requirements can be accommodated.

The explanation in Chapter 19 assumed that payment will be made in return for the documents, but this is not necessarily so. The seller may be prepared to give credit to the buyer, requiring payment only after the passage of a fixed period of time, say thirty, sixty, or ninety days after delivery of the documents. While this is simple, it also leaves the seller exposed to the possibility that the buyer will not pay because he is insolvent or pays late, perhaps only after the resolution of a contractual dispute. To an extent, the autonomy of payment of bills of exchange can help to solve the late payment problem if the contract of sale requires the buyer to accept a bill of exchange drawn on him by the seller in return for the shipping documents. Thus the seller might forward a bill of exchange[129] to the buyer with the shipping documents on the basis that unless the buyer accepts the bill and returns it to the seller for presentation, all documents must be returned. The advantage to the seller is that once the bill has been accepted, the buyer has only a very limited number of defences to a Part 24 claim for summary judgment, thus insulating the payment obligation from contractual disputes. The disadvantage is that, even if the parties agree that title to the goods does not pass to the buyer until the bill is actually paid, the shipping documents are nevertheless in his possession and he can give good title to a third party under one of the exceptions to the *nemo dat* rule, particularly under s 25 of the Sale of Goods Act 1979 or s 9 of the Factors Act 1889. Indeed, this would be true even if the buyer decides not to accept the bill but still retain the other documents.[130] The use of banks as collecting agents can avoid this problem, as the following ComCorp example illustrates.

Exceptions to the nemo dat rule are discussed at p 273

---

129. The bill could be payable on sight or be a term bill, the term selected to give the buyer the agreed period of credit.

130. *Cahn & Meyer v Pocketts Bristol Channel Steam Packet Co Ltd* [1899] 1 QB 643 (CA).

> ### Eg ComCorp Ltd
>
> ComCorp's bank, Banco Rico, suggests the use either of a letter of credit or the use of themselves as collecting agent. Under this latter mechanism Comcorp will pass the shipping documents and the bill of exchange to the bank. The bank, as ComCorp's agent, will send these to its Mumbai branch and will release the shipping documents to the buyer only once the buyer has tendered the bill of exchange duly accepted. The bank will then purchase the bill from ComCorp and credit ComCorp's account with the discounted value of the bill.[131] The bank points out that since ComCorp has not yet agreed a price for the goods, it might offer them at a price which reflected their additional costs of funding in giving credit to the buyer.

If the seller's bank does not have a branch at a location convenient for the buyer, it can arrange for collection by another bank as its agent, called a 'Collecting Bank'. The International Chamber of Commerce has promulgated a standard set of rules to govern the relations between the seller and its bank, which remits the documents (the remitting bank) and the bank that actually effects the collection (the Collecting Bank), known as the Uniform Rules for Collections (URC).[132] These will apply if expressly incorporated by the parties and it has been held that international banking custom will apply unless expressly excluded.[133] While it seems clear under the normal law of agency that there is no privity of contract between the seller and the Collecting Bank,[134] and it has been held that the URC do not affect this,[135] it may be arguable that the URC may create such a direct contractual relationship.[136]

This process does not deal with the creditworthiness of the buyer; it might still be insolvent when the bill is presented for payment. This risk can be reduced if the bill is to be accepted by the buyer's bank, the bank's credit thus replacing the buyer's. Nevertheless, even this does not completely insulate the seller from the risk of non-payment. First, the buyer may instruct its bank not to accept the bill for whatever reason after all the bank will have no obligation to accept it) or, second, by the time the bill is received for acceptance, the bank may not wish to accept it for reasons of its own, in either case leaving the seller with the goods in a ship bound to a foreign destination and only a cause of action against the buyer for breach of contract.

---

131. It can be seen that the bank might also have a pledge over the shipping documents, thus securing borrowings ComCorp may have taken from it to fund the manufacture and export of the goods. If the collecting bank were also the buyer's own bank, that bank too might take a pledge over the shipping documents once the bill of exchange had been accepted, to secure borrowings by the buyer to fund the purchase of the goods.

132. The latest revision in 1995 is URC 552.

133. *Harlow & Jones Ltd v American Express Bank Ltd* [1990] 2 Lloyd's Rep 343 (QB) 349 (Gatehouse J). The editor of *Benjamin* adopts this analysis, stating that '[a]lthough the Uniform Rules apply only in the absence of intention to the contrary by the parties, they are departed from in very few cases'. See Michael G Bridge, *Benjamin's Sale of Goods* (8th edn, Sweet & Maxwell 2010) [22-076].

134. Unless the remitting bank carries out an instruction, as the seller's agent, to enter the seller into a direct contract with the collecting bank. See *Calico Printers' Association Ltd v Barclay's Bank Ltd* (1931) 39 Ll L Rep 51 (CA).

135. *Grosvenor Casinos Ltd v National Bank of Abu Dhabi* [2008] EWHC 511 (Comm), [2008] 1 CLC 399 [157].

136. *Bastone & Firminger Ltd v Nasima Enterprises (Nigeria) Ltd* [1996] CLC 1902 (QB) 1908 (Rix J).

Documentary credits—outline of process

Consider the following example.

> **Eg   ComCorp Ltd**
>
> As an alternative, Banco Rico suggests to Comcorp that it should require the buyer to open a letter of credit in ComCorp's favour. Once opened, the buyer's bank is legally committed to ComCorp to pay in whatever way is agreed, for example by accepting a bill of exchange payable in ninety days, once it receives specified documents—typically including a clean transferable bill of lading and a policy of marine insurance. The buyer's bank (known as the 'Issuing Bank') will arrange for Comcorp to be notified, by its agent, another bank with an office in UK (the 'Advising Bank') that the credit has been opened. ComCorp can then safely ship the goods and send the shipping documents to Banco Rico, who, as ComCorp's agent, will tender them to Advising Bank and receive a ninety-day bill of exchange accepted by Issuing Bank in return. Banco Rico will then buy the bill and credit ComCorp's account with the discounted proceeds. The Advising Bank will forward the specified documents to the Issuing Bank, which will debit the buyer's account when it pays on the bill and thus reimburse itself.

The contractual relationships between the parties are shown in Figure 24.3.

Documentary credits, as outlined in the ComCorp example, provide a solution to these final problems, insulating the seller almost entirely from the underlying contract of sale and totally from the credit of the buyer, since, as we shall see, the credit is itself not only an autonomous undertaking but also one to which there is only a very limited number of defences. It should be noted that, although there is no need for the completion of the sale to be effected by the seller's bank, this is certainly convenient, as well as providing security for the bank through its possession of the documents. Similarly, the beneficiary of the credit (ComCorp) can be given greater assurance if the Advising Bank itself agrees to accept the bill of exchange. It would then also be a 'Confirming Bank', so that both it and the Issuing Bank have an obligation to ComCorp.

In the ComCorp example, the Advising Bank is (as normal) also the bank specified in the credit to effect payment (known as the 'Nominated Bank'), which it does in the example by tendering a bill accepted by the Issuing Bank in return for the specified documents. But it may be agreed by the buyer and seller, and thus be reflected in the letter of credit, that, for example, the Nominated Bank will accept a sight or term bill

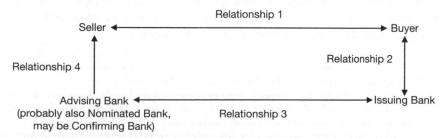

FIGURE 24.3 Relationships with letters of credit

of exchange (called an 'acceptance credit'), or purchase a bill of exchange drawn on the Issuing Bank, or, more rarely, a third party (called a 'negotiation credit'). In these and similar cases, the Nominated Bank will make payment from its own resources and look to the Issuing Bank for reimbursement against the shipping documents and, in the case of a negotiation credit, the bill of exchange. However, the Advising/Nominated/Confirming bank will not be entitled to reimbursement by the Issuing Bank for the payment it has made unless the shipping documents strictly conform to the stipulations in the credit. So, too, the Issuing Bank will not be entitled to reimbursement by its customer, the buyer, unless the documents conform. Once the Issuing Bank has received and accepted the shipping documents, it may well retain these until reimbursed by the buyer, since the bank may have financed the entire purchase. If the buyer must re-sell the goods before it can reimburse the Issuing Bank, then the bank can release the documents, enabling the buyer to take possession of them from the carrier. The bank will require the buyer to give it a 'trust receipt', and until then, if the documents include a shipped transferable bill of lading, it will have a pledge over the goods.

⬩ The use of bills of lading to provide security interests and the use of trust receipts are discussed at p 687

The International Chamber of Commerce has promulgated a set of rules for documentary credits called the UCP, the latest edition of which, the UCP 600, took effect on 1 July 2007. Like the UCR, these rules require incorporation into the contractual relationships by the parties, but by analogy to *Harlow & Jones Ltd v American Express*,[137] probably apply unless expressly or impliedly excluded.[138]

It should be noted that letters of credit may be used in transactions that do not require the presentation of documents. This chapter is concerned only with those letters which do require such a presentation; that is to say, 'documentary credits'.

The relationships between the parties to a letter of credit

Figure 24.3 illustrates the relationships between the parties. Each of the relationships will be considered in turn.

Contract 1: The relationship between buyer and seller under the contract of sale

Even in Cif or other contracts which lend themselves to a documentary sale, there is no obligation to pay by documentary credit unless the contract of sale for the goods so requires. The contract of sale may call for a revocable or irrevocable credit. Revocable credits allow the banks to revoke (end) their payment obligations at any time before they accept the documents. They provide little additional security to the seller over a documentary bill and are so rarely used that the UCP 600 does not apply to them.[139] The contract of sale for the goods will also state whether the credit is to be confirmed by Advising Bank or remain unconfirmed.

---

137. *Harlow & Jones v American Express Bank Ltd* [1990] 2 Lloyd's Rep 343 (HC).
138. See Roy Goode and Ewan McKendrick, *Goode on Commercial Law* (4th edn, Penguin Books 2010) 1077. However, Art 1 of the UCP 600 states that the UCP apply 'to any documentary credit ... when the text of the credit expressly indicates that it is subject to these rules'.
139. Article 1 of the UCP 600 states that UCP 600 applies to 'credits', which are defined in Art 3 as 'irrevocable arrangements'.

Whatever the specification of the credit agreed between the buyer and the seller, its opening is normally a condition precedent to the seller's obligation to ship the goods,[140] as the seller may be relying on the credit to finance the transaction and/or seeking to minimize costs by not shipping the goods until the issue of the credit ensures that the transaction will result in payment.[141]

 Trans Trust SPRL v Danubian Trading Co Ltd [1952] 2 QB 297 (CA)

FACTS: Danubian agreed to buy a quantity of steel from Trans Trust. Trans Trust in turn had to buy the steel from a Belgian company. Danubian was to open an irrevocable credit immediately, which it failed to do. Trans Trust did not ship the goods on the agreed date but extended the period for opening the credit. Danubian still failed to perform and Trans Trust sued it for breach of contract for its loss of profit on the transaction. Danubian argued that:

1. when it agreed to open the letter of credit this was like an agreement 'subject to contract'—that is, the opening of the credit was a condition precedent to the existence of a contract;

2. alternatively, by not shipping the goods on the agreed date, the seller was in breach of contract;

3. the credit was no more than a way of paying the price and in any contract a seller who is not paid the price must minimize his loss by selling to another party. In this case, since the price of steel had risen over the contract price, it could have done so at an even greater profit.

HELD: The Court held that:

- properly construed, the buyer had offered to purchase the steel and had promised to open a letter of credit and this offer had been accepted, therefore the opening of the credit was not a condition precedent to the existence of the contract;

- the seller was under no obligation to ship the goods before the credit was arranged. If the buyer fails to provide the credit, the seller could treat himself as discharged from any further performance of the contract and sue the buyer for damages for not providing the credit;

- the obligation to open a credit is not the same thing as an obligation to pay the price. Once it has been opened, the seller can use a credit to raise finance which he may need in order to purchase the contract goods, and in its absence he cannot purchase the goods and so cannot benefit from the rise in the market price. The buyer knew that Trans Trust was reliant on the credit to finance its own purchase, so that the loss of profit was not too remote.

---

140. *Garcia v Page & Co Ltd* (1936) 55 LlL Rep 391 (KB). See also Mance LJ in *Kronos Worldwide Ltd v Sempra Oil Trading Sarl* [2004] CLC 136 (CA) [19]. See Malcolm Clarke, 'Bankers Commercial Credits among High Trees' (1974) 33 CLJ 260, 264–9 for the alternative analyses of the effect of not opening the credit. Typically, the court will not treat the opening as a condition precedent to the existence of a contract: see *Trans Trust SPRL v Danubian Trading Co Ltd* [1952] 2 QB 297 (CA).
141. [1952] 2 QB 297 (CA).

If, as in *Trans Trust*, the contract requires the credit to be opened 'immediately', 'that means that the buyer has such time as is needed by a person of reasonable diligence to get that credit established'.[142] If the contract is silent as to the timing of the opening of the credit, the courts will imply that it must be opened within a reasonable time,[143] which is dependent on all of the circumstances and is at the latest by the first day of the shipping period, and probably sufficient time before that date to enable the seller to take advantage of the whole of that period.[144] Although this principle was established in relation to Cif contracts, where it is the seller who decides when shipment will actually take place, it appears to apply equally to Fob contracts, where the buyer makes that decision.[145]

As between buyer and seller, the doctrine of substantial not strict compliance applies in relation to the credit, so that minor differences between the terms of the credit and its specification in the contract of sale do not constitute a breach of contract by the buyer.[146] Thus, so long as the credit does not conflict with the express terms of the contract then, if the terms of the credit are fair and reasonable, the sellers must accept the credit as against the buyers, and tender documents in accordance with its terms in order to procure payment.[147] Thus in *Soproma v Marine & Animal By-Products Corp*,[148] where the contract of sale was silent on the matter whether the bills of lading should be 'freight prepaid' or 'freight unpaid', and the credit stated that the sellers must tender 'freight prepaid' bills, it was held that the buyers were not in breach of contract in procuring the credit in the form they had. By contrast, sellers in a Fob contract were entitled to treat as non-conforming, and so reject, a letter of credit opened which called for tender of freight pre-paid bills of lading.[149]

Under normal contractual principles,[150] a party can waive a contractual requirement which is wholly for his own benefit. For example, in *Soproma v Marine*, it was held that even if the credit had been non-conforming, the seller had waived his rights to object to the alleged non-conformities since he had re-negotiated some unconnected variations to its terms, thus leading the buyers to conclude he would not rely on his contractual rights.[151] However, in *LORICO*,[152] the sellers rejected a non-conforming credit and the buyer arranged for another to be opened. This, too, was non-conforming, to which the seller raised no objection, but they demanded

---

142. *Garcia v Page & Co Ltd* (1936) 55 Ll L Rep 391 (KB) (Porter J).

143. ibid applying to letters of credit the general principle established in *Hick v Raymond & Reid* [1893] AC 22 (HL).

144. *Pavia & Co SpA v Thurmann-Neilson* [1952] 2 QB 84 (CA), as interpreted by Denning LJ in *Sianson-Teicher Inter American Grain Corp v Oilcakes and Oilseeds Trading Co Ltd* [1954] 1 WLR 1394 (CA) (1400).

145. *Ian Stach Ltd v Baker Bosley Ltd* [1958] 2 QB 130 (QB).

146. *Bunge Corp v Vegetable Vitamin Foods (Pte) Ltd* [1985] (QB).

147. *Soproma SPA v Marine & Animal By-Products Corporation* [1966] 1 Lloyd's Rep 367 (QB).

148. [1966] 1 Lloyd's Rep 367 (QB).

149. *Glencore Grain Rotterdam BV v Lebanese Organisation for International Commerce* [1997] 4 All ER 514 (CA). The difference, of course, being that the essence of a Cif contract is that the seller pays for the cost of carriage, whilst in Fob it is the buyer who must meet this cost.

150. The principles of waiver as established in cases such as *Hickman v Haynes* (1875) LR 10 CP 598, seem indistinguishable from promissory estoppel.

151. In fact, there were two very clear non-conformities apart from the freight paid/unpaid issue—the contract of sale required confirmed credits, but the credit opened was unconfirmed and it was opened after the commencement of the shipping period.

152. *Glencore Grain Rotterdam BV v Lebanese Organisation for International Commerce* [1997] 4 All ER 514 (CA).

a price increase. It was held that it had not waived its right to reject the credit, as silence in these circumstances could not amount to a representation that it were content with the non-conforming credit on which the buyer had relied. On the other hand, where there is an alteration in the terms of a contract which is to both parties' advantage, then that mutual advantage constitutes consideration for the variation and is consequently binding on them. However, it may be very difficult to determine whether the parties have varied the contract or if instead one of the parties has waived his rights.[153]

WJ Alan & Co Ltd v El Nasr Export and Import Co [1972] 2 QB 189 (CA)

FACTS: The contract price of the goods was in Kenyan shillings, but the credit was expressed in sterling. The Alans, the sellers, did not object and presented invoices expressed in sterling and were paid in sterling under the credit, both before and after the date when sterling was devalued by 14 per cent against the shilling. However, the Alans sued El Nasr, the buyer, for the 14 per cent shortfall between the contract price and the amount, converted to Kenyan shillings at the new exchange rate, that it received under the credit.

HELD: Lord Denning held that there had been a waiver of the contractual right to payment in shillings; Stephenson LJ, that either there had been a waiver or a variation of contact; and Megaw LJ, that the contract had been varied, making the price payable in sterling; but whatever the reason, each judge agreed that the seller could not claim a price in shillings.

COMMENT: It was also argued that once a buyer had arranged for a credit to be issued, it had met its payment obligation under the contract, whether payment was actually made under it or not. However, the Court held that, like a bill of exchange, a letter of credit is presumed to be conditional payment only, and does not discharge the payment obligation absolutely. Theoretically this presumption can be rebutted.[154] In *Alan*, Lord Denning suggested that it might be rebutted where the seller 'stipulates for the credit to be issued by a particular bank in such circumstances where it is to be inferred that the seller looks to a particular banker to the exclusion of the buyer'.[155] There is logic in this since, normally, the issuing bank is selected by the buyer and the seller ought not to be required to take the risk of the bank's collapse. However, as *Man v Nigerian Sweets & Confectionery*[156] demonstrates, the fact that the parties agree the identity of the bank is insufficient to rebut the presumption.[157]

---

153. *WJ Alan & Co Ltd v El Nasr Export and Import Co* [1972] 2 QB 189 (CA).

154. For arguments in support of this approach see Malcolm Clarke, 'Bankers Commercial Credits Among High Trees' (1974) 33 CLJ 260 at 274–6. For cases applying the principle, see *ED & F Man Ltd v Nigerian Sweets & Confectionery Co Ltd* [1977] 2 Lloyd's Rep 50 (QB) and *Maran Road Saw Mill v Austin Taylor & Co Ltd* [1975] 1 Lloyd's Rep 156 (QB). These cases were distinguished by the Court of Appeal in *Re Charge Card Services Ltd* [1989] Ch 497 (CA), where payment by charge card was held to be an absolute payment.

155. *WJ Alan & Co Ltd v El Nasr Export and Import Co* [1972] 2 QB 189 (CA) 210.

156. *ED & F Man Ltd v Nigerian Sweets & Confectionery Co* Ltd [1977] 2 Lloyd's Rep 50 (QB).

157. Paul Todd, *Cases and Materials in International Trade Law* (Sweet & Maxwell 2002) 450 points out that in *Man v Nigerian Sweets & Confectionery*, the facts suggest that the seller merely acquiesced in the selection of the bank.

It has been held that the buyer owes a duty to the seller to 'provide a reliable and solvent paymaster'.[158] Thus if the bank wrongfully fails to pay under the credit, the seller may either pursue the bank on the credit or the buyer under the contract of sale. If he sues the buyer, the seller also has a choice to either insist on performance by tendering the documents and, if refused, suing for the price, or, alternatively, to accept non-payment as a repudiatory breach and sue for damages, mitigating his loss in the normal way.[159] Suing for the price would normally generate a higher sum, but the seller might terminate the contract and, in a rising market, sell elsewhere at a higher price.

Finally, on the buyer/seller relationship, once the documents have been accepted by the Advising/Nominated Bank, the buyer cannot then reject them as against the seller, and he must accept conforming goods; his remedy is against Issuing Bank if the documents did not conform.

Contract 2: The relationship between the buyer and the Issuing Bank

Almost inevitably the contract between the buyer and the Issuing Bank will be on the bank's standard terms incorporating the UCP 600. The buyer completes an application form for the issue of a credit, which will require him to specify the conditions which the seller must fulfil in order to induce payment, in particular stipulating the necessary documents. If the buyer is to meet his contractual duty to the seller, these stipulations must conform to their contract for the sale of goods. Likewise, since under the terms of the credit the bank is entitled to be reimbursed by the buyer only if there is a presentation of conforming documents, the buyer owes a duty to the bank to give clear instruction[160] and accurately specify the documents required to induce payment.

 Commercial Banking Co of Sydney Ltd v Jalsard Pty Ltd [1973] AC 279 (PC)

FACTS: The credit called, *inter alia*, for tender of a 'Certificate of Inspection' in respect of some electrical goods. A Certificate of Inspection was tendered, stating that the surveyors had checked the quantity and condition of the contents. If the goods had been tested it would have been clear they were defective, and the buyer, Jalsard, argued that a Certificate of Inspection meant a document certifying that the goods were of acceptable standard and conformed to the requirements of the contract under which they were sold.

HELD: The Privy Council held that a Certificate of Inspection merely required a statement that the goods had been inspected; if the buyer wanted a more detailed certificate it must specify one. Lord Diplock, in delivering the judgment also pointed out that banks are not merchants and are in no position to determine the commercial purpose of a specified document; they have only a short time in which to determine whether the documents tendered conform to the credit, and consequently, in cases of ambiguity, are required only to construe the credit's stipulations reasonably.[161]

---

158. *WJ Alan & Co Ltd v El Nasr Export and Import Co* [1972] 2 QB 189 (CA) 210 (Lord Denning).
159. *ED & F Man Ltd v Nigerian Sweets & Confectionery Co* [1977] 2 Lloyd's Rep 50 (QB).
160. *Midland Bank v Seymour* [1955] 2 Lloyd's Rep 147 (QB).
161. Returning to points he had first raised in *Midland Bank Ltd v Seymour* [1955] 2 Lloyd's Rep 147 (QB).

> **COMMENT:** It has been suggested that if the ambiguity is obvious a bank may not be acting reasonably if it does not consult the customer as to the meaning.[162]

Under previous editions of the UCP 600, the bank was required to inspect the documents with reasonable care. This requirement is missing from UCP 600; instead, Art 14 requires the Nominated Bank to 'examine a presentation to determine on the basis of the documents alone whether the documents appear on their face to constitute a complying presentation'. Whether this imposes strict liability on the bank, so that, for example, it would not be entitled to reimbursement for payments made against forged documents is unclear,[163] though it should be noted that Art 34 of the UCP 600 states that '[a] bank assumes no liability or responsibility for the form, sufficiency, accuracy, genuineness, falsification or legal effect of any document'.

Clearly, when the Issuing Bank opens the credit, it is acting on the instruction of its customer, the buyer. However, once the credit is opened it is not the customer's agent such that the customer can instruct the bank not to pay save in the case of fraud or other exception to the principle of the autonomy of the credit, since under the credit the bank has given its undertaking to the seller to pay as principal. However, if payment is refused against a conforming presentation, the Issuing Bank must indemnify the buyer against any liability the buyer incurs with the seller and other foreseeable losses. On the other hand, if there is a payment against non-conforming documents, the buyer has the following options:

- reject the documents—this case, the buyer is under no duty to reimburse the Issuing Bank for the payment it has made but abandons the goods to the bank for it to dispose of them on its own account. The buyer may also claim damages for foreseeable loss caused by the breach, but normally the buyer will suffer no greater loss by not paying for the goods and abandoning them to the bank than if the bank had rejected the documents, as it ought to have done in the first place;
- accept the documents and waive the breach by the bank;
- accept the documents without prejudice to his right to claim damages from the bank.

Contract 3: The relationship between the Issuing Bank and the Advising/Nominated/Confirming Bank

The function of the Advising Bank is simply to advise the beneficiary that the credit has been opened. However, almost inevitably the Advising Bank will also be the Nominated Bank for receiving and checking the stipulated documents and effecting payment. In what follows, the assumption is that this is the case. The relationship between the Issuing Bank and the Advising Bank is one of principal and agent in

---

162. Goff LJ in *European Asian Bank AG v Punjab and Sind Bank (No 2)* [1983] 1 WLR 642 (CA) 656. Though see Art 16(b) of the UCP 600, which gives a discretion to the bank whether to consult the buyer on whether to waive strict compliance. It is therefore strange if the bank has no discretion on whether to consult the buyer in interpreting the terms of the credit.

163. See Peter Ellinger, 'The Uniform Customs and Practice for Documentary Credits (UCP): Their Development and the Current Revisions' [2007] LMCLQ 152, 166. For the position under the 1962 edition, see *Gian Singh & Co Ltd v Banque de l'Indochine* [1974] 1 WLR 1234 (PC), where payment against a forgery did not prevent the issuing bank from recovering from its customer the sum paid under the credit.

the absence of agreement to the contrary.[164] However, where the Advising Bank is requested by the Issuing Bank to confirm the credit, then as the Confirming Bank, it is not acting solely as agent since it has a separate obligation to the buyer as principal. Consequently, if the Advising Bank is instructed by the Issuing Bank not to make a payment, then it must comply with that instruction under normal agency principles. However, if it is also the Confirming Bank, then it is entitled (and has a duty) to make a payment against conforming documents.

Article 7(c) of the UCP 600 contains an undertaking by the Issuing Bank to reimburse the Advising/Confirming Bank, which has honoured a presentation which is compliant on its face once it has forwarded the documents to the Issuing Bank. The Advising/Confirming Bank is entitled to reimbursement even if the documents are forgeries, but not if the documents are discrepant on their face, unless the Issuing Bank has waived its rights to compliant documents.[165] However, if the Advising/Confirming Bank pays against non-conforming documents, it has no right of reimbursement and instead is left to dispose of the goods on its own account.

Contracts 4 and 5: The relationship between the Issuing/Advising/Nominated/Confirming Banks and the seller

Under Art 7 of the UCP 600, the Issuing Bank undertakes to the seller that payment will be made on presentation of conforming documents to the Nominated Bank, and Art 8 contains an identical undertaking by the Confirming Bank.[166] Although the liability of the Issuing and Confirming Banks in respect of their respective undertakings to pay given to the seller by virtue of Arts 7 and 8 of the UCP 600 is undeniable, it is also inexplicable, since it is difficult to see what consideration the seller has given them in order to induce such undertakings. The seller gives no promise to the bank to tender the documents, and whilst the seller clearly relies on the bank's undertaking, thus suggesting an estoppel, the bank's obligation arises as soon as the seller is notified that the credit has been opened, not when he acts upon it, which is when an estoppel would arise. Nor does the Contract (Rights of Third Parties) Act 1999 assist, since it does not explain how the undertakings were binding prior to the Act's effective date, and in any event its effect is excluded by the operation of Art 4(a) of the UCP 600.[167]

Nevertheless, the undertakings are binding, probably through mercantile usage,[168] and the Nominated Bank has five banking days after the date of presentation to examine the documents and determine whether they constitute a conforming presentation. Once it has determined that the presentation is compliant, payment must take place as provided for in the credit.[169]

---

164. *Bank Melli Iran v Barclays Bank DCO* [1951] 2 Lloyd's Rep 367 (KB).

165. See *Habib Bank Ltd v Central Bank of Sudan* [2006] EWHC 1767 (Comm) [2006], [2007] 1 All ER (Comm) 53 for an example where the issuing bank was held to have waived its rights. The defendant was not represented. If it had been, it may have questioned whether the evidence showed a waiver in this case.

166. Typically, the Advising Bank will not only be the Nominated Bank but if there is a Confirming Bank it will be the Confirming Bank too. However, this need not be the case and the UCP 600 takes account of that fact.

167. For an analysis of the problem see Roy Goode, 'Abstract Payment Undertakings' in Peter Cane and Jane Stapleton (eds), *Essays for Patrick Atiyah* (Clarendon Press 1991).

168. See *Hamzeh Malas & Sons v British Imex Industries Ltd* [1958] 2 QB 127 (CA) 129 (Jenkins LJ).

169. UCP 600, Art 15.

By virtue of Art 16 of the UCP 600, if the bank determines that the presentation is non-conforming, it must give a single notice of refusal to honour to the presenter by 'telecommunication or, if that is not possible, by other expeditious means', stating each discrepancy and what it will do with the documents. By virtue of Art 16(f) of the UCP 600, failure to give such a notice within the five days precludes the bank from claiming the documents are non-conforming. However, it would appear that if a compliant notice is given, a bank may rely on discrepancies not on the list contained in the notice.[170]

It was estimated that approximately 70 per cent of presentations are non-conforming on first presentation,[171] and indeed one of the objectives of the UCP 600 was to reduce this percentage. However, the non-conformity is often of a minor or technical nature. Banking practice is to contact the buyer wherever possible to ask whether he is prepared to waive the discrepancy, and Art 16(b) of the UCP 600 facilitates this by providing that the Issuing Bank may approach the buyer for this purpose. However, the consultation process does not extend the five-day decision-making period.

Should the Issuing or Confirming Bank refuse to meet its obligations the seller has two options; he can either accept this as a repudiatory breach of the credit contract and sue for loss, or alternatively insist on performance and sue to recover the sum due under the credit. In the latter case, since disposal of the documents would indicate he has accepted the breach, the seller will need to retain them (and consequently the goods), rather than dispose of them elsewhere.[172] On the other hand, if payment is made against non-conforming documents such that the paying bank is unable to obtain reimbursement, it may seek repayment from the seller under a restitutionary claim for money paid under a mistake.[173] *Lipkin Gorman*[174] established the 'change of position' defence to such a claim so that a seller who had disbursed money which he would otherwise not have spent will not be liable unless he acted in bad faith; for example, by forging the documents or tendering them knowing they were forged or were otherwise false. In any event, in such a situation he would be liable for damages for deceit.[175] Under the UCP 600 it may well be that the Issuing or Confirming Bank would be prevented from making any restitutionary claim in the absence of fraud by the seller, since they would need to prove that the documents were non-conforming, something Art 16(f) of the UCP 600 precludes them from doing.

It should be noted that the UCP 600 imposes no duty on the Advising/Nominated Bank to pay the seller; a failure to pay gives him a claim, if at all, against Issuing and Confirming Banks only.

---

170. *Kydon Compania Navierra SA v National Westminster Bank Ltd, The Lena* [1981] 1 Lloyd's Rep 68 (QB), a case decided on common law principles. See Charles Debattista, 'The New UCP—Changes to the Tender of the Seller's Shipping Documents under Letters of Credit' [2007] JBL 329, who suggests the position under UCP 600 may be different.

171. UCP 600, Foreword.

172. *Belgian Grain & Produce Co Ltd v Cox & Co (France) Ltd* (1919) 1 Ll L Rep 256 (KB).

173. *Bank Russo–Iran v Gordon Woodroffe & Co Ltd* (1912) 116 Sol Jo 921 (KB).

174. *Lipkin Gorman v Karpnale Ltd* [1991] 2 AC 548 (HL).

175. *KBC Bank v Industrial Steels (UK) Ltd* [2001] 1 All ER (Comm) 409 (QB). See also *Standard Chartered Bank v Pakistan Shipping Corpn (No 2)* [2002] UKHL 4, [2002] 2 All ER (Comm) 931, where the claimant had itself deceived the issuing bank but succeeded in an action for deceit against a carrier who had falsely dated a bill of lading.

The relationship between the buyer and the Advising/Nominated and/or Confirming Banks

As Figure 24.3 demonstrates, there is no contractual relationship between the buyer and any bank other than the Issuing Bank. Consequently, in the absence of a claim in tort on *Hedley Byrne*[176] principles, which is doubtful,[177] the buyer cannot make the Advising/Nominated and/or the Confirming Bank liable to him for loss caused, for example through the rejection of conforming or the acceptance of non-conforming documents and must look to the Issuing Bank for remedy. However, Art 37 of the UCP 600 provides a disclaimer whereby the use of another bank to carry out the buyer's instruction is at the buyer's risk and the Issuing Bank has no liability if the instructions are not carried out by that other bank. The breadth of the exclusion is so wide as to render it susceptible to possible challenge by virtue of s 3 of the Unfair Contract Terms Act 1977, and banks tend not to rely on it.[178] However, the buyer is under no obligation to accept and pay for non-conforming documents tendered by the Issuing Bank,[179] so that he has no duty to reimburse the Issuing Bank in respect of a negligent acceptance of non-conforming documents by the nominated bank.

The key characteristics of credits

Strict compliance

The doctrine of strict compliance requires that all documents tendered under the credit 'must appear on their face to be precisely in accordance with the terms and conditions of the credit'.[180] Thus, in *Moralice (London) Ltd v ED & F Man*,[181] the bank was held to be entitled to reject shipping documents showing that 499.7 tonnes of sugar had been loaded, when the credit required documents showing shipment of 500 tonnes,[182] while in *Equitable Trust Co of New York v Dawson Partners Ltd*,[183] the buyers were entitled to reject a certificate of quality issued by a single expert when the credit called for one issued by 'experts' and thus were not obliged to reimburse the bank which had paid under the credit.

From a practical viewpoint the acts of rejection may appear unmeritorious,[184] but there are good practical and legal reasons for the stringency of the rule. First, the bank is treated as the buyer's agent for the purposes of making payment and

---

176. [1964] AC 465 (HL).

177. *GKN Contractors Ltd v Lloyds Bank plc* (1985) 30 BLR 48 (CA). But see *United Trading Corp SA v Allied Arab Bank Ltd* [1985] 2 Lloyd's Rep 554 (CA).

178. See Roy Goode and Ewan McKendrick, *Goode on Commercial Law* (Penguin 2010) 1082.

179. *Crédit Agricole Indosuez v Generale Bank* [2000] 1 Lloyd's Rep 123 (KB).

180. *Seaconsar Far East Ltd v Bank Markazi Jomhouri Islami Iran* [1998] CLC 1543 (CA) 1545 (Sir Christopher Staughton).

181. [1954] 2 Lloyd's Rep 526 (QB).

182. See now Art 30(b) of the UCP 600, which permits a 5 per cent tolerance more or less in quantities, (but not in numbers of packages or items).

183. [1927] 27 Ll L Rep 49 (HL).

184. But as Sir Christopher Staughton said in *Seaconsar Far East Ltd v Bank Markazi Jomhouri Islami Iran* [1998] CLC 1543 (CA) 154: 'letter of credit law is and has to be precise; it is not concerned with merits'.

therefore must act only within the authority it has been given; and second, banks cannot be required to understand the underlying contract of sale; they deal in documents, not goods,[185] and must judge them in isolation by reference to the specification in the credit,[186] as illustrated in *Rayner v Hambros Bank*.[187]

 JH Rayner & Co Ltd v Hambro's Bank Ltd [1943] KB 37 (CA)

FACTS: The letter of credit called for bills of lading and an invoice for 'Coromandel ground nuts'. Rayner, the seller and beneficiary under the letter of credit, presented an invoice for 'Coromandel ground nuts' and bills of lading for 'machine-shelled groundnut kernels'. Hambros rejected the documents and Rayner sued for payment, arguing that it was well known in the trade that 'Coromandel ground nuts' and 'machine-shelled groundnut kernels' were synonymous.

HELD: It was immaterial that both terms meant the same thing: the credit had to be construed in isolation from the underlying contract of sale. The issue was not 'Has the seller shipped goods corresponding to the contractual description?' but 'Has the seller presented documents which correspond with the description in the credit?' Consequently, since the words in the bill of lading were clearly not the same as those required by the letter of credit, the bank was entitled to reject the documents. If it had accepted them, it was at its own risk, as the buyer would have had no duty to accept them and so would have had no obligation to reimburse the bank. Adapting the words of Lord Sumner in *Equitable Trust Co of New York v Dawson Partners*,[188] there is no room for documents which are almost the same, or which will do just as well. The bank's branch abroad, which knows nothing officially of the details of the transaction thus financed, cannot take upon itself to decide what will do well enough and what will not.

COMMENT: Mackinnon LJ partly relied on the fact it was impractical to expect bankers to be aware of jargon used in every trade they financed. However, Goddard LJ concluded that even if the bank had known that the disputed terms were interchangeable, it would still have had the right to reject the documents. It is now clear that whilst the impracticality of the alternative justifies the strict compliance rule, it is not the basis of it.

Article 18(c) of the UCP 600 specifies that the description of the goods in the commercial invoice must correspond with that in the credit, but Art 14(e) states that in other documents 'the description of the goods, if stated, may be in general terms not conflicting with their description in the credit'. However, it seems unlikely that had these provisions applied in *Rayner* they would have affected the outcome. See *Astro Exito Navegacion SA v Chase Manhattan Bank NA (The Messiniaki Tolmi)*,[189] where Leggatt J held in the corresponding (though slightly differently worded) article in a previous edition of the UCP that a 'description in general terms not inconsistent with the description in the credit' suggests that correspondence in description requires all the elements in the description to be present.

---

185. See Art 5 of the UCP 600.
186. Reflected in Art 14(a). Banks are to determine 'on the basis of the documents alone, whether or not the documents appear on their face to be compliant'.
187. *JH Rayner & Co Ltd v Hambro's Bank Ltd* [1943] KB 37 (CA).
188. (1927) 27 Ll L Rep 49 (HL).   189. [1986] 1 Ll Rep 455 (QB) 458.

The strictness of the rule is tempered both at common law by the fact that 'trivial' discrepancies can be ignored and also by provisions in the UCP 600. At common law, clear typographical errors have been held to be trivial,[190] but typically not where a party's name is mis-stated[191] and what amounts to trivial is not easy to determine. In some instances where the discrepancies do not appear trivial but which nevertheless have departed from the principle that, in effect, the documents presented must 'mirror' the specification in the credit can be explained because the specification itself required the bank to exercise judgement. Thus in *Kredietbank Antwerp v Midland Bank plc*,[192] the credit called for a '[d]raft survey report issued by Griffith Inspectorate'. The report as tendered was issued by 'Daniel C Griffith (Holland) BV', stating it was a 'member of the worldwide inspectorate group'. In fact, there is no such person as 'Griffith Inspectorate', which is in effect a trading name of a network of loosely affiliated companies, and the Court of Appeal concluded that the bank ought to have interpreted the credit as requiring 'a document issued by a Griffith company, a member of the Inspectorate Group'.

As noted earlier, part of the objective of revising the UCP 600 was to reduce the number of non-compliant first presentations. Thus Art 14(d) of the UCP 600 states that data in a document need not be identical to data elsewhere in the specified documents, though it must not conflict. Likewise, Art 14(f) states that, apart from transport and insurance documents and invoices, banks will accept documents if they fulfil the function of the specified document, regardless of the content of the data contained in it or by whom it was issued, unless the credit specifies otherwise. Thus if the draft survey report in *Kredietbank Antwerp* had been issued by a surveyor which was not part of the Griffiths network, then Art 14(f) would not have been of assistance, but if the report had indicated that the goods were not of the contractual quality, Art 14(f) would require the bank to accept it unless the credit also specified that the goods must pass the survey tests.

The definition of a complying presentation in the UCP 600 is one 'in accordance with the terms and conditions of the credit, the applicable provisions of these rules and international standard banking practice', and the ICC has issued the International Standard Banking Practice for the Examination of Documents under Letters of Credit[193] (ISBP) to accompany the UCP 600. The ISBP 'explains, in explicit detail, how the rules set out in the UCP 600 are to be applied on a day-to-day basis',[194] and clearly will be influential in determining whether a presentation of documents is compliant.

Autonomy of the credit

As noted earlier, a bill of exchange, while insulating a holder in due course from the impact of some disputes arising from the underlying contract of sale, is open to some defences. Consequently, receipt of a bill of exchange, drawn on however solvent a payer, does not ensure payment. However, a letter of credit creates an

---

190. See e.g. *Bankers Trust Co v State Bank of India* [1991] 2 Lloyd's Rep 443 ('3' substituted for '8' in the buyer's telex number).
191. See *United Bank Ltd v Banque Nationale de Paris* [1992] 2 SLR 64 (High Court of Singapore); *Beyene v Irving Trust Co Ltd* (1985) 762 F 2d 4 (US Court of Appeals for the Second Circuit). However, it was accepted hypothetically in *Beyene* that misspelling 'Smith' as 'Smithh' would be trivial.
192. [1999] 1All ER (Comm) 801 (CA).   193. ICC Publication 681 (2007).   194. ibid 3.

abstract payment obligation entirely divorced from the underlying contract, as Art 4 UCP 600 states '[a] credit by its nature is a separate transaction from the sale…on which it is based…Consequently, the undertaking of a bank…under the credit is not subject to claims or defences by the applicant.' Similarly, the credit is separate from the bank–buyer relationship, the bank cannot refuse to pay because the buyer cannot or will not reimburse it.

The autonomy of the credit is well illustrated by the following case.

 ### *Hamzeh Malas & Sons v British Imex Industries Ltd* [1958] 2 QB 127 (CA)

FACTS: Hamzeh Malas, the buyer, agreed to buy a large quantity of steel reinforcing rods, to be delivered in two instalments. Payment was by two letters of credit, one for each instalment. The seller, Imex, shipped the first instalment and were paid under the first credit. However, Hamzeh Malas complained the goods were defective and sought to injunct Imex from claiming on the second letter of credit.

HELD: The injunction was refused; the contract of sale was a separate contract to the contract between the bank and the seller. The credit imposed an absolute duty on the bank to pay against compliant documents, regardless of whether the goods meet the contractual requirements, and to grant an injunction would be to circumvent this obligation.

COMMENT: The application in this case was an attempt to evade a long series of authorities which had held that the bank must pay against a conforming presentation by seeking to prevent the seller from making such a presentation. It is not surprising that it failed, but part of the reasoning of the Court is instructive. Jenkins LJ recognized that very often a seller is himself simply intermediate in a supply chain, and uses the credit to finance his purchase for onward sale to the buyer. Once the credit has been opened in his favour, his own bank being assured that its customer will receive payment from a reputable paymaster is more prepared to advance funds to the seller to finance its purchase. This practice would be impaired and the absolute assurance of payment would be lost were it possible to block payment.

⭐ See Aubrey Diamond, 'Clean Bills of Lading' (1958) 21 MLR 306

There are, however, exceptions (some disputed) to the autonomy principle, which are set out in the paragraphs that follow.

Agreement not to claim under the credit

It was held in the Court of Appeal in *Sirius International Insurance Corpn (Publ) v FAI General Insurance Co Ltd*,[195] that where the beneficiary of the credit had agreed not to claim under the credit without the consent of a third party, the court would be likely to grant an injunction to prevent a presentation.

---

195. [2003] EWCA Civ 470, [2003] 1 WLR 2214. On appeal to the House of Lords, it was held that the condition in the agreement had been satisfied, so that there was no need to consider the issue of an injunction.

Unconscionability

In both Singapore[196] and in Australia[197] courts have granted injunctions against beneficiaries making 'unconscionable demands', but what might amount to unconscionability is far from clear, though a number of the cases have involved breaches of an agreement, as in *Sirus International*, not to claim on the credit and the uncertainty such a doctrine creates may prevent its adoption in England.[198] It should also be noted that the cases in which unconscionability has been accepted as warranting an injunction against a beneficiary typically involve bank guarantees, and this point of distinction may also inhibit the extension of the doctrine to letters of credit in England and Wales.[199]

Fraud in the presentation of the documents

Where there is fraud in relation to the documents presented[200] by the person seeking payment under the credit, the bank is entitled to refuse payment.

United City Merchants (Investments) Ltd v Royal Bank of Canada. The American Accord [1983] 1 AC 168 (HL)

FACTS: The seller invoiced the buyer at twice the agreed amount to enable the Peruvian purchasers to evade Peruvian exchange control law. Payment was by a letter of credit, under which the last day for shipping was 15 December. The seller transferred the letter of credit to United City Merchants (Investments) Ltd (UCM) as security for loans UCM had made to it. The goods were shipped on 16 December but, unknown to the seller and UCM, the carrier's agent dated the bills of lading 15 December. When UCM presented the bills for payment to Royal Bank of Canada (RBC), which had confirmed the credit, RBC refused payment on the grounds that the documents were inaccurate.

HELD: The bank is entitled to refuse payment 'where the seller, for the purpose of drawing on the credit, fraudulently presents to the confirming bank documents that contain, expressly or by implication, material representations of fact that to his knowledge are untrue'.[201] UCM was unaware of the fraud and consequently was entitled to payment.

---

196. *Bocotra Construction Pte Ltd v A-G (No 2)* [1995] 2 SLR 733 (Singapore Court of Appeal). Here Karthigesu JA treated an application for payment as unconscionable where the applicant had undertaken not to make an application in an agreement to submit a dispute, alleging the applicant had impeded performance of the underlying contract to arbitration.

197. *Olex Focas Pty Ltd Skodaexport Co Ltd* [1998] 3 VR 380 (High Court of Victoria). Decided primarily on the basis of an Australian statute. See also the recent decision of the Supreme Court of South Africa, *Kwikspace Modular Buildings Ltd v Sabodala Mining Company Sarl* (173/09) [2010] ZASCA 15, involving a contract incorporating Western Australian law.

198. There may be a glimmer of an indication that English law may adopt it. See *Montrod Ltd v Grundkotter Fleischvertriebs GmbH* [2001] EWCA Civ 1954, [2002] 1 WLR 1975 [59–60] (Potter LJ), and, more obviously, *TTI Team Telecom International Ltd v Hutchison 3G UK Ltd* [2003] EWHC 762, [2003] 1 All ER (Comm) 914 [37] and [46] (Judge Thornton QC).

199. Though the same issues of autonomy of payment would seem to apply equally to guarantees as to letters of credit.

200. *United City Merchants (Investments) Ltd v Royal Bank of Canada (The American Accord)* [1983] 1 AC 168 (HL).

201. [1983] 1 AC 168 (HL) 183 (Lord Diplock).

> **COMMENT:** The House rejected the argument that the documents could be rejected if, although conforming on their face with the terms of the credit, they contained a misstatement of a material fact, even where the person who issued the document (in this case the carrier) knew it to be false.
>
> Although Lord Diplock referred to the seller's fraud, it extends to any party who presents the document for payment or reimbursement,[202] and it is clear that the 'fraud' need not amount to criminal behaviour, just that it amounts to the tort of deceit. It would also seem that the fraud must be in relation to letter of credit, since in this case the seller was complicit in what was probably an illegal act by the buyer under Peruvian law, but this did not affect its right to claim under the credit.[203] It also seems clear that only the state of mind of the claimant at presentation is relevant.[204]
>
> Lord Diplock left open the issue of whether, if a document is a complete nullity though conforming on its face, it gives the seller the right to payment under the credit, though he seems to suggest that it would.

★ See Anthony Walker, 'American Accord-Third Party Fraud and Letters of Credit' (1982) 6 IFL Rev 4

Although there is no clear English authority on the point,[205] it may be that the fraud exception is not confined to fraud in relation to the documents alone, so that if, for example, the underlying contract has been induced by a clear fraudulent misrepresentation, that might be sufficient ground for the bank to refuse payment, though this clearly infringes the autonomy principle.

There is a problem for a bank when its customer presents evidence of fraud by the seller.[206] If the bank refuses payment, it not only risks its reputation, but will also be faced at trial with having to prove fraud, admittedly on the balance of probabilities, but in the knowledge that civil courts resist making such findings, since it is a serious allegation.[207] On the other hand, if it does pay, it risks not being able to claim reimbursement unless the customer acquiesces. Thus typically the bank will invite its customer to seek an interlocutory injunction either injuncting the bank from paying or, if the seller has not already made a presentation, injuncting the seller. In cases involving injunctions against banks, the courts have devised a number of formulations to describe the standard of proof required, but it is only in wholly exceptional circumstances that an injunction will be granted, since the courts have set a relatively

---

202. *Standard Chartered Bank v Pakistan National Shipping Corp (No 2)* [2001] QB 167(CA), where the confirming bank falsely represented to the issuing bank the documents had been presented in accordance with the credit and so was refused reimbursement by the issuing bank.

203. Though it also breached a now repealed piece of UK legislation which rendered part of the credit void.

204. See *Group Josi Re v Walbrook Insurance Co Ltd* [1996] 1 WLR 1152 (CA) 1161 (Staughton LJ).

205. *Themehelp Ltd v West* [1996] QB 84 (CA) suggests (in the context of a performance guarantee to which identical considerations apply) that fraud in the underlying transaction would warrant an injunction against the seller from making an application for payment. The Canadian Supreme Court has accepted that fraud in the underlying transaction of such a character as to make the demand for payment under the credit a fraudulent one is a defence. See *Bank of Nova Scotia v Angelica-Whitewear Ltd* [1987] 1 SCR 59 (Supreme Court of Canada).

206. The word 'seller' is used because the assumption throughout is that there is an underlying sale, but the correct term is 'beneficiary'.

207. Proof that it had grounds at the time of refusal for a reasonable belief that there was fraud is insufficient (*Society of Lloyds v Canadian Imperial Bank of Commerce* [1993] 2 Lloyd's Rep 579 (Comm)).

high standard requiring compelling evidence.[208] Whilst injuncting the seller from claiming under the credit does not literally interfere with the autonomy principle,[209] it clearly interferes with its underlying commercial justification of certainty of payment, and it would appear that identical principles apply in such a case.[210] In either case, even where fraud has been proved to the appropriate standard, on *American Cyanamid*[211] principles, the balance of convenience must favour the granting of the injunction. This will rarely be the case, since if the bank is allowed to pay and fraud is proved at trial, the buyer need not reimburse the bank, while blocking payment will seriously hinder the seller.

Illegality in the underlying contract

Although not completely developed, there appears in English law to be a ground for rejection of documents based on the illegality in the underlying contract. The origin for the suggestion that underlying illegality provides an exception to the autonomy of payment principle is *The American Accord*,[212] though here the credit was in any event rendered unenforceable by English legislation to the extent that it constituted a financial contract to evade exchange control regulations in Peru. Nevertheless, in *Group Josi Re v Walbrook Insurance Co*,[213] Staughton LJ suggested, *obiter*, that if the letters of credit were a means of effecting payment in respect of an illegal underlying contract, the court would either restrain the bank from paying or the seller from claiming under the credit. However, in *Mahonia Ltd v JP Morgan Chase Bank*,[214] Colman J drew a distinction between letters of credit which were an integral part of an illegal scheme and which would be unenforceable and those which were simply a facility which assisted performance in a manner not specifically rendered illegal, as in *Group Josi*, which he implied would not.[215] How one distinguishes between an integral and peripheral letter of credit is not clear.

The documents are a nullity

For some while it was open to question whether payment must be made under a credit which, instead of containing a misrepresentation, was a nullity, through, for example, being issued without authority or by being a forgery. The issue was considered by the Court of Appeal in *Montrod Ltd v Grundkotter Fleischvertriebs GmbH*.[216]

---

208. See e.g. 'established or obvious fraud' in *Edward Owen Engineering Ltd v Barclays Bank International Ltd* [1978] QB 159 (CA), and 'a good arguable case that the only realistic inference is that the demands were fraudulent' in *United Trading Corporation SA v Allied Arab Bank Limited* [1985] 2 Lloyd's Rep 554n (CA).
209. *Themehelp Ltd v West* [1996] QB 84 (CA).
210. See *Group Josi Re v Wallbrook Insurance Co Ltd* [1996] 1 WLR 1152 (CA) 1161 (Staughton LJ). See Agasha Mugasha 'Enjoining the Beneficiary's Claim on a Letter of Credit or Bank Guarantee' [2004] JBL 515, 525–33.
211. *American Cyanamid v Ethicon Ltd* [1975] AC 396 (HL), the case which established the principles on which an interlocutory injunction will be granted.
212. [1983] 1 AC 168 (HL).
213. [1996] 1 WLR 1152 (CA).
214. [2003] EWHC 1927 (Comm), [2003] 2 Lloyd's Rep 911.
215. ibid [66], a view Cooke J seemed to adopt in *Mahonia Ltd v JP Morgan Chase Bank (No 2)* [2004] EWHC 1938 (Comm).
216. [2001] EWCA Civ 1954, [2002] 1 WLR 1975. Here the document was signed by an unauthorized person and technically may not have been a nullity, but it is difficult to see how the applicant for credit could have been estopped from denying the signatory's authority.

Here the stipulated documents included a certificate of inspection signed by a company helping to finance the buyer. The buyer fraudulently informed the seller that he could sign it on the finance company's behalf and the Court of Appeal, following the reasoning of Lord Diplock in *United City Merchants*, held that an innocent seller could demand payment even against a nullity. The primary justifications given for the decision was the necessity to preserve the autonomy principle and to increase commercial certainty, but it seems peculiar that a seller can require payment against a piece of paper which, though appearing to be compliant, is not. There seems to be some confusion in the minds of the court both in *The American Accord* and *Montrod* between the need to protect a bank which makes a payment against a document it is not aware is nullity and requiring it to make a payment against one that it knows is.[217] As Chao LJ said in *Beam Technology (MFG) PTE Ltd v Standard Chartered Bank*, requiring payment in such a situation 'defies reason and good sense'.[218]

Conclusion

In this chapter we have considered the nature of an instrument as a document which embodies payment obligations and examined in detail one important instrument, the bill of exchange. The key issues of negotiability both in terms of the means of transferring rights under the instrument and of improving them, so that a transferee has greater immunity from defences than the transferor, have been explored through a focus on the rights and duties of the parties to a bill of exchange. In this way, both the legal concepts which underpin the concept of an instrument and potential commercial applications of instruments have been examined.

This examination was extended with the discussion of letters of credit, since commonly the obligation of the relevant bank is to accept a 'time' bill of exchange in return for a conforming tender of documents. Although not specifically highlighted, bills of exchange, whether in conjunction with a letter of credit or not, ensure that the act of completing a documentary sale of goods is effected entirely by the exchange of documents, often in the absence of both buyer and seller, thus facilitating both the legal logistics and the financing of international sales.

Practice questions

1. Explain the following terms:

    *   negotiability;
    *   an instrument;
    *   a bill of exchange;

217. For further criticisms of *The American Accord* see Roy Goode, 'Abstract Payment Undertakings' in Peter Cane and Jane Stapleton (eds), *Essays for Patrick Atiyah* (Clarendon Press 1991) 228–33. Also Roy Goode and Ewan McKendrick, *Goode on Commercial Law* (4th edn, Penguin 2010) 1105–6. See also Richard Hooley's criticism of *Montrod* in 'Fraud and Letters of Credit: Is there a Nullity Exception?' (2002) 61 CLJ 279–81.

218. [2003] 1 SLR 597 (Singapore Court of Appeal) [34]. Here it was held that there is a nullity exception to the autonomy principle.

- a letter of credit;
- Issuing Bank, Advising Bank, Confirming Bank, Nominated Bank.

2. Discuss and illustrate with examples the proposition that, notwithstanding the fact that the juridical basis for the Issuing Bank's obligation to the beneficiary and the fraud and illegality defences are entirely unclear, letters of credit provide a secure payment mechanism for both buyer and seller of goods in international sales.

3. Xavier wishes to buy some goods from Gordon, but Gordon will only sell to him if Alexander will accept a bill of exchange, payable to Gordon in 120 days. Xavier draws the bill in Gordon's favour, which he gives to Gordon with A's signature on it as acceptor. Gordon sells the goods to Xavier. Gordon later gives the bill to Henry.

   As a result of his investigations into Xavier's finances, Gordon becomes concerned because he has sold goods in the past to Xavier on credit and he owes Gordon a lot of money as a result. Gordon indicates to Xavier that he is concerned about this and Xavier gives him a second bill of exchange with Alexander's signature as acceptor, again payable to Gordon in 120 days. To procure this bill, Xavier promised Alexander that he will repay him with interest. A little later, in identical circumstances to the first bill, Gordon receives a third bill with Alexander's signature on it as acceptor.

   Henry presents the three bills to Alexander for payment but Alexander refuses. Henry claims summary judgment against him and Alexander raises the following defences:

   (a) Defence 1—In relation to bill number 1, Alexander received no consideration for his accepting the bill.

   (b) Defence 2—In relation to bills 1 and 2, Alexander accepted the bill only because Xavier had threatened to ruin him financially if he did not.

   (c) Defence 3—In relation to bill 3, Alexander's signature was forged by Xavier.

   (d) Defence 4—In relation to bills 1 and 2, the date on the bill has been altered.

   Are these defences valid against Henry? Would they have been valid against Gordon if he had not given the bill to Henry?

Further reading

JR Adams, **'The Vagliano Case'** (1891) 7 LQR 295
- Although only a casenote, it explains very well the principle on which the rule that a banker is not entitled to debit his customer when the bank has paid on a bill of exchange which has a forged indorsement. It also explains why in Vagliano's case, since the acceptor had no liability to anyone on the bill, that principle did not apply. As an aside, the text at the bottom of p 296 gives a wonderful insight into the insularity of Victorian English lawyers.

Hugh Beale and Lowri Griffiths, **'Electronic Commerce: Formal Requirements in Commercial Transactions'** [2002] LMCLQ 467
- Summarizes the findings of the Law Commission on facilitation of e-commerce in relation to international trade. In particular, it looks at electronic signatures. The article goes far beyond the 'e issues' in relation to bills of exchange and letters of credit, but is a fascinating study on how to move from a world where paper represented goods and obligations to one where electrons might do the same thing.

Malcolm Clarke, 'Bankers Commercial Credits among High Trees' (1974) 33 CLJ 260
- Deals, among other things with the competing explanations why an Issuing Bank has an obligation to pay the seller, the effect of not opening a credit in the time provided in the contract of sale, whether a letter of credit is an absolute of conditional payment, and the issues involved in waiver and estoppel and the opening of a non-conforming credit.

Roy Goode, 'Abstract Payment Undertakings' in Peter Cane and Jane Stapleton (eds), *Essays for Patrick Atiyah* (Clarendon Press 1991)
- Among other things, this essay contains a careful analysis of the problems with attempting to explain how the Issuing or Confirming Bank can be under an obligation to pay the beneficiary under a letter of credit and deals with the conceptual difficulties with the current form of the fraud and illegality exceptions to the autonomy of credit principle.

LP Hitchens, 'Holders for Value and their Status: Clifford Chance v Silver' [1993] JBL 571
- Until *Clifford Chance*, writers had assumed that to be a holder in due course under s 29(1) of the Bills of Exchange Act 1882, the person must themselves have given value and not be deemed to have done so by virtue of s 27(2). Hitchens explores the rationale for the decision in *Clifford Chance* that this was not the case.

Richard Hooley, 'Fraud and Letters of Credit: Is There a Nullity Exception?' (2002) 61 CLJ 279
- Provides a number of reasons, both legal and commercial, why the law ought not to require banks to accept documents, though conforming on their face, but which the bank knows to be void in the context of the *Montrod* case.

AH Hudson, 'Time and Promissory Notes' (1962) 25 MLR 593
- Although primarily an analysis of *Williamson v Rider* [1962] All ER 268 (CA), this note deals with the requirements for the certainty of the date for payment under a bill of exchange, noting how the courts seem to have varied the degree of precision required.

Agasha Mugasha, 'Enjoining the Beneficiary's Claim on a Letter of Credit or Bank Guarantee' [2004] JBL 515
- Explores the grounds for injuncting a bank from paying or restraining the beneficiary from claiming under a letter of credit including nullity, unconscionable conduct, and defects in the underlying contract. There is also consideration of the standard of proof required.

Peter Ellinger, 'The Uniform Customs and Practice for Documentary Credits (UCP): Their Development and the Current Revisions' [2007] LMCLQ 152
- A full and scholarly analysis of the UCP 600, in contrast to previous editions and in the context of banking and commercial practice.

The following articles are also worth considering in relation to understanding the UCP 600:

Ebenezer Adodo, 'A Presentee Bank's Duty when Examining a Tender of Documents Under the Uniform Custom and Practice for Documentary Credits 600' [2009] JIBLR 566

Charles Debattista, 'The New UCP 600—Changes to the Tender of the Seller's Shipping Documents under Letters of Credit' [2007] JBL 329

Koji Takahashi, 'The Introduction of Article 12(b) in the UCP 600: Was it Really a Step Forward?' [2009] JIBLR 285

Security interests in property

- The elements of security and security interests
- Attachment and perfection
- Pledges
- Liens
- Mortgages
- Charges

INTRODUCTION

In Chapter 2, ownership rights in personal property were discussed, but reference was also made to limited rights over property. This chapter is concerned with those limited rights. These limited rights enable a person who is owed a personal obligation by someone with ownership of an asset to exercise powers over that asset, should the personal obligation not be fulfilled. These limited rights are known as 'security interests'—their effect is to provide additional remedies in the event of breach of the personal obligation and so make performance more secure. The assumption in this chapter is that the obligation secured is a debt, but there is no reason why security cannot be taken in order to secure any obligation. Consequently, whilst the words 'lender', 'creditor', 'borrower', and 'debtor' will be used, strictly speaking the terms used should be 'obligee' and 'obligor'. The words 'lender' or 'creditor' are also used to indicate the person taking the security, and 'borrower' or 'debtor' the person over whose property it is exercisable.

This chapter introduces the types of security interest and considers the essential elements of their creation and the steps that may be necessary in order for the interest to have priority over competing claims to the secured property. It then examines the main types of security interest, focussing on the mode of creation, the nature of the interests, and the rights over the property which the interest gives to the lender. The chapter ends by mentioning briefly how similar economic effects to taking security can be obtained by employing techniques which do not involve the creation of security interests.

The elements of security and security interests

The terms on which a lender is prepared to advance money or to allow credit to a counterparty, or whether he is prepared to lend or advance credit at all, is partially dependent on his assessment of the risk that the other party will not meet the personal obligation to pay/repay the money in accordance with the terms of their agreement. In other words, does he believe (credit) the borrower's promise to repay. As a result, the prudent lender will go through a process of investigation to reassure himself that the borrower is likely to repay. The care with which this process of investigation is undertaken may vary, from a cursory glance at the borrower's accounts and/or a look at any credit reference available from a reference agency, to a detailed process of financial analysis and face-to-face interviews with the proprietors and senior management of the borrower.

Nevertheless, however carefully a lender may be in analysing the risk involved in advancing credit to a borrower, the process is not foolproof; there is always a risk of default, however strong the credit of the borrower looks, and at worst there is a risk that the borrower will become insolvent before he performs the personal repayment obligation.

In an insolvency, the insolvent person's assets are gathered in and realized, with the proceeds being distributed *pari passu*[1] amongst the ordinary creditors.[2] But property owned or in the possession of the insolvent person to which a third party can assert proprietary rights, whether by way of ownership (e.g. beneficiaries under a trust) or a security interest, does not form part of insolvent's assets for distribution *pari passu*. Instead this property will be made available exclusively to the third party until his claim has been satisfied. Consequently, the claim of an ordinary, or more correctly 'unsecured' creditor will only be met once the claims of preferred and secured creditors have been paid in full. Typically, unsecured creditors will receive very little once proprietary claims have been satisfied and debts ranking ahead of their own have been paid.

➡ *pari passu*: 'with equal step' — on an equal footing, each creditor shares proportionately in the loss

It should be noted that, if having pursued his proprietary rights, the creditor's claim is still not fully satisfied, then he can pursue a personal claim along with the debtor's unsecured creditors. So the proprietary rights against the debtor's property exist in parallel with the rights against him personally. Thus a lender will often seek to reduce the likelihood of his suffering financial loss in the event of a default by seeking some form of security in the form of proprietary rights over the assets of the borrower.

In *Bristol Airport plc v Powdrill*,[3] Sir Nicolas Browne-Wilkinson adopted the following as delineating the minimum comprehended by the term 'security':

> Security is created where a person ('the creditor') to whom an obligation is owed by another ('the debtor') by statute or contract, in addition to the personal promise of the debtor to discharge the obligation, obtains rights exercisable against some property in which the debtor has an interest in order to enforce the discharge of the debtor's obligation to the creditor.

---

1. For personal insolvency, see Insolvency Act 1986, s 328. For corporate insolvency, see Insolvency Act 1986, s 107.

2. Some creditors are 'preferred' by statute (e.g. unpaid employees (Insolvency Act 1986, ss 175, 386)), so that these debts rank ahead of unsecured (and some secured) creditors for payment. Some debts are deferred (e.g. spouses' debts, Insolvency Act 1986, s 329), so that they will be paid only once all other creditors have been paid.

3. [1990] 2 All ER 493 (CA) 502.

The key, therefore, is that a valid security creates additional rights exercisable in respect of property in which the borrower has an absolute interest, but once the obligation is satisfied these rights terminate.

An example of a security interest

Consider the following example.

> ### Eg ComCorp Ltd
>
> ComCorp has a large overdraft with the bank, which is repayable 'on demand'. The bank is prepared to maintain the overdraft facility but only if it can have security. ComCorp wishes to know what type of security the bank is likely to require.

Businesses commonly are 'asset rich' but 'cash poor'; in other words, they have valuable property but need to retain this in order to run the business. They must meet invoices from suppliers as they are presented, but may not be paid themselves by their own customers for many months. In order to ease this 'cash flow' problem, the bank may offer an overdraft facility on the bank account of the business, enabling it to pay suppliers from the account even when there are insufficient funds available, and then reduce or eliminate the debt by paying funds into the account as they are received from customers. The business has a personal obligation to repay the debt, but the bank will normally require security, typically in the form of a charge over the assets of the business. Charges are dealt with later in this chapter, but, in brief, a charge typically gives the lender (the chargee) the right to sell the secured assets and apply the proceeds of sale in satisfaction of the debt; any money not so applied will be paid back to the business. However, should the bank account come back into credit when the business's receipts exceed its payments then the charge will terminate—there is no debt to secure—only to revive if the account again becomes overdrawn.

The attachment and reattachment of security interests is discussed at p 682

Quasi-security[4]

Consider the following example.

> ### Eg ComCorp Ltd
>
> In order to secure its overdraft ComCorp has charged its assets to the bank under the terms of an arrangement by which it cannot grant any security interest over its goods and the bank has indicated it will not lend any more money. ComCorp wishes to acquire some goods from a trade supplier but cannot afford to pay until it has sold the goods to its customers, and the supplier will not agree to this. ComCorp has found a

---

4. See Louise Gullifer, 'Quasi Security Interests, Functionalism and the Incidents of Security' in Ian Davies (ed), *Issues in International Commercial Law* (Ashgate 2005).

company prepared to lend the money it needs, but only if the lender can have the right to take possession of the goods and sell them to repay the debt if ComCorp defaults on the loan. Unfortunately, these rights are typical of charges, which are security interests. ComCorp wishes to know whether there is any way in which this financing can be arranged.

Other forms of arrangement exist which, while giving a creditor a sense of security, are not strictly security interests at all. In hire purchase, chattel leasing, and retention of title, the creditor has proprietary rights, but in each case the proprietary rights are those of an owner of an absolute interest who has parted with possession to the debtor, rather than the debtor having ownership of property over which he has granted a limited security interest to the creditor. For example, in a case of title retention, the seller of goods transfers possession of the goods to the purchaser, giving the purchaser time to pay, but the seller retains ownership of the goods until payment. If effective, such a title retention clause enables the seller to recover his goods from the purchaser and sell them to a third party if the purchaser fails to pay for them. The economic effect is much the same as if the purchaser acquired both ownership and possession at the outset, but granted a charge over the goods to the seller. However, here the buyer grants a security interest in goods he owns, rather than getting possessory title only, as with the title retention clause. Consequently, there has been some statutory intervention to provide a more equal treatment in corporate insolvencies of these mechanisms which give certain creditors advantages without their resorting to security interests. Similarly, there have been convincing calls to limit the expansion of proprietary rights.

Chattel leasing is discussed at p 722, and retention of title is discussed at p 255

Outline of the different forms of security interest

The main types of security interest known in English law are outlined in Figure 25.1 and fall into two main categories: possessory and non-possessory securities.

Possessory security interests rely on the lender having possession of the property over which the security interest exercisable. Thus, for example, in a pledge, property is deposited with the lender as security for a loan and so is a possessory security, but the security interest is lost if the lender loses possession; while in a mortgage, the mortgagee's security exists whether he is in possession of the property or not and so

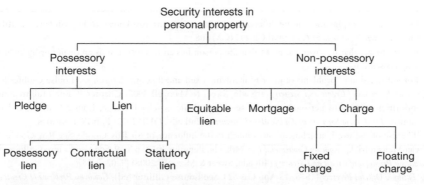

FIGURE 25.1 Security interests in personal property

is non-possessory.[5] These security interests will be discussed in detail a little later, but for the moment it is only important to recognize that some security interests are dependent on possession of the property, whilst others are not.

Attachment and perfection

The essence of security interests is that they give rights over property to the person with title to the security interest which are enforceable not merely between the parties to the security, but also by others claiming rights to the property, either because they own it[6] or because they, too, have a competing security interest in it. The following example demonstrates this.

Eg ComCorp Ltd

ComCorp Ltd grants a charge over a piece of machinery to White Bank plc. ComCorp then grants another charge over the same piece of machinery to Black Bank plc, and then sells the machinery to Spartan Ltd. Clearly, White Bank will want its security interest to give it rights over the property ahead of Spartan Ltd and Black Bank. Putting it another way, White Bank wants its charge to have priority over these third party rights. In order to do this, White Bank must show that its charge has attached to the property and that it has taken any other necessary steps to ensure that it is enforceable against third parties. It will also need to show that the rules for ranking security interests give it priority, but priority of interests is beyond the scope of this book.[7]

Attachment[8]

Attachment is the process whereby the security interest becomes fastened to the property to which it relates. Attachment involves four elements: first, valid creation; second, that the interest relates to an identifiable asset or assets or to an identifiable fund; third, the grantor must have power to grant the security; and finally, there must be some current debt to secure. Once attachment (or reattachment) takes place, the effective date of attachment is the date of the agreement unless agreed otherwise,[9] but until attachment there is no security interest.

---

5. For a succinct explanation of the different types of security interest known to English law, see Millett LJ in *Re Cosslett (Contractors) Ltd* [1998] Ch 495 (CA) 508.

6. Do not forget that by 'own' we mean that the person has an interest in it as an owner or by virtue of having possession.

7. For a discussion of problems of priority involving fixed and floating charges, see Louise Gullifer (ed), *Goode on Problems of Credit and Security* (4th edn, Sweet & Maxwell 2008) Chapter V. For a full treatment of priorities relating to personal property see Hugh Beale, Michael Bridge, Louise Gullifer, and Eva Lomnica, *The Law of Security and Title-Based Financing* (2nd edn, OUP 2012) Part IV Priorities.

8. The use of the word 'attachment' owes much to the influence of Sir Roy Goode. See Roy Goode and Ewan McKendrick, *Goode on Commercial Law* (4th edn, Penguin 2010) 670–9. See also Louise Gullifer (ed), *Goode on Problems of Credit and Security* (4th edn, Sweet & Maxwell 2008) [2-02–2-15].

9. *Tailby v Official Receiver* (1888) 13 App Cas 523. See Louise Gullifer (ed), *Goode on Problems of Credit and Security* (4th edn, Sweet & Maxwell 2008) [2-11].

Mode of creation

The mode of creation for each type of security interest varies from interest to interest and each is dealt with as we cover each type of security interest individually. Except for securities which rely on possession of the property, a specifically enforceable agreement to create a security interest will create a security interest in the shape of an equitable mortgage or charge and this matter is also dealt with later.

Identification

Except where the Bills of Sale Acts apply, there is no requirement that specific items of property be identified, generic descriptions suffice—for example 'all plant and machinery at such and such a location' is adequate. An agreement to grant security over property to be acquired in the future is effective even though, at the time of the agreement, no one can know what debts might become owed.[10] Similarly, a man may charge his income present and future;[11] however, an agreement to grant security over 'half the debts owing to me' cannot attach until the debts to which the security relates have become identifiable in some way.

Property with a right to dispose

Clearly, there must be a capable grantor, the grant must not be *ultra vires* the borrower. Equally, the borrower must have some title to the property, whether possessory or absolute, or at least the right to dispose of it under some exception to the *nemo dat* rule. Therefore where there is an agreement to grant security over future property, the security remains incomplete, at least until the property described in the security is acquired.[12]

➜ *ultra vires*: acting 'beyond one's powers'

🔗 The *nemo dat* rule is discussed at p 272

A debt to secure

There must also be some current indebtedness to secure. Thus in a mortgage granted to secure an overdraft facility, the security is incomplete until the account actually becomes overdrawn, when the security then attaches. Indeed, should that account then come back into credit, the security interest again detaches, only to reattach when the account again becomes overdrawn.

Perfection

Attachment creates a security interest between the parties, but normally third parties will not be bound unless the interest is perfected by the performance of some act which gives notice to the third party of the existence of the security interest. Some security interests do not require perfection (an oral chattel mortgage or charge by an individual automatically binds third parties),[13] as will charges created by companies

---

10. *Tailby v Official Receiver* (1888) 13 App Cas 523. This would create either an equitable mortgage or an equitable charge, depending on the details of the agreement.

11. *Syrett v Egerton* [1957] 3 All ER 331(DC). The court left open the issue of whether charging all of his property might be contrary to the principles of equity, since enforcement would leave him destitute. No point was taken that such a charge would be unenforceable under the Bills of Sale Acts.

12. In a floating charge (see pp 702) the parties agree that there is no attachment as such until crystallization.

13. See Roy Goode and Ewan McKendrick, *Goode on Commercial Law* (4th edn, Penguin 2010) 689, fn 2, though see the effect of Sale of Goods Act 1979, s 24.

which do not require registration under s 860 of the Companies Act 2006 or elsewhere, but such security interests are rare. There are three methods of perfection which apply, dependent on the type of security interest being perfected.

Perfection by possession

Where a security interest is created by the lender taking possession of the property, a person dealing with the debtor in relation to the property will be put on inquiry if the debtor does not have physical possession of it. However, possession can be constructive, as where a debtor pledges goods or the title documents to goods (which requires possession of the goods/documents to pass to the lender), but is permitted to regain physical possession of them in order to carry out some function for the lender, for example to take physical possession of the goods from a carrier and to sell.[14] Here the lender remains in constructive possession and retains his pledge intact.[15]

Perfection by registration

Statute typically requires non-possessory security interests be registered in order to bind third parties, so that a search of the relevant register will alert a person dealing with the debtor. Goode notes that there are at least eleven registers for different types of security, so that the utility of a registration system is somewhat diminished.[16] Specialist works should be consulted, therefore, to obtain detailed information on mortgages and charges over land, mortgages of ships and aircraft, and mortgages and charges over intellectual property rights, and such issues will not be mentioned further in this chapter.

Mortgages and charges created by companies of the types listed in s 860 of the Companies Act 2006 are void as against a liquidator, administrator, or creditor of the company unless registered in the company's Register of Charges, even if they are registered elsewhere.[17] Only security interests created by the company need to be registered, so that possessory liens (which arise by operation of law) are not caught, and nor are contractual liens, even when accompanied by a contractual right of sale, since these are not charges.[18] An unregistered charge is void only as against the persons listed in s 860; it remains valid against the company so that the lender can exercise its rights under the charge—for example the power of sale—and thus give good title to a purchaser.

The Bills of Sale Acts 1878 and 1882 require registration of bills of sale. The 1878 Act deals with absolute bills of sale where absolute interests in personal chattels are transferred but where possession remains with the seller. Both Acts in effect apply to security bills of sale where security interests in personal chattels are created. A security bill of sale is a document created by an individual borrower which grants

---

14. *North Western Bank Ltd v Poynter* [1895] AC 56 (HL).

15. The borrower will be required to sign a 'trust receipt' declaring he is a trustee over the documents of title, the goods to which they relate, and any insurance monies recoverable in respect of them. The receipt will also make the documents returnable on demand. See Peter Ellinger, 'Trust Receipt Financing' [2003] JIBLR 305.

16. Roy Goode and Ewan McKendrick, *Goode on Commercial Law* (4th edn, Penguin 2010) 692.

17. Companies Act 2006, s 874(1).

18. *Trident International Ltd v Barlow* [1999] 2 BCLC 506 (CA) applying *Great Eastern Railway Company v Lord's Trustee* [1909] AC 109 (HL).

to a lender the right to take possession of personal chattels belonging to the borrower, by way of security.[19] The bill of sale is void if not in the form set out in the schedule to the 1882 Act,[20] which requires attestation by 'two credible witnesses' plus identification of specific goods, and is also void if not registered within seven days of creation.[21] It is important to note that the Bills of Sale Acts only apply to documents, so security granted orally is unaffected, and they only apply when possession remains with the borrower, so possessory security is unaffected. Finally, the Bills of Sale Acts apply to individuals and not to companies or limited liability partnerships, and only apply to chattels, not things in action.

Perfection by notice

Where the secured property is a thing in action, perfection can be effected by giving notice to the person who owes the obligation, as the following example demonstrates.

Eg ComCorp Ltd

ComCorp Ltd is owed money by Tempest Ltd and assigns this debt to Prospero plc absolutely or by way of security. Prospero perfects its interest by giving Tempest notice of the assignment to it. Tempest will not be discharged of the assigned debt if it pays ComCorp.

Pledges[22]

Pledges are contractual securities under the terms of which the debtor/borrower as bailor parts with possession of the property for the purpose of creating a security interest. The lender as bailee has a right to retain possession of the goods until he is paid. The lender can sell the asset if the borrower defaults,[23] but it has been held that the lender holds any surplus beyond that needed to repay the debt on trust for the borrower.[24] There is no right of foreclosure as there is in a mortgage; either the pledge is redeemed or the property is sold.[25]

Pawnbroking provides an example of how pledges operate. A person seeking a loan leaves property with the pawnbroker, who will retain it until the debt is redeemed,

🔗 Bailment is discussed at p 34

19. Bills of Sale (1878) Amendment Act 1882, ss 3 and 17.   20. ibid s 9.   21. ibid s 8.

22. See Norman Palmer and Alistair Hudson, 'Pledge' in Norman Palmer and Ewan McKendrick (eds), *Interests in Goods* (2nd edn, LLP 1988).

23. *Re Morritt* (1886) 18 QBD 222. Cotton LJ held that the power of sale arose not by virtue of the creditor having possession, but by virtue of a 'special property' to sell on default in payment and after notice to the debtor, who nevertheless may redeem at any moment up to sale.

24. *Mathew v TM Sutton Ltd* [1994] 4 All ER 793 (Ch). This seems unlikely; pledges are of common law origin. The preferable analysis would appear that there is a personal obligation to account to the borrower for the surplus.

25. *Carter v Wake* (1877) 4 ChD 605 (Ch).

and in the case of a default he will sell the property and use the proceeds of sale to satisfy his debt, any surplus on sale accruing to the benefit of the debtor.[26] However, this example demonstrates the problems with pledges, since in principle they rely on the debtor parting with possession so that only assets which are not needed on a daily basis can be pledged—an unlikely circumstance in most businesses.[27]

Possession involves transferring control over the property to the pledgee. This might be done by the lender securing the property in his own premises, but this is not necessary. For example, in *Wrightson v McArthur and Hutchisons*,[28] the borrower placed the goods in two otherwise empty locked rooms and gave the lender the only keys. This granting of symbolic control was regarded as a pledge.[29] However, where the key does not give the lender access without the consent of a third party, then it would appear that this is insufficient to give possession.[30] Possession may also be constructive. In *Official Assignee of Madras v Mercantile Bank of India Ltd*,[31] Lord Wright insisted that goods in the possession of a third party who is holding them to the order of the borrower would be pledged if the borrower and third party attorned to the lender, assuming, of course, that the intention of the borrower and lender was to create a pledge.[32] However, the property must be capable of being possessed, so a pledge may only be created over tangible property and documentary intangibles, such as bills of exchange, bills of lading,[33] and bearer bonds,[34] and not over pure intangibles.[35]

Pledges are potentially an inconvenient form of security, since normally the borrower will be deprived of use of the goods and the lender will have to store them. However, as *The Odessa*[36] illustrates, the ability to pledge documents of title to goods which are not in the physical possession of the borrower can provide a suitable means of providing trade finance. Similarly, a pledge of documentary intangibles may well not hinder the borrower.

 Attornment is discussed at p 38

 Documentary intangibles are discussed at p 43

The Odessa v The Woolston (In Prize) [1916] 1 AC 145 (PC)

FACTS: The German purchaser of goods in transit from Chile to Europe pledged the bill of lading to a firm of London bankers, who then paid the purchase price to the seller. Thus a pledge was used to provide security in the finance of the transaction when the goods were beyond commercial exploitation in the hold of the ship. The goods were seized by the Crown at the outbreak of the First World War, and question arose whether the pledge gave

---

26. It should be noted that pawnbroking is regulated under the Consumer Credit Act 1974 and pledges are regulated agreements. Pledges by companies and credit agreements for greater than £25,000 which relate to the debtor's business are exempted by ss 16A, 16B. See JK Macleod, 'Pawnbroking: A Regulatory Issue' [1995] JBL 155 for a critique of the legislation regulating pawnbroking.

27. But see *Reeves v Capper* (1836) 132 ER 1057.

28. *Wrightson v McArthur and Hutchisons (1919) Ltd* [1921] 2 KB 807 (KB).

29. See also *Hilton v Tucker* (1888) 39 ChD 669 (Ch).

30. *Dublin City Distillery Ltd v Doherty* [1914] AC 823 (HL).

31. [1935] AC 53 (PC).   32. ibid 58–9.   33. ibid.

34. *Carter v Wake* (1877) 4 ChD 605 (Ch).

35. *Harrold v Plenty* [1901] 2 Ch 314 (Ch). Here the deposit of share certificates was construed as an equitable mortgage of the shares.

36. *The Odessa v The Woolston (In Prize)* [1916] 1 AC 145 (PC)

the bankers possessory title to the goods or simply rights over them. If the banker had title to the goods, then the seizure was unlawful.

HELD: A pledge of documents of title also acts as a pledge of the goods they represent and thus gives rights over the goods in order to realize their value, but does not create a possessory title to them. The pledge gives the lender a 'special property' (better called a 'special interest') in the property to sell, but that right of sale is exercisable by virtue of an implied authority from the debtor, not by virtue of possession. Lord Mersey also held *obiter* that the power of sale must be used for the benefit of both parties, and consequently the lender owes a duty to take care that the sale is on a reasonable basis, that no more of the goods are sold than is reasonably necessary to enable him recoup the debt, and that he must account to the debtor for any surplus.[37]

COMMENT: Thus, while the lender/pledgee has possession of the goods, this is not like the possessory title of a normal bailee, which is certainly a right in the property; it seems to be more akin to a personal right arising out of contract, but one which will bind third parties. It is therefore surprising that in the *Jag Shakti*,[38] the Privy Council held that the pledgee of a bill of lading could maintain an action in conversion against the carrier of the goods who had released them to the buyer without production of the bill of lading; conversion after all protects proprietary rights to possession. It should also be noted that, according to Lord Mersey, the lender must account for any surplus; there is no suggestion that he is a trustee of it.

Since possession is the essence of a pledge, once possession of the property is lost, so is the pledge. But in *Reeves v Capper*,[39] the lender, Capper, returned the goods to the borrower to enable him to use it for a specific purpose. The borrower then wrongfully pledged the goods to Reeves. Tindall CJ held that the original pledge was not destroyed; the borrower was not in possession, but simply had custody of the goods; consequently, Capper's pledge remained enforceable. Similarly, in *North Western Bank Ltd v Poynter*,[40] judicial recognition was given to a common trade practice where the lender returns bills of lading to the borrower in return for a 'trust receipt' under which the borrower declares he holds the documents to the order of the lender, so that the lender retains constructive possession of the documents of title.[41] This arrangement enables the borrower to recover the goods from the carrier and to sell them under the terms of the trust receipt, holding the proceeds of sale on trust for the lender. However, in *Babcock v Lawson*,[42] the lender, Babcock, returned bills of lading to the borrowers who had fraudulently represented that they needed the documents because they had sold the goods and that they would pay the proceeds of sale to Babcock. The borrowers used the bills to pledge the goods to Lawson. It was held that Babcock had lost his pledge, so that Lawson's claim had priority to his own. It remains open whether a purchaser from a borrower in possession under a trust receipt who sells in breach of duty would obtain good title.[43]

The difference between custody and possession is discussed at p 32
Bills of lading are discussed in Chapter 19

---

37. ibid 159.   38. [1986] AC 337 (PC).   39. (1836) 132 ER 1057.   40. [1895] AC 56 (HL).
41. The borrower also declares himself trustee over the documents of title, the goods to which they relate, and any insurance monies recoverable in respect of them. See Peter Ellinger, 'Trust Receipt Financing' [2003] JIBLR 305.
42. (1880) 5 QBD 284 (CA).
43. In *Lloyds Bank Ltd v Bank of America* [1938] 2 KB 147 (KB), the borrower obtained possession of the bills under a trust receipt and was held to give good title, but here he was a factor within s 2 of the Factors Act 1889, which provides an exception to the *nemo dat* rule (see p 287).

Finally, in relation to constructive possession it has been suggested that it may not even be necessary for the lender even momentarily to gain physical possession over the goods or documents of title if the borrower accepts that he is holding them to the order of the lender.[44]

Pledges are not registrable under the Bills of Sale Acts[45] nor under the Companies Act 2006;[46] they are perfected by possession. It should be noted that a contract to create a pledge does not create a pledge,[47] and so until possession is taken by the pledgee, no security interest is created.[48]

Finally, it should be noted that the bundle of rights making up the pledge is itself a piece of property which may be transferred to a third party.

Liens

Possessory liens

Liens give a creditor the right to detain the debtor's goods as security for payment where goods have been delivered to the creditor under a contract for purposes other than the creation of a security interest, typically a contract for storage, transport, or repair. Possessory liens arise by operation of law[49] and not contract, though the terms of the contract may prevent a possessory lien from arising.[50] The lien gives no rights in the property itself, simply providing a defence to an action for conversion against the possessor, and consequently will not give the creditor the right to sell unless the underlying contract so provides,[51] or where he has the right by virtue of ss 12 and 13 of the Torts (Interference with Goods) Act 1977 (sale of uncollected goods and sale by order of the court).

The lien may give the holder the right to detain the asset as security for all debts outstanding between the parties (a general lien), or alternatively only as security for payment of charges incurred in relation to the property itself (a special lien). General

---

44. *Meyerstein v Barber* (1866) LR 2 CP 38.

45. *Re Hardwick ex p Hubbard* (1886) 17 QBD 690 (CA). The Acts require more than the 'special property' in a pledge to pass under the document. In any event, in this case the pledge was complete on delivery of possession of the goods; the document was merely evidence. But suppose the borrower remained in physical possession, having attorned to the pledgee, would a written attornment be a bill of sale, since it is this that gives possession to the pledgee? See Hugh Beale, Michael Bridge, Louise Gullifer, and Eva Lomnica, *The Law of Personal Property Security* (OUP 2007) [3.20]. Similarly, would a trust receipt issued before the documents were pledged require registration as a charge? Beale et al answer this at [3.23].

46. *Wrightson v McArthur and Hutchisons (1919) Ltd* [1921] 2 KB 807 (KB). Since an instrument of pledge made by an individual does not require registration as a bill of sale, one created by a company does not fall under s 860(7)(b) of the Companies Act 2006, as a 'charge created or evidenced by an instrument which, if executed by an individual, would require registration as a bill of sale'.

47. *Dublin City Distillery Ltd v Doherty* [1914] AC 823 (HL). Though Alistair Hudson and Norman Palmer suggest possibilities to the contrary. See 'Pledge' in Norman Palmer and Ewan Mc Kendrick (eds), *Interests in Goods* (2nd edn, LLP 1998) 976.

48. Though in the appropriate circumstances the arrangement might be construed as an agreement to create a charge or mortgage.

49. *Re Bond Worth Ltd* [1980] Ch 228 (Ch). 50. *Tappenden v Artus* [1964] 2 QB 185 (CA).

51. The inclusion of such a right of sale does not of itself convert a lien into a charge (*Great Eastern Railway Co v Lord's Trustee* [1909] AC 109 (HL)).

liens which arise by virtue of customary practice exist in favour of solicitors,[52] bankers,[53] insurance brokers,[54] and stockbrokers,[55] though the position in relation to accountants[56] is less clear. Typically, these general liens will be exercised over securities or other documents held by the creditor in the course of the performance of their professional duties, though it can extend to money held in a client account. The issues were recently revisited in relation to the solicitors' lien, but the principles are, with suitable adaptation, applicable to other similar liens.

Withers LLP v Rybak and others [2011] EWCA Civ 1419

FACTS: Withers were Rybak's solicitors. Rybak owed Withers over £400,000 in legal fees. Rybak had settled a case with a third party (Langbar) by an agreement that he would pay a substantial sum to Langbar, which would be funded partly by a sale of a flat, and the court ordered that the sale proceeds be paid into Withers' client account to ensure the money would be available to Langbar. Rybak's assets were later made subject to a general freezing order, which specifically included the client account money. Withers claimed it had a possessory lien or alternatively an equitable lien or charge over the proceeds of sale of the flat held in the client account as security for the outstanding fees.

HELD: Although a solicitor is entitled to a retaining lien which extends over any documents or goods which come into his possession in his capacity as solicitor and which is the client's property, the lien does not extend to property, including money he receives with a fiduciary duty to apply for a purpose.[57] Nor does it extend to property not subjected to such a fiduciary duty, but which nevertheless comes into his hands for a special purpose where the purpose is inconsistent with a lien arising. Here, the money had been paid into the client account to ensure it was available to Langbar to satisfy its claim, and this purpose was inconsistent with the solicitors' claim to a lien.

COMMENT: Withers' secondary argument, that it had an equitable charge in the account, also failed because, on the facts, Rybak had not directed Withers to pay itself out of the monies in the client account, nor had they undertaken to pay the fees out of the fund. Similarly, the freezing order created no charge in favour of Langbar because an equitable charge can only arise if the arrangement imposes an obligation on the debtor (Rybak) to pay the debt out of the fund, and here the freezing order was not in that form, nor indeed would that be the form of a normal freezing order. It also should be noted that solicitors are officers of the court, and consequently may be required to surrender their lien if it relates to papers needed in the preparation of a case, though the former clients may be required to provide alternative security.[58]

For a discussion on the creation of equitable charges, see p 700

---

52. *Stevenson v Blakelock* (1813) 1 M&S 535 (exercisable over a lease document).
53. *Brandao v Barnett* (1846) 3 CB 519 (HL) (exercisable over securities but not where deposited for safe-keeping only).
54. *Eide UK Ltd v Lowndes Lambert Group Ltd* [1998] 1 All ER 946 (CA).
55. *Re London and Globe Finance Corp Ltd* [1902] 2 Ch 416 (Ch).
56. *Woodworth v Conroy* [1976] QB 884 (CA).
57. The Court uses the words 'purpose trust', but this is misleading as literally non-charitable trusts for purposes cannot exist (*Morice v Bishop of Durham* (1805) 10 Ves 522).
58. See *Ismail v Richards Butler* [1996] QB 711 (QB). See generally, Alistair Hudson 'Solicitors' Liens' in Norman Palmer and Ewan McKendrick (ed), *Interests in Goods* (2nd edn, LLP 1998).

Although general liens arise in only a limited number of contractual relationships, special liens will commonly be implied between parties. Consequently, a warehouseman has a lien over the deposited good as security for his storage charges,[59] a repairer for the costs of repair and associated costs,[60] and a carrier for freight charges.[61]

Eg ComCorp Ltd

ComCorp Ltd grants a lease of some industrial cleaning machinery to Leona, under the terms of which she had no right to grant any security interest. The goods bear a plate which states 'Leased from ComCorp Ltd'. Leona has to have the equipment repaired at a cost of £3,000 and the repairer allows her to recover the equipment, giving her fourteen days to pay. Two weeks later further repairs are needed which cost £1,000. This time the repairer will not release the equipment until he is paid. Leona explains that she needs the equipment to earn the money in order to pay his bills, and the repairer relents so long as Leona returns the equipment to him every night and only takes it away when she needs it for a job. Leona soon defaults on the lease and ComCorp wants possession, but the repairer refuses unless they receive £4,000. ComCorp points out that Leona had no authority to grant a lien, refuse to pay, and threaten proceedings for conversion. What are ComCorp's prospects of success?

The essence of a lien is that lawful possession is voluntarily surrendered to the creditor, so that where the creditor has possession through self-help measures under a contract,[62] fraud, or otherwise without the authority of a person with title to the goods, he has no lien. Similarly, if the creditor gives up possession he loses his lien and where it is a special lien he does not recover it in relation to pre-existing debt, even if later he regains possession of the goods. Thus in *Hatton v Car Maintenance Ltd*,[63] a garage stored, maintained, and repaired a motorist's car and provided one of their own employees as a driver whenever she wanted to go for an occasional drive. It was held that, since she was free to take the car out and go as she pleased, this amounted to possession, and each time she took possession of the car, this released the garage's lien securing its charges. This case can be compared with *Albemarle Supply Co Ltd v Hind & Co*,[64] where a garage's possession was not lost even though the debtor used the property on a daily basis.

---

59. It appears warehousemen may have a general lien if they can establish that this is a custom in this particular trade or through an implied term in the warehouse contract arising by the practice of the parties: *Chellaram (K) & Sons (London) Ltd v Butlers Warehousing and Distribution Ltd* [1977] 2 Lloyd's Rep 192 (QB).

60. *Albermarle Supply Co Ltd v Hind & Co* [1928] 1 KB 307 (CA).

61. See e.g. *Great Eastern Railway Company v Lords Trustee* [1909] AC 109 (HL).

62. *Re Cosslett (Contractors) Ltd* [1998] Ch 495 (CA).   63. [1915] 1 Ch 621 (Ch).

64. [1928] 1 KB 307 (CA).

Albemarle Supply Co Ltd v Hind & Co **[1928]**
1 KB 307 (CA)

FACTS: A debtor, Botfield, had possession of some taxicabs through a hire purchase agreement with Albemarle, but ownership remained with Albemarle. Botfield garaged his cabs with Hind & Co and fell into arrears with his garage bills. Hind agreed to allow him to take the cabs out each day to ply for hire, but only on the basis that he returned them each night to the garage. Botfield fell into arrears with his hire purchase agreement and Albemarle claimed possession of the cabs from the garage, which refused until its bills for storage and repair were paid.

HELD: The Court of Appeal held that by virtue of the agreement to return the cabs each night, the garage's special lien was maintained, presumably because Botfield had accepted that he was in possession under the direction of Hinds, in other words an attornment. Consequently, Hinds need not release the cabs to the owner until he was paid his charges.

> 🔗 Attornment is discussed at p 38

COMMENT: It was not the owner of the goods who entered into the contract underlying the lien, but the hirer, and under the terms of the hire purchase agreement, he had no authority to create a lien. However, the Court held that, although the garage knew the cabs were on hire purchase, that did not give it notice of the terms, and the owner, by giving the debtor possession of the goods, was representing that he had authority to have them garaged and repaired.[65] However, it has been suggested that simply allowing the hirer to have possession is not itself a representation, and something more is needed, so that in *Albemarle*, since the garaging was not a 'one-off' occurrence, by not interfering with the arrangement the owner was representing that the hirer had the necessary authority.[66]

> 🔗 On the similar issue of apparent authority of agents, see p 96

Contractual liens

As the name suggests, contractual liens arise by agreement of the parties and are dependent on the creditor having physical possession of the goods. Contractual and possessory liens may arise in relation to the same circumstances, in which case the contractual lien supersedes the possessory lien.[67]

 George Barker Transport Ltd v Eynon **[1974]**
1 All ER 900 (CA)

FACTS: George Barker Transport Ltd (Barker) was a road haulier. It did regular business with Eynon under the terms of a haulage contract, which gave the haulier a general lien over the goods carried. After entering into the haulage agreement, Eynon created a floating charge in favour of the bank under the terms of which they could not create charges having priority to the bank. Some time later, Eynon, who owed Barker over £3,000, asked it to

---

65. See also *Tappenden v Artus* [1964] 2 QB 185 (CA), where Diplock LJ explains this issue by reference to the apparent authority principles applicable in agency which are based on estoppel.
66. Len S Sealy and Richard JA Hooley, *Commercial Law Text, Cases and Material* (4th edn, OUP 2009) 117. See also other cases concerning liens binding owners who did not make the underlying contract.
67. *Fisher v Smith* (1878) 4 App Cas 1 (HL).

→ receiver: a person appointed by a creditor under a mortgage or charge to take possession of and administer the encumbered assets

collect 316 cartons of frozen meat from a ship in which they had been transported, but before Barker took physical possession of the meat, the bank appointed a **receiver**. The receiver agreed that Barker should collect and deliver the meat to the Eynon's customers without prejudice to Barker's general lien. When the receiver refused to pay the £3,000 bill, Barker sued, arguing that because Eynon had given it the documents necessary to effect the release of the meat from the ship, it had constructive possession of it and so had a perfected lien before the receiver was appointed. Alternatively, it argued that in collecting the meat, it was acting under the terms of the haulage agreement which gave it a general contractual lien, and once it took physical possession that lien was perfected.

HELD: The Court of Appeal held that Barker did not have constructive possession of the meat through being given the documents (which did not include a bill of lading) so the carrier would have had to attorn to the Barker that it was holding the meat to the claimant's order. However, the receiver must take the debtor's business as he finds it, and here the haulier was acting under the haulage agreement, which gave a lien that was perfected once it took physical possession.

COMMENT: This case illustrates three important points: first, that liens can prejudice the rights of a floating chargee; second, that constructive possession can be enough to support the lien, though there was no constructive possession in this case, since the documents the hauliers were given were not documents of title to the goods; and third, that possession is the essence of contractual and possessory liens.

Statutory liens

As the name suggests, these are liens created by statute. The most obvious example is the unpaid seller's lien under s 41 of the Sale of Goods Act 1979. It should be noted that this lien, too, is dependent on the seller remaining in possession of the goods (s 43), though it is supplemented by the seller's right of stoppage in transit (ss 44–46).

⌘ The unpaid seller's lien is discussed at p 393

The requirement of possession is not necessary in relation to all statutory liens, since the statute may provide otherwise.

⌘ The question whether the lessee's right under a chattel lease is proprietary or not is discussed at p 27

Bristol Airport plc v Powdrill [1990] 1 Ch 744 (CA)

FACTS: The owner of an airport exercised a right to detain two aircraft leased to the debtor by the owner for unpaid airport charges by virtue of s 88 of the Civil Aviation Act 1982. The debtor was in administration. Under s 11(3)(c) of the Insolvency Act 1986, the administrator's consent is needed before anyone can enforce 'a lien or other security over the company's property'. The issue was therefore whether the aircraft were the property of the debtor and whether the statutory right of detention was a lien or other security interest.

HELD: Browne Wilkinson V-C stated that although in a chattel lease, the right to possession is *prima facie* only contractual; since a contract to lease an aircraft would be specifically enforceable, equity would treat the contractual right to possession as creating an equitable interest in the plane. He added that although the airport did not have possession of the aircraft, nevertheless the right to detain was analogous to a possessory lien and was a security interest. The administrator's consent was therefore required before the security could be exercised.

COMMENT: Treating specifically enforceable rights to possession of a chattel as 'equitable possession' is surprising, since this is the first case in which this principle has been accepted and Goode indeed still insists that there is no such thing.[68] In any event, there seems little need for it in relation to chattel leasing, since the more obvious route would be to hold that the lessee has not merely a contractual, but a proprietary right to possession, thus giving him a possessory title.

It should be noted that, as Sir Nicolas Browne Wilkinson pointed out, this statutory right of detention had many features of the possessory lien, and there are equitable liens which do not depend on possession, so that treating this statutory right as a statutory lien was not unreasonable. The case is also authority for the proposition that exercise of a contractual or possessory lien falls under s 11(3)(c) of the Insolvency Act 1986,[69] thus requiring the consent of an administrator before it can be exercised.

⭐ See Graham McBain, 'Aircraft Liens Under English Law' (1990) 15 Air Law 79

Equitable liens[70]

Whereas possessory liens arise consensually and are dependent on possession, equitable liens arise by operation of law, are not dependent on possession, and give the holder the same rights in property as an equitable charge. There appears to be little principle involved in determining when such liens arise—the list of equitable liens is a 'seamless ragbag',[71] but the typical example is the unpaid vendor's lien in relation to a sale of land or personal property,[72] where possession has been given to the purchaser which lien secures the right to be paid the purchase price.[73] Similarly, a purchaser of land who has pre-paid has a lien over the land securing the return of the purchase price should the vendor fail to transfer title.

🔗 Equitable charges are discussed at p 699

Termination of liens

A lien may be terminated in the following ways:

- the creditor commits a serious breach of the terms on which he is holding the property;
- the creditor fails to provide the debtor with details of the sum due;
- the creditor asserts the lien over a greater sum than it covers, though it has been held that where the creditor has provided details to the debtor which would enable him to calculate the correct sum secured, the lien is not lost;[74]
- payment of the debt is tendered or the debt is otherwise satisfied;
- the creditor loses possession of the property.

---

68. Roy Goode and Ewan McKendrick, *Goode on Commercial Law* (4th edn, Penguin 2010) 44.
69. See also *Euro Commercial Leasing Ltd v Cartwright & Lewis* [1995] 2 BCLC 618 (Ch).
70. See Sarah Worthington, 'Equitable Liens in Commercial Transaction' (1994) 53 CLJ 263.
71. J Phillips, 'Equitable Liens—A Search for a Unifying Principle' in Norman Palmer and Ewan McKendrick (eds), *Interests in Goods* (2nd edn, LLP 1998) 976.
72. Though perhaps not where the Sale of Goods Act 1979 statutory lien applies, see *Transport and General Credit Corporation Ltd v Morgan* [1939] Ch 531 (Ch). Sarah Worthington, 'Equitable Liens in Commercial Transaction (1994) 53 CLJ 263, 269–70 argues to the contrary.
73. See Ian Hardingham, 'Equitable Liens for the Recovery of Purchase Money' [1985] MULR 65.
74. See *Albermarle Suply Co Ltd v Hind* [1928] 1 KB 307 (CA), where the creditor claimed security for petrol and oil which are not covered by a repairer's lien, but provided a full breakdown of his bill to the debtor.

The following case provides an interesting example of the termination and revival of liens.

 Euro Commercial Leasing Ltd v Cartwright & Lewis [1995] 2 BCLC 618 (Ch)

FACTS: Carwright and Lewis, a firm of solicitors, were owed legal fees by Euro Commercial, a company in administration. The solicitors held some of the company's money in their client account and transferred the money to its general account in satisfaction of the debt. They re-transferred the money when the administrator objected that he had not given consent to the transfer under s 11(3) of the Insolvency Act 1986. The question was whether the solicitors had lost their lien.

HELD: Although the lien had been terminated when the initial transfer had been made, it revived when the money was paid back into the client account.

COMMENT: This seems to be correct where a general lien is terminated either, as here, by provisional satisfaction, or where possession of property is lost, but later other property falls into possession.[75] Once the conditions for a fresh general lien are again satisfied (re-emergence of the debt or re-establishment of possession of property), a new lien arises. Arguments that the creditor waives his right to a general lien when releasing possession of property over which the lien is secured seem incorrect.[76]

Mortgages

A mortgage is a transfer of ownership of property to a creditor by way of security on the basis that it will be re-transferred to the mortgagor on repayment of the debt, known as 'redemption'. Until redemption, the mortgagee is in theory entitled to possession of the property, but typically, under the terms of the mortgage the mortgagor will remain in possession.

The mortgage will contain a date for redemption and although at common law a refusal by the mortgagee to re-convey the property gave rise only to a right to damages, equity would award specific performance so that in equity, the mortgagor has a bundle of rights, themselves a piece of property, known as the 'equity of redemption', by far the most important of these being the right to redeem the mortgage. Equity recognized that what on its face was a sale with a right of re-purchase was in fact a security transaction. One of the consequences of this is that, while typically the mortgage will stipulate that a failure by the mortgagor to repay

---

75. *George Barker Transport Ltd v Eynon* [1974] 1 All ER 900 (CA) (discussed on p 691).
76. This case should be contrasted with *Pennington v Reliance Motor Works Ltd* [1923] 1 KB 127 (KB) and *Hatton v Car Maintenance* Co Ltd [1915] 1 Ch 621 (Ch). Alistair Hudson suggests in 'Solicitors' Liens' in Norman Palmer and Ewan McKendrick (eds), *Interests in Goods* (2nd edn, LLP 1998) 651, that the difference relates to the fact that the lien in *Euro Commercial* related to things in action, but perhaps it is better understood to lie in the fact that the repairers in *Pennington* would have had only a special lien.

all sums due under the mortgage on the due date will terminate the mortgagor's right to redeem, the court will only permit effect to be given to it through an order of foreclosure.

Creation of mortgages

In relation to personal property there is no general requirement as to the form of a mortgage, since it involves transfer of ownership, so that if the parties intend to create a mortgage, any transfer appropriate for the type of property mortgaged is sufficient. Thus an oral mortgage of goods is possible, though if it is made in writing it will be a security bill of sale and have to meet the requirements of the Bills of Sale Act 1882.

There are exceptions. In each of the examples that follow, the mortgage must be in writing:

- a mortgage of an equitable interest in whatever type of property;[77]
- mortgages of intellectual property;[78]
- mortgages of British registered ships,[79] but not aircraft;[80]
- a legal mortgage of a thing in action.[81]

As a point of clarification, mortgages of land can now only be effected where title to the land is not registered, and even then will take effect not as a conveyance of the fee simple, but as a grant of a 3,000-year lease.[82] Consequently, the overwhelming majority of 'mortgages' over land are 'charges by way of legal mortgage' under s 87 of the Law of Property Act 1925.

Legal and equitable mortgages

Mortgages can exist at law and in equity. A mortgage of an equitable interest in property—for example of a beneficial interest under a trust[83]—must be equitable; the mortgagor has nothing recognized at law to transfer to the mortgagee. Similarly, the common law did not recognize a mortgage over property to be acquired in the future, while, after *Holroyd v Marshall*,[84] equity did. Equity also held that a specifically enforceable contract to create a mortgage was itself a mortgage, equity looking on as done those things that ought to have been done—the mortgagor ought to have executed a mortgage, so equity treated him as if he had. In relation to mortgages of land, this contract must now be in writing signed by both parties,[85] but for personal property, once the mortgagee has advanced the funds, the contract is enough, since

---

77. Law of Property Act 1925, s 53(1)(c).

78. For patents, see Patents Act 1977, s 30(6). For copyright, see Copyright Designs and Patents Act 1988, s 90(3). For trade marks, see Trade Marks Act 1994, s 24(4).

79. Merchant Shipping Act 1995, s 16 and Sch 1.

80. Though it is assumed it will be, see Mortgaging of Aircraft Order 1972 (SI 1972/1268).

81. Law of Property Act 1925, s 136.   82. ibid s 87(1).

83. Or a mortgage of the equity of redemption by a mortgagor, since this piece of property is only recognized in equity.

84. (1862) 11 ER 999 (HL).   85. Law of Property (Miscellaneous Provisions) Act 1989, s 2(1).

such a contract will always be specifically enforceable.[86] However, there must be a new advance; an agreement to create a security interest to secure pre-existing debts is not specifically enforceable and so creates no security in equity.[87] In such a case the interest must meet the legal requirements for creation. Additionally, the contract must constitute an agreement to create an immediate security, not merely a promise to create one in the future, for example on the happening of a contingency other than the acquisition of the property which is to provide the security.[88]

Simply depositing title documents with the lender as security for a loan is an accepted means whereby an equitable mortgage of the property could be effected. As noted earlier, this is now no longer possible in relation to land, but remains possible in relation to bills of lading and documentary intangibles. Typically, courts will treat the deposit of a bill of lading as security for a loan as a pledge, rather than a mortgage, in the absence of evidence to the contrary, but in *Harrold v Plenty*,[89] Cozens-Hardy J accepted that a deposit of share certificates as security for a loan necessitated a finding of mortgage, since if this were a pledge, the creditor would not be able to exercise a power of sale, the only remedy to a pledgee, since transfer of registrable securities required a signed document of transfer.

Rights of the mortgagee

Although a typical mortgage will include other rights, the four principal remedies of a mortgagee are:

1. foreclosure;
2. taking possession;
3. sale;
4. appointing a receiver.

Eg ComCorp Ltd

Blanko Ltd, one of ComCorp's customers, owed ComCorp £100,000. It was agreed that in return for ComCorp not demanding the money for a year, Blanko Ltd would grant a mortgage over a boat it owned. Lee liked boats, and soon after the mortgage was agreed he decided to take the boat out, and indeed has sailed it every weekend for the last year and now has it secured at a new marina at Portsmouth. Blanko failed to pay the debt on the due date and ComCorp wishes to foreclose on the boat, which is worth £200,000. Blanko claims that Comcorp has committed the tort of conversion by sailing the boat.

---

86. See *Swiss Bank Corp v Lloyds Bank Ltd* [1982] AC 584 (CA) 595 (Buckley LJ). The underlying obligation for which the mortgage is security need not be specifically enforceable—after all, a breach of a contract to lend money, the typical case, sounds in damages (*Rogers v Challis* (1859) 27 Beav 175) but the *agreement* to create *security* must be specifically enforceable. This requires valuable consideration on the basis of *Re Lucan (Earl)* (1890) 45 ChD 470 (Ch), and even an agreement to create a mortgage contained in a deed will not suffice (*Meek v Kettlewell* (1842) 1 Ph 342).

87. *Tailby v Official Receiver* (1888) 13 App Cas 523 (HL).

88. Though see Tan Chen-Han, 'Charges, Contingencies and Registration' (2002) 2 JCLS 191.

89. [1901] 2 Ch 314 (Ch).

> ComCorp wants to know what it should do next. Lee is especially anxious to buy the boat and has offered £150,000 for it.

Foreclosure

Foreclosure determines the mortgagor's right to redeem and vests the property in the mortgagee freed from the mortgagor's rights.[90] The debt is extinguished since the mortgagee is electing to take the property in satisfaction of the debt, and if the property realizes more on sale than the outstanding debt, the surplus is retained by the mortgagee.

Foreclosure requires an order of the court, which will not be granted until the court has given the mortgagor the opportunity to redeem, since almost inevitably the mortgagee will only wish to exercise the power where the value of the property exceeds the amount of the debt. Foreclosure proceedings are extremely rare,[91] since the court will normally exercise its power under s 91 of the Law of Property Act 1925, to order sale rather than foreclosure if an interested party so requests.

Taking possession

The right to possession will almost certainly be contained in the mortgage document itself, but even without it, a legal mortgagee is *prima facie* entitled to possession 'before the ink is dry on the mortgage, unless there is something in the contract, express or by implication, whereby he has contracted himself out of that right'.[92] This is because the legal mortgagee is the owner of the property (if personal property[93]), or treated as if he were a tenant of the mortgagor (if the property is land). The position is less clear in the case of an equitable mortgagee.[94] Providing for repayment by instalments, which of course is typical of the standard domestic house mortgage, is enough to contract out of the right to immediate possession.

The mortgagee may be able to take possession of the property peacefully as a self-help remedy, but typically will seek a court order. Where the mortgaged property includes a dwelling house, the court may, among other things, postpone possession[95] where it appears that the mortgagor will be able to repay any arrears within a reasonable time. Where the mortgage is of land and secures a regulated agreement under the Consumer Credit Act 1974, a court order is necessary.[96] Section 7 of the Bills of Sale (Amendment) Act 1882 requires that, where the mortgage falls under the Act, possession can only be taken, among other things, if the mortgagee has defaulted in payment, or there has been 'fraudulent' removal of the property from the premises. Section 13 provides that the goods cannot be removed from the place at which they were taken into the possession of the mortgagee for five clear

---

90. *Heath v Pugh* (1881) 6 QBD 346 (CA) 360 (Lord Selbourne LC).

91. *Palk v Mortgage Services Funding plc* [1993] Ch 330 (CA) 336 (Sir Donald Nicholls V-C).

92. *Four-Maids Ltd v Dudley Marshall Properties Ltd* [1957] Ch 317 (Ch) 320.

93. Cotton LJ in *Re Morrit* (1886) 18 QBD 222 (CA) 232 said '[a] mortgage of personal chattels involves in its essence, not the delivery of possession, but a conveyance of title as a security for the debt', which seems to indicate that the right to immediate possession does not apply to such a mortgage in the absence of a contractual term expressly giving such a right. However, *Watkins v Evans* (1886) 18 QBD 386 (CA) suggests that s 7 of the Bills of Sale Act 1882 implies such a power, at least where the Act applies—but only after an event of default as set out in the section.

94. See HRW Wade, 'An Equitable Mortgagee's Right to Possession' (1955) 71 LQR 204.

95. Administration of Justice Act 1970, s 36.   96. Consumer Credit Act 1974, s 126.

days. It can therefore readily be understood that chattel mortgages to which the Bills of Sales Acts apply are not popular forms of security for lenders today.

Sale

Taking possession is generally a first step towards effecting a sale. Normally the mortgage will expressly contain a power of sale, but even in the absence of agreement, it may be implied.

Where the mortgage (legal or equitable) is created by deed, s 101 of the Law of Property Act 1925 grants a power of sale over the mortgaged property once the legal date for redemption has passed, but this statutory power is not exercisable unless notice has been served on the debtor requiring redemption and three months have passed, or interest is at least two months overdue, or the mortgagor has committed some other breach of the mortgage.[97]

It was held in *Re Morrit*[98] that the equivalent provision in the Conveyancing Act 1881 to s 101 of the Law of Property Act 1925 did not apply to chattel mortgages to which the Bills of Sale (Amendment) Act 1882 applied,[99] but that either a power of sale was implied at common law after default in payment, and if the mortgagor has been given a reasonable time to pay,[100] or by s 7 of the Bills of Sale (Amendment) Act 1882.[101] Where the 1882 Act does apply, the mortgagee cannot sell the goods for five days after he has taken possession.[102]

Assuming the power of sale has arisen and is exercisable, the mortgagee is entitled to act in his own best interest in carrying out the sale, even though the debtor and any other incumbrancers (that is to say, other persons with security interests in the property) may be financially affected by the outcome. Consequently, there is no duty in negligence to the mortgagor or other incumbrancers,[103] though equity has imposed certain duties, for example to pay the rent on leasehold premises and to keep the premises in good repair, along with an equitable[104] duty to take reasonable care to obtain a proper price.[105] However, even here it is for the mortgagee to decide, acting honestly, when to sell, even if an improvement in price was foreseeable were sale delayed.[106] However, a mortgagee 'owes a general duty to subsequent incumbrancers and to the mortgagor to use his powers for the sole purpose of securing repayment of the moneys owing under his mortgage and a duty to act in good faith'.[107] Consequently, using the powers as in *Downsview Nominees*[108] in order

---

97. Law of Property Act 1925, s 103.   98. (1886) 18 QBD 222 (CA).

99. Or perhaps that it did not apply if the mortgage itself contained provisions which made the statutory power unnecessary—see Fry and Bowen LJJ in *Re Watkins* (1886) 18 QBD 386 (CA).

100. As held by Cotton, Lindley, and Bowen LJJ. But see *Deverges v Sandeman Clark & Co* [1902] 1 Ch 579 (CA).

101. As stated by Lord Esher MR and Lopes LJ.   102. Bills of Sale (Amendment) Act 1882, s 13.

103. *Downsview Nominees Ltd v First City Corp Ltd* [1994] 1 BCLC 49 (PC) 63. This case has been criticized: see Ian Fletcher, Gavin Lightman, and Gabriel Moss (eds), *Lightman and Moss The Law of Administrators and Receivers* (5th edn, Sweet & Maxwell 2011) [10-013]. It clearly imposes a lower duty on the mortgagee than on an administrator who, in seeking to achieve his objectives under Sch B1 para 3 of the Insolvency Act 1986, must not 'unnecessarily harm the interests of the creditors of the company as a whole' (para 3(4)). *Downsview* concerns the acts of an administrative receiver, but identical principles apply.

104. *Parker-Tweedale v Dunbar Bank plc* [1991] Ch 12 (CA).

105. *Re Cuckmere Brick Co Ltd v Mutual Finance Ltd* [1971] Ch 949 (CA).   106. ibid.

107. *Downsview Nominees Ltd v First City Corp Ltd* [1994] 1 BCLC 49 (PC) 63 (Lord Templeman).

108. [1994] 1 BCLC 49 (PC).

to injure a second mortgagee is actionable; however, an honest act which disregards and damages the interests of others is not.[109]

The mortgagee is accountable to the mortgagor (or any subsequent incumbrancer) for surplus in his hands after the debt has been repaid and all the costs of realization have been met.

Appointing a receiver

The function of a receiver is principally to receive the income arising from the mortgaged asset and apply it in meeting interest and repaying capital. A modern mortgage will not rely on the statutory power in s 109 of the Law of Property Act 1925, but will grant larger powers, potentially permitting a receivership to continue for years if necessary.[110] Notwithstanding the fact that the receiver will be deemed to be the agent of the mortgagor in managing the property, 'the primary duty of the receiver is to try and bring about a situation in which interest on the secured debt can be paid and the debt itself repaid [and]…[s]ubject to that primary duty, the receiver owes a duty to manage the property with due diligence'[111] by analogy to the duty on sale.[112]

Charges

Introduction

Unless created by statute,[113] charges are equitable interests[114] and do not involve the transfer either of ownership or possession of the property to the creditor, unlike a mortgage. Instead, the creditor is granted a new proprietary interest—a charge over the property—which gives him a right to realization of his security, for example by a court order for the appointment of a receiver or for sale, though charges typically give express powers without the need for a court order. Technically, therefore, a charge does not create a proprietary right in the charged property, but the effect of the availability of equitable remedies 'has the effect of giving the chargee a proprietary interest by way of security in the property charged'.[115]

The charge itself, being an item of equitable property, can itself be dealt with, for example by sale, though any transfers would need to be in writing.[116]

---

109. See e.g. *Palk v Mortgage Services Funding* Ltd [1993] Ch 330 (CA), where there was no suggestion that the bank's decision to retain the property and in effect try to 'trade out' of the negative equity which would increase the mortgagor's debt by £30,000 per year was improper, though here the Court exercised its power under s 91(2) of the Law of Property Act 1925 to order sale.

110. The power of a floating chargee to appoint an administrative receiver has been abolished save for minor exceptions (Insolvency Act 1986, s 72A).

111. *Medforth v Blake* [1999] 2 BCLC 221 (CA) 237 (Sir Richard Scott V-C).

112. But see *Silven Properties Ltd v Royal Bank of Scotland plc* [2004] 1 WLR 997 (CA), affirming that timing of a sale is a matter for the receiver and that the fact that he is the agent of the mortgagor does not affect his duties.

113. See e.g. Law of Property Act 1925, ss 85–87.   114. *Re Cosslett Contractors Ltd* [1998] Ch 495 (CA).

115. *Re Charge Card Services Ltd* [1987] Ch 150 (Ch) 76 (Millett J). In the case of a charge made by deed, s 101 of the Law of Property Act 1925, would give a chargee a right to sell without judicial order.

116. Law of Property Act 1925, s 53(1)(b).

The difference between charges and mortgages

As noted earlier, a mortgagee's rights in respect of the mortgaged property derive from the fact that a mortgage transfers ownership of the property to the mortgagee for the purpose of providing security for an underlying obligation. That ownership can be either legal, where the legal requirements for title transfer have been met, or equitable, where they have not, but equity would treat ownership as having passed. A chargee's rights derive solely from the availability of equitable remedies and arises 'when property is expressly or constructively made liable, or specially appropriated, to the discharge of a debt or some other obligation',[117] but in the absence of an intention to pass ownership to the chargee. An example might be where the borrower agrees simply that the debt will be paid out of an identifiable fund; equity will enforce this agreement specifically, typically by ordering sale so that the debt can be satisfied from the proceeds of sale.

Whilst there is a clear conceptual difference between charges and mortgages, actual differentiation is sometimes difficult where there is no express agreement. The intention that ownership of an asset should pass as security for an obligation (and thus create an equitable mortgage) need not be evidenced expressly, but may be inferred, so that if a debtor agrees to segregate a fund or other asset and to pay the debt out of that asset, 'the inference may be drawn, in the absence of any contra indication, that the parties' intention is that the creditor should have such a proprietary interest in the segregated fund or asset'.[118] Consequently, segregation of an asset for the purpose of providing security will normally create a mortgage, but not always, as the following case demonstrates.

Swiss Bank Corporation v Lloyds Bank plc [1982] AC 584 (HL)

FACTS: This case dates from the time that Bank of England consent had to be obtained for certain transactions involving foreign currencies. Swiss Bank Corporation (SBC), agreed to lend 10.5 million Swiss francs to IFT to enable it to buy some shares. IFT covenanted that it had all necessary consents and would comply with all Bank of England conditions, and repay the loan in a way approved by the Bank of England. The Bank of England conditions were that the loan would be used to purchase the shares, which would be held in a segregated account, and that interest on the loan and its eventual repayment was to come from the securities or their proceeds of sale. The account was opened at Lloyds Bank.

HELD: Lord Wilberforce (agreeing with Buckley LJ in the Court of Appeal) held that, barring evidence to the contrary, where a loan agreement imposes a positive obligation to (1) segregate property; and (2) use it for repayment of the loan and for no other purpose, this evidences that ownership of the property should pass to the lender as security for the loan, thus creating an equitable mortgage once the loan has been made.

However, on the facts of the case: first, the segregation was not in order to provide security, so there was no intention that ownership of the asset should pass to the lender, (i.e. there was no equitable mortgage); second, properly understood, the covenants in

---

117. *Swiss Bank Corporation v Lloyds Bank plc* [1982] AC 584 (CA) 595 (Buckley LJ).   118. ibid.

the loan agreement were not that IFT would repay the loan from the fund, simply that IFT would repay the loan as permitted by the Bank of England. Consequently, there was no specifically enforceable duty to pay from the fund and so no equitable charge over the share account either.

COMMENT: The outcome of the case is not surprising; the terms of the Bank of England consent were in common form and intended to protect sterling from external economic forces and not to provide lenders with security over the borrower's assets. In other words, the parties would have had to have intended that the lender have security over the fund, and while segregating a fund is evidence that the parties intend it to provide security for a loan, there was another more convincing explanation for the segregation.

In fact, in *Swiss Bank Corporation*, both Buckley LJ and the House of Lords concluded that no security interest at all had been created. However, the case demonstrates that a charge may be arise very easily: no special words are needed,[119] the parties need not understand the legal effect of their intentions,[120] and, as noted earlier, an agreement to grant security is enough.

Although a charge can be created orally,[121] typically it will be created in writing and will be registrable as a Bill of Sale in the appropriate circumstances.[122] Normally, the charge will grant an express power of sale, but the chargee can apply to the court for an order of sale where there is no express power, while a charge created by deed attracts the statutory power of sale.[123] Clearly, the property to be subjected to the charge must be identifiable, but a charge may relate to property in which the borrower currently has an interest or to property not yet owned by him.[124] In the case of current property, the charge gives the lender an immediate security interest over it, even if enforcement is contingent on obtaining a court order. In the case of future property, where the agreement is supported by valuable consideration, the right to the security is specifically enforceable the moment the property vests in the borrower and otherwise meets the description of the encumbered property.[125] However, it appears that the charge exists in an inchoate form *before* the property to which it attaches,[126] and the attachment relates back to the date of the agreement.[127]

---

119. *Cradock v Scottish Provident Institution* (1894) 70 LT 718 (CA); *National Provincial and Union Bank of England v Charnley* [1924] 1 KB 431 (CA) 440 (Bankes LJ).

120. *Swiss Bank Corporation v Lloyds Bank plc* [1982] AC 584 (CA) 595–6 (Buckley LJ).

121. Law of Property (Miscellaneous Provisions) Act 1989, s 2(6) requires a charge over land to be in writing. However, in the case of other property, Law of Property Act 1925, s 53(1)(c) (transfer of an equitable interest to be in writing) does not apply, since a charge does not transfer an equitable interest but creates one.

122. Bills of Sale Act 1878, s 4 defines bills of sale as including charges.

123. Law of Property Act 1925, s 101.

124. *Holroyd v Marshall* (1862) 11 ER 999 (HL).

125. ibid where security was taken over the current and future contents of a woollen mill. Presumably property passed on delivery to the mill—but what would the situation have been if the borrower had acquired title before the machinery was placed in the mill? See also Roger Gregory and Peter Wilson, 'Fixed and Floating Charges—A Revelation' [2001] LMCLQ 123, who demonstrate the principles lie in the sixteenth/seventeenth centuries.

126. *Re Lind* [1915] 2 Ch 345 (CA). But see Paul Matthews, 'The Effect of Bankruptcy upon Mortgages of Future Property' [1981] LMCLQ 40, who argues to the contrary.

127. *Tailby v Official Receiver* (1888) 13 App Cas 523 (HL).

Finally, as with agreements to create mortgages, for the charge to arise from the date of the agreement, the arrangement must be one which is intended to give the lender an immediate security, and not one where, for example, the borrower agrees to grant security once he acquires property or if required to do so in the future.[128]

Fixed and floating charges

Consider the following example.

> ### Eg ComCorp Ltd
>
> ComCorp Ltd supplies goods to a retailer who now owes Comcorp a considerable sum of money. Before it will continue to trade with the retailer, ComCorp wants security over the retailer's assets, which consist in the main of the stock of goods in its shops, much of which ComCorp sold to the business, as well as debts owed to the retailer by its own customers. There is a constant turnover in the stock, so it is impractical for ComCorp to have a normal mortgage over the property, as it would need to agree every time an item of stock was sold and as new stock comes in it would be free of the mortgage. Similarly, the retailer needs to be able to collect its debts and use the proceeds in running its business. ComCorp wants to know its options.

Originally, only charges which attached to specific fixed assets were recognized. Under these, known as 'fixed charges' the lender's permission would be needed before any affected asset could be disposed of. However, in *Holroyd v Marshall*,[129] the House of Lords established that a charge (or a mortgage as was the case there) can exist over future property, and a security interest attaches to the property as soon as ownership of it vests in the borrower. In *Holroyd*, the property was plant and machinery (i.e. **fixed capital**) then or in the future to be found in a factory, so that there was no problem with impracticality of obtaining the lender's permission to dispose of it. But *Re Panama, New Zealand and Australia Royal Mail Co*[130] recognized that a charge can exist over the revolving assets of a company. Here the charge was over the borrower company's 'undertaking and all sums of money arising therefrom', but the lender agreed that the borrower could acquire and dispose of its property in the ordinary course of its business until the company was wound up, when the charge would attach to all of the property of the company at that time. The Court of Appeal in Chancery held that the charge was over the company's assets present and future, and was effective to give the chargee the right to be repaid out of the assets before the unsecured creditors.

➡ fixed capital: property which a business normally retains as part of its infrastructure, in contrast to circulating capital, which is property which is acquired and disposed of on a regular basis

In these 'floating charges', the security does not attach to the property until an event occurs which the charge states will cause attachment, when the charge is then said to 'crystallize'. In effect, it is a charge over a fund of assets,[131] which for these

---

128. *National Provincial and Union Bank of England v Charnley* [1924] 1 KB 431 (CA).
129. (1862) 11 ER 999 (HL). 130. (1870) 5 Ch App 318.
131. Though see Richard Nolan, 'Property in a Fund' (2004) 120 LQR 108, who insists that property can only subsist in specific assets.

purposes is treated as an entity in its own right, but affects no specific asset until crystallization, when it becomes a fixed charge from that date over whatever is comprised in the fund. As Buckley LJ said:

> A floating charge is not a future security; it is a present security, which presently affects all the assets of the company expressed to be included in it...A floating security is not a specific mortgage of the assets, plus a licence to the mortgagor to dispose of them in the course of his business, but is a floating mortgage applying to every item comprised in the security but not specifically affecting any item until some event occurs...which causes it to crystallise into a fixed security.[132]

There is some dispute about the true nature of the floating charge and in particular whether the chargee has any interest in the charged property before crystallization. The fact that there are four plausible competing theories—that there is no interest until crystallization; that there is an interest of some sort with a licence in the borrower to deal with the assets in the ordinary course of business; the defeasible charge theory; and the overreaching theory—demonstrates that nearly 150 years after *Holroyd*, the floating charge is a 'manifestation of English genius',[133] but without knowing quite how it works!

To enforce his security, a floating chargee may appoint a receiver over the asset or sell it. However, since the charge may extend over all or a significant part of a company's assets, typical floating charges extended the powers of the receiver to allow him to run the business with a view to realizing the maximum sum for the lender. This power to appoint a receiver and manager (now called an 'administrative receiver') under a floating charge has been removed by statute.[134] The chargee, whether fixed or floating, can now appoint an administrator whose initial duty is to preserve the business as a going concern where possible, and not 'unnecessarily' damage the interests of creditors.

The difference between fixed and floating charges[135]

Although an individual can create a fixed charge over a chattel,[136] he cannot create a floating charge. All charges by an individual over personal chattels must not only be registered under the Bills of Sale Acts,[137] they must also be in the statutory form,[138] which requires description of the property[139] and cannot include future property,[140] other than property substituted for plant or machinery originally subjected to the charge.[141] This latter issue is in practice unimportant, since taking security over

---

132. *Evans v Rival Granite Quarries Ltd* [1910] 2 KB 979 (CA) 999.

133. Roy Goode and Ewan McKendrick, *Goode on Commercial Law* (4th edn, Penguin 2010) 722. For a brief summary of the first two alternatives followed by her own view see Sarah Worthington, *Proprietary Interests in Commercial Transactions* (Clarendon Press 1996) 78–86. For the final theory, see Richard Nolan, 'Property in a Fund' (2004) 120 LQR 108.

134. Insolvency Act 1986, s 72A.

135. See Louise Gullifer and Jennifer Payne, 'The Characterization of Fixed and Floating Charges' in Joshua Getzler and Jennifer Payne (eds), *Company Charges Spectrum and Beyond* (OUP 2006) 51.

136. After all, the borrower in *Holroyd* was an individual.

137. It is now established that both Acts only apply to individuals (*Slavenburg's Bank NV v Intercontinental Natural Resources Ltd* [1980] 1 WLR 1076 (QB)).

138. Bills of Sale (Amendment) Act 1882, s 9.   139. Bills of Sale (Amendment) Act 1882.

140. ibid s 5 and Schedule 1.   141. ibid s 6(2).

chattels owned by individuals is unusual. However, there is no obvious reason why an individual cannot create a floating charge over things in action.

There are a number of statutory reasons why distinguishing between fixed and floating charges is important. For example, some fixed charges are not registrable under the Companies Act 2006.[142] Similarly, while a fixed charge ranks ahead of preferred creditors in a receivership, administration, or winding up, a floating charge does not,[143] and preferred creditors have priority even in respect of debts accruing after the charge crystallized.[144] Additionally, floating charges are postponed to the costs of liquidation,[145] remuneration, and expenses of an administrator,[146] and if created within twelve months of the commencement of a winding up, are void except to the extent of any 'new value' provided under the charge.[147] Section 176A of the Insolvency Act 1986 also provides that a prescribed part of assets subject to a floating charge must be made available to unsecured creditors.[148]

The statutory subordination of floating charges gives an incentive for the lender to seek a fixed charge wherever possible, and often a 'fixed and floating' charge will be created in order to attempt to get the best of both worlds. The main difficulties emerged in connection with charges over **book debts**, since receivables are clearly an item of property and may comprise the most valuable asset of a business, yet the company needs to be able to collect its debts and use the proceeds in its business if it is to operate efficiently. Following *Siebe Gorman & Co Ltd v Barclays Bank Ltd*,[149] it was believed that a fixed charge could be created over book debts while preserving the freedom of the borrower to deal with the debts once they had been collected. This case was overruled in *Re Spectrum Plus Ltd*,[150] but the principles to be applied in order to characterize a charge as either fixed or floating were perhaps best explained in an earlier case, *Agnew v Commissioner of Inland Revenue*.[151] The Court first determines 'the nature of the rights and obligations which the parties intended to grant each other', not 'whether they intended to create a fixed or floating security in respect of the charged assets'.[152] Then the Court examines these rights and obligations to determine whether they are inconsistent with the nature of a fixed charge.

→ book debts: debts owed to the company by its clients or customers

Romer LJ provided the 'classic and frequently cited'[153] typical characteristics of a floating charge, though he was careful to avoid attempting a definition:

1. They are charges on a class of assets of a company present and future.
2. The assets include property which in the ordinary course of the business of the company would be changing from time to time.
3. Until crystallization, the company may carry on its business in the ordinary way as far as concerns the particular class of assets.[154]

---

142. Companies Act 2006, s 860, in particular charges on shares and documentary intangibles.

143. Insolvency Act 1986, ss 40, 175(2)(b) and Sch B1, para 65(2).

144. Through the combined effect of the Companies Act 2006, s 754(1), (2) and the Insolvency Act 1986, s 25.

145. Insolvency Act 1986, s 176ZA.   146. ibid s 19(4).   147. ibid s 245.

148. Insolvency Act 1986 (Prescribed Part) Order 2003—50 per cent of the first £10,000 and 20 per cent thereafter, up to a limit of £600,000.

149. [1979] 2 Lloyd's Rep 142 (Ch).   150. [2005] UKHL 41, [2005] 2 AC 680 (HL).

151. [2001] 2 BCLC 188 (PC).   152. ibid [32].

153. *Re Spectrum Plus Ltd* [2005] UKHL 41, [2005] 2 AC 680 [99].

154. *Re Yorkshire Woolcombers Association Ltd* [1903] 2 Ch 284 (CA) (295).

In fact, floating charges have been held to have been created over present property alone and future property alone,[155] and solely over part of the company's fixed capital.[156] Consequently, while it is clear that these characteristics constitute the normal 'badges' of a floating charge, so that a charge over fixed capital is *prima facie* a fixed charge and one over circulating capital is floating,[157] the key differentiator between fixed and floating charges is the third characteristic. Indeed, in *Agnew*, Lord Millett concluded that perhaps the sole issue is whether the borrower is 'free to deal with the charged assets and withdraw them from the security without the consent of the holder of the charge',[158] and this approach was adopted by the House of Lords in *Re Spectrum Plus*.

 Re Spectrum Plus Ltd [2005] UKHL 41

FACTS: Spectrum Plus created a 'specific charge' as security for debts it owed to its bank, National Westminster. The charge was in favour of the bank and given over Spectrum Plus's book debts. Spectrum Plus was allowed to collect the debts in the ordinary course of its business and agreed to pay the money as received into its current account with National Westminster and not to give third party rights over the debts without the bank's consent. Spectrum Plus also agreed, if asked, to assign the book debts to the bank. Spectrum Plus was free to operate the current account normally up to its credit limit. When Spectrum Plus went into liquidation, the current account was overdrawn. The liquidators refused to account to National Westminster for the debts they collected, claiming the charge was a floating charge, and so postponed to preferred creditors' claims.

HELD: Under a fixed charge, the charged assets were permanently appropriated to the charge and the borrower's use of the asset is thereby restricted. By contrast, with a floating charge the assets were not appropriated to the charge until crystallization, and until then the borrower was free to use them and in the ordinary course of business withdraw them from the scope of the security. Here, although the borrower was not free to deal with the unpaid book debts, once the debt had been collected the charge placed no restriction on the borrower's use of the money; consequently, the borrower was permitted by the charge to withdraw the debts from the security without the consent of the lender. Therefore this was a floating charge.

COMMENT: The form of the charge in *Spectrum Plus* was standard in the banking industry and closely modelled on one which Slade J had held at first instance to create an effective fixed charge.[159] Nevertheless, the House overruled the case and refused to apply the ruling prospectively only, even though many thousands of charges were in this form.[160]

---

155. *Re Bond Worth Ltd* [1980] Ch 228 (Ch) (a charge over the goods supplied (exclusively present property) and the proceeds of sale (exclusively future property)).

156. *Welch v Bowmaker (Ireland) Ltd* [1980] IR 251 (Irish Supreme Court).

157. See Louise Gullifer (ed), *Goode on Legal Problems of Credit and Security* (4th edn, Sweet & Maxwell 2009) [4-21].

158. *Agnew v Commissioner of Inland Revenue* [2001] 2 BCLC 188 (PC)[32].

159. *Siebe Gorman & Co Ltd v Barclays Bank Ltd* [1979] 2 Lloyd's Rep 142 (Ch).

160. For the retrospective impact, see Ken Baird, 'Statement on Behalf of HM Revenue & Customs and the DTI Insolvency Service (The Crown Departments) in Light of the House of Lords' Judgment in the Case of National Westminster Bank plc v Spectrum Plus Limited and Others [2005] UKHL 41 (Spectrum Plus)' [2005] Insolv Int 159.

⭐ See Christopher Hare, 'Charges Over Book Debts: The End of an Era' [2005] 4 LMCLQ 440

> Clearly, there were restrictions on alienability of the uncollected debts, but the obvious means of realization of them was by collection which the borrower controlled, and once collected they could use the money freely. Thus the borrower could withdraw the individual debts from the security and had free use of the proceeds.[161]

Re Spectrum Plus establishes that, while a fixed charge over book debts is possible, a floating charge is created if the borrower can collect the debts (and thus with-draw—actually extinguish—the assets subject to the charge) unless he must pay the proceeds into an account to which he has no or perhaps only limited right of recourse.[162] If this right of withdrawal from the subject of the charge is the mark of a floating charge, did that make the charge in *Holroyd* floating? Writers generally seem convinced it was a fixed charge, yet the borrower could remove and replace machinery which was the subject matter of the charge apparently without reference to the mortgagee.[163] Perhaps the reason it was fixed was that the borrower could only withdraw assets in order to replace them.[164]

How can a bank have a charge over a customer's bank account?

📎 *Re Charge Card Services* concerning receivables financing and the issue of 'charge backs' in receivables financing is considered on p 716

In *Re Spectrum Plus*, the bank had a charge over the uncollected book debts of the bor-rower, i.e. debts owed to it by third parties and over the proceeds, which were paid into the borrower's current account with the bank. That account was at all relevant times overdrawn, but had it been in credit, could the bank have had a charge over the debt it owed to the borrower? In *Re Charge Card Services Ltd*,[165] Millett J held that such an arrangement was 'conceptually impossible'; after all, how could the creditor realize his security? As we have seen, the essence of a charge is the appropriation of an asset to satisfy a debt so that the chargee can realize it—yet how can the bank realize a debt it owes itself? However, in *Re Bank of Credit and Commerce International (No 8)*,[166] Lord Hoffmann stated (*obiter*) that, while it is true that the bank could not realize its security in the normal way because it could not claim money from itself, it could enforce it simply by debiting the customer's balance on the account in credit and crediting the customer's balance on the account in debit. This seems a pragmatic conclusion, which accords with commercial practice.

---

161. See Sarah Worthington, 'Floating Charges: The Current State of Play' [2008] JIBFL 467.

162. Although pre-dating *Re Spectrum Plus*, Sarah Worthington's article 'An "Unsatisfactory Area of the Law"—Fixed and Floating Charges Yet Again' (2004) 1 Int CR 175 is a clear and practical exposition of the alternatives for a bank seeking a fixed charge. On the degree of a borrower's control in a fixed charge see Louise Gullifer (ed), *Goode on Legal Problems of Credit and Security* (4th edn, Sweet & Maxwell 2009) [4-21].

163. See Sarah Worthington, 'Fixed Charges over Book Debts and other Receivables' (1997) 113 LQR 562, 565–6; WJ Gough, *Company Charges* (LexisNexis 2007) 82; Roy Goode and Ewan McKendrick, *Goode on Commercial Law* (Penguin 2010) 721. Though see Robert Pennington, 'The Genesis of the Floating Charge' (1960) 23 MLR 630, 634.

164. Though of course the same could in a sense be said of the book debts in *Re Spectrum Plus*—the money realized was ploughed back into the business in order to sell goods and so generate a new book debt.

165. [1987] Ch 150 (Ch).   166. [1998] AC 214 (HL) 225–8.

Conclusion

Consider the following example.

 ComCorp Ltd

ComCorp Ltds's customer referred to in the previous ComCorp example (on p 702) turns out to be an individual, and so a floating charge will probably be ineffective. Greg suggests that it might be sensible to review the terms of business and ensure that when ComCorp Ltd supplied goods to the customer, ownership of the goods remains with ComCorp Ltd until its invoice for the goods was paid, and that after the cloth had been turned into the dresses, ComCorp Ltd should own the dresses as well until payment was received.

The advantage of taking security is that the secured lender, whether pledgee, lienee, mortgagee, or chargee will be beyond the *pari passu* rule in an insolvency of the debtor. Each depends on the debtor granting a security interest in property in which the debtor has an absolute interest and, apart from the charge and the equitable lien, this is effected by transferring some sort of property rights to the creditor. But the English law of security is unsatisfactory, since it has grown up in a piecemeal fashion and lacks a logical structure. First, the same economic effect as granting a security interest may be achieved by other means, for example hire purchase, chattel leasing, or title retention. But this anomaly gives rise to issues of characterization, since what looks like a sale or a lease may in reality be a charge. Second, statute has intervened to reduce the effectiveness of floating charges, so that it may become important to differentiate between fixed and floating charges, yet the same property may be capable of being subjected to either type of charge, and while all floating charges are registrable under s 860 of the Companies Act 2006 some fixed charges are not, while others may need registering in a number of registers. Third, because of the nature of the types of security interest, some types of creditor can readily obtain security by pledge or lien, while for others, taking security is almost impossible. Finally, trade creditors who have supplied goods to the insolvent business may be owed considerable sums, yet where another creditor (normally the debtor's bank) has taken a floating charge, those goods, if they are owned by the debtor, will be subject to the charge, and the proceeds of sale will be used to reduce the chargee's debt, not repay the creditor who provided the value.

Calls for reform have resulted, focussing principally on proposals to abolish the floating charge,[167] and suggestions that the economic function of an arrangement should determine its legal and regulatory treatment and not the legal structure adopted. Reviews of security interests in property have been undertaken, notably by the Crowther Committee, which reported as long ago as 1971.[168] A good summary of the issues is contained in the Law

---

167. A main proponent being Professor Sir Roy Goode. See e.g. Roy Goode, 'Proprietary Rights and Unsecured Creditors' in Barry Rider (ed), *The Realm of Company Law* (Kluwer 1998) and 'The Case for the Abolition of the Floating Charge' in Joshua Getzler and Jennifer Payne (eds), *Company Charges Spectrum and Beyond* (OUP 2006). New Zealand and Australia have abolished the floating charge, as have several Canadian provinces.

168. Department of Trade and Industry, *Report of the Committee on Consumer Credit* (Cm 4596, 1971).

Commission Consultation Paper on company security interests, which is available from the Law Commission website.[169]

As matters stand, it seems unlikely that there will be a wholesale reform of the English law of security which, although it allows security to be taken over almost anything, does not always make it apparent which method of taking security is appropriate, whether, where, and how the interest is to be perfected, and which can act very unfairly in burdening perfectly honest purchasers of goods with security interests about which it may have been impossible or at least very difficult to discover.

Practice questions

1. Explain the difference between and, where appropriate, give examples of the following:

   - security and quasi-security;
   - possessory and non-possessory security;
   - attachment and perfection;
   - a pledge and a lien;
   - a mortgage and a charge;
   - a fixed charge and a floating charge.

2. 'The English law of security is unsatisfactory since it has grown up in a piecemeal fashion and lacks a logical structure.'

   Do you agree?

3. Security+ Ltd holds a portfolio of investments in shares and bonds. It has granted a mortgage over the securities in favour of the bank, so that Security+ cannot deal with the investments without the consent of the bank. Each year, the issuers of the securities pay the interest and dividends into a special investment account Security+ has with the bank. Security+ has granted a charge over that account in favour of the bank. The bank wants to know the legal effect of this arrangement. Security+ Ltd is being pressed for payment by a trade creditor. Security+'s managing director says to the creditor, 'Look, you know we are about to get planning permission to redevelop our office site as high-quality apartments and we've got a buyer lined up—you'll get paid out of that deal.' The trade creditor extends even more credit on the strength of this assurance.

   Might Security+ have created a charge over the land? Security+ recently lent some money to one of its employees, Reg, who gave it the keys to his lock-up garage where a car he was restoring was stored, saying that Security+ should have the car as security for the debt. Reg signs a document which records all of this and states that he holds the car to Security+'s order. Reg leases the garage from a company and to get to it you have to drive over the landlord's land. Reg has since sold the car to Percy. Security+ wants to know if they have to allow Percy to take the car away. Security+ agreed that it would transfer the contents of its office building to Credito, to which it owes a lot of money, if Credito wanted it as security for the debt. Credito never asked for a transfer, but became anxious, and seeing the building was unlocked one morning, removed all of the PCs and office furniture and sold it all. Security+ wants to know whether Credito is entitled to do this.

---

169. Law Commission, *Registration of Security Interests: Company Charges and Property Other than Land* (Law Com CP No 164, 2008).

Further reading

Peter Ellinger, 'Trust Receipt Financing' [2003] JIBLR 305
- Although sea waybills and other forms of document are increasingly being used, the bill of lading retains a role in providing a convenient mechanism for secure lending in international trade. This article describes and analyses the issues, particularly where the debtor seeks to transfer title to goods pledged to a lender.

Joshua Getzler and Jennifer Payne (eds), *Company Charges Spectrum and Beyond* (OUP 2006)
- The chapters in this book all repay careful reading. On the need for reform in English security law, Roy Goode's 'The Case for Abolishing the Floating Charge' and Michael Bridge's 'The Law Commission's Proposals' provide an accessible but authoritative summary of the issues. On the nature of the charge, Louise Gullifer and Jennifer Payne's 'The Characterisation of Fixed and Floating Charges' covers a range of theories as to the nature of mortgages and charges, and examines why the differences matter, but also points to the distortions the division causes.

Louise Gullifer (ed), *Goode on Problems of Credit and Security* (4th edn, Sweet & Maxwell 2008)
- Originally deriving from a series of lectures, this book covers the nature of security interests, attachment and perfection, and fixed and floating charges, exploring unresolved problems with insight and clarity.

Norman Palmer and Ewan McKendrick (eds), *Interests in Goods* (2nd edn, LLP 1998)
- The chapters 'Pledge' by Norman Palmer and Alistair Hudson, 'Equitable Liens—A Search for a Unifying Principle' by J Phillips, and 'Solicitors' Liens' by Alistair Hudson are all worth reading (as indeed are all the chapters in this wonderful book). Possessory security has received relatively little attention compared with the wealth of literature on charges in particular, and these chapters explore a number of issues which have long deserved consideration.

Sarah Worthington, 'Equitable Liens in Commercial Transaction' (1994) 53 CLJ 263
- Equitable liens comprise a body of disparate security interests which have features more characteristic of charges than liens. The writer provides a structure for these interests, which enables a rational approach to be made to what might become a 'growth area' for the recognition of such liens in novel situations.

26 Forms of title-based financing

- Alternative methods of business financing
- Receivables financing
- The finance lease

INTRODUCTION

Chapter 2 discussed the two types of personal property recognized in English law, namely tangible items of property which are capable of being physically possessed (known as things in possession), and property which can only be enforced through legal action, (known as things in action) such as a debt. In this chapter, we will examine how the ways in which goods and things in action can be dealt with can be used to facilitate the financing of business. After a brief survey of the financing mechanisms available to businesses, this chapter will discuss receivables financing, where a succession of debts owed to a business (an income stream) can either be sold outright or subjected to a security interest in favour of a financier, focussing specifically at outright sale. The chapter will then move on to discuss how the fact that title to an asset can be split between an 'owner' and a person with physical possession of it can be used to advantage in financing the acquisition of capital items for use in a business.

In a sense, the chapter shows how the legal theory underpinning property and security concepts can be applied commercially to achieve business objectives. In each case, the underlying idea is that the finance provider obtains rights over property and does not have to rely solely on the personal obligation of the business. Throughout the chapter, the word 'business' is used to denote the finance taker, and typically this will be a company; indeed, financing through the use of floating charges is only available to companies. The word 'borrower' is not used in this chapter to indicate the taker of finance, as not all financing is by way of loan; likewise the finance provider is called 'the financier' rather than the lender.

Charges and mortgages are discussed in Chapter 25, and the reason why floating charges can only be granted by companies at p 703

Alternative methods of business financing

Typically, a financier will seek to improve the risk he is taking that he will not recover his money by acquiring rights beyond the simple obligation of a business to repay a loan. These additional rights may either be exercisable against a third party or against property owned or in use by the business. Thus, for example, the financier might obtain a guarantee from a third party so that if he cannot recover his money from the business itself, he can pursue a personal claim against the guarantor. Thus one or more of the owners of a business operated by a company may be prepared to personally guarantee the payment obligations of the company. Alternatively, the financier might obtain rights over property to which he can have recourse for payment, for example by taking a charge or mortgage over it or by having title to it, but permitting the business to use the property. To a great extent, the method that a business might employ in order to finance itself will depend on the purpose of the finance and its current financial position. For example, the business might wish to finance the purchase of new business premises, in which case it might be possible to borrow the money and grant a charge over the land. Similarly, it may already own other valuable fixed assets over which it can grant security. Alternatively, it may have a substantial stock of goods for re-sale over which it can grant a floating charge.

The following example demonstrates the typical problem that can arise.

Eg ComCorp Ltd

Comcorp manufactures and sells computers and has for some time been offering credit facilities through **hire purchase**[1] to its customers, who are primarily young people on low wages. ComCorp's finance director has pointed out that the company can no longer fund this activity from its own resources and that it needs to receive full value for the computers shortly after sale. He wants to know how ComCorp can find the necessary funding. ComCorp has already granted a charge over all of its tangible assets, which forbids the granting of security over any of its assets.

> ➡ hire purchase: a method of financing where the financier purchases goods selected by its customer who takes possession of them, agrees to make a number of periodic payments to the financier, and has the option but not the duty to purchase the goods outright

---

In ComCorp's situation, there are two alternatives: either find a financier who is prepared to finance the purchase of the computers by new customers, perhaps by hire purchase;[2] or a financier who is prepared to finance ComCorp so that it can in turn finance new customers. Since ComCorp already has a 'book' of debtors under its existing hire purchase arrangements, financing ComCorp rather than the new customers appears the preferred option; the issue is to identify an asset over which the financier can obtain rights. The debts owed to ComCorp by its customers under the hire purchase agreements are property, things in action, and these can either be assigned outright by way of sale to the financier, who then pays the purchase price to ComCorp, or subjected to a charge in favour of the finance provider as security for a loan. Financing supported by property rights like these is called 'receivables financing'; the company is using debts receivable by it as support for the finance.

🔗 The nature of things in action and their assignment is discussed at p 42

---

1. See Consumer Credit Act 1974, s 189.
2. Notice here that the financier is seeking to reduce the risk of default by acquiring rights over property in the possession of the customer.

Receivables financing

The economics of receivables financing

In simple terms, the business is entitled to a stream of cash from its debtors which can be given a capital value. Clearly, the financier will not pay the face value of the amount due, but will apply a discount rate reflecting what return it wants to make on its money. Also, because some of the debts may not be paid by the customers, an adjustment may be made to allow for this. Finally, the financier may take over the process of recovery of the debts and will need to make a charge for this, which may be reflected in the discount rate, or it may make a direct charge to the business for its services. As a result, the business will receive a discounted price for the cash flow it was entitled to receive.

Sale or charge?

A sale of receivables may be with or without recourse. In non-recourse financing, the business simply assigns the receivables, leaving the financier to bear the risk of default by the debtors. Since the financier is taking the credit risk, he will typically be prepared to pay a lower price for the debt than in recourse financing, where he has a claim against the assignor in the event that less is recovered from the debtors than was assumed in the process of determining the price paid for the debts. There is very little economic difference between recourse financing by outright sale of the receivables and a loan secured by a charge on them, since in either case, if the financier is not paid by the debtor, the assignor must make up the difference; but in legal terms the difference is substantial.

In a sale, property passes to the buyer and the buyer will enjoy the benefits of ownership and will benefit from any increase or suffer from any drop in its value. In the case of the granting of security, the relationship is between a debtor and a creditor, with the property acting as a 'fall back' should the debtor default on the loan; any change in the value of the property is for the benefit of the debtor.

The issue of how to characterize financing by outright assignment of book debts was first considered in the following case, where the Court of Appeal held that such arrangements did not create security interests.

 ***Re George Inglefield Ltd* [1933] Ch 1 (CA)**

FACTS: George Inglefield Ltd had entered into a number of hire purchase agreements with its customers and intended to enter into more. It assigned the debts owed by its customers under the existing agreements to the financier in return for a percentage of their face value, and the financier agreed that if the business offered to assign the benefit of hire purchase agreements entered into in the future, it would consider purchasing them on the same terms. It was held at first instance that the arrangement was simply a disguised loan of money secured on the debts under the hire purchase agreements, and the financier appealed.

HELD: The arrangement was a sale of the debts, not the creation of a charge or mortgage over them.

> **COMMENT:** In the course of his judgment, Romer LJ outlined what he saw as the three key differences between a sale and a security interest:
>
> > In a transaction of sale the vendor is not entitled to get back the subject-matter of the sale by returning to the purchaser the money that has passed between them. In the case of a mortgage or charge, the mortgagor is entitled, until he has been foreclosed, to get back the subject-matter of the mortgage or charge by returning to the mortgagee the money that has passed between them. The second essential difference is that if the mortgagee realizes the subject-matter of the mortgage for a sum more than sufficient to repay him, with interest and the costs, the money that has passed between him and the mortgagor he has to account to the mortgagor for the surplus. If the purchaser sells the subject-matter of the purchase, and realizes a profit, of course he has not got to account to the vendor for the profit. Thirdly, if the mortgagee realizes the mortgage property for a sum that is insufficient to repay him the money that he has paid to the mortgagor, together with interest and costs, then the mortgagee is entitled to recover from the mortgagor the balance of the money & If the purchaser were to resell the purchased property at a price which was insufficient to recoup him the money that he paid to the vendor, of course he would not be entitled to recover the balance from the vendor.[3]

However, the financing in *Re George Inglefield* was not only on a recourse basis, but the agreement provided that if the financier recovered more than the face value of the debts assigned to it, the assignor was entitled to the excess, thus suggesting a mortgage or charge on the basis of two of the three essential differences between sales and charges set out by Romer LJ in his judgment.[4] Yet the Court of Appeal unanimously decided that the arrangement was one by way of sale, though recognizing that the label the parties put on the agreement was not conclusive; the matter is one of substance not form. In fact, though not mentioned in the case, the 'security-like' characteristics in *Re George Inglefield* could quite legitimately form part of a sale agreement (admittedly a rather unusual one), where the seller guarantees that the purchaser will make a given profit from the transaction, but in return requires payment to him of any 'overage'.[5]

In fact, the courts have consistently construed as sales, receivables financing agreements expressed as sales,[6] unless the written agreement does not reflect the true agreement between the parties.[7]

The characterization of the arrangement can have important repercussions, since a sale of book debts by a company requires no registration to render them enforceable, whilst a charge almost certainly will have to be registered under s 860 of the Companies Act 2006 to remain valid in an insolvency of the chargor.[8] Book debts are debts owed to a business arising in the ordinary course of business and which would

---

3. [1933] Ch 1 (CA) 27.   4. The second and third differences are set out in the case box.

5. In fact, there are financial derivative 'collar and cap' contracts, which admittedly do not involve sales, to like effect where *A* promises *B* that it will pay the amount by which an investment owned by *B* is worth less than £*X* at a certain date, but that *B* must pay *A* the amount by which the investment exceeds £*X* at that date.

6. Also, it seems a similar approach applies where the assignment is stated to be as security: see *Orion Finance Ltd v Crown Financial Management Ltd (No 2)* [1996] 2 BCLC 382 (CA).

7. *Olds Discount Co Ltd v Cohen* [1938] 3 All ER 281n (KB); *Olds Discount Co Ltd v Playfair Ltd* [1938] 3 All ER 275 (KB), and *Lloyds & Scottish Finance Ltd v Cyril Lord Carpets Sales Ltd* [1992] BCLC 609 (HL).

8. In the case of individuals, a general assignment of book debts, whether by sale or by way of security, is void against the person's trustee in bankruptcy unless registered under the Bills of Sale Act 1878.

be entered in well-kept books of account relating to that business, whether actually so entered or not.[9] Similarly, the terms of other obligations of the company may forbid the granting of security, but may not forbid outright sales.

The type of receivables financing considered in this chapter operates by using outright sale of the debts to the finance provider. However, it is common for a bank to take a charge over a company's book debts as security for overdrafts or other bank loans, and this, too, is a form of receivables financing. However, if the company retains control of any money paid by the debtors, the charge will be characterized as 'floating',[10] significantly reducing the effectiveness of the security created.

🔗 Fixed and floating charges are discussed at p 702

Common provisions in receivables financing by sale

The form of the transaction in *Re George Inglefield*, the earliest reported case involving receivables financing by outright sale, is in many ways characteristic of such transactions even today, and it is helpful to examine some of these characteristics in order to obtain an understanding of the financial structure and possible variants. In transactions like this, the financier is often called a factor, and some agreements 'factoring agreements', but the word 'financier' will continue to be used in this book. The issue facing the assignor in *Re George Inglefield* is identical to that facing ComCorp in the example given on p 711: the company had an income stream but was short of capital. What it needed was a cash sum to use to finance its business, the financier had cash on which it wanted a return: receivables financing met both of their requirements.

Documentation

In *Re George Inglefield*, the parties entered into an agreement which was 'elaborate in its terms',[11] under which there was an actual assignment of the debts.[12] Commonly today, although the business offers to sell the debts, no assignment is actually executed. Such an agreement does not meet the requirements of s 136 of the Law of Property Act 1925, and so has no effect at law, but it does operate as an equitable assignment on the basis that equity looks on as done those things that ought to have been done. The only disadvantage of this equitable status, that the assignee may be required to join the assignor as claimant in any enforcement proceedings,[13] is readily countered by making the financier the agent of the company for the purpose of litigation. In any event, a modern agreement will provide for a legal assignment if the financier requests this.

---

9. *Independent Automatic Sales Ltd v Knowles & Foster* [1962] 1 WLR 974 (Ch). Book debts clearly has a narrower meaning than 'receivables', but there is no doubt that the sorts of debts which are the subject of normal receivables financing are book debts. Whether a charge over a company's bank accounts requires registration under s 860 is unclear: see *Re Brightlife Ltd* [1987] Ch 200 (Ch). See also Lord Hoffmann in *Re Bank of Credit and Commerce International SA (No 8)* [1998] AC 214 (HL) 227.

10. *Re Spectrum Plus Ltd* [2005] UKHL 41, [2005] AC 680.

11. *Re George Inglefield Ltd* [1933] Ch 1 (CA) 18 (Lord Hanworth). Modern agreements are much more elaborate.

12. The sale also included the goods which were hired to the customers.

13. See Civil Procedure Rules, r 19.4.

Facultative or 'whole turnover'?

The agreement in *Re George Inglefield* permitted but did not oblige the company to offer further eligible debts for purchase, nor was the financier obliged to purchase debts offered to him. This was therefore what is known as a 'facultative agreement'. Although not entirely clear from the case, it was probably what is now called a 'block discounting' agreement,[14] where the company submits a batch of debts to the financier for acceptance and so the sale of each batch constitutes a separate assignment, the original contract acting as a master agreement. The alternative to a facultative agreement is a 'whole turnover' agreement, where all eligible debts vest in the financier on coming into existence. Clearly, such agreement seeks to effect assignment of future assets. This is possible only in equity,[15] and then only if consideration is given for the contract.[16] Consequently, there must be a promise to purchase by the financier, not just a right to accept or reject an offer if a whole turnover agreement is to operate as an equitable assignment. The effect of an inchoate assignment, as in a whole turnover agreement, seems in relation to an assignment by way of charge, at least, to cause the security to attach as at the date of the agreement, not the date when the debt actually arose.

Similar issues which concern the creation of security interests are discussed at p 701

Recourse or non-recourse?

The agreement in *Re George Inglefield* was typical, being on a recourse basis, with the assignor being required to guarantee that the debts would be paid in full, but it seems there was no requirement that it repurchase bad debts at their face value at the date of repurchase, though this is now common.[17] Although this duty to repurchase has characteristics reminiscent of the duty to redeem a security, such terms are unobjectionable,[18] though the situation may well be different were there a duty to repurchase all debts assigned.[19]

Collection of the debts

In *Re George Inglefield*, the company continued to operate its sales ledger and collect the debts as it had before; indeed, payment of 25 per cent of the purchase price of the debts was deferred and the company was authorized to retain 25 per cent of all collections and remit only the remainder to the financier. Clearly, since the debts

---

14. For a description of block discounting, see Lord Scarman in *Lloyds & Scottish Finance Ltd v Cyril Lord Carpets Sales Ltd* [1992] BCLC (HL).

15. *Tailby v Official Receiver* (1888) 13 App Cas 523 (HL), which concerns future book debts, following *Holroyd v Marshall* (1862) 10 HL Cas 191 (HL), which involved goods.

16. An agreement by deed does not perfect this problem, since equity is not interested in form, only in substance, and equity does not normally assist a person giving no consideration: see *Meek v Kettlewell* (1842) 1 Hare 464.

17. In fact, it seems the company was required to accept bills of exchange drawn on them for the amount due under each assigned debt, presumably to be presented for payment by the company in the event of default. No comment was made that this is *prima facie* a security device. For an example of an agreement involving a right to require the company to repurchase debts in default, see *Re Charge Card Services Ltd* [1987] Ch 150 (Ch).

18. *Lloyds and Scottish Finance Ltd v Cyril Lord Carpets Sales Ltd* [1992] BCLC 609 (HL).

19. See Fidelis Oditah, *Legal Aspects of Receivables Financing* (Sweet & Maxwell 1991) 38–9. See also *Re Charge Card Services Ltd* [1987] Ch 150 (Ch), where, if the company went into liquidation, it had to repurchase all outstanding debts.

belong to the financier, the company is collecting the debts and presumably 'paying' themselves on his behalf.

Notification or non-notification of debtors?

In *Re George Inglefield*, the debtors were not notified of the assignment unless they went into default.[20] There is some advantage to the assignor in this arrangement, since the fact that it has factored its debts is not made known to its customers but non-notification financing increases the legal risk to the financier, since until then debtors will be making payments to the assignor, not the financier, and the debtor or third parties may obtain defences or claims which are binding on the financier. These issues are explained in more detail later in this chapter. Non-notification financing is sometimes called 'invoice discounting'.

Finance charges and retentions

In *Re George Inglefield*, the purchase price was 100 per cent of the face value of the debts from which the financier was entitled to deduct a 'finance charge' calculated as an interest rate, and the financier was a money-lending institution. However, the fact that the finance provider is in the business of lending money and uses an interest rate to calculate the discount on the face value of the assigned debts does not turn a sale into a money-lending arrangement;[21] as Porter J suggested in *Olds Discount Co Ltd v Cohen*, the question is not with what object the financiers employ their money, but the method they have of employing it.[22]

The retention of 25 per cent of the purchase price of the debts by the financier in *Re George Inglefield* was unlikely to have been construed as a security device securing the company's warranty that 100 per cent of the face vale of the debts would be collected; it was simply expressed as deferred consideration and indeed even operated as such. However, in *Re ChargeCard Services Ltd*,[23] the court held that even if the retention was neither deferred consideration nor part of a mechanism for establishing the quantum of the amount of money immediately due for payment under the agreement, it nevertheless could not amount to a security for the company's obligations, since a creditor cannot charge a debt in favour of the debtor.

 Re Charge Card Services Ltd [1987] Ch 150 (Ch)

FACTS: Charge Card Services Ltd ('CCS') entered into an invoice discount agreement with Commercial Credit. Each month CCS would offer a batch of debts owed to it by its customers for purchase. Commercial Credit would accept or reject them, and then

---

20. Consequently, the assignment in *Re George Inglefield* initially took effect in equity only, since s 136 of the Law of Property Act 1925 requires express notice of the assignment to be given to the debtor.

21. See *Lloyds & Scottish Finance Ltd v Cyril Lord Carpets Sales Ltd* [1992] BCLC 609 (HL) 619 (Lord Scarman).

22. *Olds Discount Co Ltd v Cohen* [1938] 3 All ER 281n (KB). For an explanation of the distinction between an interest charge and a discount, see *Welsh Development Agency v Export Finance Co Ltd* [1992] BCLC 148 (CA) 165–6 (Dillon LJ).

23. [1987] Ch 150 (Ch).

make a payment to CCS. Under the terms of the agreement, Commercial Credit was to maintain an account which would be credited with the purchase price of the debts assigned to it and debited with the value of bad debts Commercial Credit required CCS to repurchase. Commercial Credit had to pay the balance on this account from time to time to CCS, less a retention 'as security for & any amount prospectively chargeable to the company as a debit' to the account. CCS went into liquidation and the liquidator argued that Commercial Credit's right to retain some of the purchase price amounted to a charge securing its right to set off any claim it had against CCS in respect of bad debts against the obligation to pay the purchase price of debts it had bought during the accounting period. As a charge, it would be void for non-registration under what is now s 860 of the Companies Act 2006.

HELD: The retention was not security for CCS's obligations but a contractual limitation on its right to require immediate payment of the whole of the purchase price of the debts. Without the retention, the account would always overstate Commercial Credit's payment obligation, which the agreement defined as the purchase price of the debts less the value of bad debts; it was therefore simply an accounting device to avoid overpayment. On this basis, CCS could not be granting a security interest (a charge) over that proportion of the purchase price of the debts which Commercial Credit had retained, since it was never entitled to receive it—there was no property to subject to the charge.

In the alternative, Millett J considered the situation if he were wrong and CCS did have a right to the whole purchase price of the debts and in turn did owe a debt to Commercial Credit for the bad debts. Clearly if this were true, it did have an asset which could be the subject matter of a charge. However, he held that 'a charge in favour of a debtor of his own indebtedness to the chargor is conceptually impossible'. Consequently, on either interpretation of the nature of the retention, it did not amount to a charge.

COMMENT: Millet J's primary reason for determining the right of retention was not a charge was in effect that Commercial Credit had agreed to pay the realized value of the debts assigned to it. That value, of course, could not be calculated at the outset, so the debits and credits to the account each month were not part of the process of calculating the price of the debts but establishing the quantum of the next monthly payment to be made to CCS.

The secondary reason, that charging the benefit of a debt to the debtor (known as a 'charge back'), is conceptually impossible, raised some concern in banking circles, since the practice of taking a charge over customers' deposit accounts was and is common practice. Nevertheless, there is some force in the argument that the property (the right to sue the financier for the money retained) can nether be assigned[24] to the debtor, since it would simply act as a release of payment obligation, nor can the property be set aside (appropriated) for the chargee to realize in order to be repaid from the proceeds, since the debtor cannot sue himself!

Chargebacks and the nature of charges are discussed further on p 706

See Roy Goode, 'Setting Off Contingent Claims' [1986] JBL 431

The conclusion that a creditor cannot charge a debt in favour of the debtor, though supported by a number of academic commentators,[25] was heavily criticized

---

24. In other words, it cannot be mortgaged, since a mortgage requires the mortgagee to have title to the mortgaged property.
25. See especially Roy Goode, *Legal Problems of Credit and Security* (2nd edn, Sweet & Maxwell 1988) 124–9. In the latest edition of what is now *Goode on Legal Problems of Credit and Security* (4th edn, Sweet & Maxwell 2008) [3-12], the editor, Louise Gullifer, writes that the conceptual and policy arguments Sir Roy Goode advanced against charge backs 'must yield to business practice and legislative developments designed to accommodate it', a point Sir Roy Goode himself acknowledged in the third edition of the book.

by Lord Hoffmann in *Re Bank of Credit and Commerce International SA (No 8)*,[26] though in a context far removed from receivables financing, leaving open the possibility that a right of retention in a poorly drafted financing documentation might be vulnerable to attack as a charge.

Relationships and priorities

Figure 26.1 sets out the basic relationships.

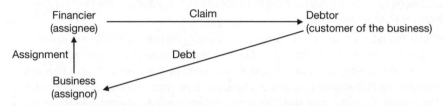

FIGURE 26.1 Legal relations in receivables financing by assignment not charge

The relationship between the financier and the assignor

Where the agreement is on an invoice discounting basis, the assignor will continue to receive payments from the debtors and indeed even where notice of the assignment has been given to the debtor, it is commonplace for payment to be made directly to the assignor by its customer by mistake.[27] The agreement will provide that the assignor will hold all receipts on trust for the financier,[28] but in effect, unless the assignor segregates and maintains such monies in a separate designated trust account,[29] or unless the bank is aware of the source of the money and knowingly assists the assignor to break its trust, the financier will probably be left with only a personal claim against the assignor, which will abate in its insolvency.

The relationship between the financier and the debtor[30]

Consider the following example.

Eg ComCorp Ltd

ComCorp decides to enter into a block discounting agreement with Avarita and assigns all of its existing hire purchase contracts to it, and each month offers a batch of new contracts for Avarita to buy. Among the existing contracts is one under which ComCorp hired a

---

26. [1998] AC 214 (HL) 225–8. On this case, see Roy Goode, 'Charge Backs and Legal Fictions' (1998) 114 LQR 178.

27. In fact less so now where, typically, payment is made through bank transfer to a designated account.

28. Roy Goode and Ewan McKendrick, *Goode on Commercial Law* (4th edn, Penguin 2010) 791 argues that no express declaration of trust is necessary; cheques and money received will be automatically held on trust citing *International Factors Ltd v Rodriguez* [1979] QB 351 (CA) as authority.

29. If the fund is not segregated, then the financier may be still be able to identify the proceeds in the hands of others through tracing.

30. See Andrew Tettenborn, 'Assignees, Equities and Cross Claims: Principles and Confusion' [2002] LMCLQ 485.

computer to Jim. The computer never works properly and Jim returns it after a couple of months, refusing to make any more payments, and claiming the return of the payments he made to ComCorp.

Jim buys another computer on hire purchase from ComCorp. A few days later, ComCorp contracts Jim to do a week's work for them at £100 per day. Two days into the contract, Jim is notified that his hire purchase agreement has been assigned to Avarita. ComCorp has refused to pay Jim the money due under the contract for services and Jim has refused to pay Avarita any of the five £100 instalments due under the hire purchase agreement.

ComCorp wants to know whether Avarita, who purchased both of the hire purchase agreements with Jim, is entitled to claim the full value of the debts from him.

The financier can obtain no better rights under the contract than the assignor. Under the *nemo dat* rule he will take, subject to the counterparty's right to terminate The *nemo dat* rule is discussed at p 272 the contract for breach of condition, any defences such as fraud, duress, or misrepresentation leading to avoidance of the contract, or other defences arising out of the contract, whether arising before or after notice is given to the debtor. Thus, for example, if the debt is due under a contract for the sale of goods which is lawfully terminated for breach of condition, then the financier cannot enforce that debt, but equally since he is not a party to the contract between the assignor and the debtor, the financier cannot incur liabilities to the debtor, including a liability to repay instalments of the debt paid by a debtor prior to termination.[31]

A debtor can also set off against the financier claims arising under separate contracts which are so closely associated with the contract giving rise to the assigned debt that it would be inequitable not to allow them, regardless of whether the claim arose before notice of the assignment had been given.[32]

Similarly, a debtor can also set off against the financier any liquidated claim against the assignor which accrued before the debtor received notice of the assignment, whether or not the claim is due for payment before or after the date of the assignment.[33] However, even where the contract under which the claim arises was made before the date of the notice, debts which accrue after that date cannot be set off against the financier.[34] This is well illustrated by the following case.

Business Computers Ltd v Anglo African Leasing Ltd [1977] 2 All ER 741 (Ch)

FACTS: Anglo African Leasing Ltd owed about £10,000 to Business Computers Ltd. In a totally separate contract, Anglo African leased a computer to Business Computers at a

---

31. *Pan Ocean Shipping Co Ltd v Creditcorp Ltd, The Trident Beauty* [1994] 1 All ER 470 (HL). For a case note, see Gregory Tolhurst, 'Assignment, Equities, the Trident Beauty and Restitution' (1999) 58 CLJ 546.

32. *Government of Newfoundland v Newfoundland Rly Co* (1888) 13 App Cas 199 (PC). For further analysis of close connections and inequitablity, see *Bim Kemi AB v Blackburn Chemicals Ltd* [2001] EWCA Civ 457, [2001] 2 Lloyd's Rep 93.

33. *Christie v Taunton Delmard, Lane & Co* [1893] 2 Ch 175 (Ch); *Business Computers Ltd v Anglo African Leasing* Ltd [1977] 2 All ER 741 (Ch).

34. *Roxburghe v Cox* (1881) 17 ChD 520 (CA).

> monthly rental of £1,500, under the terms of which, if the agreement were terminated, all future rental instalments would become payable. One instalment of rent was outstanding on the day that notice of assignment by of the £10,000 debt was given to Anglo African. Anglo African terminated the lease of the computer so that the £30,000 in future rent became immediately payable.
>
> **HELD:** While Anglo African could set off the £1,500 rental instalment due at the time the notice of assignment was given against the £10,000 debt which had been assigned, it could not set off the £30,000 that became payable after the date of notification, nor indeed could it set off any part of a rental instalment which was due the day after the notice.
>
> **COMMENT:** The assignment of the £10,000 debt took place when a floating charge granted by Business Computers crystalized when a receiver was appointed under the charge. This illustrates the point that the granting of a floating charge is to effect what Edmund Davies LJ characterized as an 'incomplete assignment'.[35] On crystallization, the charge then attaches to all of the property subject to the charge being converted into a completed equitable assignment.

🔗 Floating charges are discussed at p 702

Until notice of assignment has been given to the debtor, he may safely pay the assignor, and has no further obligation even if the payment does not reach the financier. However, once notice has been given, payment to the assignor will not normally discharge the debtor's liability until the financier receives it. A prudent financier will ensure that agreement between the assignor and the debtor permits free assignability of the debt before he purchases the debt, since any dealings in the debt in breach of the agreement may not be effective.[36] Thus in *Helstan Securities Ltd v Hertfordshire County Council*,[37] an assignment of the benefit of a contract contrary to a non-assignability clause was rendered ineffective as between the financier and the debtor such that the financier could not claim payment from them. The decision leaves open the question of the effect of the assignment as between the assignor and the financier, in particular whether an appropriately drafted non-assignability clause could render the assignment void as between them and, if not, whether the financier has a proprietary claim against payments received by the assignor and if so whether it takes effect as a security.[38]

The relationship between the financier and third parties—priorities

It is always open for a business which has entered into a receivables financing agreement to assign or charge the debts to another person, though this would be in breach of the master agreement.[39] Under the much-criticized rule in *Dearle v*

---

35. *George Barker (Transport) Ltd v Eynon* [1974] 1 WLR 462 (CA) 467.
36. See Roy Goode, 'Contractual Prohibitions against Assignment' [2009] LMCLQ 300.
37. [1978] 3 All ER 262 (QB).
38. See the note on *Helstan Securities* by Roy Goode, 'Inalienable Rights?' (1979) 42 MLR 553. His analysis was accepted by Lord Browne-Wilkinson in *Linden Gardens Trust Ltd v Lenesta Sludge* Ltd[1994] 1 AC 85 (HL) 104. See also *Don King Productions Inc v Warren* [2000] Ch 291 (Ch), where Lightman J held that in the circumstances of the case, a purported assignment in breach of a non-assignability clause effected a declaration of trust over the benefit of the contract.
39. Restricting the ability of a party to grant security over or dispose of assets is a normal provision in a security transaction, and this provision in *Re George Inglefield* was partially responsible for Eve J at first

Hall,[40] priority is given to the rights of the first bona fide purchaser for value without notice of any prior interest to give notice to the debtor regardless of whether the assignments are legal or equitable.[41] The legal problems which have arisen all relate to successive assignments where the assignor has also charged its assets to a third party, or, where there is a title retention clause rather than in cases of outright fraud. Nevertheless, the same principles apply where there are competing equitable interests, whether they arise out of an assignment by way of security, outright assignment, or under a trust, as illustrated in the following case.

Compaq Computers Ltd v Abercorn Group Ltd [1993] BCLC 602 (Ch)

FACTS: Compaq sold computers to Abercorn subject to a title retention clause under an arrangement whereby Abercorn would sell the computers to sub-purchasers. Abercorn would hold the goods it purchased as bailee for Compaq until sale, and hold the proceeds of the sub sales for Compaq until Compaq had been paid. Abercorn later entered into an invoice discounting agreement in respect of the debts due to it from sub-purchasers of the computers. When Abercorn went into receivership, the financier, Kellock, gave notice to the sub-purchasers that their debts had been assigned to it. The question was whether Compaq or Kellock was entitled to the proceeds of sale of the computers to the sub-purchasers.

HELD: Mummery J held that the retention of title clause created a charge over the debts due from the sub-purchasers. Alternatively, had the charge been valid as against Kellock, or if the beneficial interest in the proceeds of sale had been in Compaq, as the clause stipulated, then the rule *Dearle v Hall* would apply and consequently on the assumption that Kellock had no notice of the agreement between Compaq and Abercorn, Kellock had priority because it had given notice first to the debtors of Abercorn of the assignment of their debts to it.

COMMENT: It should be noted that the charge created by the title reservation clause was not registered as required by s 860 of the Companies Act 2006 and so was void against Kellock for want of registration by virtue of s 874, since Kellock was a creditor. However, had the invoice discounting been by way of outright sale, the charge would not have been void as against Kellock—s 874 avoids charges against creditors, not purchasers.

The rule in *Dearle v Hall* displaces the basic rule that competing equitable interests rank in the order of their creation. If Kellock had notice of the beneficial interest of Compaq (for example, because the charge had been registered), then it could not have relied on the *Dearle* rule and the basic rule would have ensured that Compaq, being first in time, had priority.

---

instance deciding that the agreement was a mortgage. The Court of Appeal did not see this aspect of the agreement as indicative of the creation of a security interest.

40. *Dearle v Hall* (1828) 3 Russ 1. For criticisms of the rule in the context of receivables financing, see DW McLauchlan, 'Priorities—Equitable Tracing Rights and Assignments of Book Debts' (1980) 96 LQR 90 and Roy Goode, 'The Right to Trace and its Impact in Commercial Transactions' (1976) 92 LQR 528, 566.

41. See *E Pfeifer Weinkellerei-Weineinkauf GmbH & Co v Arbuthnot Factors Ltd* [1988] 1 WLR 150 (QB). Where the debt is non-assignable it would appear that notice of assignment will not fix the priorities, since the debtor is under no duty to accept the notice.

★ See Len Sealy, 'Retention of title— Rule in Dearle v Hall' (1992) 51 CLJ 19

> Mummery J adopted the reasoning in *E Pfeifer Weinkellerei-Weineinkauf GmbH & Co v Arbuthnot Factors Ltd*[42] that, although the assignment to the financier met the requirements of s 136 of the Law of Property Act 1925, once notice had been given to the debtors and so effected a legal assignment, for the purposes of establishing priorities, s 136 cannot give an assignee greater rights than if the assignment had been equitable only. Thus the doctrine that a bona fide purchaser for value of a legal interest without notice of a prior equitable right is entitled to priority in law and in equity cannot benefit an assignee of a thing in action.

The finance lease

Chapter 2 discussed two essential ideas of the English law of personal property, title, and interest, and that one may have either a 'full' (often called absolute) or a possessory title to a chattel and that one's interest may either be 'absolute' or by way of security. The chapter also discussed the concept of 'bailment', where the possession of a chattel is in one person ('the bailee'), whilst ownership in the sense of full title to an absolute interest is in another ('the bailor').[43] This part of the chapter will explore one way, the 'chattel' or 'finance' lease, in which bailment is used to reduce the impact of a default in a financial transaction.

The essence of all chattel leasing is that the owner parts with possession in favour of another person. Although the arrangement may be called a 'lease 'or a 'hire', there is no legal difference between the two (and we will use the word 'lease'), but the essence is that at the end of the arrangement the lessee must deal with the goods as directed by the lessor. It is important to note that if the lessee had an option to purchase the goods, this would be a contract of hire purchase, whilst if he had a duty to buy, it would be a **conditional sale**.

Consider the following example.

➔ conditional sale: a sale of goods superficially resembling hire purchase where title remains in the seller until the purchase price is paid, normally by instalments

Eg ComCorp Ltd

ComCorp Ltd has decided that it needs to acquire a new powerful and very expensive computer for a new venture. Because of the costs of setting up this new venture, the finance director anticipates that ComCorp will not make a profit on its whole activities for some years and he is loathe to use the company's reserves to meet the cost of the new machine. Also, the company provides cars for its senior employees and its salesmen, which it replaces every three years, and this year the whole fleet is up for renewal and the finance director would like to find a means of financing this cost too. Finally, ComCorp has decided to digitize all of its paper records. It anticipates it will need a state-of-the-art digital scanner for the length of the project, which will take about six months. The finance director does not want to incur the capital cost of purchase and the economic uncertainty of its resale value once the project is over.

---

42. [1988] 1 WLR 150 (QB).

43. In fact, there is no reason why a financier need be the owner in this sense; he may himself have had the goods bailed to him and, indeed, in many finance leases the end user does not have a direct contractual relationship with the person with full title (i.e. the owner). However, because possession is indivisible (see p 41) the owner will be bailing the goods to the end user.

There is a whole industry dedicated to providing asset-backed finance and, whilst there are a myriad of financial products available, the market typically divides leases into two main types: the operating lease; and the finance lease. In a finance lease, the assumption is that at the end of the lease the asset will have a comparatively low capital value, consequently the rental payments are calculated so as to cover the capital cost and return on capital required by the lessor. Normally at the end of the lease, all or a significant proportion of the proceeds of sale by the lessor will be rebated to the lessee. Alternatively, the lessee may be given an option to renew the lease at a significantly reduced rent. During the period of the lease, the duty to repair and maintain the goods will fall on the lessee. In an operating lease on the other hand, the rentals are calculated as the use value of goods, which are anticipated to continue to have a commercial value when the lease has expired. The key reason for differentiating between the two is their accounting treatment. A finance lease is entered on the lessee's balance sheet as an asset with an accompanying liability to meet the rental payments, with the finance charges being expensed through the profit-and-loss account, while the obligations under an operating lease are profit-and-loss items only.[44]

In ComCorp's case, a finance lease seems the likely financing mechanism for the acquisition of the computer, since Comcorp will require the asset throughout its economic life, while vehicle leasing for periods such as is contemplated by ComCorp can be structured as either finance or operating leases. Clearly, the digital scanner will have an economic life beyond the six-month project and so its use is probably better acquired under an operating lease. It might be thought that there is little difference between a finance lease and a conditional sale or hire purchase, since the rental payments are calculated on the assumption that in each case the lessee has funded its purchase entirely, along with providing the financier with his desired return on capital. Why not buy the asset outright and pay for it in instalments of capital and interest rather than have someone else buy it and lease it to you, because the rental you will pay will be materially the same? In fact, if the lessee's business is unlikely to be profitable for some while, it will be advantageous for the capital allowances, which a business can deduct for tax purposes to be claimed by the financier. In a conditional sale or hire purchase agreement, capital allowances are available to the end user; in a finance lease the capital allowances are available to the lessor and the tax benefit can in effect be used to reduce rental payments.

The remainder of this chapter will be devoted to the finance lease rather than the operating lease, but many of the same legal principles apply to both.

The legal relationships in a finance lease—lessee and supplier

Although the business will select the assets and will negotiate the principal terms of the contract of sale without relying on the skill and judgment of the lessor, it will be the lessor who enters into the contract to purchase with the supplier

---

44. Statements of Standard Accounting Practice, SSAP 21, *Accounting for Leases and Hire Purchase Contracts* issued by the Accounting Standards Committee of the Institute of Chartered Accountants for England and Wales. SSAP 21 defines a finance lease as 'a lease that transfers substantially all of the risks and rewards of ownership of an asset to the Lessee'. Such a transfer is to be presumed if, at inception of the lease, the present value of the payments under the lease amounts to substantially all (normally 90 per cent or more) of the fair value of the asset.

(as in Fig. 26.2), and consequently the lessee will have some difficulties in enforcing his rights against the supplier should the goods prove to be unsatisfactory, since there is no direct contractual relationship between them. There are four possible approaches to this problem.

The lessor agrees to enforce his rights against the supplier for the benefit of the lessee

Clearly, the lessor has entered into a contract, the performance of which benefits a third party to that contract, namely the lessee. The leasing agreement will almost certainly exempt the lessor from liability arising out of breach by the supplier of the underlying contract of sale,[45] so that even assuming that the supplier knows about the lessee (which normally it will), it is probably not reasonably foreseeable that the lessor will suffer any loss through having to compensate the lessee by virtue of the supplier's breach of contract.[46] The issue therefore arises whether the lessor can sue and recover damages assessed by reference to the lessee's loss. In *Beswick v Beswick*,[47] the majority of the House of Lords concluded that, on general contractual principles, in a contract for the benefit of a third party, a claimant can recover nominal damages only, since he suffers no personal loss. Likewise, in *Woodar Investment Development Ltd v Wimpey Construction Co Ltd*,[48] the House of Lords disapproved of Lord Denning's contention in *Jackson v Horizon Holidays Ltd*[49] that there was no such general principle, explaining that decision as either an example where the damages awarded represented the contracting party's own loss or that a special rule applies in relation to contracts intended to provide enjoyment for the contracting party and his family. Nevertheless, this situation creates a 'legal black hole'[50] in which the person with the right to sue suffers no loss, while the person who suffers loss has no right to sue. The existence of this black hole may well have provided an incentive to the courts, initially in relation to contracts of carriage of goods by sea[51] and then construction

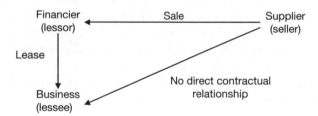

FIGURE 26.2 Legal relations in a finance lease

45. This will have to meet the test of reasonableness under the Unfair Contract Terms Act 1977. For an example of where a blanket exclusion of rights under ss 8–10 of the Supply of Goods and Services Act 1982 was held unreasonable, see *Lobster Group Ltd v Heidelberg Graphic Equipment Ltd* [2009] EWHC 1919 (TCC).

46. Though, of course, adapting Lord Griffith's reasoning in *Linden Gardens Trust Ltd v Lenesta Sludge Disposals Ltd* [1994] AC 85(HL) 97, the lessor does suffer financial loss because he has to spend money to give him the benefit of the bargain which the defendant had promised but failed to deliver.

47. [1968] AC 58 (HL).   48. [1980] 1 WLR 277 (HL).   49. [1975] 1 WLR 1468 (CA).

50. *Darlington BC v Wiltshier (Northern) Ltd* [1995] 3 All ER 895 (CA) 906 (discussed on p 726).

51. *Albacruz (Cargo Owners) v Albazero (Owners) (The Albazero)* [1977] AC (HL) 774. Now no longer much of an issue in this context after the Carriage of Goods by Sea Act 1992 (see p 502).

contracts,[52] to establish an exception to the general rule, explained in the following way by Lord Diplock in *The Albazero:*

> [I]n a commercial contract concerning goods where it is in the contemplation of the parties that the proprietary interests in the goods may be transferred from one owner to another after the contract has been entered into and before the breach which causes loss or damage to the goods, an original party to the contract, if such be the intention of them both, is to be treated in law as having entered into the contract for the benefit of all persons who have or may acquire an interest in the goods before they are lost or damaged, and is entitled to recover by way of damages for breach of contract the actual loss sustained by those for whose benefit the contract is entered into.[53]

In *Linden Gardens Trust v Lenesta Sludge Disposals Ltd*,[54] the majority adopted this principle in determining that a building contractor was liable to a subsequent purchaser of the land. Although there has been no reported case in which this narrower ground for the decision in *Linden Gardens* has been applied to finance leases, there seems no reason why in principle it should not, at least if there is no other way in which the lessee can acquire rights against the supplier.[55] There may be difficulty in showing that the parties to the sale contract had the intention that the purchase was for the benefit of another, but in *Linden Gardens* the fact that title to the property was likely to be transferred seemed to be enough to raise this presumption. In a typical finance lease case, the fact that the purchaser is interposed by the lessee who, up until the last, has been negotiating the purchase, may well make the likelihood of subsequent transfer[56] clear, even if the lessee has not specifically disclosed the nature of the purchase, while in any event, the names of finance companies usually make their function obvious.

In *Linden Gardens*, Lord Griffiths, as part of the minority, concluded that the contracting party himself suffers financial loss in having to put right the defects in the sale goods in order to obtain what he had bargained for and so can sue personally for damages in respect of that loss.[57] Although this 'broader ground' for the decision in the case was not adopted by the majority in *Linden Gardens*, it was accepted in two of the dissenting judgments in *Panatown Ltd v Alfred McAlpine Construction Ltd*.[58] If this broader ground were to be adopted generally, it may provide a more convenient means by which the lessee could be compensated, since it is dependent neither on the knowledge nor the intention of the parties to the sale contract. Although it is not completely clear, it seems likely that the lessor cannot benefit personally from an

---

52. *Linden Gardens Trust v Lenesta Sludge Disposals Ltd* [1994] AC 85 (HL).
53. [1977] AC 774 (HL) 847.
54. [1994] AC 85 (HL).
55. Where there is another way in which the lessee can obtain the benefit of the right to claim compensatory damages against the supplier, then there is no reason to suppose that the parties to the sale intended the lessor to be contracting for the benefit of the lessee, nor indeed any incentive for the court to extend the exceptions to the general rule, since there is no 'black hole'.
56. In this case, a transfer of possession only.
57. *Linden Gardens Trust Ltd v Lenesta Sludge Disposals Ltd* [1994] AC 85 (HL).
58. [2000] 3 WLR 946 (HL) discussed by Brian Coote, 'The Performance Interest, Panatown, and the Problem of Loss' (2001) 117 LQR 81. The majority in *Panatown* did not comment adversely on the idea of the performance interest.

action based on the broader ground, since in *Linden Gardens* Lord Griffiths required the claimant either to have repaired or intended to repair the property or to have agreed with the third party that he would be responsible for the condition of the property.[59]

The lessor assigns his rights to the lessee, who then sues the supplier

Assuming, of course, that the *Linden Gardens* exception can apply to finance leases, assignment of the lessor's rights to the lessee is an alternative and probably preferable approach to the lessor suing directly, as the following case demonstrates.

 Darlington Borough Council v Wiltshier Northern Ltd [1995] 3 All ER 895 (CA)

FACTS: Wiltshier Northern Ltd agreed with Morgan Grenfell to carry out building work on land belonging to Darlington BC. Morgan Grenfell was financing the project but had no interest in the land. Under the terms of the finance contract, and known to Wiltshier, Darlington could call on Morgan Grenfell to assign to it all of Morgan Grenfell's rights against Wiltshier. Defects in the building appeared. Morgan Grenfell assigned its rights under the building contract to Darlington, who sued Wiltshier for its loss. Wiltshier argued that an assignee of a contract can be in no better position than the assignor, and since Morgan Grenfell had suffered no financial loss, the assignee, Darlington could recover no more than nominal damages.

HELD: The Court of Appeal held, applying the narrower ground in *Linden Gardens*, that the financier had the right to recover substantial damages and had assigned this right to Darlington, who were entitled to pursue that claim.

⭐ See Michael P Furmston, 'Damages for Loss Suffered by Someone Else' (1996) 6 Cons Law 201

Although there is no reason why the lessor should not assign its rights against the supplier to the lessee in the lease agreement, there would appear to be no objection if they are assigned later, following the decision in *Offer-Hoar v Larkstore Ltd*[60] that the purpose of the rule that an assignee cannot recover more than an assignor of a thing in action is to protect the debtor from increased liability caused by the assignment.

The lessee acquires rights under the Contracts (Rights of Third Parties Act) 1999

There is no reason why the lessor and the supplier should not specifically agree in the sale contract that the lessee is to have the right to claim under the contract by

---

59. In relation to finance leases, Lord Griffith's second alternative is unlikely to apply, since liability of the lessor for defects in the goods is always excluded. The reason for insisting on these alternatives is that they prevent the lessor from pocketing the damages and thus improving his financial position because the goods were defective. The same objective could be achieved if the leasing agreement provided that the lessor has a duty to pursue remedies against the supplier (at the lessee's risk) and to account to the lessee for the proceeds of that suit. For a discussion of the issues arising generally in relation to contracts for the benefit of third parties, see Hugh Beale (ed), *Chitty on Contracts* (31st edn, Sweet & Maxwell 2012) [18-51-63].

60. [2006] EWCA Civ 1079, WLR 2926 (CA).

virtue of s 1(1)(a) of the Contracts (Rights of Third Parties Act) 1999. However, this term does not appear to be common in practice, and consequently the lessee will have to rely on s 1(1)(b), under which he may enforce a term which 'purports to confer a benefit on him', unless the lessor and supplier intended it not to be enforceable by him.[61] The problem for the lessee is that, in the words of Christopher Clarke J:

> [a] contract does not purport to confer a benefit on a third party simply because the position of the third party will be improved if the contract is performed. The reference in the section to the term purporting to 'confer' a benefit & [connotes] that the language used by the parties shows that one of the purposes of their bargain (rather than one of its incidental effects if performed) was to benefit the third party.[62]

Consequently, for s 1(1)(b) to apply, the terms of the contract of sale would need to deal specifically with the issue of third party rights. Contracts for the sale of goods will be conducted almost inevitably on the seller's standard terms, and since the lessor is disinterested in their content, it is essential during the negotiation process for the lessee to require the supplier to amend those terms in order to afford it rights under the 1999 Act.

Where there is an international sale and the lessor, lessee, and supplier are resident in a 'contracting state' or the proper law of the contract is that of a contracting state,[63] the UNIDROIT Convention on International Financial Leasing provides a lessee with all of the rights he would have had as a party to the contract and as if the goods were supplied directly to him.[64] However, fewer than a dozen states have ratified the convention[65] and it has not been ratified by the UK.

There is a collateral contract between the supplier and the lessee

Where the lessee is induced to enter into the leasing agreement by a false statement of fact by the supplier, then if this representation is intended to have contractual effect, it can be treated by the lessee as a collateral warranty by the supplier, the consideration for which is his (the lessee's) entry into the leasing agreement.[66]

Also, in the fairly atypical circumstances where the lessee is misled into believing that he is leasing from the supplier, the lessor will be estopped from denying that representations made by the supplier were made by him or with his authority.[67]

---

61. Contracts (Rights of Third Parties) Act 1999, s 1(2).

62. *Dolphin Maritime and Aviation Services Ltd v Sveriges Angfartygs Forening* [2009] EWHC 716 (Comm), [2010] 1 All ER (Comm) 473 [74].

63. UNIDROIT Convention on International Financial Leasing, Art 3(1).   64. ibid Art 10.

65. Though some countries, although not ratifying the convention, have incorporated some of its principles into their domestic law. See e.g. the Tanzanian Financial Leasing Act 2008.

66. See *Andrews v Hopkinson* [1957] 1 QB 229 (QB). See also *Yeoman Credit Ltd v Odgers* [1962] 1 All ER 789 (CA), where the lessee successfully claimed damages to compensate him for his liability under the finance agreement. Both of these cases involved hire purchase, but the same principles will apply to finance leases.

67. *Lease Management Services Ltd v Purnell Secretarial Services Ltd* [1999] 1 WLR 263 (CA), a case where a clause in the lease agreement excluding liability for representations made about the goods (a photocopier) was held to be unreasonable under the Unfair Contract Terms Act 1977.

The legal relationships in a finance lease—lessee and lessor

Since the relationship between lessor and lessee is one of hire not sale, the implied terms under the Sale of Goods Act 1979 will not apply, though potentially their counterparts under the Supply of Goods and Services Act 1982 may. That said, since the lessee does not normally rely on the skill and judgment of the lessor in selecting the goods, the term as to fitness for purpose under s 4(5) of the Supply of Goods and Services Act 1982 will not be implied into the contract between them, though the term for satisfactory quality under s 4(2) of the Supply of Goods and Services Act 1982 *prima facie* will.[68] However, since the lessor is not involved in the specification or selection of the goods, it does not seem unreasonable for him to exclude liability in relation to their quality. As noted earlier, this leaves the lessee in the 'black hole' without obvious recourse in respect of defects in the goods, and this has been held to be sufficient to render an exclusion of the implied term unfair.[69] Consequently, it is potentially advantageous to both lessor and lessee if the contract of sale for the goods specifically gives the lessee the right to enforce it.

While considering *Business Computers Ltd v Anglo African Leasing Ltd*[70] earlier, we encountered a typical provision in a finance lease, namely that on early termination, whether by the lessee or by the lessor, where the lessee has committed a breach which permits termination,[71] the lessee is liable for all future rental payments. This is necessary for the lessor since the second-hand value of the goods plus rentals paid is unlikely to be sufficient to enable it to recover the cost of purchase until close to the end of the lease. The problem is that the lessor must ensure that this provision is not struck down as a penalty, as in *Lombard North Central plc v Butterworth*,[72] consequently, it must amount to a genuine pre-estimate of loss for the failure of the lessee to make all contractual payments. In fact, there is no method for reaching the 'correct' answer. Consequently, the suggestion that 'the court ought to recognise any stipulated loss value formula that as seen at the time when the agreement was made is likely to do substantial justice between the parties'[73] is eminently sensible.

The legal relationships in a finance lease—the lessor and the supplier

The lessor and supplier are simply buyer and seller. However, the measure of damages payable to the lessor in the case of breach of contract by the supplier is complicated by the existence of the lease. If, as would be normal, the supplier knows that the lessor is not the end user, then the supply of goods in such a way as to permit the lessee to refuse to accept them as against the lessor should, on normal *Hadley v*

---

68. *Lobster Group Limited v Heidelberg Graphic Equipment Limited* [2009] EWHC 1919.
69. ibid [147].   70. [1977] 2 All ER 741 (QB).
71. See the drafting device in *Lombard North Central plc v Butterworth* [1987] QB 527 (CA).
72. [1987] QB 527 (CA).
73. Roy Goode and Ewan McKendrick, *Goode on Commercial Law* (4th edn, Penguin 2010) 774. There is an excellent discussion on the problems in Roy Goode, *Hire Purchase Law and Practice* (2nd edn, Butterworth & Co 1970) 887ff.

Baxendale[74] grounds, enable the lessor to recover damages reflecting its loss of profit through loss of bargain with the lessee, assuming that the profit is not extraordinary and so not foreseeable. However, as noted earlier, since the lessor is insulated from claims from the lessee based on defects in the goods, it is only by virtue of an exception to the rule barring claims in respect of losses by third parties that the supplier can be liable to the lessor for the lessee's losses.

The legal relationships in a finance lease—the lessee and third parties

It is by no means clear whether the lessee would be able to retain the leased good were the lessor to sell them to a third party. As against the lessor he is a bailee, and he has possessory title to the goods, and, assuming that he does not breach the lease agreement, cannot be required to give up possession to the lessor/bailor. However, if the lessor sells the goods to a third party who is unaware of the lease, that person will acquire full title to the goods, but on normal contractual principles cannot be bound by the terms of the lease. Thus if the lessee is to resist a claim to possession by the third party, he must have a proprietary interest which is capable of binding a third party with full title to the goods, and it is by no means clear that he has such a proprietary right.

The issue of proprietary interests is referred to in Chapter 2 at p 26

The legal relationships in a finance lease—the lessor and third parties

Save temporarily in the case where the lessee acts as undisclosed principal in the sale, the lessee cannot pass title to the goods to a third party, since none of the exceptions to the *nemo dat* rule can apply.

Exceptions to the nemo dat *rule are discussed at p 273*

Complicating factors

Although the three-party relationship described earlier is by far the most common in the UK, some finance leases have more complicated structures, some of which, for the sake of completeness, are listed here:

- The lessee completes the purchase from the supplier as agent for the lessor. The lessor may either be disclosed as principal to the supplier or be undisclosed, as where the lessee wishes to hide the fact he is employing a finance lease. In either case, the lessor is exposed to liability if the lessee/agent exceeds his authority. In the case of an undisclosed principal, title to the goods will vest in the lessee initially, requiring some act on his part to vest them in the lessor; until then the lessee may pass title to a third party.

The liability of an agent to a third party is discussed in Chapter 8

- The lessee purchases the goods in his own name and on his own behalf. In such a case the parties have two options. First, the supplier may agree to cancel this purchase with the consent of the lessee and novate it in favour of the lessor. Alternatively, if this is not possible, and especially where the goods have been acquired some time ago by the lessee, the lessor may agree to a 'sale and lease back'. Clearly, the lessee must deliver the goods to the lessor for title to pass, but of course will remain in physical possession throughout. This delivery is effected by an attornment by the lessee in favour of the lessor giving him

Attornment is discussed at p 38

---

74. (1854) 9 Exch 341—enshrined in SGA 1979, s 50.

constructive possession followed immediately by the granting of the lease.[75] The clear danger with sale and leaseback is its being characterized as a disguised security device, which will require registration to be effective in an insolvency of the lessee, but it is established that where there is a bona fide sale and lease-back, it will be treated as such.[76]

- The financier purchases the goods, leases it to the lessor, who subleases it to the lessee. Normally, a finance lease forbids the lessee from dealing in the goods, but here the lessor is expressly given the right to grant sub-leases and the arrangement is designed to provide an outside financing source. Normally, the financier/head lessor will take an assignment of the rental payments from the lessee, either by way of charge or under a block discounting.

Conclusion

This chapter has considered in detail two methods by which a business might acquire finance in ways which, to an extent, protects the finance provider from the consequences of financial failure of the business, using two property concepts, assignment of things in action and bailment. The finance industry is extremely inventive and these are but two of the ways in which a financier can obtain shelter while the storm of insolvency of the business bursts around him. However, this invention is born out of an understanding of the property concepts underpinning the products it creates, so that understanding these is of vital importance.

However, as we have seen, the products are not entirely successful in protecting the financier, whilst sometimes leaving the business with potential problems. Thus with finance leases there are genuine legal difficulties in providing the business with remedies against a supplier of deficient goods. Whilst the Contracts (Rights of Third Parties Act) 1999 provides a solution, the difficulty is that it involves action by the business in order to protect its interests, and very few businesses have the capability of doing this, whilst the financier has probably provided himself with a suitable exclusion clause and so is not personally involved in the problem.

With receivables financing, the issues are rather different. Here the requirements of the industry militate in favour of loan agreements with customers, which permit assignment since without such a clause, the business will not be able to factor its debts. The customer, including substantial enterprises, is probably unconcerned by the prospect of assignment of the debt. But not only does the assignment change the dynamics of any dispute with the assignor arising over a separate contract, but it may find dealing with a financier, expert in debt collection and only concerned about recovery of the money, rather different to dealing with a business with which it has an on-going commercial relationship.

Consequently, this chapter has sought to demonstrate how, from the building blocks of legal theory, financial products can be created, which, although far from perfect looked at from the viewpoints of all those concerned in them, nevertheless operate effectively as a basis for providing sources of finance for businesses.

---

75. *Michael Gerson (Leasing) Ltd v Wilkinson* [2001] QB 514 (CA).

76. See *Yorkshire Railway Wagon Company v Maclure* (1882) LR 21 ChD 309 (CA), where initially the parties created a charge over the assets, but on the advice of counsel unwound the arrangement and effected a sale and leaseback, which was upheld as such by the Court of Appeal.

Practice questions

1. (a) Describe the features of and differences between:
   - hire purchase;
   - conditional sale;
   - a finance lease;
   - an operating lease.
   (b) Describe the legal effect of the differences between:
   - receivables financing by charge and by outright sale;
   - block discounting and whole turnover financing;
   - a legal and equitable assignment of a debt.

2. 'The lack of recourse by a lessee under a finance lease to anyone other than his lessor can be readily cured through careful documentation.'
   Discuss.

3. You are an in-house lawyer for FinHoCo Ltd, a finance house which does receivables financing. You receive an urgent phone call from the finance director at about 7.00pm, just as you were about to go home early. He says that one of the company's clients, BusiCo Ltd, has just notified them that it is insolvent. The finance director tells you FinHoCo has bought over £10 million of debt owed to BusiCo from its clients and wants to know whether FinHoCo's agreement with BusiCo Ltd will 'stand up'. You can't access the BusiCo file until tomorrow morning, but have a copy of FinHoCo's standard receivables financing agreement.

   The agreement is headed 'Master Factoring Agreement'. Under its terms, FinHoCo agrees to 'consider purchasing debts offered to it by the Business' (meaning BussiCo in this instance) 'from time to time'. If FinHoCo agrees to purchase the offered debts, then by clause 10 of the agreement, the business warrants that the debts will be paid in full by its customers and that it would re-purchase any bad debts at face value. The 'purchase price' for the debts is 'the discounted value of the block of debts'. The agreement then stated that FinHoCo would pay 'the Purchase Price to the Business on the last working day of every month'. A little later on, the agreement stated that FinHoCo was:

   > entitled to retain a percentage of the Purchase Price, calculated in its sole discretion as security for the Business' obligations arising under clause 10 hereof ('the Retention'). The Retention shall be used in the first instance to meet the Business' re-purchase obligations under clause 10 in respect of the block of debts to which it relates but to the extent that the amount recovered in respect of that block of debt is greater than that assumed by FinHoCo in determining the amount of the Retention, the Retention shall be returned to the Business.

   You analyse the agreement to determine:

   (a) Is this a whole turnover or block discounting agreement?
   (b) Is this intended by the parties to be an outright sale of the debts or to operate as a security?
   (c) Regardless of what the parties intended, might the court characterize the whole agreement or part of it as an assignment by way of security?
   (d) If it is a security, what would the impact be on the validity of the agreement?

You check the Companies Register online and discover to your horror that BusiCo Ltd granted a floating charge over its whole undertaking over a year ago and the charge was duly registered. However, the charge permits BusiCo to enter into receivables financing. You then consider the effect of this charge on priorities between the Master Agreement and the charge assuming the Master Agreement takes effect as an outright sale.

What advice should you give to the finance director?

Further reading

Hugh Beale, Louise Gullifer, and Eva Lomnicka, *The Law of Personal Property Security* (OUP 2007)
- A comprehensive and scholarly work, which covers the range of security issues, but Chapter 5 contains much useful material on receivables financing and finance leases.

Brian Coote, 'The Performance Interest, Panatown, and the Problem of Loss' (2001) 117 LQR 81
- Although in the form of a long casenote, this article provides a clear exposition of the issues which *McAlpine v Panatown* raises in relation to the protection of the 'performance interest' by damages in contract. It does not address how the principles might be adapted, if at all, in the context of the finance lease, but provides material for thought.

Roy Goode, 'Inalienable Rights' (1979) 42 MLR 553
- Where a debt contains a non-assignability clause, the effect of that clause is of vital importance to a financier contemplating purchasing or taking a charge over it. The ways in which such a clause might affect the rights of a transferee are explored in this casenote on *Helstan Securities Ltd v Hertfordshire County Council*.

Roy Goode, 'Charge Backs and Legal Fictions' (1998) 114 LQR 178
- This casenote provides a critique of the decision in *Re BCCI (No 8)* concerning the conceptual possibility of charge backs. It is a succinct exposition of the issue and careful reading facilitates an understanding of the nature of a charge—a key issue when considering receivables financing.

DW McLauchlan, 'Priorities—Equitable Tracing Rights and Assignments of Book Debts' (1980) 96 LQR 90
- Although somewhat overtaken by events, this is an article which investigates the application of the Rule in *Dearle v Hall* in relation not only to tracing rights but title retention and provides insights into how the rule actually works, with trenchant criticism of its use in the world of receivables financing.

Simon Mills (ed), *Goode on Proprietary Rights and Insolvency in Sales Transactions* (3rd edn Sweet & Maxwell 2009)
- The effectiveness of receivables financing and finance leases is tested in the context of the insolvency of the business seeking financial accommodation. Many of the difficult issues raised in this chapter receive analysis in this expanded version of Professor Goode's original work, looking at the ways in which a proprietary claim can insulate the financier for claims of creditors in such an insolvency.

Fidelis Oditah, *Legal aspects of Receivables Financing* (Sweet & Maxwell 1990)
- Although now a little old, the book is not out of date and is a constant companion for practitioners in the field.

Andrew Tettenborn, 'Assignees Equities and Cross Claims: Principles and Confusion' [2002] LMCLQ 485
- Discusses the effect of the range of cross claims which might be made by a debtor as against the assignee of the debt.

index

Introductory note

References such as '178–9' indicate (not necessarily continuous) discussion of a topic across a range of pages. Wherever possible in the case of topics with many references, these have either been divided into sub-topics or only the most significant discussions of the topic are listed. As the entire work concerns 'commercial law', the use of this term (and certain others which occur constantly throughout the book) as an entry point has been restricted. Information will be found under the corresponding detailed topics.